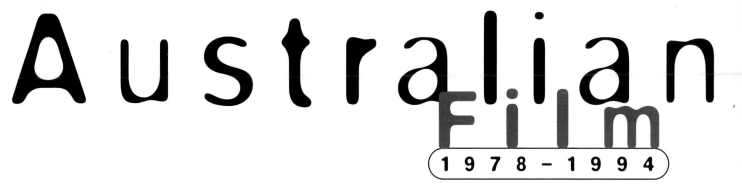

Australian Film

1978 - 1994

A Survey of Theatrical Features

D1208822

Compiled and edited by
Scott Murray

Editorial Assistants
Raffaele Caputo
(1978–92)
Alissa Tanskaya
(1993–94)

Melbourne

OXFORD UNIVERSITY PRESS

in association with

THE AUSTRALIAN FILM COMMISSION
and
CINEMA PAPERS

OXFORD UNIVERSITY PRESS AUSTRALIA

Oxford New York
Athens Auckland Bangkok Bombay
Calcutta Cape Town Dar es Salaam Delhi
Florence Hong Kong Istanbul Karachi
Kuala Lumpur Madras Madrid Melbourne
Mexico City Nairobi Paris Singapore
Tapei Tokyo Toronto
and associated companies in
Berlin Ibadan

OXFORD is a trade mark of Oxford University Press

National Library of Australia
Cataloguing-in-Publication Data

Australian Film 1978–1994: a survey of
theatrical features.

2nd ed.
Bibliography.
Includes index.

ISBN 0 19 553777 7

1. Motion pictures – Australia – History.
2. Motion pictures, Australian – History.
I. Tanskaya, Alissa II. Murray, Scott, 1951–
III. Caputo, Raffaele.
IV. Australian Film Commission
V. Title: Cinema Papers.
VI Title: Australian film 1978–1994.

791.430994

Written and published with the assistance of
the Australian Film Commission

Front cover: Bernadette (Terence Stamp), Felicia (Guy
Pearce) and Mitzi (Hugo Weaving) in Stephan Elliott's
The Adventures of Priscilla, Queen of the Desert;
photograph   by Elise Lockwood, courtesy of Al Clark

Proof-reader: Arthur Salton
Oxford editor: Ruth Siems
Cover and text design by Steve Randles
Printed by Impact Printing Victoria Pty Ltd
Published by Oxford University Press,
235 Normanby Road, South Melbourne, Australia

CONTENTS

1981

69

1982

89

1983

119

1984

141

Annie's Coming Out
The Camel Boy
The Coolangatta Gold
Dot and the Bunny
Fast Talking
Future Schlock
Melvin: Son of Alvin
My First Wife
One Night Stand
Razorback
The Settlement
Silver City
The Slim Dusty Movie
Stanley: Every Home Should Have One
Street Hero
Strikebound
"Undercover"
Where the Green Ants Dream
The Wild Duck

1985

163

Bliss
Burke & Wills
The Coca-Cola Kid
Emoh Ruo
The Empty Beach
Epic
Fran
An Indecent Obsession
Mad Max Beyond Thunderdome
Morris West's The Naked Country
Rebel
Robbery Under Arms
The Still Point
A Street to Die
Tail of a Tiger
Warming Up
Wills & Burke
The Winds of Jarrah

1986

183

Backlash
The Big Hurt
Cactus
Cool Change
Crocodile Dundee
Dead-End Drive-In
Death of a Soldier
Dot and Keeto
Dot and the Koala
Dot and the Whale
Fair Game
For Love Alone
Fortress
The Fringe Dwellers
Frog Dreaming
Jenny Kissed Me
Malcolm
The More Things Change…
Playing Beatie Bow
Short Changed
Sky Pirates
Traps
Unfinished Business
Windrider
Wrong World

1987

1988

1989

1990

1991

1992

FOREWORD

Australian Film 1978–1994 chronicles the feature films made by an industry striving to find its footing after the initial flush of success enjoyed by the likes of **Picnic At Hanging Rock** and **My Brilliant Career**. But more was happening than the maturing of the film industry. These seventeen years saw the focus of the debates shift from a preoccupation with production and how films came to be made to an engagement with a concept of audience and the development of Australian audiences for Australian films.

Integral to both debates is the shifting spectre of cultural authenticity, characterised in the earlier films by an attachment to a costumed nationalism, which gave way to an engagement with contemporary issues emerging from a diverse and multi-cultural society. Changing representations have in no small way been brought about by women, Aborigines and people from multi-cultural backgrounds telling their own stories.

The features made during the period from 1978 to 1994 attest to the critical rôle government intervention plays in ensuring that Australians continue to enjoy making and watching films about stories which are their own. Government assistance to the industry changed significantly during the period. The Australian Film Commission (AFC), established in 1975, formed the core of financial support until the Division 10BA tax concessions were introduced on 24 June 1981. The generosity of these concessions were progressively reduced during the course of the decade from 150/50 to 100 per cent by mid 1988. At this time, the Australian Film Finance Corporation was established.

Government involvement with film has not been limited to the provision of funds for production. This book is itself a testament to the rôle the AFC plays in engendering a viable cultural milieu which has an impact on both the films and the society from which they emerge. A vital film culture serves to invigorate the creative process as well as the society in which such creativity is situated. Film publications, film festivals and events, distribution and exhibition opportunities, including home video, have been on the rise over the past seventeen years and have enabled Australians to view and contextualise their own cinema.

The output of the Australian film industry over the period 1978 to 1994 has been prolific and exciting. The feature films included in *Australian Film 1978–1994* bear witness to the energy, creativity and particular perspective that Australian films have to present to national and international audiences. Ours is a dynamic industry with a pivotal part to play as Australia moves towards a new century.

Cathy Robinson
Chief Executive
Australian Film Commission

1

PREFACE

Australian Film 1978–1994: A Survey of Theatrical Features is a revised and expanded edition of *Australian Film 1978–1992*, which was released in November 1993. Rather than just reprint (with minor corrections), it was decided to add two additional chapters for the years 1993 and 1994.

Australian Film 1978–1994 is primarily a reference work. As with the pioneering *Australian Film 1900–1977: A Guide to Feature Film Production,* by Andrew Pike and Ross Cooper[1], it aims to record all the theatrically-released Australian features of a given period. It has been compiled independently of the first, but hopefully carries on the spirit and principal aims.

Understandably, given the dramatic changes in the film industry in the past decade or so, there have been some adjustments of approach. For example, whereas many film lovers in the early 1970s saw most Australian features that were made, that is not the case today. The mid-1980s burst of activity saw so many films being produced that many disappeared quickly from view; others were never even sighted. Listing each theatrical feature here, then, becomes a kind of verification of its very existence.

The primary aim of both editions of this book has been to record a film's major technical and cast credits. These are presented in a block at the beginning of each film entry. They are as comprehensive and accurate as possible, and taken directly from the film itself (or a video copy).

Following the credits block, there is a critical text of generally three- to five-hundred words. Whereas Pike and Cooper concentrated mostly on plot summary, basic production information and a sampling of newspaper criticism, adding their own critical opinions where deemed appropriate, that approach has been changed here.

First, the sampling of newspaper reviews has been omitted. Before 1970, and save for a few brave exceptions, newspapers were the major source of film criticism in Australia. That is no longer the case. Australia is quite well served with film journals, ranging from *Cinema Papers* to *Metro* and *Exposure*. Then there is the growing number of books on the Australian film industry, many offering critical perspectives. These range from *The New Australian Cinema*, through the works of Susan Dermody and Liz Jacka, to those of Brian McFarlane and David Stratton. In short, the publication of film criticism has changed dramatically and, with a few exceptions, newspaper reviewing is no longer at the forefront.

Second, important production information (budget, location, when shot, etc.) is incorporated in the credits block, where known. Additional information only appears in the text if the specific author feels it relevant.

Third, there is a consistency of critical approach in Pike and Cooper that is not appropriate here. In Australia, there are almost as many critical approaches as there are writers on film, and to reflect that very diversity this book has deliberately opted for a wide range of authors. (Readers looking for a single-perspective overview could consult McFarlane, Stratton or this author's 'Australian cinema in the 1970s and 1980s' in *Australian Cinema*.)

Some may argue that a reference book has no need to make evaluative judgements, but it is clearly impossible not to do so, no matter how cunningly or unconsciously opinions may be disguised. Such an argument also supposes that one person's view of a film is something more than that – a definitive statement etched in metaphoric stone. But film criticism, by its very nature, is testament to the fact that films are open texts which invite an infinitude of readings. Printing only one evaluation per film in this book in no way suggests there aren't many other (even better) ways of writing about that film.

At the same time, authors were requested to include a plot description and be as non-pejorative as possible.

As to pairings between author and film, prospective authors were invited by the editor to select which films they wished to cover. Where overlaps occurred, or no film garnered a volunteer, selections were made by the editor and/or editorial assistants.[2]

All the credit entries were compiled by the editor or (in a few cases) an editorial assistant.

In closing, it should be gratefully noted that the research and production of the first edition of this book was in part financed by the Australian Film Commission (AFC). While such an acknowledgment usually only appears in small print on the copyright page, it is recorded here because without the AFC's kind support this book, like so many others, would not have been written. Particular thanks go to Kim Williams, who while Chief Executive of the AFC first backed the project, and Cathy Robinson, the present Chief Executive, who enthusiastically continued that commitment.

Scott Murray
Editor

---

[1] Andrew Pike and Ross Cooper, *Australian Film 1900–1977: A Guide to Feature Film Production*, Oxford University Press, in association with The Australian Film Institute, Melbourne, 1980.

[2] The first edition of this book was intended only to cover ten years (that is, to 1987), but the scope was (at the relative last minute) extended. Given the tight deadlines that resulted, it was decided that the entries for 1991 and 1992 be based on those reviews already printed in *Cinema Papers*. The original authors were asked to cut them down (or rewrite, if they preferred). Where that was not possible, the cut-down was done in-house. In a few other cases, too, where a film was unavailable for viewing or a review fell through, extracts from *Cinema Papers* were used. All these cases are duly noted.

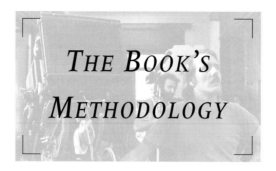

THE BOOK'S METHODOLOGY

To aid readers in the use of this book, what follows is a description of the methodology used in the selection of entries and the reproduction of credits.

WHAT IS AN AUSTRALIAN THEATRICAL FEATURE FILM

Features and tele-features are defined here, in accord with the world archivist standard, as dramas of more than 60 minutes which have been shot and/or projected on 16, 35 or 65/70mm film.

Super 8 works are not usually considered by archivists. However, two Super 8 features were theatrically released in 1993–94, and both are covered in Appendix B.

Video features are not covered in the main text as they are not *film*. They are, however, dealt with in Appendix C.

Drama content

By definition, a feature must have a considerable amount of 'acted' drama. **The ABC of Love and Sex Australia Style** is included because, although a documentary in some senses, it is almost entirely enacted by paid performers. Equally, **The Good Woman of Bangkok** is included because, while having the appearance of a documentary, much of it is actually staged, and the lead actress (Yagwalak Chonchanakun) plays a character other than herself (named Aoi).

On the other hand, **Vincent: The Life and Death of Vincent Van Gogh** is not listed, as the dramatic element is very small and is in the traditional style of a documentary that dramatises odd moments.

Animated

Unlike some other reference works, this book includes animated features as they meet all archivist definitions of what constitutes a feature. However, because all the animated features listed in this book are by Yoram Gross and employ similar techniques, making individual reviews liable to restatement, an overall critical analysis of his work appears as Appendix A. The titles and credits of each film, however, are included in the year-by-year groupings.

Is it Australian?

This is the hardest determination to make. Production standards have changed since Pike and Cooper's *Australian Film 1900–1977: A Guide to Feature Film Production* and traditional delineations have become blurred.

The country where principal photography took place has been often used as one test, while other archivists have argued for the origin of financing. The location standard falls down with what are obviously Australian films that are largely shot off-shore (**Far East**, for example). Then again, most films today have a mix of financing from various world territories and that latter criterion is also confusing.

Equally, there are problems with a determination based on the nationality of the production company. Film companies are sometimes set up to maximise tax benefits and the location may reflect neither where a film was shot nor who financed it. Even more troublesome, most films have more than one production company, and they may well be (and often are) spread wide across the globe.

Some critics prefer to determine a film's nationality from that of the director. But this is self-defeating as it would mean, for example, that many of the great American films of the 1930s couldn't be called American because their directors were European émigrés. Likewise, Tim Burstall's and John Duigan's Australian work would have to be discounted because they were born in Britain, Paul Cox's because he was born in The Netherlands, and so on.

Despite its self-evident problems, this nationality-of-the-director syndrome is surprisingly strong among Australian writers, especially when it comes to *American* film-makers, and some disagreed loudly with the inclusion in the first edition of **The Salute of the Jugger** (as the editor forewarned). Yet, it was shot entirely in Australia, with an almost exclusively Australian crew and cast. From any objective stand-point, it is, like **Walkabout** and **"Wake in Fright"**, more 'Australian' than **Green Card** (also included), which was made without any Australian cast and very few Australian crew entirely in New York.

In this second edition, the most controversial entry is probably **Lorenzo's Oil**. But **Lorenzo's** falls into exactly the same category as **Green Card**, which almost every local author seems happy to call Australian. Both were written by Australians in Australia, shot and financed in the US, and post-produced back in Australia. Some might argue **Green Card** has the added bonus of being an official co-production, but what has an essentially arbitrary bureaucratic ruling to do with the renegade world of cinema?

Finally, some writers opt for where the copyright of a film is held. This, too, has many problems, the most obvious being that copyright is usually not held by a single entity but by several, representing more than one different nationality.

Ultimately, there is no foolproof way of setting in stone what constitutes an Australian film. After all, a film like **The Piano** can rightly be claimed by New Zealanders as their own — or even by the French, who financed it! Common sense must be applied, with all its attendant flaws. If some feel the coverage of the book is too wide-ranging, then surely that is preferable to a selection that is too narrow.

Theatrical or non-theatrical

An equally difficult determination to make is whether a film is a feature or tele-feature. In past eras, this was easier as there was little confusion between the two: tele-features were made exclusively for television screening and, although usually shot on film, tended to be completed on video (particularly the titles).

But as production escalated in the 1980s, the demarcation lines shifted. Whereas in the 1970s almost every Australian feature received a theatrical release, by the end of the 1980s that was true of less than 50 per cent. Many films went straight to video, others to television, some to oblivion. A new determination was required.

In the first edition of this book, a two-category system was adopted. Films were divided into:
1 Features that were theatrically released in Australia (each of which was included with major credits and a critical appraisal); and
2 Feature-length films that were released on video or television, or not at all (each of which was listed with basic credits in an appendix: 'Non-theatrical Features 1978–92').

Such an approach meant deciding what constituted a theatrical release. The rule adopted was at least one cinema screening where tickets were sold for that film. That did not include a festival screening, where tickets are usually sold for a number or series of films.

In some cases, a cinema may have been hired to release a film (**Snow: The Movie**), which some may feel is not a proper release. But this was once a common practice in Australia known as 'four-walling'.

The same criteria of theatrical release hold in this edition, but, as an exhaustive book on unreleased and tele-features is presently being researched, the former appendix on non-theatrical features has been omitted. In its place is Appendix D, which lists (with major credits and synopses) every feature completed or started since 1992 which had not been shown in a cinema by the end of 1994.

Date

Of the many alternative dating systems, the one chosen here is the year of Australian theatrical release. Films have been chaptered accordingly, in alphabetical order.

A different standard that could have been adopted is commercial world release but this has not been used as information about those Australian films which premiered overseas is not always readily available or easily verified.

Some authors prefer to quote the year of completion. That date is included as part of the copyright information. (For ease of reference, the date is always placed immediately after the © symbol, no matter how that credit is worded on the film.)

A note of caution

The first edition of this book carried the following disclaimer:

> While every attempt has been made to be comprehensive and accurate, it is possible that a film believed not to have been released may have been so unnoticed. So far, all reference books on Australian cinema have had significant omissions, deliberate or otherwise. While this book aims to be comprehensive, the particular problems of the mid-1980s boom may have led to the odd regrettable slip-up.

So far, no film has been found to be omitted. All the same, the disclaimer still holds.

THE CREDITS

Reproduced below is a typical set of credits, followed by an explanation of various key entries.

I G O R   A U Z I N S

THE COOLANGATTA GOLD

Michael Edgley International and Hoyts Theatres in association with Peter Schreck, Igor Auzins and John Weiley present THE COOLANGATTA GOLD. © 1984 Angoloro, Michael Edgley International and Hoyts Theatres. *Budget:* $7 million. *Location:* Coolangatta and the Gold Coast (Queensland). *Australian distributor:* Hoyts. *Opened:* 22 November 1984. *Video:* RCA–Columbia Hoyts. *Rating:* PG. 35mm. Panavision. 112 mins.

Producer: John Weiley. *Associate producer:* Brian Burgess. *Executive producers:* Terry Jackman, Michael Edgley. *Scriptwriter:* Peter Schreck. Developed from an idea by Max Oldfield and a story by Ted Robinson and Peter Schreck. *Director of photography:* Keith Wagstaff. *Camera operator:* David Burr. *Production designer:* Bob Hill. *Costume designers:* Lea Haig, Camilla Roun-

tree. *Editor:* Tim Wellburn. *Composer:* Bill Conti. *Sound supervisor:* Phil Judd. [*Sound recordist:* not credited.] *Sound editors:* Marc van Buuren; Karin Whittington, Tim Jordan (dia.). *Mixers:* Phil Judd, Julian Ellingworth.

Cast

Joss McWilliam (Steve), Nick Tate (The Father: Joe), Colin Friels (Adam), Josephine Smulders (Kerry), Robyn Nevin (The Mother: Roslyn), Grant Kenny (Grant), Melanie Day (Gilda), Melissa Jaffer (Ballet Teacher), Paul Starling (Karate Teacher), Brian Syron (The Entrepreneur); Wilbur Wilde, Paul Clark, Martin Holt, Marlon Holden, Scott Thompson (The Band); Robert Brough (Commentary [sic; Commentator]), Graduates of the Australian Ballet School (Dancers).

The director

The name above the title is that of the director. This graphic high-positioning in no way preferences auteurism (though there is much to be said for it), but recognises that most people interested in cinema connect films with their directors, and vice versa.

The title

A film's title is that recorded on a print of the film, not that listed in press material (they often differ). Thus, it is **Hightide** (one word) and **Star Struck** (two), not as press materials (and many critics) might mis-title them.

Equally, it is **Sumner Locke Elliott's Careful He Might Hear You**, with the authorial possessive the film-makers intended, but without a comma after **Careful**, which most film writers insist on adding (the novel has it).

Possessives

The issue of authorial possessives is an interesting one. Possessives staked their claim in titles when film-makers began adapting plays and novels to the screen. The novelist's or playwright's name was often felt to be an inducement to ticket sales. Thus, one has **Tennessee Williams' A Streetcar Named Desire** and **Ian Fleming's Dr. No**, among countless others.

This predilection for adaptation became so prevalent that the populist press opted to abbreviate titles and omit the possessive. This practice is still seen today, though fortunately it is on the wane. The full titles of **Mary Shelley's Frankenstein** and **Bram Stoker's Dracula** were, in the main, accurately rendered in the press and by reviewers.

Being a reference work, this book has naturally no desire other than to faithfully record what is on the screen. Thus the reader will find entries for **David Williamson's The Club** and **Morris West's The Naked Country**. (The index also includes abbreviated versions for those unfamiliar with the full titles.)

An interesting corollary are the two Australian films with authorial possessives which are *not* based on extant plays or novels: **Peter Kenna's The Umbrella Woman** (or **Peter Kenna's The Good Wife**, as it was retitled in the US) and **David O'Brien's Shotgun Wedding**.

In the first case, the scriptwriter contracted his name to be in the main title, although this was ignored by almost every critic in this country. In the second, **David O'Brien's** appears on the card before **Shotgun Wedding**, but the sense of title is clear:

Aden Young [and] Zoë Carides in David O'Brien's

new card

Shotgun Wedding

Graphics

Another key issue is how to take into account the graphic design of a title. The standard chosen here is to reproduce all titles in the critical texts in upper-and-lower case.[1] (As entry headings have been capitalised, slightly larger type on some letters mirrors the upper-and-lower-case rendition.)

At the same time, an approximation of the actual title is made in the credits block prior to the copyright symbol: e.g., 'THE delinquents' or, as above, 'THE COOLANGATTA GOLD'.

In the rare cases where a film has a subtitle, the standard archivist style of a colon (as opposed to a dash) is used to separate the two. The three principal types are:

1 A main title and an additional one in smaller type. For example, with **Doctors & Nurses: A Story of Hopes**, the 'DOCTORS & NURSES' appears in large letters, the 'a story of hopes' in smaller script on a bandaid placed across the main title;

2 Titles where the two or more parts do not form a continuous statement without punctuation, as with **Against the Grain: More Meat than Wheat**; and

3 Where the wording flows normally, though different type faces are used in the title, as with **Mad Max Beyond Thunderdome**.

The line-break symbol used in poetry [/] is employed on occasion in the credits block listing of the title where knowledge of a line break is deemed helpful in comprehending a title's representation. Equally, [//] is used to indicate a change from one title card to another.

In the critical texts, all theatrical film titles are bold; novels, magazines, plays, other films and television programmes are in italics; short stories, poems, etc., are in single quotes.

Choosing credits

The decision as to which credits to list, from the hundreds a film may have, was based on standard practice and an observance of, and participation in, film production. Most entries need no explanation, but some may. The first, and one of the most problematic, concerns the production company. Nowhere on a film is there such a credit. Instead, there is the opening production credit (prior to the main title) and, usually at the end, the copyright credit.

In the case of **The Coolangatta Gold**, the first title on the film reads:

Michael Edgley International
and
Hoyts Theatres
in association with

Followed on the next title card by:

Peter Schreck, Igor Auzins
and
John Weiley
present

Then, on the next:

THE COOLANGATTA GOLD

If that isn't complex enough, at the end of the film the copyright credit reads:

© 1984 Angoloro P/L, Michael Edgley International and
Hoyts Theatres.

Despite the complex legalities involved and a genuine confusion as to what can be rightfully called the production company/ies, some authors have tried to render a production company credit as a single entry (one reference book has 'p.c.: Hoyts–Edgley' for the above).

A credit for financial assistance by one or more government funding bodies (the Australian Film Commission, Film Victoria, etc.) is only included if actually credited on the film.

Budgets are given only where known. Given the producer's eye is generally on what sounds or reads well in the media, published budgets should be treated with caution.

The dates of location filming and of theatrical release are only listed where known; the same for location details.

Among the crew credits, one of particular interest is 'Camera operator'. Although usually not credited in reference works, the camera operator plays a vital, and usually unheralded, rôle in maintaining and defining a director's visual concept. Where there is no entry for 'Camera operator', that is because the director of photography also operated, a fairly-common practice in Australia.

Even more undervalued by critics is the contribution of the sound department (how often is a reader's attention drawn to sound in a review or article?). Yet, the sound editors (also known as dubbing editors), for example, can work on a film for longer than anyone else and do much to shape a film's tone. That is why all the principal sound contributors are recorded here.

Since the first edition was published in late 1993, it has been interesting to note the increased importance given on film credits to sound people. 'Sound designer' is now a quite common credit. Going even further, but provoking audience mirth, was the credit 'Audiographer' on **Broken Highway**. It has not been sighted since, but just as 'cinematography' has increasingly replaced 'director of photography' in some circles, so may 'Audiographer' gain substantial ground.

A few other clarifications: the terms 'Production designer' and 'Art director' have been used interchangeably on Australian productions (though the former seems to be taking hold). For this book, 'Production designer' is used for the principal person, regardless of how the film credits that rôle.

Sometimes there is no costume designer on a film, in which case the highest-rated worker in wardrobe is credited under his/her specific title.

Where no credit appears on the screen, the entry is recorded in brackets, as with [*Production designer:* not credited.]. If the film carries no credit, but it is known who performed that task, the entry reads, as on **Palm Beach**: [*Editor:* not credited; Albie Thoms.]. Where an assumption is made, the shorthand 'atb' for 'assumed to be' is used.

In the case of animated films, the credits are understandably of a different form.

Spellings

All names are taken from the credits and reproduce exactly those spellings. This can lead to a variation from film to film. For example, director of photography Garry Wapshott has a double 'r' in his **The ABC of Love and Sex Australia Style** credit but only one on **Felicity**. Equally, the director of **Felicity** is listed as 'John D. Lamond', but the co-scriptwriting credit drops the 'D.'.

Some directors, too, change their name from film to film. **My Brilliant Career** is directed by Gill Armstrong, but **Hightide** (and others) by Gillian Armstrong; Jacki McKimmie directed **Australian Dream**, but Jackie McKimmie is credited for **Waiting**.

Where a spelling is known to be wrong ('Brian Brown' in **The Chant of Jimmie Blacksmith**), or a variant spelling of the most common form, there is either a footnote or a [sic]. In all cases, it is assumed that a reader has just consulted a single entry and not read the book from start to finish.

Abbreviations and punctuation are as given on the film. With **Bullseye**, for example, the opening credits refer to 'P.B.L. Productions', but the copyright at the end deletes the full stops and refers to 'PBL Productions'. Both forms are reproduced as is.

The George Millers

As many readers would know, there are two George Millers working as directors. Most books attempt to differentiate between the two names, prefixing a 'Dr' to one or inserting the initial 'T' into the other. As both directors sign their films simply 'George Miller', no alteration of name is used here. (See Appendix E for filmographies of both directors.)

Rating

This is the censorship rating given by the Australian Film Censorship Board and (formerly) published in the *Australian Government Gazette*.

Some years ago, the traditional 'NRC' (Not Recommended for Children) became 'PG' (Parental Guidance), resulting in differing terminology over the course of the book. The recent and redundant 'clarifying' notations, such as '15+', have not been included.

A film's length in metres, where given after the date of the censorship decision, is that recorded in the published censorship lists. Usually, this figure is accurate, though variations do occur. Sometimes producers alter a film after it has been rated and without resubmitting it to the censor, and sometimes there is a typographical error in the published lists. All known variations are noted.

Running time

There are often many quoted running times for a film. For example, the Censorship Board recorded the length of **Mad Max** at 2486.35m, or 91 mins. The press release in Australia lists it at 90 mins; the highly-reliable *Monthly Film Bulletin* increased it to 101 mins; Leonard Maltin and Steven H. Scheuer go for 93. According to director George Miller, 91 mins is correct.

One reason for the confusion is that films are often cut just before or after release, but the press material is not amended. So, it must be taken as read that a listed running time is in many cases only a best guess.

Cast credits

The minimum of actors listed is twenty, unless the film contains fewer rôles. In those few cases where the total cast list is only slightly more than twenty, it is included in full.

The order of the credits is that shown on the end credits, except where the film lists them alphabetically or in order of appearance. In these latter cases, the credits are run per the order of whoever is listed on the front credits, then (after a separating semicolon) as per the end credits. This is not the situation with **My Brilliant Career** which, uniquely, has no actor credits at the start of the film.

The character names are per the credits, not the press material, as with most books. Thus, for **Backlash**, one reference work credits actor Anne Smith as 'Mrs Smith', but the film, and this book, have her as 'Publican's Wife'. (Where a descriptive character name is more than one word, the first letter in each key word is capitalised.)

This approach is not always as easy as it sounds. On **Travelling North**, the end credits list Graham Kennedy's character as 'Freddy', yet the opening credits have the name as 'Freddie'. (Variants, where spotted, are noted.)

Often, too, a film will only credit a character's first name, whereas the press release (and some books) will include a surname. The self-evident problem with uncredited names is determining the correct spelling. A character may say in a film, 'Mrs Stephens', but, without a credit at the end, should that be 'Mrs Stevens'? And a press kit is no guide. Though in **Cool Change** the lead female character is called 'Joanna', and is so credited at the end, the stills for the film caption her as 'Joanne'.

Even worse, take the case of **Fortress**, where the press book and film credits rarely agree:

Actor	Character (as per film)	Character (as per press book)
Kurtwood Smith	Prison Officer Poe	Prison Director Poe
Alan Zitner	Claustrophobic Prisoner	Camper
Denni Gordon	Karen's Cellmate	Lydia
Eric Briant Wells	Border Guard Friendly	Border Guard
Peter Marshall	Travel Authorization Guard	Travel Agent

References

Key references are given for major articles, reviews and interviews in *Cinema Papers*, Australia's major critical and historical film journal, and, for most of the period covered by this book, the only Australian publication continuously indexed by the *International Index of Film Periodicals*.

References are also given for *Filmnews*, a monthly newspaper which concentrated on political and union issues, and alternative cinema, until its demise in May 1994.[2]

Other Australian publications of interest, but not referenced here, are the sadly-defunct *Freeze Frame* and *Filmviews* (which merged with *Cinema Papers*), and the extant *Metro*, *Exposure* and *Continuum*.

No book references are cited because they would take up too much space; each book has its own index and often a reference is only a line or two long. Relevant books and periodicals are listed in Appendix F.

All cited references standardise film titles in article headings in bold.

FINAL NOTE

Despite every effort to record a film's credits accurately, this is sometimes very difficult. Some films have credits which are readable only on a big screen (if then), and sadly too many transfers to video in this country are of dreadful quality. Like **The Earthling**'s, they are ungraded, making one shot over-exposed, the next impenetrably murky. As well, Panavision films (for example, **Crosstalk**) tend not to be scanned, resulting in not only half the (often key) action going missing, but also the edges of the credits. In Europe, every scope and widescreen film is letterboxed on video (and on television). Hopefully, that will become the standard here. Certainly, Ronin is to be applauded for its recent releases of **Broken Highway** and others in a masked format.

Future editions of this book will record any significant new or clarifying information that comes to light.

---

[1] Worldwide, critics adopt upper-and-lower case for all film titles with one bizarre exception: **sex, lies, and videotape**. Even though it is only one of thousands of films with lower-case titles (**sweetie, the coca-cola kid** and **single white female**, to name but a few), it is the only one critics reproduce this way.

[2] It was relaunched by the AFC in March 1995, but closed again in July 1995.

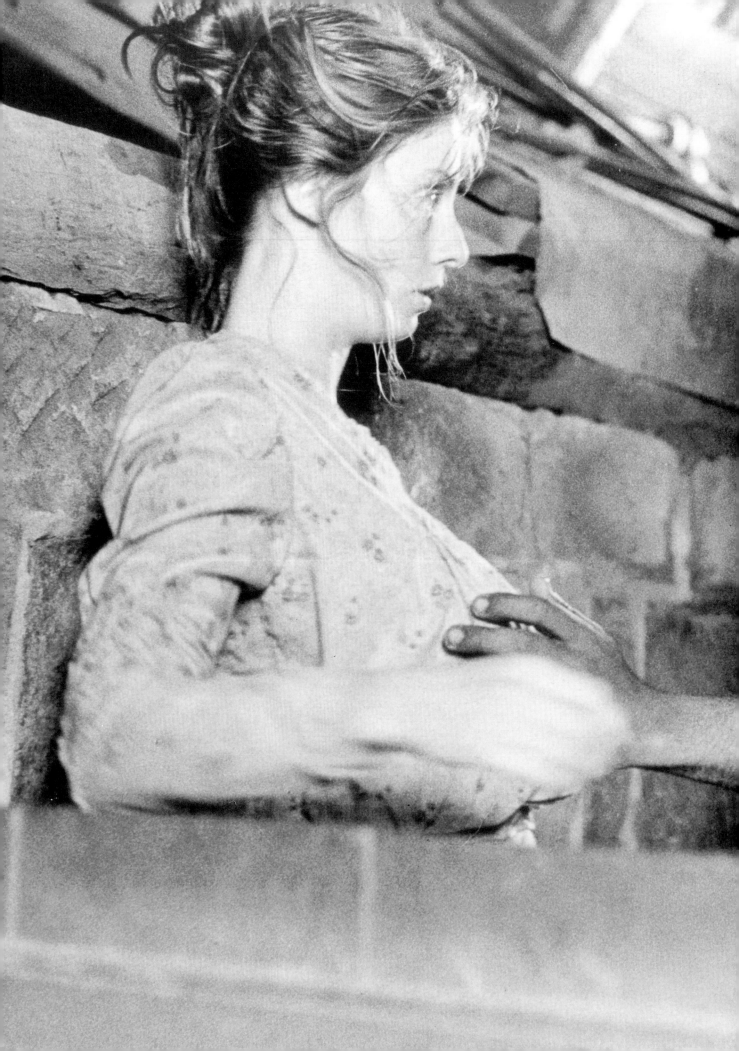

Jimmie (Tommy Lewis), right, and wife Gilda (Angela Punch). Fred Schepisi's The Chant of Jimmie Blacksmith.

JOHN D. LAMOND

THE ABC OF LOVE AND SEX AUSTRALIA STYLE

[No opening production company credit.] the ABC of Love and Sex Australia Style. © 1977 ABC of Love and Sex Film Productions. *Budget:* $70,000. *Locations:* Melbourne; Stockholm (Sweden). *Australian distributor:* Roadshow. *Video:* Roadshow. *Rating:* R (March 1978, after 3 mins and 36 secs were cut; 2387m). 35mm. 87 mins.

Producer: John D. Lamond. *Scriptwriters:* John Lamond, Alan Finney. *Director of photography:* Garry[1] Wapshott. *Production designer:* Stephen Walsh. [*Costume designer:* not credited.] *Editor:* Russell Hurley. [*Composer:* not credited.] [*Sound recordist:* not credited.] *Sound editor:* Russell Hurley. *Mixer:* Bob Gardiner.

Cast

Maj. Briht Bergström-Walan; Birgitta Almstrom[2], Robyn Bartly, Bettina Borer, Rosemarie Borg, Ian Broadbent, Leon Cosak, Ian Crow, Catherine Diás, Elizabeth Fetherstone, Marie Louise Forse, Flavio Giovangnoli, Loiuse [sic] Hemmingway, John Michael Howson, Susan Hunter, Nicholas Kislinsky, Katie Morgan, Brigid O'Donoughue, Marilyn Rodgers, Kenth Schönning, Gillian Seamer, Mawd Sundling, Peter Thompson, Stephen Walsh; Sandy Gore, Michael Cole (Narrators).

A 'liberated' young woman[3] (Katie Morgan).

The Australian film renaissance of the 1970s began with John B. Murray's **The Naked Bunyip** (1970), which proved that Australians were, after all, interested in seeing locally made films – especially if they were about sex.

Other film-makers soon followed. Tim Burstall released **Stork** in 1971 and then the enormously successful sex comedy, **Alvin Purple**, in 1973. That same year saw the release of another sex documentary, Chris Carey's **An Essay on Pornography**.

In part, these and other films reflected the liberating climate of the time, and the partial dismantlement of the previously draconian approach to film censorship. Many local films revelled in full nudity, treating sex with humour and arguing that it was not 'dirty' but life-affirming.

In 1975 came yet another documentary, John D. Lamond's **Australia After Dark**, a light-hearted look at various exotica, including nude painting, mud bathing and satanic rituals. Lamond had been an industry stalwart during the early renaissance, having been a projectionist on **The Naked Bunyip**'s country tour and working for Roadshow Film Distributors.

Following **Australia After Dark**'s commercial success, Lamond made **The ABC of**

Love and Sex Australia Style, a film even less bound by strict notions of documentary form. In fact, almost every scene is acted out by performers, from the modern and oft-naked young couple to the leotarded girls who dance around alphabet cubes and a giant phallus. The major exception is an interview with the staggeringly solemn Swedish sex researcher, Maj. Briht Bergström-Walan.

The film has an alpha-to-omega approach (A=Anatomy, B=Babies, etc.), though poor V gets ignored (surprising since Voyeurism is a concept about which director Lamond seems particularly well-suited to comment).

What is notable about this film, and others like it, is the joyousness it attributes to free sexuality, in all its forms. Though such films are viewed by many today as sexist and catering solely to male fantasies (a view contradicted by the ticket sales), films like **The ABC of Love and Sex Australia Style** were important in liberalising community attitudes to sexual matters. For example, when talking of H=Homosexuality, the narrator remarks:

Homosexuals cannot be blamed for having different sex lives. The same love, tenderness and warmth that exists in a satisfac-

tory heterosexual relationship can exist in a homosexual relationship. And, of course, there will always be a problem with homosexuality as long as an intolerant attitude to it exists.

Apart from the misguided 'with', such liberal sentiments were most welcome in antipodean Australia. All the same, the free-spirit approach does seem a touch naïve in the era of Brett Easton Ellis ('masochism is a harmless sex activity' and 'some say a good bout of masochism is hard to beat').

Still, given the American cinema's obsession in the 1980s with naked bodies as objects to be abused and mutilated, to be pierced violently by knives and cut apart by chainsaws, there is much to applaud in the 1970s' almost mystical adoration of nude bodies and sex.

SCOTT MURRAY

---

[1] On other films 'Garry' is usually spelt with only one 'r'.
[2] No character names are given in the credits.
[3] See footnote 2.

Reference
'John Lamond', an interview by Scott Murray on director John D. Lamond's work up to **Felicity**, *Cinema Papers*, no. 18, October–November 1978, pp. 94–8, 157.

BLUE FIN

South Australian Film Corporation and McElroy and McElroy present BLUE FIN. © 1978 South Australian Film Corporation. *Budget:* $750,000. *Locations:* Streaky Bay, Adelaide (South Australia). *Filmed:* June 1978. *Australian distributor:* Roadshow. *Opened:* December 1978. *Video:* Star Video. *Rating:* G (November 1978; 2413m). 35mm. 88 mins.

   Producer: Hal McElroy. *Executive producer:* Matt Carroll. *Scriptwriter:* Sonia Borg. Based on the novel by Colin Thiele. *Director of photography:* Geoffrey Burton. *Camera operator:* John Seale. *Production designer:* David Copping. [*Costume designer:* not credited.] *Editor:* Rod Adamson. *Composer:* Michael Carlos. *Sound recordist:* Don Connolly. *Sound editors:* Paul Maxwell (dia.); Ted Otton[2] (fx). *Mixer:* Phil Judd.

Cast

Hardy Kruger (Pascoe), Greg Rowe (Snook), John Jarratt (Sam), Liddy Clark (Ruth), Hugh Keays-Byrne (Stan), Alfred Bell (Geordie), Ralph Cotterill (Herbie), George Spartels (Con), Jock Owen (Jock), Elspeth Ballantyne (Mrs Pascoe), John Godden (Ockie), John Thompson (Snitch), Kelly Aitken (Pam), John Frawley (Sir Oswald), Graham Rouse (Bellamy), Terry Camilleri (Lofty), Wayne Rodda (Radio Operator), Peter Crossley (Minister), Brian Moore (Oil Company Man), Anne Mullinar (Lady Henry); the townspeople of Streaky Bay, South Australia; Max Cullen (The Pensioner).

Blue Fin is based on the Colin Thiele novel about a budding young fisherman called Snook who faces the ultimate challenge at sea when his father's tuna boat is destroyed in a cyclone. The central relationship is a strained one between the eleven-year-old Snook (Greg Rowe) and his edgy father, Pascoe (Hardy Kruger), who is set in the belief that his son will never make a fisherman. At sea, Snook finds solace in the friendship of a crewman, Sam (John Jarratt), who, as it turns out, also has a soft spot for Snook's sister, Ruth (Liddy Clark).

   While the film has the early makings of a great adventure yarn, director Carl Schultz's exploration of dramatic events and their consequences is too shallow and lacking in detail. Schultz is also too nonchalant in his treatment of a number of life-endangering incidents, including the final catastrophe. A boat fire which claims an important character is acknowledged only fleetingly by way of a radio news broadcast, then by a half-hearted search. And, later, when a number of crewmen are lost overboard, it is as if their lives were never of any consequence.

   The screenplay by Sonia Borg is somewhat too economic and does not allow much more than a superficial exploration of character and token recognition of several generic themes. The script also contains a 'mandatory' romance to help the plot along. At the same time, there are some poignant exchanges between the characters. In one scene, Mrs Pascoe (Elspeth Ballantyne) is asked what she did when her fisherman husband once went missing at sea. 'Waited', she replies in a dead-pan manner, which elucidates a universal lament of fishermen's wives. And there is an amusing moment of working-class Australians celebrating a 'Miss Tuna' ball.

   But the strengths of **Blue Fin** have much more to do with its solid production values and Geoff Burton's calm and evocative photography. Burton is particularly sensitive to the moods of the sea and those who live by it, as in the scene when a crowd of townsfolk gathers on the end of a pier to mourn the dead. In another scene, the image of bored youngsters slurping milkshakes outside a pizza shop captures precisely the monotony of life in a remote coastal town.

   For children and patient adults, the film eventually satisfies a popular cinema formula: the child who overcomes the odds and earns his rite of passage. Greg Rowe is steadfast as the young hero, though his part is lacking a wholeness that would have been achieved through more solid interaction with other characters, particularly with his aloof father.

                                    GREG KERR

----

[1] Bruce Beresford directed (uncredited) the reshoot of the key cabin sequence (see David Stratton, *The Last New Wave: The Australian Film Revival*, Angus & Robertson Publishers, Sydney, 1980, pp. 217–22).
[2] Usually spelt 'Ötton'.

References
'Sonia Borg', an interview with the scriptwriter by Paul Davies, *Cinema Papers*, no. 18, October–November 1978, pp. 108–11, 162.
'Production Report: **Blue Fin**', *Cinema Papers*, no. 19, January–February 1979, comprising an interview with director Carl Schultz, by Peter Beilby and Rod Bishop, pp. 208–9, 242–3, and an interview with composer Michael Carlos, by Rod Bishop and Cameron Allan, pp. 210–13.
'**Blue Fin**', a review by Brian McFarlane, ibid., p. 221.
'Bob Saunders', an interview with the man behind Pact Productions, one of the film's investors, by Peter Beilby, *Cinema Papers*, no. 31, March–April 1981, pp. 26–9, 100.

Pascoe (Hardy Kruger) and son Snook (Greg Rowe).

THE CHANT OF JIMMIE BLACKSMITH

[No opening production credit.[1]] THE CHANT OF JIMMIE BLACKSMITH. [© not given; atb 1978.] Produced with the assistance of the Australian Film Commission and the Victorian Film Corporation. *Budget:* $1.28 million. *Locations:* Dubbo, Gulgong, Scone, Armidale, Kempsey, Dorrigo, Bundarra, Mudgee (New South Wales); Melbourne. *Filmed:* August–November 1977. *Australian distributor:* Hoyts. *Opened:* 22 June 1978. *Video:* Thorn EMI Video. *Rating:* M (classified R in April 1978, but rating reduced to M on 3 May; 3284m). 35mm. Panavision. 120 mins.

Producer: Fred Schepisi. *Associate producer:* Roy Stevens. *Scriptwriter:* Fred Schepisi. Based on the novel by Thomas Keneally. *Director of photography:* Ian Baker. *Production designer:* Wendy Dickson. *Costume designer:* Bruce Finlayson. *Editor:* Brian Kavanagh. *Composer:* Bruce Smeaton. *Sound recordist:* Bob Allen. *Sound editors:* Peter Burgess, William Anderson, Dean Gawen. *Mixer:* Gerry Humphries.

Cast

Tommy Lewis [Jimmie[2]], Freddy Reynolds [Mort], Ray Barrett [Farrell], Jack Thompson [Rev. Neville], Angela Punch[3] [Gilda]; Steve Dodds; Peter Carroll [McCready]; Don Crosby [Newby], Elizabeth Alexander [Miss Graf], Peter Sumner [Dowie Stead], Tim Robertson [Healey], Ray Meagher [Dud Edmonds], Brian Anderson [Hyberry], Jane Harders [Mrs Healey], Jack Charles [Uncle Tabidgi], Arthur Dignam [Man in Butcher Shop], Robyn Nevin [Mrs McCready], Brian[4] Brown [Shearer], Ian Gilmour [Eddie], John Jarratt[5] [Michaels].

Jimmie Blacksmith[6] (Tommy Lewis) is inevitably and tragically caught between the white society to which he aspires and the Aboriginal life which the white man has irreversibly corrupted. As a half-caste, Jimmie is constantly being exploited by the white bosses whose approval he so conscientiously seeks and is cut off from the natural world of his black ancestors. Pushed beyond endurance when his latest employers, the Newbys, withhold food from him and his hapless white wife, Gilda (Angela Punch), in an attempt to persuade her to leave Jimmie, he embarks on a bloodbath from which there is no turning back. Taking to the bush with his full-black half-brother Mort (Freddy Reynolds), Jimmie finds only temporary concealment but no comfort, and

his bloody end coincides with the birth of Australian nationhood and talk of federation.

Fred Schepisi's film version of Thomas Keneally's spare, powerful novel is passionately committed to its subject. Unlike most of the other period pieces of the late 1970s, **The Chant of Jimmie Blacksmith** deals with a matter of pressing moral concern – the destruction of a race – rather than nostalgic re-creation of times past. The film's imagery powerfully evokes Jimmie's oppression by the white world and his estrangement from the grimly beautiful landscape through which he flees. Schepisi's screenplay was sometimes criticised for announcing its themes with an undue explicitness, the more apparent by contrast with the mute eloquence of the film's *mise-en-scène*.

The Chant of Jimmie Blacksmith, budgeted at more than $1.2 million, was the most expensive Australian film made up to that time. As well as the Australian Film Commission and the Victorian Film Corporation (now Film Victoria), the film's financial backers included Hoyts Theatres, making its first production investment in the New Australian Cinema. However, despite the publicity attending the film's making and despite generally glowing reviews, the film failed commercially. It may be that it touches too raw a communal nerve for box-office popularity, or that its protagonist's failure to find a way out of his dilemma makes it too downbeat for ready identification. For whatever reason, the film has been under-valued by Australian audiences; overseas, it was highly praised by British and American critics, including

Pauline Kael who excepted it from her judgement of the overall blandness of Australian films. And it secured a *succès d'estime* for itself and created a major breakthrough in overseas recognition of the New Australian Cinema when it was invited into the official Competition at Cannes in 1978.

BRIAN MCFARLANE

1 There is an end credit which reads, 'Produced through The Film House[,] Melbourne, Australia, with the assistance of The AFC[,] The Victorian Film Corporation [and] Hoyts Theatres Ltd'.
2 There are no character names given in the end film credits. These are taken from press material and should be 'read' accordingly. They are listed in the order of actors given on the film.
3 Later to be known as the sometimes hyphenated Angela Punch McGregor.
4 Usually spelt 'Bryan Brown'.
5 Usually spelt 'John Jarratt'.
6 See footnote 2.
7 See footnote 2.

References
'Production Report: **The Chant of Jimmie Blacksmith**', *Cinema Papers*, no. 15, January 1978, incorporating an interview with scriptwriter–producer–director Fred Schepisi, by David Rowe and Scott Murray, pp. 244–6, 269, and an interview with director of photography Ian Baker, by Scott Murray, pp. 247–9.
'**The Chant of Jimmie Blacksmith**', a review by Brian McFarlane, *Cinema Papers*, no. 17, August – September 1978, pp. 58–9.
'Fred Schepisi: Pushing the Boundaries', a career interview by Scott Murray, *Cinema Papers*, no. 80, August 1990, pp. 28–42.
'The **Jimmy** [sic] **Blacksmith** Ban', a report on union action by the ATAEA by Martha Ansara, *Filmnews*, May 1978, p. 1.

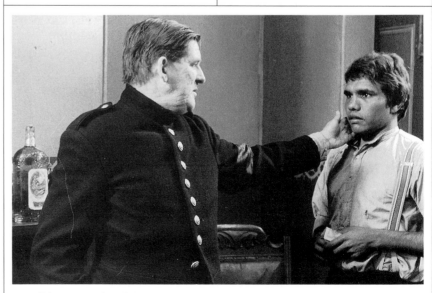

Farrell (Ray Barrett) and Jimmie[7] (Tommy Lewis).

THE IRISHMAN

Michael (Simon Burke) and Paddy Doolan (Michael Craig).

Australian Film Commission [and] GU Film Distributors present A Forest Home Films–South Australian Film Corporation Production. THE IRISHMAN. © 1978 A Forest Home Film. *Budget:* $767,000. *Locations:* Charters Towers, Bluff Downs, Mingela, Ravenswood (Queensland). *Filmed:* May–July 1977. *Australian distributor:* GUO. *Opened:* 28 February 1978. *Video:* Australian Video. *Rating:* NRC (December 1977; 2963m[1]). 35mm. 108 mins.

Producer: Anthony Buckley. *Scriptwriter:* Donald Crombie. Based on the novel by Elizabeth O'Conner. *Director of photography:* Peter James. *Camera operator:* John Seale. *Production designer:* Owen Williams. *Costume designer:* Judith Dorsman. *Editor:* Tim Wellburn. *Composer:* Charles Marawood. *Sound recordist:* Gary Wilkins. *Sound editor:* Bob Cogger. *Mixer:* Peter Fenton.

Cast

Michael Craig (Paddy Doolan), Simon Burke (Michael Doolan), Robyn Nevin (Jenny Doolan), Lou Brown (Will Doolan), Tui Bow (Granny Doolan), Andrew Maguire (Grandpa Doolan), Gerard Kennedy (Chad Logan), Tony Barry (Robert Dalgleish), Marcella Burgoyne (Mrs Dalgleish), Bryan Brown (Eric Haywood), Roberta Grant (Mrs Bailey Clark), Tina McMahon (Bo-Bo).

Teamster Paddy Doolan (Michael Craig) is unwilling to admit that the days of the Clydesdale-hauled wagons are numbered, their function about to be supplanted by the likes of the transport lorries owned by Eric Haywood (Bryan Brown). Paddy is a man locked in a more heroic past, as he sees it, and this brings him into conflict, not only with the changing, more mechanised times, but with his family as well. His older son, Will (Lou Brown), has left home, refusing to join Paddy in partnership; his younger son, Michael (Simon Burke), remains loyal to Paddy, whose death in an accident pushes Michael into premature manhood and responsibility.

The Irishman has a good deal in common with the mainstream of the New Australian Cinema of the 1970s. Its great strength is in the visual beauty of its evocation of recent Australian history: the earlier years of this century in outback Queensland are given a golden glow of affectionate recollection. Adapted from a novel (like many films of its period), it is set in a past which is depicted with nostalgia rather than sharp scrutiny; and, again like many key films of the revival, it is centred on a youthful search for adulthood. Perhaps in a burgeoning national cinema, such as Australia in the later 1970s seemed to be aspiring to, it is not surprising to find a pre-occupation both with its past and with the processes of maturation.

The film also shares the episodic structuring principles of other rites-of-passage fictions of the New Australian Cinema. The fact that it is not as dramatically strong as it is visually impressive may perhaps be attributed to its failure to locate more centrally the figure of Michael, under pressure to assume a premature responsibility. The character of Paddy, vigorously played by British actor Michael Craig, dominates the first half of the film, then disappears for most of the second half while Michael searches literally for him and metaphorically for replacement father figures. It is, therefore, Michael who alone might have pulled together the often attractive, affectionately observed pictures of a disintegrating family life.

BRIAN MCFARLANE

---

[1] The Censorship bulletin lists the length at 2907.58m but an AFC brochure gives it as 2963m, which appears correct.

References

'The Irishman', a production report by Barry Tucker (with extracts from reports to the investors), *Cinema Papers*, no. 15, January 1978, pp. 117–20.

'The Irishman', a review by Susan Dermody, *Cinema Papers*, no. 16, April–June 1978, pp. 355.

LITTLE BOY LOST

Summit (International) Films presents LIT-TLE BOY LOST. © 1978 John Powell Productions and Others Limited, Partnership. *Budget:* $395,000. *Location:* Armidale (New South Wales). *Filmed:* April–June 1978. *Australian distributor:* Filmways. *Opened:* 16 November 1978 (Armidale); 1979 in Sydney. *Video:* Filmways. *Rating:* G (November 1978; 2468.7m). 35mm. 90 mins.

Producer: Alan Spires. *Scriptwriter:* Terry Bourke. Based on the story by John Powell and Suzanne Taylor. *Director of photography:* Ray Henman. *Camera operators:* Bob McDonald, Kevan Lind, Louis Irving. *Production designer:* Bruce Barber. *Wardrobe:* Robyn Hall, Robyn Schuurmans, Lesley McLennan. *Supervising editor:* Ron Williams. *Editor:* Doris Haller. *Composer:* Bob Young. *Sound recordists:* Phil Judd, Ron Green. *Sound editors:* Max Lemon, Andrew Stuart. *Mixer:* Phil Heywood.

Cast

John Hargreaves (Jacko Walls[2]), Nathan Dawes (Stephen Walls), Lorna Lesley (Dorrie Walls), Tony Barry (Sergeant Jack O'Dea), James Elliott (Harry Tickle), Les Foxcroft ('Grumps'), John Jarratt (Vic Tanner), Robert Quilter (Roy Grills), Don Crosby (Cyril Grills), John Nash (Wally Westley), Brian Anderson (Sergeant Fred Mason), Redmond Phillips (Canon Pritchard), Bernadette Hughson (Aunt Pat), Ray Marshall (Hotelkeeper), Julie Dawson (Ruth Tanner), Max Osbiston (Inspector James), Steve Dodd (Tracker Bindi), Mark Hashfield (Reporter).

Based on a true story, Terry Bourke's **Little Boy Lost** is not a film one will be lost in. The story focuses not so much on the misadventure of four-year-old Stephen Walls (Nathan Dawes), when he gets lost in the outback, as on the simpleness and essentially stereotyped nature of the country people.

All the people of Stephen's town, and the neighbouring ones far and wide (an element of a fairy-tale here), gather to search for the boy. Many have come from downing the odd beer and they produce such a noise as they yodel, stumble and curse their way through the bush that Stephen goes into hiding. Without this fateful element, the search would be over. In fact, the search takes four days, the length of time Stephen is able to successfully evade his rescuers. With so many people around, he ceases to be lost and is in fact playing a not-so-funny game of hide-and-seek.

The two recurring motifs in this film are an eagle and religion. The sudden close-ups of the eagle and the less subtle ploy of over-emphasised symbolism, coupled with loud **Psycho**-style music[3], makes an uncomfortable connection between life and death and the boy and his searchers. Religion, the other motif, is looked at through a cynical eye. When Canon Pritchard (Redmond Phillips) visits Dorrie Walls (Lorna Lesley), the insignificant and helpless mother of the boy, his bland dialogue is not reassuring in the circumstances: 'Stephen could be with our heavenly father'; 'I notice you haven't wept. I think you should'; and 'It's God's will.' Shots of the country folk praying and exercising faith are juxtaposed with Pritchard's pre-empting death.

There are many irrelevant scenes, the most obvious one being where Tracker Bindi (Steve Dodd), an Aboriginal, is introduced – yet another tired reinforcement of a false stereotype. By the middle of the film, the benign conversations ensure that boredom has set in. Bourke's attempts at tension, when the rescuers are close to Stephen, also fail. What was possibly an endearing true-life story has no cinematic energy here to propel it along.

SUZANNE BROWN

---

[1] Bourke replaced the original director, John Powell, during filming. Some of Powell's work remains.

[2] Some of the character names come from a cast list supplied by the director, as not all of the credits on the available video were readable.

[3] The music for **Psycho** (Alfred Hitchcock, 1960) was by Bernard Hermann.

Reference
'Little Boy Lost', a review by Margaret McClusky, *Cinema Papers*, no. 20, March–April 1979, pp. 305–6.

Jacko Walls (John Hargreaves) and Stephen (Nathan Dawes).

MOUTH TO MOUTH

Vega Film Productions presents MOUTH to MOUTH. [© not given; atb 1978.] *Budget:* $129,000. *Location:* Melbourne. *Filmed:* June–July 1977. Made with the assistance of the Victorian Film Corporation. *Australian distributor:* Greg Lynch Film Distributors. *Opened:* July 1978. *Video:* Greg Lynch. *Rating:* M (May 1978; 2633m). 16mm (blown up to 35mm). 96 mins.

Producer: John Sainken. *Co-producer:* John Duigan. *Scriptwriter:* John Duigan. *Director of photography:* Tom Cowan. *Production designer:* Tracey Watt. *Wardrobe:* Christina MacKay. *Editor:* Tony Paterson. *Composer:* Roy Ritchie. *Sound recordist:* Lloyd Carrick. [*Sound editor:* not credited.] *Mixer:* Steve Edwards.

Cast

Kim Krejus (Carrie), Sonia Peat (Jeanie), Ian Gilmour (Tim), Sergio Frazzetto (Serge), Walter Pym (Fred), Michael Carmen (Tony); Roz de Winter, Thea Pritchard (Social Welfare Officers); Neil McColl (Mangles), Peter Finlay (Daryl), Robynne Bourne (Susan), Lorraine West (Anne), Dominic Marafioti (Giovanni), Peter Ashby (Milkshake Customer); Janys Hayes, Shona Stephen, Jayne Craig (Girls in Training Centre); Jack Brown (Jeanie's Customer), Joan Letch (Jeanie's Neighbour), Stacey Malinoff (Cashier), Joanne Barker (Salesgirl), Roy Edmonds (Shop Detective), Shirley Lester (Woman in House), Mary Charleston (Massage Parlour Girl); Peter Felmingham, Tom Broadbridge (Detectives).

M ore than any other of John Duigan's films of the 1970s, **Mouth to Mouth** best represents the transitional stage of much of the thematic preoccupations that have given his work commercial and critical success through the 1980s. **The Firm Man** (1975) and **The Trespassers** (1976) are not unlike **Mouth to Mouth** in that all are predominantly concerned with interpersonal relationships, yet the story environments of the former are somewhat vacuous in terms of how the action unfolds. **Mouth to Mouth**, on the other hand, fills out the screen with strong elements of social determinism affecting the relationships of four outcast teenagers. Later in his career, in films such as **The Year My Voice Broke** (1987) and **Flirting** (1991), interpersonal relationships develop through vaguely spiritual and psychological forms of determinism.

The film revolves around four homeless, unemployed youths attempting to scratch an emotional and reasonably 'civil' existence

Tim(Ian Gilmour) and Carrie (Kim Krejus) .

out of the wasteland of a heavily industrialised urban environment. The four characters consist of two boys from the country, Serge (Sergio Frazzetto) and Tim (Ian Gilmour), in the city to find work, and two girls, Carrie (Kim Krejus) and Jeanie (Sonia Peat), who are runaways from a girls' reformatory. They meet and, due to their difficult social positions, form an alliance in order to provisionally keep at bay the harsh realities of an indifferent and uncaring society.

Duigan is acutely watchful of character development and character interaction in respect of the paradoxes these four youngsters face when confronting the vicissitudes of a hostile, emotionally and intellectually alienating society. Not only are they forced into an alternative niche of existence, the parameters of which are established by the environment, they find themselves continually drawn out of their 'haven' by the elements that place them there in the first place.

Furthermore, Duigan is also acutely aware of accommodating his subject matter to the limitations of budget. **Mouth to Mouth** was made for $129,000 and yet

Duigan is able to achieve a sense of social and ideological critique, and maintain dramatic tension with subject matter that is well served by an *art brut* style: gritty surface, disconcerting compositions, episodic development, rapid cutting of sequences (as opposed to the distinctive use of long takes in his later films), atonal use of natural sound, and juicing baroque sensibilities out of minimalist acting.

RAFFAELE CAPUTO

References

'John Duigan on **Mouth to Mouth**', an interview with the scriptwriter–director by Scott Murray, *Cinema Papers*, no. 16, April–June 1978, pp. 312–15, 377.

'**Mouth to Mouth**', a review by Jack Clancy, ibid., p. 356.

'Greg Lynch: The Middle Ground', an interview with the distributor by Scott Murray, *Cinema Papers*, no. 31, March–April 1981, pp. 36–9, 71.

'**Mouth to Mouth**', reviewed by Steven Wallace, *Filmnews*, September 1977, p. 18.

'Ethics of the Outsider', an interview with John Duigan by Albert Moran, *Filmnews*, April 1984, pp. 10–12.

NEWSFRONT

Palm Beach Pictures in association with [the] N.S.W. Film Corporation[,] Australian Film Commission [and] Village Roadshow presents NEWSFRONT. © 1978 Palm Beach Pictures. *Budget:* $600,000. *Locations:* Sydney, Narrabeen, country New South Wales. *Filmed:* October–November 1977. *Australian distributor:* Roadshow. *Opened:* 29 July 1978. *Video:* CEL Australian Video. *Rating:* NRC (May 1978; 3018.3m). 35mm. Colour and B&W. 110 mins.

Producer: David Elfick. *Associate producer:* Richard Brennan. *Scriptwriter:* Phillip Noyce.[1] Based on an original screenplay by Bob Ellis. From a concept by David Elfick [and, uncredited, Philippe Mora]. *Director of photography:* Vincent Monton. *Camera operator:* Louis Irving. *Production designer:* Lisa[2] Coote. *Costumes:* Norma Moriceau. *Editor:* John Scott. *Composer:* William Motzing. *Sound recordist:* Tim Lloyd. *Sound editor:* Greg Bell. *Mixers:* Peter Fenton, Julian Ellingworth, Berry Van Bronkhorst.

Cast

Bill Hunter (Len Maguire), Wendy Hughes (Amy McKenzie), Gerard Kennedy (Frank Maguire), Chris Haywood (Chris Hewitt), John Ewart (Charlie Henderson), Angela Punch[3] (Fay Maguire), Don Crosby (A. G. Marwood), Bryan Brown (Geoff the Editor), John Clayton (Cliff the Production Manager), Lorna Lesley (Ellie), John Dease (Ken the Narrator), Drew Forsythe (Bruce the Second Editor), Tony Barry (Greasy the Sound Mixer), Mark Holden (Len's New Assistant), Alexander Archdale (Sir Charles), Bill Lyle (Macka the Projectionist), Paul Jones (Charlie's Assistant); Bruce Spence, Les Foxcroft (Redex Trial Drivers); Robyn Moase (Dinah), John Flaus (Father Coughlan), Chad Morgan (Redex Singer).

After opening with a spectacular montage of newsreel footage, Newsfront establishes a rivalry between two newsreel companies. The leading cameraman for Cinetone is Len Maguire (Bill Hunter). Around him are, among others, his ambitious brother, Frank (Gerard Kennedy), Frank's girlfriend, Amy (Wendy Hughes), and the 'hard but fair' studio boss, A. G. Marwood (Don Crosby), who represent some of the particular traits of working Australians. The rival company, Newsco, is personified by an irascible cameraman, Charlie Henderson (John Ewart).

The film moves through several time spans, each focusing on a major item of news in Australia: the referendum to ban the Communist Party, the Redex round-Australia car trial, the Maitland floods and the Olympic Games. Parallel with this are the events of Len's personal life, including the birth of his children and the deteriorating relationship with his strict Catholic wife, his brother's decision to head for America and his relationship with his young assistant, Chris (Chris Haywood), an English migrant whose fling with a girl (Lorna Lesley) in the outback leads to a quick marriage before the lad dies accidentally during the floods.

By the mid-1950s, television has arrived and Newsco has been forced to merge with its rival, though Len, on the brink of resignation and in a now unsatisfying relationship with Amy, is offered a major opportunity to film the Olympic Games in Melbourne. Finally, Len finds himself alone, with his integrity intact, as all about him have 'fallen', and he marches off to an uncertain future holding the most valuable scoop footage he has ever shot.

Newsfront is constructed from newsreel footage and newly-filmed material which is integrated with seamless effect into a continuous narrative. It also incorporates characters closely based on some of the leading figures of the film industry, with the most easily recognisable being Ken G. Hall personified as the studio head A. G. Marwood.

The film employs effective shorthand methods of dramatising issues, largely through the dialogue by Bob Ellis (who removed his name from the credits but took out newspaper advertisements reclaiming his work when the film won the AFI Award for Best Film). This allows for a certain glibness and facility with argumentation that is not exactly common among ordinary working Australians. Nevertheless, it is extraordinarily effective. Equally important is the film's easy and laconic humour,
making it one of the few films to capture the Australian ability to use a low-key sarcasm for humour.

Essentially, Newsfront encapsulates the passing of an earlier time. It is a lament for the prickly working man of deep integrity and loyalty, the man doing his job with a sense of honour. It represents a passing era as loud-mouthed American multinationals take over our industry (brilliantly captured in the return of brother Frank, complete with American accent and mispronouncing 'Mel-bourne'). Newsfront remains luminous in the memory, standing the test of time better than almost any other film from that golden mid-'70s period of youthful exuberance and vitality.

GEOFF GARDNER

---

[1] Despite the fact all the other major credits are at the front, the scriptwriter credit is at the end.
[2] Usually spelt 'Lissa'.
[3] Punch later changed her surname to the sometimes hyphenated Punch McGregor.

References
'Phil Noyce: Interview', an interview with the co-scriptwriter–director by Mary Moody, *Cinema Papers*, no. 14, October 1977, pp. 111–13, 191.
'Production Report: **Newsfront**', *Cinema Papers*, no. 17, August–September 1978, comprising an account of the filming by Phillip Noyce, p. 46, and a storyboard of the Maitland flood sequence, pp. 47–9.
'**Newsfront**', a review by Keith Connolly, ibid., pp. 57–8.
'Selling **Newsfront**', a marketing analysis by Michael Harvey, *Cinema Papers*, no. 22, July–August 1979, pp. 436–9, 477.
'Bob Ellis', a career interview with the co-scriptwriter by Richard Brennan, *Cinema Papers*, no. 29, October–November 1980, pp. 314–19, 386.
'**Newsfront**: an interview with Phil Noyce', Ken Cameron, *Filmnews*, August 1978, pp. 10–12.

Frank Maguire (Gerard Kennedy) and Amy McKenzie (Wendy Hughes).

Cameramen Len Maguire (Bill Hunter) and Chris Hewitt (Chris Haywood).

RICHARD FRANKLIN

PATRICK

AIFC [and] Antony I. Ginnane in association with Filmways Australia presents [sic] for Australian International Film Corporation PATRICK. © 1977 AIFC. Made in association with the AFC and the Victorian Film Corporation. *Budget:* $400,000. *Location:* Melbourne. *Filmed:* late 1977. *Australian distributor:* Filmways. *Opened:* 1 October 1978. *Video:* Video Classics. *Rating:* M (May 1978; 3154m). 35mm. 115 mins.

Producers: Antony I. Ginnane, Richard Franklin. *Executive producer:* William Fayman. *Scriptwriter:* Everett de Roche[1]. *Director of photography:* Don McAlpine. *Camera operators:* Dan Burstall, John Endacott. *Production designer:* Leslie Binns. *Wardrobe:* Kevin Regan. *Editor:* Edward McQueen-Mason. *Composer:* Brian May. *Sound recordist:* Paul Clark. *Sound editor:* Edward McQueen-Mason. *Mixer:* Peter Fenton.

Cast

Susan Penhaligon (Kathy Jacquard), Robert Helpmann (Dr Roget), Rod Mullinar (Ed Jacquard), Julia Blake (Matron Cassidy), Helen Hemingway (Sister Williams), Bruce Barry (Brian Wright), Robert Thompson (Patrick), Maria Mercedes (Nurse Panicale), Walter Pym (Captain Fraser), Frank Wilson (Detective Sgt. Grant), Carole-Ann Aylett (Patrick's Mother), Paul Young (Lover), Marilyn Rodgers (Day Desk Nurse), John Murphy (Barman), Ray Chubb (S.E.C. Worker), Everett de Roche (S.E.C. Worker), Peter Culpen (Detective), Gillian Seemer (Nurse).

'One hundred and sixty pounds of limp meat hanging from a comatose brain' is how Dr Roget (Robert Helpmann) diagnoses Patrick (Robert Thompson), who has been in this death-in-life condition for three years in a hospital for the psychologically disturbed. Having electrocuted his mother and her lover by throwing a glowing radiator into their bath, he now makes contact with the world only through the typewriter operated by nurse Kathy Jacquard (Susan Penhaligon), for whom he appears to have conceived a passion. This passion leads to various psychokinetic phenomena involving staff and patients at the hospital.

A synopsis of the plot of **Patrick** scarcely does it much service and a dozen years after its release it still looks like one of the liveliest films of the Australian revival. Unlike many of its contemporaries, it simply trusts the narrative structures and paraphernalia of melodrama. Director Richard Franklin, scriptwriter Everett de Roche and director of photography Don McAlpine all know how to maximise the twin elements of suspense and surprise; and the cast enters engagingly into vivifying such stereotypes as the plucky heroine, the neurotic matron and the eccentric doctor. There are pleasing Gothic touches in the setting and in the juxtaposition of the everyday and the bizarre.

No Australian film-maker deserves a more thorough-going critical rehabilitation than Richard Franklin. Never attracted to lofty themes, nostalgic period pieces or to celebrations of local mythology, Franklin has persistently shown himself one of the most adroit directorial talents of the revival. His films have been obdurately underrated, dismissed as transPacific, as being patently commercial – as if either of those epithets (if true) precluded quality. What he does offer is a cinephile's pleasure in the exercise of the medium and a firm grasp of its narrative traditions: he can tell a story fluidly and wittily, and he can invoke a whole range of film experience without succumbing to mere homage. **Patrick**, **Roadgames** (1981), **Psycho II** (1983), **Cloak and Dagger** (1984) and **Link** (1986): not many directors have made five such lively entertainments in the past decade or so.[2]

BRIAN MCFARLANE

---

1 One of several spellings (de Roche, De Roche, DeRoche). Usually De Roche.
2 Franklin has since directed, in the US, **FX/2** (1991), oddly re-titled **FX2: The Deadly Art of Illusion** in Australia.

References

'**Patrick** – Special Effects: An Interview with Conrad Rothman', the special effects supervisor, by Dennis Nicholson, Peter Beilby and Scott Murray, *Cinema Papers*, no. 16, April–June 1978, pp. 303–5, 377.

'Brian May', an interview with the conductor by Ivan Hutchinson, *Cinema Papers*, no. 17, August–September 1978, pp. 32–3.

'**Patrick**', a review by Brian McFarlane, *Cinema Papers*, no. 18, October–November 1978, pp. 141–2.

'Antony I. Ginnane', an interview with the producer by Peter Beilby and Scott Murray, *Cinema Papers*, no. 19, January–February 1979, pp. 174–9, 234–7.

'Everett De Roche', a career interview with the scriptwriter by Paul Davies, *Cinema Papers*, no. 25, February–March 1980, pp. 30–3, 76, 78.

'**Patrick** – another step-sister', a review by Martha Ansara, *Filmnews*, November 1978, p. 11.

Electrocuted: Patrick's Mother (Carole-Ann Aylett) and Lover (Paul Young).

SOLO

A Hannay–Williams Production. SOLO.
© 1977 David Hannay–Tony Williams
Productions Pty Ltd. *Budget:* $250,000.
Location: Waimarama (New Zealand).
Filmed: February–March 1977. An
Australia–New Zealand Co-production.
Australian distributor: Film Scholars.
Opened: June 1978. *Video:* CEL. *Rating:*
NRC (March 1978; 2688m). 35mm. 96 mins.

Producers: David Hannay, Tony
Williams. *Executive producers:* Bill Sheat,
John Sturzaker. *Associate producer:* Tony
Troke. *Scriptwriters:* Tony Williams, Martyn
Sanderson. *Director of photography:* John
Blick. *Production designer:* Paul Carvell.
Wardrobe supervisor: Christine Reynolds.
Editor: Tony Williams. *Music:* Robbie Laven
& Marion Arts; Dave Fraser; Furber Meyer
& Charig. *Sound recordist:* Robert Allen.
Sound editor: Dell King. *Mixers:* Phil Judd;
Phil Heywood (asst).

Cast

Martyn Sanderson (Jules), Lisa Peers (Judy
Ballantyne), Jock Spence (Radio Operator),
Vincent Gil (Paul Robinson), Perry
Armstrong (Billy Robinson), Frances
Edmund (School Teacher), Uncle Roy (Man
on Bike), Davina Whitehouse (Rohana
Beaulieu), Maxwell Fernie (Crispin
Beaulieu), Gillian Hope (Woman on Train),
Veronica Lawrence (Sue), Val Murphy
(Anita).

Judy Ballantyne (Lisa Peers) and Paul Robinson (Vincent Gil).

Solo, the first Australian–New Zealand
feature co-production, is a deceptively
straightforward film. It contains an unconventional aerial courtship, the obligatory
romantic idyll, exotic settings, and the regrettable but necessary separation. What is most
noteworthy is the way in which these elements weave through a series of interlocking
motifs and metaphors which examine
notions about the past and present, and
about self-isolation and mutual needs.

Paul Robinson (Vincent Gil), an aerial
spotter pilot, spends most of his working life
in the solitary confines of his cockpit, flying
over the vast pine forests of New Zealand's
north island. One day, he almost arrests Judy
Ballantyne (Lisa Peers), a young hitch-hiker,
for illegally lighting a fire. Then, when Judy
is stranded on a highway outside a nearby
town, Paul's precocious adolescent son, Billy
(Perry Armstrong), invites her to spend the
night at their house. The next day, after some
reluctance on Judy's part, she and Bill set off
with Paul on a trip in his restored Tiger
Moth.

It is on this journey that the relationships

begin to alter. An oil leak forces the plane
down and they spend time with the
Beaulieus, an eccentric, cultured old couple
struggling to run an organic farm.

Sensing an intimate bond developing
between his father and Judy, Billy steals the
plane and crash-lands, narrowly escaping
injury. Judy returns home and begins to
question her intentions in relation to Paul,
and, after an emotionally explosive confrontation verging on violence, she flees into
the night.

Although the details of Paul's past remain
purposely obscure – except for a photograph
hinting at a previous marriage – it emerges
that he is a man whose expectations and
codes of conduct have been shaped by the
cultural sensibilities prevalent in the 1950s.
In contrast, Judy is a young woman clearly
linked to some of the major preoccupations
of the flourishing counterculture of the late
1960s.

Solo is a film as much concerned with
detailing personal relationships as it is with
situating those relationships in some kind
of temporal process – the past confronting
the present with the resulting uncertainty
and contradictions in behaviour. Some of
the most engaging and sensitively drawn
sequences are directly related to the effort
necessary to manage the interplay between
self-containment and a desire for personal
contact.

The use of landscape and space also plays
an important part in conveying the solitude
that pervades the lives of these people. It
must, however, be added that there are
sequences in the film which are not completely successful and detract appreciably
from the overall atmosphere generated: the
opening scene comes across like a car chase
out of *Homicide* and the lengthy speech on
the 'romantic period' is unnecessarily
explanatory.

Perhaps the most satisfying aspect of **Solo**
is the exploration of what C. Wright Mills
has called the intersection of biography and
history, the fact that individual circumstances
and problems are linked inextricably with
larger social ones. Mills writes that people
'do not usually define the troubles they
endure in terms of historical change or institutional contradiction'. In a small way, the
film attempts to redress this situation.

JOHN LANGER[1]

---

[1] Extracted from Langer's review in *Cinema Papers*
(see References).

References
'Solo', a production report by Mary Moody, comprising interviews with producer David Hannay,
director Tony Williams and actors Lisa Peers
and Vincent Gil, *Cinema Papers*, no. 13, July
1977, pp. 62–6.
'Solo', a review by John Langer, *Cinema Papers*,
no. 17, August–September 1978, p. 63.

THIRD PERSON PLURAL

[No opening production company credit.] THIRD PERSON PLURAL. *Alternative title*: 'Volita' (working). © 1978 Abraxas Films. *Budget*: $35,600. *Location*: Sydney. *Australian distributor*: Abraxas Films. *Video*: not released. *Rating*: M (classified June 1978 at 1086m, then in July 1978 at 1009m). 16mm. 92 mins.

Producers: Greg Ricketson, John Weiley. *Scriptwriter*: James Ricketson, in association with the actors. *Director of photography*: Tom Cowan. [*Production designer*: not credited.] [*Costume designer*: not credited.] *Editor*: Christopher Cordeaux. [*Composer*: not credited.] *Sound recordist*: Kevin Kearney. [*Sound editor*: not credited.] *Sound mix*: A.P.A. Leisure Time International.

Cast

Bryan Brown (Mark), Margaret Cameron (Beth), George Shevtsov (Terry), Linden Wilkinson (Danny), David Cameron (Toby), Elaine Hudson (Girl in Park), Martha Ansara (Video Assistant), Joachim McLean (Joachim), Naomi Kelly (Naomi Kelly).

In **Third Person Plural**, four young people 'get to know each other' through ceaseless conversation during weekends away on a yacht. There is Beth (Margaret Cameron) – naïve, not-too-bright, whose greatest dream is to have a farm with goats and make patchwork quilts; Danny (Linden Wilkinson) – the do-gooder and documentary filmmaker, who is working on a video about old people; Mark (Bryan Brown) – serious, self-absorbed, very concerned about 'the meaning of it all'; and Terry (George Shevtsov) – the carefree, good-natured boat owner.

After some time in the boat, Beth realises she is in love with Terry, which causes some problems as she also loves her husband, Toby (David Cameron), who stays at home on weekends, presumably to finish off work for Monday and look after the baby. She arranges to leave home so she can be with Terry, but finds he isn't that serious – all of which is not particularly traumatic, because everyone is very gentle and understanding, or perhaps too bland, for any other reaction.

Meanwhile, things are developing between Danny and Mark. But there is some conflict when Mark questions Danny's motives in her documentary film-making. He regards the work as insensitive and challenges the sureness of her opinion that people can be made happier if they only work to bring about change. 'But what *is* happiness? How do you define it?', he asks earnestly.

The script was devised by director James Ricketson and the actors during a workshop, and some of the dialogue appears to have been improvised at the time of filming. The conversation (and there certainly isn't much else occurring) tends to centre on the inconsequential ('Who brought the watermelon?' 'Have you seen my glass?' 'Shall I tie the knot here?') or attempts to shed light on the grand issues ('But why are we *here*?' 'What's the reason for it all?' 'I can't help asking why.'), with little else in between.

The dialogue is frequently clumsy, boring and/or irritating. Mark's anxious expression and constant harping on 'What does it all mean?' eventually becomes quite absurd. Surely people concerned with such matters just don't talk about them in this way.

There is not much subtlety, a lot of repetition and the little that happens is predictable and unilluminating. What we learn about the characters is from their conversation only – there are few situations or incidents which allow their reactions to be revealed.

ROBIN ANDERSON[1]

---

[1] Extracted from Robin Anderson's review in *Cinema Papers* (see References).

References

'Poor Cinema', an analysis of low-budget filmmaking, including notes on the making of **Third Person Plural**, then called 'Volita', by scriptwriter–director James Ricketson, *Cinema Papers*, no. 16, April–June 1978, pp. 316–17.

'Third Person Plural', a review by Robin Anderson, *Cinema Papers*, no. 19, January–February 1979, pp. 223–4.

'Bryan Brown', a career interview with the actor by Barbara Alysen, *Cinema Papers*, no. 31, March–April 1981, pp. 14–19.

'Towards a Poor Cinema', James Ricketson, a precursor to his *Cinema Papers* article and written before filming, *Filmnews*, November 1977, p. 9.

Terry (George Shevtsov), Danny (Linden Wilkinson) and Mark (Bryan Brown).

WEEKEND OF SHADOWS

Samson Productions [and the] South Australian Film Corporation in association with [the] Australian Film Commission present WEEKEND OF SHADOWS. © 1977 Samson Productions Pty Limited. *Budget:* $500,000. *Location:* Macclesfield (South Australia). *Filmed:* July–August 1977. *Australian distributor:* Roadshow. *Opened:* 12 April 1978. *Video:* Australian Video. *Rating:* M (February 1978; 2605.85m). 35mm. 95 mins.

Producers: Tom Jeffrey, Matt Carroll. *Associate producer:* Sue Milliken. *Scriptwriter:* Peter Yeldham. Adapted from the novel *The Reckoning* by Hugh Atkinson. *Director of photography:* Richard Wallace. *Camera operator:* John Seale. *Production designer:* Christopher Webster. *Costume designer:* Anna Senior. *Editor:* Rod Adamson. *Composer:* Charles Marawood. *Sound recordist:* Ken Hammond. *Sound editor:* Greg Bell. *Mixer:* Peter Fenton.

Cast

John Waters (Rabbit), Melissa Jaffer (Vi), Wyn Roberts (Sergeant Caxton), Barbara West (Helen Caxton), Kevin Miles (The Superintendent), Graham Rouse (Ab Nolan), Audine Leith (Kathy Nolan), Graeme Blundell (Bernie), Keith Lee (Wayne), Bill Hunter (Bosun), Les Foxcroft (Badger), Kit Taylor (Ryan), Don Barker (O'Dowd), David Hursthouse (Smith), Bryan Brown (Bennett), Rob George (Constable Forest), Ken Weaver (McCord), Lesley Dayman (Riley), Hedley Cullen (Vi's Father), Tony Barry (Wallace), Mark Gawenda (The Pole), Richard Lane (Young Harry), Stuart Campbell (Gibb), Tony Allison (Hennessy), Faith Kleinig (Mrs Foster).

Vi (Melissa Jaffer) and Rabbit (John Waters).

Weekend of Shadows confronts the audience with compelling moral questions. It makes a plea for the individual and proclaims the unfortunate consequences of going along with the masses – the loss of individuality and the ability to determine one's fate.

Set in 1930s small-town Australia, this is a film of the past, but the issues addressed remain in the present. Peter Yeldham's script from Hugh Atkinson's novel, *The Reckoning*, begins with the discovery of a murder. The murder, however, is significant to the story only for the repercussions it brings to the town. The prime suspect is The Pole (Mark Gawenda) – a foreigner, an outsider, a man who is believed to enjoy the company of women – who has conveniently disappeared. A manhunt is organised by Sergeant Caxton

(Wyn Roberts), who seizes the opportunity to try and reclaim the respect of his superiors and his former city posting. He is driven on by the desperate ambition of his wife, Helen (Barbara West).

At the same time, the story of Rabbit (John Waters) begins to unfold. Rabbit is another outsider, whose 'strangeness' is revealed in his preference for spending time with his wife and son, rather than drinking in the pub 'with the boys'. He is also pressured by his ambitious wife, Vi (Melissa Jaffer), to sign up for the manhunt, against his wishes and better judgement. Her desire is that they are simply seen to be like everyone else in the community.

The night search turns into a weekend, the men becoming drunker and wilder, and Sergeant Caxton more anxious. When the men finally find The Pole, they taunt him terribly. Rabbit, who has increasingly come to identify with this victimised figure, shoots The Pole dead to prevent his further suffering. However, the greater tragedy is that The Pole is later found to be not guilty in a surprising, but totally credible, conclusion.

The narrative is constructed through parallels of similarity and difference: Rabbit and The Pole, both innocent victims of a consensus society; the two wives, whose desires become instruments in the demise of their

own husbands: Sergeant Caxton and Vi, both with a past to overturn; Rabbit and the sergeant, one meek, the other strong. Through such comparisons one comes to understand character and motivation.

The different characters' pasts and aspirations are further illuminated through flashbacks. These are some of the most engaging moments in the film. One learns, for example, about Vi's sexual encounters with every young man in town and how Rabbit became 'father' of her child through the chance drawing of straws. And yet, despite such a dubious beginning, they come to build a life together.

Not at all well received on its release, **Weekend of Shadows** was heavily criticised for heavy-handedness. As a morality play, however, it succeeds admirably.

ANNA DZENIS

References
'Tom Jeffrey', an interview with the director by Richard Brennan, *Cinema Papers*, no. 16, April–June 1978, pp. 324–7.
'Weekend of Shadows', a review by Jack Clancy, *Cinema Papers*, no. 17, August–September 1978, p. 61.
'Peter Yeldham', a career interview with the scriptwriter by Paul Davies, *Cinema Papers*, no. 27, June–July 1980, pp. 176–9, 214.

Sybylla Melvyn (Judy Davis) contemplates a diary entry. Gill Armstrong's My Brilliant Career.

APOSTASY

Ukiyo Films presents a twice told tale in Black Red White. APOSTASY.[1] © 1978 Ukiyo Films. Produced with the assistance of the Creative Development Branch of the Australian Film Commission. *Budget:* $50,000. *Location:* Melbourne. *Australian distributor:* Australian Film Institute. *Opened:* 19 May 1979. *Video:* not released. [*Rating:* not known.[2]] 16mm. 108 mins.

Producer: Don McLennan. *Executive producers:* David Thomas, Stewart Hornsey, Virginia Brook. *Scriptwriter:* Zbigniew Friedrich. *Director of photography:* Zbigniew Friedrich. [*Production designer:* not credited.] [*Costume designer:* not credited.] *Editor:* Zbigniew Friedrich. *Song:* 'What Do You Know' written by Joe Creighton. *Sung by:* Joe Creighton, Ross Hannaford. *Chilean song:* Isabelle Parrar. *Violin music:* Eric Gradman. *Sound recordist:* Lloyd Carrick. [*Sound editor:* not credited.] [*Mixer:* not credited.]

Cast

Rod McNicol (The Man), Juliet Bacskai (The Woman), Phil Motherwell (Madman on the Street), Alan Money (Old Man in Cafe); Gemal Fikret Rabit, Josef Pernar, Dimitri Kioursidis, Gianni Micallef (Boys in Street); Ross Skiffington (Magician), Irene Barberis (Woman at the Table), Richard Doctors (Concertina Player), J. J. Jannu (Wood Sculptor), Paul Cox (Photographer); Charles Wallman, Stewart Hornsey, David Thomas, Adrian Smith, Peter Wakeham, Zena Lester, Pam Adena, Anada Li, Maxine Rosewall, Russell Goldthorpe, Jeremy Stanford, Stephen Stanford, Rod McLennan, Linda Craig.

Zbigniew Friedrich's **Apostasy** is typical of many low-budget films made during the 1970s. Shot on 16mm, with an essentially unprofessional cast and inexperienced crew, it is very personalised and personal film-making.

It begins with an elliptical scene between The Man (Rod McNicol) and a Madman (Phil Motherwell), which involves a labyrinthine journey through Melbourne streets while various spiritual issues are voiced.

The Woman (Juliet Bacskai) then enters a room in an ornate Victorian mansion (Labassa in Melbourne). Her clothes change, as does the film's colour, to black and white. Perhaps all that follows is a flashback, for at the end of the film the colour returns as The Woman leaves the room, which now seems more a shrine than the chaotically lived-in space of before.

The Woman (Juliet Bacskai) and The Man (Rod McNicol).

In the room is The Man, who reluctantly agrees to photograph her. But first he makes her deface one side of her face with make-up. As she turns one profile to the camera, then the other, he begins a discussion on duality (beauty/ugliness; rough/smooth; man/woman) that continues intermittently throughout the film.

The Man and The Woman drift into a short affaire, but they are increasingly revealed to be very different. The Man is notable mostly for his extremely pessimistic muttering about all and sundry; he sounds as if he has been shut up with a vast library of 1970s New Age books and is now released on speed. One's reaction to the film depends almost exclusively on how interesting one finds his verbosity. A typical conversation runs as follows:

'You don't say much, do you?', says The Woman.

'Every time I open my mouth I speak to myself […] My everyday life is a confession. Sometimes I sit here at the table and the only things between me and the desperate swine of death are my pens, my pads, my writing gear, a bottle of Coke, a bottle of rum […]'

While this portentousness, let alone pretentiousness, is hard to digest, it is still preferable to the downright silliness of some dialogue: 'Have you ever thought that without the rest of your body your head wouldn't be able to think?' (The Woman). Such exchanges remind one of the equally stilted conversations typical of films of the period – most specifically, the late-1970s films of Paul Cox. In fact, Cox's presence hovers over this film (he is also a participant, recounting his traumatising encounter with a tram conductor on his first or second day in Australia).

As the film is set during the 1975 elections, when Whitlam was defeated by Fraser, there are several political observations and tirades against the military–industrial complex. But it is the media which cops the greatest scorn for the way it corrupts totally acquiescent adults and innocent children. This leads to a fantastical ending where some boys play with The Man's discarded gun and one boy is bloodily killed, only to rise miraculously.

SCOTT MURRAY

---

[1] The title is also given in Greek.
[2] Can find no record of the film's censorship rating in the official list. Assume it to be 'M'.

Reference

'Apostasy', a review by Steve Wallace, *Filmnews*, May 1980, p. 6.

CATHY'S CHILD

AFC[,] NSW Film Corporation [and] Roadshow present a CB Films Production. CATHY'S CHILD. © 1978 C.B. Films Pty. Ltd. Produced with the assistance of the Australian Film Commission. *Budget:* $325,000. *Locations:* Sydney; Athens (Greece). *Filmed:* June–July 1978. *Australian distributor:* Roadshow. *Opened:* 12 July 1979. *Video:* Australian Video. *Rating:* NRC (May 1979; reduced version of 2469m; originally 2661m). 35mm. 90 mins.

Producers: Errol Sullivan, Pom Oliver. *Scriptwriter:* Ken Quinnell. Based on the novel *A Piece of Paper* by Dick Wordley. *Director of photography:* Gary Hansen. *Production designer:* Ross Major. *Wardrobe:* Sally Campbell. *Editor:* Tim Wellburn. *Composer:* William Motzing. *Sound recordists:* Tim Lloyd, Thanassis Arvanitis. *Sound editors:* Tim Wellburn, Vicki Ambrose. *Mixer:* Peter Fenton.

Cast

Michele Fawdon (Cathy²), Alan Cassell (Dick Wordley), Bryan Brown (Paul Nicholson), Arthur Dignam (Minister), Willie Fennell (Gordon Cooper), Flavia Arena (Irene), Kay Yates (Mrs Green), Jim Karangis (Mario), Judy Stevenson (Barmaid), Mike Harris (Foyer Attendant), Linda Newton (Vicki), Vic Rodney (Sgt. Newberry), Lex Marinos (Con Havros), Bob Hughes (Mike), Anna Hruby (Delia), Frankie J. Holden (Det. Plummer), Barry

Eaton (Newsreader), Gerry Gallagher (Smedley), Robert Alexander (Bernhard), Annibole Miglucci (Perelli), Sophia Haskas (Angelina), Petros Printzis (Landlord), Sally McKenzie (Young Nun), Liz Marshall (Old Nun), Harry Michaels (Greek Taxi Driver), Bernadette Scarcella (Maris).

After the lush, art-house quality of Donald Crombie's two period films, **Caddie** (1976) and **The Irishman** (1978), the no-frills realism of **Cathy's Child**, a film about a Maltese woman in multi-cultural Australia, comes as a welcome surprise.

The film is based on a true story. Cathy (Michele Fawdon), a Maltese national married to an Australian Greek, approaches a Sydney newspaper for help in seeking the return of her three-year-old daughter, Maris (Bernadette Scarcella), taken out of the country illegally by her estranged husband, to live with his family in Greece.

Alan Cassell and Bryan Brown play two journalists, Dick Wordley and Paul Nicholson, who help her break through bureaucratic red tape in the race to secure her Australian citizenship and thwart her husband's plans. Cassell is particularly good as Wordley, the burnt-out alcoholic who recovers his zest for journalism when he falls in love with Cathy, but Brown's supporting rôle is too slender to allow him to extend himself.

Contrasted with the clutch of period films that preceded it, **Cathy's Child** is refreshingly contemporary. The storyline develops deftly, with pace, and the use of bright, flat lighting gives the film its sense of urgency and reportage. Cathy in her high boots and shabby coat has all the feel of the real world and its problems. The film is pared down to essentials, and triteness and sentimentality are avoided through the integrity of the acting.

Crombie treats his subject seriously: the attempt by men from old-world cultures to continue the subjugation of women and children. He focuses on the rôle played by men in the Greek and Australian communities in both causing, and in helping to rectify, injustice. But this laudable, even-handed approach to deeply-entrenched cultural problems leads to dissipation of the film's energy. The dramatic pulse is diluted by Crombie's concern to deal fairly with what, in fact, is a blatant misuse of male power.

Once Cathy is reunited with her child, and romance precluded between Wordley and Cathy, the film has nowhere to go and the ending is strangely anti-climactic. A more adventurous approach may have been to pursue the unpleasant underpinnings of the plot. A more critical investigation of the conflict between the transplanting of old-world patriarchy into Australia, and a mother's love and rights, could have sustained the film's initial power.

However, **Cathy's Child** remains a moving, skilful and edifying portrayal of a mother's negotiating her way in a foreign culture, one of the first Australian films of its kind to tackle social issues of this sort head-on.

JAN EPSTEIN

---

¹ Usually spelt 'Donald'.
² Writers usually refer to this character as 'Cathy Baikas', but there is no surname on the film.

References

'Production Report: **Cathy's Child**', *Cinema Papers*, no. 18, October–November 1978, comprising an interview with co-producer Errol Sullivan by Peter Beilby and Scott Murray, pp. 128–30, and an interview with director Donald Crombie by Murray and Beilby, pp. 131–3.
'**Cathy's Child**', a review by Barbara Alysen, *Cinema Papers*, no. 22, July–August 1979, p. 467.
'Ken Quinnell – Hooked on Working with Real Characters', an interview with the scriptwriter by Tina Kaufman and Barbara Alysen, *Filmnews*, August 1979, pp. 5–6.
'**Cathy's Child**', a review by Denise Hare, ibid., p. 17.

Cathy (Michele Fawdon) and daughter Maris (Bernadette Scarcella).

DAWN!

Aquataurus Film Productions in association with the South Australian Film Corporation presents Joy Cavill's production of Dawn!. © 1978 Aquataurus Film Productions Pty Ltd. Made with the assistance of the Australian Film Commission and The Seven Network. *Budget:* $762,391. *Locations:* Adelaide, Sydney, Melbourne, Townsville. *Filmed:* September–November 1978. *Australian distributor:* Hoyts. *Opened:* 8 March 1979. *Video:* Star Video. *Rating:* NRC (January 1979; 2989m[1]). 35mm. 109 mins.

Producer: Joy Cavill. *Executive producer:* Jill C. Robb. *Associate producer:* Sandra McKenzie. *Scriptwriter:* Joy Cavill. *Director of photography:* Russell Boyd. *Camera operator:* John Seale. *Production designer:* Ross Major. *Costume designer:* Judith Dorsman. *Editor:* Max Lemon. *Composer:* Michael Carlos. *Sound recordist:* Ken Hammond. *Sound editor:* Bob Cogger. *Mixer:* Alasdair MacFarlane.

Cast

Bronwyn Mackay-Payne (Dawn), Tom Richards (Harry), John Diedrich (Gary), Bunney Brooke (Mum), Ron Haddrick (Pop), Gabrielle Hartley (Kate), Ivar Kants (Len), David Cameron (Joe), Kevin Wilson (Bippy), Lyndall Barbour (Edie), John Clayton (Syd), Go Mikami (Police Inspector), Judith Fisher (Chaperone), Reg Gillam (1st Board Member), Bill Charlton (Johnno), John Armstrong (Dusty), Judi Farr (New Resident), Wayne Anthony (Garage Customer), Richard Hill (Ken), John Jamieson (Reporter), Robert Davis (2nd Board Member).

As a biopic of one of Australia's best-loved sporting personalities, **Dawn!** is fairly satisfying, though less-than-captivating, cinema.

The central problem is the casting of a non-professional actress, Bronwyn Mackay-Payne, in the title rôle of champion swimmer Dawn Fraser. She looks the part, in spite of being quite a bit taller than the real-life Fraser, but her acting range is too limited for some of the film's more demanding scenes.[2]

This failing is most tested in the latter part of the film, when, after tracing the rise and rise of Dawn Fraser from rebellious teenager to world's greatest female swimmer, it begins to examine the private person. Not that co-producer Joy Cavill's screenplay delves at all deeply, but it does endeavour to present the disappointments and frustrations behind a career marked by constant triumph in the pool and almost-as-frequent clashes with authority out of it.

The swimmer's fierce attachment to her working-class origins in Balmain – she subsequently became an independent MP for the area – is well established, concluding with an effective sequence showing Dawn moving among her peers in the local pub. (Director Ken Hannam here reminds one of some of the best scenes in his **Sunday Too Far Away**, 1975.) Dawn's marriage and other attachments are also dealt with fairly effectively, in a frank enough manner to meet the demands of factual and dramatic credibility without undermining the film's basically worshipful approach.

There are many good supporting performances, notably Bunney Brooke as Dawn's mother, Ron Haddrick as her ailing father and Lyndall Barbour as Edie, a neighbourhood friend, although some of the other characters are rather superficially drawn.

The many swimming scenes are well-staged, imaginatively shot and, to the uninitiated eye at least, seem quite authentic.

KEITH CONNOLLY

---

[1] An AFC brochure has it one metre longer at 2990m.
[2] This writer was informed several years after the film's release that a pre-production decision to dub Mackay-Payne's dialogue with the voice of a professional actress was abandoned, with obviously detrimental results.

References

'Production Report: **Dawn!**', *Cinema Papers*, no. 16, April–June 1978, comprising an interview with writer–producer Joy Cavill by Peter Beilby and Scott Murray, pp. 338–9, 347, an interview with director Ken Hannam by Murray and Beilby, pp. 340–3, and an interview with production designer Ross Major by Beilby and Murray, pp. 344–7.
'**Dawn!**', a review by Meaghan Morris, *Cinema Papers*, no. 21, May–June 1979, pp. 386–7.
'**Dawn!**', a review by Nick Herd, *Filmnews*, April 1979, p. 6.

Mum (Bunney Brooke) and daughter Dawn (Bronwyn Mackay-Payne).

DIMBOOLA

[No opening production credit.[1]] DIMBOOLA. © 1979 Pram Factory Productions. *Budget:* $350,000. *Location:* Dimboola. *Filmed:* June–July 1978. *Australian distributor:* GUO. *Opened:* 11 May 1979. *Video:* Videoscope. *Rating:* M (March 1979; 2386.41m). 35mm. Panavision. 94 mins.

Producer: John Weiley. *Associate producers:* John Timlin, Max Gillies. *Scriptwriter:* Jack Hibberd. Adapted from the play by Jack Hibberd. *Director of photography:* Tom Cowan. *Production designer:* Larry Eastwood. *Costumes:* Rose Chong, Margot Lindsay. *Editor:* Tony Paterson. *Composer:* George Dreyfus. *Sound recordist:* Lloyd Carrick. [*Sound editor:* not credited.] *Mixer:* Julian Ellingworth.[2]

Cast

Bruce Spence [Morrie[3]], Natalie Bate [Maureen], Max Gillies [Vivian Worcester-Jones], Bill Garner [Dangles], Jack Perry [Horrie], Dick May [Shovel], Esme Melville [April], Terry McDermott [Darcy], Allan[4] Rowe [Angus], Irene Hewitt [Florence], Kerry Dwyer [Shirl], Val Jellay [Aggie], Barry Barkla [Rev. Potts], Tim Robertson [Father O'Shea], Laurel Frank [Jackleen], Sue Ingleton [Marilyn], Claire Dobbin [Worms], Chad Morgan [Bayonet], Max Cullen [Mutton], Paul Hampton [Ambrose], Evelyn Krape [Monica], Helen Sky [Astrid], Max Fairchild [T-Bone], Phil Motherwell [Sniper], Claire Binney [Angelique].

Dimboola is generally regarded as one of the film industry's biggest disappointments. Based on the smash-hit play by Jack Hibberd, where the audience participates at a country wedding celebration, the film is an unfunny collection of caricatures overplayed by members of Carlton's pioneering Pram Factory theatre group.

Morrie[5] (Bruce Spence) works on the railways with his mate Dangles (Bill Garner). Theirs is a languorous employment (Morrie has a keenness for reading *Phantom* comics on the job), which not even the arrival of an eccentric British journalist, Vivian Worcester-Jones (Max Gillies), can ruffle. But it is just a few days to Morrie's wedding and his last days of 'freedom' must, one presumes, be spent as he wishes.

What follows is partly narrated by Vivian Worcester-Jones, who is on assignment for a British newspaper, and who finds the country folk quite peculiar: ocker Aussie males with an interest in bashing a Pom; waitresses at the milkbar who long to be singers (called The Milkshakes!); the town drunks who make extraordinary contortions

Newlyweds: Maureen[6] (Natalie Bate) and Morrie (Bruce Spence).

with their facial muscles; silly clergymen who frown on dancing; and so on.

With so many eccentrics on the loose, it is hardly surprising that things start going horribly wrong: the hairdryer incinerates the scalp of Aunt Aggie (Val Jellay); Morrie is photographed at his bucks' night in a compromising position with the stripper, Angelique (Claire Binney); Morrie's mum, Florence (Irene Hewitt), becomes drunk and reveals to her startled husband that she had a pre-marital fling with Bayonet (Chad Morgan), which may mean Maureen and Morrie are first cousins. And so it goes ...

The real pity is that none of this is funny (a view shared, it seems, by almost everyone). Much of the cause can be located in the way the Pram Factory cast appears to be making up for all those actors over the decades who felt their best work had been repressed by film directors. Here, they seem to have a completely free rein and the results are absurd and unhumorous. Had this film been cast with actual country people, instead of Carlton thespians pretending to be them (with the inevitable tone of condescension), it may well have worked better. (It should be noted that the film's director, John Duigan, was rumoured to be at loggerheads with many at the Pram Factory during production.)

The other major mistake, as most writers have commented, was the decision to rewrite the play – a play which had been the most successful ever staged in Australia to that point. The reworked film is too diffuse, it attempts too many comedy styles and it misses out on the claustrophobic tension of the original. Many film adaptations of plays have been severely debilitated by being 'opened out'; this is no exception.

SCOTT MURRAY

[1] At least on the supplied video, but it goes straight into the first (?) shot, so something may be missing.
[2] This is an assumption. There is a credit for 'assistant dubbing mixer' but nothing else in the sound mixing area.
[3] There are no character names in the cast credits; these are assembled from various sources.
[4] Usually spelt 'Alan'.
[5] See footnote 3.
[6] See footnote 3.

References

'**Dimboola**', a production report by Jack Clancy, *Cinema Papers*, no. 18, October–November 1978, pp. 99–101.

'**Dimboola**', a review by Sue Adler, *Cinema Papers*, no. 21, May–June 1979, p. 384.

'**Dimboola**', a review by Barbara Alysen, *Filmnews*, July 1979, p. 11.

'Ethics of the Outsider', an interview with writer–director John Duigan by Albert Moran, *Filmnews*, April 1984, pp. 10–12.

FELICITY

[No opening production credit.] FELICITY. © 1978 Krystal Motion Picture Productions. *Budget*: $200,000. *Locations*: Melbourne; Hong Kong. *Australian distributor*: Roadshow. *Opened*: 5 July 1979. *Video*: Roadshow. *Rating*: R (December 1978 at 2550.99m; April 1979 at 2487m). 35mm. 90 mins.

Producers: Russell Hurley, John Lamond. *Executive producer*: William Marshall. [*Scriptwriter*: not credited; atb John D. Lamond.] *Director of photography*: Gary Wapshott. *Production designer*: Stephen Walsh. *Wardrobe*: Diane Morris. *Editor*: Russell Hurley. [*Composer*: not credited.] *Sound recordist*: John Phillips. *Sound editor*: Lindsay Parker. [*Mixer*: not credited.]

Cast

Glory Annen (Felicity Robinson), Christopher Milne (Miles), Joni Flynn (Me Ling), Jody Hanson (Jenny); Marilyn Rodgers [Christine[1]], Gordon Charles [Stephen]; John Michael Howson (Adrian); David Bradshaw [Andrew], Christine Calcutt [Nun], Angela Menzies Willis [Bathhouse Girl 1], Sarah Lee [Bathhouse Girl 2], Charles Gilroy [Mr Jacobs]; Toni Maines, Ted Kwok, Joe Lin, Arlene Andrewartha, Michael Leong, Merryn Anslee, Rachel Yared, John Stewart, Catrina Chong.

After the commercial success of his two sex 'documentaries', **Australia After Dark** (1975) and **The ABC of Love and Sex Australia Style** (1978), John D. Lamond decided to move into more mainstream fiction. He thus devised the story of a schoolgirl's discovering all about sex and true love.

The film begins with Felicity (Glory Annen) at Willows End, an up-market Catholic ladies college (the oft-used Montsalvat), where tentative lesbianism and nude showers are the main excitement for participants and a peeping-Tom gardener (spiritedly played by an uncredited Lamond).

Felicity then receives a letter from daddy and news of a holiday in Hong Kong with two of his friends. After a plane trip where fellow passengers act out the **Emmanuelle**[2] fantasy of doing it mid-air, a servant drives Felicity to her hosts' (rather Melbournian-looking) mansion, intoning on the way that, 'Things happen here that we'd never dream of.' In Lamond's case, that means secretly watching people make love, wearing black lingerie, having full body massages and indulging in 'zipless fucks'. And in the background are the thrumming markets of Asian exoticness.

But sex, Felicity learns, is not everything, and Miles (Christopher Milne), the youth who saves her from some Chinese attackers, helps open her up emotionally. Theirs is a shared and equal relationship and not at all monogamous, Felicity doing it with several who cross her path.

Felicity is easy to make fun of, for it is rather basically produced and the **Emmanuelle**-style genre seems to lock it in a 1970s time warp. Despite that, **Felicity** has its value. As Meaghan Morris has percipiently pointed out:

Felicity [...] take[s] up a positively pedagogical tone, emphasizing the desirability of a tolerant and understanding attitude to sex [...It] ends with a hymn to the virtues of a fusion of love and sex at the centre of a liberated life.

Felicity, interestingly, is the only [Australian] narrative film [up till 1980] to point to a sexuality free of conflict and antagonism of interests between men and women [...][3]

Felicity does, however, reflect its time in favouring female nudity to male and having the sex act performed with a dispiriting listlessness decreed by the censorship standards then in force. It is certainly curious to see a woman sit near motionless on a man and have both partners look as if nirvana has descended on them.

Interestingly, Lamond refers to his early work quite explicitly in this film. When Felicity and Miles go to a cinema, **The ABC of Love and Sex Australia Style** is what they see. More intriguingly, Lamond has a montage of the young lovers impatiently making love in public places: the cinema, on a tram and in an ascending lift. In the **The ABC of Love and Sex**, Lamond gives as examples for 'D=Dreams' couples making it in a lift, on a plane and in the cinema. There is clearly some form of erotic auteurism at work here.

SCOTT MURRAY

---

1 Apart from five principal rôles, no character names are given in the end credits. Those listed above are taken from spoken dialogue and publicity material.
2 *Emmanuelle* (Just Jaeckin, 1974).
3 Meaghan Morris, 'Personal Relationships and Sexuality', in *The New Australian Cinema*, Scott Murray (ed.), Thomas Nelson Australia and Cinema Papers, Melbourne, 1980, p. 138.

Reference

'John Lamond', an interview with the producer–director by Scott Murray on the director's work up to **Felicity**, *Cinema Papers*, no. 18, October–November 1978, pp. 94–98, 157.

Jenny (Jody Hanson) and Felicity Robinson (Glory Annen).

IN SEARCH OF ANNA

Storm Productions, in association with the Australian Film Commission and the Victorian Film Corporation[,] presents IN SEARCH OF ANNA. © 1978 Storm Productions. Made in association with the Australian Film Commission and the Victorian Film Corporation. *Budget:* $231,000. *Locations:* on the road from Melbourne to Surfers Paradise. *Filmed:* February–April 1977. *Australian distributor:* GUO. *Opened:* 28 July 1979. *Video:* Videoscope. *Rating:* M (May 1978; 2621m; later cut to 2496m[1]). 35mm. 91 mins.

Producer: Esben Storm. *Associate producer:* Natalie Miller. *Scriptwriter:* Esben Storm. *Director of photography:* Mike Edols. *Production designer:* Sally Campbell. [*Costume designer:* not credited.] *Editor:* Dusan Werner. *Musical director:* Michael Norton. *Sound recordist:* Lawrie Fitzgerald. *Sound editor:* Haydn Keenan. *Mixers:* Peter Fenton, Julian Ellingworth.

Cast

Richard Moir (Tony), Judy Morris (Sam), Bill Hunter (Peter), Alex Taifer (Tony's Father), Ian Nimmo (Buzz), Gary Waddell (Maxie)[2]; Richard Murphett (Undertaker); Shuvus, Lou Brown (Country Boys); Maurie Fields (Taxi Driver), Mrs Penini (Cafe Proprietor); Merle Keenan, Lily Vargersen (Gossiping Women); Chris Haywood (Jerry), Rick Ireland (Man at Crown St House), Martin Sharp (Eternity Man), Helen Wall (Photographic Model).

In Search of Anna, written, produced and directed by Esben Storm, is a poetic moment in Australian cinema. The title recalls the search for another Anna who was never found – in *L'Avventura* (Michelangelo Antonioni, 1960). The significance of this reference lies in the European art-cinema traditions that it invokes, the cinema of film-makers such as Antonioni and Alain Resnais. It is an auteurist cinema of poetic images whose preoccupations with time, memory, history and the struggle for self are also concerns central to Storm's film.

Yet what is even more interesting about **In Search of Anna** is not its possible European antecedents, but that it is a very Australian film. Made in a market when films of Australia's historical past were getting a lot of attention, **In Search of Anna** is located in contemporary 1970s Australia.

Filmed on the road from Melbourne through Sydney to Queensland, the film-maker and his crew travelled this route with their characters. The changing landscape from Melbourne's industrial wastelands to

Sam (Judy Morris) and Tony (Richard Moir).

Sydney's narrow streets and terrace houses, from cliff-face highways and stretches of ocean to the lush foliage of the tropical North, all add to the visual pleasure of the journey. Similarly, cultural landmarks like the music of Australian bands AC/DC, The Angels, Stiletto, Rose Tattoo and Steve Wright dominate the soundtrack. Such details make the film a real time piece.

The story being told is a simple one. It is about starting over again. Tony (Richard Moir) has just been released from prison after serving a six-year sentence for armed robbery. However, the narrative structure is complex and ambitious. Tony's return to his past is interwoven with scenes from the present as he hitches a rides with Sam (Judy Morris) in a 1938 Buick, in search of his old girlfriend, the elusive Anna.

Paralleling past and present sets up a series of enigmas but not as a source of confusion. It becomes an unexpectedly engaging and seductive strategy, functioning to illuminate character and action. Jerry (Chris Haywood) defines Tony's youthful, urban, violent past. Returning to this life, Tony confronts his immobilised Greek father, the pain and responsibility of his mother's suicide, and a violent reckoning with his childhood friend, Jerry. Sam, on the other hand, is the spirit of the present, a self-possessed, hip photographer's model who questions Tony's

naïve romanticism, and through whom he can tell his story.

This is also a film which is heard as much as it is seen. Conversations in the car, the reading aloud of Anna's letters, Tony's mother's suicide note – voices from the past, all densely layered over and around the images, heighten our sense of how the past informs the present and the dreams we pursue.

Hardly a commercial success on its initial release, **In Search of Anna** is a film just waiting to be rediscovered and appreciated for the mini-masterpiece it is.

ANNA DZENIS

1 This shorter version appears not to have been resubmitted for censorship.
2 Order of the head credits; the end credits are in order of appearance.

References
'Production Report: **In Search of Anna**', *Cinema Papers*, no. 13, July 1977, pp. 51–5, comprising an interview with producer–director Esben Storm by Gordon Glenn and Scott Murray.
'In Search of Anna', a review by Barbara Boyd, *Cinema Papers*, no. 21, May–June 1979, p. 385.
'Ken Cameron talks to Esben Storm about **In Search of Anna**', *Filmnews*, June 1979, pp. 1, 5–9.
'In Search of Anna', a review by Ken Quinnell, ibid., p. 12.

THE JOURNALIST

New South Wales Film Corporation [and] FJF Promoters presents [sic] THE JOURNALIST. © 1979 FJ Films Pty Ltd. *Budget:* $400,000. *Locations:* Sydney; Hong Kong. *Filmed:* January–February 1979. *Australian distributor:* Roadshow. *Opened:* 15 November 1979. *Video:* Australian Video. *Rating:* M (May 1979; 2314.7m). 35mm. 83 mins.

Producer: Pom Oliver. *Scriptwriters:* Edna Wilson, Michael Thornhill. *Director of photography:* Don McAlpine. *Camera operator:* David Burr. *Production designer:* Jenny Green. *Costumes:* Anna Senior. *Editors:* Tim Wellburn, Ron Williams. [*Composer:* not credited.] *Song:* 'The Fancy Dancer'. *Music and lyrics:* Wayne Kent-Healing. *Music coordinators:* David White, Tom Zelinka. *Sound recordist:* Tim Lloyd. *Sound editor:* Dean Gawen. *Mixer:* Peter Fenton.

Cast

Jack Thompson (Simon Morris), Elizabeth Alexander (Liz Corbett), Sam Neill (Rex), Carol Raye (Maggie Nicholson), Penne Hackforth-Jones (Gillie Griffiths), Charles "Bud" Tingwell[1] (Sid Mitchell[2]), Stuart Wagstaff (Courtney Lewers), Slim De Grey[3] (Senior Interviewer), Candy Raymond (Sunshine), Jane Harders (Wendy), Michele Jarman (Susie), Margo Lee (Editor), Victoria Nicolls (Phillipa Richards), Sandra Lee Paterson (Marriage Celebrant), Frank Wilson (Vic Parsons), Beryl Cheers (Regina Brown), Ken Goodlet (Editorial Director), Frankie J. Holden (2nd Investigator), Ray Meagher (1st Investigator), Ray Marshall (Senior Investigator), Laurel McGowan (Jane Furlong), Vic Rooney (Bert), Walter Sullivan (Charles Nicholson).[4]

Jack Thompson introduced a new phrase to the speech of many Australians in the late 1970s when he intoned in a television soft-drink commercial: 'Clayton's…the drink I'm having when I'm not having a drink.'

The expression, though not the drink, was soon on everyone's lips. Compering the 1979 Australian Film Awards, Graham Kennedy brought the house down when he described Michael Thornhill's The Journalist as 'the movie Jack Thompson makes when he's not making a movie!' It was a stinging crack, but not undeserved.

The film, the nadir both of Thornhill's directorial career and the production–sponsorship of the short-lived New South Wales Film Corporation, is a derivative sex comedy with few laughs, little narrative structure beyond a schematic predictability

Journalists: Gillie Griffiths (Penne Hackforth-Jones), Simon Morris (Jack Thompson) and Rex (Sam Neill).

and some astonishingly mechanical performances from a top-level cast, headed by Thompson. (The supporting cast reads like a roll call of Australian acting talent of the day: Elizabeth Alexander, Sam Neill, Carol Raye, Charles "Bud" Tingwell, Frank Wilson, Jude Kuring, Dennis Miller, Ray Meagher, Candy Raymond, et al.)

Thompson plays Simon Morris, a self-delighted Sydney newspaper reporter with an Alvin Purple-type problem: women find him irresistible, and vice versa. Separated from wife and daughter, he has an ongoing relationship with a colleague, Liz Corbett (Elizabeth Alexander), and numerous other affaires. Juggling this complicated life, he encounters further difficulty when a pompous political writer, Sid Mitchell (Tingwell), becomes editor of his newspaper. Simon resigns, can't get another job for a while and is shadowed by two dim-witted ASIO spooks after applying for a government information service posting.

Practically nothing in this lightweight piece hangs together – the scenes of

Thompson's extremely undemanding working life, his amatory escapades or his interchanges with wives, lovers, friends, enemies or workmates, headed by Rex (a somewhat apologetic Sam Neill).

Thompson portrays Simon with a dash of the boyish insouciance of his performance as Foley in **Sunday Too Far Away** (Ken Hannam) four years before, but none of its appeal. The script and direction here are too inept and the film as a whole is altogether too phoney.

KEITH CONNOLLY

---

[1] On the front credits, the name is rendered as 'Charles (Bud) Tingwell'.
[2] On the front credits, Tingwell's character is called 'The Dean'.
[3] Spelt 'Slim DeGrey' on the opening credits.
[4] As the end credits are in order of appearance, this ordering is per the opening credits.

Reference
'The Journalist', a review by Meaghan Morris, *Cinema Papers*, no. 22, July–August 1979, pp. 464–5.

JUST OUT OF REACH

Portrait Films presents JUST OUT OF REACH. © 1979 Portrait Films. Produced with the assistance of the Creative Development Branch of the Australian Film Commission. *Budget:* $41,000. *Location:* Sydney. *Filmed:* February–March 1979. *Australian distributor:* Sydney Filmmakers Co-operative. *Opened:* November 1979. *Video:* not released. *Rating:* M (March 1980; 691.11m). 16mm. 62 mins.

Producer: Ross Matthews. *Scriptwriter:* Linda Blagg. *Director of photography:* Russell Boyd. *Camera operator:* Nixon Binney. *Production designer:* Grace Walker. [*Costume designer:* not credited.] *Editor:* Ted Ötton. *Composer:* William Motzing. *Sound recordist:* Kevin Kearney. [*Sound editor:* not credited.] *Mixer:* Peter Fenton.

Cast

Lorna Lesley (Cathy), Sam Neill (Mike), Martin Vaughan (Father), Judi Farr (Mother), Ian Gilmour[1] (Steve), Lou Brown (John), Jackie Dalton (Jenny), Liz Kidney (Susan), Martin Rooke (Boyfriend), Carl Harrison-Ford (Tutor), Roger Hudson (Man at Party), Barbara Gibbs (Nurse); Year 11 Hunters Hill High School (Class).

Just Out of Reach is Linda Blagg's ninth film and first feature. Her earlier work includes the shorts *Birthplace* (1975) and *Just Me and My Little Girlie* (1976), and four documentaries in Film Australia's Our Multicultural Society series.[2]

Loosely based on Blagg's own experiences, **Just Out of Reach** deals with a young woman's attempted suicide after the breakdown of her marriage. It begins and ends with Cathy (Lorna Lesley) being admitted to hospital after slashing her wrists, and in between examines her family life, early relationships and marriage in an attempt to show the forces that create a depressive personality.

Cathy is the elder daughter of British migrant parents. Her father works on mining sites and is often away from home, leaving family discipline to his wife. Badly out of tune with the mores of their daughter's generation, Cathy's parents use threats, violence and the withdrawal of affection to cajole her into conformity. She in turn looks outside the family for the love and approval they fail to provide. But the people she turns to – her boyfriend, a teacher who later becomes her husband, and her sister – are unable to help.

For a woman incapable of dealing with her problems alone, suicide seems the only answer.

The motivation for Cathy's often infuriating behaviour is dealt with by having her speak her thoughts in a voice-over. This technique invites comparison with other discourses on suicide and family breakdown, particularly John Hopkins' television plays *Talking to a Stranger* and *Stevie*. But where these are articulate and profound, Cathy's teenage monologues on the meaning of life border on the banal. The naïveté of Cathy's thoughts, however, is exactly what makes them real.

Like *Just Me and My Little Girlie*, which deals with father–daughter incest, **Just Out of Reach** has a brave choice of subject. One of the most compelling notions our society has thrown up is the idea that psychological well-being is a matter of personal choice. It is no accident that this theory goes hand-in-hand with the notion that wealth and material success accrue from individual initiative and hard work. Both are part of an ideology which denies that luck and inherited background play a rôle in an individual's life.

A film like **Just Out of Reach** could easily have become an extended commercial for Lifeline, but Blagg avoids this by concentrating on motivations and outside pressures, rather than a solution to the problem. Blagg says the film is about loneliness and alienation rather than suicide. Describing it as a 'kitchen sink drama', she says that in it she wanted to explain self-destructive behaviour through family background.

BARBARA ALYSEN[3]

---

[1] On the front credits Gilmour's surname is spelt 'Gilmore'.
[2] *Flo and Marianna, Kamahl, Betty* and *EBR* (1977–78).
[3] Extracted from Alysen's article in *Cinema Papers* (see References).

References
'Just Out of Reach, Morris Loves Jack, Conman Harry and Others', a composite review by Barbara Alysen, *Cinema Papers*, no. 24, December 1979–January 1980, pp. 662–3.
'Women in Drama: Linda Blagg', an interview with the writer–director by Mark Stiles, *Cinema Papers*, no. 35, November–December 1981, pp. 456–7, 513.
'Linda Blagg – explaining people's behaviour', an interview with the writer–director by Tina Kaufman and Stephen Wallace, *Filmnews*, October 1979, pp. 8–9.
'Just Out of Reach', a review by Denise Hare, *Filmnews*, November–December 1979, p. 14.

Cathy (Lorna Lesley) and her father (Martin Vaughan).

THE KING OF THE TWO DAY WONDER

[Unchecked.[1]] [© atb 1979.] Made with the assistance of the Creative Development Branch of the Australian Film Commission. *Location:* Melbourne. *Australian distributor:* Vincent Film Library (AFI). *Opened:* 28 May 1979. *Video:* not released. *Rating:* M (May 1979; 724.02m). 16mm. 66 mins.

Producers: Kevin Anderson, Walter Dobrowolski. *Scriptwriter:* Kevin Anderson. *Director of photography:* Kevin Anderson. [*Production designer:* not known.] [*Costume designer:* not known.] *Editors:* Kevin Anderson, Tony Stevens. *Composer:* Gregory Sneddon. *Sound recordists:* Phil Stirling, Nick Alexander, Lloyd Carrick, John Phillips. *Sound editors:* John Phillips, John Rowley. *Mixer:* Les McKenzie.

Cast

Walter Dobrowolski [Robert Damian; Blake], Sigrid Thornton [Christy], Allen Bickford [Barry], James Robertson [Assassin], Maureen O'Loughlin [Ondine]; John Matyear, Ron Macris, Dianne Giulieri, Daryl Gladwin, Ian Blake, Ron Watkins, Andrew Robertson.

The King of the Two Day Wonder, written, directed, photographed and co-produced by Kevin Anderson, is an extremely ambitious film. It experiments with time and narrative, and even with notions of character. It presents the kind of complex, even baffling, surface which makes one applaud its daring, while retaining the uneasy suspicion that not all of its apparent complexities are fully under directorial control.

The film begins with the very nice idea of a writer, Robert Damian[2] (played effectively, if a touch narcissistically, by co-producer Walter Dobrowolski), completing his latest pulp-fiction novel involving a detective called Blake. Having met his two-day deadline, he delays submitting the manuscript to his publisher because he is not satisfied with the ending.

Damian is not concerned so much with multiple possibilities of narrative as with the inter-relation between the narrative and his own life. In re-examining the novel, he becomes involved in a re-examination of his own life, to the point where the two become interchangeable. He sits at his typewriter smoking endless Gauloise cigarettes, while in intercut scenes we see aspects of his previous life, and the lives of the characters in the novel.

One of the most striking, even haunting, moments in the film is when Damian looks out through the window and sees himself (Blake or Damian?) leaving the building. The two selves exchange looks of awareness.

On the level of literal realism, it is of course absurd. However, the film is not concerned with presenting, but with commenting on, forms of realism, and it is particularly effective because it presents the sense of a divided self that has been implicit in the portrait of Damian the writer so far.

Even the resolution of Damian's dilemma has a divided, ambivalent tone to it. He takes the manuscript with him down to the beach and in a gesture of independence and defiance throws it to the waves. But the waves bring it back to him and he scrambles after the sheets of paper – we gather, too late.

The detective story provides opportunities enough for a film-maker to parody, pay homage to, or simply make references to other films, and the number and breadth of these references in The King of the Two Day Wonder indicates a love of cinema which is so often a feature of young film-makers' work, and a self-indulgent eclecticism which so frequently flaws it. This eclecticism is equally evident in the cinematic style (or styles), and in the use of music.

The ending of the film returns us to one of its motifs: Damian meets a girl playing, very tentatively and imperfectly, the Albinoni melody which has so frequently recurred. It is the kind of open ending from which the viewer can take his or her own meaning.

The scene is touching, beautifully shot, yet puzzling, suggesting a comment on creative activity that becomes a comment of the film itself. Like the playing, **The King of the Two Day Wonder** is uncertain, not totally in command, but full of promise.

JACK CLANCY[3]

---

[1] The credits and title could not be checked as no print or video of the film was available.
[2] See footnote 1.
[3] Extracted from Clancy's review in *Cinema Papers* (see Reference).
[4] See footnote 1.

Reference
'The King of the Two Day Wonder', a review by Jack Clancy, *Cinema Papers*, no. 22, July–August 1979, pp. 465–7.

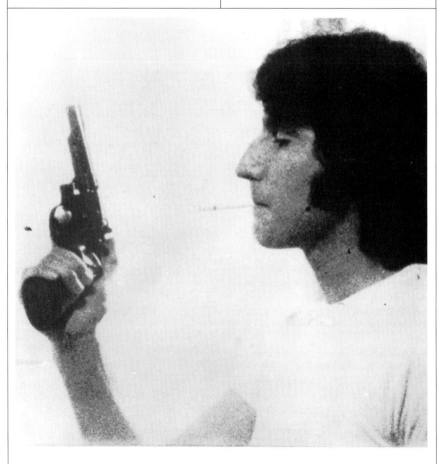

Robert Damian/Blake[4] (Walter Dobrowolski).

KOSTAS

Victorian Film Corporation and Illumination Films present KOSTAS. © 1979 Kostas Film Productions. *Budget:* $224,000. *Location:* Melbourne. *Filmed:* March 1979. *Australian distributor:* Greg Lynch Film Distributors. *Opened:* 16 August 1979. *Video:* Videoscope. *Rating:* M (June 1979 at 2880m; in August 1979 reduced by producer to 2578m). 35mm. 94 mins.

Producer: Bernard Eddy. *Executive producer:* Kostas Kallergis. *Associate producer:* Tony Llewellyn-Jones. *Scriptwriter:* Linda Aronson. Based on an original concept by Paul Cox. *Director of photography:* Vittorio Bernini. *Production designer:* Alan Stubenrauch. *Wardrobe:* Carol Devine. *Editor:* John Scott. *Composer:* Mikis Theodorakis. *Sound recordist:* Lloyd Carrick. *Sound editor:* Bruce Lamshed. *Mixer:* David Harrison.

Cast

Takis Emmanuel (Kostas), Wendy Hughes (Carol), Kris McQuade (Jenny), Sophia Harrison (Lucy), Tony Llewellyn-Jones (Tony), Sakis Dragonas (Mihali), Ahmet Ozirmak (Turkish Boy), Dawn Klingberg (Landlady), Peter Thompson (Landlord), Chris Haywood (Martin), Maurie Fields (Taxi Boss), Nick Skiadopolous (Criticos), Graeme Blundell (John), Norman Kaye (Passenger), Lakis Kantzipas (Petros), Amalia Vassiliadis (Anna), Myron Kougioum (Haralambo); Antonius Baxevandis, Arthur Fidigiannis, Basil Vassos (Interrogators).[2]

Kostas (Takis Emmanuel) is a Greek refugee journalist now living in Melbourne and working without enthusiasm as a taxi-driver. At the airport, he is transfixed by Carol (Wendy Hughes) and sets out, with considerable urgency, to seduce her. Carol, a Toorak divorcée with a young daughter, Lucy (Sophia Harrison), works in a commercial art gallery and organises social functions. Kostas and Carol are star-crossed lovers from different worlds, and it is their difference that forms the substance of the story.

Although this plot summary may suggest a somewhat clichéd story, the telling isn't. A photographer-turned-film-maker, Paul Cox's images poignantly evoke the things that separate people. This is a narrative that begins and ends with airport departures, and that is structured around the climax motivated by the death of Kostas' mother. Characters are often framed by windows, inside looking out, or conversing at

Carol (Wendy Hughes) and Kostas (Takis Emmanuel).

doorways which function as borders, boundaries, separations.

But it is really the social spaces and cultural milieus the central characters inhabit that keeps them apart. We see Kostas in his rooming house, also occupied by other lonely and isolated people, watching his home movie footage of Greece – a past and a history, the images of his dreams and memories. He frequents the Greek coffee shop run by his cousins, where sub-titled conversations are spoken in their native language. He takes Carol to a Greek restaurant, where group dancing and wild plate-breaking are the norm. His heritage has formed him but it also inhibits him.

Carol's world, on the other hand, is élite, privileged and genteel: a well-to-do house and a commercial gallery in an upper-class suburb. It is a world of social engagements and polite conversations. A dinner party at her house pits Martin (Chris Haywood) at his manic, ocker best against Kostas in a dispute about Greek history; the culmination is a fist-fight which breaks unspoken proprieties. Rather than empathise with her Greek lover, Carol temporarily decides he does not fit into her life.

The fact that Cox is a cultured migrant himself, born in The Netherlands, suggests there are elements of autobiography in this tale. And it is true that, while the most haunting and disturbing images belong to Kostas,

they are also among the most passionate and poetically rendered.

Kostas opened the 1979 Melbourne Film Festival, the first time an Australian feature was bestowed with this honour. However, the climate of criticism – the sway of 'correct ideological practices' – saw many critics judge the film harshly. For some there was a lack of detail about the Greek political situation. Others felt that more attention should be paid to the issue of migration and the problems migrants faced in Australia. At the best, it was argued that Cox was Australia's Michelangelo Antonioni who would achieve success once he found a social theme.

With hindsight, it is necessary to see **Kostas** not for what it isn't, but for what it is – an emotional and very personal film – and value it as such.

ANNA DZENIS

---

[1] There is no director credit, just 'A Film by Paul Cox'.
[2] As the end credits are in order of appearance, this ordering is per the opening credits.

References
'Kostas', a review by Keith Connolly, *Cinema Papers*, no. 22, July–August 1979, pp. 463–4.
'Greg Lynch: The Middle Ground', an interview with the distributor by Scott Murray, *Cinema Papers*, no. 31, March–April 1981, pp. 36–9, 71.

THE LAST OF THE KNUCKLEMEN

Hexagon presents in association with the Victorian Film Corporation and the New South Wales Film Corporation THE LAST OF THE KNUCKLEMEN. © 1979 A Hexagon Production. Produced with financial assistance from the Victorian Film Corporation, the New South Wales Film Corporation and the Australian Film Commission. *Budget:* $460,000. *Locations:* Andamooka (South Australia); Melbourne. *Filmed:* September–October 1978. *Australian distributor:* Roadshow. *Opened:* 12 July 1979. *Video:* Roadshow Home Video. *Rating:* R (May 1979; appeal against rating rejected same month; 2538m). 35mm. 93 mins.

Producer: Tim Burstall. *Associate producer:* Byron Kennedy. *Scriptwriter:* Tim Burstall. Based on the play by John Powers. *Director of photography:* Dan Burstall. *Production designer:* Leslie Binns. *Wardrobe:* Kevin Regan, Norma Pollard. *Editor:* Edward McQueen-Mason. *Composer:* Bruce Smeaton. *Sound recordist:* John Phillips. *Sound editor:* Edward McQueen-Mason. *Mixer:* Peter Fenton.

Cast

Gerard Kennedy (Tarzan), Michael Preston (Pansy), Peter Hehir (Tom), Dennis Miller (Horse), Michael Caton (Monk), Steve Rackman (Carl), Michael Duffield (Methuselah), Stephen Bisley (Mad Dog), Stewart Faichney (Tassie); Sean Myers (Engineer), Gerry Duggan (Old Arthur), Ross Skiffington (Second Engineer), Les James (Barman), Tim Robertson (Man in Bar), Saviour Summit (Cook), Margaret Buza (Postmistress), James Parker (Pinip), Saltbush (Band in Pub), Denise Drysdale (Whore), Helen Watts (Second Whore).

Based on John Powers' lively three-act play set on a north-west drilling site (the film changes the locale to Central Australia), The Last of the Knucklemen is a simplistic but interesting film within narrow confines.

Director Tim Burstall's screenplay is surprisingly faithful to the ascending theatrical pitch of the original, but the film's trouble lies not so much in the script as in the tenacity with which, in almost every expository scene, Burstall goes for the dramatic jugular. The exceptions to this stridently elemental approach help prove the point. The best thing in the film is a high-stakes card game between Methuselah (Michael Duffield), a sick old gambler, and Pansy (Michael Preston), the camp stirrer – characters granted a greater dimension in Burstall's conception (and very well played).

Mad Dog (Stephen Bisley) watches Pansy (Michael Preston) fight Tarzan (Gerard Kennedy).

When Methuselah enunciates his limited remaining ambitions, only to see them blighted in one hand of poker, the film gains in warmth and substance.

By comparison, the other characters, even that of Tarzan (Gerard Kennedy), the legendary knuckleman of the title, are patently basic theatrical devices. Tarzan, the crew foreman, is fiercely possessive of his 'turf', a squalid little domain he dominates by force of personality and reminders of his fading physical prowess. As Methuselah explains to newcomer Monk (Michael Caton), knucklemen like Tarzan are relics of 'the old days' when the riff-raff had to be held in check by men good with their fists.

At bottom, The Last of the Knucklemen is a morality tale in which flawed but humane Good triumphs over cracked and sneaky Evil. It is not hard to identify the Good Guys: they smile more, swear less and are passing fair in appearance. The Baddies scowl darkly, curse horribly and probably pull the wings off live flies. What's more, one of them, Carl (Steve Rackman), is a German of quite grotesque Hunnishness (again untypically, only two immigrants are sighted throughout the film).

Carl is brought to the camp by Pansy to 'do' Tarzan with big money wagered on the result. Both baddies get their come-uppance when the enigmatic Tom (Peter Hehir), a fugitive payroll robber and karate expert, fights in Tarzan's stead, proving that nice guys *can* finish first – if they have a black belt.

In the main, the film is commendable, if unadventurous, technically. Leslie Binns' functionally theatrical bunk-house set is sparsely claustrophobic, as befits the cockpit of nearly all significant action. The tensions and temper of the plot originate there and Burstall wisely confines most of the exterior sequences to background authentication – the men at work, visits to the small town, swimming in a muddy stream.

In sum, **The Last of the Knucklemen** is disappointing, not for any marked defect of rendition, but rather because Burstall keeps his sights too low.

KEITH CONNOLLY[1]

[1] Extracted from Connolly's review in *Cinema Papers* (see References).

References
'Tim Burstall', a career interview with the director by Scott Murray, *Cinema Papers*, no. 23, September–October 1979, pp. 490–6, 576–7.
'**The Last of the Knucklemen**', a review by Keith Connolly, *Cinema Papers*, ibid., pp. 563–4.

THE LITTLE CONVICT

Yoram Gross presents The Little Convict. © 1979 Yoram Gross Film Studio. *Budget:* $423,467. *Australian distributor:* Roadshow. *Opened:* 20 December 1979. *Video:* CEL. *Rating:* G. 35 mm. 80 mins.

Producer: Yoram Gross. *Associate producer:* Sandra Gross. *Scriptwriter:* John Palmer. Based on an original story by Yoram Gross. *Lighting:* Madd Lighting. *Live-action photography:* Brian Probyn, Chris Ashbrook, Frank Hammond. *Animation photography:* Jenny Ochse, Bob Evans, Graham Sharpe, Ted Northover. *Wardrobe:* Judith Dorsman. *Editor:* Rod Hay. *Composer:* Bob Young. *Lyrics:* Rolf Harris, Harry Butler, Barry Booth, John Palmer, Davey & Hughes, Frank Roosen. *Songs performed by:* Rolf Harris. *Sound recordists:* Phil Judd, Laurie Napier, David McConnachie. *Sound editor:* Rod Hay. *Mixers:* Phil Heywood, Julian Ellingworth.

Animation director: Paul McAdam. *Character design:* Athol Henry, Paul McAdam. *Storyboard:* Laurie Sharpe. Background layouts: Amber Vellani. *Casting:* Richard Meikle. *Animators:* Athol Henry, John Hill, Cynthia Leech, Wal Logue, Paul McAdam, Ray Nowland, Vivien Ray, Irena Slapczynski, Kay Watts. *Inbetweeners:* Mark Benvenuti, Maria Brinkley, Jan D'Silva, Rodney D'Silva, Dianne Farrington, Wal Logue, Helen McAdam, Kay Watts, Milan Zahorski. *Colour design:* Carmel Lennon. Painters: Nancy Anning, Christopher Cole, Kim Craste, Ruth Edelman, Gail Engel, Murray Griffin, Seiko Kanda, Jane Kinny, Chris Long, Sue Mason, Krystyna Mikita, Belinda Price, Wende Weis.

Cast

Rolf Harris [The Old Storyteller[1]].

Voices

Sean Hinton (Toby), Kerry McGuire (Polly), Paul Bertram (Silly Billy), Shane Porteous (Jack Doolan), Harry Lawrence (Dipper), Gary Marika (Wahroonga), Anne Haddy (Augusta), Brian Harrison (Big George), Paul Bertram (Corporal Weazel Wesley), Gary Files (Governor Lightfoot), Richard Meikle (Sergeant Bully Langden), Ronald Falk (Pertwee).

[See Appendix A, pp. 352–4, for discussion of all the Yoram Gross films.]

---

1 Character name taken from press kit.

References
'The Little Convict', a review by Antoinette Starkiewicz, *Cinema Papers*, no. 26, April–May 1980, p. 141.
'Yoram Gross', an interview by Antoinette Starkiewicz, *Cinema Papers*, no. 48, October–November, 1984, pp. 334–8, 390.

The Old Storyteller (Rolf Harris), centre, with Governor Lightfoot and Augusta.

COLIN EGGLESTON

LONG WEEKEND

Dugong Films presents LONG WEEKEND. © 1977 Dugong Films. Produced with financial assistance from the Australian Film Commission and the Victorian Film Corporation. *Budget:* $420,000. *Locations:* Melbourne, Phillip Island (Victoria). *Filmed:* April–May 1977. *Australian distributor:* Roadshow. *Opened:* 29 March 1979. *Rating:* M (July 1978, 2578m). *Video:* CBS–Fox Video. *Video rating:* M (February 1984). 35mm. 92 mins.

Producer: Colin Eggleston. *Executive producer:* Richard Brennan. *Scriptwriter:* Everett De Roche. *Director of photography:* Vincent Monton. *Camera operator:* Louis Irving. *Production designer:* Larry Eastwood. *Wardrobe:* Kevin Reagan. *Editor:* Brian Kavanagh. *Composer:* Michael Carlos. *Sound recordist:* John Phillips. *Sound editor:* Peter Burgess. [*Mixer:* not credited.]

Cast

John Hargreaves (Peter), Briony Behets (Marcia), Mike McEwen (Truckie), Roy Day (Old Fisherman), Michael Aitkens (Barman), Sue Kiss von Soly (City Girl).

Long Weekend is a well-crafted thriller which very knowingly uses the conventions of a certain sub-genre of the *fantastique*. It is in the tradition of Hitchcock's **The Birds** (1963), Graham Baker's **Impulse** (1984) and J. G. Ballard's fiction (whose stories about beaches and drowning are especially recalled by the undead dugong of this film). In this tradition, unusual and eventually fatal events occur which seem to have a supernatural cause: here, nature takes revenge on a brutish city couple, Peter (John Hargreaves) and Marcia (Briony Behets).

While the viewer is clearly, almost emphatically, directed to this 'reading' of the story, it is never straightforwardly or unambiguously confirmed. The special cinematic potential of such stories comes from the fact that they simultaneously tend towards over-determined 'meaningfulness' (with every image and sound labouring to hint at allegorical or symbolic points) and its opposite: a sort of queer, flat, surrealistic literalness, meaning nothing. De Roche's work as a screenwriter (**Patrick**[1], *Heart of Midnight*) has often exploited this dual tendency, but **Long Weekend**, in its filmic realisation of the necessary ambiguity, remains a fairly unique achievement in Australian cinema.

As Meaghan Morris has observed, it is one of many local films (e.g., **Picnic at Hanging Rock**, **Peter Kenna's The Umbrella Woman**[2]) that 'makes poetry out of sexual polarization'[3]. The film is structured upon several sequences that intercut Peter and Marcia absorbed, alone, in the pursuits deemed appropriate to their respective genders: masculinity is equated with 'outdoors' activities (rugged mountaineering, hunting, loud exhibitionism, phallic gunplay and surfing), while femininity is equated with 'indoors' life (cooking, comfort, reading and auto-eroticism). Although this rigid polarisation, plus the thread of allegorical incidents and symbols suggesting that Marcia's abortion (resulting from a marital infidelity) is the principal 'crime' which nature is avenging, indicates a rather conservative view of contemporary sexual politics, it must be conceded that the film is hardly flattering to either character (in a sense condemning both to death), and that it glancingly portrays their 'malaise' as social in origin.

Any unilateral interpretation of the film is in fact difficult to sustain, given its consistent and often minute exploitation of the modern *fantastique* style. Ambiguities are generated everywhere, and different symbolic possibilities are tried out in the course of the film. For most of the story, for instance, it is suggested that only Marcia can hear the wail of the baby dugong (this 'subjectivity' signalled through clever aural treatments), because of its significance to her, but at the end it seems that Peter hears it as well.

Long Weekend succeeds as a film because it cleverly restricts its elements and articulates them exhaustively. The numerous cutaways to 'ominous' glimpses of the natural environment, employing extreme close-up and variable focus, are often effective. There are a number of strikingly dramatic camera movements, such as the one that first reveals the beach, or that which simulates Peter's slow discovery of Marcia's dead body in the morning light. The soundtrack integrates music and sound effects in a stylised, dramatic way, employing sonic surges, rumbles, reverberations and shock punctuations in the best contemporary thriller fashion.

ADRIAN MARTIN

[1] **Patrick** (Richard Franklin, 1978).
[2] **Picnic at Hanging Rock** (Peter Weir, 1975) and **Peter Kenna's The Umbrella Woman** (Ken Cameron, 1987).
[3] Meaghan Morris, 'Personal Relationships and Sexuality', in *The New Australian Cinema*, Scott Murray (ed.), Thomas Nelson and Cinema Papers, Melbourne, 1980, p. 143.

References

'**Long Weekend**', a review by Scott Murray, *Cinema Papers*, no. 20, March–April 1979, pp. 303–4.
'Everett De Roche', a career interview with the scriptwriter by Paul Davies, *Cinema Papers*, no. 25, February–March 1980, pp. 30–3, 76, 78.

Peter (John Hargreaves) searches for the dugong.

MAD MAX

Kennedy Miller present[s] MAD MAX. © 1979 Crossroads International Finance Co. N V. *Budget:* $380,000. *Locations:* Melbourne, Sunbury, Clunes (Victoria). *Filmed:* November–December 1977. *Australian distributor:* Roadshow. *Opened:* 12 April 1979. *Video:* Roadshow Home Video. *Rating:* R (April 1979; 2486.35m). 35mm. Todd AO. 91 mins.

Producer: Byron Kennedy. *Associate producer:* Bill Miller. *Scriptwriters:* James McCausland, George Miller. Based on a story by George Miller and Byron Kennedy. *Director of photography:* David Eggby. *Production designer:* Jon Dowding. *Costume designer:* Clare Griffin. *Editors:* Tony Paterson, Cliff Hayes.[1] *Composer:* Brian May. *Sound recordist:* Gary Wilkins. *Sound editor:* Ned Dawson (fx). *Mixer:* Roger Savage.[2]

Cast

Mel Gibson [Max Rockatansky[3]], Joanne Samuel [Jessie Rockatansky], Roger Ward [Fifi Macafee], Steve Bisley [Jim Goose], Tim Burns [Johnny], Hugh Keays-Byrne [The Toecutter]; Lisa Aldenhoven (Nurse), David Bracks (Mudguts), Bertrand Cadart (Clunk), David Cameron (Underground Mechanic), Robina Chaffey (Singer), Stephen Clarl (Sarse), Mathew Constantine (Toddler), Jerry Day (Ziggy), Reg Evans (Station Master), Howard Eynon (Diabando), Max Fairchild (Benno), John Farndale (Grinner), Peter Flemington (Senior Doctor), Sheila Florence[4] (May Sawaisy), Nic Gazzana (Starbuck), Hunter Gibb (Lair), Vince Gil (Nightrider).

A particular sequence of plot events in Mad Max leads to a moment when Jim Goose[5] (Steve Bisley) boards his motorbike, not knowing that it has been tampered with by members of the gang headed by The Toecutter (Hugh Keays-Byrne). The audience knows something terrible is going to happen to him, but can't be sure exactly what, so the film goes for a 'slow burn' of cinematic suspense: a montage of shots of Goose innocently riding down the highway before he reaches his fate. George Miller includes no less than fourteen shots (in little over a minute) in this exquisitely tense passage. This sequence is not usually cited among the film's bravura action 'set pieces', but, like them, it shows why Miller is perhaps Australia's most completely cinematic film-maker, and certainly the only one to have influenced film-making internationally (see, for instance, the subsequent

Jessie Rockatansky[7] (Joanne Samuel) and her baby try to escape a bikie gang.

work of the Coen brothers, Sam Raimi, John Carpenter and Tsui Hark).

This first film in the Mad Max series is less culturally dense, and less self-consciously 'mythic', than its sequels. Its principal narrative and iconographic elements have been cleanly abstracted from mainly contemporary, international traditions of action-adventure fiction: a lawless, broken-down society (reminiscent of the 'pioneer' setting of many Westerns), divided between leather-clad, nastily 'perverse' (i.e., homo-erotic) bikies and somewhat mercenary, law-enforcing trouble-shooters; a heroic 'lone warrior' (Mel Gibson as Max Rockatansky) who embodies 'decent' morality but, in his righteous, vengeful rage, comes to resemble the villains he fights; a pleasurably masochistic dwelling on the injuries of the male star (as in the star vehicles of Stallone, Norris and Eastwood).

Less well-recognised is the extent to which the film draws on contemporaneous horror-thriller movies (such as Tobe Hooper's **Texas Chainsaw Massacre**, 1975, and John Carpenter's **Halloween**, 1978) for its moments of gore (flashes of severed or charred body parts) and its insistent setting-up of women and children as imminent targets for violence.

Beyond this generic, 'intertextual' play, it is also undoubtedly true that **Mad Max**, in an unselfconscious, spontaneous, almost dreamlike way, taps into many aspects of what has been called the 'social imaginary' of Australia. The film captures many of the social and personal 'phantasms' that are embodied in what Miller himself has referred to as the nation's 'car culture': complex, collective ideas and emotions relating to freedom, space, community, speed, confinement, escape, risk, threat and gender rôles.

The film is uniquely powerful in its meshing of this 'social imaginary' with the intricate textual mechanics of modern action cinema. Too often reduced to its bare 'mythic' structure, **Mad Max** is most fully realised on the minute, material level of image-sound relations. As Alain Garel[6] has argued, the film's near-abstract, 'kinetic' thrust is certainly more historically important and internally successful (as is clear in retrospect) than its more conventionally dramaturgical side. This is a tension with which Miller will grapple in all his subsequent directorial projects. This writer, however, has no hesitation in celebrating the radical 'play' with form that **Mad Max** helped foster in 1980s mainstream cinema.

ADRIAN MARTIN

1 The front credits list only Tony Paterson as editor. Hayes is listed at the end when the editor credit is repeated.
2 The credit reads 'Post-production sound: Roger Savage'.
3 There are no character names on the credits for the first six actors; the names given are from various sources.
4 Should be spelt 'Florance'.
5 See footnote 3.
6 Alain Garel, 'George Miller', *La Revue du Cinéma*, no. 409, October 1985.
7 See footnote 3.

References

'Production Report: **Mad Max**', *Cinema Papers*, no. 21, May–June 1979, comprising an interview with producer Byron Kennedy by Peter Beilby and Scott Murray, pp. 366–8, and an interview with director George Miller, by Murray and Beilby, pp. 369–71.
'**Mad Max**', a review by Geoff Mayer, ibid., p. 383.
'Film Production Design…And the Word was Light', John Dowding, the film's production designer, *Cinema Papers*, no. 36, February 1982, pp. 426–31, 90–2, 94.
'Mel Gibson', an interview with the actor by Margaret Smith, *Cinema Papers*, no. 42, March 1983, pp. 12–17.
'We Need George Miller', Dave Maher, *Filmnews*, June 1979, p. 16.
'**Mad Max**: Another Rider of the Silver Screen', an interview with George Miller by Peter Page and Tina Kaufman, *Filmnews*, July 1979, pp. 8–10.
'Mad Max & The Warriors…The Seduction of Machismo', Karl Blond & Frank Watters, and '….or innocuous fantasy?', Barbara Alysen, *Filmnews*, October 1979, p. 14–15.

MONEY MOVERS

South Australian Film Corporation presents MONEY MOVERS. © 1978 South Australian Film Corporation. Made with the assistance of the New South Wales Film Corporation. *Budget:* $536,861. *Location:* Adelaide. *Filmed:* February–March 1978. *Australian distributor:* Roadshow. *Opened:* 1 February 1979. *Video:* Star Video. *Rating:* R (October 1978; 2551.82m; an appeal against the rating was rejected; reduced to 2525.82m at same rating in January 1979). 35mm. 92 mins.

Producer: Matt Carroll. *Scriptwriter:* Bruce Beresford. Based on the novel, *The Money Movers*, by Devon Minchin. *Director of photography:* Don McAlpine. *Camera operator:* John Seale. *Production designer:* David Copping. *Wardrobe:* Anna Senior. *Editor:* William Anderson. [*Composer:* not cred-ited.] *Sound recordist:* Don Connolly. [*Sound editor:* not credited.] *Mixers:* Peter Fenton, Julian Ellingworth.

Cast

Terence Donovan (Eric Jackson), Tony Bonner (Leo Bassett), Ed Devereaux (Dick Martin), Charles (Bud) Tingwell (Jack Henderson), Candy Raymond (Mindel Seagers), Bryan Brown (Brian Jackson), Alan Cassell (Sammy Rose), Lucky Grills (Robert Conway), Jeanie Drynan (Dawn Jackson), Gary Files (Ernest Sainsbury), Hu Pryce (David Griffiths), Frank Wilson (Lionel Darcy), Ray Marshall (Ed Gallagher), Tony Allison (Man at Bank), Brian Anderson (Technician), Kevin Brenner (Youth), Terry Camilleri (Dino), Bill Charlton (Second Guard), Kathy Dior (Managing Director's Secretary), Graham Gow (First Detective), James Elliot (Ben Lancer), Robert Essex (Tony Duggan), Max Fairchild (Toecutter).

Rather neglected at the time, Bruce Beresford's **Money Movers** remains one of the better action–thrillers made in this country.

Eric Jackson (Terence Donovan), a security supervisor at Darcys Security Services, plans to rob the 'counting house' of $20 million. His gang includes his brother, Brian (Bryan Brown), and union leader Ed Gallagher (Ray Marshall), whose ability to call a work stoppage at the right moment is a key to the robbery's success.

Unfortunately, the plan comes to the notice of a corrupt cop, Sammy Rose (Alan Cassell), and a grisly businessman, Mr Henderson (Charles (Bud) Tingwell). With the help of some extra pressures (wire-cutters lop off one of Eric's toes), Henderson muscles in. There is also the problem of

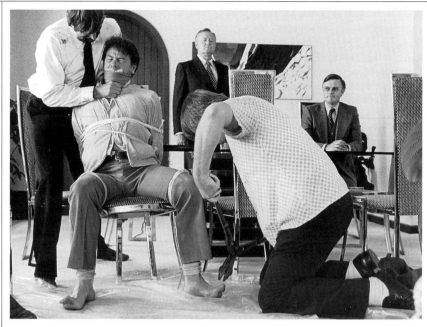

Eric Jackson (Terence Donovan) is tortured by Toecutter (Max Fairchild). Jack Henderson (Charles (Bud) Tingwell) and Ernest Sainsbury (Gary Files) watch.

an undercover insurance investigator, Leo Bassett (Tony Bonner), and an ex-cop, Dick Martin (Ed Devereaux).

All these narrative strands come together in a violent and well-staged finale. It caused alarm in 1979 over its 'excessive' violence, but had the critics known what Martin Scorsese had in store they might have been less vocal.

Running parallel with the action story are several depictions of Australian character. Foremost is the view of corruption in all spheres of life and how the average Aussie takes this for granted (no one, for example, shows surprise that the cop is bent). The film also plays with this notion by having the audience on side with Eric Jackson at the start, then slowly shifting sympathy to Dick Martin (who even admits to having been a bit on the take while in the police force).

A second undercurrent concerns homosexuality. The film depicts a very male world and the principal men live with no reference to heterosexuality (Henderson, Dick, Darcy (Frank Wilson)) or with bored disinterest (Eric). The only exceptions are Brian, who has a young blonde girlfriend, and Leo, who goes to bed with Mindel Seagers (Candy Raymond), but obviously as part of his investigation.

As well, Leo is accused of being a homosexual because he likes poetry; Henderson is shown to live alone with his aged mum (a staple image of homosexual gangsters in British crime films); and David Griffiths

(Hu Pryce) makes a pass at Eric, which is rejected and may part explain why David so over-kills Eric in the climax.

It is hard to determine any specific theme behind all this, except for the obvious mistrust of homosexuals Aussie males have, at least on the surface, and that homosexuality is more prevalent than its detractors may suppose. While some may find a slight tone of homophobia in the film, Beresford plays fair by having homosexuals on both sides of the law (David and Henderson).

Like Beresford's later **Puberty Blues** (1981), the film is shot by Don McAlpine to highlight the Australian ugliness. The interior light is harsh (and overhead), the colour schemes spectacularly vulgar.

The actors are so uniformly good it is unfair to highlight any, but Ed Devereaux was so under-used by the Australian cinema that, when he gives a performance like this, one misses acutely what else he could have done.

SCOTT MURRAY

References
'Money Movers', a review by Denise Hare, *Cinema Papers*, no. 22, July–August 1979, pp. 467–9.
'Bob Saunders', an interview with the man behind Pact Productions, one of the film's investors, by Peter Beilby, *Cinema Papers*, no. 31, March–April 1981, pp. 26–9, 100.
'The [sic] **Money Movers**', a review by Stuart Green, *Filmnews*, March 1979, p. 5.

MY BRILLIANT CAREER

The New South Wales Film Corporation and GUO Film Distributors present Margaret Fink's Production of My Brilliant Career. © 1979 Margaret Fink Films. *Budget:* $925,000. *Location:* Monaro region (New South Wales). *Filmed:* October–November 1978. *Australian distributor:* GUO. *Opened:* 17 August 1979. *Video:* Australian Video. *Rating:* G (July 1979; 2795m). 35mm. 100 mins.

Producer: Margaret Fink. *Associate producer:* Jane Scott. *Scriptwriter:* Eleanor Witcombe. Based on the novel by Miles Franklin. *Director of photography:* Don McAlpine. *Camera operators:* Peter Moss, Louis Irving. *Production designer:* Luciana Arrighi. *Costume designer:* Anna Senior. *Editor:* Nicholas Beauman. *Composer:* Nathan Waks. *Sound recordist:* Don Connolly. *Sound editor:* Greg Bell. *Mixer:* Peter Fenton.

Cast

Judy Davis (Sybylla Melvyn), Sam Neill (Harry Beecham), Wendy Hughes (Aunt Helen), Robert Grubb (Frank Hawden), Max Cullen (Mr McSwat), Aileen Britton (Grandma Bossier), Peter Whitford (Uncle Julius), Patricia Kennedy (Aunt Gussie); Possum Gully: Alan Hopgood (Father), Julia Blake (Mother), David Franklin (Horace), Marion Shad (Gertie), Arron Wood (Stanley), Sue Davies (Aurora), Gordon Piper (Barman), James Moss (Pub Drinker); Caddagat: Bill Charlton (Joe), Suzanne Roylance (Biddy), Zelda Smith (Ethel), Bobbie Ward (Mrs Butler); Five Bob Downs: Basil Clark (Butler), Amanda Pratt (Blanche Derrick), Dorothy St Heaps (Mrs Derrick), Gerry Duggan (Squatter), Babs McMillan (Miss Benson); McSwats: Carole Skinner (Mrs McSwat), Tony Hughes (Peter), Tina Robinson (Lizer), Aaron Corrin (Jimmy), Sharon Crouch (Sarah), Robert Austin (Willie), Mark Spain (Tommy), Simone Buchanan (Mary Anne), Hayley-Joye (Rosie Jane), Kathleen Percival (Baby).[2]

Just when the Australian cinema-going public seemed to have had its fill of period pieces, and just as 1979 looked like a bad year for local movies, Gill Armstrong's version of the turn-of-the-century classic by Miles Franklin gave the industry a shot in the arm critically and commercially. (George Miller's **Mad Max** was the only other major success of the year.)

Franklin's heroine, Sybylla Melvyn, predates the 1970s feminist movement by seven decades, but anticipates it in her determination to assert her own identity and her

own independence. She hankers for a literary career and the film, which begins with Sybylla (Judy Davis) announcing her intentions, ends with the consignment of her manuscript to Blackwood's, Edinburgh. Along the way she has left the genteel poverty of her home to live in the gracious comforts of her grandmother's house where her cultural leanings are fostered. She stays long enough at the opulent property Five Bob Downs for its owner, Harry Beecham (Sam Neill), to fall in love with her. Tempted as she is by his proposal and tested as she has been by a stint as governess with the teeming, squalid McSwats, she opts nevertheless to take her future into her own hands.

Much was made of the female-dominated production personnel – director, producer, associate producer, screenwriter and production designer – and the rôle of Sybylla of course launched Judy Davis as a major star of the new Australian cinema.[3] Her performance is resourceful and varied as she moves touchingly from egotistic yearnings through witty rebellion and awakened sexuality to an acceptance of her own individuality and a value for this. By allowing Sam Neill to present a more attractive Harry than Franklin's novel suggests, it might be argued that Armstrong and scriptwriter Eleanor Witcombe have pandered to the box-office value of a romantic hero. Equally, though, it might be said that Sybylla's feminist determination is made more persuasive if the man she renounces is handsome, kind

Harry Beecham (Sam Neill) and Sybylla Melvyn (Judy Davis).

and tolerant. The screenplay (and there is some contention about degrees of responsibility for it) in some ways sharpens and toughens Franklin's often callow and gushy novel. Witcombe and Armstrong, in shearing Sybylla of the novel's jaunty excesses, have enabled Davis to create a really substantial rôle, and one which still informs her screen persona.

The literary adaptation was a staple of Australian film production in the latter half of the 1970s, though public taste was no longer excited by it in 1979. However, **My Brilliant Career** showed the sub-genre at its best. It took a well-loved classic, discreetly updated it ideologically, gave it a narrative coherence not always apparent in the original, and, through a sumptuous visual style, ensconced the whole in a *mise-en-scène* that worked dramatically rather than merely pictorially. In these ways it encapsulates some of the key virtues of late '70s Australian filmmaking.

BRIAN McFARLANE

---

[1] Armstrong would credit herself on subsequent films as Gillian Armstrong.

[2] The lengthy end cast credits (oddly, there are none at the start) are grouped according to location ('Five Bob Downs', 'McSwats', etc.), so this ordering is but an attempt at fairness.

[3] Davis had appeared in one previous film, **High Rolling** (Igor Auzins, 1977), but she drew little attention.

References

'Production Report: **My Brilliant Career**', *Cinema Papers*, no. 20, March–April 1979, comprising an interview with producer Magaret Fink by Peter Beilby and Scott Murray, pp. 288–90, 319, and an interview with director Gill Armstrong by Beilby and Murray, pp. 291–3, 319.

'Luciana Arrighi', an interview with the production designer by Sue Adler, *Cinema Papers*, no. 22, July–August 1979, pp. 421–4.

'**My Brilliant Career**', a review by Brian McFarlane, *Cinema Papers*, no. 23, September–October 1979, pp. 564–5.

'Judy Davis', a career interview with the actor by John Ley and Steve Bisley, *Cinema Papers*, no. 32, May–June 1981, pp. 116–21.

'Wendy Hughes', an interview with the actor by Richard Brennan, *Cinema Papers*, no. 40, October 1982, pp. 428–32.

'Coming in from the Cold', an article (with quotes) on Gillian Armstrong by Debi Enker, *Cinema Papers*, no. 52, July 1985, pp. 26–9.

'Gillian Armstrong talking about her brilliant career', an interview by Barbara Alysen, Jeni Thornley and Tina Kaufman, *Filmnews*, October 1979, pp. 10–13.

TOM JEFFREY

THE ODD ANGRY SHOT

A Samson Film. THE ODD ANGRY SHOT. © 1979 Samson Productions Pty Ltd. *Budget:* $600,000. *Location:* Canungra (Queensland). *Filmed:* August–September 1978. *Australian distributor:* GUO. *Opened:* 1 March 1979. *Video:* Thorn EMI Video. *Rating:* M (January 1979; 2468.70[1]). 35mm. 92 mins.

Producers: Sue Milliken, Tom Jeffrey. *Scriptwriter:* Tom Jeffrey. Based on the novel by William Nagle. *Director of photography:* Don McAlpine. *Camera operator:* John Seale. *Production designer:* Bernard Hides. *Costume designer:* Anna Senior. *Editor:* Brian Kavanagh. *Composer:* Michael Carlos. *Sound recordist:* Don Connolly. *Sound editors:* Dean Gawen, Paul Maxwell. *Mixer:* Peter Fenton.

Cast

Graham Kennedy (Harry), John Hargreaves (Bung), John Jarratt (Bill), Bryan Brown (Rogers), Graeme Blundell (Dawson), Richard Moir (Medic), Ian Gilmour (Scott), Graham Rouse (The Cook), John Allen (Lieut. Golonka), Tony Barry (Black Ronnie), Brandon Burke (Isaacs), John Fitzgerald (Intelligence Corporal), Mike Harris (Sergeant Major), Johnny Garfield (Padre), Ray Meagher (Range Corporal), Frankie J. Holden (Spotted Soldier), Roger Newcombe (Lieut. Clifford), Brian Evis (Mayberry), Rose Ricketts (Nurse), Chuck McKinney (1st Marine), Freddie Paris (2nd Marine), Sharon Higgins (Bill's Girl).

When Tom Jeffrey's film was released in 1979, it came in for a good deal of misdirected critical flak because it wasn't a different kind of film about Vietnam. It was chided for not mounting a more obvious case against Australia's involvement in the Vietnam war.

The point that was often missed by reviewers brandishing their own liberal sensibilities was that **The Odd Angry Shot** is less a war film than a study, often played for comedy, of a group of soldiers coping with boredom and each other. Its concern is not so much to offer a critique of the Vietnam war as to examine certain kinds of Australian male humour and camaraderie in circumstances that, increasingly, place a great strain on these qualities. The best of the film is in the way it eventually finds these qualities inadequate.

A small group of the Special Air Services Regiment, 21 Patrol, led by the cynical Harry (Graham Kennedy), who is in flight from a broken marriage, is joined by another Australian, Bung (John Hargreaves), when his own group is disbanded. The members of 21 Patrol (played by a strong male ensemble also including Bryan Brown, John Jarratt, Graeme Blundell and Ian Gilmour) spend their time playing cards, drinking beer, nursing their tinea, and making routine jokes about masturbation and 'queens'. From time to time, they are sent off on a raiding party; they have leave in Saigon; they receive the odd disturbing bit of news from home; and,

in a final skirmish around a bridge, Bung is killed and the others exact revenge on the Viet Cong. The film's last moments, in which Harry and Bill (Jarratt) sit silently in a Sydney bar, suggest the sobering nature of the experience.

What is really wrong with the film is an absence of narrative thrust. There is little shape, little tension, little building of episodes, so that the film's pleasures remain those of incidental observation. If it aspires to the satire of **M.A.S.H.** (Robert Altman, 1970), it lacks the necessary harshness and black vision. **The Odd Angry Shot** is sometimes moving and sometimes comic but the whole is considerably less than the sum of the parts. It nevertheless scored reasonable financial success on its first release.

BRIAN MCFARLANE

---

[1] An AFC brochure lists the length at 2524m.

References
'Vietnam on Film', includes discussion of the film by Keith Connolly, *Cinema Papers*, no. 21, May–June 1979, pp. 334–8.
'**The Odd Angry Shot**', a review by Susan Dermody, ibid., pp. 387, 391.
'Bryan Brown', a career interview with the actor by Barbara Alysen, *Cinema Papers*, no. 31, March–April 1981, pp. 14–19.
'Men in Recent Oz Films', Glen Lewis, *Filmnews*, January–February 1980, p. 9.

Bill (John Jarratt), Bung (John Hargreaves), Rogers (Bryan Brown) and Harry (Graham Kennedy).

Special Air Services: Harry (Graham Kennedy) and Bung (John Hargreaves).

PATRICK WHITE'S THE NIGHT THE PROWLER

A New South Wales Film Corporation Presentation. PATRICK WHITE'S THE NIGHT THE PROWLER. © 1978 Chariot Films Pty. Ltd. *Budget:* $400,000. *Location:* Sydney. *Filmed:* November–December 1977. *Australian distributor:* Australian Film Institute. *Opened:* 15 June 1979. *Video:* Australian Video. *Rating:* M (May 1978; 2743m). 35mm. 90 mins.

Producer: Anthony Buckley. *Scriptwriter:* Patrick White. Based on the play by Patrick White. *Director of photography:* David Sanderson. *Camera operator:* Kevan Lind. *Production designer:* Luciana Arrighi. *Wardrobe:* Anna Senior. *Editor:* Sara Bennett. *Composer:* Cameron Allan. *Sound recordist:* Don Connolly. *Sound editor:* Paul Maxwell. *Mixer:* Peter Fenton.

Cast

Ruth Cracknell (Doris Bannister), John Frawley (Humphrey Bannister), Kerry Walker (Felicity Bannister), John Derum (John Galbraith), Maggie Kirkpatrick (Madge Hopkirk), Terry Camilleri (Prowler), Harry Neilson (Old Man), Peter Collingwood (Dr. Herborn), Robbie Ward (Mrs. Burstall), Merv Lillie (Alcoholic Man), Dorothy Hewitt (Alcoholic Woman), Ray Marshall (Detective 1), Robert Baxter (Detective 2), Paul Chubb (Policeman 1), John Cobley (Policeman 2), Ray Bennett (Sergeant), Alexander Archdale (Sir Roland Duddleston), Doris Fitton (Lady Duddleston), June Collis (Jill Pegley), Maggie Blinco (Patti Stevens), Roger Carroll (Harv), Paddy Madden (Dave).

Felicity Bannister (Kerry Walker) and Prowler (Terry Camilleri).

Patrick White's The Night The Prowler is about the dark side of suburban family life. The critical fortunes of the film also have their dark side. Selected to open the 1978 Sydney Film Festival, reviewers' reactions were scathing and vitriolic. David Stratton, however, was to later argue that this criticism was 'one of the most shameful and saddening chapters in the history of the new Australian cinema'[1]. Adrian Martin, in his turn, applauded the film in 1980 as 'the most ambitious film involving family relationships yet produced in Australia'[2].

The story begins as a tragi-comedy, focused on the hysterical reactions of Doris (Ruth Cracknell) and Humphrey Bannister (John Frawley) to an alleged sexual attack on their plain, overweight daughter, Felicity (Kerry Walker). Only much later, through flashback, is the truth of the incident involving the prowler and Felicity revealed. A complex narrative structure weaves between the present of Felicity's liberation and the past of the family.

It is this family which is the focus of an acerbic attack on middle-class attitudes and values. Ruth Cracknell's portrait of the oppressive, obsessive, incessantly cleaning mother is both comic and chilling. Endlessly gossiping to her friend Madge Hopkirk (Maggie Kirkpatrick) over the phone, she seems to get vicarious pleasure from recounting the rape of her daughter. The father's concern for his daughter's virginity also seems to veil a more fundamental sexual repression. The home's *mise-en-scène* further adds to the feelings of claustrophobia: kitschy baroque mirrors, copper fry-pan clocks, reproduction prints of young girls, chintzy wallpaper, bottles of 4711 cologne and Old Spice after-shave.

The film, however, changes from a comedy of manners into a journey of revelation as Felicity exploits the attack to break free from family, fiancé and lifestyle. In a poetic, surreal, blue-filtered dark night, Felicity dons black leather and becomes a prowler herself, menacing mainly men in streets and parks. She breaks into houses similar to her own to wreak revengeful havoc.

Stylistically, Felicity's night wanderings are so strange and fantastic they invite neither identification nor empathy. Even more bewildering is the film's closing sequence. It is implied that wisdom and realisation come to Felicity when she encounters a naked old man who is lying on a mattress on the ground in a rat-infested, derelict house, dreaming only of the past pleasures of easy bowel movements. After this encounter, so she says, Felicity is 'released'.

Patrick White's The Night The Prowler is a film that plays with expectations. It is alternatively comic and serious; sometimes a social document, at other times a thriller. It succeeds in bringing to the surface some of the darkest recesses of suburban family life. But the alternatives that could lie beyond are less than clear.

It is possible, however, that the film's inability to find convincing images of liberation may be a way of saying that escape from the family is unimaginable.

ANNA DZENIS

1 David Stratton, *The Last New Wave: The Australian Film Revival*, Angus & Robertson, Sydney, 1980, pp.168–9.
2 Adrian Martin, 'Fantasy', in *The New Australian Cinema*, Scott Murray (ed.), Thomas Nelson Australia and Cinema Papers, Melbourne, 1980. p. 111.

References
'The Night The Prowler', a review by Brian McFarlane, *Cinema Papers*, no. 20, March–April 1979, pp. 301–2.
'Jim Sharman', an interview with the director by Robyn Anderson and Sue Adler, *Cinema Papers*, ibid., pp. 268–71, 318.

SNAPSHOT

Antony I. Ginnane and William Fayman present for Australian International Film Corporation (a division of Filmways Australia) SNAPSHOT. [© not given; atb 1979.] Made in association with the Australian Film Commission and the Victorian Film Corporation. *Budget:* $310,000. *Location:* Melbourne. *Australian distributor:* Filmways. *Opened:* 1 June 1979. *Video:* Video Classics. *Rating:* M (December 1978; 2523m). 35mm. 92 mins.

Producer: Antony I. Ginnane. *Executive producer:* William Fayman. *Associate producer:* Barbi Taylor. *Scriptwriters:* Chris de Roche, Everett de Roche[1]. *Director of photography:* Vincent Monton. *Camera operator:* Louis Irving. *Production designers:* John Dowding, Jill Eden. *Costume designer:* Aphrodite Jansen[2]. *Editor:* Philip Reid. *Composer:* Brian May. *Sound recordist:* Paul Clark. *Sound editor:* Dean Gawen. *Mixer:* Peter Fenton.

Cast

Chantal Contouri [Madeline[3]], Robert Bruning (Elmer), Sigrid Thornton (Angela), Denise Drysdale (Lily), Vincent Gil (Daryl), Jon Sidney (Mr Pluckett), Jacqui Gordon (Becky), Julia Blake (Mrs Bailey), Hugh Keays-Byrne (Linsey), Peter Stratford (Roger), Christine Amor (Paula), Lulu Pinkus (Wendy), Bob Brown (Captain Rock), Stewart Faichney (Peter), Chris Milne (Book Marker), Peter Felmingham (Boris).

Two firemen walk into a burning building and douse a smouldering human corpse; on the pavement outside, a hysterical woman screams a name and is dragged away by police … These are the tantalising clues to the plot of this psychological thriller.

Screenwriters Chris and Everett de Roche and director Simon Wincer have endeavoured to create an after-dark nail-biter. By foretelling a final, violent act, **Snapshot** sets itself the task of maintaining a dramatic edge and satisfying viewer expectations to its conclusion. Wincer has all the ingredients to work with. It starts out (as suspense movies often do) with an innocent whose life is about to take an unforeseeable, sinister turn. The central character is Angela (Sigrid Thornton), a young hairdresser who gets lured into modelling by a bitchy magazine model, Madeline[4] (Chantal Contouri), who talks Angela into stripping for a perfume advertisement. This gets her noticed in the industry and that is when her problems start.

At this plot juncture, the naïve Angela is mixed up with some dicey characters: a sleazy film producer, Elmer (Robert Bruning); an eccentric magazine photographer, Linsey (Hugh Keays-Byrne); and an obsessive ex-boyfriend, Daryl (Vincent Gil). When horrible things start to happen – the discovery of a pig's head in her bed, for one – the viewer has good enough reason to believe someone wants Angela dead. The question is who and why?

Snapshot has a number of redeeming features, including some entertaining dialogue and a plot which offers some interesting twists. But anyone who has seen **Psycho** (Alfred Hitchcock, 1960), **Play Misty For Me** (Clint Eastwood, 1971), **The Godfather** (Francis Ford Coppola, 1972) or even **Duel** (Steven Spielberg, 1971) will know this is not a particularly inspired piece of cinema. Its camera work and, to a lesser extent, sound effects are unashamedly redolent of Hitchcock's suspense-building techniques. And while **Snapshot** builds into an adequate climax, it is flawed by a lull in momentum midway through.

In trying to fix the structural problems, Wincer has gone to great lengths to get the most out of his cast. Sigrid Thornton is convincing, particularly in her vulnerable moments, but most of the supporting actors overdo their parts to the point where they leave no room for interpretation. A male hairdresser is nothing other than a raving 'faggot'; Angela's schoolgirl sister is predictably po-faced and malicious; and it seems just a matter of time before the shonky film producer gets his new discovery to remove her blouse.

Most attempts to develop psychological idiosyncrasies of character are either flimsy or too familiar. But the script does offer some oddities of its own, the most obvious being the use of an omnipresent 'Mr Whippy' ice-cream truck, of all things, as a supposedly menacing element to the story.

Brian May's instrumental score features prominently during the film's tenser moments but, after a while, it is debatable how much suspense is aroused by the tinkling of an ivory key.

GREG KERR

---

[1] One of several variant spellings (De Roche, DeRoche, etc.)

[2] Later known as Aphrodite Kondos.

[3] Chantal Contouri's character name is not credited on the film. Contouri is credited at the beginning of the film but, puzzlingly, not at the end with all the other actors (and character names). In the film, her character is called 'Madeline', but should that be spelt 'Madelaine', etc.?

[4] See footnote 3.

References

'Snapshot', a review by Brian McFarlane, *Cinema Papers*, no. 21, May–June 1979, pp. 385–6.
'Everett De Roche', a career interview with the co-scriptwriter by Paul Davies, *Cinema Papers*, no. 25, February–March 1980, pp. 30–3, 76, 78.

Angela (Sigrid Thornton) and the sleazy Elmer (Robert Bruning).

THIRST

NSW Film Corporation[,] Antony I. Ginnane & William Fayman present THIRST. © 1979 F. G. Film Productions. Made in association with the New South Wales Film Corporation and the Victorian Film Corporation. *Budget:* $750,000. *Location:* Montsalvat, Melbourne. *Australian distributor:* GUO. *Opened:* 28 September 1979. *Video:* Video Classics. *Rating:* M (May 1979; 2538m). 35mm. 93 mins.

Producer: Antony I. Ginnane. *Executive producer:* William Fayman. *Associate producer:* Barbi Taylor. *Scriptwriter:* John Pinkney. *Director of photography:* Vincent Monton. *Camera operator:* Louis Irving. *Production designer:* Jon Dowding. *Costume designer:* Aphrodite Kondos. *Editor:* Philip Reid. *Composer:* Brian May. *Sound recordist:* Paul Clark. *Sound editors:* Terry Rodman, Peter Burgess. *Mixer:* Peter Fenton.

Cast

Chantal Contouri (Kate Davis), Shirley Cameron (Mrs Barker), Max Phipps (Mr Hodge), Henry Silva (Dr Gauss), Rod Mullinar (Derek), Amanda Muggleton (Martha), Robert Thompson (Sean), Rosie Sturgess (Lori), David Hemmings (Dr Fraser), Walter Pym (Dichter), Lulu Pinkus[1] (Nurse), Chris Milne (David), Jacqui Gordon (Leah), Val Christensen (Toni), Glenys O'Brien (Guide), Ben Nightingale (Tourist Driver), Stephen Clark (Barman), Stewart Faichney (Security Man), David Vella (Security Man), Paddy Burnet (Blue Rinse Lady), Yvette Rees (Nurse), Vicki Andonopoulos (The Child Kate).

One morning, Kate Davis (Chantal Contouri), a successful young career woman, is shocked to discover that the milk carton which has just spilt on the kitchen floor contains blood. Immediately afterwards she is drugged and abducted by members of a mysterious sect called 'The Brotherhood', and taken to a secret location.

Kate awakens some time later in what appears to be a hospital ward where a nurse offers her blood to drink, which she refuses. Scared and confused, she is told by her captors that she is descended from an ancient, aristocratic family of vampires, and that her destiny is preordained. But Kate's refusal to accept such a notion compels her prisoners to use drastic measures to break down her resistance. The sadistic Mrs Barker (Shirley Cameron) advocates the use of drug-induced brainwashing and, although the urbane Dr Fraser (David Hemmings) opposes such a course of action, he is outnumbered by his colleagues.

The 'farm' on which Kate is now a prisoner is a kind of human dairy where human 'cattle' are kept docile and regularly milked of their blood. Vampirism has come a long way since Count Dracula's day: the human blood is pasteurised in sanitary, high-tech surroundings and then packaged in milk-cartons for mass distribution. When Kate discovers what is going on here, she immediately flees. She steals a truck, but is soon recaptured.

In spite of Dr Fraser's misgivings about the possible psychological consequences, Kate is administered powerful hallucinogenic drugs and subjected to a series of nightmarish encounters. When she is finally unable to distinguish fantasy from reality, Kate submits to her captors' will and is delivered from her terrors.

Once she has undergone an initiation ceremony into The Brotherhood, where she feasts on a chosen victim's blood, she is returned to her normal, everyday life. Although she is unaware of her previous ordeal, she is plagued with persistent nightmares and a compulsive thirst for blood.

One day her lover, Derek (Rod Mullinar), is abducted and taken to the farm for conditioning, but Dr Fraser decides to help him escape to a secret hideout in the woods. Kate is later taken to be reunited with Derek, but when she arrives at the hideout, Dr Fraser's true motives are revealed. He, like Kate, is descended from a long line of aristocratic vampires and seeks to unite their respective blood lines (get it?). Hence, a glorious destiny is about to be fulfilled.

Thirst is a variation on the popular 1970s 'vampire' genre, which seems to have drawn on certain elements of science fiction – especially the American film **Soylent Green** (Richard Fleischer, 1973) – for its inspiration. The theme of unspeakable evil lurking beneath surface normality was a common preoccupation of science-fiction horror in the 1970s. As a horror film, **Thirst** is somewhat lacking: only the hallucination sequence is really effective in conveying a sense of paranoid disorientation.

BRUCE SANDOW

Kate Davis (Chantal Contouri) contemplates escape from the 'farm'.

---

[1] Now known as 'Lulu Serious'.

References

'Thirst', a review by Geoff Mayer, *Cinema Papers*, no. 23, September–October 1979, p. 571.
'Bob Saunders', an interview with the man behind Pact Productions, one of the film's investors, by Peter Beilby, *Cinema Papers*, no. 31, March–April 1981, pp. 26–9, 100.

TIM

Satori presents Pisces Productions in association with Australian Film Commission[,] G.U.O. Film Distributors Pty Ltd [and the] Nine Television Network of Australia presents Tim. © 1979 Pisces Productions Pty Ltd. *Budget:* $650,000. *Location:* Sydney. *Filmed:* August–September 1978. *Australian distributor:* GUO. *Opened:* 13 July 1979. *Video:* Thorn–EMI. *Rating:* M (April 1979; 2984m). 35mm. 109 mins.

Producer: Michael Pate. *Associate producer:* Geof Gardiner. *Scriptwriter:* Michael Pate. Based on the novel by Colleen McCullough. *Director of photography:* Paul Onorato. *Camera operator:* Frank Hammond. *Production designer:* John Carroll. *Costume designer:* Pat Forster. *Editor:* David Stiven. *Composer:* Eric Jupp. *Sound recordist:* Les McKenzie. *Sound editor:* Bob Cogger. *Mixer:* Peter Fenton.

Cast

Piper Laurie (Mary Horton), Mel Gibson (Tim Melville), Alwyn Kurts (Ron Melville), Pat Evison (Em Melville), Peter Gwynne (Tom Ainsley), Deborah Kennedy (Dawnie Melville), David Foster (Mick Harrington), Michael Caulfield (John Harrington), Margo Lee (Mrs Harrington), James Condon (Mr Harrington), Brenda Senders (Mrs Porter), Kevin Leslie (Curly), Allen Penney (Mr Thompson), Brian Barrie (Dr Perkins), Geoff Usher (Minister), Bill Charlton (Builder), Sheila McGuire Taylor (Celebrant), Doris Goddard (Maud), Catherine Bray (Mrs Martinson), Arthur Faynes (Ambulance Attendant).

Tim Melville (Mel Gibson) and Mary Horton (Piper Laurie).

As the 1970s drew to a close and the New Australian Cinema looked sure to remain for the long haul, one began to witness an odd spectacle: a handful of films started to emerge which cast off the shackles of historical drama and looked at the contemporary world. **Mad Max** (George Miller, 1979), **The Odd Angry Shot** (Tom Jeffrey, 1979) and **Tim**, among others, are memorable examples.

But whereas **Mad Max** went on to become one of the most successful action films in the world at the time, and **The Odd Angry Shot** was one of the first films to address the question of the Vietnam experience, **Tim** works on the less exciting, but still potentially rewarding, ground of Australian social realism.

The film brings together the intellectually-handicapped Tim Melville (Mel Gibson), and a cultured, middle-aged American business woman, Mary Horton (Piper Laurie).

As Tim, Mel Gibson offers a plausible performance, having to rely for much of the film on displaying his physique to the fascinated Mary. Piper Laurie, too, is impressive, as Mary wrestles with the idea of her attraction to Tim, who is 'not the full quid' as his father, Ron (Alywn Kurts), quickly tells her, and the fact that in her world she is going to look strange.

Director Michael Pate, making one of his few forays to the other side of the camera, makes the most of the two worlds represented by the co-stars. This is particularly evident by his initial juxtaposition, and then merging, of these worlds (when the lovers eventually marry). Where Pate disappoints, however, is in not going further with the examination of prevailing attitudes to sexual stereotypes, particularly in relation to the middle-aged Mary. Instead, he opts for the happy-ever-after ending, more in keeping with the original material, written by popular novelist Colleen McCullough.

Woven around Tim and Mary's slowly developing romance is a portrait of Tim's family, his aged parents worrying for his future and his sister about to get married. These secondary characters provide the film with its real strength, particularly in the scenes shot in the family home, where Tim's new-found interest generates both amusement and pathos.

Though at various moments during the film's duration it actually gets there, overall **Tim** is a disappointment, reverting to melodrama where the potential to address interesting if not important issues remains just that: potential.

PETER LAWRANCE

References

'Michael Pate', an interview with the director by Peter Beilby and Scott Murray, *Cinema Papers*, no. 21, May–June 1979, pp. 346–9, 401.
'Tim', a review by Dorothy Hewett, *Cinema Papers*, no. 23, September–October 1979, pp. 567–8.
'Mel Gibson', an interview with the actor by Margaret Smith, *Cinema Papers*, no. 42, March 1983, pp. 12–17.

Lt. George Witton (Lewis Fitz-Gerald), Lt. Peter Handcock (Bryan Brown) and Harry 'Breaker' Morant (Edward Woodward). Bruce Beresford's 'Breaker' Morant.

BLOOD MONEY

[No opening production company credit.] BLOOD MONEY. © [date not given; atb 1980] GL Film Enterprises Pty Ltd. Produced with the assistance of the Creative Development Branch of the Australian Film Commission. *Location:* Melbourne. *Australian distributor:* Greg Lynch Film Enterprises. *Opened:* 23 October 1980. *Video:* GL Video. *Rating:* M¹ (October 1980; 691.11m). 16mm. 63 mins.

Producers: Tom Broadbridge, Chris Oliver. *Scriptwriters:* Chris Fitchett, John Ruane, Ellery Ryan. *Director of photography:* Ellery Ryan. [*Production designer:* not credited.] [*Costume designer:* not credited.] *Editor:* Chris Oliver. *Composer:* Mark McSherry. *Sound recordist:* Lloyd Carrick. *Sound editor:* Chris Warner. [*Mixer:* not credited.]

Cast

John Flaus (Pete Shields), Chrissie James (Jeannie), Bryan Brown (Brian Shields), Sophie Murphy (Kathy), John Proper (Jack), Peter Curtin (Dan), Sue Jones (Doctor), Jay Mannering (Jim), Peter Stratford (Curtis), Caroline Cassidy (Lisa Curtis), Michael Carmen (Assistant Manager), Garry Metcalf (Anderson), Tom Broadbridge (Parking Officer), Joanne Baker (Salesgirl), Nigel Broadbridge (Tony), Peter Tammer (Laurie), Peggy Nicholls (Lady), Ron Brierley (Taxi Driver), Dean Carey (Young Policeman), Murray Crawford (Gunman).

Blood Money is a fine, economic piece of crime fiction. Unusually for a local film coming at the start of the 1980s, it draws knowingly on a wide range of situations, characters and themes beloved of the crime genre both in cinema and 'pulp' literature.

The plot centres on an ageing criminal, Pete Shields (John Flaus), who re-enters the 'underworld' only to find that its values and manners have changed radically. Modern crime is corporate, mercenary, full of conniving entrepreneurs and trigger-happy 'punks'; Shields' way is straight, tough, true.

Facing death through cancer, Shields kidnaps the daughter of the criminal kingpin Curtis (Peter Stratford), and elaborately stage-manages his own death. (For a late 1980s American B-movie variation on this classic generic premise, compare Eric Red's **Cohen and Tate**, 1989.)

Beyond these action elements, the film's principal dramatic resonance emerges from the tense and ambiguous familial relation between Shields, his brother Brian (Bryan Brown), Brian's wife Jeannie (Chrissie James) and their daughter Kathy (Sophie Murphy). The dramatic 'subtext' haunting the film, surfacing only in hints and allusions, is the possibility that Kathy is in fact Pete's child from his past affaire with Jeannie. This brings into play a complex swirl of emotions, particularly between the brothers – love and hate, loyalty and resentment.

In this emotional context, Pete's final 'suicide' is especially ambiguous. On the one hand, his act cements Brian's established nuclear family unit by providing money for Kathy's future, and removing himself as the point of 'trouble', the lurking, repressed element from the past threatening the family's stability. On the other hand, his act may be bitterly ironic: the gift of 'dirty' criminal money, and the fact that he arranges for Brian to see him die, suggest a cruel symbolic gesture against the 'sanctified' façade of the family that has excluded him. Which is to say, **Blood Money** draws on the rich thematic matrix of 'the home' and 'the outsider' present not only in crime dramas, but more especially in Westerns like John Ford's **The Searchers** (1956), the ambiguous resolution of which is echoed in Brian's final line, 'We're going home.'

Blood Money is notable mainly for these thematic complexities structured carefully into the script and skilfully executed by the cast. For a crime-thriller, its action scenes are rather tentative, and it is somewhat under-stylised in the use of lighting, composition and sound effects. Like the later directorial work of co-writer John Ruane (*Feathers*, short, 1986; **Death in Brunswick**, 1991), it tends more towards good literature than good cinema, but this is a virtue that perhaps should not be too underestimated.

ADRIAN MARTIN

¹ The video cover wrongly states the rating to be 'NRC'.

Reference
'**Blood Money**', a review by Adrian Martin, *Cinema Papers*, no. 30, December 1980–January 1981, pp. 479–80.

Pete Shields (John Flaus) and brother Brian (Bryan Brown).

'BREAKER' MORANT

South Australian Film Corporation presents 'Breaker' Morant. © 1979 South Australian Film Corporation. Made with the assistance of the Australian Film Commission, The Seven Network and PACT Productions. *Budget:* $800,000. *Location:* Burra (South Australia). *Filmed:* May–June 1979. *Australian distributor:* Roadshow. *Opened:* 16 May 1980. *Video:* Australian Video. *Rating:* NRC (February 1980; 2928.24m). 35mm. 104 mins.

Producer: Matthew Carroll. *Scriptwriters:* Jonathan Hardy, David Stevens, Bruce Beresford. Based on the play by Kenneth Ross. *Director of photography:* Don McAlpine. *Camera operator:* Peter Moss. *Production designer:* David Copping. *Costume designer:* Anna Senior. *Editor:* William Anderson. *Musical arranger:* Phil Cuneen. *Sound recordist:* Gary Wilkins. [*Sound editor:* not credited.] *Mixers:* Phil Judd, Phil Heywood.

Cast

Edward Woodward (Harry 'Breaker' Morant), Jack Thompson (Major J. F. Thomas), John Waters (Capt. Alfred Taylor), Bryan Brown (Lt. Peter Handcock), Charles Tingwell (Lt. Col. Denny), Terence Donovan (Capt. Simon Hunt), Vincent Ball (Col. Ian (Johnny) Hamilton), Ray Meagher (Sgt. Maj. Drummond), Chris Haywood (Capt. Sharp), Russell Kiefel (Christiaan Botha), Lewis Fitz-Gerald (Lt. George Witton), Rod Mullinar (Maj. Charles Bolton), Alan Cassell (Lord Kitchener), Rob Steele (Capt. Robertson), Chris Smith (Cameron Sergeant), Bruno Knez (Rev. Hesse), John Pfitzner (Boer Leader), Frank Wilson (Dr. Johnson), Michael Procanin (Visser), Ray Ball (Court Reporter), Halifa Cisse (Black Guide), Norman Currer (Boer Singer), Bridget Cornish (Hunts [sic] Sister), Judy Dick (Mrs. Shiels), Barbara West (Mrs. Vanderberg).

I n Pietersburg, Transvaal, in 1901, three officers of the Bushveldt Carbineers are being court-martialled for the shooting of Boers, who had killed and mutilated a British captain, and the killing of a German missionary, before he could spread word about the Carbineers. The film, based on this episode of the Boer War, alternates between the trial and the events which gave rise to it.

Essentially, the three Carbineers are being sacrificed by the British imperialist powers in the hope of preventing Germany from entering the war on the side of the Boers. Two of the Carbineers are Australian, Lt. Peter Handcock (Bryan Brown) and Lt. George

Lt. Peter Handcock (Bryan Brown) and Mrs Vanderberg (Barbara West), with daughter.

Witton (Lewis Fitz-Gerald); the third is the eponymous British adventurer long associated with Australia. The outcome of the court-martial is the execution of Harry 'Breaker' Morant (Edward Woodward) and Handcock, and the imprisonment of Witton.

'Breaker' Morant is one of a series of films directed by Bruce Beresford in which he examines the play of loyalties in a hierarchical set-up, and in which he deplores the effects of a self-serving authoritarianism. Films as diverse as **The Getting of Wisdom** (1977) and **David Williamson's The Club** (1980) are further examples. In 'Breaker' Morant, the milieu is that of the army and Beresford several times shows himself a perceptive chronicler of social groups. Here, he sees the gap between the British who represent authority, vested especially in the duplicitous figure of Lord Kitchener (Alan Cassell), and the colonial soldiers, on whom the imperial enterprise depends, as a space permitting manipulation and treachery. By contrast with the way in which the three officers realise they have been betrayed by their superiors is the growing trust and respect they feel for their Australian defence counsel.

The British and British attitudes have not often been favourably represented in new Australian cinema, but **'Breaker' Morant** is no mere anti-British tirade. Its strength is in the network of relationships it creates: between the three officers under trial and their counsel, between the latter and his English counterpart, between the soldiers and their peace-time intimates. The film pre-

sents the facts of the case with considerable regard for authenticity and its anti-British feeling represents 1980 thinking even more strongly than 1901 facts. However, the film's success was more likely due to its finely-acted human drama and to Beresford's skill in maintaining fluidity in an often static setting.

BRIAN MCFARLANE

References

'Breaker [sic] Morant', a review by Jack Clancy, *Cinema Papers*, no. 28, August–September 1980, p. 283.

'Edward Woodward', an interview with the actor by Tom Ryan, *Cinema Papers*, no. 29, October–November 1980, pp. 332–3.

'Breaker [sic] Morant Rethought or Eighty Years On, The Culture Still Cringes', Stephen Crofts, *Cinema Papers*, no. 30, December 1980–January 1981, pp. 420–1.

'Ellis Vs Crofts', incorporating a letter from scriptwriter Bob Ellis in reference to Crofts article (see above), followed by Crofts' reply, *Cinema Papers*, no. 31, March–April 1981, pp. 11–13.

'Bryan Brown', a career interview with the actor by Barbara Alysen, *Cinema Papers*, ibid., pp. 14–19.

'Bob Saunders', an interview with the man behind Pact Productions, one of the film's investors, by Peter Beilby, ibid., pp. 26–9, 100.

'Breaker [sic] Morant: Patterns of Heroism', Thelma Ragas, *Cinema Papers*, no. 36, February 1982, pp. 48–9, 53.

'Going South: The Adelaide Connection', an article on the SAFC by Philippa Hawker, *Cinema Papers*, no. 61, January 1987, pp. 20–3.

'Where the Boys Are', Jeni Thornley, *Filmnews*, February 1981, p. 10.

THE CHAIN REACTION

A Palm Beach Picture. THE CHAIN REACTION. *Alternative title:* 'The Man at the Edge of the Freeway' (working). © 1980 Palm Beach Pictures. *Budget:* $450,000. *Location:* Glen Davis (New South Wales). *Filmed:* September–October 1979. *Australian distributor:* Hoyts. *Opened:* 25 September 1980. *Video:* Australian Video. *Rating:* M (April 1980; 2509.90m). 35 mm. 92 mins.

Producer: David Elfick. *Associate producers:* Ross Matthews, George Miller. *Scriptwriter:* Ian Barry. *Director of photography:* Russell Boyd. *Camera operator:* Nixon Binney. *Production designer:* Graham Walker. *Costume designer:* Norma Moriceau. *Editor:* Tim Wellburn. *Composer:* Andrew Thomas Wilson. *Sound recordist:* Lloyd Carrick. *Sound editors:* Lindsay Frazer (dia.); Anne Ohlsson, Greg Bell, Tim Wellburn (fx). *Mixers:* Phil Judd, Phil Heywood.

Cast

Steve Bisley (Larry), Arna-Maria Winchester (Carmel), Ross Thompson (Heinrich), Ralph Cotterill (Gray), Hugh Keays-Byrne (Eagle), Lorna Lesley (Gloria), Richard Moir (Constable Piggott), Patrick Ward (Oates), Laurie Moran (Sergeant McSweeney), Michael Long (Doctor), Bill McCluskey (Ralph), Margo Lloyd (Molly), Tim Burns (Survey Driver), Arthur Sherman (Byron Langley), Barry Donnelly (Gateman), P. J. Jones (Bernie the Beater), David Bracks (Spray Painter), Jore Winchester (Marcia), Joshua Ward (Jason Stillson), Ryan McKibbon (Stephen Stillson), Kim Gyngell (Crabs), Roger Ward (Moose), Sal Sarah (Pellegrini), Frankie J. Holden (Farts).

The Chain Reaction arrived on the heels of **Mad Max** (George Miller, 1979) – including chase scenes supervised by George Miller himself – and was enthusiastically linked to it by critics demanding a vigorous 'genre' cinema in Australia, free of the obligation to be sedately naturalistic and earnestly 'meaningful' like so many films of the early-1970s 'renaissance'. Although seldom cited with such ardour in the intervening years, it now deserves to be rated (as Carol Barker suggests in a 1991 issue of *Continuum*) as one of the richest and most appealing Australian features related to 'exploitation' cinema.

Writer–director Ian Barry (whose subsequent career sadly did not follow the kind of path signposted by this film) seems to know both the narrative structures and æsthetic mechanisms of the various action genres very well indeed. The film economically ties together a number of classical plot

Larry (Steve Bisley), Heinrich (Ross Thompson) and Carmel (Arna-Maria Winchester).

devices – a race against time, loss of memory, imminent catastrophe, the clash of innocent bystanders and a sinisterly ubiquitous State system – around the central premise of a leak in a nuclear power plant. The innocents are played colourfully by Steve Bisley and Arna-Maria Winchester, incarnating amid the explosive mayhem various 'typically Australian' attitudes and reactions (such as anti-authoritarianism) that work to 'customise' an American film model to a local sensibility.

The film's cinematic style is rigorous and consistently inventive, full of attention-grabbing visual and aural effects. In the images there is a well-thought-out use of slow tracking shots, gothic shadows and a play between foreground and background spaces; and on the soundtrack, a multi-functional synthesised score that mixes conventional music, the 'treated' sounds of objects within the fiction, and a range of intermediate sound effects that disorientate and intrigue the viewer.

Predictably, the film was criticised on its initial release for its 'shallow', functional characterisation – in fact perfectly suited to the æsthetic needs of a genre movie – and for its 'sensationalist' treatment of a topical political issue. As in so much exploitation cinema, the 'big theme' (here, the nuclear question) indeed functions as a mere pretext, a device for generating thrilling structures and effects. And yet the aura of gothic menace and paranoia that the film exudes is surely not an entirely inappropriate artistic response to one of the principal terrors of our age. In retrospect, **The Chain Reaction** looks to be not only a cinematically exciting, but also a culturally apposite expression of collective dread.

ADRIAN MARTIN

References

'Chain Reaction [sic]', a production report by Graham Shirley, *Cinema Papers*, no. 25, February–March 1980, pp. 15–19.
'The Chain Reaction', a review by Rick Thompson, *Cinema Papers*, no. 30, December 1980–January 1981, pp. 476–7.

DAVID WILLIAMSON'S THE CLUB

South Australian Film Corporation and the NSW Film Corporation present David Williamson's the club. © 1980 South Australian Film Corporation. *Location:* Melbourne. *Australian distributor:* Roadshow. *Opened:* 18 September 1980. *Video:* Australian Video. *Rating:* M (September 1980; 2633.28m). 35mm. 96 mins.

Producer: Matt Carroll. *Associate producer:* Moya Iceton. *Scriptwriter:* David Williamson. Based on the play, *The Club*, by David Williamson. *Director of photography:* Don McAlpine. *Production designer:* David Copping. *Wardrobe:* Ruth de la Lande. *Editor:* William Anderson. *Composer:* Mike Brady. *Sound recordist:* Gary Wilkins. *Sound editor:* William Anderson. *Mixers:* Phil Judd, Phil Haywood[1].

Cast

Jack Thompson (Laurie Holden), Harold Hopkins (Danny Rowe), Graham Kennedy (Ted Parker), John Howard (Geoff Hayward), Frank Wilson (Jock Riley), Alan Cassell (Gerry Cooper), Maggie Doyle (Susy), Lou Richards (Commentator), Toni Gay Shaw (Stripper), Jack Harris (1st Club Official), Frank Haggart (2nd Club Official), Jim Cain (3rd Club Official), Gary Files (2nd Football Commentator), Ed Turley (Tony), Scot Palmer (Newspaper Reporter 1), Ron Carter (Newspaper Reporter 2), Nick Harvey (MC at Ballroom), Ann Henderson (Geoff's Sister), Diana Greentree (Geoff's Mother), John Proper (Rostoff), Susan Hopkins (Danny's Girlfriend).

Bruce Beresford's adaptation of David Williamson's *The Club* takes one back to a time when sport, especially the local version of football, was seen as a recreational activity by both players and supporters alike. This is not to suggest the game of football and the various clubs that surround Melbourne have been breeding grounds for fierce loyalty and, in the process, created a strong sense of identity for those involved. Since the VFL went national, and encouraged corporate involvement, it would seem the notion of a 'club' in the aforementioned context is an anachronism.

Thus, on one level at least, Beresford's film offers a nostalgic view of the passionate game of football. On another level, **David Williamson's The Club** shows the machinations of a 'fictional' team and a sample of the internal politicking from which the narrative structure is generated. Through a diverse array of characters – and through

scriptwriter David Williamson's acute understanding of human greed and opportunism – the film becomes an intriguing and often witty examination of the forces that motivate those involved.

In a story that plots the slow rise of a football club at the base of the ladder, a feature of the film is the interplay that takes place between the actual games and boardroom shuffling, where personalities are toppled at an alarming rate. As a film that tackles the game of football at a parochial level, the director creates an understanding of the game that can be clearly understood by audiences living beyond Australian shores.

For all that, much of the credit must be directed at Beresford's cast, who include Graham Kennedy as president Ted Parker, who gets shafted, and Frank Wilson as Jock Riley, whose scheming, nasty approach is the cause for much of the film's comic achievement. Also notable are Jack Thompson as coach Laurie Holden, and John Howard as Geoff Hayward, a new

Tasmanian recruit with exceptional football skills and a penchant for arguing with the board members. Alongside these characters is a select cast of 'real' footballers drawn from the then Collingwood football team.

The combination of behind-the-scenes drama and insertion of actual football footage creates a fast-paced and often amusing vision of how things once were in this arena of sport.

PETER LAWRANCE

---

[1] Should be spelt 'Phil Heywood'.

References

'The Club', a review by Keith Connolly, *Cinema Papers*, no. 29, October–November 1980, pp. 377–8.

'David Williamson', an analysis of the work of the playwright and scriptwriter by Cecilia Rice, *Cinema Papers*, no. 32, May–June 1981, pp. 122–7.

'Where the Boys Are', Jeni Thornley, *Filmnews*, February 1981, p. 10.

Scheming Jock Riley (Frank Wilson) and fiery coach Laurie Holden (Jack Thompson).

P E T E R   C O L L I N S O N

THE EARTHLING

Samuel Z. Arkoff presents THE EARTH-LING.[1] © 1980 Filmways Pictures Inc. *Locations:* Blue Mountains, Barrington Forest (New South Wales). *Filmed:* September–October 1979. *Australian distributor:* Roadshow. *Opened:* 24 July 1980. *Video:* Roadshow. *Rating:* NRC (July 1980; 2660.71m). 35mm. 97 mins.[2]

Producers: Elliot Schick, John Strong. *Executive producer:* Stephen W. Sharmatt. *Scriptwriter:* Lanny Cotler. *Director of photography:* Don McAlpine. *Camera operator:* John Seale. *Production designers:* Bernard Hides, Bob Hilditch, David Copping. *Costume designer:* Judith Dorsman. *Editor:* Frank Morriss. *Composer:* Dick De Benedictis. *Sound recordist:* Don Connolly. *Sound editors:* Bill Stevenson, Bob Biggart. *Mixers:* Bill Varney, Steve Maslow, Gregg Landaker; Willie Schmidt (music).

Cast

William Holden (Patrick Foley), Ricky Schroder (Shawn Daley), Jack Thompson (Ross Daley), Olivia Hamnett (Bertina Daley), Alwyn Kurts (Christian Neilson), Pat Evison (Mrs Neilson), Redmond Phillips (Buddy Burns), Ray Barrett (Parnell), Tony Barry (Red), Allan Penney (Harlan), Willy Fennell (R. C.), Walter Pym (Uncle), Cul Cullen (Dawson), Dawn Schroder (Dalton), Maggie Blinco (Jessica), Tui Bow (Lyla), Danny Adcock (Bus Driver).

Of those Australian films about figures 'lost' in the landscape, two which stand out are **Walkabout** (1971) and **The Earthling**. Both were made by foreigners (Nicolas Roeg and Peter Collinson) and both were vilified on their release. The former has since gained its deserved status in the pantheon, but the more minor **The Earthling** remains ignored to this day.

Patrick Foley (William Holden), dying presumably of cancer, returns from America to his outback country town. There, after the briefest of conversations with long-lost acquaintances, he sets off over the mountains to a remote and hidden valley where his father once carved out a small farm.

On his way, he comes across Shawn Daley (Ricky Schroder), who has just seen his father and mother die in a campervan accident. Lost, hungry and afraid, Shawn seeks Patrick's help but is coldly rebuffed. The irascible Patrick wants nothing to do with anybody else and tells the boy he must fend for himself. Shawn has no choice but to keep hounding Patrick, and the rest of the film is the changing relationship between this dying man and a dependent child.

Patrick is the wise teacher–not only about how to survive on and understand the land, but, much more important, how to face life itself. Patrick impresses on Shawn that all struggle must be faced openly and courageously, that every second must be fully lived. While Patrick's methods may sometimes seem brutal (as when he makes no move to protect the boy from wild dogs), they have a clear mythic dimension.

While some critics have criticised the film for being sentimental, this is a toughly told story that brooks no Hollywood soppiness (save for the treacle-ish closing song, typical of the period). Where Collinson could have gone for the sentimental jugular, in what proves to be the last scene between Patrick and Shawn, his direction is a model of restraint. The resonance in Holden's voice when Patrick speaks of the need to openly express one's love is much more than a mere actor's fine reading of a line. Holden, who like Collinson died soon after the film's completion, captures that precious sense of passing on life's knowledge to other generations, to children perhaps not had.

The Earthling, as much as one can tell from the ungraded video commercially available, is beautifully shot by Don McAlpine in the most stunning of locations. Peter Collinson's direction (and the script) is a little jerky at times; at others, it is precise and powerful. Get rid of the end song and a very average film score, smooth out the few glitches, project it in a cinema where it belongs and one has an always interesting exploration of the heroic journey. As George Miller would later describe his magisterial **Lorenzo's Oil** (1992), **The Earthling**, in a far more minor key, is 'a companion manual for courageous human conduct'[3].

SCOTT MURRAY

Irascible Patrick Foley (William Holden) and the lost Shawn Daley (Ricky Schroder).

---

1 An end credit reads 'An Earthly Associates Film'.
2 Later recut and lengthened to 102 mins.
3 'George Miller's **Lorenzo's Oil**', an interview with Miller by Scott Murray, *Cinema Papers*, no. 92, April 1993, p. 17.

Patrick Foley (William Holden) and Uncle (Walter Pym).

M A U R I C E   M U R P H Y

FATTY FINN

C.F.C. Children's Film Corporation presents in association with The Australian Film Commission and Film Productions FATTY FINN. © 1980 Childrens [sic] Film Corporation. *Budget:* $350,000. *Location:* Glebe (Sydney). *Australian distributor:* Hoyts. *Opened:* 18 December 1980. *Video:* Syme Home Video. *Rating:* G (July 1980; 2509.92). 35mm. 91 mins.

Producer: Brian Rosen. *Executive producer:* John Sexton. *Scriptwriters:* Bob Ellis, Chris McGill. From an idea by Bob Ellis. Based on 'the much[-]loved comic book characters created by Syd Nicholls'. *Director of photography:* John Seale. *Production designer:* Lissa Coote. *Costume designer:* Norma Moriceau. *Editor:* Robert Gibson. *Composers:* Grahame Bond, Rory O'Donohue. *Sound recordist:* Tim Lloyd. *Sound editors:* Greg Bell; Helen Brown (asst). *Mixers:* Peter Fenton; Gethin Creagh (asst).

Cast

Bert Newton (John Finn), Noni Hazlehurst (Myrtle Finn), Gerard Kennedy (Tiger Murphy), Lorraine Bayly (Maggie McGrath), Ben Oxenbould (Fatty Finn), Greg Kelly (Bruiser), John Smythe (Pawnbroker), Henri Szeps (Mr. Zilch), Peter Carroll (Teacher), Richmond Young (Claffey), Tony Llewellyn-Jones (Dunny Man), Frank Wilson (Lord Mayor), Ross Higgins (Radio Announcer); Rebecca Rigg (Tilly), Jeremy Larsson (Headlights), Martin Lewis (Skeet), Hugo Grieve (Seasy), Sandy Leask (Lolly Legs), Melita Simec (Bruiser's Girl), Christian Robinson (Squizzy), Murray Shultz (Flies), Miguel Lopez (Mac).

Myrtle (Noni Hazlehurst), Fatty (Ben Oxenbould) and John Finn (Bert Newton).

Children's films had little prominence in the Australian film industry until the Australian Children's Television Foundation was established in 1982. The immediate impact of that initiative seemed to be that television received a boost while feature films languished.

Somewhere between the end of ABC radio's *Children's Hour* as entertainment and the late 1980s, children got Disney cartoons and probably too many Donald Ducks. **Fatty Finn** challenged that with its awkwardly constructed story about the suburban redhead with freckles who was really a good kid – he just had to prove himself.

Set as a period piece at a time when children played in back lanes and never seemed to swear, **Fatty Finn** indulges a sort of bourgeois fantasy of childhood while relishing the wonders of antipodean suburban life. Its narrative confusion and simplistic storyline

is sentimental in an old-fashioned way, but that was precisely its appeal.

Based on an Australian comic-strip character originated in the 1930s, the film tries to make a point about popular children's history in Australia. That made it an important, and certainly a brave, project.

The time of its release was probably the last chance to make movies for children before the contemporary adventure filmmaking techniques of George Lucas and friends sent movies into a remarkable international adventure land that Australia's suburban sentimentality could not touch. **Fatty Finn** just predated this onslaught and is important for that reason.

Bert Newton's appearance as an older, sillier male character, John Finn, provides added entertainment, although children, the

audience at which the film was aimed, could not care less about the moon-faced Newton's appearance. But he, too, is part of that Australia of the past – the family values that suppress the bold free thinking under pressure that makes Fatty Finn such a good kid after all.

MARCUS BREEN

References

'Bob Ellis', a career interview with the co-scriptwriter by Richard Brennan, *Cinema Papers*, no. 29, October–November 1980, pp. 314–19, 386.

'Fatty Finn', a review by Geoff Mayer, *Cinema Papers*, no. 31, March–April 1981, pp. 66–7.

'Maurice Murphy', an interview by Dave Sargent, *Cinema Papers*, no. 35, November–December 1981, pp. 444–7, 514.

FINAL CUT

Wilgar Productions present[s] FINAL CUT. © 1980 Wilgar Productions. Produced with the assistance of The Queensland Film Corporation and the Australian Film Commission. *Location:* Surfers Paradise (Queensland). *Australian distributor:* GUO. *Opened:* 17 October 1980. *Video:* Syme Home Video. *Rating:* M (June 1980; 2231.04m). 35mm. 81 mins.

Producer: Mike Williams. *Executive producer:* Frank Gardiner. *Scriptwriters:* Jonathan Dawson, Ross Dimsey. Based on an original idea by Jonathan Dawson. *Director of photography:* Ron Johanson. *Production designer:* Philip Warner. *Costumes:* Camilla Rountree. *Editor:* Tony Paterson. *Composer:* Howard J. Davidson. *Sound recordist:* John Rowley. [*Sound editor:* not credited.] *Mixers:* Julian Ellingworth, Phil Heywood.

Cast

Lou Brown [Chris[1]], David Clendinning [Dominic], Jennifer Cluff [Sarah], Narelle Johnson [Yvette]; Thaddeus Smith, Carmen J. McCall, Amanda MacTaggart, Jan Goebel, Peter Shorter, Toula Levonis, Leo Wockner, Christine Broadway, Robin Bishop, Lee Jackson, Karen Warden, Lyn Barron, Bob Lemmon, Julie Teale, Anna Christison, John Christison.

Dominic[2] (David Clendinning), a music industry magnate, is the subject of a documentary being made by a film journalist, Chris (Lou Brown), and his journalist girlfriend, Sarah (Jennifer Cluff). Chris believes Dominic may be involved in making blue movies, particularly ones where people get killed, and he sets out to investigate. But Dominic guards his private life jealously.

Nonetheless, and for reasons not well explained, Chris and Sarah are given permission not only to interview Dominic in his penthouse, but to spend the weekend. From being an enigma, Dominic loses whatever air of mystery was established in the early scenes on his yacht as a sudden familiarity between the characters takes over. This simply jars and saps the relationships of any tension.

A central flaw is that Chris is not the probing type. He handles his proximity to his subject as if he were a friend visiting from out of town, not a journo doing an exposé. Sarah is lifeless and Dominic's mistress, Yvette (Narelle Johnson), even more so. Hence, when it comes to the killing and Chris's unwitting involvement in a 'snuff' movie, you care so little for any of them that you kind of hope they all get one in the forehead. As it turns out, this eventually happens, and not before time. The relatively short running time of 81 minutes seems interminable.

There are some Hitchcock touches in the film (the inevitable shower scene, the camera under the glass table) but that's as good as the visuals get.

There is, however, a revealing, hilarious moment towards the end which accurately indicates where the film stands. After a minor-league bloodbath, Dominic is pushed into his large pool. As he thrashes around he pleads with gulping gasps, 'I can't swim!' So why have a pool, stupid?

JIM SCHEMBRI

---

1 The credits do not list character names. These are taken from press material.
2 See footnote 1.

Dominic (David Clendinning) and Chris (Lou Brown).

HARD KNOCKS

Andromeda Productions presents HARD KNOCKS[1]. *Alternative title:* 'Sam' (working). © 1980 Andromeda Productions. *Budget:* $35,000. *Location:* Melbourne. *Australian distributor:* Greg Lynch Film Distributors. *Opened:* 23 October 1980. *Video:* VCA. *Rating:* M (June 1980; 2304.12). 16 mm. 85 mins.

Producers: Don McLennan, Hilton Bonner. *Associate producer:* Sonny Naidu[2]. *Scriptwriters:* Don McLennan, Hilton Bonner. *Director of photography:* Zbigniew Friedrich. [*Production designer:* not credited.] *Wardrobe:* Julie Cutler. *Editor:* Zbigniew Friedrich. *Sound recordist:* Lloyd Carrick. [*Sound editor:* not credited; atb Zbnigiew Friedrich.] [*Mixer:* not credited personally; R. G. Film Services.]

Cast

Tracy Mann [Sam[3]], Bill Hunter [Brady], Kirsty Grant [Debbie], Penelope Stewart [Raelene], John Arnold [Wally[4]]; Kim Rushworth; Hilton Bonner [Frank]; Elizabeth Stevenson; Jack Allen [Father]; John Murphy; Max Cullen [Newman], Tony Barry [Barry]; Suzanne Dudley; Rennie Ellis [Photographer], Murielle Salter [Robbery Victim]; Debbie Conway, John Shavas; David McKinley [Station Attendant]; Anne Phelan, Tony Bonner.

Wally[5] (John Arnold), Sam (Tracy Mann).

Women have been portrayed in Australian feature films as the great saviours of Australian country life and their settler men, but rarely as focal points of urban anguish. **Hard Knocks** makes a concerted effort to portray a young, single Australian woman as a survivor in a repressive, patriarchal society. While the film flounders towards its subject rather than engaging it convincingly, there is a sense of desperation that makes it a worthy testament to women's place in Australia.

Unfortunately, it baulks at incorporating the necessarily strident feminist construction of women in Australia, or a feminist reading of Australia per se. Nevertheless, as Sam, Tracy Mann gives the film a fragile strength that wilfully asserts itself when the men inevitably try to exploit her.

Sadly, **Hard Knocks** did not attract much attention at the time of its release. The explicit sexism of so much cinema in the 1980s did not help the film to reach an audience. After the growth of the Australian 'art house' and independent cinema circuit later in the decade, a film like **Hard Knocks** may have received a better run, or have been marketed with more conviction by the major distributors.

Hard Knocks shares its realist tragedy with at least two other Australian feature films, **Fran** (Glenda Hambly, 1985) and to a lesser extent **Monkey Grip** (Ken Cameron, 1982). All three films traced through the embers of urban feminist fires and made a mark. Of the three, **Hard Knocks** maintains a harder edge that importantly looks beyond the prevailing middle-class concerns of many Australian feature film-makers. Its concerns with class and women in Australia give it a place in the historical lexicon of Australian film.

MARCUS BREEN

---

[1] An end credit reads, 'An Andromeda Production for Taren Point Traders'.
[2] Usually 'Santhana Naidu'.

[3] Character names were unreadable on the viewed copy due to an uncorrected video scan leaving much information off the edge of the screen. Where possible, names have been taken from a variety of sources.
[4] The press notes give Arnold's character as 'Munch', but the credits opt for 'Wally'.
[5] See footnotes 1 and 4.

References

'Hard Knocks', a review by Almos Maksay, *Cinema Papers*, no. 29, October–November 1980, pp. 378–80.

'Don McLennan and Peter Friedrich', an interview with the director and the director of photography by Rod Bishop, *Cinema Papers*, no. 30, December 1980–January 1981, pp. 412–16, 505–7.

'Greg Lynch: The Middle Ground', an interview with the distributor by Scott Murray, *Cinema Papers*, no. 31, March–April 1981, pp. 36–9, 71.

HARLEQUIN

William Fayman presents Antony I. Ginnane's Production. HARLEQUIN. © 1980 Farlight Investments. *Budget:* $850,000. *Location:* Perth. *Filmed:* late 1979. *Australian distributor:* GUO. *Opened:* 20 March 1980. *Video:* Video Classics. *Rating:* M (February 1980; 2593.58m). 35mm. Panavision. 95 mins.

Producer: Antony I. Ginnane. *Executive producer:* William Fayman. *Associate producer:* Jane Scott. *Scriptwriter:* Everett De Roche. *Director of photography:* Gary Hansen. *Camera operator:* Peter Moss. *Production designer:* Bernard Hides. *Costume designer:* Terry Ryan. *Editor:* Adrian Carr. *Composer:* Brian May. *Sound recordist:* Gary Wilkins. *Sound editor:* Stephen Lambeth. *Mixer:* Peter Fenton.

Cast

Robert Powell (Gregory Wolfe), David Hemmings (Nick Rast), Carmen Duncan (Sandra Rast), Broderick Crawford (Doc Wheelan), Gus Mercurio (Mr Berger), Alan Cassell (Mr Porter), Mark Spain (Alex Rast), Alyson Best (Alice), Sean Myers (Benny Lucas), Mary Simpson (Zoe Cayce), Bevan Lee (Mr Robinson), Neville Teedy (Dr Barthelemy), Mary Mackay (Miss Edith Twist), John Frawley (Dr Lovelock), Nita Pannell (Mabel Wheelan), David Hough (Mr Jepson), Klaus Schultz (Arthur), Peter West (Godfrey), Maurie Ogden (Prison Officer), Jack Ferrari (Ell Steele).

For Nick Rast (David Hemmings), wife Sandra (Carmen Duncan) and their leukæmia-ridden son, Alex (Mark Spain), the 'harlequin' is Gregory Wolfe (Robert Powell). Faith healer, magus and entertainer, he miraculously appears to cure the young boy, becoming his companion–mentor and Sandra's lover. However, the political heavies who are grooming Nick Rast for a figurehead position try to convince him that Gregory is really a fraud – a secret agent. In a sequence of terror and special effects, Gregory is killed. But while Nick starts to doubt the political machine, we are left to ponder the nature and identity of Gregory Wolfe.

The idea behind **Harlequin** was to take the Rasputin story about the mad monk who held great sway over the family of Tsar Nicholas in pre-revolutionary Russia and place it in a contemporary context. The way this translates and is retold, however, was the source of some critical dissatisfaction. There are two key areas of concern.

The first is a function of the international aspirations of the producer, Antony I. Ginnane. His late-1970s and early-'80s films followed a formula of sex, violence, the supernatural and a handful of low-profile overseas stars. Loosely defined as indigenous productions, any Australianness was deliberately neutralised. Although **Harlequin** was shot in Perth, there is little that locates it there, or anywhere else for that matter. It is primarily an interior drama with a cast of mixed accents. The political system is vaguely American, with key figures being referred to by such titles as 'senator' and 'governor'.

Second, the script has too many loose ends and red herrings, and a conclusion that provides few answers.

In its defence, **Harlequin** does spin out before our eyes an intriguing performance of power. Robert Powell's Gregory Wolfe is a statuesque, enigmatic, piercing presence who commands time, sound and the appearance of objects. There is also the power of the backroom boys. Broderick Crawford's Doc Wheelan is the weighty, manipulative politician who murderously plots and schemes. Magic and politics are suggestively linked. But what this amounts to, at worst, is some pretentious philosophising; at its best, to something mysterious for which there are no simple answers.

With all its enigmas, **Harlequin** does place many questions before us. The doctors condemn the frail, pallid nine-year-old boy to death – modern medicine can help him no more. But Gregory Wolfe cures him, or at least appears to. Nick Rast believes the truth of the photographs that are placed before him – he acts and decides on what he hears and sees. But this truth is also uncertain. Such questions of belief and faith are important but the film needs to do more than merely state them; it needs to invoke them so that we feel their weight and significance.

ANNA DZENIS

References

'Production Report: **Harlequin**', *Cinema Papers*, no. 24, December 1979–January 1980, comprising an interview with director Simon Wincer by Peter Beilby and Scott Murray, pp. 638–42, an interview with associate producer Jane Scott by Beilby and Murray, pp. 643–5, and an interview with production designer Bernard Hides by Murray and Beilby, pp. 646–7, 680.

'Everett De Roche', a career interview with the scriptwriter by Paul Davies, *Cinema Papers*, no. 25, February–March 1980, pp. 30–3, 76, 78.

'**Harlequin**', a review by Jack Clancy, *Cinema Papers*, no. 26, April–May 1980, pp. 140–1.

'Bob Saunders', an interview with the man behind Pact Productions, one of the film's investors, by Peter Beilby, *Cinema Papers*, no. 31, March–April 1981, pp. 26–9, 100.

Mr Berger (Gus Mercurio) watches Gregory Wolfe (Robert Powell) hold Alex Rast (Mark Spain).

MANGANINNIE

Tasmanian Film Corporation presents MANGANINNIE. © 1980 Tasmanian Film Corporation. Made in association with the Australian Film Commission, GUO Film Distributors, Examiner Northern TV, Tasmanian Television and Tasmanian Drive-In Theatre Holdings. *Budget:* $481,000. *Location:* central and west-coast Tasmania. *Filmed:* November–December 1979. *Australian distributor:* GUO. *Opened:* 10 July 1980. *Video:* not known. *Rating:* G (April 1980; 2482m[1]). 35mm. 90 mins.

Producer: Gilda Baracchi. *Executive producers:* Gil Brealey, Malcolm Smith. *Scriptwriter:* Ken Kelso. Based on the novel by Beth Roberts. *Director of photography:* Gary Hansen. *Production designer:* Neil Angwin. *Wardrobe master:* Graham Purcell. *Editor:* Mike Woolveridge. *Composer:* Peter Sculthorpe. *Sound recordist:* John Schiefelbein. *Sound editor:* Peter Burgess. *Mixer:* Peter Fenton.

Cast

Mawuyal Yanthalawuy (Manganinnie), Anna Ralph (Joanna), Phillip Hinton (Edward Waterman), Elaine Mangan (Margaret Waterman – Joanna's Mother); Mana Mana Dhamarrandji, Jarrka Dhamarrandji, Len Burarrapuwuy Dhamarrandji, Makultja Bapali Dhamarrandji (Aboriginal Children); Gunjalk, Dharnabariniy, Banarraba Bukaltjpi (Aboriginal Women); Mununbatijiwuy Munyaryun, Paul Spearin, Michael Yawunydjurr, Gutiwa Dhamarrandji, Murguluma Dhamarrandji, Malana Dhamarrandji, Stan Roach, Charles Yunupinga (Aboriginal Warriors); Barry Pierce (Captain), Hazel Alger (Housemaid), Don Evans (Convict 1), Bill McCluskey (Convict 2), Elaine Mangan (Joanna Waterman – Voice Over).

At a time when too many Australian films were hyped far beyond their worth, John Honey's **Manganinnie** was grievously undervalued. A child's-eye view of the most shameful episode in Australia's history – the virtual wiping-out of the Aborigines – it has an artful innocence that makes the dreadful events of the 1830s seem all the more terrible. The first feature film from the Tasmanian Film Corporation, it was, correctly, classified G, and, quite wrongly, dismissed as a children-only film as a result.

As the British colonial forces make their notorious clearances of the Aboriginal population, the heroine of the title, played by Mawuyal Yanthalawuy – then a 36-year-old Darwin pre-school teacher – is seen hiding in the bush after a redcoat raid has swept away her small tribe.

As guileless as the small white girl, Joanna (Anna Ralph), she then looks after, Manganinnie also possesses a deep, sad wisdom. The original Tasmanians either did not know how to make fire, or had lost the knack, and Manganinnie, keeper of the flame for her group, entrances the child with her glowing fire-stick.

As this odd couple moves through the country, director John Honey doesn't ask too much of his amateur actors and Ken Kelso's script, adapted from a novel by Beth Roberts, pares the dialogue to essentials and fills in many details with voice-over recollections by the child in later life. Thus, the implications of the hopeless search by the woman and the girl as they trek from the mountains to the sea in search of the vanished tribe are explained and expanded.

The poignancy of Manganinnie's gradual realisation that her people, and, therefore, her way of life, are gone forever is underscored in Gary Hansen's quietly modulated photography and Peter Sculthorpe's spare background music. This basic seriousness conflicts at times with more conventional touches, such as interludes with a pet wombat, a brush with brutish convicts, the Victorian formality of the girl's home and lapses into some rather obvious narrative devices. But a moving final sequence, in which Joanna stares into the flames of Manganinnie's funeral pyre, transcends all.

KEITH CONNOLLY

---

[1] An AFC brochure lists the length at 2469m.

References

'Malcolm Smith', an interview with the director of the Tasmanian Film Corporation by Peter Beilby and Scott Murray, *Cinema Papers*, no. 26, April–May 1980, pp. 112–15, 153.

'Manganinnie', a review by Virginia Duigan, *Cinema Papers*, no. 29, October–November 1980, pp. 380–1.

Joanna (Anna Ralph) and Manganinnie (Mawuyal Yanthalawuy).

CHRIS McGILL

... MAYBE THIS TIME

NSW Film Corporation presents a Cherrywood Film. ...maybe this time. © 1980 Cherrywood Film Productions Pty Ltd. *Budget:* $460,000. *Locations:* Sydney, Canberra, the south coast of New South Wales. *Australian distributor:* Roadshow. *Opened:* August 1980. *Video:* CEL. *Rating:* M (August 1980; 2621.47m). 35 mm. 96 mins.

Producer: Brian Kavanagh. *Scriptwriters:* Anne Brooksbank, Bob Ellis. *Director of photography:* Russell Boyd. *Camera operator:* Nixon Binney. *Production designer:* Christopher Webster. *Costume designer:* Anna Senior. *Editor:* Waynelle Clos[1]. *Composer:* Bruce Smeaton. *Sound recordist:* Lloyd Carrick. *Sound editor:* Dean Gawen. [*Mixer:* not credited.]

Cast

Judy Morris (Fran), Bill Hunter (Stephen), Mike Preston (Paddy), Jill Perryman (Fran's Mother), Ken Shorter (Alan), Michele Fawdon (Margo), Leonard Teale (The Minister), Chris Haywood (The Salesman), Rod Mullinar (Jack), Jude Kuring (Meredith), Lorna Leslie (Susy Williams), Lyndall Barbour (Miss Bates), Celia de Burgh (Paddy's Girl), Lyn Collingwood (Myrtle), Gillian Hyde (Miss Peterson), John Clayton (Estate Agent), Tim Burns (Student 1), Willie Fennell (Mr Todd), Tessa Mallos (Sarah), Madeleine Blackwell (Bronwyn).

Set in the years of the Whitlam government, Chris McGill's ... **Maybe This Time** stars Judy Morris as Fran, a trendy young woman of the time, who can get neither her act nor her aspirations together. It asks the audience to laugh ruefully with, not at, her attempts to live independently of men, while enjoying close relationships with them. She goes some of the way to achieving this aim, but ultimately suffers disappointment and disillusion.

The main trouble with the film is that these permutations are depicted with varying degrees of credibility. Some of the situations are real and convincing, others verge – presumably unwittingly – on farce. Nevertheless, scriptwriters Anne Brooksbank and Bob Ellis create an appealing, and generally believeable, character in their protagonist, and Judy Morris portrays her winningly.

Fran, 29 and dreading 30, is assistant to history professor Paddy (Mike Preston) at one of the newer universities. She is having an affaire with a cynically ambitious federal minister's aide, Stephen (Bill Hunter), but ultimately befriends his estranged wife, Meredith (Jude Kuring).

Alan (Ken Shorter) and Fran (Judy Morris).

Proud of, yet not fully satisfied with, her independent status, Fran returns to her home in the country. But she gets little comfort or support from disapproving mother (Jill Perryman) and unhappily married sister, Margo (Michele Fawdon); even worse is a sexually-disastrous reunion with an old flame, Alan (Ken Shorter), scion of a wealthy squatter family. The whole country episode serves to rub in the film's theme: women may strive to be independent, but it's still a man's world. Fran's male relationships are all dependent, involving surrender to some degree: Stephen uses her, Paddy patronises her and Alan seems unaware that he seeks to impose the very subordination from which she originally had fled.

In some respects, ... **Maybe This Time** is unusual among Australian features of the day in attempting a commentary–comedy that is both provocative and thoughtful. The attempt is not all that successful, in part because the serious comment is, in places, couched in terms more suited to television sitcom (as when Stephen, in bed with Fran, invites his estranged wife to join them), and the pace varies from desultory to brisk and beyond. But the overall tone of generous observation matches the script's wry wit.

KEITH CONNOLLY

---

[1] Usually spelt 'Wayne Le Clos'.

References

'Maybe This Time [sic]', a review by Rod Bishop and Fiona Mackie, *Cinema Papers*, no. 28, August–September 1980, pp. 280–1.

'Bob Ellis', a career interview by Richard Brennan, *Cinema Papers*, no. 29, October–November 1980, pp. 314–19, 386.

'Maybe This Time [sic]', a brief review by Adrienne Parr, *Filmnews*, June 1981, p. 17.

NIGHTMARES

Murdered George D'alberg (Max Phipps) and panic-struck Judy (Nina Landis).

Bioscope presents a John Lamond Picture[–]Enterprises Production. NIGHT-MARES. © 1980 Movityme. *Location:* Melbourne. *Australian distributor:* Roadshow. *Opened:* November 1980. *Video:* Roadshow Home Video. *Rating:* R (October 1980; 2258.93m). 35mm. Panavision. 82 mins.

Producers: John Lamond, Colin Eggleston. *Scriptwriter:* Colin Eggleston. Based on an original idea by John Lamond and John-Michael Howson. *Director of photography:* Garry Wapshott. *Production designer:* Paul Jones. *Wardrobe:* Aphrodite Kondos, Jan Barkell. *Editor:* Colin Eggleston. *Composer:* Brian May. *Sound recordist:* John Phillips. [*Sound editor:* not credited.] *Mixer:* Phil Judd.

Cast

Jenny Neumann (Helen Selleck), Gary Sweet (Terry Besanko), Nina Landis (Judy), Max Phipps (George D'alberg), John-Michael Howson (Bennett Collingswood), Edmund Pegge (Bruce), Sue Jones (Gay), Adele Lewin (Sue), Briony Behets (Angela), Maureen Edwards (Mother), Byron Williams (Father), Peter Tulloch (Brian), Malcolm Steed (Doctor), Denise Peterson (Bad Auditionee),

Tania Uren (Policeman No. 1), Gary Day (Policeman No. 2), Joy Westmore (Matron), Lise Rodgers (Mousy Auditionee), Doug Bowles (Baby Sitter), Rossana Zuanetti (Girl in Lane), Gene Van Dam (Boy in Lane), Angela Menzies-Willis (Lover in Bed).

A small girl walks sleepily down the corridor to her parents' bedroom. Silently opening the door, she finds her father (Byron Williams) in bed with a blonde (Angela Menzies-Willis). A month later, Cathy and her mother (Maureen Edwards) leave to visit Granny. Cathy falls asleep on the back seat. When she awakes, she notices her mother is kissing a man in the front while driving. When Cathy physically intervenes, the car crashes and Cathy is tossed through the car window (shades of Phil Noyce's **Dead Calm** ten years on). After extricating herself from the wreck, Cathy drags her mother away to safety. But a slither of glass catches in her mother's throat and kills her. So begins the trauma and the nightmares which will continue to haunt Cathy and send her, sixteen years later, on a savage murder spree.

Surprisingly, director John Lamond makes no attempt to pretend anyone but Cathy, now strangely renamed Helen Selleck[2]

(Jenny Neumann) and now an actress, is the murderer. Though she is not seen during the killing scenes (it is all wobbly cam and heavy breathing), she has visual flashes of things only the murderer could know.

One result of this don't-hide approach is that there is no tension in the film. Equally, one knows each potential victim is certainly done for; maybe director John Lamond felt the entertainment comes from watching numerous naked bodies get stabbed or castrated. And even if Lamond never actually shows a glass spike rip into flesh, most viewers will find the murders quite disturbing, especially since most occur during sex.

The only two things that single **Nightmares** out from the plethora of horror films that would come over the next decade is the characterisation of vile theatre critic Bennett Collingswood (John-Michael Howson). When George D'alberg (Max Phipps), Helen's theatre director, confronts Bennett after an opening night performance, there is this memorable exchange.

'What lies, slanders and half-truths are you perpetrating tonight, Bennett, in the guise of fair criticism? [...] I suppose you panned us all, you crippled old queen.'
'Save one shining light.'
'Whose knickers you want to get into, no doubt.'

Not only is it rare for a film-maker to rail so vehemently against critics, but many people at the time took Bennett Collingswood to be an attack on the (heterosexual) film reviewer for *The Age*, Colin Bennett. Bennett angered large sections of the film industry with an intemperate panning of Tim Burstall's pioneering **2000 Weeks** (1969). For this, he was never forgiven (nor for preferring foreign art movies to the oft-crude attempts at commercialism by battling Australian film-makers).

Every industry has its *roman-à-clefs*[3], but this caricature in **Nightmares** must rank as one of the most vitriolic.

SCOTT MURRAY

---

[1] John D. Lamond dropped the 'D.' on this film.
[2] There is nothing which actually states that Cathy becomes Helen, but Lamond seems to expect us to assume this.
[3] Another *cause célèbre* was the shooting script of Michael Thornhill's **Between Wars** (1974), which was reputed to have several outrageous send-ups of staff at the then Australian Film Development Corporation.

PALM BEACH

[No opening production company credit.] © 1979 Albie Thoms Productions. *Budget:* $100,000. *Location:* Palm Beach (Sydney). *Australian distributor:* Albie Thoms. *Opened:* January 1980. *Video:* Video Classics. *Rating:* M (July 1979; 2370²). 16mm (blown up to 35mm). 88 mins.

[*Producer:* Albie Thoms.] [*Scriptwriter:* Albie Thoms.] *Director of photography:* Oscar Scherl. [*Production designer:* not credited.] [*Costume designer:* not credited.] [*Editor:* Albie Thoms.] *Composer:* Terry Hannigan. *Sound recordists:* Michael Moore, Rick Creaser. [*Sound editor:* not credited.] *Mixer:* Julian Ellingworth.

Cast

Nat Young (Nick Naylor), Ken Brown (Joe Ryan), Amanda Berry (Leilani Adams), Bryan Brown (Paul Kite), Julie McGregor (Kate O'Brien), John Flaus (Larry Kent), Bronwyn Stevens-Jones (Wendy Naylor), David Lourie (Zane Crean), Peter Wright (Rupert Roberts), John Clayton (Eric Tailor), Lyn Collingwood (Mrs Adams), Adrian Rawlins (David Litvinoff), P. J. Jones (Det. Sgt Robinson), Mick Eyre (Magazine Editor), Jim Roberts (Art School Dean), Kathy Power (Art School Student), Mick Winter (Board Polisher), Tony Wicks (Board Shop Owner), David Elfick (Projectionist), Sandra Alexandra (University Lecturer), Bruce Gould (Antique Dealer).

Palm Beach is set in the northern beach suburbs of Sydney, and introduces and interconnects a dozen or more characters by following the efforts of Joe Ryan (Ken Brown), an outsider who has turned up in Palm Beach to seek the assistance of an old surfing mate in paying off a debt. The two men surf and drive rather aimlessly around the suburb trying to locate drugs and, over a day and a night, encounter a number of other residents each with a personal drama. In particular, there is Paul Kite (Bryan Brown), out of work and down on his luck, who resorts to robbery and bungles the job, killing a policeman in the process, and Leilani (Amanda Berry), a runaway teenager who eventually puts Joe in touch with a drug dealer.

These are the elements of an authentic Australian drama – a story of sex and drugs with a soundtrack of rock 'n' roll blaring ceaselessly from radios, record players and live bands. The denizens of the beach suburb, a rare mix of rich and poor, straight and crooked, are peculiar not just to Australia but to this northern area of Sydney. They offer authentic Australian voices and sounds, though the improvised dialogue has a halting quality that bespeaks non-actors trying a little too self-consciously to articulate a plot.

This is a film which takes its time to get to its points. Thoms uses a static camera,

often fixed quite simply in the back seat of the car, to give the impression of real time passing. The film celebrates a kind of comic/pathetic ordinariness in so much of the daily life of Australians, with odd highlights of quirks and jokes. There is a tracking shot past a stripper to a lighted portrait of the Queen in an RSL Club, a digression into a humorously heated discussion about women's rôle in the surfing culture.

Finally, there is the extraordinary character of Larry Kent (John Flaus), named after the fictional private detective who featured in pulp novels and a radio serial in the 1950s, stories of a suave detective immersing himself in cases inevitably involving glamorous women. Here, in a remarkable and comic piece of revisionism, Kent is reduced to a man out of time and place, playing poker machines and discussing Rugby League heroes of many moons past, living in a house unchanged since the 1950s, removing his hairpiece and, in a nod to Chandler's *The Long Goodbye* surely, elaborately fiddling with his coffee percolator to produce the perfect brew.

Palm Beach is a film of casual but cunning construction. But Thoms was not prepared to forsake completely his past as a film-maker interested in formally exploring the potential of the medium. But despite being an auspicious debut, **Palm Beach** remains the sole feature film made by Thoms. It is a terrible reminder that there are people of great ability who have never been able to pursue their craft in the Australian film industry, while dozens of mediocrities have had the chance to squander countless dollars and a multitude of opportunities.

GEOFF GARDNER

---

¹ The film begins 'PALM BEACH [/] by Albie Thoms'. There are no director, producer, scriptwriter, etc., credits.
² An AFC brochure gives the length as 2414m, which appears to be correct.

References
'Albie Thoms', an interview with the film's maker by Rod Bishop and Fiona Mackie, *Cinema Papers*, no. 22, July–August 1979, pp. 429–31, 471–2.
'Palm Beach', a review by Noel Purdon, *Cinema Papers*, no. 24, December 1979–January 1980, p. 660.
'Talking to Albie Thoms, Director of **Palm Beach**', an interview by Martha Ansara, Nick Herd and Tina Kaufman, *Filmnews*, May 1979, pp. 6–8.
'**Palm Beach**', Barrett Hodsdon, *Filmnews*, January–February 1980, p. 6.

Paul Kite (Bryan Brown), the bungling robber.

STIR

The NSW Film Corporation presents STIR. *Alternative title:* 'The Promotion of Mr Smith' (working). © 1980 Smiley Films Pty Ltd. *Budget:* $485,000. *Location:* Gladstone (South Australia). *Filmed:* October–November 1979. *Australian distributor:* Hoyts. *Opened:* 23 October 1980. *Video:* Australian Video. *Rating:* M (rated R in August 1980 but changed after appeal in September 1980; 2770.43m). 35mm. 101 mins.

Producer: Richard Brennan. *Scriptwriter:* Bob Jewson. *Director of photography:* Geoff Burton. *Production designer:* Lee Whitmore. *Wardrobe:* Edie Kurzer. *Editor:* Henry Dangar. *Composer:* Cameron Allan. *Sound recordist:* Gary Wilkins. *Sound editor:* Andrew Steuart. *Mixers:* Phil Judd, Phil Heywood.

Cast

Bryan Brown (China Jackson), Max Phipps (Norton), Dennis Miller (Redford), Gary Waddell (Dave), Phil Motherwell (Alby), Edward Robshaw (Partridge), Michael Gow (Andrew), Robert 'Tex' Morton (The Governor), Ray Marshall (Chalmers), Syd Heylen (Old Bob), Robert Noble (Riley), Paul Sonkkila (McIntosh), Keith Gallasch (Tony), Les Newcombe (Hogan), James Marsh (Webster), Peter Kowitz (Lewis), Tony Wager (Visiting Justice), Maurice Saidi (Barker), Kevin Storey (Chickenman), Chris Smith (Warder with Baton).

Stir opens with a violent scene of prison warders systematically assaulting inmates which is intercut with a sequence where one of the prisoners, China Jackson (Bryan Brown), goes public on television about the bashings, watched by an anxious prison warder, Norton (Max Phipps), the leader of the group of warders responsible for the assault. The film then cuts to three years later and to a prison van returning Jackson to the same prison with the dialogue containing many foreboding comments about the potential for an explosive situation to develop.

Jackson's return is looked on with relish by the brutally sadistic warders, Partridge (Edward Robshaw) and McIntosh (Paul Sonkkila). It brings to a head simmering tensions between the prisoners and the administration, the latter characterised by the stupidity of The Governor (Robert 'Tex' Morton), a bungling, bureaucratic fool who turns a blind eye to the violence of his staff.

An attempt by Norton to reconcile his differences with Jackson is rejected and slowly Jackson is drawn into the activities of the hotheads who want to rebel. Despite his reluctance, due in part to the short term he is serving, Jackson eventually leads a rebellion which ends in the prison being gutted by fire. The prisoners give up, are herded into a pen and are again brutally bashed.

Stir is a film that confronts a thorny and constant aspect of Australian life: the treatment of our prison population since European settlement which has been characterised by violence, with a brutal few rendering docile an intimidated group by terror. It was made during a period when a number of ex-prisoners wrote and spoke about their experiences through plays and journalism. Bob Jewson, who wrote the script, was a prisoner in Bathurst gaol during a riot and his script is based on this and other similar events. It is straightforward, laconic and forthright about the brutality that occurred. To its credit, it resolutely refuses to analyse its situation politically or apportion blame on those in authority.

Where the film is less effective is in its portrayal of an essential 'niceness' about prison life. There is a camaraderie among the inmates rather too close to the stiff upper lip POW movies of the 1950s (and a long way from life portrayed in John Hillcoat's Ghosts...Of the Civil Dead, 1989). About the only nod to the grimmer realities of prison life and relationships is the constant foul language. Prison sexuality is only rendered via the comic seduction of a first-timer by an old fag with no reference to the more usual rape and violent ownership.

As well, the narrative development has a static quality and the direction and the editing could have usefully used the sort of energy that a director like Sidney Lumet might have brought to it. But this is probably a rather harsh criticism of a director making his first feature and getting stuck into a brutal and neglected aspect of modern Australian life.

GEOFF GARDNER

References

'Production Report: **Stir**', *Cinema Papers*, no. 25, February–March 1980, comprising an interview with producer Richard Brennan by Barbara Alysen, pp. 46–9, 75, and an interview with scriptwriter Bob Jewson by Alysen, pp. 50–3.
'**Stir**', a review by Brian McFarlane, *Cinema Papers*, no. 28, August–September 1980, pp. 279–80.
'Stephen Wallace', an interview by Barbara Alysen, *Cinema Papers*, no. 29, October–November 1980, pp. 341–3.

Prisoner China Jackson (Bryan Brown) and Norton (Max Phipps), the sadistic warder.

TOUCH AND GO

The Bank Manageress (Pamela Martin) is held to ransom by one of the gang.

Maxwell-Pellatt in association with The Queensland Film Corporation and the Australian Film Commission presents TOUCH AND GO. *Alternative title:* 'Friday the Thirteenth' (working). © 1980 Mutiny Pictures. Made with the assistance of the Queensland Film Corporation and the Australian Film Commission. *Budget:* $541,000. *Locations:* Maroochydore, Noosa Heads (Queensland); Sydney. *Filmed:* November–December 1979. *Australian distributor:* GUO. *Opened:* 12 June 1980. *Video:* Syme Home Video. *Rating:* NRC (May 1980; 2550.99m). 35 mm. 93 mins.

Producer: John Pellatt. *Executive producers:* Peter Maxwell, Peter Yeldham. *Scriptwriter:* Peter Yeldham. *Director of photography:* John McLean. *Camera operator:* Kevan Lind. *Production designer:* David Copping. *Wardrobe:* Kate Duffy. *Editors:* Sarah Bennett, Paul Maxwell. *Composers:* Jon English, Charlie Hull. *Sound recordist:* Brian Morris. *Sound editors:* Paul Maxwell, Sara Bennett. *Mixers:* Peter Fenton, Gethin Creagh.

Cast

Wendy Hughes (Eva), Chantal Contouri (Fiona), Carmen Duncan (Millicent), Jon English (Frank), Jeanie Drynan (Gina), Liddy Clark (Helen), Christine Amor (Sue), John Bluthal (Anatole), Brian Blain (George), Vince Martin (Steve, Policeman), Barbara Stephens (Julia, Head Mistress), Pamela Martin (Bank Manageress), Joe James (Radio Producer), Roger Ward (Wrestler), Lex Foxcroft (Husband), Beryl Cheers (Wife), Alan Wilson (Freddie, the Voice), Bevan Lee (Fisherman), Marcus Hale (Waiter), Adrian Bernotti (Taxi Driver), Sally Anning (Telephonist); Gavan Arden, Geoff Mills, Peter Molineux (Policemen at Roadblock).

This disastrously unfunny comedy... thriller concerns three attractive young society sophisticates working for charity, who turn to robbery at a luxurious island resort on the Great Barrier Reef to keep a special primary school for underprivileged children in operation. It is a slapdash attempt at the caper genre, relying on the gimmick of its main female cast, but it resembles a hand-me-down rip-off of television's *Charley's Angels*.

Chief investors were the fledgling Queensland Film Corporation, backing only its second major feature in that state (the other was the equally unsatisfying **Final Cut**, Ross Dimsey, 1980), Greater Union and the Australian Film Commission.

A month's shooting began in November 1979 at Maroochydore and Noosa Heads in Queensland, with eight weeks of night filming in Sydney. Scenes supposedly set on a Barrier Reef island were shot at a Maroochydore hotel for budgetary reasons.

English expatriate producer John Pellatt had previously worked on **Age of Consent** (Michael Powell, 1969) and was associate producer on **They're a Weird Mob** (Michael Powell, 1966).

The film was initially shot under the working title 'Friday the Thirteenth', but it was changed when the producers were informed about the horror film of the same name then being made in the US.

Much play was made of the fact that the film was unashamedly commercial and boasted the strongest female cast of any Australian movie (Wendy Hughes, Chantal Contouri, Carmen Duncan, Jeanie Drynan). But it closed in June 1980 after only three weeks of release in Brisbane.

PAUL HARRIS

References

'Peter Yeldham', a career interview with the scriptwriter by Paul Davies, *Cinema Papers*, no. 27, June–July 1980, pp. 176–9, 214.

'Wendy Hughes', an interview with the actor by Richard Brennan, *Cinema Papers*, no. 40, October 1982, pp. 428–32.

1981

Frank (Mel Gibson) and Archy (Mark Lee).
Peter Weir's Gallipoli.

TIM BURNS

AGAINST THE GRAIN: MORE MEAT THAN WHEAT

[No opening production company credit.[1]] AGAINST THE GRAIN [/] MORE MEAT THAN WHEAT. [© not given; atb 1980.] Funded by the Australian Film Commission. *Budget:* $30,000. *Australian distributor:* Sydney Film-makers Co-operative. *Video:* not known. *Rating:* not known. 16mm. 76 mins.

[*Producer:* not credited.] [*Scriptwriter:* not credited.] *Director of photography:* Louis Irving. *Additional camera:* Brendan Stretch, John Clark. [*Production designer:* not credited.] [*Costume designer:* not credited.] *Editors:* Peter Gailey, Melissa Woods, Chris Cordaux.[2] *Composer:* Nick Lyons. *Sound recordists:* Dasha Ross (loc.); Laurie Fitzgerald (post-prod.). *Sound editor:* Laurie Fitzgerald. [*Mixer:* not credited.]

Cast

Michael Callaghan (Ray Unit), Sandy Edwards (Paula Oid), Joy Burns (Joy Unit), Mary Burns (Mary Unit), Letham Burns (Letham Unit), George Sutton (Devac); Lindsay Smith[3], Ry Callaghan, Marie McMahon, Earth Works-Poster Collective, Louis Irving, Mental as Anything, Robert Burns, Jack Cullity, Jim McDonnell, Victoria Middleton, Helen Grace, Michael Shelling, Ian Millis, Peter Gailey, Langdon Philip Jack, Kay Burns, Sharon Burns, Bradley Burns, James Dibble and the Extended 'Nuclear' Family.

A gainst the Grain: More Meat than Wheat is a film with a staunch political agenda. It is a feature-length experimental narrative produced and directed by Tim Burns with the assistance of the Australian Film Commission.

The focus of the story is Ray Unit (Michael Callaghan), whom we first encounter making a smoke-bomb which he explodes at an Anzac Day March in Sydney. Now a wanted man, he changes his appearance and escapes via a long train trip across the Nullarbor to his family home in Perth.

The film is also an investigation of social and political contradictions. Ray's plans, his travels and encounters are constantly under surveillance by the State. His attempts to seek political asylum and to gain entry into Lucas Heights are even supported by the State which merely seeks to use him as a public example to justify further repressive social controls.

The film compares individual acts of violence with institutional brutality through complex visual and aural juxtapositions. The servicemen march to celebrate their heroism in returning from a war of excessive weaponry and widespread slaughter. Yet, ironically, it is Ray's bomb, planted in a wreath, disruptive but hardly deadly, which is seen as a significant act of violent terrorism. The mythologised rural farming community, 'the backbone of Australia', is

shown to be a place of cold, clinical killing which is performed without remorse or question. Ray's mother's demonstration of baking bread with revolutionary yeast that rises in an hour recalls her son's manufacture of his bomb. These parallels invite us to question 'the difference'.

The film also self-consciously investigates issues of representation: the construction, use and dissemination of images. It uses excerpts from advertisements, television news, fictional films, still photographs and a continual return to multiple monitor surveillance.

Another key character is the photographer Paula Oid (Sandy Edwards). Paula is concerned with the politics of the image. Ray tells her that the camera, like a gun, is a predatory weapon. Photographing people turns them into objects; it is a kind of sublimated murder.

Paula concedes that the camera is a tool of aggression, invoking *Playboy*-type magazines and sexist advertising as examples. In attempting to redress the balance, she orchestrates a photo-shoot using men as sex objects in a rôle reversal of traditional advertisements. However, Paula's own images are also used to betray Ray. The work of well-intentioned photographers, let alone revolutionary artists, can also be co-opted and used to further the ideological ends of the State.

The problem with this rich juxtaposition of images and ideas is that, ultimately, the film's political analysis is neither profound nor useful, where one interpretation is as valid as another and open-endedness is everything. It is never clear whom this film is addressing, or whom it is hoping to convert. It reinforces ideological stereotypes while failing to create real change. For a film which wears its political heart on its sleeve, this would have to be considered a major flaw.

ANNA DZENIS

---

[1] At the end there is the following credit: 'A Nightshift Production'.
[2] Usually spelt 'Cordeaux'
[3] No character names are given on the film for the rest of the cast.

References

'Tim Burns', an interview with the director by Noel Purdon, *Cinema Papers*, no. 28, August–September 1980, pp. 266–9, 300.
'The New Generation', John Fox, *Cinema Papers*, no. 31, March–April 1981, pp. 34–5, 99.

Terrorist Ray Unit (Michael Callaghan).

ALISON'S BIRTHDAY

An Australian Film Commission [and] Fontana Films Presentation [of] A David Hannay Production. ALISON'S BIRTHDAY. © 1979 David Hannay Productions Pty Limited. Produced in association with the Australian Film Commission, Fontana Films Pty Limited and The Seven Network. *Locations:* south coast of NSW; Sydney. *Filmed:* January–February 1979. *Australian distributor:* Filmways. *Video:* CEL. *Rating:* NRC (April 1980; 1064.09m). 16mm (blown up to 35mm). 97 mins.

Producer: David Hannay. *Associate producer:* Michael Falloon. *Scriptwriter:* Ian Coughlan. *Director of photography:* Brian Bansgrove. *Camera operator:* Kevan Lind. *Production designer:* Bob Hilditch. *Wardrobe:* Robert Lloyd. *Editor:* Tim Street. *Composers:* Brian King, Alan Oloman. *Mirne's Theme* by Ian Coughlan. *Sound recordist:* Phil Judd. *Sound editor:* Tim Street. *Mixers:* Phil Judd, Phil Heywood.

Cast

Joanne Samuel (Alison Findlay), Margie McCrae (Chrissie Willis), Julie Wilson (Maureen Fate), Martin Vaughan (Mr Martin), Rosalind Spears (Maggie Carlyle), Robyn Gibbes (Helen McGill), Lou Brown (Pete Healey), Ian Coughlan (Dave Ducker), Bunney Brooke (Jennifer Findlay), John Bluthal (Dean Findlay), Ralph Cotterill (Brian Healey), Marion Jones ('Grandmother' Thorne), George Carden (Druid Leader), Belinda Giblin (Isabel Thorne), Vincent Ball (Dr Jeremy Lyall), Brian Wenzel (Police Sergeant), Bernard Lewis (Michael), Lisa Peers (Sally Brown), Sonia Peet (Hospital Clerk), Eric Oldfield (Priest), Brian Blain ('Uncle' Patrick), Adam Bowen ('Cousin' Richard), Stephen O'Rourke (Detective).

'Grandmother' Thorne (Marion Jones).

A lison's Birthday passed almost unnoticed in 1981 and falls into Adrian Martin's category of the 'unloved'. It has barely been written about, even though it compares well to the many horror-thrillers that came in the 1980s. Not that this is to say the film succeeds, for it doesn't – it is too slow and suspenseless – but it has a coherent narrative and is well cast in parts.

When 16, Alison Findlay (Joanne Samuel) is warned during a seance not to go to her 19th birthday party. Despite this omen, she agrees to a party when cajoled by her 'aunt', Jennifer Findlay (Bunney Brooke), and 'uncle', Dean (John Bluthal), who have looked after her since her parents were killed soon after her birth.

Alison returns to Sydney with her boyfriend, Pete Healey (Lou Brown). Like many other cinematic boyfriends, he is rebuffed at the front door by Alison's overly-protective guardians. At first, this means little, but slowly Pete suspects something more sinister is afoot, especially when Alison explains that there is a miniature Stonehenge at the bottom of the garden. Pete tries to break into the house and take Alison away, but he is outwitted by this most sinister of charming old couples. He turns to a psychic friend for help, but the forces of evil (Jennifer and Dean belong to a coven of Druids obsessed with preserving the life of Mirne, a spirit goddess) are too strong to combat.

Alison's Birthday is atypical of late 1970s horror-thrillers in that it concerns subtle manipulations of the soul, with only rare interest in violence or terror. The calm surface and even pacing do not represent a lack of energy, as first appears, but a way of suggesting how the subtle forces of evil can work quietly and undetected.

The ending is certainly the opposite of many American thrillers where good prevails (even if the last shot invariably suggests evil hasn't given up yet). And the last subtitle ('Alison – 104 years old') has a chilling black humour very rare in Australian cinema.

Bunney Brooke and John Bluthal are excellent as Alison's false relatives: all cloying charm and middle-class repressiveness. Joanne Samuel does her best as Alison, even though she is years too old and has trouble making convincing the odd long monologue. And Lou Brown's Pete makes a perfect foil to the druids: decent but not overly so; capable of making errors of judgement but without the total stupidity usually demanded of lead characters in order to keep creaky narratives ticking.

Ian Coughlan, who has made no feature since, directs in a fairly standard manner. But to his credit, the film is never silly, in the way the truly dreadful **Spook** (David Anthony Hall, unreleased, 1986) and **Frenchman's Farm** (Ron Way, 1987) are, and the dark tone is convincing. If his film reminds one of anything, it is the much-later **Sporloos** (**The Vanishing**, George Sluizer, 1988), where a husband searches obsessively for his kidnapped wife and ends up being overwhelmed by a force he fails to fully understand.

SCOTT MURRAY

References

'Production Report: **Alison's Birthday**', *Cinema Papers*, no. 22, July–August 1979, comprising an interview with The Seven Network's John Sturzaker, an investor, by Peter Beilby and Scott Murray, pp. 446–8, 479, and an interview with director Ian Coughlan, by Murray and Beilby, pp. 449–51.

'**Alison's Birthday**', a brief review by Peter Kemp, *Filmnews*, May 1981, p. 13.

CENTRESPREAD

Australian Film Distributors in association with Greg Lynch Film Distributors present[s] a Wayne Groom Production. CENTRESPREAD. © 1981 Australian Film Productions Pty Ltd. *Budget:* $600,000. *Location:* Adelaide, Surfers Paradise (Queensland). *Australian distributor:* Greg Lynch Film Distributors. *Video:* VCA. *Rating:* R (July 1981; 2256.93m). Super 16mm (blown up to 35mm). 82 mins.

Producer: Wayne Groom. *Scriptwriters:* Michael Ralph, Robert Fogden. *Director of photography:* Geoffrey Simpson. *Set designers:* Michael Ralph, Robert Fogden, Keith Bradford. *Costume designer:* Mark Holliday. *Editor:* Tony Paterson. *Composer:* John Sharp. *Sound recordist:* James Currie. [*Sound editor:* not credited; atb Tony Paterson.] *Mixer:* Bruce Lamshed.

Cast

Kylie Foster (Niki), Paul Trahir (Gerard), Mark Watson (Mark), Ivor Louis (Editor), Jack Neate (Old Man), Edson Annan (Boss), Paula Carter (Waitress), John Nobbs (Droog 1), Colin Moglia (Droog 2), Sarah Collins (Cafe Model), Carmen McCall (House Model), Helina McCall (Bald Lady), Mark Bonnet (Rapist), Brenda Knowles (Motorbike Girl); Simone Boyce, Jullie Christy (Seducers); Amber, Julie Sims (Paint Girls); Teresa Hamilton Small, Lyn Barron (Beach Girls); Ann Jones, Sue Kem, Jackie Oakden, Sharon McCarthy (Shower Girls); Sue Woods, Margaret Dupre, Lee Zand, Helen Herbetson (Waterfall Girls); Pam Walker, Jane McIntosh (Animal Girls).

Gerard (Paul Trahir) and his 'nice' girlfriend, Niki (Kylie Foster).

Gerard (Paul Trahir) is the privileged, star photographer for Central, a computer which controls the totalitarian near-future. Gerard's speciality is images of violent sexuality.

At his first photo session, Gerard photographs a Droog (John Nobbs) as he threatens a nude Bald Lady (Helina McCall) with two machetes. But just as the Droog is about to decapitate her, she vanishes.

In the next shoot, a Rapist (Mark Bonnet) on a motorbike rides past Motorbike Girl (Brenda Knowles); both are wearing black leather. The girl pulls out a knife and cuts the man as he zips past. He falls off and lies apparently dead on the desert ground. The girl goes over to him, but the man is still alive and promptly strips and rapes her. At one point, he mauls her breasts with blood-stained hands in a particularly gruesome image that would probably not pass the Film Censorship Board today.

Of course, as the film goes along, all these images are 'deconstructed' by Gerard's finding his better emotions stirred by a young woman, Niki (Kylie Foster), who is as if from an earlier and finer time (partially signified by her preferring feminine underwear).

Gerard increasingly feels antipathy with the images he is supposed to create. In a conversation with Niki, he explains that violent pornography is Central's way of appealing to, and satiating, what is base in all of us, like the Romans did at the Colosseum. He then argues, somewhat evangelistically, that if he can replace violent images with beautiful ones, then the masses out there will become finer human beings.

Made on a shoe-string budget, mostly at the South Australian Film Corporation's studio in Adelaide, the film is ultimately little more than an exercise in full nudity and simulated sex in the soft-porn tradition. Unlike many others of this type, it has a coherent narrative. But many will feel that, while it in

the end criticises violent sexuality, the depiction of such images is not distanced but lascivious. An overall lack of conviction in the performances (particularly by Kylie Foster and the nude models who act as if they'd be happier in a silent film) does not help.

Where **Centrespread** is of most critical interest today is in the heaviness of some of its imagery, which is sure to offend many people, and in how, like most sex films, it is a masturbatory fantasy that pretends at the end to endorse true love above free sex.

SCOTT MURRAY

References
'Greg Lynch: The Middle Ground', an interview with the investor–distributor by Scott Murray, *Cinema Papers*, no. 31, March–April 1981, pp. 36–9, 71.
'Tony Paterson', an interview by Fred Harden, *Cinema Papers*, no. 36, February 1982, pp. 456–7, 513.

DOCTORS & NURSES: A STORY OF HOPES

A Universal Entertainment Corporation Production in association with [the] AFC & FINN Productions. Doctors & Nurses [/] a story of hopes.[1] © 1981 Universal Entertainment Corporation. *Budget:* $400,000. *Australian distributor:* Classic Films. *Opened:* December 1981. *Video:* Syme Home Video. *Rating:* G (November 1981; 2454.14m). 35mm. 89 mins.

Producer: Brian Rosen. *Scriptwriters:* Maurice Gleitzman, Doug Edwards, Robyn Moase, Tony Sheldon, Maurice Murphy. Based on an original idea by Maurice Murphy. *Director of photography:* John Seale. *Production designer:* Bob Hill. *Costume designer:* Judith Dorsman. *Editor:* Gregory Ropert. *Composer:* Mike Harvey. *Sound recordist:* Tim Lloyd. *Sound editor:* Greg Ropert. *Mixers:* Peter Fenton, Gethin Creagh.

Cast

Pamela Stephenson (Permanent Wave), Bert Newton (Mr Cody), Richard Meikle (The President), Drew Forsythe (Katz), Andrew McFarlane (Milligan), Graeme Blundell (Mr X), June Salter (Lady Cliquot), Terry Bader (Mr Gleeson), Bill Young (Agent 1), Lance Curtis (Agent 2), Bill McCluskey (Producer), Rebecca Rigg (Mercia King), Jason Samuels (Bud Abel), Miguel Lopez (Juan Peron), Jeremy Larsson (Rupert Young), Brent Gowland (Bernard Christian), Sarah Lambert (Mary Grey), Paris Burnett (Vicki Sweetacre), Larissa Burnett (Belinda Sweetacre), Mary Anne Davidson (Isabel Gold).

Ideas for children's television shows are fine in their place, which is on television in 30-minute blocks, not on the cinema screen in 90-minute features. Maurice Murphy had a nice comic idea with **Doctors & Nurses: A Story of Hopes**, which was to shoot a hospital soapie with child actors playing the medical staff and adults playing the patients. The downfall of the endeavour is that, after the novelty value wears off in the first ten minutes, there is too little to replace it.

The storylines predictably involve relationships between the staff, administration problems (they are trying to get a grant from Lady Cliquot (June Salter)), some weird patients (Bert Newton, Andrew McFarlane, Graeme Blundell and Pamela Stephenson do forgettable turns as derelict, crim and rock star, respectively) and a visit from the President of the United States. It sounds busier than it is, and the plotlines are basically dull, none of which is helped by the film's largely inert shooting style. Most scenes

are filmed flatly in front of camera, with few long shots or camera movements to shake the feeling that the film is a whole series of one-off sketches.

The film also suffers from conceptual confusion. The chief purpose behind having children in adult rôles would surely have been one of two options: the children acting incredibly adult and (mock) seriously, or having them inhabit a child's world in which they are the authority figures with adults at their mercy. The film simply doesn't know what to do, swinging wildly and nervously from one concept to the other. For instance, at one stage a character says, 'There's a finger that should have been kissed better an hour ago', while at others there are allusions to the sexual promiscuity of one of the nurses who is dating the Vienna Boy's Choir and the Harlem Globetrotters. The film tries to have it both ways, but fails.

And having adults play adults also undermines the whole idea of having children play adults in the first place. Certainly, the characters played by June Salter and Richard Meikle (The President) should logically have been done by children, but internal logic is the one thing the film lacks and needs most. (There is even an incredibly clumsy scene where an adult/adult tells a child/adult about being a kid!)

To its credit, there are some funny monologues which are handled surprisingly well by some of the child actors, such as the plot exposition given by a nurse to a heavily bandaged patient. However, in a lot of cases, some of the children appear to have been given the singularly onerous task of spouting jokes they do not quite understand.

Overall, not enough happens in **Doctors & Nurses: A Story of Hopes** to justify the exercise or the length lavished on it. The basic idea was fine (it worked for Alan Parker in **Bugsy Malone**, 1976), but the underlying concept and direction were simply not thought through well enough. It might have been much funnier if it had been taken more seriously.

JIM SCHEMBRI

---

[1] 'Doctors & nurses' appears first, then a bandaid carrying the words 'a story of hopes' is placed across the title on a diagonal.

References

'Maurice Murphy', an interview by Dave Sargent, *Cinema Papers*, no. 35, November–December 1981, pp. 444–7, 514.
'Doctors and Nurses [sic]' a review by Debi Enker, *Cinema Papers*, no. 36, February 1982, pp. 75, 76, 83.

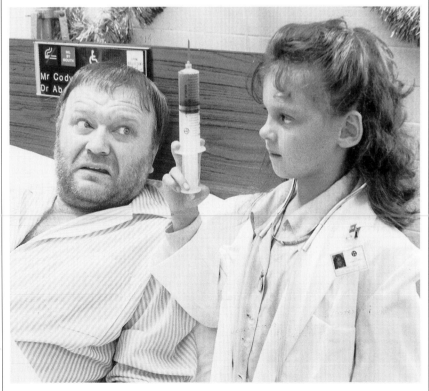

Mr Cody (Bert Newton) and Dr Isabel Gold (Mary Anne Davidson).

GALLIPOLI

Robert Stigwood–Rupert Murdoch for Associated R & R Films Pty Ltd present[s] Gallipoli. © 1981 Associated R & R Films Pty Ltd. Thanks to the Australian Film Commission and the South Australian Film Corporation. *Budget*: $2.6 million. *Locations*: Port Lincoln (South Australia); Egypt. *Australian distributor*: Roadshow. *Video*: Roadshow Home Video. *Rating*: NRC (May 1981; 3011.90m). 35mm. Panavision. 110 mins.

Producers: Robert Stigwood, Patricia Lovell. *Executive producer*: Francis O'Brien. *Associate producers*: Martin Cooper, Ben Gannon. *Scriptwriter*: David Williamson. Based on a story by Peter Weir. *Director of photography*: Russell Boyd. *Camera operator*: John Seale. *Design co-ordinator*: Wendy Weir. *Art director*: Herbert Pinter. *Wardrobe co-ordinator*: Terry Ryan. *Editor*: William Anderson. *Additional music*: Brian May. *Sound recordist*: Don Connolly. *Sound supervisor*: Greg Bell. *Sound editors*: Helen Brown (dia.); Peter Burgess (fx). *Mixers*: Peter Fenton, Ron Purvis, Gethin Creagh.

Cast

Mel Gibson (Frank Dunne), Mark Lee (Archy), Bill Hunter (Major Barton), Robert Grubb (Billy), Bill Kerr (Jack), John Morris (Col. Robinson), Harold Baigent (Camel Driver), Tim McKenzie (Barney), David Argue (Snowy), Harold Hopkins (Les McCann), Charles Yunupingu (Zac), Heath Harris (Stockman), Ron Graham (Wallace Hamilton), Brian Anderson (Railway Foreman), Reg Evans (Athletics Official 1), Jack Giddy (Official 2), Dane Peterson (Announcer), Paul Linkson (Recruiting Officer), Jenny Lovell (Waitress), Steve Dodd (Billy Snakeskin), Robyn Galwey (Mary), Don Quin (Lionel), Phyllis Burford (Laura), Marjorie Irving (Gran), John Murphy (Frank's Father), Diane Chamberlain (Mrs Barton), Gerda Nicolson (Rose Hamilton).

Gallipoli begins with images of a young man, Archy (Mark Lee), practising his sprint in the West Australian dawn in May 1915. It ends with a frozen frame which holds him in the heroic posture of the military runner, now streaked with blood, cut down in his youthful prime at Gallipoli. The earlier half of the film has to do with Archy's career as a sprinter and his meeting with the cynical Frank Dunne (Mel Gibson), whom he defeats at an athletic meeting. Their friendship is sealed in a trek across a vast, dry lake-bed as they make their way to Perth to 'join up' and, after separation, they are reunited in Egypt before their running prowess secures them a transfer to Gallipoli.

It is possible to be critical of **Gallipoli** on ideological grounds: it doesn't, for instance, adopt a clear anti-war stance; it acquiesces too easily in the myth-making resonance of the Anzac story; and so on. Nevertheless, it remains one of the flagships of the new Australian cinema, and deservedly so, for it has virtues that set it well above the level of Boys Own Adventure (as it was sneeringly described in a recent book). If it is not especially an anti-war film, it is certainly not pro-war, and certainly does not approve of Australia's participation in World War I. Its interest is, rather, in the way people react to the idea of war, and of this war in particular, and how they behave *in* war.

Peter Weir and his scriptwriter David Williamson have dramatised and examined ideas like mateship, competitiveness and sporting spirit, which are elements popularly associated with the national character. Beside these, Archy's mindless patriotism and Frank's pragmatism in response to Britain's war diminish in importance as their friendship is strengthened in exotic places and dangerous engagements. Perhaps it is at heart the male love story some have claimed it to be; whether or not this is true, the film unequivocally celebrates the bond of mateship without recourse to either sentimentality or tiresome buddy-ism.

Gallipoli, along with **Mad Max** (George Miller, 1979), was one of the first Australian films to achieve mainstream North American distribution. It was distributed by Paramount in the US where it did quite well without reproducing its great success in Australia. Given the unsympathetic representation of the British in the film, it is not surprising to note that it provoked dissentient voices to air their outrage in the correspondence columns of *The Times*.

BRIAN MCFARLANE

References

'Gallipoli', a review by Brian McFarlane, *Cinema Papers*, no. 33, July–August 1981, pp. 285–6.

'Peter Weir: Towards the Centre', an interview with the director by Brian McFarlane and Tom Ryan, *Cinema Papers*, no. 34, September–October 1981, pp. 322–9.

'Mel Gibson', an interview with the actor by Margaret Smith, *Cinema Papers*, no. 42, March 1983, pp. 12–17.

'Peter Weir', an interview with the director by Katherine Tulich, *Cinema Papers*, no. 80, August 1990, pp. 6–10.

'Gallipoli: You are Being Told What You are to Remember', Sylvia Lawson, *Filmnews*, November–December 1981, p. 11.

Archy (Mark Lee) and Frank (Mel Gibson).

GRENDEL GRENDEL GRENDEL

A presentation of The Victorian Film Corporation[,] Hoyts Theatres Ltd [and] TVW Enterprises Ltd. GRENDEL [/] GRENDEL [/] GRENDEL. © 1983 (1980) Animation Australia Pty Ltd[2]. *Budget:* $566,000. *Australian distributor:* Hoyts. *Opened:* August 1981. *Video:* not known. *Rating:* G. 35mm. 88 mins.

Producers: Phillip Adams, Alexander Stitt. *Associate producer:* Greg Terry. *Scriptwriter:* Alexander Stitt. Based on the novel, *Grendel*, by John Gardner. *Director of photography:* John Pollard. *Animation director:* Frank Hellard. [*Editor:* not credited.] *Composer:* Bruce Smeaton. *Recording supervisor:* Alf Bean. *Recording engineer:* Graham Owens.

Voices

Peter Ustinov, Keith Michell, Arthur Dignam, Ed Rosser, Bobby Bright, Ric Stone, Ernie Bourne, Rho Schepisi, Colin McEwan, Alison Bird, Barry Hill, Peter Aanensen, Jack Brown, Julie McKenna.

Grendel's mother loved him, according to the title song. But in 1981, audiences didn't respond to Alexander Stitt's animated monster, and neither did most critics who deigned to notice it. Exactly why this should have been so isn't easy to determine,

although the difficulty some reviewers seemed to have in putting a handle on Stitt's inspired version of a celebrated legend was undoubtedly a factor.

Like **Manganinnie** (John Honey, 1980), **Grendel Grendel Grendel** was dismissed in some quarters as 'kiddie stuff', although it was clearly more than that. It was, indeed, a lively, witty, superbly crafted adaptation of the Beowulf legend, based on the American novelist John Gardner's version of a story that has descended to our time through much minstrelsy and literary reworking.

Stitt tells it from the viewpoint of Grendel, regarding him as a sentimental, troubled creature and Man the insensitive monster. Poor Grendel is seen as something of a ninny in a cruel, largely uncaring world. He yearns for love, beauty and understanding, but doesn't appreciate his own physical strength, or the effect it, and his appearance, have on others.

The script avoids the philosophic depths of the Gardner novel, while plainly adopting its basic sentiments: tolerance and justice, against violence and superstition. Grendel *does* eat the odd human, but only after the rude rustics who invade his domain scorn and reject him.

The insecure, boorish king Hrothgar and his minions get into such a panic over 'the great boogy' that they call in the mighty

monster-slayer, Beowulf, and there is a mother of a showdown.

All this is depicted in artistically superb, conventional (though unDisneyish) animation graced by an excellent soundtrack. The voices are splendid, most notably Peter Ustinov as Grendel, Arthur Dignam as Beowulf, Keith Michell as Shaper the balladeer and Ed Rosser as Hrothgar, with songs and background music by Bruce Smeaton setting a complementary, sardonic tone.

The only false note in this department is a sudsily-inappropriate theme song. Other miscalculations are a less-than-helpful introduction by producer Phillip Adams and an unsatisfying conclusion.

KEITH CONNOLLY

---

[1] Credit reads, 'Designed & directed by Alexander Stitt'.
[2] The odd dating, '© 1983', is probably due to the later video release. One presumes the original film is © 1980.

References
'An Animated Progress Report on **Grendel Grendel Grendel**', Alex Stitt, *Cinema Papers*, no. 20, March–April 1979, pp. 339–41.
'An Animated Progress Report on Grendel Grendel Grendel: Part Two', Alex Stitt, *Cinema Papers*, no. 27, June–July 1980, pp. 184–6.

Grendel, right, and his mother.

HOODWINK

The New South Wales Film Corporation present[s] a CB Films Production. HOOD-WINK[1]. © 1980 CB Films Pty Ltd. *Budget:* $1 million. *Location:* Sydney. Made with the financial assistance of Faywin Investments Pty Ltd and The New South Wales Film Corporation. *Australian distributor:* Hoyts. *Video:* Australian Video. *Rating:* M (June 1981; 2432.88m). 35mm. 89 mins.[2]

Producers: Pom Oliver, Errol Sullivan. *Scriptwriter:* Ken Quinnell. Story inspired by Carl Synnerdahl. *Director of photography:* Dean Semler. *Production designer:* Ross Major. *Wardrobe:* Robyn Schuurmans. *Editor:* Nicholas Beauman. *Composer:* Cameron Allan. *Sound recordist:* Gary Wilkins. *Sound editors:* Andrew Steuart; Penn Robinson (fx); Lindsay Frazer (dia.). *Mixer:* Peter Fenton.

Cast

John Hargreaves (Martin), Judy Davis (Sarah), Dennis Miller (Ralph), Wendy Hughes (Lucy), Max Cullen (Buster), Paul Chubb (Reid), Michael Caton (Shapley), Wendy Strehlow (Martin's Sister), Kim Deacon (Marian), Les Foxcroft (Baldy), Colin Friels (Robert), Ralph Cotterill (Shakey), Brian McDermott (Collins), Paul Sonkilla[3] (Lancaster), Geoffrey Rush (Detective 1), Tony Strachan (Chicka), Willie Fennell (Bank Manager), Ray Meagher (Shaw), Neil Redfern (Jimmy), Martin Vaughan (Solicitor).

Martin (John Hargreaves) and Sarah (Judy Davis).

Hoodwink fits into the romantic–crime genre, focusing on an individual anti-hero. Most of his behaviour is interpreted in psychological terms, and most strikingly (but not surprisingly) there is little attempt to situate his story in a social context (i.e., sex, class, etc.). This could be explained as 'giving the audience what they want', but it is really nothing less than distorting the social and political practice of cinema in the name of 'entertainment'. **Hoodwink** might have been more than just another 'entertaining' film with 'popular' appeal if its film-makers had tried to tell the story from a different perspective, or had employed a non-conventional narrative form which might have opened it up for more levels of interpretation.

John Hargreaves plays Martin, a con(victed) man who bluffs a number of people into thinking that he is blind to gain a reduced prison sentence. It is a rôle that would be a challenge to any actor, and Hargreaves succeeds well, giving Martin a rough-diamond physicality and a 'likeable larrikin' presence.

This very characterisation is arguably a reflection of a cultural stereotype linked with Australia's convict past and she'll-be-right present, and one which many film-makers have gone to great lengths to construct as being part of the national male identity. Whether it is or not is extremely contentious.

The characters of Lucy (Wendy Hughes), Marian (Kim Deacon) and Sarah (Judy Davis) are all reflective of cultural stereotypes of another kind. They are 'three women who help create the problems' for Martin. Lucy deserts him for the 'security' of life as a croupier and a flat of her own. Marian, a voluptuous dancer and 'pick up', betrays him. And Sarah, wife of a lay preacher – 'quiet, religious, sexually repressed' – falls in love with him. Love creates the 'biggest difficulty of all'.

Hughes' and Deacon's performances, though suitably executed, are limited by the constraints of a narrative that constructs their characters like cut-out paper dolls – as women are often (mis)represented in film. As for Judy Davis, she proves her ability to develop a character with a quirk, but the rôle is really too small for her talents and magnitude; she virtually disrupts the film. It is also particularly distressing that the narrative resolves Sarah's conflict and struggle in a very conservative manner.

British director Claude Whatham injects a vaguely British tone in the film's style, mood and pace. As a visitor to this country, he is able to take a fresh look at the Australian landscape and have it photographed to convey symbolic meaning. This is especially noticeable in a scene in Sarah's house where a picture window neatly frames the splendour of Australia's roaming outback in all its glory.

However, Whatham doesn't seem to make any significant commentary in relation to the cultural specificity of the story. This might be understandable, considering that he did not originate the project, but it has resulted in a film that is great to look at but has little substance.

DAVE SARGENT[4]

---

[1] The double 'O' in the title is, in fact, interlocking handcuffs.
[2] Stratton quotes the length at 93 mins, while the video slick states 99 mins.
[3] Usually spelt 'Sonkkila'.
[4] Extracted from Sargent's review in *Cinema Papers* (see References).

References
'Judy Davis', a career interview with the actor by John Ley and Steve Bisley, *Cinema Papers*, no. 32, May–June 1981, pp. 116–21.
'Hoodwink', a review by Dave Sargent, *Cinema Papers*, no. 34, September–October 1981, pp. 397–8.
'Wendy Hughes', an interview with the actor by Richard Brennan, *Cinema Papers*, no. 40, October 1982, pp. 428–32.
'Captain of the Clouds', an article (with quotes) on actor John Hargreaves by Gail McCrea, *Cinema Papers*, no. 56, March 1986, pp. 38–9, 40.

THE KILLING OF ANGEL STREET

Forest Home Films presents in association with [the] Australian Film Commission[,] G.U.O. Film Distributors [and] Endeavour Communications Corporation The Killing of ANGEL STREET. © 1982 Forest Home Films. *Budget:* $1.5 million. *Location:* Sydney. *Australian distributor:* GUO. *Opened:* October 1981. *Video:* Thorn–EMI. *Rating:* M (September 1981; 2770.43m). 35mm. 96 mins.

Producer: Anthony Buckley. *Executive producer:* Jim George. *Scriptwriters:* Evan Jones, Michael Craig, Cecil Holmes. Based on an original story by Michael Craig. *Director of photography:* Peter James. *Camera operator:* Danny Batterham. *Production designer:* David Copping. *Costume designer:* Judith Dorsman. *Editor:* Tim Wellburn. *Composer:* Brian May. *Sound recordist:* John Phillips. *Sound editor:* Peter Burgess. *Mixers:* Peter Fenton, Phil Heywood.

Cast

Elizabeth Alexander (Jessica Simmonds), John Hargreaves (Elliott), Reg Lye (Riley), Alexander Archdale (B. C. Simmonds), David Downer (Alan Simmonds), Gordon McDougall (Sir Arthur Wadham), Ric Herbert (Ben), Brendon Lunney (Scott), Caz Lederman (Nancy), Allan Bickford (Collins), Pnina Bloch (Zoe), John Stone (Mr Benson), Arkie Whiteley (Tina Benson), Norman Kaye (Mander), Peter De Salis (Melville), David Waters (Ric James), Peter Collingwood (Government Minister), Anthony Martin (Les).

In intention, **Angel Street** is a political thriller. It is based quite openly on the Juanita Nielsen case, about the Sydney woman who disappeared in 1975 at the height of her involvement in the struggles of King's Cross residents and their supporters against a large-scale development project.

Elizabeth Alexander plays Jessica Simmonds, a Juanita-style character, and John Hargreaves' Elliott is obviously based on Jack Mundey, though he, too, is shown to be 'fiction', being bumped off by the developers' underworld allies rather than being expelled from the union. Jessica is a rather unworldly scientist who has returned from overseas to find her father, retired professor B. C. Simmonds (Alexander Archdale), and the harbourside terrace house where she grew up at the centre of resistance to the scheme. The old man is clearly having the time of his life ('Why should the young have all the good causes?'), encouraging his

Elliott (John Hargreaves) and Jessica Simmonds (Elizabeth Alexander).

working-class neighbours to hang on to their homes.

Then B. C. dies in a mysterious fire that almost certainly wasn't an accident and Jessica becomes his surrogate. In the process, she is brutally introduced to links between organised crime, the police, the developers and highly-placed state government officials. She is wheedled, threatened, conned and finally abducted by the underworld heavies, employees of a casino operator busily ploughing his illegal profits into more conventionally legitimate enterprises like the Angel Street development. But, having been drawn into the battle without really understanding what is at stake, Jessica becomes committed to it body and soul.

How and why she does so is the stuff of nicely-attuned, understated character development, for which Crombie, the writers and, above all, Alexander deserve great credit. Her Jessica stands triumphantly with Helen Morse's Caddie and Michele Fawdon's Cathy, other Crombie heroines who grow in stature as they combat a hostile world.

Crombie tells what is essentially a dark, grim story in colourful, populist tones, the style in which he is most fluent. It worked very well for **Caddie** (1976) and **Cathy's Child** (1979), and the same may be said about **Angel Street.** But because of the more 'public' nature of the subject, he has been subjected to critical scoldings about 'a soapy sort of social comment'[1]. This and similar comments do insufficient justice to a gifted

director who consistently and conscientiously aims his social-realism at the broadest-possible audience.

Crombie is at fault, however, when **Angel Street** occasionally lapses into mannered slickness, typified by some *Sweeney*-ish police behaviour and a tendency to telegraph the film's dramatic punches with anticipatory over-use of Brian May's rather transparent score. He must also, of course, take ultimate responsibility for deficiencies in the narrative and supporting performances.

The film's weaknesses, however, are hugely outweighed by its many strengths. These include a sound factual basis for a thriller-type plot, convincing central performances, direction nicely balanced between reportage and drama, a suitably atmospheric harbourside location for the main action and Peter James' ingeniously contrasted photography.

KEITH CONNOLLY[2]

---

[1] Meaghan Morris, *Financial Review*, 2 October 1981.

[2] Extracted from Connolly's review in *Cinema Papers* (see References).

References

'The Killing of Angel Street', a review by Keith Connolly, *Cinema Papers*, no. 35, November–December 1981, pp. 499–500.

'The Killing of Angel Street', a brief review by AP [Adrienne Parr], *Filmnews*, October 1981, p. 13.

MAD MAX 2

Kennedy Miller presents MAD MAX 2. *Alternative title:* The Road Warrior (US). © 1981 Kennedy Miller Entertainment Pty. Ltd and Others. *Budget:* $4.5 million. *Location:* environs of Broken Hill (New South Wales). *Australian distributor:* Roadshow. *Opened:* December 1981. *Video:* Warner Home Video. *Rating:* M (December 1981; 2593.58m, but cut to 2565.70m after being classified R and appeal rejected; all same month). 35mm. Pananvision. 94 mins.

Producer: Byron Kennedy. *Scriptwriters:* Terry Hayes, George Miller, Brian Hannant. *Director of photography:* Dean Semler. *Production designer:* Graham "Grace" Walker. *Costume designer:* Norma Moriceau. *Editors:* David Stiven, Tim Wellburn, Michael Balson. *Composer:* Brian May. *Sound recordist:* Lloyd Carrick. *Supervising sound editor:* Bruce Lamshed. *Sound editors:* Mark Van Buuren, Penn Robinson, Andrew Stewart[1]. *Mixers:* Roger Savage, Bruce Lamshed, Byron Kennedy.

Cast

Mel Gibson (Max), Bruce Spence (The Gyro Captain), Mike Preston (Pappagallo), Max Phipps (Toadie), Vernon Wells (Wez), Emil Minty (The Feral Kid), Kjell Nilsson (The Humungus), Virginia Hey (Warrior Woman), William Zappa (Zetta), Arkie Whiteley (The Captain's Girl), Steve J. Spears (Mechanic), Syd Heylen (Curmudgeon), Moira Claux (Big Rebecca), David Downer (Nathan), David Slingsby (Quiet Man), Kristoffer Greaves (Mechanic's Assistant), Max Fairchild (Broken Victim), Tyler Coppin (Defiant Victim), Jimmy Brown (Golden Youth), Tony Dearay (Grinning Mohawker), Kathleen McKay (Victim), Guy Morris (Bearclaw Mohawk); Annie Jones, James McCardell (Tent Lovers); Harold Baigent (Voice of Narrator).

Although it is not generally discussed in this way, one reason for the phenomenal international commercial success of **Mad Max 2** is clearly that it was one of the first 'high concept' movies of the 1980s. Its genius lay in its unlikely (even illogical) combination of elements: first, the extrapolation of the hero, Max (Mel Gibson), into a savage, post-apocalyptic landscape; second, and most decisively, the imagining of this futuristic world in the purest 'post punk' (or, more exactly, 'neo romantic') style of early 1980s music, fashion and design. In this way, as Philip Brophy has suggested, **Mad Max 2** amply filled the bill for many 'cult movie' fans around the world as 'a new slant on the gaudy and grotesque in cinema'[2].

The cultural legacy of **Mad Max 2**'s high concept was extraordinarily extensive and diverse. In cinema, it created a veritable 'post-apocalypse' genre and has been parodied, 'quoted' and ripped-off in everything from teen movies to music videos.

The virtues of **Mad Max 2** as a film are many. Suffice to say, it is an action epic of extraordinary craft and art. To the extreme, no-nonsense economy of the narrative and the marvellous 'graph' of violent setpieces alternating with quieter scenes mastered in **Mad Max** (George Miller, 1979), Miller adds a more florid, emotive style, particularly via elaborate camera movements (compare the classic low dolly into Max as he intervenes in the unfolding crisis by sparely intoning, 'You want to get out of here, you talk to me'). In the large spread of iconic character-groupings – monstrous, sado-masochistic punk villains and strapping, blonde-haired 'good citizens' – there is a very large dose of droll, ocker humour. Indeed, one of the film's finest achievements is its balancing of a comic-strip-like High Camp flamboyance with a genuinely affecting air of 'pulp' or B-movie poetry and grandeur.

Many critics (including this one) regard **Mad Max 2** as one of the finest films ever made in Australia. In fact, on its release it helped precipitate a shift in film criticism towards a celebration of formal play, pure filmic effect and the kinetic, performative engagement of savvy spectators in a popular culture context. For not only was the film far beyond the ken of old-fashioned 'lit crit' approaches to cinema (its 'themes' are

simple, even banal, mere pretexts for action), it also seemed to mock and outrun the mode of ideological critique that had risen to prominence in the 1970s.

Perhaps too much emphasis has been placed, over the years, on the supposedly timeless and universal 'mythical' aspect of **Mad Max 2**, with particular reference to Miller's own favourite citation, Joseph Campbell's *The Hero With a Thousand Faces*. A truer view might be that the enduring greatness and fascination of **Mad Max 2** comes from the fact that it is not pure but impure myth-making, performed at a dizzy height of cinematic invention. It is simultaneously, and shamelessly, a visionary kinetic experience, a tacky music video, a classically moral action epic, a gleefully amoral exploitation movie, and a stirring mythic tract. What more could one ask for from a single film?

ADRIAN MARTIN

---

1 Usually spelt 'Steuart'.
2 'Tales of Terror' (see References).

References
'Mad Max 2', a review by Almos Maksay, *Cinema Papers*, no. 36, February 1982, pp. 74–5.
'Mel Gibson', an interview with the actor by Margaret Smith, *Cinema Papers*, no. 42, March 1983, pp. 12–17.
'Tales of Terror: the Horror Films You Think You Know', Philip Brophy, *Cinema Papers*, no. 49, December 1984, p. 404.
'Brian May', an interview with the composer by Ivan Hutchinson, *Cinema Papers*, no. 50, February–March 1985, pp. 47–9, 88

Feral Child (Emily Minty) and Max (Mel Gibson) flee from Humungus' gang.

The Gyro Captain (Bruce Spence).

JOHN D. LAMOND

PACIFIC BANANA

[No opening production company credit.[1]]
PACIFIC BANANA. © 1980 Pacific Banana Pty Ltd. *Locations:* Huahine, Tahiti and Adelaide. *Australian distributor:* Roadshow. *Video:* Australian Video, through Star Video. *Rating:* R (October 1980; 2258.93m). 35mm. 82 mins.

Producer: John D. Lamond. *Associate producer:* John Pruzanski. *Scriptwriter:* Alan Hopgood. *Director of photography:* Gary Wapshott. *Wardrobe:* Dianne Smith, Ruth De La Lande. *Editor:* Russell Hurley. [*Composer:* not credited.] Title song written and sung by Deborah Gray and Luan Peters. *Sound recordist:* John Phillips. *Sound editor:* Lindsay Parker. *Mixer:* Bob Gardiner.

Cast

Graeme Blundell [Martin[2]], Robin Stewart [Paul], Deborah Gray [Sally], Alyson Best [Mandy], Helen Hemingway [Julia Blandings]; Manuia Taie (Laya), Luan Peters (Candy Bubbles); Audine Leith [Lady Blandings], Alan Hopgood [Sir Harry Blandings]; Graeme Duckett, Joy Thompson, Renata McLachlan, Angela Menzies-Wills, Violet Waieria, Leonora Jackson, Mary McGregor.

Pacific Banana is an attempt by director John D. Lamond to revive the soft-core sex film of the 1970s, most specifically the highly-successful **Alvin Purple** (Tim Burstall, 1973). Lamond even went so far as to employ **Alvin Purple**'s scriptwriter, Alan Hopgood, and its star, Graeme Blundell.

Blundell's character, Martin[3], is somewhat different to Alvin: rather than being able to seduce every woman he comes across, he sneezes whenever he is aroused and immediately loses his erection. This tends to get Martin into constant trouble, as when Lady Blandings (Audine Leith) tries unsuccessfully to seduce him on her husband's corporate jet. Martin is immediately redeployed to another of the businesses owned by Sir Harry Blandings (Alan Hopgood), the phallically named Banana Airlines. Using a brightly painted DC3, it plies the route to Tahiti with rather sex-starved passengers and crew. The two stewardesses, Sally (Deborah Gray) and Mandy (Alyson Best), for example, are joint fiancées of the pilot, Paul (Robin Stewart), whom they share by roster. He is the real Alvin character, with more than one 'opening' (as Hopgood's script would have it) in every port.

The style of comedy is all double-entendre ('Right now Sally's reconsidering her position.' 'Oh, which one? I thought she enjoyed all of them', *ad nauseam*) and much nudity – though, as was the style at the time, only the women go full frontal and the sex is most vaguely simulated. Even more to type, Martin finds true love at the end (with Blandings' daughter) and his erection returns.

There is little to be said for the film because it fails in its two key concerns by being neither erotic nor funny. It is also sexist in the most numbing way, and the attempt to acknowledge this by having the stewardesses tell the pilot at the end that they consider him a sex object is particularly dispiriting.

The only attempt at humour that comes close to raising a smile on this viewer's face is in the scene where Martin indulges in some nude body-painting. After the inevitable debilitating sneeze, he mutters to the disappointed women, 'I better go. I've got to go and visit an art gallery.' A slim picking indeed.

The film-makers, seemingly aware of the paucity of humour, added a voice-over, presumably to spice it up. Unfortunately, the narrator lowers the tone even more: when a priest looks up Sally's dress, the narrator chuckles most smuttily.

Even Lamond seems to have got cold feet in one scene: as an elderly citizen walks to the plane, Martin mumbles: 'Probably writing a book on sex for the senile.' The narrator jumps in, 'Oh, Martin that was terrible.' Rightly so, but how is one supposed to take constructive criticism from a smutty pervert?

SCOTT MURRAY

---

[1] The production company was the South Australian Film Corporation, but, apparently unhappy with having made a sex film, it kept its name off the credits. The only reference to the SAFC is at the beginning of the commercially released video which states that the SAFC has licensed the use of this motion picture on video.
[2] Few character names are given on the film. Some of those given are taken from what is said in the film. There can be no guarantee on spellings.
[3] See footnote 2.
[4] See footnote 3.

Publicity still of Alyson Best, Robin Stewart, Deborah Gray, Luan Peters and Graeme Blundell.

PUBERTY BLUES

Limelight Productions presents Puberty Blues. © 1980 Limelight Productions Pty Ltd. *Budget:* $890,000. *Location:* Cronulla (Sydney). Made in association with the Australian Film Commission. *Australian distributor:* Roadshow. *Video:* Roadshow. *Rating:* M (September 1981; 2276.69m). 35mm. Panavision. 87 mins.[1]

Producers: Joan Long, Margaret Kelly. *Scriptwriter:* Margaret Kelly. Based on the novel by Kathy Lette and Gabrielle Carey. *Director of photography:* Don McAlpine. *Production designer:* David Copping. *Wardrobe mistress:* Sue Armstrong. *Editors:* William Anderson, Jeanine Chialvo. *Composers:* Les Gock; Tim Finn (theme song). *Sound recordist:* Gary Wilkins. [*Sound editor:* not credited.] *Mixers:* Douglas Turner, Julian Ellingworth.

Cast

Nell Schofield (Debbie), Jad Capelja (Sue), Geoff Rhoe[2] (Garry), Tony Hughes (Danny), Sandy Paul (Tracey), Leander Brett (Cheryl), Jay Hackett (Bruce), Ned Lander (Strach), Joanne Olsen (Vicki), Julie Medana (Kim), Michael Shearman (Glenn), Dean Dunstone (Seagull), Tina Robinson (Freda), Nerida Clark (Carol), Kirrily Nolan (Mrs Vickers), Alan Cassell (Mr Vickers), Rowena Wallace (Mrs Knight), Charles Tingwell (The Headmaster), Kate Shiel (Mrs Velland), Pamela Gibbons (Jazz Ballet Teacher), Lyn Murphy (Mrs Hennessy), Andrew Martin (Mr Berkhoff), Rob Thomas (Car Salesman), Brian Harrison (Mr Little), Brian Anderson (Drive-In Attendant).

When this film was released in 1981, it was seen as a teen-flick, surfie-style comedy. And, perhaps at the time, the film's comedy was immediately apparent. Teenagers would have identified with the characters and the surf culture portrayed would have been more meaningful. A decade later, the film presents a rather dark and disturbing vision of a pathetic and often less-than-wholesome moment in the development of Australian national identity.

Puberty Blues, based on a novel by Kathy Lette and Gabrielle Carey, tells a story of two teenagers, Debbie (Nell Schofield) and Sue (Jad Capelja), whose main aim at the beginning of the film is to become accepted into a surfie clique on the most 'prestigious' spot on the beach. After getting into the group, the girls become completely initiated into its rules and rituals. These include smoking dope, drinking, wild partying, compulsory 'screwing' with compulsory 'boyfriends' and maintaining a level of such utter boredom

Sue (Jad Capelja) and Debbie (Nell Schofield).

that it eventually drives them away. However, none of this is as 'fun' as it sounds. The savage futility of these teenagers' lives, the disturbing boredom of their daily routine that provokes senseless and dangerous behaviour, the oppressive, almost tribal, chauvinism of their male companions, and the girls' easy, grateful welcome of this attitude all add up to a very grim picture.

The banal, conservative attitudes and the placid naïveté of their parents and school teachers can do little to change this situation. When in the end of the film, Debbie and Sue 'break out' of and 'challenge' the clique and its traditions by getting up on the surf board (only Debbie does this; Sue merely tags along) and doing what the boys do best, it does not seem like a great victory. By all means, the girls finally do something that they previously would have been too scared to do, but so what? This step is too small and its optimistic symbolism gets lost amid the prevalent futility and hopelessness of the film.

All that is not to say that **Puberty Blues** is not a powerful film. It churns out its social realism with an uncomfortable matter-of-factness. Nell Schofield, directed with great

understanding of the subject matter, gives a subtle and all-too-believable performance of a confused and insecure teenager. Bruce Beresford and cinematographer Don McAlpine choose to frame the less attractive aspects of Australian life in a most unexciting way, and it works to prove their point with great consistency. **Puberty Blues** will probably never again be classified as comedy, but it does make for a solid piece of gritty realist drama.

ANNA GUL

[1] The AFC's press sheet on the film gives the length as 2386m, or 87 mins. This seems more likely.
[2] The opening credits drop the 'h'.
[3] See footnote 2.

References

'**Puberty Blues**: Margaret Kelly & Joan Long', an interview with the scriptwriter and the producer by Miranda Brown, *Cinema Papers*, no. 35, November–December 1981, pp. 432–7.
'**Puberty Blues**', a review by Jim Schembri, *Cinema Papers*, no. 36, February 1982, pp. 72–3.
'**Puberty Blues**', a short review by Peter Kemp, *Filmnews*, November–December 1981, p. 13.

RACE FOR THE YANKEE ZEPHYR

Hemdale, Pact Productions and Fay, Richwhite present a First City Film. RACE FOR THE YANKEE ZEPHYR[1]. *Alternative title:* Treasure of the Yankee Zephyr (US). © [date not given; atb 1981] Gupta Film Services Pty Ltd[,] Pellinto Investments NV, Drake Films Ltd.[2] An Australia–New Zealand Co-production. *Budget:* $6 million. *Australian distributor:* Greater Union. *Video:* Thorn EMI. *Rating:* NRC (October 1981; 2962.44m). 35mm. 108 mins.

Producers: Antony I. Ginnane, John Barnett, David Hemmings. *Executive producers:* John Daly, Michael Fay, William Fayman. *Associate producer:* Brian W. Cook. *Scriptwriter:* Everett De Roche. *Director of photography:* Vincent Monton. *Camera operator:* Freddie Cooper. *Production designer:* Bernard Hides. *Costume designer:* Aphrodite Kondos. *Editor:* John Laing. *Composer:* Brian May. *Sound recordist:* Graham Morris. *Sound editors:* Don Reynolds; Derek Monton (dia.). *Mixer:* Brian Shennan.

Cast

Ken Wahl (Barney), Lesley Ann Warren (Sally), Donald Pleasence (Gibbie), George Peppard (Brown), Bruno Lawrence (Barker), Grant Tilly (Collector), Robert Bruce (Barman), Harry Rutherford-Jones (Harry); Tony Sparks, Clark Walkington, Frank Taurua, Steve Nicolle, Dick Jones, Dennis Hunt (Brown's Henchmen).

David Hemmings' Race for the Yankee Zephyr opens with a fake newsreel of money being loaded onto a World War II plane, the 'Yankee Zephyr', just before it takes off for one of General MacArthur's bases in New Zealand. Aloft, the plane begins to trail smoke and drifts off into the clouds. It and its $50 million payload of gold are lost, its mysterious disappearance the stuff of legend to this day. (This in itself is rather unbelievable because the plane from which the newsreel is being shot need only have followed the plane to where it crashed and there would be no mystery!)

The film then cuts to the daredevil Barney (Ken Wahl) and his ever-drunk companion, Gibbie (Donald Pleasence), hunting deer from a helicopter. The scene ends with Gibbie's being dropped from beneath the chopper into a mountain lake where he is left to spend the night.

When Gibbie awakes, he finds the once-submerged wreck of the lost 'Yankee Zephyr' next to him. Inside, he discovers crates of Old Crow whiskey and various medals. What

he does not notice is the box of gold he uses as a platform to help carry stuff out of the plane. But Gibbie's good fortune means he becomes even drunker than usual (and actor Donald Pleasence even more excessive in his performance). This over-extended comic sequence is far too laboured and Brian May's quirky music is irritating. In all, it is an inauspicious start to a film, and a plot, with much promise.

Once the action-adventure aspects take over, however, the film does gather pace and interest. At its best, it is a solid attempt at that most internationalist of genres, the action-adventure. However, for too much of the time believability is suspended by a hail of bullets that fail all too often to hit their easy targets. Gibbie's aside that 'They aren't exactly marksmen' doesn't go anywhere near far enough in covering up the implausibility, which also renders the otherwise well-staged action sequences (particularly those involving helicopters) less than convincing. The spectacular scenery of New Zealand's South Island is compensation only in short bursts.

What also annoys is dialogue which goes to extraordinary lengths to be descriptive ('You're about as warm as Friday's deer dung', Gibbie mutters). This flippancy is matched by characterisations that are parodies of parodies. One can't help but feel sorry for George Peppard, whose Brown is a blond-

haired gay based quite clearly on Dirk Bogarde's Gabriel in **Modesty Blaise** (Joseph Losey, 1966). All that is missing is a goldfish swimming around in those endless martinis Brown carries around – even in a rubber dinghy down a rapid.

Clearly, this is a film that does not take itself, or its genre, seriously. Regrettably, director David Hemmings' own sense of fun is rarely infectious.

SCOTT MURRAY

---

1 There is a star between the last two words of the title. As well, it should be noted that some press books for the film give the title as 'Race to the Yankee Zephyr', which has led many film writers to adopt that incorrect title.
2 This is a best guess at a quite unreadable copyright credit.

References
'David Hemmings', an interview with the director by Ross Lansell, *Cinema Papers*, no. 20, May–June 1979, pp. 351–5.
'Everett De Roche', a career interview with the scriptwriter by Paul Davies, *Cinema Papers*, no. 25, February–March 1980, pp. 30–3, 76, 78.
'Bob Saunders', an interview with the man behind Pact Productions, one of the film's investors, by Peter Beilby, *Cinema Papers*, no. 31, March–April 1981, pp. 26–9, 100.
'Soundtracks', with review of the film's score by Ivan Hutchinson, *Cinema Papers*, no. 89. August 1992, pp. 62–3.

Gibbie (Donald Pleasence) beside the 'Yankee Zephyr'.

ROADGAMES

Pat Quid (Stacy Keach), Boswell and Hitch (Jamie Lee Curtis).

[No opening production credit.[1]] ROADGAMES. [© not given; atb 1981.] *Budget:* $1.75 million. *Locations:* Melbourne; Nullarbor Plain (South Australia). *Australian distributor:* GUO. *Opened:* September 1981. *Video:* Star Video. *Rating:* M. 35mm. 101 mins.

Producer: Richard Franklin. *Executive producer:* Bernard Schwartz. *Co-producer:* Barbi Taylor. *Scriptwriter:* Everett De Roche. *Director of photography:* Vincent Monton. *Camera operator:* Louis Irving. *Production designer:* Jon Dowding. *Costume designer:* Aphrodite Kondos. *Editor:* Edward McQueen-Mason. *Composer:* Brian May. *Sound recordists:* Paul Clark, Raymond Phillips. *Sound editors:* Louise Johnson, Lon E. Bender. *Mixers:* John Keene Wilkins, Robert W. Glass Jnr., Robert M. Thirlwent.

Cast

Stacy Keach (Pat Quid), Jamie Lee Curtis (Hitch), Marion Edward (Frita), Grant Page (Smith or Jones), Thaddeus Smith (Police [sic]), Stephen Millichamp (Police [sic]), Alan Hopgood (Lester), John Murphy (Benny Balls), Bill Stacey (Captain Careful), Robert Thompson (Sleezy Rider), Colin Vancao (Fred Frugal).

Richard Franklin's **Roadgames** teams up Pat Quid (Stacy Keach), a truck driver, and Hitch (Jamie Lee Curtis), a hitch-hiker, as victims of seemingly alien forces in a strange and often hostile environment. As the title suggests, the film is set out on the road – the long road which links East and West. Along the way, there is a series of games that ultimately become menacing.

Pat amuses himself on the long hauls between Australian cities by indulging in his passion for word games. These he plays with a wry use of his immediate environment: other cars, the CB radio, the news, hitch-hikers. But the 'other world' outside the truck poses threats and dangers that he cannot control; indeed, one suspects that as an American in an Australian setting these are dangers he cannot quite understand.

The film begins with Pat and his erst-while companion, Boswell (a dingo), unknowingly witnessing a murder and then taking on an assignment which entails transporting a load of meat to the West. It so happens a union dispute has caused a shortage of meat, and out of this the issue of a 'truckie' as a kind of strike-breaker emerges. To some extent this proves to be a red-herring, yet it is this seemingly inconsequential narrative device that leads the character into a more dangerous 'game'.

Director Richard Franklin rapidly builds up a romantic image of a man who refuses to categorise himself as a truck driver, who recites poetry and reads literature, yet who is running away from an unspecified fear (his darker side perhaps?). Similarly, Hitch is unhappy, though her reasons are specifically family orientated, and takes to the road and Pat as a means of escape.

Juxtaposed with their plight is the real danger, the psychopath with a strong incli-nation for dismembering women and dis-tributing body parts along the highway. One senses that Keach wills this figure into his world and, in so doing, forces himself to confront that hidden, unspecified fear within himself. Thus, for the first half of **Roadgames**, the audience is treated to a kind of inverted, minimalist narrative pattern of Steven Spielberg's **Duel** (1971), where the truck driver is stalked by an ever-present van and a psychopath who reaches telepathi-cally into Keach's disturbed psyche.

Franklin, whose penchant for the thriller genre combines effectively with his obvious admiration for Hitchcockian methodology, has set out to play with film for the sake of film. (See Brian McFarlane's vigorous analy-sis in *Cinema Papers*.[2])

PETER LAWRANCE

---

[1] At the end there is this credit: 'An Essaness Pictures Presentation'. The video slick also car-ries the message: 'A Quest Film Production'.
[2] 'Roadgames' (see References).

References
'Production Report: **Roadgames**', *Cinema Papers*, no. 28, August–September 1980, comprising an interview with actor Stacy Keach by Peter Beilby, Scott Murray and Tom Ryan, pp. 238–41, 294, 296, and an interview with producer–director Richard Franklin by Murray and Ryan, pp. 242–6, 299.
'Roadgames', a review by Brian McFarlane, *Cinema Papers*, no. 33, July–August 1981, pp. 288–9.
'Soundtracks', with review of the film's score by Ivan Hutchinson, *Cinema Papers*, no. 89, August 1992, pp. 62–3.

SAVE THE LADY

McDuff (Bill Kerr), the ship's engineer, and Captain Playfair (Desmond Tester).

[Unchecked.[1]][© atb 1981] Tasmanian Film Corporation. *Location:* Hobart. *Australian distributor:* Young Australia Films. *Rating:* G. 16mm. 76 mins.

Producer: Barry Pierce. *Executive producer:* John Honey. *Scriptwriters:* John Palmer, Yoram Gross. Based on the novel, *Save the Lady,* by Yoram Gross. *Director of photography:* Gert Kirchner. *Production designer:* Jon Bowling. *Wardrobe:* Kay Alty. *Editor:* Mike Woolveridge. *Composer:* Peter McKinley. *Sound recordist:* John Schiefelbein. *Sound editor:* Mike Woolveridge. *Mixers:* Peter McKinley, John Schiefelbein.

Cast

Wallas Eaton (Trotter), John Ewart (Uncle Harry), Bill Kerr (McDuff), Desmond Tester (Captain Playfair), John Coleby (Menial), Robert Clarkson (Specs), Miranda Cartledge (Jo), Matthew Excell (Ben), Kim Clifford (Gina); Frankie Davidson, John Unicomb, Barrie Rugless.

Save the Lady is a children's film directed by Leon Thau, based on a novel by the noted animator, Yoram Gross. It was also the second and final feature financed by the short-lived Tasmanian Film Corporation.

Established in 1977, the TFC was one of the first film bodies to be set up by a state government. Apart from numerous documentaries, it produced the acclaimed but little-seen **Manganinnie** (John Honey, 1980), one of the few Australian films to deal with Aboriginal issues at that time.

A year or so after **Save the Lady** was finished, the TFC was sold off to private investors. The minister in charge, Robert Robson, said, 'The decision was a regrettable one, but unavoidable in the state's current economic plight.' The TFC's demise was, in fact, a forerunner of the problems that would face state film bodies in New South Wales, Queensland and South Australia. The TFC's financial problems may also have helped keep **Save the Lady**'s theatrical release to a minimum.

At time of this book's going to press, no film or video copy was found to be available for viewing. However, according to various other sources, the story concerns an 80-year-old ferryboat, *Lady*, which is about to be destroyed by the modern-minded and heartlessly bureaucratic Transport Commission.

Four children–Specs (Robert Clarkson), Jo (Miranda Cartledge), Ben (Matthew Excell), Gina (Kim Clifford)–decide to fight back and, with the help of Captain Playfair (Desmond Tester) and the engineer, McDuff (Bill Kerr), save the ferry. They are greatly aided by Uncle Harry (John Ewart), a cleaner at the Transport Commission who acts as a much-needed spy.

According to David Stratton, 'After the motley group sets sail with *Lady,* and they are pursued by police boats, all ends well and the vessel will sail on.'[2]

SCOTT MURRAY

[1] No copy of the film was available for viewing.
[2] David Stratton, *The Avocado Plantation: Boom and Bust in the Australian Film Industry,* Macmillan, Sydney, 1990, p. 343.

THE SURVIVOR

Antony I. Ginnane and William Fayman present in association with Laurence Myers A Tuesday Films Production.[1] THE SURVIVOR.[2] © 1980 Pact Productions Pty Ltd. *Budget:* $1.3 million. *Location:* Adelaide and country South Australia. *Australian distributor:* GUO. *Video:* Thorn EMI Video. *Rating:* M (October 1980; 2705.14m, but cut in June 1981 to 2386m). 35mm. 99 (then 87) mins.

Producer: Antony I. Ginnane. *Executive producer:* William Fayman. *Associate producer:* Jane Scott. *Scriptwriter:* David Ambrose. Based on the novel by James Herbert. *Director of photography:* John Seale. *Camera operator:* Peter Moss. *Production designer:* Bernard Hides. *Costume designer:* Terry Ryan. *Editor:* Tony Paterson. *Composer:* Brian May. *Sound recordist:* Tim Lloyd. *Sound editor:* Bruce Lamshed. *Mixer:* Peter Fenton.

Cast

Robert Powell (Keller), Jenny Agutter (Hobbs), Joseph Cotten (Priest), Angela Punch-McGregor (Beth), Peter Sumner (Tewson), Lorna Lesley (Susan), Robert Cotterill (Slater), Adrian Wright (Goodwin), Tyler Coppin (Boy), Kirk Alexander (Dr Martindale), Jon Nicholls (Jackson), Roger Cardwell (Flight Engineer), Jenufa Scott-Roberts (Stewardess), John Edmund (Goswell), Denzil Howson (Rogers), Edwin Hodgman (Bain), Heather Steen (Allens), Brenton Whittle (Thornton), Geoff Pullan (Osborne), Robin Bowring (Stuart).

Almost incomprehensible for most of its cut-down 87 minutes, The Survivor was British actor David Hemmings' fourth film as director, though his first in Australia. The plot, such as there is, concerns the attempts of a pilot, Keller (Robert Powell), to understand why he has survived a plane crash which destroyed a 747 and killed every other person aboard. His search for an answer takes him repeatedly to the crash site. On one flight over it in a light aircraft, he notices a strange woman, Hobbs (Jenny Agutter), standing at the head of a group of small children, but no wreckage.

This supernatural thriller is loaded with references to other films of the genre. Joseph Cotten appears as a priest (echoes of the Exorcist and Omen cycles); an opportunistic photographer is mysteriously murdered when his lens appears to have captured something it shouldn't have (ditto); Keller seems to have been spared death only to be dragged back into it by mental torture and the collective will of those who did not survive (**Carnival of Souls**, Herk Harvey, 1962; Zombie movies); and the lost children in the wilderness image is central to much colonial folklore and was used most famously in Peter Weir's **Picnic at Hanging Rock** (1975).

Indeed, **Picnic at Hanging Rock** seems to have influenced **The Survivor** in another sense, insofar as the suspense and horror generated by the film depend more on sound than on visual effects. Only the well-orchestrated crash sequence which opens the film strives for a presentation of the underlying horror in a more tangible way. The attempt to intellectualise a scenario which might easily have lent itself to the splatter-movie genre reflects a deliberate decision on the part of producer Antony I. Ginnane and director Hemmings to eschew 'gore' in favour of 'cerebral', in anticipation of a change of direction in audience expectations which never eventuated (see David Stratton's *The Avocado Plantation*[3]). But the film doesn't fail because Hemmings and Ginnane misread audience expectations; it fails because they did not have the courage to develop the psychological elements of the script to their full potential, and because they lacked the clarity of vision to bring some sense to this muddled story.

Instead of using the device of Keller's temporary amnesia to address the issue of guilt (at having survived), the film posits Keller as a supernatural detective, granted a temporary reprieve from the death he has in reality already suffered, so that he might discover the identity and motivation of the real killer. This turns out to be the man who owns the airline, who appears to have blown up his own plane simply to prove that he could. His speech is reminiscent of Orson Welles' ferris-wheel speech as Harry Lime in Carol Reed's **The Third Man** (1949), but whereas Lime is operating out of a post-war milieu in which morality has been severely skewed, the airline owner is speaking out of a vacuum which in no way connects with the rest of the film.

KARL QUINN

1 An end credit reads: 'Made in association with Pact Productions Pty Ltd.'
2 The end of the film adds double quote marks to the opening title; thus, "THE SURVIVOR".
3 David Stratton, *The Avocado Plantation: Boom and Bust in the Australian Film Industry*, Macmillan, Sydney, 1990, pp. 298-300.

Reference
'Bob Saunders', an interview with the man behind Pact Productions, one of the film's investors, by Peter Beilby, *Cinema Papers*, no. 31, March–April 1981, pp. 26–9, 100.

Keller (Robert Powell) and Priest (Joseph Cotten).

WINTER OF OUR DREAMS

Vega Film Productions presents Winter of our Dreams. © 1981 Vega Film Productions Pty Ltd. *Budget:* $350,000. *Location:* Sydney. Made in association with the Australian Film Commission, GUO Film Distributors, Spectrum Films and Winta Investments. *Australian distributor:* GUO. *Opened:* August 1981. *Video:* Thorn EMI. *Rating:* M (June 1981; 2454.14m). 35mm. 89 mins.[1]

Producer: Richard Mason. *Scriptwriter:* John Duigan. *Director of photography:* Tom Cowan. *Camera operator:* Nixon Binney. *Production designer:* Lee Whitmore. *Wardrobe:* Helen Parry (Cathy Downes'). *Editor:* Henry Dangar. *Composer:* Sharon Calcraft. *Sound recordist:* Lloyd Carrick. *Sound editor:* Andrew Steuart. *Mixers:* Phil Judd, Phil Haywood[2].

Cast

Judy Davis (Lou), Bryan Brown (Rob), Cathy Downes (Gretel), Baz Luhrmann (Pete), Peter Mochrie (Tim), Mervyn Drake (Mick), Margie McCrae (Lisa), Mercia Deane-Johns (Angela), Joy Hruby (Marge), Kim Deacon (Michelle), Caz Lederman (Jenny), Virginia Duigan (Sylvia), Rosemary Lenzo (Girl in Bookshop), Alex Pinder (Terry), John Smythe (Jan Hertz), Bill Garner (Zoe Lake), Robert Hughes (Martin Harris), Bassia Carole (Tom McCarthy), Helen Pankhurst (Dolly Brukman), Craig Lambert (Jeremy Connolly), Arthur Pease (Sno Norton Sinclair).

In a brief establishing sequence, a distraught young woman, Lisa (Margie McCrae), tries unsuccessfully to contact an old friend, Rob (Bryan Brown), and leaves her guitar with a King's Cross prostitute, Lou (Judy Davis). Later, when Rob, proprietor of an alternative bookshop, learns of Lisa's suicide, he decides to investigate. This leads to a meeting with Lou, and a relationship develops around recollections of Lisa.

Rather unrealistically, Lou sees in Rob a saviour from her drug-ridden, desperate life – not that he gives her much encouragement. When Lou attempts to deepen their rapport with a few spicy confidences about her trade, Rob cuts her short. Later, he not unkindly declines her sexual advances.

Rob is more complex and psychologically interesting, but a good deal less sympathetic, than Lou. He is a detached, rather than disillusioned, not-so-old Leftie, in student days a red-hot activist, now materially comfortable but given to moments of self-reproach. He lives in a trendy Balmain home with Gretel (Cathy Downes), his sexually liberated, academic wife. These days,

Rob has little better to do than contemplate his own emotional and spiritual inadequacy; his only challenge is a computer chess set.

Brown plays Rob with the quizzically troubled air of self-doubt, furthering the script's suggestion of self-protective ambivalence in his attitude to both women.

Lou is all up-front, or nearly all. Judy Davis portrays beautifully her easily cracked bravado, her tremulous aspirations, her gawkiness, her pathetic mixture of ignorance and insouciance.

Lou's dislocation is heightened by glimpses of Gretel and Rob's culturally (and materially) rich lifestyle – insights that undermine her ability to go on with her own ugly existence. So she takes the plunge, putting Rob and Gretel's professed liberalism to the test by cold-turkeying out of heroin addiction while staying in their house. Not altogether happily, they look after her. The ordeal reinforces Lou's resolve to make a fresh start.

There have been few more quietly moving scenes in an Australian film than the final sequence of **Winter of our Dreams**. Writer–director John Duigan craftily arouses one's fears that Lou is about to take her identification with Lisa to its ultimate conclusion. He is carefully subtle about it, though. Audiences seem equally divided between those who draw a pessimistic conclusion from the final shot and those who find it emotionally uplifting.

Duigan maintains an unhurried pace throughout, in keeping with the tenor of his naturalistic purpose. If some characters

behave just a little too sweetly (as when the McGregors look after Lou, and in the 'come-and-join-us' bonhomie of the uranium demonstrators), such behaviour is not inconsistent with such people, or at least with their self-image.

Winter of our Dreams is a wry contemplation of the disturbing nexus between self-expression and personal responsibility in social relationships. In examining this by means of two unusual but by no means unique Australians, Duigan is beating the bounds of naturalism that had been his *métier*.

KEITH CONNOLLY[3]

---

[1] The AFC press notes list the film as 93 minutes or 2551m.
[2] Usually spelt 'Heywood'.
[3] Extracted from Connolly's review in *Cinema Papers* (see References).

References

'Judy Davis', a career interview with the actor by John Ley and Steve Bisley, *Cinema Papers*, no. 32, May–June 1981, pp. 116–21.

'John Duigan and **Winter of our Dreams**', an interview with the writer-director by Scott Murray, *Cinema Papers*, no. 33, July–August 1981, pp. 226–9, 299.

'**Winter of our Dreams**', a review by Keith Connolly, *Cinema Papers*, no. 34, September–October 1981, pp. 395–6.

'Life of Bryan', an article (with quotes) on actor Bryan Brown by Dorre Koeser, *Cinema Papers*, no. 53, September 1985, pp. 16–19.

'Ethics of the Outsider', an interview with director John Duigan by Albert Moran, *Filmnews*, April 1984, pp. 10–12.

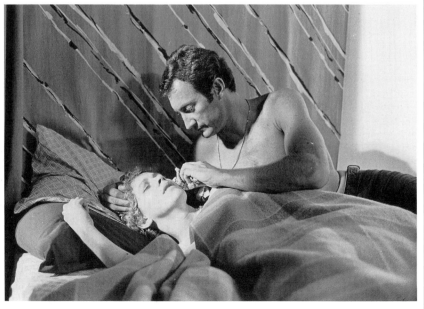

Lou (Judy Davis), a prostitute, and Rob (Bryan Brown).

WRONG SIDE OF THE ROAD

[No opening production company credit.] WRONG SIDE OF THE ROAD. © 1981. *Location:* Point Pearce (South Australia). Produced with the assistance of the Creative Development Branch of the Australian Film Commission, the Aboriginal Art Board and the Aboriginal Advancement League of South Australia. *Australian distributor:* Sydney Film-makers Co-operative. *Video:* Home Cinema Group. *Rating:* M (August 1981; 855m). 16mm. 79 mins.[1]

Producers: Ned Lander, Graeme Issac. *Scriptwriters:* Graeme Issac, Ned Lander, in collaboration with cast. *Director of photography:* Louis Irving. *Production designer:* Jan Mackay. *Wardrobe:* Jan Mackay. *Editor:* John Scott. *Music:* No Fixed Address, Us Mob. *Sound recordist:* Lloyd Carrick. *Sound editor:* Peter Butt. *Mixer:* Peter Fenton.

Cast

No Fixed Address: Leslie Graham (Les Stevens), Chris Jones (Ricky), Veronica Rankine (Vonnie), Bart Willoughby (Bart), John Miller (John John); Us Mob: Ronnie Ansell (Ronnie), Peter Butler (Pedro), Carol Karpanny (Carroll), Wally McArthur (Wally); John Francis, Noel Pommery, Rob McGregor, Craig Tidswell, Frank Malony, Mark Thompson, Franco Carli, Richard Shoesmith, Christian Jocumsen (City Policemen); Leilal Rankine (Amy Smith), Veronica Brodie (Aunty Veronica), Gayle Rankine (Gayle), Donna Drover (Donna); Donald Freshwater, Ken Hampton Jr, Edward Love (Roadies); Sam Cohen, Phillip Rehn, Chris Haywood, Emu Nugent (Country Policemen).

This docu-drama launched Aboriginal rock music into the public domain. Its uncompromising examination of the treatment of black musicians in the bands Us Mob and No Fixed Address was a challenge to white Australia, whose perceptions of Aboriginal music and people had been restricted to the sounds and images of tribal Australians. Here was a story of urban Aboriginal Australia, with the vicious teeth of racism cutting deep. Here also was a delightful insight into the new generation of Aboriginal and black consciousness regenerating itself through rock music.

The remarkable music, combined with the unquestioned politics of the film, pointed towards the explosion of Aboriginal aspirations that developed in the late 1970s and exploded into full view with the election of the Hawke Labor Government in 1983, two years after **Wrong Side of the Road** was released.

A country cop (Chris Haywood), right, arrests Ronnie (Ronnie Ansell).

The film's appeal was its conscious blurring of documentary and fictional styles. Producer–director Ned Lander was determined to get under the fingernails to examine the dirt of white Australia's treatment of Aborigines while introducing filmgoers to Aboriginal rock. In the early 1980s, Aboriginal rock was a remarkable, new popular music form. The combination of the portrayal of despair and injustice directed at Aborigines and the exciting prospect of their voice (and their political campaign) being heard through this new music moved beyond the prevailing depictions of Aborigines as suffering victims of white oppression.

The sight of socially competent young Aboriginal men and women fighting for fundamental human rights – for example, 'the right' to perform in a hotel after the publican discovered the band he had booked was black and threw them out – was and is shocking. But the Aboriginal music that cut across this unsightly scenario has become a focal point of the ongoing Aboriginal struggle for identity and meaning that was captured, in a less material level (or with some spiritual empathy), at about the same time, in Peter Weir's **The Last Wave** (1977).

In the years since this film was made, the subsequent use of popular music as a source of empowerment for Aborigines indicates that the film marked a significant turning point in Australian film and musical history.

MARCUS BREEN

---

[1] Video cut in June 1982 to 76 mins.

References

'**Wrong Side of the Road**', a review by Almos Maksay, *Cinema Papers*, no. 35, November–December 1981, pp. 503, 504.

'**Wrong Side of the Road**', an interview with Ned Lander, producer Graeme Issac, Veronica Brodie (Aboriginal Sobriety Group) and Leila Rankine (Centre for Aboriginal Studies) by Annie Bickford, Gilly Leahy and Tina Kaufman, *Filmnews*, October 1981, pp. 8–9, 11.

'**Bloody Captain Cook Bastards Coming Here**', a review of **Wrong Side of the Road** by Annie Bickford and Jeni Thornley, ibid., pp. 10, 12.

1982

Guy Hamilton (Mel Gibson), Colonel Henderson (Bill Kerr), Billy Kwan (Linda Hunt) and Jill Bryant (Sigourney Weaver). Peter Weir's The Year of Living Dangerously.

AROUND THE WORLD WITH DOT

Yoram Gross presents Dot and Santa Claus[1]. *Alternative titles:* 'Dot and Santa Claus' (video) and 'The Further Adventures of Dot and the Kangaroo' (working). © 1982 Yoram Gross Film Studio. *Australian distributor:* Hoyts. *Video:* VSA (Roadshow). *Rating:* G (May 1982).[2] 35mm. 72 mins.

Producer: Yoram Gross. *Associate producer:* Sandra Gross. *Scriptwriters:* John Palmer, Yoram Gross. Based on original story by Yoram Gross. *Photography:* John Barnard, Chris Ashbrook. *Animation photography:* Jenny Ochse, Bob Evans. *Editors:* Des Horne, Colin Waddy, Jennifer Kretzschmar, Chris Plowright. *Composer:* Bob Young. *Lyrics:* John Palmer. *Sung by:* Drew Forsythe, Barbara Frawley, Ross Higgins. *Sound recordists:* John Holling-worth, John Franks. *Mixer:* Martin Benge.

Animation director: Ray Nowland. *Storyboard and character design:* Nicholas Harding, Athol Henry, Ray Nowland, Andrew Szemenyei. *Layouts:* Ray Nowland. *Backgrounds:* Amber Ellis, Abignew Dromirecki (Kolorkraft Laboratory). *Animators:* Nicholas Harding, Athol Henry, John Hill, Cynthia Leech, Paul Marron, Chris Minos, Ray Nowland, Kevin Roper, Andrew Szemenyei, Kaye Watts. *Assistant animators:* Lynda Amos, Elizabeth Goodwin, Lyn Hennessy, Ted Hennessy, Tony Hill, Sharyn Jackson, I. B. Kazda, Boris Koslov, Ginnady Koslov, Babetta Latooy, Svetlana Lin, Glen Lovett, Narelle Neils, Dagmar Persan, Ann Rossell, Vaclav Smejkial, Robyn Smith, Michael Sutton, Jeanette Toms, Maria Venness, Bruce Warner, Fiona Warner, Olga Zahorsky.

Cast

Drew Forsythe (Santa Claus).

Voices

Drew Forsythe, Barbara Frawley, Ron Haddrick, Anne Haddy, Ross Higgins.

[See Appendix A for overview on all the Gross films, pp. 352–4.]

---

[1] The only available video had 'Dot and Santa Claus' as the title.

[2] Rated as 'Dot and Santa Claus'.

Reference

'Yoram Gross', an interview with the producer–director by Antoinette Starkiewicz, *Cinema Papers*, no. 48, October–November, 1984, pp. 334–8, 390.

Santa Claus and Dot.

ATTACK FORCE Z

John McCallum Productions [and] Central
Motion Picture Corporation presents [sic]
ATTACK FORCE Z[1]. *Alternative title:* 'Z-
Men' (working). © 1980 John McCallum
Productions[–]Central Motion Picture
Corporation Co-production. *Location:*
Taiwan. Made in association with the
Australian Film Commission. *Australian
distributor:* Roadshow. *Opened:* June 1982.
Video: Roadshow. *Rating:* M (December
1980; 2621.47m but cut in May 1982 to
2541.53m). 35mm. 93 mins.

   Producer: Lee Robinson. *Executive pro-
ducers:* John McCallum, George F. Chang.
Scriptwriter: Roger Marshall. *Director of
photography:* Lin Hun-Chung. *Production
designer:* Bernard Hides. *Wardrobe:* Byi Syou
Jen. *Composer:* Eric Jupp. *Editor:* David
Stiven. *Sound recordists:* Don Connolly, Tim
Lloyd. *Sound editors:* Lindsay Frazer, Stuart
Armstrong, Denise Haslem, Penn Robinson.
Mixer: Peter Fenton.

Cast

John Phillip Law (Jan Veitch), Mel Gibson
(Paul Kelly), Sam Neill (Danny Costello),
Chris Haywood (Sparrer Bird), John Waters
(Ted King), Ned Chun (Rice Farmer), Sylvia
Chang (Chien Hau), O Ti (Shaw Hu), Koo
Chuan Hsiung (Lin Chan-Lang), Lung
Shuan (Watanabe), Vi Yuan (Imanaka), Wei
Su (Wong Chong), Hsa Li-Wen (Lee Chang),
Val Champion (Ed Ayres), Wang Yu (Oshiko
Imoguchi).

*Danny Costello (Sam Neill), Sparrer Bird (Chris Haywood), Jan Veitch (John Phillip Law)
and Paul Kelly (Mel Gibson).*

Attack Force Z has lived its life mainly on
video, where it acquired a market value
due to those cast members who subsequently
ascended to stardom: Mel Gibson, Sam Neill,
John Waters and, to a lesser extent, Chris
Haywood. Perhaps equally prescient, in a
less spectacular way, was the attempt of the
film to plug into an 'Australasian' production base, something which John McCallum
and Lee Robinson (a film director from the
1950s) had already explored in their television series, *Bailey's Bird* (1976–77), and
were to do so again in another Force Z story.

   The film itself, set during World War II,
mixes progressive and reactionary elements
in a curious and contradictory way. From
one angle, it is an entirely conventional,
even backward-looking generic war drama –
authorised and authenticated (as a pre-
credit title card informs us) by the veterans
of the Z Force Association. Beginning *in
medias res* like Samuel Fuller's **The Big Red
One** (1980), the Force lands on an island
held by the Japanese. Gradually its
mission is revealed to us: to safely transport
two diplomats who are being hidden and

protected by the local 'resistance'. The film
makes a laborious and somewhat suspect
distinction between the nasty Japanese –
cold-blooded, snivelling, robotic – and those
stoic, dignified, mystical islanders who follow
Chinese traditions.

   The film has a high dose of traditional
'gung ho' war film heroics. Yet, at the same
time, it is also a film in the Gallipoli tradition
about Aussie losers – only Paul Kelly (Mel
Gibson) gets out alive, and even the diplomat
he presumes to have rescued turns out to be
dead – and about a rapprochement and co-
operation between Western and Oriental
societies that is tragically cut short by the
relentless atrocities of war. This latter theme
is specifically dramatised through the love
story of Jan Veitch (John Phillip Law) and
Chien Hau (Sylvia Chang), and finds its most
affecting expression in the final shot where
a lifting camera surveys, with Chien, the carnage and waste precipitated by the Force's
operation.

   Tim Burstall took over as director from
Phillip Noyce shortly before shooting
started. According to David Stratton's
account in *The Avocado Plantation*[2], the film
was originally intended to 'explore aspects
of colonialism', the outline of which one can
dimly imagine from the film as it is. Burstall's
direction is crisp in an unfussy action-movie
fashion, with character relations and
dramatic tensions sketched economically
and confidently; his unmistakeably 'old fashioned' approach, however, is underlined by
Eric Jupp's appallingly clichéd score (oriental chimes and gongs for the islanders,
military brass and drums for the soldiers).
Overall, **Attack Force Z** is an interesting and
somewhat overlooked film.

ADRIAN MARTIN

1 The 'Z' has a vertical sword through it.
2 David Stratton, *The Avocado Plantation:
Boom and Bust in the Australian Film Industry*,
Macmillan, Sydney, 1990, pp. 42–4.

THE BEST OF FRIENDS

The NSW Film Corporation presents A Friendly Film. The Best of Friends. © 1981 A Friendly Film Company P/L. *Location:* Sydney. *Australian distributor:* Hoyts. *Video:* Australian Video. *Rating:* M (August 1981; 2621.47m). 35mm. 97 mins.

Producer: Tom Jeffrey. *Scriptwriter:* Donald MacDonald. *Director of photography:* David Gribble. *Camera operator:* Nixon Binney. *Production designer:* John Carroll. *Costume designer:* Carol Berry. *Editor:* Ron Williams. *Composer:* Brian King. *Sound recordist:* Tim Lloyd. *Sound editor:* Paul Maxwell. *Mixers:* Peter Fenton, Gethin Creagh.

Cast

Angela Punch McGregor (Melanie), Graeme Blundell (Tom), Ruth Cracknell (Iris), Henri Szeps (Lilo), Graham Rouse (Father James), Moya O'Sullivan (Mrs Malone), Les Foxcroft (Mr Malone), Mark Lee (Bruce), Sonja Tallis (Pammie), Deborah Grey (Grace), Serge Lazareff (Colin), Alan Becher (Tim), Ron Falk (Waiter), Maggie Dence (Shop Assistant), Gordon McDougall (Doctor), Meg Graham (Singing Telegram Girl), Christine Jeston (Secretary), Lynette Haddrick (T.V. Receptionist).

This film attempts to address the eternal question: Can friends who, after a long time as friends, have sex and still be friends? Unfortunately, although perhaps appropriately, the film seems to spend an eternity musing without saying anything much.

Approaching this subject as a comedy may have seemed like the logical way to go, but the film-makers may have laboured under the same misapprehension as those who made **Luigis Ladies** (Judy Morris, 1989) at the other end of the decade: that comedy films are a cinch to make.

The first stumble happens within about the first three minutes, when the film's chief theme is announced with the subtlety of a party whistle. The second stumble comes within fifteen minutes when best friends Melanie (Angela Punch McGregor) and Tom (Graeme Blundell) do the deed after a particularly liquid dinner at which Melanie gets comprehensively smashed. By playing its cards so early, the film sets itself up to deal with the consequences of the deed (possessiveness, jealousy) which it does with an alarming lack of humour, drama or charm. It simply doesn't live up to its promise.

There is absolutely no sense of comic pacing in what follows. The film seems to jerk from one poorly-handled confrontation

Melanie (Angela Punch McGregor) orders Tom (Graeme Blundell), right, from her bedroom, watched by Bruce (Mark Lee).

to another. Similarly, there is a dearth of comic inspiration. This is clear from an early shot featuring a pool at a restaurant. Sure enough, by film's end, the pool is fallen into.

The film makes the fatal mistake, particularly symptomatic in poor comedy, of treating things too lightly. There are no dramatic weightings placed on the events, nothing to invite the viewer to care. It is also simply stupid in places. Several of the key questions raised early in the film are: Why does Tom have sex with Melanie when she is so drunk? What kind of a friend is he? What kind of a person is she? The issues are never resolved.

The soundtrack sounds as if it were lifted straight off a television soap opera, and indicates a post-production which was fraught with the realisation by director Michael Robertson that what he had wasn't

very good, and needed some exclamation points.

The film is significant in that it marked a major career change for Angela Punch McGregor. Her experience on it prompted her to steer largely clear of comedy, a decision which her subsequent dramatic triumphs have proved to have been a very wise one.

JIM SCHEMBRI

References

'The Best of Friends', a review by Jim Murphy, *Cinema Papers*, no. 37, April 1982, p. 171.

'Best (of) Friends', Geoff Mayer, *Cinema Papers*, no. 43, May–June 1983, pp. 123–5.

'Angela Punch McGregor', an interview with the actor by Jim Schembri, *Cinema Papers*, no. 49, December, 1984, pp. 418–21, 471.

'The Best of Friends', a short review by Kathe Boehringer, *Filmnews*, January–February 1982, p. 13.

BREAKFAST IN PARIS

Cinema Enterprises presents Breakfast In Paris. © 1981 'Breakfast in Paris' Pty Ltd. *Locations:* Paris; Melbourne. *Australian distributor:* Roadshow. *Video:* Roadshow Home Video. *Rating:* M (January 1982; 2593.29m). 35mm. 94 mins.

Producer: John D. Lamond. *Associate producer:* Michael Hirsh. *Scriptwriter:* Morris Dalton. *Director of photography:* Ross Berryman. *Production designer:* Stephen Walsh. *Wardrobe co-ordinator:* Jane Howat. *Editor:* Jill Rice. *Composer:* Brian May. *Sound recordist:* John Rowley. *Sound editor:* Ross Hamilton. *Mixers:* Ron Purvis, Les McKenzie.

Cast

Barbara Parkins (Jackie Wyatt), Rod Mullinar (Michael Barnes), Jack Lenoir (Pierre), Elspeth Ballantyne (Millie), Jeremy Higgins (Marcel), Graham Stanley (Henri), Christopher Milne (Craig), Jennie Lamond (Flower Girl); Mary Amphlett, Graham Barker, Adrienne Barrett, Edna Bartlett, Evelyne Bisarre, Lyn Brodie, Doug Bowles, Paula de Burgh, Helen Callanan, Jean Caniel, Melinda Collette, Ramsey Collins, Marcel Cugola, Gary Dean, Lisa Dombroski, Michelle Downes, Allan Easther, Darryl Emerson, Kim Formosa, Fabrice Grandou, Judy Green, Christine Gilligan.

Jackie Wyatt (Barbara Parkins), a successful fashion executive in Melbourne, cuts work early to go home and cook dinner for her lover. They have been together for one year and it is time, she feels, to momentarily put aside the demands of being an independent career woman and think of him. But in her bedroom she finds both her lover and a bath-towelled blonde.

Putting love behind her, Jackie decides to head off for Paris but at Melbourne airport bumps into photographer, Michael Barnes (Rod Mullinar). Not only is he accident-prone (as spilt cups of coffee and a lost breakfast egg will later reinforce), he is a terrible flirt with an atrocious opening line. As he picks up Jackie's handbag from the ground, he remarks, 'Now I've met your handbag, I'd like to meet the rest of you.'

On the plane, in the first of the film's many non-surprises, Jackie and Michael are seated together. She tries to work and read, he to chat her up. Michael is the sort of Old Age male who takes a loud 'no' as positive encouragement.

Maybe it is the magic of the romantic city, but once in Paris Jackie finds Michael increasingly attractive and romance finally blossoms. This is particularly surprising because Michael's incessant pursuit of Jackie has been little short of sexual harassment, not what one imagines she would admire.[1] Director John D. Lamond tries to sidestep this problem by going for humour, Michael popping up to proposition Jackie in all sorts of places. Some of the locations are so ridiculous (amidst a clothes rack, in a cupboard) that he rather resembles the uncatchable rat in *Fawlty Towers*.

Once Jackie and Michael are lovers, many additional problems intervene: they range from jealousy and a fear of commitment (one must trust whom one loves) to stolen letters (one must not trust others). There is even a car accident straight out of Leo McCarey's **Love Affair** (1933). But they add no convincing drama to this predictable tale of trust regained. The romance between Jackie and Michael never ignites, due more to bad dialogue and a jerky narrative than to the efforts of the actors.

Most disappointing, Lamond having gone all the way to Paris, is his inability to bring the city alive. His footage is just dreary travelogue (generally without dialogue but with a scandalously ersatz Francis Lai score from Brian May). Unlike **Once in Paris…** (Frank D. Gilroy, 1978) and **Until September** (Richard Marquand, 1984), to name two similar films of the same era, Paris just doesn't *colour* the story; the film could equally be set in Tierra del Fuego, for all that one gets from the city.

In part, this is due to an unwise reliance on bad sets built in Port Melbourne studios for a Paris café, street and two hotel rooms. The whiff of Port Phillip Bay is sadly far stronger than that of the River Seine.

SCOTT MURRAY

---

[1] For a parallel, see Rose Lucas's analysis of sexual harassment in **'Frankie and Johnny'**, *Cinema Papers*, no. 87, March-April 1992, pp. 61-3.

Jackie Wyatt (Barbara Parkins) and Michael Barnes (Rod Mullinar).

JAMES CLAYDEN

CORPSE

[No opening production credit.] CORPSE. © 1982 James Clayden. *Location:* Melbourne. *Australian distributor:* James Clayden. *Video:* not released. *Rating:* not rated. 16mm. 111 mins.

Producer: James Clayden. *Scriptwriter:* James Clayden. *Director of photography:* James Clayden. [*Production designer:* not credited.] [*Costume designer:* not credited.] *Editor:* James Clayden. *Composer:* Christopher Knowles. [*Sound recordist:* not credited.] [*Sound editor:* not credited.] [*Mixer:* not credited.]

Cast

Ann Eckersley, Christopher Knowles, David Maher, Michael Dunn.

James Clayden's film was made over several years and is in the tradition of films by film-makers who have worked extensively in other areas of the visual arts. There is no narrative to the film; rather, it presents images and sequences of the Australian landscape interspersed with some interiors. The human figure is present to some degree, being seen in black flitting through certain scenes and in some of the interiors.

The viewer of the film sees sequence after sequence, for this is a very long film, shot in remarkable landscapes, which give the effect of rendering nature as dark, bleak and forbidding. The intense colour photography concentrates on details and forms, and one's appreciation depends on the degree to which one finds these images fascinating.

On the soundtrack is a variety of music motifs and some somewhat rambling and difficult to comprehend prose, which the viewer may have difficulty in remembering.

It has to be acknowledged that Clayden's photographic skills are superb. He has a painter's eye and brings it to bear on the creation of some luscious landscapes. The shots in one sequence of silted lakes harbouring dead trees are magnificent and this sequence gives us the most precise clue as to Clayden's meaning. He is rendering the earth itself as a corpse and the film's images progressively come to focus with greater intensity on the devastation wreaked by man. Hence the fleeting appearance of the black-clad figure (a nod to F. W. Murnau's 1921 **Nosferatu: Eine Symphonie Des Grauens**?), a vampire feeding directly from it. As well, one is reminded of Werner Herzog's **Fata Morgana** (1971), a film noted for evoking not the end of the world, but its beginning, with images similar in their intense rendering of aridity.

It should be said that the interior sequences seem much more contrived: the shots which need lighting have little subtlety and their meaning is obscure, especially in relation to the clarity of the exteriors and the meaning associated with them.

Watching this film, all two hours of it, is not the easiest experience and its rewards and virtues are modest. Nevertheless, it remains a work of interest and, in the context of the small amount of genuine experimental film-making done in this country, it remains a key work of its time.

GEOFF GARDNER

Reference

'Clayden', unsigned, *Filmnews*, November 1985, p. 19.

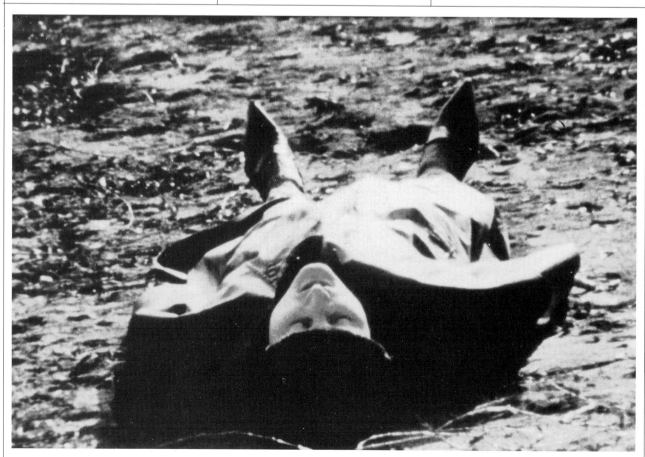

The black-clad figure.

CROSSTALK

The New South Wales Film Corporation presents CROSSTALK. *Alternative titles:* 'High Rise' and 'Wall to Wall' (working). © 1982 Wall to Wall Ltd [Nam]. *Budget:* $1.2 million. *Location:* Sydney. *Filmed:* May–June 1981. *Australian distributor:* GUO. *Video:* Australian Video. *Rating:* M (May 1982; 2203m). 35mm. 83 mins.

Producer: Errol Sullivan. *Executive producer:* Ross Matthews. *Scriptwriters:* Linda Lane, Mark Egerton, with additional material by Denis Whitburn. [Based on an original idea and screenplay by Keith Salvat, with assistance from Bob Jewson and Byron Kennedy; uncredited.] *Director of photography:* Vincent Monton. *Camera operator:* David Williamson. *Production designer:* Larry Eastwood. *Wardrobe:* Jenny Miles. [*Editor:* not credited.] *Composer:* Chris Neal. *Sound recordist:* John Phillips. *Sound editors:* Jeanine Chialvo, Vicki Ambrose. *Mixer:* Julian Ellingworth.

Cast

Gary Day (Ed Ballinger), Penny Downie (Cindy), Brian McDermott (Whitehead), Peter Collingwood (Hollister), Kim Deacon (Jane), Jill Forster (Mrs Stollier), John Ewart (Stollier), Judith Wood (Clair).

Jane (Kim Deacon), with Mrs Stollier (Jill Forster) in the dryer.

There is a point beyond which homage becomes usurpage, where a film becomes more notable for what it 'borrows' than for any ideas of its own. Such, sadly, is the case with Mark Egerton's Crosstalk.

The film from which the 'inspiration' comes is, yet again, Alfred Hitchcock's 1954 **Rear Window** (not that there is even a hint of an acknowledgement in the credits to Hitchcock, scriptwriter John Michael Hayes or source novelist William Irish (Cornell Woolrich)).

In **Rear Window**, photographer L. B. Jeffries (James Stewart) is confined to a wheelable chair by a broken leg. Frustrated, he scans the neighbouring flats with binoculars and deduces that a murder has occurred in a flat opposite. Both his fiancée, Lisa Fremont (Grace Kelly), and his nurse, Stella (Thelma Ritter), think him crazy till they, too, are caught up in a deadly game.

In **Crosstalk**, Ed Ballinger (Gary Day), a computer expert, is confined to a wheelchair after the brakes on his car fail. Frustrated, he scans the neighbouring flats with his powerful I-500 computer and deduces a murder has occurred in the flat above. Both his wife, Cindy (Penny Downie), and his nurse, Jane (Kim Deacon), think him crazy till they, too, are caught up in a deadly game.

The parallels are so close that when **Crosstalk** varies from its predecessor one blinks in shock. For example: it is the Jane/Stella character who goes to investigate the murderer's flat, instead of Cindy/Lisa. But hopes that this may have been playfulness on the film-makers' part are dashed by a passage in David Stratton's *The Avocado Plantation* which reveals that some of Cindy's scenes were given over to Jane when the actress playing Cindy was no longer available.[1]

Such complaints aside, **Crosstalk** is, on several levels, one of the better Australian thrillers of the 1980s. After a particularly dull opening that adds nothing of value, the film is quite gripping, even tense. Egerton's evocation of a computer-controlled universe is highly atmospheric and the alienation of life in inner-city high-rises is eerily conveyed.

As well, there is a welcome scarcity of dialogue which makes this a film one must listen to: considerable meaning is conveyed by the strange noises of the computer, the synthesised music, the playing back (with distortion) of sounds and conversations secretly recorded.

The ending, however, is silly: the computer takes control, killing one of the bad guys. Ed is left alive, but the murderer is not and Cindy is quite mad. While it is true we live in an impersonal world, with good reason to be paranoid about electronic surveillance, something a little less trite would have helped.

A final note: it is not recommended that anyone view the commercially distributed video. The film was shot in Panavision and the video transfer is unscanned, which sometimes means that all one gets of some two-shots is the space between the characters.

SCOTT MURRAY

---

[1] For a full account of the film's troubled production (including the sacking of the film's original director and originator, Keith Salvat), see David Stratton, *The Avocado Plantation: Boom and Bust in the Film Industry*, Macmillan, Sydney, 1990, pp. 255–61.

Reference

'Crosstalk', a short review by Peter Kemp, *Filmnews*, October 1982, p. 17.

A DANGEROUS SUMMER

Filmco Limited present[s] A McElroy & McElroy Production. A DANGEROUS SUMMER. © 1982 Filmco Limited. *Budget:* $2.3 million. *Locations:* Blue Mountains, Sydney. *Australian distributor:* Roadshow. *Video:* Roadshow Home Video. *Rating:* M (May 1982; 2441.27m). 35mm. 88 mins.

Producer: James McElroy. *Scriptwriters:* David Ambrose, Quentin Masters. Based on an original idea by Kit Denton, James McElroy. *Director of photography:* Peter Hannan. *Camera operators:* Keith Wood, David Eggby. *Production designers:* Bob Hilditch, John Carroll. *Costume designer:* Marta Statescu. *Editor:* Ted Ötton. *Composer:* Groove Myers. *Sound recordists:* Don Connolly, Mark Lewis. *Sound editors:* John Foster, John Hackney, Michael Norton. *Mixers:* Phil Judd, Ron Purvis.

Cast

Tom Skerritt (Howard Anderson), Ian Gilmour (Steve Adams), James Mason (George Engels), Wendy Hughes (Sophie McCann), Ray Barrett (F. C. O. Webster), Kim Deacon (Maggie Anderson), Guy Doleman (Julian Fane), Giselle Morgan (Girl in Van), Shane Porteous (Sgt. Goodwin), Peter Lawless (Webster's Driver), Ronald Falk (Clive Bennett), Stephen Leeder (Construction Foreman), Ian Mortimer (Joe), Michael Petrovitch (Joe Laliniei), Peter Rowley (Immigration Officer), Geraldine Ward (Sarah Hart), Norman Kaye (Percy Farley), Mary-Lou Stewart (Ann Hendricks), Martin Harris (Curly Chester), Gemma Masters (Fane's Daughter), Lynn Collingwood (Woman in Van), Phillip De Carle (Man in Van), Charlie Masters (Boy on Beach).

In the Menzies Hotel bar: George Engels (James Mason) and Howard Anderson (Tom Skerritt).

Howard Anderson (Tom Skerritt) is designing and building a resort complex in the fragile, bushfire-prone area of the Blue Mountains. While he may be driven by a (misdirected) desire to create, his partner, Julian Fane (Guy Doleman), is concerned only with profit from insurance fraud. The many bushfires that are ravaging the area are but a prelude to the resort's destruction and a hoped-for $10 million payout.

Sophie McCann (Wendy Hughes), an insurance lawyer, uncovers evidence of a fraud, but she is drowned early on at Manly Beach (quite a shock, given that one expects an actor of Hughes' standing to stay around longer). More alert to the dangers of exposé investigations is George Engels (James Mason), from Lloyds of London. He teams up with a conscience-stricken Howard, now fully aware of his partner's duplicitous plans, and together they work to flush out the arsonist and stop the carnage.

Inspired by the many bushfires that rage around Sydney in summer, this film has a 1970s quality of movie-making on the run. Some of the footage was actually second-unit work done before principal photography started, while other fire sequences have a documentary feel of grab-it-while-you-can. The performances sometimes look like 'first takes' and often the coverage is scrappy and confusing. Editing has also left several scenes absurdly short: Maggie Anderson (Kim Deacon) and Steve Adams (Ian Gilmour) outside Luna Park; Howard in a Kings Cross bar.

As a result, there is little tension to the film; the arsonist is easy to pick; and the resolution inevitable (Howard contributing to burning down the resort), given his was a wrong-headed plan to begin with.

The principal interest of the film, apart from being another of the many 1980s films about Sydney corruption, comes not from its story, nor the craft (though the burning train sequence is a *tour de force* of Australian action cinema), but from one performance: James Mason's. Made near the end of his career, this is something of a side-light, though it does have some stunning moments. The best is in the bar of the Menzies Hotel where the English George leaves some buddies discussing cricket (Larwood, of course!), and ventures across to introduce himself to Howard. The change in personality, the querying, perceptive looks, the edge of joviality: this is sublime acting.

Many critics, while rightly singling out Mason, have tended to damn the rest. But Tom Skerritt, a fine American actor, does well with his muddled part. If there are far too many shots of him moping around with a troubled conscience, that is hardly his fault. What Skerritt does, he does well. Perhaps the anger at the time at casting Americans in Australian films clouded judgment.[1] It is easier to be objective today with many of the harshest critics of internationalist casting now living and working in America.

SCOTT MURRAY

---

[1] The hysteria also led authors Liz Jacka and Susan Dermody to denounce the film for having an American director, yet Quentin was the son of Australian novelist Olga Masters.

Reference

'Wendy Hughes', an interview with the actor by Richard Brennan, *Cinema Papers*, no. 40, October 1982, pp. 428–32.

DUET FOR FOUR

[No opening production credit.[1]] DUET FOR FOUR. *Alternative titles:* 'Toy Man' and 'Partners' (working titles). © 1981 Burstall Nominees Pty Ltd. Made in association with the Victorian Film Corporation and the Australian Film Commission. *Locations:* Melbourne, Queenscliff. *Australian distributor:* GUO. *Opened:* March 1982. *Video:* Syme Home Video. *Rating:* M (September 1981; 2621.47m).[2] 35mm. Panavision. 97 mins.

Producers: Tom Burstall, Tim Burstall. *Scriptwriter:* David Williamson. *Director of photography:* Dan Burstall. *Production designer:* Herbert Pinter. *Costume designer:* Jane Hyland. *Editor:* Edward McQueen-Mason. *Composer:* Peter Sullivan. *Sound recordist:* Phil Stirling. *Sound editors:* Edward McQueen-Mason, Louise Johnson. *Mixer:* Peter Fenton.

Cast

Mike Preston (Ray Martin), Wendy Hughes (Barbara Dunstan), Michael Pate (Al Geisman), Diane Cilento (Margot Martin), Gary Day (Terry Byrne), Vanessa Leigh (Dianne Sanders), Warwick Comber (Cliff Ingersoll), Sigrid Thornton (Caroline Martin), Clare Binney (Jacki Nesbitt), Peter Aanensen (Senior Detective), Arthur Dignam (Doug Quincey), Peter Statford[3] (Bernie Crittendon), Rod Mullinar (Ken Overland)[4]; John Proper (Foreman), David Morley (Dougal Dunstan), Justin Morley (Erik Dunstan), Leah Steventon (Mary Dunstan), Doug Bowley (Toby Carroll), Joseph Donghia (Unemployed Young Man), Jenta Sobbott (Unemployed Young Woman), Roy Edmonds (Advertising Man).

Duet for Four is clearly Tim Burstall's attempt to make a 1980s version of **Petersen** (1974). It shares many of the earlier film's themes – the 'mid-life crisis' of earthy, working-class Ray Martin (Mike Preston) struggling with the middle-class milieu (corporatism, the art world, bourgeois sexual manners) into which he has reluctantly but inevitably ascended. David Williamson's script was in fact written in the mid-1970s, and the film betrays a 1970s (even a 1960s) sensibility, particularly in the representation of the foppish young artist, Cliff Ingersoll (Warwick Comber), lover of Ray's wife, Margot (Diane Cilento), and the student bohemia in which his daughter, Caroline (Sigrid Thornton), lives.

Petersen's romantic celebration of its earthy, ocker hero was politically contentious, but at least the film vividly dramatised the various sides of its argument. **Duet for Four**,

by contrast, is a dull film, and Burstall's familiar view of class conflict seems no longer provocative or even accurate. Partly this is because the 'male pathos' here is far softer. Ray's central drives are towards harmony and reconciliation in his family relations, and a return to his former glory days when he worked on the preservation of fine old trains – a dramatically leaden symbol of old-style masculine individualism – rather than squandering his life away as a 'toy man' (Williamson's original title) selling mere commodities.

The film attempts to build a two-tier dramatic metaphor, paralleling the moves in a corporate take-over with the vicissitudes of personal–sexual relations. Just as the expatriate Aussie-turned-American Al Geisman (Michael Pate) is criticised by the film for his aggressive, 'invasive' business tactics, he also embodies predatory sexuality. (In an Australian vs American joke typical of many films of the period, Geisman extols a porno video – 'the screwing's great' – while the locals regard it with wry, unaroused bemusement). All the film's representative bourgeoisie are also faulted (Margot, Cliff, Caroline's bohemian companions) for being selfishly possessive or cold in relationships. The 'haven' the film creates for its hero in this heartless world is his relationship with Caroline – as strangely charged as it is unexplored, particularly in the absurd scene where Ray, in a rage, breaks into Caroline's house to seize her childhood doll and bring it to her hospital bed.

Duet for Four lacks Burstall's customary directorial flair. Its disconcertingly television-like, perfunctory stylisation earns

Brian McFarlane's derogatory comparison with 'American soap opera'[5]; Peter Sullivan's blandly tuneful musical score is especially irritating. It must be mentioned, however, that this same 'flatness' – the reduction of *mise-en-scène* and plot to minimal permutations of characters and motives, as in Mark Rappaport's avant-garde films – inspired perhaps the only favourable account of the film, Sam Rohdie's review in *Cinema Papers*. Unlikely as it may seem in hindsight, Burstall's method (here and in other films) fleetingly encountered its true echo in the academic practice of structuralist-semiotic film analysis. I don't think Petersen (Jack Thompson) would approve.

ADRIAN MARTIN

---

1 An end title reads 'Made in association with Victorian Film Corporation, Australian Film Commission, Temjad, Greater Union Organisation, L. Ian Roach, Tim Burstall and Associates.'
2 Made and rated under the title 'Partners'. The AFC brochure on the film cites the length as 2661m.
3 The front credits have surname as 'Stratford', which is correct.
4 The end credits are given in order of appearance; up to this point, credits are in the order on the front credits.
5 Brian McFarlane, *Australian Cinema 1970–1985*, William Heinemann Australia, Melbourne, 1987, p. 130.

References
'**Duet for Four**', a review by Sam Rohdie, *Cinema Papers*, no. 37, April 1982, pp. 169–70.
'**Duet for Four**', a review by Peter Kemp, *Filmnews*, March 1982, p. 13.

Al Geisman (Michael Pate), right, makes a pass at Jacki Nesbitt (Clare Binney).

JOHN DUIGAN

FAR EAST

Filmco Australia presents An Alfred Road Films production. FAR EAST. © 1982 Alfred Road Films Limited. *Budget:* $1.3 million. *Locations:* Manila (The Philippines); Sydney. Made in association with the Australian Film Commission. *Australian distributor:* Roadshow. *Opened:* 30 July 1982. *Video:* Roadshow Home Video. *Rating:* M (July 1982; 2935.01m). 35mm. 102 mins.

Producer: Richard Mason. *Associate producer:* John Masson. *Scriptwriter:* John Duigan. *Director of photography:* Brian Probyn. *Camera operator:* Peter Moss. *Production designer:* Ross Major. *Costume designer:* Jan Hurley. *Editor:* Henry Dangar. *Composer:* Sharon Calcraft. *Sound recordist:* Peter Barker. *Sound editor:* Andrew Steuart. *Mixers:* Peter Fenton, Gethin Creagh, Annie Cocksedge.

Cast

Bryan Brown (Morgan Keefe), Helen Morse (Jo Reeves), John Bell (Peter Reeves), Raina McKeon (Rosita Constanza), Henry Duval (Rodolfo De Cruz), Sinan Leong (Nene), Bill Hunter (Walker), John Clayton (Tony Alsop), Duc Sanh Lieu (Kip), Anna Rowena (Julia), Clive Marshall (Vinar), Allen Leong (Lieutenant Gregorio), Francis Yin (Arnulfo), John Krummel (Simon Talbot), Charito Ortez (Penny Alsop), Tony Barraga (Priest), Arthur Sherman (Bill Williamson), John Alansu (Jose), Lam Duong (Alejo), Lambert Feist (Roberto), Warwick Moss (Barry).

Far East depicts an unidentified South-East Asian country fractured with polarities of wealth and deprivation, and victimised by a brutal and repressive military government. It exposes a society where government and industry are synonymous with exploitation and corruption, but chooses to develop this theme with a narrative structure popularised by Hollywood films of the 1940s.

From the moment Jo Reeves (Helen Morse) glides into Morgan Keefe's (Bryan Brown) Koala Klub, with her husband Peter (John Bell) in tow, it is **Casablanca** (Michael Curtiz, 1942) revisited. Outside the Klub the world is a dangerous and turbulent place, but within its confines Keefe is the arbiter of authority and morality. He, like his predecessors Rick (Humphrey Bogart) and Rob McGregor (Bryan Brown) in **Winter of our Dreams** (John Duigan, 1981), has carved a niche from which he can view the surrounding world with ambivalence, and from a distance.

Morgan is lured from cynical passivity by his love for Jo and a memory of the relationship that they shared while he was stationed in Saigon during the Vietnam war. His commitment to help Jo, by rescuing her husband, activates a chain of events that not only jeopardises his business and his relationship with his mistress Nene (Sinan Leong), but also imperils and ultimately claims his life.

It is often difficult to empathise with Keefe (though precedent suggests that we should). His rekindled love for Jo is understandable and his wry pursuit of her attentions quite romantic. Yet his willingness to barter with the lives of his employees, and brusquely ignore Nene's pain, ascribes a type of callousness and a dubious morality that seems malevolent, except by the cosmetic construction of a personal, if idiosyncratic, moral code.

Jo is in many respects a replication of the female characters created by Howard Hawks in **To Have and Have Not** (1944), **Rio Bravo** (1959) and **Ball of Fire** (1941). Her effortless transition through a male world, characterised by card games, darts and an admirable capacity for liquor, is invigorated by consummate feminity and defiant self-expression. Helen Morse exudes an air of elegance and glamorous sexuality, whether she is lounging on a loo or bluffing her way through a poker hand. Finally, however, forcing her to forfeit Keefe, as Ilsa (Ingrid Bergman) did Rick, and contrasting her with the quiet, yet formidable, determination of Rosita Constanza (Raina McKeon), the activist with whom Reeves becomes involved, diffuses the potency of her character and unsatisfactorily resolves its ambiguities.

Ultimately, the film's attempt to probe the instigators of injustice and produce 'a protest against the treatment of the poor and powerless' lacks cohesion. Its convictions are continually undermined by a style and structure that inhibit both the development of its characters and the proven skills of its director. The marriage of Duigan's concerns with a Hollywood love story results in an unconvincing romance and a simplistic political thriller.

DEBI ENKER[1]

---

[1] Extracted from Enker's review in *Cinema Papers* (see References).

Reference:
'Helen Morse and Richard Mason', an interview with the actor and the producer by George Tosi, *Cinema Papers*, no. 39, August 1982, pp. 310–15.
'**Far East**', a review by Debi Enker, ibid., pp. 363–4.
'Ethics of the Outsider', an interview with director John Duigan by Albert Moran, *Filmnews*, April 1984, pp. 10–12.

Casablanca revisited: Morgan Keefe (Bryan Brown) and Jo Reeves (Helen Morse).

FREEDOM

South Australian Film Corporation and Endeavour Communications Corporation Limited present FREEDOM[1]. © 1981 South Australian Film Corporation and Endeavour Communications Corporation Limited. *Location:* Adelaide and surrounds. *Filmed:* May–June 1981. *Australian distributor:* Roadshow. *Opened:* 1 April 1982. *Video:* Star Video. *Rating:* M (February 1982; 2788.80m). 35mm. 102 mins.

Producer: Matt Carroll. *Executive producer:* Jim George. *Scriptwriter:* John Emery. *Director of photography:* Ron Johanson. *Production designer:* Herbert Pinter. *Wardrobe:* Ruth de la Lande. *Editor:* Phil Reid. *Composer:* Don Walker. *Sound recordist:* Tim Lloyd. *Sound editor:* Andrew Prowse. *Mixers:* Phil Judd, Phil Heywood, Jim Currie.

Cast

Jon Blake (Ron), Candy Raymond (Annie), Jad Capelja (Sally), Charles 'Bud' Tingwell (Cassidy), Max Cullen (Factory Clerk), Chris Haywood (Phil), Reg Lye (Old Farmer), John Clayton (C.E.S. Officer), Greg Rowe (Bowser Boy), Rob Steele (Salesman), Tony Blackett (Salesman), Paul Sonkkila (C.E.S. Officer), Katie Edwards (Ron's Mother), Louise le Nay (Margie), Stuart McCreery (Worker), Paul Churlish (Foreman), Bob Barrett (Tow Truck Driver), Julie Dawson-Daniels (Foster Mother), Dulcie Davenport (Old Woman), Judy Dick (Waitress), Domenico Spadavecchia (Aristotle), Joe di Sario (Italian Worker), James Cameron (John Doniger), Chris Crowe (Youth), John Fenton (Brian Samuels), Glynn Nicholas (Busker).

One can perhaps be thankful that, in spite of its symptomatic fast vehicles, high-speed chases, beautiful women and excellent stuntwork, Scott Hicks' ironically titled **Freedom** does not subscribe to the car-film syndrome.

Ron (Jon Blake) is an unemployed youth whose domestic tension and dismal prospects on the job market nourish an increasingly bewildering and engrossing fantasy, which he later realises. Although occasionally ostentatious, some well-directed scenes in the early part of **Freedom** align viewer empathy with Ron as they depict the gnawing frustrations, the inability to fulfil modest ambitions and the stunted opportunities that combine to nurture his corresponding desire to escape these pressures.

Ron displaces the ego-crushing frustrations of his reality with a corresponding

Ron (Jon Blake), Sally (Jad Capelja) and a white Porsche.

ego-enforcing fantasy. Dressed in the height of fashion at the wheel of a Porsche, he glides effortlessly along a country road, a beautiful woman (Candy Raymond) by his side, but pursued by an ominous black car. The Porsche and the woman have a basis in reality: she is Annie Martin, an old friend of Ron's.

Arriving at Annie's apartment for a date, Ron overhears her phone conversation with her lover and is angered to learn that she plans to use him to tease her lover. In response to yet another scheme to exploit him, Ron steals her keys and speeds off with her car to no place in particular.

It is from here that a combination of elements effectively inhibits any chance of taking the film seriously. Ron's unsavoury character reversal into his fantasy image, his association with Sally (Jad Capelja), a thinly drawn runaway mother in search of her child, a squad of incapable, moronic policemen and the ultimate pointlessness of Ron's trek through the countryside sap the subsequent developments in **Freedom** of the slightest tension or concern.

The futility of Ron's escapade is painfully stated toward the end of **Freedom**. Having left Sally sleeping on a hill, Ron tries to outrun the police through countryside which he soon recognises as the locale of his fantasy. Predictably, he comes across a snapped railing, stops the Porsche and stares down at the wreckage of the ominous black car. Realising nothing, he heaves the empty

shell of his dream car over the edge and down the crevasse.

Finally, in an incredibly unconvincing dénouement, a little van, proclaiming that 'Jesus Saves', conveniently chugs up to Ron's rescue. 'Where are you headed?', the driver asks. Ron's reply is a precise 'I don't know.' Nor does the viewer know – or indeed care.

Freedom is a technically proficient film with clear, sharp pictures, some acute editing, fluent, imaginative direction and an atmospheric soundtrack by Don Walker. Impressive packaging, however, cannot compensate for the manner in which **Freedom** disregards the promise cultivated at the start in the pursuit of ideas that are rendered sterile by a lack of coherence and purpose.

JIM SCHEMBRI[2]

---

[1] There has been a tendency among critics to include a closing exclamation mark as part of the title. However, while there is such an exclamation in the title on the cover of the video slick, there is none on the film.

[2] Extracted from Schembri's review in *Cinema Papers* (see 'References').

References

'Bob Saunders', an interview with the man behind Filmco, one of the film's investors, by Peter Beilby, *Cinema Papers*, no. 31, March–April 1980, pp. 26–9, 100.

'Freedom', a review by Jim Schembri, *Cinema Papers*, no. 38, June 1982, pp. 269–71.

'Freedom' a short review by Peter Kemp, *Filmnews*, April 1982, p. 13.

GINGER MEGGS

John Sexton presents GINGER MEGGS.[1] [© not listed; atb 1982.] *Budget:* $1.3 million. *Location:* Bowral (New South Wales). *Australian distributor:* Hoyts. *Opened:* 9 December 1982. *Video:* Hoyts Polygram Video. *Rating:* G (July 1982; 2770.43m). 35mm. 100 mins.

Producer: John Sexton. *Co-producer:* Michael Latimer. *Scriptwriter:* Michael Latimer. Based on a story by Michael Latimer and John Sexton. [Based on a comic strip created by Jim Bancks.] *Director of photography:* John Seale. *Production designer:* Larry Eastwood. *Wardrobe co-ordinator:* Miranda Skinner. *Editor:* Philip Howe. *Composer:* John Stuart. *Sound recordist:* Tim Lloyd. *Sound editors:* Vicki Gates, Denise Hunter, Claire O'Brien. *Mixer:* Brian Shennan.

Cast

Garry McDonald (Mr Meggs), Ross Higgins (Mr Floggswell), Gwen Plumb (Miss Leach), Harold Hopkins (Mr Fox), John Wood (Constable Brady), Hugh Keays-Byrne (Captain Hook), John Clayton (Mr Wentworth), Terry Camilleri (Mr Crackett), Coral Kelly (Mrs Meggs), Candy Raymond (Alex's Mother), Drew Forsythe (Tiger Kelly), Paul Daniel (Ginger Meggs), Mark Spain (Benny), Daniel Cumerford (Eddie Coogan), Shelley Armsworth (Minnie Peters), Rowan Hillard (Dudley Meggs), Adrian McLeod (Ocker), Mark Kounnas (Raggsy), Kristian Harper (Darkie), Darren Flynn (Joey), David Hanning (Sammy), Andrew Heard (Jacky), Miranda Latimer (Polly).

Ginger Meggs (Paul Daniel) wreaks some havoc.

Producer John Sexton, who had also made **Fatty Finn** (Maurice Murphy, 1980), has been constantly attracted to themes that chronicle Australian folklore, such as Simon Wincer's **Phar Lap** (1983) and Ian Barry's **Minnamurra** (1989).

The much-beloved comic-strip character of Ginger Meggs had been around since 1921, but seemed unlikely material for a feature aimed at juvenile audiences raised on **Star Wars** (George Lucas, 1977) and Space Invaders. Scriptwriter Michael Latimer, married to the daughter of Ginger's creator, Jim Bancks, failed to lick the problem of how to adapt material which was firmly rooted in a bygone era, namely the Depression years.

Filmed on location in the New South Wales rural town of Bowral, the storyline seems to be taking place in a nostalgically realised never-never world, prior to the introduction of television and other forms of mass entertainment.

Ginger Meggs (Paul Daniel) is faithfully depicted as the red-headed larrikin lad, perpetually confronted by bullies and parental authority. But his suburban adventures are of a mundane and uncomplicated variety that rely too much on naïve, homespun humour, self-consciously harking back to a simpler era. The episodic plot advances in fitful fashion as Ginger promises his girlfriend, Minnie Peters (Shelley Armsworth), that he will give up fighting, wags school and dodges his nemesis, the perennial bully, Tiger Kelly (Drew Forsythe).

Ostensibly designed for kids, the primary appeal seems to be for adults of nostalgic temperament, although even this effect is undercut by an inappropriate and bland 1980s rock score. Like the recent **Dick Tracy** (Warren Beatty, 1990), another comic strip adaptation, the film's exteriors are bathed in bold, primary colours while the interiors are also stylised in browns and golds.

Ginger, played by Paul Daniel in his screen debut, is singularly lacking in comic personality and the adult figures are encouraged to mug for the camera as though this were some kind of unwritten rule for comic-strip characters. A prime offender in this regard is Garry McDonald as Ginger's disciplinarian and eye-rolling dad.

Debuting director Jonathan Dawson, a film lecturer and co-writer of the dire **Final Cut** (Ross Dimsey, 1980), does not appear to have made another film since.

PAUL HARRIS

---

[1] The title is followed, on a different card, by 'created by bancks'.

Reference

'Ginger Meggs', a review by Geoff Mayer, *Cinema Papers*, no. 42, March 1983, p. 65.

HEATWAVE

Preston Crothers in association with M&L Pty Ltd present HEATWAVE. © 1981 Heatwave Films. *Budget:* $1.5 million. *Location:* King's Cross (Sydney). *Australian distributor:* Roadshow. *Opened:* March 1982. *Video:* Roadshow. *Rating:* M (December 1981; 2509.92m). 35mm. 91 mins.

Producer: Hilary Linstead. *Co-producer:* Ross Matthews. *Scriptwriters:* Marc Rosenberg, Phillip Noyce. Based on an original screenplay by Mark Stiles, Tim Gooding. *Director of photography:* Vince Monton[1]. *Camera operator:* Louis Irving. *Production designer:* Ross Major. *Costume designer:* Terry Ryan. *Editor:* John Scott. *Composer:* Cameron Allan. *Sound recordist:* Lloyd Carrick. *Sound editors:* Greg Bell, Helen Brown, Stella Savvas. *Mixers:* Peter Fenton, Gethin Creagh, Philip Heywood.

Cast

Judy Davis (Kate Dean), Richard Moir (Stephen West), Chris Haywood (Peter Houseman), Bill Hunter (Robert Duncan), John Gregg (Phillip Lawson), Anna Jemison[2] (Victoria West), John Meillon (Freddy Dwyer), Dennis Miller (Mick Davis), Peter Hehir (Cigar-smoking Bodyguard), Gillian Jones (Barbie Lee Taylor), Frank Gallacher (Dick Molnar), Tui Bow (Annie), Don Crosby (Jim Taylor), Lynette Curran (Evonne Houseman), Graham Rouse (Detective 1), Paul Chubb (Detective 2), Vic Rooney (Building Supervisor), P. J. Jones (Bodyguard), Gary Waddel (Florist Messenger), Alastair Duncan (American Speaker).

Heatwave is Phillip Noyce's second feature film, after **Newsfront** (1978), and it chooses as its subject the events surrounding a grandiose property development in Sydney.

The development is to be built on an old area of the city whose inhabitants are old and/or working class. The project is opposed by a coalition of local interests and, after a woman activist who publishes a local radical newspaper disappears, much of the opposition is organised by a young middle-class woman, Kate Dean (Judy Davis in what is one of her best film performances). The events in the film recall the life and disappearance of a Sydney activist–journalist, Juanita Nielsen, whose life also obliquely provided the background to another film made in Sydney around the same time, **The Killing of Angel Street** (Don Crombie, 1981).

In Noyce's film, the focus is on both the development and the relationship between its architect, Stephen West (Richard Moir), and anarchist/terrorist/murderer Kate Dean. The architect, an obsessive about his work and its value, sees his project both as something for the well-off in this instance and as a model for low-cost housing in the future.

In the background of this drama is a detailed description of the political, business and law enforcement machinations that are going on to ensure that the development goes ahead, producing a subversive view of the corrupt nature of politics and business in Sydney. This involves a fearless exposition of these matters, one rarely echoed in Australian feature film-making, though not without antecedents in such dramas as *Scales of Justice* (television series, Michael Jenkins, 1983) and the Kennedy Miller tele-feature *The Clean Machine* (tele-feature, Ken Cameron, 1988), neither of which, however, is handled with the same sense of skilled *mise-en-scène*.

In particular, attention should be paid to the quality of Cameron Allan's score, the use of 'shock' slow-motion, the method of moving the narrative forward by the overlaid sound of news reports and the superbly created sense of oppressive summer heat during which the action takes place, an oppression that is broken by the downpour at the climax but which is totally cyclical, as befits a tale of institutional corruption and cronyism. **Heatwave** has always been a film to match the highest achievements of world cinema.

All these virtues of bold and audacious subject matter and the acute sense of film style would, however, matter far less if they had not been applied to the drama of a relationship between West and Dean that contains considerable thought and is rendered with great credibility.

Heatwave has inspirational qualities that derive from its desire to tackle a tough theme and subject with direct and uncompromising force, as well as considerable elegant grace. It is similarly game enough to do this from a multi-faceted viewpoint which allows character and drama to be explored in a totally cool and distanced manner. It remains discomforting, making its audience feel, even today, that little has changed and that the lives of ordinary men and women are still manipulated by social forces dominated by greed and self-interest.

GEOFF GARDNER

---

1 Usually 'Vincent Monton'.
2 Later known as 'Anna Maria Monticelli'.

References

'Judy Davis', a career interview with the actor by John Ley and Steve Bisley, *Cinema Papers*, no. 32, May–June 1981, pp. 116–21.

'Heatwave', a review by Geoff Gardner, *Cinema Papers*, no. 37, April 1982, pp. 163–4.

'Heatwave: Director Phil Noyce', an interview by Arnold Zable, *Cinema Papers*, no. 38, June 1982, pp. 220–4.

Kate Dean (Judy Davis) comforts Annie (Tui Bow), a victim of an inner-city development.

LONELY HEARTS

[No opening production credit.[1]] LONELY HEARTS. © 1981 Adams Packer Film Productions. *Budget:* $648,000. *Location:* Melbourne. *Australian distributor:* Murray Mancha. *Video:* Filmpac. *Rating:* M (February 1982; 2621.47m). 35mm. 95 mins.

Producer: John B. Murray. *Executive producer:* Phillip Adams. *Associate producer:* Erwin Rado. *Scriptwriters:* Paul Cox, John Clarke. *Director of photography:* Yuri Sokol. *Camera operator:* Barry Malseed. *Production designer:* Neil Angwin. *Wardrobe:* Frankie Hogan. *Editor:* Tim Lewis. *Music arranged and performed by:* Norman Kaye. *Sound recordist:* Ken Hammond. *Sound editor:* Peter Burgess. *Mixer:* Peter Fenton.

Cast

Wendy Hughes (Patricia), Norman Kaye (Peter), Jon Finlayson (George), Julia Blake (Pamela), Jonathan Hardy (Bruce); Irene Inescort and Vic Gordon (Patricia's Parents); Ted Grove-Rogers (Peter's Father), Ronald Falk (Wig Salesman), Chris Haywood (The Detective), Diana Greentree (Sally Gordon), Margaret Steven (The Psychiatrist), Kris McQuade (Rosemarie), Maurie Fields (The Taxi Driver); Laurie Dobson, Myrtle Roberts, Irene Hewitt, Jean Campbell, Ernest Wilson, Tony Llewellyn-Jones.

Lonely Hearts is a story about the human heart and its need to find a home. It begins with the funeral of the mother of Peter (Norman Kaye), an affable, toupeed piano tuner and teacher. The death, one week away from his fiftieth birthday, liberates Peter and he starts living a little.

Peter contacts a dating agency and is offered an introduction to Patricia (Wendy Hughes). She is a sexually repressed thirty-year-old bank clerk, who has just left her overbearing parents to tentatively begin an independent life in her own apartment. **Lonely Hearts** is their love story.

The great appeal of the film is in its celebration of the 'ordinariness' of this love story. These characters are anti-heroes with an easily understood awkwardness. These are people we might know.

Wendy Hughes, usually an image of poise and sophistication, is cast against type. Patricia's self-conscious, awkward demeanour, her unflattering haircut, glasses and dowdy clothes, her nervous child-like obedience in the face of her parents and her sexual panic are all agonisingly felt.

Norman Kaye's Peter, on the other hand, is curiously likeable. Part of the reason is that his nervousness, his occupation, his family and the odd situations he gets himself into are littered with numerous comic possibilities of which Cox makes good use.

This may be tragi-comedy, but there is a lot to smile about as Peter is talked into buying a tacky new toupee from the supercilious Wig Salesman (Ronald Falk), or when Peter, ever the furtive schoolboy, is entertained by Rosemary (Kris McQuade), a prostitute from an agency called Call-A-Kitten. Then there is his friend, George (Jon Finlayson), the hysterical amateur theatre director of the production of Strindberg's *The Father*, which itself is a source of comedy. And there are also Peter's histrionic, overbearing sister, Pamela (Julia Blake), and his brother-in-law, Bruce (Jonathan Hardy), the henpecked husband and theatre aspirant.

As well, there are a number of sight gags on the perimeter that remind us not to take even the most serious things too seriously. In the opening sequence, the mourners overtake the hearse, so the hearse has to chase them through traffic to again take the lead. And in a madly eccentric interlude, Peter poses as a blind piano tuner who startles his client by driving off in a car.

Despite all these odd characters and situations falling into the path of these two lonely hearts, somewhere along the way they still manage to fall in love. **Lonely Hearts** has warmth, sadness, quirkiness and humour, but it does not leave you weeping. It is a film that touches you without tearing you apart. This is one of its greatest achievements.

ANNA DZENIS

---

[1] The producer credit reads: 'Produced for Adams Packer Films by John B. Murray'.

References

'Wendy Hughes', an interview with the actor by Richard Brennan, *Cinema Papers*, no. 40, October 1982, pp. 428–32.

'Paul Cox', an interview with the director by Debi Enker, *Cinema Papers*, no. 46, July 1984, pp. 122–9.

'Dutch Threat', an interview with director Paul Cox by Carol Bennetto, *Cinema Papers*, no. 59, September 1986, pp. 18–22.

'Yuri Sokol', an article (with quotes) on the director of photography by Mary Colbert, *Cinema Papers*, no. 74, July 1989, pp. 26–30.

'**Lonely Hearts**', a short review by Kathe Boehringer, *Filmnews*, November–December 1982, p. 25.

Tentative lovers: Peter (Norman Kaye) and Patricia (Wendy Hughes).

THE MAN FROM SNOWY RIVER

Michael Edgley International and Cambridge Films present A Geoff Burrowes–George Miller Production. THE MAN FROM SNOWY RIVER. © 1982 Snowy River Investment Pty Ltd and Others. *Budget:* $3 million. *Locations:* Mansfield and environs, Central Victoria. *Australian distributor:* Hoyts. *Opened:* March 1982. *Video:* CEL. *Rating:* NRC (December 1981; 2908m). 35mm. Panavision. 106 mins.

Producer: Geoff Burrowes. *Executive producers:* Michael Edgley, Simon Wincer. *Scriptwriter:* John Dixon. From a script by Fred Cul Cullen. Based on the poem by A. B. 'Banjo' Paterson. *Director of photography:* Keith Wagstaff. *Camera operators:* Dan Burstall, David Eggby, Malcolm Richards, Keith Wagstaff. *Production designer:* Leslie Binns. *Costume designer:* Robin Hall. *Master of the Horse:* Charlie Lovick. *Editor:* Adrian Carr. *Composer:* Bruce Rowland. *Sound recordist:* Gary Wilkins. *Sound editor:* Terry Rodman. *Mixers:* Robert J. Litt, David J. Kimball, Elliot Tyson.

Cast

Kirk Douglas (Spur; Harrison), Jack Thompson (Clancy), Tom Burlinson (Jim Craig), Sigrid Thornton (Jessica), Lorraine Bayly (Rosemary), Terence Donovan (Henry Craig), June Jago (Mrs Bailey), Gus Mercurio (Frew), David Bradshaw (Banjo Paterson), Tony Bonner (Kane), Chris Haywood (Curly), Tommy Dysart (Mountain Man), Bruce Kerr (Man in Street), Kristopher Steele (Moss), Howard Eynon (Short Man), John Nash (Tall Man); Jack Lovick, Charlie Lovick, John Lovick, Frank Hearn, Jack Purcell (Mountain Horsemen).

The Man from Snowy River is a shamelessly opportunist pandering to the box office and to American film markets in particular. It is worthy of note only insofar as the enormity of its popular success requires some critical and political attention.

Based on A. B. 'Banjo' Paterson's poem about the recapture of a runaway colt, the narrative consists of an awkward attempt to marry the myths of the so-called 'national cultures' of Australia and America. Harrison (Kirk Douglas), the cattle baron, embodies the 'going west' pioneer mentality of early America and of the self-righteous, imperialistic rhetoric of the classic Western genre film in particular – a 'going west' that can cynically be seen as echoed in the imposition of Hollywood values and conventions onto a 'virginal' Australian cinema.

Jessica (Sigrid Thornton) and Jim Craig (Tom Burlinson) in the high country.

With Harrison occupying the position of coloniser, some of the heat is taken off our fine Australian pioneers, who are in fact involved in an identical process of encoding the landscape within their own territorial and ideological parameters. There is much talk about the 'wildness' of the landscape, yet it is appropriated within the film's representational economy primarily as the proving-ground for an ethos of dominant masculinity and the cult of male-to-male or patrilineal bonding.

The land 'opening' activities of the American Western are played out over the loose structural framework of A. B. Paterson's ballad of the noble bushman, of the camaraderie of men on and against the landscape, and of the glorification of the underdog. The film thus treads an often uneasy line between a eulogising of the ostensibly egalitarian bonding between mates, and a privileging of the individual male hero or leader of men which can be seen in the rite of passage of young Jim Craig (Tom Burlinson) from untried son of the father to a manhood that is evidenced through his power over nature in the form of horses, landscape and women.

Indeed, one of the more objectionable aspects of the film is its stereotypical equation of women with a passive landscape to be cultivated or a horse to be ridden. The love interest, Jessica (Sigrid Thornton), is virtually indistinguishable from Bess, the missing horse, in a similar way that the male narrative may be seen as crudely encapsulated in the correspondence between Jim, the Man from Snowy River, and the greatly prized 'colt from Old Regret' which will challenge and eventually replace the stallion/father.

ROSE LUCAS

References

'Geoff Burrowes and George Miller: Two Men Behind **Snowy River**', an interview with the producer and the director by George Tosi, *Cinema Papers*, no. 38, June 1982, pp. 206–12, 283.

'**The Man from Snowy River**', a review by Arnold Zable, ibid., pp. 261–2.

'**The Man from Snowy River**: Parents and Orphans', an article by Jack Clancy, *Cinema Papers*, no. 42, March 1983, pp. 50–2.

'The Sound of Music', an interview with composer Bruce Rowland (and others) by Jenni Gyffyn, *Cinema Papers*, no. 69, May 1988, pp. 10–15.

'**Man from Snowy River** [sic]' a review by Denise Hare, *Filmnews*, April 1982, p. 13.

'Ride the High Country: **The Man from Snowy River** & Australian Popular Culture', Tom O'Regan, *Filmnews*, September 1982, pp. 8–9.

KEN CAMERON

MONKEY GRIP

Pavilion Films presents Monkey Grip. © 1981 Pavilion Films. *Budget:* $1.17 million. *Location:* Sydney. *Australian distributor:* Roadshow. *Video:* Roadshow Home Video. *Opened:* June 1982. *Rating:* M (February 1982; 2788.80m, but cut to 2743m in March after being classified R). 35mm. 99 mins.

Producer: Patricia Lovell. *Executive producer:* Danny Collins. *Associate producer:* Treisha Ghent. *Scriptwriter:* Ken Cameron, in association with Helen Garner. Based on the novel by Helen Garner. *Director of photography:* David Gribble. *Camera operators:* Nixon Binney, Danny Batterham. *Production designer:* Clark Munro. *Wardrobe:* Kathy James. *Editor:* David Huggett. *Composer:* Bruce Smeaton. *Sound recordist:* Mark Lewis. *Sound editor:* Ashley Grenville. *Mixer:* Peter Fenton.

Cast

Noni Hazlehurst (Nora), Colin Friels (Javo), Alice Garner (Gracie), Harold Hopkins (Willie), Candy Raymond (Lillian), Michael Caton (Clive), Tim Burns (Martin), Christina Amphlett (Angela), Don Miller-Robinson (Gerald), Lisa Peers (Rita), Cathy Downes (Eve), Justin Ridley (Roaster), Pearl Christie (Juliet), Vera Plevnik (Jessie), Jamie Fonti (Ramondo), Esben Storm (Record Producer), Phil Motherwell (Actor 1), Dana Auzins (Actor 2), Gary Waddell (Actor 3), Bill Charlton (Truck Driver), Carole Skinner (Waitress), Vincent Lovegrove (Dave).

By the early 1980s, Australian cinema had begun a self-conscious move away from the constraints of costume drama and period recreation. While there had always been the odd foray into the realm of the present in the 1980s, it seemed producers couldn't get enough contentious 'current' issues or the prospect of reflecting a real, happening Australian culture.

Given the number of films being produced (or the number that failed to emerge, particularly as the tax incentives picked up), it followed that producers would chase original sources for script material. Suddenly Australian writers whose work had achieved some level of success or recognition were to be translated to the big screen.

Monkey Grip is no exception to that trend; indeed, in some ways it could be seen as a forerunner. The film is adapted from Helen Garner's largely autobiographical novel of the same name and, like the book, sets out to document the lives of a group of inner-city dwellers caught on a merry-go-round of parties, drugs and sexual manoeuvres. The film also contains a liberal dose of rock 'n' roll.

While Monkey Grip appears to go nowhere quite slowly, there is a thread of continuity set up as the film's narrator, Nora (Noni Hazlehurst), contemplates – via her journal – some of the complexities of the lifestyle and in the process tackles certain questions of identity. Her quest is made that much more difficult as she slowly falls in love with a junkie, Javo (Colin Friels), who, predictably, isn't too concerned with commitment.

Garner's interpretation of this 'glorious' period of free love and a little bit of so-called anarchy does little more than highlight the joys of life inner-city style: working on creative 'Left' newspapers, living in large communal houses where tensions are rarer than children misbehaving, doing dope, alcohol and smack, if you're that way inclined, swapping sexual partners and finally drying each other's tears, after the event(s).

The film does showcase the superb acting talents of Noni Hazlehurst and Colin Friels, and the lesser-known but equally interesting performance of Christina Amphlett. Indeed, her part as a scorned lover trying to make it in a rock band and desperate to keep her emotional cool threatens to eclipse other aspects of the story. The inclusion of the 'rock' band – a thinly disguised Divinyls – creates the most interesting sub-plot in an otherwise tepid evocation of this small group of people.

PETER LAWRANCE

Nora (Noni Hazelhurst) and her junkie boyfriend, Javo (Colin Friels).

References

'Monkey Grip', a review by Brian McFarlane, *Cinema Papers*, no. 38, June 1982, pp. 366–7.

'Words and Images: Monkey Grip', Brian McFarlane, *Cinema Papers*, no. 44–5, April 1984, pp. 16–21.

'Monkey Grip', a review by Peter Kemp, *Filmnews*, June 1982, p. 15.

'A Film About Communicating with Other People', an uncredited interview with actor Noni Hazlehurst, *Filmnews*, October 1982, pp. 10–11.

'Ken Talking', an interview with director Ken Cameron by Tim Burns and Tina Kaufman, *Filmnews*, August–September 1984, p. 10–12.

NEXT OF KIN

A Film House/SIS Production. NEXT OF KIN. © 1982 S.I.S. Productions Pty Ltd and Filmco Limited. Produced with financial assistance from the New Zealand Film Commission and the New South Wales Film Corporation. *Locations:* Melbourne, Sydenham, Clarkefield (Victoria). *Australian distributor:* Roadshow. *Video:* Roadshow Home Video. *Rating:* M (June 1982; 2454m). 35mm. 89 mins.

Producer: Robert Le Tet. *Co-producer:* Timothy White. *Scriptwriters:* Michael Heath, Tony Williams. *Director of photography:* Gary Hansen. *Production designers:* Richard Francis, Nick Hepworth. *Wardrobe:* Jenny Arnott. *Editor:* Max Lemon. *Composer:* Klaus Schulze. *Sound recordist:* Gary Wilkins. *Sound editors:* Louise Johnson, Frank Lipson; Ross Chambers (asst). *Mixer:* Julian Ellingworth.

Cast

Jackie Kerin (Linda), John Jarratt (Barney), Alex Scott (Dr. Barton), Gerda Nicolson (Connie), Charles McCallum (Lance), Bernadette Gibson (Rita/Mrs. Ryan), Robert Ratti (Kelvin), Vince Deltito (Nico), Tommy Dysart (Harry), Debra Lawrance (Carol), Kristina Marshall (Linda (aged 4)), Simon Thorpe (C.F.A. Speaker); David Allshorn, Alan Rowe (Service Club Men); Matt Burns (Mr. Collins), Daphne Miller (Freda), Isobel Harley (Paula), Eunice Crimp (Cockoo), Irene Hewitt (Maid); Myrtle Woods, Vic Gordon, Peter Lord, Ernest Wilson, Bill Mars (Montclare Residents); John Bishop (Truckie), Mitchell Faircloth (Cafe Man).

A young woman's journey into her mother's horrifying past is a key theme in this taut suspense film directed by Tony Williams.

Linda (Jackie Kerin) inherits her mother's property, once a manor but now converted into a nursing home for the aged. Her return to the town she grew up in is met with a mixture of curiosity and hostility. Apart from discovering a mass of debts and the home filled with eccentric folk, Linda is tormented by a murderous presence which lurks within the bowels of the manor.

Things go bump in the night, candles are mysteriously relit and bodies are found drowned in baths or with their throats slashed in fountains. None of these phenomena makes much sense until Linda reads her mother's diaries, and learns along the way that her mother's spurned, mentally sick sister is still alive and intent on revenge.

The plot may be a little hokey, and has more red herrings than an Agatha Christie novel, but this spooky yarn is slickly

Four-year-old Linda (Kristina Marshall).

directed, intriguing and at times visually reminiscent of Stanley Kubrick's **The Shining** (1980).

Via Linda's journey, the film explores the nature of blood ties, whether it be between mother and daughter or sibling rivalry between sisters; acceptance, as seen in the return home of a 'prodigal' daughter and her re-assimilation into country life; and, finally, deprivation of rights, exemplified by Linda's aunt's incarceration in a mental institution which prompts her desire for revenge.

While on one hand Linda's free spirit is weighed down by the daily routine of running a nursing home, her maternal instincts are activated and find solace in caring for the old, particularly war veteran Lance (Charles McCallum), and hanging out with her old sweetheart, Barney (John Jarratt). Like Ripley (Sigourney Weaver) from **Alien** (Ridley Scott, 1979), Linda is a loner. She stands apart from other women who, in the film, are represented as either homely and dumb or cruel and catty. Like Ripley, Linda fights to uncover the truth and destroy the evil force, in this instance, her aunt.

On another level, the film deals with primal, power/rivalry relationships between women, exemplified in Linda's relationship with nursing home manager, Connie (Gerda Nicolson), her mother's repressive relationship with her sister, and Linda's relationship with Barney's love interest. Linda views Connie, her aunt's alter ego, with some suspicion, despite Connie's attempts to be

helpful and motherly. Their relationship becomes more fragmented when Linda suspects Connie and the lying Dr. Barton (Alex Scott) of contributing to her mother's breakdown. The film also touches on her mother's relationship with her sister, their closeness cut asunder when her mother put her sister into a mental institution.

As testimony to the saying 'Each man kills the thing he loves', her mother's sister seeks justice through a series of psychological cat-and-mouse games which result in murder.

By contrast, the male characters are essentially token rôles: Barney is dumb but nice, Dr Barton is slightly sleazy, Lance is an eccentric, harmless old fogey. None of the males poses any threat to the relationships females have with them.

During the final, bloody dénouement, Linda stakes out in her local coffee shop, waiting for her foe with a shotgun and accompanied by the shop owner's child. Interestingly, although she finally stabs and shoots her assailants, there is no sense of catharsis–the viewer is left with the disconcerting feeling that one can destroy the past but never get rid of it. She is next of kin, set to inherit a past which shrouds her future.

PAT GILLESPIE

Reference

'Next of Kin: Tony Williams', an interview with the director by Scott Murray, *Cinema Papers*, no. 38, June 1982, pp. 242–5, 291.

HENRI SAFRAN

"NORMAN LOVES ROSE"

Norman Films presents "NORMAN LOVES ROSE"[1]. © 1982 Norman Films Pty Ltd. *Budget:* $1.3 million. *Location:* Sydney. *Australian distributor:* GUO. *Video:* CIC-Taft. *Rating:* M (April 1982; 2660.71m). 35mm. 98 mins.

Producers: Henri Safran, Basil Appleby. *Executive producer:* Max Weston. *Scriptwriter:* Henri Safran. *Director of photography:* Vince Monton. *Camera operator:* Nixon Binney. *Production designer:* Darrell Lass. [*Costume designer:* not credited.] *Editor:* Don Saunders. *Composer:* Mike Perjanik. *Sound recordist:* Ross Linton. *Sound editor:* Ian Munro. *Mixer:* Peter Fenton.

Cast

Carol Kane (Rose), Tony Owen (Norman), Myra De Groot (Mother), David Downer (Michael), Barry Otto (Charles), Sandy Gore (Maureen), Warren Mitchell (Morris), Virginia Hey (The Girlfriend), Louise Pajo (Shirley), Valerie Newstead (1st Lady), Betty Benfield (2nd Lady), Julie Herbert (Daily), Olivia Brown (Nurse), Harold Newstead (Sid), Sid Feldheim (David), Johnny Lockwood (Sam), Arthur Sherman (Presser), Gypsy Dorney (Jennifer), Aaron Hitties (David), Theo Stevens (Orthodox Jew), Gary Kuiger (Cantor), Jozef Drewniar (Psychiatrist), Geoffrey Smith (Doctor), Sue Stenmark (Woman on Bus), Michael Adams (Rich Gentleman), Shane Tapper (Youth).

The New Australian Cinema was not so prolific of comedies that audiences could afford to neglect so engaging a film as "Norman Loves Rose". The Norman (Tony Owen) of the title is the adolescent son of a middle-class Jewish family, and Rose (Carol Kane) is the sister-in-law he adores and quickly impregnates. In doing so, he succeeds where his dentist brother, Michael (David Downer), has been so signally failing. At Norman's barmitzvah celebration, Michael intones, 'You will assume duties which up to now have been my father's and mine', unaware that Norman has already well and truly done so.

The basis for this graceful comedy may sound tasteless, but the film is not. Its central plot manœuvre is executed gracefully so that none of the three principals loses sympathy. David Downer's Michael is indeed a figure touched with genuine pathos, desperately trying to measure up to his family's expectations, and envious of the apparently adventurous sex life of his randy partner, Charles (Barry Otto). The family pressures may derive from certain Jewish stereotypes,

Norman (Tony Owen) and Maureen (Sandy Gore).

but they are sketched with sympathetic detail so that even the possessive mother emerges as more than a caricature. Similarly, Charlie's swinging life-style is eloquently presented as a façade for the pain of his wrecked marriage.

In one sense, "Norman Loves Rose" belongs with those other Australian features about boys hovering on the brink of manhood, caught up in the exhilaration and pain of sexual maturation. However, it is perhaps unique in seeing that this situation may be the occasion for comedy as well as for more solemn rites-of-passage drama. It is not a film which spells out its meanings: it is satisfied to dramatise Norman's passion and Michael's frustrations, and their parents' varied obsessions and anxieties. In doing so, the film achieves a warmth and non-didactic

lightness of touch that distinguishes it from the few other Australian ventures in the field of romantic comedy. Henri Safran's tactful direction of his own screenplay provides a touching and funny criticism and vindication of family life.

BRIAN MCFARLANE

---

[1] The 'O' in 'ROSE' is actually a heart.

References

'Henri Safran talks about **Norman Loves Rose** [sic]', an interview with the director by Margaret Smith, *Cinema Papers*, no. 40, October 1982, pp. 408–12.
'**Norman Loves Rose** [sic]', a review by Brian McFarlane, ibid., pp. 465–6.
'**Norman Loves Rose** [sic]', a short review by Kathe Boehringer, *Filmnews*, September 1982, p. 13.

THE PIRATE MOVIE

David Joseph presents THE PIRATE MOVIE. © 1982 Joseph Hamilton International Productions Pty Ltd. *Budget:* $6 million. *Locations:* Port Campbell, Werribee, Melbourne (Victoria). *Australian distributor:* Fox–Columbia. *Video:* CBS–Fox. *Rating:* NRC (July 1982; 2880m). 35mm. 105 mins.[1]

Producer: David Joseph. *Executive producer:* Ted Hamilton. *Associate producer:* David Anderson. *Scriptwriter:* Trevor Farrant. Based on the operetta *The Pirates of Penzance* by W. S. Gilbert and A. S. Sullivan. *Director of photography:* Robin Copping. *Camera operator:* David Burr. *Original concept and design:* Jon Dowding. *Production designer:* Tony Woollard. *Costume designer:* Aphrodite Kondos. *Editor:* Kenneth W. Zemke. *Original songs:* Terry Britten; Kit Hain, Sue Shifrin, Brian Robertson. Incidental music and adaptations arranged and conducted by Peter Sullivan. *Choreography:* David Atkins. *Sound recordist:* Paul Clark. *Sound editors:* Terry Rodman, Peter Burgess, Andrew Steuart, Bruce Lamshed. *Mixers:* Ron Purvis (sup.); Phil Heywood (fx); Gethin Creagh (music).

Cast

Kristy McNichol (Mabel), Christopher Atkins (Frederic), Ted Hamilton (The Pirate King), Bill Kerr (Major General), Maggie Kirkpatrick (Ruth), Garry McDonald (Sergeant; Inspector), Chuck McKinney (Samuel), Marc Colombani (Dwarf Pirate), Linda Nagle (Aphrodite), Kate Ferguson (Edith), Rhonda Burchmore (Kate), Cathrine Lynch (Isabel), John Allansy (Chinese Captain); Paul Graham, Nic Gazzana, Chris Hession, Kjell Nilsson, Tony Deary, Roy Dudley, Gene Del'Mace, George Novak, Kurt Schneider, Bernard Ledger, Richard Boué, Stephen Fyfield, Peter Pantellic, Harry Morris, Roger Ward, Ian Mortimer, George Zakaria, Zev Eletheriou, Edward Brodsky-Schuster (The Pirates).

The Pirate Movie, while ostensibly based on *The Pirates of Penzance*, is a magpie collection of Gilbert and Sullivan, modern pop songs, slapstick, in-jokes and filmic references.

The film begins in modern times when a class of girls goes to visit a 'pirate' ship on Melbourne's Yarra River. One of the girls, good and plain Mabel (Kristy McNicol), wanders round with a 'ghetto blaster', ignored by her pretty companions. After a demonstration of sword fighting by a young man (Christopher Atkins), the girls are invited to go sailing with him. But Mabel is left behind by her scheming friends and her attempt to catch up by wind-surfer leaves her near drowned and dreaming on the water's edge…

It is now the 1880s and the young man has become Frederic, an apprentice to The Pirate King (Ted Hamilton) on his ship. Frederic feels it is time to branch out on his own and bids his rough-and-tough crew-mates goodbye. Unceremoniously made to walk the plank ('Hang five, honky', one crew member shouts), he plunges into the sea.

Frederic swims to shore, where a group of girls in period bathing clothes flee in fright. But Mabel does not.

The dialogue that follows sets the tone of the rest of the film: jokey, irreverent, post-modern and often silly. After Mabel and Frederic walk love-struck towards each other and have conversed for but ten seconds, Frederic says he thinks he wants to marry her. Mabel replies most self-referentially, 'God, that was a short love scene.' They then burst into song ('My First Love').

Mabel is the daughter of 'a very modern' Major General (Bill Kerr) and the rest of the film charts Frederic's battle to win Mabel's hand, defeat The Pirate King and retrieve lost treasure. Along the way, there are more songs, some Feydeu-like farce and an over-extended sword fight. But despite the best efforts of Mabel and Frederic, The Pirate King emerges victorious and orders the good guys to be put to death. Fortunately, at this very moment Mabel is reminded that it is all her dream and she demands a 'happy ending'.

Unfortunately, the various strains of comedy and genre do not always sit comfortably with each other, the modernisation of the Gilbert and Sullivan songs lacks wit ('I straighten more piratical erections than Bo Derek')[2] and the double entendres wouldn't be out of place in a 'Carry On' movie ('You'll be hung.' 'Oh, I am, I am. And very well, thank you').

Still, this is a film of enormous energy and bravado (except for the laborious skit in The Pirate King's boudoir and the very messy closing fight). It is hard to imagine many film-makers attempting so hybrid a film with so little reserve. The result, mostly, is silly and unfunny. Nevertheless, it is a hard film to dismiss totally. After all, can one think of many local films where the narrative, full of heroic and violent men, is actually controlled by so feisty a young woman?

SCOTT MURRAY

Mabel (Kristy McNichol) and The Pirate King (Ted Hamilton).

---

[1] The video runs only 95 mins.
[2] But are well sung. Bill Kerr's rendition of 'A Modern Major General' is actually far superior, and much snappier, than that in a recent production by the Victorian State Opera.

THE PLAINS OF HEAVEN

[No opening production credit.] the plains of heaven. © 1982 Seon Film Productions. *Location:* Victorian alps. *Australian distributor:* AFI. *Video:* Syme Home Video. *Rating:* M (July 1982; 855.66m). 16 mm. 80 mins.

Producer: John Cruthers. *Associate producer:* Brian McKenzie. *Scriptwriters:* Ian Pringle, Doug Ling, Elizabeth Parsons. *Director of photography:* Ray Argall. *Production designer:* Elizabeth Stirling. [*Costume designer:* not credited.] [*Editor:* not credited; Ray Argall.] *Composer:* Andrew Duffield. *Sound recordist:* Bruce Emery. *Sound editors:* Ray Argall, Bruce Emery. *Mixers:* Bruce Emery, Tony Paterson.

Cast

Richard Moir (Barker), Reg Evans (Cunningham), Gerard Kennedy (Lenko), John Flaus (Landrover Owner), Jenny Cartwright (Nurse), Brian McKenzie (Lewis), Adam Biscombe (Soldier on Train), Joe Ford (Video Producer), Bryce Menzies (ISC Man), Bid Nosal (Secretary).

Few recent Australian films have explored the national obsession with space and the uncertainty it generates in the national psyche as emphatically as **The Plains of Heaven**.

As a film, it marked the opening stanza of Ian Pringle's move into an intensely European style of film-making that seemed especially comfortable in Melbourne. By the end of the 1980s, it had taken root in Berlin, with Pringle and his colleagues working under the enthusiastic wing of Wim Wenders.

The Plains of Heaven is set in the Victorian alps, where two isolated men fight with technology and the alpine environment for meaning. The film treats the increasingly complicated relationship of the male characters with a vigour that signalled a determined enthusiasm for the film-making craft. Often linear, bordering on the clinical, the characters become motifs for a larger examination of isolation, although an eerie supernaturalism almost pushes the film into the terrain of the gothic nightmare.

The somewhat grand European approach proves to be the film's weakness. Pringle loses sight of the ideas he seemed keen to explore. The relationship between Barker (Richard Moir) and Cunningham (Reg Evans), while in part an enthralling study in the anxiety of isolation in the Australian wilderness, ultimately seems short on insights, with resolutions generated through melodrama and an ultimate retreat into a nihilistic fatalism. Nevertheless, the rare, even vicious,

natural scenery of the film generates an unsettling sense of place, although, importantly, Pringle's obsessive use of alpine Australia does not sit well with the rural, isolationist mythology of Australia's vast 'dead heart'.

The Europeanisation of Australian films, rather than a concentration on everyday American life, has not had an easy time and Pringle is something of an unsung hero for his pursuit of big themes. At the time it was made, **The Plains of Heaven** represented a bold attempt to examine psycho-social issues in a European style of film-making in the Australian context.

MARCUS BREEN

References

'The Plains of Heaven: Ian Pringle', an interview with the director by Mark Stiles, *Cinema Papers*, no. 42, March 1983, pp. 26–9.

'The Plains of Heaven', a review by Jim Schembri, ibid., pp. 65–7.

'The Films of Ian Pringle', John O'Hara, *Cinema Papers*, no. 50, February–March 1985, pp. 16–21.

'The Plains of Heaven', a short review, uncredited, *Filmnews*, November–December 1982, p. 25.

'The Plains of Heaven: Plane of Expression – Plane of Content – Plane of Heaven?', Mark Jackson, *Filmnews*, August–September 1983, p. 19.

Barker (Richard Moir) in the Victorian alps.

JOHN CLARK

RUNNING ON EMPTY

The Film Corporation of Western Australia presents Running On Empty. *Alternative titles:* 'Fast Lane Fever' and 'Wild Wheels' (working). © [date not given; atb 1982] Film Corporation of Western Australia. *Budget:* $2 million. *Locations:* Sydney, Cobar (New South Wales). *Australian distributor:* Roadshow. *Video:* Roadshow Home Video. *Rating:* M (June 1982). 35mm. Panavision. 83 mins.

Producer: Pom Oliver. *Executive producer:* David Roe. *Associate producer:* Mark Egerton. *Scriptwriter:* Barry Tomblin. Based on an original idea by John Clark. *Director of photography:* David Gribble. *Camera operator:* David Burr. *Production designer:* Greg Brown. *Wardrobe:* Roger Monk. *Editor:* Stuart Armstrong. *Composer:* Peter Crosbie. *Sound recordist:* Syd Butterworth. *Supervising sound editor:* Marc Van Buuren. *Sound editor:* Tim Jordan (dia.). *Mixer:* Julian Ellingworth.

Cast

Terry Serio (Mike), Deborah Conway (Julie), Max Cullen (Rebel), Richard Moir (Fox), Penne Hackforth-Jones (Dave), Vangelis Mourikis (Tony), Grahame Bond (Jagger), Bob Barrett (Workman), Warren Blondell (Lee), Jon Darling (Workman), Peter Davies (Ram's Mate), Kristoffer Greaves (Starter), Paul Johnstone (Lecherous Garage Attendant), Chris Haywood (Photographer), Maurice Hughes (Foreman), Tim McLean (Photographer's Assistant), Brian McNevin (Fox's Timer), Sno Norton-Sinclair (Starter's Mate), Robin Ramsay (Dad), Geoff Rhoe (Ram), Keli Roberts (Sheryl), Anne Semler (Joan), Jacki Simmons (Nurse), Gerard Sont (Victor).

Running on Empty makes its relationship to **Rebel Without a Cause** (1955) unashamedly clear: it takes the chicken-run elements of Nicholas Ray's film and inflates them; it traces the relationship between a young and restless trio; and it even has a character called Rebel, a rocker whose golden era was the Dean age, and who still behaves as if he's living in the 1950s.

But the film never attempts to match the mood and intensity of its precursor. As Meaghan Morris in the *Australian Financial Review* said, perhaps over generously:

> There is a uniquely suburban spirit of fantasy at work in **Running on Empty** which puts it at a cultural distance from the Hollywood models it lovingly works over. Rather than a gang film it would just as well be called – to use an old-fashioned term – a larrikin film.[1]

Julie (Deborah Conway), Mike (Terry Serio) and Tony (Vangelis Mourikis).

For Morris, the gang-member, Hollywood style, is a creature ruled by a single code of survival, while the larrikin is, above all, inconsistent: a cheerful street lout one minute, a murderous thug the next.

You could certainly find inconsistency in **Running on Empty**. It teeters between myth and parody, niceness and nastiness, and its characters oscillate between dangerous and ludicrous, mostly the latter. Sometimes it appears like a cross between a cartoon and a commercial. Adding to the sense of stylistic confusion, Grahame Bond and Penne Hackforth-Jones play a pair of comically sinister cops who have strayed in from an entirely different film, amusing but bewildering punctuation points.

But the film's main character, Mike (Terry Serio), is a larrikin in the most basic sense of the word. He is no Jim Stark (James Dean) from **Rebel Without a Cause**, anguished, intense, passionate, locked in a struggle with his parents for their love and approval, putting adults to shame with his more-than-adult intensity and earnestness. Mike likes cars, and speed, and that is the most complicated that it gets, despite occasional declarations suggesting a desire to avoid conformity or coercion.

Mike's automotive duel, a development of the Jim-Buzz (Corey Allen) rivalry in **Rebel Without a Cause**, is with gang-leader Fox, played with leering, pantomime wickedness by Richard Moir. And like Jim, Mike links up with his rival's girl, Julie (Deborah Conway). Mike and Julie are an unlikely couple, hampered by some clumsy dialogue.

In films like **Freedom** (Scott Hicks, 1982), **The FJ Holden** (Michael Thornhill, 1977), **Dead-End Drive-In** (Brian Trenchard Smith, 1986) and **The Big Steal** (Nadia Tass, 1991), the boy-meets-car element is tied to something more substantial or coherent. **Running on Empty** looks good – it was photographed by David Gribble, who also worked on **The FJ Holden**. But its resolution is completely arbitrary. It is a film without a navigator or a map, a 1950s vehicle with no place to go.

PHILIPPA HAWKER

---

[1] *Australian Financial Review*, 20 August 1982.

References

'**Running on Empty**', a review by Mark Spratt, *Cinema Papers*, no. 40, October 1982, pp. 467–8.
'**Running on Empty**', a short review by Peter Kemp, *Filmnews*, August 1982, p. 16.

SNOW: THE MOVIE

Darren (David Argue), Wayne (Lance Curtis) and Bruno (Peter Moon).

Snowfilm Productions presents SNOW [/] THE MOVIE. © 1982 Snowfilm Productions Pty Ltd. *Budget:* $420,000. *Location:* Falls Creek (Victoria). *Australian distributor:* Snowfilm Productions. *Opened:* 13 June 1982. *Video:* not released. *Rating:* M (June 1982; 91 mins). 85 mins.

Producer: Eve Ash. *Scriptwriters:* Lance Curtis, Geoff Kelso, Peter Moon, David Argue, Robert Gibson. *Directors of photography:* Martin McGrath, Tim Smart. *Camera operators:* Martin McGrath, Tim Smart, Butch Sawko. [*Production designer:* not credited.] [*Wardrobe:* not credited; Yvonne Visser.] *Editor:* Robert Gibson. *Composer:* George Worontschak. *Sound recordist:* Steve Edwards. *Sound editor:* Steve Edwards. *Mixer:* Steve Edwards.

Cast

David Argue (Darren), Lance Curtis (Wayne), Peter Moon (Bruno), Peppie Angliss (Pepi), Jeannie O'Donnell (Pam), Tom Coltrane (Bruce), Geoff Kelso (Uncle Jack), Eddie Zandberg (Hamish McAlpine), Ian McFadyen (Ian), Scott Fulmer (Ski Instructor), Angela Rea (Mrs Castellucia), Totty (Fony), Yvonne Visser (Ms Mountain), Jenny King (Girl).

Filmed on location at Falls Creek, **Snow: The Movie**, directed by Robert Gibson, is an attempt to create comedy that capitalises on the then-emerging talent from Melbourne's comedy cabaret circuit.

A tedious comedy, consisting of feeble attempts at satire and recycled stand-up routines, the film reaches its nadir with a tired and sexist wet T-shirt segment. What enjoyment can be derived from the experience can be attributed to the cast's valiant efforts to transcend the non-existent plot and lack of production values.

The seemingly improvised storyline follows the misadventures of two friends, Darren (David Argue, fresh from Peter Weir's **Gallipoli**, 1981) and Wayne (Lance Curtis), who win a competition and head off on their first skiing holiday.

Making her debut as a feature producer, Eve Ash, who specialises in documentaries and corporate videos for the business and educational sector, was confident of attracting a large, if specialised, audience. ('There are over half a million skiers in Australia – that is our market.')

The world premiere was held at one of the film's main locations, the Sundance Inn at the start of the skiing season in June 1982, and the only theatrical screenings were some Longford late shows in Melbourne.

PAUL HARRIS

SQUIZZY TAYLOR

Roger Simpson & Roger Le Mesurier present Squizzy Taylor. © 1982 Simpson Le Mesurier Films (Melbourne). Made in association with the Victorian Film Corporation. *Budget:* $1.7 million. *Location:* Melbourne. *Australian distributor:* Filmways. *Rating:* M (March 1982; 2673.5m). 35mm. 97 mins.

Producer: Roger Le Mesurier. *Executive producer:* Roger Simpson. *Scriptwriter:* Roger Simpson. *Director of photography:* Dan Burstall. *Production designer:* Logan Brewer. *Costume designer:* Jane Hyland. *Choreography:* David Atkins. *Editor:* David Pulbrook. *Composer:* Bruce Smeaton. *Sound recordist:* Phil Stirling. *Sound editors:* Louise Johnson, Steve Lambeth. *Mixer:* Peter Fenton.

Cast

David Atkins (Squizzy Taylor), Jacki Weaver (Dolly), Alan Cassell (Det. Brophy), Michael Long (Det. Piggott), Kim Lewis (Ida Pender), Robert Hughes (Reg Harvey), Cul Cullen (Henry Stokes), Steve Bisley ('Snowy' Cutmore), Peter Hosking (Angus Murray), Tony Rickards (Dutch), Simon Thorpe (Paddy), Paul Trahair (Young Detective), Peter Paulson ('Long' Harry Slater), David Scott ('Bunny' Whiting), Jenni Caffin (Tart), John Larking (Superintendent); Hardy Stow, Ian Clutterham, Adam Joseph (Reporters).

Like most things that pass via folklore into history, the real life of Arthur 'Squizzy' Taylor was hardly as colourful as legend would have us believe. In actuality, Taylor was little more than a minor hoodlum in Melbourne's criminal world of the 1920s—that is, until the print media of the day got their hands on him. Responding to America's attention-grabbing Prohibition gangland headlines, the media, with Taylor's complicity, made of him a local front page Al Capone. The 'crime czar' tag sold newspapers and titillated the imagination of the predominantly middle-class reading public.

Screenwriter Roger Simpson, whose *Power Without Glory* screenplay deals with the same era, and director Kevin Dobson have retained a few actual events in Taylor's life and fashioned around them a largely fictional plot which chronicles a rogue's progress from petty hood to the seat of power and wealth amongst the Melbourne underworld.

Squizzy Taylor (David Atkins) begins his 'career' by pitching two rival gangs into warfare. In the aftermath, he steps into the power vacuum. Along the way he falls in love with a young dancer, Ida Pender (Kim Lewis), and befriends a journalist, Reg Harvey (Robert Hughes), who inscribes the underworld fable. Concurrently, Squizzy is used as a pawn in a battle of wills between two police officers who hold differing ideas about law enforcement. One, Det. Piggott (Michael Long), follows the letter of the law–uncompromising and stern, for whom Squizzy is the nemesis to be destroyed. The other, Det. Brophy (Alan Cassell), a policeman with underground connections, sees the agents of both the law and the criminal world as locked in a symbiotic relationship. Eventually, much of Squizzy's fate is held in the hands of the law and the media.

At first, **Squizzy Taylor** seems a rarity for the Australian cinema: that is, a gangster film in the mould of the Hollywood crime dramas of the 1930s. Certainly, its plot trajectory is that of the classic 'rise and fall of the hero' structure common to so many of the American gangster films. As well, there is a fair use of genre iconography and milieu: gangland vendettas, guns blazing from speeding vintage cars, gambling dens, brothel houses, dance halls, and so on. But it is a facile use of iconography and it quickly becomes apparent that the film's relation to the genre is superficial and decorative. Dobson's direction often sacrifices narrative drive for lingering shots of the production design. This can only lead to dramatic inertia.

Nor does it help that Squizzy is fundamentally a reactive character - really a pawn in someone else's story. The classic gangster hero's ascension to power is propelled by a remarkable force of will, an internal, almost psychic will to power which in turn energises the very narrative used to convey the story. Dobson's direction loses that energy and so too does the hero and the urgency of his drama.

ROLANDO CAPUTO

References

'Kevin Dobson', an interview with the director by Scott Murray, *Cinema Papers*, no. 36, February 1982, pp. 410–15, 97.

'Jacki Weaver', an interview with the actor by Tom Ryan, *Cinema Papers*, no. 37, April 1982, pp. 120–4, 185.

'Squizzy Taylor', a review by Jim Schembri, *Cinema Papers*, no. 39, August 1982, pp. 367–9.

Gangster Squizzy Taylor (David Atkins).

STAR STRUCK

Palm Beach Pictures presents STAR STRUCK.[1] © 1982 Palm Beach Pictures. *Budget:* $2.5 million. *Location:* Sydney. Made in association with the Australian Film Commission. *Australian distributor:* Hoyts. *Video:* Star Video. *Rating:* NRC (December 1981; 2880.15m). 35mm. 105 mins.

Producers: David Elfick, Richard Brennan. *Associate producer:* Stephen MacLean. *Scriptwriter:* Stephen MacLean. *Director of photography:* Russell Boyd. *Camera operator:* Nixon Binney. *Production designer:* Brian Thomson. *Costume designers:* Luciana Arrighi, Terry Ryan. *Editor:* Nicholas Beauman. *Musical director:* Mark Moffatt. *Choreographer:* David Atkins. *Sound recordist:* Phil Judd. *Sound editors:* Paul Maxwell, Helen Brown, Marc Van Buuren, Anne Breslin, Peter Forster. *Mixers:* David Dockendorf, Peter Fenton, Gethin Creagh.

Cast

Jo Kennedy (Jackie), Ross O'Donovan (Angus), Margo Lee (Pearl), Pat Evison (Nana), John O'May (Terry), Ned Lander (Robbie), Max Cullen (Reg), Dennis Miller (Lou), Norman Erskine (Hazza), Melissa Jaffer (Mrs Booth); Phil Judd, Dwayne Hillman, Ian Gilroy (The Swingers); Mark Little (Carl), Ian Spence (Spider), Kerry McKay (Phil), Peter Davies (Timpany), Carol Burns (Teacher), Max Simms (Window Dresser), Pat Rooney (Bouncer), Vola Vandere (Flamenco Dancer), Giselle Morgan (Wilma), Ken Lambeth (Schoolboy Bully), Jamie Campbell (Schoolboy 1), Warren Lewis (Schoolboy 2), Lucky Grills (Brewery Truckdriver), Syd Heylen (Pub Regular), Rainee Skinner (Rock Photographer).

Though made by the usually competent Gillian Armstrong, **Star Struck** is a disappointing and gaudy musical comedy. It includes many lengthy song-and-dance routines choreographed by David Atkins and attempts to be funny in that tried-and-true Aussie mode of 'quirky'. Therefore, it is at least true to the genre, but that's about it, because the music and the comedy just don't gel in this film's gappy storyline.

Jo Kennedy, in a less than simply naïve performance, plays Jackie, a barmaid at the Harbourview Hotel – a kitschy, low-class pub. She looks like a twelve-year-old's concept of punk and often acts like one, though we are supposed to believe that she's eighteen. Her best friend is her fourteen-year-old cousin, Angus (Ross O'Donovan), a most annoyingly precocious youth, who,

like Jackie, lives above the pub with the rest of their motley family.

The teenagers, bored with their lives, dream of bigger and better things: namely of Jackie's becoming a rock star. The gag here is that 'Life's just a matter of what you want', as Angus aptly puts it. 'Start out wanting a Volkswagen and you'll end up with a Volkswagen. If you start out wanting a Jag, you'll end up with a Jag.' So, Angus encourages Jackie to capture the attention of a rock-show host, Terry (John O'May), by making her walk on a tightrope between two city buildings, wearing a 'topless-woman' costume. The trick works, with Jackie's stunt screening on the evening news and Jackie ending up at a police station, only to be bailed out by Terry himself.

Terry is impressed and promises that Jackie, and The Wombats – a band she has literally 'picked up' earlier on in the film – will feature on his show. Jackie falls in love with Terry. However, when it comes to the crunch, The Wombats are banned from the show, Jackie features in an idiotic act completely unsuited to her style and Terry reveals that he is gay – this, one fears, is supposed to be a major joke.

All ends up well after Jackie and The Wombats 'kidnap' the stage at a major band contest at the Opera House on New Year's Eve and win – fireworks and all. A number of sub-plots involving a liaison between

Jackie's mum and Angus' father, the pub business going to financial ruin and Jackie's relationship with the leader of The Wombats, Robbie (Ned Lander), are also tied up neatly with the winning of the contest.

Unfortunately, the only quality of those implied by the plot that actually surfaces is the raw animal energy. Otherwise, the jokes and the stunts are not funny. The music is annoying and the dance numbers are very dull, resembling the 1980s American television show, *Solid Gold*. The acting style is, one supposes, meant to be farcical, but this does not come off, either. It's not funny; it just looks like bad acting. Even Russell Boyd, usually a brilliant director of photography, fails to do anything worthy for this picture. The garish costumes designed by Luciana Arrighi and Terry Ryan are the final straw.

ANNA GUL

---

[1] Although many writers may make the title one word, it is two on the film.

References

'Starstruck [sic]: Stephen MacLean', an interview with the scriptwriter by Scott Murray, *Cinema Papers*, no. 37, April 1982, pp. 110–16.
'Starstruck [sic]', a review by Debi Enker, ibid., pp. 166–7.
'Starstruck [sic]', a review by Peter Kemp, *Filmnews*, May 1982, p. 13.
'Starstructure', Stuart Cunningham and Tom O'Regan, *Filmnews*, March 1983, p. 13.

Robbie (Ned Lander) and Jackie (Jo Kennedy) dance on the pub bar.

SWEET DREAMERS

[No opening production credit.[1]] Sweet Dreamers. © 1981. T. C. Productions. Made with assistance of the Creative Development Branch of the Australian Film Commission. *Location:* Sydney; London (2nd unit shot). *Australian distributor:* AFI. *Opened:* May 1982. *Video:* not released. *Rating:* M (July 1981; 888.57m). 16mm. 96 mins.

Producer: Lesley Tucker. *Scriptwriters:* Tom Cowan, Lesley Tucker. *Director of photography:* Brian Probyn. *Production designer:* Lesley Tucker. [*Costume designer:* not credited.] *Editors:* Tom Cowan, Lesley Tucker. *Composer:* Brett Cabot. *Sound recordist:* Paul Schneller. *Sound editor:* Peter Sommerville. *Mixers:* Julian Ellingworth; Alisdair MacFarlane (music).

Cast

Richard Moir [Will Daniels[2]], Sue Smithers [Josephine Russell]; Adam Bowen (Stuart), Frankie Raymond (Landlady), Richard Tipping (Busker), Karen Turner (Actress); Paul Blackwell, Tony Johnson (Train Louts); Gabriel (Waitress), Gypsy Rose (Little Girl).

This little-known film is a highly autobiographical account of the trials of making films by director Tom Cowan and producer Lesley Tucker. It begins in London, where Will Daniels[3] (Richard Moir), an Australian director of photography, has just begun a relationship with Josephine Russell (Sue Smithers). At the same time, Will is trying to complete a personal script. But Will is somewhat under-motivated and, while Josephine is at work, he tends to drift around her flat, looking for signs to her inner life.

Josephine is a script reader for a commercial production firm, setting up the first of many contrasts between sectors of the film industry. Will aims to 'make original films in Australia', but worries that 'So many young people with brilliant ideas just don't get a chance.' Will and Josephine's 'honest', non-exploitative approach to cinema is contrasted to the opposing realities of the commercial film world (typified by the sold-out director for whom Will unsatisfactorily works), and, far worse, of government film bureaucracies. Not only are there such remarks as 'Jerks like Goldman manipulating the Film Commission', Will even raises a call to arms: 'We should seize the cinemas. We've paid for them many times over.' The irony, of course, is that the much-maligned Australian Film Commission actually financed the film.

After the disappointments of London, Will and Josephine up stakes for Australia. 'I think that we're home', Will says on the

Josephine Russell[4] (Sue Smithers) and Will Daniels (Richard Moir).

ride into Sydney from the airport. This is despite Will's having already accurately proclaimed that 'Australia is not love-story territory.'

In Sydney, things tend to parallel in reverse aspects of the couple's London life: for example, Will is out much of the day and Josephine is left to explore his (far more spartan) flat. Despite the opportunity, the film makes little of Josephine's sacrificing a solid job in London for career-less prospects in Sydney (she shows great resolve by opening her own little restaurant).

Despite Will and Josephine's many ups and downs (he is staggeringly selfish around the house and has an outdated view of gender rôles that is nicely subverted when Josephine dresses him up as a girl), the film ends happily. The completed script, 'I Ching on a Double Bed', is now being shot in their flat. (Rather too cutely, there are some shots of Tom Cowan and Lesley Tucker playing crew members.)

While many may find it too navel-gazing, there is much to like about this gentle film. It has a great delicacy of tone and the relationship has a warmth rare in Australian cinema (aided greatly by the cosy patina of Brian Probyn's lighting). And even if the blaming of others for slow career advancement is a little tiresome at times, at least Cowan allows Will a degree of self-perception.

Cowan is one of Australia's better-known directors of photography, particularly for his work on the early films of John Duigan, but his four films as director (there are also **The Office Picnic**, 1973, **Promised Woman**, 1976, and **Journey Among Women**, 1977) are of note for their sweetness of tone, skilled marshalling of limited resources and a commitment to personalised film-making.

SCOTT MURRAY

---

1 At least on the 16mm print viewed, which was missing a leader.
2 There are no character name credits on the film for Moir's and Smithers' parts. These names are renditions of what is spoken in the film.
3 See footnote 2.
4 See footnote 2.

Reference
'Sweet Dreamers', a review by Stephen Wallace, *Filmnews*, March 1982, p. 11.

TURKEY SHOOT

Hemdale and FGH present for Filmco TURKEY SHOOT. *Alternative title:* Escape 2000 (US). © 1981 Second FGH Film Corporation Pty. Limited. *Budget:* $3.2 million. *Location:* Cairns (Queensland). *Australian distributor:* Roadshow. *Video:* Roadshow Home Video. *Rating:* M (April 1982; 2496.13m). 35mm. Panavision. 93 mins.

Producers: Antony I. Ginnane, William Fayman. *Executive producers:* John Daly, David Hemmings. *Associate producer:* Brian W. Cook. *Scriptwriters:* Jon George, Neill Hicks. *Based on a story by:* George Schenck. *Director of photography:* John McLean. *Camera operator:* David Burr. *Production designer:* Bernard Hides. *Costume designer:* Aphrodite Kondos. *Editor:* Alan Lake. *Composer:* Brian May. *Sound recordist:* Paul Clark. *Sound editor:* Lee Smith. *Mixer:* Peter Fenton.

Cast

Steve Railsback (Paul Anders), Olivia Hussey (Chris Walters), Michael Craig (Charles Thatcher), Carmen Duncan (Jennifer), Noel Ferrier (Mallory), Lynda Stoner (Rita Daniels), Roger Ward (Ritter), Michael Petrovich (Tito), Gus Mercurio (Red), John Ley (Dodge), Bill Young (Griffin), Steve Rackman (Alph), John Godden (Andy), Oriana Panozzo (Melinda).

Ritter (Roger Ward) and Chris Walters (Olivia Hussey) .

Turkey Shoot purports to represent a nightmarish vision of 1995, a time when henchmen from a dictatorship are rounding up dissidents and malcontents into re-education camps. The $3.2 million splatter fantasy centres on 'Re-Ed Camp 47', a type of tropical Gulag where commanders espouse hard-core Communist ideology and think up novel ways to slaughter their captives.

To ease the boredom, the captors release five troublesome 'deviates' into the wilds and set out to hunt them to the death. Hereafter, the film preoccupies itself with a series of unintentionally comical cat-and-mouse chases, and a blood-letting spree that is gratuitous to the point of being absurd. It borrows the plot-line of **The Most Dangerous Game**[1] (Ernest B. Schoedsack, Irving Pichel), a 1932 film about a count who hunts criminals on a remote island.

In translation, **Turkey Shoot** botches the hunter-versus-hunted scenario with an over-emphasis on violence, appalling acting and a plot that is no more advanced than a boys' adventure comic. The prison brass go out on the hunt with all sorts of gadgets, including machine-guns and arrows that explode.

One of the pursuers even has an ape-man called Alf to help dispose of victims. The story abounds with sinister intention, but, with the way the hunters bungle around, they really aren't much nastier than the German POW guards in *Hogan's Heroes*.

The villains end up easy picking for the 'heroes' of the show, Paul Anders (Steve Railsback) and Chris Walters (Olivia Hussey), who go back to main camp and inspire the other captives to insurrection.

Turkey Shoot never stands a chance of being taken seriously in either the choice or treatment of its subject matter. The notion of re-education camps in western democracies (the pawns of the dictatorship have either Australian or American accents) is about as likely as Elvis Presley turning up on Mars.

Apart from a far-fetched storyline, the film is riddled with sight misrepresentation and flaws in plot, editing and continuity. In one scene, Gus Mercurio, who plays a gammy-legged prison guard, forgets he has a limp. In another, the single-shot rifle of Charles Thatcher (Michael Craig) mysteriously acquires a semi-automatic capacity.

The dialogue is hollow, clichéd and laced with cheap sexual innuendo that would not be out of place in a garage porno flick. Brian May's music creates a foreboding mood dur-

ing the opening credits, though later his garbled synthesiser arrangements are snuffed out by torrents of gunfire and screaming.

During the making of the film in northern Queensland, director Brian Trenchard-Smith was quoted as saying, 'The name of the game is blood and guts.' The finished product excels in nothing more, but even its gory special effects are messy and Monty Pythonesque in flavour.

Turkey Shoot is so incompetent and over-indulged that one cannot be altogether sure that its creators did not have some tongue-in-cheek intentions. Unfortunately, though, the film is laughable for all the wrong reasons.

GREG KERR

[1] Also known as **The Hounds of Zaroff** (UK).

References

'Brian Trenchard Smith', a career interview with the director by Richard Brennan, *Cinema Papers*, no. 24, December 1979–January 1980, pp. 598–603, 674.

'Bob Saunders', an interview with the man behind Filmco, one of the film's investors, by Peter Beilby, *Cinema Papers*, no. 31, March–April 1981, pp. 26–9, 100.

'Turkey Shoot', a review by Geoff Mayer, *Cinema Papers*, no. 42, March 1983, pp. 69, 70.

WE OF THE NEVER NEVER

Adams Packer Film Productions and Film Corporation of Western Australia. WE OF THE NEVER NEVER. © [date not given; atb 1982] Adams Packer Film Productions, Film Corporation of Western Australia, General Television. *Budget:* $3 million. *Location:* Mataranka (Northern Territory). *Australian distributor:* Hoyts. *Video:* Australian Video. *Rating:* G (August 1982; 3840.20m). 35mm. Technovision. 134 mins.

Producer: Greg Tepper. *Executive producer:* Phillip Adams. *Co-producer:* John B. Murray. *Associate producer:* Brian Rosen. *Scriptwriter:* Peter Schreck. Based on the book by Mrs Aeneas Gunn. *Director of photography:* Gary Hansen. *Camera operators:* Peter Van Santen, Chris Cain, Phil Cross. *Production designer:* Josephine Ford. *Costume designer:* Camilla Rountree. *Editor:* Clifford Hayes. *Composer:* Peter Best. *Sound recordist:* Laurie Robinson. *Sound editors:* Frank Lipson, Hugh Waddell, Beth Harrison. *Mixers:* Phill Judd, Jim Currie.

Cast

Angela Punch McGregor (Jeannie), Arthur Dignam (Aeneas Gunn), Tony Barry (Mac), Tommy Lewis (Jackeroo), Lewis Fitz-Gerald (Jack), Martin Vaughan (Dan), John Jarratt (Dandy), Tex Morton (Landlord), Donald Blitner (Goggle Eye), Kim Chiu Kok (Sam Lee), Mawuyul Yanthalawuy (Rosie), Cecil Parkee (Cheon), Brian Granrott (Neaves), Danny Adcock (Brown), John Cameron (Jimmy Dodd), Sibina Willy (Bett Bett), Jessie Roberts (Nellie), Christine Conway (Judy), Ray Pattison (Johnny Wakelin), George Jadarku (Charly), Sally McKenzie (Carrie), Sarah Craig (Liz), Fincina Hopgood (Dot), Lise Rodgers (Friend 1), Dayle Alison (Friend 2), Jenni Cunningham (Friend 3); and the people of Bamyili, Djembere, Beswick, Roper Valley and Ngukkur.

We of the Never Never revives the story of Jeannie Gunn, who in 1901 left Melbourne to live with her pioneer husband in Australia's Northern Territory. The story is by no means astonishing from a historical point of view. Mrs Gunn was, after all, an ordinary woman making do in adverse and isolated surroundings as many non-Aboriginal women did before her during the gold rushes and squatting era.

We of the Never Never rightly avoids any claims to seminal importance, which is why it is able to so effectively recreate Mrs Gunn's diaries of her one cathartic year on the frontier. The casting of Angela Punch McGregor as Mrs Gunn is as interesting as it is affecting. She is at once a woman clinging on to the niceties of her Victorian heritage; later, and largely through her empathy with local Aborigines, the Englishness of her old persona gives way to the subtle emergence of someone new – the Australian outback woman.

Arthur Dignam excels as Aeneas Gunn, the manager of the station which becomes home to him and his new wife. It is difficult to imagine too many actors who could match Dignam's reserved emotional range before the camera. His quiet, self-doubting air is also important to the film because it offsets the monosyllabic roughness of the station hands (played by Tommy Lewis, Tony Barry and Lewis Fitz-Gerald).

The film takes up with the Gunns on their 'honeymoon' journey to the Northern Territory. Right from the moment the newly-weds step off a train into a torrential downpour, director Igor Auzins does well to avoid the outback clichés perpetrated in some films. The film, which was shot where the Gunns' story unfolded at Elsey Station near Katherine, pays careful attention to the nuances of the land, its textures, moods and sounds. The late Gary Hansen won an AFI award for his photography on the film, and his use of natural lighting is at times brilliant.

Hansen's work helps build some of the film's most memorable moments. A Christmas Day celebration on the verandah of the Gunn homestead is portrayed in vivid, affectionate detail. Hansen's skill also adds a surreal dimension to a camp-fire discussion that becomes one of the most potent scenes in the film.

We of the Never Never pays as much attention to its characters as it does to their surroundings. The characters are able to take form through a rich and often humorous script, which plays upon the idiomatic language of the 'Capricornia' region.

The film documents the Australian Aboriginal experience at a crucial period, and seems to make a genuine effort to give its black characters a meaningful voice. The Aborigines at Elsey Station still nurture their primitive links with the land but the link is weakening because of their vulnerability to the interference and influence of white Europeans. The subject is handled sensitively without shirking things as they really were.

We of the Never Never is a wonderful-looking film that covers plenty of emotional terrain without getting maudlin. Best of all, it never loses sight of telling the story of ordinary people in somewhat extraordinary circumstances.

GREG KERR

References:
'Angela Punch McGregor', an interview with the actor by Jim Schembri, *Cinema Papers*, no. 49, December, 1984, pp. 418–21, 471.
'We of the Never Never', a review by Almos Maksay, ibid., pp. 422–4, 472.
'Peter Schreck', an interview with the scriptwriter by Jim Schembri, *Cinema Papers*, no. 50, February–March 1985, pp. 34–7, 84.
'We of the Never Never', a short review by Kathe Boehringer, *Filmnews*, November–December 1982, p. 25.

Jeannie Gunn (Angela Punch McGregor) is 'admired' by Rosie (Mawuyul Yanthalawuy) and other tribal Aborigines.

ESBEN STORM

WITH PREJUDICE

[No opening production company credit.] © 1982 Sirocco Visual Programming Pty. Ltd. *Budget:* $250,000. *Location:* Sydney. *Australian distributor:* AFI. *Video:* Ronin (AFI Collection). *Rating:* M. 16mm. 72 mins.

Producer: Don Catchlove. *Executive producer:* Jim George. *Scriptwriter:* Leon Saunders. *Director of photography:* Peter Levy. *Production designer:* Bob Hill. *Standby wardrobe:* Lyn Askew. *Editors:* Michael Norton, Peter Fletcher. *Composer:* Ralph Tyrrell. *Sound recordist:* Mark Lewis. [*Sound editors:* not credited.] [*Mixer:* not credited.]

Cast

Scott Burgess [Ross Dunn[1]], John Ley [Tim Anderson], Terry Serio [Paul Alister], David Slingsby [Richard Seary], Max Cullen [Krawczyk], Richard Moir [Middleton], Chris Haywood [Rogerson], Tony Barry [Adams, Defence for Dunn], David Downer [Eindfeld, Defence for Anderson], Phillip Hinton [Gregory, Crown Prosecutor], Paul Sonkila[2] [Gilligan], Peter Whitford [Bodor, Defence for Anderson], Leslie Dayman [Shadbolt, Defence for Alister], Redmond Phillips [Nagle, Judge], Ian Nimo [O'Brien], Brian McDermott [Howard], Kevin Healey [Perrin], Robert Noble [Cook], John Clayton [Burke], Tim McKenzie [Tueno][3].

With Prejudice is a dramatisation of the trial in 1979 of Paul Alister, Timothy Anderson and Ross Dunn for conspiracy to murder Robert Campbell, leader of the National Alliance. The accused were all members of the Ananda Marga, which the press and the judicial system successfully portrayed as a fanatical religious cult bent on violent revolution.[4]

The trial is a classic instance of Australian justice denied, where a police informer's frame-up convinced a jury and sent three innocent men to gaol. It took many years for the legal system to correct the wrong, and this dramatised documentary, made for television but gaining a theatrical release, was a significant contributor in bringing the case to greater public light.

As detailed in the film, the prosecution's case is based largely on the testimony of Richard Seary[5] (David Slingsby), the informer who had infiltrated the sect. Seary claims he drove Dunn and Alister to Campbell's house with the clear intention of bombing Campbell and, if need be, his family. Short of their destination, however, they were arrested by the police who had been alerted by Seary. (Throughout all this Anderson was at the sect's headquarters.)

The only material evidence of any worth is a blue bag containing a bomb taken from the back seat of the car, and the two letters in Anderson's jacket which allegedly set forth the sect's revolutionary agenda. As well, there are the police notes of interviews which claim to record accurately the mad revolutionary ravings of the accused.

It is stated near the start of this dramatisation that all the dialogue 'has been taken from a transcript of that trial', which is a clear attempt on director Esben Storm's part to give the film an aura of objectivity. But that statement is misleading for several reasons. How does one know that the many dramatic recreations outside the courtroom are a fair and objective interpretation of the spoken evidence? Equally, how much can one trust in the actors' representations of their characters? Is the emphasis on certain words, the facial gestures, the twitching hands, accurate and fair?

Richard Seary, for one, is portrayed as a slimy, near certifiable, (former?) drug addict with psychotic delusions of grandeur. Likewise, the police are rendered as collusive, corrupt and brutal, with a clear enthusiasm for framing the innocent.

All this may have a solid basis in reality, but it undermines the drama. The bad guys are so sinister, the accused so stoically good, that the audience has little choice but to read the proceedings as a paranoia piece about 'us' and 'them'. Storm even shows Seary, after the trials, carrying a blue bag under his arm, just like the one that contained the bomb.

This cannot possibly be based on the trial record, so one has to ask when that implied guarantee of truthfulness expired?

With Prejudice has many parallels with Fred Schepisi's Evil Angels (1988): both examine serious failings of the judicial system, catalysed by public and media distrust of religious cults. But whereas Schepisi explores society's participation in that miscarriage, Storm sees the Ananda Marga error as purely the result of police corruption. The way he presents the case is such that no sane man or woman could have proclaimed the men guilty.

This raises a related issue: Why does Storm recreate the February trial, which was aborted, and not the retrial which resulted in the guilty verdicts? Showing one trial but asking the audience to distrust the verdict of a quite different one is simply disingenuous, yet another example of pejorative in a film with pretensions to objectivity, but only propaganda at its heart.

SCOTT MURRAY

---

1 There are no character names on the credits. These are taken from a press sheet.
2 Usually spelt 'Sonkkilla'.
3 There are no credits on the video copy of the film suplied by the director for John Clayton and Tim McKenzie.
4 The sect would always claim the only revolution it was interested in was spiritual.
5 See footnote 1.
6 See footnote 1.

Paul Alister [6] *(Terry Serio), Tim Anderson (John Ley) and Ross Dunn (Scott Burgess).*

THE YEAR OF LIVING DANGEROUSLY

Metro–Goldwyn–Mayer presents A Freddie Fields Presentation [of] A McElroy & McElroy Production. THE YEAR OF [/] LIVING DANGEROUSLY. © 1982 MGM/UA Entertainment Co. *Budget:* $6 million. *Location:* Manila (The Philippines). *Australian distributor:* UIP. *Video:* MGM/UA Home Video. *Rating:* M (December 1982; 3211m). Panavision. 35mm. 117 mins.

Producer: Jim McElroy. *Scriptwriters:* David Williamson, Peter Weir, C. J. Koch.[1] Based on the novel by C. J. Koch. *Director of photography:* Russell Boyd. *Camera operator:* Nixon Binney. *Design co-ordinator:* Wendy Weir. *Production designer:* Herbert Pinter. *Costume designer:* Terry Ryan. *Editor:* William Anderson. *Composer:* Maurice Jarre. *Sound recordist:* Gary Wilkins. *Sound editor:* Andrew Steuart. *Mixers:* Peter Fenton (dia.), Phil Heywood (fx), Gethin Creagh (music).

Cast

Mel Gibson (Guy Hamilton), Sigourney Weaver (Jill Bryant), Linda Hunt (Billy Kwan), Bill Kerr (Colonel Henderson), Noel Ferrier (Wally O'Sullivan), Paul Sonkkila (Kevin Condon), Bembol Roco (Kumar), Kuh Ledesma (Tiger Lily), Domingo Landicho (Hortono), Cecily Polson (Moira), Michael Murphy (Pete Curtis), Hermino de Guzman (Immigration Officer), Ali Nur (Ali), Joel Agona (Palace Guard), Mike Emperio (Sukarno), Bernardo Nacilla (Dwarf), Coco Marantha (Pool Waiter), Norma Uatuhan (Ibu), Lito Tolentino (Udin), David Oyang (Hadji), Mark Egerton (Embassy Aide), Joonee Gamba (Naval Officer), Pudji Waseso (Officer in Café), Joel Lamangan (Security Man No. 1), Mario Layo (Security Man No. 2), Jabo Djohansjan (Doctor), Agus Widjaja (Roadblock Soldier), Chris Quivak (Airport Official).

The Year of Living Dangerously marks a turning point in the career of director Peter Weir. Following this film, he made a break for the US, from where he has worked ever since. Up to the time of the film's release, Weir's work had been notable for its penetrating insight into aspects of Australia's cultural heritage, in particular his ability to hone in on bizarre and extreme elements in films such as **The Cars That Ate Paris** (1974), **Picnic at Hanging Rock** (1975) and **The Last Wave** (1977), films which created much attention both locally and overseas.

With **The Year of Living Dangerously**, taken from a novel by C. J. Koch, Weir appeared to deviate somewhat from his earlier work. Certainly the film's setting –

Jill Bryant (Sigourney Weaver) and Guy Hamilton (Mel Gibson).

Indonesia during the Sukarno crisis – suggests his interests were changing, at least on the surface. However, Weir's fascination with the individual pitted against a transient world (a theme he would explore consistently in the US) is particularly pronounced here.

In **The Year of Living Dangerously**, Weir has been coupled with a largely American central cast, including Mel Gibson, who was almost re-Americanised by then. In this context, the film can be seen to embody an American approach, particularly as the politically violent place appears to become 'background', for a while at least, to the developing romance of the central characters.

However, where much American cinema that addresses the Western presence in Asia and the Third World opts for a romantic element, and ending, Weir's film creates a see-saw effect as the narrative swings between romance and political turmoil.

Weir's interests go beyond the level of day-to-day existence, breaching 'other realms' that characterise his earlier work: characters forced to deal with situations they can't comprehend, or worlds that are alien. From this background, Weir draws out people who are freakish (Linda Hunt playing a male Indonesian photographer whose knowledge of the 'events' is, ultimately, the most dangerous weapon anyone can have) or committed to something they don't

understand (Mel Gibson as an ABC foreign correspondent) or simply an array of Western low-lifes (diplomats, embassy personnel and journalists awash in a sea of alcohol and cynicism, and a determination to maintain their own Western standards).

In this respect, Weir's ability to penetrate character to perceive and portray a darker, foreboding side of human nature is fundamental to any reading of his films. The politics of that year are thus rendered secondary (although it should be said that the film does not surrender to a complete romantic sell-out at the end). These are characters who lived dangerously and managed to survive. What remains is the unerring sense that part of them was left behind.

PETER LAWRANCE

---

[1] See letter from. C. J. Koch in *Cinema Papers* over the script credit dispute (see References).

References
'Letter to Editor', by the scriptwriter C. J. Koch, *Cinema Papers*, no. 42, March 1983, p. 10.
'Mel Gibson', an interview with the actor by Margaret Smith, ibid., pp. 12–17.
'The Year of Living Dangerously', a review by Debi Enker, ibid., pp. 64–5.
'The Year of Living Dangerously', a short review by Peter Kemp, *Filmnews*, January–February 1983, p. 17.

BMX BANDITS

BUDDIES

BUSH CHRISTMAS

THE CLINIC

DOUBLE DEAL

DUSTY

FIGHTING BACK

GOING DOWN

GOODBYE PARADISE

HOSTAGE: THE CHRISTINE MARESCH
    STORY

KITTY AND THE BAGMAN

MAN OF FLOWERS

MIDNITE SPARES

MOLLY

MOVING OUT

NOW AND FOREVER

PHAR LAP

THE RETURN OF CAPTAIN INVINCIBLE

SARAH

SUMNER LOCKE ELLIOTT'S CAREFUL
    HE MIGHT HEAR YOU

Lila (Robyn Nevin). Carl Schultz's Sumner
Locke Elliott's Careful He Might Hear You.

BMX BANDITS

Nilsen Premiere presents BMX BANDITS. © 1983 BMX Bandits Pty Ltd. *Location:* Sydney's nothern beaches. *Australian distributor:* Filmways. *Video:* K-Tel. *Rating:* G (*video:* February 1984). 35mm. 91 mins.

Producers: Tom Broadbridge, Paul F. Davies. *Associate producer:* Brian D. Burgess. *Scriptwriter:* Patrick Edgeworth. Based on a screenplay by Russell Hagg. *Director of photography:* John Seale. *Production designer:* Ross Major. *Wardrobe mistress:* Lesley McLennan. *Editor:* Alan Lake. *Composers:* Colin Stead, Frank Strangio. *Sound recordist:* Ken Hammond. *Sound editor:* Andrew Steuart. *Mixers:* Gethin Creagh, Phil Judd.

Cast

David Argue (Whitey), John Ley (Moustache), Nicole Kidman (Judy), Angelo D'Angelo (P. J.), James Lugton (Goose), Bryan Marshall ("The Boss"), Brian Sloman (The Creep), Peter Brown (Police Constable), Bill Brady (Police Sergeant), Linda Newton (Policewoman), Bob Hicks (Heavy 1), Guy Norris (Heavy 2), Chris Hession (Heavy 3), Norman Hodges (The Drunk), Tracy Wallace (Buxom Lady), Michael Gillette (Vicar), Brian Best (Supermarket Manager), Jerry D'Angelo (Boy 1), Malcolm Day (Boy 2), Ray Marshall (Foreman), Patrick Mansfield (Crane Driver), Alan McQueen (Workman).

Goose (James Lugton), Judy (Nicole Kidman) and P. J. (Angelo D'Angelo).

The opening establishing shot of BMX Bandits is a typical panorama of a North Sydney beach suburb. The image then jumps to a stylised montage of close-up detail, as a young BMX rider straps on his gear and launches himself into the world.

This wonderful beginning places the film firmly in the tradition of those teen movies worldwide which are about ordinary, suburban kids 'working' their city, intimately knowing its streets, escape routes, nooks and crannies. The downbeat reality of workaday suburban life is thus played off against the momentary, ecstatic 'transcendence' provided by bike riding. (For an American treatment of this theme, compare Tom Donnelly's **Quicksilver**, 1986.)

The film relates to a teen road-movie tradition inaugurated by **American Graffiti** (George Lucas, 1973), rather than the 'high energy' teen movies of John Hughes. It shows teenagers not in the home but perennially 'cruising' streets, diners and secret haunts. A special feature of this tradition is the affectionate, whimsical, slightly radical emphasis on the open, shifting 'group' relations of people in their early teens, as distinct from the one-on-one sexual attachments of later

adult life. As Judy (Nicole Kidman) says of her friendship with P. J. (Angelo D'Angelo) and Goose (James Lugton), 'You know what they say: two's company, three gets us talked about.'

Like most of Brian Trenchard-Smith's films, it is fast, well-modulated and very economically devised. The central narrative device (again familiar from teen road movies like **The Legend of Billie Jean**, Matthew Robins, 1985) is a simple communications gadget (the walkie-talkie) which links all the characters, allowing them to 'cover' their town. Since their signal can also be picked up by the police and villains alike, the 'action-adventure' moves in the story are extremely well articulated, setting up several thrilling chase sequences.

One of the most notable and pleasurable aspects of the film is the way it weaves references to movies, television and popular culture into the integral fabric of the story. Early on, Goose relates his love of gory 'horror road movies', cueing a comic-eerie chase scene set in a cemetery at night. Later, Judy

invents a hilarious pastiche of teen horror movies in order to distract her captors. And many of the film's 'bad guys' – whether criminals or cranky, unjust bosses at suburban worksites – seem culled from British television, a source cued by the *Minder* T-shirt worn by Whitey (David Argue). This perceptive mix of American and British pop culture references is rare in Australian cinema.

As in many a teen movie, the tone is kept light, whether a scene is devoted to bloodless action, mild slapstick comedy or 'innocently' romantic character interaction. Such lightness of tone has, of course, consigned **BMX Bandits** to critical oblivion as a mere 'kids' film' lacking drama or meaning. Yet, appreciated as a teen movie, it is intricate, entertaining and often disarming. Within its own terms, it is one of the most perfectly realised Australian films of the 1980s.

ADRIAN MARTIN

---

[1] There is no director's credit, just 'A Film by Brian Trenchard-Smith'.

BUDDIES

J. D. Productions presents BUDDIES. © 1983 J. D. Productions Pty. Ltd. *Locations:* Emerald, Rubyvale (Queensland). Produced with the assistance of the Queensland Film Corporation. *Australian distributor:* J. D. Productions. *Video:* not known. *Rating:* PG. 35mm. Panavision. 97 mins.

Producer: John Dingwall. *Associate producer:* Brian D. Burgess. *Scriptwriter:* John Dingwall. *Director of photography:* David Eggby. *Camera operator:* Clive Duncan. *Production designer:* Philip Warner. *Costume designer:* Jane Hyland. *Editor:* Martyn Down. *Composer:* Chris Neal. *Sound recordist:* Peter Barker. *Sound editors:* Marc Van Buuren; Karin Whittington (asst.). *Mixer:* Julian Ellingworth.

Cast

Colin Friels (Mike), Harold Hopkins (Johnny), Kris McQuade (Stella), Norman Kaye (George), Bruce Spence (Ted), Dennis Miller (Andy), Dinah Shearing (Merl), Simon Chilvers (Alfred), Lisa Peers (Jennifer), Andrew Sharp (Peter), Rob Steele (Policeman), Ralph Albring (Hans), Bob Hicks (Gorilla); Hermie De Guzman, Michael Anderson (Thai Buyers); John Millroy (Clerk), Rhonda Carling-Rogers (Andy's Woman), Michael Terry (Nick), Kevin Dean (Bus Driver), Jack Gorman (Sam), Allan Kemp (Musician at Pub).

John Dingwall's excellent screenplay for **Sunday Too Far Away** (Ken Hannam, 1975) should have made his next projects bankable, but **Buddies** had a very tough time. First set in South Australia's opal fields, it finally found a home years later in central Queensland's sapphire country around Emerald.

Mike (Colin Friels) and Johnny (Harold Hopkins) are buddies, sharing the same tin hut and small sapphire claim. Theirs is a typically Australian male closeness, which the arrival of a girl, Jennifer (Lisa Peers), inevitably destroys.

They are also likeable battlers who take on and, if not beat, at least hold at bay the mean-spirited bigger guys. The worst is Andy (Dennis Miller), who represents the future: bulldozers instead of shovels, and market manipulation to improve profitability. Unlike **Sunday Too Far Away**, where Dingwall's Aussie heroes refuse to play the capitalist game and go on strike, Mike is a more likely lad who plays the same games as Andy.

This is made abundantly clear not only in the scenes of price rigging, but in the battle over the new claim. Mike arrives with Johnny to stake a bit of land, only to find most of it already staked. They move to one side and start pegging there, but Andy comes along and orders them off the site. Mike says he got there first, but the existing pegs clearly prove Andy did. Mike is blatantly in the wrong, yet the film asks one to side with him, even down to cheering him and Johnny when they blow up the watertank and other targets around Andy's house.

If this isn't puzzling enough, the film indulges in some pedestrian anti-intellectualism. Jennifer (Lisa Peers) dumps her academic boyfriend, Peter (Andrew Sharp), for Mike after she sees Mike being a real man by driving a bulldozer half-naked. (Similarly, the film sneers at Jennifer's middle-class mother for looking down on these hard-working, if crude, Aussie lads.)

The film has a few loose ends and some rather careless direction. For example, after a rather tedious drunk-pilot sequence, Nicholson cuts to two of Mike's mates watching the plane spin on the bush runway, even though it is several forested miles away from where they are standing. Likewise, Mike is appallingly rude to Stella (Kris McQuade) for being jealous of Jennifer, saying, 'I'm tired of the performance', yet Stella could hardly have made a habit of it as Jennifer and her family are the first visitors in some time.

These and other moments aside, the film has a cheery charm, helped greatly by another winning performance from Colin Friels. The dialogue is spiced with some crisp lines and the various partings at the bus stop are rather touching. It is a great pity the film continues on with an exceedingly dull fight between two bulldozers.

SCOTT MURRAY

Reference
'Buddies', Tom O'Regan, *Filmnews*, January–February 1984, p. 7.

Mike (Colin Friels) and close friend Johnny (Harold Hopkins).

BUSH CHRISTMAS

Barron Films presents BUSH CHRISTMAS. © 1983 Barron Films Limited[,] Bush Christmas Productions Limited and the Unitholders of 'Bush Christmas'. Developed with the assistance of the Australian Film Commission, in association with the Film and Television Institute (W.A.) Inc. Produced in association with the Queensland Film Corporation. *Location:* Beaudesert Shire (Queensland). *Australian distributor:* Hoyts. *Opened:* December 1983. *Video:* Kids Classics. *Rating:* G (2486m). Super16 (blown up to 35mm). 91 mins.

Producers: Gilda Baracchi, Paul Barron. *Executive producer:* Paul Barron. *Scriptwriter:* Ted Roberts. Based on the Rank Organization's original film, Bush Christmas [Ralph Smart, 1947]. *Director of photography:* Malcolm Richards. *Production designer:* Darrell Lass. *Wardrobe:* Utopia Road. *Editor:* Ron Williams. *Composer:* Mike Perjanik, featuring "The Bushwackers". *Sound recordists:* Don Connolly; Phil Judd (post-synch). *Sound editor:* Penn Robertson. *Mixer:* Julian Ellingworth.

Cast

John Ewart (Bill), John Howard (Sly), Mark Spain (John Thompson), James Wingrove (Michael), Peter Sumner (Ben Thompson), Nicole Kidman (Helen Thompson), Manalpuy (Manalpuy), Vineta O'Malley (Kate Thompson), Maurice Hughes (Carrol); Roger Corbet, Michael Harris, Luis McManus, Dobe Newton, Anthony O'Neill, Fred Strauks (The Bushwackers Band); Bob Hunt (Jack), Brian Thompson (Bookmaker), Liam Maloney (Derby Mulcahy).

Bush Christmas is set in the Australian outback during the early 1950s and the simple story consists of two strands. The first concerns the mortgage debt of Ben (Peter Sumner) and Kate Thompson (Vineta O'Malley), a debt which must be paid by the first day of January or the Thompsons will lose their homestead to the local stock-and-station agent.

The second strand, which occupies the bulk of the film and dovetails with the first, follows the activities of Bill (John Ewart) and Sly (John Howard), the manager and lead singer of a struggling bush band. Stranded and broke after the Christmas dance in Tullageal, the two rogues decide to 'borrow' the Thompsons' prize racehorse and enter it in country-race circuits in an effort to recoup their fortunes. However, the two Thompson children, Helen (Nicole Kidman) and John (Mark Spain), together with their British cousin, Michael (James Wingrove), and Aboriginal hand, Manalpuy (Manalpuy), decide to follow the thieves, while Ben Thompson is away attempting to sell cattle to raise the mortgage.

The bulk of the film cuts back and forth between the largely comic attempts of Sly and Bill to cross the ranges with the horses and the desperate attempts of the four youths to follow them. Their trek climaxes when Manalpuy, Michael and Helen fall into a deserted mine shaft which soon becomes flooded. The last section of the film, after the recapture of the horses, deals with the last-ditch attempt by the Thompsons to raise money by racing their horse in the New Year's Day cross-country race.

Within the essentially 19th-century melodramatic conventions of the story, scriptwriter Ted Roberts has injected a consistent stream of humour, largely focusing on the relationship between Sly and Bill. Sly, in particular, has a number of very funny lines, with one of the best being his horrified reaction that Bill's killing of a bush rabbit will antagonise the Aborigines watching their progress ('You've shot one of their pets'). There are also some nice throwaway lines, such as Howard muttering 'Taxi!' as he stumbles through the dense bush. Even the children share in the comedy, particularly that potential scene-stealer Mark Spain as John, who downs a witchetty grub with relish as his conservative British cousin is heard retching off-screen.

Credit must go to director Henri Safran, and director of photography Malcolm Richards. Their expertise is particularly evident in the climactic cross-country race which is captured largely in longshot during the first half, reserving the close-ups of jockey Manalpuy and Prince to generate excitement and tension during the closing part. Similarly, this expertise is obvious when the children stumble upon a supposedly deserted shack and find a couple of unwelcome visitors, and again when they are trapped in the mine shaft. In fact, it permeates the entire film.

Bush Christmas retains interest throughout with a deft blend of humour, action and attractive characterisations.

GEOFF MAYER[1]

---

[1] Extracted from Mayer's review in *Cinema Papers* (see References).

References

'**Bush Christmas** and **Molly**', a joint review by Geoff Mayer, *Cinema Papers*, no. 44–5, April 1984, pp. 88–9.

'**Bush Christmas**', a review by Penny Davies, *Filmnews*, November–December 1983, p. 17.

Manalpuy (Manalpuy) and Helen Thompson (Nicole Kidman) search for the thieves.

THE CLINIC

The Film House & Generation Films present THE CLINIC. © 1982 The Film House and Generation Films. *Budget:* $1 million. *Location:* Melbourne. *Australian distributor:* Roadshow. *Video:* Australian Video. *Rating:* M (July 1982; 2550.99m). 35mm. 93 mins.

Producers: Robert Le Tet, Bob Weis. *Scriptwriter:* Greg Millin. *Director of photography:* Ian Baker. *Production designer:* Tracy Watt. *Wardrobe:* Rose Chong. *Editor:* Edward McQueen-Mason. *Music director:* Redmond Symons. *Sound recordist:* John Rowley. *Sound editors:* Terry Rodman, Frank Lipson, Peter Burgess. *Mixer:* Roger Savage.

Cast

Chris Haywood [Dr Eric Linden[1]], Simon Burke [Paul Armstrong], Gerda Nicolson [Linda], Rona McLeod [Dr Carol Young], Suzanne Roylance [Pattie], Veronica Lang [Nancy], Pat Evison [Alda], Max Bruch [Hassad], Gabrielle Hartley [Gillian], Jane Clifton [Sharon], Ned Lander [Warwick], Martin Sharman [Carl], Tom Travers [Phil], Tony Rickards [Chris], Mark Little [Basil], Betty Bobbitt [Wilma], Marilyn O'Donnell [Simone], Geoff Parry [Charlie], Laurence Mah [Sun Ho], Paul Kuek [Hi Choong], Danny Nash [Hippy], Alan Pentland [Bill].

Dr Eric Linden[3] (Chris Haywood) instructs Pattie (Suzanne Roylance), a nursing sister.

The Clinic takes the unlikely subject of a day spent in a clinic for the treatment of venereal disease and other sexual problems. It focuses on the four doctors, the ancillary staff, a medical student visiting for the day and a bevy of patients, perhaps a couple of dozen in all.

Paul Armstrong[2] (Simon Burke) is the medical student, young, priggish and very unsure of himself. He very quickly reveals a degree of homophobia. He sits in with Eric Linden (Chris Haywood), a blasé young doctor who has seen it all and is as relaxed as Paul is tense, except for having a giant hangover.

There are two other doctors: an Indian, Hassad (Max Bruch), and Dr Carol Young (Rona McLeod), a young woman going through some marital discord because her husband does not want children. The group is completed by a kindly woman counsellor, Alda (Pat Evison).

The plot consists of vignette after vignette from the patients, with the petty dramas of the staff each coming to some resolution. (One patient commits suicide and there is a bomb threat from some lunatic religious fundamentalist, which at one stage forces the building to be emptied.)

A film of no over-reaching ambition, **The Clinic** is refreshingly comic in its approach, building its lines and gags straight out of personal experience, but never causing the characters to fall into slapstick situations nor allowing the audience to indulge in any sense of nudging superiority. It never resorts to innuendo or bad taste, and its ability to allow the audience to share a joke is quite remarkable.

This refreshingly direct but comic approach causes the film to be entirely non-judgemental about any predicament presented no matter what it might relate to. We are not sniggering as we hear of disease, impotence, ejaculation and erection – all the anxieties of the male (of all preferences) and many of those of the female – casually and honestly revealed. We can accept quite easily a homosexual's throwaway parting words to a worried female patient as she goes off to consult the doctor, 'Here's looking up you kid', for exactly what it is: a superbly timed and delivered one-line joke. And there are a lot more equally well-delivered exchanges, jokes and bits of banter.

Confined in its space, cutting between characters with virtually no introduction or transition, **The Clinic** employs the methods of television soap opera and simply asks the audience to hang on as it breathlessly rushes through its narrative. This involves a risk because it might seem flimsy, as if the film is all middle and no end, even with the very minor revelation of Paul's own problem being solved (a sequence preceded by a wonderful joke involving Eric and a pub toilet, one that the audience picks up on very quickly.) It has few false moves, perhaps confined only to the medical student's rather-too-sudden conversion to tolerance.

GEOFF GARDNER

---

[1] No character names are given in the opening or closing credits. These are taken from *Monthly Film Bulletin.*
[2] See footnote 1.
[3] See footnote 1.

References

'Voyages of Discovery', an interview with director David Stevens by Debi Enker, *Cinema Papers*, no. 44–5, April 1984, pp. 10–15, 106.
'The Clinic', a review by Debi Enker, ibid., pp. 92–4.
'The Clinic', a short review by Peter Kemp, *Film-news*, March 1983, p. 17.

DOUBLE DEAL

A Rychemond Film. DOUBLE DEAL[1]. ©
1981 Rychemond Film Productions. *Budget:*
$1 million. *Location:* Melbourne. *Australian
distributor:* Roadshow. *Video:* Roadshow
Home Video. *Rating:* M. 35mm. Panavision.
90 mins.

Producers: Brian Kavanagh, Lynn Barker.
Associate producer: Carlie Deans. *Script-
writer:* Brian Kavanagh. *Director of
photography:* Ross Berryman. *Production
designer:* Jill Eden. *Wardrobe:* Anna Jakab;
Pat Forster (for Angela Punch McGregor).
Editor: Tim Lewis. *Composer:* Bruce
Smeaton. *Sound recordist:* John Phillips.
Sound editors: Dean Gawen; Frank Lipson
(asst). [*Mixer:* not credited.]

Cast

Louis Jourdan (Peter Sterling), Angela
Punch McGregor (Christine Sterling), Diane
Craig (Miss Stevens), Warwick Comber
(Young Man), Peter Cummins (Detective
Mills), Bruce Spence (Doug Mitchell), June
Jago (Mrs Coolidge), Kerry Walker (Sibyl
Anderson), Joan Letch (Mum), Danee
Lindsay (Junior Secretary), Sean Myers
(Freddie), Robin Cumming (James), Harold
Baigent (Sir Henry), Kerry Daniel (Doug's
Girl), Brenda Beddison (Old Lady), Don
Bridges (Station Assistant).

Fashion model Christine Sterling (Angela
Punch McGregor) is bored with her
marriage to rich businessman Peter (Louis
Jourdan) and ripe for any sexual adventure.
As the film establishes this situation, we are
also informed of the presence, via a series of
quick cuts to a parallel action, of a mysterious silver-suited, motorbike-riding Young
Man (Warwick Comber), who is clearly up
to no good.

After stealing a Rolls-Royce, the Young
Man tracks Christine to her home, then induces her to run away with him and, shortly
thereafter, has her join him in robbing a post
office. From here on the film follows a series
of double- and triple-crosses between the
Young Man, Peter, Christine and Peter's secretary, Miss Stevens (Diane Craig), and the
audience is treated to a guessing game as to
who is manipulating whom.

These are the elements of the British
whodunnit, a genre stretching back to the
beginning of narrative cinema and here re-
assembled somewhat lethargically with
hardly a nod to the shock, frisson-producing,
tactics applied in the best films of their kind.
(Terence Young's **Wait Until Dark**, 1967,
Joseph L. Mankiewicz's **Sleuth**, 1972, and
Richard Fleischer's **Blind Terror**, 1971, spring
to mind as good examples.)

Christine Sterling (Angela Punch McGregor) in disguise.

Double Deal lumbers through its plot
with a reasonable degree of efficiency but
with increasing implausibility. As a result, it
fails to involve its audience or invite any sense
of complicity with Christine's plight. It simply doesn't deliver the shocks and surprises
necessary to keep the viewer guessing,
whether these be through the introduction
of some black humour or some real terror.
Such elements would seem essential to keep
the audience interested in guessing as to who
is doing what to whom, up to an ending
which neatly explains 'why'.

There are some incidental pleasures,
however, most notably the final shots of the
film with Peter and Christine inadvertently
and silently reconciling on a train ride home,
both abandoned by their accomplices and
each able to manage a half smile as they face
the prospects of a future apparently to be
shared despite their new-found knowledge of
each other's behaviour. As well, there is Peter
Cummins as Detective Mills, an archetypal
Inspector Plod laboriously chasing up 'clues'
and, for the most part, keeping his Akubra
hat on indoors.

GEOFF GARDNER

---

[1] The title is repeated upside down so that the
four words make a square. One could argue,
therefore, that the correct title is **Double Deal
Double Deal**.

References

'Bob Saunders', an interview with the man behind
Pact Productions, one of the film's investors,
by Peter Beilby, *Cinema Papers*, no. 31, March–
April 1980, pp. 26–9, 100.
'Angela Punch McGregor', an interview with the
actor by Jim Schembri, *Cinema Papers*, no. 49,
December, 1984, pp. 418–21, 471.

DUSTY

Kestrel Films (Australia) in association with Dusty Productions presents Dusty. © 1982 Dusty Productions. *Australian distributor:* Filmways. *Opened:* 1 April 1983. *Video:* K-Tel. *Rating:* G (July 1982; 2413.84m). 35 mm. 88 mins.

Producer: Gil Brealey. *Associate producer:* David Morgan. *Scriptwriter:* Sonia Borg. Based on the novel by Frank Dalby Davison. *Director of photography:* Alex McPhee. *Editor:* David Greig. *Production designer:* Robbie Perkins. *Wardrobe:* May Harris. *Composer:* Frank Strangio. *Sound recordist:* John Phillips. *Sound editors:* Louise Johnson, Steve Lambeth. *Mixer:* John Phillips.

Cast

Bill Kerr (Tom Lincoln), Noel Trevarthen (Harry Morrison), Carol Burns (Clara Morrison), John Stanton (Railey Jordan), Nick Holland (Jack Morrison), Dan Lynch (Ron Morrison), Kati Edwards (Mrs Muspratt), Will Kerr (Jim Logan), Ed Thurley (Fred Patterson), Mary Howlett (Mrs Patterson), Peter Aanensen (Mr Brownless), Pam Murphy (Mrs Brownless), Reg Gorman (Watson), Nevil Thurgood (Arch Jackson), Kim Trengrove (Barmaid), Andrea Butcher (Sally), Terry Trimble (Commentator); Phillip Day, Andrew Clement (Shearers): John Stanton [Reader of Prologue].

Dusty is something of a surprise. With its unpretentious style, this gently paced feature emerges as a significant contribution to those films that tackle aspects of Australian bushlore.

In his novel, *Dusty*, Frank Dalby Davison touches on universal themes: the relationship between man and animal, and man's attitude to the environment. He has a deep empathy for his animal and human characters, and director John Richardson remains faithful to that spirit. As in *Man-Shy*, much of the story is told from the animal's point of view.

The film's prologue depicts the mating of homestead kelpie and dingo bitch. The dingo bitch is killed by a youth who stumbles on her lair of pups. The surviving pup, in appearance a kelpie, is sold to Tom Lincoln (Bill Kerr), a former drover who now works as a hired hand for sheep farmer Harry Morrison (Noel Trevarthen). Tom trains the pup into a fine, prizewinning sheep dog, highly sought after by the farmers in the district. But it soon becomes apparent that Dusty has also retained the hunting instincts of his dingo mother: he becomes a sheep killer, a menace to the local farmers who

must now remove him. Tom's great attachment to the dog sees him leave the Morrisons and his secure job.

Harry Morrison's son, Jack (Nick Holland), is portrayed as a young man with a love for the land, one drawn to the wisdom and free nature of the ageing Tom. Harry respects Tom as a reliable worker, but measures success in terms of property and family; for him, Tom is essentially an outsider and an example of failure in life. The crisis caused by Dusty affects the relationships among all the central characters: it brings to the surface tensions between father and son, husband and wife (Carol Burns), farmer and hired hand.

Highlights of the film are Bill Kerr's beautifully controlled portrayal of Tom Lincoln and John Stanton as Railey Jordan, the professional dog-hunter. Railey is another complex character of the Australian bush and, in a sense, a younger version of Tom Lincoln: a loner, with a deep knowledge of bushcraft and a feeling for the delicate balances in nature.

But the film belongs mainly, as it should, to Dusty. He is brought to life in a way that does justice to Davison's account. The Dusty of the film was specifically prepared for the rôle for more than 18 months by skilled dog trainer Mary McCrabb.

Richardson's documentary skills are in evidence in his portraits of country life. And director of photography Alex McPhee, working on his first feature, is able to employ the patience and experience gained from his previous work in current affairs and documentaries to capture the atmosphere.

Dusty is a film of understanding, patience, restraint and deep commitment; it touches on the spiritual intimations that lie just beneath the surface of human beings.

ARNOLD ZABLE[1]

---

[1] Extracted from Zable's review in *Cinema Papers* (see Reference).

Reference

'Dusty', a review by Arnold Zable, *Cinema Papers*, no. 43, May–June 1983, pp. 157–8.

Farm-hand Tom Lincoln (Bill Kerr) and his beloved Dusty.

FIGHTING BACK

Adams Packer present[s] A Samson Film. FIGHTING BACK. © 1982 Samson Productions. *Location:* Sydney. *Australian distributor:* Roadshow. *Video:* CEL. *Rating:* M (July 1982; 2726.97m). 35mm. 100 mins.

Producers: Sue Milliken, Tom Jeffrey. *Executive producer:* Phillip Adams. *Scriptwriter:* Michael Cove, Tom Jeffrey. Based on the novel, *Tom*, by John Embling. *Director of photography:* John Seale. *Production designer:* Christopher Webster. *Costume designer:* Robyn Schuurmans. *Editor:* Ron Williams. *Composer:* Colin Stead. *Sound recordist:* Tim Lloyd. *Sound editor:* Les Fiddess. *Mixers:* Peter Fenton, Phil Heywood.

Cast

Lewis Fitz-Gerald (John), Paul Smith (Tom), Kris McQuade (Mrs Goodwood), Caroline Gillmer (Rosemary), Robyn Nevin (Mary), Wyn Roberts (Payne), Ben Gabriel (Moreland), Gillian Jones (English Teacher), Ray Bennett (Headmaster 1), Derek Barnes (Headmaster 2), Don Reid (Fred Spalding), Rob Steele (Truscott), John Darling (Teacher 1), Neil Stevens (Teacher 2), Maurie Fields (Police Sergeant), Anne Haddy (Magistrate), Michael Cove (Jesus Freak), Michael Smith (Lee), Robert Beaven (Sammy), Dave Godden (Mike), Joe Rawson (Jim), Stephen Gray (Drew), Leanne Ellis (Brenda), Stephanie Wishart (Kate).

Michael Caulfield's **Fighting Back** is an earnest, but not wholly successful, attempt to flesh out in cinematic terms the true story of teacher John Embling's fight to reclaim a disturbed boy, told in his book, *Tom*.

Embling, a teacher of remedial English in Melbourne's western suburbs, became concerned about Tom, a surly, aggressive thirteen-year-old who was the despair of his deserted mother. Tom often played truant, was given to violent rages and had already spent six months in a juvenile institution.

The film, Caulfield's first as screen director (he had previously directed for the stage and tutored young actors for screen rôles in **Storm Boy**, **The Chant of Jimmie Blacksmith** and **My Brilliant Career**[1]), transfers the action to the industrial suburbs around Botany Bay, Sydney.

A respectful screenplay, by Michael Cove and co-producer Tom Jeffrey, reflects some of the difficulties the film-makers faced in bringing this disturbing story to the screen.

Probably because Embling – portrayed by Lewis Fitz-Gerald as a young man of gentle fortitude – is reticent about himself in the book (though his ideas on the needs and rights of disturbed children are clear enough), he emerges in the film as little more than a didactic cipher.

On the other hand, Tom, played by young Sydneysider Paul Smith, bursts upon us as a kicking, screaming, scratching bundle of resentments. He is a textbook case of the utterly alienated urban child, product of a broken home who is abused and misunderstood at school, in trouble with the law, loved but at odds with his mother.

The film never quite overcomes this dramatic imbalance between the presentation of its leading characters.

Of the other principal characters, Kris McQuade is highly convincing as the mother. Scenes in which she attempts to explain her helpless frustration are among the most effective in the film, while Robyn Nevin adds a world-weary touch as the school's other remedial teacher.

By contrast, the portrayal of Tom's outbursts and faltering attempts at self-examination are, in the main, unconvincing.

KEITH CONNOLLY

[1] **Storm Boy** (Henri Safran, 1976), **The Chant of Jimmie Blacksmith** (Fred Schepisi, 1978) and **My Brilliant Career** (Gill Armstrong, 1979).

References
'Fighting Back', a review by Jim Schembri, *Cinema Papers*, no. 43, May–June 1983, pp. 161, 163.
'Fighting Back', a short review by Kathe Boehringer, *Filmnews*, April–May 1983, p. 17.

Rosemary (Caroline Gillmer) and John (Lewis Fitz-Gerald) oversee a pillow fight.

GOING DOWN

X Productions presents GOING DOWN. © 1982 X Productions. *Budget:* $400,000. *Location:* Sydney. *Australian distributor:* Haydn Keenan. *Opened:* July 1983. *Video:* Australian Video. *Rating:* M. 16mm. 94 mins.

Producer: Haydn Keenan. *Associate producer:* Julie Barry. *Scriptwriters:* Melissa Woods, Julie Barry, Moira MacLaine-Cross. Based on an original idea by Moira MacLaine-Cross. *Director of photography:* Malcolm Richards. *Camera operator:* Race Gailey. *Production designer:* Melody Cooper. [*Costume designer:* not credited.] *Editor:* Paul Healy. *Music co-ordinator:* Kim Chesire. *Emulated sound:* Andrew Thomas Wilson. *Sound recordist:* Lloyd Carrick. *Soundtrack:* Lloyd Carrick, Little Ashley. *Sound editors:* Little Ashley, Paul Healy, Peter Gailey, Peter Fletcher. *Mixers:* Peter Fenton, Gethin Creagh.

Cast

Tracey Mann (Karli), Vera Plevnik (Jane), Julie Barry (Jackie), Moira MacLaine-Cross (Ellen), Esben Storm (Michael), David Argue (Greg; Trixie), Ian Gilmour (Shadow), Lou Brown (Adam), Mercia Dean-Jones (Ned), Ian Nimmo (John), Henk Johannes (Ian), Michael Callaghan (Boris), Tim Burns (Newlywed Dave), Anna Healy-North (Newlywed Deidre), Richard Brennan (Chemist), Richard Moir (Hotel Night Manager), Ralph Cotterill (Karli's Father), Hugh Keays-Byrne (Bottom the Biker), Julie Allan (The Dealer), Steve J. Spears (Trendy at Party), Barbara Fitzgerald (Policewoman), Leila Burke (Madame).

Haydn Keenan made this film over a number of years, under funding and production conditions that would normally deter tougher mortals. As a result, **Going Down** represented a remarkable landmark in Australian independent film-making. Unfortunately, it is a landmark that few people noticed.

As a film that took its inspiration from inner-city communal households of Australia's 1970s counter-culture – in a considerably more optimistic, less drug-oriented sense than **Pure S...** (Bert Deling, 1975) or **Dogs in Space** (Richard Lowenstein, 1987) – **Going Down** penetrated Australian youth culture with bold disregard for convention.

It combined documentary and *cinéma verité* with Super 8 earthiness, pushing it into areas that are now common to the quick-edited excitement of rock-music film clips. More important, **Going Down** followed its title, watching the gutter and late-night parties through a bottle of vodka.

When the dim light of dawn brings its heartache, headaches and hangovers, the glossy, material world of Sydney seems irrelevant. Indeed, in many ways it is Keenan's determination to describe contemporary Australian life, without the predictable affectations of careerist film-makers looking over their shoulder at their next project, that gives this film bite.

Appearing seriously dated in the 1990s, **Going Down** is one of the independent films that put the true grit of Australian life on the screen in the early 1980s.

That Keenan has not had a prolific career making feature films in Australia represents the failure of the funding establishment to acknowledge the important contribution the Keenans of the Australian film-making community can and should be making.

MARCUS BREEN

Reference

'Going Down', a short review by Ross Gibson, *Filmnews*, July 1983, p. 15.

Jane (Vera Plevnik) and Jackie (Julie Barry) on the town.

GOODBYE PARADISE

Petersham Pictures in association with The NSW Film Corporation present[s] GOODBYE PARADISE. © 1982 Petersham Pictures Pty Ltd. *Budget:* $1.8 million. *Location:* Gold Coast. *Australian distributor:* Filmways. *Video:* Australian Video. *Rating:* M (May 1982; 3291.60m). 35mm. 119 mins.

Producer: Jane Scott. *Scriptwriters:* Bob Ellis, Denny Lawrence. Original idea by Denny Lawrence. *Director of photography:* John Seale. *Camera operator:* Danny Batterham. *Production designer:* George Liddle. *Costume designer:* Kate Duffy. *Editor:* Richard Francis-Bruce. *Composer:* Peter Best. *Sound recordist:* Syd Butterworth. *Sound editor:* Andrew Steuart. *Mixers:* Peter Fenton, Phil Heywood, Gethin Creagh.

Cast

Ray Barrett (Michael Stacey), Robyn Nevin (Kate), Carole Skinner (Landlady), Peter Lawless (Soldier), Lex Marinos (Con), Ray Shaw (Entertainer), Don Pascoe (Les McCredie), Holly Brown (Drag Queen), Kris McQuade (Hooker), Frank Gallacher (Keith), Kate Fitzpatrick (Mrs McCredie), Wallas Eaton (Clyde), Grant Dodwell (Seaworld Boy), Mark Hembrow (Igor), Geoff Healey (Temple Receptionist), Kareen Michelle (Crystal Mountain), Mervyn Drake (Temple Teacher), Hugh Arnold (1st Disciple), Michael Lynch (2nd Disciple), Shawn Thorburn (3rd Disciple), Waverney Ford (Lonely Buffalo), Paul Chubb (Curly), Stew McAllister (Bluey), Jay Jay Bailey (Con's Girlfriend), Janet Scrivener (Kathy), John Benton (Reporter), Ron Mee Lee (Kim Long Sam), Guy Doleman (Quiney).

Goodbye Paradise, one of the most underrated films of the post-1970s revival, begins with one of the hardest-to-master film stylistics: the voice-over. Here it belongs to Michael Stacey (Ray Barrett):

The winter sun was going down on Surfers Paradise. It was my 98th day on the wagon and it didn't feel any better than the 97th. I missed my hip-flask of Johnnie Walker, my ex-wife Jean, my pet dog Somari and my exorbitant salary as Deputy Commissioner of Police. I wasn't sure any more I was cut out to be a writer of controversial exposés of police corruption. At the moment, I couldn't lift the lid off a can of baked beans. I wanted to be 12 years old again and the best spin bowler at Southport High…

This opening introduces the world-wise and -weary tone of the film. It borrows knowingly from the genre standard of a

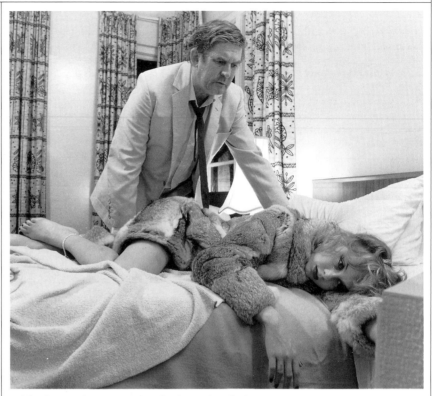

Michael Stacey (Ray Barrett) and a drugged Kathy (Janet Scrivener).

decent man down and out because of evil forces outside his control. Not that he won't fight back…and well.

Most telling is the nostalgic touch about cricket being played at a time when Australia was 'a country I used to be proud of', as Stacey later puts it. In the film, Australia (specifically, Queensland) is a no-man's land of exploitation by developers, politicians and police (a sort of militarised 'Saigon'). The old come to die expensively in the sun and the youth are preyed upon and corrupted, by age-old pressures of drugs and prostitution and by the new-age ones of pseudo-mystical retreats into nature.

Stacey stumbles through it all in an alcoholic haze, the effects of booze a telling metaphor for a world-view increasingly askew. As the film makes all too clear at the end, many of the evils of free-enterprise capitalism are the result of old men refusing to relinquish control, of trying to regain their youth through the exercise of power.

Energising the plot is Stacey's search for a senator's wayward daughter, Kathy (Janet Scrivener). On the way, he uncovers a military coup that plans to restore order in a way beneficial to Americans who want to drill for oil in the Barrier Reef and Asians who have land and people exploitation in mind. More out of control than in, he helps null-

ify the right-wingers. In a gloriously over-the-top sequence, freedom prevails and Stacey ends up a little wiser, if still broke.

Goodbye Paradise is a very clever piece of controlled fabulation which bursts out of genre strictures into liberating anarchy. Having the absolute courage of its convictions, it takes ideas and boldly pushes them beyond the safe and into a poetic and powerful hyper-realism. (Stacey's musing about the destroyed crop of rhubarb somehow reminding him of 'human potential' ranks as one of the finest and most powerful moments in all Australian cinema.)

But for all the wisdom and wit behind the script, the film really belongs to Ray Barrett. Long one of Australia's few actors properly labelled great, here he has the part of a lifetime. The supporting cast are all fine (particularly a glowing Robyn Nevin), but this is a film where watching Barrett is the centre-piece.

SCOTT MURRAY

References

'Ray Barrett', an interview by Mark Stiles, *Cinema Papers*, no. 40, October 1982, pp. 438–41.

'Denny Lawrence', an interview with the co-scriptwriter by Cristine Cremen, *Cinema Papers*, no. 43, May–June 1983, pp. 112–15.

'**Goodbye Paradise**', a short review by Kathe Boehringer, *Filmnews*, July 1983, p. 15.

HOSTAGE: THE CHRISTINE MARESCH STORY

Frontier Films presents HOSTAGE [/] the christine maresch story. A KLEJAZZ Production. © 1983. *Locations:* Munich; Broken Hill, Sydney (New South Wales). *Australian distributor:* Roadshow. *Opened:* 5 May 1983. *Video:* Roadshow Home Video. *Rating:* R. 35mm. 90 mins.

Producer: Frank Shields. *Associate producer:* Basil Appleby. *Scriptwriters:* Frank Shields, John Lind. Based on a true story by Christine Maresch. *Director of photography:* Vincent Monton. *Camera operator:* David Williamson. *Production designer:* Phil McLaren. *Costume designer:* David Rowe. *Editor:* Don Saunders. *Composer:* Davood Tabrizi. *Sound recordist:* Bob Allen. *Sound editor:* Greg Bell. *Mixer:* Julian Ellingworth.

Cast

Kerry Mack (Christine Maresch), Ralph Schicha (Walter Maresch), Gabriella Barraket (Child), Judy Nunn (Mrs Lewis), Vic Robins (Mr Lewis), Doris Goddard (Mrs Hoffman), Michael Harrs (John Hoffman), Claire Binney (Freda Hoffman), Henk Johann (Wolfgang), Burt Cooper (Helmut), Ian Mortimer (Gary), Moshe Kedem (Zaiter), Benno Sterzenbach (Mr Maresch), Lydia Kreibohm (Heidi Maresch); Maximilian Wolters (Reisenberg).

From its furiously sudden opening, intercutting the wheels of a truck barrelling down the highway and quick flashes of Christine Maresch (Kerry Mack) suffering domestic violence, **Hostage: The Christine Maresch Story** is one of the very few tough, lively 'exploitation' films to have emerged in Australia. Shamelessly 'sensationalist', graphic and melodramatic, it reaches some of the expressive heights cinephiles know from the 'B' films of Edgar Ulmer, Joseph H. Lewis or Sam Fuller. Yet these very qualities have condemned it, in more conservative and genteel circles of film culture, to being ignored or merely faintly praised.

Christine Maresch's true-life story is Australia's equivalent to America's Patty Hearst saga. Indeed, as an example of what Robin Wood calls 'the woman's nightmare', **Hostage: The Christine Maresch Story** anticipates Paul Schrader's treatment of similar material in **Patty Hearst** (1988). The logic and drive of both films is truly nightmarish.

Christine finds herself coerced into marrying a deranged, suicidal immigrant, Walter (Ralph Schicha), with a sinister priest advising, 'It's a godly act.' Then, once Walter has persuaded her (by this stage she is pregnant) to relocate to Germany with him,

she discovers he is part of a neo-Nazi movement (the film's gloriously unsubtle insertion of archival sound and image of Nazism recalling especially Fuller's **Verboten**, 1959). At the height of her increasingly doped-out misery, Christine becomes Walter's accomplice in a dangerous series of robberies.

One of the points made with great precision by the film is the extent to which Walter's psyche is a mass of unfounded projections and delusions, both sexual (romanticising Christine's 'purity' and then exploding with paranoiac possessiveness and jealousy) and political (his father, in whose name he continues the Nazi cause, simply informs him that 'the war is over'). Even his eagerness to rob banks seems fuelled by the newspapers' description of him and Christine as a modern-day Bonnie and Clyde, and later he eulogises the team of Baader and Meinhof: 'Now there's a relationship that worked!'

Shields has a strong understanding of the kind of characterisation best employed in genre films of this sort: strong, elemental

lines of ambivalent conflict between the protagonists (love/hate, trust/suspicion/, sadism/masochism) are dramatised, and then shifted or redefined at key turning points (such as when Christine 'softens' towards Walter after his act of compassion in Turkey, and his resolution to give up his past). Often the film milks its thrills from tense triangular situations: Will Walter's Nazi comrades support or dump Christine? Will their baby go towards him or her during their final shipboard confrontation (a finale that anticipates Phillip Noyce's **Dead Calm**, 1989)? On a more culturally specific plane, the film uses wonderfully the resilience and droll humour of Christine as an iconic Australian working-class woman, fiercely clutching her baby and deflating Walter's absurd ego even in the midst of events most debilitating to her body and spirit.

Hostage: The Christine Maresch Story is one of the most explosive, enduring and significant movies of Australian cinema in the 1980s.

ADRIAN MARTIN

Walter Maresch (Ralph Schicha), right, threatens wife Christine (Kerry Mack).

KITTY AND THE BAGMAN

Adams Packer Film Productions in assoc. with Forest Home Films. KITTY AND THE BAGMAN. © 1982 Forest Home Films Pty Ltd for Adams Packer Film Productions. *Budget:* $2.5 million. *Location:* Melbourne. *Australian distributor:* GUO. *Video:* CEL. *Rating:* M (June 1982; 2660.71m). 35mm. 97 mins.

Producer: Anthony Buckley. *Executive producer:* Phillip Adams. *Scriptwriters:* John Burney, Philip Cornford. *Director of photography:* Dean Semler. *Camera operator:* Danny Batterham. *Production designer:* Owen Williams. *Costume designer:* Judith Dorsman. *Editor:* Tim Wellburn. *Composer:* Brian May. *Sound recordist:* John Phillips. *Sound editor:* Vicki Ambrose. *Mixers:* Peter Fenton, Alasdair MacFarlane.

Cast

Liddy Clark (Kitty O'Rourke), John Stanton (The Bagman), Val Lehman ('Big' Lil Delaney), Gerard Maguire (Cyril Vickers), Collette Mann (Doris de Salle), Paul Chubb (Slugger), Danny Adcock (Detective Thomas), David Bradshaw (Larry O'Rourke), Anthony Hawkins (Simon Mornington), John Ewart (The Train Driver), Reg Evans (Chicka Delaney), Kylie Foster (Sarah Jones), Edward Hepple (Sam), Doug Ramsey (Inspector), Barry Donnelly (Sergeant Pete), David Slingsby (Johnny Williams), Terry Camilleri (Railway Detective), Roger Carroll (Police Commissioner), Alan McQueen (Fireman), Clive Marshall (Train Guard).

Kitty O'Rourke (Liddy Clark), an English seamstress, arrives in Australia with her new husband only to find him instantly arrested by a thuggish policeman (John Stanton), later to be known as 'The Bagman', who enlightens Kitty as to her husband's earlier nefarious activities. Kitty drifts into the criminal world and is pursued by her husband's lawyer. But The Bagman, who organises the illicit vice trade on behalf of unseen political masters, spots Kitty's strength of character and sets her up as a brothel manager and a rival to 'Big' Lil Delaney (Val Lehman), a tough no-nonsense competitor.

Kitty slowly falls for Cyril Vickers (Gerard Maguire), the man who introduced her to crime, but he has other plans, including a train robbery which goes wrong because he has been betrayed to 'Big' Lil. This brings The Bagman into vicious action while around them a gang war breaks out. It is now obvious that The Bagman is in love with

Kitty. After she discovers Vickers' deception, she humiliates him in public and responds to 'Big' Lil's final taunt with a two-fingered salute and leaves with The Bagman for a new life.

This attempt at a boisterous costume drama, dominated by attempts to be funny, colourful and fast moving at all costs, suffers from a certain confusion of intentions. One suspects that the script, by John Burney and Philip Cornford, was written with a darker purpose than displayed here. After all, it covers a broad canvas of political and police corruption, something that has remained endemic in Sydney for decades.

Alongside this, there is the portrayal of the Sydney vice scene as a place unrelentingly devoted to a good time populated by whores with hearts of gold and smiles on their faces. Apart from The Bagman's perpetual glower, and the stylistic device of never having him take his hat off (except after he has been to bed with Kitty), the characters, men and women alike, would seem to be just boys and girls out for fun, surrounded by crowds of happy, laughing extras peering out of their windows at the jolly goings-on.

Nobody suffers too seriously, even if a couple of extras get shot.

In a way, this film represented the end of the Australian period film that its producer Anthony Buckley and executive producer Phillip Adams milked throughout the 1970s. It was a cycle that exhausted itself and one feels that exhaustion in this movie. Its determined niceness, its characters in their impeccably recreated period costumes and settings, with their excellent, accentless speech, are derived one suspects from other movies rather than reality.

As well, the casting leaves a lot to be desired. Liddy Clark, eternally smiling, is unconvincing. John Stanton, with the same impeccable accent he employed later in his portrayal of Malcolm Fraser[1], is hardly everyone's model of the rough-and-tumble corrupt cop and Val Lehman's portrait of a tough 'Big' Lil Delaney suffers from being a reprise of her part in the television soap *Prisoner*.

GEOFF GARDNER

---

[1] In the television mini-series, *The Dismissal* (1983).

Kitty O'Rourke (Liddy Clark), Slugger (Paul Chubb) and Cyril Vickers (Gerard Maguire).

MAN OF FLOWERS

[No opening production credit.] Man of Flowers. © 1983 A Flowers International Pty Ltd Production. *Budget:* $3.2 million. *Location:* Melbourne. *Australian distributor:* Roadshow. *Video:* Roadshow Home Video. *Rating:* M (June 1982). 35mm. 91 mins.

Producers: Jane Ballantyne, Paul Cox. *Associate producer:* Tony Llewellyn-Jones. *Scriptwriter:* Paul Cox. *Dialogue:* Bob Ellis. *Director of photography:* Yuri Sokol. *Camera operator:* Gaetano Martinetti[2]. *Production designer:* Asher Bilu. *Wardrobe:* Lirit Bilu. *Editor:* Tim Lewis. *Sound recordist:* Lloyd Carrick. *Sound editor:* Terry Rodman. *Mixer:* James Currie.

Cast

Norman Kaye (Charles Bremer), Alyson Best (Lisa), Chris Haywood (David), Sarah Walker (Jane), Julia Blake (Art Teacher), Bob Ellis (Pyschiatrist), Barry Dickins (Postman), Patrick Cook (Coppershop Man), Victoria Eagger (Angela), Werner Herzog (Father), Hilary Kelly (Mother), James Stratford (Young Charles); Eileen Joyce, Marianne Baillieu (Aunts); Lirit Bilu, Juliet Bacskai (Florists); Dawn Klingberg (Cleaning Lady), Tony Llewellyn-Jones (Church Warden).

Charles Bremer (Norman Kaye) is an intriguing character: he is initially presented in an almost comic fashion as an unblinking, small man who derives pleasure from watching an artist's model, Lisa (Alyson Best), do a striptease in his living room. He then marches into a church across the road to play the organ (visual pun intended, surely). As the film progresses, however, Charles becomes less and less a harmless figure of fun.

Kaye's portrayal of tortured sensibility, deliberateness and delicate naïveté is a perfect echo of the dramatic flashback sequences Paul Cox uses to recall Charles' boyhood. With quavering, slow-motion images reminiscent of a nightmare, these scenes are a powerful evocation of a misunderstood childhood.

The need for and fascination with sensuality and beauty by the boy is ignored by a stern, authoritarian Father (Werner Herzog) and catered for by a beautiful, if overprotective, Mother (Hilary Kelly). Gradually, the boy turns away from his father, retreating psychologically and raising claims of retardation from one of his aunts. The latter, over-blown and fleshy, are the incarnation of the women in a Titian

painting and a stark contrast to the lean, ascetic lines of Charles' mother. The nightmarish evocation explains why Charles grows up with obsessions about naked women, flowers and sculpture.

However, the character Charles is not as much a study of a distorted psyche as it is a representation of an attitude to art. Charles is a strong advocate of a classical school of thought on art. The questioning of artistic (and other) values is presented as a simplistic conflict between the traditional and the avant-garde, the old and the nouveau.

The attractiveness of **Man of Flowers** is due, in part, to the minor characters. Created by Cox and fellow scenarist Bob Ellis, they are delightful diversions that also serve to add interest to the character of Charles. There is a diverse community of equally lost souls: guilt-ridden, self-pitying Psychiatrist (Bob Ellis); Postman (Barry Dickins), with theories on the meaning of life who never writes letters; Coppersmith (Patrick Cook), with intriguing ideas about society's disposal of its dead; and shy Church Warden (Tony Llewellyn-Jones). It is also a welcome absurdity rather than pretentiousness that these characters are played respectively by a well-known scriptwriter, a playwright, a cartoonist and the associate producer of the film.

The film is also enhanced by the stunning photography of Yuri Sokol, a lush operatic score and beautiful art direction by Asher Bilu, replete with allusions to Titian paintings, Caravaggio-inspired sets and the Magritte-like character of Charles himself.

Man of Flowers manages to satisfy the senses, provide disarming wit and tease the mind with provocative images, drawing the audience in and convincing it that the film is challenging the intellect, when, in fact, it is merely teasing and disarming the converted.

HELEN GREENWOOD[3]

---

[1] There is no director's credit, just 'A Film by Paul Cox'.
[2] Later known as just 'Nino Martinetti'.
[3] Extracted from Greenwood's review in *Cinema Papers* (see References).

References
'Man of Flowers', a review by Helen Greenwood, *Cinema Papers*, no. 44–5, April 1984, pp. 85–6.
'Paul Cox', an interview with the director by Debi Enker, *Cinema Papers*, no. 46, July 1984, pp. 122–9.
'Yuri Sokol', an article (with quotes) on the director of photography by Mary Colbert, *Cinema Papers*, no. 74, July 1989, pp. 26–30.
'Man of Flowers', a short review by John Conomos, *Filmnews*, October 1983, p. 16.

Jane (Sarah Walker) and Lisa (Alyson Best).

MIDNITE SPARES

[No opening production credit.[1]] MIDNITE SPARES. © 1982 Wednesday Investments Pty Ltd and Filmco Ltd. *Budget:* $2.6 million. *Location:* Sydney. *Australian distributor:* Roadshow. *Video:* Roadshow Home Video. *Rating:* M (December 1982; 2386.41m). 35mm. 87 mins.

Producer: Tom Burstall. *Executive producer:* John Fitzgerald. *Scriptwriter:* Terry Larsen. Based on an idea of John Fitzgerald. *Director of photography:* Geoff Burton. *Production designer:* George Little. *Wardrobe:* Ruth de la Lande. *Editor:* Andrew Prowse. *Composer:* Cameron Allan. *Sound recordist:* Lloyd Carrick. *Sound editors:* Greg Bell, Helen Brown, Hugh Waddell, Peter Foster. *Mixers:* Phil Judd, Phil Heywood.

Cast

James Laurie (Steve), Gia Carides (Ruth), Max Cullen (Tomas), Bruce Spence (Wimpy), David Argue (Rabbit), Tony Barry (Howard), Graeme Blundell (Sidebottom), John Clayton (Vincent), Terry Camilleri (Harry Diaz), John Godden (Chris the Rat), Jonathan Coleman (Wayne Grubb), Amanda Dole (Janelle), Ray Marshall (Panton), Tessa Mallos (Maria Mintos), Deborah Masters (Sophie Diaz), Lou Brown (Young Detective), Moya O'Sullivan (Caravan Lady), Maggie Blinco (Carol), Larry Crane (Jolly Offsider), Chris Lewis (Joe Diaz), Ray Mizzi (Diaz Rat).

If there were ever a persuasive argument for clear-headedly venturing into the much-derided '10BA days' of Australian cinema, it is **Midnite Spares**. It is certainly a modest 'genre film' (as action–thrillers are often dismissively labelled), but it is far from being the 'dull and soporific' work that David Stratton finds 'typical of the early 80s'[2].

Watched today with a generous spirit, **Midnite Spares** seems like a homage to a phantom subterranean body of Australian 'exploitation' movies. With its cagey crossbreeding of different genres, its veritable gallery of flamboyant character actors (including Tony Barry, Max Cullen, David Argue and Bruce Spence), its proudly 'parochial' touches of suburban realism and its spectacularly brutal car-smash set-pieces, **Midnite Spares** sets in motion an always lively mix of elements, at moments anticipating the texture of far more highly regarded later films like **Nirvana Street Murder** (Aleksi Vellis, 1991) and **Death In Brunswick** (John Ruane, 1991).

In its story of a rugged blond hero (James Laurie as Steve) pushed 'over the edge' into a mission to avenge his dead father, **Midnite**

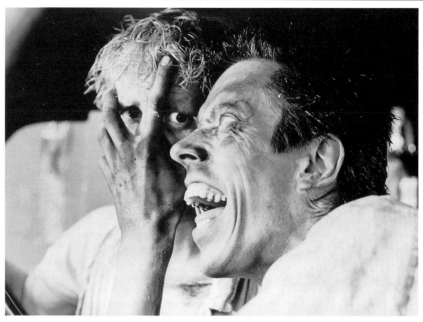

Rabbit (David Argue) and Wimpy (Bruce Spence).

Spares is clearly in the wake of the first two Mad Max films.[3] More broadly, it reworks many elements from a rich cross-genre in Australian cinema: the 'car movie'. From **The Cars That Ate Paris** (Peter Weir, 1974) and **The FJ Holden** (Michael Thornhill, 1977) to **Dead-End Drive-In** (Brian Trenchard Smith, 1986) and **Running On Empty** (John Clark, 1982), to cite only a few, Australian car movies have delved deeply into the collective 'phantasms' of contemporary, urban, industrialised Australia.[4] **Midnite Spares** conjures that fringe world of 'savage' capitalism, a world of spare parts, auto theft and 'repo mongrels', both good and evil, that we know well from the car movie – a fantasy world far from any 'normal' structures of law, family and nine-to-five work.

Yet, for all its feverish, melodramatic carmovie imaginings, **Midnite Spares** also has a line into certain, very interesting social realities. Before the third Mad Max instalment[5], this is one of the first 'genre movies' of the 1980s to openly and warmly reflect a new, suburban multi-culturalism, with Greek–Australians (among others) joining the Aussie heroes on their final knightly smash-'em-up quest, and old-style white-Australia racists (such as the sleazy entrepreneur played by Jonathan Coleman) unambiguously denounced throughout.

Even within the core group of main characters, there is an unusual and endearing diversity at work. **Midnite Spares** (like Brian Trenchard-Smith's 1983 **BMX Bandits**) joins an international 'democratic–populist' trend

in genre cinema (including other car movies of the period like Jonathan Demme's **Handle With Care,** 1977, and Joel Schumacher's **D.C. Cab,** 1983), celebrating the 'everyday differences' between ordinary people. So, alongside the conventionally 'good-looking' hero and heroine (Gia Carides as Ruth), the film makes room for the garrulous immigrant-loner Tomas (Max Cullen), and even semi-retarded, sexually backward hangers-on like Wimpy (Bruce Spence) and Rabbit (David Argue), who endlessly equate sexual intercourse with working on (or getting run over by) a car. Even the 'love interest' between Steve and Ruth is presented with wonderfully 'daggy' dramatic understatement, and a sense of the makeshift, mobile nature of contemporary relations.

ADRIAN MARTIN

---

1 At least on the video, which gives the feeling of being a little truncated at the start. The video slick says 'Filmco Australia presents'.

2 David Stratton, *The Avocado Plantation: Boom and Bust in the Australian Film Industry,* Macmillan, Sydney, 1990, p. 276.

3 **Mad Max** (George Miller, 1979) and **Mad Max 2** (Miller, 1981).

4 For an illuminating discussion, see Meaghan Morris, 'Fate and the Family Sedan', in *East-West Journal,* vol. 4, no. 1, December 1989.

5 **Mad Max Beyond Thunderdome** (George Miller and George Ogilvie, 1985).

Reference

'Midnight [sic] Spares', a short review by Kathe Boehringer, *Filmnews,* April–May 1983, p. 17.

MOLLY

The New South Wales Film Corporation [and] Greater Union Film Distributors–M&L present MOLLY. © 1983 Troplisa Pty Ltd. *Budget:* $1 million. *Locations:* outback NSW. *Australian distributor:* Greater Union Distributors. *Video:* CEL. *Rating:* G. 35 mm. 88 mins.

Producer: Hilary Linstead. *Executive producer:* Richard Brennan. *Associate producers:* Phillip Roope, Mark Thomas. *Scriptwriters:* Phillip Roope, Mark Thomas, Hilary Linstead, Ned Lander. *Director of photography:* Vincent Monton. *Art director:* Robert Dein. *Costume designer:* Laurel Frank. *Dog Handler:* Don Tregear, for Vera's Animal Agency. *Editor:* Stewart Young. *Musical director:* Graeme Issac. *Sound recordist:* Lloyd Carrick. *Sound editor:* Greg Bell. *Mixer:* Phil Judd.

Cast

Claudia Karvan (Maxie Ireland), Garry McDonald (Jones), Molly (Molly), Reg Lye (Old Dan), Melissa Jaffer (Aunt Jenny), Ruth Cracknell (Mrs Reach), Leslie Dayman (Bill Ireland), Robin Laurie (Stella), Tanya Lester (Gina), Jake Blundell (Rudi), Microphone Conway (Neville), Jim Conway (Roy), Ray Marshall (Errol), Ken Snodgrass (Laurie), Michael O'Neill (Lyle), Kerry Dwyer (Sister Carmel). Lucky Grills (Dog Catcher), Slim de Grey (Tommy); members of the Flying Fruit Fly Circus; Los Trios Ringbarkus.

Molly has a lot going for it, notably a photogenic dog which 'sings' and a virtually foolproof plot situation involving a little girl's attempt to recover the dog after it has been stolen. But the film also demonstrates a recurrent weakness in many Australian films: a reasonable basis for a film but insufficiently detailed script preparation resulting in a repetitive middle section after a strong opening.

The film is at its best at the start when Old Dan (Reg Lye) takes Molly into a country pub and cons the locals with his singing dog. The whole sequence comes off particularly well – acting, atmosphere and tension – and Lye is most authoritative in these surroundings, especially when Old Dan orders a triple whisky with a beer chaser.

Old Dan travels to Sydney with his dog and he befriends young Maxie Ireland (Claudia Karvan), who is moving to Coogee to live with her aunt after the death of her mother. Dan suffers a heart attack and entrusts Molly to Maxie's protection. The bulk of the film concerns the repeated attempts of Jones (Garry McDonald) to steal the dog, together with Maxie's attempts to find a home for the animal.

Rather than revitalising familiar conventions with humour, **Molly** opts for rather sinister overtones. If one walked in late one could be excused for thinking one was watching, on occasions, the build-up for a 'splatter' movie. The villain's obsession with becoming a performer dictates his single-minded efforts to steal Molly, a reasonable plot device to generate some tension. But director Ned Lander and director of photography Vincent Monton repeatedly emphasise the psychotic disturbance of the villain: shots of his boarding-house room with its show-business fetish; a protracted sequence of Jones applying clown make-up to his face, or shaving his head with a barber's cut-throat razor (and in one gruesome scene he accidentally steps on the blade).

The only explanation I can offer for the rather radical shift in tone between the girl and her dog in sunny Coogee and the demented villain is the desire to approximate the threatening qualities of the fairy-tales gathered by the Brothers Grimm, and publicity for the film describes **Molly** as a 'modern fairy-tale about a dog with a rare gift'. Certainly fear is a key ingredient as the villain prowls the alleys of Coogee at night with his cane rattling the corrugated iron fences near Maxie's bed, or his sinister observation of a lonely little girl walking the dark streets illuminated by a single street light. Late in the film, in a bizarre sequence, he even terrorises young Maxie dressed in a nun's outfit.

Graeme Issac's music and the Flying Fruit Fly Circus represent an appealing counterpoint to McDonald's villain and it is unfortunate that a little more thought was not given to the script as there is much in the film to appeal to young children.

GEOFF MAYER[1]

---

[1] Extracted from Mayer's joint review in *Cinema Papers* (see Reference).

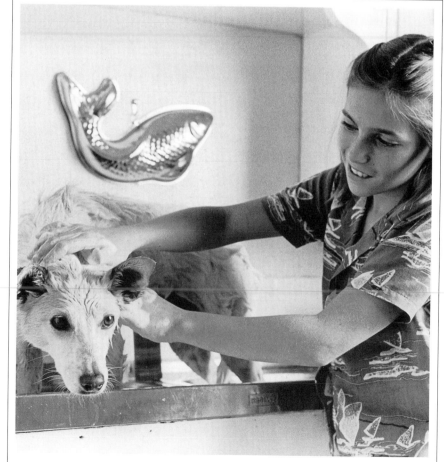

Maxie Ireland (Claudia Karvan) washes Molly.

Reference
'**Bush Christmas** and **Molly**', a joint review by Geoff Mayer, *Cinema Papers*, no. 44–5, April 1984, pp. 88–9.

MICHAEL PATTINSON

MOVING OUT

A Pattinson Ballantyne Production MOVING OUT. © 1982 Pattinson Ballantyne Film Productions. *Budget:* $600,000. *Location:* Melbourne. *Australian distributor:* Greater Union Distributors. *Opened:* March 1983. *Video:* Roadshow Home Video. *Rating:* M (July 1982; 2468.70m). 35mm. 91 mins.

Producers: Jane Ballantyne, Michael Pattinson. *Associate producer:* Julie Monton. *Scriptwriter:* Jan Sardi. *Director of photography:* Vincent Monton. *Production designer:* Neil Angwin. *Costume designer:* Frankie Hogan. *Editor:* Robert Martin. *Composer:* Danny Beckerman. *Sound recordist:* Geoff White. *Sound editor:* Martin Jeffs. *Mixer:* Julian Ellingworth.

Cast

Vince Colosimo (Gino), Maurice Devincentis (Renato), Tibor Gyapjas (Allan), Sally Cooper (Sandy), Desiree[1] Smith (Helen), Nicole Miranda (Maria), Santina Failla (Franca), Julio Dalleore (Pippo), Peter Albert Sardi (Gino's Father), Kate Jason (Gino's Mother), Luciano Catenacci (Maria's Father), Sylvie Fonti (Maria's Mother), Brian James (Mr. Aitkens), Sandy Gore (Miss Stanislaus), Ivar Kants (Mr. Clarke), Tony Volpe (Tony), Alan Crapper (Peter), Vince Moro (Nick), Charles Garzarella (Joe), Guido Romano (Boy 1), Steve Rizzolio (Boy 2), John Cassagranda (Boy 3), Morris Delmonte (Boy 4).

Moving Out centres on Gino (Vince Colosimo), the adolescent son of Italian immigrants. The family has been in Australia for sufficient time to have saved enough to buy a house in the outer suburbs after spending years living in cramped accommodation in an inner northern suburb of Melbourne.

Gino is the family's sole go-between with 'Australian' society. During the film, he negotiates the arrival of relatives, the last two weeks of school term, the start and sudden end of a tentative relationship with an Australian girl and the family's move to what a delinquent Australian friend describes as 'wogsville'.

From these situations there emerges a series of pressures on Gino. The pangs of an alienated adolescent are overlaid with the pangs of the alienated immigrant. He has a massive lack of self-esteem deriving from a view of himself which requires him to denounce his mother tongue as 'wog' and to refuse to speak Italian even to his parents, who speak little else. Adding to the depression, bordering on self-disgust, which results

are an education system teaching nothing of interest or value, a home featuring a father who spends most of the time away at work, a comatose grandmother and, finally, some desultory out-of-hours adventures with Australian girls and beer.

This is an acute observation of the life of the immigrant in the inner city. It is rendered with utter fidelity in its patterns of speech, movement, geography, decor and dress, not fashionable virtues easily found in Australian films. In its presentation of the cultural confrontation between Italian peasant stock, dominated by insular and rigorous family values, and the panzer battalions of Australia desperate to impose their ignorance on any new arrival, we can discover a battle between cultures that ends with both sides alienated and confused. The sub-text is a radical critique of an immigration programme which, at least until our manufacturing industry fell apart in the early 1980s, was based on the need to import factory fodder.

While this may sound grim, one of the film's many virtues is to render this material with humour, even to the extent of slowly building a gag about the boy who is renovating his school desk with screws stolen from the school lavatories.

Moving Out was a film made outside the dominant modes of Australian representa-

tion. One assumes its writer Jan Sardi has been more and better influenced by the major neo-realist works of his country of birth rather than by the rather more prissy products of Australia's cinema, with their insistence on elegant decor and design, and a photographic 'look' that emphasises the hazy and circumspect nature of the subjects.

Modest works of realism which record some penetrating insights into one of the key developments in post-war Australian society are few and far between. Those who have lived in and watched our inner working class suburbs change since World War II will most appreciate the film's skills and virtues. For others, it should serve a very educational purpose.

GEOFF GARDNER

---

[1] Usually spelt 'Desirée'.
[2] See footnote 1.

References
'**Moving Out**', a review by Geoffrey Gardner, *Cinema Papers*, no. 42, March 1983, p. 63.
'**Moving Out**: Scripting and Casting', Marcus Breen, *Cinema Papers*, no. 43, May–June 1983, pp. 116–17.
'**Michael Pattinson and Jan Sardi**', an interview with the director and the scriptwriter by Debi Enker, *Cinema Papers*, no. 48, October–November, 1984, pp. 314–18, 383.

Allan (Tibor Gyapjas), Renato (Maurice Devincentis) and Gino (Vince Colosimo).

A D R I A N   C A R R[1]

NOW AND FOREVER

[No opening production credit.] NOW AND FOREVER. © 1982 Now and Forever Film Partnership. *Location:* Sydney. *Australian distributor:* Roadshow. *Video:* Roadshow Home Video. *Rating:* M (July 1982; 2770.43m). 35mm. Panavision. 89 mins.

Producers: Treisha Ghent, Carnegie Fieldhouse. *Associate producer:* Rea Francis. *Scriptwriter:* Richard Cassidy. Based on the novel by Danielle Steel. *Director of photography:* Don McAlpine. *Camera operator:* Danny Batterham. *Production designer:* Rene and Rochford. *Costume designer:* Rene and Rochford. *Editor:* Adrian Carr. *Composer:* Bruce Rowland. *Supervising sound recordist:* Kevin Kearney. *Sound recordist:* John Franks. *Supervising sound editor:* Bruce Lamshed. *Sound editors:* Peter Burgess, Glen Martin. *Mixers:* Robert J. Litt, Elliot Tyson, David J. Kimball.

Cast

Cheryl Ladd (Jessie Clarke), Robert Coleby (Ian Clarke), Carmen Duncan (Astrid Bonner), Christine Amor (Margaret Burton), Aileen Britton (Bethanie), Alex Scott (Andrew Wyndham), Kris McQuade (Matilda Spencer), John Allen (Martin Harrington), Rod Mullinar (Geoffrey Bates), Kevin Healy (Jock Martin), Michael Long (William Horton), Tim Burns (Kent Adams), Henri Szeps (Barry York), Redmond Phillips (Judge), Amanda Ma (Kat), Sarah de Teliga (Zina), Ray Marshall (Harvey Green), Paul Bertram (James Eaton), Alan Tobin (Wayne Buttery), Reg Gillam (Magistrate).

Husband and wife: Ian (Robert Coleby) and Jessie Clarke (Cheryl Ladd).

Now and Forever, adapted from a novel by Danielle Steel, is the story of a woman's faith in a husband wrongly convicted of rape. In some ways, it is one woman's rebuke of aspects of late-1970s feminism.

Jessie Clarke (Cheryl Ladd) is a modern, independent woman who runs a fashion boutique (i.e., she supplies 'image' to women). At home is her 'kept' husband, Ian (Robert Coleby), a writer with one novel and several short stories to his published credit.

While Jessie is off in New York buying fashion, Ian sits drinking wine by Sydney Harbour. There he is picked up by a most-forward Margaret Burton (Christine Amor), who all but drags him to her apartment where she aggressively straddles the inebriated author. That afternoon, Jessie returns home; the next day, Ian is arrested for rape.

The first problem is bail ($15,000), which Jessie must raise herself. The bank refuses and she has to brow-beat a loan shark into advancing it: this is a woman who will stand by her man, no matter how horrible the accusation.

Despite irrefutable evidence that Margaret is a nut case seeking revenge on her former husband, who looks like Ian and drives the same Morgan sports car, the jury convicts Ian. (Like **Evil Angels**, **With Prejudice**[2] and several others, this is not a film to strengthen one's belief in the jury system in this country.)

In gaol, Ian finds a sort of peace: he writes well and finds friendship with an old prisoner, whom he (quite touchingly) teaches to read. Back at home, Jessie, after showing such early strength, cracks up and turns to drink. She is rescued by a friend, Astrid Bonner (Carmen Duncan), and bundled off to the country where she is attracted to Geoffrey Bates (Rod Mullinar), a squatter type. But, at the very last minute of his gentlemanly seduction, she realises she is in love with Ian–now and forever.

The film is interesting for the issues it raises, but disappointing for doing so little with them. The expense of defending oneself is raised, but only as an obstacle for a determined woman to overcome. The film can be seen to indirectly criticise exorbitant legal costs, but it does no more than suggest. And it fails to grasp the equally relevant issue (though understandable ten years ago) of charging people for false accusations.

Many, of course, will find the whole subject of a false rape claim counter-productive in a climate where too few actual rapes are reported. Still, the Tyson case and others are a reminder of how allegedly perjured evidence can sway ill-informed juries into making dubious verdicts (guided by a dislike, if not worse, of a defendant).

But this is not a film to find such issues debated in depth: it is essentially a 'women's film' for the Mills & Boon crowd. It also values old-fashioned female strengths as more important than those social ills targeted by feminists.

SCOTT MURRAY

---

[1] Adrian Carr, the editor, took over during shooting. There is a credit on the film for 'Additional material directed by Richard Cassidy'.
[2] **Evil Angels** (Fred Schepisi, 1988), **With Prejudice** (Esben Storm, 1982).

PHAR LAP

John Sexton Productions in association with Michael Edgley International present[s] PHAR LAP. © 1983. *Budget:* $7 million. *Locations:* Melbourne, Victoria; New South Wales. *Australian distributor:* Hoyts. *Opened:* 11 August 1983. *Video:* RCA–Columbia–Hoyts. *Rating:* PG. 118 mins.

Producer: John Sexton. *Executive producer:* Richard Davis. *Scriptwriter:* David Williamson. *Director of photography:* Russell Boyd. *Camera operators:* Nixon Binney, Russell Boyd, Bill Grimmond, Keith Lambert, Dan Burstall, David Connell. *Production designer:* Laurence Eastwood. *Costume designer:* Anna Senior. *Editor:* Tony Paterson. *Composer:* Bruce Rowland. *Sound recordist:* Gary Wilkins. *Sound editors:* Terry Rodman, Peter Burgess. *Mixers:* Peter Fenton, Phil Heywood.

Cast

Tom Burlinson (Tommy Woodcock) Martin Vaughan (Harry Telford), Judy Morris (Bea David), Celia de Burgh (Vi Telford), Ron Leibman (Dave Davis), Vincent Ball (Lachlan McKinnon), John Stanton (Eric Connolly), Peter Whitford (Bert Wolfe), Robert Grubb (William Nielson), Richard Morgan ("Cashy" Martin), Georgia Carr (Emma), James Steel (Jim Pike), Steven Bannister (Younger Cappy Telford), Richard Terrill (Older Cappy Telford), Warwick Moss (McCready), Henry Duvall (Mr Ping), Pat Thompson (Edith), Redmond Phillips (Sir Samuel Hordern), Maggie Miller (May Holmes), Anthony Hawkins (Guy Raymond).

Tommy Woodcock (Tom Burlinson) puts a bridle on Phar Lap.

Australian popular heroes seem to generate enormous adoration from their simplicity, their apparent innate sense of fair play and a sense of democratic optimism. But when a horse and its trainer become the focus for such values, it is necessary to see Australia as quite a strange place indeed. But this is the stuff of popular culture. Its success lies in its nationalistic passion for identifying the essential characteristics of Australian cultural life and hammering them home with almost wilful abandon.

It is difficult not to enjoy **Phar Lap**, such is its enthusiasm for its subject. In identifying the passions of horse trainer Tommy Woodcock (Tom Burlinson) with the greatest Australian[1] racehorse of all time, **Phar Lap** indulges itself in a decisive, nostalgic replay of popular emotion. The 1930s setting of the film provides a focus for the rapidly disappearing cultural values of the past. Certainly director Simon Wincer is able to encapsulate frontier values like mateship, honesty and egalitarianism in a story that has added bite because those values are a part of Australian folklore.

The story of Phar Lap's phenomenal rise to fame on the racetrack and the love that Tommy Woodcock had for the horse incorporates enormous drama. The drama takes on national and class overtones, as Woodcock, the poor young stable-hand, sees his cherished dreams ruined by ambition and hollow promises of vast amounts of American money.

But the real focus and power of the film is its relentless, sentimental indulgence in the values that once seemed to make Australia a great country. This is the sort of film that assists the development of national identity, by offering up real stories with a none-too-subtle thematics. That its focus is a horse and an otherwise simple stable-hand serves to suggest that popular culture may yet be the best means of identifying Australian cultural and political identity in film.

MARCUS BREEN

---

1 Phar Lap was actually a New Zealand horse, but Australia seems to have adopted it.

References
'Simon Wincer', an interview by Scott Murray, *Cinema Papers*, no. 44–5, April 1984, pp. 28–31, 102.
'**Phar Lap**', a review by Keith Connolly, ibid., pp. 87–8.

PHILIPPE MORA

THE RETURN OF CAPTAIN INVINCIBLE

Andrew Gaty presents a Seven Keys Production. THE RETURN OF CAPTAIN INVINCIBLE. © 1982 Willarra Pty Ltd. *Budget:* $7 million. *Locations:* Sydney, the Blue Mountains (New South Wales); New York. *Australian distributor:* Seven Keys. *Video:* Seven Keys Video. *Rating:* NRC. 35mm. Panavision. 91 mins.

Producer: Andrew Gaty. *Associate producer:* Brian D. Burgess. *Scriptwriters:* Steven de Souza, Andrew Gaty. *Director of photography:* Mike Molloy. *Camera operator:* Lou Irving. *Production designer:* David Copping. *Costume designer:* Katy Duffy. *Editor:* John Scott. *Composer:* William Motzing. *Sound recordist:* Ken Hammond. *Sound editor:* John Foster. *Mixers:* Phil Judd; Phil Heywood (fx); Gethin Creagh (music).

Cast

Alan Arkin (Captain Invincible), Christopher Lee (Mr Midnight), Kate Fitzpatrick (Patty Patria), Bill Hunter (Tupper/Coach), Michael Pate (President), David Argue (Italian Salesman), John Bluthal (Deli Owner), Chelsea Brown (Tour Guide), Max Cullen (Italian Man), Arthur Dignam (Lawyer), Noel Ferrier (Air Force General), Hayes Gordon (Kirby), Chris Haywood (Maître d'), Graham Kennedy (Prime Minister), Gus Mercurio (Noisy Garbageman), Max Phipps (Admiral), Alfred Sandor (New York Police Captain), Brian Adams (Reporter), Vince Aloschi (Deli Assistant), Ron Beck (Black Salesman).

The premise of **The Return of Captain Invincible** is not a bad one. It concerns an early-day superhero, past his prime, Captain Invincible (Alan Arkin), who fell victim to the HUAC and McCarthyism in the 1950s and ended up a drunken bum in the Australian outback. He is now summoned to make a comeback and defeat an old enemy, Mr Midnight (Christopher Lee), a villain in the tradition of Hitler, who continues white supremacist practices.

The film is an ambitious, multi-million-dollar production designed for the international market place, with the objective of having the broadest possible appeal: hence, overseas actors (Alan Arkin and Christopher Lee), special effects 'better than those in **Superman**'[1] and American as well as Australian locations. The film was conceived by its makers as an escapist fantasy, a political satire, a nostalgic comedy. But in their desire to make a film that pleased everybody, they pleased no one. Critics called it a spectacular debacle, and audiences stayed away.

Yet the film is not without potential. The opening moments are full of promise. The 'News on the March' sequence, reminiscent of **Citizen Kane** (Orson Welles, 1941), consummately constructed by director Philippe Mora (director also of the highly reputed documentary, *Brother Can You Spare a Dime?*, 1974), has the gritty, nostalgic realism of old newsreels while economically and humorously constructing the Captain's heroic past.

There are other notable sequences as Captain Invincible learns to be a hero again – flying in a harness in front of rear-projected scenes, reciting scripting dialogue, just to get back the old feelings. In its difference from traditional superhero images, this could almost be described as post-modern pastiche.

However, the choice to make the film a modern musical fantasy seems ill-conceived. Three of the ten songs are written by Hartley and O'Brien, the composing team from **The Rocky Horror Picture Show** (Jim Sharman, 1975). But what may have worked for **Rocky Horror** does not work here. Captain Invincible himself croons like Frank Sinatra, bemoaning a past when his stature was unquestioned. It's all a bit too much to take.

But ultimately it is the oft-repeated desire for a return to the past – a past of 'french fries rather than bean curd and sprouts', of 'policewomen rather than policepersons' and of good old fashioned patriotic songs – that remains most problematic. After beginning amid the nightmare of the Cold War, HUAC and McCarthyism, one would think the film would hold such values in question. But any suggestion of irony, satire or even the most basic political analysis quickly disappears. Instead, the Captain's simplistic, patriotic sentimentality triumphs, inspired by the sounds of 'God Bless America'. You can see why many Australians have experienced difficulty with this film.

ANNA DZENIS

[1] Quote from press material. **Superman** (Richard Donner, 1978).

Patty Patria (Kate Fitzpatrick) and Captain Invincible (Alan Arkin).

SARAH

Yoram Gross presents SARAH. *Alternative titles:* 'The Seventh Match' (working) and Sarah and the Squirrel (US). © 1983 Yoram Gross Film Studio. *Budget:* $583,000. *Australian distributor:* CEL. *Video:* CEL. *Rating:* G (May 1980; 57 mins).[1] 80 mins.

Producer: Yoram Gross. *Associate producer:* Sandra Gross. *Screenplay:* Yoram Gross. Based on an original story by Yoram Gross. *Animation photography:* Jenny Ochse, Bob Evans. *Animation camera operator:* Jenny Ochse. *Director of photography (New York):* Lloyd Freidus. *Wardrobe (for Mia Farrow):* Marsha Patten. *Art director:* Athol Henry. *Editor:* Christopher Plowright. *Music:* Vivaldi's Four Seasons. *Performed by:* I Musici. *Music for clarinet performed by:* Giora Feidman. *Sound recordist:* Gary Rich (New York). *Mixer:* Phil Judd.

Animation director: Athol Henry. *Background layouts:* Athol Henry, Amber Vellani. *Principal animators:* Athol Henry, Cynthia Leech, Andrew Szemenyei. *Animators:* Nicholas Harding, Ray Nowland, Kevin Roper. *Assistant animators:* Astrid Brennan, Maria Brinkley, Marian Brooks, Diane Farrington, Eva Helischer, Brenda McKie, Paul Marron, Kaye Watts. *Additional animation:* Irena Slapczynski, Ty Bosco. *Colour design:* Susan Speer.

Cast

Mia Farrow (Sarah).

Voices

Joan Bruce, John Faassen, Ron Haddrick, Shane Porteous.

[See Appendix A on all the Gross films, pp. 352–4.]

___

[1] Rated as 'The Seventh Match' in a shorter version.

___

Reference
'Yoram Gross', an interview by Antoinette Starkiewicz, *Cinema Papers*, no. 48, October–November, 1984, pp. 334–8, 390.

Sarah (Mia Farrow) and friend.

Sumner Locke Elliott's Careful He Might Hear You

Syme International Productions in assoc. with [the] NSW Film Corporation presents Sumner Locke Elliott's CAREFUL HE MIGHT HEAR YOU. © 1983 Syme Entertainment Pty Ltd. Made with the assistance of the Australian Film Commission. *Location:* Sydney. *Australian distributor:* Hoyts. *Opened:* September 1983. *Video:* RCA–Columbia Pictures–Hoyts Video. *Rating:* M. 35 mm. 110 mins.

Producer: Jill Robb. *Scriptwriter:* Michael Jenkins. *Director of photography:* John Seale. *Production designer:* John Soddart. *Costume designer:* Bruce Finlayson. *Editor:* Richard Francis-Bruce. *Composer:* Ray Cook. *Sound recordist:* Syd Butterworth. *Sound editor:* Andrew Steuart. *Mixers:* Roger Savage, Julian Ellingworth.

Cast

Wendy Hughes (Vanessa), Robyn Nevin (Lila), Nicholas Gledhill (PS), John Hargreaves (Logan), Geraldine Turner (Vere), Isabelle Anderson (Agnes), Peter Whitford (George), Colleen Clifford (Ettie), Edward Howell (Judge), Jacqueline Kott (Miss Pile), Julie Nihill (Diana), Michael Long (Mr Hood), Len London (Mr Gentle), Beth Child (Mrs Grindel), Colin Croft (The Magician), Virginia Portingale (Miss Colden), Steve Fyfield (Chauffeur), Pega Williams (Winnie Grindel), Kylie Burgess (Cynthia), Tony Blanchard (Ian).

Set in Sydney during the Great Depression, Sumner Locke Elliott's Careful He Might Hear You tells the story of the six-year-old PS (Nicholas Gledhill), whose mother is dead and whose father has disappeared. PS's peaceful and happy life with his working-class Aunt Lila (Robyn Nevin) and Uncle George (Peter Whitford) is interrupted by the arrival of wealthy, Anglophile Aunt Vanessa (Wendy Hughes) from England. A battle over the custody of PS ensues in which Vanessa is successful. However, PS rebels against this decision and is finally allowed to live with the couple who raised him.

The acting by all members of the cast is generally admirable, though at times overly histrionic, with an exceptional performance from Wendy Hughes, whose character is snobbish, neurotic and sexually repressed, and a subtle, well-balanced performance from Nicholas Gledhill, who gives many a wistful, soulful gaze past the camera during the film.

The film is in the genre of unabashed melodrama which plays on four main themes: the Anglo-Australian dichotomy of Australian culture, growing up and the loss

PS (Nicholas Gledhill) with Aunt Vanessa (Wendy Hughes).

of innocence, the effects of the Great Depression on Australian society and an analysis of male–female interaction and sexual repression.

Director Carl Schultz is comfortable with the melodrama genre, aptly guiding it through the nostalgia that is on a par with the best tear-jerkers. The lush period art direction and John Seale's poetic cinematography make this film a beautiful visual experience.

What is particularly interesting is that an extra effort has been made to reinforce the fact that what is happening is seen from a child's point of view. The movement of the camera, often flowing and swirling, captures not only what the boy sees, but also how his observations make him feel. The framing is often quirky, and the action is sometimes seen through or over objects such as grass, trees, house partitions and blinds. This reminds us of the fact that a child's perspective of the world is a markedly different one from that of adults.

Sound editing and effects also contribute to the consistency of PS's point of view. Sound is often muddled, multi-layered and somewhat confusing, so that if the viewer does not understand then neither does PS.

The film's preoccupation with PS's perspective is one of the most attuned and perfected examples of this style.

Overall, the film attempts to grapple with sensibilities that are rare in Australian cinema, and sometimes it loses the necessary subtlety, looking more like a parody of what it should really be. Ray Cook's score is at times emotionally excessive; the more sombre, brooding moments in the film are perhaps too Gothic to be relevant; and some of the performances are too emotional to be believable. However, the flaws in this picture are insufficient to harm the final result, which is that this is one of the better-made period films of the Australian cinema.

Anna Gul

References

'Wendy Hughes', an interview with the actor by Richard Brennan, *Cinema Papers*, no. 40, October 1982, pp. 428–32.

'Careful, [sic] He Might Hear You', a review by Jim Schembri, *Cinema Papers*, no. 44–5, April 1984, pp. 86–7.

'Captain of the Clouds', an article (with quotes) on actor John Hargreaves by Gail McCrea, *Cinema Papers*, no. 56, March 1986, pp. 38–9, 40.

'Careful He Might Hear You', a short review by Penny Davies, *Filmnews*, October 1983, p. 16.

1984

Jake (Bill Kerr) gets ready to face the giant pig. Russell Mulcahy's Razorback.

ANNIE'S COMING OUT

Film Australia presents Annie's Coming Out. © 1984 Film Australia [and] Australian Film Commission. *Location:* Melbourne. *Australian distributor:* Hoyts. *Opened:* 27 September 1984. *Video:* RCA–Columbia–Hoyts. *Rating:* NRC (March 1984; 2441.27m). 35mm. 96 mins.

Producer: Don Murray. *Executive producer:* Don Harley. *Scriptwriters:* John Patterson, Chris Borthwick. Based on the true story of [and a book by] Rosemary Crossley and Anne McDonald. *Director of photography:* Mick Von Bornemann. *Camera operator:* Bruce Hillyard. *Production designer:* Robbie Perkins. *Wardrobe:* Lucinda McGuigan. *Editor:* Lindsay Frazer. *Composer:* Simon Walker. *Sound recordist:* Rodney Simmons. *Sound editor:* Tim Jordan. *Mixer:* John Herron.

Cast

Angela Punch McGregor (Jessica Hathaway), Drew Forsythe (David Lewis), Liddy Clark (Sally Clements), Monica Maughan (Vera Peters), Philippa Baker (Sister Waterman), Tina Arhondis (Annie O'Farrell), Mark Butler (Dr John Monroe), John Frawley (Harding), Wallas Eaton (Dr Rowell), Lyn Collingwood (Mrs O'Farrell), Laurie Dobson (Mr O'Farrell), Carl Bleazby (Bill Hathaway), Esme Melville (Mrs Arnold), Judith Graham (Mrs Hathaway), Alastair Duncan (Hopgood), Simon Chilvers (Warren Metcalf), James Wright (Douglas), Charles Tingwell (Judge), Brett Reynolds (Timmy), Matthew Simpson (Stephen).

Annie's Coming Out is based on 'the story of Anne McDonald', whose physical disability caused her to be misdiagnosed as intellectually disabled. But it is not only from the position of Annie O'Farrell (Tina Arhondis) that the audience is drawn into the film; the third-person, observing camera gives the audience another means of identification. It merges the first-person story of Annie *and* Jessica Hathaway (Angela Punch McGregor), in 'real life' Rosemary Crossley, and the events surrounding the development of their teacher–student, symbolic mother–daughter relationship.

The reason for bringing Annie's story to the screen seems more than clear: to point out the plight of disabled people whose lives are shaped mainly by the appalling conditions of institutionalisation, in a society which actively encourages such structures and activity. However, despite the fact that the film has such a strong commitment to an important set of issues, it leaves one feeling discontented. Much of this has to do with the emphasis on heroics which (over)determines the enunciation of 'Annie's story'.

Admittedly, the highly charged performance of Angela Punch McGregor, crisp photography by Mick Von Bornemann, swift editing by Lindsay Frazer and the stirringly melodramatic score by Simon Walker are all superb. And it is true that some of the incisive narration of Annie, along with several unsettling images, gives one insight into an institution. Yet, all of these aspects basically work to reduce the complex elements of a 'real-life story' such as Annie's to a series of screen clichés. The poetic, though alluring, style of 'Annie's voice' and the sometimes 'too-clean' images almost undermine the impact of some representations, which in real life are far more disturbing.

Annie's Coming Out, at times, seems to want to safeguard the audience by not presenting sights that are too shocking while, at other times, it seems to want to leave things glaringly unsaid. This may relate also to not wanting to cause further controversy among the story's real life participants; in the film, the conflict of Annie, her parents and Jessica's intervention is delicately sidestepped. But, more important, this cautiousness seems to have to do with certain assumptions in the film about the way in which films change people's attitudes.

Films can be, and often are, a source of inspiration, and sometimes may help to change people. But the question must also be asked: Why is there a tendency in film narrative to reduce the stories of the disabled to 'individual against society', 'triumph against all odds' and 'winning', especially when in 'real life' the difficulties and conflicts that disabled people have to contend with are rarely resolved so neatly or so triumphantly? This should not be read as a demand for realism in films, but rather as a demand for film-makers to interpret complex stories in more complex ways.

DAVE SARGENT[1]

---

[1] Extracted from Sargent's review in *Cinema Papers* (see References).

References

'Annie's Coming Out', a review by Dave Sargent, *Cinema Papers*, no. 46, July 1984, p. 177.

'Angela Punch McGregor', an interview with the actor by Jim Schembri, *Cinema Papers*, no. 49, December 1984, pp. 418–21, 471.

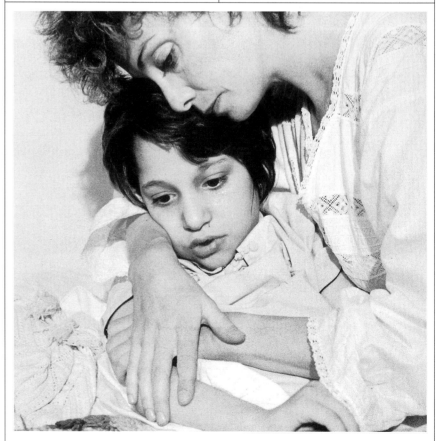

Annie O'Farrell (Tina Arhondis) and Jessica Hathaway (Angela Punch McGregor).

THE CAMEL BOY

Yoram Gross presents THE CAMEL BOY. © 1984 Yoram Gross Film Studio. *Australian distributor:* Yoram Gross. *Video:* CEL. *Rating:* G (July 1984; 1837.81m; longer version 790m on 16mm in October 1984). 35mm. 75 mins.

Producer: Yoram Gross. *Associate producer:* Sandra Gross. *Scriptwritwer:* John Palmer. Based on an original idea by Yoram Gross. *Photography:* Graham Sharpe, Jenny Ochse. *Editors:* Philippe Vignes, Christopher Plowright. *Composer:* Bob Young. *Lyrics:* John Palmer. *Sung by:* Robyn Moore. *Sound editor:* Ray Thomas. *Mixer:* Peter Fenton.

Animation director: Ray Nowland.

Background layouts: Amber Ellis, Gennady Kozlov. *Animators:* Gairden Cooke, Ariel Ferrari, Murray Griffen, Nicholas Harding, Lianne Hughes, Charles McRae, Robert Malherbe, Don McKinnon, Ray Nowland, Andrew Szemenyei, Eva Szabo, Szabalos Szabo. *Additional animators:* Paul Barker, Zbigniew Bilyk, Lucinda Clutterbuck, Max Gunner, Eva Helischer, Koichi Kashiwa, Wayne Kelly, Boris Kozlov, Domingo Rivera, Vicky Robinson, Liu Ruo, Phillip Scarrold, Jan de Silva, Bela Szeman, Min Xu, Gennady Kozlov. *Painters:* Belinda Bateman, Maria Haren, Mimi Intal, Corallee Munro, Wendy Munro, Eva Wajs, Li Yang. *Backgrounds:*

Amber Ellis, Gennady Kozlov. *Models:* Leaf Nowland. *Graphics:* Eric David. *Special fx painting:* Amber Ellis, Jeanette Toms, Gennady Kozlov.

Cast

Ron Haddrick (O'Connell).

Voices

Barbara Frawley, Ron Haddrick, John Meillon, Robyn Moore, Michael Pate.

[See Appendix A on all the Gross films, pp. 352–4.]

Ali and Binta, the baby camel.

THE COOLANGATTA GOLD

Michael Edgley International and Hoyts Theatres in association with Peter Schreck, Igor Auzins and John Weiley present THE COOLANGATTA GOLD. © 1984 Angoloro, P/L, Michael Edgley International and Hoyts Theatres. *Budget:* $7 million. *Location:* Coolangatta and the Gold Coast (Queensland). *Australian distributor:* Hoyts. *Opened:* 22 November 1984. *Video:* RCA–Columbia–Hoyts. *Rating:* PG. 35mm. Panavision. 112 mins.

Producer: John Weiley. *Associate producer:* Brian Burgess. *Executive producers:* Terry Jackman, Michael Edgley. *Scriptwriter:* Peter Schreck. Developed from an idea by Max Oldfield and a story by Ted Robinson and Peter Schreck. *Director of photography:* Keith Wagstaff. *Camera operator:* David Burr. *Production designer:* Bob Hill. *Costume designers:* Lea Haig, Camilla Rountree. *Editor:* Tim Wellburn. *Composer:* Bill Conti. *Sound supervisor:* Phil Judd. [*Sound recordist:* not credited.] *Sound editors:* Marc van Buuren; Karin Whittington, Tim Jordan (dia.). *Mixers:* Phil Judd, Julian Ellingworth.

Cast

Joss McWilliam (Steve), Nick Tate (The Father: Joe), Colin Friels (Adam), Josephine Smulders (Kerry), Robyn Nevin (The Mother: Roslyn), Grant Kenny (Grant), Melanie Day (Gilda), Melissa Jaffer (Ballet Teacher), Paul Starling (Karate Teacher), Brian Syron (The Entrepreneur); Wilbur Wilde, Paul Clark, Martin Holt, Marlon Holden, Scott Thompson (The Band); Robert Brough (Commentary [Commentator]), Graduates of the Australian Ballet School (Dancers).

Twenty years earlier, Joe (Nick Tate) has been beaten in the Gold Coast Iron Man contest. Now, all his hopes are centred on his son, Adam (Colin Friels), whom he is training relentlessly to defeat Grant (Grant Kenny), son of the man who defeated Joe. In his obsession with Adam's winning, he cruelly neglects the needs and achievements of his younger son, Steve (Joss McWilliam), who seeks success as a karate expert and a rock musician. Steve finally rebels against the injustice of his father's treatment and decides to win the Coolangatta Gold Triathlon himself. In the last minutes of the race, he shows that he could have…and goes off to join his ballerina girlfriend, Kerry (Josephine Smulders).

The male competitive instinct, so endemic as a source of conflict in Australian fiction as to qualify it as an element of the

Steve (Joss McWilliam) and Adam (Colin Friels).

national mythology, is at the heart of this film's meaning. In this way it is linked with such notable Australian films as **Gallipoli** (Peter Weir, 1981) and **Newsfront** (Phillip Noyce, 1978) and with the British **Chariots of Fire** (Hugh Hudson, 1981). Joe Lucas' insistence on the importance of winning has distorted his own life and that of his sons. The film presents the activities of competitiveness with often bravura effectiveness, making much use of helicopter shots, tracking and zooming, and agile editing procedures to give a sense of the sheer expenditure of physical energy involved. It offers, too, a persuasive sense of the rigorous discipline demanded by the activities it depicts: the triathlon (running, swimming and surf-board-riding), ballet and karate. It presents the exertion and physical challenge with a corresponding visual and kinetic panache.

The film was not critically well received largely on the grounds that neither screenplay nor direction was able to give the human conflicts a psychological interest to match the film's physical qualities of image and sound and movement. Though it is true that the film is not clear or detailed enough about motives or shades of affection and resentment, for much of the time it succeeds in distracting attention from its thin spots. **The Coolangatta Gold** needs to be seen on a large screen for the full impact of what it does best, but even in the reduced form of video it is enjoyably far from the decorous school of tasteful Australian film-making.

BRIAN MCFARLANE

References

'Peter Schreck', an interview with the scriptwriter by Jim Schembri, *Cinema Papers*, no. 50, February–March 1985, pp. 34–7, 84.

'The Coolangatta Gold', a review by Brian McFarlane, ibid., pp. 68–9.

'Leap Year', an article (with quotes) on actor Colin Friels by Debi Enker, *Cinema Papers*, no. 56, March 1986, pp. 14–15.

'The Coolangatta Gold', a short review by Kathe Boehringer, *Filmnews*, November–December 1984, p. 19.

DOT AND THE BUNNY

Yoram Gross presents DOT and the BUNNY. © 1983 Yoram Gross Film Studio. Produced in association with Dot & the Rabbit Pty Ltd and the Australian Film Commission. *Australian distributor:* Yoram Gross. *Video:* CEL and VSA. *Rating:* G. 35mm. 81 mins.

Producer: Yoram Gross. *Associate producer:* Sandra Gross. *Screenplay:* John Palmer. Based on an original idea by Yoram Gross. *Animation photography:* Jenny Ochse, Graham Sharpe. *Editor:* Christopher Plowright. *Composer:* Bob Young. *Lyrics:* A. B. (Banjo) Paterson, John Palmer. *Sung by:* Barbara Frawley, Ross Higgins, Robyn Moore. *Sound recordist:* Black Inc Recorders, Sound on Film. *Sound editor:* Tomas Pokorny. *Mixers:* Peter Fenton; Martin Benge (music).

Animation director: Athol Henry. *Story and character design:* Athol Henry, Andrew Szemenyei. *Layouts:* John Bunge, Laurie Sharpe. *Backgrounds:* Amber Ellis, Zbigniew Dromirecki, Gennady Kozlov. *Animators:* Ty Bosco, John Burge, Ariel Ferrari, Murray Griffen, Nicholas Harding, Eva Helischer, Athol Henry, Lianne Hughes, Victor Johnson, Cynthia Leech, Chris Minos, Pere van Reyk, Laurie Sharpe, Eva Szabo, Szabalos Szabo, Andrew Szemenyei. *Inbetweeners:* Eva Helischer, Wayne Kelly, Robert Malherbe, Dariusz Polkowski, Vicki Robinson, Philip Scarrold, Paul Stibal, Bela Szeman.

Cast

Anna Quinn.

Voices

Drew Forsythe, Barbara Frawley, Ron Haddrick, Anne Haddy, Ross Higgins, Robyn Moore.

[See Appendix A on all the Gross films, pp. 352–4.]

Reference

'Yoram Gross', an interview by Antoinette Starkiewicz, *Cinema Papers*, no. 48, October–November, 1984, pp. 334–8, 390.

Dot and Bunny.

KEN CAMERON

FAST TALKING

[No opening production credit.] FAST TALKING. © 1983 Oldata Pty Ltd. *Location:* Sydney. *Australian distributor:* Filmways. *Video:* Filmways VTC, marketed by K-TEL Video. *Rating:* M (January 1984). Super 16 mm. 95 mins.

Producer: Ross Matthews. *Scriptwriter:* Ken Cameron. *Director of photography:* David Gribble. *Production designer:* Neil Angwin. *Costume designer:* Terry Ryan. *Editor:* David Huggett. *Composer:* Sharon Calcraft. *Sound recordist:* Tim Lloyd. *Sound editors:* David Huggett, Marc van Buuren, Susan Midgley. *Mixers:* Julian Ellingworth, Mike Thomas.

Cast

Rod Zuanic (Steve Carson), Toni Allaylis (Vicki), Chris Truswell (Moose), Gail Sweeny (Narelle), Steve Bisley (Redback), Peter Hehir (Ralph Carson), Tracy Mann (Sharon), Dennis Moore (Yates), Julie McGregor (Steve's Mother), Garry Cook (Al Carson), Peter Collingwood (Principal), Ron Hackett (Woodwork Teacher), Ric Carter (Geography Teacher), Frank Lloyd (Careers Adviser), John Cobley (Roll Call Teacher), Bill McCluskey (Swinton), Alistair Duncan (School Inspector), Genevieve Moy (Yates' Secretary), Mariette Rups-Donnelly (School Secretary), Ellen Wilson (Kate Archer).

On its initial Australian release, a *Cinema Papers* cover story[1] grouped **Fast Talking** with two other contemporaneous films about 'rebels, rumbles and motor-cycle boys': James Foley's **Reckless** (1984) and Francis Ford Coppola's **Rumble Fish** (1983). While the latter two works circulated easily in the film and video markets as vivid, all-American 'teen movies', Ken Cameron's film refuses a complicity with the more commercial end of this genre. **Fast Talking** is more a 'social realist' teen drama, a culturally respectable 'issue' like Ken Loach's **Kes** (1969) or Stanley Kramer's **Bless the Beasts and the Children** (1972) – and, also like those, it seems a film made more for secondary school classroom discussion than for mass audience-divertissement.

This distance from the more 'vulgar' American teen-movie model is not total. There are some lively, exhilarating moments of teen high jinks and rebellion, a number of classic caricatures of authoritarian, narrow-minded adults, and a character (Chris Truswell as Moose) who does a running impression of Michael Crawford from the popular television series *Some Mothers Do 'Ave 'Em*. But the film's tone is generally downbeat, especially in the bland, dreamy, jazzy musical score used in place of the rock tracks so typical of the genre (even a cameo appearance in a school dance scene by the band Eurogliders is underplayed).

The film's themes are the classic ones of the social-realist teen drama. Steve Carson (Rod Zuanic), a livewire hero deprived of proper social opportunity because of his violent, broken home environment, becomes a 'trouble maker' as he instinctively defies the authoritarian structures of school and society. The only 'rôle model' Steve can respect is the bike mechanic, Redback (Steve Bisley), a sage ex-con who tries, gently and unsuccessfully, to guide the boy away from a life of crime.

In the typically pessimistic manner of social realism, Cameron matter-of-factly paints a fatalistic, 'no future' social backdrop that the hero will likely never alter, even if he could develop a greater consciousness of his social position. Yet the film is dialectical at least to the extent that it grants some weight and reality to gestures and moments of impulsive resistance. The title indicates all the 'fast moves' – talking, stealing, running away, playing tricks – which, however doomed or ineffectual in the final instance, nonetheless express a spirit of revolt, and spontaneously renew the broken history of anarchist resistance.

Although **Fast Talking** is ultimately a fairly middle-of-the-road social issue film, and one that has been little cited critically since its release, it does have a number of distinctive, original elements that anticipate subsequent realist teen films, especially Jean-Claude Brisseau's **De bruit et de fureur** (**The Sound and the Fury**, 1988). Like Brisseau, Cameron draws on his own experience as a secondary-school teacher for some sharp, realistic depictions of classroom life. Most remarkably, the film has a shadowy subplot involving the sexual liaison between a 'progressive' middle-class teacher (Tracy Mann) and a student – an interesting antidote to the soft, asexual humanism of so many films about classroom interaction in the manner of **Dead Poets Society** (Peter Weir, 1989).

ADRIAN MARTIN

---

[1] 'Rebels, Rumbles and Motor-cycle Boys' (see References).

References
'Fast Talking', a review by Geoff Mayer, *Cinema Papers*, no. 47, August 1984, p. 269.
'Ken Cameron', an interview with the writer-director by Scott Murray, *Cinema Papers*, no. 48, October–November 1984, pp. 302–7.
'Rebels, Rumbles and Motor-cycle Boys', Mark Spratt, *Cinema Papers*, ibid., pp. 308–13.
'Ken Talking', an interview with Ken Cameron by Tim Burns and Tina Kaufman, *Filmnews*, August–September 1984, pp. 10–12.
'Fast Talking', a short review by Cathy Wright, *Filmnews*, ibid., p. 17.

Redback (Steve Bisley) and Steve Carson (Rod Zuanic).

FUTURE SCHLOCK

[No opening production credit.] FUTURE Schlock. © 1984 The Ultimate Show Pty Ltd. *Budget:* $80,000. *Location:* Melbourne. *Australian distributor:* Valhalla. *Opened:* Easter 1984. *Video:* THG Video (CIC–Taft). *Rating:* M (July 1984; 833.72m). 16mm. 85 mins.[1]

Producers: Barry Peak, Chris Kiely. *Scriptwriters:* Barry Peak, Chris Kiely. *Director of photography:* Malcolm Richards. *Production designer:* Ian McWha. *Costumes:* Karen Merkel. *Editors:* Robert Martin, Ray Pond. *Composers:* John McCubbery, Doug Saunders. *Sound recordists:* Murray Tregonning, Lindsay Wray, Don Borden. [*Sound editor:* not credited.] [*Mixer:* not credited.]

Cast

Maryanne Fahey (Sarah), Michael Bishop (Bear), Tracey Callander (Ronnie), Tiriel Mora (Alvin), Simon Thorpe (Sammy), Peter Cox (Cap'n Fruitcake), Keith Walker (Sgt. Tatts), Evan Zachariah (Skunk), Gary Adams (Bob), Deborah Force (Trish), Mitchell Faircloth (Dr Allen), Jason van de Velde (Simon), Tracey Harvey (Lois), Effie James (Mrs Christie), Ron Granger (Mr Christie), Peter Moon (Minister), Tom Elovaris (Il Revolto), Michael Eckersall (School Teacher), Paul Harris (Newsreader), Alec Guinness (Man in the White Suit), Nellie Metcalf (Ticketseller), Phillip Zachariah (Scruff), Drago Spina (Man with Tongue; Man without Tongue), David J. G. Hirst (Police Captain), Peter Thompson (Mervyn), Axe Palling (Lizard of Oz), Susie Plisken (Carnal Miranda).

From a starting point of announcing the 'first Australian new-wave comedy', Barry Peak and Chris Kiely of the Valhalla Cinema have produced, on a shoestring ($80,000) budget, a film tailor-made for that cinema's audience.

Future Schlock is built around dozens of passing references to films familiar to Valhalla patrons, notably John Carpenter's **Escape From New York** (1981) and John Waters' **Desperate Living** (1977), though Mike Nichols' **The Graduate** (1967) may be harking back a bit far. A barrage of visual and verbal information establishes that Melbourne has been the site of a middle-class revolt in 1990. Freaks, perverts, dope fiends and the like have been walled into an inner-city ghetto, while the suburban bourgeoisie carries on outside to the words of a revised national anthem extolling the joys of Australian middle-class life.

The ghetto dwellers are kept passively drugged via their water supply, except for a few with a private supply of wine, including Sarah (Maryanne Fahey) and Bear (Michael Bishop), performers at Alvin's Hole night-club by night. Posing as the Cisco Kid and Pancho by day, they sneak into suburbia disguised as 'subbies' to perform acts of sabotage. Voice-over narration by Alvin (Tiriel Mora) and inter-titles smooth over the cracks.

A tolerance, indeed love, of Z-grade film-making is necessary to appreciate **Future Schlock**. The budgetary restrictions call for much invention and imagination in location work, and devices such as bricks being placed on a map to represent the ghetto. However, the claustrophobic shooting style gives little real sense of the geography of the film. The ghetto doesn't exist as a place beyond a few exteriors, and the fact that most of its inhabitants are perpetually doped saves having to make them do anything. Cisco and Pancho are folk heroes, according to the narrator, but nobody appears to notice or celebrate their activities, many of which are merely mildly amusing.

On stage at Alvin's, though, Sarah and Bear have an engaging act, pouncing on sub-urbanites surreptitiously slumming as raw material.

The law is represented by a bunch of thuggish cops, trained to beat up 10 or 12 people a day, and a special squad to capture the two bandits. These two officers, Cap'n Fruitcake (Peter Cox) and Sgt. Tatts (Keith Walker), perpetually dream of transvestism, etc., in the voice-over.

The most disappointing aspect is the film's failure to pinpoint its comic vision, which runs a gamut of styles from cheap satire and self-mockery through gross effects to goonish surrealism. This lack of unity in the material, coupled with performances ranging from spirited in the leads to downright amateur, results in a fairly benign film against all intentions. Sarah and Bear's final coup, springing a ludicrous 'Revised Standard of Guidelines' on the gullible middle class, seems more a good-natured prank than an angry blow for freedom for the underdogs who remain unliberated while the hero and heroine venture forth to infiltrate the Vatican and the White House.

MARK SPRATT[2]

---

[1] The commercially released video gives the length as 74 mins.
[2] Extracted from Spratt's review in *Cinema Papers* (see References).

References

'Future Schlock', a review by Mark Spratt, *Cinema Papers*, no. 46, July 1984, pp. 181, 182.

'Future Schlock', a short review by Ross Gibson, *Filmnews*, August–September 1984, p. 17.

Bear (Michael Bishop), a ghetto dweller.

MELVIN: SON OF ALVIN

A McElroy & McElroy Production. Melvin [/] Son of ALVIN. © 1984 Melvin, Son of Alvin Film Partnership. *Location:* Sydney. *Australian distributor:* Roadshow. *Opened:* December 1984. *Video:* Roadshow Home Video. *Rating:* M. 35mm. 85 mins.

Producer: James McElroy. *Associate producers:* Tim Sanders, Wilma Schinella. *Scriptwriter:* Morris Gleitzman. *Director of photography:* Ross Berryman. *Camera operator:* Stephen Dobson. *Production designer:* Jon Dowding. *Costume designers:* Marta Statescu, Sandra Tynan. *Editor:* John Hollands. *Composer:* Colin Stead. *Sound recordist:* John Rowley. *Sound editor:* Penn Robinson. *Mixer:* Julian Ellingworth.

Cast

Gerry Sont (Melvin), Lenita Psillakis (Gloria), Jon Finlayson (Burnbaum), Tina Bursill (Dee Tanner), Col McEwan (Mr Simpson), Abigail (Mrs Simpson), David Argue (Cameraman), Arianthe Calani (Mrs Giannis), Graeme Blundell (Alvin), Patsy Martin (Matron), Wayne Tomczyk (Melvin, aged 3), Michael Shaw (Melvin, aged 7), Silas Kincott (Melvin, aged 11), Marianne Collopy (Miss Fosdyke), Adair Stagg (School Crossing Lady), Steve Bastoni (Bullo), Greg Stroud (Ferret), David Beresh (Streaky), Geoff Parry (Science Teacher), Peter Harvey-Wright (TV Producer), Lazar Rodic (Porter with Suitcases).

Gloria (Lenita Psillakis), Mrs Giannis (Arianthe Calani) and Melvin (Gerry Sont).

This second and final sequel to the 1973 hit comedy **Alvin Purple** (Tim Burstall) was packaged by producer James McElroy, who was not involved with the original. Prior to this project there had been both an **Alvin Rides Again** (David Bilcock jun. and Robin Copping, 1974) and a short-lived *Alvin Purple* television series produced by the ABC.

Gerry Sont, who had played minor rôles in **Early Frost** (no director credit, 1982) and **Running on Empty** (John Clark, 1982), was best known in the television soap, *Waterloo Station*.

Sont plays the virginal Melvin, who works as a teenage car-wash attendant. He is attractive to women but cannot understand why, as he does not realise that he is the son of Alvin (Graeme Blundell). He becomes friendly with a Greek usherette, Gloria (Lenita Psillakis), who rescues him from marauding women and becomes his well-meaning girlfriend. Eventually, a reunion of the Purple clan takes place where all is revealed.

Graeme Blundell reprises his Alvin persona, now sadly middle aged and burnt out,

working as a singer in a purple jumpsuit on the league-clubs circuit, singing schmaltzy ballads to his adoring women fans.

Melvin: Son of Alvin is John Eastway's feature debut. Eastway and scriptwriter Morris Gleitzman were both major contributors to the Norman Gunston television programmes and the sketch comedy format is very evident. All that is missing is the laugh track.

Psillakis, a former model, plays a rôle not too dissimilar to that of Sophie (Zoë Carides) in **Death in Brunswick** (John Ruane, 1991) and Helen (Mary Coustas) in **Nirvana Street Murder** (Aleksi Vellis, 1991), except that in this particular case she plays an ethnic stereotype. In thankless support rôles, Tina Bursill as a crusading *60 Minutes*-style reporter and David Argue as her bumbling cameraman are teamed as comedy relief.

Gleitzman's screenplay is almost like a Mel Brooks scattergun spoof which prompts the obvious question: How does one parody

that which is already parody? The humour is curiously old-fashioned and replete with poofter jokes and sexual sniggering of the Benny Hill variety, the only topicality being a dubious gag reference to the emerging AIDS epidemic.

Production was twice delayed when major backers suddenly pulled out prior to the scheduled commencements of shooting in December 1983, and January 1984. Before the film's commercial release three cuts were ordered by the censor in order for the film to gain an M certificate. The material snipped featured nudity and a simulation of oral sex. What remained in the final cut was innocuous enough to ensure a brief theatrical run and public indifference.

PAUL HARRIS

Reference

'Melvin, Son of Alvin', a review by Dave Sargent, *Cinema Papers*, no. 50, February–March 1985, pp. 73–4.

MY FIRST WIFE

[No opening production company credit.] My First Wife. © 1984 Dofine Ltd. Made with the assistance of Film Victoria. *Location:* Williamstown (Melbourne). *Australian distributor:* Roadshow. *Opened:* 13 September 1984. *Video:* Palace Academy Video. *Rating:* M (August 1984; 2633m). 35mm. 95 mins.

Producers: Jane Ballantyne, Paul Cox. *Associate producer:* Tony Llewellyn-Jones. *Scenario:* Paul Cox. *Screen adaptation:* Paul Cox, Bob Ellis. *Director of photography:* Yuri Sokol. *Camera operator:* Gaetano Nino Martinetti[1]. *Production designer:* Asher Bilu. [*Costume designer:* not credited.] *Editor:* Tim Lewis. *Sound recordist:* Ken Hammond. *Sound editor:* Craig Carter. *Mixer:* James Currie.

Cast

John Hargreaves (John), Wendy Hughes (Helen), Lucy Charlotte Angwin (Lucy), David Cameron (Tom), Anna Jemison[2] (Hilary), Betty Lucas (Helen's Mother), Lucy Uralov (John's Mother), Robin Lovejoy (John's Father), Charles Tingwell (Helen's Father), Jon Finlayson (Bernard), Julia Blake (Kirstin), Ron Ralk (Psychiatrist), Xenia Groutas (John's Sister), Reg Roddick (Priest), Renée Geyer (Barmaid), Sabrina Lorenz (Barbra), Christopher Holligan (Bar Singer), Linden Wilkenson (Doctor), Tony Llewellyn-Jones (Doctor), Symonetta Dennis (Nurse), Jentah Sobott (Nurse).

My First Wife is recognisably a Paul Cox film, perhaps his most personal. Cox himself admits, 'It was inspired by the breakup of my marriage [...] The character of the husband, with all his weaknesses and bad behaviour, was based on me.'[3]

The credit sequence is layered over a montage of enigmatic images, evoking a landscape of emotions. A train crawls horizontally across the screen. Other trains pass in opposite directions. It becomes mesmeric, one train following another. The cycles of life, of love and of loss, of passing, are foregrounded. A child will be born, a father will die, one love replacing another.

The camera sweeps down a hallway through a well-to-do house. Portraits on the wall drag the past into the present. A couple make passionate love. We then see another man, who, like the viewer, is also watching, contemplating. But he is not there, in his house, witnessing as we are his wife's adultery. He is elsewhere. This is John (John Hargreaves), the husband, a composer and host of a late-night classical-music radio pro-

gramme. The steps we are tracing are through his world, his reality, his life and his marriage.

The film begins with an ending: John unwittingly confronting his wife, Helen (Wendy Hughes), with statistics on marital infidelity. Of course he'd know if she were having an affaire. He is, after all, her husband. 'Has she ever had an affaire?', he asks provocatively. He is blinkered, possessed, self-righteous and definitely not expecting her reply. 'I don't love you any more. I haven't loved you for a long time.' And with this she announces her intention to leave him. It is the moment of dissolution.

John's excessive grief and self-righteous rage explode from hysteria, violence, emotional blackmail and attempted suicide to the kidnapping of their only child, Lucy (Lucy Angwin). At the same time, John's father is in hospital dying of cancer. During one of John's visits, his father proclaims that, in the end, the family is all that matters. It is the most pivotal of all the messages in this bitter-sweet moral tale.

We come to understand these emotional and moral values that the film holds so dear through the parallels and contrasts set up within the families, between children and their parents, between different generations and cultures.

Thus, the final image of the family together, walking away from the grave, is

simultaneously of reconciliation and irrevocable loss. It is both an uncertain and tentative end, yet resolute in the affirmation of the importance of families, and the irreplaceable bonds they share.

The real power of this film lies in such stolen moments, in the poetry of such images. The magical, almost hypnotic repetition and rhythm of these images and sounds encourage us to share and recall, to interweave our own lives, thoughts and memories with those of the film, making it a rare, sensitive and challenging artistic achievement.

ANNA DZENIS

---

1 Later known as just 'Nino Martinetti'.
2 Later known as 'Anna Maria Monticelli'.
3 Quoted in David Stratton, *The Avocado Plantation: Boom and Bust in the Australian Film Industry*, Macmillan, Sydney, 1990, pp. 99–100.

References

'Paul Cox', an interview with the director by Debi Enker, *Cinema Papers*, no. 46, July 1984, pp. 122–9.
'My First Wife', a review by Brian McFarlane, *Cinema Papers*, no. 48, October–November 1984, pp. 358–9.
'Yuri Sokol', an article (with quotes) on the director of photography by Mary Colbert, *Cinema Papers*, no. 74, July 1989, pp. 26–30.
'My First Wife', a review by Ross Gibson, *Film-news*, August–September 1984, p. 17.

John (John Hargreaves), Lucy (Lucy Charlotte Angwin) and Helen (Wendy Hughes).

ONE NIGHT STAND

Michael Edgley International [and] Hoyts Theatres present an Astra Film Production. ONE NIGHT STAND.[1] © 1984 Astra Film Productions Pty Ltd. Produced with the assistance of the Australian Film Commission. *Locations:* Sydney, New York, Paris. *Australian distributor:* Hoyts. *Opened:* 5 May 1984. *Video:* RCA–Columbia–Hoyts. *Rating:* M (March 1984; 2568m). 35mm. 94 mins.

Producer: Richard Mason. *Executive producer:* Simon Wincer. *Associate producer:* Julia Overton. *Scriptwriter:* John Duigan. *Director of photography:* Tom Cowan. *Editor:* John Scott. *Production designer:* Ross Major. *Costume designer:* Ross Major. *Music:* William Motzing. *Sound recordist:* Peter Barker. *Sound editor:* Marc van Buuren. *Mixer:* Julian Ellingworth.

Cast

Tyler Coppin (Sam), Cassandra Delaney (Sharon), Jay Hackett (Brendon), Saskia Post (Eva), David Pledger (Tony); Todd Boyce, Michael Cloyd, Justin Monjo (American Sailors); John Krummel (News Personality), Richard Morecroft (First Newsreader), Helen Pankhurst (Second Newsreader), Frankie Raymond (Frankie), Tsukasa Fruya (Robot Dancer), Peggy Thompson (Sam's Mother), Monica McDonald (Sam's U.S. Girlfriend), Ian Gilmour (Sharon's Ex Boyfriend), Tom Appleton (Thug), Lois Ramsey (Salvation Army Woman), Michael Conway (Security Guard), Jennifer Miller (Teacher), Alec Morgan (Scottish Piper).

John Duigan has argued that his intention in making **One Night Stand** was to show how people might behave in the face of a nuclear attack and to explore the sense of powerlessness experienced by many in the shadow of this threat.

In attempting to fulfil these aims, Duigan has adopted an episodic structure which largely eschews a more traditional, linear narrative with its strong emphasis on cause-and-effect elements building to a powerful conclusion. However, in rejecting this narrative structure, Duigan sacrifices tension and suspense, and one is left mostly watching for transformation in the characters and for insights generated through them.

Duigan attempts to alter the audience's perception of the reactions to a nuclear confrontation by initially establishing the stereotypical characteristics of three of the teenagers, excluding Sam (Tyler Coppin), who are primarily interested in the opposite sex and having fun. The regeneration and (perhaps) growth in their reactions comes about slowly and it is probably hoped that the target audience will also change its attitude accordingly.

Once the film moves into the Opera House, Duigan adopts two seemingly contradictory approaches to the drama. First, the Opera House is used as a theatrical metaphor in which the four characters perform a play within a play, unaware of the significance of the events of this drama and without any control over what is taking place around them. The irony of this is heightened by the use of the innocent resonance in the early 1960s song, 'It Might as Well Rain Until September', near the beginning of the film and as the bomb drops at the end.

Duigan's somewhat absurdist approach in the Opera House is heightened by the use of Fritz Lang's 1926 German film **Metropolis** throughout and at the end of the film. Yet, among these distancing devices, the film uses a series of sentimental and banal flashback sequences. Most of these seem rather pointless except to sentimentalise the characters and support one of their cries in the Opera House that, 'I dunno what you're supposed to do in life but whatever it is I don't reckon I've done it.'

The confusion in the aims of the approaches adopted by Duigan is readily apparent at the conclusion of the film. Surely the purpose of this film is to mark its social discourse as existing outside the film text – hence, the possibility of audience discussion and, hopefully, action in accordance with the film's social message. To achieve this, the film should not be viewed as a fiction nor the activities of the teenagers as a game. Yet the cross-cutting from the scenes of chaos in **Metropolis** to the Australians running to an underground railway station only heightens the fictionality of **One Night Stand** and indicates that, like **Metropolis**, it is only a movie, a science-fiction fantasy.

GEOFF MAYER[2]

---

[1] The title is a mix of upper and lower case. This is an approximation.
[2] Extracted from Mayer's review in *Cinema Papers* (see References).

References

'One Night Stand', a review by Geoff Mayer, *Cinema Papers*, no. 46, July 1984, pp. 178–9.

'Ethics of the Outsider', an interview with writer-director John Duigan by Albert Moran, *Filmnews*, April 1984, pp. 10–12; plus an interview with John Duigan by Dave Sargent, pp. 11–12.

Brendon (Jay Hackett), Sharon (Cassandra Delaney), Sam (Tyler Coppin) and Eva (Saskia Post)

RAZORBACK

Western Film Productions (No.1) [and] UAA. *Razorback*. © 1983 UAA Films Limited. *Budget:* $4.3 million. *Australian distributor:* GUO. *Opened:* April 1984. *Video:* Roadshow. *Rating:* M (March 1984; 2578.42m).[1] 35mm. Panavision. 95 mins.

Producer: Hal McElroy. *Associate producer:* Tim Sanders. *Scriptwriter:* Everett de Roche. Based on the novel by Peter Brennan. *Director of photography:* Dean Semler. *Production designer:* Bryce Walmsley. *Costume designer:* Helen Hooper. *Razorback designer:* Bob McCarron. *Editor:* William Anderson. *Composer:* Iva Davies. *Sound recordist:* Tim Lloyd. *Sound editors:* Greg Bell, Helen Brown, Ashley Grenville, Karin Whittington, Anne Breslin. *Mixers:* Ron Purvis, Peter Fenton, Phil Heywood.

Cast

Gregory Harrison (Carl Winters), Arkie Whiteley (Sarah Cameron), Bill Kerr (Jake Cullen), Chris Haywood (Benny Baker), David Argue (Dicko Baker), Judy Morris (Beth Winters), John Ewart (Turner), John Howard (Danny), Don Smith (Wallace), Mervyn Drake (Andy), Redmond Phillips (Magistrate), Alan Beecher (Counsel), Peter Schwartz (Lawyer), Beth Child (Louise Cullen), Rick Kennedy (Farmer), Chris Hession (Television Cowboy), Brian Adams (Male Newscaster), Jinx Lootens (Female Newscaster), Angus Malone (Scotty), Peter Boswell (Wagstaff), Don Lane (Himself).

Razorback was a bid by producer Hal McElroy and video-clip-maker Russell Mulcahy to crack the international film market. Mulcahy, who began his career on the ABC television programme, *Countdown*, has subsequently made three big-budget international epics, **Highlander** (1986), **Highlander II: The Quickening** (1991) and **Ricochet** (1991). High on style and minimal on content, Mulcahy's films could be termed video-clip horror.

Razorback, a surreal send-up of the classic horror genre, is a mix of **Jaws** (Steven Spielberg, 1975), **Evil Angels** (Fred Schepisi, 1988), **Deliverance** (John Boorman, 1972) and **The Cabinet of Dr Caligari** (Robert Wiene, 1919) – with rock clip effects thrown in. Smoke machines and synthesisers work overtime to provide erratic weather and nightmare visions, which are complemented by a haunting synthesiser soundtrack from Iva Davies.

Set in the desert, with whacky characters, Dean Semler cinematography and **Mad Max 2**-style cars, it is easy to compare **Razorback** to the George Miller film made

Turner (John Ewart) and Sarah Cameron (Arkie Whiteley).

three years earlier. However, while **Mad Max 2** has a kind of cowboys-and-indians logic – and a good-looking, sensitive hero – **Razorback**'s world is much less tangible, more ethereal, a world where the baddies outsmart the goodies.

Though Mulcahy's dark post-apocalyptic vision does employ real Australian elements, a kind of hyper-reality, the outback, looms large and untameable, with florid sunsets, barren salt plains, dust storms, barbed wire, gnarled branches – and exaggerated pig noises.

Constrained by a relatively small budget ($4.3 million), the film-makers opted for an arty approach to horror. Although at times gratuitously tacky, **Razorback** is a hilariously funny send-up, seemingly incorporating anything the film-makers could get their hands on.

From the opening shot of a windmill and a foregrounded kangaroo, it is difficult to take the film seriously. A young boy is abducted by a razorback – normally an aggressive, disease-ridden animal that hunts in packs and engorges horses. This one, however, has developed monster proportions.

Into this wild arena Mulcahy then throws a few urbane Americans: the environmentalist, Beth Winters (Judy Morris, with a dreadful American accent), and her mild-mannered husband, Carl (US television star Gregory Harrison), who comes to investigate her death. The film's only true-to-life character is the boy's grandfather, Jake (Bill

Kerr), who seeks revenge on the razorback. But the film's best performances come from Chris Haywood and David Argue as the black-comic brothers, Benny and Dicko Baker. Hardened survivors – probably inbreds – they work in an abattoirs processing kangaroo meat for petfood (PETPAK). The scene of much blood and gore, the abattoirs is a fabulous setting to catch a view of the obviously fake razorback – when it eats Benny, bit by bit.

While American critic Leslie Halliwell refers to the film's 'grim images of Australian life', Americans themselves are hardly unscathed by **Razorback**'s satire: the husband and wife characters are veritable caricatures. Mulcahy is not merely concerned with social critique, he parodies issues as broad as the dingo baby case, environmental protests and film-making traditions. With the current fad of satirical comedy on television (*The Big Gig, Fast Forward*), **Razorback**'s outrageous visual style is probably more accessible now than when it was made.

HELEN BARLOW

---

1 The video is rated 'R' for some reason.

References

'Russell Mulcahy', an interview with the director by Jim Schembri, *Cinema Papers*, no. 46, July 1984, pp. 138–41.

'Razorback', a review by Jim Schembri, ibid., p. 178.

'Razorback', a short review by Ross Gibson, *Filmnews*, April 1984, p. 17.

THE SETTLEMENT

The Queensland Film Corporation presents A Robert Bruning Production. *The Settlement.* © 1983 Robert Bruning Productions Pty Ltd. Script developed with assistance from the Australian Film Commission. *Locations:* Marburg, Samford, Rosewood, Ipswich (Queensland). *Australian distributor:* Ronin. *Video:* Australian Video. *Rating:* M. 35mm. 98 mins.

Producer: Robert Bruning. *Associate producer:* Anne Bruning. *Scriptwriter:* Ted Roberts. *Director of photography:* Ernest Clark. *Production designer:* John Watson. *Wardrobe:* Ron Reid. *Editor:* Henry Dangar. *Composer:* Sven Libaek. *Sound recordist:* Max Bowring. *Sound editors:* Ashley Grenville, Anne Breslin. *Mixer:* Julian Ellingworth.

Cast

Bill Kerr [Kearney[1]], John Jarratt [Martin], Lorna Lesley [Joycie], Tony Barry [Crowe], Katy Wild [Mrs Crowe], David Downer [Father Kleran], Elaine Cusick [Mrs Lohan], Alan Cassell [Lohan], Babette Stephens [Mrs Gansman]; Neil Fitzpatrick, Dudley Hogarth, Dennis Grosvenor, Maurice Hughes, Vanessa Wilkinson, Harry Lawrence, Malcolm Gork, Jim Sharman, Robert Janssen, Robert Eastgate, Peter Merrill, Stu Cochrane, Peter Armstrong, Tony King.

Kearney[3] (Bill Kerr) and Martin (John Jarratt).

Howard Rubie's **The Settlement** is an exception among Australian films, being a celebration of sexual preference and of individualism over conservative repression.

Kearney[2] (Bill Kerr) and Martin (John Jarratt) work the sideshows of rural Australia in the 1950s. Martin is a pugilist and Kearney tries to hustle a few side bets. But as the film opens, Martin has underestimated his opponent and is flattened. Unable to pay out the wager, Kearney and Martin scramble out under the boxing tent as a fight ensues.

Kearney and Martin wander the lonely country road, sleeping out at night. But Kearney's health is worsening and, when they reach the town of Cedar Creek, Martin's outburst of concern sees them spend the night at the home of the local copper, Crowe (Tony Barry), and his repressed Catholic wife (Katy Wild).

The next morning the men move on, finding shelter in a wreck of a cabin on Crown land. Martin returns to town where he befriends the recently arrived barmaid, Joycie (Lorna Lesley). She senses a decency in Martin and buys him the brandy he can't afford for his ailing mate. Joycie also agrees

to come and tend Kearney, going so far as to undress and sleep with him in an effort to keep him warm. Later that night, an envious Martin overhears them make love.

One now has the beginnings of a *ménage à trois* that eventually stirs the townswomen to violent action (specifically, Mrs Crowe) and deprives the extended family of the home, the settlement, they have so lovingly created.

What is unusual, as mentioned earlier, is that Rubie and writer Ted Roberts have the trio refuse to split up in accord with community pressures. They walk off into the future together, a future glimpsed briefly at the close where they are making a living in the side-show business – successfully this time. Quite clearly, Rubie and Roberts are arguing that the threesome's very success (all have been losers before) is because they are living their lives exactly as they wish, not as others may demand. This is a stirring and most welcome message.

Rubie, who directs in a totally unaffected manner, is aided by an excellent cast. Lesley plays the girl with a prostitute past without even the slightest nod to stereotype. John

Jarratt has long excelled at playing the basic, good Aussie fella, and he is again excellent here. Bill Kerr, too, makes Joycie's interest in the aged Kearney believable, and his pairing with Jarratt has resulted in an intriguing depiction of mateship. Tony Barry, as well, is perfect as the cop with a hard exterior but a 'decent' core.

The mechanics of the structure do become a little too obvious in the latter part (is there no wife in Australia who is not repressed sexually?), but mostly this is a precise and true study of character and a telling depiction of Australian society at less than its finest.

SCOTT MURRAY

---

[1] The film provides no character names on the credits. These have been assembled from various sources.
[2] See footnote 1.
[3] See footnote 1.

References
'The Settlement', a short review by Sally Stockbridge, *Filmnews*, July 1984, p. 20.
'The Settlement', a review by Penny Davies, *Filmnews*, October 1984, p. 19.

SILVER CITY

Limelight Productions presents SILVER CITY. © 1984 Limelight Productions. *Australian distributor:* Filmways. *Video:* CBS–Fox. *Rating:* NRC (September 1984; 2743m). 35mm. Panavision. 101 mins.

Producer: Joan Long. *Scriptwriters:* Sophia Turkiewicz, Thomas Keneally. *Director of photography:* John Seale. *Camera operator:* Danny Batterham. *Art director:* Igor Nay. *Costume designer:* Jan Hurley. *Editor:* Don Saunders. *Composer:* William Motzing. *Sound recordist:* Mark Lewis. *Sound editor:* Les Fiddess. *Mixer:* Julian Ellingworth.

Cast

Gosia Dobrowolska (Nina), Ivar Kants (Julian), Anna Jemison[1] (Anna), Steve Bisley (Viktor), Debra Lawrance (Helena), Ewa Brok (Mrs Bronowska), Joel Cohen (Young Daniel), Tim McKenzie (Mr Roy), Halina Abromowicz (Ella), Dennis Miller (Max), Annie Byron (Dorothy), Adam Brown (Man on Train), Cheryl Walton (100,000th Displaced Person), Ron Blanchard (Arthur Calwell), Noel Hodda (Estonian Man), Robert Newman (Customs Official 1), Samantha Marshall (Woman with Quilt), Thomas Zentai (Husband), Russell Newman (Customs Official 2), Wenanty Nozu (Leon), Ron Graham (Director), Karen Peterson (Interpreter).

Australia 1962: a chance encounter on a Sydney-bound train between former lovers Nina (Gosia Dobrowolska) and Julian (Ivar Kants) results in an extended flashback tracing not only the story of their romance, but also the broader socio-cultural experiences of a group of post-war Polish migrants.

This opening sequence of **Silver City** is perhaps its most poignantly successful, touching carefully on a number of themes which are progressively drawn out in the ensuing narrative. For, as the characters' words skirt the real issue, their gestures betray the memory of a former intimacy – a love affaire never satisfactorily resolved – of aspirations fulfilled and unfulfilled. It is Nina's words ('Remember Silver City?') which draws the story back twelve or so years to the dock-side debarkation of the newly arrived. This scene introduces the core group of Polish characters whose saga of cultural integration we bear witness to.

Together with Nina and Julian, it comprises Julian's wife, Anna (Anna Jemison[2]), their children, a mother-in-law, Mrs Bronowska (Ewa Brok), and fellow traveller-come-friend, Viktor (Steve Bisley). They are

soon transported inland to an isolated migrant hostel made of large corrugated-steel dormitories – thus the 'silver city' of the title. After a lengthy stay at the hostel, some of the characters' lives take different paths, but their destinies all finally cross again as they accede to the lure of the big city.

Silver City is the debut feature of Australian Film and Television School graduate Sophia Turkiewicz, herself an immigrant child of Polish parents. Her short student film, *Letters From Poland* (1978), had already introduced the themes that would find deeper and more extended treatment in **Silver City**.

The screenplay – written by Turkiewicz, with contributions by novelist Thomas Keneally – while, for the most part successfully balancing the love story and the wider social drama of the group, seems altogether heavy handed in its depiction of Australian culture. For the most part, the locals are shown to be intolerant of the 'new Australians', especially officials who are painted as petty bureaucrats, overtly stern or somewhat corrupt – the hostel Director (Ron Graham) being a case-study in 'commandant mentality'. The few that escape the taint of intolerance – such as Nina's prospective beau Mr Roy (Tim McKenzie) or a friendly ocker neighbour and his wife – are little more than Aussie caricatures.

A fairer social portrait could only have enriched the drama, as it is the Polish char-

acters who come across as having an undue condescension towards the local culture. Their cultural arrogance seems altogether strange given that they are post-war refugees with the dream of a new future in their hearts, escaping the ravages of a war-torn Europe, and, given the time and their Polishness, a country experiencing political and religious oppression. But this is precisely where Turkiewicz's direction of the drama fails her, for she cannot make us fully understand the psychological trauma they inherited from the war and how it shaped their mentality in a new land. This is perhaps inevitable given that Turkiewicz finally favours the love story between Nina and Julian, and the consequences it has on the family. The social dimension of the drama recedes, leaving the film as just another melodrama about lovers and family conflict.

ROLANDO CAPUTO

---

1 Later known as 'Anna Maria Monticelli'.
2 See footnote 1.

References

'Sophia Turkiewicz', an interview with the director by Christine Cremen, *Cinema Papers*, no. 47, August 1984, pp. 236–9, 287.
'Silver City', a review by Helen Greenwood, *Cinema Papers*, no. 48, October–November 1984, pp. 362–3.
'Silver City', a review by Penny Davies, *Filmnews*, October, 1984, p. 18.

Julian (Ivar Kants), Nina (Gosia Dobrowolska) and Customs Official 1 (Robert Newman).

THE SLIM DUSTY MOVIE

[No opening production credit.] THE SLIM DUSTY MOVIE. © 1984 The Slim Dusty Movie Ltd. *Australian distributor:* GUO. *Opened:* 18 October 1984. *Video:* Thorn EMI. *Rating:* G (2935.01m). 35mm. 107 mins.

Producer: Kent Chadwick. *Associate producer:* Brian Douglas. *Scriptwriter:* Kent Chadwick. *Director of photography:* David Eggby. *Additional photography:* Dan Burstall. *Camera operators:* Clive Duncan, David Connell, Gaetano Nino Martinetti[1]. *Production designer:* Leslie Binns. *Costume designer:* Jane Hyland. *Editor:* Ken Sallows. *Location sound supervisor:* Paul Clark. *Sound recordist:* Steve Haggerty. *Sound editors:* Dean Gawen, Ken Sallows, Rob Scott. *Mixers:* Gethin Creagh; Martin Oswin (2nd); Clive Jones (concert sound).

Cast

Slim Dusty, Joy McKean, Anne Kirkpatrick, The Travelling Country Band, David Kirkpatrick, Gordon Parsons, Lew Williams, Buck Taylor (as Themselves); Jon Blake (Slim Dusty as a Young Man), Dean Stidworthy (Slim Dusty as a Boy), Sandy Paul (Joy McKean as a Young Woman), Mary Charleston (Heather McKean as a Young Woman), Beverley Phillips (Slim's Mother), Tom Travers (Slim's Father), Brett Lewis (Slim's Young Mate, Shorty Rangers), Earl Francis (Country Radio Announcer); James Wright (City Radio Announcer); Frank Foster, Jim Sharman (Showground Spruikers); Johnny Brady (Whipcracker), Jeanette Leigh (Milkbar Waitress).

This is an expertly executed documentary-drama on Australia's one and only country music legend. The film records the annual travels across Australia of Slim Dusty, his wife Joy McKean, daughter Anne Kirkpatrick, and The Travelling Country Band, from one small country hall to another, from carnival shows to rodeo performances, and from outback concerts under the sky to shows in a major city concert hall.

The film also dramatically recreates the early years of Slim Dusty, who was born David Gordon Kirkpatrick. The dramatised sequences open from a decisive moment on a small dairy farm at Nulla Nulla Creek in New South Wales in 1937, when an eleven-year-old boy decided to change his name and become a country music star. The film then charts a story through the war years and Slim's first recording hopes, his courtship of Joy McKean, their struggle through lean years, right up to their performances in travelling sideshows of the 1950s.

Like Slim's own travels, **The Slim Dusty Movie** looks like a long, wearisome haul, yet it studiously avoids the bipartisan concept that is often a typical all-embracing feature of the musical bio-pic: that is, where the talent of an individual is placed against the conventions of a prevailing musical form in order to highlight his or her uniqueness. As a documentary, it also avoids the convention of a narrator or authoritative voice; authority is generated rather through the juxtaposition of images. This allows a particular depth and freedom to the form: the film is a documentary bio-pic, yet it is a road movie; it concerns one man, yet it embraces a vast cross-section of Australian life.

There is a sense that several local and colourful histories are told as Slim Dusty travels to each new destination. At times, the film dwells on extraordinary outback characters such as Lew Williams, a bush balladeer who has given inspiration to Slim's music; at other times, brief visual interludes of places far from Slim's travels are enough to realise the extent to which Slim's music is ingrained in the remotest corner of Australia.

The film hardly finds any need for dialogue, commentary or words, apart from those that are sung. In an early dramatic sequence, for example, only a brief exchange of glances is necessary to establish Slim's desire to take up the guitar.

Overall, it is an incredibly graphic film, relying a good deal on movement within the frame as well as between images. Movement is of course a large part of the lifestyle of Slim Dusty and The Travelling Band. The movement of an object or person within one shot is always balanced in the next with movement in an opposite direction. Moving vehicles, for instance, are often cues into the past – the dramatic sequences – and for returning to the present.

Moreover, the songs usually deal with memories, a time perhaps forgotten by the majority of Australians; and just as often a song sets in train a visual complex of shots equivalent to its mood – a slouch hat, fingers rolling a cigarette, the lines on a man's face.

Perhaps all that **The Slim Dusty Movie** finally reveals is the simplicity of Slim Dusty's lifestyle, a man hardly changed in a career spanning more than 50 years. Yet it is a simplicity captured most eloquently.

RAFFAELE CAPUTO

Lew Williams and Slim Dusty (as themselves).

---

[1] Later known as just 'Nino Martinetti'.

Slim Dusty as a boy (Dean Stidworthy) and Slim's father (Tom Travers).

STANLEY: EVERY HOME SHOULD HAVE ONE

Andrew Gaty presents A Seven Keys production. Stanley [/] EVERY HOME SHOULD HAVE ONE. © 1983 Benley Films and Others Pty. Ltd. and Seven Keys Pty. Ltd. *Budget:* $4 million. *Location:* Sydney. *Australian distributor:* Seven Keys. *Video:* Seven Keys Video. *Rating:* M. 35mm. 93 mins.

Producer: Andrew Gaty. *Executive producer:* Brian Rosen. *Associate producer:* Warwick Ross. *Scriptwriter:* Esben Storm. Based on a story by Esben Storm and Andrew Gaty. *Director of photography:* Russell Boyd. *Camera operator:* Nixon Binney. *Production designer:* Owen Williams. *Costume designer:* Robyn Richards. *Editor:* William Anderson. *Musical director:* William Motzing. *Sound recordist:* Mark Lewis. *Sound editors:* Andrew Steuart, Lee Smith, Jeanine Chialvo, Peter Burgess. *Mixers:* Peter Fenton (dia.); Phil Heywood (fx).

Cast

Graham Kennedy (Norman Norris), Nell Campbell (Amy), Peter Bensley (Stanley), Michael Craig (Sir Stanley), Leonard Teale (1st Detective), Harold Hopkins (Harry), Susan Walker (Doris Norris), Max Cullen (Berger), David Argue (Morris Norris), Lorna Lesley (Cheryl), Betty Lucas (Lady Dunstan), Adam Bowen (Head Waiter), Allan Dargin (Bobby), Rupert Burns (Vince), Jon Ewing (Reg), Johnny Lockwood (Flasher), Joy Smithers (Patty Norris), Tony Ward (Gary), Leslie Dayman (2nd Detective), Willie Fennell (Herb the Fisherman), Esben Storm (Menswear Attendant).

Stanley (Peter Bensley) pitches His Master's Choice dog food.

Esben Storm's comedy, **Stanley: Every Home Should Have One**, attracted a certain amount of notoriety (both good and bad, depending on your view of what constitutes worthwhile publicity) during its 1983 pre-production, thanks to a tussle between Actors Equity and producer Andrew Gaty over who was to play the title rôle.

Equity vetoed Gaty's stated preferences for English stars Tom Conti and Anthony Andrews. In the end, Gaty settled for Australia's Peter Bensley, then starring in the trash-time television serial *The Young Doctors*, to play the off-the-rails scion of an industrial tycoon. Bensley is supported by a quality cast that includes Graham Kennedy, Max Cullen, Michael Craig and David Argue. The resultant film, however, is an embarrassing throwback to **The Adventures of Barry McKenzie** (Bruce Beresford, 1972)

and **Alvin Purple** (Tim Burstall, 1973) days of the previous decade.

The idea is not at all bad: Stanley, an eccentric in the vein of Dudley Moore's character in **Arthur** (Steve Gordon, 1981), flees to suburbia when his stern parent threatens to have him 'put away' after one madcap escapade too many, but finds that the 'ordinary' suburban family with whom he takes refuge (chosen as 'most typical' by the firm's computer) is anything but normal.

There is easy-going Norman (Graham Kennedy) and Doris Norris (Susan Walker), pillars of the local bowling club, and their teenage children, Morris (David Argue, doing his popular truculent crazy act) and Patty (Joy Smithers).

At first, Stanley settles in well. He gets a job in a shop and starts to hit it off with a girl, Amy (Nell Campbell), who seems as

overwhelmingly 'normal' as the host family. Then things start to go awry.

The main trouble with the film is that Storm's treatment (he also wrote it from a story conceived with the producer) reduces a promising premise to a chaotic mishmash of slapstick, crudity and offensive satire. From the frenetic anarchy of an early sequence in which Stanley tries to talk his father's firm into marketing dog food for humans, the film rampages through a ragbag of basic sight-gags, sitcom clichés and even a few elementary social comments.

Most audiences – and they were few – yawned more than they laughed.

KEITH CONNOLLY

Reference

'Stanley [sic]', a review by Mark Spratt, *Cinema Papers*, no. 46, July 1984, pp. 180–1.

STREET HERO

Paul Dainty presents Street Hero. © 1984 Paul Dainty Films Ltd. Produced with assistance of Film Victoria. Developed with the assistance of the Australian Film Commission. *Location:* Melbourne. *Australian distributor:* Roadshow. *Opened:* 16 August 1984. *Video:* Roadshow Home Video. *Rating:* M (August 1984; 2743m). 35mm. 100 mins.

Producer: Julie Monton. *Executive producer:* Paul Dainty. *Scriptwriter:* Jan Sardi. *Director of photography:* Vincent Monton. *Camera operator:* David Williamson. *Editor:* David Pulbrook. *Production designer:* Brian Thomson. *Wardrobe:* Norma Moriceau. *Music co-ordinator:* Anthony A. O'Grady. *Composer:* Bruce Smeaton. *Sound recordist:* Gary Wilkins. *Sound editors:* Terry Rodman, Bruce Lamshed, Craig Carter. *Mixers:* Roger Savage, Bruce Lamshed, David Harrison.

Cast

Vince Colosimo (Vinnie), Sigrid Thornton (Gloria), Sandy Gore (Bonnie Rogers), Bill Hunter (Det. Fitzpatrick), Ray Marshall (George), Amanda Muggleton (Miss Reagan), Peta Toppano (Vinnie's Mother), Peter Albert Sardi (Joey), Luciano Catenacci (Ciccio), Robert Noble (Mick O'Shea), Noel Browne (Det. Richards), Tibor Gyapjas (Freddo), Darren Boyd (Karl), Jim Fotopoulos (Billy), Vince D'Amico (Nino), John Lee (Vice Principal), Max Davidson (Principal), Fincina Hopgood (Trixie), Samuel Hopgood (Mickey), David Colosimo (Vince six years old), Steve Hammond (Tony Romano).

Street Hero is one of several Australian films made in the early-to-mid 1980s which explicitly deal with the world of contemporary urban youth culture.

The film's non-conformist hero, Vinnie (Vince Colosimo), is beset with problems from all sides. At once the school outcast at odds with teachers and peer group, Vinnie spends his nights as a runner for the local mafia and pursuing a boxing career which is going nowhere. His home life fares no better. Living together with his mother and two siblings in cramped government housing, domestic life is fraught with tension due to his mother's live-in lover, whose homicidal behaviour leads to fatal consequences.

As if that were not enough, the screenplay burdens the hero with an Oedipal drama that manifests itself through sporadic flashbacks/hallucinations of his dead father – whom we learn was both a boxer and mafioso. Vinnie is obviously heading down

George (Ray Marshall) and Vinnie (Vince Colosimo).

the same road, but his subsequent involvement with the school band, the understanding of his girlfriend, Gloria (Sigrid Thornton), and the commitment of his arts/music teacher, Bonnie (Sandy Gore), help him to slowly reassess his world.

Scriptwriter Jan Sardi has produced a screenplay which seems altogether too narratively congested. Sub-plots and incidents leak out from all angles. For example, while an extended high-school staffroom scene may offer an accurate observation on the world of teachers in a stifling education system, it remains only arbitrarily connected to the trajectory of the hero's drama. Equally tenuous, though more integrated, are the storylines dealing with a good/bad policeman (Bill Hunter), and the mutual attraction between Vinnie and his teacher Bonnie. At times, one cannot but feel that Sardi's screenplay is at best a concoction of sub-plots straining to gel into a seamless whole.

If Sardi's screenplay lacks finesse and a certain subtlety of intention, then Michael Pattinson's direction only compounds problems. They, together with lead actor Vince Colosimo and other members of cast and crew, had previously collaborated on the social–realist drama **Moving Out** (1982). **Street Hero** retains some of that film's world and look, but grafts onto the social–realist

style some jazzy MTV-derived visuals and an upfront pop soundtrack, resulting in a disconcertingly hybrid *mise-en-scène* which oscillates between realism and artifice.

The centre of the film's nightlife is Easy Street – a multi-purpose narrative space which accommodates both the criminal underworld's base of operation and a strip of glitzy cafés where the teenagers hang out. The film's production design team has rendered the space as a highly-stylised, theatrical, neon-lit set. The intention no doubt is to consciously contrast this space with, say, the visually impoverished space of the Commission housing. But the effect is at best overstated.

In essence, **Street Hero** is a synthetic teen movie made by film-makers who do not fully understand what drives the genre. **Secrets** (1992), their most recent attempt at a teen movie 'in the American vein', seems destined to a similar fate.

ROLANDO CAPUTO

References
'Michael Pattinson and Jan Sardi', an interview with the director and the scriptwriter by Debi Enker, *Cinema Papers*, no. 48, October–November 1984, pp. 314–18, 383.
'**Street Hero**', a review by Dave Sargent, ibid., pp. 366–7.

STRIKEBOUND

[No opening production credit.] STRIKE-BOUND. © 1983 TRM Productions Pty. Ltd. Made with the assistance of Film Victoria. *Locations:* Toongabbie, Wonthaggi, Korumburra, Maldon, Toora (Victoria). *Australian distributor:* Ronin Films. *Rating:* M. *Video:* CBS–Fox. 16 mm (blown up to 35mm). 101 mins.

Producers: Miranda Bain, Timothy White. *Executive producers:* Erik Lipins, Miranda Bain. *Scriptwriter:* Richard Lowenstein. Adapted from the book *Dead Men Don't Dig Coal* by Wendy Lowenstein. *Director of photography:* Andrew De Groot. *Camera operator:* Paul Elliot. *Production designer:* Tracy Watt. *Costume designer:* Jennie Tate. *Editor:* Jill Bilcock. *Composer:* Declan Affley. *Sound recordist:* Dean Gawen. *Sound editors:* Dean Gawen, Frank Lipson. *Mixers:* Gethin Creagh, Martin Oswin.

Cast

Chris Haywood (Wattie Doig), Carol Burns (Agnes Doig), Hugh Keays-Byrne (Idris Williams), Rob Steele (Charlie Nelson), Nik Foster (Harry Bell), David Kendall (Birch), Anthony Hawkins (Police Sergeant), Marion Edward (Meg), Lazar Rodic (Yugoslav Scab), Reg Evans (Ernie), Rod Williams (Tom); Ian Shrives, Tiriel Mora (Militant Miners); May Howlett (Salvation Army Captain), Declan Affley (Welsh Singer), Denzil Howson (Politician), Charles Gilroy (Grocer), Ivor Bowyer (Rev. Busby), Kirsty Grant (Mrs King), Alice Lowenstein (Josie); Wattie Doig, Agnes Doig [as themselves].

Unlike the shearers' strike which is used as a mechanism to wind up the plot of **Sunday Too Far Away** (Ken Hannam, 1975), the miners' strike on the South Gippsland coalfields in the 1930s is the essential subject of this film. The events of the 1930s are recalled by Wattie and Agnes Doig, Scottish immigrants who were closely involved.

Wattie (Chris Haywood) leads the miners of the Sunbeam Colliery in protest against inadequate wages and appalling conditions. Scab labour is called in but the strikers flood them out, then barricade themselves in the mine until the company agrees to meet their demands. Agnes (Carol Burns), meanwhile, forms the Korumburra Women's Auxiliary which shows its militancy in boycotting shopkeepers who sympathise with the company. Fifty years later they recall the events of the strike with pride.

Richard Lowenstein's first feature film, based on his mother's book, *Dead Men Don't Dig Coal*, is one of the very few Australian films to take working-class life seriously. It

doesn't sentimentalise working-class heroism – Wattie is allowed his share of bloody-mindedness – but it does take a serious interest in the day-to-day lives of people doing dangerous, ill-rewarded work, and applauds the warmth and solidarity they find in the face of privation. Its sympathies are clear-cut: without unity and unionism, without loyalty to their class, the workers are powerless against their employers. In this sense, the film is not afraid of being didactic and this probably accounts for its chief weakness, too, which is the crudely melodramatic way in which the management figures are presented.

There are senses in which **Strikebound** is an important film other than for its preoccupation with a cinematically neglected class and subject. (The neglect may be commercially well-judged; **Strikebound** did not do well at the box office.) It is a film which focuses on a movement, on a group of people rather than on an individual protagonist in the classical Hollywood manner. The

Doigs' personal story is subordinated to a major political struggle. Further, in its use of the real-life figures of Wattie and Agnes Doig and through other non-diegetic inserts, the film also breaks with the Hollywood narrative model by drawing explicit attention to its processes of narration. It is one of the most daring and most undervalued films of the Australian revival.

BRIAN McFARLANE

References

'Strikebound', a production report containing an interview with director Richard Lowenstein by Scott Murray, *Cinema Papers*, no. 47, August 1984, pp. 210–13, 291, and an interview with director of photography Andrew de Groot by Murray, pp. 214–15, 287, and an interview with Dean Gawen, Gethin Creagh and Richard Lowenstein on sound by Pat Fiske, pp. 216–17, 288.

'Strikebound', a review by Dave Watson, *Cinema Papers*, no. 48, October–November 1984, pp. 357–8.

Wattie Doig (Chris Haywood) and Idris Williams (Hugh Keays-Byrne).

"*UNDERCOVER*"

A Palm Beach Picture.[1] "Undercover". © 1982 Palm Beach Pictures (Undercover) and Filmco Limited. Made in association with the Australian Film Commission. *Location:* Sydney, country New South Wales. *Australian distributor:* Roadshow. *Video:* Roadshow. *Rating:* NRC (July 1983 at 2605m; reduced by producer in January 1984 to 2428m). 35mm. 100 mins.

Producer: David Elfick. *Executive producer:* Richard H Toltz. *Scriptwriter:* Miranda Downes. *Director of photography:* Dean Semler. *Production designer:* Herbert Pinter. *Costume designer:* Kirstin Fredrikson. *Editor:* Tim Wellburn. *Musical director:* William Motzing. *Composer:* Bruce Smeaton. *Additional music:* William Motzing. *Sound recordist:* Peter Barker. *Sound editors:* Marc van Buuren; Tim Jordan (dia.). *Mixer:* Roger Savage.

Cast

Genevieve Picot (Libby), John Walton (Fred), Michael Pare[2] (Max), Sandy Gore (Nina), Peter Phelps (Theo), Andrew Sharp (Arthur), Caz Lederman (May), Wallas Eaton (Mr Breedlove), Susan Leith (Alice), Nicholas Eadie (Frank Bugden), Barry Otto (Professor Henckel), Midge Dempsey (Gladys), Debbie Baile (Mona), Ian Gilmour (Simmo), Lyn Lovett (Miss Barton), Phillip Ross (Mason), Bill McCluskey (Glover), John Barnes (League President), Isabelle Anderson (Enchantress).

Frustrated by the confines of life in Mudgee during the 1920s, where things are anything but roaring, and by her bleak employment prospects as a fitter with the local firm of corsetiers, a plucky Libby (Genevieve Picot) sets off for Sydney. On the train voyage, she flings her corset, the symbol of her own former employment and some of the conventions of her age, out the window.

Once in Sydney, it is not long before she is knocking on the door of Unique Corsets, to find work in the only field she knows. A further display of pluckiness, when she discovers that the company only wants to interview males, impresses the young Fred (John Walton) and secures her a position as a trainee designer.

Libby and a fellow apprentice, Alice (Susan Leith), are taken under the awesome but ever-so-stylish wing of Nina (Sandy Gore) and trained in the finer points of corsetry ('Remember, displaced flesh must go somewhere') and life itself ('It doesn't matter what you do as long as you do it *brilliantly*').

Along with Nina and the young impractical Fred, who dreams of a time when people overseas will demand to be able to buy Australian-made, the driving force of the company is the American marketing strategist, Max (Michael Pare[3]). Finding his swagger and confidence abrasive, Libby becomes quite hostile towards him. She has a tentative and seemingly experimental relationship with a sales representative to the company, Theo (Peter Phelps), which evaporates as soon as her career becomes more involving and demanding, and her interest in and admiration for Fred increase.

To satisfy notions of the excellence of imports, Unique Corsets undergoes a name change and, emulating the French, becomes the House of Berlei. Ironically, at the same time, Fred launches a campaign to 'buy Australian' which culminates in the voyage of the Great White Train, transporting an exhibition of Australian-made goods across the countryside.

The film takes full advantage of the cultural and historical curiosities which surround the Berlei story and the era in which it is set, such as the Train and the Great Anthropometric Survey, when thousands of women presented themselves to be measured for the statistics necessary to design the new range of Berlei underwear. These details are woven well into the texture of the film which on the whole works on an intimate and compassionate level.

One imbalance in the film is its approach to the fashion and underwear industry. Although perhaps taking too whimsical a look at an industry which has served as a stern master to countless women, it does not glamorise it in any way. The opening credits are backed by shining satin, but the camp side of fashion is not really introduced again until the Busby Berkeley-like finale where the costumes of the dancers and their routines dominate the stage.

It is otherwise an entertaining, compassionate and sensitive film with several fine performances, in particular from Sandy Gore as the irrepressible siren of style, Nina.

SUSAN TATE[4]

---

1 An end credit reads: 'A Palm Beach Picture– Filmco Production in association with the AFC'.
2 Usually spelt 'Paré'.
3 See footnote 2.
4 Extracted from Tate's review in *Cinema Papers* (see References).

References

'Voyages of Discovery', an interview with director David Stevens by Debi Enker, *Cinema Papers*, no. 44–5, April 1984, pp. 10–15, 106.
'Undercover', a review by Susan Tate, *Cinema Papers*, no. 46, July 1984, p. 185.
'Undercover', a very brief review by Kathe Boehringer, *Filmnews*, March 1984, p. 16.

Nina (Sandy Gore), the irrepressible siren of style.

WHERE THE GREEN ANTS DREAM

A Coproduction of Werner Herzog Filmproduktion and ZDF.[2] WHERE THE GREEN ANTS DREAM. [© not given; atb 1984.] Special thanks to the Australian Film Commission. *Locations:* Coober Pedy (South Australia); Melbourne. *Australian distributor:* Newvision Film Distributors. *Video:* Home Cinema Group. *Rating:* NRC (July 1984; 2688.14m). 35mm. 90 mins.

Producer: Lucki Stipetic. [*Scriptwriter:* not credited; atb Werner Herzog.] Additional dialogue: Bob Ellis. *Director of photography:* Jörg Schmidt-Reitwein. *Set designer:* Ulrich Bergfelder. *Wardrobe:* Frances D. Hogan. *Editor:* Beate Mainka-Jellinghaus. [*Composer:* not credited.] *Sound:* Claus Langer. [*Sound editor:* not credited.] [*Mixer:* not credited.]

Cast

Bruce Spence [Lance Hackett[3]], Wandjuk Marika [Miliritbi], Roy Marika [Dayipu], Ray Barrett [Cole], Norman Kaye [Baldwin Ferguson], Ralph Cotterill [Fletcher], Nicolas Lathouris [Arnold], Basil Clarke [Blackburn], Ray Marshall [Coulthard], Dhungala I. Marika [Malila], Gary Williams [Watson], Tony Llewellyn-Jones [Fitzsimmons], Robert Brissenden [Prof. Stanner], Bob Ellis [Supermarket Manager], Michael Edols [Young Attorney], Susan Greaves [Secretary], Marraru Wunungmurra [Daisy Barunga], Max Fairchild [Police Officer], Noel Lyon [Bailiff], Trevor Oxford [Worker], Hugh Keays-Byrne [Ayers Mining Exec.], Andrew Mack [Protocol Officer], Paul Cox [Ayers Mining Photographer].

Miliritbi[5] (Wandjuk Marika), Lance Hackett (Bruce Spence), Dayipu (Roy Marika) and Baldwin Ferguson (Norman Kaye).

Werner Herzog is a true internationalist, a journeyman film-maker who has filmed in many of the world's remotest and most spiritual places. He is a European romanticist with a passion for Old World mythologies. Long before New Age became trendy, he was exploring non-Western philosophies, especially the dreamings of 'primitive' cultures.

In 1983, Herzog ventured to Australia to make **Where the Green Ants Dream**, about a confrontation between white and Aboriginal Australians over the mining of a sacred site. In the process, he contrasts Western despoliation with a 40,000-year-old attunement with nature.

Lance Hackett[4] (Bruce Spence) is doing sonic testing of a new zone in Coober Pedy when several Aborigines interrupt the detonations. They claim the area is where the green ants dream and disturbing them will bring havoc to the world. Lance's company, Ayers Mining, tries to buy the Aborigines off, but gets nowhere. It even donates a Hercules aeroplane, which the Aborigines think is a giant green ant: they just use the interior as a camp site and the cockpit as a place to stare east, from where the ants will reputedly come.

The cross-purposes result in a court case, the aged judge being overwhelmingly sympathetic to the Aborigines during the hearing, only to rule definitively against them. A drunk Aborigine then flies the plane off into the mountains, where it crashes, and Lance quits his job, and, like a predecessor, opts for shelter in a disused water tank.

One reason the film passed with little attention is that it is totally flat dramatically. Almost no scene succeeds in creating tension and the confrontations – physical and ideological – lack resonance. Worse, the scenes where characters sit slowly expounding ideology are difficult to take, even though they have been a staple of all Herzog films (but usually in sub-titled German).

That said, the film is of interest for many reasons: apart from the obvious one of its topicality (and yet again here is a situation where an overseas director has come to make a film Australians should have), this is a film which struggles to deal with ideas. A certain archness in dialogue cannot detract significantly from the fact that Herzog examines concepts Australian film-makers have generally shied away from: the nature of being; how Western man seems to have lost direction, futile speculations about far-off universes covering for lost communion with a land it has so violated.

There is a certain romanticism in the way Herzog films the Aborigines – noble faces stark against the harsh sky – but this is typical of all his work. Anyway, one cannot deny that the European tradition of idealising ethnic cultures has been crucial in attempts by Westerners to understand ethnic societies and help prevent their wholesale destruction.

At times obscure, at others gloriously eloquent (the old lady waiting for her dog at the mine entrance, her multi-coloured umbrella behind her, is as striking and powerful an image as any the Australian cinema has conjured), **Where the Green Ants Dream** may not be major Herzog, but it need not be ignored, either.

SCOTT MURRAY

---

1 The credit reads 'A Film by Werner Herzog'.
2 This does not appear before the opening title (nothing precedes it) but as the last credit of the opening credits. There are no end credits.
3 There are no character names on the credits. These are taken from the press book and should be viewed accordingly.
4 See footnote 3.
5 See footnote 3.

References

'Where the Green Ants Dream', a review by Dorre Koeser, *Cinema Papers*, no. 48, October–November 1984, p. 367.
'Where the Green Ants Dream', a review by John Conomos, *Filmnews*, August–September 1984, p. 17.

THE WILD DUCK

Phillip Emanuel presents in association with Film Bancor of Australia The Wild Duck. © 1983 Tiazu Pty Ltd. *Location:* Sydney. *Australian distributor:* Roadshow. *Video:* Palace Academy Video. *Rating:* PG. 35mm. 92 mins.

Producer: Phillip Emanuel. *Co-producer:* Basil Appleby. *Scriptwriters:* Tutte Lemkow, Dido Merwin, Henri Safran. Additional material by Peter Smalley. Based on the play by Henrik Ibsen. *Director of photography:* Peter James. *Camera operator:* Danny Batterham. *Production designer:* Darrell Lass. *Costume designer:* David Rowe. *Editor:* Don Saunders. *Composer:* Simon Walker. *Sound recordist:* Syd Butterworth. *Sound editor:* Les Fiddess. *Mixer:* Julian Ellingworth.

Cast

Liv Ullman (Gina), Jeremy Irons (Harold), Lucinda Jones (Henriette), John Meillon (Old Ackland), Arthur Dignam (Gregory), Michael Pate (Wardle), Rhys McConnochie (Mr Roland), Colin Croft (Mollison), Marion Edward (Mrs Summers), Peter de Sahs (Peters), Jeff Truman (Johnson), Clive Marshall (Gray), Robert Bruning (Large Gentleman), Desmond Tester (Elderly Guest), Georgie Stirling (Caretaker).

The plays of the great 19th-century Norwegian dramatist Henrik Ibsen are full of cinematically appealing melodrama, but screen transcription has seldom been wholly successful. Henri Safran's 1983 version of *The Wild Duck*, a darkly tragic, deeply symbolic tale of human frailty, self-sacrifice and guilt, transposes the plot to turn-of-the-century Australia, while remaining faithful to the essentials of the original.

The screenplay, by Safran, Tutte Lemkow, Dido Merwin and Peter Smalley, never mentions the Australian locale, and overseas audiences probably were unaware of it. French-born Safran had a magnificent cast headed by international stars Liv Ullman, as Gina Ackland, sorely-tried wife with a 'scandalous' past, and Jeremy Irons as her wimpish husband, Harold.

The Australian supporting players are led by Arthur Dignam as Gregory, the well-meaning but insensitive friend who is the catalyst of the tragedy, and John Meillon, playing the disgraced old soldier who relives happier days by shooting wild game in his son's attic.

Within 24 hours of Gregory's coming into the humdrum life of the Acklands (Ibsen's Ekdals), Gregory perceives subterfuges, secrets and illusions that poor old Harold hasn't rumbled (or refused to

concede) for 15 years. Gregory is such a self-righteous prig that he sees it as his duty to open his friend's eyes…with inevitably tragic consequences.

To modern eyes, the husband's reaction, and its shocking dénouement, when daughter Henriette (Lucinda Jones) self-immolates, are incredibly over-the-top. But that's the way one of the greatest of all dramatists wrote it, for his time, and the respectful Safran certainly wasn't likely to revise Ibsen's structure.

Where he *does*, perhaps unwittingly, depart from Ibsen is in the very literalness of a reading that tends to gloss over the difficult questions – on the real nature of truth, happiness and reality – that are at the heart of the original drama.

The performances are good (though it might be said that Ullman puts too much of her own patent intelligence into the downtrodden Gina), Peter James' camera makes the locale believable and Darrell Lass' production designs are quietly authentic.

KEITH CONNOLLY

References

'The Wild Duck', a review by Paulo Weinberger, *Cinema Papers*, no. 46, July 1984, pp. 184–5.
'The Wild Duck', a short review by Penny Davies, *Filmnews*, March 1984, p. 16.

Harold (Jeremy Irons), Henriette (Lucinda Jones) and Gregory (Arthur Dignam).

Aunty Entity (Tina Turner) and her Imperial Guards. George Miller and George Ogilvie's Mad Max Beyond Thunderdome.

163

BLISS

Window III Productions & New South Wales Film Corporation present Bliss. © 1985 A Window III Production. Financed by The Quantum Group in association with the New South Wales Film Corporation. *Budget:* $3.4 million. *Location:* Sydney. *Australian distributor:* New South Wales Film Corporation. *Opened:* 19 September 1985. *Video:* CEL. *Rating:* M. 35mm. 110 mins.[1]

Producer: Anthony Buckley. *Scriptwriters:* Ray Lawrence, Peter Carey. Based on the novel by Peter Carey. *Director of photography:* Paul Murphy. *Camera operator:* David Williamson. *Design consultant:* Wendy Dickson. *Art director:* Owen Paterson. *Editor:* Wayne Le Clos. *Composer:* Peter Best. *Sound recordist:* Gary Wilkins. *Sound editor:* Dean Gawen. *Mixers:* Peter Fenton, Phil Heywood.

Cast

Barry Otto (Harry Joy), Lynette Curran (Bettina Joy), Helen Jones (Honey Barbara), Gia Carides (Lucy Joy), Miles Buchanan (David Joy), Jeff Truman (Joel), Tim Robertson (Alex Duval), Bryan Marshall (Adrian Clunes), Jon Ewing (Aldo), Kerry Walker (Alice Dalton), Paul Chubb (Reverend Des), Sara de Teliga (Harry's Mother), Saski[2] Post (Harry's Daughter), George Whaley (Vance Joy), Robert Menzies (Damian), Nique Needles (Ken McLaren), Marco Colombani (Dwarf), Tommy Dysart (De Vere), Les Foxcroft (Paul Bees), Alexandra Hey (Nursie), Manning Clark (Preacher).

Harry Joy (Barry Otto) suffers a heart attack and is 'dead' for four minutes. During that time, he has an out-of-body experience (a virtuoso sequence where the camera 'floats' aloft), before returning (descending) to his body a different man.

After hospitalisation, Harry goes through what is usually termed a mental breakdown and becomes suspicious of those around him. He is more than justified given that his wife, Bettina (Lynette Curran), is screwing his American partner, Joel (Jeff Truman); his son, David (Miles Buchanan), is a coke dealer and his daughter, Lucy (Gia Carides), gives her brother blow jobs in lieu of cash for drugs.

These early sequences are unusually structured. Apart from a narrative line that is close to 'real' (Harry's illness), there are Harry's dreams (awakening from an anæsthetic during an operation to push his organs back in), and the dreams/imaginings of others. Most unusual, there are also scenes of fabulation that come from no clear point

Harry Joy (Barry Otto), Aldo (Jon Ewing), Dwarf (Marco Colombini) and De Vere (Tommy Dysart).

of view: the restaurant scene where Bettina and Joel bonk à la carte; the change mid-fellatio of David into a Nazi uniform. (Is this his perception? Lucy's? The film-maker's?)

One is asked to take on faith this fractured approach. But while it has odd moments of successful shock, and others of plain silliness (the sardines), it tends to sap the film of all narrative flow. Director Ray Lawrence is unable to stop his film jerking along, and often just dying.

But then things change: the film starts concentrating on Harry and his love for Honey Barbara (Helen Jones), a hippy prostitute from a country valley who inspires Harry to break free of the cancer-ridden hell of city life and live among the trees and birds. Not that it is easy for Harry, for he is first committed to an asylum by his avaricious family and the only way out is a usury deal with Bettina. This means reneging on Honey Barbara, and she leaves him. But Bettina then learns she has cancer and explosively self-destructs.

Harry is free now to abandon city life and start anew in the bush, but the angry Honey Barbara will still have nothing to do with him. Harry waits, writing a love letter that takes eight years to be sent – trees that first must grow before her bees can savour its

delicious scent and then sweeten her honey. Tasting her unexpectedly glorious honey, Honey Barbara walks through the forest to Harry and says, 'I'm not going to spend the rest of my life hating you.'

This is one of the finest romantic resolutions in Australian cinema, not only for seeing a romance through to a happy ending (and that makes it rare), but also for the imaginativeness of the reconciliation.

When Harry later dies, killed by one of his trees, he floats free again. This time he does not return. With the excellent music of Peter Best (surely the most underrated of all Australian film composers), a soaring camera now loaded with meaning and a sense of a life having finally been well lived, this is a most touching and poignant ending.

SCOTT MURRAY

---

1 Shown at the 1985 Cannes Film Festival at 135 mins. This long version was screened on SBS.
2 Usually spelt 'Saskia'.

References

'Bliss in a Sometimes Joyless World', a brief article (with quotes) on producer Anthony Buckley by Peter Galvin, *Cinema Papers*, no. 54, November 1985, pp. 16–17.
'A Matter of Life and Death: **Bliss**', a review by David Stratton, ibid., p. 65.

BURKE & WILLS

Hoyts Edgley presents Burke & Wills. © 1985 Australian Film Investment Corporation. Made with the assistance of the Australian Film Commission. *Budget:* $8.9 million. *Locations:* Melbourne; South Australia; Northern Territory; England. *Australian distributor:* Hoyts. *Opened:* 7 November 1985. *Video:* RCA–Columbia–Hoyts. *Rating:* PG. 35mm. Panavision. 140 mins.

Producers: Graeme Clifford, John Sexton. *Executive producers:* Terry Jackman, Michael Edgley. *Scriptwriter:* Michael Thomas. *Director of photography:* Russell Boyd. *Camera operator:* Nixon Binney. *Production designer:* Ross Major. *Costume designer:* George Liddle. *Editor:* Tim Wellburn. *Composer:* Peter Sculthorpe. *Sound recordist:* Syd Butterworth. *Sound editor:* Jeanine Chialvo; Lee Smith (fx). *Mixers:* Peter Fenton, Ron Purvis, Phil Heywood.

Cast

Jack Thompson [Robert O'Hara Burke[1]], Nigel Havers [William John Wills], Greta Scacchi [Julia Matthews], Matthew Fargher [John King], Ralph Cotterill [Charley Gray], Drew Forsythe [William Brahe], Chris Haywood [Tom McDonagh], Monroe Reimers [Dost Mahomet], Ron Blanchard [Bill Patton], Barry Hill [George Landells], Roderick Williams [Bill Wright], Hugh Keays-Byrne [Ambrose Kyte], Arthur Dignam [Sir William Stawell], Ken Goodlet [Dr John Macadam], Edward Hepple [Ludwig Becker], Peter Collingwood [Dr William Wills], Susanna Harker [Bessie Wills], Martin Redpath [The Mayor of Melbourne], Julia Hamilton [Mrs Kyte].

Tackling the untimely deaths of historical figures has always presented film-makers with a dilemma. The makers of **Gandhi** (Richard Attenborough, 1982) and **Phar Lap** (Simon Wincer, 1983), for example, resigned themselves to the fact that audiences were aware of the plights of their title characters, stuck the deaths at the head of the film to stop the suspense and opted for the flashback approach.

The approach adopted by writer Michael Thomas and director Graeme Clifford in **Burke & Wills**, however, refuses this *fait accompli* attitude to historical fact. It takes a more ambitious, and ultimately more effective, path: that of creating an attachment, even an ambivalence, to the lead characters, and then recounting their last moments through the anguish of the expedition's lone survivor, John King[2] (Matthew Fargher). The

result is something of a double-whammy for the viewer, who discovers that, in spite of hours of primary school tutelage on the outcome of the ill-fated journey, it comes as a moving revelation.

It is precisely this approach that lends the film much of its considerable emotional clout. A refusal to be intimidated by either the magnitude of the mistakes or history's glowing eulogies to pioneering spirit lends the saga a new lease of life. The myths are humanised; errors in judgement that have been magnified to monumental sins over the passage of time are reduced to digestible human foibles.

Visually, structurally and in terms of many of its characterisations, the film resembles a Western, but a Western of the period when cowboys were becoming oddities on the periphery of a developing society. While Russell Boyd's majestic cinematography adeptly captures the expansive outback, the characters sway between stoicism, short-sightedness and indefatigable spirit. The Aborigines become synonymous with the Indians: noticeably passive, but clearly in and of the land, amused, confused and suspicious of the alien intruders.

Jack Thompson's Robert O'Hara Burke wears his badge of courage and his individual moral code proudly, but Thompson allows his character to trespass into less charismatic territories. He is seen to be vain, bombastic and prone to rely on impulses that he should have learned are too often misguided. And, while Nigel Havers' gently blossoming portrait of the refined, strait-laced William John Wills provides the necessary contrast, conflict and compassion

of any great mateship, Greta Scacchi as Burke's fiancée, Julia Matthews, supplies the romantic interest – the spirited woman waiting in vain for the boys to come home.

The emotional thrust of **Burke & Wills** is built on intensity rather than subtlety. The unconcealed admiration for individuals willing to go out on a limb is at the film's core, as is the outrage, eventually vocalised by King, at a sedentary middle-class happy to bathe in the glory but ready to assume none of the responsibility of achievement.

While the passion for this brand of heroism can occasionally overflow into a heavy-handed outburst unnecessarily identifying Right and Wrong, it is generally powerful and poignant. This tale of an epic historical journey has a perspective that is both reverent and refreshing.

DEBI ENKER[3]

---

[1] The cast credits are white against a bleached sky and on video are totally unreadable. These come from *Monthly Film Bulletin*.
[2] See footnote 1.
[3] Extracted from Enker's review in *Cinema Papers* (see References).
[4] See footnote 1.

References

'Making Treks', an article (with quotes) on director Graeme Clifford by Debi Enker, *Cinema Papers*, no. 54, November 1985, pp. 18–19.
'Once Upon a Time in the North: **Burke & Wills**', a review by Debi Enker, ibid., p. 69.
'Jack from Dick to Joe', an article (with quotes) on actor Jack Thompson by Nick Roddick, *Cinema Papers*, no. 56, March 1986, p. 15.
'Burke and [sic] **Wills**', a review by Ross Gibson, *Filmnews*, December 1985, p. 14.

Robert O'Hara Burke[4] (Jack Thompson) and William John Wills (Nigel Havers).

THE COCA-COLA KID

Cinema Enterprises and David Roe present the coca-cola kid. © 1985 Grand Bay Films International Pty Ltd. *Budget:* $3 million. *Locations:* Sydney, the Blue Mountains (New South Wales). *Australian distributor:* Roadshow. *Video:* Premier Home Entertainment. *Rating:* M. 93 mins.

Producer: David Roe. *Executive producer:* Les Lithgow. *Co-producer:* Sylvie le Clezio. *Scriptwriter:* Frank Moorhouse. Based on short stories in *The Americans, Baby* and *The Electrical Experience* by Frank Moorhouse. *Director of photography:* Dean Semler. *Production designer:* Graham (Grace) Walker. *Costume designer:* Terry Ryan. *Editor:* John Scott. *Composer:* William Motzing. *Original songs:* Tim Finn. *Sound recordist:* Mark Lewis. *Sound editors:* Dean Gawen, Helen Brown. *Mixers:* Gethin Creagh, Martin Oswin.

Cast

Eric Roberts (Becker), Greta Scacchi (Terri), Bill Kerr (T. George McDowell), Max Gillies (Frank), Kris McQuade (Juliana), Tony Barry (Bushman), Chris Haywood (Kim), Paul Chubb (Fred), David Slingsby (Waiter), Tim Finn (Philip), Colleen Clifford (Mrs Haversham), Rebecca Smart (DMZ), Esben Storm (Country Hotel Manager), Steve Dodd (Mr Joe), Ian Gilmour (Marjorie), David Argue (Newspaper Vendor); Linda Nagle, Julie Nihill, Fiona Halett (Marching Girls); Ricky Fataar, Mark Moffatt, Paul Hester, Rex Goh (Rock Musicians).

The Coca-Cola Kid has gone down in the folklore of the Australian film industry as a prime example of a project which looked great at the outset, but went horribly wrong in the making. It promised not only the meeting of an internationally acclaimed, radical film-maker (Dusan Makavejev) with one of the most respected Australian fiction writers (Frank Moorhouse), but also a definitive treatment of a theme beloved of Australian cinema: the uneasy, often hostile, tortuously ambivalent relation between American and Australian societies, allegorised in a tale of the 'stranger in a strange land'.

However, Makavejev reportedly had a very difficult time both on set and with his producers, and the finished film betrays fundamental uncertainties of conception, tone and pitch. (For one colourful account of the problems of its making, see Moorhouse's *Lateshows*.[1])

It is a difficult film to discuss because, thematically, it is completely incoherent. The meanings of individual scenes and certain thematic threads are quite clear, but taken together they make no sense. In the first 'act' (generally agreed to be the most successful), the film seems bent on a heavy-handed satire of the corporate, fast-talking, tight-assed, fundamentalist American way of life, incarnated in Becker (Eric Roberts in a rather overwrought performance). To this repressive, 'control-freak', hyper-capitalist mode of existence, Makavejev interestingly opposes (as he does in his other films) a (peculiarly Australian) 'schizo system' of being – loose, eccentric, merrily inefficient, spontaneously mixing up the public and private spheres of life.

These thematic developments are abruptly aborted with the introduction of T. George McDowell (Bill Kerr), the last remaining small-time 'bush capitalist', who manufactures his own cola. Not merely switching at this point into what Ross Gibson calls a 'politically vulgar drama of nostalgic nationalism versus empire'[2], the film attempts to work up a sympathetic 'mirror relation' between the 'frontier' styles of Becker and McDowell, with urban Australia now cast as a hellish site of sexual ambiguity and treachery (for example, the terrible scene of Terri's 'decadent' inner-city party). We are asked as viewers both to approve the necessary 'degradation' of Becker as he learns to loosen up, and to feel sorry for his plight as a beleaguered 'outsider' with some fine 'old fashioned' ideas of progress. Onto all this is superimposed an unreadable Oedipal plot, with McDowell as the father who must be 'transgressed' by the son, Becker, to win the mother/daughter figure, Terri.

The meaning of many passing details and sub-plots in the film seems wildly unfixed. Early on is a neat joke about a 'savage', didgeridoo-playing Aborigine who turns out to have a showbiz agent, signalling a witty and knowing subversion of conservative stereotypes. But, later, a conniving waiter at Becker's hotel is portrayed, in a completely reactionary fashion, as the classic 'insane' (and similarly crypto-gay) Left-wing terrorist; and Terri throughout is sadly made the repository of an assortment of backward male projections: randy secretary, earth-mother-showering-with-child, ditsy airhead, 'life force', source of redemption for the battered hero…

Perhaps the most charitable notion that could be advanced to defend the film is that Makavejev's celebration of anarchic 'schizo systems' naturally extends to the film-making process itself, resulting in a work that is perhaps deliberately 'decentred', shifting and blissfully contradictory.

ADRIAN MARTIN

---

1 Frank Moorhouse, *Lateshows*, Wild and Wooley, Sydney, 1990.
2 Ross Gibson, '**The Coca Cola** [sic] **Kid**' (see References).

References

'The Reel Thing', an article by director Dusan Makavejev, *Cinema Papers*, no. 51, May 1985, pp. 60–2.

'Mysteries of the Organization: **The Coca-Cola Kid**', a review by John Baxter, *Cinema Papers*, no. 54, November 1985, pp. 69–70.

'**The Coca Cola** [sic] **Kid**', a short review by Ross Gibson, *Filmnews*, September 1985, p. 17.

Cross-cultural lovers: Becker (Eric Roberts) and Terri (Greta Scacchi).

EMOH RUO

UAA Films presents A Palm Beach Picture. EMOH RUO. © 1985 Western Film Productions No. 7 Pty Limited. *Budget:* $1.7 million. *Location:* Baulkham Hills, Sydney. *Australian distributor:* GUO. *Video:* Roadshow Home Video. *Rating:* M. 35mm. 93 mins.

Producer: David Elfick. *Executive producers:* David Thomas, John Picton-Warlow. *Associate producer:* Steve Knapman. *Scriptwriters:* Paul Leadon, David Poltorak. *Director of photography:* Andrew Lesnie. *Production designer:* Robert Dein. *Costume designer:* Anthony Jones. *Editor:* Ted Ötton. *Composer:* Cameron Allan. *Sound recordist:* Paul Brincat. *Sound supervisor:* Roger Savage. *Sound editors:* Les Fiddess (dia.); Bruce Emery (fx). *Mixers:* Roger Savage, Bruce Emery, David Harrison.

Cast

Joy Smithers (Terri Tunkley), Martin Sacks (Des Tunkley), Jack Ellis (Jack Tunkley), Philip Quast (Les Tunkley), Louise Le May (Helen Tunkley); Joanna Burgess, Natalie Burgess (Tunkley Twins); Genevieve Mooy (Margaret York), Max Phipps (Sam Tregado), Bill Young (Wally Wombat), Helen McDonald (Pat Harrison), Mervyn Drake (Warren Harrison), Noel Hodda (Pete), Ric Carter (Thommo), Di Smith (Cheryl Mason), Lance Curtis (Wayne Mason), Joy Dobson (Narelle), Garry Who (Policeman), Charito Ortez (Sam's Receptionist), Rainee Skinner (Teller), John Spicer (Magistrate), Ray Marshall (Clarrie).

Des (Martin Sacks) and Terri Tunkley (Joy Smithers) are a young, happily-married but struggling couple about to take the big plunge and buy into the Great Australian Dream. Falling under the spell of a television advertisement extolling the joys of home ownership, Terri cajoles Des into making their first big financial commitment.

At first, Des is none too enthusiastic about leaving their carefree, downwardly mobile lifestyle in a caravan park by the sea, and neither is their young son, Jack (Jack Ellis). The good life for Des is embodied in his beloved, as-yet-to-be-restored motor-boat. Here then lies a basis for conflict between Terri's desire for the domestic comforts of a 'real' home, and Des' dream of sailing away to the West Indies.

Undeterred by her husband's initial reluctance, Terri calls on Austral Finance for a housing loan. Now more determined than ever to realise her dream, Terri becomes frustrated by Des' lack of interest. When things finally come to a head between them one

Des (Martin Sacks) and Terri Tunkley (Joy Smithers).

rainy afternoon, Des relents and sells his boat to raise the loan deposit. Immediately, the family packs up and sets off for their brand new home in a far-flung housing estate on the city's fringe.

Not long after they settle into their new life, things begin to go awry: not only are their only neighbours dreadful nerds, but Des and Terri are also forced to work interminable hours to meet the repayments. Worse still, their 'dream' home turns out to be a complete lemon.

These unforeseen difficulties begin to take their toll and, when Des loses his licence and they are served with an eviction notice, their happy marriage is threatened. But just as things appear to hit rock bottom, Des, goaded on by his wife's accusation that he never completes anything he starts, labours day and night on a backyard barbecue to prove her wrong.

When friends and family drop over and marvel at Des' masterpiece, Sam Tregado (Max Phipps), the shonky developer who sold the Tunkleys their jerry-built house, arrives unannounced with some prospective buyers and receives a less-than-welcome reception from a now-overwrought Terri.

The young couple eventually settle their differences and agree to quit the suburban life, just in time to see their house collapse into a pile of rubble. Soon afterwards, Des goes on to become a successful entrepreneur of custom-built barbecues, and in the final scene the Tunkley family sets off with their new caravan in tow on an endless holiday.

More light-hearted situation comedy than biting satire, the film has its amusing moments. Competently made and entertaining in a lowbrow way, it has no pretensions to social comment. But its resorting to well-known Australian stereotypes is more often witless than inspired.

The ending is pure wish fulfilment, an embodiment of that other great Australian dream.

BRUCE SANDOW

References

'Seeing Stars', an article about the actors Joy Smithers and Martin Sacks by Nick Roddick, *Cinema Papers*, no. 51, May 1985, pp. 20–21.

'On Our Selection: **Emoh Ruo**', a review by Christine Cremen, *Cinema Papers*, no. 54, November 1985, pp. 67, 69.

CHRIS THOMSON

THE EMPTY BEACH

A Jethro Films Production. THE EMPTY BEACH. © 1985 Jethro Films Pty Ltd. *Budget:* $1.8 million. *Location:* Sydney. *Australian distributor:* Hoyts. *Opened:* 12 September 1985. *Video:* RCA–Columbia–Hoyts. *Rating:* M. 35mm. 89 mins.

Producers: Timothy Read, John Edwards. *Executive producer:* Bob Weis. *Scriptwriter:* Keith Dewhurst. Based on the novel by Peter Corris. *Director of photography:* John Seale. *Production designer:* Lawrence[1] Eastwood. *Costume designer:* Miranda Skinner. *Editor:* Lindsay Frazer. *Composers:* Martin Armiger, Red Symons. *Sound recordist:* Max Hensser. *Sound editor:* Greg Bell. *Mixer:* Gethin Creagh.

Cast

Bryan Brown (Cliff Hardy), Anna Maria Monticelli[2] (Anne Winter), Belinda Giblin (Marion Singer), Ray Barrett (McLean), John Wood (Parker), Peter Collingwood (Ward), Nick Tate (Henneberry), Kerry Mack (Hildegard), Joss McWilliam (Tal), Sally Cooper (Sandy Modesto), Rhys McConnochie (Garth Green), Steve Rackman (Rex), Robert Alexander (Bob), Bob Barrett (Johnno), Christopher Lewis (Aldo), Steve J. Spears (Manny), Kerry Dwyer (Mary Mahoud), Dean Nottle (Mercer), Robert Noble (Pinball Manager), Simone Taylor (Sharon), Harry Lawrence (Leon), Alexander Hay (Edgar Montefiore).

Cliff Hardy (Bryan Brown) drags the corpse of Henneberry (Nick Tate) from the ocean.

The Empty Beach indelicately taps into a particularly American tradition of crime fiction, even though Australian cinema and culture has very little expertise with it. What the film-makers have overlooked is that the moral universe of the American detective, because of all its socio-historical and æsthetic complexity, cannot be simply and easily transposed to the Australian cultural and social context.

Set in and around Sydney's Bondi, The Empty Beach has Cliff Hardy (Bryan Brown), divorced and a recent non-smoker, employed by Marion Singer (Belinda Giblin), widow of a wealthy real-estate businessman, John Singer (Barry Leane). A man whose business transactions were not always above board, John Singer disappeared two years earlier off Bondi beach. Though his body was not recovered, a suicide note was found in the cabin of his yacht. But Marion has recently received anonymous information that her husband is still alive, and she hires Hardy to discover the truth. This leads Hardy through a minute (criminal) web of Singer's former business associates now masquerading as part of Bondi's respectable and élite class.

This story has the bare bones of many a crime fiction, and unfortunately it is mostly at this level of plot, stock character and iconic reference that **The Empty Beach** operates. If Cliff Hardy is in the line-up with the figures of Philip Marlowe, Lew Archer, Sam Spade, et al., then the implications of discovering, developing, accommodating and translating this figure and his universe within the Australian urban environment, and within the Australian vernacular, are not attended to. For example, Bondi beach becomes the California coastline and the film is replete with 'tough talk' that appears to extend from the hard-boiled school. But this is all they can ever be: elements which look to be something else. What remains absent is the poetic laconicism of the detective's universe.

Although these elements are tangible and recognisable, and bear much resemblance to other places, characters, situations and figures of speech, there are also poetic, mythic, philosophical associations that can-not be ignored or merely duplicated. The laconic brevity of the American detective's language, for instance, alludes to so much within his fatalistic vision of the world. It is not merely 'tough talk' as it is in **The Empty Beach**.

Director Chris Thomson and scriptwriter Keith Dewhurst certainly know the elements of the tradition, but they have not understood the flexibilities and inflexibilities of the stylistic and philosophical resonances of them.

RAFFAELE CAPUTO

---

[1] Usually spelt 'Laurence'.
[2] Formerly known as 'Anna Jemison'.

References

'Life of Bryan', an article (with quotes) on actor Bryan Brown by Dorre Koeser, *Cinema Papers*, no. 53, September 1985, pp. 16–19.
'The Long G'day: **The Empty Beach**', a review by Paul Kalina, *Cinema Papers*, no. 54, November 1985, p. 66.
'**The Empty Beach**', a short review by Kathe Boehringer, *Filmnews*, September 1985, p. 16.

EPIC

Yoram Gross presents Epic. © Yoram Gross Film Studio. *Australian distributor:* Yoram Gross. *Video:* CEL and VSA. *Rating:* G. 35mm. 75 mins.

Producer: Yoram Gross. *Associate producer:* Sandra Gross. *Scriptwriter:* John Palmer. Based on original story by Yoram Gross. *Photography:* Graham Sharpe, Jan Carruthers, Ricky Vergara. *Editor:* Y. Jerzy. *Composer:* Guy Gross. *Sound editors:* Arne Ohlsson, Lee Smith. *Mixers:* Peter Fenton, Phil Heywood.

Animation director: Athol Henry. *Animators:* Gairden Cooke, Ariel Ferrari, Murray Griffen, Nicholas Harding, Andrew Szemenyei, Rowen Avon. *Additional animators:* Paul Baker, Zbigniew Bilyk, Lucinda Clutterbuck, Koichi Kashiwa, Wayne Kelly, Boris Kozlov, Domingo Rivera, Vicky Robinson, Liu Ruo, Phillip Scarrold, Jan de Silva, Bela Szeman, Min Xu, Gennady Kozlov, Maria Haren. *Painters:* Mimi Intal, Corallee Munro, Robyn Drayton, Joseph Cabatuan. *Backgrounds:* Amber Ellis, Gennady Kozlov, Norman Yeend, Graham Binding. *Graphics:* Eric David. *Special fx painting:* Amber Ellis, Jeanette Toms, Gennady Kozlov.

Voices

Ross Higgins, Robyn Moore, Benitta Collins

[See Appendix A on all the Gross films, pp. 352–4.]

References
'Yoram Gross', an interview with the producer-director by Antoinette Starkiewicz, *Cinema Papers*, no. 48, October–November 1984, pp. 334–8, 380–1.
'Yoram Gross', Raffaele Caputo, *Cinema Papers*, no. 86, January 1992, pp. 36–42.

Benitta Collins and dingoes.

FRAN

Barron Films presents Fran. © 1985 Bush Christmas Productions Ltd. and the Unit Holders in 'Fran'. Produced with financial assistance from the Western Australian Film Council and developed with assistance from the Australian Film Commission. *Budget:* $700,000. *Location:* Perth. *Australian distributor:* Barron Films. *Opened:* 14 November 1985. *Video:* CBS–Fox. *Rating:* M. 16mm. 94 mins.

Producer: David Rapsey. *Executive producer:* Paul Barron. *Scriptwriter:* Glenda Hambly. *Director of photography:* Jan Kenny. *Camera operator:* Jan Kenny. *Production designer:* Theo Mathews. [*Costume designer:* not credited.] *Editor:* Tai Tang Thein. *Composer:* Greg Schultz. *Sound recordist:* Kim Lord. *Sound editors:* Glen Martin, Glenda Hambly. [*Mixer:* not credited.]

Cast

Noni Hazlehurst (Fran), Annie Byron (Marge), Alan Fletcher (Jeff), Narelle Simpson (Lisa), Travis Ward (Tom), Rosie Logie (Cynthia), Danny Adcock (Ray), Steve Jodrell (Michael Butlin), Penny Brown (Sally Aspinal), Faith Clayton (Waigani Supervisor), Richard Tulloch (Peter Cook), Colin McEwan (Graham Brooks), Rosemary Harrison (Carol Brooks), Paul Rella-Marta (Tony Simpson), Tina Wunderberg (Annie Simpson), Ross Coli (Weed), Ken Smith (Mr Pearce), Bruno Napolitano (Deli Owner), Jeremy Higgins (Welfare Officer), Michael Muntz (Collection Agent).

Fran (Noni Hazlehurst) is a likeable, vivacious, madcap, irresponsible and negligent mother of three children, each from a different relationship. She is a product of the welfare system and several foster homes, and of an alcoholic mother and a father she never knew. Passionate about protecting her children from the community welfare authorities, whom she paints as the enemy, she nevertheless fails to do so.

Fran's own self-esteem requires a man in her life and, after the violent end of one relationship, she desperately picks up Jeff (Alan Fletcher), a wayward barman. To secure her relationship with Jeff, she holidays with him, deserting her children for weeks. In her absence, the children become wards of the state, and it is claimed that Jeff has sexually interfered with Fran's eldest daughter, Lisa (Narelle Simpson). The story is about cycles and the painful, inexorable way the past keeps repeating itself.

Fran is the first feature of writer–director Glenda Hambly, who previously worked with documentaries. The idea for the film grew out of research Hambly was doing for the West Australian Department of Community Welfare, which was planning a documentary to support the implementation of a new child welfare scheme. When the controversial scheme and the documentary fell through, Hambly developed the material into a feature-length script. It constructs a complex portrait of a woman and the social structure incapable of supporting her. Both humorous and tragic, this is not a film of simple solutions.

Though the power of the film may come from the issues it addresses, they are made particularly compelling through the strength and credibility of many fine performances. Hazlehurst's laconic vernacular empowers the rhythms and attitudes of working-class dialogue. She walks, wiggles and dances with an audacious, adolescent sexuality that invites you to love her as you loathe her. She is endearing despite her mistakes. Our reactions to her are complex – alternately forgiving and judgemental.

Annie Byron, as Fran's homely neighbour, Marge, puts in another excellent performance. Marge is a single mother, too, but, unlike Fran, she fears men. She offers Fran support and camaraderie, but her lifestyle is not an enviable one. And, of course, there is Lisa, the daughter too young to play mother, whose looks and face tug at your heart as you watch her become the victim of a past not of her making.

Fran is one of the first Australian features to credit a female director of photography, Jan Kenny, and this is quite significant. While social–realist subject matter doesn't always invite attention to the image or *mise-en-scène*, this is often because of the way form supports function. Yet the look of **Fran**'s world is pivotal in the credibility we attribute to her story: the drab, uninspiring suburbia of housing commission estates, harsh Australian sunshine, bland backyards, parched streets dotted with souped-up cars and dreary pubs full of lonely people. There is nothing romantically dark, mysterious or tantalising here like the suburbs of David Lynch's America. However, **Fran**'s world is all the more chilling and disturbing for it.

ANNA DZENIS

Refereces
'Noni's Choice', an article on the actor Noni Hazlehurst by Dorre Koeser, *Cinema Papers*, no. 51, May 1985, pp. 50–3.
'Fear and Loathing in WA: **Fran**', a review by Paul Byrnes, *Cinema Papers*, no. 55, January 1986, p. 62.

Fran (Noni Hazlehurst) and Jeff (Alan Fletcher).

AN INDECENT OBSESSION

Hoyts/Michael Edgley International presents A P.B.L. Production. An Indecent Obsession.[1] © 1985 P.B.L. Productions Pty. Ltd. *Budget:* $2.1 million. *Location:* Lord Howe Island. *Australian distributor:* Hoyts. *Opened:* 23 May 1985. *Video:* RCA–Columbia–Hoyts. *Rating:* M. 35mm. 106 mins.

Producer: Ian Bradley. *Executive producers:* Michael Edgley, John Daniell. *Associate producer:* Maura Fay. *Scriptwriter:* Denise Morgan. Based on the novel by Colleen McCullough. *Director of photography:* Ernest Clark. *Camera operator:* David Foreman. *Production designer:* Michael Ralph. *Costume designer:* Graham Purcell. *Editor:* Philip Howe. *Composer:* Dave Skinner. *Sound recordist:* Ken Hammond. *Sound editor:* Tony Vaccher. *Post-production sound:* Max Hensser. *Mixer:* Gethin Greagh[2].

Cast

Wendy Hughes (Honour Langtry), Gary Sweet (Michael Wilson), Richard Moir (Luce Daggett), Jonathan Hyde (Neil Parkinson), Bruno Lawrence (Matt Sawyer), Mark Little (Benedict Maynard), Tony Sheldon (Nugget Jones), Bill Hunter (Colonel Chinstrap), Julia Blake (Matron), Caroline Gillmer (Sally Dawkins), Marina Finlay (Sue Peddar), John Sheerin (R.S.M.), Andrew Martin (Pennyquick), Mark David (Colin), Masayuki Fujioka (Japanese Soldier).

Committed though one may be to the notion that there is no necessary correlation between the quality of a film and that of the novel from which it is adapted, **An Indecent Obsession** must give one pause. Directed by Lex Marinos, it offers persuasive evidence of the intransigence of trash. The situations, the characters and the dialogue are instinct with the unmistakable sensibility of the original author, Colleen McCullough.

Sister Honour Langtry (Wendy Hughes) runs, with remarkable incompetence, the psychiatric ward of a military hospital on a Pacific island during World War II. All the inmates, in their variously bizarre ways, dote on 'Sis', as they affectionately call her.

The inmates – just an ordinary cross-section of cranks – include a rowdy officer-type, Neil Parkinson (Jonathan Hyde), who comes from The Same Background as Sis, something which he believes gives him the edge over mad-eyed Luce Daggett (Richard Moir), a former actor of lowly social origins and sexual ambiguities. Then there is a religious nut and mother's boy called Benedict

Honour Langtry (Wendy Hughes), an incompetent nursing sister.

Maynard (Mark Little); Nugget Jones (Tony Sheldon), a hypochondriac who is forever reading medical works in search of new symptoms; and Matt Sawyer (Bruno Lawrence), who may or may not be blind.

Tensions run high, and Sis gets no support from Colonel Chinstrap (Bill Hunter) or Matron (Julia Blake). In fact, they, not unreasonably, get very tired of her.

Into this seething microcosm of lunatic fancies and unrequited passions comes handsome young Michael Wilson (Gary Sweet), who is apparently normal. What, then, is he doing in Ward X? Well, it transpires – via a feverish dream sequence – that the RSM whom he'd tried to kill had made some very indecent suggestions to him. The same thing happens again when Luce does something provocative to him under the showers.

This time, though, Mike finds refuge in Langtry's bed. And, while they're making some love, something very nasty is happening to Luce. You can just imagine how Sis blames herself for this next day.

An Indecent Obsession is the sort of film where to outline the main events is virtually an art of criticism. But plenty of enjoyable – even remarkable – films have taken preposterous plots and manipulated them so as to foreground striking dramatic patterns (Jacques Tourneur's **Experiment Perilous**, 1944, and Otto Preminger's **Angel Face**, 1953, to name but two).

Here, however, Marinos simply lets McCullough's bunch of cardboard loonies gather round a table or on a verandah until someone drives someone else into a frenzy.

It is not just the money that is wasted (though that matters, too), it is the spectacle of usually competent actors demeaning themselves in such hysterical twaddle. Richard Moir curls his lip (above which sprouts a cad's moustache), Gary Sweet ripples his chest muscles, Wendy Hughes again bares her left breast, and Bill Hunter and Julia Blake fume and fret.

Not that **An Indecent Obsession** is really any worse than television's *The Thorn Birds* or **Tim** (Michael Pate, 1979) the movie. All of which leads me to believe that McCullough, like blood, will out.

BRIAN MCFARLANE

---

[1] Title is preceded, on a separate card and after the principal cast, with 'in Colleen McCullough's'.
[2] Should be 'Gethin Creagh'.

References
'M*U*S*H: **An Indecent Obsession**', a review by Brian McFarlane, *Cinema Papers*, no. 53, September 1985, p. 64.
'An Indecent Obsession', a review by Kathe Boehringer, *Filmnews*, May 1985, p. 13.

MAD MAX BEYOND THUNDERDOME

Kennedy Miller presents MAD MAX [/] BEYOND THUNDERDOME.[1] © 1985 Kennedy Miller Productions Pty Ltd. *Locations:* Coober Pedy (South Australia); Blue Mountains, Camperdown (New South Wales). *Australian distributor:* Roadshow. *Opened:* 8 August 1985. *Video:* Warner Home Video. *Rating:* M. 35mm. Panavision. 106 mins.

Producer: George Miller. *Co-producers:* Doug Mitchell, Terry Hayes. *Associate producers:* Steve Amezdroz, Marcus D'Arcy. *Scriptwriters:* Terry Hayes, George Miller. *Director of photography:* Dean Semler. *Camera operators:* Toby Phillips, David Burr, Louis Irving, Richard Merryman. *Production designer:* Graham 'Grace' Walker. *Costume designer:* Norma Moriceau. *Editor:* Richard Francis-Bruce. *Composer:* Maurice Jarre. *Sound supervisor:* Roger Savage. *Sound design:* Bruce Lamshed. *Production sound recordist:* Lloyd Carrick. *Additional sound:* Phil Judd. *Sound editors:* Tim Jordan, Karin Whittington, Annabelle Sheehan (dial.); Frank Lipson, Craig Carter, Tim Chau (fx). *Mixers:* Roger Savage, Bruce Lamshed.

Cast

Mel Gibson (Mad Max), Tina Turner (Aunty Entity), Helen Buday (Savannah Nix), Frank Thring (The Collector), Bruce Spence (Jedediah the Pilot), Robert Grubb (Pig Killer), Angelo Rossitto (The Master), Angry Anderson (Ironbar), George Spartels (Blackfinger), Edwin Hodgeman (Dr Dealgood), Mark Spain (Skyfish), Mark Kounnas (Gekko), Rod Zuanic (Scrooloose), Justine Clarke (Anna Goanna), Shane Tickner (Eddie), Tom Jennings (Slake), Adam Cockburn (Jedediah Jnr.), Bob Hornby (Waterseller), Andrew Oh (Ton Ton Tattoo), Toni Allaylis (Cusha…the Pregnant Girl), James Wingrove (Tubba Tintye), Adam Scougall (Finn McCoo), Adam Willits (Mr Scratch).

One of the most striking features of the Mad Max cycle is the manner in which its instalments take place in starkly different (even incommensurable) fictional universes. From each film to the next there is a quantum leap; effectively, only the character of Max[2] (Mel Gibson) binds them – and even he is scarcely the same kind of 'hero' in the third film as in the first.

Mad Max Beyond Thunderdome has a much more elaborately conceived fictional world than its two predecessors. This is because, instead of the largely mobile battles between individuals or social groups, **Mad Max Beyond Thunderdome** is largely an essay on the nature of civilisation, with

The 'blood and shit' economy of Bartertown.

Max still the archetypal wanderer who allows us to traverse and compare different modes of social life. Bartertown, in particular, is a fascinating conception, with its economy running on 'blood and shit'.

The film is unusual and ambitious in many respects, and on its release certainly disconcerted those critics and viewers expecting a 'topper' to the pure cinematic kineticism of **Mad Max 2** (1981). The film has its spectacular set-pieces (particularly the final chase), but they are distributed throughout a rather reflective three-part story structure, each part taking place in a different natural or social environment. The second part – featuring the long, theatrical, 'dreamtime' recitation on the origins of civilisation by the 'Children of the Crack' (clearly the model for the Lost Boys in Steven Spielberg's **Hook**, 1991) – is the least action oriented, and (to this critic among others) the most archly self-conscious moment in the film's 'essayistic' trajectory.

George Miller has been aware at least since **Mad Max 2** of the potently 'mythic' dimension of his work, with its iconic character archetypes (such as the outsider-hero) and 'universally' recurring themes. In **Thunderdome**, this dimension is foregrounded; the film is, in Ross Gibson's words, 'unequivocally mythological'. Gibson has provided what is without doubt the fullest and most perceptive account of **Thunderdome**[3] – which has the great virtue of linking 'timeless' mythologies (as Miller might see them) with historical, political and national ones.

According to Gibson, the film is a primary, Genesis myth: the birth of a civilisation. Although dismissed by some as a purely 'internationalist' project with little

Australian specificity and resonance, Gibson convincingly argues that the film gathers 'leitmotivs and icons from white Australian history' relating to the national myth of 'transcendental failure' (which includes figures such as Leichhardt, Burke and Wills, and Patrick White's *Voss*). Yet the film's 'utopian' force comes from the way it twists and renegotiates this myth. Instead of the grandly pathetic spectacle of the Gallipoli myth, we are offered a vision of social growth and integration based on pervasive strategies of improvisation, adaptation and the canny reassemblage of all signs, props, meanings and situations to hand.

The vast transformations wrought upon the 'heroic function' of Max constitute one of the major fascinations of the whole cycle of Mad Max films. From family man to revenger, survivor to nomad, hired gun to wasteland philosopher, Max has often been a reluctant and ambiguous hero, with the requisite dark hints that he could just as easily be a murderous mercenary, a ruthless scavenger or a psychotic, death-driven loner. His ambiguities are partly 'classic', familiar from such cinematic legends as Akira Kurosawa's samurai heroes; but they are also modern, finely in tune with the amorality of contemporaneous heroes like Snake Pliskin in John Carpenter's **Escape From New York** (1981). **Thunderdome** bravely closes the Mad Max cycle by, in essence, erasing Max's heroic status almost completely. At the end, Max is really only making his way, like anyone else, through the surreal signs and settings of a world yet-to-be.

ADRIAN MARTIN

---

[1] The opening credit reads, 'Warner Bros. Pictures[,] A Warner Communications Company'.

[2] In **Mad Max** (1979), the character is 'Max Rockatansky'; in **Mad Max 2** (1981) he is 'Max'; in **Mad Max Beyond Thunderdome** he is 'Mad Max'.

[3] Ross Gibson, 'Yondering: A Reading of **Mad Max Beyond Thunderdome**', *Art & Text*, no. 19, October–December 1985.

References

'On the Road Again', a location report by Paul Kalina, *Cinema Papers*, no. 51, May 1985, pp. 38–9, 41.

'Mel's Way: **Mad Max: Beyond Thunderdome**', a review by Debi Enker, *Cinema Papers*, no. 53, September 1985, p. 61.

'Miller's Tale', an interview with director George Miller by Tom Ryan, *Cinema Papers*, no. 67, January 1988, pp. 12–16.

'**Mad Max Beyond Thunderdome**', a short review by Ross Gibson, *Filmnews*, September 1985, pp. 16–17.

MORRIS WEST'S THE NAKED COUNTRY

Naked Country Productions presents A Ross Dimsey Production. MORRIS WEST'S THE NAKED COUNTRY. © 1985 Naked Country Productions. *Budget:* $2.75 million. *Location:* Charters Towers (Queensland). *Australian distributor:* Filmpac. *Video:* K-Tel. *Rating:* M. 35mm. 92 mins.

Producer: Ross Dimsey. *Executive producers:* Mark Josem, Bill Marshall, Peter Sherman, Robert Ward. *Scriptwriters:* Ross Dimsey, Tim Burstall. Based on the novel by Morris West. *Director of photography:* David Eggby. *Production designer:* Philip Warner. *Costume designers:* Ron Williams, Robyn Hall. *Editor:* Tony Paterson. *Composer:* Bruce Smeaton. *Sound recordist:* Max Bowring. *Sound editors:* Pippa Anderson, Geoff Hill. *Mixer:* Julian Ellingworth.

Cast

John Stanton (Lance Dillon), Rebecca Gilling (Mary Dillon), Ivar Kants (Sgt Neil Adams), Tommy Lewis (Mundara), Simon Chilvers (Inspector Poole), John Jarratt (Mick Conrad), Neela Dey (Menyan), Hector Thomas (Willinja), Donald Blitner (Billy-Jo), Kevin McKellar (Jacky-Boy), Marlene Bell (Big Sally), Malcolm Cork (Constable Des O'Day), Michael Cockatoo (Tanglefoot), Roger Cox (Publican), Peter Noble (Gilligan), Peter Graham (Driver), Neville Jingles (Tjumi), Curtis Kelly (Yandedah), Kenneth Jacob Jnr. (Billabura), Lloyd Chong (Pithinjarii), Albert Wilson (Tjuputee).

Based on a novel about the relations between whites and Aborigines written in the 1950s, **Morris West's The Naked Country** (like Bruce Beresford's **The Fringe Dwellers**, 1986) takes one back to social attitudes circulating at the time of Charles Chauvel's **Jedda** (1955). But whereas Beresford's film takes the path of naturalistic 'social realism', Burstall and his collaborators continue Chauvel's exploration in a direct and daring way. For this is a full-blooded melodrama painting, in broad strokes, the conflicts and contradictions of white rule; not 'quality' melodrama (like Alan J. Pakula's **Sophie's Choice**, 1982) but 'trashy' soap opera which affronts (as Chauvel did) genteel bourgeois æsthetic and moral standards with its 'transgressive' sexual couplings and ethically complex system of eye-for-eye killings.

Burstall establishes with characteristic economy the virtually iconic characters and their social interrelations. In the first scene,

land-owning farmer Lance Dillon (John Stanton) confronts proud young Mundara (Tommy Lewis), who speaks for the Aborigines' sacred ownership of their land. Scenes then introduce Lance's politically troubled, emotionally dissatisfied wife Mary (Rebecca Gilling) and the equally ill-at-ease Sgt Neil Adams (Ivar Kants), who has a drinking problem and a sympathetic understanding of black law. The 'semantic diagram' of the film is in fact far from being either artistically crude or mindlessly racist, as a number of commentators have imputed. As well as characters initially embodying the extremes of white and black values, there are key in-between figures (like Neil and the blacks living in and helping the white community) who at the same time bridge these extremes, and indicate the ironic limitations of racial 'assimilation' (as when a black 'maid' suggests that all Mary needs to be happy is a 'piccaninny').

Most important, all the characters are subjected, in the course of the narrative, to an elegant process of contrast and comparison typical of the melodramatic form, bringing out the various affinities and differences between the white and black social systems. For instance, Mundara's violation of tribal law in 'demanding' Menyan (Neela Dey), the woman he loves, is rhymed with Mary's and Neil's 'cross-class' affaire. Mundara is likened to Neil in that both are rebellious, somewhat hot-headed, restless in

their prescribed social place. But where Neil is weak and pathetic, Mundara is strong and noble. Lance's more profound symbolic kinship is ultimately to his sworn enemy, Mundara. Both are described as 'determined characters', and Mundara's rhetorical condemnation of Lance in the first scene – that he could not last three days living off the land alone as blacks do – is pointedly disproved by the main stretch of the film's action, with an 'exiled' Lance surviving numerous spear attacks and eating nutritious bugs. The final, sublimely homoerotic rapprochement of Lance and Mundara, with the latter (half-killed by his elders) pleading 'Kill me, please, boss Dillon', is as complex a swirl of personal and political determinations as occurs at the end of other profoundly expressive 'trash' masterpieces like Richard Fleischer's **Mandingo** (1975) and King Vidor's **Duel in the Sun** (1946). The final shots of Lance, now symbolically part-black as be buries Mundara and proudly swinging his tribal implement, are particularly moving.

ADRIAN MARTIN

References

'Burstall & Dimsey go West', Ewan Burnett, *Cinema Papers*, no. 51, May 1985, pp. 48–9.
'Where no Culture Flies: **Morris West's The Naked Country**', a review by John Baxter, *Cinema Papers*, no. 53, September 1985, pp. 62–3.

Farmer Lance Dillon (John Stanton).

REBEL

Phillip Emanuel presents in association with The Village Roadshow Corporation. REBEL. © 1985 Phillip Emmanuel Productions Limited. *Budget:* $5 million. *Australian distributor:* Roadshow. *Opened:* December 1985. *Video:* Roadshow Home Video. *Rating:* M. 35mm. 93 mins.

Producer: Phillip Emanuel. *Executive producers:* Robyn Campbell-Jones, Bonnie Harris. *Associate producer:* Susan Wild. *Scriptwriters:* Michael Jenkins, Bob Herbert. Based on the play *No Names, No Pack Drill* by Bob Herbert. *Director of photography:* Peter James. *Camera operator:* Danny Batterham. *Production designer:* Brian Thomson. *Costume designer:* Roger Kirk. *Editor:* Michael Honey. *Composer:* Chris Neal. *Original songs:* Peter Best. *Sound recordist:* Mark Lewis. *Sound editor:* Penn Robinson. *Mixers:* Julian Ellingworth; Peter Fenton, Ron Purvis, Phil Heywood (asst.).

Cast

Matt Dillon (Rebel), Debbie Byrne (Kathy McLeod), Bryan Brown (Tiger), Bill Hunter (Browning), Ray Barrett (Bubbles), Julie Nihill (Joycie), John O'May (Bernie), Kim Deacon (Hazel), Isabelle Anderson (Mrs Palmer), Sheree Da Costa (Barbara); Joy Smithers, Cassandra Delaney, Antoinette Byron, Nicky Crayson, Nikki Coghill, Sally Phillips, Betti Summerson, Lissa Ross (All Girl Band); Chris Hession (Lambert), Spike Cherrie (Wood), Tom Appleton (Tiger's Heavy 1), James Marsh (Tiger's Heavy 2).

The depiction of Australians at war is one genre in which local film-makers have excelled, primarily because of their attention to fact and storyline. The theatrically inclined **Rebel** appears to have tried in these departments, but it is a film lacking substance and credence.

Matt Dillon plays Rebel, a wounded US marine who deserts the army while recuperating in Sydney in 1942, and falls in love with a cabaret singer, Kathy McLeod (Debbie Byrne). The film traces the messy liaison between the pair against a backdrop of glitzy nightclubs and wartime uncertainty.

The storyline has plenty of potential. Rebel is a man on the run from both the military police and his past as a soldier. Kathy has the inner conflict of loving a stranger while her own soldier–husband is away fighting the Japanese.

For the most part, the film is big on colour, noise and action, but thin on character development, script and direction. It would appear not much thought has gone into developing the love interest. Attempts at bonding the pair on screen are layered with banal familiarity and corniness.

The script is an adaptation of a play, Bob Herbert's 1979 *No Names, No Pack Drill.* The sets and musical sequences are elaborate to the point that the film never quite lifts itself from an atmosphere of stagey claustrophobia. Many of the scenes are filmed either at night and/or indoors, and little has been done (not even a glimpse of the Harbour Bridge) to convey a sense of local geography that may have helped to shape the story.

Much of the eye-play between soldier Rebel and stage queen Kathy takes place at gaudy nightclub settings where an all-female review group packs in big crowds of servicemen. At least a quarter of the film is devoted to songs and dancing, making it a wartime musical of sorts.

The songs are written by Peter Best, and there is no doubting the quality of his work and the scope it affords Debbie Byrne to deliver her singing talents. One wonders, though, whether the lyrics in some of the songs ('You drop a grenade in an enemy tank…') were written by martial strategists.

The casting of US actor Matt Dillon is justifiable given the steady presence of American soldiers on Australian shores during WWII. Notwithstanding this, more could have been made of the friction that existed between American servicemen and Australian soldiers who are conspicuously absent in the film. Rebel's Americanness opens the way for some amusing cultural juxtapositions, mostly through the interaction of a natty con-artist, Tiger (Bryan Brown), who promises to get the soldier a safe passage out of Sydney – for a price.

Although Dillon's brooding is well suited to his Rebel persona, some major plot flaws make his character a little too hard to believe in the long run. And the film ends without answering a nagging question: Why wouldn't a war deserter so intent on hiding his identity trade his uniform for civilian dress?

GREG KERR

References

'Living with the Camera', an article (with quotes) on actor Debbie Byrne by Debi Enker, *Cinema Papers*, no. 55, January 1986, pp. 18–20.

'Seeing Red', an article (with quotes) on production designer Brian Thomson by Paul Kalina, ibid., pp. 22–3, 35.

'Kings Cross Melody of 1942: **Rebel**', a review by Paul Kalina, ibid., p. 61.

'**Rebel**', a review by Susan Charlton, *Filmnews*, December 1985, p. 13.

Kathy McLeod (Debbie Byrne) and Rebel (Matt Dillon).

D O N A L D   C R O M B I E   A N D   K E N   H A N N A M

ROBBERY UNDER ARMS

S.A.F.C. Productions in association with ITC Entertainment presents ROBBERY UNDER ARMS. © 1985 S.A.F.C. Productions Ltd. *Budget:* $7.3 million. *Location:* Flinders Ranges (South Australia). *Australian distributor:* ITC Entertainment. *Video:* CEL. *Rating:* PG. 35mm. 141 mins.

Producer: Jock Blair. *Executive producer:* John Morris. *Associate producers:* Pamela H. Vanneck, Bruce Moir. *Scriptwriters:* Graeme Koetsveld, Tony Morphett. Based on the novel by Rolf Boldrewood. *Director of photography:* Ernest Clark. *Camera operator:* David Foreman. *Production designer:* George Liddle. *Costume designer:* Anna Senior. *Editor:* Andrew Prowse. *Composers:* Garry McDonald, Laurie Stone. *Sound recordist:* Lloyd Carrick. *Sound editors:* Peter Burgess, Frank Lipson, Craig Carter, Glenn Martin, Stephen Lambeth. *Mixers:* James Currie (chief); David Harrison (fx); Peter Smith (music).

Cast

Sam Neill (Captain Starlight), Steven Vidler (Dick), Christopher Cummins (Jim), Liz Newman (Gracey), Jane Menelaus (Aileen), Andy Anderson (George), Deborah Coulls (Kate), Susie Lindeman (Jeannie), Elaine Cusick (Mum), Ed Devereux (Ben), Tommy Lewis (Warrigal), Robert Grubb (Morringer), David Bradshaw (Goring), John Dick (Trooper Fall), Michael Duffield (Mr. Falkland), Keith Smith (Trooper Smith), Don Barker (Wilson), Roger Ward (McIntyre), Paul Chubb (Mungo), Conor McDermottroe (Catholic Priest), Wan Thye Liew (Chinese Merchant).

Captain Starlight, the semi-mythical hero from the Rolf Boldrewood novel, has now been the subject of at least four film versions of *Robbery Under Arms*.[1] The latest (a cut-down of the mini-series) is a fairly conventional exercise in storytelling, galvanised by an impressive mixture of romance, adventure and morality. Sam Neill plays the Englishman who has forsaken his aristocratic past, made for Australia and assumed the identity of Starlight – cattle rustler, cad and petty bushranger.

The film opens with the immaculately dressed Starlight leaping from a horse onto a fast-moving train where he befriends a group of highbrow diners before robbing them. Starlight and an Aboriginal accomplice, Warrigal (Tommy Lewis), then propose a toast to the Queen. With this far-fetched, comical beginning, directors Donald Crombie and Ken Hannam set the tone for

Captain Starlight (Sam Neill) and Ben (Ed Devereux).

a movie that holds no serious claims to hard fact and historical detail.

Robbery Under Arms is more a rollicking yarn which – in the spirit of the book – is told with abiding affection. Although a little overlong, the film has an excellent cast, a plot that rarely slackens and a strong visual panorama, thanks to the photography of Ernest Clark of the Flinders Ranges of South Australia.

The film is set around 1880 in semi-outback Australia where Starlight is making a few sly dollars with the help of two inseparable brothers, Dick and Jim Marston (Steven Vidler and Christopher Cummins). Just who Starlight was and what he actually did are questions subject to contention to this day. The celebrated Peter Finch played the mysterious bushranger in the 1957 version, but there is no doubting the charismatic Sam Neill brings the character to life in a convincing manner. His smooth performance is accentuated by the interaction of a colourful stream of colonialists who empathise with his anti-establishment leanings.

A screenplay by Graeme Koetsveld and Tony Morphett allows the plot to take some worthwhile turns, not least when the Marston boys face the repercussions of flirting with two sisters at a cattle sale. Characters are developed well through the film; two who stand out are the big-hearted Dick Marston and Morringer (Robert Grubb), an officious police chief. The minor characters are shaped nicely into the milieu of the era; some are also given an important voice. One thinks of Warrigal's soliloquy on Aboriginal land rights, and an Irish Catholic priest's denunciation of the British Empire.

Robbery Under Arms has a habit of romanticising the colonial days and goes way over the top during a prison breakout scene. Its depictions are nonetheless informative and entertaining, especially when Starlight and the gang take to the goldfields. One amusing scene with an underlying historical irony involves Starlight playing cricket with Warrigal along the mullock heaps.

If one were to offer criticism of Starlight, it is that his motives for becoming a bushranger are barely touched. He is mysterious, laconic, courageous – all of the things which help shape a screen enigma. But in the sociological context of the Australian bushranger experience, too much is assumed rather than explained about this film's romantic hero.

GREG KERR

[1] **Robbery Under Arms**: Charles Macmahon, 1907; Kenneth Brampton, 1920; and Jack Lee, 1957.

References

'Arms & Men', a production report containing an article (with quotes) on producer Jock Blair and co-director Donald Crombie by Nick Roddick, *Cinema Papers*, no. 51, May 1985, pp. 54–5, 57–8, and an article (with quotes) on co-director Ken Hannam by Sheila Johnston, p. 58.

'Riders of the Ranges: **Robbery Under Arms**', a review by Nick Roddick, ibid., pp. 81–2.

'Going South: The Adelaide Connection', an article on the South Australian Film Corporation by Philippa Hawker, *Cinema Papers*, no. 61, January 1987, pp. 20–3.

'Soundtracks', with a review of the film's score by Ivan Hutchinson, *Cinema Papers*, no. 89., August 1992, pp. 62–63.

BARBARA BOYD-ANDERSON

THE STILL POINT

Colosimo Film Productions present THE STILL POINT. © 1985 Colosimo Film Productions Pty Ltd. *Budget:* $262,000. *Location:* Melbourne. *Australian distributor:* Colosimo Film Productions. *Video:* VCA. *Rating:* PG. 16mm. 85 mins.

Producer: Rosa Colosimo. *Scriptwriters:* Rosa Colosimo, Barbara Boyd-Anderson. *Director of photography:* Kevin Anderson. *Production designer:* Paddy Reardon. *Costume designer:* Frankie Hogan. *Editor:* Zbigniew Friedrich. *Composer:* Pierre Pierre. *Sound recordist:* Geoffrey White. [*Sound editors:* not credited.] *Mixer:* Peter Frost.

Cast

Nadine Garner (Sarah), Lyn Semmler (Barbara), Robin Cuming (Mr Warren-Smith), Steve Bastoni (David), Alex Menglet (Paul), Kirstie Grant (Simone), Gregory Fleet (Tony), Alisa Meadow (Chris), Ben Mendelsohn (Peter), Jodie Yemm (Bianca), Dianne Parrington (Dance Teacher), Rona McLeod (Art Teacher), Angioletta Shwarz (Pamela), Johnny Quinn (Bill), Gerry Mertagh (Walter), Melissa Colosimo (Girl at Desk), Sassy Hayyatt (Helen), Katrina Logan (Chloe), Sarah Lassez (Jane), Marcus White (Andrew).

The Still Point belongs not in the 'teen movie' tradition of American pop cinema (e.g., the work of John Hughes), but squarely in the tradition of humanist literature written for teenagers, particularly teenage girls. Although there are perfunctory details of modern pop music and teenage fashions, the themes focused on by the film are the 'timeless', universal ones of teenage literature: youthful alienation, the generation gap, the modern condition of the single-parent family and the problem of introducing new lovers into the picture – the confused burgeoning of teen sexuality. Emphasised are the optimistic themes of personal growth, effort and compromise between parent and child in order to reach mutual understanding, and integration into a supportive community.

The teenage alienation of Sarah (Nadine Garner) finds a vivid dramatic correlative in her deafness (although this condition is rather poorly established in the story's exposition). Barbara Boyd-Anderson's direction is undynamic, particularly in the early interior scenes detailing Sarah's fraught relations with her mother, Barbara (Lyn Semmler), her lover, Paul (Alex Menglet), and her distant businessman father, although the script gestures towards some interesting emotional knots: Sarah blaming herself for

Sarah (Nadine Garner) and David (Steve Bastoni).

the failure of her parents' marriage, and her playing an almost maternal rôle with her father ('I could look after you'). Least well dramatised is Paul's function as a spontaneous 'life force' reinvigorating Barbara (it is an unfortunately passionless film), and the fleeting 'transcendence' Sarah experiences in a music-box with a rotating figurine of a ballet dancer, an image repeated rather too often.

The narrative device of a country idyll, in which the protagonist is thrown into a new world and makes new friends, is beloved of both teen movies and teen literature. When Sarah visits her grandfather, Mr Warren-Smith (Robin Cuming), the film moves into the livelier territory of first love with the sensitive David (Steve Bastoni), the various social pressures exerted by teen peer groups, and the gradual bridging of the generation gap, mediated through loveable, understanding Granddad. But key scenes, such as the teenage party, have little direc-

torial colour, and the climactic emotional confrontations between family members make strange use of slow zooms and tensely silent *temps mort*.

The film has its notable qualities. Garner's ability to convey the 'pissed off', exasperated emotional states peculiar to teenagers is wonderful, and the final scene (complete with a quotation from T. S. Eliot's 'Burnt Norton') is strikingly irresolute, refusing the expected tie-up of all emotional problems. **The Still Point** is true to the 'teen literature' genre, and has probably been successfully used as a discussion-starter on typical adolescent problems in secondary-school classrooms. As a contemporary teen movie, however, it scarcely gets off the ground.

ADRIAN MARTIN

Reference
'Careful, She Can't Hear You: **The Still Point**', a review by Mark Spratt, *Cinema Papers*, no. 55, January 1986, pp. 70–1.

A STREET TO DIE

Mermaid Beach Productions and Multifilms present A STREET TO DIE. © 1985 Mermaid Beach Productions. *Australian distributor:* Octopus. *Video:* Supreme Entertainment. *Rating:* PG. 16mm (blown up to 35mm). 91 mins.

Producer: Bill Bennett. *Associate producer:* Jenny Day. *Scriptwriter:* Bill Bennett. *Director of photography:* Geoff Burton. *Camera operator:* Geoff Burton. *Production designer:* Igor Nay. *Costume designer:* Magi Beswick. *Editor:* Denise Hunter. *Composers:* Michael Atkinson, Michael Spicer. *Sound recordist:* Leo Sullivan. *Sound editor:* Fiddess Films. *Mixer:* Brett Robinson.

Cast

Chris Haywood (Colin Turner), Jennifer Cluff (Lorraine Turner), Peter Hehir (Peter Townley), Andrew Chirgwin (Paul Turner), Peter Chirgwin (Jason Turner), Malcolm Keith (Real Estate Boss), Robin Ramsay (Tom), Steven Shaw (Factory Worker), Susannah Fowle (Julie), Peter Kowitz (Craig), Marion Chirgwin (Kathy), Joy Hruby (Maureen), Jane Burton-Taylor (Betty), Christopher Morton (Christopher), Brigid Gregg (Janet), Arianthe Galani (Dr Walsea), Lian Lunson (Receptionist), John Black (Clinic Doctor), Pat Evison (Sister Sweet), Deborah Kramer (Dr Hamilton).

Bill Bennett's dramatisation of the events in the shortened life of Vietnam veteran Colin Simpson – Colin Turner (Chris Haywood) in the film – has many self-set obstacles to hurdle. The subject itself – the crippling and carcinogenic effects of Agent Orange – has become well known through the media and presenting an 'exposé' about it risks joining the dots perfunctorily together, with no power to move or shock.

While A Street to Die doesn't entirely overcome this difficulty, it is evident that writer–director Bennett has used his skills to create a cinema film that is subtle and unsensationalist. It is more of a personal story and less of a 'big issue' film.

The film establishes an important sense of geography in its opening shots. The Turner family – Colin and Lorraine (Jennifer Cluff) and their two children – drive into suburbia to a new home in an ex-servicemen's housing area. As the Turners pull to a stop, a neighbour's child smashes glass on the road – the first of many economical visual signs to suggest growing abnormality and discord in the apparently placid and well-kept suburb.

Colin's first symptoms (rashes, glandular lumps) are initially ignored by him and his doctor. Then, amid scenes of relatively normal family routines, comes the realisation of a gradually worsening physical condition and the knowledge that other families on the Turners' side of the street also have problems: children with brain dysfunctions, husbands prone to violent and irrational behaviour. Following diagnosis of his probable leukemia or lymphoma, Colin begins gathering evidence of the effects of chemical spraying in Vietnam.

Colin's acknowledgement of his condition is manifested in several ways: his anger at a council worker spraying pesticides on a children's playground; his obsession with fixing everything in the house (which provokes Lorraine into a rage of denial that this is necessary; she wants everything to remain the same).

After Colin's death, Lorraine continues her fight for compensation and acknowledgement of the effects of Agent Orange, and discovers that Colin's medical records have vanished. The final enquiry sequence is a headlong bolt into the brick wall of bureaucracy, from which Lorraine and her legal adviser (Peter Hehir) emerge triumphant.

The last sequence has a marvellously controlled sense of *mise-en-scène*. In an earlier scene, shot from medium distance, we have seen Lorraine bury Colin's ashes in the garden and plant a tree over them. When she ultimately receives a telegram advising her of success at the enquiry, we see her call out, 'We've won!', ostensibly to her son. Then a camera movement reveals that she is touching Colin's tree and is, of course, talking to him.

A Street to Die is clearly a labour of love, and the two lead performances display an admirably unsentimentalised feeling of ordinary people at the focal point of a far-reaching and far-from-ordinary story.

MARK SPRATT[1]

---

[1] Extracted from Spratt's review in *Cinema Papers* (see Reference).

Reference

'Bringing it all Back Home: A Street to Die', a review by Mark Spratt, *Cinema Papers*, no. 54, November 1985, pp. 66–7.

Lorraine (Jennifer Cluff) and Colin Turner (Chris Haywood).

TAIL OF A TIGER

The Producers' Circle presents TAIL OF A TIGER. © 1984 Pijelo Pty. Limited. *Location:* Balmain (Sydney). *Australian distributor:* Roadshow. *Video:* Roadshow Home Video. *Rating:* G. 35mm. 80 mins.

Producer: James M. Vernon. *Executive producer:* Grahame Jennings. *Scriptwriter:* Rolf De Heer. Based on an original work by Peter Hubbard. *Director of photography:* Richard Michalak. *Production designer:* Judith Russell. *Wardrobe:* Clarrissa Patterson. *Editor:* Suresh Ayyar. *Composers:* Steve Arnold, Graham Tardif. *Sound recordist:* Kevin Kearney. *Sound editor:* Penn Robinson. *Mixer:* Alasdair MacFarlane.

Cast

Grant Navin (Orville), Gordon Poole (Harry), Caz Lederman (Lydia), Peter Feeley (Spike), Gayle Kennedy (Beryl), Walter Sullivan (Stan), Basil Clarke (Jacko), Norm Gobert (Albert), Dylan Lyle (Rabbit), Louise Darcy (Wilma), Adrian Cirrillo (Spider), Peter Fogarty (Otto), Kristian Verega (Wombat), Michael Young (Blue), Sue Collie (Teacher's Voice).

Every young boy, it seems, wishes to fly at some point. Rolf De Heer's **Tail of a Tiger** is the story of a boy who fights the odds and ends up piloting a Tiger Moth (hence the title) he has helped rebuild.

Orville (Grant Navin) is the class nerd: bright with big-rimmed glasses and buck teeth. Whereas the members of the tough gang run by Spike (Peter Feeley) all fly expensive, remote-controlled planes, all poor Orville can do is build miniatures out of balsa wood. His many attempts at joining the gang are rebuffed and he feels quite isolated. Orville's mistake, of course, is that he foolishly craves peer acceptance and as a result suffers rejection. Orville's lesson in life will be to not pretend he is someone else, but dare to be different, to let people take him as he is.

Orville's stocks are soon improved when he discovers the local drunk, Harry (Gordon Poole), has a broken-down Tiger Moth. Once a war hero, Harry has sunk into an alcoholic haze of self-pity and rejects the enthusiastic pleas of Orville to fix the plane. But, this being a moralistic children's film, goodness wins, the plane is fixed and both take to the skies of Sydney. A reformed Spike (he has just called Orville 'mate'!) watches enviously from the ground.

The dilemma of the children's film is whether to make a film kids will want to watch or one educators feel they should. Where the former may present life as it is, with unpredictable twists and turns, and no sense of a supreme being in control of all outcomes, the latter prefers a universe where goodness always prevails, where everyone learns something important about themselves and others, where Christian-approved morals hover near or on the surface.

The problem with this 'parenting' approach is that the films are often rejected by kids whose sophistication is often far above that of the adult film-makers who 'preach down'. They are also not easy for childless adults to sit through, especially if as lifeless as **Tail of a Tiger**. Very few scenes work dramatically (the acting is amateur) and Rolf De Heer does very little to energise his film.

This is a pity because after a tedious opening, where everything is so basically spelt out, the script expands and mutates in potentially interesting ways. Harry says that his old plane has a soul (one that refuses to allow itself to be restored), but this notion is all but dropped and little made of the interesting notion of inanimate objects having personalities. Then, dead war pilots return to help out Orville and Harry, sometimes as ghosts with magical powers, and sometimes personified as neighbours with hearts of gold. But, again, little is made of this and the sub-plot looks like an incongruous bit of sci-fi tossed in to spice the brew.

Tail of a Tiger, like many Australian films, is testimony to under-achievement.

SCOTT MURRAY

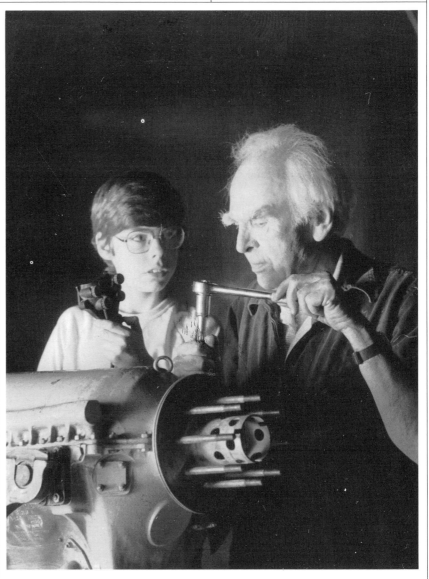

Orville (Grant Navin) and Harry (Gordon Poole).

WARMING UP

JNP. WARMING UP. © 1984 JNP Films Pty Ltd. *Locations:* Wilgunyah, Sydney (New South Wales). *Australian distributor:* Hoyts. *Video:* Thorn EMI. *Rating:* PG. 35 mm. 94 mins.

Producer: James Davern. *Associate producer:* Terry Vincent. *Scriptwriter:* James Davern. *Director of photography:* Joseph Pickering. *Production designer:* Michael Ralph. *Costume designer:* Helen Hooper. *Editor:* Zsolt Kollanyi. *Composer:* Mike Perjanik. *Sound recordist:* Ross Linton. *Sound editor:* Zsolt Kollanyi. *Mixer:* Julian Ellingworth.

Cast

Barbara Stephens (Juliet Cavanagh-Forbes), Henri Szeps (Peter Sullivan), Queenie Ashton (Mrs Marsh), Adam Fernance (Randolph Cavanagh-Forbes), Lloyd Morris (Ox), Tim Grogan (Snoopy); Bruce Wedderburn, Tom Appleton, Peter Blackburn, Colin Morganti, Wayne Pigram, Gray Wilson, Aldo King, Angus Gamson, Robert Fisher, Trevor Musty, Damien Bray, Adam Bray, Steve Bradmore ("The Wombats"); Ron Blanchard (Len), Martin Harris (Dinny), Lester Morris (Henry), Patrick Ward (Watney), Kevin Golsby (Splinter), Sally Gilbertson (Marilyn), Jacqui Peters (Charlene).

Despite a premise that may not appear all that appealing–a country football team learns ballet–Bruce Best's **Warming Up** turns out to be an intermittently charming and funny comedy. While no lost gem, it can rightly claim to have been overlooked.

After an exhausting early morning jog, Juliet Cavanagh-Forbes (Barbara Stephens) decides to abandon her exercise-obsessed boyfriend and head up country with her son, Randolph (Adam Fernance). On the outskirts of Wilgunyah, she feels harassed by some young bikies and fights back, strewing the road with ballet costumes and sending the riders crashing across roads, streams and paddocks. Juliet has made her arrival in town very apparent, for this is an Australian country town where the men rule and the only gods are football and the pub. Having already taken on the bikies, who turn out to be the town's football team, Juliet then goes into the men's bar and orders a beer, which is refused. Her disappointment is loudly voiced and soon she is under arrest. Then begins a long-running confrontation with Peter (Henri Szeps), the local cop and team's coach.

Juliet wants to run a ballet school, with the help of Mrs Marsh (Queenie Ashton),

and that means sharing the town's one free hall with the macho footballers. This leads to one of the film's best set-pieces: a 'battle' between the young ballet dancers on one side of a portable screen and the footballers doing exercises on the other. It is a beautifully orchestrated sequence, with the tension, noise and confrontation building dramatically.

The footballers' greatest fear is having it revealed that Juliet is secretly giving them ballet exercises to improve their fitness, without their coach's knowledge. So successful are her 'feminine' methods that within weeks they defeat last year's premiers. No one can stop the team now, though their style of play is becoming so balletic that one wonders how long the umpires will allow them on the ground. (The director's inability to convincingly show how the footballers can jump high also renders the comedy here a touch silly.)

The most unusual aspect of this film is its portrayal of Juliet. She is one of the feistiest spirits in Australian cinema. She is brash, temperamental and confused, hellbent on

never letting anyone control or restrict her. She bristles against male authority and has the subtlety of a tank in changing things ('a bulldozer with brain damage' as Peter gruffly labels her).

In many ways, Juliet's recent cinematic antecedent is Goldie Hawn's many characters, with one significant difference. In **Wildcats** (Michael Ritchie, 1986), where Hawn's character trains a male football team, she resorts to male training methods and her motivation is an obsession for winning. In **Warming Up**, Juliet uses 'poofter' ballet to get her team fit and she has no interest in the team's winning (other than to win a dare); she is totally against all competitive sport. Though Hawn's characters are often touted as modern, independent women, they are actually far more regressive than Juliet.

Warming Up, then, is an often amusing tale of stereotyped sex rôles and one woman's desire to change things. Along the way, Juliet discovers much about herself and, at film's end, she is more at ease with herself and those around her.

SCOTT MURRAY

Juliet Cavanagh-Forbes (Barbara Stevens), Randolph (Adam Fernance) and Peter Sullivan (Henri Szeps).

WILLS & BURKE

Stony Desert presents Wills & Burke[1]. ©
1985 Stony Desert Limited. *Budget:* $1.75
million. *Locations:* Cranbourne, Melbourne
(Victoria). *Australian distributor:* GUO.
Opened: 24 October 1985. *Video:* Premiere.
Rating: PG. 35mm. Panavision. 101 mins.

   Producer: Bob Weis. *Co-producer:*
Margot McDonald. *Scriptwriter:* Philip
Dalkin. *Director of photography:* Gaetano
Nino Martinetti[2]. *Production designer:* Tracy
Watt. *Costume designers:* Rose Chong, Karen
Merkel. *Editor:* Edward McQueen-Mason.
Composers: Paul Grabowsky, Red Symons.
Sound recordist: Ian Ryan. *Sound editors:*
Glen Martin (fx); Livia Ruzic (dia.). *Mixers:*
David Harrison, Roger Savage.

Cast

Garry McDonald (Robert O'Hara Burke),
Kim Gyngell (William John Wills), Peter
Collingwood (Sir William Stawell), Roderick
Williams (George James Landells), Jonathon
Hardy (John Macadame), Mark Little (John
King), Roy Baldwin (Charlie Gray), Alex
Menglet (William Brahe), Tony Rickards
(Patton), Simon Thorpe (McDonough),
Daryl Prasad (Dost Mohammed), Wyn
Roberts (William Wright), Dalibor Satalic
(Beckler), Nicole Kidman (Julia Mathews),
Henry Maas (Charles), Chris Haywood
(Constable), Paul Pryor (Michael), Kirk
Alexander (Mr Lewis), Stephen Kearney
(Ambrose), Neil Gladwin (Godfrey), Colin
Haye (Publican), Mark Mitchell
(Carpenter), Jay Mannering (Menindee
Local), Andrew Martin (Welch).

Robert O'Hara Burke (Garry McDonald) and William John Wills (Kim Gyngell).

This isn't the place to go into the absurd
timing of Bob Weis' Pythonesque spoof,
Wills & Burke, which opened a week before
the premiere of Graeme Clifford's reverent
epic on the 19th-century explorers (**Burke
& Wills**). It could be claimed that the clash
is at least appropriate to the lunatic conduct
and incredible lack of perception of the real-
life expedition itself. Philip Dalkin's screenplay, directed and produced by Weis, presents the tragedy of the worst foul-up in the
history of Australian exploration as theatrical farce.

   Garry McDonald plays Irish-born police
superintendent Robert O'Hara Burke as a
dashing nincompoop who unerringly leads
the party to utter disaster. His second-in-
command, well-born Englishman William
John Wills, is portrayed by Kim Gyngell as a
self-effacing, serious young man, dressed
throughout in full morning suit.

   The trouble, however, is that the spoof
doesn't work. The film is almost as flat as
the terrain the explorers crossed, the few

good gags, visual and verbal, overwhelmed
by others that are obvious and overdone.

   Jonathon Hardy is the Royal Society's
John Macadame, who prefers Burke to a
more qualified leader, because the other
applicant lacks theatrical training. He is
much more impressed by Burke's dashing
pursuit of actress Julia Mathews (Nicole
Kidman).

   One of the script's better inventions is to
present the eminent judicial and political
figure Sir William Stawell (Peter Collingwood) as a grandee utterly convinced that
the populace loves him to distraction. One
could speculate on the target of the satire,
with Prime Minister Hawke (then at the
height of his opinion-poll popularity) a likely candidate.

   Budgeted at less than $2 million, **Wills
& Burke** is a quite expansive and good-

looking film, shot by Gaetano Nino
Martinetti and designed by Tracy Watt. It
was originally conceived as a television mini-
series and probably should have been
produced as one – or left in the 'not-such-a-
good-idea' basket.

KEITH CONNOLLY

---

[1] The film is often incorrectly referred to as 'Wills
& Burke: The Untold Story', but this is a confusion resulting from a publicity tag-line.
[2] Later known as 'Nino Martinetti'.

References

'History Lessons', an article (with quotes) on
producer Bob Weis by Nick Roddick, *Cinema
Papers*, no. 54, November 1985, pp. 22–4.
'Norman Gunston's Australia: **Wills and** [sic]
Burke', a review by Nick Roddick, ibid., p. 67.
'**Wills and** [sic] **Burke**', a short review by Ross
Gibson, *Filmnews*, November 1985, p. 21.

MARK EGERTON

THE WINDS OF JARRAH

Film Corporation of Western Australia Limited presents The Winds of Jarrah. © 1983 Film Corporation of Western Australia Limited. Developed with the assistance of the Australian Film Commission. Produced by the Film Corporation of Western Australia. *Budget:* $2.5 million. *Location:* Dorrigo (New South Wales). *Filmed:* January-February 1983. *Australian distributor:* Filmways. *Video:* Filmpac. *Rating:* M (October 1984; 2194.40m reduced version). 35mm. Panavision. 80 mins.

Producers: Mark Egerton, Marj Pearson. *Associate producer:* Cara Farnes. *Scriptwriter:* Mark Egerton. Based on a storyline, characters and screenplay by Bob Ellis and Anne Brooksbank. Based on the Harlequin/Mills & Boon novel, *The House in the Timberwoods*, by Joyce Dingwell. *Director of photography:* Geoff Burton. *Camera operator:* David Williamson. *Production designer:* Graham "Grace" Walker. *Costume designer:* David Rowe. *Editor:* Sara Bennett. *Composer:* John Steuart. *Sound recordist:* Gary Wilkins. *Sound editors:* Paul Maxwell, Peter Foster, Anne Breslin, Emma Hay. *Mixers:* Gethin Creagh; Martin Oswin (2nd).

Cast

Terence Donovan ("Timber" Marlow), Susan Lyons (Diana Venness), Harold Hopkins (Jack Farrell), Steve Bisley (Clem Mathieson), Martin Vaughan (Ben), Dorothy Alison (Mrs Sullivan), Isabelle Anderson (Helen Marlow), Steven Grives (Kevin), Emil Minty (Andy Marlow), Nikki Gemmell (Kathy Marlow), Mark Kounnas (Peter Marlow), Les Foxcroft (Woody Gunner), Michael Long (Paul Marlow), Ray Marshall (Man in Train), Kati Edwards (Lady in Train), Bill McClusky (Tall Soldier).

The Winds of Jarrah bears the dubious novelty value of being the first film to be adapted from a Mills & Boon novel: in this case, *The House in the Timberwoods* (1959), by the prolific Australian author, Joyce Dingwell.

Set in 1946, this florid melodrama, exquisitely shot by Geoff Burton, centres on the relationship between the boss of a sawmilling operation, "Timber" Marlow (Terence Donovan), and a young English governess, Diana Venness (Susan Lyons), recently jilted in love, whom "Timber" employs to look after his three children.

The producers had optimistically hoped for a glossy romantic epic in the style of **Ryan's Daughter** (David Lean, 1970), but

the resulting film, adapted by director Mark Egerton from a script by Bob Ellis and Anne Brooksbank, is full of risible dialogue which defeats the cast's best efforts at creating plausible characters, leaving only the lush scenery to be admired.

Susan Lyons, a NIDA graduate, had previously worked mainly on stage and had appeared in the mini-series, *For the Term of His Natural Life* (Rob Stewart, 1982), whereas Egerton had worked with Terence Donovan when the former worked as first assistant director on **Money Movers** (Bruce Beresford, 1979).

Financed by the Film Corporation of Western Australia, of which Geoff Pearson, co-producer, was the head, it was the Corporation's second wholly backed feature following **Running on Empty** (John Clark, 1982).

The seven-week shoot began in January 1983 and concluded at the end of February on a $2.5 million budget. Although filming was originally proposed for Western Australia (Pemberton) locations, similar vegetation and spectacularly photogenic rainforest country were found in northern New South Wales in the dairy and timber country of Dorrigo.

Three years after the film's completion, an announcement was made that the film would be theatrically released after extensive recutting. It had a short run in outback New South Wales before eventually turning up in video stores.

PAUL HARRIS

Diana Venness (Susan Lyons).

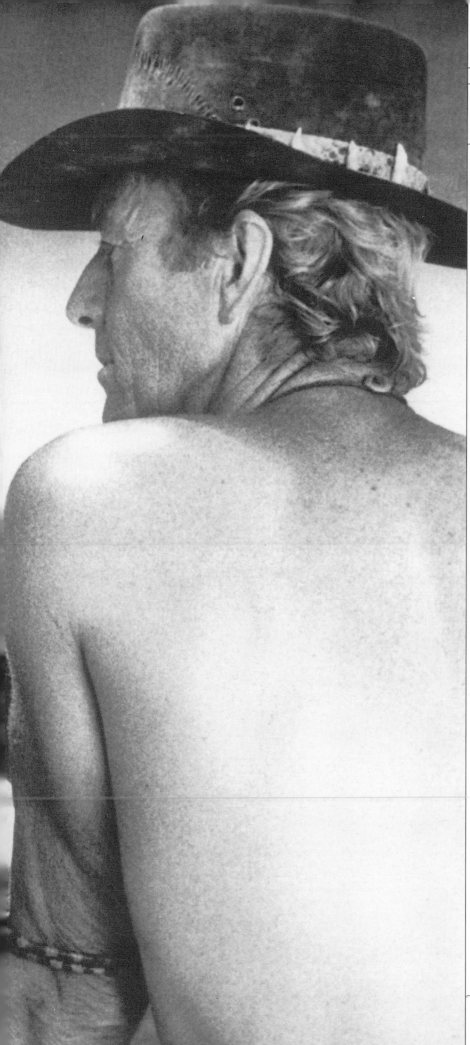

1986

Sue Charlton (Linda Kozlowski) and Mick 'Crocodile' Dundee (Paul Hogan). Peter Faiman's Crocodile Dundee.

BACKLASH

Mermaid Beach Productions. BACKLASH. © 1986 Mermaid Beach Productions. *Budget:* $275,000. *Location:* western New South Wales. *Australian distributor:* Dendy. *Video:* Virgin. *Rating:* M. Super 16mm (blown up to 35mm). 89 mins.

Producer: Bill Bennett. *Scriptwriter:* Bill Bennett. *Dialogue:* David Argue, Gia Carides, Lydia Miller, Brian Syron, Bill Bennett. *Director of photography:* Tony Wilson. [*Production designer:* not credited.] *Wardrobe:* Martin Wright, Louise Fischer. *Editor:* Denise Hunter. *Composers:* Michael Atkinson, Michael Spicer. *Sound recordist:* Leo Sullivan. *Sound editor:* Brett Robinson. [*Mixer:* not credited.]

Cast

David Argue (Trevor Darling), Gia Carides (Nikki Iceton), Lydia Miller (Kath), Brian Syron (The Executioner), Anne Smith (Publican's Wife), Don Smith (Publican), Jennifer Cluff (Waitress), George Skiadas (Cook), Mary Prentice (Motel Receptionist), John Lawrence (Property Owner), Greg Lawrence (Owner's Son), Garry Jackson (1st Policeman), Gregory McMahon (2nd Policeman), Barry Mackaness (Petrol Pump Attendant), Anthony Holmes (Detective).

Two white cops escort an Aborigine from Sydney to Broken Hill to stand trial for the alleged murder of a small-town publican. Since it is obvious from the opening sequence that the woman is innocent, **Backlash** is more a study of white-versus-black justice than an Aboriginal whodunit. However, a thriller element is introduced via the film's cleverly disguised sub-plot concerning the death of an Aboriginal youth.

Former journalist and documentary-maker Bill Bennett wrote, directed and co-produced the film. Something of an Australian auteur, Bennett favours improvised performances. With **Backlash**, he spent two weeks with the cast, discussing the film's 26-page scene breakdown, before proceeding to Broken Hill for the shoot. The pivotal characters—the two cops played by David Argue and Gia Carides—are superbly realised. Bennett says they came up with ideas that would not have been possible had they used a script. Both Argue and Carides had had experience with improvisation.

Argue is ideal for the part of the hardened, streetwise bigot, Trevor Darling. Fresh from his demotion to the uniform section after killing an Aboriginal youth in a shoot-out, Darling epitomises the sleazy cop who drinks and smokes dope on duty. 'I didn't smoke dope 'til I was in the drug squad. It

was compulsory', he says. He intimidates his buddy cop, Nikki Iceton: 'Sit back Icebox and put your belt on…Jesus, Freud would love you.'

A regular of Theatresports and fresh from her rôle in **Bliss**, Carides is convincing as the rookie cop. The Aboriginal woman, Kath, is played by Lydia Miller, at the time a nurse, but who has since become one of Australia's more accomplished actresses.

Most of **Backlash** takes place in western New South Wales. After taking a wildly miscalculated short-cut, the unlikely trio becomes stranded in near-desert conditions with only Fantales and windscreen-washer water for nourishment. In this harsh setting, Kath's bush survival skills earn the two cops' respect, and, when they are rescued, Darling and Iceton take up her cause. Determined to gain a confession from the Publican's Wife (Anne Smith), they return to the scene of the crime—the film's one unconvincing moment. Aboriginal payback law has the last say in the film, when the Aboriginal youth's father avenges his son's death.

Despite a few continuity and technical gaffs, the $275,000 film exudes a strange

power, and is immensely entertaining. As one of several films released in 1986 on an Aboriginal theme (Bruce Beresford's **The Fringe Dwellers** is another), **Backlash** had its world premiere in the Un Certain Regard section of the 1986 Cannes Film Festival. As with his previous feature, the award-winning Agent Orange drama, **A Street to Die**, **Backlash** was shot on Super 16 and blown up to 35mm. Bennett raised money for both films by knocking on doors in North Queensland. While at the time Bennett claimed that he would never use improvisation again, he did so to great effect in the two tele-features he directed in 1989, *Malpractice* and *Mortgage*.

Helen Barlow

References

'Bill Bennett', an article (with quotes) about the director by Kathy Bail, *Cinema Papers*, no. 60, November 1986, pp. 28–31.

'Backlash', a review by David Stratton, *Cinema Papers*, no. 61, January 1987, p. 45.

'Black Heroines White Directors', Tim Rowse, *Filmnews*, November 1986, p. 11.

Nikki Iceton (Gia Carides) and Trevor Darling (David Argue).

THE BIG HURT

Lisa (Lian Lunson), Price (David Bradshaw) and two Tank Girls.

[No opening production company credit.] THE BIG HURT. © 1986 The Big Hurt Ltd. *Budget:* $690,000. *Location:* Melbourne. *Australian distributor:* Valhalla. *Video:* CIC-Taft Video. *Rating:* R. Super 16. 93 mins.

Producer: Chris Kiely. *Executive producer:* Phillip J. Dwyer. *Scriptwriters:* Barry Peak, Sylvia Bradshaw. *Director of photography:* Malcolm Richards. *Production designer:* Paddy Reardon. *Costume designer:* Anna Jakab. *Editor:* Ralph Strasser. *Composer:* Allan Zavod. *Sound recordist:* John Rowley. *Sound editor:* Neil Brown. *Mixer:* David Harrison.

Cast

David Bradshaw (Price), Lian Lunson (Lisa), Simon Chilvers (Algerson), John Ewart (Harry[1]), Nick Waters (McBride), Alan Cassell (Blake), Alethe McGrath (Mrs Trent), Joanne Canning (Ballerina), Syd Conabere (O'Neal), Tommy Dysart (Schwartz), Dorothy Cutts (Rachel), Gary Adams (Fletch), Abbe Holmes (Jenny), Robin Cuming (Monk), Julie Jones (Wendy), Paul Young (Smudge), Julie du Rieu (Street Whore), Paul Russell (David Myles), Mira Babic (Temptress), Yvonne Braumann (Human Ashtray[2]), John Allan (Jagger), James McRae (News Editor).

Price (David Bradshaw) is a bachelor and a characteristically heavy-drinking journalist who has recently been released from gaol where he spent 12 weeks for malicious libel. He returns to *The Melbourne Star* newspaper only to find that his job, desk and regular lover have all been taken care of while he has been away. He has been demoted to doing the police rounds and immediately stumbles upon some bizarre murders.

Price is approached by Lisa (Lian Lunson), a tall, mysterious woman whose stability and credibility are questionable, as she has also spent some time away—in a mental hospital. She enlists Price's help to find her scientist father—though her father reportedly committed suicide 15 years earlier. Price's investigations lead him through the sleazy underworld of Melbourne's nightlife and he unearths the previous scandal attached to Lisa's father.

Barry Peak, the director, opens this traditionally structured mystery film with a long-winded attempt at artistic symbolism: a ballerina is dancing alternately on flowers (death lilies) and broken glass. This is meant to denote a later part in the plot where we learn that the scientists have been experimenting with a drug that transposes pleasure and pain. These experiments are conducted on female prostitutes from St Kilda, de-picted as expendable, desperate and voiceless members of the community.

Lisa and the other female characters portrayed are not attributed any more value than the prostitutes: they are flat, one-dimensional characters used to furnish this sub-standard script. The attention is focused on Price's dragging this crime story forward and surrounding him are a variety of unsatisfactory relationships.

Uncreative camera work and stilted acting result in some extraordinarily still interchanges which make it difficult for viewers to lose themselves in the story. Added to this is dull dialogue, which is occasionally out of synch. Peak, however, has made good use of a number of eternally topical issues: corruption in high organisations (in this case, ASIO), government cover-ups, the ethics of journalism, the ethics of drug testing, and the perception of pleasure and pain. But none of these themes is pursued to any notable degree and instead we are left with a tired, unsubtle plot which is visually unrewarding.

SUZANNE BROWN

---

[1] The front credits give the character name as 'Harry Gregory'.

[2] Braumann is also credited further on in the end credits as 'Tank Girl #4'.

CACTUS

[No opening production company credit.]
CACTUS. © 1986 Dofine Limited. Made with the assistance of Film Victoria and the Australian Film Commission. *Budget:* $1.5 million. *Location:* Dandenong Ranges (Victoria). *Australian distributor:* Roadshow. *Opened:* 4 September 1986. *Video:* Premiere. *Rating:* M. 35mm. 92 mins.

Producers: Jane Ballantyne, Paul Cox. *Associate producer:* Tony Llewellyn-Jones. *Scriptwriters:* Paul Cox, Bob Ellis, Norman Kaye. *Additional dialogue:* Morris Lurie. Based on an original scenario by Paul Cox. *Director of photography:* Yuri Sokol. *Camera operator:* Gaetano Nino Martinetti[1]. *Production designer:* Asher Bilu. *Wardrobe:* Aphrodite Kondos. *Editor:* Tim Lewis. *Composers:* Asher Bilu (fx); Elsa Davis (party songs). *Sound recordist:* Ken Hammond. *Sound editors:* Frank Lipson, Tim Chau. *Mixer:* James Currie.

Cast

Isabelle Huppert (Colo), Robert Menzies (Robert), Norman Kaye (Tom), Monica Maughan (Bea), Banduk Marika (Banduk), Sheila Florance (Martha), Peter Aanensen (George), Julia Blake (Club Speaker), Lionel Kowal (Eye Specialist), Jean-Pierre Mignon (Jean-François), Elsa Davis (Elsa), Ray Marshall (Kevin), Maurie Fields (Maurie), Sean Scully (Doctor), Dawn Klingberg (Pedestrian), Curtis Easton (Young Robert), Kyra Cox (Sister), Tarni James (Mother), Tony Llewellyn-Jones (Father).

Cactus is one of Paul Cox's most likeable, emotionally satisfying and unpretentious films. Set in the Dandenong Ranges just outside Melbourne, the story is told straightforwardly, despite an underlying elusive symbolism.

Colo (Isabelle Huppert), a young Frenchwoman holidaying in Australia with friends Tom (Norman Kaye) and Bea (Monica Maughan), is forced to re-evaluate her life and failing marriage when a piece of glass pierces her eye in a car accident. She is told that if her damaged eye is not removed soon, she will also lose the vision in her good eye from sympathetic opthalmitis, but Colo wavers (the reasons why she procrastinates are never made clear).

Colo is then introduced by her friends to Robert (Robert Menzies), a withdrawn, tense young man, blind from birth, who grows cacti. They become lovers and, through the relationship which develops, Colo learns to adjust to her impairment, and her view of the world begins to change.

Robert (Robert Menzies) and Colo (Isabelle Huppert).

Cox always elicits honest, warm performances from his actors, and Cactus is no exception. Menzies is completely believable as the defensive, vulnerable, prickly Robert, while Huppert as Colo registers emotion with understated, subliminal power. Cox uses her Frenchness—her outsider status—to great effect, as a lens through which to filter his own perceptions of Australian culture and people. Through her we see ourselves, and Cox details with great affection a raft of off-beat characters—all friends and collaborators of Cox—who give the film emotional depth and a quirky originality.

Cactus has all the elements that make Cox's films so distinctive: strong psychological interest, and a mix of narrative realism with experimental sequences bordering on documentary which provide textural contrasts (flickering 'home movie' and dream sequences), as well as a palpable sense of place. Cox's civilised community of eccentrics, the panning of gum trees and sky, the sounds of the bush and Pergolesi's *Stabat Mater*—the nexus between Australia and Europe, and the particularity of a pocket of local Melbourne culture, has never been so precisely captured on film.

Cox's odd choice of the cactus as a symbol was, one suspects, instinctive, but it seems right. It grows and can flower while seemingly deprived of nourishment, and it has connotations of transplanted loneliness and prickliness. It also has strong tactile connotations which are particularly apt for people with diminished vision.

Although Cactus lacks the dramatic intensity of Paul Cox's better-known films (**Lonely Hearts**, 1982; **Man of Flowers**, 1983; and **My First Wife**, 1984), it is appealingly languid, non-judgemental and cohesive, one of Cox's finest and most memorable films.

JAN EPSTEIN

---

[1] Later known as just 'Nino Martinetti'.

References

'**Cactus** Flower', an article (with quotes) on actor Isabelle Huppert by Nick Roddick, *Cinema Papers*, no. 57, May 1986, pp. 36–8.
'Dutch Threat', an interview with director Paul Cox by Carol Bennetto, *Cinema Papers*, no. 59, September 1986, pp. 18–22.
'Seeing I: **Cactus**', a review by David Stratton, ibid., p. 43.
'**Cactus**', a review by Adrian Martin, *Filmnews*, September 1986, p. 17.

COOL CHANGE

Geoff Burrowes & George Miller present COOL CHANGE. © 1985 Delatite Productions. *Location:* Mansfield and Victorian Alps. *Australian distributor:* Hoyts. *Opened:* 10 April 1986. *Video:* RCA-Columbia-Hoyts. *Rating:* PG. 35mm. 88 mins.

Producer: Dennis Wright. *Executive producer:* Geoff Burrowes. *Scriptwriter:* Patrick Edgeworth. *Director of photography:* John Haddy. *Production designer:* Leslie Binns. *Wardrobe:* Jeannie Cameron. *Editor:* Philip Reid. *Composer:* Bruce Rowland. *Sound recordist:* Lloyd Carrick. *Sound supervisor:* Terry Rodman. *Sound editor:* Peter Burgess. *Mixer:* James Currie.

Cast

Jon Blake (Steve), Lisa Armytage (Joanna), Deborra-Lee Furness (Lee), David Bradshaw (James Hardwicke), Alec Wilson (Bull Raddick), James Wright (Snr Ranger), Mark Albiston (Frank Mitchell), Alan Fletcher (Rob Mitchell), Marie Redshaw (Helen Mitchell), Clive Hearne (Ray Regan), Christopher Stevenson (Jim Regan), Jennifer Hearne (Jennifer Regan), Robert Bruning (Minister), Wilbur Wilde (Wally West), Alister Neely (Joanna's Child), Chris Waters (Stock & Station Agent), Ray Pattison (Curly), Terry Brittingham (Greenie), Meryl McColl (Punk Girl Greenie), Bob Halsall (Frank's Mate), Robert Ratti (Yobbo Leader), Angela Gigliotti (Yobbo Girl).

The promotional material for **Cool Change** need not have alluded to the fact it was produced by the makers of **The Man From Snowy River** (George Miller, 1982). The film is a virtual sequel to the Banjo Paterson-inspired epic of 19th-century cattlemen in the high plains of Australia. Although the films are set a century apart, they are remarkably similar in theme and context. They are both, essentially, about men (and women) and their cattle-grazing vocations, and embattled individuals battling against external forces, be they human or otherwise.

Cool Change tells of the struggle of high-country cattlemen to resist state government pressure to turn high-country grazing runs into a national park, a move which would preclude livestock grazing and a historic livelihood.

The central figure is Steve (Jon Blake), a parks-and-wildlife ranger who gets seconded against his wishes to the high country as a pawn for the city conservation bureaucrats. He is an ambiguous, likeable

kind of hero who puts out fires with a foam extinguisher and who is all smiles while chopping down snow gums (an image that would offend Australia's new-age environmentalism). Ironically, Steve's roots go back to the region of his posting, where his family grow beef and where he runs into an old flame, Joanna (Lisa Armytage).

Cool Change is one of the few contemporary Australian films to tackle a political issue, and there are no doubts that its makers have a deep empathy for the high country and its cattlemen. But most of its characters are stunted by a hackneyed 'them-versus-us' plot which is always going to make the greenies and bureaucrats out to be a pack of mugs. A scene that comes to mind is when conservation minister's bimbo offsider, Lee (Deborra-Lee Furness), turns up for a field tour of the alpine region dressed in high heels and carrying a picnic basket. Notwithstanding this, many of the country dwellers are also portrayed in an unfavourable light reminiscent of the ugly Australian primitiveness in Ted Kotcheff's "Wake in Fright" (1971).

To its credit, **Cool Change** tries to authenticate its story in terms of place and

contemporary events. It tackles an environmental issue and, for once, it is the man on the land who is getting a decent hearing, albeit a biased one.

The main actors do a serviceable job given the film's self-imposed limitations, and John Haddy's camera captures both the grandeur of the alpine country and **The Man from Snowy River**-inspired horse stunts. However, the visual continuity of the film is hampered by some sloppy editing, giving the impression that the film was put together in a hurry. The script has its humorous moments but is hollow in too many places, and has a tendency to stretch believability. The climax is ruined by a highly inflamed, inaccurate portrayal of government rangers heading for the mountains in paramilitary formation—and armed with M-16 machine guns—to meet their adversaries on horseback. Of course, there is no need to guess who outwits whom in the end.

GREG KERR

Reference

'Cattle Cry: **Cool Change**', a review by Nick Roddick, *Cinema Papers*, no. 57, May 1986, p. 84.

Joanna (Lisa Armytage) and Steve (Jon Blake).

CROCODILE DUNDEE

A Rimfire Films production. CROCODILE DUNDEE. *Alternative title:* "Crocodile" Dundee (US). © 1986 Rimfire Films Limited. *Locations:* Queensland, Northern Territory, Sydney; New York. *Australian distributor:* Hoyts. *Opened:* 24 April 1986. *Video:* CBS-Fox. *Rating:* M. Panavision. 35mm. 102 mins.

Producer: John Cornell. *Line producer:* Jane Scott. *Associate producer:* Wayne Young. *Scriptwriters:* Paul Hogan, Ken Shadie, John Cornell. *Director of photography:* Russell Boyd. *Camera operator:* Peter Menzies Jnr. *Production designer:* Graham (Grace) Walker. *Costume designer:* Norma Moriceau. *Editor:* David Stiven. *Composer:* Peter Best. *Sound recordists:* Gary Wilkins (Aust.), Bill Daly (US). *Sound editors:* Karen Whittington, Craig Carter, Adrian Carr (dia.); Bruce Lamshed, Louise Johnson, Tim Chau (fx). *Mixers:* Roger Savage, Bruce Lamshed.

Cast

Paul Hogan (Mick 'Crocodile' Dundee), Linda Kozlowski (Sue Charlton), John Meillon (Walter Reilly), David Gulpilil (Neville Bell), Ritchie Singer (Con), Maggie Blinco (Ida), Steve Rackman (Don), Gerry Skilton (Nugget), Terry Gill (Duffy), Peter Turnbull (Trevor); Mark Blum (Richard Mason), Michael Lombard (Sam Charlton), Irving Metzman (Doorman), Reginald Veliohson (Gus), Rick Colitti (Danny), John Snyder (Pimp), J. J. Cole (Buzzy), Gwyllum Evans (Wendell Wainwright), Clarie Hague (Dorothy Wainwright), Jan Saint (Wino), Peter Bucossi (Subway Creek [sic]), Sullivan Walker (Tall Man).

Crocodile Dundee's legend in the Australian film industry is as great as the legend of Mick 'Crocodile' Dundee is in the film itself. Paul Hogan wanted to make 'a *proper* movie' and ended up with a mega-hit blockbuster and, more surprising for an Australian film, an international success. The formula here seems to have been a charming, unpretentious simplicity of story and style, high production values and an abundance of tried-and-true basic humour.

This is a fairy-tale adventure-romance for the young and old, with many a reference to Tarzan and Jane. Linda Kozlowski and Paul Hogan are perfect together as the sophisticated, tough American reporter Sue Charlton and the laconic, easy-going bushman Mick 'Crocodile' Dundee.

Sue has been working in Sydney, and travels west to pursue a claim that a certain Mick was attacked and mauled by a crocodile in the remote outback, but managed to drag himself to safety through the bush over several days. After meeting Wally Reilly (John Meillon), Mick's friend, more-words-than-action assistant and partner in a venture called Never Never Tours, and listening to yarns of Mick's mythic bravery, Sue finally meets the man himself, who at first seems to be just another ocker yobbo. But once Sue sets out with him to retrace his steps to safety during his crocodile incident, he begins to present a different picture. Behind the façade of facetious behaviour, Mick is wise and strong, and his knowledge of the bush and his ability to communicate with animals astounds Sue. Besides that, Mick charms her and the audience with his lack of sophistication and unpretentiousness.

After their adventures in the outback, Sue decides that it might be fun for her personally, and interesting for her story on Mick, if he comes to New York with her. And here the film and its humour become a touch more sophisticated. Mick's naïveté during his sojourn in New York makes him successful in a lifestyle where even the natives often fail. He is untouchable, a holy innocent, and finds burden with neither crime nor corruption nor the twisted and manipulative behaviour of the New Yorkers. But he also becomes a celebrity through Sue's articles in the newspaper. His only problem is that he has fallen in love with Sue and she becomes engaged to a most unlovable colleague, Richard Mason (Mark Blum). In the end Sue realises that she too is in love with Mick, and, in what has to be one of the best sequences in Australian cinema, she declares her love for him in an overcrowded subway station.

Crocodile Dundee is a true feel-good pic. It doesn't attempt to be anything else, but it achieves its goal so well that its success is easy to understand. But also, and perhaps more important, no matter what critics may have written about it, no matter what calculations might have been made during the production of the film, there are no real reasons for the film's success. This is one Aussie film that simply got lucky.

ANNA GUL

References
'A Fistful of Koalas', John Baxter, *Cinema Papers*, no. 57, May 1986, pp. 26–9.
'Crocs Away: **Crocodile Dundee**', a review by Nick Roddick, *Cinema Papers*, no. 58, July 1986, p. 40.
'The Sound of Music', an interview with composer Peter Best (and others) by Jenni Gyffyn, *Cinema Papers*, no. 69, May 1988, pp. 10–15.
'"Crocodile" Dundee Overseas', Stephen Crofts, *Cinema Papers*, no. 77, January 1990, pp. 16–19.

Mick 'Crocodile' Dundee (Paul Hogan) surveys New York.

BRIAN TRENCHARD-SMITH

DEAD-END DRIVE-IN

Springvale Productions in association with New South Wales Film Corporation present DEAD-END Drive-In[1]. © 1986 Springvale Productions and New South Wales Film Corporation. *Budget:* $2.3 million. *Location:* Sydney. *Australian distributor:* GUO. *Video:* Australian Video. *Rating:* M. 35mm. 90 mins.

Producer: Andrew Williams. *Co-producer:* Damien Parer. *Scriptwriter:* Peter Smalley. [Uncredited: based on a story by Peter Carey.] *Director of photography:* Paul Murphy. *Camera operator:* Kevan Lind. *Production designer:* Larry Eastwood. *Costume designer:* Anthony Jones. *Editors:* Alan Lane, Lee Smith. *Composer:* Frank Strangio. *Sound recordist:* Leo Sullivan. *Sound editors:* Lee Smith, Les Fiddess. *Mixer:* Martin Oswin.

Cast

Ned Manning (Crabs), Natalie McCurry (Carmen), Peter Whitford (Thompson), Wilbur Wilde (Hazza), Dave Gibson (Dave), Sandie Lillingston (Beth), Ollie Hall (Frank), Lyn Collingwood (Fay), Nikki McWaters (Shirl), Melissa Davis (Narelle), Margi di Ferranti (Jill), Desiree[2] Smith (Tracey), Murray Fahey (Mickey), Jeremy Shadlow (Jeff), Brett Climo (Dog); Alan McQueen, Ken Snodgrass (Accident Cops); Bill Lyle, Garry Who (Drive-in Cops); Bernadette Foster (Momma), Ron Sinclair (News Reporter), Ghandi McIntyre (Indian), David Jones (T.V. Newsreader).

Dead-End Drive-In is adapted from a Peter Carey story, and went into production in the same year that Bliss (Ray Lawrence), adapted from a Carey novel, was released. The opening titles set the scene: race wars in South Africa, a second Wall Street crash and huge riots during Australia's bicentennial year, a prelude to the use of emergency powers by the government.

In urban Australia in the 1990s, the streets are combat zones, dominated by marauding gangs of 'Karboys', vultures on wheels. Their only competition is provided by parasitic tow-truck drivers and television crews who rush from accident to accident.

Crabs (Ned Manning) is eager to be part of the tow-truck scene like his muscle-bound brother, Frank. Slight, enthusiastic, puppyish, he exercises and builds up his body so that he will be strong enough for a stint on the trucks. After a trip out to an accident scene with his brother—an energetic, comical scene that sets the tone for the whole film—he borrows Frank's Chevy to go to the drive-in. But during the show, as Crabs and

The Karboys, who terrorise the highways.

his girlfriend Carmen (Natalie McCurry) make out in the back seat, the wheels are stolen.

The unctuous, unflappable manager, Thompson (Peter Whitford), tells an outraged Crabs to stay the night. The next day Crabs finds that he is part of a captive audience: the drive-in is a kind of containment camp for the young. They will remain there 'until the government decides what to do with you', Thompson tells them.

So the Star Drive-In becomes a kind of punk suburbia, a holiday resort with an electrified fence, a caravan park–prison. The cars are converted into dwellings, and the only fuel is fast food at the Eazy Eatin.

Production designer Larry Eastwood brought in local graffiti artists to help give the abandoned Sydney drive-in the authentic late 20th-century tribal look, a punk bower-bird style that could be called Delinquent Domestic. Carmen adapts to the environment, to the food vouchers and the subcultures that spring up: she finds companions who tell her that she is better off inside than outside. But Crabs chafes. He is not prepared to stay in the camp, and he plans his escape.

As he plots his departure, Asian families are brought into the camp, and the Star's inhabitants respond by forming a White Australia Committee and holding a rally. Crabs does not become involved. It is not that he is particularly tolerant or understanding; rather, his whole life now revolves around escape and he sees the new arrivals in one light only: 'They're not the enemy. They're prisoners just like us.'

Dead-End Drive-In is faithful to the tone and many of the details of Carey's story, although the escape attempt, in the hands of an action director like Trenchard-Smith, is prolonged and exciting, with a terrific cli-

mactic stunt. The film is full of sharp, witty touches that are never gratuitous. One example is the drive-in fare: several of Trenchard-Smith's films can be seen on the drive-in screens, notably **Turkey Shoot**, his far more violent 1981 feature about a futuristic prison camp.

The film was one of four productions in 1985 to be assisted by the New South Wales Film Corporation. At that stage, Michael Jenkins, who had directed the mini-series *Scales of Justice*, was named as director. The film was underwritten by merchant bankers Capel Court Corporation Ltd and CCF Australia Securities Ltd. It was Capel Court's first venture into film underwriting.

The film was acquired by New World at Cannes in 1986. But unfortunately **Dead-End Drive-In** did not find the Australian audience it deserved, and it disappeared after a short theatrical release. In mid-1987, the film's actors got together to promote the film, approaching independent cinema owners to screen it. Lead actor Ned Manning criticised the distributor, Greater Union, for not giving **Dead-End Drive-In** enough support. It had received a two-week season in Sydney and equally brief seasons in Adelaide and Brisbane. In Melbourne, ironically, it was a supporting feature at the drive-in.

PHILIPPA HAWKER

[1] On the end credits, the first hyphen is dropped from the title, its being rendered as 'Dead End Drive-In'.
[2] Sometimes 'Desirée'.

References
'Anyone Can Do a Stunt Once…', an article on the stunts by Nick Roddick, *Cinema Papers*, no. 56, March 1986, pp. 17–20.
'A Horse for all Courses', an article (with quotes) with Brian Trenchard-Smith by Brian Jones, ibid., pp. 26–8.

PHILIPPE   MORA

DEATH OF A SOLDIER

Suatu Film Management presents A William Nagle-David Hannay Production. DEATH OF A SOLDIER. © 1985 Suata Management Limited on behalf of the investors. *Budget:* $3 million. *Location:* Melbourne. *Australian distributor:* Open Eye. *Opened:* October 1986.[1] *Video:* CBS-Fox. *Rating:* M (February 1987; 2605.85m). 35mm. Panavision. 105 mins.

Producers: David Hannay, William Nagle. *Associate producers:* Honnon Page, Richard Jabara. *Executive producers:* Oscar Scherl, Richard Tanner. *Co-producer:* Lance Reynolds. *Scriptwriter:* William Nagle. *Director of photography:* Louis Irving. *Production designer:* Geoff Richardson. *Costume designer:* Alexandra Tynan. *Editor:* John Scott. *Composer:* Allan Zavod. *Sound recordist:* Geoff White. *Sound design:* Greg Bell. *Sound editor:* Helen Brown (dia.). *Mixer:* Julian Ellingworth.

Cast

James Coburn (Major Patrick Dannenberg), Bill Hunter (Detective Sergeant Fred Bluey Adams), Reb Brown (Private Edward Leonski), Maurie Fields (Detective Sergeant Ray Martin), Max Fairchild (Major William Fricks), Belinda Davey (Margot Saunders), Randall Berger (Private Anthony Gallo), Michael Pate (Major Gen. Richard Sutherland), Jon Sidney (General Douglas MacArthur), Nell Johnson (Maisie), Pippa Wilson (Singer in Boomerang Bar), Kim Rushworth's Maple Leaf Jazz Band (Band in Bar), John McTiernan (Colonel Williams), Ron Pinnell (Mr. Harmon), Len Kasserman (Major Gen. Eichelberger), Lisa Aldenhoven (1st Girl in Bar), Nigel Bradshaw (Sergeant Rothgerber).

Philippe Mora is a generally underrated Australian director, doubtless because his garish 'pop culture' sensibility is virtually antithetical to the more sedate, naturalistic values ruling much Australian drama, particularly during the 1970s 'renaissance'.

Death of a Soldier represents in Mora's career a strange rapprochement between the familiar Australian 'period' film (based in this case on a true event, the Leonski murders of the 1940s) and his own characteristic sensibility. Those who have written approvingly of the film (e.g., John Baxter in *Cinema Papers*) praise the provocative way it introduces strong elements of conflict and violence into what Pauline Kael called our cinema of 'good housekeeping' (or, alternatively, what Susan Dermody and Liz Jacka dub the 'AFC genre'). By the same token, for a Mora movie it is rather restrained, more

Margot Saunders (Belinda Davey) and Major Patrick Dannenberg (James Coburn).

respectful of conventional dramatic unities and motivations than his usual 'pop' work— so much so that Mora fan Philip Brophy finds it 'painfully conventional'[2].

The film is structured along two central, interwoven lines. The first charts the increasing madness of soldier Leonski (American actor Reb Brown), as he murders a string of women. Mora modulates from naturalism into more expressionistic passages (involving, for instance, blaring jazz music of the era) to evoke Leonski's rising hysteria, and his barely contained, bull-like sexual violence. For most of the film, Leonski is portrayed as a straightforward 'psycho'; but in the final scenes there is an interesting shift in tone, suggesting that he may be, rather, a victimised 'innocent', akin to a child (such shifts in dramatic perspective are characteristic of Mora's pop sensibility).

The film's simultaneous second line, detailing the complex bureaucratic mechanisms of investigation and punishment set in train by the American army (James Coburn plays the central American official with his familiarly beguiling air of world-weariness) and the Australian army. In the often tense clashes between these two bureaucracies, we are invited to read an allegory of the relationship between America and Australia as nations, a relationship fraught with (again, barely contained) colonial envy, resentment and violence. (This particular allegorical conflict is dear to much Australian cinema in the 1980s.[3]) The film's setpiece of a shoot-out between Australians and Americans at a train station is presented powerfully as an eruption of a national hysteria and will-to-power usually avoided or 'repressed' by our more 'respectable' period films and their famous 'recessive' heroes.

Although less deliberately excessive in its stylistic mannerisms than Mora's other films, **Death of a Soldier** is nonetheless full of typically spectacular touches. Due to the æsthetic constraints imposed by the nominal naturalism of this project, Mora restricts such touches mainly to scene transitions. Many scenes begin abruptly on surprising, disorientating 'shock' cuts, with a sound whose source is locatable somewhere in the shot (e.g., steam from a train) and also extravagantly 'treated' (in terms of echo, volume and so on) for maximum visceral impact.

Overall, the film is an oddity; not entirely successful (in normative, generic terms) as either 'straight' drama or perverse exploitation, but nonetheless an intriguing, messy mixture of elements and impulses from both tendencies.

ADRIAN MARTIN

---

[1] Even though the film was rated in February 1987, the producer, David Hannay, is sure the film was first released in October 1986 at the Stanmore Cinema, Sydney, by Independent Exhibitors.
[2] *Filmviews* (Winter 1987).
[3] For example, **Razorback** (Russell Mulcahy, 1984), **Crocodile Dundee** (Peter Faiman, 1986) and **The Coca-Cola Kid** (Dusan Makavejev, 1985).

References
'Mora Way of Life', an article (with quotes) on director Philippe Mora by Nick Roddick, *Cinema Papers*, no. 61, January 1987, p. 9.
'Philippe Mora: What Can We Do to Help You Stop Screaming?', John Baxter, *Cinema Papers*, no. 74, July 1989, pp. 14–17.
'**Death of a Soldier**', a review by Michael Healy, *Cinema Papers*, no. 62, March 1987, p. 53.

DOT AND KEETO

Yoram Gross presents DOT and Keeto. © 1985 Yoram Gross Film Studio. *Australian distributor:* Yoram Gross. *Video:* CEL. *Rating:* G. 35mm. 70 mins.

Producer: Yoram Gross. *Associate producer:* Sandra Gross. *Scriptwriter:* John Palmer. *Director of photography:* Graham Sharpe. *Photographers:* Jan Carruthers, Ricky Vergara. *Composers:* Guy Gross, Bob Young, John Sangster, John Levine, John Zulaikha, Paul Adolphus.

Animation director: Ray Nowland. *Animators:* Ray Nowland, Andrew Szemenyei, Ariel Ferrari, Nicholas Harding, Rowen Avon, Paul McAdam, Stan Walker,

John Berge, Wal Logue. *In-betweeners:* Paul Baker, Jenny Barber, Mark Benvenuti, Rodney Brundsdon, Hanka Bilyk, Barbara Coy, Greg Farrugia, Murray Griffin, Max Gunner, Debbie Horne, Joseph Cabatuan, Domingo Rivera, Wayne Kelly, Sarah Lawson, Julie Peters, John Robertson, Vicky Robinson, Jan Stephen, Bela Szeman. *Painters:* Robyn Drayton, Mimi Intal, Corallee Munro, Joseph Cabatuan. *Backgrounds:* Amber Ellis. *Graphics:* Eric David. *Special fx painting:* Jeanette Toms.

Voices

Robyn Moore, Keith Scott.

[See Appendix A on all the Gross films, pp. 352–4.]

References
'Dot Dot Dot: **Dot and Keeto**', a review by Sophie Cunningham, *Cinema Papers*, no. 58, July 1986, pp. 51–2.
'Yoram Gross', an interview with the producer-director by Antoinette Starkiewicz, *Cinema Papers*, no. 48, October–November 1984, pp. 334–8, 380–1.
'Yoram Gross', Raffaele Caputo, *Cinema Papers*, no. 86, January 1992, pp. 36–42.

A miniaturised Dot and her pal, Keeto, the mosquito.

DOT AND THE KOALA

Yoram Gross presents DOT AND THE KOALA. © 1984 Yoram Gross Filmstudio Pty Ltd. Produced by Yoram Gross Filmstudios in association with Dot & the Koala Pty Ltd. *Australian distributor:* Yoram Gross. *Video:* CEL. *Rating:* G. 35mm. 75 mins.

Producer: Yoram Gross. *Associate producer:* Sandra Gross. *Scriptwriters:* Greg Flynn, Yoram Gross. Based on an original idea by Yoram Gross. *Director of photography:* Grahame Sharpe. *Photography:* Jan Carruthers, Ricky Vergara. *Editors:* Neil Thumpston, Ted Otton[1], Ian Spruce. *Composers:* Bob Young, John Sangster. *Lyrics:* Gairden Cooke. *Sound editor:* Andrew Plain. *Mixers:* Gethin Creagh, Sid McDonald.

Animation director: Gairden Cooke. *Storyboard and character design:* Gairden Cooke. *Animators:* Paul McAdam, John Berge, Gairden Cooke, Joanna Fryer, Nick Harding, Wal Logue, Jacques Muller, Stan Walker, Andrew Szemenyei. *In-betweeners:* Paul Baker, Steve Becker, Karen Boubouttis, Bela Szeman, Julie Peters, Lu Rou, Vicky Robinson, Maria Haren, Domingo Rivera, Wayne Kelly, Denise Kirkan, Jan Stephen, Rodney Brunsdon, Judy Howieson, Murray Griffen, Joanna Fryer, Greg Farrugia. *Painters:* Robyn Drayton, Mimi Intal, Corallee Munro, Joseph Cabatuan. *Backgrounds:* Amber Ellis. *Graphics:* Eric David. *Special fx painting:* Christiane van der Casseyen, Jeanette Toms. *Graphics:* Eric David.

Voices

Robyn Moore, Keith Scott.

[See Appendix A on all the Gross films, pp. 352–4.]

---

[1] Should be 'Ötton'.

References
'Yoram Gross', an interview with the producer-director by Antoinette Starkiewicz, *Cinema Papers*, no. 48, October–November 1984, pp. 334–8, 380–1.
'Yoram Gross', Raffaele Caputo, *Cinema Papers*, no. 86, January 1992, pp. 36–42.

Dot and her animal friends.

DOT AND THE WHALE

Yoram Gross presents Dot and the Whale. © 1986 Yoram Gross Film Studio. *Australian distributor:* Yoram Gross. *Video:* CEL. *Rating:* G. 35mm. 75 mins.

Producer: Yoram Gross. *Associate producer:* Sandra Gross. *Scriptwriter:* John Palmer. Based on an original idea by Yoram Gross. *Director of photography:* Graham Sharpe. *Photography:* Ricky Vergara, Erik Bierens, Graham Binding. *Composers:* Guy Gross, Bob Young. *Lyrics:* John Palmer. Sung by: Kim Deacon, Robyn Moore, Keith Scott. *Sound editors:* Rod Hay, Derek Wenderski. *Mixers:* Paul Heywood, Ron Purvis.

Animation director: Ray Nowland. *Animators:* Wal Logue, Nick Harding, John Burge, Stan Walker, Ariel Ferrari, Paul McAdam, Andrew Szemenyei, Bela Szeman, Rowen Smith, Gairden Cooke. *In-betweeners:* Paul Baker, Steve Becker, Clare Lyonette, Kathie O'Rourke, Lu Rou, Vicky Robinson, Maria Haren, Domingo Rivera, Jan Stephen, Judy Howieson, Murray Griffen, Joanna Fryer, Greg Farrugia, Hanka Bilyk. *Layout artists:* Ray Nowland, Nobuko Yuasa. *Painters:* Robyn Drayton, Mimi Intal, Corallee Munro, Joseph Cabatuan, Paulette Martin, Annamaria Dimmers. *Backgrounds:*

Amber Ellis, Sheila Christofides, Barry Dean. *Special fx painting:* Christiane van der Casseyen, Jeanette Toms. *Graphics:* Eric David.

Voices

Robyn Moore, Keith Scott.

[See Appendix A on all the Gross films, pp. 352–4.]

Reference

'Yoram Gross', Raffaele Caputo, *Cinema Papers*, no. 86, January 1992, pp. 36–42.

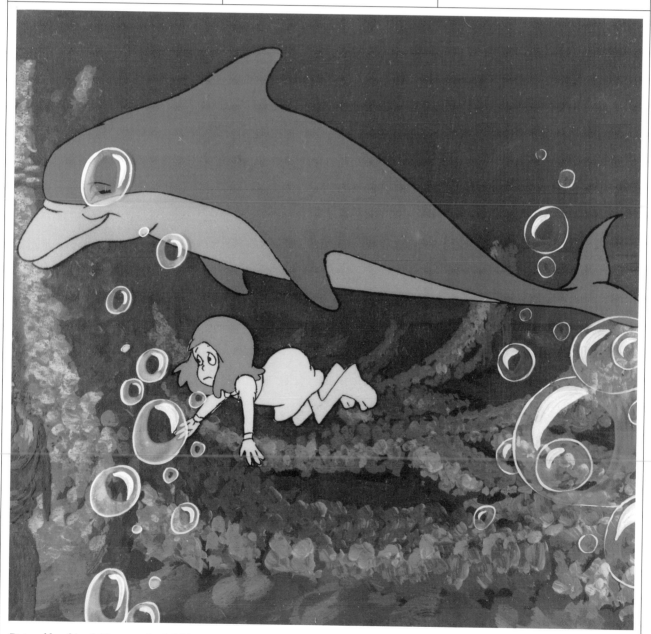

Dot and her friend, Neptune, the dolphin.

FAIR GAME

Southern Films International presents FAIR GAME. © 1985 Southern Films International Limited. Made with the assistance of the AFC. *Budget:* $1.26 million. *Location:* South Australia. *Australian distributor:* CEL. *Video:* CEL. *Rating:* M. 35mm. 85 mins.

Producers: Ron Saunders, Harley Manners. *Scriptwriter:* Rob George. *Director of photography:* Andrew Lesnie. *Production designer:* Kimble Hilder. *Wardrobe supervisor:* Peter Bevan. *Editor:* A. J. Prowse. *Composer:* Ashley Irwin. *Sound recordist:* Toivo Lember. *Sound editors:* Frank Lipson, Steve Lambeth. *Mixers:* James Currie, Peter Smith.

Cast

Cassandra Delaney (Jessica), Peter Ford (Sunny), David Sandford (Ringo), Garry Who (Sparks), Don Barker (Frank), Carmel Young (Moire), Adrian Shirley (Victor), Wayne Anthony (Derek), Kyle (Dog).

In an isolated wildlife sanctuary in outback Australia, there is a woman alone (her husband is at a conference). This would be no cause for alarm if it were not for the three bored and malevolent men—Sunny (Peter Ford), the ringleader, and Ringo (David Sandford) and Sparks (Garry Who), the simpletons—who are shooting protected kangaroos and skinning them. Jessica (Cassandra Delaney) tries to get help from the police, but is treated in a patronising manner. The three men then focus their attention on Jessica and she becomes 'fair game'.

This sexist film was written by Rob George and directed by Mario Andreacchio. The first instance of male fantasy is created when Ringo sticks his head out from underneath Jessica's car and takes a photo of her crutch; Jessica is wearing only a shirt and no underwear. This submissive and unaccountable sexuality continues with Jessica taking off all her clothes and lying naked on the bed. While she is asleep, the men again photograph her.

The film contrives female vulnerability and insinuates that the ultimate expression of male sexuality is to force a woman into sex, which she secretly wants. The connotations of rape are explicit and the images presented encourage the audience to assume it has taken place. Given the continued truculent behaviour, it would be hard to believe otherwise.

There are some passing allusions to other sources, but whether or not they are intentional is unclear. There are echoes of Henry

Jessica (Cassandra Delaney) hides from Ringo (David Sandford) and Sunny (Peter Ford).

Lawson's 'The Drover's Wife', with its story of a woman alone in the outback and open to harassment while her husband is away working, and to **Mad Max** (George Miller, 1979), with the warrior-type clothing and car.

The film repeats the same patterns, and voyeurism and eroticisation of violence against women are complicit and fundamental to the story. This is a misogynistic and unartistic film, and the predictable ending gives one no feeling of justice—the damage has already been done.

SUZANNE BROWN

Reference
'Truck All: **Fair Game**', a review by Nick Roddick, *Cinema Papers*, no. 59, September 1986, pp. 44–5.

FOR LOVE ALONE

UAA presents FOR LOVE ALONE. © 1985 Western Film Productions No. 6 Pty Ltd. *Budget:* $3.8 million. *Location:* Sydney. *Australian distributor:* GUO. *Opened:* 22 May 1986. *Video:* Roadshow. *Rating:* PG. 35mm. 104 mins.

Producer: Margaret Fink. *Executive producer:* David Thomas. *Scriptwriter:* Stephen Wallace. Based on the novel by Christina Stead. *Director of photography:* Alun Bollinger. *Camera operator:* Danny Batterham. *Production designer:* John Stoddart. *Costume designer:* Jennie Tate. *Editor:* Henry Dangar. *Composer:* Nathan Waks. *Sound recordist:* Syd Butterworth. *Supervising sound editor:* Greg Bell. *Sound editor:* Karin Whittington (dia.). *Mixers:* Peter Fenton, Phil Heywood, Ron Purvis.

Cast

Helen Buday (Teresa), Sam Neill (James Quick), Hugo Weaving (Jonathan Crow), Huw Williams (Harry), Hugh Keayes-Byrne (Andrew), Odile Le Clezio (Kitty), John Polson (Leo), Nicholas Opolski (Lance), Judi Farr (Aunt Bea), Anna Phillips (Anne), Tracey Higginson (Mali), Gary Smith (Mali's Husband), Regina Gaigalas (Jean), Naomi Watts (Leo's Girlfriend), Linden Wilkinson (Miss Haviland), Susie Lindeman (Clara), Jenny Vuletic (Elaine), Fiona Stewart (1st Teacher), Marcelle Schmitz (2nd Teacher), Jennifer Hagan (Manette), Anna North (Lucy), Renee Wray (English Landlady), Kate Raison (English Waitress).

Producer Margaret Fink attempted to repeat the success of her earlier production, **My Brilliant Career** (Gill Armstrong, 1979), in this screen adaptation of Christina Stead's 1940 novel. However, **For Love Alone** is no such masterpiece. Written and directed by Stephen Wallace, **For Love Alone**'s story is tedious and its dialogue stilted. Certainly if the script were as well crafted as the film's AFI Award-winning production and costume design, **For Love Alone** may have had a greater impact.

An exploration of a woman's ideas about love, the film loosely follows the early years of Stead's life as she strives to be a writer and find happiness with a man. The character, Teresa (Helen Buday), is obsessed with love. Seeking refuge from her repressive family and the drudgery of work in a city office, she pins her hopes on the first man she meets, her intense, handsome Latin teacher, Jonathan Crow (Hugo Weaving). She has a romantic ideal that he cannot fulfil. An independent, imaginative woman, Teresa is committed to Jonathan, but he treats her

badly. His inability to love in fact compels him to destroy her innocent love.

Eventually, Teresa gains her independence through another man, James Quick (Sam Neill), who really loves her ('a true gentleman', according to the film's press notes). Under Quick's guidance, Teresa attends boisterous socialist meetings and elegant restaurants, and is no longer a naïve romantic, but a maturing young woman and writer. Advocating avant-garde views, Quick even allows Teresa to experience passion with another man before he marries her.

While the book aimed to be a feminist treatise—portraying an independent woman born into the wrong era—in the film Teresa spends too much of her time accommodating the whims of men. The film would have achieved more depth if the idea of a Bohemian underclass with avant-garde views on life and love had been further developed.

Hugo Weaving is suitably morose in his soulful, dour portrayal of the man born on the wrong side of the tracks; he could well have been rehearsing his later blind photographer rôle in **Proof** (Jocelyn Moorhouse,

1991). Interestingly, Genevieve Picot (Weaving's romantic (dis)interest in **Proof**) auditioned for the rôle of Teresa, but she was considered too old. After a two-and-a-half-year search, Helen Buday was chosen for the part. In her first major screen rôle (after a minor part in **Mad Max Beyond Thunderdome**, George Miller and George Ogilvie, 1985), Buday is sufficiently wistful as the idealistic young Teresa. However, her narration throughout the film is stoic and over-used. Sam Neill exudes his usual charisma as the cultured James Quick.

HELEN BARLOW

References

'Stephen Wallace', an interview with the director by Paul Kalina, *Cinema Papers*, no. 50, February–March 1985, pp. 10–15.

'David Stratton Talks to Producer Margaret Fink about her Long-awaited Project', *Cinema Papers*, no. 57, May 1986, p. 42.

'Love's Labour's Won: For Love Alone', a review by Tony Mitchell, ibid., p. 82.

'Cracking Bollinger', an interview with director of photography Alun Bollinger by Erika Addis, *Filmnews*, September 1986, p. 13.

Harry (Huw Williams) and Teresa (Helen Buday).

FORTRESS

Crawford Productions presents FORTRESS. © 1985 Crawford Productions. *Locations:* Bairnsdale, Buchan Caves, The Grampians (Victoria). *Australian distributor:* UIP. *Opened:* 26 June 1986. *Video:* CBS-FOX. *Rating:* M. 35mm. 88 mins.

Producer: Raymond Menmuir. *Executive producers:* Hector Crawford, Ian Crawford, Terry Stapleton. *Associate producer:* Michael Lake. *Scriptwriter:* Everett de Roche. Based on the novel by Gabrielle Lord. *Director of photography:* David Connell. *Production designer:* Philip Warner. *Wardrobe supervisor:* Clare Griffin. *Editor:* Ralph Strasser. *Composer:* Danny Beckerman. *Sound recordist:* Andrew Ramage. *Sound editors:* Mike Woolveridge, Fiona Strain; Robert Grant, Ross Chambers, Glenn Newnham (dia.). *Mixer:* Phil Judd.

Cast

Rachel Ward (Sally Jones), Sean Garlick (Sid), Rebecca Rigg (Narelle), Robin Mason (Derek), Marc Gray (Tommy), Beth Buchanan (Leanne), Asher Keddie (Sue), Bradley Meehan (Richard), Anna Crawford (Sarah), Richard Terrill (Toby), Peter Hehir (Father Christmas), David Bradshaw (Pussy Cat), Vernon Wells (Dabby Duck), Roger Stephen (Mac the Mouse), Elaine Cusick (Mrs O'Brien), Laurie Moran (Mr O'Brien), Ray Chubb (Publican), Wendy Playfair (Old Woman), Ed Turley (Old Man), Nick Waters (Det Sgt Cotter), Terence Donovan (Det Sgt Mitchell).

Fortress is based on the Faraday kidnapping of 1972, where John Francis Eastway and others kidnapped the children and teacher of the small, multi-class school.

The beginning of the film is quite eerie, even if the omens of trouble ahead (the shooting of a fox, etc.) are a little too obvious. But from the moment the masked gang arrives at the lonely school and kidnaps Sally Jones (Rachel Ward) and her class, the film works well as a 'true-life' re-creation.

That sense of verisimilitude continues in the scenes in the cave where the hostages are held, especially when they find a way out via an underground lake. The walk to the lonely farmhouse, too, is quite tense, for one knows that something bad will happen (the film is, after all, only half way through), but not exactly how. When an old lady answers her front door, one's mind races through the possibilities: she is part of the gang, she won't believe their story and will send them away, etc. It turns out that the gang has her hostage too, and the children and Sally are locked up in a barn and the old lady and her husband are callously killed.

This is a key moment for many reasons: not only is the old man's death the first truly explicit violence (unfortunately let down by weak make-up and effects), but the film turns decidedly darker. It is no longer a Boys' Own adventure but *Lord of the Flies*.

For the next thirty minutes or so, one regrets this new direction: there is a dulling sense of *déjà vu* as the children build booby-traps around the cave to which they have escaped, as they put on war paint and turn into little savages. It is not surprising, then, that so many critics turned against the film at this point: one has simply seen it all (and better) before. Not only that, a genuinely fascinating and true story has been tossed aside for the conventions of violence-demanding Hollywood (a habit of scriptwriter Everett de Roche).

But even given all that, the resolution of the film still works. It has a very dark edge: the children, now back in society, carry beneath their calm surfaces a new, more savage, way of being. The violence of the kidnap-pers really has begat violence. Whereas in American cinema, people return to their normal lives virtually unchanged by battles with evil, here that is not so. These children are a frightening presence, and evidence of how any violence in society sets up reverberations that extend far beyond the original villains' deaths or incarcerations.

While overextended, and sometimes overwrought, **Fortress** remains one of the better and darker thrillers made in this country.

SCOTT MURRAY

Reference
'Mutton Dressed as Rambo: **Fortress**', a review by Tony Drouyn, *Cinema Papers*, no. 59, September 1986, p. 51.

Sally Jones (Rachel Ward).

THE FRINGE DWELLERS

Fringe Dwellers Productions Pty. Ltd. in association with Ozfilm Limited presents The Fringe Dwellers. © 1986 Fringe Dwellers Productions Pty. Ltd. *Budget:* $1.26 million. *Locations:* Murgon, Cherbourg (Queensland). *Australian distributor:* Roadshow. *Opened:* October 1986. *Video:* Roadshow Home Video. *Rating:* PG. 98 mins.

Producer: Sue Milliken. *Executive producer:* Damien Nolan. *Scriptwriters:* Bruce Beresford, Rhoisin Beresford. *Based on the novel by* Nene Gare. *Director of photography:* Don McAlpine. *Camera operator:* Darrin Ballangarry. *Production designer:* Herbert Pinter. *Costume designer:* Helen Watts. *Editor:* Tim Wellburn. *Composer:* George Dreyfus. *Sound recordist:* Max Bowring. *Sound editor:* Penn Robinson. *Mixers:* Peter Fenton, Phil Heywood.

Cast

Kristina Nehm (Trilby Comeaway), Justine Saunders (Mollie Comeaway), Bob Maza (Joe Comeaway), Kylie Belling (Noonah Comeaway), Denis Walker (Bartie Comeaway), Ernie Dingo (Phil), Malcolm Silva (Charlie), Marlene Bell (Hannah), Michelle Torres (Audrena), Michele Miles (Blanchie), Kath Walker (Eva), Bill Sandy (Skippy), Maureen Watson (Rene), Robert Ugle (Tim), Alan Dargin (Bruce), Terry Thompson (Horrie), Anne Saward (May), Dianne Eden (Matron), Wilkie Collins (Dr Symons), Lisa-Jane Stockwell (Nurse McCarthy).

Joe Comeaway (Bob Maza) and daughter Trilby (Kristina Nehm).

An Aboriginal girl, Trilby (Kristina Nehm), and her younger brother, Bartie (Denis Walker), attend a high school in an outback town and live in a dilapidated riverbank settlement with their family. Trilby's sister, Noonah (Kylie Belling), is training to be a nurse at the local hospital. Her father, Joe (Bob Maza), always finds excuses as to why he can't look for a job. Trilby's ambitions run to seeing her family move to a Housing Commission home in the town, a goal that requires her father to find a job so that a deposit can be made.

After the family moves in, there are problems in adjusting to more middle-class lifestyles. Trilby discovers that the dreams of middle-class well-being are constantly undermined by her increasing identification with the general oppression of her race, and the injustice and intolerance directed toward Aborigines by her peers at school and whites in authority. As well, she discovers an incomprehension of her pride by her white neighbours, who themselves seem rather bet-

ter spoken and more middle class than might otherwise be living in a Housing Commission area. Trilby also begins a relationship with Phil (Ernie Dingo), a young horseman with a wanderlust who eventually gets her pregnant and then disappears.

Trilby and the family face crises which relate to their Aboriginality and their status. The father loses the rent money in a card game and the family is evicted. Trilby gives birth but, in one of several 'mystical moments', the baby dies. There is then a moment of family reconciliation and Phil returns. The next morning, with her mother's tacit consent, Trilby leaves for the city.

Adapted from a novel written in 1961 by Nene Gare, a European and a woman closely connected with what was then called Native Welfare, the film of *The Fringe Dwellers* is an uneasy attempt to make a novel written in a specific time relate to the situation of black Australians today. Certainly there is a positive view taken of their personal lives: unending hospitality and sharing of whatever is at hand; libertarian personal relationships conducted without guilt, blame or remorse; goals subordinated to ensuring that others can share any benefits. This lifestyle is portrayed positively, contrasted humorously with a stiff, over-mannered and repressed white society populated by children who goad blacks for their difference and adults who bend over backwards to be tolerant.

Clearly director Bruce Beresford felt that here there was some truth about the Aboriginal experience today to be explored in this film. He wanted to tell of the difference between black and white in Australia and, in the character of Trilby, there is a conduit for contradictory impulses in the black character, at least as Beresford perceives it. The choice of a novel from the 1960s makes this task more difficult. There is too much made of the character of the happy black layabout, as personified by Trilby's father, and by his brother and family who also move in to the new house.

The Fringe Dwellers is earnest, but finally it is backward looking and complacent rather than being a dynamic film which, as the book was in its time, is controversial and inspirational. It introduces much too much sentimentality and hits some very jarring notes. Finally, it simply does not have the impact of many other smaller, less prominent documentaries and dramas that cover the same thematic ground.

GEOFF GARDNER

References

'Fringe Benefits', Kathy Bail, *Cinema Papers*, no. 58, July 1986, pp. 14–17.
'Ordinary People: **The Fringe Dwellers**', a review by Nick Roddick, *Cinema Papers*, no. 60, November 1986, p. 39.
'Black Heroines White Directors', Tim Rowse, *Filmnews*, November 1986, p. 11.

FROG DREAMING

[No opening production credit.[1]] FROG DREAMING. *Alternative title:* The Spirit Chasers (US). © 1985 Western Film Productions No. 12 Pty. Ltd. Developed with the assistance of Film Victoria. *Budget:* $388,000. *Locations:* Moorooduc Quarry, Woods Point, Frankston, Healesville (Victoria). *Australian distributor:* GUO. *Opened:* 1 May 1986. *Video:* Roadshow Home Video. *Rating:* PG. 35mm. 93 mins.

Producer: Barbi Taylor. *Executive producers:* David Thomas, John Picton-Warlow. *Co-producer:* Everett DeRoche[2]. *Scriptwriter:* Everett DeRoche. *Director of photography:* John McLean. *Camera operator:* Danny Batterham. *Production designer:* Jon Dowding. *Costume designer:* Aphrodite Kondos. *Editor:* Brian Kavanagh. *Composer:* Brian May. *Sound recordist:* Mark Lewis. *Sound editors:* Craig Carter; Ken Sallows (dia.); Tim Chau, Rex Watts (fx). *Mixer:* Roger Savage.

Cast

Henry Thomas (Cody), Tony Barry (Gaza), Rachel Friend (Wendy), Tamsin West (Jane), John Ewart (Ricketts), Dennis Miller (Mr Cannon), Katy Manning (Mrs Cannon), Dempsey Knight (Charlie Pride), Chris Gregory (Wheatley), Mark Knight (Henry), Laurie Dobson (Gleeson), Jay Mannering (Haggard), Tim Hughes (Beilby), Howard Eynon (Ranger), David Ravenswood (Kauffman), Peter Cummins (Neville), Amanda Fernbach (Becky), Marcus Eyre (Doctor), Glen Hunt (Tobins), Kevin King (Opah), Vince Quayle (Barney), El Prezzos (Band at Dance); Hugh Bryant, Renae Carol, Laura Christie (Children).

Frog Dreaming is a fanciful story about an American-born orphan, Cody (Henry Thomas), a child inventor of the precocious variety, whose father was killed in Vietnam. Cody is brought up by his Australian guardian, Gaza (Tony Barry), a likeable yobbo, in a small bush town where he sets out to discover the 'secret' of an eerie body of water that doesn't appear on any map.

The water, declared to be an Aboriginal taboo area, is actually a pond in a quarry, but to Cody's young mind it is haunting, magical and mysterious. (The title actually refers to an area of special ground that is supposedly haunted by malevolent spirits and the home of a fire-breathing bunyip called Donkegin.)

A distribution deal had been negotiated with 20th-Century Fox, which had recently enjoyed minor success with the pick-up of

Cody (Henry Thomas).

The Man from Snowy River (George Miller, 1982) for international release, but the negative pick-up deal collapsed when Fox pulled out during shooting.

Financed by UAA Films, the troubled production commenced in October 1984 on a budget of $388,000. Two weeks into the shoot director Russell Hagg departed citing 'creative differences' and was replaced by Brian Trenchard-Smith. Filming recommenced afresh and the schedule was trimmed so that it could still come in on budget.

Trenchard-Smith's touch is apparent in the action set-pieces, particularly the exhilarating scene where Cody adapts his bike to ride on a railway track and takes it out for a test spin.

Producer Barbi Taylor, a longtime associate of Richard Franklin, had met Thomas when she worked on Franklin's **Cloak and Dagger** (1984) as a production consultant. Actors Equity approved the importing of Thomas under its 'exceptional circumstances'

clause, when argument was put forward that it was difficult to find an appropriate actor in the right age group from the pool of local actors in his age range. In retrospect, his casting seems to have been purely for marketing reasons as his performance is stiff and inexpressive.

The script, by American expatriate Everett DeRoche, frequently deploys American slang expressions and the film has largely irrelevant shots of Australian wildlife, presumably with overseas markets in mind.

PAUL HARRIS

---

[1] On the video slick it reads, 'UAA Films presents […] A Middle Reef Production.'
[2] One of various spellings. Most often it is 'De Roche'.

Reference
'Childhood's End: **Frog Dreaming**', a review by Raffaele Caputo, *Cinema Papers*, no. 59, September 1986, p. 50.

JENNY KISSED ME

Nilsen Premiere presents JENNY KISSED ME. © 1985 Nilsen Premiere. *Australian distributor:* Hoyts. *Opened:* 6 February 1986. *Video:* RCA-Columbia-Hoyts. *Rating:* M. 35mm. 98 mins.

Producer: Tom Broadbridge. *Scriptwriter:* Warwick Hind. Based on a screenplay by Judith Colquhoun. *Director of photography:* Bob Kohler. *Production designer:* Jon Dowding. *Wardrobe:* Aphrodite Kondos. *Editor:* Alan Lake. *Composers:* Trevor Lucas, Ian Mason. *Sound recordist:* Paul Clark. *Sound editor:* Penn Robinson. *Mixer:* Phil Heywood.

Cast

Ivar Kants (Lindsay Fenton), Deborra-Lee Furness (Carol Grey), Tamsin West (Jenny Grey), Paula Duncan (Gaynor Roberts), Steven Grives (Mal Evans), Mary Ward (Grace), Nicki Paul (Policewoman Moore), Meg Clancy (Matron at Childrens [sic] Home), Tim Robertson (Sergeant Blake), Peter Black (Sergeant Thompson), Edward Hepple (Judge Halliday), Nicholas Eadie (Steve Anderson), Louise Le Nay (Welfare Officer), Jillian Murray (Lindsay's Doctor), Wayne Cull (Rosewarne), Terry Gill (Des Ormonde), Maureen Edwards (Magistrate), Wilbur Wilde (Telecom Repairman), David Bergin (Drug Cop 1), Christopher Barry (Drug Cop 2), Gennie Nevinson (Drug Cop 3).

In an essay in *The Australian Screen*[1], William Routt explores the frequently intense, ambiguous and perverse relations between fathers and daughters in Australian cinema, particularly in the 1920s and 1930s. Routt refers to **Jenny Kissed Me** as 'perhaps the single most extreme example of the father–daughter sub-genre'.

The film plunges right from the start into a volatile character triangle: Carol Grey (Deborra-Lee Furness), a frustrated housewife stagnating in a sleepy country town; her moody young daughter, Jenny (Tamsin West); and her de facto partner, Lindsay Fenton (Ivar Kants), who appears to care more for Jenny (even though he is not her real father) than for Carol—with Jenny reciprocating the preference. Urged on by her old friend Gaynor Roberts (Paula Duncan), a high-class prostitute from the city, Carol has a tryst with her neighbour while a storm rages, and Jenny is left alone, crying out for 'Dad'. Lindsay is moved to such rage by this and by other actions he takes to be proof of Carol's inability to be a 'proper mother' that their relationship becomes violent and impossible. Carol runs

to the city with Jenny, becoming a prostitute and getting entangled with a drug-pushing pimp. Meanwhile, Lindsay searches the city in vain for Jenny, as he slowly dies of cancer. Finally, after an emotional court battle, Carol and Lindsay are married at his deathbed and, in a coda back at the country house, mother and daughter are finally united in love.

Beyond its crisp and efficient direction (with much spectacular cutting on movement), what makes the film interesting is its B-movie melodrama touch: there is virtually no conventional character psychology, only a series of action-packed, sometimes barely-motivated 'moves'. The film's moral stance towards what it shows is extremely opaque and fluctuating. The script would seem to essentially take Lindsay's side, as loving, caring, selfless father-figure, against Carol's, as philandering, whoring, selfish 'bad mother'. As it plays, however, the film's triangle is much more ambiguous. Carol is an extremely sympathetic character at times, while Lindsay's single-minded obsession for Jenny registers as somewhat excessive and 'unnatural' (as Carol suggests). Thus, the film trembles with a strange, largely unspoken incest theme. When, finally, Carol

simply takes Lindsay's place in Jenny's affections by repeating his earlier words and rituals of love, the film seems not resolved, but still open and trembling, as if now the mother–daughter relation has become just as perversely charged as the father–daughter one.

The film's curious and compelling level of intensity is caught in the 18th-century ode by J. H. Leigh Hunt that is written on the screen at the start, and spoken (by Lindsay) over the end:

Say I'm weary, say I'm sad
Say that health and wealth have missed me
Say I'm growing old, but add:
Jenny kissed me.

ADRIAN MARTIN

---

[1] 'The Fairest Child of the Motherland: Colonialism and Family in Australian Films of the 1920s', William Routt, in *The Australian Screen*, Albert Moran & Tom O'Regan (eds), Penguin, Melbourne, 1989, p. 35.

Reference
'Modern Crimes: **Jenny Kissed Me**', a review by Debi Enker, *Cinema Papers*, no. 56, March 1986, p. 76.

Lindsay Fenton (Ivar Kants) and Carol Grey (Deborra-Lee Furness).

MALCOLM

Cascade Films present[s] MALCOLM. © 1986 Cascade Films. *Budget:* $999,000. *Location:* Melbourne. *Australian distributor:* Hoyts. *Opened:* 18 September 1986. *Video:* Hoyts Polygram Video. *Rating:* PG. 35mm. 90 mins.

[*Producers:* not listed; atb Nadia Tass, David Parker.] *Executive producer:* Bryce Menzies. *Associate producer:* Timothy White. *Scriptwriter:* David Parker. The character of Malcolm was inspired by John Tassopoulos. *Director of photography:* David Parker. [*Production designer:* not listed.] *Wardrobe:* Lucinda McGuigan. *Editor:* Ken Sallows. *Composer:* Simon Jeffes. *Sound recordist:* Paul Clark. *Sound editors:* Craig Carter, Dean Gawen. *Mixers:* Roger Savage, Bruce Emery.

Cast

Colin Friels (Malcolm), John Hargreaves (Frank), Lindy Davies (Judith), Chris Haywood (Willy), Charles 'Bud' Tingwell (Tramways Supervisor), Beverley Phillips (Mrs T.), Judith Stratford (Jenny), Heather Mitchell (Barmaid), Tony Mahood (Tram Conductor), David Lander (Restaurant Hoon #1), David Letch (Restaurant Hoon #2), Mike Bishop (Armed Guard), David Johnston (TV Announcer), Katerina Tassopoulos (Jenny's Mother), Ian McFadyen (Model Shop Salesman), Ian Shrives (Split Car Cop #1), David Gray (Split Car Cop #2), Roy Edmonds (Highway Patrol Cop #1), John Raaen (Highway Patrol Cop #2), Peter Hosking (Bank Nightwatchman).

There will always be a place for fantasy and always a time for laughter. **Malcolm**, Nadia Tass' first feature, gives us an abundance of both.

The apparently simple-minded Malcolm (played with pathos and jocularity by Colin Friels) is a maintenance man on the tramways. Fired after he takes his own jerry-built tram out for a joyride through the streets of Melbourne, he retreats into his fantasy world at home.

Malcolm's small weatherboard house is cluttered with weird and wonderful gadgets: his letter box is on model-railway tracks; the cage of his pet cockatoo is attached to wires (he travels flying-fox style); and the kitchen is like a miniature tramways depot, trams shuttling between pots and pans. Even sending for the milk is a complex operation. The milk bottle container is on the roof of a toy car which runs by remote control and trundles down to the local milk bar.

It is a game that landlady Mrs T. (Beverley Phillips) has been playing along with for some time. And, when Malcolm can't pay up, she insists that he take in a boarder. Handing him an elaborate questionnaire ('Are you neat and tidy?', 'Do you have a job?'), she leaves him to contend with his first caller, Frank (John Hargreaves), a not-so-sharp crim who's as rough as rough.

When Frank moves in with his adoring and provocative moll, Judith (Lindy Davies), Malcolm is completely bamboozled and is immediately dismissed by his new tenant as a moron. But when Frank pulls off a warehouse robbery with his mate, Willy (Chris Haywood), it becomes apparent that he has the same knack for tricks, or rather need for them, as Malcolm.

Much of the humour comes from the way in which Tass treats the relationship between Malcolm and Frank, in particular the situations in which Malcolm disarms Frank with his sincerity and honesty.

The way in which Malcolm takes to crime is orchestrated beautifully, especially the staging of his own remote-control robbery. Frank is impressed, and the three join forces in planning an operation involving the Anglo-Swiss Bank. This event is the climax of the film. Malcolm's whacky ideas come to the fore, revealing a genius hitherto unrecognised. Even morality is taken care of, because, as Judith says, 'It's all crooks' money anyway.'

Malcolm is not a complex story and its 'message' is an old-fashioned one: that there are positive qualities, even genius, to be tapped in everyone—in outsiders like Frank, or those labelled as backward, like Malcolm.

Even so, stories can be lost in the way they are told. And the fact that, in **Malcolm**, we find both a comic and a cinematic flair sets it apart and makes it work.

KATHY BAIL[1]

---

[1] Extracted from Bail's review in *Cinema Papers* (see References).

References

'Leap Year', an article (with quotes) on actor Colin Friels by Debi Enker, *Cinema Papers*, no. 56, March 1986, pp. 14–15.

'On the Right Track: **Malcolm**', a review by Kathy Bail, *Cinema Papers*, no. 59, September 1986, p. 41.

'Cinema in the Round', an article (with quotes) on director Nadia Tass by Kathy Bail, *Cinema Papers*, no. 60, November 1986, p. 11.

'**Malcolm**', a review by Peter Kemp, *Filmnews*, September 1986, p. 17.

Malcolm (Colin Friels), the mechanical whizz.

Malcolm (Colin Friels) takes his home-made tram for a run.

THE MORE THINGS CHANGE...

Syme International Productions and New South Wales Film Corporation present THE MORE THINGS CHANGE.... © 1985 Syme International Entertainment Pty Ltd and New South Wales Film Corporation. *Budget:* $2.32 million. *Location:* Melbourne and environs. *Australian distributor:* Hoyts. *Opened:* 20 March 1986. *Video:* RCA-Columbia-Hoyts. *Rating:* PG. 35mm. Panavision. 94 mins.

Producer: Jill Robb. *Associate producer:* Greg Ricketson. *Scriptwriter:* Moya Wood. *Director of photography:* Dan Burstall. *Production designer:* Josephine Ford. *Wardrobe supervisor:* Anje Bos. *Editor:* Jill Bilcock. *Composer:* Peter Best. *Sound supervisor:* Roger Savage. *Sound recordist:* John Phillips. *Sound editors:* Steve Lambeth, Steve Burgess. *Mixers:* Roger Savage, Bruce Emery.

Cast

Judy Morris (Connie), Barry Otto (Lex), Victoria Longley (Geraldine), Lewis Fitz-Gerald (Barry), Peter Carroll (Roley), Louise Le Nay (Lydia), Owen Johnson (Nicholas), Brenda Addie (Angela), Joanne Barker (Bridesmaid 1), Adrienne Barrett (Karen), Bill Bennett (Eric), Paddy Burnet (Mim), John Egan (Vince), Chris Gaffney (Sponge), Joan Harris (Matron), Robert McGregor (Baby), Margo McLennan (Barbara), Alex Menglet (Telecom Man), Robert Ratti (Jollian), Colwyn Roberts (Truck Driver), Malcolm Robertson (Sam), Harriet Spalding (Bridesmaid 2), George Trotman (Edgar), Joy Westmore (Mrs Degan), Eddy Zlaty (Michael).

Distinguished stage and film actor Robyn Nevin made her debut as a film director with **The More Things Change…**. In fact, **The More Things Change…** is very much a film made by women: it was produced by Jill Robb, whose previous success had been **Sumner Locke Elliott's Careful He Might Hear You** (Carl Schultz, 1983), written by Moya Wood, edited by Jill Bilcock and with Josephine Ford as production designer. The resulting film is likeable, serious, low-key and well-observed. In the end, it is perhaps a little too quiet, too lacking in narrative thrust for its own good, and this perhaps helps to account for its failure at the box office, though it might have done better in an arthouse setting than as a mainstream Hoyts release.

There are really two main strands to the film's story. Connie (Judy Morris) works in a Melbourne publishing house while husband Lex (Barry Otto) tries to make a go of

Geraldine (Victoria Longley), Connie (Judy Morris) and Barry (Lewis Fitz-Gerald).

running the neglected farm they have bought some distance from Melbourne. This is essentially a drama of rôle-reversal, of exploring gender functions, as Connie becomes the breadwinner while Lex is left to play 'mother' to their small son, Nicholas (Owen Johnson). Increasingly, Connie comes to feel that, 'I'm just the one who brings home the pay packet', and this feeling is intensified when she hires a pregnant 19-year-old, Geraldine (Victoria Longley), to look after Nicholas. Connie is torn between wanting (and needing) to maintain her career and her sense of being marginalised in the household she maintains.

All of this is done with care and convincing detail. What is less satisfactory is Geraldine's own story. She is engaged to Barry (Lewis Fitz-Gerald) who is not the father of her child but who still wants to marry her, and she is determined to conceal her pregnancy from her family, go ahead with plans to have the baby adopted and follow this with a big white wedding. Despite Geraldine's apparently clear-headed plans,

things do not turn out quite as expected. The film suffers somewhat when interest is diverted to Geraldine and Barry's story. The film's makers seem to want to establish a parallel between the two couples, so that the hopeful outcome for Geraldine and Barry provides a comment on the precarious balance between Lex and Connie. In the interests of narrative tightness, it might have been better to maintain the focus more firmly on the older couple. Their rôles are conceived in more detail and are played by Barry Otto and Judy Morris with sympathy and understanding.

BRIAN MCFARLANE

References

'Changes…', an article by Debi Enker, *Cinema Papers*, no. 56, March 1986, pp. 35–7.
'Cold Comfort Farm: **The More Things Change …**', a review by Paul Kalina, *Cinema Papers*, ibid., p. 71.
'**The More Things Change** [sic]', a short review by Margaret Lupton, *Filmnews*, May 1986, p. 17.

PLAYING BEATIE BOW

SAFC Productions Ltd present[s] Playing Beatie Bow. © 1985 S.A.F.C. Productions Ltd. Made in association with the Australian Film Commission. *Budget:* $4.4 million. *Location:* the Rocks (Sydney); Adelaide. *Australian distributor:* CEL. *Opened:* 7 August 1986. *Video:* Australian Video. *Rating:* PG. 35mm. 93 mins.

Producer: Jock Blair. *Associate producer:* Bruce Moir. *Executive producer:* John Morris. *Scriptwriter:* Peter Gawler. Based on the novel by Ruth Park. *Director of photography:* Geoffrey Simpson. *Camera operator:* David Foreman. *Production designer:* George Liddle. *Wardrobe:* Anna Wade. *Editor:* A. J. Prowse. *Composers:* Garry McDonald, Laurie Stone. *Sound recordist:* Robert Cutcher. *Sound editors:* Frank Lipson, Glenn Newnham, Dean Gawen. *Mixers:* James Currie; David Harrison (fx); Peter Smith (music).

Cast

Imogen Annesley (Abigail), Peter Phelps (Judah; Robert), Mouche Phillips (Beatie), Nikki Coghill (Dovey), Moya O'Sullivan (Granny), Don Barker (Samuel), Lyndel Rowe (Kathy), Barbara Stephens (Justine), Damian Janko (Gibbie), Phoebe Salter (Natalie), Su Cruickshank (Madam), Henry Salter (Swanton), Jo England (Doll), Edward Caddick (Legless), Edwin Hodgeman (Sir), Glenn Boswell (Parrot), Richard Boue (Fidge), Michaele Read (Blackie), Johnny Hallyday (Ben), Tim Perry (Jacko), Perri Hamilton (Singer).

The whimsical **Playing Beatie Bow** is one of the few Australian fantasy films to explore the notion of time travel. It does so with some panache and style given the magnitude of the task it sets itself.

It tells the story of Abigail (Imogen Annesley), a discontented Sydney teenager whose special powers bring her into contact with a ghost-like girl, Beatie (Mouche Phillips), who can't find her way 'back home' to the 19th century. Somehow, the little girl has been washed up in modern-day Sydney, and it is not clear how, until Abigail accidentally travels back through time with her to 1873. Then, according to the film, Sydney's Rocks area was densely populated with an eccentric and seedy mix of colonialists.

Abigail gets injured immediately upon her 'arrival' and wakes up in the care of an Irish family who, for reasons unknown, regard her with prophetic awe. Later, one begins to see why.

Playing Beatie Bow is based on the novel of the same name by Ruth Park, who had input into Peter Gawler's script. Director Don Crombie maintains the momentum of Park's novel, although the first twenty minutes of the film are rather tedious and prosaic. In the opening frames, for instance, it is hard to decipher the relevance of a crumpled Coke can to the plot, other than it being a symbol of 20th-century consumerism. And a series of flashes of a railway bridge are more distracting than poignant.

The logistics of Abigail's time journey leave plenty to the imagination but it is worth remembering that the film is in the same escapist vein as **Back to the Future** (Robert Zemeckis, 1985). Its atmospherics are Walt Disney in flavour, and a rather animated brothel sequence is the closest it gets to warranting anything harsher than a PG rating. On the whole, the characters are inoffensive and colourful if not a little overdone. Judah (Peter Phelps), for instance, has a huge set of sideburns, speaks with a rich Irish accent and tells his love interest, 'You make me want to jump over the moon.'

The 'old Sydney' scenes are limited in scale but realistic enough ($400,000 of the production budget was allocated to reconstruct the Rocks in a disused industrial site in South Australia). During the period scenes, director of photography Geoffrey Simpson conveys a mood of dark, omnipresent squalor which is effective but over-exaggerated at times.

The lead actress Imogen Annesley holds her own in the film without blossoming, and her part is helped along by Abigail's romance of sorts with Judah and Robert (also played by Peter Phelps). The scriptwriters have done well to extract some solid themes out of a story that is ostensibly a fantasy. It covers the effects of war on a disillusioned ex-Light Horseman, Samuel (Don Barker), the social ostracism of the underprivileged and minority groups, family breakdown and universal alienation.

Playing Beatie Bow finishes on a much stronger note by drawing out its plot to a satisfactory conclusion upon Abigail's return to the present day.

GREG KERR

References

'Time and Again: **Playing Beatie Bow**', a review by Paul Kalina, *Cinema Papers*, no. 59, September 1986, p. 49.

'Going South: The Adelaide Connection', an article on the South Australian Film Corporation by Philippa Hawker, *Cinema Papers*, no. 61, January 1987, pp. 20–3.

'**Playing Beatie Bow**', a review by Susan K. Charlton, *Filmnews*, October 1986, p. 13.

Abigail (Imogen Annesley) in 1873 Sydney.

SHORT CHANGED

The New South Wales Film Corporation and Magpie Films presents [sic] SHORT CHANGED. © 1985 Magpie Films and New South Wales Film Corporation. Produced with the assistance of the Australian Film Commission. *Budget:* $1.2 million. *Location:* Sydney. *Filmed:* May–June 1985. *Australian distributor:* Greater Union. *Opened:* 13 November 1986. *Video:* Roadshow Home Video. *Rating:* M (2853m). 35mm. 104 mins.

Producer: Ross Matthews. *Associate producer:* Barbara Gibbs. *Scriptwriter:* Robert J. Merritt. Based on a screenplay by Ken Quinnell and Robert J. Merritt. *Director of photography:* Peter Levy. *Production designer:* Kristian Fredrikson. *Wardrobe supervisor:* Anna French. *Editor:* Richard Francis-Bruce. *Composer:* Chris Neal. *Sound recordist:* Peter Barker. *Sound editors:* Tim Jordan, Richard Francis-Bruce. *Mixers:* Julian Ellingworth, Mike Thomas.

Cast

David Kennedy (Stuart Wilkins), Susan Leith (Alison Wilkins), Jamie Agius (Tommy Wilkins), Ray Meagher (Marshall), Mark Little (Curly), Wanjum Carpenter (Tommy, Aged 2), Steve Dodd (Old Drunk), Athol Compton (Bruiser), Mac Silva (First Friend), Sylvia Scott (Nan), Timothy Hornibrook (Preacher), Ronald Merritt (Uncle), Ken Radley (Sergeant, Land Rights March), Jim Holt (Serizio), Donnie Prior (Policeman, City Lock-up), Rhys McConnochie (Headmaster), Ron Haddrick (Garrick), "Lucky" Wikramanayake (Gopowalla), Alan McQueen (Cummings), Daphne Grey (Judge), Denis MacKay (Edwards), Lyndel Rowe (Counsellor), James Robertson (Brian), Michael Gow (Sinclair).

Tommy Wilkins (Jamie Agius) is the 'magpie' son of a young Aborigine, Stuart (David Kennedy), and a white middle-class woman, Alison (Susan Leith). Tommy is only two when his parents begin to drift apart—a suggestion of the ultimate incompatibility of two worlds. Believing that Stuart is always going to play the rôle of the victim (like his father who died in jail), Alison leaves with her son after she sees Stuart arrested at a land-rights demonstration.

The narrative is then picked up seven years later. Alison is living with her father, a strict, domineering man who wants everyone (including his grandson whom he has sent to a Catholic school) to know that he's worked for every dollar. Tommy knows nothing of his father until Stuart drunkenly arrives at the boarding school in the middle of the night and cries out for his son.

Short Changed is about Stuart's attempt to win custody of his child and, more important, the way in which he establishes their relationship by teaching Tommy about his Aboriginal heritage. As this journey progresses, misconceptions and blindnesses are broken down. Tommy learns to see Stuart as his father, rather than Stuart's mate Curly (brilliantly played by Mark Little), whom Tommy immediately warms to. Curly is a tragi-comic character, who brings to the film a welcome humour and, in a wry, fully handled scene, he tells Tommy to be glad that he has a father, for he never had one.

If a theme can be traced in this film, it would centre on the notion of belonging, whether it be to the land, to a cultural tradition, or perhaps to a family. The strength of the film is its ability to express the complexities of race and heritage.

With **Short Changed**, scriptwriter Bob Merritt obviously knew exactly what he wanted to say and does so bluntly. The speech given by Stuart's lawyer in the Family Court is straight polemic and it is at this point that one feels that black, red and yellow flags should be flying. We are, in fact, left with little choice but to cheer from the sidelines, the consequence being that the details of the story are occasionally lost to these larger issues.

Ogilvie has inspired a spirited performance from Jamie Agius, who makes an extraordinary acting debut (he received the Aboriginal Artist of the Year Award). David Kennedy also gives a very forthright performance, rising to the demands of a carefully written, often contradictory, character. Through the character of Stuart, we develop an understanding of the position of the urban black and, on another level, the position of a man who finally transforms rage and despair into positive action.

KATHY BAIL[1]

---

[1] Extracted from Bail's review in *Cinema Papers* (see Reference).

Reference
'Short Changed', a review by Kathy Bail, *Cinema Papers*, no. 61, January 1987, p. 43.

Stuart Wilkins (David Kennedy), Alison (Susan Leith) and the two-year-old Tommy (Wanjum Carpenter).

SKY PIRATES

[No opening production credit.] SKY PIRATES. © 1985 Sky Pirates Limited–John Lamond Motion Pictures. *Location:* Bora Bora; Melbourne. *Australian distributor:* Roadshow. *Opened:* 16 January 1986. *Video:* Roadshow. *Rating:* M. 35mm. Panavision. 86 mins.

Producers: John Lamond, Michael Hirsh. *Scriptwriter:* John Lamond. Additional material written by Rob Moubray, Peter Herbert. *Director of photography:* Garry Wapshott. *Camera operator:* Malcolm Burrows. *Production designer:* Kristian Fredrickson[1]. *Costume designer:* Kristian Fredrickson. *Editors:* John Lamond, Michael Hirsh. *Composer:* Brian May. *Sound recordist:* Gary Wilkins. *Sound design-supervising sound editor:* Bruce Lamshed. *Sound editors:* Peter Burgess, Craig Carter, Tim Chau, Terry Rodman (fx); Adrian Carr (dia). *Mixers:* Roger Savage, Phil Judd.

Cast

John Hargreaves (Harris), Meredith Phillips (Melanie), Max Phipps (Savage), Bill Hunter (O'Reilly), Simon Chilvers (Rev. Mitchell), Alex Scott (General Hackett), David Parker (Hayes), Adrian Wright (Valentine), Peter Cummins (Colonel Brien), Tommy Dysart (Barman), Wayne Cull (Logan), Alex Menglett (Sullivan), Nigel Bradshaw (Spencer), Chris Gregory (Appleton), John Murphy (Gus), Victor Kazan (Sir Manning Benson), Clive Hearne (Captain Fisher), Bill Fozz (Armed Sentry); Hayes Gordon [Narrator].

'The Ark has been Raided and The Stone Romanced. Now let the Real Adventure begin'. The video slick for **Sky Pirates** indicates blatantly enough the popular American successes of the 1980s it is trying to emulate, albeit on a much smaller budget. The adventure genre has always been an extremely elastic one, and **Sky Pirates** joins an international host of post-**Raiders of the Lost Ark**[2] projects drawing on an eclectic set of plot elements and atmospheric devices from the horror, thriller, war and romantic comedy genres (among others). With many 1980s adventure films (whether about Indiana Jones, Biggles, Allan Quartermain or Buckaroo Banzai), **Sky Pirates** shares a jokey attitude towards heroism (John Hargreaves as Harris climbs onto a plane wing whilst declaring that he is afraid of heights); spectacular scenes of violence ranging from the brutal to the comic; a nostalgic attitude towards old Hollywood values and stereotypes (Meredith Phillips plays Melanie, a faintly discernible mixture of feisty Hawksian

Harris (John Hargreaves) and Melanie (Meredith Phillips) on Easter Island.

woman-in-uniform and sultry Hitchcockian heroine); and a quasi-Nazi evil villain, Savage (Max Phipps), trying to get his hands on the 'ultimate power' (perhaps an unconscious or veiled symbol for nuclear power). A special touch of **Mad Max**-influenced[3] 'Australian gothic' is added in the scene of O'Reilly (Bill Hunter), lord of a punkish Central Australian community, playing Russian roulette with Harris.

The story moves around a great deal, on planes, trains, automobiles and boats, back and forth from Australia to Bora Bora. Discharged for military insubordination from the army (making him the archetypal law-enforcing loner), Lt Harris teams up with Melanie and tracks her father, Rev. Mitchell (Simon Chilvers), from the 'Australian Institute of Theology' who is on the trail of the separated pieces of a powerful mystical tablet. At every turn, he does battle with Savage, who wants the tablet's power (presumably to rule the world). As in **Raiders of the Lost Ark**, the final climax momentarily unleashes the force of the tablet (burning Savage to a frazzle) in order to maintain a cosmic status quo: the tablet dormant below the earth, humans looking after their own business above.

Of course, **Sky Pirates** suffers by comparison with Spielberg's adventure epics, with their kinetic direction (Colin Eggleston delivers little on the promise of his im-

pressive **Long Weekend**, 1978), vivid characterisation, and lavish sets and special effects. However, if one chooses to see the film, say, in the tradition of Italian 'exploitation' cinema with its 'rip-offs' of box-office formulæ like that engendered by **Raiders of the Lost Ark**, then one can take an appropriately surrealist delight in the 'pulp poetry' of its sudden, arbitrary transitions (two characters simply die off-screen early on), cheap effects (a plane superimposed on a map signifies a journey), and erratic fluctuations in technique and style (including the bizarrely grotesque death of a cleaning woman down an elevator shaft handled in the excessive manner of Dario Argento).

Ultimately, **Sky Pirates** is not a particularly accomplished film in a conventional sense, but it is far from negligible as a ramshackle 'pop' curiosity, perfectly suited for the more fragmentary viewing connoisseurship of the video age.

ADRIAN MARTIN

---

[1] Usually spelt 'Fredrikson'.
[2] **Raiders of the Lost Ark** (Steven Spielberg, 1981).
[3] **Mad Max** (George Miller, 1979).

References
'Captain of the Clouds', an article (with quotes) on actor John Hargreaves by Gail McCrea, *Cinema Papers*, no. 56, March 1986, pp. 38–9, 40.
'Plumbing the Heights: **Sky Pirates**', a review by Peter Krein, ibid., p. 79.

TRAPS

[No opening production credit.] TRAPS. © 1985 John Hughes. Produced with the financial assistance of the Creative Development Branch of the Australian Film Commission. *Location:* Melbourne. *Australian distributor:* AFID. *Video:* not known. *Rating:* not known. 16mm. 98 mins.

Producer: John Hughes. *Scriptwriters:* Paul Davies, John Hughes. *Director of photography:* Jaems Grant. *Camera operator:* Erika Addis. *Production designers:* Clare Jager, Susan Weis. *Editor:* Zbigniew Friedrich. *Sound recordists:* Pat Fiske, Lou Hubbard, Jack Holt, John Cruthers, Laurie Robinson. *Mixer:* David Harrison.

Cast

Carolyn Howard (Jude Campbell), Gwenda Wiseman (Gwenda Wiseman), Paul Davies (George), John Flaus (Father Coughlan), Peter Sommerfield (Father in Plane), Jessie Hughes (Girl in Plane); Lou Weis, Tao Weis (Two Boys); Drew Cottle (Man in Pub), Lesley Stern (Librarian).

Jude Campbell (Carolyn Howard).

If Australian political intrigue were ever presented in film, it would be in the form of the standard docu-drama, the equally conventional feature film or the difficult innovation that combines those two established genres.

Traps tries to light the fuse for a political bomb with this combination, adding fictional scenarios for effect. It is a technique that few other Australian film-makers have tried. The result is a heavy, often confused, but engrossing attempt to give colour and meaning to the cut and thrust of everyday 'small' personal politics and 'big' federal government politics.

Based on the experiences of a female journalist, the film works its way through conspiracy theories involving the Australian Labor Party and the demise of reformist Australian governments through the efforts of the CIA. This was a popular conspiracy theory after the fall of the Whitlam Labor Government in November 1975, and it is told by intermixing a journalist's search for an answer to the conspiracy with interviews with working journalists and political activists.

The sense of desperation experienced by traditional Labor voters in the mid-1980s as the Hawke Labor Government became increasingly conservative is a further aspect of the film and its study of power and corruption.

The analysis of power that **Traps** attempts draws from ideas that have flourished in the Left, but need refinement. This includes the important task of identifying the media as a major subverter of meaning: the personal as a confused and frequently compromised space; the political as power relations that required geo-political considerations, especially for Australia after the debacle of the Whitlam sacking of 1975.

These themes may be vast and more suited to the conventions of talking heads, but director John Hughes tries techniques here that offered genuine and often exciting potential. Borrowing frequently from the European feature film style of the discontinuous narrative, and at other times from the avant-garde of the 1970s, the result was too vigorously criticised for its failures, rather than congratulated for its effort.

Traps never received much support from demanding Australian critics whose passion for narrative or avant-gardist forms did not have much tolerance for eclectic methodologies. Hughes has an important place in the Left, where his films have found something of a home – perhaps a dubious resting place.

Nevertheless, Hughes makes demands on his audiences and tries new ideas in film-making techniques. **Traps** put him on the map, offering a different approach to politics in a country that was threatened with more committed yet boring political docu-dramas than it needed.

MARCUS BREEN

References
'End Game: **Traps**', a review by Annette Blonski, *Cinema Papers*, no. 57, May 1986, p. 85.
'**Traps**: A Sympathetic Joke on Its Audience', Tim Rowse, *Filmnews*, February–March 1986, p. 15.

UNFINISHED BUSINESS

[No opening production credit.[1]] Unfinished Business. © 1985 Unfinished Business Pty Ltd. *Budget:* $102,000. *Location:* Sydney. *Australian distributor:* Lipsync. *Video:* CBS-Fox. *Rating:* M. 35mm. 78 mins.

Producer: Rebel Penfold-Russell. *Executive producer:* Andrena Finlay. *Co-producer:* Patric Juillet. *Scriptwriter:* Bob Ellis. *Director of photography:* Andrew Lesnie. *Production designer:* Jane Johnston. *Wardrobe:* Jane Johnston. *Editor:* Amanda Robson. *Musical arranger:* Norman Kaye. *Sound recordist:* Gerry Nucifora. *Sound editors:* Fiona Strain, Ashley Grenville. *Mixer:* Mike Thomas.

Cast

Michele Fawdon (Maureen), John Clayton (Geoff), Norman Kaye (George), Call Ricketson (Alice Benson); Jack and Jennie Ellis and Katie Hughes (Her Children); Tom Ellis (Baby), Andrew Lesnie (Telegram Boy).

After becoming known as a playwright, scriptwriter and provocative essayist, Bob Ellis turned his hand to directing a script of his own, the artfully written and produced **Unfinished Business.** In all his writing, Ellis has taken an interest in, indeed contributed to at some public length, the war of the sexes. His film debut has much in it that comes directly from his own experiences of first-time fatherhood, particularly the attention given to detail about the best times for conception of children of certain sex, a situation which, in the film, leads to much frustration on the part of the male and some hilarity on the part of the audience.

This low-budget film, for the most part having only two characters on screen, concerns a couple accidentally reuniting after fifteen years apart. They quickly tumble into bed and, after the first occasion, Maureen (Michele Fawdon) confesses that her husband is sterile and she desperately wants to bear him a child. Geoff (John Clayton), the former lover, seeing the opportunity for the relationship to reignite, reluctantly agrees to impregnate her. They go off to an idyllic setting at Palm Beach and set about the conception, she with clinical calm, he with lust in his heart. They talk, they banter, they bicker, she conceives, they inevitably argue and make up, and both go back to their normal lives. A year later, Geoff visits Maureen and, in the presence of her husband, George (Norman Kaye), holds the baby for a moment.

Played as a gentle comedy with much time spent on the delivery of jokes, moral fables, aphorisms ('I like aphorisms. They are like a heart starter in the morning', says Geoff), this is a kind of revisionist rewrite of the romantic comedies of the 1930s and 1940s when the codes prevented actual sexual intercourse, naked bodies and discussions of sex. Here all those are in evidence, but all in the service of the same bitter-sweet, slightly remorseful narrative that finally has to say only that you can't go on forever with illicit behaviour.

Perhaps this modest endeavour is finally too light to bear the weight of all those aphorisms about love and sex and life that Ellis puts down. Certainly, the going does get a little heavy as sequence after sequence starts with a medium close-up of Geoff beginning another of his little speeches, and this is despite John Clayton's doing a great job of fleshing out a character with a range of grumpy mannerisms that play very well against the well-conveyed sense of insecurity that Michele Fawdon conveys.

Ellis' abilities as an inventor of odd relationships that come surrounded with an aura of jokes, references, *bon mots* and so on is probably seen to better effect in his work with Paul Cox (**Man of Flowers**, 1983; **My First Wife**, 1984) than here. As a director, he doesn't appear to know when to let the moment go and when to reject what might not have been such a great idea (the musical leitmotif of Peter Dawson singing 'I'll walk beside you' being one such). His work is always of interest and merit, though the jury is still out on whether he can profitably direct his own scripts.

GEOFF GARDNER

---

[1] The film does state at the start that it is 'a film by Bob Ellis, Andrew Lesnie, Michele Fawdon, John Clayton, Norman Kaye, Rebel Penfold-Russell, Andrena Finlay, Patric Juillet, Jake Atkinson, June Henman, […]' et al.

Reference
'**Unfinished Business**', a review by Peter Kemp, *Filmnews*, October 1986, p. 12.

Geoff (John Clayton) and Maureen (Michele Fawdon).

WINDRIDER

Barron Films presents Windrider. *Alternative title:* 'Making Waves' (working). © 1986 Bush Christmas Productions Pty Ltd. *Budget:* $2.5 million. *Location:* Perth. *Australian distributor:* Hoyts. *Opened:* 25 December 1986. *Video:* RCA-Columbia-Hoyts. *Rating:* M. 35mm. 92 mins.

Producer: Paul D. Barron. *Associate producer:* Bonnie Harris. *Scriptwriters:* Everett DeRoche[1], Bonnie Harris. *Director of photography:* Joseph Pickering. *Camera operator:* Simon Akkerman. *Production designer:* Phil Peters. *Costume designer:* Noel Howell. *Editor:* John Scott. *Composer:* Kevin Peek. *Sound recordist:* Mark Lewis. *Sound editors:* Ashley Grenville, Helen Brown. *Mixers:* Julian Ellingworth, Michael Thomas.

Cast

Simon Chilvers (Howard), Tom Burlinson (P. C. Simpson), Nicole Kidman (Jade), Jill Perryman (Miss Dodge), Charles Tingwell (Stewart Simpson Snr.); At the Beach: Kim Bullard (Coyote), Graeme (Stig) Wemyss (Ratso), Mark Williams (Mangle), Alastair Cummings (Rabbit), Robin Miller (Wally), Matt Parkinson (Lurch), Lorraine Webster (Mud); The Band: John Ryan (McBride), Lance Karapetcoff (King), Ric Whitte (Ross), Andy Copeman (Hayes), Trevor Spencer (Engineer); The Office: Alistair Browning (Cram), Penny Brown (Kate), Peggy Walker (Tea Lady); Here and There: Roger Watkins (Barman), Jerry Thomas (Bouncer), Maurie Ogden (Marco).

Windrider is a modest, youth-oriented entertainment, the debut feature by director of photography Vincent Monton (**Newsfront, Heatwave**[2]). Scripted by Everett DeRoche (**Roadgames, Patrick**[3]), it is notable for the way it emulates the American 'teen movie' model more successfully than strained, uncertain teen entertainments made in Australia like **Street Hero** (Michael Pattinson, 1984) or **The Delinquents** (Chris Thomson, 1989). Specifically, it achieves that light-hearted, pacey cinematic treatment of 'everyday' actions (like making breakfast or racing to get to work on time) which audiences know from, for instance, John Hughes' teen movies. Indeed, **Windrider** indicates the potentially winning formula that **The Big Steal** (Nadia Tass, 1990) was later to perfect: the combination of a typically Australian, whimsical comic sensibility ('daggy' and droll) with the impulse in American popular entertainment to 'energise' (without completely glamorising or making spectacular) the mundane lives of ordinary people.

Like an American teen movie, it has clear, driving plot and theme 'set-ups' or 'hooks' which are cleanly resolved by the end (Monton has cited Paul Brickman's **Risky Business**, 1983, as a model he had in mind).

P. C. Simpson (Tom Burlinson) executes a 360 degree arc one fine morning as he windrides the surf; but to verify this to others he must track down the one person who witnessed it, the pop singer Jade (Nicole Kidman). Their relationship follows a typical romantic comedy line: initial antagonism, resistances and obstacles to be overcome, mis-understandings, final rapprochement—with a special Australian emphasis on his sexual immaturity ('I suppose a quickie in the back is out of the question?').

In his work life, P. C. is an energetic young company executive of the kind we know from post-Brat Pack American films like **From the Hip** (Bob Clark, 1987). In this arena, what he lacks is a sufficiently understanding and empathetic relationship with his father, Stewart Simpson Snr (Charles Tingwell), who is also his boss. As P. C.'s helpfully wise and witty secretary, Miss Dodge (Jill Perryman), puts it, 'How do you expect to have a stable relationship with a woman when you can't communicate with your own father?' Classically, all the divided characters move to a 'middle ground' position where they learn what they have in common, accept the 'ordinary' but satisfying achieve-

ments of their lives, and grow just a little as human beings.

Critical reaction to **Windrider** has been predictably snobbish and dismissive. While for Brian McFarlane its 'mixture of 1950s and 1980s plot conventions is uniquely repellent'[4], for David Stratton its 'overall slightness' and 'basically rather bland' material is relieved only by the prurient interest of Kidman's 'first nude scenes'[5] (clearly a historic event). It would be fairer to say that it is an efficient, diverting pop culture youth entertainment like many others, offering the same smorgasbord of touristic delights, rock-video segments, low humour, ordinary glamour and an obligatory edifying moral message. No more, but no less.

ADRIAN MARTIN

1 One of several spellings.
2 **Newsfront** (Phillip Noyce, 1979), **Heatwave** (Noyce, 1982).
3 **Roadgames** (Richard Franklin, 1981), **Patrick** (Franklin, 1978).
4 Brian McFarlane, 'Washed Out: **Windrider**', *Freeze Frame*, vol. 1 no. 4, July 1987, pp. 44–5.
5 David Stratton, *The Avacado Plantation: Boom and Bust in the Australian Film Industry*, Macmillan, Sydney, 1990, p. 152.

Reference
'Windrider', a review by Philippa Hawker, *Cinema Papers*, no. 61, January 1987, p. 41.

Lovers Jade (Nicole Kidman) and P. C. Simpson (Tom Burlinson).

WRONG WORLD

[No opening production company credit.] WRONG WORLD. © 1984 Seon Film Productions. Produced with the assistance of Film Victoria and the Australian Film Commission. *Locations:* Melbourne, Nhill (Victoria). *Australian distributor:* AFID. *Video:* Ronin. *Rating:* M. 16mm (blown up to 35mm). 97 mins.

Producer: Bryce Menzies. *Executive producer:* John Cruthers. *Associate producer:* Basia Puszka. *Scriptwriters:* Doug Ling, Ian Pringle. *Director of photography:* Ray Argall. *Production designer:* Christine Johnson. *Wardrobe:* Jane Howat. *Editor:* Ray Argall. *Composer:* Eric Gradman, with Dave Cahill, Nick Rischbieth. *Sound recordist:* Bruce Emery. *Sound editor:* Rebecca Grubelich. [*Mixer:* not credited.]

Cast

Richard Moir [David Trueman[1]], Jo Kennedy [Mary]; Nicolas Lathouris (Rangott), Robbie McGregor (Robert), Esben Storm (Lawrence), Tim Robinson (Psychiatrist), Cliff Ellen (Old Man), Elise McCleod (Girl at Service Station).

David Trueman[2] (Richard Moir), a socially committed medical doctor, dulls with morphine his pain at not becoming 'the Albert Schweitzer of Bolivia'. Addicted, he drifts through New York and the American mid-west, finally referring himself to a drug withdrawal clinic in his home town of Melbourne.

While going cold turkey, David meets the streetwise junkie, Mary (Jo Kennedy). Their relationship, made necessary by a mutual desire to escape the institution, is instinctively testy and suspicious: they behave like threatened, feral animals, despite their individually felt desires for warmth and affection.

They begin to drive in a state of suspension—even trance—towards Mary's home town of Nhill, isolated on a desolate stretch of the Victoria-South Australia border. Their intimacy grows, but the affection is checked by one unstated condition: their eventual, unavoidable separation.

Director Ian Pringle and co-writer Doug Ling have given David an omnipresent voice-over. By turns humorous, depressively egocentric and strained by flowery literacy, it is nevertheless a structural link for the entire script. What is more, it serves to enrich David's character. 'The problem', he declares, 'is how to stop thinking. America has cracked it. If you start thinking in America, all you have to do is turn on the television or go for a drive. If reincarnation is true, then I want to come back as an American.'

Mary[4] (Jo Kennedy).

Without the benefit of a voice-over, Jo Kennedy must capitalise on every moment of her screen time. Her *tour-de-force* of a performance should also be judged against the masculine bias of the screenplay. (Kennedy won Best Actress at the 1985 Berlin Film Festival.)

Mary's relationship with David slowly thaws, but the delicate webs they build to connect their lives are still encircled by their transitory experiences. To hope for more would be unrealistic. Never promising more than it can deliver, **Wrong World** refuses to cajole or seduce its audience by compromising its realism. The slowly melting cores within its initially icy characters are drawn out by Mary, and we realise we are seeing both characters during a period of rare mutual warmth and compassion. It is a pleasurable hiatus in the futile, even cynical, melancholia of their lives.

Apart from Kennedy's remarkable performance, Pringle is well served by Ray Argall's sumptuous cinematography and decisive editing; by Eric Gradman's sparsely evocative soundtrack; by memorable secondary characters; and by a controlled per-formance from Richard Moir, given the task of creating a credible character out of an amorphous, slippery and tortured protagonist with a burnt-out centre.

ROD BISHOP[3]

---

[1] Character names for Richard Moir and Jo Kennedy are not given in the credits. These are taken from captioned stills.
[2] See footnote 1.
[3] Extracted from Bishop's review in *Cinema Papers* (see References).
[4] See footnote 1.

References

'The Films of Ian Pringle', John O'Hara, *Cinema Papers*, no. 50, February–March 1985, pp. 16–21.

'On Dangerous Ground: **Wrong World**', a review by Rod Bishop, *Cinema Papers*, no. 56, March 1986, p. 69.

Danny (Noah Taylor). John Duigan's
The Year My Voice Broke.

211

JACKI McKIMMIE [1]

AUSTRALIAN DREAM

[No opening production company credit.] AUSTRALIAN DREAM. © 1986 Filmside Ltd. *Budget:* $870,000. *Location:* Brisbane. *Australian distributor:* Ronin. *Video:* Roadshow Home Video. *Rating:* M (February 1987; 2331.55m). 16mm (blown up to 35mm). 85 mins.

Producers: Sue Wild, Jacki McKimmie. *Executive producer:* Ross Matthews. *Scriptwriter:* Jacki McKimmie. *Director of photography:* Andrew Lesnie. *Production designer:* Chris McKimmie. [*Costume designer:* not credited.]. *Editor:* Sara Bennett. *Musical director:* Colin Timms. *Sound recordist:* Ian Grant. *Sound editor:* Sara Bennett. [*Mixer:* not credited.]

Cast

Noni Hazlehurst (Dorothy), Graeme Blundell (Geoffrey), John Jarratt (Todd), Barry Rugless (Sir Bruce), Margaret Lord (Demonstrator), Jenny Mansfield (Tracey), Caine O'Connel (Jason), Ruth Barraclough (Sharon), James Ricketson (Bill (the Baby)), Lil Kelman (Sandra (the Bride)), John Kerr (Frank (the Swaggie)), Jenny Kubler (Betty (the Poodle)), Meg Simpson (Joy (the Angel)), Marlon Holden (John (the Devil)), Jill Loos (Barbara (Virgin Mary)), Tony Bellette (Ted (the Aborigine)), Craig Cromin (Don (Errol Flynn)), Peter Sherry (Ron (Miss Australia)), Alexandra Black (Shirley (Norm)), Di Fuller (Rita (the Peanut)), Peter Fuller (Joe (the Banana)), Gabrielle Lanbrose (Mary (the Mummy)), Brian Hinselwood (Greg (the Shark)).

After making an award-winning short film, *Stations* (1983), with Noni Hazlehurst in the lead, Queensland filmmaker Jacki McKimmie chose to put the official morals and mores of her home state under scrutiny in her feature-film debut.

Hazlehurst plays Dorothy, a suburban housewife whose butcher husband, Geoffrey (Graeme Blundell), is standing for election to state parliament for the Prosperity Party. (It quickly becomes evident that the Prosperity Party is a code-name for the then dominant National Party.)

The film starts on a Friday afternoon and ends on the next Sunday morning. Dorothy first attends a party for women where sex aids and lingerie are sold and Todd (John Jarratt), a near-naked male dancer, entertains. Dorothy then goes off to her creative writing class where an appalling academic makes appalling suggestions. She comes home to her suburban battleground of identical houses where her husband whisks her off to a political rally.

Saturday is spent in the usual activities with their children, as well as in preparations for the monthly street barbecue which they are hosting. She meets up again with Todd, who is starting to dominate a fantasy life rendered on the soundtrack by a reading of the Mills-&-Boonish novel she is writing. In one of an increasing number of acts of petty rebellion against her circumstances, she invites Todd and his band to play at the party. The party turns into a shambles, made worse by the fact that Geoffrey has been subject to one humiliation after another. Dorothy runs away with Todd and the final shots show her achieving her longed-for ecstasy in the back of a panel van.

Australian Dream set out to pillory the Queensland establishment, a male-dominated body of massive hypocrisy and gargantuan desire to press a strait-laced orthodox morality into the service of those able to make any sort of dollar. The establishment, represented here by the gross Sir Bruce (Barry Rugless), is determined to keep the population very quiet, hence the continued references to having the police and the media on side and the population acquiescent. This is drawn with broad brush but the arrows of satire go straight to the heart of a political system in terminal malaise, one that would be swept away only a few years later.

This satire is presented from Dorothy's viewpoint, the view of a woman suffering terminal frustration but unable to express herself in any coherent way. She fantasises about sexual pleasure taking her away from all the humdrum activities she is forced to undertake, much of it in the service of her husband's ambitions. He, in fact, is the most repressed character of all, typical of the suburban New Right, filled with hatred of socialists and homosexuals, absolutely fearful of any sexual activity outside marriage and, in a lovely satirical shaft about the stupidity of his obsessions, totally transfixed by meat.

The film is cruel and, for the Australian cinema (as opposed to its theatre and television), most unusual, its desire to flamboyantly expose to ridicule quite untrammelled. It has moments of total hilarity and one's only complaint is that the opportunity was eschewed to build the gags more slowly so as to be even more cataclysmic. The film tends to favour an episodic presentation which probably caused it to forgo an even more cutting and anarchic style.

GEOFF GARDNER

---

[1] Jacki McKimmie later appended an 'e' to her first name.

References

'Dream Maker', an article (with quotes) on writer–director Jackie [sic] McKimmie by Mary Colbert, *Cinema Papers*, no. 56, March 1986, p. 14.

'Australian Dream', a review by Helen Garner, *Cinema Papers*, no. 62, March 1987, p. 55.

'Australian Dream: The Jackie [sic] McKimmie Interview', an interview with the writer–director by Anna Grieve and Tina Kaufman, *Filmnews*, March 1987, p. 7.

A fantasy life: Todd (John Jarratt) and Dorothy (Noni Hazlehurst).

BUSHFIRE MOON

Entertainment Media presents BUSHFIRE M.O.O.N.[1] © 1987 Entertainment Media. Produced with the assistance of Film Victoria. *Location:* Melbourne. *Australian distributor:* Roadshow. *Opened:* December 1987. *Video:* Roadshow Home Video. *Rating:* G (November 1987; 2386.41m). 35mm. 87 mins.

Producers: Peter Beilby, Robert Le Tet. *Scriptwriter:* Jeff Peck. *Director of photography:* David Connell. *Production designer:* Otello Stolfo. *Costume designer:* Rose Chong. *Editor:* Tim Wellburn. *Composer:* Bruce Rowland. *Sound recordist:* Andrew Ramage. *Sound supervisor:* Richard Brobyn. *Sound editors:* Glenn Newman, Gavin Myers. [*Mixer:* not credited; Richard Brobyn.]

Cast

Dee Wallace Stone (Elizabeth), John Waters (Patrick), Charles Tingwell (Max Bell), Bill Kerr (Watson), Nadine Garner (Sarah), Grant Piro (Angus), Andrew Ferguson (Ned), Francis Bell (Sharkey), Christopher Stevenson (Jamie), Kim Gyngell (Hungry Bill), David Ravenswood (Mr Gullett), Maggie Millar (Mrs Gullett), Francine Ormrod (Penelope Gullett), Bruce Kilpatrick (Adam McKimmie), Callie Gray (Pip McKimmie), Christine Keogh (Heather McKimmie), Neil Melville (Mr Potts), Martin Redpath (Sgt Gibbs), Rosie Sturgess (Miss Daly), John Heywood (Tom Murchie).

In outback Australia, Christmas 1891 is bushfire season and, for the O'Day[2] family, problem time. After a dust storm sweeps over the countryside and turns their swamps to mud, Patrick (John Waters) is faced with a decision: either slaughter the thirsty sheep and admit defeat or ask Mr Watson (Bill Kerr), the wealthy landowner of the next property, for help. Eight-year-old Ned (Andrew Ferguson) unknowingly applies more pressure to the situation by mistaking Max Bell (Charles Tingwell)—an ex-miner who is on his way to Mr Watson's to collect a debt—for Father Christmas.

The original story and screenplay, written by Jeff Peck and directed by George Miller, has a definite moral concern about the pleasure of giving—even to those who don't deserve it—rather than receiving. The pivotal characters, Mr Watson, the rich man who is a miser, and his ex-partner Max Bell, the thief, are perfect candidates for reform. Mr Watson's characterisation alludes to Scrooge, the main character in the Charles Dickens story, 'A Christmas Carol': Scrooge awakens on Christmas Day a changed man, as does Mr Watson. Ned, the main catalyst to

Ned (Andrew Ferguson).

the action, is portrayed as an angelic and endearing little boy, but at times Andrew Ferguson pushes 'congenial' to the limit with his pleading soprano voice.

Patrick met his American wife, Elizabeth (American actress Dee Wallace Stone), in San Francisco and brought her to Australia. The myth that Australia was a prosperous country around the gold rush era is explored. 'This is not the paradise I promised you', Patrick says to his wife as he feels the pinch of a harsh and relentless environment he cannot control.

The photography (David Connell) of the dusty brown land is clear and simple, and the music (Bruce Rowland) is neither overstated nor understated in comparison to the visual image presented. Dramatically this film is natural and believable, even if some of the direction appears to be too positioned.

The ending pushes one's belief too far, however, by endowing Max Bell with some magical Father Christmas qualities. But if the aim of the film was to create a heart-warming family tale, the film-makers have succeeded.

SUZANNE BROWN

---

[1] There is an end credit which reads, 'Produced in association with The Disney Channel, PBS Wonder Works, Revcom Productions. Produced with the assistance of Film Victoria, The Film House, Australian Children's Tele-vision Foundation.'

[2] There is no reference to 'O'Day' on the credits, but that is the name said in the film and the spelling in the press book.

Reference

'**Bushfire Moon**', a review by Sarah Guest, *Cinema Papers*, no. 67, January 1988, pp. 38–9.

DOGS IN SPACE

An Entertainment Media and The Burrowes Film Group production. *Dogs in Space.* © 1986 Central Park Films Pty Ltd. *Location:* Melbourne. *Australian distributor:* Hoyts-Ronin. *Opened:* 1 January 1987. *Video:* RCA-Columbia-Hoyts. *Rating:* R (January 1987; 2825.29m; appeal against rating rejected). 35mm. 103 mins.

Producer: Glenys Rowe. *Executive producers:* Robert Le Tet, Dennis Wright. *Executive in charge of production:* John Kearney. *Scriptwriter:* Richard Lowenstein. *Director of photography:* Andrew de Groot. *Camera operator:* Paul Elliot. *Production designer:* Jody Borland. *Wardrobe:* Lynn-Maree Milburn, Karen Ansell. *Editor:* Jill Bilcock. *Musical director:* Ollie Olsen. *Sound recordists:* Dean Gawen, Stephen Vaughan. *Sound editors:* Dean Gawen, Steve Lambeth, Tim Chau, Louise Johnson. *Mixers:* Roger Savage, Bruce Emery.

Cast

Michael Hutchence (Sam), **Saskia Post** (Anna), **Nique Needles** (Tim), **Deanna Bond** (The Girl), **Tony Helou** (Luchio), **Chris Haywood** (Chainsaw Man), **Peter Walsh** (Anthony), **Laura Swanson** (Clare), **Adam Briscomb** (Grant), **Sharon Jessop** (Leanne), **Edward Clayton-Jones** (Nick), **Martii Coles** (Mark), **Chuck Meo** (Charles), **Caroline Lee** (Jenny), **Fiona Latham** (Barbara), **Stephanie Johnson** (Erica), **Glenys Osborne** (Lisa); **Allanah Hill, Robyn McLellan** (Anna's Girlfriends); **Troy Davies** (Skinhead); **John Murphy, Owen Robertson, Troy Davies** (Leanne's Brothers); **Helen Phillips** (Stacey), **Kelly Hoare** (Chainsaw Woman), **Robyn Lowenstein** (Chainsaw Baby).

Dogs in Space ostensibly concerns a share-household in which a variety of characters' lives overlap in the context of a somewhat carefree, subcultural lifestyle. The swirl of characters and events, however, actually pivot around the story of Sam (Michael Hutchence) and Anna (Saskia Post), and their relationship is partly conditioned by Sam's use of drugs.

Sam, a lead member of a small band, Dogs in Space, has all the makings of a primal being. He seems to communicate through grunts rather than coherent speech, crawls about the floor most of the time, is completely indifferent to the world outside the front doorstep, and seems to survive only on drugs and television. His is the world of the punk-music scene in Melbourne.

Anna, on the other hand, is a vivacious suburban girl, who seeks a career and has a life independent from that of the share-household. Her connection to the punk scene is uncertain apart from her love for Sam, even though she detests his drug-taking. Her death at the end of the film by a drug overdose is tragic in a Christ-like manner: she is the sacrifice to the failure of a generation.

Director Richard Lowenstein based his script on stories, experiences and incidents from a range of individuals and groups active in the new music scene at the time, many of whom appear in the film. In retrospect, however, the mantle of a definitive statement actually seems to result from the pot-boiler aspect of the film's setting.

The house serves to epitomise an era and to encapsulate its lifestyles and attitudes. The film's vision of this era is best summed up at the opening with the quote from an Iggy Pop song: 'We eat dog food. So what!' This is an attitude Lowenstein has called the 'Who gives a fuck' mentality, and it is what holds the group together.

But this catch-all vision is ultimately reductionist: characters become token characters, relating to one another through slogans, or as types rather than people from particular backgrounds with something to say and the need to be heard. There is no sense that their cohesion (or divisiveness) is based upon political, social and cultural realities.

The film's saving grace is Andrew de Groot's camerawork, which drifts in and out of situations as though the camera were a character, and is closely aligned with the film's motif of space travel and lifestyle. (Moreover, if the lifestyle of the inner-city house is in likeness to life in space, then the constant references to Skylab are the grim anticipation of the household's fate.) The camera often captures the house in a dream-like, fluid style, with its stream of characters flowing in and out. At times, the movements of characters resemble the weightless, free-floating movements of the space footage. De Groot's camera serves well the trajectory of a particular world in decline, and the film's references to space travel are its most salient symbolical features.

RAFFAELE CAPUTO

References

'Putting the Bite into **Dogs in Space**', a report by Kathy Bail (and Fred Harden on the titles), *Cinema Papers*, no. 61, January 1987, pp. 14–18.

'**Dogs in Space**', a review by Vikki Riley, *Cinema Papers*, no. 62, March 1987, pp. 44–5.

'Wayward Haywood', an article (with quotes) on actor Chris Hawood by Joanna Murray-Smith, *Cinema Papers*, no. 63, May 1987, pp. 38–9.

'**Dogs in Space**', a short review by Kathe Boehringer, *Filmnews*, December 1986, pp. 12–13.

Anna (Saskia Post) and Tim (Nique Needles).

Sam (Michael Hutchence) and Anna (Saskia Post).

DOT AND THE SMUGGLERS

Yoram Gross presents Dot and the Smugglers. *Alternative titles:* 'Dot and the Bunyip' and 'Dot and the Lake Monster' (working). © 1987 Yoram Gross Film Studios Pty Ltd. *Australian distributor:* Yoram Gross. *Video:* CEL. *Rating:* G (February 1987; 1536.08m). 35mm. 75 mins.

Producer: Yoram Gross. *Associate producer:* Sandra Gross. *Scriptwriter:* Greg Flynn. *Additional dialogue:* Rod Hay. *Director of photography:* Graham Sharpe. *Photography:* Ricky Vergara, Erik Bierens, Graham Binding. *Editor:* Rod Hay. *Composer:* Guy Gross. *Lyrics:* John Palmer, Bob Young, Chris Harriott. *Sound editor:* Rod Hay. *Mixers:* Phil Judd, Martin Oswin.

Animation director: Jacques Muller. *Character design:* Jacques Muller. *Colour design:* Jeanette Toms, Chris V. D. Casseyen. *Animators:* John Burge, Nick Harding, Athol Henry, Wal Logue, Brenda McKie, Jacques Muller, Rowen Smith, Bela Szeman, Andrew Szemenyei, Stan Walker. *In-betweeners:* Paul Baker, Steve Becker, Lu Rou, Vicky Robinson, Maria Haren, Domingo Rivera, Jan Stephen, Judy Howieson, Murray Griffen, Joanna Fryer, Greg Farrugia, Hanka Bilyk, Roland Chat, Clare Lyonette, Kathie O'Rourke, Paul Stilbal, Peter McDonald. *Layout artists:* Nobuko Yuasa, Brenda McKie, Jacques Muller. *Painters:* Robyn Drayton, Mimi Intal, Corallee Munro, Joseph Cabatuan, Paulette Martin, Annamaria Dimmers. *Backgrounds:* Amber Ellis, Sheila Christofides, Barry Dean. *Special fx painting:* Jeanette Toms. *Graphics:* Eric David.

Voices

Robyn Moore, Keith Scott.

[See Appendix A on all the Gross films, pp. 352–4.]

Reference
'Yoram Gross', Raffaele Caputo, *Cinema Papers*, no. 86, January 1992, pp. 36–42.

Dot and a koala.

Dot Goes to Hollywood

[No opening production credit.[1]] DOT GOES TO HOLLYWOOD. *Alternative titles:* 'Dot in Good Old Hollywood' and 'Dot in Concert' (working). © 1987 Yoram Gross Film Studio. A Dot in Concert Production. *Australian distributor:* Yoram Gross. *Video:* CEL. *Rating:* G. 35mm. 75 mins.

Producer: Yoram Gross. *Associate producer:* Sandra Gross. *Screenplay:* John Palmer. *Animation photography:* Joseph Cabatuan, Ngoc Minh Nguyen, Graham Sharpe. *Editor:* Rod Hay. *Composer:* Guy Gross. *Lyrics:* John Palmer, Bob Young, Guy Gross. *Sung by:* Robyn Moore. *Music performed by:* Guy Gross. *Sound editors:* Rod Hay, Nicki Roller, Guy Gross. *Mixer:* Phil Judd.

Animation director: Athol Henry. *Backgrounds:* Sheila Christofides, Amber Ellis, Gennady Kozlov, Dixon Wu. *Colour designers:* Amber Ellis, Jeanette Toms. *Special fx painting:* Sheila Christofides, Amber Ellis, Jeanette Toms. *Animators:* Junko Aoyama, Paul McAdam, Nobuko Burnfield, Ray Nowland, Ariel Ferrari, Darek Polkowski, Nicholas Harding, Bela Szeman, Athol Henry, Andrew Szemenyei, Wal Logue, Stan Walker. *Character designers:* Nobuko Burnfield, Ray Nowland, Stan Walker. *Layouts:* Athol Henry, Ray Nowland. *In-betweeners:* Mark Benvenuti, Peter McDonald, Joseph Cabatuan, Kathie O'Rourke, Yukiko Davis, Jun Rivera, Phillip Einfield, Vicki Robinson, Gennady Kozlov, Dixon Wu, Sophia Rou Lui, Antony Zmak, Clare Lyonette, Jaime Cabatuan. *Painters & Tracers:* Jaime Cabatuan, Cindy Luckwell, Anna Maria Dimmers, Paulette Martin, Mimi Intal, Jung-Ae Ro, Elizabeth Jamsik, Carlos Rodrigius, Xi Kang Lin, Charlie Scapellato. *Animation aid:* Bernard Vidal.

Voices

Robyn Moore, Keith Scott.

[See Appendix A on all the Gross films, pp. 352–4.]

---

[1] There is an opening statement which reads: 'Dot and the Kangaroo salute One Hundred Years of Hollywood.'

Reference
'Yoram Gross', Raffaele Caputo, *Cinema Papers*, no. 86, January 1992, pp. 36–42.

Dot and friends.

FRENCHMAN'S FARM

A Mavis Bramston Production. FRENCH-MAN'S FARM. © 1986 Mavis Bramston Productions Ltd. *Location:* outback Queensland. *Australian distributor:* CEL. *Video:* CEL. *Rating:* M. 35mm. 100 mins.

Producers: James Fishburn, Matt White. *Executive producer:* Colson Worner. *Scriptwriters:* James Fishburn, Ron Way, Matt White. Based on an original script by William Russell. *Director of photography:* Malcolm McCulloch. *Camera operator:* Henry Pierce. *Production designer:* Richard Rooker. *Wardrobe supervisor:* Maureen Klestov. *Editor:* Pippa Anderson. *Composer:* Tommy Tycho. *Sound recordist:* Max Bowring. *Sound editor:* Greg Bell. *Mixers:* Julian Ellingworth, Alasdair MacFarlane.

Cast

Ray Barrett [Harry Benson[1]], Norman Kaye [Reverend Aldershot], John Meillon [Bill Dolan]; David Reyne (Barry Norden); Tracey Tainsh [Jackie Grenville]; Phil Brock (John Hatcher), Andrew Blackman (John Mainsbridge), Andrew Johnston (William Morris); Errol O'Neill, Penny Jones (Programmers); Jennifer Flowers (Mrs. Grenville), Kym Lynch (George Slater), Ian Leigh-Cooper (Librarian), Lynne Schofield (Madame Cheveraux), Rod Warren (Television Newsreader), Alexander Black (Archives Clerk), Robert Eastgate (Second Detective), Keith Scott (Radio Announcer), Maurice Hughes (Country Policeman), Laurence Hodge (Man at Telephone), Bill Watson (Farmer), Himself (Swaggy), Tui Bow (Miss Morton).

Reverend Aldershot[3] (Norman Kaye), Barry Norden (David Reyne) and Jackie Grenville (Tracey Tainsh).

It is 1984 and Jackie Grenville[2] (Tracey Tainsh), a law student, is returning from her parents' house in country Queensland, when her car breaks down on a bridge. A strange phenomenon occurs and Jackie is transported back 40 years in time to 1944. She witnesses a murder on 'Frenchman's Farm' and the murderer tries to kill her, too. Fortunately, Jackie is transported forward in time to 1984.

The bewildering experience, coupled with the sceptical reaction of her boyfriend, Barry Norden (David Reyne), prompts her to look up old newspapers and search for clues relevant to the murder. When Jackie discovers some intriguing information, she persuades Barry to accompany her on her return to Harrisville, the scene of the crime.

The screenplay was originally written by William Russell and was adapted by Ron Way (the director), Matt White (a film critic) and James Fishburn. The underlying idea may have been better suited to another medium, for example a book, where all the intricacies of dates and ancestors could be explained slowly and clearly. The police, for example, are introduced into the plot by the fact that the unsolved murder-case file in the archives has a memorandum attached to it directing that the police department be notified if anyone looks at it.

The murder case is inexplicably wiped off the computer and an unusual smell recurs at strategic moments in the film to signify a spiritual presence. The film continually cuts from Harrisville and then back to the police station, and it imitates an investigative style with Jackie and Barry as the detectives.

Singing voices are heard when an eerie atmosphere is depicted and to indicate that something strange is about to happen. At some stages, the crescendo of orchestral music is incompatible with the action.

The photography is clear and light but there is not much the actors can do with the unfortunate dialogue. An example of this is when Barry decides to have a night at home with Jackie: 'Tonight it's wine, woman and song', he says, and Jackie replies, 'Yes, and I know who will be supplying the wine and the woman.'

The plot relies on a lot of tying up and matching of dates, and in the end there is too much information to digest. What may have had potential on paper has lost much in its transition to the screen.

SUZANNE BROWN

---

[1] There are no character names given in the credits for Barrett, Kaye, Meillon and Tainsh. These are taken from a press release.
[2] See footnote 1.
[3] See footnote 1.

Reference
'Frenchman's Farm', a short review by Adrienne McKibbins, *Filmnews*, May 1987, p. 12.

GOING SANE

[No opening production company credit.] GOING SANE. © 1985 Sea-Change Films Pty. Limited and New South Wales Film Corporation. *Budget:* $2.1 million. Script developed with the assistance of the Australian Film Commission and the New South Wales Film Corporation. *Australian distributor:* GUO. *Video:* Applause. *Rating:* M (November 1986; 2441.27). 35mm. 89 mins.

Producer: Tom Jeffrey. *Executive producer:* John Sandford. *Scriptwriter:* John Sandford. *Director of photography:* Dean Semler. *Camera operator:* David Williamson. *Production designer:* Igor Nay. *Costume designer:* Jan Hurley. *Editor:* Brian Kavanagh. *Composer:* Cameron Allan. *Sound recordist:* Syd Butterworth. *Sound editor:* Penn Robinson. *Mixers:* Julian Ellingworth, Michael Thomas.

Cast

John Waters (Martin Brown), Judy Morris (Ainslie Brown), Linda Cropper (Irene Carter), Kate Raison (Nosh), Frank Wilson (Sir Colin Grant), Jim Holt (Irwin Grant), Maggie Blinco (Miss Griffiths), Brett Climo (Matthew Brown), Robyn Moase (Marcia), Tim Robertson (Owen Owen), Anne Semler (Marta Owen), Rob Steele (Sergeant at Office), Terry Brady (Big Cop at Office), Paul Booth (Engineer), Ron Stephenson (Unionist), Allan McFadden (Management Man), Beth Child (Hospital Sister), Jim Kemp (Dr Frankel), Denise Roberts (Hospital Clerk), Richard Healy (Norm), Brian Anderson (Old Dero).

Michael Robertson's **Going Sane** was one of a small crop of mid-1980s Australian films about male mid-life crisis in which successful men quit the urban rat-race to seek peace and enlightenment in the countryside.

It has something in common with Ray Lawrence's **Bliss**, although John **Sandford**'s poorly resolved screenplay for **Going Sane** is not a patch on Lawrence and Peter Carey's adaptation of the latter's novel.

John Waters plays Martin Brown, a successful 40-year-old mining engineer who tosses aside job, wife Ainslie (Judy Morris) and family, has a brief affaire with his secretary, Irene Carter (Linda Cropper), then heads for the hills.

Once there, he has hair-raising encounters with a nuttily homicidal Welshman, Owen Owen (Tim Robertson), and the man's amorous wife, Marta (Anne Semler), is hospitalised and encounters a sympathetic greenie, Nosh (Kate Raison), who whisks him off to her family's lush cattle property. Then his old mining corporation, run by a tyrant, Sir Colin Grant (Frank Wilson), casts its greedy eyes on the rural haven's verdant paddocks and the escapee is back fighting his former employer.

Like the protagonist of **Bliss**, Martin infuriates family and business associates by his rejection of material values, but, apart from some self-righteous fuming by the wife and ex-boss, the confrontations do not amount to much. Nor do several plot-lines, such as the drop-out's relationships with wife, son and girlfriends.

Robertson's exposition of all this is lucid, but plodding. In a number of scenes, the talented cast no doubt would have been grateful for brisker dispatch of some notably banal dialogue.

KEITH CONNOLLY

Martin Brown (John Waters) and wife Ainslie (Judy Morris).

GROUND ZERO

Avenue Pictures presents GROUND ZERO.[1] © 1987 BDB Production and Distribution Pty Ltd. *Budget*: $7 million. *Locations*: Coober Pedy, Woomera (South Australia); Melbourne. *Australian distributor*: Hoyts. *Opened*: 1 October 1987. *Video*: Vestron Video International. *Rating*: M (February 1988[2]). 35mm. Panavision. 109 mins.

Producer: Michael Pattinson. *Executive producers*: Kent Lovell, John Kearney, Dennis Wright. *Scriptwriters*: Mac Gudgeon, Jan Sardi. *Director of photography*: Steve Dobson. *Camera operator*: Ian Jones. *Production designer*: Brian Thomson. *Wardrobe supervisor*: Margot Lindsay. *Editor*: David Pulbrook. *Composer*: Chris Neal [Tom Bähler is so credited on the American version[3]]. *Sound recordist*: Gary Wilkins. *Supervising sound editor*: Craig Carter. *Sound editors*: Livia Ruzic (dia.); Craig Carter, Peter McBain, Frank Lipson, Lindsay Frazer, Steve Burgess (fx); Bruce Lamshed, Steve Burgess (foley). *Mixers*: Roger Savage, Bruce Emery.

Cast

Colin Friels (Harvey), Jack Thompson (Trebilcock), Donald Pleasence (Prosper), Natalie Bate[4] (Pat), Burnham Burnham (Charlie), Simon Chilvers (Commission President), Neil Fitzpatrick (Hocking), Bob Maza (Walamari), Beverley Dunn (Commissioner #1), Alan Hopgood (Commissioner #2), Peter Cummins (Australian Veteran), Brian James (Vice-Admiral Windsor), Steve Dodd (Freddy Tjapalijarri), Alfred Austen (Aboriginal Elder), Muade [sic] Pepper (Aboriginal Witness), Beryl Brunette (Aboriginal Woman), Julius Szappanos (Bailiff); Greg Carroll, Dean Nottle (Agents); Kim Gyngell, Mark Mitchell (Detectives).

The background to **Ground Zero** lies in the Australian government's decision to set up a Royal Commission into allegations made that atomic bomb tests conducted in Australia in the early 1950s had led to deaths. The film suggests that the real cover-up was the countless numbers of Aborigines living in the desert who were victims of the blast.

This is a powerful subject, filled with pungent observation of government policy, the conduct of investigations and the operation of the security services.

The device chosen to dramatise these issues is a film cameraman, Harvey (Colin Friels), whose father filmed the blasts and died mysteriously. Harvey's apartment is broken into and his estranged wife, Pat

(Natalie Bate[5]), a television news reporter, tells him of a 'D' Notice on certain matters. This leads Harvey to the headquarters of ASIO where he manages to confront the smooth-talking Trebilcock (Jack Thompson).

Various sinister forces are at work attempting to suppress the truth, with physical violence occurring between ASIO and its British counterparts. Eventually, Harvey comes to believe that the truth will be found by visiting Prosper (Donald Pleasence), a former soldier and now a reclusive painter living in an outback cave, who, when he needs to move around, is carried on the back of a blind Aboriginal victim of the blasts.

Ground Zero set out with some ambition to make a dramatic film about a subject of some political and social interest. It levels accusing fingers at the operations of the security services and the way the establishment closes ranks to deny any admission of past guilt or error. It does this in a format which, while not original, has the virtue of the best modern thrillers in that while presenting a fast-moving and violent narrative it allows itself speculation on and satire of modern politics.

But despite this background of up-to-the-moment political intrigue married to a narrative derived from the formulæ of the pulp detective story, **Ground Zero** is a somewhat uneasy mixture which probably needed to be better in both these areas to be acceptable to those audiences interested in either its politics or its thrills. As a thriller, possibly because it gets carried away with dazzling the audience with some displays of the latest

technology (even including a chess computer which is registering 'CHECKMATE' when Harvey finally returns home defeated), it lacks the frenetic pace and slam-bang action scenes of the kind that might be rendered by Walter Hill or John McTiernan. And as a political pamphlet, it fails to make real revelations or accusations that might have provoked some reaction from government or even the public. On that level, the film has a rather costly degree of ambiguity. It seems difficult to be sure whether the Commission President (Simon Chilvers) has become part of the conspiracy, as the ASIO man sits smugly beside him at the end, or has simply had the truth withheld or has been barking up the wrong tree.

GEOFF GARDNER

---

1 There is an end credit which reads, 'Presented by Michael Pattinson and The Burrowes Film Group'.
2 Even though the film was rated in February 1988, it was released in 1987.
3 According to David Stratton, a shortened version of the film with Tom Bähler's score is the one shown on Australian television. The locally released video has Chris Neal's score.
4 Natalie Bate is dubbed by Sandy Gore on the video version (and, presumably, the American). This is not credited.
5 See footnote 4.

References

'Ground Zero', a review by Mick Broderick, *Cinema Papers*, no. 65, September 1987, pp. 51–2.
'Ground Zero: Top Thriller', a review by Liz Jacka, *Filmnews*, October 1987, p. 11.

The eccentric Prosper (Donald Pleasence).

HIGHTIDE

Hemdale Film Corporation presents an FGH/SJL Production. HIGHTIDE.[1] © 1987 SJL Productions Pty Ltd. *Locations:* Eden, Merimbula, Sydney (New South Wales). *Australian distributor:* Filmpac. *Opened:* August 1987. *Video:* Filmpac. *Rating:* M (June 1987; 2852.72m). 35mm. 104 mins.

Producer: Sandra Levy. *Executive producers:* Antony I. Ginnane, Joseph Skrzynski. *Associate producer:* Greg Ricketson. *Scriptwriter:* Laura Jones. *Director of photography:* Russell Boyd. *Additional photography:* David Gribble. *Production designer:* Sally Campbell. *Costume designer:* Terry Ryan. *Editor:* Nick Beauman. *Composer:* Peter Best. *Sound recordist:* Ben Osmo. *Supervising sound editor:* Tim Jordan. *Sound editors:* Anne Breslin, John Paterson. *Mixers:* Peter Fenton, Phil Heywood, Martin Oswin.

Cast

Judy Davis (Lilli), Jan Adele (Bet), Claudia Karvan (Ally), Frankie J. Holden (Lester), John Clayton (Col), Colin Friels (Mick), Toni Scanlon (Mary), Monica Trapaga (Tracey), Barry Rugless (Club Manager), "Cowboy" Bob Purtell (Joe), Mark Hembrow (Mechanic), Emily Stocker (Michelle), Marc Gray (Jason), Sarah Oord (Nicole), Jan Boreham (Mona), May Howlett (Mick's Mum), David Attrill (Band Member), Charles Camilleri (Band Member), Robert Carlton (Pinball Boy), Kathryn Chalker (Teacher).

An atmospheric film set on the far south coast of New South Wales, **Hightide** effectively captures the isolated mood of small-town Australia. Rather than a backdrop of sizzling summer beaches, director Gillian Armstrong's wintry, windswept locations provide the ideal environment to explore the lives of three women: Bet (Jan Adele), the hardened old survivor; Ally (Claudia Karvan), her surfie teenage granddaughter; and Lilli (Judy Davis), the girl's mother.

Lilli is a drifter, a back-up singer for an Elvis Presley imitator, Lester (Frankie J. Holden). When she loses her job, her car breaks down and she has to wait for it to be repaired. She stays at the local caravan park, where she befriends a daughter she has long abandoned. While Lilli is irresistibly drawn to her daughter, she has always distanced herself from responsibility; **Hightide** is the story of Lilli's personal journey to accepting commitment and the past she has left behind.

Sometime mother: Lilli (Judy Davis).

Hightide is a collaboration between Armstrong, writer Laura Jones and producer Sandra Levy. Stemming from Armstrong's desire to make a film about surfing culture, the Lilli character was originally written as a male surfer drifting up and down the coast. However, in the final draft Armstrong decided that a woman would be much more interesting. Perhaps this accounts for the strength and complexity of Lilli's character. As Davis wryly noted at the time, 'Maybe all women's parts in future could be written as if for men and then changed.'

While filming, Armstrong opted for constant camera movement. In many ways, the fluidity of the camera parallels the lives of the characters. Laura Jones' spare dialogue complements Armstrong's textured cinematic style: we are never given too much information. In the opening moments, the camera pans across its subjects: timeless images of a body half-submerged in water are juxtaposed with the aimless life on the road; the camera speeds along a deserted beach and cuts to the centre lines of a highway. The film is full of contrasts: a contemporary rock 'n' roll and saxophone soundtrack plays against life in the sleepy fishing village, the pastel colours of nature exaggerate the glaring red hues of the nightclub scenes, the gritty ugliness of man-made buildings is set against the natural beauty of the ocean.

A study of loneliness, lost youth and how people survive, the film never lapses into sentimentality; instead, the audience is engrossed in the characters, caught up in their lives. So enigmatic is Davis' AFI Award-winning performance that, right till the end, Lilli's final decision is never certain. (Jan Adele also won the 1987 AFI Award for Best Supporting Actress.)

HELEN BARLOW

---

[1] The poster, the press books and almost all writers render the title in two words, but the film clearly has it as one.

References

'Gillian Armstrong Returns to Eden', an interview with the director by Anna Grieve, *Cinema Papers*, no. 63, May 1987, pp. 30–3.
'**High Tide** [sic]', a review by John Baxter, *Cinema Papers*, no. 65, September 1987, p. 45.
'**High Tide** [sic]', a review by Liz Jacka, *Filmnews*, August 1987, pp. 12–13.

KANGAROO

Ross Dimsey presents a Tim Burstall Film. KANGAROO. © 1986 Naked Country Productions. *Budget:* $3.3 million. *Location:* Melbourne. *Australian distributor:* Filmways. *Video:* Filmpac. *Rating:* M (March 1987; 2962.44m reduced version). 35mm. Panavision. 108 mins.

Producer: Ross Dimsey. *Executive producers:* Mark Josem, William Marshall, Peter Sherman, Robert Ward. *Scriptwriter:* Evan Jones. Adapted from the novel by D. H. Lawrence. *Director of photography:* Dan Burstall. *Production designer:* Tracy Watt. *Costume designer:* Terry Ryan. *Sound recordist:* Paul Clark. *Editor:* Edward McQueen-Mason. *Composer:* Nathan Waks. *Sound editors:* Ross A. Porter (fx); Livia Ruzic (dia.). *Mixer:* Peter Fenton.

Cast

Colin Friels (Richard Somers), Judy Davis (Harriet Somers), John Walton (Jack Calcott), Julie Nihill (Vicki Calcott), Hugh Keays-Byrne (Kangaroo), Peter Hehir (Jaz), Peter Cummins (Struthers), Tim Robertson (O'Neill), Malcolm Robertson (Publisher), David Hutchins (Cornwall Detective), Victor Kazan (Army Captain), Bill Richardson (Army Sergeant), Alan Lee (Collier), Richard Moss (Major), Howard Priddle (1st Doctor), Denzil Howson (2nd Doctor), Ron Pinnell (Dug), Geoff Brooks (Taxi Driver), Bob Butcher (Drummer).

Harriet (Judy Davis) and Richard Somers (Colin Friels).

D. H. Lawrence spent three months in Australia in 1922 and in the following year appeared *Kangaroo*, the novel based on his experiences there.

Richard Somers and his German-born wife Harriet, essentially portraits of Lawrence and his wife Frieda, leave the narrow bigotry of English provincial life, in which her nationality and his reputation as a non-patriot and 'a writer of filth' make them deeply suspect. They go to Sydney, hoping for a new freedom from petty restraint. Instead, they find, on the one hand, a vulgar suburbia (their house is called 'Torestin') and, on the other, a dangerous conflict of political passions. Their neighbour, John Calcott, tries to draw Somers into a fascist organisation run by ex-diggers led by Kangaroo, but Somers is ultimately as repelled by this as he is unmoved by the socialist rhetoric of Struthers, the trade union leader. After a bloody battle between these two factions, a disillusioned Somers and Harriet leave Australia.

For years, it seemed, Tim Burstall was reported to be about to film *Kangaroo* and the prospect of two kinds of abrasiveness—

Burstall's and Lawrence's—in conjunction whetted the appetite. In the event, the film, while far from negligible, does less than justice to either. The best of Lawrence's novel may well be in the sensuous particularity with which he rendered the strangeness and beauty of the Australian landscape. The film is oddly restrained about this. There is a cut from a shot of Richard (Colin Friels) and Harriet Somers (a superb Judy Davis) walking away from the camera down a bleak, foggy English street to the blaze of light and colour which accompanies the caption 'SYDNEY 1922'. But the opposition thus set up is not really followed through: the odd shot of a broad, sunswept beach tends to emphasise how *enclosed* is most of the Australian section of the film.

The narrative content of the novel, in both matters, is often either murkily indistinct or gratingly explicit, but inevitably graced with those touches of illumination that mark Lawrence at his most powerful.

Burstall's direction and Evan Jones' screenplay both pull together the political events and render them more crudely melodramatic than they are in the novel. The film's major triumph is in the relationship between Somers and Harriet, and in the curious feeling of attraction and contempt which exists between Somers and Jack Calcott (John Walton). The oppositions of male and female, and male and male, of passion and inhibition, define the contours of Burstall's—and the film's—strength.

BRIAN McFARLANE

References

'Leap Year', an article (with quotes) on actor Colin Friels by Debi Enker, *Cinema Papers*, no. 56, March 1986, pp. 14–15.

'Love, Marriage, Life and the Whole Damn Thing', an uncredited location report, ibid., p. 42.

'**Kangaroo**', a review by Peter Craven, *Cinema Papers*, no. 63, May 1987, pp. 57–8.

'**Kangaroo**', a short review by Adrienne McKibbins, *Filmnews*, May 1987, p. 13.

LES PATTERSON SAVES THE WORLD

Diane Millstead presents a Barry Humphries Fillum. Les Patterson SAVES THE WORLD. © 1987 Humpstead Productions Pty Limited. Produced with the assistance of the Australian Film Commission. *Locations:* Australia, Morocco; the US. *Australian distributor:* Hoyts. *Opened:* 9 April 1987. *Video:* Premiere Home Video. *Rating:* M (April 1987; 2687m). 35mm. Panavision. 98 mins.

Producer: Sue Milliken. *Executive producer:* Diane Millstead. *Scriptwriters:* Barry Humphries, Diane Millstead. *Director of photography:* David Connell. *Camera operator:* David Williamson. *Production designer:* Graham (Grace) Walker. *Costume designer:* Anna Senior. *Editor:* Tim Wellburn. *Composer:* Tim Finn. *Sound recordist:* Syd Butterworth. *Sound editors:* Penn Robinson, Jeanine Chialvo. *Sound mixers:* Peter Fenton, Phil Heywood, Ron Purvis.

Cast

Himself[1] (Sir Les Patterson), Herself (Dame Edna Everage), Pamela Stephenson (Veronique Crudite), Thaao Penghlis (Col. Richard Godowni), Andrew Clarke (Neville Thonge), Henri Szeps (Dr Herpes; Desiree), Hugh Keays-Byrne (Inspector Farouk), Elizabeth McIvor (Nancy Borovansky), Garth Meade (Mustafa Toul), Arthur Sherman (General Evans), Josef Drewniak (Mossolov), Esben Storm (Russian Scientist), Joy Westmore (Lady Gwen Patterson), Connie Hobbs (Madge Allsop); Christine Hill, Kati Edwards, Julie Godfrey, Patricia Howson, Penny Stehli, Sue Ingleton (The Possums for Peace); Paul Jennings (Prime Minister), Graham Kennedy (Brian Lannigan), John Clarke (Mike Rooke).

Les Patterson Saves the World presents a curious case study. Much publicised before its release, it 'bombed' at the box office within six weeks, and was damned by virtually all reviewers, who evoked the inevitable unfavourable comparisons and associations. Australian cinema was returning it seemed, in the unsubtle hands of actor–writer–satirist Barry Humphries, to the 'ocker' comedies it had left behind with the advent of **Picnic at Hanging Rock** (Peter Weir, 1975). Moreover, beside its predecessor **Crocodile Dundee** (Peter Faiman, 1986)—that other big-budget comedy aimed at the international market—this seemed a charmless, bombastic, carelessly put-together work, incapable of 'winning' audiences either locally or overseas.

The plot is indeed crowded (centring on Humphries' famous character Sir Les Patterson as Australian ambassador in a fermenting Middle East), and the tone is high farce, loud and spectacular. Part of the problem of its construction stems from the fact that it aims to be a multi-genre 'action comedy' with a bit of everything thrown in, so that one passes uneasily from elaborately staged gags (such as the revolving restaurant finale) to 'dramatic' (i.e., perfunctory) chase-fight-explosion sequences, and from broad comic performers (including Humphries, Henri Szeps and Pamela Stephenson) to 'straight', po-faced ones (Andrew Clarke).

There is an intriguing strain of misanthropy in the film. Giving full vent to the darkest side of Humphries' humour, it mercilessly pillories 'ordinary' people and the cultured bourgeoisie alike, all institutions and values—and even its own status as an 'export commodity' on the international market, offering parodic 'tourist' images of Australia (e.g., kangaroos on tram tracks in city streets). The film's humour—the complete antithesis of the American 'feel good' style mastered by the makers of **Crocodile Dundee**—is at every moment cruel, solipsistic, scatological and deliberately tasteless, culminating in a running gag about characters catching a grotesque AIDS-style disease from toilet seats.

Indeed, those local commentators who cautiously praised the film—this writer[2] and the soundtrack composer Martin Armiger[3]—linked it to the tradition of vulgar 'low comedy' that includes Benny Hill and some 'exploitation' cinema, and argued that the film be respected as an instance of such comedy. (On the other hand, the 'low' humorist Barry Dickins curtly pronounced, '**Les Patterson Saves the World** is crap.'[4]) Armiger hypothesised, 'this is a humour so weird that it might take a few years to sink in', and suggested the film 'may prove to have legs'. However, the film had to wait five years for a video release and has not had even a single theatrical screening in Australia subsequent to its initial run.

ADRIAN MARTIN

---

1 The end credits get the first two character entries round the wrong way. Presumably, the film-makers meant 'Sir Les Patterson as Himself', etc.
2 Adrian Martin, *Freeze Frame*, May 1987, p. 39.
3 Martin Armiger, *Xpress*, June–July 1987, p. 11.
4 Barry Dickins, *Cinema Papers*, no. 64, July 1987, p. 46.
5 See footnote 1.

Reference
'Les Patterson Saves the World', a review by Barry Dickins, *Cinema Papers*, no. 64, July 1987, p. 46.

Sir Les Patterson (Himself[5]), Dr Herpes (Henri Szeps) and Veronique Crudite (Pamela Stephenson).

THE LIGHTHORSEMEN

An RKO Pictures–FGH Presentation. A Picture Show Production. THE LIGHTHORSEMEN. © 1987 International Film Management Limited. *Budget:* $10.5 million. *Locations:* Hawker and Port Lincoln (South Australia); Corryong, Geelong and Melbourne (Victoria). *Filmed:* September–October 1986. *Australian distributor:* Hoyts. *Opened:* 10 September 1987. *Video:* RCA–Columbia–Hoyts. *Rating:* PG (August 1987; 3586m). 35mm. Panavision. 131 mins.

Producers: Ian Jones, Simon Wincer. *Executive producer:* Antony I. Ginnane. *Associate producers:* Jan Bladier, David Lee. *Scriptwriter:* Ian Jones. *Director of photography:* Dean Semler. *Camera operators:* Dean Semler; Ian Jones, Richard Merryman. *Production designer:* Bernard Hides. *Costume designer:* David Rowe. *Supervising editor:* Adrian Carr. *Editors:* Adrian Carr, Peter Burgess. *Composer:* Mario Millo. *Sound recordist:* Lloyd Carrick. *Sound editors:* Peter Burgess, Craig Carter, Livia Ruzic. *Mixers:* James Currie; Phil Heywood (fx); Peter D. Smith (music).

Cast

Jon Blake (Scotty), Peter Phelps (Dave), Tony Bonner (Bourchier), Bill Kerr (Chauvel), John Walton (Tas), Gary Sweet (Frank), Tim McKenzie (Chiller), Shane Briant (Reichert), Serge Lazareff (Rankin), Sigrid Thornton (Anne), Anthony Andrews (Meinertzhagen), Nick Waters (Lighthorse Sgt.), John Larking (Station Master), John Heywood (Dave's Dad), Di O'Connor (Dave's Mum), Ralph Cotterill (Von Kressenstein), Grant Piro (Charlie), Matthew Randell (British Sgt.), Peter Douglas (Cockney Lance Corp.), Patrick Frost (Sgt. Ted Seger), Adrian Wright (Lawson), Jim Willoughby (Farrier Sgt.), Iain Strutt (Armourer Sgt.), Anne Scott-Pendlebury (Sister).

The Lighthorsemen is an account of the lead-up to an Australian Light Horse charge at Beersheba during World War II. The British, with 60,000 men, had repeatedly failed to take the Turkish town. In one hour, 800 Australian Light Horse did, with 30 fatalities. This victory remains one of the decisive moments of Australians at war and far more worthy of celebration than the failure at Gallipoli (where some Light Horse had already served). Perhaps it is the spirit of self-deprecation, which Simon Wincer's film celebrates, that finds defeat so easy to discuss and record.

When The Lighthorsemen was released, many critics derided the ninety or so minutes before the climactic charge. They suggested the story was thin, melodramatic and sentimental.

In part, the extended build-up does have elements of melodrama, but intelligently and subtly so. The Lighthorsemen owes much to the traditions of The Lives of a Bengal Lancer (Henry Hathaway, 1935) and Gunga Din (George Stevens, 1939), but whereas they are blatantly sentimental, with classic stereotypes, Wincer's film is different. (After all, how many films about man's heroism in war has a lead character who refuses to kill a man.)

True there are some awkward moments (such as the explanatory dialogue between the two Germans at the start), and the odd clichéd delivery, but Wincer generates great impact from this very reticence. Wincer also uses classic stereotypes only to a point, and allows each major character a moment to reveal the degree to which he is acting out a self-protecting rôle.

Wincer reveals this explicitly in one very moving scene, where Anne (Sigrid Thornton) is asked to write a fake letter by Meinertzhagen (Anthony Andrews) as part of an intelligence ploy. She is told to imagine she is a woman who has just given birth in London, and that she is writing to her husband stationed in Turkey whom she may never see again, and who may never see his child. A tear runs down Anne's face as she writes, for this very act of writing is forcing her to face what, in wards full of dying men, she has naturally tried to avoid.

Equally moving is the scene where Tas (a brilliant John Walton) writes a letter home the night before he is killed (earlier he has referred to his children as 'bloody kids', but behind the very flatness of delivery there is great affection). Wincer avoids all the clichés of the situation, playing it right down: Tas merely hands the letter the next morning to a mate, for him to post.

But even if critics could not be moved by such scenes, there is no explanation for their lack of acclaim for the action sequences and the stunning visual look. Wincer shoots characters and movement in a landscape better than most other Australian directors. His compositions are beautiful without being obvious, his camera work always elegant and his editing crisp. He also understands the uses of individual lenses and the effects cutting between can do. In terms of confident use of craft, his only Australian equal is George Miller.

SCOTT MURRAY

References

'Getting Set to Raise the Hackles in Hawker', an uncredited article, *Cinema Papers*, no. 60, November 1986, pp. 36–7.

'The Lighthorsemen', a review by Brian Courtis, *Cinema Papers*, no. 66, November 1987, pp. 40–1.

'Simon Wincer: Trusting His Instincts', an interview with the director by Scott Murray, *Cinema Papers*, no. 76, November 1989, pp. 6–12, 78–9.

Scotty (Jon Blake), Tas (John Walton), Chiller (Tim McKenzie) and Dave (Peter Phelps).

K E N   C A M E R O N

PETER KENNA'S THE UMBRELLA WOMAN

Laughing Kookaburra Productions in association with Michael Nolan presents Peter Kenna's THE UMBRELLA WOMAN. *Alternative title:* Peter Kenna's The Good Wife (US and UK). © 1986 Laughing Kookaburra Productions. Produced with the assistance of the Australian Film Commission. *Location:* Bowraville (New South Wales). *Australian distributor:* Roadshow. *Opened:* 14 May 1987. *Video:* Premier. *Rating:* M (March 1987; 2605.85m). 35mm. 95 mins.

Producer: Jan Sharp. *Associate producer:* Helen Watts. *Scriptwriter:* Peter Kenna. *Director of photography:* James Bartle. *Camera operator:* Peter Menzies. *Production designer:* Sally Campbell. *Costume designer:* Jennie Tate. *Editor:* John Scott. *Composer:* Cameron Allan. *Sound recordist:* Ben Osmo. *Sound editors:* Liz Goldfinch (dia.); Annie Breslin (fx); Steve Burgess (foley). *Mixer:* Roger Savage.

Cast

Rachel Ward (Marge Hills), Bryan Brown (Sonny Hills), Steven Vidler (Sugar Hills), Sam Neill (Neville Gifford), Jennifer Claire (Daisy), Bruce Barry (Archie), Peter Cummins (Ned), Carole Skinner (Mrs Gibson), Clarissa Kaye-Mason (Mrs Jackson), Barry Hill (Mr Fielding), Susan Lyons (Mrs Fielding), Helen Jones (Rosia), Lisa Hensley (Sylvia), May Howlett (Mrs Carmichael), Maureen Green (Sal), Garry Cook (Gerry), Harold Kissin (Davis, Station Master), Oliver Hall (Mick Jones), Sue Ingleton (Rita), Robert Barrett (Heckler at Bar).

In an important essay on personal relationships and sexuality, Meaghan Morris comments:

> ...Australian cinema could scarcely be accused of promoting the virtues of life-long love and marriage. There is little or no glorification of full-blown romantic love, for example, and none of the heightened respect for the eternal drama of the couple that defines the themes of so much European and American cinema. Instead, there is a fascination with group behaviour, and with relationships seen in the context of social institutions.[1]

There is no grimmer or more salutary demonstration of this prevalent dramatic attitude than **Peter Kenna's The Umbrella Woman**.

It is a widely misunderstood and underrated film. Perhaps its makers started out consciously with the humanist piety to which David Stratton reduces it: 'Even if you find

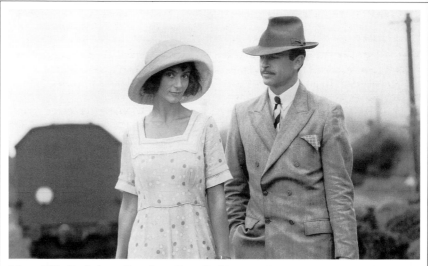
Marge Hills (Rachel Ward) and Neville Gifford (Sam Neill).

out what you want most in life, you cannot always get it.'[2] Yet this story of the unquenchably frustrated Marge Hills (Rachel Ward) pursuing a number of disastrous relationships with a succession of variously unsatisfying men—husband Sonny (Bryan Brown), his brother Sugar (Steven Vidler) and erotic vagabond Neville Gifford (Sam Neill)—paints a much darker, because utterly social, picture of the relations that pertain between men and women.

The film rigorously traces the social conditions that constrain, stultify and pervert a woman's sexual and romantic drives. From the opening crosscut montage, society is shown as completely segregated according to gender: Marge performs as solitary midwife while Sonny fells trees and engages in hostile camaraderie with his mates. Corresponding to the available conformist gender rôles are starkly circumscribed social spaces, such as the 'Ladies Parlour' in the local pub. In the no-less socialised internal, psychological landscape of the characters, the woman is always cast in an impossible position: to her husband she must be a 'good', obedient wife; to his brother a selfless sexual tutor; to the vagrant misogynist an unsentimental whore. Even Marge finds herself disgusted by the 'unladylike', openly libidinal behaviour of her mother. After leaving her husband, experiencing brutal rejection from her lover, and dragging herself back to home and her 'proper' rôle, Marge is of course left, in the final shots, still longing hopelessly for release.

In *The Imaginary Industry*, Elizabeth Jacka yokes the film to her (and Susan Dermody's) polemic against the so-called 'AFC-genre', citing it as a late, hangover ex-

ample of a project 'rendered bland, flat and unconvincing by the conventions of the AFC-genre', in which 'the film-makers opt for a literal AFC-genre style of attack[3]. This account of the film is hard to sustain. A typical scene, intercutting one of Neville's casual sex encounters with Marge's lonely, dreamy gaze (as if she were seeing, or even conjuring, the former), is anything but 'literal'; Ken Cameron's direction throughout is heightened and intense, suffused with the complex drives that are the film's subject.

Peter Kenna's The Umbrella Woman does not deserve its composite reputation as a conservative, conventional, bland 'costume drama' in the style of some Australian films of the 1970s; it is a corrosive, despairing, highly 'materialist' portrayal of certain values underlying Australian life.

ADRIAN MARTIN

---

[1] Meaghan Morris, 'Personal Relationships and Sexuality', *The New Australian Cinema*, Scott Murray (ed.), Thomas Nelson and Cinema Papers, Melbourne, 1980, p. 135.

[2] David Stratton, *The Avocado Plantation: Boom and Bust in the Australian Film Industry*, Macmillan, Sydney, 1990, p. 160.

[3] *The Imaginary Industry: Australian Film in the Late '80s*, Susan Dermody and Elizabeth Jacka (eds), AFTRS Publications, Sydney, 1988, pp. 83, 85.

References

'The Umbrella Woman [sic]', a review by Christina Thompson, *Cinema Papers*, no. 63, May 1987, pp. 54–5.

'Cameron Allan: What's the Score?', an interview with the composer by Felicity Fox, *Cinema Papers*, no. 69, May 1988, pp. 16–17.

THE PLACE AT THE COAST

The NSWFC & Daedalus II present The Place at the Coast. *Alternative title:* 'The Bee-Eater' (working). © 1986 Daedalus II Films Pty Ltd and NSWFC. *Location:* New South Wales Coast. *Australian distributor:* Ronin. *Opened:* 18 September 1987. *Video:* First Release. *Rating:* PG (June 1987; 2550.99m). 35mm. 92.5 mins.

Producer: Hilary Furlong. *Scriptwriter:* Hilary Furlong. Based on the novel by Jane Hyde. *Director of photography:* Jeff Darling. *Production designer:* Owen Paterson. *Costume designer:* Anna French. *Editor:* Nicholas Beauman. *Composer:* Chris Neal. *Sound recordist:* Phil Stirling. *Sound editors:* Tim Jordan, Anne Breslin, Karin Whittington, David Rae. *Mixer:* Phil Heywood.

Cast

John Hargreaves (Neil McAdam), Tushka Bergen (Ellie McAdam), Aileen Britton (Gran), Willie Fennell (Fred Ryan), Michele Fawdon (Aunt Helen), Julie Hamilton (Enid Burroughs), Sue Ingleton (Nan Montgomery), Margo Lee (May Ryan), Garry McDonald (Dan Burroughs), Ray Meagher (Uncle Doug), Brendon Lunney (Seymour Steele), Dora Batt (Marnie), Kate Beattie (Young Ellie), Beverley Bergen (Mum), Heather Mitchell (Margot Ryan), Rod Zuanic ("King"), Emily Crook (Julie Montgomery), Alexander Broun (Bob Montgomery), Lillian Crombie (Mrs Lundy).

Teenager Ellie McAdam (Tushka Bergen) and her father, Neil (John Hargreaves), take their long Christmas holiday at their house on the coast. On the way, the memory of Ellie's mother's death in a car accident is relived.

Once there, while looking forward to the solitude ('Six whole weeks with just us', she exclaims), Ellie renews her acquaintance with several of the local families. Her father, though, is stand-offish and prefers to spend time fishing with just one of them, the eccentric Dan Burroughs (Garry McDonald) whose wife, Enid (Julie Hamilton), runs the general store and tends for the most part to be a comic ditherer.

Over the summer, developments slowly emerge. Ellie learns of a motel development that she feels will threaten the ecology of the area. She is also threatened by the slowly blossoming romance between her father and Margot Ryan (Heather Mitchell), the daughter of one of the locals, who has returned from overseas to visit her family. Somewhat slowly all these matters resolve themselves over the course of the summer, Ellie and her father leaving with her slowly coming to terms with the prospect of her father's re-marrying and the development remaining a vague threat.

This somewhat meagre plot is the background to a character study of the kind that flourished in the Australian cinema for a short time. It was a style of film-making that rarely found favour with the public and most of the films of this kind, including this one, were box-office failures. The carefully studied creation of atmosphere of beach and forest, the somewhat laborious creation of character and the less-than-diverting eccentricities some of the supporting characters evince are all evidence of a method of film-making that takes as its model the most refined (and dull) practices of the British BBC model.

As well, George Ogilvie, in his second solo work as a feature director[1], employs a camera that relentlessly tracks its characters at a discreet distance, slowly moving around inside the ramshackle house, peering out from darkened interiors and discovering characters only after some time is spent tracking. It is slow and tidy, and rather too predictable.

There are, though, some effective moments. The scene when Ellie is brought home suspiciously late crackles with shifting tension between the characters as their sympathies and antipathies change during the course of the confrontation, perhaps because there is some editing to match the flow of the words rather than a slow track into medium shot. But this is too rare a moment, and it ends with a slow track, in a film which seems to take a very long time to tell a very short story. The supposed virtues of good taste and the display of delicate sensibilities are not enough to save the film from tedium.

GEOFF GARDNER

---

[1] George Ogilvie had previously co-directed with George Miller **Mad Max Beyond Thunderdome** (1985) and, by himself, **Short Changed** (1986).

References
'The Place at the Coast', a review by Melinda Houston, *Cinema Papers*, no. 65, September 1987, pp. 44–5.
'The Place at the Coast', an unsigned [Shelley Kay?] review, *Filmnews*, October 1987, p. 13.

Neil McAdam (John Hargreaves), Margot Ryan (Heather Mitchell) and Ellie McAdam (Tushka Bergen).

DI DREW

THE RIGHT HAND MAN

Lord Harry Ironminster (Rupert Everett) and fiancée Sarah Redbridge (Catherine McClements).

UAA presents a Yarraman Film Production. THE RIGHT HAND MAN. © 1986 UAA (Australasia) Limited. *Budget:* $5.5 million. *Location:* Bathurst (New South Wales). *Australian distributor:* GUO. *Opened:* 21 November 1987. *Video:* Hoyts Polygram Video. *Rating:* M. 35mm. Panavision. 97 mins.

Producers: Steven Grives, Tom Oliver, Basil Appleby. *Executive producer:* David Thomas. *Scriptwriter:* Helen Hodgman. Based on the novel by Kathleen Peyton. Story developed by Steven Grives. *Director of photography:* Peter James. *Camera operator:* Danny Batterham. *Production designer:* Neil Angwin. *Costume designer:* Graham Purcell. *Editor:* Don Saunders. *Composer:* Allan Zavod. *Sound recordist:* Syd Butterworth. *Sound editors:* Stephanie Flack (dia.); Phil Heywood (fx); Ron Purvis (music). *Mixer:* Peter Fenton.

Cast

Rupert Everett (Lord Harry Ironminster), Hugo Weaving (Ned Devine), Arthur Dignam (Dr Redbridge), Jennifer Claire (Lady Ironminster), Catherine McClements (Sarah Redbridge), Ralph Cotterill (Sam), Adam Cockburn (Violet Head), Tim Elliott (Lord Ironminster), Jack Allen (Shopkeeper), John Spicer (Publican), Brian

Scrymgeour (Yard Boss), Les Ash (1st Postilion), Tamas Szegedi (2nd Postilion), Tony Ash (Black Coach Driver), Bruce Stewart (Minister), Anna Lee (Worn Woman), Syd Smith (Local), Keith Smith (Sickly Man); Pat Bishop, Amy Blanchard.

One of the handful of Australian films made under 10BA for the Perth-based production company UAA (as distinct from its tax-funded investment in overseas productions), Di Drew's dark costume drama stars elegant Englishman Rupert Everett, quite appropriately, as Lord Harry Ironminster, the aristocratic scion of a well-to-do squatter in 19th-century New South Wales.

The bleak story, adapted for the screen by Helen Hodgman from a novel by Kathleen Peyton, has Lord Harry, semi-invalid son of a rural grandee, responsible for his father's death in a coaching accident which also costs him his right arm. Guilt-stricken Harry lapses into ever-deeper melancholy because he can no longer ride the horses that have been his chief interest. Then he employs saturnine tearaway Ned Devine (Hugo Weaving), former driver of a giant coach called the Leviathan that roars symbolically through the nearby bush at night. Ned, literally, becomes the languish-

ing young master's right-hand man, even bedding the boss' fiancée, Sarah Redbridge (Catherine McClements), at his request. When she becomes pregnant, Harry decides it's time to go—as had many members of the audience during the film's sparse commercial season.

An intensely atmospheric and good-looking film (Peter James took the 1986 AFI Best Cinematography award and Neil Angwin's production design was highly praised), **The Right Hand Man** seemed almost out of place in the 1980s, its high-camp melodrama belonging more to the 1940s and British films like Leslie Arliss' **The Man in Grey** (1943).

Some of the most dramatic scenes seem to come from that era, too. But few Australian films have captured more effective images than the shots of the thundering, swaying coach, implying an apocalyptic significance that the story signally fails to deliver.

KEITH CONNOLLY

References
'Sticking to the Ley-lines', an uncredited article about the film's period design, *Cinema Papers*, no. 55, January 1986, p. 44.
'Right Hand Man [sic]', a short review by Adrienne McKibbins, *Filmnews*, December 1987, p. 16.

RUNNING FROM THE GUNS

The Burrowes Film Group presents RUN-NING FROM THE GUNS. *Alternative title:* 'Free Enterprise' (working). © 1987 The Burrowes Film Group. *Budget:* $6.6 million. *Location:* Docklands, Port Melbourne. *Australian distributor:* Hoyts. *Opened:* 16 September 1987. *Video:* Hoyts–Columbia–RCA. *Rating:* M (September 1987; 2386.41m). 35mm. 87 mins.

Producer: Geoff Burrowes. *Executive producers:* Dennis Wright, Kent Lovell. *Scriptwriter:* John Dixon. *Director of photography:* Keith Wagstaff. *Camera operator:* John Haddy. *Production designer:* Leslie Binns. *Wardrobe supervisor:* Jenny Arnott. *Editor:* Ray Daley. *Composer:* Bruce Rowland. *Sound recordist:* John Schiefelbein. *Sound supervisor:* Terry Rodman. *Sound editors:* Gary Woodyard, Tim Chau. *Sound mixers:* James Currie, David Harrison, Peter Smith.

Cast

Jon Blake (Davie), Mark Hembrow (Peter), Nikki Coghill (Jill), Terence Donovan (Bangles), Peter Whitford (Terry), Patrick Ward (Mulcahy), Warwick Sims (Simon Martin), Bill Kerr (Gilman), Gerard Kennedy (Big Jim), Toni Lamond (Davie's Mum), Gus Mercurio (Chazza), Ken Snodgrass (Ocker), Nick Waters (Raeburn), David Bickerstaff (Cranston), Greg Ross (Mallard), Barry Hill (Sir Julian), Delilah (Marathon Mandy), Susan Lee Masterton (Madame), Ben Michaels (Spanner), Ray Rivamonte (Muppet).

Davie (Jon Blake) and Peter (Mark Hembrow) are two likely lads who run a car repair shop in the industrial part of Port Melbourne. They are working-class boys of the type Australian cinema regularly tries to lionise, as if in their larrikin approach to life they epitomise true Aussie maleness. They may love hot cars, like to bend the law a little and even carry unlicensed guns, but they are always nice to mum and have a highly defined sense of mateship.

On the look-out for a good deal, Davie and Peter purchase some toys from a bankrupt firm in Taiwan, but at the docks their container is switched for another, by Bangles (Terence Donovan), and they end up with a load of koalas (or 'bears', Peter calls them). When Bangles tries to have his hoons take possession of the container, they lose out in a spectacular car crash. Negotiation with the container's real owner proves even more difficult and Bangles find himself out of his league (ending up a charred corpse).

Likely lads: Davie (Jon Blake) and Peter (Mark Hembrow).

Davie and Peter manage to escape many close shaves (one by having Peter drive a diesel engine into a warehouse hide-out of some crims where blow-torch is the preferred method of torture), and there are many car chases. They are joined in their adventures by Jill (Nikki Coghill), who works for a federal crime commission, and seems to be the one honest person there.

The film portrays society as totally corrupt, from the small-time crim who works the pub with goods off the back of a truck to one of Australia's most powerful companies (Auspac) running an enormous criminal network. The infiltration by Auspac's tentacles is staggering: they seem to have cars instantly ready for tailing on all major roads, and, when Jill and Peter leave her office at the crime commission, they can travel only a couple of floors in the lift before being apprehended by disguised bad guys. Does this mean Auspac has suitably attired associates at the ready in every key building in Melbourne?

Against these forces of corporate evil rise up the working class (referred to as 'grubby little workers' by the crime boss), and its waterside union. But even if the union does

finally come to the aid of the good guys, the film-maker sends it up by having its members storm Auspac's offices with such 'timely' placards as 'Out of Korea'.

Even though caricature is the order of the day, the way director John Dixon represents the wealthy is the most ludicrous. Almost without exception in Australian cinema, the powerful and titled are absurdly caricatured, inappropriately cast.

But the biggest problem viewers of **Running from the Guns** face is the lack of tension or excitement in the many action sequences. The first (on the docks) is ruined, despite some good stunts, by Dixon's silly portrayal of the hoons; the lengthy car chase down the Great Ocean Road has no drama; and the shoot-out at the end resorts to the most desperate of editing tricks—cutting frames out of the middle of a shot—to speed things along.

SCOTT MURRAY

Reference

'**Running from the Guns**', a review by Melinda Houston, *Cinema Papers*, no. 66, November 1987, p. 41.

SLATE WYN & ME

Hemdale Film Corporation presents An FGH Presentation for International Film Management [of] An Ukiyo Films Production. Slate Wyn & Me. © 1987 International Film Management Limited. Script developed with the assistance of Film Victoria. *Location:* Swan Hill and environs (Victoria). *Australian distributor:* Filmpac. *Video:* Vestron Video International. *Rating:* M (April 1987; 2386.41m[1]). 35mm. Panavision. 87 mins.

Producer: Tom Burstall. *Executive producers:* Antony I. Ginnane, William Fayman. *Line producer:* Brian D. Burgess. *Scriptwriter:* Don McLennan. Based on the novel *Slate & Wyn and Blanche McBride* by Georgia Savage. *Director of photography:* David Connell. *Production designer:* Paddy Reardon. *Costume designer:* Jeanie Cameron. *Editor:* Zbigniew Friedrich. *Composers:* Trevor Lucas, Ian Mason. *Sound recordist:* Andrew Ramage. *Sound editor:* Zbigniew Friedrich. *Mixer:* Bruce Emery.

Cast

Sigrid Thornton (Blanche), Simon Burke (Wyn), Martin Sacks (Slate), Tommy Lewis (Morgan), Lesley Baker (Molly), Harold Baigent (Sammy), Michelle Torres (Daphne), Murray Fahey (Martin), Taya Straton (Pippa), Julia MacDougall (Del Downer), Peter Cummins (Old Man Downer), Reg Gorman (Wilkinson), Warren Owens (Tommy); Eric McPhan, Simon Westaway (Policemen); Kurt Von Schneider (Truck Driver).

Slate (charismatically played by Martin Sacks) and Wyn (Simon Burke) are the Jackson[2] brothers, in the tradition of, but without the popular mystique of, the Kellys.

Slate is a Vietnam veteran with danger on his mind and a chip on his shoulder. Equipped with a pair of mean 1960s sideburns, Slate is a bit of a rough diamond in the sleepy hollow of Mowbray. This isn't small-town America but it might as well be: the boys skol beer at the local dance and the girls mooch around them in smart frocks. Only the fairy lights lend it Aussie nostalgia.

Wyn is the typical younger brother: thicker in flesh and mind, he reveres Slate, who has seen action he could only dream of and who knows how to chase it. When Slate suggests ripping off the local bank, Wyn's in like Flynn.

The hold-up is interrupted by the local inspector. Wyn panics, his gun goes off and the thrill seekers turn fugitive. But there's a witness, Blanche (Sigrid Thornton), and so the boys chuck her in the boot and head north.

Thornton seems endlessly destined to play the well-heeled horse-riding type who redeems herself by virtue of her fiery independence. As Blanche, she competently moves from pristine school marm to whisky-swilling co-rebel as the boys promote her from kicked-around to sidekick.

Switching Wyn's fab red Valiant for the all-time fantasy car—a blue-finned convertible which is handily waiting in the outback to be stolen—the trio trek along endless dirt tracks, beside endless rivers and through endless campsites. This allows for lots of gorgeous sunsets and meaningful looks over flickering camp fires.

As Blanche becomes increasingly more beautiful and matey, there is cause for the only tension apparent in the film. The big worry is who gets Blanche and how the other brother deals with it. With her perfect pout and a deft little manipulative touch, she crushes the mateship bond between two men who only had each other. Isn't that just like a woman?

Every turn of the plot runs true to course: the switching allegiances, the tension of isolation, the adrenalin of the open road, a tale of basically sweet boys who inadvertently treat the law the way fortune has treated them and find themselves on a one-way highway straight to hell.

Along the predictable road of events are various illogical and unconvincing turns, including Wyn's panic-less shooting of a cop, a moment dependent on convincing terror and around which the whole plot turns.

Don McLennan's script is often laboured and occasionally banal, given to patchy delivery and providing little complexity for the actors to sink their teeth into. It is not really anybody's story, although the title (reworked from Georgia Savage's novel on which the film is based) suggests it belongs to Blanche.

Despite all this, **Slate Wyn & Me** is curiously enjoyable, saved by some hard-to-define, low-key, sardonic self-mockery.

JOANNA MURRAY-SMITH[3]

---

[1] *Monthly Film Bulletin* gives the length at 2501m (8207 ft), or 91 mins.
[2] There is no mention of 'Jackson' in the credits, but the name is used throughout the film and is spelt thus in the press material.
[3] Extracted from Murray-Smith's review in *Cinema Papers* (see References).

References

'Slate, Wyn and Me [sic]', a review by Joanna Murray-Smith, *Cinema Papers*, no. 65, September 1987, pp. 53–4.
'Don McLennan', an interview with the director by Rod Bishop, *Cinema Papers*, no. 77, January 1990, pp. 22–7.

Blanche (Sigrid Thornton) slugs Wyn (Simon Burke).

THOSE DEAR DEPARTED

Phillip Emanuel·presents THOSE DEAR DEPARTED. © 1987 Phillip Emanuel Productions Limited. Script developed with the assistance of the Australian Film Commission. *Location:* Sydney. *Australian distributor:* Roadshow. *Opened:* 13 August 1987. *Video:* Premiere. *Rating:* M (August 1987; reduced version 2397m). 35mm. 88 mins.

Producer: Phillip Emanuel. *Associate producers:* Barbara Gibbs, Ted Robinson. *Scriptwriter:* Steve J. Spears. *Director of photography:* David Burr. *Production designer:* Roger Ford. [*Costume designer:* not credited.] *Editor:* Robert Gibson. *Composer:* Phillip Scott. *Sound recordists:* Phil Keros, Mark Lewis. *Sound editor:* Helen Brown. *Mixers:* Ian McLoughlin, Phil Judd.

Cast

Garry McDonald (Max Falcon), Pamela Stephenson (Marilyn Falcon), Su Cruickshank (Norda), Marian Dworakowski (Richard), Ritchie Singer (Gordon), John Clarke (Jerry—the Inspector), Jonathon Biggins (Steve—the Sergeant), Arthur Dignam (Producer), Ignatius Jones (Phil), Antonia Murphy (Phoebe), Connie Hobbs (Ruth), Peter Pedachini (Milton Shaver), Peter Rowley (Prophet), Graeme Blundell (Dr Howie[1]), Benjamin Griffith (Tiny Max), Patrick Cook (Stage Manager), Vicki Bonnet (Angel), Len Peihopa (Reg), Maureen O'Shaughnessy (Bronwyn), Steve J. Spears (Dangerman), George Pollock (Rabbi), Frank Lloyd (Catholic Priest), Geoff Kelso (Man in Transit Lounge), Jozef Drewiak (Freud).

It would be fair to say that the makers of this film were attempting to produce a black comedy. But in no way have they succeeded, which is a pity because the plot has much potential.

Marilyn Falcon (Pamela Stephenson) is the beautiful but scheming wife of a 'well-known stage and screen actor', Max Falcon (Garry McDonald), who is starring in a show called *Freud—The Musical*. While her unsuspecting husband is singing and dancing his heart out, Marilyn is in the midst of a steamy affaire with the family chauffeur and a well-known 'European poet', Richard (Marian Dworakowski). Together, they are also plotting Max's murder. All this Marilyn tells us right from the start when she 'confesses', after most of the events have taken place, into a tape recorder.

As her narration continues, we learn that after numerous, but rather lame, attempts she finally succeeds in killing Max. In the process, she also manages to 'murder' Max's big-hearted, Mother-Earthish agent, Norda (Su Cruickshank)—by accident; Phil (Ignatius Jones) and Phoebe (Antonia Murphy), Max's co-stars—because they were going to tell the police she killed her husband; Richard, who is forced into committing suicide—because of the situation she led him into; and the two policemen, Jerry (John Clarke) and Steve (Jonathon Biggins)—who are after her. Correction: Marilyn actually kills Jerry when she comes back in her next life as none other than a dog.

The main gag of this homicidal fiasco is that each person comes back to haunt Marilyn after going to a special 'mid-way' audition to Heaven and discovering that they still have some unfinished business back on earth: that is, to make Marilyn confess and eventually bring her back with them.

This should have provided a fertile ground for a very black comedy and, were it in the hands of someone like Michael Lehmann (**Heathers**, 1989; **Meet the Applegates**, 1991; **Hudson Hawk**, 1991), it might have done so. Unfortunately, it's not funny; it's sad, because so many people are trying so hard and ending up with a film that falls totally apart.

For example, the (deliberately) jagged editing, particularly in the first third, acts against, rather than with, the film, continually disorienting and unnerving the viewer. The dialogue is not great, but bearable, made less so by the over-the-top histrionics of the actors. Why do they need to grimace (Garry McDonald, Su Cruickshank, Marian Dworakowski) and pout (Pamela Stephenson) so much? Do they and the director really think it funny?

As for *Freud—The Musical*, the idea is funny, a clever comment on our society's weird trend to enjoy gaudy musical productions of just about anything famous or infamous. But does the film have to show quite so much of this loud and annoying farce? We get the point after only one scene.

Those Dear Departed is ultimately one of those unfortunate Australian attempts at a witty comedy that ends up being neither a comedy nor even a film of interest.

ANNA GUL

---

[1] On the opening credits Blundell's character is called 'The Psychiatrist'.

Marilyn Falcon (Pamela Stephenson) and husband Max (Garry McDonald).

THE TIME GUARDIAN

Hemdale Film Corporation presents An FGH Presentation for International Film Management Ltd and Chateau Productions Investments. THE TIME GUARDIAN. © 1987 International Film Management Ltd. *Budget:* $8 million. *Locations:* Port Adelaide, Adelaide. *Australian distributor:* Filmpac. *Video:* Filmpac. *Rating:* PG (September 1987; 2386.41m). 35mm. 87 mins.

Producers: Norman Wilkinson, Robert Lagettie. *Co-producer:* Harley Manners. *Executive producer:* Antony I. Ginnane. *Scriptwriters:* John Baxter, Brian Hannant. *Director of photography:* Geoff Burton. *Camera operator:* David Foreman. *Production designer:* George Liddle. *Costume supervisor:* Jean Turnball. *Editor:* A. J. Prowse. *Composer:* Allan Zavod. *Sound recordist:* Toivo Lember. *Supervising sound editor:* Frank Lipson. *Sound editors:* Steve Lambeth, Glenn Martin (fx); Andrew Plain (dia.). *Mixer:* James Currie (chief); Bruce Lamshed (fx); Peter Smith (music).

Cast

Tom Burlinson (Ballard), Nikki Coghill (Annie), Dean Stockwell (Boss), Carrie Fisher (Petra), Peter Merrill (Zuryk), Tim Robertson (McCarthy), Jim Holt (Rafferty), Wan Thye Liew (Sun-Wah), Damon Sanders (Smith), Tom Karpanny (Tracker), Henry Salter (Prenzler), Peter Healy (Wayne), Adrian Shirley (Counihan), Don Barker (Undertaker), Terry Crawford (Tucker), Micheale D. Read (Snowy), Jo Fleming (Wounded Jen-Diki), Bernard David (Danny), John Clark (Didgeridoo Player), Ray Kearns (Warrior), Jimmy James (Stick Clapper), Kirk Alexander (Narrator).

Time guardian: Ballard (Tom Burlinson).

The Time Guardian, Australia's first attempt at high-technology science fiction, is one of those unfortunate formula films betrayed by a serious misunderstanding of the genre. It follows the typical 'adventure film' graph: a battle in the first five minutes, a handsome hero who meets a beautiful girl, wretched villains and a fight for survival against time. But it neglects the more fundamental concerns of a plausible plot, character-defining dialogue, convincing acting and coherent direction.

The opening voice-over and titles tells us that, in the aftermath of global nuclear destruction in the 24th century, one city survives by learning to travel through time. It is pursued by the villainous Jen-Diki, a race of cyborgs (part human, part machine) who, having no home of their own, are bent upon ransacking the City.

In the penultimate battle, Ballard (Tom Burlinson), the stoical macho hero, is forced to blow up one of the City's legs (it is has four). It cannot land in the next era, so Ballard and Petra (Carrie Fisher) are sent as the advance guard to build a mound of rocks for the City to land on. They are beamed into a pond near an outback town called Midas where they are immediately befriended by Aboriginal men doing a corroboree, then attacked by the Jen-Diki, who have followed them. Somehow they destroy the Jen-Diki time-travel device.

Petra is wounded in the battle but Ballard finds female companionship with a beautiful geologist, Annie (Nikki Coghill). Ballard and Annie then escape to where the City has landed. But despite having surrendered thei time-travel device, Jen-Diki appear from every nook and cranny, besieging the City in the final showdown.

Science fiction, like any other form of narrative cinema, must establish an internal consistency in its logic to keep the audience satisfied. A problem with **The Time Guardian** is that its plot devices lack subtlety or coherent integration into the dramatic structure. The film also has an unfortunate tendency to substitute confusion for intrigue. This is partly due to Brian Hannant's direction. Not enough attention is given to important plot points and too much time is wasted on red herrings.[1]

The actors would have been better off if they had not taken their dialogue so seriously. Tom Burlinson, determined to break out of the 'cute' mould, snarls at everyone indiscriminately but has problems finding a further dimension. Nikki Coghill is competent, says her lines with a smile, but has the sincerity and conviction of a *Vogue* cover. The only areas which come away unscathed are technical ones such as the photography, the special effects, make-up and sound.

TONY AYRES[2]

[1] The film was recut and partially reshot after Brian Hannant left the film. He disowns much of what is left.

[2] Extracted from Ayres' review in *Cinema Papers* (see Reference).

Reference
'The Time Guardian', a review by Tony Ayres, *Cinema Papers*, no. 67, January 1988, p. 44.

TO MARKET TO MARKET

Goosey Limited presents TO MARKET [/] TO MARKET. © 1987 Goosey Limited. Produced with the assistance of Film Victoria and the Australian Film Commission. *Location:* Melbourne. *Australian distributor:* Goosey Limited. *Video:* not released. *Rating:* M. 35mm. 88 mins.

Producer: Virginia Rouse. *Associate producer:* Trish Carney. *Scriptwriter:* Virginia Rouse. *Director of photography:* Jaems Grant. *Production designer:* Virginia Rouse. *Wardrobe:* Michele Leonard. *Editor:* Tony Paterson. *Music consultant:* Erwin Rado. *Sound recordist:* Laurie Robinson. *Sound editors:* Tony Paterson, Mark Atkin. *Mixer:* James Currie.

Cast

Philip Quast (Edward), Maureen Edwards (Valerie), Noel Trevarthan (William Senior), Kate Reid (Jackie), Tony Llewellyn-Jones (Richard), Genevieve Picot (Suzanna), Wayne Cull (William), Fincina Hopgood (Finci), Derek Yuen (Farid), Philippa Griffin (Edward aged 10 months), Marcus Gollings (Edward aged 13), Paul Morris (William aged 14 years), Natalie Kemp (Suzanna aged 14), Lucy Sherman (Friend), James Brook (Moore), Douglas Brook (Soclest), Justin Newman (Kelly), Andrew Gough (Paterson), Paul Cox (Mortician), Danielle Kemp (Nanny).

Edward aged 13 (Marcus Gollings), right, with mother Valerie (Maureen Edwards).

Virginia Rouse's **To Market To Market** is one of the blackest views of family life ever seen in this country. This is not rich melodrama about family turmoil (à la Ray Lawler), but a minimalist and chilling look at the subtle power games family members use to manipulate and destroy others.

The film opens with a baby suspended over a table by someone in shadow; the film ends with a puppet child climbing a ladder, before floating in space, free. **To Market To Market** is the story of a boy/man's journey to that freedom, which comes from his leaving a family he has fought so hard to be part of. The irony is that it is the sinister machinations of his sister and brother that ensure his departure, not self-will.

The film is divided into two parts. The first, set in Melbourne in 1965, concerns 13-year-old Edward (Marcus Gollings) who yearns to be close to his parvenu-ish mother (a shop assistant married into titled society). His father is a stern disciplinarian who even insists Edward practise bowel control by breaking each stool into at least four pieces while defecating. Nothing can save him from paternal contempt, or from the sinister sibling games.

At a draconian private boarding school, Edward fares a little better—until, that is, a much discriminated-against Chinese boy Edward has helped 'acclimatise' to school life hangs himself (after climbing a ladder which prefigures the one in the end sequence). There are also suggestions, here and elsewhere, of auto-erotic asphyxiation, but, like many intriguing aspects of the film, they are not specifically resolved.

The narrative then jumps 22 years to 1987. Edward (Philip Quast) is a very successful lawyer in his father's firm, but he is no closer to either parent. Sister Suzanna (Genevieve Picot) and brother William (Wayne Cull) tolerate him only in so far as they can use him. For William, that means forcing his brother into making an illegal (and vaguely described) cash transfer to Hong Kong, which instigates a police investigation.

It is Edward's parents' belief that he is responsible (William and Suzanna, who have a disturbing sexual ambience together, say it is all Edward's fault). As the reputation of the family firm has been besmirched, Edward must go, but he beats them to the punch by resigning—from the firm and the family, after having taken one last, calm look around the family home, a barren space with no evidence of human habitation (a stylistic of the living and work areas in the film: bare walls, bare tables, all clean and sterile).

Rouse shares Jocelyn Moorhouse's interest in appalling women: the mother and sister are as cruel and frustrated as Celia (Genevieve Picot) in **Proof** (1991); the only other character, Jackie (Kate Reid), Edward's sort of girlfriend, is a target for petty feminine wiles.

The men aren't much chop, either, though Edward remains vaguely sympathetic throughout. The big problem is Rouse's inability to convince one that the principled Edward would do so corrupt a deed for his slimy brother, no matter how much he desires filial acceptance.

The film is also let down by a too-measured slow pace, an acting standard in places more reminiscent of a student film, the odd indulgence (Kate's dancing), lighting that is far too murky and a lack of narrative drive, especially in the vignette-structured first part.

Still, this is a film with a definite and bold perspective, a commitment to personal cinema outside genre codings, based on a script full of ideas and originality.

SCOTT MURRAY

CARL   SCHULTZ

TRAVELLING NORTH

Ben Gannon presents TRAVELLING NORTH. © 1986 View Pictures Limited. *Budget:* $2.5 million. *Locations:* Melbourne; Port Douglas (Queensland). *Australian distributor:* CEL. *Opened:* 19 June 1987. *Video:* CEL. *Rating:* PG (January 1987; 2633.28m). 35mm. 96 mins.

Producer: Ben Gannon. *Scriptwriter:* David Williamson. Based on the play by David Williamson. *Director of photography:* Julian Penney. *Production designer:* Owen Patterson. *Costume designer:* Jennie Tate. *Editor:* Henry Dangar. *Music co-ordinator:* Alan John. *Sound recordist:* Syd Butterworth. *Sound editors:* Karin Whittington (dia.); Penn Robinson (fx). *Mixer:* Julian Ellingworth.

Cast

Leo McKern (Frank), Julia Blake (Frances), Henri Szeps (Saul), Michele Fawdon (Helen), Diane Craig (Sophie), Andrea Moor (Joan), Drew Forsythe (Martin), John Gregg (Jim), Graham Kennedy (Freddy[1]), Rob Steele (Syd), John Black (Alan), Roger Oakley (Stan), Joe MacColum (Boat Owner), Nicholas Holland (Waiter), Steve Shaw (Estate Agent), Genevieve Mooy (Gallery Attendant), Beavan Wilson (Celebrant); Kym Herbert, Amy Fuller, Rebecca Fuller, Andrew McMahon, Mitchell McMahon, Jessica McMahon, Angie Thompson (Children).

The adaptation of theatre to the cinema can be dicey, one that raises a variety of problems and, predictably, a variety of comparisons. The most commonly discussed issue is that of realising a world which will not visually swamp the work's central thematic concerns. Conversely, it can be excruciating watching a film that is in essence confined to two or three locations in an attempt to retain a sense of the original.

Such problems had seemed to dog the first batch of films using David Williamson's plays as a source: **The Removalists** (Tom Jeffrey, 1975) in the former category, **Don's Party** (Bruce Beresford, 1976) in the latter. Since then Williamson's own awareness has developed considerably, along with his proliferative style. The result has seen a great improvement in filmic adaptations of his plays, often with Williamson doing the written adaptation.

Travelling North initially appears to be no exception. Under the direction of Carl Schultz, who utilises a variety of locations and creates a sense of wide open space, there is an expectation of filmic style initiated. Williamson's gallery of ambivalent characters soon puts paid to the possibility. The film is rapidly tied down by scenes reliant on dialogue to move the story along, rather than developing character and a natural flow through deployment of a visual style.

The film centres on Frank (Leo McKern) and Frances (Julia Blake) who move up north from Melbourne to spend their final years together. Their union is based on the notion of romance and civilised lifestyle. Both have left their respective families. Frances' married daughters are unhappy about their mother's 'deserting' them, as she did when they were children, while Frank's daughter sometimes hints at his estranged son and the nasty treatment he gave his first wife. Frank is not a nice person; but he tries—at least until his angina deteriorates. His relationship with Frances takes a similar dive. The term 'his' is used deliberately here to point to the film's remarkable one-sidedness. Everything is Frank. Frances loves him (he insists she spell that out), and other characters are concerned about him. But apart from Frances' love, it is difficult to ascertain any sense of her character. Is she there for the ride? Perhaps. The only other trait pertaining to Frances is her welling sense of guilt, the result of leaving her daughters.

For all this, Frances is a well-liked, attractive person. She develops friendships with the northern neighbour, Freddy[2] (Graham Kennedy, giving a performance notable for its alacrity), and Frank's doctor, Saul (Henri Szeps, in an amusingly wry role). This aside, we see no real development of the character, which is a major flaw given the film's focus on her and Frank's relationship.

Director Carl Schultz does attempt to brighten a generally gloomy script with a relatively tight pace and sense of visual expanse. But it is difficult to shake the sense that this work belongs to the stage. The issues, questions and responses are spelt out via dialogue as characters go through their motions. There is little sense of these people having an inner dimension or a particularly real life.

PETER LAWRANCE

---

[1] The front credits list Graham Kennedy's character as 'Freddie'.
[2] See footnote 1.

References
'Travelling North', a review by James Waites, *Cinema Papers*, no. 63, May 1987, pp. 59–60.
'Travelling North', a short review by Kathe Boehringer, *Filmnews*, Late July 1987, p. 12.

Sophie (Diane Craig), Helen (Michele Fawdon) and Frances (Julia Blake).

TWELFTH NIGHT

[No opening production company credit.] Twelfth NIGHT. © 1986 Twelfth Night Pty Ltd. *Budget:* $590,000. *Location:* Sydney (studio). *Australian distributor:* Greater Union. *Video:* not released. *Rating:* PG. 35 mm. 117 mins.

Producer: Don Catchlove. *Executive producer:* Tom Stacey. *Scriptwriter:* Neil Armfield. Based on the play by William Shakespeare. *Director of photography:* Louis Irving. *Production designer:* Stephen Curtis. *Costume designer:* Anthony Jones. *Editor:* Nicholas Beauman. *Composer:* Alan John. *Sound recordist:* Rob Stalder. *Sound editors:* Karen[1] Whittington, Annie Beslin, Phil Dickson. *Mixer:* Julian Ellingworth.

Cast

Gillian Jones [Viola; Sebastian; Cesario[2]], Ivar Kants [Orsino, Duke of Illyria], Jacqy Phillips [Countess Olivia], Peter Cummins [Malvolio], Kerry Walker [Feste], John Wood [Sir Toby Belch], Geoffrey Rush [Sir Andrew Aguecheek], Tracy Harvey [Maria]; Igor Sas; Stuart MacCreery [Antonio]; Russell Kiefel (Sea Captain), Jim Holt (Valentine), Paul Williams (Curio), Alan David Lee (Messenger), Odile le Clezio (Maid), Richard Healy (Police Officer), Tony Martin (Police Officer), Bob Baines (Priest), Mark McManus (Sailor), Curtis Weiss (Sailor).

P utting any stage play on the screen is hard enough, but Shakespeare, in Australia, in 1986, 400 years and 10,000 miles from home base, poses even more problems. Here is a production that does not come out unscathed in the struggle, but in some very real ways is a victor.

In the circumstances, it is hard to forget the stage production which inspired this film, a production which acknowledged the above and much more. A young director confirmed his talent, and the idiosyncratic team of actors, working together under the banner of Jim Sharman's Lighthouse Company in Adelaide, confirmed the virtue of ensemble. It was one of those rare combinations of excellent application of creative intelligence, with a wave of that rare wand called 'magic over the top'. As a record of that success, the film is valuable. But, of course, film is film also, and here Armfield makes some bold choices, though not all work as well as he might have hoped.

The wonderful setting, somewhere between the Gold Coast and Pinacoladaland, more or less survives. At least acknowledgement is made of the fact that what we see is not meant to be mistaken for the real world. Artifice itself is one of the fundamental building blocks of this play's themes; sweeping scenes of a castle by the sea would not have helped. But the price Armfield pays is, almost unavoidably, a cramped feeling.

A more particular problem has arisen out of a decision to have the twin brother and sister played by one actor, Gillian Jones. Since the sister is, for the most part, in disguise as a boy, a godlike performance of three in one is required.

Perhaps the biggest hurdle lies in the fact that Shakespeare's art is fundamentally to do with words in a three-dimensional space (a theatre). Shakespeare's audience looked with their ears. So what can a camera do: lavish its interrogating eye on these invisible sound waves flowing voluptuously out of actors' mouths? One can see Armfield has attempted to embrace the possibilities of the lens. But what is gained is unclear, and all the conceits, so delicious on stage, are lost.

Then there are the performances. There is a lot of pleasure in Ivar Kants and Jacqy Phillips playing the young royals as cool modern yuppies; John Wood, Peter Cummins, Geoffrey Rush and Tracy Harvey in some of the raciest low-life comedy you'll see in a while; and Kerry Walker on a marvellous razor's edge in the tragi-comic rôle of the wise clown, Feste. In lesser rôles, well played, are Igor Sas, Stuart McCreery and Russell Kiefel (sadly, giving over his excellent rendition of the twin brother Sebastian[3] to Gillian Jones).

This is the only significant flaw in the film; a whole homosexual sub-plot is lost, and something even of the significance of Jacqy Phillips' rendition of Olivia is undermined. But, thankfully, the audience is repaid with some glorious acting from Gillian Jones in the triple rôles of Viola, Cesario and Sebastian.

JAMES WAITES[4]

---

[1] Usually spelt 'Karin'.
[2] No character names for the principal cast are given on the film, though they are for the secondary cast. The character names printed here are taken from captioned stills.
[3] See footnote 2.
[4] Extracted from Waites' review in *Cinema Papers* (see Reference).
[5] See footnote 2.

Reference
'Twelfth Night', a review by James Waites, *Cinema Papers*, no. 64, July 1987, pp. 48–9.

Sea Captain (Russell Kiefel) and Viola[5] (Gillian Jones).

WITH LOVE TO THE PERSON NEXT TO ME

Standard Films presents WITH LOVE TO THE PERSON NEXT TO ME. © 1986 Standard Films Ltd. Produced with financial assistance from Film Victoria and the Creative Development Branch of the Australian Film Commission. *Budget:* $120,000. *Location:* Melbourne. *Australian distributor:* AFID. *Video:* AFI. *Rating:* M (October 1987; 1042m). 16mm. 98 mins.

Producer: John Cruthers. *Scriptwriter:* Brian McKenzie. *Director of photography:* Ray Argall. *Production designer:* Kerith Holmes. *Wardrobe:* Keith Holmes. *Editors:* David Greig, Ray Argall. *Sound recordist:* Mark Tarpey. *Sound editor:* Andrew Plain. *Mixer:* David Harrison.

Cast

Kim[1] Gyngell (Wallace), Sally McKenzie (Gail), Paul Chubb (Syd), Barry Dickins (Bodger), Daniel Scharf (Mechanic); Terry Gill, Peter Black (Punters in Taxi); Dallibor Satallic (European Man), Cliff Heard (Man at Show), Pat Elischer (Betty), Patsy Martin (Jean), Beverley Gardiner (Irene), Vince D'Amico (Man with Greyhound), Terry Gill (Security Guard), Simon Wilmot (Unknown Soldier); Tibor Gyapjas, Roger Stephen, Chris Hunter (Louts in Taxi); Adrian Rawlins, Geoffrey Barry (Men in Bed); Karl Price (Businessman in Taxi); Peter Sardi, Sydney Jackson, Peter Hosking, Mark Mitchell (Salesmen in Taxi); Phil Motherwell (Drunk in Taxi); Neville Stonehouse, Peter Swindon (Derelict Men).

Wallace (Kim[3] Gyngell) replays his tape recordings.

Brian McKenzie's first feature, **With Love to the Person Next to Me**, is a downbeat, grainy mood piece. It is nicely structured and shot atmospherically in well-chosen, off-beat locations: a run-down block of flats in St Kilda, the Altona power station lit up like a Christmas tree in Melbourne's western suburbs, a weatherboard hovel in one of Richmond's meaner streets. Against this background, McKenzie explores the down-at-heel world of the emotionally dispossessed with compassion, an ear and eye for accuracy, and no hint of condescension.

Wallace (Kim[2] Gyngell) is a taxi driver who makes cider in his small flat by day, and by night ferries passengers in his cab through Melbourne's inner city. Wallace is curious about people, but he's inept and shy. His neighbours in the apartment block live mysterious lives behind closed doors. His only conduit to people is his taxi. Wallace secretly tapes the stories passengers tell him in his cab, and plays them back during the day in his room. Their sad, sometimes funny, confessions fascinate him.

However, real life impinges on Wallace when against his will he is drawn into the shady dealings of two neighbours, the hectoring, bullying Syd (Paul Chubb), and his taciturn side-kick, Bodger (Barry Dickins). He is also drawn into a relationship of sorts with Syd's worldly-wise girlfriend, Gail (Sally McKenzie), who works in a local shoe factory. The film ends somewhat inconclusively—'a slice from life'—but suggests that important insights are gained along the way. No one can remain isolated forever.

Ray Argall's photography adds a moody romanticism to the realism of the world inhabited by McKenzie's characters, who use language which is shocking to middle-class ears. 'Nice' people do not swear, and the strings of expletives at times make what the characters say impenetrable. Then the realisation sets in that language can divide us into classes, even castes.

Language is the currency of a culture, and much of the dialogue in this film comes from tape recordings made by McKenzie himself when he drove taxis like Wallace. These conversations, uttered in the confessional of a taxi, and later replayed as disembodied voices, reverberate with authenticity—sad, tragic, confusing stories of people struggling to make sense from loneliness, disappointment and all the impoverishment of existence in a fractured society.

With Love to the Person Next to Me is a funny, unsentimental film about losers and loners, odd-bods and dreamers like Wallace and Gail, and the young woman in the taxi—not defeated, yet.

JAN EPSTEIN

---

[1] Usually spelt 'Kym'.
[2] See footnote 1.
[3] See footnote 1.

Reference
'With Love to the Person Next to Me', a review by Anne Marie Crawford, *Filmnews*, November 1987, p. 11.

WITH TIME TO KILL

[No opening production company credit.] WITH TIME TO KILL.[2] © 1987 James Clayden. Produced with the assistance of the Australian Film Commission and Australian Film Television & Radio School. *Location:* Melbourne. *Australian distributor:* Australian Film Television & Radio School. *Video:* Roadshow. *Rating:* M. Shot on Super 8 and finished on 1" video. 71 mins.

Producer: James Clayden. *Scriptwriter:* James Clayden. *Director of photography:* Laurie McInnes. [*Production designer:* not credited.] [*Costume designer:* not credited.] *Editor:* Gary Hillberg. *Composer:* Chris Knowles. *Sound:* Steve Burgess. [*Sound editor:* not credited; atb Steve Burgess.] [*Mixer:* not credited; atb Steve Burgess.]

Sgt. Max Clements (James Clayden) and Lt. Nick Yates (Ian Scott).

Cast

Ian Scott (Lt. Nick Yates), Elizabeth Huntley (Louise Yates), Jan Freidel (Voice), James Clayden (Sgt. Max Clements), John Howard (Adam Sayer), Janet Golding (Lin Van Hek), Peter Green ('The Laundryman'), Barry Dickins (Terry Bendix), Tim Robertson (Jack Keane), Stephen Cummings (Tony Shaw), Val Kirwan (Clairvoyant), Phil Motherwell (Frank Williams), Marie Hoy (Sarah Davis), Sarah Mogridge (Voice), Lorender Freeman (Martin Ludlow), Peaches La Creme (Victoria Clements), David Brown (Brendon Golding), Rhonda Wilson (Actress (rehearsing)), Richard Lee (Lenny Loyd), Joe Dolce (Frank Isaccs), Nigel Buesst (Wilson Manning), Neil Gladwin (Andrew Bryce), Colin Talbot (Voice).

With Time To Kill is surely one of the most unusual features ever to achieve a theatrical and video release in Australia. Beginning life as a very low-budget Super-8 project funded by the Australian Film Commission's 'No Frills Fund', it ended up as a short feature post-produced on video. (A complete account of the film's making can be found in the AFTRS publication *Taking Care of Business*, 1988.)

The film is the work of the well-known painter and avant-garde dramatist James Clayden, whose important experimental films include *The Ghost Paintings* (short, 1986) and the feature-length **Corpse** (1982). Although clearly drawing from the 'visionary', poetic art-cinema tradition of F. W. Murnau, Werner Herzog and Andrei Tarkovsky, Clayden seems equally interested in the hard-edged, kinetic, downbeat mainstream experimentation of Martin Scorsese and John Cassavetes, and of Ridley Scott's **Blade Runner** (1982).

Accordingly, in line with the strange, self-reflexive 'thrillers' created by Jean-Luc Godard (**Détective**, 1985) or Rainer Werner Fassbinder (**Der Amerikanische Soldat**, 1970), **With Time to Kill** is a 'mutant' genre film, deliberately 'making strange' conventional elements and mixing them (with equally deliberate incongruity) with avant-garde elements. As in many a *nouvelle vague* film, brutish gangsters quote Dostoevsky, and violence is both treated playfully (as an obvious screen illusion) and fetishised as a dark, spellbinding, almost abstract spectacle.

Clayden takes the modernist celebration of the near-impenetrability of classic thriller plots (e.g., Howard Hawks' **The Big Sleep**, 1946) to a dizzy extreme—indeed, many of the plot 'links' joining improvised scenes appear to have been devised arbitrarily, at the post-production stage of voice-over narration. The story, and the precise narrative status of many individual incidents, remain resolutely murky, but the overall theme is clear: the creeping corruption and evil that spreads from the criminal underworld to envelop first the trigger-happy 'psycho' cop Sgt. Max Clements (Clayden), and eventually even his initially decent, sane partner, the narrator Lt. Nick Yates (Ian Scott). Madness and perversity overtake all the characters, who utter sombre existentialist maxims like 'all is pain and fear' before being wasted.

The film can be appreciated as a vivid document of a certain inner-city Melbourne cultural 'underground'—indeed, it is far more faithful, in its way, to the spirit and letter of that underground than **Dogs In Space** (Richard Lowenstein, 1987), which misguidedly tries to re-stage and dramatise the life of the scene, or even **Ghosts…of the Civil Dead** (John Hillcoat, 1989). Clayden utilises contributions from a large network of

innovative theatre actors (Val Kirwan, Phil Motherwell), independent film-makers (Nigel Buesst) and post-punk musicians (Chris Knowles, Ollie Olsen), and mixes these with the work of more 'above ground' figures like comedian Barry Dickins, singer–songwriter Stephen Cummings, actor Tim Robertson and cinematographer Laurie McInnes (director of the short, *Palisade*, 1987, and the feature, **Broken Highway**, 1993).

Indeed, the wilful incoherence of the film largely derives from the fact that it gleefully accommodates an unwieldy 'intertext' of fragments from other works, particularly John Howard's and Rhonda Wilson's performance of Daniel Keane's play *The Hour Before My Brother Dies* (filmed by Clayden for ABC television), and Marie Hoy's rough, confrontational video *Informo* (documented in *Cantrills Filmnotes* 51/52, 1986). The 'storyline' is conjured as much from these fragments as from the loose generic premise.

With Time to Kill is not an easy or even particularly pleasurable film to watch, but it is a subversive oddity now lurking in many a video shop, and for that reason (at least) it demands a special footnote in Australian film history.

ADRIAN MARTIN

---

[1] There is no director credit, just 'A Film by James Clayden'.

[2] The title is graphically rendered so that several letters in green read as 'HELL'.

References

'The Maltese Ford Falcon', Joanna Murray-Smith, *Cinema Papers*, no. 66, November 1987, pp. 26–7.

'Clayden', unsigned, *Filmnews*, November 1985, p. 19.

THE YEAR MY VOICE BROKE

A Kennedy Miller production. The Year My Voice Broke. © 1987 Kennedy Miller. *Location:* Braidwood (New South Wales). *Australian distributor:* Hoyts. *Opened:* 17 October 1987. *Video:* First Release. *Rating:* M (September 1987; 2797.86m). 35mm. 105 mins.

Producers: Terry Hayes, Doug Mitchell, George Miller. *Associate producer:* Barbara Gibbs. *Scriptwriter:* John Duigan. *Director of photography:* Geoff Burton. *Production designer:* Roger Ford. *Costume designers:* Lyn Askew, Fiona Nicolls. *Editor:* Neil Thumpston. *Sound recordist:* Ross Linton. *Sound editors:* (dia.) Karin Whittington, Tim Jordan. *Mixer:* Phil Judd.

Cast

Noah Taylor (Danny), Loene Carmen (Freya), Ben Mendelsohn (Trevor), Graeme Blundell (Nils Olson), Lynette Curran (Anne Olson), Malcolm Robertson (Bruce Embling), Judi Farr (Sheila Embling), Tim Robertson (Bob Leishman), Bruce Spence (Jonah), Harold Hopkins (Tom Alcock), Anja Coleby (Gail Olson), Kylie Ostara (Alison), Kelly Dingwall (Barry), Dorothy St. Heaps (Mrs Keith), Emma Lyle (Lisa), Louise Birgan (Lyn), Mary Regan (Miss McColl), Matthew Ross (Malseed), Allan Penney (Martin), Queenie Ashton (Mrs O'Neil).

For many, John Duigan's **The Year My Voice Broke** came to epitomise the archetypal 'rites of passage' story in an Australian context. There is certainly a strong sense that the three central characters—Danny (Noah Taylor), Freya (Loene Carmen) and Trevor (Ben Mendelsohn)—are at a sensitive and crucial stage of their lives, partly embattled by the restrictive mores and attitudes of their rural, small-town setting, and reaching out to each other and to the horizon of adulthood. The notion of a 'rites of passage' is invariably and intimately connected with sex, a subject central to the film's triangle of characters, particularly the younger Danny. Thus, it is easy to view **The Year My Voice Broke** in the mode of, say, Scott Murray's **Devil in the Flesh**, made two years earlier[1], another archetypal 'rites of passage' film where a young boy's sexual awakening is on the fringe of manhood.

But there is another sense in which one could say that in **The Year My Voice Broke** the three characters tend to preserve their childhood longer than the other people of the township. Each retains a more primal experience of the world: Trevor is inno-

cently and charismatically anti-authoritarian, a mass of unsocialised, destructive urges, who steals cars for the sheer pleasure of it; Freya, who is enamoured of Trevor, is earthy for she is mystically connected with the land around the town, and, in particular, the abandoned ghost-like home on the hill; and Danny, who is enamoured of Freya, moves away from experiencing his world as a social totality, but as one in continuous flux between the material and a supernatural–spiritual understanding.

Like Duigan's previous films, the characters in this film are outsiders, estranged from their society-in-miniature. But **The Year My Voice Broke** is unlike his previous films in that the connection between the outsider and society is not based on harsh political and social realities—realities which cannot be transcended and which have often been fatalistic for Duigan's characters. This move away from a sense of fatalism is a major shift of perspective across John Duigan's body of films.

Perhaps one reason for this shift is Duigan's association with Kennedy Miller. **The Year My Voice Broke** has mythical elements, particularly in respect of Freya's mystical connection with the ever-present, ghost-like home on the hill. The film reveals that the one-time inhabitant of the house

was Freya's mother, a prostitute who has become the small community's unspoken guilt. Freya is a reminder of that guilt. This sub-plot of an absent mother's having some mythical influence on the community through her daughter strongly parallels the myth of Persephone and Demeter in reverse (the absent daughter influencing the life of the mother and her community). Given George Miller's well-known appreciation of the work of Joseph Campbell on primitive mythology, it would not be unlikely to think Miller had a hand in subtly influencing **The Year My Voice Broke** into the area of Greek mythology.

RAFFAELE CAPUTO

---

[1] Not released in Australia until 1989.

References

'Miller's Tale', an interview with producer George Miller by Tom Ryan, *Cinema Papers*, no. 67, January 1988, pp. 12–16.
'John Duigan's Moral Tales', Christina Thompson, ibid., pp. 17–19.
'The Year My Voice Broke', a review by John Nicoll, ibid., pp. 43–4.
'John Duigan: Awakening the Dormant', an interview by Scott Murray, *Cinema Papers*, no. 76, November 1989, pp. 30–5, 77.
'The Year My…[sic]', a review by Kathe Boehringer, *Filmnews*, November 1987, p. 13.

Danny (Noah Taylor) and Freya (Loene Carmen).

1988

Albert Einstein (Yahoo Serious) perfects a surfboard. Yahoo Serious' Young Einstein.

239

STEPHEN MacLEAN

AROUND THE WORLD IN 80 WAYS

Palm Beach Entertainment[,] Australian European Finance Corporation Ltd [and] Commonwealth Bank of Australia present Around the World in 80 Ways. © 1986 Australian European Finance Corporation Limited. *Budget:* $2.25 million. *Location:* Sydney. *Australian distributor:* Hoyts. *Video:* First Release. *Rating:* M (February 1987; 2335.98m). 35mm. 86 mins.

Producers: David Elfick, Steve Knapman. *Scriptwriters:* Stephen MacLean, Paul Leadon. *Director of photography:* Louis Irving. *Production designer:* Lissa Coote. *Costume designer:* Clarrissa Patterson. *Editor:* Marc van Buuren. *Composer:* Chris Neal. *Sound recordist:* Paul Brincat. *Sound editors:* Karin Whittington (dia.), Steve Burgess, Nicki Roller (fx), Andrew Stewart (foley). *Sound supervisor:* Roger Savage. *Mixers:* Roger Savage, Bruce Emery.

Cast

Philip Quast (Wally Davis), Allan Penney (Roly Davis), Diana Davidson (Mavis Davis), Kelly Dingwall (Eddy Davis), Gosia Dobrowolska (Nurse Ophelia Cox), Rob Steele (Alec Moffatt), Judith Fisher (Lotta Boyle), Jane Markey ("Miserable" Madge), John Howard (Doctor Proctor), Frank Lloyd (Mr Tinkle), Cathren Michalak (Mrs Tinkle); Nicki Gardner, Helen Simons, Elizabeth Burton (Geisha Girls); Ric Carter (Financier).

Roly Davis (Allan Penney) and Nurse Ophelia Cox (Gosia Dobrowolska).

Given its relatively small budget, **Around the World in 80 Ways** is an adventurous comedy with a highly convoluted plot that shifts gears around a number of themes, sub-themes and extemporaneous gags, and is host to a string of clownish characters.

The adventure begins with Wally Davis (Philip Quast) who runs a failing small-time tourism business in Queensland. He is also homosexual, which seems to account for much of the film's campy gesturing and decor. But Wally's homosexuality is also a point of slight contention with his family in Sydney, particularly his father Roly (Allan Penney), a man verging on senility: he is virtually blind and bound to a wheelchair.

One day, just as creditors are dismantling his business, Wally receives a letter from his mother, Mavis (Diana Davidson), explaining she has had enough of playing the long-suffering wife, has placed Roly in an old people's home and is heading off on a round-the-world tour. In desperate need of funds, Wally heads back to Sydney to intercept her departure, but is too late.

Roly, however, learns that his ex-business partner and next-door neighbour, Alec

Moffatt (Rob Steele), is booked on the same tour as Mavis. Many years ago, Moffatt cheated Roly out of their car business, and, while Moffatt prospered, Roly's health deteriorated. Roly now believes Moffatt is out to cheat him of his wife. He convinces his younger son, Eddy (Kelly Dingwall), an unemployed sound-effects genius, to escort him on the same itinerary in search of his wife, and reveals a stash of $20,000 he has been building up secretly over the years.

Wally, however, in order to rescue himself from financial woes, contrives with Eddy to make Roly believe an imaginary trip of sound effects and smells is the real thing. Eddy, who is smitten by Nurse Ophelia Cox (Gosia Dobrowolska), also procures her help because she believes a lively atmosphere is the best form of therapy for retiring types, yet she is unaware of Eddy and Wally's embezzling scheme.

As it happens, the imaginary trip turns out to be more fun and beneficial to Roly than the real trip is to Mavis, eventually leading to the liberation of the other inhabitants from the old people's home.

Around the World in 80 Ways is a rather inventive attempt at social farce, but it is a comedy out of step with the tendency of a more sophisticated brand of social satire that emerged in Australian film around the mid-

1980s. In different ways, **Emoh Ruo** (Denny Lawrence, 1985), **Malcolm** (Nadia Tass, 1986) and **Young Einstein** (Yahoo Serious, 1988) are three notable examples of the sophisticated trend.

Interestingly, David Elfick, producer of **Around the World in 80 Ways**, was also producer on **Emoh Ruo**, which has a greater satiric bite because its honed-down plot becomes a wit-sharpened scalpel on a treasured Australian philosophy–institution—the dream of owning a home. Unlike **Emoh Ruo**, **80 Ways** is in the vein of the epic, escapist comedy like Stanley Kramer's **It's a Mad Mad Mad Mad World** (1963), or even this film's name-sake comedy adventure, **Around the World in 80 Days** (Michael Anderson, 1956). But the film falls into easy traps which replace potential archaic slapstick with crude comic elements that indeed support racial and sexual stereotypes. Even the use of character names like Ophelia Cox is indicative of the film's lack of sophistication. This aside, the film still manages to retain some comic inventiveness, especially in respect of social criticism. The film's finale is a nod to the Eddie Cantor style of the down-and-outer coming to the rescue of the poor.

RAFFAELE CAPUTO

AS TIME GOES BY

Valhalla presents AS TIME GOES BY. *Alternative title:* 'The Cricketer' (working). © 1987 Monroe Stahr Productions Limited. *Locations:* Silverton (New South Wales); Melbourne. *Australian distributor:* Valhalla The Other Films. *Video:* The Home Cinema Group. *Rating:* PG (February 1988). Super 16 (blown up to 35mm). 96 mins.

Producer: Chris Kiely. *Executive producer:* Phillip J. Dwyer. *Scriptwriter:* Barry Peak. *Director of photography:* John Ogden. *Production designer:* Paddy Reardon. *Wardrobe superviser:* Carolyn Nott. *Editor:* Ralph Strasser. *Composer:* Peter Sullivan. *Sound recordist:* Steve Hagerty. *Sound editors:* Tim Chau (fx); Ralph Strasser (dia.). *Mixers:* Peter Frost, Tim Chau, John Wilkinson.

Cast

Nique Needles (Mike), Bruno Lawrence (Ryder), Marcelle Schmitz (Connie), Ray Barrett (J. L. Weston), Max Gillies (Joe Bogart[1]), Mitchell Faircloth (McCauley), Deborah Force (Cheryl), Christine Keogh (Margie), Don Bridges (Ern), Ian Shrives (Greaser), Jane Clifton (Mechanic), Mitch Harrison (Crim), Fred Peter (Boreman), John Barrett (Sandhill Bob), Rex Greeney (Town Drunk); Mathew King (Additional Voices).

As Time Goes By, written and directed by Barry Peak, is a good-natured science-fiction comedy about the encounter between a young surfie and an alien in the outback of Australia.

Mike (Nique Needles) crosses the outback with his surfboard en route to a rendezvous in the middle of nowhere with someone he has never met before, called Joe Bogart (Max Gillies). Details of the meeting are contained in a note left to Mike, twenty-five years earlier, by his now dead mother.

Mike finds Bogart, an alien time-traveller, living stranded in the desert in a spacecraft that looks like a 1940s diner and bar. Joe needs Mike's help to recover a power capsule for the spacecraft so that he can return to his own galaxy far, far away.

In his travels through the dusty outback town of Dingo, Mike meets a brooding policeman called Ryder (Bruno Lawrence), and an attractive station owner, Connie (Marcelle Schmitz). When the time comes to wrest the power capsule from the grasping hands of evil-doers—a greedy land baron, J. L. Weston (Ray Barrett), who wants to turn the desert into a tropical playground for the rich, and McCauley (Mitchell Faircloth), a fanatical scientist obsessed with UFOs—the race is on to the film's conclusion. It sees Ryder resurrected from the dead

in the nick of time (he turns out to be Mike's long-lost Dad), and Mike joining his mad mate Joe on very foreign soil.

What can one say about a film that has Max Gillies playing an alien with what looks like an umbilical cord attached to his neck, who speaks in lines from old movies in the impersonated voices of Cagney, Bogart, Garbo, George Brent and others, except that it's absurd and thoroughly endearing? Gillies is a delight; quite inimitable.

Bruno Lawrence and Nique Needles play their rôles straight, while Barrett, Faircloth and Don Bridges as Ern, a Dingo shop-keeper obsessed with dust, go over the top with theirs.

As Time Goes By, following **Future Schlock** (Barry Peak and Chris Kiely, 1984) and **The Big Hurt** (Peak, 1986), was made in association with the Valhalla Cinema Group. Destined, even designed, for cult moviedom, it is a genuine local oddity, as amusing and improbable as Gillies' cocktail shaker, which moves him backwards and forwards in time.

JAN EPSTEIN

---

[1] The front credits give Max Gillies' character as 'The Alien'.

Reference
'**As Time Goes By**', a review by Melina Houston, *Cinema Papers*, no. 70, November 1988, p. 29.

J. L. Weston (Ray Barrett), Greaser (Ian Shrives) and Ern (Don Bridges).

BACKSTAGE

The Burrowes Film Group presents BACK-STAGE. © 1987 The Burrowes Film Group. *Locations:* Melbourne; New York. *Australian distributor:* Hoyts. *Video:* RCA–Columbia–Hoyts. *Rating:* PG. 35mm. 94 mins.

Producer: Geoff Burrowes. *Co-producer:* Frank Howson. *Executive producers:* Kent C. Lovell, Dennis Wright, John Kearney. *Associate producers:* Peter Boyle, John Powditch. *Scriptwriters:* Jonathan Hardy, Frank Howson. Based on an original idea of John Lamond. *Director of photography:* Keith Wagstaff. *Camera operator:* David Eggby. *Production designer:* Leslie Binns. *Costume designer:* Jane Hyland. *Editor:* Ray Daley. *Composer:* Bruce Rowland. *Sound recordist:* John Schiefelbein. *Sound editors:* Gary Woodyard, Tim Chau. *Mixer:* James Currie, David Harrison, Peter D. Smith.

Cast

Laura Branigan (Kate Lawrence), Michael Aitkens (Robert Landau), Noel Ferrier (Mortimer Wynde), Rowena Wallace (Evelyn Hough), Phillip Holder (Bill French), Len Kaserman (Milton), Kym Gyngell (Paarvo), David Letch (Steven Williams), Mary Ward (Geraldine Woollencraft), Henry Cuthbertson (Myles Frewe), John Tarrant (Bruce Tendon), James Condon (Frank Turner), Penelope Stewart (Mary Foote), Ian Mune (Mangin), Nancy Kiel (Evie), John Frawley (Metheny), Robin Dene (Bollinger), Randall Berger (Roger Weiss), Les Terrill (Lawyer—Manhattan Bar), Nadine Wells (Secretary—Manhattan Bar).

At least one aspect of the generally lowly regarded œuvre of producer Frank Howson deserves discussion—the aspiration of several of his projects (**Boulevard of Broken Dreams, Heaven Tonight, What the Moon Saw**[1]) to dramatise the conditions of Australian culture. That is, the principal subject of his films—often overriding the nominally central but usually rather pale character relationships—ends up being the drama of cultural values and tastes: 'high' vs 'low' art, 'fake' vs 'authentic' creative expression, art vs criticism, national vs international culture, and so on. These cultural fault-lines are traced in various interrelations of the worlds of theatre, pop music, film, radio, newspapers and television. **Backstage** (although it was reportedly taken out of Howson's hands by the Burrowes Film Group and subsequently disowned by him) is a poor film by any standards, but a fascinating case study in its portrayal of cultural attitudes.

Inadvertently, the film is deeply revealing of a number of entrenched cultural attitudes. Ostensibly, its stance is 'anti-imperialist', with its theatre critic-hero, Robert Landau (Michael Aitkens), speaking out against both American import stars and the dominance of British traditions in Australian theatre. The film's real animus, however, is reserved for 'vulgar', shallow, garish popular culture—Robert endlessly denounces the 'superficiality' and 'insulting triviality' of the play that Kate Lawrence (Laura Branigan) stars in (and commercial television), and asks for great, serious, 'meaningful' work to appear (unsurprisingly and stereotypically, he eventually swaps criticism—or 'necrophilia', as Kate calls it—for playwriting). His (and the film's) 'high cultural' values are in fact wholly British in inspiration (and therefore just as 'imperial' as those it denounces), as evidenced in the very casting of Aitkens, the climactic stage performance of Chekov and the affectionate celebration throughout of the witty, 'professional', no-nonsense acting style of British-style comic actors like Noel Ferrier, as opposed to the emotional excesses of the American 'method' (and the intellectual 'wanking' of the avant-garde, embodied in Kym Gyngell as a fey, hippie director).

Yet, as a confused, schizophrenic film, **Backstage** cannot be ultimately read as properly upholding even these 'high' cultural values. As commercial entertainment, its *modus operandi* is the amelioration of all conflicts, and the creation of strained 'midway' compromises between different cultural values. Thus, the love story between Robert and Kate, besides turning her into a 'real' actress and him into a 'real' writer, also produces new rock songs with 'meaningful' lyrics; and the ultimate Chekov performance is indeed a bizarre hybrid of art and showbiz, subdued 'theatrical' acting and spectacularly 'vulgar' display (with the crowd going wild exactly as it did in the opening rock concert scene). Not since the days of Rooney and Garland in the Andy Hardy films has there been such a flagrant example of popular culture's defensive, unrequited drive to be taken as 'more' than just pop—and of the fascinating, extravagant failure of such a dream.

ADRIAN MARTIN

---

[1] **Boulevard of Broken Dreams** (Pino Amenta, 1988), **Heaven Tonight** (Amenta, 1991), **What the Moon Saw** (Amenta, 1990).

Reference
'Backstage', a review by Adrienne McKibbins, *Filmnews*, May 1988, p. 9.

Robert Landau (Michael Aitkens) and Laura Branigan (Kate Lawrence).

BELINDA

Fontana Productions. Belinda. © 1987
Fontana Production[s]. *Location:* Sydney.
Filmed: August–October 1986. *Australian
distributor:* Greater Union. *Video:* CBS-Fox.
Rating: M. 35mm. 97 mins.

Producer: Bedrich Kabriel. *Scriptwriter:*
Pamela Gibbons. *Director of photography:*
Malcolm McCulloch. *Production designers:*
Bedrich Kabriel, Herbert Pinter. *Costume
designer:* Bruce Finlayson. *Editor:* David
Huggett. *Musical director–composer:* Les
Gock. *Choreography:* Robyn Moase. *Sound
recordist:* Tim Lloyd. *Sound editors:* David
Huggett (dubbing); Glen Auchinachie (fx).
Mixers: Martin Oswin, John Herron.

Cast

Deanne Jeffs (Belinda), Mary Regan
(Crystal), Kaarin Fairfax (Sandra), Joy
Smithers (Liz), Elizabeth Lord (Mandy),
Kahti (Helen), Robyn Moase (Brenda),
Kathryn Walker (Kathy), John Jarratt
(Graeme), Hazel Phillips (Doreen), Gerda
Nicolson (Belinda's Mother), Alan Cassell
(Belinda's Father), Nicos Lathouris (Benny
Rose), Bart Pavlovich (Brazda), Robert
Simper (Brazda's Bodyguard), Armando
Hurley (Billy James), Ricky May (Jackie
Cole), Caz Lederman (Rhonda), Jeffery
Rhoe (Timothy), Tim Burns (Jamie).

Publicity still: *Robyn Moase (who plays Brenda), Mary Regan (Crystal), Elizabeth Lord
(Mandy), Joy Smithers (Liz), Ricky May (Jackie Cole), Kahti (Helen), Deanne Jeffs
(Belinda) and Kaarin Fairfax (Sandra).*

Pamela Gibbons' largely autobiographical film tells of a dramatic period in the
life of a young, aspiring ballerina. It has the
many awkwardnesses of a first film, but its
increasingly dark story has moments of real
power.

Sixteen-year-old Belinda (Deanne Jeffs)
attempts to expand the boundaries of her
life and career outside the rarefied confines
of her ballet school. She tries for a job in the
theatre, but she is too young and has to
settle for a position as a showgirl at the
Paradise Club nightclub.

At this point, the film appears a light-
hearted tale of backstage life, with the
humour and camaraderie of an eccentric
group of long-time showgirls (a 'pack of
molls' one character labels them). But the
atmosphere slowly darkens as the internal
pain of several women is gradually revealed:
Crystal (Mary Regan), for example, is saving all she can in a desperate bid to go to
Switzerland and reclaim her estranged young
son.

Some will find the opening out of the
characters' stories a bit melodramatic, and
the film telescopes its dramatic points too
concisely into the final night of the Paradise
Club before it becomes a disco. But it does

manage to create a quite harrowing atmosphere and tension.

Belinda, for one, is wrongly accused by
a waitress, Rhonda (Caz Lederman), of hit-
ting up on her love interest, Timothy (Jeffery
Rhoe). Rhonda and two fellow waitresses
lure her into the backyard, where Rhonda
rips Belinda's costume open. Calling her a
virgin and a cock-teaser, Rhonda then rup-
tures Belinda's hymen with her hand.

This is a very tough scene and quite unlike anything else in Australian cinema.
While hardly conforming to strict feminist
notions about how women should be positively represented in cinema, this scene rings
true and is courageous for its boldness.

One undercurrent of the film, and this
scene in particular, is a sense of repressed
lesbianism among several of the girls. There
are many scenes in Australian films where
male violence against other males carries
connotations of the repressed homosexuality of some mateship (Ted Kotcheff's **"Wake

in Fright"**, 1971, etc.), but this is perhaps
the sole female case.

The film closes, after this female violence
and Crystal's suicide, with an uncomfortable scene with Belinda's dance instructor,
Graeme (John Jarratt). Seeing her upset, he
explains how many people carry great pain
within them and that the rôle of art is to
reflect the soul. If one does it with sufficient
clarity, that can light up the world. It is easy
to jeer at the pretentiousness of the dialogue
and stilted performance here, but one
senses the cathartic feeling that lies behind it.

Belinda is very much a first film and there
is much that can be criticised. But the journeys Belinda and Crystal take are told with
such feeling that the film ends up as a not-
ineffective tribute to some brave spirits.

SCOTT MURRAY

Reference
'**Belinda**', a review by Adrienne McKibbins, *Filmnews*, September 1988, p. 13.

BOULEVARD OF BROKEN DREAMS

A Boulevard Films Production. Boulevard of Broken Dreams. © 1988 Boulevard Films Pty Ltd. *Budget:* $2 million. *Locations:* Melbourne; Los Angeles. *Australian distributor:* Hoyts. *Video:* RCA–Columbia–Hoyts. *Rating:* M. 35mm. 94 mins.

Producer: Frank Howson. *Executive producer:* Peter Boyle. *Associate producer:* Barbi Taylor. *Scriptwriter:* Frank Howson. *Director of photography:* David Connell. *Production designer:* Otello Stolfo. *Costume designer:* Cheryl McCloud. *Editor:* Philip Reid. *Composer:* John Capek. *Sound recordist:* Andrew Ramage. *Sound editors:* Craig Carter, Glenn Martin. *Mixer:* James Currie.

Cast

John Waters (Tom Garfield), Penelope Stewart (Helen Garfield), Nicki Paull (Suzy Daniels), Kim[1] Gyngell (Ian McKenzie), Andrew McFarlane (Jonathon Lovell), Ross Thompson (Cameron Wright), Jacinta Stapleton (Jessie Garfield), Kevin Miles (Geoff Bormann), William Ten Eyck (Michael Orrloff), Helen McDonald (Dr. Goldstein), Ian Catchlove (Bookstore Manager), Jeremy Kewley (Waiter), John Samaha (Cab Driver), Ian McFadyen (Hotel Clerk), John Concannon (Bellboy), Peter Lindsay (William Walshe), Lance Strauss (Steward), Sally-Ann Read (Hooker), John Smith (Barman), James Lee Stanley (Adam Verona), Elizabeth Lamers (Laura Graham), Jess Harnell (Benny Dimase), Biggles (Ian's Dog).

Tom Garfield (John Waters) is an Australian playwright living in California who has made the big time. He has a string of successes to his name and the ultimate accolade of being featured on the cover of *Rolling Stone*. The price he pays is estrangement from his wife, Helen (Penelope Stewart), and young daughter, Jessie (Jacinta Stapleton), and a propensity to pill-popping.

This is the film's backdrop, conjured effortlessly before and during the credits, with shots of Tom in his car on a Los Angeles freeway, lazy drifts of the camera through Tom's apartment, settling on objects which tell the story (the magazine cover, photos) and cuts to a weary Tom being pressured by his agent not to abandon writing and fly home to Australia.

Characterisation, with a few exceptions, is the strength of the film, which is generally engaging and interesting. Andrew McFarlane does well with the difficult character of Jonathon, Helen's new boyfriend, giving depth to a largely unsympathetic per-

Tom Garfield (John Waters), the Melbourne playwright returned home.

sonality. Jacinta Stapleton gives a strong, unaffected performance, as does Nicki Paull as Suzy Daniels, a young actress just starting her career and who has the lead rôle in a production of Tom's latest hit.

Frank Howson has written some convincing scenes between the actress and playwright, and Suzy and Tom represent a nice juxtaposition of jaded appetite and one that has just been whetted. The sexual tension between the enthusiastic Suzy, and Tom, whose emotions are battered and straining in another direction, are nicely understated.

The pity is that the film ultimately falls victim to unevenness in other areas, notably the intrusive interruption of mood by an insensitive soundtrack, a lack of courage in pushing the film as far as the material could go, and hammy acting by Kevin Miles and Ross Thompson (*Carson's Law* revisited).

According to the production notes, director Pino Amenta allowed Miles to have his head in portraying Geoff Bormann, the theatrical producer of Tom's play. While the portrayal is, in its way, a comic tour de force, it is also a mistake. It undermines the film as a serious examination of the downside of fame, if this was the film's intention. Miles and Thompson are playing a different film from Waters, Paull and co. The degree to which their approach to humour does the film a disservice can be measured by the performance of Kim[2] Gyngell as Ian McKenzie,

Tom's old Carlton mate. Gyngell's McKenzie is pure joy to watch. He's funny, vulnerable and immensely real, a 'type', though Gyngell never deserts the authenticity of his character for a cheap laugh.

One of the other pleasures of the film is the idiosyncratic representation of Melbourne as a backdrop: Port Melbourne, the Yarra, Parliament House, Canterbury and Carlton, an unusual slice of the city skyline from the roof of the Regent Hotel. There is a genuine sense of the mood and place here that at times is reminiscent of Paul Cox's films.

The twist in the tale of **Boulevard of Broken Dreams** is another illustration of chances lost. This drive for neatness and catharsis robs the film of its initial realism and turns it into a weepie.

JAN EPSTEIN

---

[1] Usually spelt 'Kym'.
[2] See footnote 1.

References
'**Boulevard of Broken Dreams**', a review by Philippa Hawker, *Cinema Papers*, no. 70, November 1988, p. 24.
'**Boulevard Films**', a report on the production company by Paul Kalina, including an interview with producer Frank Howson, *Cinema Papers*, no. 76, November 1989, pp. 42–6, 77.
'**Boulevard of Broken Dreams**', a review by Barbra Luby, *Filmnews*, October 1988, p. 13.

ROD HAY

BREAKING LOOSE

Misfit (Dar Davies) pursues Ross (Peter Phelps), obscured, in car.

Avalon Films presents A Phil Avalon Production. BREAKING LOOSE. © 1988 Avalon Film Productions. *Locations:* Sydney, central coast (New South Wales). *Australian distributor:* Hoyts. *Video:* First Release. *Rating:* M (August 1988). 35mm. 87 mins.

Producer: Phil Avalon. *Executive producers:* Eric Jury, James Michael Vernon. *Scriptwriter:* Rod Hay. From an original idea by Phil Avalon. *Director of photography:* Richard Michalak. *Camera operator:* John Brock. *Art director:* Andrew Paul. *Costume designer:* Jenny Campbell. *Editor:* Ted Otton[1]. *Composer:* Jan Preston. *Sound recordist:* Bob Clayton. *Sound editors:* Sue Metcalfe (dia.); Nicky Roller (fx). *Mixers:* Phil Judd, Ian McLoughlin.

Cast

Peter Phelps (Ross), Vince Martin (Robbie), Abigail (Helen), David Ngoombutjarra (Davie), Shane O'Connor (Sampson), Angela Kennedy (Jacky), John Clayton (Neville), Sharon Tamlyn (Tammie), Gary Waddell (Copper), Carlo Bianchino (Junior), Sandra Lee Paterson (Caroline), Tom Richards (Rick), Kristoffer Greaves (Skunk), Kate Grusovin (Crystal), Dee Krainz (Shazar), Patch (Hooter the Dog).

For every action there is an equal and opposite reaction. That is a law of physics.

It is also a law of film. In 1981, Bruce Beresford made **Puberty Blues**, an intelligent, funny, touching look at Australian beach culture. In 1988, Rod Hay and Phil Avalon made **Breaking Loose**, a stupid, unfunny look at the surfie lifestyle.

The story concerns young Ross (Peter Phelps), who leaves home to join up with his surfboard-making friend on the coast. Before he leaves, however, he has a run-in with a gang of bikies, a member of which he totals in a macho duel. While Ross is on the beach trying to learn about growing up, the bikies trundle around on their Harleys looking for him.

If this film had been made ten years before it actually was, there might be some excuse for it. As it is, it is a distressing sign that something so immature could find its way onto film. This kind of thing would have worked much better as a comedy, an 'intentional' comedy. As it is, its attempts at raising tension and fear and some sort of romantic yearning for the life of the beach bum fall flat and raise many derisive chuckles.

The main problem is that the characters suffer from a terminal lack of character. Director Rod Hay, who also wrote the piece, may have a great ear for dialogue, but not from what you hear here. When the emotionally constipated Ross utters, 'I need some time and space to myself', you know you're in trouble. Things don't improve.

The bikies, supposedly intended to strike fear into the hearts of Ross, his friends and the audience, are monumentally unconvincing. They are akin to the ones in the Clint Eastwood vehicles **Every Which Way But Loose** (James Fargo, 1978) and **Any Which Way You Can** (Buddy Van Horn, 1980). The difference is that Eastwood's bikies weren't desperately looking for credibility, although they probably would have had more luck finding it.

However, the beach, not the road, is the focus of the film. Hence, there are lashings of cinematography straight out of the 'do what feels easy' book of shoreline photography. It is immensely boring surf footage, awash with crashing waves, surf skis and the inevitable sunsets.

When the bikies do turn up, there is a violent showdown of sorts in which Ross proves his manhood by blowing the bikies up. The moral of the story, presumably, is that there is nothing wrong with Australian beach culture that a Molotov cocktail can't solve.

JIM SCHEMBRI

---

[1] Should be 'Otton'.

Reference
'Breaking Loose', a short review by Adrian Martin, *Filmnews*, October 1988, p. 13.

JOHN CORNELL

"CROCODILE" DUNDEE II

Paramount Pictures presents a Rimfire Films production. "Crocodile" DUNDEE II. © 1988 Rimfire Films Limited. *Locations:* New York; Northern Territory. *Australian distributor:* Hoyts. *Opened:* 20 May 1988. *Video:* CBS-Fox. *Rating:* PG. 35mm. Panavision. 112 mins.

Producers: John Cornell, Jane Scott. *Executive producer:* Paul Hogan. *Associate producer:* Mark Turnbull. *Scriptwriters:* Paul Hogan, Brett Hogan. *Director of photography:* Russell Boyd. *Camera operator:* Peter Menzies. *Production designer:* Lawrence[1] Eastwood. *Costume designer:* Norma Moriceau. *Editor:* David Stiven. *Composer:* Peter Best. *Sound recordists:* Gary Wilkins, Terry Annesley (Australia); Tom Brandau (New York). *Sound supervisor:* Penn Robinson. *Supervising sound editor:* George Waters III. *Supervising ADR editor:* Lettie Odney. *Supervising foley editor:* Victoria Martin. *Mixers:* John Reitz, David Campbell, Gregg Rudloff.

Cast

Paul Hogan (Mick 'Crocodile' Dundee[2]), Linda Kozlowski (Sue Charlton), John Meillon (Walter Reilly), Ernie Dingo (Charlie), Steve Rackman (Donk), Gerry Skilton (Nugget), Gus Mercurio (Frank), Jim Holt (Erskine), Alec Wilson (Denning), Maggie Blinco (Ida), Bill Sandy (Teddy), Mark Saunders (Diamond), Betty Bobbitt (Meg); Jim Cooper and Sam Cooper (Dorrigo Brothers); Fernando Segura (Hotel Manager), Mark Blum (Richard Mason), Hechter Ubarry (Rico), Juan Fernandez (Miguel), Charles Dutton (Leroy Brown).

Following in the superbly successful footsteps of its predecessor, Crocodile Dundee (Peter Faiman, 1986), this film continues the story of the laconic, bush-wise character Mick 'Crocodile' Dundee (Paul Hogan) and his tough and adventurous lady, the New York reporter Sue Charlton (Linda Kozlowski). Having declared their love for each other in the previous pic, the couple are now living together in a New York apartment. While Sue is busy with her career, Mick is beginning to feel homesick and generally uneasy with hanging around and doing nothing in particular in this gigantic foreign city. Meanwhile, Sue's ex-husband, Richard Mason (Mark Blum), is in Colombia, spying on Rico (Hechter Ubarry), a drug-dealer. He mails vital evidence to Sue in New York, but is murdered soon afterwards.

Back in New York, Rico kidnaps Sue and instructs Mick about delivering the evidence.

Mick refuses to comply and, after organising his own posse of decidedly questionable characters, rescues Sue from Rico's fortified mansion. The problem solved, Mick and Sue's life seems to be back to normal, until bullets start flying through their windows. And so they go into hiding, back into the good old Aussie bush.

Until this part of the film, "Crocodile" Dundee II is competent but nothing special. The plot is clichéd and the humour, though still plentiful, is of a much lower standard than in Crocodile Dundee. Back on Australian soil, however, the story picks up quite a bit. Rico and his sidekicks have finally tracked down Mick and Sue, but they significantly underestimate Mick's power and cunning when he is in his element. Unnerved by the mystery and seeming treachery of the Australian bush, frightened and embarrassed by Mick and his fellow Aborigines' endless game of bush-scare tactics, Rico's gang is finally captured and Rico ends up dead. Mick is plainly the victorious hero, but, more important, he is finally back home and Sue joyfully declares that she is, too.

It is not only the story which becomes wittier or the humour which becomes quirkier in the 'Australian' section of the film. The cinematography, particularly the use of light in the bush, increases in skill, and the film begins to look beautiful. The editing is almost flawless, creating a very definite mood, particularly in the sequence when Mick disappears to contact his Aboriginal mates, and a bizarre frightening sound drifts through the dusk over the landscape and its inhabitants. The editing in this 'outback' section also needs to be crystal clear as Mick and his friends play numerous tricks on the bad guys; there should be no room for confusion in the audience as to who is doing what, and successfully there is not.

Because of the various disparities between the 'Australian' and the 'American' sections, the film is uneven and the level of interest tends to drop in some crucial moments. Nevertheless, "Crocodile" Dundee II is still a basically good-value old-fashioned adventure, of the kind that possesses a timeless quality and can be enjoyed by various generations.

ANNA GUL

---

[1] Usually spelt 'Laurence'.
[2] Although the film's title puts "Crocodile" in double quotes, the cast credits give the nickname single quotes.

References
'Hogan's Heroes', Steven J. Spears, *Cinema Papers*, no. 70, November 1988, p. 22.
'"Crocodile" Dundee Overseas', Stephen Crofts, *Cinema Papers*, no. 77, January 1990, pp. 16–19.

Sue Charlton (Linda Kozlowski), Mick 'Crocodile' Dundee (Paul Hogan) and shopper (Dianne Derfner).

ECHOES OF PARADISE

Laughing Kookaburra Productions in association with Australian European Finance Corporation Limited present[s] Echoes of PARADISE. *Alternative titles:* 'Promises to Keep' and 'Shadows of the Peacock' (working). © 1987 Laughing Kookaburra Productions Pty Ltd. *Locations:* Phuket (Thailand); Sydney. *Australian distributor:* Roadshow. *Video:* Roadshow. *Rating:* M (February 1988). 35mm. 92 mins.

Producer: Jane Scott. *Executive producer:* Jan Sharp. *Scriptwriter:* Jan Sharp. *Additional material:* Anne Brooksbank. *Director of photography:* Peter James. *Camera operator:* Danny Batterham. *Production designer:* Judith Russell. *Costume designer:* Clarrissa Patterson. *Composer:* William Motzing. *Editor:* Frans Vandenburg. *Sound recordist:* Tim Lloyd. *Supervising sound editor:* Greg Bell. *Sound editors:* Danielle Wessner (dia.), Sally Fitzpatrick (fx). *Mixers:* Peter Fenton, Phil Heywood, Martin Oswin.

Cast

Wendy Hughes (Maria), John Lone (Raka), Steven Jacobs (George), Peta Toppano (Judy), Rod Mullinar (Terry), Gillian Jones (Mitty), Claudia Karvan (Julie), Rebecca Smart (Tessa), Matthew Taylor (Simon), Vithawat Bunnag (Sali), Prasert (Kasem), Lynda Stoner (Beth Mason), Ray Harding (Paul Mason), Penny Stehl (Mrs. Evans), Dibbs Mather (Rev. Whiteley), Don Pascoe (Senator Blayney), Jan Boreham (Nun), Ruth Caro (Nurse); Samantha Barber, Sabrina Bourdot (American Tourists); John Spicer (Club Porter), Marjorie Child (Maria's Mother).

A scorned and lonely wife: Maria (Wendy Hughes).

Syrupy dialogue and a clichéd scenario mar this quasi-romantic melodrama about the sexual awakening of a married woman. Maria (Wendy Hughes) is a devoted wife and mother, who, traumatised after hearing of her husband's infidelities, heads off to Thailand to focus her thoughts and heal. While holidaying, she meets and falls in love with a Balinese dancer, Raka (John Lone), and realises how shallow and unfulfilled life with her husband George (Steven Jacobs) has been. In the interim, George arrives in Bali and attempts somewhat passionlessly to woo her back. Maria is faced with the dilemma of surrendering her past in the pursuit of self-fulfilment or returning to her family and husband.

Through Maria's eyes, director Phillip Noyce takes the viewer into two worlds: an urban jungle, where money, infidelity, insincerity and hypocrisy are the norm; and a tropical paradise, where people go to retreat from the rat-race, heal and rebirth. But while Maria is cajoled into a sense of false comfort in Bali, the reality is that its idyllic charms mask tensions: people who stay at the resort are deep down no different to those she seeks to flee.

In the film, people are driven by material wealth, such as George and his friends, and the Thai resort owner, Terry (Rod Mullinar). They lose emotional perspective in their ruthless pursuit of money and its associated benefits. It is the old chestnut of money doesn't buy love. In George's and Terry's world, insincerity comes easily, as do hypocrisy and double standards.

Maria and Raka are kindred souls, both embracing old-fashioned values of respect, fidelity and commitment. Their attraction is more than physical; each finds in the other a catalytic release. For Raka, it is the ability to dance again and return home to Bali to repair his relationship with his father; for Maria, it is coming to terms with her inner self. When Maria first encounters Raka, he reminds one of a bird dancing in a wooden cage. Although Terry regards Raka as a 'prize possession' and treats him lavishly, Raka has to pay a price: surrendering his freedom. This is no different from Maria's situation: she is trapped in a life-style and married to a man who views her as an asset. While to date she has sublimated her feelings into a selfless love of her children, it is only when she meets Raka that both can escape the ties that bind them.

Maria's strong maternal instincts set her apart from other women—a quality which George takes for granted. It is only when Maria and Raka leave that Terry and George realise how empty their lives have become.

While the concept behind **Echoes of Paradise** is admirable, the execution is weak. The film is a very mediocre **Shirley Valentine** (Lewis Gilbert, 1989) weighed down by a poor script, a lush film score and some ham acting. A little less cliché and a little more sensitivity might have salvaged some of its sentiment.

PAT GILLESPIE

EMMA'S WAR

Curzon Film Distributors and Belinon Productions present Emma's War. © 1985 Belinon Productions Ltd. *Australian distributor:* Clytie Jessop. *Video:* not released. *Rating:* M. 35mm. 94 mins.

Producers: Clytie Jessop, Andrena Finlay. *Executive producer:* Robin Dalton. *Associate producer:* David Hannay. *Scriptwriters:* Peter Smalley, Clytie Jessop. *Director of photography:* Tom Cowan. *Production designer:* Jane Norris. *Costume supervisor:* Miv Brewer. *Editor:* Sonia Hoffman. *Composer:* John Williams. *Sound recordist:* Ross McKay. *Sound editors:* Ashley Grenville, Andrew Cunningham, Sally Fitzpatrick, Fiona Strain, David Bracks. *Mixer:* Julian Ellingworth.

Cast

Lee Remick (Anne Grange), Miranda Otto (Emma Grange), Mark Lee (John Davidson), Terence Donovan (Frank Grange), Donal Gibson (Hank), Bridey Lee (Laurel Grange), Pat Evison (Miss Arnott), Grigor Taylor (Dr Friedlander), Noelene Brown (Mrs Mortimer), Rebel Russell (Miss Gunz), Mervyn Drake (Iceman), Ashley Grenville (Brian), Kay Eklund (Miss Clewes), Jean Calver (Old Woman, Grog Shop), David Cahill (Headmaster, Country School), Sky Carter (Girl 1, Balliantyne), Rita North (Girl 2, Balliantyne), Jason West (Spectacled Boy), Tara Rajkumar (Indian Dancer); Helen McDonald (Narrator).

Idyllic childhood: Laurel Grange (Bridey Lee) and Emma Grange (Miranda Otto).

From its opening images of a mother and her two daughters picnicking in a pastoral setting reminiscent of a lower form of French Impressionism, one immediately suspects that first-time writer–director Clytie Jessop frames her shots with a conscious eye for painterly compositions. Not surprisingly, then, the quasi-autobiographical story that unfolds deals with a middle-class family of quietly artistic sensibilities.

Set in the war years of the 1940s, **Emma's War** is intermittently narrated in voice-over by Emma Grange, who, together with her younger sister, Laurel (Bridey Lee), attended a boarding college presided over by educational free-thinkers.[1]

Nestled amongst the scenic beauty of the Blue Mountains, Balliantyne College seems a utopian dream, a timeless world sealed off from the harsher reality of the wider world at war. It evokes a kind of Rousseauian universe in which students pass idyllic days in pursuit of the higher ideals of art and nature.

These days come to an end for Emma and Laurel when their mother, Anne Grange (Lee Remick), frustrated and alone in suburban Sydney, decides to move the family to

a small bush town. This relocation causes an inevitable resentment on the part of Emma, who pines for Balliantyne as one would for a paradise lost.

Unwilling to adapt to the academic impoverishment of bush schooling, Emma (Miranda Otto) plays truant and, in the course of her wanderings, encounters a young, unwilling conscript, John Davidson (Mark Lee), who has taken refuge in the town's backwoods. But what seems at first to be the beginning of a romantic sub-plot is quickly aborted as he is discovered and dragged off.

Ostensibly the story of a young girl's rites of passage, **Emma's War** has an unfortunate episodic quality. This is less the result of a controlled elliptical narrative style than a foreshortening of the dramatic components of the plot. The story initiated by the film is never fully told and one is left with the impression of having seen a series of sketches for a canvas that never materialises.

Such a metaphor is apt in other ways, for Jessop and director of photography Tom Cowan seem to *a priori* favour the pictorial

ambience and resonance of the image over and above its need to carry the story. This art-book rendering of images is especially true of the film's first half and no more so than in the scenes at Balliantyne College.

For all its visual niceties, though, there is a darker tone eating away at the edges of this film. If Emma's sexual world—her longings, desires, fantasies—remain obscured in half-light, her mother's sexuality is both at once more overt and deeply enigmatic. And while the plot can conveniently excuse her sexual frustration, her drunkenness, her sometime irrational fits as justifiably those of a woman under stress (war-time, absent husband), there is a residual meaning in Lee Remick's performance in certain scenes which suggest other psychological undercurrents at work. But, like Emma's wistful, melancholic voice-over, Jessop's clean, poetic imagery holds the darker, murkier undercurrents of real life in abeyance.

ROLANDO CAPUTO

---

[1] The narration is that of an older, unseen, Emma (Helen McDonald).

MICHAEL THORNHILL

THE EVERLASTING SECRET FAMILY

Hemdale Film Corporation presents An FGH Presentation for International Film Management Limited. THE EVERLASTING SECRET FAMILY. © 1987 International Film Management Limited. *Location:* Sydney. *Australian distributor:* Filmpac. *Video:* Filmpac. *Rating:* M (September 1987; 2468.70m). 35mm. 94 mins.

Producer: Michael Thornhill. *Executive producer:* Antony I. Ginnane. *Co-producer:* Sue Carleton. *Scriptwriter:* Frank Moorhouse. Based on Moorhouse's book of short stories, *The Everlasting Secret Family & Other Secrets. Director of photography:* Julian Penney. *Production designer:* Peta Lawson. *Costumes:* Graham Purcell; Anthony Jones (Heather Mitchell's and Beth Child's). *Editor:* Pam Barnetta. *Composer:* Tony Bremner. *Sound recordists:* John Schiefelbein, Grant Stuart. *Sound editor:* Andrew Plain. [*Mixer:* not credited.]

Cast

Arthur Dignam (The Senator), Mark Lee (The Youth), Heather Mitchell (The Wife), Dennis Miller (Eric, the Chauffeur), Paul Goddard (The Son), Beth Child (The Pottery Woman), John Clayton (The Mayor), Nick Holland (The New Chauffeur), Bogdan Koca (The Medical Specialist), Michael Kozuki (Mr Akutangana), Tim Page (The New Judge), Anna Volska (The Wife's Friend), Michael Winchester (The School Teacher), John Meillon (The Judge), James Maddox (Pianist), John Paramor (Barrister), Vicki Luke (Political Secretary), Tony Bremner (Piano Singer).

Backed by ponderous religious music, the camera picks up a school sports day. Beautiful youths pose in white athletic gear. A man, The Senator (Arthur Dignam), emerges from a chauffeur-driven car at St Michael's School for Boys (presumably a Catholic institution) and, after a succession of knowing looks, speaks to one particular boy, The Youth (Mark Lee). Next, the same boy abruptly leaves his classroom, is driven away and is then seen naked to the waist being questioned by The Senator, who is in a bathrobe. A love scene between the two follows and The Youth is then installed in a flat as a kept man ('It's your job to be; to give pleasure'), and slowly drawn into a secret and conspiratorial homosexual world.

Based on Frank Moorhouse's story of the same name, the film appears to have undergone extensive revision, removing itself further from the very explicit description the story contained. Both book and film,

however, have as their starting point innuendo and gossip about conservative politics in Australia over a period from the late 1950s to the present, particularly gossip about the secret sexual preferences of a number of powerful figures in conservative politics and the law.

The film follows the relationship of the two males and sets it against a background of politics—not politics of the big issues, but of the day to day, the secret deals, the personal lives given over to school assemblies and meetings of the party faithful.

Each man develops other interests. The Senator feels obliged to marry and father a child. The Youth has a fling with a voluptuous and ageing art teacher. But both their lives are finally dominated by the membership of a society, The Rose. Vaguely Masonic in its practices, the society's members do a dance while dressed in white and masked. They are then addressed by The Judge (John Meillon), who makes sexual claims on the new young members. Although secret, the society sees itself as providing the nation's moral and political leadership.

This is the stuff of conspiracy theory run rampant, but it is not filmed with any hysteria or sense of revelation. Rather, the film moves throughout its scenes with a sense of

stately calm. The camera moves with elegant, studied grace, the editing is seamless and shock is totally absent, even in the scenes with Meillon as a judge who is into bondage.

The film contains a remarkable view of modern Australian politics, positing, by its desire to generalise, that Australian conservatism is dominated by a clique of homosexual conspirators seeking to exert their influence through a secret old-boy network.

If audiences find difficulty in accepting this 'explanation' of Australian politics, then they will probably find that the film essentially reveals an intolerance of homosexuality that would seem at odds with the libertarian views known to be held by the director and writer. Furthermore, there seems a deep contradiction between the essentially anti-homosexual viewpoint and the lusciously photographed images of masculine men involved in a series of homo-erotic interludes.

GEOFF GARDNER

References
'The Everlasting Secret Family', a review by Anne McDonald, *Cinema Papers*, no. 69, May 1988, pp. 48–50.
'The Everlasting Secret Family', a review by Liz Jacka, *Filmnews*, March 1988, p. 13.

The Senator's Wife (Heather Mitchell) and The Son (Paul Goddard).

EVIL ANGELS

Warner Bros. presents A Cannon Entertainment Inc/Golan-Globus Production in association with Cinema Verity. EVIL ANGELS. *Alternative title:* A Cry in the Dark. © [date not given; atb 1988] Evil Angels Films. *Locations:* Melbourne; Darwin, Ayers Rock, Alice Springs (Northern Territory). *Australian distributor:* Warner Bros. *Opened:* 4 November 1988. *Video:* Warner Home Video. *Rating:* M (September 1988). 35mm. Panavision. 121 mins.

Producer: Verity Lambert. *Executive producers:* Menahem Golan, Yoram Globus. *Line producer:* Roy Stevens. *Scriptwriters:* Robert Caswell, Fred Schepisi. Based on the book *Evil Angels* by John Bryson. *Director of photography:* Ian Baker. *Camera operator:* Ian Jones. *Production designers:* Wendy Dickson, George Liddle. *Costume designer:* Bruce Finlayson. *Editor:* Jill Bilcock. *Composer:* Bruce Smeaton. *Supervising sound recordists:* Craig Carter, Terry Rodman. *Sound recordists:* Gary Wilkins; Peter Fenton (dia.); Martin Oswin, Robin Gray (music). *Sound editors:* Livia Ruzic, Glenn Newnham, Tim Chau, Gary Woodyard.

Cast

Meryl Streep (Lindy Chamberlain), Sam Neill (Michael Chamberlain), Bruce Myles (Barker), Neil Fitzpatrick (Phillips), Charles Tingwell (Justice Muirhead), Maurice Fields (Barritt), Nick Tate (Charlwood), Lewis Fitz-Gerald (Tipple); Lauren Shepherd, Bethany Ann Prickett, Alison O'Connell and Aliza Dason (Azaria); Peter Hosking (Macknay), Matthew Barker (O'Loughlin), Dennis Miller (Sturgess), Brendan Higgins (Kirkham), Ian Swan (Cavanagh), Robert Wallace (Pauling), Sandy Gore (Joy Kuhl), Kevin Miles (Professor Cameron), Jim Holt (John Eldridge), John Howard (Lyle Morris), Frank Holden (Leslie Thompson), Tim Robertson (Wallace), Patsy Stephen (Anne Houghton), Ian Gilmour (John Buckland), Mervyn Drake (Gilroy), Vincent Gil (Roff), Burt Cooper (Gilligan), Mark Little (Constable Morris).

Evil Angels performs a number of dexterous moves to discredit the media and legal constructions of the Chamberlain story and produce an overriding sense of shame. By simple juxtaposition of scenes of media manipulation with scenes of popular myth-making, the film implies that jokes and news reports belong to the same order of exploitation. Similarly, intercutting simple exchanges between Lindy (Meryl Streep) and Michael Chamberlain (Sam Neill) with courtroom drama makes the police–forensic–judicial processes seem ridiculous, even malevolent.

Michael and Lindy emerge as survivors of a nightmare journey from an initial stage of innocence to a determination to prove their innocence. The opening scenes of the film celebrate an innate goodness at the heart of family life, captured in that quintessential Australian family experience: the camping holiday. All the ingredients for a popular mythology are firmly in place by the time Michael is busily barbecuing vegetarian sausages at the fateful campsite. Enter the dingo; exit Azaria. The end of innocence begins.

From this point, the film begins to function as some kind of avenging angel, swooping into pubs, press rooms and dinner parties across Australia, singling out bad taste and media hype for judgement and censure. The Chamberlains, meanwhile, struggle to maintain a sense of bemused incredulity as their own image is fed back to them via local gossip and national headlines. Part of their painful emergence from the cocoon of small-town family life into national prominence involves putting aside their faith in straight talk and learning to play by the media's rules.

For the film's purposes, the media and the myth-making process become mere sideshows for the real drama going on in the bedroom and the courtroom. Time and again, **Evil Angels** falls back on the behind-the-scenes drama of a disrupted family life as its real focus. What emerges is the sense that a marriage contract based on a shared faith in the will of God has been tried, tested and not found wanting. Michael's darkest hour occurs during the Alice Springs trial. As he falls apart from anxiety and misery, Lindy grows more ironic, more stolid, encasing her monumental anger in an expanding body to produce the film's most biting moments of black comedy.

Meryl Streep's performance tics, not to mention her accent, function like a mask which keeps us caught up in the unwinnable game of trying to catch a glimpse of the real Lindy behind the media image. Sam Neill's performance provides a neat foil: his image blends into Michael Chamberlain's, producing a perfect fit.

From the guilty verdict to Lindy's release from prison, **Evil Angels** covers a lot of ground in a very short time. And while the condensation of the events enables a number of issues to be neatly sidestepped, the implication that this extraordinary saga could have taken over the life of any helpless family on holiday in the Australian outback induces both fear and shame.

FELICITY COLLINS[1]

---

[1] Extracted from Collins' review in *Cinema Papers* (see References).

References

'The Making of **Evil Angels**', Philippa Hawker, *Cinema Papers*, no. 70, November 1988, pp. 8–13.

'Evil Angels', a review by Felicity Collins, *Cinema Papers*, no. 71, January 1989, pp. 55–6.

'Fred Schepisi: Pushing the Boundaries', a career interview with the director by Scott Murray, *Cinema Papers*, no. 80, August 1990, pp. 28–42.

Lindy (Meryl Streep) and Michael Chamberlain (Sam Neill).

GRIEVOUS BODILY HARM

International Film Management Limited presents a Smiley Films Production for FGH. *Grievous Bodily Harm*. © 1988 International Film Management Limited. Produced with the assistance of the Australian Film Commission. *Location:* Sydney. *Australian distributor:* Filmpac. *Opened:* September 1988. *Video:* Filmpac. *Rating:* M (August 1988). 35mm. 96 mins.

Producer: Richard Brennan. *Executive producers:* Antony I. Ginnane, Errol Sullivan. *Scriptwriter:* Warwick Hind. *Director of photography:* Ellery Ryan. *Camera operator:* David Williamson. *Production designer:* Roger Ford. *Costume designer:* Roger Ford. *Editor:* Marc van Buuren. *Composer:* Chris Neal. *Sound recordist:* Andrew Ramage. *Sound editors:* Karin Whittington, Phil Dickson, Rick Lisle. *Mixer:* Ian McLoughlin.

Cast

Colin Friels (Tom Stewart), John Waters (Morris Martin), Bruno Lawrence (Ray Birch), Shane Briant (Stephen Enderby), Caz Lederman (Vivian Enderby), Sandy Gore (Barbara Helmsley), Kerry Armstrong (Annie), Joy Bell (Claudine), Kim[1] Gyngell (Mick), John Flaus (Neil Bradshaw), Craig Ashley (Agostino), Gary Waddell (Eddie Weaks), Gary Stalker (Derek Allen), Marisa Wipani (Suzie), Saskia Schlict (Natalie), Dominic Gowans (Prentice), Don Reed (Headmaster), Ric Carter (Les), Sheridan Murphy (Katherine), Vic Rooney (Pellegrini).

Crime reporter Tom Stewart (Colin Friels) watches a stake-out.

Tom Stewart (Colin Friels) is a journalist with a nose for the crime beat and a lack of conscience when it comes to reporting the facts. He has just written a book about police corruption in a murder case, even though he suspected the convicted man to be guilty (as turned out to be the case). And when he has a chance to secretly pocket almost $300,000 of stolen money from a wrecked car, he takes it.

On the other side of the law, so to speak, is Ray Birch (Bruno Lawrence), a detective-sergeant who is not averse to shooting a man in cold blood and then calling it self-defence. Clearly, he and Tom are brothers of a sort and, in a spirit of mutual distrust common to the law and the press, they help each other out.

But false friendship is strained when they investigate the murder spree by Morris Martin (John Waters), a deranged school teacher on the trail of his supposedly dead lover, Claudine (Joy Bell). Morris thinks he has seen her and he's prepared to kill anyone in his way.

After a minor-key opening where Morris fixatedly watches a porno video he shot of Claudine and two friends, the film cuts to a brisk crime-scene sequence where, amidst masses of rain and the blue-grey light director of photography Ellery Ryan so loves, Tom steals the money. Director Mark Joffe cleverly leads one to think that Tom is at first a cop, then a likeable journalist, then finally an unscrupulous thief. It is crisp and to the point.

But the film, having established Morris and Tom, then predictably does the same with Ray. At the beginning of a stake-out sequence where a gunman is holding a girl hostage, Ray is shown as a good cop doing an honest job; he even calls on Tom's help to diffuse a dangerous situation. But this is just a ruse to get the gunman to the door so that Ray can kill him. He then fires his rifle into the ground and says the gunman fired first. After a bit of pressure, Tom agrees to go along with the cover-up.

This is where the film stalls (and from where it only fitfully recovers). The scripting is far too obvious and the structure dully predictable: set up a character, then undermine audience expectation; then set up another and play a similar twist. By the end of the stake-out, the audience knows too much and has too little to look forward to. What 'surprises' director Mark Joffe and scriptwriter Warwick Hind do toss up (sexual perversity, Claudine's still being alive, etc.) lack dramatic pay-off.

The dialogue, too, is not always comfortable, especially when the film ventures into the realms of dark sexuality (as where Morris near-throttles an ex-lover; she complains, but he says that is how she taught him). In fact, the film's handling of sexuality is rather naughty schoolboyish and is a very pale version of, say, *Miami Vice* where the perversity truly unsettles.

There are problems, too, in Morris' characterisation: there is no dramatic interest in his going mad; no sympathy, no revulsion. It is just predictable and, at times, a bit silly (especially when poor Morris reappears near the end after a car accident).

Where the film works best is in the portrayal of Claudine, a very much alive and cold-hearted prostitute. Given that the thriller genre has been heavily populated over the decades by whores with hearts of gold, the icy manipulations of Claudine make a rewarding variant—so much so that her departure to New York with the gullible Ray Birch is the film's one truly chilling moment. One certainly doesn't need the newspaper headline to tell us of Ray's fate.

Compared to other Australian thrillers, the slimmest of all genre pickings, **Grievous Bodily Harm** is of interest for some well-scripted scenes, a winning performance from Colin Friels and a stylish look to some scenes (particularly night exteriors). What lets it down mostly is the unnecessary explicitness and resultant lack of tension.

SCOTT MURRAY

_____
[1] Usually spelt 'Kym'.

_____
References
'**Grievous Bodily Harm**', a review by Peter Lawrance, *Cinema Papers*, no. 71, January 1989, p. 56.
'**Grievous Bodily Harm**', a review by Liz Jacka, *Filmnews*, November 1988, p. 13.

HAYDN KEENAN'S PANDEMONIUM

Smart St. Films in association with Tra La La Films Limited present[s] HAYDN KEENAN'S PANDEMONIUM. © 1987 K.F.M. Pandemonium Pty Ltd. *Budget:* $600,000. *Location:* Bondi (Sydney). *Australian distributor:* Smart St. Films. *Video:* not released. *Rating:* R. 35mm. 88 mins.

Producers: Alex Cutler, Haydn Keenan. *Executive producer:* Patric Juillet. *Co-executive producers:* Malcolm Olivestone, Anthony James. *Line producer:* Helen Boyd. *Scriptwriters:* Peter Gailey, Haydn Keenan. *Director of photography:* David Sanderson. *Production designer:* Melody Cooper. *Costume designer:* Melody Cooper. *Editor:* Paul Healy. *Composer:* Cameron Allan. *Sound recordist:* Phillip Keros. *Sound editors:* Philippa Harvey, Helen Brown. *Mixers:* Paul Huntingford, Peter "Chuck" Fenton, Phil "Randy" Heywood, Martin "Buzz" Oswin.

Cast

David Argue (Kales Leadingham; Ding the Dingo), Amanda Dole (The Dingo Girl), Esben Storm (E. B. DeWoolf), Arna-Maria Winchester (P. B. DeWoolf), Lex Marinos (Det. Sgt. Dick Dickerson); Rainee Skinner, Kerry Mack (The Twins); Ian Nimmo (Mr. David), Ashley Grenville (Little Adolph; The Paperboy), Mercia Deane-Jones (Morticia), Henk Johannes (The Count), Pete Smith (Peter Kong), Gary Foley (The Holy Ghost), Haydn Keenan (Dr. Doctor; Adrian), Ignatius Jones (Director; Marriage Celebrant; Auctioneer), Greg Ham (Marvo the Magician), Kate Reid (Mother Witness), Robert Kewley (Father Witness), Rupert Reid (Child Witness), Robyn Gibbes (Police Constable).

Haydn Keenan's Pandemonium opens with Kales Leadingham (David Argue), a babbling and crazed young man, escaping from a lunatic asylum. Sitting on a bus stop, he begins to tell a tale of 'love, sacrifice and revenge so startling that, had I not been there personally to experience it, I would have dismissed it'.

The film goes into flashback, opening on Bondi Beach where a semi-naked woman making animal noises appears. The Dingo Girl (Amanda Dole) and Kales then appear on the step of a bizarre warehouse, a disused movie studio where a weird collection of inhabitants ('a few trusted tenants') are up to perverse and violent no good. Among them is a group involved in some idiotic insemination plot involving Adolph Hitler.

P. B. DeWoolf (Arna-Maria Winchester).

A dozen or so characters roam through the building and the plot, deliberately committing acts of violence and seduction, and coming up with some moments that are extremely distasteful: a fœtus is put in a blender; Little Adolph (Ashley Grenville) has his penis unceremoniously sliced off; the naked girl turns out to have been raised by dingoes, leading to many jokes referring to the Chamberlain case. Along the way, there are songs and some sort of 'happy' ending.

Haydn Keenan directed the film and appears in it as a moustachioed villain involved in cloning experiments (his long-time collaborator and partner Esben Storm plays a similarly sleazy film producer mostly determined on seducing The Dingo Girl, played with stoic lack of expression by Amanda Dole). It is clearly an attempt by Keenan to make a bad-taste box-office success, deliberately shocking and involving much in the way of humour designed to make its audience give the groan of sick delight that characterises the most successful long-running cult movies.

Haydn Keenan's Pandemonium has the blood of **The Rocky Horror Picture Show** (Jim Sharman, 1975) coursing through its exploitative veins. That is not necessarily a bad model (or even a bad thing!). The film,

however, failed to get a proper release and it may have been that its elements were simply too distasteful (too 'gross' in common parlance) for those attempting to assess its commercial potential.

What may have inhibited its distribution was the fact that, while its subject and plot have a massive component of black humour and perversion, the shooting of the film conforms to far more tasteful rules and thus avoids the truly exploitationist elements associated with it: the relished close-ups of sex and violence. Perhaps the film-makers were aware of the essence of exploitation without being aware of the rules developed to analyse it (by Joe Bob Briggs, perhaps).

This is pure speculation and does not detract from the fact that this is probably the least boring Australian film ever made. No matter how much the viewer may writhe and groan at its excess, the film never lets up on its momentum and its desire to hurtle down those vulgar paths without regard to any other matters…such as reputation or taste.

GEOFF GARDNER

Reference
'Cameron Allan: What's the Score?', an interview with the composer by Felicity Fox, *Cinema Papers*, no. 69, May 1988, pp. 16–17.

THE MAN FROM SNOWY RIVER II

The Burrowes Film Group and Hoyts Entertainment. THE MAN FROM SNOWY RIVER II. *Alternative title:* Return to Snowy River Part II (US). © 1982 The Burrowes Film Group. *Location:* Mansfield and environs (Victoria). *Australian distributor:* Hoyts. *Opened:* 25 March 1988. *Video:* Hoyts Polygram Video. *Rating:* PG. 35mm. Panavision. 97 mins.

Producer: Geoff Burrowes. *Executive producers:* Dennis Wright, Kent Lovell, John Kearney. *Scriptwriters:* John Dixon, Geoff Burrowes. *Director of photography:* Keith Wagstaff. *Camera operator:* David Williamson. *Production designer:* Leslie Binns. *Costume designer:* Jenny Arnott. *Editor:* Gary Woodyard. *Composer:* Bruce Rowland. *Sound supervisor:* Terry Rodman. *Sound recordist:* Gary Wilkins. *Sound editors:* Peter Burgess, Tim Chau. *Mixers:* David Harrison, Ron Purvis, Terry Rodman.

Cast

Tom Burlinson (Jim), Sigrid Thornton (Jessica), Brian Dennehy (Harrison), Nicholas Eadie (Alistair Patton), Mark Hembrow (Seb), Bryan Marshall (Hawker), Rhys McConnochie (Patton Snr), Peter Cummins (Jake), Cornelia Francis (Mrs Darcy), Tony Barry (Jacko), Wyn Roberts (Priest), Alec Wilson (Patton's Crony), Peter Browne (Reilly), Alan Hopgood (Simmons), Mark Pennell (Collins), Charlie Lovick (Jacko's Son), Greg Stroud (Jockey), Nick Waters (Announcer at Harrison's), Cae Rees (Barmaid), John Raaen (Lout in Bar), Bruce Clarkson (Bystander at Harrison's), Peter Tulloch (Bystander outside Church), Christopher Stevenson (Harrison's Waiter), Geoff Beamish (Frank), Gerald Egan (Jamie McKay).

There have been some changes from the original in this sequel: Geoff Burrowes is now the director, and Kirk Douglas has, in true soapie fashion, metamorphosed into Brian Dennehy as Harrison. However, other than that, this film continues in the blatant myth-making tracks of its predecessor in its attempts to delineate what it means to be a 'real' Australian and, almost tautologically, what it means to be a 'real' Australian male.

Jim (Tom Burlinson) is still having to prove his incipient manhood and, once again, his final success in this is mirrored in his mastery over the landscape, the wild horses and the woman, Jessica (Sigrid Thornton). While he must still do battle with the powerful father—a battle that is finally won when he saddles up and rides the hitherto malevolent black stallion—the struggle in this film is largely figured in the terms of an egalitarian ethos which is pitted against the traditions and hierarchies of a European culture. Jim's 'dry-as-a-bone' feats on horseback are finally seen as superior to those of his rival for Jessica, the wealthy young cavalry officer Alistair Patton (Nicholas Eadie); his mateship with Seb (Mark Hembrow), and his good relations with the high country men and the simple working folk (who 'have no bosses') is privileged over Patton's 'lord of the manor' attitude to them; and the genuine emotion implicit in his cross-class union with Jessica is seen as preferable to any money-based perpetuation of aristocratic families.

Sentimentally framed against the magnificent backdrops of the high country, the film asks one to see Jim and Jessica as parents of a nation which upholds anti-authoritarian values, which privileges a virtually sacred bond between a man, his horses and his physical environment, and in which a concept of manhood is established through a taming of the 'high stepping fillies' and an ostensibly 'natural' patrilineal inheritance of power from stallion to colt.

ROSE LUCAS

Reference
'The Man from Snowy River II', a review by Freda Freiberg, *Cinema Papers*, no. 69, May 1988, pp. 51–2.

Patton Snr (Rhys McConnochie) and Harrison (Brian Dennehy).

VINCENT WARD

THE NAVIGATOR: A MEDIEVAL ODYSSEY

Arenafilm and the Film Investment Corporation of New Zealand present [...] with the assistance of the AFC [and] the NZ Film Commission THE NAVIGATOR [/] A medievAl odyssey.[1] © 1988 Arenafilm Pty Ltd. A New Zealand-Australia Co-production. *Budget:* $4.3 million. *Locations:* Auckland, Mount Ruapehu, Waitomo, Southern Alps (New Zealand). *Australian distributor:* Ronin. *Opened:* December 1988. *Video:* The Home Cinema Group. *Rating:* PG (August 1988). 35mm. 91 mins.

Producer: John Maynard. *Co-producer:* Gary Hannam. *Scriptwriters:* Vincent Ward, Kely Lyons, Geoff Chapple. From an original idea by Vincent Ward. *Director of photography:* Geoffrey Simpson. *Camera operator:* Allen Guilford. *Production designer:* Sally Campbell. *Costume designer:* Glenys Jackson. *Editor:* John Scott. *Composer:* Davood A. Tabrizi. *Sound recordists:* Dick Reade; Richard Lush (music). *Sound editors:* Liz Goldfinch (dia.); Peter Townsend, Lee Smith (fx). *Additional sound editors:* Danielle Wiessner, Greg Bell. *Mixers:* Phil Judd; Richard Lush, Davood A. Tabrizi (music).

Cast

Bruce Lyons (Connor), Chris Haywood (Arno), Hamish McFarlane (Griffin), Marshall Napier (Searle), Noel Appleby (Ulf), Paul Livingston (Martin), Sarah Pierse (Linnet), Mark Wheatley (Tog 1), Tony Herbert (Tog 2), Jessica Cardiff-Smith (Esme), Roy Wesney (Grandpa), Kathleen-Elizabeth Kelly (Grandma), Jay Saussey (Griffin's Girlfriend), Charles Walker (Old Chrissie), Desmond Kelly (Smithy), Bill Le Marquand (Tom), Jay Lavea Laga'aia (Jay), Norman Fairley (Submarine Captain), Alister Babbage (Grigor).

There are many ways of noting parallels between today's world and a former time. In the case of Vincent Ward's **The Navigator: A Medieval Odyssey**, it has the brilliant conceit of having five men and a boy tunnel from a Middle Ages ravaged by Black Death to a present day of industrial horror and reflecting glass.

It is 1348 and Connor (Bruce Lyons) returns from out of the wasteland to his poor Cumbrian mining village to warn of pestilence sweeping the land. A boy, Griffin (Hamish McFarlane), then dreams that his village can be saved if they dig through the centre of the earth to where a great cathedral stands. There they must cast and restore the copper spike before the sun rises.

As the boy recounts his dream, one sees its visualisation as flash forwards in time. On tunnelling through to 1980s Auckland, the six Cumbrians face the obstacles of crossing a busy freeway, convincing some foundry workers (on their last night of employment) to cast a copper spike, crossing a sea as a submarine surfaces and climbing the cathedral steeple.

Throughout his tale, Griffin also sees flashes of someone's death, his reading of which keeps changing until he realises it is his own. He then discovers he is infected with the plague that Connor has brought back, and dies.

Ward sets up many readings of these parallel times: Black Death and AIDS; a joint fear of annihilation (plague and nuclear); an interest in one's antecedents/descendants; and so on. In substance, these readings don't amount to more than notions, and one's response is more intuitive than anything else. Such frissons do, however, cumulate into a rather powerful experience, where the mythic elements work directly on the viewer. (Perhaps the only exception is the putting of the spike on the cathedral, which is curiously flat dramatically given all that has preceded it.)

Ward's greatest strength (and weakness) is his visual imagery. At best, as in the black-and-white scenes of a snow-bound Cumbria, it is breathtaking and proof of a talented director with clear vision and the technical skill to achieve it.

At the same time, too many images and stylistics in the film are 'borrowed' from filmic predecessors—in particular, Andrei Tarkovsky's **Andrei Rublev** (1966) and **Ivanovo Detstvo** (**Ivan's Childhood**, 1962). The stark close-ups of Griffin, the wheel over the pit, the very contrast of black clothes against white snow, the floundering white horse and the final shouting about 'The bells, the bells' go beyond mere homage to an unnerving preferencing of another's work above one's own. (As well, the staging of several scenes, and the theatrical performances, bespeak the influence of Peter Brook.)

However, all this is not to deny that **The Navigator: A Medieval Odyssey** is one of the finer and more striking films of Australian (and New Zealand) cinema.

SCOTT MURRAY

---

[1] This title is hard to reproduce because 'a medieval odyssey' is all lower-case except for the 'a's.

References

'**The Navigator** [sic]: Vincent Ward's Past Dreams of the Future', an article on Ward (with quotes) by Michele Nayman, *Cinema Papers*, no. 69, May 1988, pp. 30–1.

'The Two Ages of **The Navigator** [sic]', an article by Peter Hughes, *Cinema Papers*, no. 72, March 1989, pp. 26–7.

'**The Navigator** [sic]', a review by Barbra Luby, *Filmnews*, December 1988, p. 10.

Griffin (Hamish McFarlane) in a modern world.

THE PURSUIT OF HAPPINESS

Jequerity Films presents The Pursuit of Happiness. © 1987 Jequerity Pty Ltd. Produced with the assistance of the Australian Film Commission and The Film & Television Institute (W.A.). *Location:* Fremantle (Western Australia). *Australian distributor:* AFI Distribution. *Video:* AFI. *Rating:* PG. 16mm. 83 mins.

Producer: Martha Ansara. *Associate producers:* Kit Guyatt, Madelon Wilkens. *Executive producer:* Richard Mason. *Scriptwriters:* Martha Ansara, Alex Glasgow, Laura Black and cast. *Director of photography:* Michael Edols. [*Production designer:* not credited.] *Costume designer:* Tish Phillips. *Editor:* Kit Guyatt. *Sound:* Pat Fiske. [*Sound editor:* not credited.] *Mixer:* George Hart.

Cast

Laura Black (Anna), Peter Hardy (John), Anna Gare (Mandy), Jack Coleman (Stan); Dennis Schultz, Alex Glasgow, Nola Edgar, David Colson; Senator Jo Vallentine, Alec Smith, Don Allison, Ex-Lt. Commander Michael Lynch, Brent Sumner, Marge Spence, Liz Woods, Rob Mann, Julie Barker, Maurice Venables, Kelli Stevens, Don Whitton, Katie and Samantha Fry (as themselves).

Anna (Laura Black) and John (Peter Hardy) are a married, middle-aged, Fremantle couple who have a 15-year-old daughter, Mandy (Anna Gare). John is on the local council and has recently gone out on his own, trying to establish a PR business. Anna, after being a housewife and mother for fifteen years, embarks on a journalistic career, and Mandy is into protesting against nuclear weapons and singing in a rock band. She has a tense relationship with her father, a confused one with her mother and prefers to spend most of her time with her grandfather, Stan (Jack Coleman), who is a war veteran and a peace activist.

The various tensions arising from the differences in political concerns, personal morals and preoccupations with social issues between the members of this family provide the patchy background for this film, which is basically a documentary on the various menaces of nuclear weapons to Australia and Australian military involvement with America. The final result is an uneven, uninvolving and unnecessarily didactic piece of mixed-genre cinema.

Attempting to be powerful in dealing with such serious issues as nuclear war, feminism and materialism, the film fails to be anything but a stream of clichés in the

Mandy (Anna Gare) and Anna (Laura Black).

'fiction' part of the film and an endless bombardment of the viewer with 'vital' facts about nuclear issues and their relevance to Australia in the 'doco' part. The main characters are never fully realised and remain mere caricatures of what they should be.

John is the 'typical' male, preoccupied with making more and more money, which, as he points out, is a way of 'winning', and the film points out is a metaphor for men fighting wars. He is completely insensitive to his wife, daughter and father. He is also, and most unsubtly so, resentful of his wife's attempting to find her true self after years of subjugation to his mores.

Anna's attempts to define herself, 'awaken' politically and rebel against being a 'good little wife' are all too obvious. But at least Laura Black can act, which is not something that can be said about the other members of the cast. Nevertheless, delivering lines such as, 'I was sick of being an empty-headed woman, all instinct and emotion', and making them sound genuine would be difficult for anyone.

Mandy, throughout the film, is kept too peripheral to make her significance believable. Besides, Anna Gare looks too old to be fifteen, and dressing her up in pony-tails or giving her dolls to play with does not change this fact.

Visually, the film is dull, perhaps deliberately so, as it is trying hard to capture the glib aspects of existence. The pace is very slow, attempting to be thought-provoking, one supposes. Overall, the relevance of the film's nuclear issues seems dated, as the world deems nuclear disarmament to be vital. But it is not impossible that this little-known film could have been a necessary drop in the ocean of protest that helps the world in general to begin to think differently.

ANNA GUL

References

'Question and Ansara', an interview with director Martha Ansara by Anna Grieve, *Cinema Papers*, no. 68, March 1988, pp. 6–7.
'Martha Ansara: Happiness', an interview by Jeni Thornley, *Filmnews*, February 1988, pp. 8–9.

RIKKY AND PETE

United Artists present[s] A Cascade Films Production. Rikky and Pete. © 1988 United Artists Pictures, Inc. Produced with the assistance of Film Victoria. *Budget:* $4 million. *Locations:* Melbourne; Broken Hill (New South Wales). *Australian distributor:* UIP. *Opened:* 10 June 1988. *Video:* Warner Home Video. *Rating:* M. 35mm. 101 mins.

Producers: Nadia Tass, David Parker. *Executive producer:* Bryce Menzies. *Co-producer:* Timothy White. *Scriptwriter:* David Parker. *Director of photography:* David Parker. *Production designer:* Josephine Ford. *Costume designer:* Phil Eagles. *Additional costume design:* Anje Bos. *Editor:* Ken Sallows. *Composer:* Eddie Raynor. *Songs:* Phil Judd. *Sound recordist:* Lloyd Carrick. *Sound editors:* Frank Lipson, Craig Carter; Ross Chambers (dia.). *Mixer:* Roger Savage.

Cast

Stephen Kearney (Pete), Nina Landis (Rikky), Bruce Spence (Ben), Lewis Fitzgerald[1] (Adam), Dorothy Alison (Mrs Menzies), Roderick Williams (Holy Joe), Tetchie Agbayani (Flossie), Bill Hunter (Whitstead), Bruno Lawrence (Sonny), Don Reid (Mr Menzies), Peter Cummins (Delahunty), Peter Hehir (Desk Sergeant), Ralph Cotterill (George Pattinger), Denis Lees (Fingers), Rod Baxter (Truckyard Man), Graham Rouse (Drunk at Winton), Roger Cox (General Store Owner), Alan Hopgood (Laughing Uncle), Burt Cooper (Gallery Weirdo), John Lee (High Ranking Officer), Richard Healy (Winton Barman), Patti Perkins (Aunt), Jaime Gough (Young Boy).

Rikky and Pete is the follow-up film to Malcolm (1986), the successful debut feature of husband-and-wife team Nadia Tass and David Parker. With an unexpected critical and box-office success, industry logic often dictates that if a formula works the first time then it will likely work again, only with a better budget and thus wider appeal next time around.

Rikky (Nina Landis) and Pete (Stephen Kearney) are brother and sister from an upper-middle-class family. Rikky is a qualified geologist unable to find suitable work in her home town of Melbourne. She also entertains a very small singing career that is going nowhere fast. Pete, like Malcolm (Colin Friels), is an inventive genius, who has a morning shift delivering newspapers in a novel way—a buggie adapted into a contraption which folds newspapers into paper planes and sends them in flight to the desired

Rikky (Nina Landis), Flossie (Tetchie Agbayani) and Pete (Stephen Kearney).

doorstep. But, by night, Pete pulls off costly pranks to taunt the local police sergeant, Whitstead (Bill Hunter), who apparently caused an accident which left Rikky and Pete's mother (Dorothy Alison) in a wheelchair.

Life for the pair in Melbourne does not seem to offer anything other than frustration: their father (Don Reid) is authoritarian and overbearing, and Whitstead is finally figuring out the identity of his prankster. Surreptitiously, the pair borrow their father's car and, with Whitstead in pursuit, head for the mining town of Mount Isa where, working together as a team, they make good.

For this second outing Tass and Parker retain much of the elements central to the success of **Malcolm**: the interpersonal relationship of a close-knit unit of people; a central character whose mode of behaviour is askance to normal social behaviour; and, of course, the inventive gadgetry. But Tass and Parker seem to have miscalculated on how these elements hold together.

To illustrate, one need only compare the opening segments of each film. Malcolm's unauthorised ride through the streets of Melbourne on his makeshift, one-man tram is pure joy for him. The ride is without use value. Only with the introduction of the incompetent crim Frank (John Hargreaves),

does Malcolm's relationship with gadgets change and, by the end of the film, it has turned into something else. Pete's delivery of newspapers, on the other hand, has use value in relation to the job. This opening is about the command of that particular situation, and in a small way reflects the position of superiority Pete can have over his world. This is indeed how **Rikky and Pete** concludes after brother and sister return to Melbourne: Pete is seen commanding a fleet of his newspaper delivery contraptions for a large newspaper firm.

In this way, Malcolm has a subtle though much greater anarchic quality than Pete clearly seems to act out. Pete merely fulfils the unconscious and contradictory logic of his anti-authoritarian position: the will to command was always there from the start.

RAFFAELE CAPUTO

[1] Usually the 'g' is capitalised; thus, 'Fitz-Gerald'.

References

'Rikky, Pete and Mine Over Matter', an article (with quotes) on director of photography–scriptwriter David Parker by Philippa Hawker, *Cinema Papers*, no. 69, May 1988, pp. 26–8.
'**Rikky and Pete**', a review by Barbra Luby, *Filmnews*, July 1988, p. 14.

SHAME

Barron Films and UAA Films. Shame. © 1987 Barron Films. *Location:* Toojay (Western Australia). *Australian distributor:* Hoyts. *Opened:* 26 February 1988. *Video:* RCA–Columbia–Hoyts. *Rating:* M (June 1987; cut to 90 mins in February 1988). Super 16 (blown up to 35mm). 94 mins.

Producers: Damien Parer, Paul D. Barron. *Scriptwriters:* Beverly Blankenship, Michael Brindley. *Director of photography:* Joseph Pickering. *Camera operator:* David Carroll. *Production designer:* Phil Peters. *Costume designer:* Noel Howell. *Editor:* Kerry Regan. *Composer:* Mario Millo. *Sound recordist:* David Glasser. *Mixers:* Michael Thomas, Julian Ellingworth.

Cast

Deborra-Lee Furness (Asta Cadell), Tony Barry (Tim Curtis), Simone Buchanan (Lizzie Curtis), Gillian Jones (Tina Farrel), Peter Aanensen (Sergeant Wal Cuddy), Margaret Ford (Norma Curtis), David Franklin (Danny Fiske), Bill McClusky (Ross), Allison Taylor (Penny), Phil Dean (Gary), Graeme "Stig" Wemyss (Bobby), Douglas Walker (Andrew), Matthew Quartermaine (Brian), Matt Hayden (Wayne), Warren Jones (Bruce), Faith Clayton (Dulcie), Mandy Henning (Rita), Julie Hudspeth (Fay), Pat Skevington (Mrs Rudolph), Robert Luobikis (Little Stevie).

Shame is a powerful example of an Australian film that attempts to use old genre and narrative conventions to stress some contemporary issues. Its central narrative focuses on the shocking predicament in a rural Western Australian town, Ginborak, where gang rape is an accepted part of 'boys being boys', and is ignored and indeed tacitly condoned by the male authorities of the town.

Asta Cadell (Deborra-Lee Furness), as the stranger who arrives upon this scene, is a blonde-haired, leather-clad, urban professional touring the apparently idyllic countryside on her expensive bike, making her a sharp class and behavioural contrast to the trapped and down-trodden women of the town. What she discovers when she rides into town, both about the gender relations there and about her own attitudes towards physical violence and justice, shocks and disturbs.

Asta befriends the most recent victim, Lizzie Curtis (Simone Buchanan), and attempts to turn the tide of male violence by encouraging Lizzie to be more assertive in the defence of both her physical and legal rights. However, this encouragement and the potential rôle-model which Asta offers to the women of Ginborak is seriously undercut by the narrative outcome which highlights the film's underlying uncertainty about the causes of such gender-based violence and the appropriate responses to it: the film concludes with a close-up of Asta's tormented face as she is forced to acknowledge that, on one level at least, Lizzie's death has occurred as a direct result of her own intervention.

This story is also overlaid by the narrative and ideological aspects of **Shame**'s genre model, the 1953 classic Western **Shane** (George Stevens). Although the events which occur are different, the structural pattern of heroic stranger riding into a strife-ridden community, winning the affection and admiration of one of its young members and inevitably riding off again, remains intact. Where this complicates **Shame**'s political message is that it tends to cast Asta as the exceptional woman and not as a possible rôle for the ordinary woman; also, as we see her literally fighting it out with the town's reprehensible louts, she becomes barely distinguishable from the maverick individual male hero, who, in the end, simply proves to be smarter and tougher than his asocial opponents.

Perhaps most worryingly, Asta's behaviour seems to suggest that the notion of power has again been represented as a conventionally masculine and physical prerogative. Despite the horror and disgust engendered by the narrative, the film has offered no real way out of the debilitating gender stereotypes of active male and passive female, as its bleak conclusion envisions no viable options for resistance to sexual attack.

ROSE LUCAS

References

'Steve Jodrell After **Shame**', an article (with quotes) by Bron Sibree, *Cinema Papers*, no. 70, November 1988, p. 32.

'Shame', the first part of the screenplay by Beverly Blankenship and Michael Brindley, ibid., pp. 34–43.

'Shame', the second part of the screenplay, *Cinema Papers*, no. 72, March 1989, pp. 61–6.

'Shame', the third part of the screenplay, *Cinema Papers*, no. 74, July 1989, pp. 61–7.

'Shame', an unsigned review, *Filmnews*, May 1988, p. 9.

'A Woman on a Motorbike', an interview with co-scriptwriter Michael Brindley by Lyndell Fairleigh, *Filmnews*, July 1988, p. 10.

Asta Cadell (Deborra-Lee Furness) and Mr Fiske (Colin McEwan).

THE SURFER

Frontier Films, in association with the Producers' Circle[,] present[s] The Surfer. © 1986 Night Flight Limited. Special thanks to the Queensland Film Corporation. *Locations:* Brisbane, Surfers Paradise (Queensland). *Australian distributor:* Frontier Films. *Video:* CBS Fox Video. *Rating:* M. 35mm. 90 mins.

Producers: James M. Vernon, Frank Shields. *Executive producer:* Grahame Jennings. *Scriptwriter:* David Marsh. Based on an original story by Frank Shields. *Director of photography:* Michael Edols. *Production designer:* Martin O'Neill. *Wardrobe:* Fiona Nicolls. *Editor:* Greg Bell. *Composer:* Davood Tabrizi. *Sound recordist:* Max Bowring. *Sound editor:* Greg Bell. *Sound mixer:* Phil Judd.

Cast

Gary Day (Sam Barlow), Gosia Dobrowolska (Gina), Rod Mullinar (Hagan), Tony Barry (Calhoun), Gerard MacGuire (Jack), Kris McQuade (Trish), Stephen Leeder (Slaney), Rose Adami (Slaney's Wife), Tony Bellette (Car Salesman), Alexandra Black (Country Barmaid), Raymond Chan (Long Hair Vietnamese), David Glendenning (Murph), Sueyan Cox (Casino Barmaid), Jose Element (Garage Boy), Joan Grimsley (Girl Guide Leader), Tyrone Hopkins (Aboriginal Passenger), Claire Hobson (Jack's Daughter), Fred Pembelton (Minister for Housing), Greg Ross (Garage Man); Bill Sandy, Nancy Mary Sandy, Linda Sandy (Aboriginal Family).

The Surfer is a low-budget action-thriller which, somewhat unexpectedly, developed a rather high-profile reputation when it was selected for the Directors' Fortnight at Cannes in 1987. Justificatory comparisons then were made, fairly diffidently, with the films of Samuel Fuller. Thus, the programme note writer for the Edinburgh Film Festival (which invited the film to participate after its Cannes screening) was able to enthuse, 'If there are to be successors to Hollywood's great action directors, Frank Shields could number among them.'

The central character is Sam Barlow (Gary Day), a Vietnam veteran, living a lazy life hiring out surfboards and betting on the races, who reluctantly accepts an invitation to attend a party thrown by old friends Trish (Kris McQuade) and Jack (Gerard MacGuire). There, a woman named Gina (Gosia Dobrowolska) asks him to carry a letter to Jack. He also meets Calhoun (Tony Barry), a hardnosed police detective.

After reading the letter, Jack asks Sam to accompany him to a mystery destination and, when they arrive, Jack is killed. Sam starts to investigate matters and, after meeting up with the mysterious Gina, they set out to unravel the mystery of Jack's death.

Sam encounters another veteran, Slaney (Stephen Leeder), once married to a Vietnamese woman, and his search brings him into contact with Hagan (Rod Mullinar), a casino operator. Sam and Gina, despite Gina's rôle in the affaire being complicated by her allegiances to the villains, discover information about a ship arriving and head north, hotly pursued by Calhoun, who dies in a vicious fight with Sam, and then by Hagan, who it turns out is involved with mysterious political forces. Finally, Sam and Gina are the last people standing and eventually leave together.

Those who saw the film as an inheritor of some noble Hollywood traditions found its straightforward brutal energy and vitality as revealing some grasp of action technique generally fairly foreign to Australian film-making. (Those qualities, in fact, were more

in evidence in Frank Shields' earlier film **Hostage: The Christine Maresch Story**, 1983, which appeared to have the advantage of a higher budget and hence rather better production values and shooting schedules.)

The Surfer's energy makes only the most modest impact and its story, its editing and its attempt to be a genre piece are not particularly effective. As well, it is neither reflexive enough to be able to contain an element of parody (Sam's few one-line ripostes just aren't slick enough to amuse: 'Have you ever been in trouble with the police before? I crashed a Policeman's Ball once' is about the best), or bold and eccentric enough in the plotting to keep the audience involved.

On the evidence of this film, Shields is another director with a desire to make the low-budget action thriller that Don Siegel or Phil Karlson could turn their hand to with ease. The comparisons with Fuller, whose work was always more baroque and extreme, particularly in its choice of both subjects and protagonists, are way off the mark.

GEOFF GARDNER

On the run and in love: Sam Barlow (Gary Day) and Gina (Gosia Dobrowolska).

THE TALE OF RUBY ROSE

Hemdale Film Corporation in association with Antony I. Ginnane and FGH, a Seon Film production. THE TALE OF RUBY ROSE. © 1987 Seon Film Productions. Produced with the assistance of Film Victoria. *Location:* Central Highlands of Tasmania. *Australian distributor:* Seon Films. *Video:* Home Cinema Group. *Rating:* PG (November 1987; 2743m). Super 16 (blown up to 35mm). Anamorphic. 100 mins.

Producers: Bryce Menzies, Andrew Wiseman. *Executive producer:* Basia Puszka. *Associate producer:* Ian Pringle. *Scriptwriter:* Roger Scholes. *Director of photography:* Steve Mason. *Production designer:* Bryce Perrin. *Wardrobe:* Helen Poynder. *Editor:* Roger Scholes. *Composer:* Paul Schutze. *Sound recordist:* Bob Cutcher. *Sound editors:* Andrew Plain, Adrienne Parr (dia.); Roger Scholes, Paul Schutze (fx). *Mixer:* Bruce Emery.

Cast

Melita Jurisic (Ruby Rose), Chris Haywood (Henry Rose), Rod Zuanic (Gem), Martyn Sanderson (Bennett), Sheila Florance (Grandma), Sheila Kennelly (Cook), John McKelvey (Tasker), Wilkie Collins (Father), Nell Dobson (Mrs Bennett), Terry Garcia (Vassi), Marie-Rose Jones (Singer), Graham Davis (Town Man), Phil Hammond (Dead Bennett).

Ruby Rose (Melita Jurisic) and Grandma (Sheila Florance).

At around the time when, according to The Tale of Ruby Rose, Ruby (Melita Jurisic) was meeting and marrying Henry Rose (Chris Haywood), the first Australian feature film to exploit the beauties of the rugged Tasmanian highlands was being produced: Louise Lovely's **Jewelled Nights** (1925), a romantic melodrama of a society heiress who ran away from a forced marriage. It was directed by its star, whose golden curls were tied severely back and hidden so she could pass as male in the all-male world of the osmiridian miners. In a typically romantic resolution, her disguise is eventually penetrated by the man with whom she has fallen in love and who rescues her from that environment.

Ruby Rose's life in the wilderness is not nearly so simple, nor her problems so easily resolved. She and Henry live with their adopted son, Gem (Rod Zuanic), in a slab hut under the Walls of Jerusalem, insulated from all but occasional contact with the outside world. Despite the grandeur of their surroundings, they eke out a subsistence by selling the skins of trapped possums and wallabies. Gem has difficulty coming to terms with Henry's pragmatic philosophy that

'things grow and you kill them'. Ruby copes well with such realities, but struggles with other demons. (The isolation and the privation of living under such extremes of climate and terrain are spectacularly captured by director of photography Steve Mason.)

In Ruby's experience, men have always controlled access to knowledge—and have not necessarily shared it. Henry did earlier teach her to read, but her father withheld knowledge of her mother and grandmother, and even Henry is now withholding information about his plans for the farm. She cannot depend on men to save her, so she saves herself. She undertakes her journey, the perils of several dark nights in the open now outweighed by her desperate need.

In contrast to the men, women share what knowledge they have. Ruby teaches Gem, but, more significantly, her physical journey takes her to the grandmother she has never met and the knowledge that has been withheld from her. The scene where the two women share a bath symbolises Ruby's spiritual rebirth, giving her strength to accept the past and to return home without fear.

Ideologically, **The Tale Of Ruby Rose** and **Jewelled Nights** may be very different, but they are uncomfortably alike in the response they have elicited from major distributors. Louise Lovely hawked her film around before finding a reluctant distributor, lost money on it and retired from production embittered by the experience. Initially, the producers of **Ruby Rose** were even less successful. No major distributor was prepared to market it, so they toured Tasmania with the film. Finally, they saw it released at the State Film Theatre, Melbourne, and the Chauvel Cinema in Sydney.

INA BERTRAND AND JAN CHANDLER[1]

---

[1] Extracted from Bertrand and Chandler's review in *Cinema Papers* (see References).

References

'Wayward Haywood', an article (with quotes) on actor Chris Haywood by Joanna Murray-Smith, *Cinema Papers*, no. 63, May 1987, pp. 38–9.

'The Sound of Music', an interview with composer Paul Schutze (and others) by Jenni Gyffyn, *Cinema Papers*, no. 69, May 1988, pp. 10–15.

'The Tale of Ruby Rose', a review by Ina Bertrand and Jan Chandler, *Cinema Papers*, no. 70, November 1988, p. 31.

BOB ELLIS[1]

WARM NIGHTS ON A SLOW MOVING TRAIN

Western Pacific Films presents A Ross Dimsey Production. WARM NIGHTS [/] on a slow moving train. © 1987 Western Pacific Films Ltd. Made with the participation of Film Victoria. *Location:* Melbourne. *Australian distributor:* Filmpac. *Video:* Filmpac. *Rating:* M (September 1987; 2468m). 91 mins.

Producers: Ross Dimsey, Patric Juillet. *Executive producers:* Ross Dimsey, William T. Marshall, Peter Sherman, Robert Ward. *Scriptwriters:* Bob Ellis, Denny Lawrence. *Director of photography:* Yuri Sokol. *Camera operator:* Nino Martinetti. *Production designer:* Tracy Watt. *Costume designer:* Alexandra Tynan. *Editor:* Tim Lewis. *Composer:* Peter Sullivan. *Sound recordist:* Gary Wilkins. *Sound editors:* Glen Newman, Ross Porter. *Mixer:* James Currie.

Cast

Wendy Hughes (Girl), Colin Friels (Man), Norman Kaye (Salesman), John Clayton (Football Coach), Lewis Fitz-Gerald (Brian), Rod Zuanic (Young Soldier), Steve J. Spears (Singer), Grant Tilly (Politician), Peter Whitford (Steward), Peter Sullivan (Piano-playing Steward), Chris Haywood (Station-master) John Flaus (Taxi Driver), Peter Carmody (Second-class Passenger).

Girl (Wendy Hughes) and Man (Colin Friels) aboard a train.

The title, with its mellow and erotic overtones, immediately promises titillation. That would also seem to be borne out when Girl (Wendy Hughes) enters the scene, an interstate train, exuding cheap glamour. She travels by train, picks up men, takes them back to her compartment and then announces there is to be a fee for her services. On each trip she assumes a different persona (different clothes, accents, disguise), no doubt to inject some variety into the scheme of things and to give some credibility to the different pick-ups. But after two such episodes we discover Girl teaching art to a class of Catholic schoolgirls and that she is undertaking her activities on the train to support a crippled brother addicted to morphine. We also realise that she is being watched by a mysterious stranger.

Only the dab and fanciful hand of Bob Ellis could dream up a combination of these elements and enliven it with his own brand of aphorisms, bantering exchanges, references and prejudices ('Everything is fated, like the course of the class struggle in these Nostradamus years.' 'Everyone has to believe their system of belief is correct. This is what whoring means.' 'In a reasonable society no man should be held responsible for what

happens after 3.00 am. And no woman either.').

The film, then, is constructed around a series of two-hander episodes between Girl, 'playing' a succession of (somewhat mindless) Australian females, and a succession of typical (somewhat lacklustre) Australian males. It has an amusement value at least while each scene is being played. Some of these exchanges even have gamely heroic dialogue which, when delivered with some conviction by Hughes and such competent character actors as John Clayton (as the out-of-work Football Coach) and Rod Zuanic (as the near-innocent Young Soldier), have a ring of truth that overcomes the somewhat tasteless/pretentious surroundings.

The film might have remained a pleasant comedy about the deceptiveness of appearances had it continued to stay within these limits. Instead, it embarks on a further plot extravagance involving the mysterious stranger, Man (Colin Friels, affecting an Irish brogue as manufactured by a NIDA graduate). Man works for some security agency

('I work in the dark. I find things out. Such as there are to be found out.') and he takes Girl to bed in what one is led to believe is true love, and then induces her to administer a death drug to a travelling politician. The film ends in betrayal and Girl remains a lonely and saddened figure.

The comedy thus moves to melodrama of the fruitiest kind and it requires a degree of aplomb and sang-froid on the part of both the film-makers and the audience to cope with its increasingly bizarre plot. That its essential risibility only becomes apparent on reflection is a further tribute to the power of the moving image to keep us transfixed no matter what is put before us.

GEOFF GARDNER

[1] The commercially released version of this film was disowned by the director when it was cut some 35 minutes by producer Ross Dimsey.

Reference

'Warm Nights on a Slow Moving Train', a review by Lorraine Mortimer, *Cinema Papers*, no. 69, May 1988, pp. 58–9.

YOUNG EINSTEIN

A Serious Film. Young Einstein. © 1988 Warner Bros. Inc. *Budget:* $2.3 million. Produced with the assistance of the Australian Film Commission. *Locations:* Sydney, Newcastle, Wollombi (New South Wales). *Australian distributor:* Roadshow. *Opened:* December 1988. *Video:* Roadshow Home Video. *Rating:* PG (October 1988). 35mm. 91 mins.

Producers: Yahoo Serious, Warwick Ross, David Roach. *Executive producers* Graham Burke, Ray Beattie. *Associate producer:* Lulu Pinkus. *Scriptwriters:* Yahoo Serious, David Roach. *Director of photography:* Jeff "Ace" Darling. *Camera operators:* Jeff Darling, John Swaffield, Garry Wapshott, Jeremy Robbins, Roger Buckingham. *Production designers:* Steve Marr, Laurie Faen, Colin Gibson, Ron Highfield; Stuart Way (addit.). *Costume designer:* Susan Bowden. *Editors:* Yahoo Serious (supervising); David Roach, Neil Thumpston, Peter Whitmore, Amanda Robson. *Composers:* William Motzing, Martin Armiger, Tommy Tycho. *Sound recordists:* Geoff Grist, Max Hensser, Paul Brincat. *Sound editors:* Annie Breslin, Ashley Grenville. *Mixers:* Richard Beggs, Dale Strumple; Angus Robertson, John Herron, Martin Oswin, Phil Heywood, Ian McLoughlin (dia.).

Cast

Yahoo Serious (Albert Einstein), Odile Le Clezio (Marie Curie), John Howard (Preston Preston), Peewee Wilson (Mr Einstein), Su Cruickshank (Mrs Einstein), Lulu Pinkus (Blonde), Kaarin Fairfax (Brunette), Michael Lake (Manager), Jonathan Coleman (Wolfgang Bavarian), Johnny McCall (Rudy Bavarian), Michael Blaxland (Desk Clerk), Ray Fogo (Bright Clerk); Terry Pead and Alice Pead (Inventor Couple); Frank McDonald (Nihilist), Tony Harvey (Bursar), Tim Elliot (Lecturer), Ray Winslade (Droving Student), Ian "Danno" Rogerson (Randy Student).[1]

Films rarely get second chances, but **Young Einstein** is a twice-told tale; its first version, finished in 1986, appeared in the Australian Film Institute Awards, where it won Best Music Award for William Motzing. Its second incarnation two years later was a marketing triumph spearheaded by the indefatigable director–leading actor–editor, who also took a producer's and screenwriter's credit.

This time, **Young Einstein** followed hot on the heels of **"Crocodile" Dundee II** (John Cornell, 1988), and comparisons between the two laconic, ingenuous and ingenious heroes were frequently made. But Serious' character was a historical figure reimagined: Albert Einstein, somehow born in Tasmania, raised among the apple orchards, who splits the atom, puts bubbles in beer, and discovers relativity and rock 'n' roll. Along the way, he falls in love with Marie Curie (Odile Le Clezio), spends time in a lunatic asylum and saves the world from nuclear destruction.

Serious, with his Struwwelpeter coiffure and gangling style, is the centre of the film, which he crams with anachronisms, sight gags, send-ups of Australian films, physical clowning, eye-catching scenery and the cream of popular Australian rock 'n' roll.

Yahoo Serious (born Greg Pead in Newcastle) was an art student, tyre fitter and maker of commercials, who got the idea for the film while travelling down the Amazon. He made a 16mm promotional short for the film, and managed to get the Australian Film Commission to support the project. By March 1984, an hour of the film had been shot, financed partly by the AFC and partly by private investment. Cast and crew worked on a deferment basis. According to David Roach, one of the film's producers, they had approached independent companies such as McElroy & McElroy and Seven Keys, but were always asked to make the comedy more American.

They then managed to persuade a US distributor, Film Accord, to come up with a $2 million pre-sale, and the film was completed. But in 1986 Film Accord sued the production to recover its distribution guarantee and the rushes, claiming that the film delivered was not the one it had contracted to buy. The dispute was settled out of court, when Village Roadshow bought out Film Accord in March 1987, after seeing the second answer print of the film.

Village Roadshow's Graham Burke was a dogged advocate of the film, and was prepared to commit more money to it. The film's original budget was spent all over again in post-production and additional filming—about an hour was reshot. Warner Brothers picked up both US and international rights, and Mark II of **Young Einstein** was released at the end of 1988. It was a critical and commercial hit in Australia. Local reviewers found it 'refreshing', 'entertaining' and 'exhilarating', and audiences followed suit.

Overseas reviewers were more restrained, but it took $13 million in the US, and was one of Warners' biggest hits of 1989.

PHILIPPA HAWKER

---

[1] This is a cut-down of a big cast list.

References

'The Sounds of Martin', an article (with quotes) on the co-composer Martin Armiger by Anna Grieve, *Cinema Papers*, no. 61, January 1987, p. 13.

'Start Laughing: This is Serious', Philippa Hawker, *Cinema Papers*, no. 71, January 1989, pp. 10–12.

'**Young Einstein**', a review by Vikki Riley, ibid., p. 55.

Albert Einstein (Yahoo Serious) and Marie Curie (Odile Le Clezio).

1989

Ray (Nicholas Eadie) and Celia Carmichael (Rebecca Smart). Ann Turner's Celia.

D A R Y L   D E L L O R A

AGAINST THE INNOCENT

Film art doco presents AGAINST THE INNOCENT. © 1988 Film Art Doco Pty. Ltd. Produced with the assistance of the Australian Film Commission and the Creative Initiatives Program of Film Victoria. *Location:* Melbourne. *Australian distributor:* AFI Distribution. *Video:* Home Cinema Group (AFI Collection). *Rating:* M. 16mm. 76 mins.

Producer: Richard Jones. *Executive producers:* Daryl Dellora, Jenny Hocking. *Scriptwriters:* Daryl Dellora, Jenny Hocking. Based on the original PhD research of Jenny Hocking. *Director of photography:* Vladimir Kromas. *Camera operator:* John Cumming. *Production designer:* Karen Von Bamberger. *Editor:* Daryl Dellora. *Composer:* Paul Schutze. *Sound design:* Paul Schutze. *Sound recordist:* Mark Tarpey. *Sound editors:* Daryl Dellora, Piers Douglas. [*Mixer:* not credited.]

Cast

Margaret Cameron (Monica Schleyer), Nicos Lathouris (Tim McKenzie), Alex Menglet (Karl Heinmann), John F. Howard (Terrorist), Robin Cuming (Hostage), Terry McDermott (Senator), Francis Bell (Brigadier de Bondage), Don Dunstan (as Himself), Salvador Cardenal (as Himself), Peter McEvoy (Rex McEvoy), Louise Smith (Bartender), Sue Byrne (Georgia), Peter Healy (Tom), Terry O'Brien (Adrian), Pamela Rabe (American Woman), Earl Francis (First Man), John Murphy (Second Man), Kurt Geyer (X), Chris Barnett (ASIO Agent), Stephen Costain (Attorney-General); Ian Scott, Richard Peach [Narrators].

In **Against the Innocent**, Daryl Dellora mixes documentary with drama, and black-and-white with colour, to argue that Australia since the Hilton bombing in 1978 faces a greater danger for counter-terrorism strategies developed by the federal government than it does from terrorism itself.

The story follows Monica Schleyer (Margaret Cameron), a German academic whose interest is in the expansion of the power of the State. She comes to Australia to give a lecture on counter-terrorism. 'There is no such thing as a terrorist', she tells her audience. 'A terrorist is whoever a government decides to prosecute as such. Terrorism is a reaction, a label that simplifies complex social and political situations.'

Monica's lecture is Dellora's chief didactic device. He intercuts it with an ongoing hostage drama, and several interviews. A German professor (Alex Menglet) explains

Tim McKenzie (Nicos Lathouris).

that terrorism is the reaction to a rigid, unresponsive political system. A senator (Terry McDermott) expresses concern at the lack of checks and balances provided for the Protective Services Co-ordinating Centre (the national anti-terrorist co-ordinating body). Brigadier de Bondage (Francis Bell) highlights the potential for abuse in the policy of 'the iron fist in a velvet glove'. There is an interview with Don Dunstan who speaks about the commissioning of Justice Hope, during Dunstan's time as Premier, to report on the activities of secret police operations in South Australia. The film ends with Monica's being arrested by police and deported, a resolution of the hostage drama, and a monologue from the revolutionary theatre piece *Ulrike Meinhof Sings*.

Dellora draws attention to the risks inherent in establishing anti-terrorist organisations: agencies set up to protect the people can be used against the people. This danger is real. Beyond this concern, however, Dellora's argument is specious. First, he denies the fact that it is impossible to conceive of a modern State that can exist without some kind of undercover agency. Second, he

assumes that all terrorist activities are morally equivalent and justified.

According to Dellora, Australia has ASIO, ASIS, SAS, SWOS, STAR and SOG to protect its interests. Therefore, the film implies, the political system in this country is no more worthy of support than countries such as China or South Africa. 'Concern for human rights', says Monica in the film, 'is an economic and political euphemism. Human rights are a mask for military and economic concerns.' This blanket, non-discriminatory view offers little to those living under repressive regimes who wish desperately (and sometimes give their lives) for the human rights that exist in liberal democracies like Australia.

Many terrorists fight just causes. Violence can sometimes be legitimated, depending on the social and political circumstances. But that does not mean it is always valid. Any argument or film that claims this to be the case must be challenged. The existence of a security organisation in a society does mean, in itself, that Australia is one step away from a totalitarian regime.

JAN EPSTEIN

BLOWING HOT AND COLD

Chancom Limited and Colosimo Film Productions present BLOWING HOT AND COLD. © 1988 Colosimo Film Productions Pty Ltd. *Locations:* Redesdale, Kyneton, Diggers Rest, Taradale, Melbourne (Victoria). *Australian distributor:* Colosimo Film Productions. *Video:* Force Video. *Rating:* M. 16mm. 85 mins.

Producer: Rosa Colosimo. *Executive producers:* Kevin Moore, Rosa Colosimo, Reg McLean. *Associate producer:* A. N. Cohen. *Scriptwriters:* Rosa Colosimo, and Reg McLean, Luciano Vincenzoni, Sergio Donati. *Additional writing:* Josie Arnold. *Director of photography:* Jaems Grant. *Production designer:* David Vassiliou. *Wardrobe supervisor:* Anita Fioravanti. *Editor:* Nicolas Lee. *Composer:* Joe Dolce. *Sound recordist:* John Wilkinson. *Sound editors:* Nicolas Lee (dia.); Annette Kelly (fx). *Mixer:* Jim Currie.

Cast

Peter Adams (Jack Phillips), Joe Dolce (Nino Patrovita), Kate Gorman (Sally Phillips), Bruce Kane (Jeff Lynch), Elspeth Ballantyne (Shelagh MacBean), Dennis Coard (Hogan), Johnny Raaen (Bartlett), Denise Drysdale (Shelley), Robin Harrison (Mr MacBean), Mary Coustas (Jenny), Wayne Hirst (Joe, The Policeman), Reg McLean (Farmer), Howard Stanley (Publican), Patricia Lyon (Lady in Garage), Michael Nasser (Drug Customer), Marc Gracie (Lead Singer); Randy, The Mechanical Dog; Leo Ransdale, Ernie Nicholls, Syd Hall, Dean Wallace, Andrew Gracie, Robyn Clancy, Trudy Lowe, Lou Anderson.

Jack Phillips (Peter Adams) is a beer-swilling lone parent who runs a service station on a very quiet road outside Redesdale (Central Victoria). His 18-year-old daughter, Sally (Kate Gorman), has run away with a drug dealer and Jack has given up on everything except the dream of seeing his Sally again.

Into his suspended life stumbles a crazy Sicilian, Nino Patrovita (Joe Dolce), a travelling salesman of brooms, brushes and pornography. Unable to pay for petrol and the tune-up of his engine, Nino speeds off, having first chained Jack's truck to a shed post. When Jack drives off in pursuit, down comes the shed.

After catching Nino, in a none-too-exciting chase, Jack puts him to work to pay off the now-owed $3045. So begins a master–servant relationship that slowly moves to friendship, superficially prefiguring Pavel Lounguine's **Taxi Blues** one year later. But

whereas Lounguine's film is a masterwork of complex psychology and subtly shifting power games, **Blowing Hot and Cold** is far more basic, playing off obvious stereotypes and opting for quirkiness instead of resonance. Sometimes the strategy is effective, but mostly the film is predictable and bogged down by a too-casual pace.

What is commendable, as with Liocha (Piotr Mamonov) in **Taxi Blues**, is how bold the scriptwriters and director Marc Gracie are in pushing the eccentricities of Nino. In no sense is Nino a New-Age man: he makes crude gestures about humping, views every women as a sexual conquest, swears prolifically, cheats and lies at will, insensitively dresses his inflatable doll in one of Sally's dresses, etc.

Obviously, the intent is to make Nino not only unlikeable but a pithy satire of the worst aspects of male Italianness so that one can slowly undermine that perception and reveal a gentle, caring soul within. It is partly effective, though Nino ends up looking a touch de-ballsed and sentimental.

Nino's Italianness is a special interest to the film and producer co-scriptwriter Rosa Colosimo makes quite clear how she feels about being of Italian heritage in Australia.

When faced with a meal of tinned baked beans, Nino says:

> Call this eating? [...] Australians are crazy [...] worry too much [...] This Australia I fall in love with it [...] She's so beautiful, big [...] rich [...] And she still no wanta me but I try again. And then [...]

This idea is then linked with a muttered comment later from Nino about Sally's being like Australia and how both can be made right again, but the concept goes nowhere meaningful.

Blowing Hot and Cold is one of several low-budget films produced by Colosimo in a burst of activity in the mid-to-late 1980s. Only this, however, seems to have secured a theatrical release.

As for the unusual title, that is taken from a Corsican proverb quoted in part by Nino during the film and printed in full at the end:

> When my fingers are cold,
> I blow on them to warm them.
> When my fingers are hot,
> I blow on them to cool them.
> If I can blow hot and cold at will,
> Then I can do anything.

SCOTT MURRAY

Jack Phillips (Peter Adams) and Nino Patrovita (Joe Dolce).

BULLSEYE

P.B.L. Productions and Dumbarton Films present in association with Brian Rosen BULLSEYE. *Alternative titles:* 'The Trailblazer', 'Trailblazer', 'Outback' and 'Birdsville' (working). © 1986 PBL Productions Pty Ltd. *Budget:* $4.3 million. *Location:* Outback Queensland. *Australian distributor:* Hoyts. *Video:* RCA-Columbia-Hoyts. *Rating:* PG. 35mm. Panavision. 93 mins.

Producer: Brian Rosen. *Scriptwriter:* Robert Wales. *Additional dialogue:* Bob Ellis. *Director of photography:* Dean Semler. *Camera operator:* David Williamson. *Production designer:* George Liddle. *Costume designer:* George Liddle. *Editor:* Richard Francis-Bruce. *Composer:* Chris Neal. *Sound recordist:* Peter Barker. *Sound editors:* Andrew Stuart (foley); Tim Jordan (dia.); Richard Francis-Bruce (fx). *Mixers:* Roger Savage, Bruce Emery.

Cast

Paul Goddard (Harry Watford), Kathryn Walker (Lily Boyd), John Wood (Bluey McGuirk), Lynette Curran (Dora McKenzie), Paul Chubb (Don McKenzie), Bruce Spence (Purdy), Kerry Walker (Mrs Goodge), John Meillon (Samuel Merrit), Jackie Guyula (Wooly), David Slingsby (Spence), Mark Pegler (Frank Murray), Alfie Bell (Hill), Jeff Truman (Sergeant Willis), Dane Gibson (Constable Hackett), Lauri Moran (Ben Deakan), Paul Keane (Constable Harris), Barry Lovett (Sergeant Liddle), John Sheerin (Bob Campbell), Rhys McConnochie (Justice Collins).

Carl Schultz, director of Sumner Locke Elliott's Careful He Might Hear You and Goodbye Paradise (both 1983), made another film deeply embedded in Australian culture with Bullseye. A romantic comedy with a farcical and satirical element, it does not have as much lift as the others and is not wrestling with any sensitive or significant issues.

Set in dusty, outback Queensland, the original story and screenplay by Robert Wales (with additional dialogue by Bob Ellis), revolves around Harry Watford (Paul Goddard), a simple and honest farmhand who 'just wants a better job'. Harry is romantically involved with Lily Boyd (Kathryn Walker), also employed 'help' on the station, who receives a letter from her deceased aunty's solicitors to inform her that there is some inheritance waiting to be collected. Lily departs for Adelaide and her imagined new life, leaving Harry in his unhappy situation. 'I'm never going to forget you Harry', she says, to which he replies, 'Maybe I'll see you in Adelaide.'

This gives a hint to the surprising change of character he goes through when he steals a few hundred cattle from his boss, Don McKenzie (Paul Chubb), and heads them across the desert with his Irish friend, Bluey McGuirk (John Wood), to Adelaide. What follows are the hiccups in his journey.

Don's prize white English bull, Lord Hampton, is determined to follow the herd of cows and won't be discouraged. The lovesick bull (the namesake of the title) is important only because, had it not followed the cows, the boss may not have noticed their being missing. Two manipulative station-hands, Purdy (Bruce Spence) and Spence (David Slingsby), force themselves along on the journey.

Lily's story is picked up again in Balmoral, South Australia, where she finds her inheritance is not quite what she had expected and she is forced to work in a brothel. It is not unexpected that Lily and Harry's paths cross again in Adelaide. Harry is the hero throughout the film, even though he is into stealing. The boss' wife, Dora (Lynette Curran), is completely on his side and the ending exaggerates the noble qualities forced upon Harry.

Carl Schultz and director of photography Dean Semler are obviously having fun with the innovative photography. In one scene, there is a close-up of the bull's head and nostrils as it walks almost over, but just to the side of, the camera, which is angled upwards. The camera then follows the jiggling male anatomy.

The film is entertaining in its contrived absurdity, but lacks any substance behind the comic send-ups.

SUZANNE BROWN

Harry Watford (Paul Goddard) and the prize bull, Lord Hampton.

CANDY REGENTAG

Rainy Day Pty Ltd presents Candy Regentag. *Alternative title:* Kiss the Night. © 1987 Rainy Day Pty Ltd. Made with the assistance of the Australian Film Commission. *Budget:* $750,000. *Location:* Kings Cross (Sydney). *Australian distributor:* Don Catchlove-Premium. *Video:* Home Cinema Group. *Rating:* R.[1] Super 16 (blown up to 35mm). 102 mins.

Producer: Graeme Isaac. *Executive Producer:* Don Catchlove. *Scriptwriter:* Don Catchlove. *Director of photography:* Michael Edols. *Production designer:* Rob Ricketson. *Costume designer:* Suzy Carter. *Editor:* Tony Stevens. *Composers:* Nigel Westlake, Phil Colson. *Sound recordist:* Ross Linton. *Sound Editor:* Ashley Grenville. *Mixer:* Julian Ellingworth.

Cast

Patsy Stephen (Candy), Warwick Moss (Reg), Gary Aron Cook[2] (Ian), Maxine Klibingaitis (Bibi), Toni Scanlon (Gail), Aussie Merciadez (Veronica), Rainee Skinner (Flour), Jacqui Phillips (Wendy), Beth Child (Lola), Pete Smith (Clayton), Christopher Lewis (Phil), Imogen Annesley (Sascha), John Polson (Cyril), Arky Michael (Franky), Lorenze Arolio (Mario), James Lugton (Greg), Chris Truswell (Leo), Peter Armstrong (Doorman), Dan Holliday (Chris), Gary Who ('Can you feel it'), Basil Clarke (George), John Ley (Client with Knife).

Bibi (Maxine Klibingaitis) and Candy (Patsy Stephen).

Candy (Patsy Stephen) is the professional name of a working girl in a busy King's Cross brothel, who makes the fatal mistake of allowing herself to become romantically involved with a middle-aged client, Reg (Warwick Moss).

Candy is relatively sophisticated compared with the other workers at the parlour. Her art-school background and unsatisfactory relationship with live-in lover indicate a desire to escape from a routine that is soul and body destroying. But when the initial attraction grows into an obsession, the master-servant distinction is blurred with disastrous results for both parties.

Clearly influenced by films like **Working Girls** (Lizzie Borden, 1987) and **Broken Mirrors** (Marlene Gorris, 1984), which chronicle the industrial and socio-political processes by which these establishments function, director James Ricketson mines familiar territory, but in an idiosyncratic manner.

Working with cinematographer Michael Edols and the Super 16 format, Ricketson has made an obvious attempt to heighten realism with the use of documentary techniques. Night-time shooting in the seamy locale of King's Cross gives the film an authenticity heightened by hand-held camera work and the presence of the night-time crowds.

Dramatically uneven and subject to variable acting quality, with long stretches of semi-improvised dialogue, the film is stylistically a second cousin to **Going Down** (Haydn Keenan, 1983) and **Tender Hooks** (Mary Callaghan, 1989), two Sydney-based low-budget productions which reflected the inner-suburban milieu with a sense of urgency missing from any number of lavishly funded projects that were produced in this period.

Producer–writer Don Catchlove, either unwilling or unable to secure interest from distributors, released the film in Sydney and Melbourne through a joint arrangement with Melbourne-based exhibitor–distributor Michael Walsh (of Premium Films).

Modestly budgeted at $750,000, the film was totally funded by the Australian Film Commission.

Despite an extensive publicity campaign, which included predictable interest from the tabloid press, the film quickly disappeared before emerging on video as **Kiss the Night**.

PAUL HARRIS

---

1 A specially modified (as opposed to cut) television version exists. The video is rated 'M'.
2 At the beginning of the film, Gary Aron Cook's name gains an 'r' and loses the middle name, becoming Garry Cook. A combination of the two, Garry Aron Cook, is believed to be correct.

Reference

'**Candy Regentag**', a review by Annabelle Sheehan, *Filmnews*, July 1989, p. 12.

CAPPUCCINO

Archer Films presents Cappuccino. © 1989 Archer Films. Produced with the assistance of the Australian Film Commission. *Location:* Sydney. *Australian distributor:* Ronin Films. *Video:* Home Cinema Group. *Rating:* M. 35 mm. 84 mins.

Producers: Anthony Bowman, Sue Wild. *Associate producers:* Danny Batterham, Jeanie Drynan, Darrell Lass, Rowena Wallace, Barry Quin, John Clayton. *Scriptwriter:* Anthony Bowman. *Director of photography:* Danny Batterham. *Production designer:* Darrell Lass. *Costume supervisor:* Edie Kurzer. *Editor:* Richard Hindley. *Composer:* William Motzing. *Sound recordist:* Ross Linton. *Sound Editor:* Andrew Plain. *Mixer:* Ian McLoughlin.

Cast

John Clayton (Max), Rowena Wallace (Anna), Jeanie Drynan (Maggie), Barry Quin (Larry), Christina Parker[1] (Celia), Ritchie Singer (Bollinger), Simon Matthew (Nigel), Saviour Sammut (Enzo), Saturday Rosenberg (Lulu), François Bocquet (Salvador), Ernie Dingo (as Himself), Louise Howitt (Nurse), Cecil Parkee (Soy), Harold Newstead (Waiter), Jim Pike (Club M.C.), Derek Amber (Jerome), Ken Porter (Big Pan), Warwick Eegg (George), Charles Little (Director), Susie Maizels (Casting Woman), Ron Simpson (Rupert), Paul Ricardi (Stagehand).

Maggie (Jeanie Drynan) and Anna (Rowena Wallace).

Anthony Bowman's **Cappuccino** aims to take a fresh stand on urban 'ultra' life. Such a change in focus was long overdue in the Australian cinema and the film must receive credit for this initiative.

Cappuccino begins with Max (John Clayton) doing a personal retrospective. His interesting face, highlighted against a background of darkness, tells his biography with vaudevillian strine to a concealed audience. We don't realise until later that Max's audience is made up of fellow inmates.

The other characters are mainly of the thespian milieu which nervously haunts Sydney's inner city. Anna (Rowena Wallace) is a successful stage actor who wants to be a director. Her friend Maggie (Jeanie Drynan) would be happy just to land a rôle. Larry (Barry Quin) is a famous soap star who lives with the constant tension of self-justification. Celia (Christina[2] Parker) represents flibbertigibbet youth in pursuit of opportunity—any opportunity. She dumps Max for 'star' Larry.

Max then inadvertently obtains a scandalous video, of the police commissioner in a pornographic performance, from a nasty detective, Bollinger (Ritchie Singer). This is stolen by opportunistic Celia, presumably sensing the likelihood of remuneration. This supposedly warrants the pernicious pursuit by Bollinger and his youthful off-sider, Nigel (Simon Matthew).

Suggestive of the milieu and the point at which the characters converge and interact is an unnamed coffee shop. Unfortunately, the frothy café conversation is weighed down with jokeless punch-lines, and Wallace and Drynan spend most of the film in a seated position doing bits of conversation. When the film does explode into action, such as the pursuit of Max by Bollinger and Nigel down Oxford Street, the director fails to make the chase intoxicating; it just fizzles out.

The film ends when Bollinger is gratuitously blown away by mercenary minx Celia. The crew then appears on screen to announce that it is a film after all. Such gestures of self-reflexivity are contingent upon grand filmic conjurors having held us spellbound in their magic. This is not the case here.

The deficiencies of script and direction make it difficult to focus on the various performances. In some instances, this is a case of being let off the hook, but in others one feels a sense of sabotage. While there are doubtless moments of viscerally cringing interaction, one feels an actor is hamstrung *ab initio* by so patchy and ill-defined a script.

There is so much happening in **Cappuccino** conversations: love affaires, chaos, investigations and intrigues, comedy, statements about the state of Sydney theatre, murder, pornography, prison and coffee. So much happens that nothing really happens. This film is flawed by its random devitalisation and a lack of focused energy.

SHELLEY KAY[2]

---

[1] Christina Parker's name drops the 'h' when listed on the front credits.
[2] See footnote 1.
[3] Extracted from Kay's review in *Cinema Papers* (see References).
[4] See footnote 1.

References

'Cappuccino', a review by Shelley Kay, *Cinema Papers*, no. 77, January 1990, pp. 64–5.

'Cappuccino', a review by Liz Jacka, *Filmnews*, December 1989, p. 16.

ANN TURNER

CELIA

Seon Films presents CELIA. © 1988 Seon Films. *Budget:* $1.4 million. *Location:* Melbourne (Victoria). *Australian distributor:* Hoyts. *Video:* First Release. *Rating:* M. 35mm. 102 mins.

Producers: Timothy White, Gordon Glenn. *Executive producer:* Bryce Menzies. *Associate producer:* Ian Pringle. *Scriptwriter:* Ann Turner. *Director of photography:* Geoffrey Simpson. *Production designer:* Peta Lawson. *Costume designer:* Rose Chong. *Editor:* Ken Sallows. *Composer:* Chris Neal. *Sound recordist:* Lloyd Carrick. *Sound Editor:* Peter Burgess. *Mixers:* James Currie, Phil Heywood, Peter D. Smith.

Cast

Rebecca Smart (Celia Carmichael), Nicholas Eadie (Ray Carmichael), Mary-Anne Fahey (Pat Carmichael), Victoria Longley (Alice Tanner), Margaret Ricketts (Granny), Alexander Hutchinson (Steve Tanner), Adrian Mitchell (Karl Tanner), Callie Gray (Meryl Tanner), Martin Sharman (Evan Tanner), Claire Couttie (Heather Goldman), Alex Menglet (Mr Goldman), Amelia Frid (Stephanie Burke), William Zappa (Sgt John Burke), Fion Keane (Soapy Burke), Louise Le Nay (Debbie Burke), Shannon McNamara (Slim), Luke Mathews (White Knight), Deborra-Lee Furness (Miss Greenaway).

Director Ann Turner's debut feature uses a striking mix of child's perspective and political persecution to present a complex, layered look at growing-up in the Australian suburbs in the 1950s.

The film is set in Melbourne in 1957, and opens with the eight-year-old Celia Carmichael (Rebecca Smart) taking breakfast to her grandmother, only to find that she has died during her sleep. After the old woman's death, Celia's parents forbid her to enter the room for fear that she will be tainted by her evil ways (she was a Marxist and a thespian). Nonetheless, Celia spends much of her time there.

Celia's parents, Ray (Nicholas Eadie) and June Carmichael (Mary-Anne Fahey), are archetypically complacent suburbanites. He works for the PMG, she is a housewife. The only spectre that haunts their cosy world view is that of Communism. Ray hates all things Red and is impassioned to speak his mind when he discovers that his new neighbours, Steve (Alexander Hutchinson) and Alice Tanner (Victoria Longley), are in fact members of the Communist Party of Australia. He forbids Celia, who adores Alice

(notice the names are anagrams of each other), from seeing the Tanners or their children.

Concomitant with this story is a parallel and apparently much simpler narrative thread in which Celia desperately desires a rabbit during the Victorian government's drive to exterminate them all at the time of the great plague. Eventually, Celia's rabbit is confiscated, but only after she has won the right to own it again. One suspects that this stands as a kind of metaphor for the passing from innocence into experience for both Celia and her newly politicised mother. But the rite of passage is considerably more hazardous for Celia, for shortly after this she enacts a violent revenge upon Ray's friend, Sgt John Burke (William Zappa), whom she sees as the embodiment of all the evil in her world.

In its weaving of apparently disparate threads into a single tale of bonding, trust and betrayal, Celia manages to be both politically astute and wonderfully naïve at the same time. To some extent, easy contrasts of innocence and experience are up-ended, with Celia's childish perspective offering a good deal more humanity and insight than the cold, inflexible precepts of Menzies-era conservatism. But while Turner is clearly pre-

senting those precepts as untenable, the oppositional values of the CPA fare little better. The Left is portrayed, in a brief but important scene, as being bound in internecine feuding over the appropriate direction of the Party in the light of Khrushchev's revelations of Stalin's atrocities.

What Turner offers in place of Communism is the possibility of women bonding together. But while the men in Celia are mostly either ineffectual or inflexible, not all the women pass muster as proto-feminists. It is this uninhibited willingness to mix the inspirational elements of Australia's past with the more mundane that makes Celia such a powerful, funny and at times unsettling film about the right of all people, whether Communists, women or children, to hold and assert opinions, even in the heart of red-tiled suburbia.

KARL QUINN

References
'Take the Bunny and Run', an interview with writer–director Ann Turner by Ron Burnett, *Cinema Papers*, no. 72, March 1989, pp. 6–10.
'Celia', a review by Ina Bertrand, *Cinema Papers*, no. 73, May 1989, p. 61.
'Celia', a review by Peter Kemp, *Filmnews*, May 1989, p. 11.

Celia Carmichael (Rebecca Smart) shoots at a monster.

DAISY AND SIMON

Executive Producers (Hong Kong) presents Daisy and Simon. Filmed by Falcon Films in association with Barron Films. *Alternative title:* Where the Outback Ends (overseas). © 1988 Executive Producers. Developed with the assistance of The Western Australia Film Council, The Australian Film Commission and The Film and Television Institute of W.A. *Australian distributor:* Hoyts. *Video:* RCA–Columbia–Hoyts. *Rating:* PG. 35mm. 106 mins.

Producers: Pamela N. Borain, Paul D. Barron. *Executive producer:* Charles E. Wolnizer. *Scriptwriter:* Anthony Wheeler. Originally developed by Hugh Kitson and Colin Borgonnan. *Director of photography:* John R. McLean. *Production designer:* Kevin Sexton. *Costume designer:* Denise Napier. *Editor:* Mark Norfolk. *Composer:* Andrew Hagan. *Sound recordist:* Don Connolly. *Sound* supervisor: Lee McKenzie. *Sound Editor:* Peter Jones. *Sound Mixers:* Dominic Ip, Michael Sin.

Cast

Jan Adele (Daisy), Sean Scully (Simon), Colin McEwan (Vince), Leith Taylor (Susy), Shaunna O'Grady (Joan), Elizabeth Caiacob (Mary), Tony Wager (Cuthbert), Peter Taylor (Doctor), Nicole Thompson (Pepper), Katie Thompson (Lee-Anne), Peter Hardy (Head Ruffian), Roy Menz (Ruffian 2), Kim Gittings (Ruffian 3), Rob Langlands (Policeman), Abe Walters (Piano Player), Fiddlers Green Bush Band (Band).

Daisy and Simon is a film full of elements pulling in different directions. The film's marketing ('an oddball comedy of eccentric proportions') would have us believe that it is a story in the tradition of the 'odd couple' genre; that is, two characters of absolutely opposite nature and temperament having to co-exist, resulting in a comedy of errors and manners. But, if anything, Stasch Radwanski Jr.'s slow, studied direction and John R. McLean's stately, and at times overtly atmospheric, photography reveal the ambitions of an art movie more interested in the introspective study of the melancholic malaise of lives gone wrong.

One suspects that the screenplay contains the seeds of a compromise in intention and approach. According to the film's credits, the project was originally developed by Hugh Kitson and Colin Borgonnan under the title 'Where the Outback Ends'—certainly a more neutral and non-comic title. The screenplay is by Anthony Wheeler, and the change in title seems to indicate a shift in emphasis. If, though, the screenplay was written essentially as a comedy with a bitter-sweet edge,

then Radwanski has intentionally directed against the grain of the comic intent.

The film opens with what are now the standard postcard-pretty images of the Australian outback. Travelling through these overtly stylised vistas of the back of beyond, Simon (Sean Scully)—a young accountant escaping the big city—breaks down en route. Seeking assistance, he comes across a ramshackle homestead owned by the bed-ridden cranky, old Daisy (Jan Adele). Simon, without any real direction in life (due to a recent troubled past slowly revealed over the course of the story), stays on and thus is formed an uneasy alliance which brings both characters back to 'life'. It is this middle section of the film which contains most of the odd-couple comic business, but neither camera placement nor editing seem to want to aid the comic momentum of shots and scenes. In fact, wherever possible, Radwanski chooses obtusely angled compositions and slow pans and dolly shots which give the film a somewhat lethargic, studied pace.

As the introspective, mild-mannered Simon, Scully gives for the most part a fine, controlled performance. He does not play at comedy, but allows the humour to be carried by the situation. Unfortunately, the same cannot be said for Jan Adele. Hers is an embarrassingly unrestrained, full-blown comic performance which borders on caricature. Her dialogue is littered with an over-ripe ocker vernacular which, given Adele's performance, comes across as less humorous than grating.

Nonetheless, it is a film of some æsthetic merit. The film's photography and art direction are very accomplished, even if at times the excess of style is not always at the service of the story. But this may all stem from Radwanski's arty compositions—the figures-in-a-landscape shots and characters framed in relation to iconoclastic outback 'architecture' of one kind or an other—which seem altogether overdone.

ROLANDO CAPUTO

Daisy (Jan Adele) and Simon (Sean Scully).

DAVID WILLIAMSON'S EMERALD CITY

Limelight Productions Pty Ltd in association with New South Wales Film Corporation presents [...] David Williamson's [/] EMERALD CITY. © 1988 New South Wales Film and Television Office. *Location:* Sydney. *Australian distributor:* GUO. *Video:* Roadshow. *Opened:* 9 February 1992. *Rating:* M (September 1988). 35mm. 92 mins.

Producer: Joan Long. *Scriptwriter:* David Williamson. Based on his play. *Director of photography:* Paul Murphy. *Camera operator:* David Williamson. *Production designer:* Owen Williams. *Costume designer:* Anthony Jones. *Editor:* Neil Thumpston. *Composer:* Chris Neal. *Sound recordist:* Ben Osmo. *Sound Editor:* Greg Bell. *Mixer:* Phil Judd.

Cast

John Hargreaves (Colin Rogers), Robyn Nevin (Kate Rogers), Chris Haywood (Mike McCord), Nicole Kidman (Helen Davey), Ruth Cracknell (Elaine Ross), Dennis Miller (Malcolm Bennett), Ella Scott (Penny Rogers), Haydon Samuels (Sam Rogers) Nicholas Hammond (Ian Wall), Michelle Torres (Kath Mitchell), Bruce Venables (Limousine Driver), Rebel Penfold-Russell (Kate's Friend), Robert Rosen (Society Photographer), Wenanty Nosul (Polish Director), Phillip Dodd ('Coastwatchers' Director), Aki Taninaka (Japanese Officer), David Hobbs (Coastwatcher), Jan Ringrose (Make-up Girl), Rocky McDonald (U.S. Airman); Dar Davies, Don Vaughan (Japanese Soldiers).

Adapted from one of David Williamson's most popular stage plays, **David Williamson's Emerald City** could also have been one of his most successful films. At first glance a story offering throwaway lines about Sydney (where business is done at cocktail parties) versus Melbourne (the home of idealists), the film cleverly deals with power and corruption, and its effect on human relationships. A verbose satire of the great Australian ambition to achieve international recognition, it even points a few barbs at the wheeling and dealing of film-making. (Perhaps Williamson was referring to his own aspirations: for several years he has had a number of projects in Hollywood.)

David Williamson's Emerald City tells the story of a thirty-something couple, Colin (John Hargreaves) and Kate Rogers (Robyn Nevin). Obsessed with dreams of harbour views and sub-tropical sunshine, Colin, a successful screenwriter, persuades his family to move from Melbourne to Sydney. In

Mike McCord (Chris Haywood) and Helen Davey (Nicole Kidman).

Sydney he meets Mike McCord (a cheeky performance from Chris Haywood). Mike is an ambitious, no-talent film hustler who hopes to make it as a producer through working with Colin. Although Colin's previous success has stemmed from more serious projects such as 'Days of Wine and Whitlam', Colin forgoes his past ideals and adopts a more supercilious style of writing.

Arguments erupt in the Rogers household. Kate—who is attempting to publish a book written by an Aboriginal woman (titled 'Black Rage')—cannot accommodate Colin's corruption of ideals. Ironically, it is Kate who achieves success, but not without a degree of compromise—and Mike's underhandedness.

With Williamson's penchant for creating larger-than-life characters, the most appealing aspect of *Emerald City* was his rapid-fire, laugh-a-minute dialogue. When Joan Long attended the second night of the Sydney Theatre Company's production of the play, she fell in love with it and decided to produce it for film.

Williamson wrote the screen adaptation—as he has done for all his filmed plays—toning down the characters for the more intimate film medium. However, problems with **David Williamson's Emerald City** arose during rehearsals when the two leading actors—Hargreaves and Nevin—wanted to include the original stage dialogue in the film. Director Michael Jenkins allowed them to do so. The resultant wordiness may have subsequently inhibited the film's success.

Other changes made to the play also simply don't work. A toning down of the female characters, for example, proves ineffective. As well, Ruth Cracknell's stage fire as film producer Elaine Ross is watered down for the big screen, to the extent that she becomes empathetic, almost nice. And Andrea Moor's sleazy stage Helen, McCord's girlfriend, is far superior to Nicole Kidman's coy film nymph.

Jarring lime green titles and Chris Neal's over-bubbly soundtrack also serve to alienate rather than entice the audience.

HELEN BARLOW

References
'Emerald City', a review by John Slavin, *Cinema Papers*, no. 73, May 1989, pp. 63–4.
'Emerald City', a short review by Barbra Luby, *Filmnews*, February 1989, p. 12.

DEAD CALM

Kennedy Miller presents DEAD CALM. © 1988 Kennedy Miller Productions. *Locations:* Whitsunday Passage, Hamilton Island (Queensland); Sydney. *Australian distributor:* Roadshow. *Video:* Warner Home Video. *Rating:* M. 35mm. Panavision. 95 mins.

Producers: Terry Hayes, Doug Mitchell, George Miller. *Scriptwriter:* Terry Hayes. From the novel by Charles Williams. *Directors of photography:* Dean Semler; Geoff Burton (opening sequence). *Production designer:* Graham 'Grace' Walker. *Costume designer:* Norma Moriceau. *Editor:* Richard Francis-Bruce. *Music:* Graeme Revell. *Sound design:* Lee Smith. *Sound recordist:* Ben Osmo. *Sound editors:* Peter Townend (fx); Annabelle Sheehan, Tim Jordan, Susan Metcalfe (dia.). *Mixers:* Roger Savage, Phil Judd.

Cast

Nicole Kidman (Rae Ingram), Sam Neill (John Ingram), Billy Zane (Hughie Warriner), Rod Mullinar (Russell Bellows), Joshua Tilden (Danny), George Shevtsov (Doctor), Michael Long (Specialist Doctor); Lisa Collins, Sharon Cook, Paula Hudson-Brinkley, Malinda Rutter ('Orpheus' Cruise Girls); Benji U.D., AD (Dog).

Rae Ingram (Nicole Kidman) threatens Hughie Warriner (Billy Zane).

A pared-down thriller with three actors, two boats and a dog, **Dead Calm** never lets up on suspense in the same way that other Kennedy Miller productions—such as **Mad Max** (George Miller, 1979)—never let up on action. While feeding off childhood stories of pirates and madmen at sea—indeed the villain's boat, 'Orpheus', resembles a pirate ship—**Dead Calm**'s setting is contemporary, evoking the beauty and the dangers of isolation.

After the death of their son in an automobile accident, veteran sailor John Ingram (Sam Neill) and his young wife, Rae (Nicole Kidman), escape to the seclusion of the Pacific Ocean on board their luxury yacht, 'Saracen'. But when they notice a man rowing towards them across the dead-flat ocean, they have no idea of the terror that will ensue.

The supposed survivor of a food poisoning epidemic on board his ship, the young American, Hughie Warriner (Billy Zane), is welcomed on board 'Saracen'. He sleeps while John—more than a tad suspicious—goes to inspect 'Orpheus', leaving his wife alone with Hughie. When John finds the occupants murdered, he peers back towards 'Saracen' with a knowing glance, then jumps back into his dinghy and rows

frenetically, heart pounding with every stroke. But he is too late: 'Saracen' pulls away just before he reaches it, a wry chuckle emanating from Hughie's demonic face.

While Rae has the chance to kill Hughie on a number of occasions, she is inhibited by her recent brush with death—and by an incredibly obedient dog, which foils several of her plans. Eventually she is forced to submit to Hughie's sexual advances in order to seize control.

Enhanced by Graeme Revell's synthesised score, the film's tension is set up in a brisk opening sequence: a busy railway station, the traumatic car accident and Rae in hospital. It then cuts to the ocean: quiet, calm and timeless. Filmed in the Whitsunday Passage aboard a veritable fleet of yachts, **Dead Calm** truly evokes the feeling of menace at sea.

On Hamilton Island the film-makers built a second sound stage housing a huge tank that doubled the action at sea, as well as interiors of both ships.

The 1989 winner of numerous AFI craft awards for cinematography, editing, music and sound, **Dead Calm** features the talents of Academy Award-winning cinematographer Dean Semler. Director Phillip Noyce—while previously known for the social conscience

films, **Newsfront** (1978) and **Heatwave** (1982)—also previously worked with Kennedy Miller on the 1984 mini-series, *The Cowra Breakout*. George Miller also contributed to **Dead Calm**'s production by directing a number of scenes after returning from shooting **The Witches of Eastwick** (1987) in the US.

Dead Calm is based on Charles Williams' 1963 novel, which in 1968 was made as **The Deep** by Orson Welles, but has never been screened.

HELEN BARLOW

---

[1] George Miller directed second unit on the film, plus (allegedly) the opening sequence (which had a different crew). He may also have directed part of the final ending, which was reworked after American test screenings. None of this work is credited.

References
'Phil Noyce: **Dead Calm**', an interview with the director by Brian McFarlane, *Cinema Papers*, no. 73, May 1989, pp. 6–11.
'**Dead Calm**', a review by Shelley Kay, ibid., pp. 61–2.
'Terry Hayes: Interweaving the Fabric', an interview with the scriptwriter by Scott Murray, *Cinema Papers*, no. 76, November 1989, pp. 24–9, 76.

John Ingram (Sam Neill) and Rae Ingram (Nicole Kidman).

CHRIS THOMSON

THE DELINQUENTS

A Village Roadshow Pictures Presentation [of] A Cutler-Wilcox Production in association with Silver Lining Entertainment. THE delinquents. © 1989 The Delinquents Pty Ltd, Village Roadshow Corporation Limited, Australian Film Finance Corporation. *Australian distributor:* Roadshow. *Video:* Roadshow Home Video. *Rating:* M (June 1982). 35mm. 101 mins.

Producers: Alex Cutler, Mike Wilcox. *Executive producers:* Graham Burke, Greg Coote, John Tarnoff. *Associate producers:* Isolar Enterprises, Inc, Robert Goodale. *Scriptwriters:* Clayton Frohman, Mac Gudgeon. Based on the novel by Criena Rohan. *Director of photography:* Andrew Lesnie. *Production designer:* Laurence Eastwood. *Costume designer:* Bruce Finlayson. *Editor:* John Scott. *Composer:* Miles Goodman. *Sound recordist:* Paul Brincat. *Sound editors:* Greg Bell (dia.); Ashley Grenville (fx). *Mixers:* Gethin Creagh, Martin Oswin.

Cast

Kylie Minogue (Lola), Charlie Schlatter (Brownie), Bruno Lawrence (Bosun), Todd Boyce (Lyle), Desirée Smith (Mavis), Angela Punch-McGregor (Mrs Lovell), Melissa Jaffer (Aunt Westbury), Lynette Curran (Mrs Hansen), Lyn Treadgold (Prison Matron), Duncan Wass (Bert), Rosemary Harris (Isobel), Yvonne Hooper (Landlady), Jonathan Hardy (Magistrate), Errol O'Neill (Theatre Manager), Rachel Szalay (Maxine); Russell Krause, Ove Altman (Sailors); Darryl Hukins (Bodgie), Robert Willox (Postman), Maurice Hughes (Bartender).

The Delinquents has the rather dishonourable place in Australian film history of being the first spectacular failure of the Australian Film Finance Corporation—and a failure because it seemed such a gross miscalculation of a 'surefire' commercial hit. Pre-publicity stressed pop star Kylie Minogue's acting debut and the romantic sparks that would fly on-screen between her and imported American actor, Charlie Schlatter. Above all, the film promised to be a savvy combination of the energy of American teen movies of the 1970s and 1980s with an Australian content and sensibility (courtesy of Criena Rohan's novel).

The film was a disappointment to public and critics alike—especially as a teen movie. The sexuality of Lola (Minogue), chafing against her bland and conformist social environment, is alluded to verbally more than it is shown cinematically. Moments of high-spirited teen rebellion (such as a riot in a girl's prison dorm) are fleeting and lead only to an extremely sanitised ending in which Lola ends up with her 'wild one' (Schlatter as Brownie) fully tamed, and an instant child to form a happy, nuclear family. The thrust of the film is marked by its use of rock 'n' roll standards—from 'Be Bop a Lula' as a sign of youth anarchy to 'Lucille' as a cute, fun song that the family unit dances to in the final frame.

The Delinquents becomes somewhat more interesting, however, if it is viewed as an old-style 'woman's melodrama' rather than a contemporary teen movie. Certainly, the film's attention is almost solely on Lola, even to the point of making Brownie a peripheral cipher. Like many of Hollywood's melodramatic heroines, Lola is presented as a woman imprisoned within a strict gender rôle. Her dreams of escape are no less socially conditioned—she is a sucker for the grand romantic fantasies contained in *Wuthering Heights* and *Romeo and Juliet*. Completing this knot of patriarchal oppression, Brownie is, for much of the story, off on his own gender trip, sailing the high seas with his symbolic father-figure, Bosun (Bruno Lawrence).

In neither script nor direction does the film properly explore these thematic possibilities. Its attitude towards the topic of romantic love is extremely confused, at one moment ironic and pointedly anti-romantic (as in the juxtaposition of flowery pop songs with the first physical fumblings of the lovers), at another sentimental and idealistic (as in Lola's opposition to her repressive aunt). The 'happy ending' already mentioned is arrived at without the slightest hint of irony or ambiguity.

Ultimately, **The Delinquents** is a weakly handled, insubstantial film. Its style wavers uneasily between the naturalism of the Australian period films of the 1970s (like **Break of Day** or **Caddie**[1]) and the 'feel good' conventions of contemporary American cinema, without entirely embracing either option. It lacks any directorial energy, and boasts a high number of puzzling plot ellipses and inconsequential secondary characters. Most painfully, it has the feel of a 'trans-Pacific' project unwisely geared for the international market—one in which the authentic 'Australianism' of Rohan's novel is reduced to a stream of mannered, ocker colloquialisms with fruity theatricality by the cast.

ADRIAN MARTIN

[1] **Break of Day** (Ken Hannam, 1976), **Caddie** (Don Crombie, 1976).

References
'The Delinquents', a location report by Patricia Amad and Philippa Hawker, *Cinema Papers*, no. 74, July 1989, pp. 4–7.
'The Delinquents', a review by Adrian Martin, *Cinema Papers*, no. 78, March 1990, pp. 50–1.
'Nice Is Not Enough in **The Delinquents**', Adrian Rawlings, *Filmnews*, May 1990, p. 10.

Lola (Kylie Minogue) and Brownie (Charlie Schlatter).

DEVIL IN THE FLESH

JCW Film Management Limited and World Film Alliance present A Collins Murray Production. DEVIL IN THE FLESH. *Alternative titles:* 'Marie Claire' (working) and 'Beyond Innocence' (US). © 1985 JCW Film Management Limited. Budget: $1.6 million. *Locations:* Castlemaine, Dunolly, Bendigo, Malmsbury, Melbourne (Victoria). *Australian distributor:* Hoyts Premium. *Video:* RCA–Columbia–Hoyts. *Rating:* M. 35mm. 104 mins (Australian version 99 mins).

Producer: John B. Murray. *Executive Producer:* Peter Collins. *Line producer:* Tom Burstall. *Scriptwriter:* Scott Murray. Based on the novel, *Le Diable au Corps*, by Raymond Radiguet. *Director of photography:* Andrew de Groot. *Camera operator:* David Williamson. [*Production designer:* uncredited; Scott Murray.] *Art director:* Paddy Reardon. *Costumes:* Frankie Hogan; Rosemary Ryan (design consultant). *Editor:* Tim Lewis. *Composer:* Philippe Sarde. *Sound recordist:* Laurie Robinson. *Sound editors:* Craig Carter, Rex Watts. *Mixer:* James Currie.

Cast

Katia Caballero (Marthe Foscari), Keith Smith (Paul Hansen), John Morris (John Hansen), Jill Forster (Jill Hansen), Colin Duckworth (Pierre Fournier), Reine Lavoie (Madelaine Fournier), Jeremy Johnson (Simon Greene), Odile le Clezio (Simone), Louise Elvin (Artists' Model), Luciano Martucci (Ermanno), Stephan Tailly (Bernard), Eldon Hogan (Train Guard), John Murphy (Brother Murphy), Jock MacRae (Mr Clarke), John Walker (Florist), Juliana Krygger (Rebecca), Milton Holden (Violin Teacher), Richard Butler (Hotel Receptionist), Benjamin Molina (Child).

Writer–director Scott Murray's first feature, **Devil in the Flesh**, is one of three films made from Raymond Radiguet's classic novel, *Le Diable au Corps*: the others are Frenchman Claude Autant-Lara's 1947 version and Marco Bellocchio's 1986 version.[1] Radiguet's novel is set during the period of World War I and tells the story of a doomed love affaire between an adolescent on the brink of manhood and a young woman engaged to a French soldier absent at the Front for much of the story. The events take place on the outskirts of Paris.

Murray—working from his own screenplay—makes some necessary changes while fundamentally remaining faithful to the spirit of the novel. He has updated the

Marthe Foscari (Katia Caballero) and Paul Hansen (Keith Smith).

period to World War II and set the events in a quietly picturesque rural Australia.

In the film, Marthe Foscari (Katia Caballero), the young woman, is the daughter of an established French immigrant family, and Paul Hansen (Keith Smith), the young lover, the son of a local middle-class family. To retain historical accuracy, Marthe's fiancé in the novel has been changed to a local Italian interned at the outbreak of war. He is not her fiancé but her husband, which further heightens the moral dilemma for the parents (if not for the lovers).

However, one significant structural change in plot between novel and film is the ending. Murray has commented on this, saying: 'In the novel, Marthe dies soon after giving birth to their child. While it is an effective literary resolution, it is a rather Victorian device. I felt the film should have its own ending, one that evolved logically and emotionally from its own structure.'[2]

From the evidence on screen Murray was justified in changing the ending, for the sequence of the lovers meeting a year or so after the break-up of their relationship provides the film with one of its very finest moments. In fact, there are many fine moments overall in Murray's handling of the theme of a free spirit changing the personality of an emotionally closed individual. Katia Caballero's performance as the independent Marthe, an emotionally mature young woman more secure in her understanding of the moral shades of grey in an adult universe, is beautifully rendered. Paul, on the other hand, is approaching manhood, entering unfamiliar territory (both sexual

and psychological) in his affaire with Marthe, stimulated and responding to new emotions. Crucially, the relationship provides Paul with a rite of passage to manhood.

From the opening image of a car moving into frame and taking with it the gaze of the audience into this imaginary world of the screen, Murray directs the drama with subtle and stylish delicacy. He is complemented by Andrew De Groot's brilliant cinematography which captures every nuance of colour—especially striking in the Balthus-inspired production design of Marthe's apartment—and aided by Philippe Sarde's quietly effective music score.

The film premiered at the 1986 Cannes Film Festival and won the praise of French (and international) critics—an honour indeed given the preciousness the French attach to their literary classics.

ROLANDO CAPUTO

---

[1] There is also a recent French television version, which in some aspects seems 'based' on Murray's film. It should also be noted that Murray's **Devil in the Flesh** pre-dates Bellocchio's by six months, even though they both premiered at Cannes in 1986 (Murray's in La Semaine de la Critique Française and Bellocchio's in Le Quinzaine des Réalisateurs).
[2] *Filmviews*, no. 134, Summer 1987–88, p. 12.

References
'**Devil in the Flesh**', a review by Rolando Caputo, *Cinema Papers*, no. 71, January 1989, pp. 54–5.
'Soundtracks', with a review of the film's score by Ivan Hutchinson, *Cinema Papers*, no. 89. August 1992, pp. 62–3.

GEORGIA

A Jethro Films Pty Ltd Production. GEORGIA. *Alternative title:* 'A Difficult Woman' (working). © 1988 A Jethro Films Production. *Location:* Melbourne. *Australian distributor:* Hoyts. *Video:* Home Cinema Group. *Rating:* M. 35mm. 93 mins.

Producer: Bob Weis. Line *Producer:* Margot McDonald. *Scriptwriters:* Ben Lewin, Joanna Murray-Smith, Bob Weis. Based on an original story by Mac Gudgeon. *Director of photography:* Yuri Sokol. *Camera operator:* Vladimir Osherov. *Production designer:* Jon Dowding. *Costume designer:* Aphrodite Kondos. *Editor:* Edward McQueen-Mason. *Composer:* Paul Grabowsky. *Sound recordist:* John Phillips. *Sound editors:* Frank Lipson (fx); Ross A. Porter (dia.); Edward McQueen-Mason (ADR). *Sound Mixer:* Roger Savage.

Cast

Judy Davis (Nina; Georgia), John Bach (Karlin), Julia Blake (Elizabeth), Alex Menglet (Lazlo), Marshall Napier (Le Mat), Lewis Fiander (Scarlatti), Roy Baldwin (Librarian), Keryn Boyer (Policewoman No. 1), Tommy Dysart (Bystander), Lynda Gibson (Policewoman No. 2), Colin Hay (Policeman), Nic Lathouris (Bystander), David Letch (Gallery Manager), Robert Meldrum (Alex), Jillian Murray (Leela), Marilyn O'Donnell (Bystander), John O'May (Mr Leonard), Holly Porter (Baby Nina), Dalibon Satalic (Clerk), David Swann (Bystander); Vichea Ten, Terry Trimble (Removalists).

Investigating the past: Nina (Judy Davis).

A notable trademark of writer–director Ben Lewin's work is his ability to create colourful, quirky, unconventional characters, and to place narrative entirely at their service. However, **Georgia**, a mystery-cum-thriller, seems to be not only a strange match of talent to a project, but an uneasy marriage of disparate genres and influences, from **Rashomon** (Akira Kurosawa, 1950) and **Blowup** (Michelangelo Antonioni, 1966) to any number of Hitchcock themes.

Nina Bailey (Judy Davis) is on the threshold of a challenging career as an investigating lawyer when she moves into a new apartment—a fancy, New York-style loft overlooking Port Phillip. On her first night there, she discovers a photograph of a woman holding a small baby. Later that night, an invitation to a retrospective exhibition of photographs by a Georgia White is slipped under her door.

Nina attends the exhibition, where she is intrigued by the photographs on show: a murder victim slumped in a blood-splattered bath; a policeman, later identified as Le Mat (Marshall Napier), inspecting the scene; the infamously shady property developer and businessman, Karlin (John Bach), trying to shield himself from the photographer; a brooding self-portrait of the photographer.

Nina is confounded, however, when she recognises her 'mother', Elizabeth (Julia Blake), and Elizabeth's lover, Lazlo (Alex Menglet), in these photographs. After confronting Elizabeth, Nina learns that Georgia was her real mother. Some say Georgia committed suicide; others say she was pushed into the water and drowned.

Nina sets forth to investigate her mother's death. Starting with Elizabeth, then Lazlo, she tracks down Le Mat, who has since been taken off the police force, and finally meets the elusive Karlin. Their stories unfold through flashback sequences, creating a conflicting and contradictory picture of the episodes leading up to the fatal moment of Georgia's death.

The film strives to draw as many parallels as it possibly can between Georgia and Nina. Aside from having the same actress play both parts, visual links are made between the view from Nina's apartment and that from the house where Georgia died. But the parallel soon becomes strained and, in any case, something of a lost opportunity. Nina's career, boldly investigating tax fraud, is dropped as an issue early in the film, making redundant an obvious similarity between Nina and Georgia as women who know/knew too much.

The characters remain shrouded in secrecy, suffocating in the burdens of the past, and little is revealed. Red herrings abound. By implication the viewer finds out how Georgia died, but the characters themselves remain sketchy, essentially one-dimensional. The stilted characterisations also occasionally veer toward caricature and the characters are rarely engaging, making it difficult to really care about their suffering or the outcome.

PAUL KALINA[1]

---

[1] Extracted from Kalina's review in *Cinema Papers* (see Reference).

Reference

'**Georgia**', a review by Paul Kalina, *Cinema Papers*, no. 75, September 1989, pp. 60–1.

GHOSTS...OF THE CIVIL DEAD

Correctional Services Inc [and] Outlaw Values present GHOSTS...OF THE CIVIL DEAD. © 1988 Correctional Services Inc. (Film Productions) Ltd. *Australian distributor:* Outlaw Values. *Video:* Home Cinema Group. *Rating:* R. 35mm. 93 mins.

Producer: Evan English. *Executive producer:* Evan English. *Associate producer:* Mike Hopkins. *Scriptwriters:* Gene Conkie, John Hillcoat, Evan English, Nick Cave, Hugo Race. *Directors of photography:* Paul Goldman, Graham Wood. *Camera operator:* (Nevada) Evan English. *Production designer:* Chris Kennedy. *Wardrobe supervisor:* Karen Everett. *Editor:* Stewart Young. *Music:* Nick Cave, Mick Harvey, Blixa Bargeld. *Sound recordist:* Bronwyn Murphy. *Sound design:* Dean Gawen. *Sound editors:* Peter Clancy, Rex Watts, Sue Lamshed. *Mixer:* Roger Savage.

Cast

Dave Field (Wenzil), Mike Bishop (David Yale), Chris De Rose (Grezner), Nick Cave (Maynard), Freddo Dierck (Robbins), Vincent Gil (Ruben), Bogdan Koca (Waychek), Kevin Mackey (Glover), Dave Mason (Lilly), M. E. Duncan (Junkie 1), Nick Seferi (Junkie 2), Tony Clark (Simone), Yilmaz Tuhan (Food King), Ian Mortimer (Jack), Mick King (Edwin Neal), Angelo Papadopoulos (John Bird), Rob Fox (Hobday), Robin Dene (Coyne), John Flaus (Armstrong), Zlato Kasumovic (Polly Borland), Mick Manzaris (Brucey Borland), Robert Scrivano (Quarnstrom), Gary Francis (Flecker).

If the glut of horror genre movies of the mid-to-late 1980s did anything, it reduced the alarming visceral response to movies that audiences could experience. But nothing could prepare an audience for the hyper-realist onslaught of **Ghosts...of the Civil Dead**. It cuts into social, personal and emotional sensibilities with an unoiled chainsaw, displaying the outrageous aberrations of modern prison life. The reform of hardened prisoners is shown to be a farce, as prison officers and correction authorities engage in a 'lock down' of a new-style high-security prison.

Based on models of prisons that really do exist in the US, the film mixes genres with disorientating disregard for tradition. This is an important feature of the film, which works to expose the audience to the deprivations that are a part of prison-life abnormality. The film is unequivocating in its exposure of the new régime of high-security prisons which must be shown for

what they are and challenged, lest civilisation, as we think we know it, becomes grossly dehumanised.

Ghosts...of the Civil Dead is a graphic and disturbing picture—a picture many people could not stand to sit through and one which only extremist psycho-pathologists could tolerate seeing again.

But it is and was an important film when it appeared mid-way through 1989 to enjoy short seasons at Australian art-house cinemas. It is directed and produced by former rock-clip film-makers John Hillcoat and Evan English, who appear to have learned a considerable amount from their days among the smoke machines, guitars and pop stars of the rock-music world.

The film maintains the intensity of a three-minute pop song for more than 90 minutes, using the ruthlessly fast editing that is a signature of film clips. Images blur into power, then into bloody hyper-realism.

The film was made as an 'issues film' with its currency accentuated by the then conservative government in Queensland opening Australia's first privately run prison, with the

implication being that prisons that are freed from the public domain of state correction authorities could become vicious bastions of a new correctional barbarity.

Australia began as a convict colony and it is appropriate that this film, as a prison film among many other things, was made by a group of committed young Australians. The remarkable thing is that **Stir** (Stephen Wallace, 1980), the only other great Australian prison film, also makes similar points about barbaric prison systems. Perhaps of all nationalities, Australians, as heirs of convicts, should and do have an intensity about prisons and their reform that few others share.

MARCUS BREEN

References
'Ghosts...of the Civil Dead', a location report (with quotes) by Jillian Burt, *Cinema Papers*, no. 68, March 1988, pp. 8–11.
'Ghosts...of the Civil Dead', a review by Shelley Kay, *Cinema Papers*, no. 74, July 1989, pp. 46–7.
'Ghosts...of the Civil Dead', a review by Hart Cohen, *Filmnews*, June 1989, p. 11.

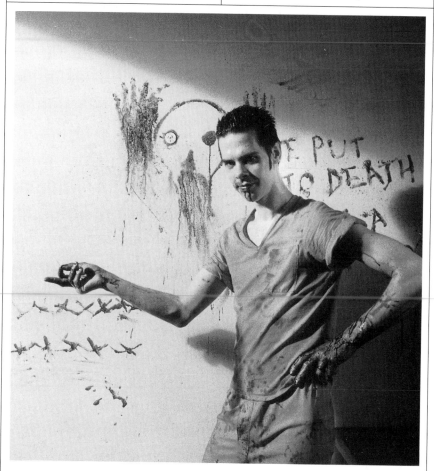

Maynard (Nick Cave) makes a protest.

INCIDENT AT RAVEN'S GATE

Hemdale Film Corporation presents An FGH Presentation for International Film Management Limited. INCIDENT AT RAVEN'S GATE. © 1988 International Film Management Limited. Made with the assistance of the South Australian Film Corporation. *Budget:* $2.5 million. *Location:* South Australia. *Australian distributor:* Filmpac. *Video:* Filmpac. *Rating:* M. 35mm. 94 mins.

Producers: Rolf de Heer, Marc Rosenberg. *Executive producer:* Antony I. Ginnane. *Scriptwriters:* Marc Rosenberg, Rolf de Heer. Adapted from an original screenplay by James Michael Vernon. *Director of photography:* Richard Michalak. *Camera operator:* Andrew Lesnie. *Production designer:* Judi Russell. *Costume designer:* Clarissa Patterson.[1] *Original music:* Graham Tardif, with Roman Kronen. *Editor:* Suresh Ayyar. *Sound recordist:* Rob Cutcher. *Supervising Sound Editor:* Andrew Plain. *Mixers:* James Currie; Phil Heywood (fx); Peter Smith (music).

Cast

Steven Vidler (Eddie), Celine Griffin (Rachel), Ritchie Singer (Richard), Vincent Gil (Skinner), Saturday Rosenberg (Annie), Terry Camilleri (Hemmings), Max Cullen (Taylor), Peter Douglas (Bruce), Ernie Ellison (George), Brian O'Connor (Bill), Sylvia Thiele (Kate), Paul Philpott (Pinhead), Max Lorenzin (Weasel), Phil Bitter (Des).

Incident at Raven's Gate is an intriguing combination of the domestic and the supernatural, and it doesn't fit comfortably into a mould. It is a film which received only a desultory theatrical release, but it is an impressive combination of genres—part supernatural thriller, part science fiction, part psychological drama—and it has a grim sense of humour.

Directed by Rolf de Heer, the film handles the transitions between domestic tension and supernatural horror with flair and plausibility; it has strong, effective performances and a particularly imaginative use of sound.

It opens with two investigations that converge on Raven's Gate, a country property in South Australia. Taylor (Max Cullen), a policeman, looks into the alleged theft of a football trophy; a mysterious stranger, Hemmings (Terry Camilleri), who claims to be an astrophysicist attached to Special Branch, is on a very different kind of mission.

The film goes back five days, showing us the inhabitants of the Raven's Gate property. Richard (Ritchie Singer) is a dull dog, irritable and serious, whose greatest passion is hydroponics; his wife Rachel (Celine Griffin) wears sleek summer dresses and scarlet silk slips; and brother Eddie (Steven Vidler), who is out on parole after a gaol term for car theft, is an unlikely country boy with his bleached crew-cut, lurid T-shirts, taste for thrash music and easygoing attitude. They do not fit in to the rural setting, and they don't seem to mix with the locals.

Eddie visits the township's pub, where he is a target of the local rednecks. He is seeing the barmaid, Annie (Saturday Rosenberg), and this makes him unpopular with the local cop, Skinner (Vincent Gil), an opera lover with a weakness for *La Traviata* and Annie. Gradually, the suppressed tensions in this are played out and the events leading up to the destruction of Raven's Gate take place.

The opening moments of the film give some oblique but unmistakeable indications that the solution will have something to do with a mysterious arrival and departure in the vicinity. The film then gradually builds up the notion that a spaceship has landed, and that an unseen presence is affecting the people and the place. This is suggested playfully at first.

Natural laws become violated: waterholes dry up overnight, a dog turns suddenly savage, dead birds rain down from the sky. Sometimes there is a comic touch. People start acting strangely, intensely, jealously. Skinner's infatuation with Annie reaches grotesque proportions. It is as if the aliens apply enormous pressure to the areas they arrive in: they soak up water, they soak up sanity.

Gradually, the manifestations become more frightening and bizarre, and the film builds to a dramatic climax. Even then, it is the distortion of the familiar that provides the element of terror: this is true of the screenplay, and of its interpretation. Sound and image create the disorientation and tension, rather than effects.

David Stratton championed the film in *Variety* and *The Sydney Morning Herald*, but it did not get the release or the acclaim it deserved.

PHILIPPA HAWKER

---

[1] Usually spelt 'Clarrissa Patterson'.

References
'Long Wait for **Raven's Gate**', Tina Kaufman, *Filmnews*, April 1989, p. 10.
'**Incident at Raven's Gate**', a short review by Andrew Frost, ibid., p. 10.

Eddie (Steven Vidler), out of gaol and out of place.

ISLAND

Illumination Films and Atlantis Releasing in association with Film Victoria presents ISLAND. © 1989 Illumination Films. *Location:* Greece. *Australian distributor:* Newvision. *Video:* Fox Columbia. *Rating:* M. 35mm. 93 mins.

 Producers: Paul Cox, Santhana K. Naidu. *Executive producers:* William Marshall, Jeannine Seawell. *Associate Producer:* Takis Emmanuel. *Scriptwriter:* Paul Cox. *Director of photography:* Michael Edols. *Production designer:* Neil Angwin. [*Costume designer:* not credited.] *Editor:* John Scott. [*Composer:* not credited.] *Sound recordist:* James Currie. *Sound Editor:* Livia Ruzic. *Mixer:* James Currie.

Cast

Irene Papas (Marquise), Eva Sitta (Eva), Anoja Weerasinghe (Sahana), Chris Haywood (Janis), François Bernard (Frenchman), Norman Kaye (Henry), Rousso Petrinolis (Rousso), Michael Psaris (Michalis), Jiannis Janakakis (Janis' Brother), Tassos Ioannides (Butcher), Nikolas Manolakis (Motorcyclist), Louise Edeleanu (Frenchman's Girlfriend); Irene Papanikola, Maria Alakioti, Michalis Alakiotis (Elderly Greek Family); Panais Patiniotis (Man with Donkey); Nikitas Kastrinos, Iordanis Markonios, Manolis Petrinolis (Musicians).

Paul Cox's **Island** is a film about emotional displacement and alienation. Three women on a Greek island are in psychological exile from a problematic world: Eva (Eva Sitta), an Australian–Czech girl, who is trying to break a drug habit; Marquise (Irene Papas), a Greek artist from the mainland and an earth mother, who is mistrustful of men and the societies they have produced; and Sahana (Anoja Weerasinghe), a Sri Lankan marooned on holiday on the island, who is waiting anxiously for the return of her husband, a political activist, from their homeland. United by their fear of the outside world, the women befriend each other.

Inhabited by warm, kindly people, the island is a paradise, but it cannot keep the world at bay. A serpent steals into this Eden, a predatory Frenchman (François Bernard), who deals in drugs. Eva is hooked again. Janis (Chris Haywood), a deaf mute and friend of the three women, discovers what the Frenchman is up to, and he is expelled from the island. When he returns and attacks Eva, Janis kills him and other islanders help to secretly dispose of the body. Shortly afterwards, Sahana learns that her husband has died in Sri Lanka. Despite danger to herself,

Marquise (Irene Papas).

she decides to return home. Before she leaves, she tells Eva, who wants to go with her, that she must 'leave the sea behind her, and go inland'.

Island experiments uncertainly with a *cinéma vérité* film style which has several of the islanders acting themselves. The inclusion of them as characters in the film's narrative embeds Cox's story in the physical and psychological reality of the island. However, even at its most affecting (the scene where Eva, toying with self-destruction, is rescued by three old people and taken into their house, where she is given biscuits and a warm shawl), this playing with the boundary between documentary and fiction is only half successful. The style distracts from the drama by drawing attention to itself.

Cox's humanistic concerns are treated with less subtlety in **Island** than usual. A moral tone intrudes as he examines ways of being through the women and the cultures they represent. This works against Cox's most distinguishing feature: his gift for lightness

and his naturalism. Papas' extrovert presence makes Marquise sound strident when Cox is speaking through her. 'I will not die for my country. I will die for my children, my mother, my lover if he's worth it. I will die for the earth, but I won't die for a flag.' Her rejection of nationalism is counterbalanced by Sahana's return to her roots: 'I'm weeping for my country. I have to go. Life has no meaning away from home.'

These clichéd characterisations, emblematic rather than original, suggest that Cox is at his best when he explores a perplexed, urban Australian consciousness.

JAN EPSTEIN

---

[1] There is no director's credit, just 'A Film by Paul Cox'.

References

'Island', a review by Anne-Marie Crawford, *Cinema Papers*, no. 76, November 1989, pp. 60–1.

'Island', a review by Liz Jacka, *Filmnews*, October 1989, p. 13.

LUIGIS LADIES

Tra La La Films Ltd presents Luigis Ladies[1]. © 1989 TRA LA LA FILMS Limited. *Location:* Sydney. *Australian distributor:* Hoyts. *Opened:* 11 May 1989. *Video:* First Release. *Rating:* M. 35 mm. Panavision. 91 mins.

 Producer: Patric Juillet. *Executive producer:* Wendy Hughes. *Associate producer:* Rachel Symes. *Scriptwriters:* Jennifer Claire, Judy Morris, Wendy Hughes, Ranald Allan. *Director of photography:* Steve Mason. *Production designer:* Melody Cooper. [*Costume designer:* not credited.] *Editor:* Pamela Barnetta. *Composer:* Sharon Calcraft. *Sound editors:* Wayne Pashley, Erin Sinclair. *Mixers:* Martin Oswin, John Herron.

Cast

Wendy Hughes (Sara), Sandy Gore (Cee), Anne Tenney (Jane), David Rappaport (Luigi), John Walton (Steve), Ray Meagher (Lance), Serge Lazareff (Trev), Joe Spano (Nick) Max Cullen (Chef), Brian Adams (Tom Stoker); Simon Angell, Alex Angell (The Twins); Prue Bassett (Nancy), Rosemary Blundo (Maria), Glenn Boswell (Kitchen Hand—stunt), Damian Cudmore (Lifesaver), Maggie Dence (Shandra), George Donikian (Australian Newsreader), Mervyn Drake (Jonathan), Roberta Grant (Shop Assistant), Johnny Hallyday (Kitchen Hand—stunt), Ric Hutton (Lord Timothy), Genevieve Lemon (Debbo).

Sara (Wendy Hughes).

There is a heartbeat of humour buried deep inside Luigis Ladies. During a send-up of a New Age meeting, people hop and skip like animals around a hall, trying to find themselves. One man in the background is a koala. He's good. He's funny. He's the one laugh in the film.

 This alleged comedy, directed and co-written by actor Judy Morris, and executive-produced by actor Wendy Hughes (who also co-wrote), is marked by scores of wasted comic opportunities and wasted talents strewn across a story of three women trying to cope with some sort of post-feminist anxiety syndrome.

 Sara (Wendy Hughes) is a magazine editor; Cee (Sandy Gore) is the dumped wife of an academic; and Jane (Anne Tenney) is the wife of an unfaithful wine merchant. They meet regularly at Luigi's, a restaurant run by the diminutive Luigi (David Rappaport), to discuss life's problems.

 In dealing with these multiple mid-life crises, the film has ample opportunity to milk humour (and drama) from things like the stock market crash of October 1987, hyperactive children, society restaurants, feminism, glitz journalism, yuppiedom, unwanted pregnancy, infidelity, sexual politics, sex, celibacy, temperamental French chefs, the New Age rage, cosmetic surgery and Sydney. But nothing is developed around these (or a number of other) narrative nuclei to make them the least bit interesting or funny.

 This appears to be the result of a directorial flatness which dogs the whole film. And many scenes of sharp emotion that would lend themselves so well to comedy or drama (or both) are diffused by poor performances, a grand lack of good, credible dialogue and some very dull photography.

 Special mention must be made of the low standard of performance from what is an obviously talented and distinguished cast. Crucial to any effective comedy film is the need of a performance to nail an emotion or a dramatic tone soundly on the head, and this must fit consistently (more or less) within an appropriate narrative context. With **Luigis Ladies**, what we basically have is an aimless mess: the performances are over-played and underplayed at all the wrong moments—monologues fall flat and attempts at a bit of good old shtick (like being drunk, overwhelmed, saddened or angry) are torpedoed by lame and unconvincing acting.

 In a word, what the film basically lacks is scope. There's not enough substance either in the material or in the performances for a failed television sitcom pilot, let alone a full-length cinema feature.

 But in all fairness, Judy Morris and Wendy Hughes deserve a toast to the future. They are two extremely talented actors who have proved themselves in front of the camera many times over. Here's to their next film collaboration. It will be better. It has to be.

JIM SCHEMBRI[2]

---

[1] Despite the need for one, the title has no apostrophe.

[2] Extracted from Schembri's review in *Cinema Papers* (see Reference).

Reference

'Luigi's [sic] Ladies', a review by Jim Schembri, *Cinema Papers*, no. 73, May 1989, p. 66.

MINNAMURRA

B. D. B. Production & Distribution presents a Burrowes Film Group [–] John Sexton Productions film. MINNAMURRA. *Alternative titles:* 'Outback' (working) and The Fighting Creed (video). © 1988 Birmarna Pty Limited. *Locations:* "Kangaroobie", Orange; "Balltrees"; Scone (New South Wales). *Australian distributor:* Hoyts. *Video:* Roadshow Home Video. *Rating:* PG. 35mm. Panavision. 92 mins.

Producer: John Sexton. *Executive producers:* Antony I. Ginnane, Kent C. Lovell. *Line producer:* Su Armstrong. *Scriptwriter:* John Sexton. *Director of photography:* Ross Berryman. *Production designer:* Owen Paterson. *Costume designer:* Terry Ryan. *Editor:* Henry Dangar. *Composer:* Mario Millo. *Sound recordist:* Ben Osmo. *Sound editors:* Peter Townend (fx); Tim Jordan, Susan Metcalf (dia.). *Mixers:* Roger Savage, Ian McLoughlin.

Cast

Jeff Fahey (Ben Creed), Tushka Bergen (Alice May Richards), Steven Vidler (Jack Donaghue), Richard Moir (Bill Thompson), Shane Briant (Allenby), Frederick Parslow (James Richards), Cornelia Francis (Caroline Richards), Michael Winchester (Rupert Richards), Sandy Gore (Maude Richards), Drew Forsythe (Henry Iverson), Robert Davis (Lord Kitchener), Andrew Sharp (Major Tim Swift), Kevin Healey (General Partington), Owen Weincott (General Smith), Colin Taylor (Taylor), Conor McDermottroe (Peagrum), James Steele (Slater), Mic Conway (Freddie), Fiona Stewart (Bessie), Derek Merdle (Butler), Laurie Moran (Auctioneer), Wallas Eaton (Grassmore), Peter Collingwood (Banker).

Class, money, sex: these classic ingredients of melodrama are the stock-in-trade of Ian Barry's **Minnamurra** and, given the new Australian cinema's extraordinary coyness about melodrama as a mode, it is perhaps not surprising that the film was a resounding failure, critically and commercially. But not only does it rework these classic ingredients quite skilfully, its range of characters and situations seems in direct line of descent from 19th-century fiction through 1940s Hollywood.

There is a high-spirited heroine, Alice May Richards (Tushka Bergen), determined to save the eponymous family home, when her ailing father (Frederick Parslow) dies; father is a gentleman locked in conflict with a robber baron neighbour who is determined to ruin him; there are two suitors to the girl's hand: Jack Donaghue (Steven Vidler), a drover who carefully drops his 'g's to suggest one-ness with the oppressed, and Ben Creed (Jeff Fahey), who knows how to behave in a drawing-room but may not be too scrupulous; and there are a Free Spirit, Aunt Maude (Sandy Gore), a leader in Melbourne's turn-of-the-century Bohemia, a snobbish mother (Cornelia Francis) and devoted family retainers.

The heroine kicks over the traces in various ways, sometimes recalling such other Australian female rebels as Sybylla Melvin (Judy Davis) in **My Brilliant Career** (Gill Armstrong, 1979) and Laura (Susannah Fowle) in **The Getting of Wisdom** (Bruce Beresford, 1977), and the matter of which suitor she will choose seems arbitrarily resolved. Many of her reactions—even to such staples of melodrama as 'Who will take over the old place now that father is dead?'—appear to belong more to the 1980s than to the 1890s, but so did the behaviours of countless heroines of Hollywood costume melodrama of the 1940s often seem to be reconciling the demands of the period of the film's making with that of its setting. In general, **Minnamurra** is not overly concerned with the period, neither in setting, dress nor mores, and it is none the worse for that. It avoids that endemic disease of new Australian cinema of lingering over the bric-à-brac while the narrative goes to pot.

The narrative, in fact, swings along. The cross-class romantic complication develops along with issues relating to the mortgage on Minnamurra, the manipulation of the Land League and the sale of horses to Lord Kitchener for service in South Africa. The film is not ashamed of bold melodramatic flourishes, and it borrows flamboyantly from the Western genre in matters of both iconography (open spaces, pounding hooves) and narrative (its romantic triangle, the conflict between father and neighbour as rival 'ranchers').

Finally, **Minnamurra**, even if one does not want to claim intellectual distinction for it, is frequently a ravishment to the eyes, and the scenes involving the moving of horses have a powerful kinetic appeal.

BRIAN MCFARLANE

The not-always-scrupulous Ben Creed (Jeff Fahey).

MULL

An International Film Management Limited Presentation [of] A Ukiyo Films Production. *Mull. Alternative title:* Mullaway (video[1]). © 1988 International Film Management Limited. *Location:* Melbourne. *Australian distributor:* Filmpac. *Video:* Filmpac. *Rating:* M. 35mm. 90 mins.

Producer: D. Howard Grigsby. *Executive producer:* Antony I. Ginnane. *Scriptwriter:* Jon Stephens. Based on the novel *Mullaway* by Bron Nicholls. *Director of photography:* Zbigniew Friedrich. *Editor:* Zbigniew Friedrich. *Production designer:* Patrick Reardon. *Costume designer:* Jeanie Cameron. *Composer:* Michael Atkinson. *Sound recorder:* Lloyd Carrick. *Sound editors:* Livia Ruzic (dia); Steve Lambeth (fx); Doron Kippen, Glenn Newnham (foley). *Mixer:* Bruce Emery.

Cast

Nadine Garner (Phoebe Mullens), Bill Hunter (Frank Mullens), Sue Jones (Deborah Mullens), Craig Morrison (Steve Mullens), Bradley Kilpatrick (Alan Mullens), Kymara Stowers (Jo Mullens), Monty Maizels (Don), Esme Melville (Fanny), Gerard Maguire (Dr Graham), Mary Coustas (Helen), Juno Roxas (Guido), Chris Tabone (Drummer), Nicholas Caruana (Bass Player), Nick Giannopoulos (George), David Cameron (Larry), Bruce Langdon (Paul), Gary Files (Brother Baxter), Jon Stephens (Waiter), Dominic Sweeney (Jim), Vince Jones (Jazz Singer).

Mull is a rites-of-passage story. It begins one parched, lazy summer at Christmas time. The Mullens family lives in St Kilda near the beach. As the youngest daughter is taking a photograph of the family with her new camera, the mother collapses. She is rushed to the hospital where they diagnose Hodgkinson's disease. Seventeen-year old Phoebe Mullens (Nadine Garner), nicknamed 'Mull', makes a decision to drop out of school to look after her family.

This is by no means an easy task. Mull's mother, Deborah (Sue Jones), is now bedridden. Her security guard father, Frank (Bill Hunter), is a fanatical born-again Christian and an ex-alcoholic always teetering on the brink of return. Her brother, Steve (Craig Morrison), plays in a band and, she discovers, is gay and experimenting with heroin. Her younger brother, Alan (Bradley Kilpatrick), is pubescent and struggling with the hypocrisy of his father's religion and his mother's terminal illness quite hysterically.

Young sister Jodie (Kymara Stowers) is demanding simply because of her age.

There are not only the internal family problems that Mull must confront, but also an awakening to what is going on in the world around her. Her fantasy romance turns out to be her gay brother's lover. Her most supportive school teacher is also involved in a homosexual relationship. Her best friend, Helen (Mary Coustas), gets pregnant and half-heartedly marries her Greek boyfriend in an extravagant Greek wedding. And Mull's first romantic relationship with a young deaf-mute causes her more problems than it does him.

The film is a social drama and director Don McLennan chose to give it a documentary feeling. Interiors are drab and depressing, and these contribute to the feeling of struggle and oppression.

There are, however, luminous moments: the crowded, sun-bleached beaches, the rocky foreshore where Mull walks with Guido (Juno Roxas), the crazy, brightly coloured fun-rides in Luna Park, the exuberant songs from Steve, Guido and their garage band, and the Fitzroy Street night club with its jazz music. This is a rich and complex world.

The greatest riches come from the young woman's inner voice. There are a number of scenes where Mull narrates the feelings she writes into her diary. In the last scene, her final words reflect on a difficult year, and her intention to return to school and to make something of her life. What exactly, she's not sure, but the film watches her with faith. We have witnessed this young woman's struggles, we have seen her grow and we believe in her.

Don McLennan has made a series of films in which there are strong young female protagonists: Sam (Tracey Mann) in **Hard Knocks** (1980), Blanche McBride (Sigrid Thornton) in **Slate Wyn & Me** (1987) and now Mull.

Despite the recognition **Mull** received in the AFI Awards (Nadine Garner won Best Actress), it was poorly distributed and did not reach a wide audience. Together with McLennan's other works, it waits to be discovered.

ANNA DZENIS

---

[1] Even though the video slick says '**Mull**', the video carries the title '**Mullaway**'.

References
'Don McLennan', an interview with the director by Rod Bishop, *Cinema Papers*, no. 77, January 1990, pp. 22–7.
'Mull', a review by Shelley Kay, *Filmnews*, May 1989, p. 12.

Jo (Kymara Stowers) and Phoebe Mullens (Nadine Garner).

THE SALUTE OF THE JUGGER

Kings Road Entertainment presents THE SALUTE OF THE JUGGER. © 1989 Kings Road Entertainment. *Location:* Coober Pedy (South Australia). *Australian distributor:* Filmpac. *Video:* Filmpac. *Rating:* M. 35mm. 100 mins.

    Producer: Charles Roven. *Executive producer:* Brian Rosen. *Scriptwriter:* David Peoples. *Director of photography:* David Eggby. *Camera operator:* Philip M. Cross. *Production designer:* John Stoddart. *Costume designer:* Terry Ryan. *Editor:* Richard Francis-Bruce. *Composer:* Todd Boekelheide. *Sound designer:* Jay Boekelheide. *Sound recordist:* Lloyd Carrick. *Sound editors:* Douglas Murray (fx); Barbara McBaine, Paige Sartorious (dia.); Luis Colina (foley). *Mixers:* Marke Berger (supervising); David Parker, Todd Boekelheide, Danny Kopelson.

Cast

Rutger Hauer (Sallow), Joan Chen (Kidda), Vincent Phillip D'Onofrio (Young Gar), Anna Katarina (Big Cimber), Delroy Lindo (Mbulu), Hugh Keays-Byrne[1] (Lord Vile), Gandhi McIntyre (Gandhi), Max Fairchild (Gonzo), Justin Monju (Dog Boy), Aaron Martin (Samchin Boy), Casey Huang (Kidda's Father), Quang Dinh (Samchin Head Elder), John Doumtsis (Samchin Timekeeper), John Biro (Samchin Peasant #1), Brian Cawley (Samchin Peasant #2), Gino Terranova (Samchin Peasant #3), Cecila Wong (Kidda's Mother), David Bookalil (Enforcement Officer #1), John Samaha (Enforcement Officer #2), Honie Robinson (Kolkan Blond Daughter).

David Peoples' The Salute of the Jugger is an undiscovered gem of the Australian cinema. An American-financed production made here with some local cast and crew, it was dismissed by most who saw it during its brief release. But this is one of the best-written and -directed films of the revival, with brilliant production design from John Stoddart and, yet again, excellent photography from David Eggby (whose superb work on Simon Wincer's **Quigley** the next year would be equally ignored). Now that Peoples is a hot property in Hollywood (due to his superb script for Clint Eastwood's **Unforgiven**, 1992), **The Salute of the Jugger** may one day be widely seen and discussed. It would be a shame if it were not.

    The time is the future, a post-apocalyptic wasteland straight out of **Mad Max Beyond Thunderdome** (George Miller and George Ogilvie, 1985), with its poverty-stricken desert towns and horrendous underground cities where the rich and privileged live on one level, and the rest below. (Peoples and Stoddart have highlighted what is the mediæval influence inherent in such a concept, even using that evocative image of tax collectors defrauding all who venture from zone to zone.)

    For the survivors of this wasteland, the central interest is The Game (shades of the Thunderdome). It is an extremely violent derivative of rugby[2] with many broken limbs and deep wounds (there are many scenes of flesh being sewn). But at the end of each game, every player treats the others with respect and friendship (the salute of the title). Despite everything, a sportsmanship survives, as if something noble in man remains resistant to destruction.

    Once a champion of The Game and an élite member of The League, made up of teams from the nine cities, Sallow (Rutger Hauer) now wanders with his motley team from one outer town to another. When the inexperienced Kidda (Joan Chen) replaces his injured runner (or 'quick'), she cajoles the group into going to the Red City and challenging The League. Sallow, who was expelled for having once courted a wealthy lady, is at first reluctant, but finally agrees.

    At the City, Sallow must beat off the sinister plans of Lord Vile (Hugh Keays-Byrne), who demands Sallow be blinded, and lead his inexperienced team to victory against the vicious and professional cruelty of The League.

    Many films gain drama from a sporting victory at the end, but few are as dramatic and exhilarating as this. Sallow's defiant instruction to Kidda to not run with the dog's head to the spike, but walk, is heroic in the most powerfully mythic of ways.

    Clearly, the film is influenced by the sort of stories retold and analysed by Joseph Campbell. The heroic journey recounted here is clearly delineated (returning to the site of defeat and facing blindness in the battle to succeed). It also has striking parallels with 'life game' novels such as Kawabata's *The Master of Go*.

    Victorious, the younger players are snapped up by The League, but Sallow is cast again into the wasteland, unforgiven, where he will continue to play The Game till totally blind and all life drained from him. That is his fate: to be the best and all but outlawed, known only through the stories that will continue to be told.

SCOTT MURRAY

---

[1] Opening credits have surname as 'Keays-Bryne'.
[2] Each side has one runner (the quick), one protector and four defenders. The aim is for the quick to grab the dog skull and, circumventing the violent attacks of the opposition (wielding padded steel bars and spiked chains), reach the end of the playing ground and place the skull on the spike. Some critics have claimed the game is incomprehensible, but it is absolutely clear in all its rules and stratagems. And all this with barely a word of explanation—yet another tribute to Peoples' skill as a director.

References

'Second Glance: **The Salute of the Jugger**', Scott Murray, *Cinema Papers*, no. 92, April 1993, p. 53.

'Briefly', letter about the film from Annie Marshall, with comment by Scott Murray, *Cinema Papers*, no. 95, August 1993, p. 2.

Gonzo (Max Fairchild) and Lord Vile (Hugh Keays-Byrne) inside the Red City.

SEBASTIAN AND THE SPARROW

The Kino Film Co. Ltd. presents A Colour and Movement Film. SEBASTIAN AND THE Sparrow. © 1989 The Kino Film Co. Ltd. Made with the assistance of the Australian Film Commission, the South Australian Film & TV Financing Fund, the South Australian Film Corporation and International Year of Youth (South Australian Committee). *Location:* Adelaide. *Australian distributor:* The Kino Film Co. *Video:* The Home Cinema Group. *Rating:* PG. 35mm. 88 mins.

Producer: Scott Hicks. *Executive producer:* Terry Ohlsson. *Associate producer:* Darryl Sheen. *Scriptwriter:* Scott Hicks. *Director of photography:* David Foreman. *Production designer:* Anni Browning. *Wardrobe:* Robin Hall. *Editor:* Pip Karmel. *Composer:* Allan Zavod. *Sound recordist:* Toivo Lember. *Sound editors:* Yvonne van Gyem, Pip Karmel. *Mixers:* James Currie, Peter Smith.

Cast

Alexander Bainbridge (Sebastian), Jeremy Angerson (Sparrow), Robert Coleby (Peter Thornbury), Elizabeth Alexander (Jenny Thornbury), Vincent Gil (Streetworker (Mick)), John Clayton (Country Cop), Alice Ramsay (Maude), Jethro Heysen-Hicks (Jethro), Chris Roberts (Turbo), Peter Crossley (Red), Patrick Frost (School Teacher); Brenton Whittle, Kathryn Fisher, Bob Newman, June Lindley, Grant Piro, Mike Norman, Rebe Taylor, Damon Sanders, Simon Cockrum, Jody Hollow, Scott Heysen, Rachel Rains, Chris Bumagia, Emily Kelly.

Sebastian and the Sparrow is an Australian children's film of rare quality. It is sensitive, but not overly sentimental. It is targeted for children, and yet, unlike most children's cinema, it does not forget about film 'quality'. Most important, it represents young teenagers without judgement or condescension. It does not pretend that young people are naïve or innocent of anything, and almost revels in the precociousness of modern teenagers. And, the plot is actually interesting and involving.

Sebastian (Alexander Bainbridge) and Sparrow (Jeremy Angerson) are two very different boys from very different social backgrounds. Sebastian, who initially seems to be a total 'sissy', comes from an affluent family. His spacious, chaotically messy home is in a wealthy, though, as the film subtly notes, rather frigid neighbourhood. He attends one of the better private schools of Adelaide, and is so bored with his perfect,

Sebastian (Alexander Bainbridge) and Sparrow (Jeremy Angerson).

over-provided existence that his family and teachers, noticing that something is wrong, decide that he might need to see a therapist.

Sparrow, on the other hand, lives in the dark and dangerous world of homelessness and street survival. He is a runaway from a foster home, because, according to him, all they cared about was the allowance cheque. He has a mother, but does not know where she is or whether she cares to see him. His father, along with his happy past and a real childhood, is dead.

One day, Sparrow and Sebastian meet at a pinball machine in a milkbar, and from there, through a series of quirky adventures, their friendship develops. Sparrow ends up staying in Sebastian's house, but there is a youth-shelter worker, Mick (Vincent Gil) after him, as Sparrow is still considered a runaway. More important, Mick has news that Sparrow's mother wants to see him, which Sparrow finds hard to believe,

The two boys set out to find more information about the mother. This is routine for Sparrow, but an adventure for Sebastian, who sees this as a way of escaping the monotony of his life. They meet up with Sparrow's

druggie friends: a petrol-head and his moll, and a graffiti artist, whose work, incidentally, Sebastian has long admired and taken many Polaroids of.

When Sparrow becomes finally convinced that his mother really does want to see him, he and Sebastian decide that she may be found out west, in a place called Cactus, where Sparrow grew up. And so the boys take off, with Sebastian becoming a runaway also. After several adventures, all ends well: Sparrow finally meets up with his mother and Sebastian returns home.

The script succeeds almost entirely in avoiding clichés. Scott Hicks directs with a careful, gentle touch, which the script requires. Visually, it is appealing and often beautifully quirky. Alexander Bainbridge, though not showing any great promise as an actor, does not really hamper the overall performances, particularly that of Jeremy Angerson, who has a magnificent ability to brood.

Sebastian and the Sparrow is a little gem, and not, one hopes, only to be enjoyed by kids.

ANNA GUL

SONS OF STEEL

James Michael Vernon presents Sons of Steel. © 1988 Big Island Pictures Pty. Ltd. Budget: $3 million. *Location:* Sydney. *Australian distributor:* James Michael Vernon. *Video:* Virgin Vision. *Rating:* M. 35mm. 104 mins.

Producer: James Michael Vernon. *Associate producer:* Penny Wall. *Scriptwriter:* Gary L. Keady. *Director of photography:* Joseph Pickering. *Camera operator:* Wayne Taylor. *Production designer:* Graham (Grace) Walker. *Costume designers:* Gary L. Keady, Nicholas Huxley, Nichola Braithwaite. *Editor:* Amanda Robson. *Music director:* Gary L. Keady. *Sound recordist:* Paul Radcliffe. *Sound design:* Paul Radcliffe. *Sound fx:* Russell Dunlop. *Mixer:* Bruce Brown.

Cast

Rob Hartley (Black Alice), Roz Wason (Hope), Jeff Duff (Secta); Dasha Blahova [Honor[1]], Ralph Cotterill [Karzoff], Elizabeth Richmond [Djard], Wayne Snell [Ex]; Machs Colombini; Mark Hembrow [Mal]; Sharlie Wetherill (Stained Class), Gordon Wood (Police Trooper Dicks), Wendy Dys (Meg), Raquel Suartzman (Prissy), Michelle Vaughan (Voluptuous), Jos O'Neill (Robert; Android), Beth Child (Matron), Jodie Andrews (Receptionist), Jeraza Green (Female Nurse), Nicholas Huxley (Male Nurse), Doug Mealing (President), Gayle-Ann (General 1), Karl Webster (General 2) .

In a not-too-distant future, South Pacific nations have merged to create a giant trading block, Oceana. When a rock singer-cum-peace activist, Black Alice (Rob Hartley), organises a flotilla to protest the arrival of a nuclear submarine, invited into port by the President (Doug Mealing) of Oceana to break the nuclear-free zone status of the region, Black Alice is trapped inside a hologram by the Fascist government's security forces. More than a century later, he is freed accidentally by a pair of post-holocaust Neanderthals only to discover Secta (Jeff Duff), the man responsible for his imprisonment, is alive in an underground bunker. Secta gleefully informs Alice that the nuclear detonation was caused ironically by his very own activism—the peace ferry colliding with the sub and unleashing the global conflagration. With less than ten hours before his metabolism decays (due to his earlier suspended animation), Black Alice is sent back in time to prevent the nuclear disaster from occurring.

With genre 'influences' ranging from **Superman II**, *Max Headroom*, **The Rocky Horror Picture Show**, **Mad Max**, **Aliens** and **Radioactive Dreams** to **The Terminator**[2], and a central character who less than successfully conflates Peter Garrett, Angry Anderson and Bon Scott, **Sons of Steel** is literally a 'fantastic' work of late 1980s pastiche.

Clearly directed at **The Rocky Horror Picture Show**'s audience, **Sons of Steel** unfortunately relies too much on scatology and limp-wristed shtick (bordering on the homophobic), ultimately wallowing in the low-brow while aiming for cult status. The entire plot premise and credibility of a street savvy, pacifist rock and roller who intervenes through wit and lyric rather than flexing his formidable brawn is quickly demolished when hero Black Alice indulges in ultra-violent screen fantasies (blowing away bureaucrats and apparatchiks à la **Billy Liar** and **A Clockwork Orange**[3]) and then later actively pursues these in the post-apocalyptic ruins ('Got any happenin' weapons?').

On paper, the scenario must have appeared a fabulous idea. Writer–director Gary L. Keady (who also co-wrote the score and supervised the inventive costume design) has forged a highly vibrant Australian film, yet, in retrospect, one perhaps better suited to animation (e.g., **Rock & Rule** or **Akira**[4]).

The strengths of **Sons of Steel** lie in the imaginative, low-budget production design, cinematography and costuming, and (partly) in a convulsive *outré* performance by Rob Hartley as Black Alice. The film's producers must also be credited for attempting a very rare thing in local cinema production: a rock-and-roll comedy that is science fiction to boot. But for all of the revelry in its comic-book construction, **Sons of Steel** nevertheless aches to be taken seriously. Here the classic exploitation equation of 'having your cake and eating it too' fails, which only serves to heighten its reactionary subtexts of vengeance, violence and nihilism.

MICK BRODERICK

---

1 The next six cast have no character names in the credits; five character names are taken from the press book.
2 **Superman II** (Richard Lester, 1980), **The Rocky Horror Picture Show** (Jim Sharman, 1975), **Mad Max** (George Miller, 1979), **Aliens** (James Cameron, 1986), **Radioactive Dreams** (Albert Pyun, 1986), **The Terminator** (James Cameron, 1984).
3 **Billy Liar** (John Schlesinger, 1963), **A Clockwork Orange** (Stanley Kubrick, 1971).
4 **Rock & Rule** (Clive A. Smith, 1983), **Akira** (Katsuhiro Otomo, 1988).

Rock singer-cum-peace activist Black Alice (Rob Hartley).

SPIRITS OF THE AIR, GREMLINS OF THE CLOUDS

A Meaningful Eye Contact Film. SPIRITS OF THE AIR ◊ GREMLINS OF THE CLOUDS. © 1988 [no company listed]. Produced in conjunction with MMA Films, Pro-Image and the Creative Development Branch of the Australian Film Commission. *Locations:* Broken Hill; Sydney (New South Wales). *Australian distributor:* Meaningful Eye Contact. *Video:* Home Cinema Group. *Rating:* M. 16mm. 93 mins.

Producers: Alex Proyas, Andrew McPhail. *Scriptwriter:* Alex Proyas. *Director of photography:* David Knaus. *Production designer:* Sean Callinan. [*Costume designers:* not credited; Angela Tonks, Mathu Anderson.] *Editor:* Craig Wood. *Composer:* Craig Wood. *Sound recordist:* David White. *Sound design:* Craig Wood. [*Sound Editor:* not credited; atb Craig Wood.] *Mixer:* Ian McLoughlin.

Cast

Michael Lake (Felix), Rhys Davis (Betty), The Norm[1] (Smith).

Out of an unnamed post-apocalyptic desert stumbles Smith (The Norm[2]), in *de rigueur* post-punk black coat, boots and gloves. On the verge of collapse, he is rescued by the wheel-chair-bound Felix (Michael Lake) and his reluctant sister, Betty (Phys Davis), then revived inside their decrepit outback homestead. After prolonged posing, mumbling and ranting, it becomes clear that taciturn Smith is on the run, Felix is a crippled amateur aviator and Betty a sexually repressed religious fanatic still traumatised by the loss of her evangelical father years before.

Felix convinces Smith to stay a while and, after a series of bumbled test flights, Smith is given the task of assembling a human-powered light plane capable of taking all three over impenetrable mountains to the north and avoiding the mysterious pursuers travelling five days behind to the south. On the day of their departure, however, Betty persuades Felix to remain, reminding him of a death-bed promise to their father never to attempt human flight again. After a sad, resigned farewell, Felix coaxes Smith into the air and freedom.

Spirits of the Air, Gremlins of the Clouds is a unique and antithetical Australian feature film. It is so far removed from the social-realist, historical or art-house genres of 1970s and 1980s Australian cinema to be instantly refreshing. Although its lame and clichéd narrative barely propels the plot along its 93 minutes, this very emptiness resonates and amplifies the film's extraordinary visual and aural texture. More like a single, extended music video (and, as it happens, 1990s television advertising), its production design, art direction, musical score, cinematography and *mise-en-scène* evoke such a powerful amalgam of myth and iconography that any disappointments with script and acting be-come marginalised. As such, it is perhaps best read as a post-modern essay synthesising a vast array of intertextual references and motifs—from **Eraserhead** (David Lynch, 1978) to **Mad Max Beyond Thunderdome** (George Miller and George Ogilvie, 1985), Salvador Dali to Sidney Nolan, Split Enz to The Cure, T. S. Eliot to J. G. Ballard.

The compelling artistic imagery created by Spirits of the Air, Gremlins of the Clouds is that of an imaginary, hyper-real space at once immediately recognisable as Australian yet with enough alien topography to create a surreal dreamscape. The piercing azure blue of the outback sky is marvellously captured, frequently dominating more than two-thirds of the frame, and evokes an immense sense of distance at the vanishing point of the desert-red horizon. Juxtaposed against this spectacular azimuth are bizarre images: twisted, hand-carved homestead gargoyles; sun-bleached cattle bones; silhouetted totemic poles and mediæval banners; and Betty, playing her Chinese violin dressed in white Victorian underwear or scarlet Asian silks aflame in the setting sun.

It is tempting to superficially reduce **Spirits of the Air, Gremlins of the Clouds** to no more than the sum of its parts; to suggest that it is all form and no content. Ah, but what form!

MICK BRODERICK

---

1 According to the press material, 'The Norm' is actually 'Norman Boyd'.
2 See footnote 1.
3 See footnote 1.

Smith (The Norm[3]), a post-apocalyptic adventurer.

A STING IN THE TAIL

Rosa Colosimo Films presents A STING IN THE TALE. *Alternative title:* 'Scorpio' (working). © 1989 Rosa Colosimo Pty Ltd. *Location:* Adelaide. *Australian distributor:* Rosa Colosimo Films. *Opened:* November 1989. *Video:* not released. *Rating:* M. 16mm. 96 mins.

Producers: Rosa Colosimo, Reg McLean. *Scriptwriter:* Patrick Edgeworth. Based on a story by Patrick Edgeworth, Eugene Schlusser, Reg McLean, Rosa Colosimo. *Director of photography:* Nicholas Sherman. *Production designer:* Lisa (Blitz) Brennan. *Wardrobe:* Anita Fioravanti. *Editor:* Zbigniew Friedrich. *Composer:* Allan Zavod. *Sound recordist:* Michael Piper. *Sound editors:* Annette Kelly, Lanni Smith. *Mixers:* James Currie, Phil Heywood.

Cast

Diane Craig (Diane Lane), Gary Day (Barry Robbins), Lynne Williams (Louise Parker), Edwin Hodgeman (Monroe), Don Barker (Prime Minister), John Noble (PM's Minder), Tony Mack (Michael Meadows), Bob Newman (Permanent Secretary), Gordon Goulding (Wilson Sinclair), Patrick Edgeworth (Editor), Gary Bishop (Leader of the Opposition), Robert Leach (Speaker of the House), Michael Norman (Police Inspector), Lyn Semmler (Interviewer), Matthew Randell (Newscaster), Joanne Cooper (Barmaid); Tony Allison, Peter Raymond Powell (Drinkers).

A Sting in the Tale is a home-grown political satire, one which announces itself in the press material as concerning itself with 'how the full force of the male-dominated world of power tries to manipulate the life and career of one woman and how she turns the tables on them'.

Scriptwriter Patrick Edgeworth (*Boswell for the Defence*) deliberately uses caricatured characters to make various telling points in his fable about the nature of political power, backroom party machinations and male sexism.

Diane Lane (Diane Craig) is the newly elected and naïve backbencher, formerly a trade-union official, who enters parliament after winning the seat of Black Stump in a by-election. With a sense of heady idealism, she ascends the corridors of power and navigates a treacherous political minefield, carrying some odd personal baggage with her along the way.

Not surprising, given the jaunty tone of the piece, she eventually becomes Australia's first female prime minister. This occurs despite obstacles placed in her ascent by

Diane Lane (Diane Craig) and a parliamentarian (uncredited).

married lover, Barry Robbins (Gary Day), a corrupt and chain-smoking Minister for Health, and the schemings of seedy media magnate, Monroe (Edwin Hodgeman), a Rupert Murdoch sound-and-lookalike character, basically your standard media baron.

Produced by the prolific Rosa Colosimo on South Australian locations to represent the federal capital, the film uneasily settles for a broad comedy style that lacks any real bite or venom with most of the characters trading quips that would seem more at home in the shorthand vocabulary of television sitcoms.

Director Eugene Schlusser, a former actor and theatre director with extensive television experience, seems to be fighting an uphill battle on obviously limited resources. The low budget frequently strains dramatic credibility, particularly in any scene that takes place in the political arena. The soundtrack suggests the presence of dozens of people, but the recurring image is limited to the same half dozen or so extras traipsing across the screen.

Intermittently amusing, A Sting in the Tale, amiable and relaxed in tone, lacks any real sense of passion or commitment to its subject matter, and seems content to straddle a dated twilight zone, which is perched uneasily between broad farce and glum earnestness.

PAUL HARRIS[1]

---

[1] Extracted from Harris' review in *Cinema Papers* (see Reference).

Reference

'A Sting in the Tale', a review by Paul Harris, *Cinema Papers*, no. 78, March 1990, p. 57.

SWEETIE

Arenafilm presents sweetie. © 1989 Arenafilm. Developed with the assistance of the New South Wales Film Corporation. Produced with the assistance of the Australian Film Commission. *Location:* Sydney. *Australian distributor:* Filmpac. *Opened:* September 1989. *Video:* Home Cinema Group. *Rating:* M. 35mm. 97 mins.

Producer: John Maynard. *Co-producer:* William MacKinnon. *Scriptwriters:* Gerard Lee, Jane Campion. *Director of photography:* Sally Bongers. *Camera operator:* Jane Castle. *Production designer:* Peter Harris. *Costume designer:* Amanda Lovejoy. *Editor:* Veronika Haussler. *Composer:* Martin Armiger. *Sound recordist:* Leo Sullivan. *Sound Editor:* Liz Goldfinch. *Mixers:* Tony Vaccher, John Dennison.

Cast

Genevieve Lemon (Sweetie), Karen Colston (Kay), Tom Lycos (Louis), Jon Darling (Gordon), Dorothy Barry (Flo), Michael Lake (Bob), André Pataczek (Clayton), Jean Hadgraft (Mrs Schneller), Paul Livingston (Teddy Schneller), Louise Fox (Cheryl), Ann Merchant (Paula), Robyn Frank (Ruth), Bronwyn Morgan (Sue), Sean Fennell (Boy Clerk), Sean Callinan (Simboo), Norm Galton (Notary), Warren Hensley (Man Handshaker), Regina Heilmann (Girl), Charles Abbott (Meditation Teacher), Diana Armer (Melony), Barbara Middleton (Clayton's Mum).

Jane Campion's first feature, **Sweetie**, is filled with disturbing images and themes that return to haunt the imagination long after the film's shortcomings are forgotten. Kay (Karen Colston) is a thin, colourless young woman who works in a bank. She is trying to live a normal life away from her family which is dominated by Kay's sister Dawn (Genevieve Lemon), nicknamed 'Sweetie', who is raucous, uninhibited, obese and prone to violent, destructive tantrums if she can't have her way. Kay, by comparison, is introverted. She is superstitious, frightened of life and in the grip of a morbid fear of trees which is ruining the relationship with her boyfriend, Louis (Tom Lycos). Louis plants a tree in their backyard which celebrates their living together, but Kay is terrified of it. It looks yellow and sickly. What if it should die? Kay pulls it out by the roots one night and next day her passion for Louis has mysteriously vanished. No amount of patience on Louis' part seems able to rekindle it. How this state of affairs might have resolved itself normally we will never know

Dawn (Genevieve Lemon) and spaced-out Bob (Michael Lake).

for, at this point, Sweetie bursts into Kay's life, and onto the screen.

Before the entry of Sweetie, Campion's film lacks focus. The acting seems desultory and of variable quality. Only Kay's obsession with trees has real power. From this point on, however, the film springs into surreal life, so much so that it forces the viewer to question the need to have delayed Sweetie's entrance for so long. Her uncontrollable presence invades every nook and cranny of Kay's carefully ordered existence, in the same way that the hairy roots of trees invade Kay's dreams and turn them into nightmares. Kay is swept back into family life with a vengeance, when Kay's mother, Flo (Dorothy Barry), leaves her father, Gordon (Jon Darling), because of Sweetie, and Gordon moves in with her. The nightmare ends in farce and tragedy when Sweetie, barking like a dog, falls naked from a tree, her body painted black.

Sweetie is a ghastly parody of the tyranny of family life. The warmth and tenderness of which Sweetie is capable can suddenly turn and devour the very people that she succours. As well as being the source of the family's energy, she is the incarnation of the 'uncertainty principle', and Kay, who yearns for continuity and certainty, is terrified.

Sweetie's potent images are a powerful reflection of the tension between individual

freedom and the profound constraints created by families. Kay becomes liberated by the death of Sweetie, who is a bizarre manifestation of social/family control. This theme jostles uncomfortably with the final sad, poignant glimpse of her lost innocence and potential: the young Sweetie performing for her father, her red hair gleaming. This is a powerful humanistic perspective, which prefigures Campion's later achievement, **An Angel at My Table** (1990).

The lensing of Sally Bongers (the first woman cinematographer to work on an Australian 35mm film) is as challenging and exciting as Campion's original, fragmented and decentred vision.

JAN EPSTEIN

References

'Jane Campion', an interview with the director by Philippa Hawker, *Cinema Papers*, no. 73, May 1989, pp. 29–30.

'Sally Bongers', an article on the DOP (with quotes) by Mary Colbert, *Cinema Papers*, no. 75, September 1989, pp. 4–8.

'Sweetie', a review by Anne-Marie Crawford and Adrian Martin, ibid., pp. 56–7.

'**An Angel at My Table**', an interview with director Jane Campion by Hunter Cordaiy, *Cinema Papers*, no. 81, December 1990, pp. 32–6.

'Sitcom of the Absurd: **Sweetie**', a review by Shelley Kay, *Filmnews*, September, 1989, p. 6.

'Once Upon a Time: Jane Campion Talks About How She Made **Sweetie**', an interview with the director by Meagan McMurchy, *Filmnews*, ibid., p. 7.

TENDER HOOKS

[No opening production company credit.] Tender Hooks. *Alternative title:* 'Contact' (working). [© not given; atb 1988.] *Location:* Sydney. *Australian distributor:* Ronin. *Video:* Home Cinema Group. *Rating:* M. 16mm (blown up to 35mm). 95 mins.

Producer: Chris Oliver. *Associate producer:* Anne Grieve. *Scriptwriter:* Mary Callaghan. *Director of photography:* Ray Argall. *Production designer:* Kerrie Brown. *Costume designer:* Kerrie Brown. *Editor:* Tony Stevens. *Musical director:* Graham Bidstrup. *Sound recordist:* Pat Fiske. *Sound editors:* Helen Brown, Tim Chau, Paul Healy, Danielle Wiessner. *Mixers:* Peter Fenton, Martin Oswin.

Cast

Jo Kennedy (Mitchell), Nique Needles (Rex Reeson), Toni Scanlon (Lorraine), Noeleen Walsh (Customer Brainwaves), Shane Connor (Wayne), Simon Westaway (Motor Cycle Cop), Robert Menzies (Yawn), Anna Phillips (Gaye), Ian Mortimer (Vic), John Polson (Tony), Brian Roberts (Yahoo Leader); Grant Page, Bob Hicks, Chris Hession (Yahoos); Liz Chance (Shirley), Jessie O'Meara Healey (Lukie), Kim Deacon (Connie), Dan Halliday (Col), John Ley (Ad Director).

Tender Hooks is a film about 'doing time', not as marked out by the passage of the sun or moon but as a succession of states. There is time on the outside and time on the inside. The cyclical path of the two is inextricably and inevitably linked, like night following day. The shadow of one is remembered in the living of the other.

On the outside, life is instantaneous. Thoughts and desires are obsessional and then become distracted, with the same erratic speed of moths mesmerised by ever-changing sources of light. On the inside, home is something to be endured in doses. 'Not much to do here except mutilate yourself', says Rex Reeson (Nique Needles) almost drily.

Tender Hooks, the first feature from Mary Callaghan, is a small story writ large with the finest of detail. One suspects the writer–director is an inveterate scribbler and note-taker with an eye like a Polaroid.

The audience's enjoyment lies in the resonance of the film's repertoire of looks, quips and body moves, rather than through a structured series of climactic moments. Rex is always on the move somewhere else, following up yet another scam. At first, this only serves to make him all the more endearing and Mitchell (Jo Kennedy) finds him implicated in her life before she has had a chance to absorb it. Rex has perfected the sheepish grin and it's a winner for him for quite some time, overriding Mitchell's doubts about his crim friends, uncertain movements and an endless stream of stolen presents (meaningless objects given as meaningful gifts).

Their lovemaking is a jumble of clothes and limbs, television and dirty dishes. 'If you hadn't stuck your tongue in my ear I could have gone on for longer', says Rex as he cleans up the results of a split condom, using Mitchell's hairdryer. All the time, marital bickering from the flat overhead sets an ominous tone.

On a 'job' at a harbourside penthouse with two mates, Rex watches porn on the home video and eats from the fridge while the work of fleecing the joint is supposed to be taking place. This kind of sensual relationship towards theft cannot last. Gradually, life on the outside heads towards its inevitable reunion with that on the inside of the prison wall.

Callaghan makes the point that crims carry their prison around with them and those who love them end up 'doing time' as well. These are the tender hooks that tear people apart at the same time as they are keeping them together.

Though the film might wish to be about Kennedy's Mitchell, it cannot help but revolve around Needles' Rex. Even though he seems powerless—shorn and made scrawny by prison life—it's still his life and experience that give structure to the narrative and to the life of Mitchell. Choices have to be made.

Callaghan's fictions have documentary intentions and every little detail must ring true—and it does.

SUSAN CHARLTON[1]

---

[1] Extracted from Charlton's review in *Cinema Papers* (see References).

References
'Tender Hooks', a review by Susan Charlton, *Cinema Papers*, no. 71, January 1989, p. 59.
'Tender Hooks', a review by Shelley Kay, *Filmnews*, March 1989, p. 13.

Mitchell (Jo Kennedy).

*Young Janet (Alexia Keogh). Jane
Campion's* An Angel at My Table.

AN ANGEL AT MY TABLE[1]

Hibiscus Films in association with the New Zealand Film Commission presents AN ANGEL AT MY TABLE. © 1990 Hibiscus Films Ltd. Produced by Hibiscus Films Ltd in association with the New Zealand Film Commission, Television New Zealand Ltd, Australian Broadcasting Corporation and Channel 4. *Location:* New Zealand. *Australian distributor:* Sharmill Films. *Opened:* 20 September 1990. *Video:* Applause Home Video. *Rating:* PG. 35mm. 150 mins.

Producer: Bridget Ikin. *Co-producer:* John Maynard. *Scriptwriter:* Laura Jones. Based on the autobiographies of Janet Frame [*To the Is-Land, Angel at My Table* and *Envoy from Mirror City*]. *Director of photography:* Stuart Dryburgh. *Production designer:* Grant Major. *Costume designer:* Glenys Jackson. *Editor:* Veronika Haussler. *Composer:* Don McGlashan. *Sound recordist:* Graham Morris. *Sound designers:* John Dennison, Tony Vaccher. *Sound editors:* John Dennison, Tony Vaccher. *Mixers:* John Dennison, Tony Vaccher.

Cast

Kerry Fox (Janet), Alexia Keogh (Young Janet), Karen Fergusson (Teenage Janet), Iris Churn (Mum), Jessie Mune (Baby Janet), K. J. Wilson (Dad), Francesca Collins (Baby Jane), Melina Bernbecker (Myrtle), Andrew Binns (Bruddle), Glynis Angell (Isabel), Sara Smuts-Kennedy (June), Martyn Sanderson (Frank Sargeson), David Letch (Patrick), William Brandt (Bernard), Katherine Murray-Cowper (Young Isabel), Mark Thomson (Billy Delaware), Brenda Kendall (Miss Botting), Ailene Herring (Teacher), Faye Flegg (Doctor), Carla Hedgeman (Young Poppy), Hamish McFarlane (Avril Luxon), Geoff Barlow (Headmaster), Samantha Townsley (Teenage Isabel), Brian Flegg (Doctor), Eileen Clark, Margaret Gordon (Neighbours).[2]

Few subjects have proved more intractable to the cinema's resources than that of a writer's life. Most attempts have settled for giving the life of the writer rather than the life of her writing or the writing in her life.

In view of the disappointing record of such attempts, it is doubly pleasing to note the success of **An Angel at My Table**, Jane Campion's film based on the autobiographies of New Zealand author Janet Frame. Essentially a 'Portrait of the Artist as a Young Woman', it offers a richly textured experience on several levels.

What is at once impressive is the way it keeps its eye on what makes its protagonist

important: that is, as a writer. She is presented as fascinated with words from the outset, in ways that are made truthful in the performances of Alexia Keogh, who plays Janet as a red-headed mop of a child, and Karen Fergusson, who takes over as teenager.

The idea of solitariness as the writer's condition is also there from the opening shot of the little girl on a straight road. It is uninsistently done, but it is enough to suggest that the solitary child is the mainspring of the gauche, likeable adult.

But if to be solitary is necessary to the writer, to have something to write about may also involve the intercourse of daily life, and one of the strengths of Campion's film is in its representation of the facts of this life. There is an unobtrusive plainness and beauty as the camera inspects kitchens and bedrooms, schools and neighbours. The episodes in the psychiatric hospital in which Janet (Kerry Fox) is given electric shock treatments are horrifying in the very plainness with which they are recorded.

There is a third key element in the mosaic of Janet's life: her sensuality. The camera takes a direct, entirely non-prurient interest in girls dressing and undressing, in slabs of thigh exposed above gartered stockings.

The three actresses who play Janet at various stages of her life are beyond praise. They provide a vital continuity; they not merely look convincingly enough like each other, but the rôles are so carefully written and the

actresses so skilfully directed that each grows seamlessly into the next.

The film's mode is essentially episodic, but Campion and scriptwriter Laura Jones have ensured that the episodes which comprise the narrative achieve a remarkable coherence. The structure is held together by the protagonist's growing awareness, not in a simplistic version of the *bildungsroman* but in a watchful, eager, easily alarmed approach. Given what life has handed out to her as well as what it has promised, such an approach is justified.

This film understands what it means to meander intelligently and observe acutely.

BRIAN MCFARLANE[3]

---

[1] Though made as a three-part mini-series, **An Angel at My Table** was released theatrically and therefore qualifies. It was also selected for the film festival in Venezia as a feature.

[2] Given the enormity of the cast list, this is a necessarily brief and reordered selection.

[3] Extracted from McFarlane's review in *Cinema Papers* (see References).

References

'An Angel at My Table', an interview with director Jane Campion by Hunter Cordaiy, *Cinema Papers*, no. 81, December 1990, pp. 32–6.

'An Angel at My Table', a review by Brian McFarlane, ibid., pp. 52–3.

'Not a Frame Out of Place: If Ever a Film Was Made in Heaven', Liz Jacka, *Filmnews*, September 1990, p. 16.

Bruddle (Andrew Binns), Mum (Iris Churn), Dad (K. J. Wilson), Janet (Kerry Fox), June (Sara Smuts-Kennedy) and Isabel (Glynis Angell).

THE BIG STEAL

Cascade Films presents THE BIG STEAL. *Alternative title:* 'Marc Van Ark' (working). © 1990 Cascade Films Pty Ltd [and] Australian Film Finance Corporation Pty Ltd. Made with the assistance of Film Victoria. Made with the participation of Australian Film Finance Corporation. *Location:* Melbourne. *Australian distributor:* Hoyts. *Opened:* 20 September 1990. *Video:* RCA–Columbia–Hoyts. *Rating:* PG. 35mm. 99 mins.

Producers: David Parker, Nadia Tass. *Co-producer:* Timothy White. *Associate producer:* Bryce Menzies. *Scriptwriter:* David Parker. *Additional scriptwriting:* Max Dunn. *Script consultants:* Bob Ellis, Andrew Knight, David Lander. *Director of photography:* David Parker. *Camera operator:* Rex Nicholson. *Production designer:* Paddy Reardon. *Costume designer:* Anje Bos. *Editor:* Peter Carrodus. *Composer:* Philip Judd. *Sound recordist:* John Wilkinson. *Sound supervisor:* Dean Gawen. *Sound editors:* Dean Gawen, Rex Watts, Paul Huntingford. *Mixer:* Roger Savage.

Cast

Ben Mendelsohn (Danny Clark), Claudia Karvan (Joanna Johnson), Steve Bisley (Gordon Farkas), Marshall Napier (Mr Desmond Clark), Damon Herriman (Mark Jorgensen), Angelo D'Angelo (Vangeli Petrakis), Tim Robertson (Mr Desmond Johnson), Maggie King (Mrs Edith Clark), Sheryl Munks (Pam Schaeffer), Lise Rodgers (Mrs Johnson), Frankie J. Holden (Frank), Mark Hennessy (Jimmy), Roy Edmunds (George), Mike Nikol (Dougy), Andrew Spence (Car Pound Policeman), Ken Radley (Arresting Policeman), Robert Meldrum (Lawyer), Robert Morgan (Stewart), Eve Von Bibra (Pam's Friend), Mark Warren (Hoon Driver).

Danny Clark (Ben Mendelsohn) and Joanna Johnson (Claudia Karvan).

There's no big secret to the appeal of The Big Steal: it is a sweet romantic comedy, a revenge fantasy, a kid's adventure film …nothing more. It is well made, well acted, sincere and endowed with enough intelligence to give it body, but not quite enough to weigh it down. Certainly, as with Nadia Tass' first film (**Malcolm**, 1986), this is not a film to get deep about.

Nervous teenager Danny Clark (Ben Mendelsohn) tries to impress Joanna Johnson (Claudia Karvan) into dating him by telling her he has a Jaguar, which he hasn't. She says yes, so he hurriedly buys one to prove he wasn't lying. But the Jag is a lemon, the car salesman, Gordon Farkas (Steve Bisley), an unashamed shyster, and Danny and his pals plot revenge.

Here we have it all: adolescent boy–girl romance; cars; adventure; and a villain on whom the heroes can exercise that invaluable maxim from **National Lampoon's Animal House** (John Landis, 1978): 'Don't get mad, get even.'

In the first few minutes, the film plugs straight into two central concerns of most Western (and probably by now Eastern) adolescent males: cars and girls. As these twin desires begin rubbing against each other, we are treated to some nicely observed hard facts about the emotional maelstrom of adolescence. The film goes on to show, with only slight exaggeration, the mammoth scale that infatuation can assume.

But the car-and-girl ethic is quickly subverted for a much nobler theme. On the way home from their date, Danny gets into a drag with a bunch of local hoons. The car blows out and ejaculates oil onto Joanna. She walks off in disgust, ridiculing the brazen display of cardboard machismo.

This singularly American value system is then replaced with something a little closer to home. The revenge plot against the lowlife car salesman serves as a minor-league consumerist fantasy about getting back at those smooth operators who have turned the art of credit squeezing into Australia's new national sport.

This narrative keystone is laced with some wonderful touches of verbal and visual humour. The film also boasts some comic devices that are as deftly and ingeniously engineered as any of the mechanical devices in **Malcolm**.

Apart from the liberal peppering of humour, there is plenty of homespun philosophical appeal in **The Big Steal**. Danny's growing sensitivity to his parents, the tension between Danny, Joanna's father and her best friend, and his taking the responsibility for his own mess may not be enough to keep a *Home and Away* script conference going for more than five minutes, but they do give the film some dramatic weight.

The film's photography (by David Parker) also deserves praise for achieving what many would have thought impossible: taking Melbourne locations and making them look interesting.

JIM SCHEMBRI[1]

---

[1] Extracted from Schembri's review in *Cinema Papers* (see References).

References

'The Big Steal', a review by Jim Schembri, *Cinema Papers*, no. 81, December 1990, pp. 53–4.
'The Big Steal', a review by Mary Colbert, *Film-news*, September 1990, p. 11.

BLOODMOON

Village Roadshow Pictures presents in association with Michael Fisher Productions BLOODMOON. © 1989 Village Roadshow Pictures (Australia) Pty Ltd. *Location:* Brisbane, Gold Coast (Queensland). *Australian distributor:* Roadshow. *Video:* Applause. *Rating:* R. 35mm. 100 mins.

Producer: Stanley O'Toole. *Executive producers:* Graham Burke, Gregory Coote. *Associate producer:* David Munro. *Scriptwriter:* Robert Brennan. *Director of photography:* John Stokes. *Camera operator:* Bradley Shield. *Production designer:* Philip Warner. *Wardrobe:* Helen Mains. *Editor:* David Halliday. *Composer:* Brian May. *Sound recordist:* Ian Grant. [*Sound Editor:* not credited.] *Mixers:* James Currie, Peter Smith.

Cast

Leon Lissek (Myles Sheffield), Christine Amor (Virginia Sheffield), Ian Williams (Kevin Lynch), Helen Thomson (Mary Huston), Craige Cronnin (Matt Desmond), Hazel Howson (Sister Mary-Ellen), Suzie MacKenzie (Michelle), Anya Molina (Jennifer), Brian Moll (Mr. Gordian), Stephen Bergin (Mark), Christophe Broadway (Scott), Samantha Rittson (Gretchen), Tess Pike (Kylie), Jo Munro (Jackie), Michelle Doake (Linda), Chris Uhlmann (Chip), Justin Ractliffe (Zits), Damien Lutz (Tom), Warwick Brown (Billy), Gregory Pamment (Rich), Sueyan Cox (Sandy Desmond).

Bloodmoon is a truly memorable cinematic experience, an unspeakably funny film in the saddest possible way. Bereft of originality or even the ability to copy with style, the story—a kind of conglomerate of *Romeo and Juliet*, **Halloween**, **Friday the 13th**, **Revenge of the Nerds**[1] and 'The Film with No Brain'—goes something like this:

The woods near an all-girl Catholic school, where the inmates seem to do nothing but sing in choirs and flash their developing breasts, is being stalked by a psycho who likes strangling teenagers with a custom-made strand of barbed wire. The Catholic girls like to have it off in the woods with the Catholic boys from the nearby Winchester school, something frowned upon by the head nun, Sister Mary-Ellen (Hazel Howson).

The posh boys from Winchester have a running war with the working-class lads from town, known as 'The Townies'. A forbidden romance blooms between one of the Townies, Kevin (Ian Williams), and the lead Catholic girl, Mary (Helen Thomson).

Mary (Helen Thomson) and Kevin (Ian Williams).

Sub-plots involving their romance, the identity of the pyscho, two girls who want to cheat on their exams, the background of the 'mysterious' married couple who run the school and the growing concern of the local policeman develop with the grace and subtlety of a surgical chainsaw to an 'action' climax.

A major problem with **Bloodmoon** is that it lacks a convincing killer who looks motivated enough to scare you. It also lacks convincing victims who look scared enough to scare you. The fact that they are played by a cast of unknowns, whose acting talents certainly have an awful lot of developing to do, doesn't help.

The easy way out of this would have been to contract some novel ways for these characters to die but the film can't even manage to do that. All one gets are a few spurts of Heinz Big Red around the neck and eyes.

Stylewise, the film is void. The biggest problem is its inability to master the basic rule of the Red Herring. Only two are set up—the psycho is either Sister Mary-Ellen or the sexually inadequate husband, Myles Sheffield (Leon Lissek)—and before long

there's no doubt who it is, hence no suspense.

Visually, the film is a disappointment. The camerawork is drab and the lighting is flat. But the biggest stylistic problem is the editing. In films of this genre, editing is where the best scares come from. The cleverest the editing gets in **Bloodmoon** is a cut from a screaming mouth in the woods to a singing mouth in the choir. Yo!

It is with films like **Bloodmoon** that people start spouting phrases such as 'It's so bad it's good' and 'At least it was funny' and 'unintentional comedy'. To say this about a $1-a-week video is fine; to say it about the first mainstream Australian film to be released in the 1990s is not.

JIM SCHEMBRI[2]

1 **Halloween** (John Carpenter, 1978), **Friday the 13th** (Sean S. Cunningham, 1980), **Revenge of the Nerds** (Jeff Kanew, 1984).
2 Extracted from Schembri's review in *Cinema Papers* (see Reference).

Reference
'Bloodmoon', a review by Jim Schembri, *Cinema Papers*, no. 79, May 1990, pp. 66–7.

BLOOD OATH

A Sovereign Pictures Release. Village Roadshow Pictures presents A Charles Waterstreet and Siege Production. BLOOD OATH. © 1990 Blood Oath Productions and The Australian Film Finance Corporation[1]. Script developed with the assistance of the Australian Film Commission. Made with the participation of Australian Film Finance Corporation. *Budget:* $7 million. *Location:* Queensland. *Australian distributor:* Roadshow. *Opened:* 26 July 1990. *Video:* Premiere. *Rating:* M. 35mm. 108 mins.

Producers: Charles Waterstreet, Denis Whitburn, Brian A. Williams. *Co-producer:* Annie Bleakley. *Executive producers:* Graham Burke, Greg Coote, John Tarnoff. *Line producer:* Richard Brennan. *Screenplay:* Denis Whitburn, Brian A. Williams.[2] *Director of photography:* Russell Boyd. *Camera operator:* David Williamson. *Production designer:* Bernard Hides. *Costume designer:* Roger Kirk. *Editor:* Nicholas Beauman. *Composer:* David McHugh. *Additional music:* Stewart D'Arrietta, Don Miller-Robinson. *Sound recordist:* Ben Osmo. *Sound editor:* Karin Whittington (fx); Tim Jordan (dia.). *Mixers:* Gethin Creagh, Roger Savage.

Cast

Bryan Brown (Captain Cooper), George Takei (Vice-Admiral Baron Takahashi), Terry O'Quinn (Major Beckett), John Bach (Major Roberts), Toshi Shioya (Lt. Tanaka), John Clarke (Sheedy), Deborah Unger (Sister Littell), John Polson (Private Jimmy Fenton), Russell Crowe (Lt. Corbett), Nicholas Eadie (Sgt. Keenan), Jason Donovan (Private Talbot), Tetsu Watanabe (Captain Ikeuchi), Sokyu Fujita (Mr. Matsugee), Ray Barrett (President of the Bench), Kazuhiro Muroyama (Lt. Noboru Kamura), David Argue (Flight Lt. Eddy Fenton), Yuichiro Senga (Lt. Shimada), Andrew Booth (Pvt. Mitchell), Malcolm Cork (Australian Soldier), Donal Gibson (Corporal Patterson).

Blood Oath is director Stephen Wallace's account of precedential war-crimes trials that took place not long after the end of World War II.

Conducted on Ambon, then still part of the Dutch East Indies, the proceedings brought 91 Japanese officers and other ranks to trial for atrocities committed against Australian prisoners, hundreds of whom had died of starvation, disease, brutal treatment—or had been cold-bloodedly murdered—in a prisoner-of-war camp on the island.

The screenplay, by Denis Whitburn and Brian A. Williams, draws heavily on the record of the trial and particularly the experiences of the latter's father, who was the chief Australian prosecutor and, in subsequent civilian life, a judge.

The narrative has harrowing and intense moments, but too much else lacks that sense of purpose and urgency necessary to compelling courtroom drama. For instance, a scapegoat/conspiracy element that suggests an incipient Cold War agenda on the part of our great and powerful ally, the US, is presented but not pursued. Along with several other plot strands, it serves only to deflect the emotional impact of the whole, and one is left somewhat dissatisfied and unconvinced.

Another problem is that **Blood Oath** never seems quite settled in style, moving as it does between documentary-drama, at best in some of the courtroom scenes, and over-emotive melodrama, such as that in which a dying Australian witness, Private Jimmy Fenton (John Polson), recalls his brother's death.

The narrative line, too, is inconsistently, and unnecessarily, diffused. The original focus, the pursuit of evidence that will enable the prosecutor, Captain Cooper (Bryan Brown), to nail perpetrators and instigators alike, is obscured, first by the sub-plot about the US-protected former commander, Vice-Admiral Baron Takahashi (George Takei), and then by a certain amount of soul-searching on the part of Cooper.

Brown is effective in the lead rôle, conveying the impression of a person very sure of himself in dealing with the law, but increasingly uncertain as to how it is to be applied in the circumstances of a pace-setting war-crimes trial. Supporting rôles by John Bach, as an Australian officer responsible to more than one agenda, John Clarke, as the journalist who twigs what is happening, and Terry O'Quinn, as the ambivalent US liaison officer, are well handled.

But **Blood Oath** is dissatisfying, not so much for what it does or does not depict or express, but for want of definition. It is a good-looking, thoroughly professional and, in general, authentic-looking piece of work (Russell Boyd's cinematography is exemplary) that doesn't quite deliver what it at first promises. Its thrust has been blunted by a desire to avoid offence, something that scarcely could be avoided in the telling of this story of terrible atrocities.

KEITH CONNOLLY[3]

---

[1] This is the only time spotted where a 'The' proceeds 'Australian Film Finance Corporation'.

[2] It is alleged that John Clarke did significant rewriting of the screenplay on location (Clarke was one of the cast). He is credited on the film as 'Script editor'.

[3] Extracted from Connolly's review in *Cinema Papers* (see References).

References

'**Blood Oath**', a production report by Andrew L. Urban, *Cinema Papers*, no. 77, January 1990, pp. 6–9.

'Scripting **Blood Oath**: Denis Whitburn and Brian Williams', an interview by Andrew L. Urban, ibid., pp. 10–15.

'**Blood Oath**', a review by Keith Connolly, *Cinema Papers*, no. 81, December 1990, pp. 54–5.

'Bloodless', a review of **Blood Oath** by Liz Jacka, *Filmnews*, August 1990, pp. 9–10.

Captain Cooper (Bryan Brown), Private Talbot (Jason Donovan), Private Jimmy Fenton (John Polson) and Sister Little (Deborah Unger).

THE CROSSING

Beyond International Group presents THE CROSSING. © 1990 Beyond Productions Pty Ltd–Australian Film Finance Corporation Pty Ltd. Script developed with assistance from the Australian Film Commission. Made with the participation of Australian Film Finance Corporation. *Locations:* Junee, Condobolin (New South Wales). *Australian distributor:* Hoyts. *Opened:* 18 October 1990. *Video:* RCA–Columbia–Hoyts. *Rating:* M. 35 mm. 92 mins.

Producer: Sue Seeary. *Executive producers:* Al Clark, Philip Gerlach. *Associate producer:* Jenny Day. *Scriptwriter:* Ranald Allan. *Director of photography:* Jeff Darling. *Production designer:* Igor Nay. *Costume designer:* Katie Pye. *Editor:* Henry Dangar. *Composer:* Martin Armiger. *Sound recordist:* David Lee. *Supervising sound editor:* Gary O'Grady. *Sound editors:* Jeanine Chialvo (dia.); Julius Chan (atmos.). *Mixers:* Phil Heywood (supervising); Ron Purvis (fx); Martin Oswin (music).

Cast

Russell Crowe (Johnny), Robert Mammone (Sam), Danielle Spencer (Meg), Emily Lumbers (Jenny), Rodney Bell (Shorty), Ben Oxenbould (Heavyfoot), Myles Collins (Stretch), Marc Gray (Nort), Megan Connolly (Kathleen), John Blair (Billy), Rani Lockland (Gail), Lee-Ann[1] Towler (Mandy), Paul Robertson (Birdie), George Whaley (Sid), Jacqy Phillips (Marion), Les Foxcroft (Pop), Daphne Grey (Jean), Patrick Ward (Nev), May Lloyd (Peg), Warren Coleman (Clag), Maroochy Barambah (Frances), Steve Dodd (Old Spider), Cathren Michalak (Mad Hilda).

The Crossing concludes in a cemetery where Meg (Danielle Spencer) brings flowers to the grave of her former lover, Sam (Robert Mammone)—a prodigal son who had returned after many years to his parochial home town in order to take Meg back to the city with him. Already at the grave site, however, is Johnny (Russell Crowe), Meg's lover during Sam's absence. That Sam is in his grave appears, of course, as the outcome of tensions augmented within this triangle. But for what does Sam's death compensate?

The Crossing is reminiscent of Nicholas Ray's **Rebel Without a Cause** (1955). The triangular formation of the three central characters in **The Crossing** draws one to the characters of **Rebel**: Judy (Natalie Wood), Jim (James Dean) and Plato (Sal Mineo). However distant these two films may at first appear, they touch one another in this respect: what seems to underpin the expression of juvenile angst in both is the teenagers' emotional distance from their parents, in particular their fathers (or lack of).

Alienation between the generations is certainly nothing new to the teen movie genre, but we can at least begin with this emphatic structural similarity between the two films: that like Judy and Jim in **Rebel**, Meg and Sam in **The Crossing** have overly strained relations with their fathers. Johnny, on the other hand, like Plato, lacks a father, and this certainly raises questions about the nuances of Johnny's position within the triangle.

By evoking **Rebel**, however, what remains to be said is that it typifies **The Crossing**'s lack of induction at the level of narrative resolution, for the terms of sacrifice for Sam, unlike Plato, dissipate into air according to the film's own logic.

Plato's death in **Rebel** is a symbolic one which relates to parental guilt, for it comes as the culmination of events that sees the threesome form a simulated family (mother, father and child) that both apes and is representative of their respective familial situations. Plato must die, for the death compensates for the formation of the couple (Judy and Jim) and bridges the emotional distance between the generations, at the same time as it is a direct consequence of this emotional distance.

In **The Crossing**, one is hard-pressed to discover symbolic links between the alienated family relations and the events that occur in and around the triangle of young lovers. The possibility of an undercurrent of emotional drives that connect the two worlds is set back into relief on Sam's return. Rather than meshing two paradoxical models that could comment on one another, the adult world becomes a mere backdrop. Sam's death does not result from a guilty unconscious set of parental values. If Plato's death is not a whitewash of parental guilt but a reaffirmation of it, Sam's is instead purely and simply an accident.

For a film that seeks to at least establish a sense of autonomy between the young and the values and concerns of the older generation, **The Crossing**, through the conceit of Sam's death, ultimately avoids it.

RAFFAELE CAPUTO[2]

---

[1] The credits are in capitals and this represents a best guess at upper and lower case.
[2] Extracted from Caputo's review in *Cinema Papers* (see References).

References

'The Crossing', a production report by Andrew L. Urban, *Cinema Papers*, no. 78, March 1990, pp. 6–9.
'George Ogilvie', an interview with the director by Andrew L. Urban, ibid., pp. 10–14.
'The Crossing', a review by Raffaele Caputo, *Cinema Papers*, no. 81, December 1990, pp. 56–7.
'The Crossing', a review by Liz Jacka, *Filmnews*, October 1990, p. 12.

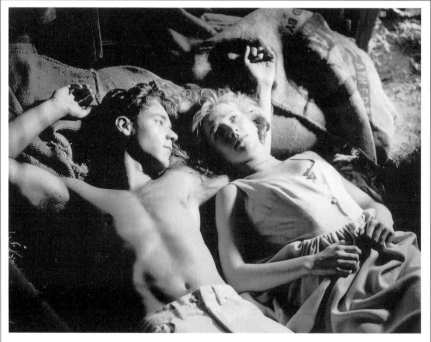

Johnny (Russell Crowe) and Meg (Danielle Spencer).

FATHER

Barron Films in association with Leftbank Productions presents FATHER. © 1989 Transcontinental Films Limited[,] Australian Film Finance Corporation [and] Film Victoria. Made with the assistance of Film Victoria. Made with the participation of Australian Film Finance Corporation. *Location:* Melbourne. *Australian distributor:* Capricorn. *Video:* Satellite Video. *Rating:* M. 35mm. 100 mins.

Producer [sic]: Damien Parer and Tony Cavanaugh, Graham Hartley, Paul D. Barron. *Executive producer:* Paul D. Barron. *Scriptwriters:* Tony Cavanaugh, Graham Hartley. *Director of photography:* Dan Burstall. *Production designer:* Philip Peters. *Costume designer:* Jeanie Cameron. *Editor:* Kerry Regan. *Composer:* Peter Best. *Sound recordist:* Andrew Ramage. *Sound editors:* Michael Thomas (dia.); Glen Auchinachie (ADR, fx). *Mixers:* Peter Fenton, Ron Purvis, Peter Sullivan.

Cast

Max Von Sydow (Joe Mueller), Carole Drinkwater (Anne Winton), Julia Blake (Iya Zetnick), Steve Jacobs (Bobby Winton), Simone Robertson (Rebecca Winton), Kahli Sneddon (Amy Winton), Nicholas Bell (Paul Jamieson), Tim Robertson (George Coleman), Bruce Alexander (Det. Sgt Racine), Denis Moore (Det. Sgt Gabriel), Jon Concannon (Ron), Reg Evans (Old Charlie), Bianca Briam (Iya Zetnick aged 12), Eve Von Bibra (Roxy), Nic Lathouris (Amos), Brenda Addie (Gloria), Kate Langbroek (TV Reporter), Colin Vancao (Judge), Nancy Black (Prosecuting Counsel); Ben Mitchell, Richard Cordner (Uniformed Police); Robert Morgan, Tibor Gyapjas (Pub Brawlers).

Father begins with a scene of a Holocaust massacre: 120 naked bodies lying in an 18m trench, out of which is crawling a survivor, 12-year-old Iya Zetnick (Bianca Briam) who will eventually track down Joe Mueller (Max Von Sydow), her parents' murderer, to Australia.

Many years later, a young woman, Anne Winton (Carole Drinkwater), much doted on by her father, Joe Mueller, finds to her shock and disbelief that he has been accused of war crimes. In spirited defence, Anne arranges legal representation for Joe, who is brought to trial swiftly in his country of adoption. Despite harassment by some elements of the public and the media, Joe is sustained by his daughter's love and the love of his grandchildren, to whom he is a revered

Rebecca Winton (Simone Robertson), Joe Mueller (Max Von Sydow) and Amy Winton (Kahli Sneddon).

figure. In the lead-up to the trial and the trial itself, Anne experiences doubts about Joe's innocence, but when he is acquitted, through the discrediting of witnesses and other evidence, she is overjoyed. Her joy, however, is short-lived. Immediately following the trial, father and daughter witness the suicide of Iya Zetnick (Julia Blake) and Anne learns that Joe is, after all, the man responsible for the crimes. Anne leaves her family home and her father forever.

However, Anne's decision to repudiate her father is not very convincing or believable. She can understand that he had to kill people, but with a smile? His answer chills her: 'I did it to survive—to prevail is everything. You think I invented the war? It surrounded us—it was my duty. I feel no shame. There's nothing special about me.' These are reasonable arguments, so why can't she forgive him?

Father is not as powerful as it should be. Unintentionally, the scriptwriters have emotionally exonerated Mueller. In analogising the massacre out of which Iya crawled to such massacres as My Lai, or Australian soldiers to Nazi collaborators, they fail to discriminate between what Iya's experience and My Lai represented.

The film portrays Mueller as elderly, frail and loving, when he had been brutal, uncaring and cruel. But, worst of all, through no fault of Julia Blake's acting, they have made Iya, the victim of a great crime, neurotic, obsessive and cunning—a pariah still, in a shabby coat and funny hat, as if she were a madwoman to be seeking justice.

Despite its attempt to be even-handed, **Father** fails to explore deeply enough the allegorical symbolism of the characters it is dealing with. Mueller is not condemned for proclaiming that 'To prevail is everything.' To prevail is not everything. Anne indicates her opposition to this belief by her departure from him, but the reason why she does so is never spelled out.

Ambiguity about Anne's leaving her father may be acceptable. What is not acceptable is that there should be any ambiguity about his being wrong. Unfortunately, **Father** conflates the two.

With more rigour, a clearer definition of the issues involved, and by allowing Iya to become a more fully developed character who can speak more articulately for herself and what she represents, **Father** could have been a major Australian contribution to the war-crimes debate.

JAN EPSTEIN[1]

[1] Extracted from Epstein's article in *Cinema Papers* (see Reference).

Reference

'Fathers & Daughters', Jan Epstein, *Cinema Papers*, no. 81, December 1990, pp. 28–31.

HEAVEN TONIGHT

Boulevard Films presents Heaven Tonight. © 1989 Boulevard Films Pty Ltd. *Location:* Melbourne. *Australian distributor:* Boulevard Films. *Video:* Warner Home Video. *Rating:* M. 35mm. 95 mins.

Producer: Frank Howson. *Executive producer:* Peter Boyle. *Line producer:* Barbi Taylor. *Co-producer:* James Michael Vernon. *Scriptwriters:* Frank Howson, Alister Webb. *Director of photography:* David Connell. *Production designer:* Bernadette Wynack. *Costume designer:* Jeanie Cameron. *Editor:* Philip Reid. *Composer:* John Capek. *Sound recordist:* Andrew Ramage. *Sound editors:* Craig Carter; Livia Ruzic (dia.). *Mixers:* James Currie (chief); Phil Heywood (fx); Peter D. Smith (music).

Cast

John Waters (Johnny Dysart), Rebecca Gilling (Annie Dysart), Kym Gyngell (Baz Schultz), Sean Scully (Tim Robbins), Guy Pearce (Paul Dysart), Sarah de Teliga (Robbins [sic] Secretary), Gary Adams (Roadie), Matthew Quartermaine (Steve), Takahito Masuda (Toshio), Tibor Gyapjas (Trevor), Nield Schneider (Man at Pub), James Boros (Paul at 15 Months), Edward Hepple (Caretaker), Reg Evans (Norm Jenkins), Lisa Colonna (Robbins [sic] Receptionist), Bryan Dawe (Steward Murchinson), Robert Morgan (Carl Bracken), Bruve Venables (Detective #1), Tim Sullivan (Detective #2), Nic Lathouris (Hot Dog Man).

Johnny Dysart (John Waters) and wife Annie (Rebecca Gilling).

In **Heaven Tonight**, co-writers Frank Howson and Alister Webb have gone to considerable lengths to develop a scenario yet to be chronicled in films exploring mainstream music: a father–son generation gap and the seemingly incompatible strains of rock music they represent.

Enter John Waters as Johnny Dysart, ageing rocker on the verge of mid-life crisis, and his budding rockstar son, Paul (Guy Pearce). Johnny was a member of the fictional Australian rock band, The Chosen Ones, which had fame in the 1960s, got into drugs and then experienced an irreparable split.

Now semi-grey-haired, Johnny lives in suburban somewhere with his wife, Annie (Rebecca Gilling), and young Paul. One soon gets an idea of what's to come when Johnny is asked by his loving, albeit doubting, wife if he is sure he is going to get that record deal, and he answers with blind self-assuredness: 'It's that close I can smell it.' Fearing her husband's inability to make a comeback, Annie suggests they buy into a Japanese

restaurant together, a proposal to which Johnny does not take kindly.

By this stage one senses the arrogant, self-possessed Johnny is unconsciously priming himself for a major emotional blow-out, and a reunion with former band crony Baz Schultz (Kym Gyngell) does little to keep the boat stable. The tragic but likeable Baz turns out to be more than just an appropriate foil for the intense Johnny. With his pock-marked skin, drug-wasted eyes and dyed-orange hair, Schultz is a symbol of wasted rockers, hopelessly displaced and disillusioned now that his brief period of glory has faded.

As for the wall of silence between father and son, it would be a risky oversimplification to suppose the two are at loggerheads because of Dad's unyielding envy over his son's developing musical ability. But that is all the viewer can assume because the script merely skims the surface of their emotional deadlock. Attempts are made to create some bonding between the pair, particularly during a tender scene when the younger one strolls in unseen to find his parents watching a home movie of him as a child. But when Paul meekly turns and walks away, still unseen, one wonders if the scriptwriters missed an opportunity for some important character development.

One of the best things about **Heaven Tonight** is how director Pino Amenta and director of photography David Connell have combined to give the film a good look and a strong sense of place; the pubs, the old rock venues and city skylines are unmistakeably Melbourne.

Another strength is its soundtrack. Most of the songs in the film were written and performed by John Waters and Guy Pearce. Experience has shown that good actors don't necessarily make good musicians and vice versa, yet in **Heaven Tonight** the music has been incorporated with a degree of competence accomplished by few actors in recent times.

At the very least, the film is an authentic document about the evolution of Australian rock 'n' roll and the people who have come and gone in it.

GREG KERR

References

'Boulevard Films', a report on the production company by Paul Kalina, including an interview with producer Frank Howson, *Cinema Papers*, no. 76, November 1989, pp. 42–6, 77.

'Heaven Tonight', a review by Greg Kerr, *Cinema Papers*, no. 82, March 1991, pp. 54–5.

'Second Glance: **Heaven Tonight**', Adrian Rawlings, *Cinema Papers*, no. 92, April 1993, pp. 52–3.

PHOBIA

Jadee Productions presents PHOBIA. ©
1989 John Dingwall. *Location:* Sydney.
Australian distributor: Jadee Productions.
Video: not released as of July 1993. *Rating:*
M. 35mm. 85 mins.

 Producer: John Mandelberg. *Executive
producer:* Will Davies. *Scriptwriter:* John
Dingwall. *Director of photography:* Steve
Newman. *Production designer:* Robert
Michael. *Wardrobe:* Ali Wais. *Editor:* John
Mandelberg. *Composer:* Ross Edwards.
Sound recordist: Brett Heath. [*Sound Editor:*
not credited.] *Mixer:* Michael Gissing.

Cast

Gosia Dobrowolska (Renata Simmons),
Sean Scully (David Simmons).

Witnessing in close-up the dwindling
hours of a marriage in tatters is not
exactly most people's idea of light-hearted
amusement. But in this, the demise of the
happy couple marks the beginning of a series
of unsettling and thoroughly engaging observations about the more sinister long-term
characteristics of contemporary relations
between the sexes.

Set almost entirely within the confines
of a comfortable suburban home-away-
from-it-all, **Phobia** presents an increasingly
suffocating scenario of unspecifiable fear,
free-floating anxiety and crushing depen-
dency.

As the quietly resolved Renata Simmons,
Gosia Dobrowolska gradually transforms
her character from agoraphobic wife to
determined woman of action. Renata's
understandably fragile psychological state
is, however, not completely of her own making. After nine years of marriage, she has
finally discovered that she has lost herself in
a relationship which, characteristically, takes
more than what it gives. The clichés associated with agoraphobia are twisted around
somewhat, and, by the final sequences, the
noose gradually tightens around her apparently stable husband's neck instead.

Co-dependent David Simmons, more
than convincingly played by Sean Scully, is
the picture of smouldering impatience,
masculine obstinance and thinly veiled
chauvinism. From the outset, it is apparent
that all is not well behind the façade of fairness and goodwill that David is so desperate
to maintain towards the emotionally black-
mailed Renata. But at the rate that whisky
bottles are drained, it is inevitable that
David's apparent benevolence turns to a bitter sarcasm associated with what is in fact
his own emotional crisis. The more Renata

struggles to escape her intolerable situation,
the more David attempts to force her into
staying with him. And this is where much
of the black humour of **Phobia** resides:
in the cynical games that such obsessives
become so expert at playing. For David, ten
years of carefully calculated 'investment'
deserves a better return than the one Renata
proposes: divorce.

Like some of the better Joseph Losey
adaptations of Harold Pinter's scripts, **Phobia**
creates a tangled psychological web of power,
co-dependency and double-binds that ultimately denies anybody the final victory. Yet
the result is not at all tragic, despite the way
the tables are eventually turned.

Shot in a straightforward, naturalistic
fashion by Steve Newman, the climactic tension of **Phobia** is nevertheless convincingly
maintained throughout. The space of the
comfortable surroundings is systematically
sketched out as a gaol-like place from which
it is difficult to escape. A high level of
performance and attention to quotidian

detail is maintained throughout the tightly
scripted drama.

In addition to these well-executed,
though cinematically conventional, devices,
there is a wilder, more renegade force that
comes through in the best moments of
Phobia. Though not exactly irreverent anarchy or youthful invention, there is certainly
something quirky (and yet familiar) about
the way Dingwall has managed to combine
psychological terror, naturalistic humour
and a narrative economy in what could quite
easily have been a nothing film about fear
and phobias in conjugal relations.

ROSS HARLEY[1]

---

[1] Extracted from Harley's review in *Cinema Papers*
 (see References).

References
'Phobia', a review by Ross Harley, *Cinema Papers*,
 no. 81, December 1990, pp. 58–9.
'Phobia', a review by Annabelle Sheehan, *Filmnews*, October 1990, p. 12.

Renata Simmons (Gosia Dobrowolska).

THE PRISONER OF ST PETERSBURG

[No opening production company credit.] The Prisoner of St Petersburg. © 1988 Seon Films Australia and Panorama Film. Produced with the assistance of the Australian Film Commission and the Berlin Film Board (FKT). An Australia–Germany Co-production. *Location*: Berlin (Germany). *Australian distributor*: Urban Eye. *Video*: not released. *Rating*: PG. 35mm. 78 mins.

Producers: Daniel Scharf, Klaus Sungen. *Scriptwriter*: Michael Wren. Based on an idea by Ian Pringle. *Director of photography*: Ray Argall. *Production designer*: Peta Lawson. [*Costume designer*: not credited.] *Editor*: Ursula West. *Composer*: Paul Schutze. *Sound recordist*: Eckhard Kuchenbecker. *Sound Editor*: Gunther Kortwich. *Mixer*: Reiner Lorenz.

Cast

Noah Taylor (Jack), Katja Teichmann (Johanna), Solveig Dommartin (Elena), René Schönenberger (Business Man), Denis Staunton (Irish Man), Johanna Karl-Lory (Old Woman), Olivier Picot (Stefan), Christian Zertz (Lorenzo), Hans-Martin Stier (Truck Driver), Efrem Accurso (Italian Truck Driver), Michael Obinja (Russian Man in Train), Lars Michalak (Russian Man Behind the Door), Ifim Bender (Russian Man with Coat), Wieland Speck (Youth in Bar), Pat O'Connell (Singing Irish Man), Ralph Wittgrebe (German Drunk).

The Prisoner of St Petersburg exemplifies director Ian Pringle's cinematic concern for physical and psychological journeys undertaken by alienated characters who are lost in the maze of post-modern life. In terms of the dominant concerns of Australian cinema, this makes him a director whose work is perceived as 'difficult' and only relevant to minority audiences. It is an undeserved reputation because his films explore the same essential imbalance in the psyche of his characters that is the basis of storytelling regardless of the context being 'minority' or 'mainstream'.

The Prisoner of St Petersburg begins with this overt sense of dislocation. A young man, Jack (Noah Taylor), travels by train to Berlin, arriving to find a suitably deserted 'old city'. This Berlin could belong to almost any year this century, a feeling enhanced by the striking black-and-white photography of Ray Argall. Such timelessness allows Jack to be established as a character trapped in an era when literature dominated the imagination—in his case by the great Russian novelists such as Gogol and Dostoevsky.

These writers, or more accurately their books, possess Jack to such a degree that his mind is tormented by their visions of the lower depths of a decaying European culture. The 'Natasha' or 'Sonja' he imagines walking past him is really Elena (played with tantalising abandon by Solveig Dommartin), who, along with her friend Johanna (Katja Teichmann in her first screen rôle), is cruising the Berlin bars. She is also trying to be free from the past, though their torment is a more contemporary angst than Jack's battle with the giants of literature.

Having established this premise, the film then follows the trio on a circular journey through the Berlin night. Their adventures are by turns poignant and humorous, dominated by the spirited performances of Dommartin and Teichmann as the two drugged and drunk women. They have a sure sense of the necessary balance between the comic and ironic, Johanna flirting with Jack who remains obsessed with Elena, convinced he's met her before, perhaps in 1866. If Elena is alluring, then Johanna is a tragi-comic figure who is enthralled with their wandering: 'I've never been so lost before', she remarks.

Unfortunately, Noah Taylor is not able to carry the rôle of the demented Jack with anything like the dramatic timing of the others, or display the sophistication needed for such a complex personality. Too often he resorts to caricature and an exaggerated rolling of his eyes to represent a disturbed mind. Because of this, the film becomes more enjoyable as a story of the two women and their bemused efforts to 'release' the prisoner Jack than of his struggle.

Even if The Prisoner of St Petersburg is not the best film Pringle has made (that honour is still reserved for Wrong World, 1986), it still points the way forward for a style of film-making which is uniquely independent in spirit.

HUNTER CORDAIY[1]

---

[1] Extracted from Cordaiy's review in *Cinema Papers* (see References).

References
'Ian Pringle: Travels to the End of the Night and **The Prisoner of St Petersburg**', an interview with the director by Hunter Cordaiy, *Cinema Papers*, no. 73, May 1989, pp. 32–4.
'**The Prisoner of St Petersburg**', a review by Hunter Cordaiy, *Cinema Papers*, no. 80, August 1990, p. 62.
'Ian Pringle: In for the Long Haul', an interview with the director by Scott Murray, *Cinema Papers*, no. 81, December 1990, pp. 6–13.
'**The Prisoner of St Petersburg**', a review by GM, *Filmnews*, April 1990, p. 13.

Jack (Noah Taylor) and Elena (Solveig Dommartin).

RAW NERVE

Lynchpin and Tosh in association with the Australian Film Commission present[s] RAW NERVE. *Alternative title:* 'Things and Other Stuff' (working). © 1988 Pyodawn Pty Ltd. Made with assistance from the Special Production Fund of the Australian Film Commission. *Location:* Sydney. *Australian distributor:* Valhalla. *Video:* Home Cinema Group. *Rating:* M. 35mm. 91 mins.

Producer: Michael Lynch. *Associate producer:* Richard Harper. *Scriptwriter:* Tony Wellington. *Director of photography:* Kim Batterham. *Production designer:* Judith Harvey. *Wardrobe:* Lyn London. *Editor:* Marcus D'Arcy. *Composer:* Dale Barlow. *Sound recordist:* Noel Quinn. *Sound editor:* Andrew Plain. *Mixer:* Ian McLoughlin.

Cast

Kelly Dingwall (David), Rebecca Rigg (Michelle), John Polson (Billy), Barry Leane (John Weatherby), Jan Kingrose (Miriam Weatherby), Kate Reid (Policeman), Sylvia Coleman (Neighbour).

R aw Nerve is clearly intended as an Australian transposition of John Hughes' American teen-movie success **The Breakfast Club** (1985). Three teens (two men and one woman) spend an intense day together, not on account of school detention (as in Hughes' film), but because they have broken into a high-bourgeois home on Sydney's North Shore. They are carefully selected character types, very different from each other: Michelle (Rebecca Rigg), older than the other two, strangely aloof and worldly-wise; David (Kelly Dingwall), like Michelle from a middle-class home, seething with unspoken resentments and frustrations; and Billy (John Polson), an extrovert working-class lad with an edge of violence. Like **The Breakfast Club**, the film moves towards the point where each teenager, in turn, lets down his or her 'mask', and reveals a painful, hidden truth. Although very much a teen movie in these respects, the film avoids close contact with contemporary popular culture (there's jazz, not rock music, on the soundtrack), and neither does it explore the surrealistic flights of fantasy common to the genre.

The film is essentially a naturalistic study of character interactions in an enclosed space. Debut feature director Tony Wellington deftly avoids the potentially 'talky', stagey, static nature of the subject by employing some classic cinematic strategies: using different rooms for different moods; distributing the three characters into successive 'twosome' scenes; dynamically

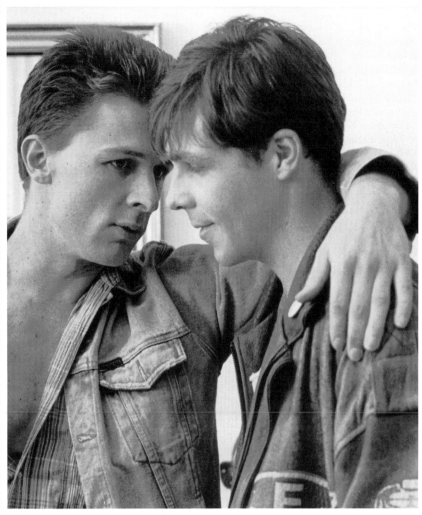

Billy (John Polson) and David (Kelly Dingwall).

cutting into the flow of events with sudden intrusions; having several of the characters perform elaborate 'play acting' dress-up rituals. In this way, the film always modulates and transforms itself, its characters, and their interrelationships. Polson, in particular, has a very cinematic performing energy: wiry, angular, mobile. Apart from a rather distracting, monotonal soundtrack, the film tries to get a similar variety and energy into its camera set-ups and editing patterns.

Thematically, the film is notable in the context of Australian cinema for its needling insistence on the class divisions between the characters—even though these are resolved rather whimsically at the end, as befits the genre. On other levels, the film's attitude can seem rather conservative and old-fashioned. The angst-ridden revelations that the teens eventually pour out might have come from a 1950s teen movie: David has seen his mother 'do it' with his Dad's boss; Michelle

has secretly given birth to a child who has been adopted out, and bears the shame of stretch marks on her young body; Billy (very like the Judd Nelson character in **The Breakfast Club**) has unloving, drunken, violent parents.

The film's 'eternal triangle' structure does not quite manage to escape, for the most part, a certain male-centred prurience. But, ultimately, the film celebrates the less sexually charged (and less ideologically loaded) space of innocent teenage friendship.

ADRIAN MARTIN[1]

---

[1] Extracted from Martin's review in *Cinema Papers* (see References).

References

'**Raw Nerve**', a review by Adrian Martin, *Cinema Papers*, no. 79, May 1990, p. 65.

'**Raw Nerve**', a short review by Michael Hutak, *Filmnews*, April 1990, p. 13.

RETURN HOME

Musical Films presents RETURN HOME. © 1989 Ray Argall [and] Musical Films Pty Ltd. Produced with the financial assistance of the Australian Film Commission and Film Victoria. *Locations:* Adelaide; Melbourne. *Australian distributor:* Urban Eye. *Opened:* 3 August 1990. *Video:* Home Cinema Group. *Rating:* M. 35mm. 87 mins.

Producer: Cristina Pozzan. *Scriptwriter:* Ray Argall. *Director of photography:* Mandy Walker. *Production designer:* Kerith Holmes. *Wardrobe:* Lucinda Clutterbuck. *Editor:* Ken Sallows. *Sound recordist:* Bronwyn Murphy. *Sound editors:* Dean Gawen, Rex Watts. *Mixers:* Dean Gawen, Rex Watts.

Cast

Dennis Coard (Noel), Frankie J. Holden (Steve), Ben Mendelsohn (Gary), Micki Camilleri (Judy), Rachel Rains (Wendy), Gypsy Lukewood (Clare), Ryan Rawlings (Wally), Paul Nestor (Brian), Alan Fletcher (Barry), Adrian Shirley (Newsagent), Michelle Stanley (Gail), Michael Coard (Paperboy), Michael Evans (Pieman), John Crouch (Angry Customer), Rory Walker (Hire Purchase Man), Liz Windsor (Mrs Walker), Joe Camilleri (Busker), Max Miller (Spanner), Joshua White (Surfie), Che Bojko (Young Boy).

Return Home is the story of one man's coming to terms with his past and the responsibility and rewards of family love. Noel (Dennis Coard), in his late thirties, is a successful insurance broker in Melbourne who returns home one summer to the Adelaide suburb of his childhood. There, he stays with his elder brother, Steve (Frankie J. Holden), Steve's wife, Judy (Micki Camilleri), and their two children. Steve runs a garage in a shopping centre that is going backwards financially in the age of American franchises and a dearth of customer service. Steve is a gifted car mechanic with a real love for his job, but it is becoming increasingly difficult to make ends meet. Both he and the ideals he stands for are on borrowed time.

Argall sets up this tale—of the negative forces of progress held tentatively at bay by one man's inherent goodness—as a metaphor for Australian society today. Values are changing in the face of altering consumer demand: local shopping centres are being replaced by impersonal supermarkets and a wasteland of drive-in food and video marts.

These 'generations' of Australian consumerism and service are linked with generations of 'family'. Argall begins his film with a brief scene of Noel, Judy and Steve in their late teens, when the local paperboy was a young Gary. Now Gary (Ben Mendelsohn) is an apprentice mechanic, when he is not absent, fretting about his stalling relationship with Wendy (Rachel Rains); Steve is his struggling boss; and Noel the emigré who left family and home. But Noel soon senses within himself emotional changes set off by the economic and social changes around him. And when he returns to his Melbourne office, the once seemingly irrelevant family snapshots now resonantly imbued with meaning, one senses a stand will be made.

Particularly intriguing is the relationship between Noel and Gary, which Argall may well have intended to serve as a companionship across generations, even somewhat father-son, but comes across at times as yet another sexless homosexual relationship (Jocelyn Moorhouse's **Proof**, 1991, et al.). It is unclear what Argall intends by this, and it does seem to distract some viewers from the more concrete issues of family and the prodigal brother.

Return Home is simply but effectively shot (Argall cuts and tracks only when he really needs to), with a subtle and affecting screenplay, and an understated level of performance rare in Australian film. That is not to say it is perfect—the otherwise carefully judged pace falters momentarily past the middle, some scenes drift a fraction too much and there is the odd gratuitous moment (as with Joe Camilleri's Busker)—but the flaws don't detract overly. **Return Home** is a significant achievement.

SCOTT MURRAY[1]

---

[1] Based in part on Murray's article in *Cinema Papers* (see References).

References

'Ray Argall: **Return Home**', an article and interview with the writer-director by Scott Murray, *Cinema Papers*, no. 78, March 1990, pp. 26–32.

'**Return Home**', a review by Peter Lawrance, *Cinema Papers*, no. 81, December 1990, p. 59.

'**Return Home**: Old Worlds, New Worlds', a review by Peter Kemp, *Filmnews*, August 1990, pp. 11–12.

Gary (Ben Mendelsohn).

Noel (Dennis Coard) and Steve (Frankie J. Holden).

SHER MOUNTAIN KILLINGS MYSTERY

Phil Avalon presents Sher Mountain Killings Mystery. © 1990 Intertropic Films Pty Ltd. *Australian distributor:* Spear Film Distributors. *Video:* First Release. *Rating:* M. 35mm. 84 mins.

Producer: Phil Avalon. *Executive producers:* Phil Avalon, Peter Taylor. *Scriptwriter:* Denis Whitburn. Based on a story by Phil Avalon. *Director of photography:* Ray Henman. *Production designer:* Keith Holloway. *Wardrobe:* Sonja Wilder. *Editor:* Ted Ötton. *Composer:* Art Phillips. *Sound recordist:* Bob Clayton. *Sound editors:* Ann Mackinolty (dia.); Carryl Irik (dubbing). *Mixer:* Martin Oswin.

Cast

Phil Avalon (Caine Cordeaux), Tom Richards (Alex Cordeaux), Abigail (Muriel Cordeaux), Ric Carter (Conrad), Ron Becks (Sole), Elizabeth McIvor (Dianne Cordeaux), Jeffrey Rhoe (Davey-Joe Cordeaux), Steven Jacobs (Billy Cordeaux), Joe Bugner (The Ranger), Amanda Pratt (Secretary), Tanya Ross (Photographic Model), David Wheeler (Wacka), Tony Fields (Photographic Model), Lucy Cooper (Schoolgirl), Peter Taylor (Max).

There is little positive to be said about this film, for it is clearly one of the least effective thrillers made in this country. Centred on a rice-paper-thin story about a stone that bestows immortality (in the right hands), it fails to create dramatic interest, tension or shock.

Davey-Joe Cordeaux (Jeffrey Rhoe) is a druggie loser who falls foul of some bad guys, Sole (Ron Becks) and Conrad (Ric Carter). He and Conrad have stolen the stone from a sleeping centenarian (Joe Bugner), but he scoots off before handing it over to Sole. He hides the stone under the bed of his idiot-mute brother, Caine Cordeaux (Phil Avalon), who takes it with him on a camping trip to Sher Mountain with brother Alex (Tom Richards).

So begins the pursuit to and over and around Sher Mountain. Apart from Alex, Caine, Davey-Joe, Conrad and Sole, there are Caine's sister, Muriel (Abigail), and Alex's near-to-estranged wife, Dianne (Elizabeth McIvor). And lurking in the bushes is the soul of the centenarian personified as The Ranger (also Bugner). The Ranger says almost nothing, fires arrows accurately, metamorphoses a corpse into fire and is capable of levitating in a creek.

The predictable result of The Ranger's intervention is that the bad guys get burned

The Ranger (Joe Bugner) and Dianne Cordeaux (Elizabeth McIvor).

(literally) and the good people plus Davey-Joe find safety and restoration of sorts.

Given this is the plot, the sole mystery is why director Vince Martin has made no discernible attempt to make any scene exciting. Where does he expect audience interest to reside? There seems little point in scripting a chase sequence if A's pursuit of B is filmed in so desultory a manner as to deny it any drama or tension.

The cast hardly helps. Producer Phil Avalon plays the idiot Caine and all sorts of politically sensitive folk will get goose bumps about his characterisation. Two of the cast are American for no narrative reason and Tom Richards, having survived the even more dreadful *Spook* (David Anthony Hall, unreleased, 1986), is burdened with a part that goes nowhere. He deserves better.

The one actor who emerges with real credit is Ric Carter, whose self-deprecating black humour is crisply delivered. Given the

ignominy of the increasing torture Conrad's poor body suffers, Carter is the only actor who manages the right tone of laconic parody.

Phil Avalon, like Rosa Colosimo, is an auteurist producer. Both their outputs have not been of the highest quality: the films are often flawed by poor scripts, listless direction and the constrictions of low budgets. Yet both, in entirely different ways, have things of value they want to say (Avalon with his interest in fringe characters at the dark edge; Colosimo in Italian-Australians and cultural differences). Avalon's best film so far is **Fatal Bond** (Vincent Monton, 1992). Hopefully, better is still to come.

SCOTT MURRAY

Reference
'Sher Mountains [sic] Killings Mystery', a short review by Paul Kalina in 'Video Releases', *Cinema Papers*, no. 84, August 1991, p. 61.

STRUCK BY LIGHTNING

Dark Horse Pictures presents STRUCK BY LIGHTNING. *Alternative title:* 'Riders on a Storm' (working). © 1990 Dark Horse Pictures Limited [and] Australian Film Finance Corporation Pty Limited. Made with the assistance of the South Australian Government through the Film and Television Financing Fund and with the assistance of the South Australian Film Corporation. Made with the participation of Australian Film Finance Corporation. *Location:* Adelaide. *Australian distributor:* Capricorn. *Video:* Satellite Entertainment. *Rating:* PG. 35mm. 105 mins.

Co-producers: Terry J. Charatsis, Trevor Farrant. *Executive producer:* Terry J. Charatsis. *Scriptwriter:* Trevor Farrant. *Director of photography:* Yuri Sokol. *Camera operator:* Vladimir Osherov. *Production designer:* Peta Lawson. *Costume designer:* Rosalea Hood. *Editor:* Simon James. *Composer:* Paul Smyth. *Sound recordist:* Toivo Lember. *Sound Editor:* Annie Breslin. *Mixers:* James Currie, Peter D. Smith, John Simpson.

Cast

Garry McDonald (Ollie Rennie), Brian Vriends (Pat Cannizzaro), Catherine McClements (Jill McHugh), Henry Salter (Noel), Denis Moore (Foster), Briony Williams (Gail), Syd Brisbane (Spencer), Brian M. Logan (Kevin), Peter Douglas (Colin), Jocelyn Betheras (Jody), Dick Tomkins (Donald), Roger Haddad (Peter), Maria Donato (Mama), Vittorio Andreacchio (Pa), David Smith (David), Jeremy Angerson (Freddy), Judith Stratford (Mrs. Reschke), Don Barker (Mr. Jeffries), Phyllis Burford (Gran), Dennis Olsen (Barnabas), Daphne Grey (PM's Wife), Su Cruickshank (Chicquita Roth), John Cousins (Charlie McCartney), Graham Duckett (Referee), Peter Green (Mr. Pink), Claire Benito (Mrs. Greatres).

Struck by Lightning, directed by Jerzy Domaradzki, and written and co-produced by Trevor Farrant, is a warm, comic, large-hearted film which features Down's Syndrome adults as actors. They not only melt the heart with their capacity to improvise and simulate characters distinct from their own, but also give the film realism and depth.

So, too, does Garry McDonald, who plays Ollie Rennie, the crusty, sour, deeply compassionate director of Saltmarsh, a sheltered workshop for retarded adults which is run on a shoestring budget in an old Adelaide mansion by the sea.

Through a humane and intelligent script, **Struck by Lightning** affirms the dignity and worth of mentally handicapped people, and tackles key issues to do with their care and protection, such as the problem of funding the programmes they need to realise their potential. It explores conflicting attitudes as to what Saltmarsh's laudable motto, 'Independence With Dignity', means.

Rennie, a middle-aged, ex-'chalky' with an ironic sense of humour and a problem with alcohol, has found his niche caring for retarded people. He may be brusque and bullying at times, but he's committed to his charges and spends much of his energy battling indifference and lobbying for money. When Rennie applies through the Saltmarsh Foundation for funding to make the workshop more self-supporting, the government responds with a grant for a physical education teacher. This is how Pat Cannizzaro (Brian Vriends), a fellow misfit fired by the Education Department for wanting to save his students rather than teach them, finds himself working at Saltmarsh.

The relationship between Rennie and Cannizzaro becomes the central dynamic for exploring the film's concerns. The partnership at first proves fruitful. Cannizzaro descends upon Saltmarsh like a lightning bolt. Young, volatile and charismatic, he energises Rennie, who is cynical about life in general and frustrated by his inability to effect change. Cannizzaro also sets out to mould Saltmarsh's motley assortment of adults into a competitive team of soccer

players that he calls, appropriately, the Heartbreakers.

Disagreement between Rennie and Cannizzaro develops over who has the correct approach. Rennie really believes that little beyond humane containment is realisable. Cannizzaro, on the other hand, believes that intellectually disabled people have a right to full self-actualisation, including sexual and artistic expression. This conflict spills over into a competition for the sexual favours of the social worker, Jill McHugh (Catherine McClements), who visits Saltmarsh regularly.

Struck by Lightning handles complex issues deftly and warmly, without didacticism or sentimentality. It has engaging characters, and is good to look at. **Struck by Lightning** is one from the heart, a fine film which one hopes will do a power of good for its subject.

JAN EPSTEIN[1]

---

[1] Extracted from Epstein's review in *Cinema Papers* (see References).

References

'Struck by Lightning', a location report by Hunter Cordaiy, *Cinema Papers*, no. 79, May 1990, pp. 24–9.

'Jerzy Domaradzki', an interview with the director by Hunter Cordaiy, ibid., May 1990, pp. 30–2.

'Struck by Lightning', a review by Jan Epstein, *Cinema Papers*, no. 83, May 1991, pp. 58–9.

'Struck by Lightning', a letter by Lorraine Zeni and Silvana Maiorana, *Filmnews*, November 1990, p. 2.

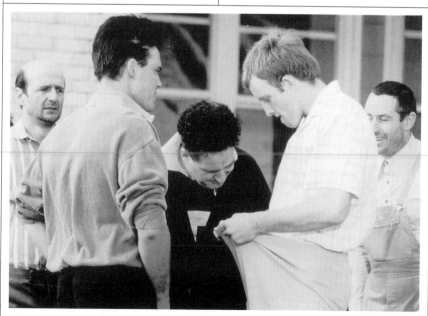

Ollie Rennie (Garry McDonald), Pat Cannizzaro (Brian Vriends), Foster (Denis Moore), Kevin (Brian M. Logan) and Colin (Peter Douglas).

MICHAEL PATTINSON

WENDY CRACKED A WALNUT

Rosen Harper Mortlock Entertainment in association with the Australian Broadcasting Corporation and Rough Diamond Productions present[s] Wendy Cracked A Walnut. © 1990 Classic Films Pty Ltd [and] Australian Film Finance Corporation Pty Ltd. Made with the participation of Australian Film Finance Corporation Pty Limited. *Australian distributor:* Hoyts. *Video:* RCA–Columbia–Hoyts. *Rating:* PG. 35mm. 84 mins.

Producer: John Edwards. *Executive producers:* Brian Rosen, Sandra Levy. *Associate producer:* Ray Brown. *Scriptwriter:* Suzanne Hawley. *Director of photography:* Jeffrey Malouf. *Camera operators:* David Williamson, Geoff Wharton. *Production designer:* Leigh Tierney. *Costume designer:* Helen Hooper. *Editor:* Michael Honey. *Composer:* Bruce Smeaton. *Sound recordist:* Nick Wood. *Supervising sound editor:* Craig Carter. *Sound editor:* Livia Ruzic (dia.). *Mixers:* Roger Savage, Julian Ellingworth.

Cast

Rosanna Arquette (Wendy), Bruce Spence (Ronnie), Hugo Weaving (Jake), Kerry Walker (Deidre), Douglas Hedge (Mr Leveredge), Doreen Warburton (Elsie), Desirée Smith (Cynthia), Jeraldine Sylbing (Mary), Betty Lucas (Mrs. Taggart), David Hoey (Sonny Taggart), Susan Lyons (Caroline), William McInnes (Ralph), Jennifer Hagan (Miss Hound), Barry Jenkins (Pierre Dalmonte), Jan Adele (Marjorie), Charles Little (Waiter), Gillian Hyde (Supermarket Demonstrator), Danny Nash (Bus Driver), Frederick Miragliotta (Aviator), Robert Price (Pirate), Toni Moran (Woman at Antoinnes [sic]), James Wardlow (Flower Man).

On paper **Wendy Cracked a Walnut** seemed a film of interesting possibilities: on the one hand, a story with an intriguing plot premise couched in a blending of style between melodrama and fairytale; on the other, the casting of a young American actor (Rosanna Arquette) of some reputation and critical acclaim. That she was to be coupled with a local actor of singular appearance and comic persona (Bruce Spence) made things all the more quirkily intriguing. It is unfortunate then that in the realised film the ingredients do not successfully blend.

Wendy (Arquette) and Ronnie (Spence) are on the eve of their tenth wedding anniversary. They share a cramped inner-city apartment—the monorail fully in view from the apartment windows as they go about their daily, working-class routines. Wendy works in the accounts division of the small Comfort Shoes factory. Ronnie peddles confectionery for Mr Jolly's Lollies on the outer country routes. Romance seems to have gone out of their marriage long ago. But if real romance is not in the air, Wendy sustains its fantasy through the avid reading of romance novels in the Mills & Boon vein. The film's lengthy opening fantasy sequence is evidence enough of Wendy's hyper-active imagination—her capacity to bring the books she reads to life.

So, when Ronnie's delivery van breaks down—in what seems like divine intervention in fairytale fashion—and he must spend the night in Lizard's Gully and thus miss their anniversary dinner, Wendy's dissatisfactions with life come to a head. Already predisposed to romantic longings, temptation soon comes her way in the form of Jake (Hugo Weaving). It is here that the narrative starts to seem awkward, for to allow the Wendy–Jake romance to develop unimpeded, Ronnie's story needs to sustain a sub-plot which feels like little more than a gimmick to keep the characters apart. So, while in the bush, Ronnie comes across a derelict road-side cafeteria whose restoration becomes his dream project. Meanwhile, back in town, Wendy is being wined and dined and danced by debonair Jake—or so it seems. Not surprisingly, as the film moves to its dénouement, the already thin line that divides fantasy from reality in Wendy's mind becomes increasingly more blurred.

In theory, the decision to cast Arquette in the girl/woman duality role seems right, for she is an actor who can convey a combination of girlish innocence and smouldering sexuality, but her performance as Wendy will not be remembered as among her best. Similarly, Hugo Weaving's rôle as a Prince Charming-type seems strained. Spence, on the other hand, is very good, but it is the kind of tailored rôle we know he could do in his sleep. The actors are not aided by a screenplay which is finally thin on plot and sketchy in its characterisations. Within its fairytale world, what seemed of allegorical relevance to real life is completely destroyed by a rather silly and inappropriate ending. All in all, the project seems more appropriate to an ABC fifty-minute tele-movie format than a feature film.

ROLANDO CAPUTO

Ronnie (Bruce Spence) and Wendy (Rosanna Arquette).

WHAT THE MOON SAW

Boulevard Films presents What The Moon Saw. © 1989 Boulevard Films Pty Ltd. *Locations:* Melbourne, Great Ocean Road (Victoria). *Australian distributor:* Boulevard Films. *Opened:* December 1990. *Video:* Warner Home Video. *Rating:* G. 35mm. 97 mins.

Producer: Frank Howson. *Executive producer:* Peter Boyle. *Line producer:* Barbi Taylor. *Co-producer:* James Michael Vernon. *Scriptwriter:* Frank Howson. [Based in part on a musical, *Sinbad's Last Adventure*, written by Frank Howson; uncredited.] *Director of photography:* David Connell. *Production designer:* Otello Stolfo. *Costume designer:* Rose Chong. *Editor:* Marc Van Buuren. *Composer:* John Capek. *Sound recordist:* Andrew Ramage. *Supervising sound editor:* Craig Carter: *Sound editor:* Livia Ruzic (dia.). *Mixers:* James Currie, Phil Heywood, Peter D. Smith.

Cast

Andrew Shephard (Steven Wilson), Pat Evison (Gran), Kim[1] Gyngell (Jim Shilling), Danielle Spencer (Emma), Kurt Ludescher (George), Mark Hennessy (Tony), Jan Friedl (Miss Melrose), Adrian Wright (Kurt), Ross Thompson (Damien Hardy), Max Phipps (Mr Zachary); Gary Sweet (Alan Wilson), Robyn Gibbs (Bev Wilson), Tibor Gyapjas (Teenager on Train), Ian McKean (Audition Pianist), Janne Coghlan (Beryl), Kalinda Ashton (Laura), Liam Magowan (Adam), Joan Brockenshire (Stage Manager), Murray Fahey (Ali), Dominic McDonald (Zachary's Assistant), Alan Fletcher (Mr Esposito), Rodney McLennan (Nigel), Shalea Lehman (Little Girl), Tommy Dysart (Skip), Nicki Paull (Night).

A young boy, Steven Wilson (Andrew Shephard), leaves the farm for a week to stay in the city with his grandmother. Gran (Pat Evison) is a one-time Tivoli showgirl who works in the ticket office at a theatre where a pantomime, *Sinbad's Last Adventure*, is showing. Steven has never seen a live show before and is greatly impressed. He is even more thrilled to meet the actors, especially the lovely Emma (Danielle Spencer), for whom he quickly develops a crush.

Over the course of the week, Steven sees the show daily, making friends with several people, but not with Mr Zachary (Max Phipps), the bad-tempered and greedy owner. Steven is upset that Mr Zachary refuses to give Emma the Friday afternoon off so that she can attend an audition, which could give her a break into 'the big time'.

On the Friday, his last day in town, Steven

Jim Shilling (Kim[4] Gyngell) and Steven Wilson (Andrew Shephard).

attends the show yet again. This time his imagination takes over, and he becomes Sinbad, overcoming his evil adversary, Mr Zachary, before living happily ever after with Emma…

Gran then wakes Steven to take him to the bus station. But before he leaves, he realises how he can thwart Mr Zachary and enable Emma to make that audition.

What the Moon Saw has obvious merits. It is an unashamedly and unselfconsciously Australian film. The central character is immediately likeable, quiet and well mannered, and Andrew Shephard brings a natural ease to the rôle. Pat Evison does a fine job as the loving Gran, and Max Phipps relishes his over-the-top part as the nasty Mr Zachary.

The essential ingredients for a successful children's movie—fantasy, adventure, humour, warmth—are all here. Even the pantomime around which the film revolves is no flimsy façade, but a show (also written by Frank Howson) which enjoyed two successful runs in Melbourne, in 1981 and 1983.

Anyone who finds the story less than

captivating, however, will quickly notice a number of gaping holes in the plot and script. For example, we have already seen Emma sing 'I Only Have Eyes For You' before the producers of the big show she is aiming at, so why is it so crucial for her to attend the Friday audition, only to sing the same song for the same people?

Equally, the delineation of several characters appears to have been given too little thought. For one, the character of Jim Shilling (Kim[2] Gyngell), the writer of *Sinbad's Last Adventure*, is confused and confusing.

Despite these and other minor flaws, most young children would find this enjoyable entertainment.

ADRIAN JACKSON[3]

---

[1] Usually spelt 'Kym'.
[2] See footnote 1.
[3] Extracted from Jackson's review in *Cinema Papers* (see Reference).
[4] See footnote 1.

Reference

'What the Moon Saw', a review by Adrian Jackson, *Cinema Papers*, no. 82, March 1991, p. 57.

1991

Thandiwe (Thandie Newton) and Nicola Radcliffe (Nicole Kidman). John Duigan's Flirting.

AYA

Goshu Films presents Aya. © 1990 Goshu Films Pty Ltd–Film Victoria [and] Australian Film Finance Corporation. Produced with the assistance of Ronin Films, the Australian Film Commission's Women's Film Fund and Film Victoria. Made with the participation of Australian Film Finance Corporation. *Locations:* Melbourne, Point Lonsdale (Victoria); Hobart (Tasmania). *Australian distributor:* Ronin. *Video:* Home Cinema Group. *Rating:* PG. 35mm. 95 mins.

Producers: Denise Patience, Solrun Hoaas. *Scriptwriter:* Solrun Hoaas. *Director of photography:* Geoff Burton. *Production designer:* Jennie Tate. *Costume designer:* Jennie Tate. *Editor:* Stewart Young. *Composer:* Roger Mason. *Sound recordist:* Ben Osmo. *Sound editors:* Peter Clancy; Tim Jordan (dia.). *Mixer:* Roger Savage.

Cast

Eri Ishida (Aya), Nicholas Eadie (Frank), Chris Haywood (Mac), Tim Robertson (Willy), Sumiko McDonald (Headwaitress), Miki Oikawa (Junko), Atsushi Suzaki (Yano), Takahito Masuda (Inoue), Christopher Parker (Ken (5 Years)), D. J. Foster (Barry), Mayumi Hoskin (Nancy), Marion Heathfield (Lorna), Jed Chegwiddon[1] (Kate), Taya Straton[2] (Tina), Nao Fakushima (Fisherman), Julie Forsyth (Mandy), Sandra Williams (Wood Chopper #1), Evelyn Johnson (Wood Chopper #2), Cathy Mundy (Wood Chopper #3), Warwick Randall (Mimicking Man), Sally Anne Upton (Pushy Woman), Howard Stanley (Spinner at Casino), Hiroshi Takayama (Two Up Player), Matthew Crosby (Punter).

Aya is an enlightened character study of a young Japanese war bride and her battle to embrace the Australian culture. It is the first feature film of Solrun Hoaas, who was born in Norway but spent eleven years in Japan, becoming fluent in the language and acquiring an understanding of its customs. She has made several films in Australia reflecting this, including the documentary, *Green Tea and Cherry Ripe* (1988).

Aya's distinctive visual style, with its rich and vividly composed images, traverses the two decades which contrast the subservience of Aya (Eri Ishida), when waitressing in a Japanese sukiyaki house, to the challenges of her assimilation as an Australian mother, wife and daughter-in-law.

The opening scene is an Australian country fair with a wood-chopping competition. Aya is now married to Frank (Nicholas Eadie), a former soldier in the occupation forces in Japan, and has only recently arrived in Australia. She performs a traditional tea ceremony and Frank's contempt for his wife's culture is made clear by his turning away uninterestedly.

As the story unfolds, we watch the earnest and accommodating Aya face not only the hostility from her family but also from the Australian government, which classifies her as an undesirable alien. The film examines her efforts to make a new life and the pressure Frank puts on her to become Australian and give up her culture. Throughout, brief extracts from letters sent home to Japan reveal a poignant cover-up as Aya disguises her unhappiness.

The turning point occurs when Frank, a successful draughtsman, has an accident and becomes withdrawn and self-pitying. Aya supports the family by working at a sukiyaki house. Their marriage slowly starts to unravel and Frank eventually becomes involved with an old acquaintance.

The changes they have gone through and the cultural barriers eventually take their toll and, after a scene of violence involving a sea egg being hurled across the kitchen, they separate. The movie ends neatly and subtly in Hobart where Mac (Chris Haywood), a close and supportive friend, finds Aya alone.

Aya is a virtuoso achievement for Hoaas. The script is the first of its kind to explore the complexities of a Japanese war bride's acculturation in Australia. The hermetic framework is carefully interwoven with artistic contrasts of the two countries. The story itself is dramatically satisfying and the editing strikes a realistic pace throughout most of the film, except in those few scenes where it becomes a little slow and loses some impact.

LISA BOWMAN[3]

---

[1] The press book has the surname as 'Chedwiggen'.
[2] The press book has the surname as 'Stratton'.
[3] Extracted from Bowman's review in *Cinema Papers* (see References).
[4] See footnote 1.

References

'Aya', a review by Lisa Bowman, *Cinema Papers*, no. 83, May 1991, pp. 52–3.

'Aya', an interview with director Solrun Hoaas by Annette Blonski and Freda Freiberg, *Filmnews*, October 1991, pp. 6–7.

'Aya', a review by Amree Hewitt, *Filmnews*, ibid., p. 12.

Frank (Nicholas Eadie), Aya (Eri Ishida) and Kate (Jed Chegwiddon[4]).

DANGEROUS GAME

Quantum Films presents a Virgo Productions Picture. DANGEROUS game. © 1988¹ Quantum Films Melbourne. Location: Sydney. *Australian distributor:* Quantum Films. *Opened:* March 1991. *Video:* Satellite Entertainment. *Rating:* M. 35mm. 98 mins.

Producers: Judith West, Basil Appleby. *Executive producer:* Robert Mercieca. *Scriptwriter:* Peter West. Based on an original script by Michael Ralph. *Additional material:* Stephen Hopkins, Jon Ezrine. *Director of photography:* Peter Levy. *Camera operator:* Bill Hammond. *Production designer:* Igor Nay. *Costume designer:* Collette Dinnigan. *Editor:* Tim Wellburn. *Composers:* Les Gock, Steve Ball. *Sound recordist:* Phillip Keros. *Sound editors:* Stephanie Flack (dia.); Les Fiddess, Simon Smithers (fx). *Mixers:* Peter Fenton, Phil Heywood, Martin Oswin.

Cast

Miles Buchanan (David), Marcus Graham (Jack), Steven Grives (Murphy), Kathryn Walker (Kathryn), Sandie Lillingston (Ziggy), John Polson (Tony), Max Meldrum (History Tutor), Raquel Suarstzman (Girl No. 1), Kerry McKay (Girl No. 2), Robbie McGregor (Police Superintendent), Christopher Dibb (Senior Officer), Susan Stenmark (T.V. Weather Girl); Peter West, Jim Richards (Cops); Terry Flanagan (Detective No. 1), Robin Menzies (Prostitute), Paris Jefferson (T.V. Movie Girl).

Kathryn (Kathryn Walker) and Jack (Marcus Graham).

D o not be surprised if you've never heard of this film. This excellent little thriller has been unnecessarily overlooked and forgotten by Australian film audiences, and that is a great pity. **Dangerous Game** is a brave, exciting and very cleverly made film. Director Stephen Hopkins and cinematographer Peter Levy made this as something of a calling card for Hollywood and it worked! They have since made **A Nightmare on Elm Street 5: The Dream Child** (1989) and **Predator 2** (1990), and though, unfortunately, these two are by no means masterpieces, they are made by a duo who have already proven their talent in their only, to date, Australian feature.

Though the action and the adventure of **Dangerous Game** are the most crucial aspects of the film, its quirky plot is what makes it all possible. David (Miles Buchanan), Jack (Marcus Graham), Kathryn (Kathryn Walker), Tony (John Polson) and Ziggy (Sandie Lillingston) are friends at Sydney University. They are basically good clean kids with a trouble-free life. Only Jack has a problem with Murphy (Steven Grives),

a policeman who takes it upon himself to harass the young lad, by giving him false parking tickets and attempting to book him for speeding, all because sometime in the past Jack's father was Murphy's superior and was responsible for his demotion. But Jack gets his own back when he reports Murphy for harassment. Murphy is subsequently suspended by his superior with a recommendation for psychiatric help, which Murphy does not accept.

When Jack and his friends get involved in a silly prank of breaking into Markwells department store, Murphy follows them, ready and waiting for revenge. He accidentally kills one of the gang and what follows in the dark, multi-storey department store between the four kids and a deranged cop makes for one of the best thrillers ever produced in Australia. The pace and timing, the acceleration of violence and the descent into the darker and scarier aspects of this adventure are perfectly judged. The frenzy that ensues emanates a brilliant, raw energy rarely captured by Australian film-makers.

Visually, the film is of great interest. Production designer Igor Nay's department

store is a grand and elaborate set, and is the film's main 'landscape'. Peter Levy cleverly adds to the terror of it all by playing with many a shade and shadow on the walls of this vast, Gothic building, with its many rows of goods, escalators, lifts and dark passages. Most of the film is set in near darkness, creating a simulation of a reverse negative effect, which makes it all even spookier. The golden light that pours over certain sections of the film glorifies the Gothic horror of its setting.

The acting is perfectly suited to the genre, and all performances are well sustained throughout. Les Gock and Steve Ball's score is compatibly bizarre and unsettling. And, apart from any political statements this film covertly makes, it is simply terrific fun to watch.

ANNA GUL

---

¹ A rough-cut of the film was completed and shown in the Marché at Cannes in 1988. The film was then reworked and finished late 1988. It was held back for release in Australia until 1991, when it opened in Queensland only.

DEATH IN BRUNSWICK

Meridian Films presents DEATH IN BRUNSWICK. © 1990 Meridian Films Pty Limited, Film Victoria [and] Australian Film Finance Corporation Pty Limited. Made with the participation of the Australian Film Finance Corporation and assistance of Film Victoria. *Location:* Melbourne. *Australian distributor:* Roadshow. *Opened:* 26 April 1991. *Video:* Applause Home Video. *Rating:* M. 35mm. 100 mins.

Producer: Timothy White. *Executive producer:* Bryce Menzies. *Associate producer:* Lynda House. *Scriptwriters:* John Ruane, Boyd Oxlade. Based on the novel by Boyd Oxlade. *Director of photography:* Ellery Ryan. *Production designer:* Chris Kennedy. *Costume designer:* Vicki Friedman. *Editor:* Neil Thumpston. *Composer:* Philip Judd. *Sound recordist:* Lloyd Carrick. *Sound editors:* Dean Gawen (supervising); Paul Huntingford (assoc.). *Mixer:* Roger Savage.

Cast

Sam Neill (Carl Fitzgerald), Zoë[1] Carides (Sophie Papafagos), John Clarke (Dave), Yvonne Lawley (Mrs Fitzgerald), Nico Lathouris (Mustafa), Nicholas Papademetriou (Yanni Voulgaris), Boris Brkic (Laurie), Deborah Kennedy (June), Doris Younane (Carmen), Denis Moore (Catholic Priest), Kris Karahisarlis (Aris), Stephen Hutchinson (Tony), Huriye Balkaya (Mustafa's Wife), Orhan Akkus (Aslan), Daniel Kadamani (Cousin Con), Sakis Dragonas (Mr Papafagos); Senol Mat, Haydar Akar, Ekrem Kuloglu (Turks); Lauchlan Jeffrey (Delinquent), Maria Beck (Maria).

Brunswick, Melbourne, is an inner-urban sprawl populated with Greeks and Turks and a few Australians, a place where each group maintains its cultural heritage amid a clutter of houses, factories and shops. This sparse setting conjures up images of a bleak world where death could be the norm.

Death in Brunswick, director John Ruane's first feature, is characterised by an economical style and a sharp talent for comedy. It moves at a rapid-fire pace which serves to create narrative tension without becoming too undermined by its comic situations.

The theme of death is central to the film. An early gag shows Carl Fitzgerald (Sam Neill) awaken one morning to find his old mother (Yvonne Lawley) head first in the gas cooker…cleaning! Her rôle in Carl's life is one of dominance and interference, precipitating the sequence of chaotic events which befall him.

Carl Fitzgerald (Sam Neill) and Dave (John Clarke).

Carl is rapidly approaching middle age and trying, at the behest of his dominating mother and his best friend, Dave (John Clarke), to get his act in life together. He is employed as a cook in a seedy nightclub and promptly becomes involved in the death of Mustafa (Nico Lathouris), a Turkish kitchen-hand who deals from the premises in hot property and drugs. Carl seeks the aid of Dave (who happens to be a grave digger) and we are entertained with a somewhat gruesome burial. Later, we hear of a headless corpse who happened to be the bouncer of the club.

All this makes for a wild, sporadic film that constantly surprises, but rarely gives away its next move. Along the way we are treated to a hot-and-fast romance between Carl and Sophie (Zoë Carides), who works in the club. It is in stark contrast to the settled, staid world occupied by Dave and his wife, June (Deborah Kennedy): she dominates him, dictates the terms and 'punishes' him for hanging around with Carl. There seems to be little space for affection and pleasure.

As the story unfolds and Carl falls deeper in love, and finds himself deeper in trouble, we are entertained with small throwaway scenes, or short visual gags. The film

is pushed relentlessly, constantly throwing out new angles, following different directions and finding new entanglements, until it reaches a point where narrative anarchy can become a strong option.

At times, however, the film does reflect some problems in bringing this somewhat complex array of characters, action and romance back home. This is evident in the central cemetery sequence. Whereas the scenes preceding it have been economical and informative, and offer a keen insight into character, here the pace falters. The playing on humour and fear is so over-extended it is almost tedious. Nevertheless, **Death in Brunswick** is infused with a joyful, celebratory feel for life.

PETER LAWRANCE[2]

<hr>

[1] The front credits give 'Zoë' an umlaut, but the end credits do not.
[2] Extracted from Lawrance's review in *Cinema Papers* (see References).

References

'Death in Brunswick', a review by Peter Lawrance, *Cinema Papers*, no. 84, August 1991, pp. 47–8.
'Death in Brunswick', an article by director John Ruane, *Filmnews*, May 1991, p. 11.
'Death in Brunswick', a review by Liz Jacka, *Filmnews*, op. cit., p. 16.

FLIRTING

Warner Bros. Kennedy Miller presents **Flirting**. © 1990 Kennedy Miller Productions Pty Limited. *Locations:* Sydney, Bathurst, Braidwood (New South Wales). *Australian distributor:* Warner Bros. *Opened:* 21 March 1991. *Video:* Warner Home Video. *Rating:* PG. 35mm. 99 mins.

Producers: George Miller, Doug Mitchell, Terry Hayes. *Associate producer:* Barbara Gibbs. *Scriptwriter:* John Duigan. *Director of photography:* Geoff Burton. *Production designer:* Roger Ford. *Costume co-ordinators:* Fiona Nicolls, Lyn Askew. *Editor:* Robert Gibson. *Sound recordist:* Ross Linton. *Sound editors:* Antony Gray, Annabelle Sheehan, Margaret Sixel, Noelleen Westcombe (dia.); Steve Burgess, Jerry Long (foley); Nicky Roller, Peter Townend (fx). *Mixer:* Phil Judd.

Cast

Noah Taylor (Danny Embling), Thandie Newton (Thandiwe Adjewa), Nicole Kidman (Nicola Radcliffe), Bartholomew Rose ('Gilby' Fryer), Felix Nobis (Jock Blair), Josh Picker ('Backa' Bourke), Jeff Truman (Mr Morris Cutts), Marshall Napier (Mr Rupert Elliott), John Dicks (Rev. Consti Nicholson), Kym Wilson (Melissa Miles), Naomi Watts (Janet Odgers), Lisa Spinadel (Barbara Howe), Francesa Raft (Fiona Spry), Malcom Robertson (Bruce Embling), Judi Farr (Sheila Embling), Freddie Paris (Solomon Adjewa), Femi Taylor (Letitia Adjewa), Gillian Hyde (Dr. Alison Pierce), Harry Lawrence (Motel Manager), Kurt Frey (Jean-Paul Sartre).[1]

In the warm after-glow of their first sexual experience, teenage lovers Danny Embling (Noah Taylor) and Thandiwe Adjewa (Thandie Newton) declare to one another, 'You're beautiful.' There is the sense that the meaning extends further than what is normally meant by 'beautiful'. It is as though their lives belong in between a recognisable reality and a mystical one, never quite settling.

It is 1965, three years after the events of **The Year My Voice Broke** (John Duigan, 1986). Although Danny now finds himself away from his small home town, he is nonetheless in a restrictive environment, trying again to transcend it through his exposure to and relationship with another person.

A minute, but significant, change in Danny's character is that he has somehow acquired a nervous stutter that hampers his attempts at communication. So, while his world apart from his small home town has grown, the possibility of expressing his place within it has regressed.

Now a resident of St Alban's College, a boys' boarding school, 17-year-old Danny exists on the fringe of this society-in-miniature. With his nervous speech and an unsportsmanlike physique, he is an object of derision for many of the other students. His sense of discovery, romance and promise comes from the view he has from his dormitory window of Cirencester College, a sister school which directly faces St Alban's across a lake.

Danny's fascination with Cirencester has more to it than an awareness of his sexual burgeoning. When one first glimpses Cirencester, the whole building looks brilliant against the night sky, as though it is propped up on stage against a painted background. There is an unreal sense, as though it isn't really there, but is the projection of one's imagination. It seems to be placed within a space that is not unlike the haunted house, or the hill and rocks, that Freya (Loene Carmen) is drawn to in **The Year My Voice Broke**. Writer–director John Duigan retains that moodiness of a 'mythical-spiritual' relationship, and it comes to the fore when Danny meets Thandiwe.

Thandiwe, although an outsider like Freya, is estranged for a whole different set of reasons, indicative of another world beyond the understanding of Danny gained from previous experiences. She is the daughter of an African nationalist on an academic post in Canberra. Because she is black, she is ostracised by most of the other girls and, thus, is on the same level as Danny in the social fabric of their respective schools.

Danny and Thandiwe are connected through an unworldly, unconsolidated view of the world. Thandiwe extends Danny's awareness of politics, race and Africa. So whereas once such elements were an encroachment on the world of Duigan's characters, they now seem to stand in a fluid, causal relation.

Flirting flirts with the other-worldliness of experiences that are sexual, emotional and sensory, in a continuum with what is perceived as the real, wider world. As Danny says at the film's completion, 'I'm looking forward to a different time. It's a big world and there's a small place for me.'

RAFFAELE CAPUTO[2]

---

[1] The cast is given according to various groupings; this represents a selection.
[2] Extracted from Caputo's review in *Cinema Papers* (see References).

References
'John Duigan: Awakening the Dormant', an interview with the writer–director by Scott Murray, *Cinema Papers*, no. 76, November 1989, pp. 30–5, 77.
'**Flirting**', a review by Raffaele Caputo, *Cinema Papers*, no. 83, May 1991, pp. 54–5.

Danny Embling (Noah Taylor) and Thandiwe Adjewa (Thandie Newton).

GOLDEN BRAID

Australian Film Commission and Film Victoria in association with Illumination Films present GOLDEN BRAID. © 1990 Australian Film Commission, Film Victoria [and] Illumination Films. *Location:* Melbourne. *Australian distributor:* Beyond. *Video:* First Release. *Rating:* M. 35mm. 91 mins.

Producers: Paul Cox, Paul Ammitzboll, Santhana Naidu. *Executive producer:* William T. Marshall. *Scriptwriters:* Paul Cox, Barry Dickins. Inspired by Guy de Maupassant's short story, 'La Chevelure'. *Director of photography:* Nino G. Martinetti. *Production designer:* Neil Angwin. *Wardrobe co-ordinator:* Gail Maes. *Editor:* Russell Hurley. *Sound recordist:* James Currie. *Sound Editor:* Livia Ruzic. *Mixer:* James Currie.

Cast

Chris Haywood (Bernard), Gosia Dobrowolska (Terese), Paul Chubb (Joseph), Norman Kaye (Psychiatrist), Marion Heathfield (Cleaning Woman), Monica Maughan (Antique Shop Owner), Robert Menzies (Ernst), Jo Kennedy (Paradise), Phillip Green (Cellist), Sheila Florance (Lady with Clock), George Fairfax (Bank Manager), Harold Baigent (Clockmaker), Barry Dickins (Barber), Victoria Eagger (Shop Assistant), Margaret Mills (Female Clerk), Dawn Klingberg (Woman in Dreams), Mark Little (Punk), Terrie Waddell (Waitress), Dr James Khong (Restaurant Owner), François[2] Bernard (Delivery Man #1), Manuel Bachet (Delivery Man #2).

Paul Cox's **Golden Braid**, based on a short story by Guy de Maupassant, continues his exploration of the human condition by highlighting lonely figures in crisis. In one way or another, his alienated characters are all searching desperately to be reunited with meaning through other people.

Bernard (Chris Haywood) is a watch-maker and restorer of old clocks, an intense man obsessed with time and locked into himself. Clocks of all descriptions crowd his house, and they glow with the golden patina that attaches to loved and cherished objects.

There is an edgy uptightness to the obsessive Bernard that makes us feel that he may have an odd sexuality. But unlike Charles (Norman Kaye) in **Man of Flowers** (1983), a film that bears some comparison to **Golden Braid**, Bernard is a sexually active man. This knowledge may surprise us, though it clearly delights Terese (Gosia Dobrowolska), whose marriage to Joseph (Paul Chubb), a

Terese (Gosia Dobrowolska) and Bernard (Chris Haywood).

Salvation Army Major and a good but dominating child-like man, is all but over.

Bernard's relationship with Terese changes him: he no longer dreams about funerals and, we learn from the Psychiatrist (Norman Kaye), he is off his medication, lithium. One day, fate decrees that Bernard be given a chance to indulge his desire to build a bridge to the dead. He takes possession of an old cabinet, said to be Venetian, and, while restoring it, discovers a secret drawer. Inside is a marvellously preserved golden braid of hair.

At first, he simply strokes the braid, inhaling the traces of the dead woman's perfume. But soon he is making love to it. He even takes it to a concert, laying it out surreptitiously on the empty seat beside him that was reserved for Terese. To all intents and purposes, Bernard has exchanged a dead woman for a living one.

In de Maupassant's story, Bernard goes mad. In Cox's film, Bernard suffers a crisis, but recovers. At first this seems inconsistent with the pathological behaviour Bernard has displayed. But the metaphor of madness as used by a novelist or film-maker is not necessarily the same as clinical madness. Cox makes clear this distinction in his style of

film-making which is at heart poetic and dreamlike, and concerned with how the mind perceives reality.

For Cox, madness is a metaphor for isolation, for being locked away in the mind from other people. Thus, Terese represents salvation to Bernard through love. That she and her harmless husband are members of the Salvation Army is, of course, a deliberate irony. Cox places no trust in the power of either conventional religions or psychiatry to help Bernard solve his problems.

Golden Braid is a simple, balanced and profound film, rich in detail, and Cox tells the story with humour and genuine eroticism, helped by a splendid cast.

JAN EPSTEIN[3]

---

[1] There is no director's credit, just 'A Film by Paul Cox'.

[2] In the credits, all names are rendered in capitals, without French accents, but on **A Woman's Tale** (see later entry) there is a 'ç' in 'François'.

[3] Extracted from Epstein's review in *Cinema Papers* (see Reference).

Reference

'Golden Braid', a review by Jan Epstein, *Cinema Papers*, no. 82, March 1991, pp. 51–2.

Bernard (Chris Haywood) and Terese (Gosia Dobrowolska).

GREEN CARD

[No opening production company credit.] GREEN CARD. © 1990 Greencard Productions Pty Limited and Australian Film Finance Corporation Pty Limited. Made with the participation of Australian Film Finance Corporation. An Australia–France Co-production. *Location:* New York. *Australian distributor:* Roadshow. *Opened:* January 1991. *Video:* Roadshow Home Video. *Rating:* PG. 35mm. 102 mins.

Producers: Peter Weir, Jean Contier. *Executive producer:* Edward S. Feldman. *Co-producer:* Duncan Henderson. *Associate producer:* Ira Halberstadt. *Scriptwriter:* Peter Weir. *Director of photography:* Geoffrey Simpson. *Camera operator:* Ken Ferris. *Production designer:* Wendy Stites. [*Costume designer:* not credited; atb Wendy Stites. *Associate costume designer:* Marilyn Matthews.] *Editor:* William Anderson. *Composer:* Hans Zimmer. *Sound recordist:* Pierre Gamet. *Sound editors:* Peter Townend, Wayne Pashley (fx); Livia Ruzic, Jeanine Chialvo, Karin Whittington (dia.). *Mixer:* Phil Judd.

Cast

Gérard Depardieu (Georges[1]), Andie MacDowell (Brontë), Bebe Neuwirth (Lauren), Gregg Edelman (Phil), Robert Prosky (Brontë's Lawyer), Jessie Keosian (Mrs. Bird), Ethan Phillips (Gorsky), Mary Louise Wilson (Mrs. Sheehan); Lois Smith, Conrad McLaren (Brontë's Neighbours); Ronald Guttman (Anton), Danny Dennis (Oscar), Stephen Pearlman (Mr. Adler), Victoria Boothby (Mrs. Adler); Ann Wedgeworth, Stefan Schnabel, Anne Shropshire, Simon James, Malachy McCourt, Emily Cho (Party Guests).

The genesis of **Green Card** began in 1983 when writer–director Peter Weir heard some of the curious stories involving 'green card' marriages—marriages for money which provide resident status in the US for one of the parties. It took another seven years to get this idea before the cameras, primarily because Weir felt that only Gérard Depardieu was suitable for the central rôle.

The story, an old staple involving opposites who discover that love transcends all geographical, social and ideological obstacles, is based on twin desires. Frenchman Georges (Depardieu) wants to stay in the US and Brontë (Andie MacDowell) wants a New York apartment with a spectacular Victorian-style greenhouse. As the apartment is only available to a married couple, her 'green card' marriage to Georges provides both the money and the necessary marital status.

Georges (Gérard Depardieu) and Brontë (Andie MacDowell).

Brontë, who finds Georges boorish, plans never to see him again. But a government investigation forces Brontë to reluctantly accept Georges into her apartment for a weekend while they fabricate a convincing history of their romance and subsequent marriage.

Brontë is a horticulturalist and a member of the 'Green Guerillas', a volunteer organisation committed to transforming the ugly urban face of New York City into community gardens and parks. Georges, on the other hand, would not know a fuchsia from a fig and has no commitment to any causes beyond himself. He provides a counterpoint to Brontë's ordered, caring world.

Brontë's social concerns, however, do not extend to the morality of marrying Georges for an apartment, and the film feels little need to explore this. Like many Weir films, there is no strong political or social subtext. The film either succeeds or fails according to the individual pleasures, or irritation, derived from the 'screwball' ramifications of their basic situation (such as constructing a fictional folio of photographs on the roof of Brontë's apartment: skiing in the 'alps', holidaying in 'Hawaii', etc.).

Because there is little surprise or pace to divert attention away from the two leads, much of the film is dependent on the 'chemistry' between Depardieu and MacDowell. His lumbering presence and hesitant English, a quality Weir apparently emphasised, certainly requires a major reorientation with anyone familiar with the screwball comedy genre, as it does not lend itself to the sparkling repartee associated with Cary Grant and other practitioners of this craft. MacDowell fulfils the requisite style and tone of a committed 'Green Guerilla', and provides a real sense of romantic vulnerability, although this is not balanced by the incisive wit and crackle of a Rosalind Russell or Carole Lombard.

There are, however, a number of compensations. The dinner party, where Weir has cleverly created a false impression with regard to Georges' musical ability, expertly fulfils its generic requirements of gently taking the mickey out of the rich.

Overall, though, there is a reluctance to draw upon the excesses of melodrama and push the film towards the outer edges of the genre. Too often Weir, as in the past, occupies the middle ground. This is apparent in his regular use of the unhappy ending that is also happy.

GEOFF MAYER[2]

---

[1] The press book incorrectly gives the spelling as 'George'.

[2] Extracted from Mayer's review in *Cinema Papers* (see References).

References

'Peter Weir', an interview with the writer-director by Katherine Tulich, *Cinema Papers*, no. 80, August 1990, pp. 6–10.

'**Green Card**', a review by Geoff Mayer, *Cinema Papers*, no. 82, March 1991, pp. 53–4.

'**Green Card**', a review by Liz Jacka, *Filmnews*, February 1991, p. 14.

HOLIDAYS ON THE RIVER YARRA

Jungle Pictures in association with the Australian Film Commission and Film Victoria presents Holidays on the River Yarra. © 1990 Jungle Pictures Pty. Ltd. Script developed with the assistance of the Australian Film Commission. *Location:* Melbourne. *Australian distributor:* Ronin. *Video:* First Release. *Rating:* M. 35mm. 88 mins.

Producer: Fiona Cochrane. *Scriptwriter:* Leo Berkeley. *Director of photography:* Brendan Lavelle. *Production designers:* Margaret Eastgate, Adele Flere. [*Costume designer:* not credited.] *Editor:* Leo Berkeley. *Composer:* Sam Mallet. *Sound recordist:* Mark Tarpey. *Sound editor:* Rex Watts. *Mixer:* not credited personally; Soundfirm.

Cast

Craig Adams (Eddie), Luke Elliot (Mick), Alex Menglet (Big Mac), Tahir Cambis (Stewie), Claudia Karvan (Elsa), Ian Scott (Frank), Sheryl Munks (Valerie), Angela McKenna (Mother); Chris Askey, John Brumpton, Jacek Koman[1] (Mercenaries); Eric Mueck (Billy), Justin Connor (Danny), Leong Lim (Shopkeeper), Robert Ratti (Nick), Arpad Mihaly (Chef), Roy Edmunds (Barry), Eddy McShortall (TAB Punter), Nick Jaye (TISM Punter), Caroline Lee (Woman in Car); David Gray, Doug Tremlett (Men at Market); John Sadler (Tram Passenger), Craig Beeby (Policeman).

Leo Berkeley's **Holidays on the River Yarra** is set within a vision of urban decay which is sometimes abstract and sometimes specific, yet always there to be escaped from.

Eddie (Craig Adams) and Mick (Luke Elliot) are unemployed teenagers, kicking their heels in a wasteland of docks, factories and new suburbs. Attracted by a promise of cash, they are enlisted to paint slogans on factory walls for Stewie (Tahir Cambis), a member of a shambling racist organisation.

Stewie introduces Mick and Eddie to a couple of his comrades, Big Mac (Alex Menglet) and Frank (Ian Scott), who are planning to lead an expedition of mercenaries on a mission to overthrow the government of a small African nation. Mick is offered a place on the mission, but the slighter Eddie appears to be of no use to them, until the rôle of cook is suggested. In the meantime, both boys must raise $500 as contribution to the mission funds and as further evidence of their commitment to the cause. In reality, neither Mick nor Eddie is really committed; rather, the mission appeals for its sense of adventure.

As hopes for raising the money fade, a desperate plan occurs to Mick: Eddie should hold up the Asian proprietor of a fish-and-chips shop. But during the robbery, Eddie becomes scared and knifes the man, who slumps to the floor in a pool of blood.

In more ways than one, this is the turning point of the film. It offers the logical conclusion of the racist ideology which informs most of the characters around Mick and Eddie. It also offers a moment of irruption, the violent incursion of action upon a film and a landscape in which action has been decidedly absent, a moment of transition for Eddie, from innocence to experience, from rebel-without-a-cause to killer-on-the-run.

The real strength of the film lies in the character of Eddie, and Berkeley is fortunate that he has in Craig Adams an actor who appears devoid of self-consciousness while playing a character who is completely self-obsessed.

But for whatever strengths Adams brings to the film, there are equal detractions. Some of the performances are not as sharp as one would hope, and the dialogue at times seems unnecessarily stilted. It is also never clear whether the mercenaries really plan to take the boys along, or if the plan is to take their money and dump them, or simply to ignore them altogether.

Equally, there are some genuinely brilliant moments—in particular, the scene in which Mick and Eddie balance precariously on a bridge, poised to jump into the river below, but neither trusting the other to join in the leap of faith—and some impressive black humour. The photography is admirable, and the scenes in which Claudia Karvan appears as Eddie's 'wannabe' friend Elsa have a lightness and sincerity about them which stands in welcome relief to the dark dishonesty of other interactions within the film.

KARL QUINN[2]

---

[1] Usually spelt 'Jacêk Kôman'.
[2] Extracted from Quinn's review in *Cinema Papers* (see References).
[3] See footnote 1.

References

'Australia at Cannes', an overview with discussion of **Holidays on the River Yarra** by Jan Epstein, *Cinema Papers*, no. 84, August 1991, pp. 32–3.

'**Holidays on the River Yarra**', a review by Karl Quinn, *Cinema Papers*, no. 86, January 1992, pp. 55–6.

"Stray Boys', an interview with director Leo Berkeley by Paul Harris, *Filmnews*, October 1991, pp. 8–10.

Eddie (Craig Adams), Mick (Luke Elliot), Mercenaries (John Brumpton, Jacek Koman[3], Chris Askey) and Big Mac (Alex Menglet).

HUNTING

Boulevard Films presents HUNTING. © 1990 Boulevard Films Pty Ltd. *Location:* Melbourne. *Budget:* $5 million. *Australian distributor:* GUO. *Video:* Warner Home Video. *Rating:* M. 35mm. Panavision. 96 mins.

Producer: Frank Howson. *Executive producer:* Peter Boyle. *Co-producer:* James Michael Vernon. *Line producer:* Barbi Taylor. *Screenplay:* Frank Howson. *Directors of photography:* David Connell, Dan Burstall. *Production designer:* Jon Dowding. *Costume designer:* Aphrodite Kondos. *Editor:* Philip Reid. *Composers:* John French, David Herzog. *Sound recordist:* John Rowley. Supervising *Sound Editor:* Craig Carter. *Sound Editor:* Livia Ruzic (dia.). *Mixers:* Roger Savage (chief); Craig Carter (fx); John French (music).

Cast

John Savage (Michael Bergman), Kerry Armstrong (Michelle Harris), Jeffrey Thomas (Larry Harris), Guy Pearce (Sharp), Rebecca Rigg (Debbie McCormick), Rhys McConnochie (Bill Stockton), Nicholas Bell (Piggott), Jacêk Kôman (Bergman's [?][1]), Stacey Valkenburg (Young Michelle), Jo Pearson (News Anchorperson), Ian Scott (Holmes), Stephen Whittaker (Robert), Des Connors (Evening Newsreader), Paige Livingston (Penny), Dale Stevens (Stockton's New Secretary), Pert Francis (Senator Hughes), Dore Kraus (Bergman's Chauffeur), George Hudley (Waiter), Lianne Bilson (Women in Block), Gareth Wilding (Forbes).

Hunting is a moody-looking picture which is hard to place in the Australian movie experience. It has the makings of a psychological drama, the atmospherics of a Romantic study and the cautionary elements of a fable. Although it is flawed along the way by some patches of weak scripting and artistic largesse, **Hunting** is still a commendable excursion into *film noir* by writer–producer–director Frank Howson.

Its central character is Michael Bergman (John Savage), an American investment mogul who moves to Melbourne to shore up his business empire. Bergman appears in a stockbroker's office 'as if by magic' to the surprise of a jittery secretary, Michelle Harris (Kerry Armstrong). After a bit of nervous eye-contact, some appallingly trite dialogue and a cup of spilt coffee, Bergman seems to have cast some sort of a spell on Michelle. Pretty soon the pair is enmeshed in an illicit affaire of far-reaching consequence. Michelle is cheating on her down-and-out

husband, Larry (Jeffrey Thomas), for one, which rekindles the guilt of her Catholic upbringing.

The affaire also reveals a darker side to quietly charismatic Bergman. By degrees, one learns he is a sybaritic egotist who harangues his associates and likes to surround himself with white candles. Initially, Savage's portrayal is stilted by a type of one-dimensional detachment and he is burdened by a script that does not offer enough insight to his motives. It is only in the latter half of the film that the character comes to life.

The turning point occurs when two of Bergman's seedy-looking minders, Sharp (Guy Pearce) and Piggott (Nicholas Bell), pay a visit to the man Bergman and his lover are cheating. It is here that Howson demonstrates his skill in front of the camera and in the editing room. To an evocative tune from Mozart's *Don Giovanni*, images of the protagonist's seducing his prey roll across the screen and are intercut with the brutal slaying of Larry, who knows too much.

Many of the scenes are embellished by operatic accentuations in lighting, sound and action. An omnipresent, sweeping darkness licks the edges of this film and shadows tend to partially obscure characters during pivotal moments.

While **Hunting** is not a happy film, it does not allow itself to become oppressed by its themes. Every so often a quirk or a clever sight-reference turns up as a counterpoint to the gloom.

One, however, does not need to look hard to find a few holes. While Savage and, to a lesser extent, Armstrong eventually fill their rôles, the performances are limited in scope and marred by overstatement. One might have expected good things from Guy Pearce as Bergman's right-hand man, but he barely intones a word, let alone a pinch of personality, through the entire film.

Hunting has a rich texture that compares with far more expensive overseas films. The camera work of David Connell and Dan Burstall gives Melbourne the look of a cosmopolitan metropolis, a fact which may have helped Boulevard package the film as an 'international' product.

GREG KERR

---

[1] Unreadable on the copy viewed and not given in press material.

Reference

'Hunting', a review by Greg Kerr, *Cinema Papers*, no. 85, November 1991, pp. 58–9.

Michelle Harris (Kerry Armstrong) and Michael Bergman (John Savage).

HURRICANE SMITH

Warner Bros. presents A Village Roadshow Pictures production. HURRICANE SMITH. © 1990 Village Roadshow Pictures (Australia) Pty Ltd. *Locations:* Marshall (Texas); Surfers Paradise (Queensland). *Australian distributor:* Roadshow. *Video:* Roadshow Home Video. *Rating:* M. 35mm. 90 mins.

Producers: Daniel O'Toole, Stanley O'Toole. *Executive producers:* Graham Burke, Gregory Coote, John Tarnoff. *Co-producers:* Sara Altshul, Kevin Dobson. *Scriptwriter:* Peter Kinloch. Based on an original idea by Kevin Dobson and Peter Kinloch. *Director of photography:* John Stokes. *Camera operator:* Bradley Shields. *Production designer:* Martin Hitchcock. *Wardrobe:* Phil Eagles. *Editor:* Pippa Anderson. *Additional editing:* Russ Woolnough. *Second assistant director and stunt co-ordinator:* Guy Norris. *Composer:* Brian May. *Sound recordist:* Ian Grant. *Sound editors:* Alan Bell; Rusty Coppleman, Richard Dunford (dia.); Teddy Mason, Chris Lancaster (footsteps). *Mixers:* Otto Snel, Michael A. Carter, Kevin Tayler.

Cast

Carl Weathers (Billy Smith), Jurgen Prochnow (Charlie Dowd), Cassandra Delaney (Julie), Tony Bonner (Howard Fenton), David Argue (Shanks), John Ewart (Dave Griffiths (Griffo)), Louise McDonald (Annabel), Suzie MacKenzie (Rachelle), Karen Hall (Francie), Johnny Raaen (Arkie Davis), Glenn Ruehland (Bernie), Matt Keys (Vince), Wayne Parry (Turbo), Ric. A. Anderson (Frank Gillespie), Charles Green (Harry Gillespie), Ian Williams (Chopper Pilot), Peter Merrill (Immigration Officer), Paula Pritchard (Secretary), Ian Cope (Cabbie No. 1), Tony Brown (Cabbie No. 2).

Billy Smith (Carl Weathers), also known as 'Hurricane', is an honest construction worker in Marshall, Texas. When he is told of his mother's death, he flies to Australia, where his long-lost sister was last seen.

In sunny Queensland, Hurricane runs into a nightmare collection of Aussies: a cabbie (Ian Cope) who is rude, unhelpful and calls him a 'septic'; Shanks (David Argue), a nutter of a brothel keeper, with a penchant for threatening people with guns; and Griffo (John Ewart), a loud-mouthed and racist publican. Also in Hurricane's way is a sinister German, Charlie Dowd (Jurgen Prochnow), henchman for the pony-tailed Howard Fenton (Tony Bonner). The only

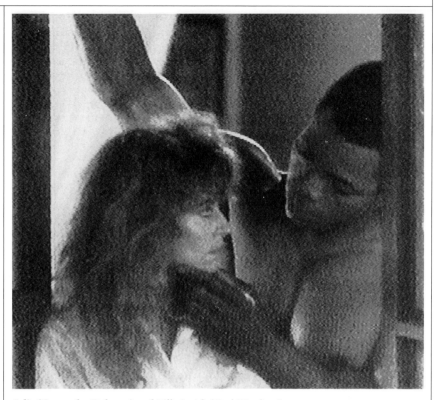

Julie (Cassandra Delaney) and Billy Smith (Carl Weathers).

shining light in this wilderness of neon and sleaze is Julie (Cassandra Delaney), yet another in that dazzlingly long line of golden-hearted whores.

In short, the film is nothing but tired cliché and Hurricane's efforts to locate his sister go through predictable moves (she, of course, is long dead). In the process, Hurricane destroys perhaps the most sinister gang ever seen in an Aussie film.

The pleasures of this routine actioner are few, and all are the responsibility of second assistant director and stunt co-ordinator Guy Norris. There is a good chase sequence where Julie tries to run away from Charlie in his Mercedes. Despite Julie's doing the inevitably stupid things 'required' by the genre (running into a deserted and enclosed carpark, etc.), the sequence is fitfully suspenseful and dramatically shot. It ends with the Mercedes being nearly totalled, which one is supposed to cheer about because, like Charlie, it is German.

The final shoot-out has an okay boat chase, but is really more notable for expending the most number of bullets since **Race for the Yankee Zephyr** (David Hemmings, 1981), with the same ludicrous marksmanship (the baddies missing from three metres with AK47s, or their like).

Other pluses of a kind include a zany and near incomprehensible performance from David Argue as Shanks, who, as usual, seems to be ad-libbing most of his lines. The best is when Hurricane calls him Damien and Shanks replies: 'Don't call me Damien. My mother's bigger than you and I decked her for calling me Damien.'

John Ewart also has a good moment when he warns Julie about going to America: 'It's full of septics over there. It's their home base.' But Julie and noble Hurricane board the plane and fly off to the good old US of A, where, as the film's prologue has it, even the local cop is a model of courteous human conduct.

Most curious of all is the film's throwbacks to the black action movies of the early 1970s, such as **Shaft** (Gordon Parks, 1971) and **Superfly** (Parks, 1972). This is particularly noticeable in the arch sex scene with its ugly red lighting, and pointed contrast of white and black skin.

Few would wish to claim **Hurricane Smith** as Australian, viewing it as an American film made on location here. However, despite its unexplained preference for American values to Australian, it has more right to be seen as a local film than some others.

SCOTT MURRAY

THE MAGIC RIDDLE

Yoram Gross presents the magic RIDDLE ☆. © 1991 Yoram Gross Films. *Australian distributor:* CEL. *Video:* Roadshow Home Video. *Rating:* G. 35mm. 93 mins.

Producer: Yoram Gross. *Executive producer:* Sandra Gross. *Scriptwriter:* Yoram Gross. Based on classical folklore and the original fairy stories of Hans Christian Andersen, Carlo Lorenzini and the Brothers Grimm. *Editor:* Rod Hay. *Composer:* Guy Gross. *Sound recordist:* John Heron. *Sound editors:* Rod Hay (dia.); Nicki Roller, Les Fiddess, Tim Ryan (fx). *Mixer:* Phil Judd.

Animation directors: Junko Aoyama, Sue Beak, Nobuko Burnfield, Nicholas Harding, Athol Henry. *Background design:* Richard Zaloudek. *Character design:* Junko Aoyama, Nobuko Burnfield, Athol Henry, Ray Nowland. *Storyboard:* Ray Nowland, Geoff Beak Productions. *Animation:* Junko Aoyama, Nobuko Burnfield, Jim Davis, Maurice Giacominto, Athol Henry, Ray Nowland, Stella Wakil, Sue Beak, Patrick Burns, Ariel Ferrari, Nicholas Harding, Victor Johnson, Darek Pierkowski, Stanley Walker.

Voices

Robyn Moore, Keith Scott.

[See Appendix A on all the Gross films, pp. 352–4.]

Reference
'Yoram Gross', Raffaele Caputo, *Cinema Papers*, no. 86, January 1992, pp. 36–42.

Phillip and Cindy.

NIRVANA STREET MURDER

[No opening production company credit.] NIRVANA STREET MURDER. © 1990 Aleksi Vellis. Funded by The Creative Development Branch of the Australian Film Commission. *Location:* Melbourne. *Australian distributor:* New Vision. *Opened:* May 1991. *Video:* Fox. *Rating:* M. 35mm. 75 mins.

Producer: Fiona Cochrane. *Executive producer:* Aleksi Vellis. *Scriptwriter:* Aleksi Vellis. *Director of photography:* Mark Lane. *Camera operator:* Paul Meulenberg. *Production designer:* Lisa Thompson. [*Costume designer:* not credited.] *Editor:* Aleksi Vellis. *Sound recordist:* Mark Atkin. *Sound Editor:* Ray Boseley. *Mixer:* Peter Frost.

Cast

Mark Little (Boady), Ben Mendelsohn (Luke), Mary Coustas (Helen), Sheila Florance (Molly), Tamara Saulwick (Penny), Yiorgo (Smeg), Roberto Micale (Hector), Russell Gilbert (Boss), Tibor Gyapjas (Vas), George Zogopoulas (Jim), Frankie Serene (Effie), Dennis Dragonas (Helen's Father), Toula Yianni (Helen's Mother), Irini Pappas (Helen's Grandmother), Nicholas Psaltopoulas (Helen's Brother), Stephen Grapsas (Spiros), Tereza Loizou (Spiros' Mother), Daniel Pollock (Derek), Randall Berger (Chemist), Desiree[1] Smith (Chemist Assistant), Vicki McGough (Schoolgirl), Paul Harris (Newsreader); John Flaus, David Roberts, Bill Bennett (Police); Joe D'Angelo (Karate Kid).

Luke (Ben Mendelsohn) and Boady (Mark Little).

There is much to praise in this modest, stylish, taut and vibrant urban black comedy. Vellis' directorial assurance and inventiveness is evident in virtually every scene, and the high-energy humour oscillates frequently between madcap bedlam and physical violence. It has a dynamic, ambivalent quality that reminds one of the absurd violent humour found in Martin Scorsese's movies, particularly in the tumultuous and sometimes pathetic relationship between the two O'Hagan[2] brothers, Boady (Mark Little) and Luke (Ben Mendelsohn).

The numerous well-choreographed scenes of irrational violence between the two hapless, free-wheeling brothers and their Greek counterparts are rich in performative nuance and subtle observations on how cultures clash in today's urban Australia.

This offbeat mixture of comedy and violence is indicative of the film-maker's supple command of his trans-generic material. What we see and hear, time and again, is Vellis' ability to blend successfully the familiar codes, icons and stylistic visuals of the old Crawford's television police dramas with the basic thematic and visual interests of the action-comedy genre.

Another finely tuned aspect is the way Vellis has represented questions of bi-cultural conflict and identity. The sequences of Luke with his Greek-Australian girlfriend, Helen (Mary Coustas), especially those at Helen's home (where her dad rules the roost with an iron fist), demonstrate a subtle and humorous understanding of the cultural and psychological mores and tensions that govern the familiar dynamics of such a household.

Another interesting feature is the emphasis placed on how Greek-Australian males interact with their Anglo-Celtic counterparts in terms of *machismo* posturings, street-wise bravado, sub-cultural rituals and anti-Anglo-Celtic obsessions. Ultimately, this leads to farce and violence.

The narrative structure of **Nirvana Street Murder** was inspired, according to Vellis, by his interest in wanting to make a movie about two brothers and by a newspaper article which dealt with a man who murdered his wife by drowning her in a waterbed. Hence the creation of the childish, unstable Boady who attempts to kill Molly (Sheila Florance) in her waterbed by cutting the bed first during one of his sleepwalking experiences.

The other important element for Vellis was the desire to construct a murder story along comic lines and everything in this black comedy of bedlam and murder stems from the stormy relationship between the two brothers. Mark Little is particularly good as Boady, while Mendelsohn gives another characteristically brilliant performance as Luke.

Vellis is not a didactic film-maker interested in giving his spectators castor oil in the hope of improving 'multi-cultural' relations in our society. Instead, what we have is a promising film-maker who raids and reworks the established movie and television genres, and popular culture, entertaining us with the rare capacity to make movie images and sounds that can astonish us for their dramatic vitality and unpredictability.

JOHN CONOMOS[3]

[1] Should be spelt 'Desirée'.
[2] There is no reference to 'O'Hagan' in the credits, but the brothers are called that in the film and the spelling comes from the press material.
[3] Extracted from Conomos' review in *Cinema Papers* (see References).

References

'Nirvana Street Murder', a review by John Conomos, *Cinema Papers*, no. 83, May 1991, pp. 57–8.
'The New Breed of Ethnic Filmmakers', Pat Gillespie, *Cinema Papers*, no. 90, October 1992, pp. 24–8.
'Nirvana Street Murder', an interview with director Alexsi [sic] Vellis and producer Fiona Cochrane by Gregory Miller, *Filmnews*, May 1991, pp. 10–12.
'Nirvana Street Murder', a review by Peter Kemp, *Filmnews*, op. cit., p. 16.

PROOF

House & Moorhouse Films presents in association with the Australian Film Commission and Film Victoria PROOF. © 1991 House & Moorhouse Films. Produced with the assistance of the Australian Film Commission and Film Victoria. *Location:* Melbourne. *Australian distributor:* Roadshow. *Opened:* 15 August 1991. *Video:* Premiere. *Rating:* M. 35mm. 86 mins.

Producer: Lynda House. *Scriptwriter:* Jocelyn Moorhouse. *Director of photography:* Martin McGrath. *Production designer:* Patrick Reardon. *Wardrobe:* Ccerri Barnett. *Editor:* Ken Sallows. *Music:* Not Drowning, Waving. *Sound recordist:* Lloyd Carrick. *Sound editor:* Glenn Newnham. *Mixers:* Roger Savage, Steve Burgess.

Cast

Hugo Weaving (Martin), Genevieve Picot (Celia), Russell Crowe (Andy), Heather Mitchell (Mother), Jeffrey Walker (Young Martin), Daniel Pollock (Punk), Frankie J. Holden (Brian), Frank Gallacher (Vet), Saskia Post (Waitress), Belinda Davey (Doctor), Cliff Ellen (Cemetery Caretaker), Tania Uren (Customer); Robert James O'Neill, Anthony Rawling, Darko Tuscan, Adele Daniele (Hoons); Roy Edmunds (2nd Policeman), Lisa Chambers (Nurse), Suzanne Chapman (Chemist Girl), Angela Campbell (High Heeled Woman), Oswaldo Maione (Waiter), Carole Patullo (Kiosk Girl), Corey (Bill, the Dog).

The blind Martin (Hugo Weaving).

Jocelyn Moorhouse's directorial debut, **Proof**, was undoubtedly the Australian success story of 1991. It is a clever, character-driven comedy underscored by a nasty touch of misogyny.

Martin (Hugo Weaving) is blind, emotionally-retarded and so distrusting of people and the world around him that he takes photographs to prove they really exist. The exercise is dependent on finding a narrator for the photographs, someone to verify that what Martin perceived was what was actually there.

Through a chance encounter, Martin finds Andy (Russell Crowe), a kitchen hand who is miles apart from him culturally, but emotionally compatible in a way that Martin's long-suffering housekeeper, Celia (Genevieve Picot), can only dream of.

Martin and Andy engage in a series of bonding exercises, including a hilarious sequence at a drive-in, and the relationship soon takes on elements of the suppressed homosexuality that seem to determine so many such friendships in Australian cinema.

When Martin invites Andy in for a drink—an innocent enough offer, certainly, but one which is complicated and loaded by the taboo nature of intimate gestures between males in Australia—the tension seems palpably sexual. Of course, it is defused, and it becomes inevitable that Andy and Celia will get together, if only so that both may experience vicariously a sexual encounter with Martin.

Martin's discovery of the liaison precipitates a crisis in this *ménage à trois*, and it looks as if Martin's sense of betrayal will lead him into further isolation. Celia is dismissed, but Andy soon works his way back into his friend's affections. The bond between the two men is finally cemented when Martin reveals the photograph which began his obsession: an image of a man in a garden raking leaves. Martin had taken the photograph as a child, in order to prove that his mother had lied when she said the man was there (he had not heard him). Andy's testimony that Martin's mother had not lied is the proof that Martin has all along been seeking.

It is unclear whether Moorhouse intended the film to be an exposé of the mis-

ogyny underlying Australian rituals of mateship, or if the film is unconsciously suffused by such values. Celia is probably the least redeemable of the characters, although ultimately the villain of the piece is not a person, but an emotion: distrust.

One also wonders how much the film's highly positive reception at Cannes influenced the widespread critical acclaim accorded the film on its Australian release. That aside, **Proof** remains an intelligent, complex film which went some way towards proving that Australia could produce entertaining, quality cinema without resorting to 19th-century rural myths.

KARL QUINN

References

'Australia at Cannes', an overview with discussion of **Proof** by Jan Epstein, *Cinema Papers*, no. 84, August 1991, pp. 32–3.
'Jocelyn Moorhouse: The Gift of **Proof**', an interview with the writer–director by Jan Epstein, *Cinema Papers*, no. 85, November 1991, pp. 4–14.
'**Proof**', a review by Karl Quinn, ibid., pp. 59–60.
'**Proof**', a review by Peter Galvin, *Filmnews*, August 1991, p. 12.

QUIGLEY

Pathe Entertainment presents QUIGLEY[1].
Alternative title: Quigley Down Under (US).
© 1990 Pathe Entertainment, Inc. *Budget:*
$18 million. *Location:* Alice Springs
(Northern Territory); Apollo Bay,
Warrnambool, Melbourne (Victoria).
Australian distributor: Greater Union.
Released: 13 June 1991. *Video:* Premiere.
Rating: M. 35mm. Panavision. 119 mins.

Producers: Stanley O'Toole, Alexandra
Rose. *Co-producer:* Megan Rose. *Script-*
writer: John Hill. *Director of photography:*
David Eggby. *Production designer:* Ross
Major. *Costume designer* (for Selleck and
Giacomo): Wayne Finkelman. *Supervising*
editor: Adrian Carr. *Editor:* Peter Burgess.
Composer: Basil Poledouris. *Sound recordist:*
Lloyd Carrick. *Supervising sound editor:* Tim
Chau. *Sound editors:* Frank Lipson, Gavin
Myers, Glenn Martin (fx); Gerry Long, John
Simpson (foley); Tom Villano (music).
Mixers: Peter Fenton, Phil Heywood, Ron
Purvis.

Cast

Tom Selleck (Matthew Quigley), Laura San
Giacomo (Crazy Cora), Alan Rickman
(Elliott Marston), Chris Haywood (Major
Ashley Pitt), Ron Haddrick (Grimmelman),
Tony Bonner (Dobkin), Jerome Ehlers
(Coogan), Conor McDermottroe (Hobb),
Roger Ward (Brophy), Ben Mendelsohn
(O'Flynn), Steve Dodd (Kunkurra); Karen
Davitt, Kylie Foster (Slatterns); William
Zappa (Reilly), Jonathan Sweet (Sergeant
Thomas), Jon Ewing (Tout), Tim Hughes
(Miller), David Slingsby (Mullion), Danny
Adcock (Mitchell), Maeliosa Stafford
(Cavanagh), Ollie Hall (Carver), Danny
Baldwin (Smythe), Jim Willoughby (Scotty),
Spike Cherrie (Hayden).

Quigley is a great-looking, well-told
Western about an American rifleman
in colonial Australia. American Tom Selleck
plays Matthew Quigley, who answers an
international advertisement to shoot vermin
at a Western Australian grazing station
owned by gun-loving, Aborigine-hating
Elliott Marston (Alan Rickman). But having witnessed Quigley's deadly eye with a
rifle, Marston has other, more sinister, plans
for his new employee: to dispatch Aborigines
who have supposedly been interfering with
the livelihood of the station. Herein lies a
moral predicament for Quigley, and the nub
of the story.

The statuesque Quigley is wise and
moralistic and not averse to inflicting his
own brand of brutality—call it justice, if you
like—when the situation warrants it. But it
is hard to imagine too many Australian filmgoers warming to the notion of an American
cowboy journeying Down Under to champion the cause of tribal Aborigines. The
notion is not only historically unlikely, it is
akin to Mick 'Crocodile' Dundee (Paul
Hogan) stepping on to the set of **Dances with
Wolves** (Kevin Costner, 1991) to lend the
Sioux Indians a hand against the American
cavalry.

That said, the film rolls along at a firm
pace. Rarely is a moment wasted on indul-
gences of script or camera, which is largely a
credit to director Simon Wincer's discipline
as a film-maker, Adrian Carr's sharp editing
and a neat screenplay by John Hill.

Within minutes of the opening, the
broad-shouldered Quigley has stepped off a
clipper, gotten into his first scrap and become
the unwilling saviour of a distressed woman,
Crazy Cora (Laura San Giacomo).

A two-day journey via bullock train to
the Marston homestead pits the American
stranger against a vast, strange land and its
more-often-than-not hostile inhabitants.
Quigley is a mere mortal in the context of
an awesome frontier, and the landscape photography of David Eggby not only reminds
us of that, it has a sweeping splendour to
rival the best in any Australian film.

Selleck is smart and equipped with just
enough cool one-liners to stop Quigley
becoming a self-important comic-book figure. The same cannot be said, though, of
Laura San Giacomo. Her part is ostensibly
a romantic foil to Quigley and, while she
demands centre focus with her paranoid
ramblings, she never quite outsteps Selleck's
shadow.

Alan Rickman shines in his bad-guy black
suit and, by the end of the show, it is hard
to imagine a screen villain more deserving
of one of his own bullets.

There are some strong local identities
in **Quigley**, too—Chris Haywood as an
officious British officer, Ben Mendelsohn as
an egotistical gunslinger (complete with dyed
red hair), and Tony Bonner and Jerome
Ehlers as two of Rickman's main lackeys—
but they are prone to copping bullets in the
back of the head or being herded off cliffs
rather than making any important acting
contributions. This is disappointing given
that **Quigley** could have been an international showcase for more Australian talent,
on and off the screen.

GREG KERR

---

[1] At the bottom of the end credits a title reads
'QUIGLEY DOWN UNDER', obviously a hangover from the American-titled version.

References
'Simon Wincer: Trusting His Instincts', an inter-
view with the director by Scott Murray, *Cinema
Papers*, no. 76, November 1989, pp. 6–12, 78–9.
'**Quigley**', a review by Greg Kerr, *Cinema Papers*,
no. 84, August 1991, pp. 53–4.

Matthew Quigley (Tom Selleck) and Crazy Cora (Laura San Giacomo).

MICHAEL JENKINS

SWEET TALKER

New Visions Pictures present[s] A New Town Film. Sweet Talker. © 1990 Confidence Productions Pty Limited. Made with the participation of Australian Film Finance Corporation Pty Limited. *Locations:* Beachport (South Australia); Sydney. *Australian distributor:* Greater Union. *Opened:* 7 November 1991. *Video:* Applause Home Video. *Rating:* PG. 35mm. 86 mins.

Producer: Ben Gannon. *Executive producers:* Taylor Hackford, Stuart Benjamin. *Scriptwriter:* Tony Morphett. Based on a story idea by Bryan Brown and Tony Morphett. *Director of photography:* Russell Boyd. *Camera operator:* David Williamson. *Production designer:* John Stoddart. *Costume designer:* Terry Ryan. *Supervising editor:* Sheldon Kahn. *Editor:* Neil Thumpston. *Composer:* Richard Thompson, with Peter Filleul. *Sound recordist:* Gary Wilkins. *Sound editors:* Robert Cornett; Jim Borgardt (ADR); Carlton Kaller, Jim Weidman (music). *Mixers:* Gregory H. Watkins, B. Tennyson Sebastian III, Dan Hilard.

Cast

Bryan Brown (Harry Reynolds), Karen Allen (Julie), Justin Rosniak (David), Chris Haywood (Bostock), Bill Kerr (Cec), Bruce Spence (Norman Foster), Bruce Myles (Scraper), Paul Chubb (Billy), Peter Hehir (Giles), Don Barker (Sgt. Watts), Bruno Lucia (Thomas), Benjamin Franklin (Larsen), Andrew S. Gilbert (Lewis), Gary Waddell (Bluey); Brian McDermott, Rob Steele (Officers); Werner Fritz Miersch (Coin Dealer); Edmund Pegge, Michael Kozuki (Businessmen); Jim Morressey (Bus Driver), Michael Kitschke (Junkie); Melissa J. Hannan, Gabrielle Watkins, Imogen Annesley, Clare Chilton (Salespersons); Peter Nikolas (Taxi Driver).

Sweet Talker begins as a sunny version of Billy Wilder's Ace in the Hole (aka The Big Carnival, 1951), with an unscrupulous man hoodwinking a gullible community for profit. By the end, the film has metamorphosed into Frank Capra territory, the simple goodness of country folk bringing about moral rejuvenation for one and bounty for all.

Harry Reynolds (Bryan Brown) is paroled from Long Bay Gaol and travels to the sleepy seaside town of Beachport. Armed with the historical research of his former cell-mate, Cec (Bill Kerr), he initiates a scam by getting the overly trusting locals to financially back his 'imminent' discovery of the Dune Ship, a Portuguese galleon that may have been wrecked nearby several centuries

Harry Reynolds (Bryan Brown).

ago. When Harry claims to have computer-enhanced satellite photographs which reveal the ship's exact location beneath the sand dunes, the money rolls in so fast he can hardly count it. All he has now to do is pick the right moment to skip town.

While staying at the Carinya Guest House (an unconvincing interior set), he befriends David (Justin Rosniak), the son of its American owner, Julie (Karen Allen). Her husband has scampered and Harry seems to provide David with the father-figure he is missing. Inevitably, it is this very sense of family which gives Harry something he has long been missing and he keeps delaying his departure. Not even the interference of the local dope grower, Cec's (hardly) unexpected arrival or a menacing real-estate tycoon (Chris Haywood, 'reprising' his Heatwave[1] rôle) make him weaken. For Harry is a new man, with new values, a Gary Cooper character reborn in Capraville.

This intermittently funny comedy has several excellent exchanges of dialogue, many crisp one-liners and a breezy charm. When he is being low-key, Bryan Brown is quite winning and it is reassuring in an Australian film to see an actor so at ease with his/her persona. It is only when he tries too consciously to act 'the seller', jumping around on tables to convince the town council, that he looks ill-at-sorts and a bit silly.

Where Sweet Talker also loses out is by making the rejuvenation of Harry too predictable and easily come by. As well, his relationship with Julie lacks spark, partially because Karen Allen is never given a scene she can do anything with. Then, too, there is the narrative predictability (few will not guess early on that the ship is found and how).

Things aren't aided, either, by Michael Jenkins' lacklustre direction: there is no perspective, the comedy uncomfortably tries to embrace all styles, and visually the film is flat (particularly in the studio).

Like Turtle Beach (Stephen Wallace, 1992), Sweet Talker was a problem film. It was mostly shot in 1989, but was in post-production for years. Some scenes were partially reshot and the script reworked.

Even so, it is an easy film to watch, Brown gives a catchy performance, the dialogue sometimes sparkles and the tone is effervescent. Had the script been a little more inventive, and the direction more focused, this might have been a small gem.

SCOTT MURRAY

---

[1] Heatwave (Phil Noyce, 1982).

Reference
'Sweet Talker', a short review by Adrienne McKibbins, *Filmnews*, November 1991, p. 17.

WAITING

A Filmside Production for the Australian Broadcasting Corporation in association with Film Four International. WAITING. © 1990 Australian Film Finance Corporation [and] Filmside Productions Pty Ltd. Developed with the assistance of the Australian Film Commission. Made with the participation of Australian Film Finance Corporation Pty. Limited. *Budget:* $1 million. *Locations:* Cessnock, Wollombi (New South Wales). *Australian distributor:* Ronin. *Video:* Applause. *Rating:* M. 35mm. 95 mins.

Producer: Ross Matthews. *Executive producer:* Penny Chapman. *Associate producer:* Wayne Barry. *Scriptwriter:* Jackie McKimmie. *Director of photography:* Steve Mason. *Camera operators:* Danny Batterham, Steve Mason. *Production designer:* Murray Picknett. *Wardrobe co-ordinator:* Colleen Woulfe. *Editor:* Michael Honey. *Composer:* Martin Armiger. *Sound recordist:* Nick Wood. *Sound supervisor:* Zsolt Kollanyi. *Sound editor:* Dorothy Welch. *Mixers:* Peter Fenton, Ron Purvis, Steve Hope.

Cast

Noni Hazlehurst (Clare), Deborra-Lee Furness (Diane), Frank Whitten (Michael), Helen Jones (Sandy), Denis Moore (Bill), Fiona Press (Therese), Ray Barrett (Frank), Noga Bernstein (Rosie), Peter Tu Tran (Tan), Brian Simpson (Booroomil), Matthew Fargher (Steve), Alan Glover (Policeman), Kaye Stevenson (Midwife), Mariette Rups-Donnelly (Gym Instructor), Justin King (Muscle Man), Jeanette Cronin (Social Worker), Connie Spinks (Woman Driver), Himself (Bazza[2]), Chloe (Scarlet).

The opening scene of **Waiting** is at once brave, confronting and humorous. A naked woman is swimming in a river surrounded by bush (and with Doris Day singing 'Que sera, sera (Whatever Will Be Will Be)' in the background). She then stands up and reveals she is far advanced in pregnancy. The woman is Clare (Noni Hazlehurst), a painter who has just won the prestigious Moët & Chandon art prize, enabling her to live in France for a year. She has booked her ticket to Paris for the first available flight—the first flight after her baby is born, that is.

At the first signs of labour pains, Clare rings friends Sandy (Helen Jones), Therese (Fiona Press) and Diane (Deborra-Lee Furness). They converge on her house in country Queensland, bringing with them three children, one husband, one boyfriend and a film camera.

In her second feature film, writer–director Jackie McKimmie tightly directs a well-written and dense script. Nearly all the action occurs within one location over twenty-four hours.

As the film unfolds, years of resentments, secrets and jealousies begin to surface. The different paths these women have chosen are indicative of the choices now available to women, and also signal the many and difficult decisions people must make.

Sandy has chosen a traditional path. She teaches kindergarten and craves motherhood. However, she is unable to have children. She comes to help deliver a baby which will become hers. Completely involved in the events emotionally, she is physically excluded from the process of procreation. The moment at which Sandy's hopes crash is impressively shot by director of photography Steve Mason, as she stands alone on a hillside masked by grey skies.

Therese is a hardened feminist. She is disillusioned with men, makes feminist films and is the mother of a teenage daughter. Throughout the pregnancy, she has interviewed Clare about surrogacy and home birth. Now she awaits the ending—the delivery itself—so she can finish her documentary.

Diane is the glamorous one. She has spent many years overseas, edits a fashion magazine and is not afraid to use her looks for her own ends. Diane has chosen to be a career woman, but not without realising some sacrifices.

Clare is the central character. She is intelligent, strong and independent. She is a talented painter who is just beginning to achieve recognition within her art community. She has chosen to live without her boyfriend. She is also beginning to question many of her beliefs.

McKimmie portrays both men and women as sympathetic, complex and human. Thus, although predominantly concerned with what are considered 'women's issues', this is not a didactic feminist tract or a sentimental portrayal of femininity, but raises issues which many women and men find problematic in a time which is trying to come to terms with the legacy of 1970s feminism, alternative lifestyles and ideological disparities.

PHILIPPA BURNE[3]

---

[1] On her first feature, **Australian Dream** (1987), Jackie McKimmie did not have an 'e' in her first name.

[2] One presumes the film-makers mean Bazza plays himself, but the credits have it the other way round.

[3] Extracted from Burne's review in *Cinema Papers* (see References).

References

'**Waiting**', a review by Philippa Burne, *Cinema Papers*, no. 83, May 1991, pp. 59–60.
'**Waiting** is Worth It', an interview with the writer–director Jackie McKimmie by Sue Pavasaris, *Filmnews*, March 1991, pp. 6–7.
'**Waiting**', a review by Annabelle Sheehan, *Filmnews*, February 1991, p. 15.

Therese (Fiona Press) and Diane (Deborra-Lee Furness).

WEEKEND WITH KATE

Phillip Emanuel presents Weekend with Kate. *Alternative title:* 'Depth of Feeling' working). © 1990 Phillip Emanuel Productions Limited. *Location:* Sydney. *Australian distributor:* Greater Union. *Video:* Premiere. *Rating:* M. 35mm. 92 mins.

Producer: Phillip Emanuel. *Co-producer:* David C. J. Douglas. *Scriptwriters:* Henry Tefay, Kee Young. *Director of photography:* Dan Burstall. *Production designer:* Laurence Eastwood. *Wardrobe supervisor:* Michelle[1] Leonard. *Editor:* Rose Evans. *Composer:* Bruce Rowland. *Sound recordist:* Tim Lloyd. *Sound editors:* Karin Whittington, Mark Van Buuren, Rick Lisle, Phil Dickson, Stella Savvas. *Mixers:* Peter Fenton, Ron Purvis.

Cast

Colin Friels (Richard Muir), Catherine McClements (Kate Muir), Jerome Ehlers (Jon Thorne), Helen Mutkins (Carla), Kate Sheil (Phoebe), Jack Mayers (Gus), Rick Adams (Ted), Emily Lumbers (Margo), Brian Vriends (Control Room Assistant), Zoe Emanuel (Girl at Airport), Bruce Venables (Bug Man), John Fielder (Fishmonger), Peter Talmacs (Jeweller), Peter Northcote (Guitarist 1), Troy Newman (Guitarist 2), Lindsay Jehan (Guitarist 3), David Wilson (Keyboard Player).

Richard (Colin Friels) and Kate Muir (Catherine McClements) organise a weekend at their 'shack' by the beach. He intends to tell her he is leaving for another woman, she intends to tell him that she wants a baby. But Richard's job as a public-relations executive with a rock-music promoter interferes, and they end up spending the weekend with world-famous rock star Jon Thorne (Jerome Ehlers). A love triangle is thus set up.

The film is set in the secluded beach shack, and there is little to interrupt the dynamics unfolding. However, a poor script leaves McClements and Ehlers adrift, and drives Friels to somewhat absurd slapstick, which at least rescues the film from drowning completely.

Friels is very funny and has all the best lines, but he is let down by the weakness of the other characters and the unevenness of tone as the film veers between comic farce and a serious look at relationships.

Stereotypes and clichés abound. Kate is the good wife, dabbling in painting and classical music. Hers is an affluent lifestyle of white houses, white clothes, white cars. She happily plays second fiddle to Richard and his career, but also realises that her life is not totally fulfilling, and decides a baby is the solution.

During the weekend, Kate discovers that Richard is having an affaire with Carla (Helen Mutkins), the stereotyped career woman: tough, manipulative, bitchy, sexual. Kate, too, is unfaithful, sleeping with Jon. So arises the biggest crisis in Kate's sheltered life. Disappointingly, she does not face up to it, running instead from one man to the other, finally settling for the security of what she already knows.

Jon Thorne is the stereotype of the rock star: self-centred and arrogant, demanding and petulant. He is the outsider who comes into the established life of Richard and Kate and threatens its stability.

Structural problems within the script undermine **Weekend with Kate**. Particularly troublesome is the ending—or 'endings'. There seems to be at least four and the actual one is disappointingly stock. (Interestingly, the production notes mention that a new ending was shot later and this is obvious when watching the film.)

The best aspect of the film is the photography. Dan Burstall manages to capture the beauty and presence of Sydney, and its northern beaches area, including the on-show affluence of Kate and Richard's lifestyle. Another strength is the soundtrack. In line with the trend in recent Australian films, it features contemporary Australian music. In this instance, this also ties in well with the rock music connection in the story.

Weekend with Kate is a film for yuppies facing crises who want to laugh and feel reassured that their lifestyles are not seriously under threat. As a film, it is safe and unthreatening, disappointing by not achieving its full potential.

PHILIPPA BURNE[2]

---

[1] Sometimes spelt 'Michele'.
[2] Extracted from Burne's review in *Cinema Papers* (see Reference).

Reference
'Weekend with Kate', a review by Philippa Burne, *Cinema Papers*, no. 82, March 1991, pp. 56–7.

Kate (Catherine McClements) and Richard (Colin Friels).

A WOMAN'S TALE

Illumination Films presents A WOMAN'S TALE. © 1991 Illumination Films [and] Australian Film Finance Corporation Pty Ltd. Made with the participation of the Australian Film Finance Corporation. *Location:* Melbourne. *Australian distributor:* Premium Films. *Video:* First Release. *Rating:* PG. 35mm. 93 mins.

Producers: Paul Cox, Santhana Naidu. *Executive producer:* William Marshall. Line *Producer:* Paul Ammitzboll. *Scriptwriters:* Paul Cox, Barry Dickins. Based on a concept by Paul Cox. *Director of photography:* Nino Martinetti. *Production designer:* Neil Angwin. *Wardrobe adviser:* Aphrodite Kondos. *Editor:* Russell Hurley. *Composer:* Paul Grabowsky. *Sound recordist:* Russell Hurley. *Sound Editor:* Craig Carter. *Mixer:* James Currie.

Cast

Sheila Florance (Martha), Gosia Dobrowolska (Anna), Norman Kaye (Billy), Chris Haywood (Jonathan), Ernest Gray (Peter), Myrtle Woods (Miss Inchley), Bruce Myles (Con 1), Alex Menglet (Con 2); François Bernard, Manuel Bachet (Neighbours); Monica Maughan (Billy's Daughter), Max Gillies (Billy's Son-in-law), Tony Llewellyn-Jones (Celebrant), David Reid (Don), Dawn Klingberg (Don's Wife), Marina Finlay (Prostitute), Victoria Eagger (Nurse 1), Marion Heathfield (Nurse 2), James Khong (Doctor), Kate Fewster (Young Martha), Carla Hoogeveen (Waitress), Nino Martinetti (Cafe Manager); Veronica Koca, Kyra Cox (Young Girls); Hal Todd (Hal Todd's Voice), Melita Jurisic (Judy's Voice).

Anna (Gosia Dobrowolska) and Martha (Sheila Florance).

Paul Cox's A Woman's Tale makes a brave attempt to tackle some difficult issues, but it also makes those difficulties obvious. It desperately wants to be an uplifting, life-affirming story about old age and death; it strives towards being profound, dialectic and spirited; but unfortunately it trips over its own well-meaning, optimistic foundations and sinks into the monotony of repetitive clichés.

Cox conceived the idea for one of the most tenacious veterans of Australian acting, Sheila Florance; he also based parts of the story on her life; and overall the film proves to be an unsettling cadence to her life and career. The dying Sheila Florance enacts herself dying. On its own, this fact holds some disturbing fascination; it is perhaps more interesting than the film itself.

One also sees the aged and ill actress at work, something that is so much more difficult to 'keep up' than her character's going

shopping, going down for a swim at the local pool or arguing with her landlord. There is a pervading sense of the real story of Sheila Florance, the woman behind the character of Martha, being so much more powerful, significant and much better able to make the film's points.

Gosia Dobrowolska, who plays Anna, the district nurse and Martha's best friend, gives a gentle and subtle performance. Anna's relationship with Martha in the film is original and beautiful. If one decides to ignore the obvious contrasts of 'this is YOUNG and this is OLD' type of iconography, the interaction of the two actresses (not the two characters) begins to convey its own significance. The enigmatically serene last scene, with Anna bending over the dying Martha to ease the old woman's final pain, suggesting the controversial euthanasia issue, is perhaps the best material in the film.

These two characters, and the character of Old Billy (Norman Kaye), are the only ones who receive the more sensitive and intelligent parts of the script. The rest of the characters are dished out the clichés available to the 'bad guys' when the 'good guys' are the aged.

The overall structure does not rescue this film from the clichés. The rather bluntly

inserted dream sequences, and the obvious imagery throughout, do not fare well; one hopes they would have some greater significance than the obvious, but they never do. Moreover, they are explained in the dialogue, just in case, one supposes, the audience missed the point.

On the favourable side, one could be grateful for the film's honesty when representing the visual qualities of age and death. The myriad of wrinkles on Martha's face and body, and all of the most unattractive features of cancer and death, are laid out bare for the viewer, no matter how disturbing and even threatening they may seem.

A Woman's Tale is not a beguiling film, but its brave attempts to make an exploration of unpleasant themes accessible are highly commendable.

ALISSA TANSKAYA[2]

---

[1] There is no director credit, just 'A Film by Paul Cox'.
[2] Extracted from Tanskaya's review in *Cinema Papers* (see References).

References

'A Woman's Tale', a review by Alissa Tanskaya, *Cinema Papers*, no. 85, November 1991, p. 59.
'A Woman's Tale', a review by Kathe Boehringer, *Filmnews*, October 1991, p. 12.

1992

*Scott Hastings (Paul Mercurio) and Liz
Holt (Gia Carides). Baz Luhrmann's*
Strictly Ballroom.

BACKSLIDING

Charles and Simon Target in association with Film Four International in association with ITEL in association with Australian Film Finance Corporation. BACKSLIDING. © 1991 CaST Films Limited and Australian Film Finance Corporation. Made with the participation of Australian Film Finance Corporation. *Location:* South Australia. *Australian distributor:* Palace. *Video:* Palace Home Entertainment. *Rating:* M. 35mm. 88 mins.

Producer: Sue Wild. *Production executive:* Basil Appleby. *Scriptwriters:* Simon Target, Ross Wilson. *Director of photography:* Tom Cowan. *Production designer:* Ross Major. *Costumes:* Andrea Hood. *Editor:* Nicholas Holmes. *Composer:* Nigel Westlake. *Sound recordist:* Ross Linton. *Sound editors:* Andrew Plain (supervising); James Manche (dia.). *Mixers:* Phil Heywood, Martin Oswin.

Cast

Tim Roth (Tom Whitton), Jim Holt (Jack Tyson), Odile Le Clezio (Alison Tyson), Ross McGregor (The Pastor), Michelle Fillery (Jerry), Patrick Duggan (Policeman #1), Jim Morlock (Policeman #2), Adrian Shirley (Radio Officer #1), Brian Knott (Radio Officer #2), Ernest Ellison (Radio Officer #3), Erik Procko (Boy), Penny McCraith (AirTraffic[1] Controller), Lee Biolos (Preacher on Tape), John Bonney (Weather Announcer), Goatee (Lilith).

Simon Target's **Backsliding** opens promisingly with a backyard baptism during which convicted felon Jack Tyson (Jim Holt), who has arrived complete with police escort, is born again. But this seemingly benign affair quickly adopts an obsessive, threatening character, and the viewer is thrown off balance. Unfortunately, Target fails to capitalise on this prologue, and his film quickly does a backslide of its own, emerging as a fairly tepid attempt at a psychological thriller.

The term 'backsliding' is employed by born-again Christians to describe the process of a repeat descent into sin. Two of the children of God who use this term with alarming frequency are Jack, now on parole and a self-professed new man, and his wife, Alison (Odile le Clezio), who first met Jack at his baptism. They run a power station in remote central Australia, with only their pet goat, Lilith (Goatee), and occasional visits by the flying pastor for company.

As one would expect, the illusory harmony of their solitary existence is irrevocably disrupted by the arrival of a stranger, Tom Whitton (Tim Roth), a drifter who has been hired by Jack's company to work as a handyman at the station. It soon becomes clear to Jack and Alison that Tom is not what he claims to be, and brooding sexual tensions among this isolated *ménage à trois* eventually lead to an explosion of violence, and a brutal confrontation between Jack and Tom.

One of the main flaws in this film is the manner in which the director handles the build-up of tension between the trio. While it is initially unsettling to witness a couple in outback Australia wandering about muttering inspirational messages like agents of the Inquisition, the script soon enters the realm of cliché.

The three central performances don't really assist the proceedings, either. Jim Holt has angular, vulpine features which prove helpful in conveying his rapid passage into lunacy, but he fails to show any of the restraint that would be necessary in making such a difficult rôle even remotely convincing. Englishman Tim Roth turns in a fatally lazy performance, apparently confusing a look of enigmatic brooding with one of bored constipation. And Odile Le Clezio's Alison looks suitably terrified when faced with her husband's murderous pursuit, but Target has failed to elicit any audience sympathy toward her character prior to this, so we don't really care when Jack threatens to do her in.

On the plus side, some of the camerawork isn't bad, though Target's direction swings between broad expressionistic techniques and those of *Matlock Police*. The conflicting use of fire and water imagery is also nicely handled, until, as with so many other aspects of this film, it is overdone.

Target also handles the violent conclusion with reasonable slickness (apart from a ludicrous and self-consciously apocalyptic false finale), and the violence, when it arrives, is well staged. But in revealing Jack to be a religious lunatic way too early in the tale's unfolding, any chance at achieving a compensating level of genuine sweat-producing tension is lost.

PAUL SALMOND[2]

---

[1] AirTraffic is rendered as one word with a capital T.

[2] Extracted from Salmond's review in *Cinema Papers* (see References).

References

'Backsliding', a location report by Mark Chipperfield, *Cinema Papers*, no. 82, March 1991, pp. 32–3.

'Backsliding', a review by Paul Salmond, *Cinema Papers*, no. 88, May-June 1992, pp. 57, 59–60.

'Backsliding', a review by Marg O'Shea, *Filmnews*, March 1992, pp. 12–13.

Jack Tyson (Jim Holt) and Alison (Odile Le Clezio).

BLACK ROBE

Laforgue (Lothaire Bluteau).

Alliance Communications & Samson Productions present A Robert Lantos Production. BLACK ROBE. © 1991 Alliance Communications Corporation in trust[,] Sampson Productions Pty Limited [and] Australian Film Finance Corporation Pty Limited. Produced with the participation of Telefilm Canada and in association with First Choice Canadian Communications Corporation with the participation of Rogers Telefund. Made with the participation of Australian Film Finance Corporation Pty Limited. A Canada–Australia Co-production. *Budget:* $11 million. *Locations:* Lac St Jean, Saguenay region, Québec (Canada); Rouen (France). *Australian distributor:* Hoyts. *Opened:* 26 February 1992. *Video:* Columbia Tristar Home Video. *Rating:* M. 35mm. 100 mins.

Producers: Robert Lantos, Stéphane Reichel, Sue Milliken. *Executive producers:* Jake Eberts, Brian Moore, Denis Héroux. *Associate producer:* Eric Norlen. *Scriptwriter:* Brian Moore. Based on his novel. *Director of photography:* Peter James. *Camera operator:* Danny Batterham. *Production designer:* Herbert Pinter. *Costume designers:* Renée April, John Hay. *Editor:* Tim Wellburn. *Composer:* Georges Delerue. *Sound recordists:* Gary Wilkins; Henri Roux (France). *Supervising sound editor:* Penn Robinson. *Sound editor:* Jeannine[1] Chialvo. *Mixer:* Phil Judd.

Cast

Lothaire Bluteau (Laforgue), Aden Young (Daniel), Sandrine Holt (Annuka), August Schellenberg (Chomina), Tantoo Cardinal (Chomina's Wife), Billy Two Rivers (Ougebemat), Lawrence Bayne (Neehatin), Harrisen Liu (Awondole), Wesley Côté (Oujita), Frank Wilson (Father Jerome), François Tassé (Father Bourque), Jean Brousseau (Champlain), Yvan Labelle (Mestigoit), Raoul Trujillo (Kiotseation), James Bobbish (Ondesson), Denis Lacroix (Tarantande), Gilles Plante (Older Workman), Gordon Tootoosis (Old Aenons), Marthe Tungeon (Laforgue's Mother), Claude Préfontaine (Old Priest).

Black Robe is a visually stunning, bloody and relentless film that tells the story of a 17th-century Jesuit priest who travels into the wilds of North America to convert the native Indians. Laforgue (Lothaire Bluteau) has been nominated by senior Jesuits to make the 2500 km journey up river to spread the word of God; 'Death is almost certain', he is told.

Shot on location in Québec, **Black Robe** marks the first Australia–Canada feature co-production. With an $11 million budget, a hard-working crew and an exceptional cast, director Bruce Beresford has created an outstanding period piece which recalls the potent eloquence of his 1980 film, '**Breaker' Morant**.

Black Robe is a big story with a big theme: the conflict of Christian ethics versus the pragmatic concerns of mortal life. The film does not break much new ground on this topic; rather, its strength lies in the manner it weaves the journey of Laforgue into the desolate and beautiful frontier it recreates.

Laforgue is a tormented hero whose ill-fated mission to show the Indians 'the way to paradise' dramatically alters the destiny of those accompanying him: a group of Algonquin Indians and a young French carpenter and translator, Daniel (Aden Young). By degrees, the black-robed Jesuit learns his mission is failing; he, too, is doubting his own faith and his ability to fend off earthly desires, such as the sin of 'intent' over an Indian girl, Annuka (Sandrine Holt), who has fallen in love with Daniel.

Ultimately, **Black Robe** becomes more a quest for survival than a journey to redemption (even though a string of Biblical allegories would have us believe the latter). Death strikes fast and brutally; the survivors are left to rely on their base instincts and an element of good fortune. As the drama escalates, so to do the themes: betrayal, honour and sacrifice, among them.

A highlight of **Black Robe** is the strength of its acting. The brooding Lothaire Bluteau is the perfect incarnation of the Jesuit martyr. Two notable secondary rôles are that of the dying Father Jerome (Frank Wilson) and Mestigoit, the dwarf sorcerer played with menacing edge by Yvan Labelle. Overall, the rôles are drawn to believable conclusions, although the unknown but seemingly gloomy fate of the lovers may leave some viewers cold.

On a technical level, the film cannot be faulted. Beresford does not deviate far from orthodox film-making techniques, yet any scenes that introduce a degree of logistical difficulty are pulled off convincingly. A taut screenplay by Brian Moore—whose novel of the same name is based on actual accounts of Jesuit missionaries—lends the film a sense of historical veracity. A thorough production team has recreated the feel of New France to the last detail, while the landscape photography of Peter James is integral to the story rather than being a brochuristic distraction.

Black Robe tells a bleak story without shirking—nothing is offered in the way of comic distraction, and the narration is free of clichéd emotions.

GREG KERR

1 Usually, spelt 'Jeanine'.

References
'Black Robe', a production report by Andrew L. Urban, *Cinema Papers*, no. 82, March 1991, pp. 6–12.
'Black Robe', a review by Greg Kerr, *Cinema Papers*, no. 87, March–April 1992, pp. 59–60.
'Black Robe', a review by Bev Tivey, *Filmnews*, December 1991, p. 15.

BLINKY BILL

[Credits not checked.[1]] Yoram Gross presents Blinky Bill. © 1992. Made with participation of Australian Film Finance Corporation Pty Ltd. Developed with the assistance of the New South Wales Television Office. *Australian distributor:* Beyond International. *Opened:* 24 September 1992. *Video:* not released as of July 1993. *Rating:* G. 35mm. 80 mins.

Producer: Yoram Gross. *Executive producers:* Sandra Gross, Tim Brooke-Hunt. *Scriptwriters:* Yoram Gross, John Palmer, Leonard Lee. Based on *The Complete Adventures of Blinky Bill* by Dorothy Wall. *Directors of photography:* Frank Hammond, Paul Ozerski. *Animation camera operators:* Margaret Antoniak, Bob Evans, Minh Nguyen, Graham Sharpe, Kevin Woodbridge. *Art director:* Ray Nowland. *Editors:* G. Y. Jerzy, Lee Smith. *Composer:* Guy Gross. *Songs:* Guy Gross. *Lyrics:* John Palmer, Mattie Porges. *Performed by:* Robyn Moore, Keith Scott. 'Sleep Bush Baby Sleep' performed by Julie Anthony. 'Frog Song' performed by Ross Higgins. *Sound supervisor:* Nicki Roller. *Dialogue engineer:* Tim Ryan. *Sound editors:* Julia Gelhard, Antony Gray. *Mixer:* Phil Judd.

Animation directors: Robert Smit, Athol Henry, Sue Beak. *Character design:* Ray Nowland, Robert Smit. *Animators:* Junko Aoyama, Sue Beak, Patrick Burns, Joshua Dodson, Donald Ezard, Gerry Grabner, Athol Henry, Nick Harding, Greg Ingram, Lui Garcia, Paul Maron, Chris Minos, Astrid Norddheim, Darek Polkowski, Warren Simpson, Andras Szemenyei, Maria Szemenyei, Stella Wakil, Stanley Walker. *Storyboard:* Robert Smit, Sue Break, Dean Taylor. *Layout artists:* Ray Van Steenwyk, Athol Henry, Steve Lumley. *Rendering supervisor:* Kerry Gulliver. *Renderers:* Jo-Anne Boag, Marzena Domaradzka, Oura Flantz, Tara Kamath, Sharon King, Vaclav Krucek, Ralph Heimens, Karen Lee, Karek Maj, Linda Mills, Janet Robinson, James Rose, Yvette Swan, Helen Connolly. *Inbetweening supervisor:* Cynthia Leech. *Inbetweeners:* Tony Ablen, Jan D'Silva, Maichael Dunn, Paul Cheng, Gary Hunter, Robert Malherbe, Stephen Moltzen, Matthew Munro, Philip Peters, Sjaojie Zheng, Adam Rapson, Stephen Robinson, Vicky Robinson, Sally Simons, Amanda Thompson, Gerard Piper, Andrew Szabo, Elizabeth Urbanczyk, Dab Huan Wu, Milan Zahorsky. *Tracing supervisor:* Kerry Martin. *Colour styling:* Belinda Price, Jeanette Toms. *Background artists:* Paul Cheng, Amber Ellis, Robert Qiu Yuan. *Paint supervisor:* Belinda Price

Voices

Robyn Moore (female characters), Keith Scott (male characters).

[See Appendix A on all the Gross films, pp. 352–4.]

---

1 No copy was available for viewing. These credits are taken from art work of the film's titles.

Reference

'Yoram Gross', Raffaele Caputo, *Cinema Papers*, no. 86, January 1992, 36–42.

Blinky Bill and friends.

BREATHING UNDER WATER

[Credits not checked.] Periscope Productions in association with Channel 4. [© atb 1992.] *Location:* Sydney. *Australian distributor:* Ronin. Opened: 15 May 1993. *Video:* not released as of July 1993. *Rating:* PG. 35mm. 78 mins.

Producer: Megan McMurchy. *Scriptwriter:* Susan Murphy Dermody. *Director of photography:* Erika Addis. *Production designer:* Stephen Curtis. *Costume designer:* Amanda Lovejoy. *Editor:* Diana Priest. *Composer:* Elizabeth Drake. *Sound recordists:* John Dennison, Tony Vaccher. [*Sound editor:* not known. *Mixer:* not known.]

Cast

Anne Louise Lambert (Beatrice), Kristoffer Greaves (Herman), Maeve Dermody (Maeve).

Maeve (Maeve Dermody).

In a discussion of Vincent Ward's **The Navigator: A Medieval Odyssey** (1988), Susan Dermody described it as a 'voyage of imagination across the face of the unconscious, which harbours within it a full embrace of death and darkness'. She ends by musing: 'Given the severe phallocentrism of the institutions of technology and geopolitics that plague our time, it is very clear to me that Griffin [Hamish McFarlane] should have been a girl.'[1] It is hard not to discern in these words the genesis of Dermody's first feature, **Breathing Under Water**.

The film can be usefully grouped with a number of quasi-experimental features funded by the Australian Film Commission in the early 1990s, including David Perry's **The Refracting Glasses** (1993) and Ross Gibson's *Dead to the World* (unreleased, 1991). These are projects with a strong 'film culture' (as opposed to 'film industry') aura, made by people with a long-standing background in criticism, teaching, script editing and various branches of 'independent' cinema.

Breathing Under Water can be understood as an 'essay film'—one that, instead of full-bloodedly telling a story, arranges the various pieces of an argument or a reverie. Like the essay films which it most resembles—those of Alexander Kluge, and especially Chris Marker's **Sans Soleil** (**Sunless**, 1982)—it unfolds across the boundaries of genre, mixing documentary with fiction, fact with whimsy, world history with personal anecdote. The film is most successful when it achieves a dreamlike, 'free associative' flow of images and sounds (including clips from classic movies, news-

reel footage and animation segments in the style of children's picture books), mimicking the 'deep logic' of the unconscious. In a strong tradition of feminist art and theory, the film searches for those illuminating moments when global politics intersects with the minute, personal experiences of desire, memory and fantasy.

In Dermody's 're-imagining' of Dante's *Inferno* via Andrei Tarkovsky, Beatrice (Anne Louise Lambert) takes her daughter Maeve (Maeve Dermody) on a journey through an imaginary landscape, combining bits of reality (like Sydney buses) with more purely fantasticated spaces. The various, allegorical zones of this world offer sights and sounds that encapsulate the madnesses and obsessions of our age—nuclear weaponry, high technology, speed, mass media. Notwithstanding the inherent 'drama' of such themes, the film is severely, deliberately de-dramatised.

This essayistic de-dramatisation is in line with Dermody's stated intention that (in the terms suggested by Ursula Le Guin) she wanted to fashion not a conventional 'hunter' narrative (on a masculine model of struggle and conquest) but a 'gatherer' narrative—hence the key visual metaphor of the protagonist's shopping bag. **Breathing Under Water** is rigorously centred on women's experience—particularly the vital bond between mother and daughter. The only significant man along for the ride is Herman (Kristoffer Greaves), whose name implies both the mythical Hermes and, more derisively, a male cipher who is merely 'Her Man'.

The central shortcoming of the film is its relentless voice-over narration, which (unlike Marker's narration for **Sunless**) fails to achieve consistent poetic effects of wit, epiphany and emotion. And, although Dermody and her colleague Liz Jacka have been inspirational in their call to Australian cinema to engage with the territory of 'the unconscious, rituals and dreams'[2], it is possible to find her film rather too conscious and over-intellectualised, its connections too pre-planned and schematic.[3]

Generally, however, **Breathing Under Water** is a confident and brave film-making debut, worthy of inclusion among the highpoints of the international genre of the essay film.

ADRIAN MARTIN

---

1   Susan Dermody, 'The Company of Eccentrics', in Dermody & Jacka (eds), *The Imaginary Industry*, AFTRS Publications, 1988, pp. 153–4.
2   Susan Dermody and Liz Jacka, *The Screening of Australia: Australian Film in the Late '80s*, Susan Dermody and Elizabeth Jacka (eds), AFTRS Publications, Sydney, 1988.
3   For an incisive critique of the film along these lines, see Vikki Riley, 'Celestial Beginnings' (see References).

References

'Breathing Under Water', a review by Pauline Adamek, *Cinema Papers*, no. 88, May–June 1992, pp. 54–5.

'Jane Freebury Finds a Film which Traces a Quest Fired by Desire: **Breathing Under Water**', an interview with writer-director Susan Murphy Dermody, *Filmnews*, May 1992, p. 12.

'Celestial Beginnings', Vikki Riley, *Filmnews*, July 1992, pp. 11–15.

COME BY CHANCE

[No opening production company credit.] Come by Chance. [© not given; atb 1992 Lara Dunston.] *Location:* Sydney. *Australian distributor:* Lara Dunston. *Opened:* 28 August 1992. *Video:* not released as of July 1993. 16mm. 85 mins.

Producer: Lara Dunston. *Co-producer:* Terry Carter. *Scriptwriter:* Lara Dunston. *Director of photography:* Lara Dunston. *Production designer:* Lara Dunston. [*Costume designer:* not credited.] *Editors:* Lara Dunston, Terry Carter. *Composer:* Terry Carter. *Sound recordist:* Terry Carter. *Sound Editor:* Terry Carter. *Mixer:* Liam Egan.

Cast

Annabel Stokes (The Girl), Simon Hann (The Boy), Kathryn Collins (Young Cowgirl), Michelle Collins (Young Cowgirl), Wendy Carnes (Shoe Store Assistant), Karen Whitney (Supermarket Cashier), Kerry McCool (Car Salesman), Terry Carter (Farmer in Field; Can-throwing Country Dude; Wig-finding Farmer; Unseen Interviewer and Additional Voice-overs); Bluey O'Brien (Man at Club Hotel Bar), Ray Polzin (Service Station Proprietor), Raife Stokes (Dude Driving Car; The Foreign Hitchhiker), Loic Guezzenec (Dude in Car), Charlie Smith (Country Friend at Rodeo), Jon Murphy (Grazier), Jayne Murphy (Grazier's Daughter), The Desert Man— Mick James (as Himself), The Pony Boys (as Themselves), Warren Dunston (D. J. Voice-overs).

Come by Chance is a first feature self-financed for around $12,000. Without the talent and labour that can be bought with government assistance, one can expect technical polish or proficiency to be of secondary importance. Some films turn this expectation into a selling point, highlighting rather than masking the 'badness' of the film. Others turn technical disadvantages into advantages of thematic and formal experimentation. Come by Chance leans toward the latter: it combines a number of documentary styles and visual textures of different film mediums.

The two lead characters, simply known as 'The Girl' (Annabel Stokes) and 'The Boy' (Simon Hann), are inner-city dwellers obsessed with country 'n' western music, who take to the road in search of 'what the west is all about', as they put it. There is the sense that the whole exercise is going to be therapeutic for both.

The comparison may seem absurd, but there is a slight echo of the theatre of Beckett,

The Girl (Annabel Stokes) and The Boy (Simon Hann).

or maybe Pirandello, in that The Boy and The Girl are really two characters in search of a story. Indeed, if there is a story to tell then it is still to be discovered somewhere in their journey out west, and it is the journey which will hopefully give their obsession a semblance of meaning.

The film swings into an interview-style documentary as the characters, shot separately, respond to questions from behind the camera. The couple are interviewed about their desire, the clothes they're wearing, how they'll live while on the road, and how they feel about each other. In most cases they contradict each other, except in their desire to discover the west.

The film then cuts between the two interview situations and what becomes a document of the actual journey, with the couple travelling along country roads in a beat-up Holden, checking into a motel room, and encountering a number of outback characters. These sequences are further intercut (occasionally) with images of the landscape that The Girl has filmed on her Super 8 camera.

In all the balancing and counterbalancing of different images and situations is discernible a perspective on the west that is always illusive. The only clue to what the

couple are actually experiencing is told through the soundtrack, the country 'n' western tunes laid over the endlessly rolling landscape. But the soundtrack has the same function as all the other western accoutrements: it doesn't quite fit together with the landscape, with the outback characters and so on.

The western elements they had traded for at the beginning of the film can just as equally be traded in. It opens out further the gap between the west of their imagination and the west they keep travelling to. To discover the west of the imagination one can only ever find it further on west. And to keep travelling further west is to return from where one started. But at $12,000 it's cheaper than a psychiatrist.

RAFFAELE CAPUTO[1]

---

[1] Extracted from Caputo's review in *Cinema Papers* (see References).

Reference
'Come by Chance', a review by Raffaele Caputo, *Cinema Papers*, no. 92, April 1993. pp. 48–9.
'No Budget to Low Budget: Pauline Adamek Finds Out How Three Feature Films Were Made on Minimal Money', with a discussion of *Come By Chance*, *Filmnews*, November 1992, pp. 6–7.

DAYDREAM BELIEVER

Beyond Films Limited presents [and] Ben Gannon presents DAYDREAM BeL-ieveR[1]. *Alternative title:* 'The Girl Who Came Late' (working). © 1991 View Films Pty. Limited and Australian Film Finance Corporation Pty. Limited. Script developed with assistance from the Australian Film Commission. Made with the participation of Australian Film Finance Corporation Pty. Limited as part of the 1990 FFC Film Fund. *Australian distributor:* Hoyts. *Video:* not released as of July 1993. *Rating:* PG. 35mm. 82 mins.

Producer: Ben Gannon. *Executive producer:* John Cooper. *Scriptwriter:* Saturday Rosenberg. *Director of photography:* Andrew Lesnie. *Production designer:* Roger Ford. *Costume designer:* Roger Ford. *Editor:* Robert Gibson. *Composers:* Todd Hunter, Johanna Pigott. *Sound recordist:* Guntis Sics. *Sound editors:* Greg Bell, Ashley Grenville, Andrew Cunningham. *Mixers:* Peter Fenton, Ron Purvis, Martin Oswin.

Cast

Miranda Otto (Nell), Martin Kemp (Digby), Gia Carides (Wendy), Anne Looby (Margo), Bruce Venables (Stu), Alister Smart (Ron), Jamie Jackson (Neville Lipsky), Geoff Morrell (Brad Hislop), Kerry Walker (Aunt Vera), George Whaley (Mike), Les Foxcroft (Perce), Katy Edwards (Young Nell), Peter Hehir (German Film Director), Russell Kiefel (Nell's Father), Keith Robinson (Commercial Director), Brian Blain (Headmaster), Howard Vernon (Dr Montgomery); Adam Cockburn, Dene Kermond, Jason Meeth (School Bullies); Emma Fowler (Schoolgirl).

Daydream Believer, Kathy Mueller's transition from children's television to feature film-making, looks just that—an in-between step. Known throughout pre-production as 'The Girl Who Came Late' (apparently a terrible pun deriving from the late-blooming sexuality of the lead character), it is the story of a young girl (Katy Edwards) who, whenever threatened, retreats into a fantasy world in which she is a horse.

This is established in the first ten minutes or so, in scenes set in 1970s rural Australia. Then, through a very strange narrative device, we move to the present day, to find our heroine, Nell (Miranda Otto), in her early twenties but not quite tired of daydreaming.

The device is strange not because it is unfamiliar, but because it is never clear if the temporal shift that the wavy screen establishes is forward to the real Nell in her present-day situation recalling her childhood (which would indicate that the opening sequence is a flashback which precedes the 'real' contemporary story) or a flashforward from the real child, Nell, to an imagined version of herself as a grown-up (which would mean that which is narratively 'real' is the first ten minutes of the film, not what comes after).

Either is possible, as the scene preceding the temporal shift has the child Nell being told that she will never find a man to love if she carries on acting like a horse; then, wavy screen cut to young woman Nell, a socially inept, unemployed aspiring actress with a car full of apples (comic suggestion that she has not yet outgrown her horseyness).

Through a series of mishaps, Nell is then involved in a collision with Digby (Martin Kemp), impresario, horse-breeder, and—surprise, surprise—the man who will see the worth in Nell in spite of (even because of) her horse fixation.

Despite the innate silliness of the premise, **Daydream Believer** comes close to being a pretty good comedy. Unfortunately, the major let-down is Kemp's character. He already seems anachronistic, a classic 1980s yuppie in a film released in mid-1992, and Kemp's performance is lacklustre at best. Miranda Otto and Gia Carides (as friend Wendy) do their best to take it seriously, but the film ultimately seems unable to resolve the conflict between its adult and childish ambitions—a conflict which finally led to the film receiving only a short Sydney release by Hoyts before being put back in the too-hard basket.

KARL QUINN

[1] The title is in upper and lower case; this is an approximation.

Reference

'Kathy Mueller's **Daydream Believer**', a production report by Eva Friedman, *Cinema Papers*, no. 88, May–June 1992, pp. 16–18.

Nell (Miranda Otto), who has a fixation with horses.

DEADLY

A Moirstorm Production. DEADLY. © 1990 Deadly Productions Pty Limited [and] Australian Film Finance Corporation Pty Limited. Script developed with the assistance of the Australian Film Commission. Made with the participation of Australian Film Finance Corporation Pty Limited as part of the 1990 FFC Film Fund. *Locations:* Wilcannia and Sydney, New South Wales. *Australian distributor:* Hoyts. *Video:* not released as of July 1993. *Rating:* M. 35mm. 99 mins.

Producer: Richard Moir. *Line producer:* Antonia Barnard. *Scriptwriters:* Esben Storm, Richard Moir, Ranald Allan. *Director of photography:* Geoffrey Simpson. *Camera operator:* Nick Mayo. *Production designer:* Peta Lawson. *Costume designer:* Terry Ryan. *Editor:* Ralph Strasser. *Composer:* Graeme Revell. *Sound recordist:* David Lee. *Sound editors:* Andrew Plain (supervising); James Manche, Jeanine Chialvo. *Mixers:* Peter Fenton, Ron Purvis, Martin Oswin, Robert Sullivan.

Cast

Jerome Ehlers (Tony Bourke), Frank Gallacher (Mick Thorton), Lydia Miller (Daphne), John Moore (Eddie), Caz Lederman (Irene), Alan David Lee (Constable Barry Blainey), Tony Barry (Deputy Commissioner Graham Stewart), Julie Nihill (Jenny), Martin Vaughan (Doctor Ward), Bill Hunter (Vernon Giles), Bruce Venables (Archie), Lillian Crombie (Sally), Steve Dodd (Kummengu), Andrew Gilbert (Constable Peter Morton), David Kennedy (Wally Nobody), Kirrily Nolan (Siobhan), Kevin Smith (Jerry), Michael Watson (Rocky), Les Shillingsworth (Singer at Funeral), Richard Moir (Willie the Pathologist), Andrew Windsor (Punk), John Gregg (Minister), Anna North (Junkie).

Deadly is essentially a run-of-the-mill good cop/bad cop story, albeit with two notable twists. The first lies in the fact that the 'good' cop has to prove that he is not in fact a 'bad' one. The second, and more significant, twist is that the site of this test of virtue is an inquest into the death of an Aboriginal man while in police custody.

This scenario clearly offers considerable potential for an invigorating exploration of the clash of cultures between black and Anglo-Celtic white Australia, but, for a variety of reasons, the overall result is less than satisfying. Perhaps the most glaring problem lies in the characterisation of the good cop, Tony Bourke (Jerome Ehlers), a detective relegated to desk duty after the accidental

shooting of a junkie during a night-time chase. Cleared of negligence by a commission of enquiry, he is given the chance to redeem himself and regain his detective status by the deputy commissioner. All he has to do is conduct a similar enquiry in the remote town of Yabbabri, the clear intention being to find the resident police officers innocent.

Director Esben Storm has obviously attempted to set up Bourke as an agent for bringing understanding to the film's (predominantly white) audience. His journey takes him from the metaphoric and literal darkness of inner-city complacency and ignorance, in which 'junkies' and 'boongs' have the same value (none), to the glaring, often unpleasant, but nonetheless illuminating light of the outback, in which the Aboriginal people are to be understood as having a dignity which the alcohol and tedium can obscure but not erase. To some extent the device works, but Bourke is never really under scrutiny in the eyes of the viewer.

The opening sequence of the film clearly establishes Bourke as a victim of circumstance. We know he didn't see the girl step out from the shadows into his line of fire; we never doubt his word. Yet, for the device of Bourke as transforming angel to be fully effective, there has to be a moment when we suspect that he is a power-hungry creep who gets off on 'accidentally' blowing away innocent bystanders.

Still, **Deadly** is not without its merits, although these reside mostly in the details: its brave depiction of alcoholism in Aboriginal and white communities, and its examination of the social implications of mixed parentage.

But perhaps the most telling moment in the film is one of little consequence to the story as a whole. It involves Mick Thorton (Frank Gallacher) taking Bourke for a spot of roo-shooting. As Bourke fixes a kangaroo in his sights, Thorton whispers, 'Let her have it. You know she wants it.' The link between so many unpalatable layers of the Australian male psyche—the desire to kill, the sexism that justifies rape in terms of 'she was asking for it', the male bonding that takes shape through rituals of violence—is drawn so deftly in this scene that, had it informed the rest of the film, **Deadly** may well have been a masterpiece.

KARL QUINN[1]

---

[1] Extracted from Quinn's review in *Cinema Papers* (see References).

References
'**Deadly**', a production report by Andrew L. Urban, *Cinema Papers*, no. 81, December 1990, pp. 14–17.
'**Deadly**', a review by Karl Quinn, *Cinema Papers*, no. 90, October 1992, pp. 51–2.
'**Deadly**', a review by Peter Galvin, *Filmnews*, August 1992, pp. 13–14.

Eddie (John Moore), Daphne (Lydia Miller) and Tony Bourke (Jerome Ehlers).

DINGO

Gevest Australia Prods presents a Gevest Productions[,] AO Productions[,] Dedra Films and Cine Cinq co-production DINGO. © 1990 Gevest Productions Pty Limited[,] Australian Film Finance Corporation Pty Limited[,] AO Productions SARI[,] Dedra SARI [and] Cine Cinq SA. *Budget:* $5 million. Made with the participation and assistance of the Western Australian Film Council, Australian Film Commission, the Centre National de la Cinématographe and Canal Plus. Made with the participation of Australian Film Finance Corporation. *Locations:* Paris; Sandstone, Meekatharra, Perth (Western Australia). *Australian distributor:* Ronin. *Opened:* 31 January 1992. *Video:* Columbia Tristar. *Rating:* PG. 35mm. 109 mins.

Producers: Rolf de Heer, Giorgio Draskovic, Marie-Pascale Osterrieth, Marc Rosenberg. *Executive producer:* Giorgio Draskovic. *Scriptwriter:* Marc Rosenberg. *Director of photography:* Denis Lenoir. *Production designer:* Judith Russell. *Costume designer:* Clarissa[1] Patterson. *Editor:* Suresh Ayyar. *Composers:* Michel Legrand, Miles Davis. *Additional music:* Tim Hood. *Sound recordist:* Henri Morelle. *Sound editors:* Ashley Grenville; Danielle Wiessner (music). *Mixers:* James Currie (chief); Peter D. Smith (music).

Cast

Colin Friels (John 'Dingo' Anderson), Miles Davis (Billy Cross), Bernadette Lafont (Angie Cross), Helen Buday (Jane Anderson), Joe Petruzzi (Peter), Steve Shaw (Archie), Helen Doig (Ruth), Daniel Scott (Young John), Chelsea Gibson (Young Jane), Ben Mortley (Young Peter), Elissa McAuliffe (Emma Anderson), Fiona Bradshaw (Jo Anderson); Dingo's Bush Band: Tim Hood (Robert—rhythm), Cyril Garnett (Mai—drums), Peter Byfield (Ned—bass); Billy Cross Jazz Band: Marcus Johnson (drums), Matthew Branston (double bass), Bill McAllister (trombone), Lee Buddle (tenor sax), Terry Thomas (alto sax), Kuki (guitar), Don Gomez (piano), Pat Crichton (trumpet).

Dreams, Freud believed, are the symbolic expressions of a person's innermost desires. Now, it must be said that filmmakers have not been slow to grasp the importance of this idea. Indeed, the links between subconscious and conscious desires, dream symbolism and wish-fulfilment are salient aspects of **Dingo**.

Marc Rosenberg, the scriptwriter, has said that the 'masterpiece' took no less than eight years to complete. The protracted effort is apparent in the final product.

The setting is Poona Flats, 1969. John Anderson (Daniel Scott), who will be known as 'Dingo', is with friends: Peter (Ben Mortley) and Jane (Chelsea Gibson), Dingo's future wife. A strange sound is heard. Significantly, John is the most sensitive to it. A jet lands on the flats and Billy Cross (the late Miles Davis), acclaimed jazzman, steps off and starts playing in front of the motley bunch of not unduly perturbed or surprised pub-goers and the children.

The effect on John is dramatic, to say the least. The whole scene is a highlight: the townspeople gather, listen and disperse as if nothing unique has happened; the arrival and departure of Billy Cross have the force almost of an epiphany, a vision in the wilderness. What is offered to John is the opportunity to transcend the banality of life as a 'dogger'; the prospect of glory—a gig with Cross in Paris.

The film, mercifully, is not just about a dream that is actualised. There are some interesting points about the tensions between ambition and family, obsession and relationships, and about the ways in which pain and adversity can lead to a greater capacity to endure (the image of the dingo is crucial). The animal is somewhat too clever for John 'Dingo' Anderson (Colin Friels); John is too clever to be what he is; both are too slow in one sense or another; both are 'too smart' in their own ways.

There are problems. There is an element of contrivance, especially towards the end, when the transformation occurs rather too quickly. And the contrasts between the naïve outback boy and Peter (Joe Petruzzi), the cynical city dweller, are too neat and familiar. Miles Davis, unfortunately, was not the most convincing of actors.

But the film stimulates on a number of levels: it has strong central performances; the drama is enriched by a mischievous streak of larrikin humour and by the use of irony; and it raises some tantalising possibilities in relation to the tension between freedom and determinism, or fatalism (though these are not really developed). Events which seem to be accidental become, in fact, parts of an overarching, enigmatic scheme which is quietly but unambiguously affirmed, at least by Billy Cross. Davis scintillates on the soundtrack, which is a vivid and vividly functional part of the drama ('The Dream', a leitmotif, a dazzling summation of the unfolding drama).

The film is attractive because of its affirmative nature: what it suggests is that John 'Dingo' Anderson and Cross are transformed by their fateful relationship and by the inscrutable workmanship that rejuvenates the one and fulfils the other.

RAYMOND YOUNIS[2]

---

[1] Usually spelt 'Clarissa'.

[2] Extracted from Younis' review in *Cinema Papers* (see References).

References
'Dingo', a review by Raymond Younis, *Cinema Papers*, no. 87, March–April 1992, pp. 60–1.
'Dingo', a review by Russell Edwards, *Filmnews*, February 1992, p. 12.

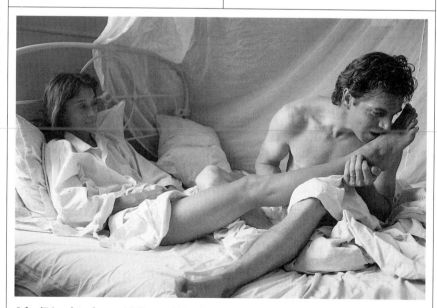

John 'Dingo' Anderson (Colin Friels) and Jane Anderson (Helen Buday).

FATAL BOND

Phillip Avalon presents fatal bond. © 1991 Avalon Films (Tovefelt Productions Pty Ltd) and Australian Film Finance Corporation Pty Ltd. Made with the participation of the Australian Film Finance Corporation. *Location:* north-central coast of NSW. *Australian distributor:* Hoyts. *Video:* First Release. *Rating:* M. 35mm. 89 mins.

Producer: Phillip Avalon[2]. *Scriptwriter:* Phillip Avalon. *Director of photography:* Ray Henman. *Production designer:* Keith Holloway. *Wardrobe:* Lyn Askew. *Editor:* Ted Ötton. *Composer:* Art Phillips. *Sound recordist:* Bob Clayton. *Sound editor:* Les Fiddess. *Mixer:* Robert Sullivan.

Cast

Linda Blair (Leonie), Jerome Ehlers (Joe Martinez), Stephen Leeder (Anthony Boon), Donal Gibson (Rocky Borgetta), Joe Bugner (Claw Miller), Caz Lederman (Detective Chenko), Teo Gerbert (Shane Boon), Penny Pederson (Bree Boon), Roger Ward (Detective Greaves), Ross Newton (Harding), As Himself [3] (Kevin Johnson), Caroline Beck (Jenny), Jan Adele (Mrs Karvan), Lyndon Harris (Joy Turner), Ken Snodgrass (Sgt. Taylor), Peter Browne (Caravan Man), Bob Barrett (Fisherman Bob), Jim Winshuttle (Fisherman), Donna Lee (Celia Boon), Ron Holbrow (Celia's Husband).

Joe Martinez (Jerome Ehlers) and Leonie (Linda Blair).

If Australia has any producer-cum-auteurs, then Phillip Avalon is certainly one. His films are preoccupied with violence bubbling to the surface in a lower-middle-class society repressed by Christian and materialist values. He has a decided affinity for the outsider, for those who refuse to play society's games and whose anti-social attitudes may, in fact, conceal a soul well attuned to life's pulses.

In Vincent Monton's **Fatal Bond**, Joe Martinez (Jerome Ehlers) is a man without a home or a known past. His only friend seems to be the Valiant car that rockets him through time and across landscape. He is a loner with a violent temper that bristles whenever he feels society is grinding down on him. If anyone encroaches upon his sense of freedom (be he a bouncer or a crim), Joe explodes—a quick headbutt followed by a frantic attack of swirling fists.

On one such occasion, he is saved from arrest by Leonie (Linda Blair), a hairdresser with an American accent and a poor love life. She is clearly attracted to Joe's sexual charisma and his anti-social nature. In some ways, Leonie personifies those women who are drawn to unlovable men, who find

reasons to stay when most others would have fled.

Monton and scriptwriter Avalon don't attempt to explain such attractions, but in the case of Leonie and Joe they make it totally believable. And this is even when Leonie chooses to live and have sex with a man whom she believes for some time to be a murderer of teenage girls.

This reticence by the film-makers to explain—why Joe is on the run from the police, what happened between him and his brother, even why Leonie is an American adrift in urban Australia—is, in fact, one of the film's strengths. It is rare in Australian cinema for a film to take on the aspects of an American-style thriller and yet avoid the banal explanation of the hows and whys.

This is not to say the structure of **Fatal Bond** is without problems. As scriptwriter, Avalon errs in not being strict enough about what perspective the film is taking. For much of the film, it reads like Joe's first-person narrative: he is clearly the protagonist (even his keeping proof of his innocence from the audience is acceptable within this style). But, in the middle of the film, Avalon abruptly abandons Joe (and Leonie) and concentrates

for a while on Anthony Boon (Stephen Leeder), a religious fanatic. Avalon also introduces Detective Chenko (Caz Lederman), whom he never properly develops.

The film is also undermined by some poor performances, particularly from the one- and two-liner actors. The major exception is Jerome Ehlers. His performance is easily one of the finest of the Australian semi-crim, existential loner. There is not a trace of sentimentality and the dark grey edge he gives everything is commanding. Ehlers shapes as one of the country's finest film actors.

SCOTT MURRAY[4]

---

[1] The end credits list the director as 'Vince Monton'.
[2] The end credits list the producer as 'Phil Avalon'.
[3] Presumably the film-makers mean 'Kevin Johnson (As Himself)'.
[4] Extracted from Murray's review in *Cinema Papers* (see Reference).

Reference
'Fatal Bond', a review by Scott Murray, *Cinema Papers*, no. 91, January 1993, pp. 45–6.

FERNGULLY: THE LAST RAINFOREST

FAI Films in association with Youngheart Productions. A Young and Faiman production. FERNGULLY: THE LAST RAINFOREST. © 1992 FAI Films Pty Ltd. A US–Australia Co-production. *Australian distributor:* Hoyts. *Video:* Fox. *Rating:* G. 35mm. 68 mins.

Producers: Wayne Young, Peter Faiman. *Co-producers:* Jim Cox, Brian Rosen, Richard Harper. *Executive producers:* Ted Field, Robert W. Cort. *Co-executive producers:* Jeff Dowd, William F. Willett. *Line producer:* Tom Klein. *Scriptwriter:* Jim Cox. Based on the stories of *FernGully* by Diana Young. *Editor:* Gillian Hutshing. *Music supervisors:* Tim Sexton, Becky Mancuso. *Composer:* Alan Silvestri.

Creative consultant: Matthew Perry. *Co-ordinating art director:* Susan Kroyer. *Animation production consultant:* Charles Leland Richardson. *Art directors:* Ralph Eggleston (colour stylist), Victoria Jenson (layout design). *Animation director:* Tony Fucile. *Special effects animation director:* Sari Gennis. *Sequence directors:* Bret Haaland, Tim Hauser, Dan Jeup, Susan Kroyer.

Voices

Tim Curry (Hexxus), Samantha Manthis (Crysta), Christian Slater (Pips), Jonathan Ward (Zak), Robin Williams (Batty Koda), Grace Zabriskie (Magi Lune), Geoffrey Blake (Ralph), Robert Pastorelli (Tony), Cheech Marin (Stump), Tommy Chong (Root), Tone-Loc (The Goanna).

Pips and Crysta.

Deep in the heart of the forest there is a place where humans exist only as characters in an almost forgotten fairy-tale. In this secret world, steeped in magic and adventure, lives a pubescent fairy named Crysta and her over-developed friend (and latent love interest), Pips; the rowdy Beetle Boys (definitely small 'h' hell's angels); Magi, the wise forest mother; and a bat named Batty Koda—as well as the rest of a wonderful and wacky crew. All is peaceful until the loggers move in, and then the fight for survival begins.

FernGully: The Last Rainforest, a feature-length animated musical fantasy, follows Crysta as she undergoes the sometimes painful transition from childhood to womanhood. It is this 'ripening', of becoming fertile, that empowers her to save FernGully.

This transition is also reflected in Zak, the human teenager, who really gets brought down to size (literally and figuratively). Zak goes from being a beach bum from Byron Bay to finally accepting responsibility and confronting himself and his destiny.

FernGully: The Last Rainforest subscribes fully to notions of 'mother' earth, and the intimate/expressive relation between women and nature. Ultimately natural wisdom and natural (magical) power lie with the feminine.

The association of the feminine with all things organic is brought into sharp relief when its antithesis arrives. The forest is invaded by 'The Leveler', a super-tech hybrid marriage of chainsaw, monster tractor and factory, which is a powerful symbol of the crushing capabilities of a mass culture which literally wants to 'level' everything in its sight.

The scene is thus set for the showdown with our forest friends, led by Crysta, whose femininity gives her the key in order to unlock the energy of life itself. Directed by Bill Kroyer, FernGully: The Last Rainforest is witty, fast-paced and packed with enough morals to keep parents happy for days.

The Australian input (apart from financial) comes not only via our spectacular rainforests but also through Wayne Young and Peter Faiman who produced the film (associate producer and director, respectively, of **Crocodile Dundee**, 1986) and Diana Young who wrote the *FernGully* stories in 1980.

The technical requirements for such a film are immense and the animators included experts in both hand-drawn and computer-enhanced animation. Computers were used for special effects, such as penetrating layers and layers of background.

The film pays extraordinary attention to detail. The colours and light infusing the forest are magnificent and characters move through the forest with a natural flow and grace that is entrancing.

The film features, among others, the voices of Samantha Manthis, Jonathan Ward, Christian Slater, Grace Zabriskie and Tim Curry. But Robin Williams manages to steal all the best laughs as the voice of the schizophrenic Batty Koda, a bat whose run-in with humans has left him just a little bewildered and maladjusted.

The upbeat nature of the whole enterprise is carried not only by the superb animation but also by the music. Songs feature prominently in the film and include performances by Sheena Easton, Tone Loc, Elton John and Johnny Clegg, with a musical score by Alan Silvestri.

JONATHAN ROPER[1]

---

[1] Extracted from Roper's review in *Cinema Papers* (see Reference).

Reference
'FernGully: The Last Rainforest', a review by Jonathan Roper, *Cinema Papers*, no. 91, January 1993, p. 47.

RON COBB

GARBO

An Eclectic Films Production. Garbo.[1] © 1990 Eclectic Films Pty Ltd [and] Australian Film Finance Corporation Pty Limited. Developed with the assistance of the Australian Film Commission, Australian Film Theatre Ltd and 'a tiny bit of assistance' from Film Victoria. Made with the participation of Australian Film Finance Corporation Pty. Limited as part of the 1990 FFC Film Fund. *Location:* Melbourne. *Australian distributor:* Hoyts. *Opened:* 21 May 1992. *Video:* Video Box Office. *Rating:* PG. 35mm. 100 mins.

Producer: Hugh Rule. *Associate producers:* Stephen Kearney, Neill Gladwin. *Line producer:* Margot McDonald. *Scriptwriter:* Patrick Cook, with Neill Gladwin and Stephen Kearney. Based on an original story by Hugh Rule, Stephen Kearney and Neill Gladwin. *Director of photography:* Geoff Burton. *Production designer:* Richard Bell. *Costume designer:* Rose Chong. *Editor:* Neil Thumpston. *Composer:* Allan Zavod. *Sound recordist:* John Phillips. *Sound supervisor:* Edward McQueen-Mason. *Sound editors:* Livia Ruzic (dia.); Ross A. Porter (fx). *Mixers:* Peter Fenton, Ron Purvis, Martin Oswin.

Cast

Stephen Kearney (Steve), Neill Gladwin (Neill), Max Cullen (Wal), Moya O'Sullivan (Freda), Imogen Annesley (Jane), Gerard Kennedy (Trevor), Tommy Dysart (Bagpipes), Max Fairchild (Big Feral), Rod Williams (The Pope), David Glazebrook (Fragile), Earl Francis (Control Tower Garbo), Ray Chubb (Garbo Foreman), Ron Bingham (Tubs), Ellen Cressey (New Driver), Cliff Ellen (Desk Sergeant), John Brumpton (Troy), Simon Chilvers (Detective—Jane's Dad), Bill Nagle (Mr Sanicleanse), Robin Cuming (Councillor), Michael Veitch (Town Clerk), Jane Clifton (Mayor).

There is nothing wrong with the 'stumbling dills' school of comedy. Neill Gladwin and Stephen Kearney have made an astonishingly successful career out of it as live-comedy duo Los Trios Ringbarkus for well over a decade. And given their stage success here and overseas, film seemed a natural progression. But it is hard to sustain a whole film where the tone of the humour is set by bumping into doors, walking through plate-glass windows, spilling drinks, falling down stairs, falling off piers and getting pissed.

The basic comedy situation set-up is this: Steve and Neill, and their Czech driver Wal (a poorly accented Max Cullen), do a garbage run that is in danger of being taken over by a much more efficient, hi-tech garbage contractor. They express their disapproval but don't actually do anything to fight it.

Neill and Steve go on holiday and leave Steve's mum at a caravan park as collateral while they return home to try and raise money to pay the bill. They confront the new garbage truck in their old one, have a chase, and eventually win the day when the Mayor (Jane Clifton) suddenly, and for no good reason, reverses her decision and decides to keep the garbos instead of taking on the new service.

Admittedly, one should not expect a high degree of sophistication in a film of this sort, but a bit of style, a touch of imagination, a skerrick of invention would have been nice. The verbal humour isn't up to much, either. There is a sparse smattering of good lines, but most are desperately unfunny, and do nothing to enhance some pretty poor attempts at visual humour. Even lines that one presumes are supposed to be one-liners fall flat.

The film is incredibly pretentious, which may be a ridiculous charge to level at a film as lame-brained as this, but something must be said when pseudo-radical Lefty clichés get bandied around. The film makes these Left-wing platitudes about the evils of big business and how technology encroaches on jobs for humans. A pretty right-thinking thing to think, you'd think. Yet the rôle of Jane (Imogen Annesley), Neill's love interest, is insultingly sexist. Jane is supposed to be an intellectual, yet she has absolutely no emotional range or depth. She is merely an attractive piece of scenery for Neill to do pratfalls around.

Director Ron Cobb missed the boat with this. A designer of enormous talent, an artist and cartoonist of great wit and perception, he has misfired in a major way. Surely someone with great visual flair should have at least made the film look interesting. The only contribution Cobb appears to have made is in the design of a garbage truck.

JIM SCHEMBRI

---

[1] There is no title in the conventional sense, merely a tilt up to the side of a truck which has 'Garbo' painted on it.

Reference

'Garbo', a review by Jim Schembri, *Cinema Papers*, no. 88, May–June 1992, pp. 60–1.

Jane (Imogen Annesley), Steve (Stephen Kearney) and Neill (Neill Gladwin).

THE GOOD WOMAN OF BANGKOK

O'Rourke & Associates Filmmakers in association with the Australian Film Commission and Channel 4. The Good Woman of Bangkok. © 1991 O'Rourke & Associates Filmmakers Pty Limited. *Location:* Bangkok (Thailand). *Australian distributor:* Ronin. Opened: 20 March 1992. *Video:* Curzon Gold (Home Cinema Group). *Rating:* M. 35mm (including blow-up from Video 8). 82 mins.

Producer: Dennis O'Rourke. *Associate producer:* Glenys Rowe. *Scriptwriter:* Dennis O'Rourke. *Director of photography:* Dennis O'Rourke. *Editor:* Tim Litchfield. *Sound recordist:* Dennis O'Rourke. *Sound editor:* Stella Savvas. *Mixer:* Gethin Creagh.

Cast

Yagwalak Chonchanakun [Aoi[1]].

The Good Woman of Bangkok is as revealing of its director, Dennis O'Rourke, as it is of its subject, Aoi (Yagwalak Chonchanakun). The film is a voyeuristic, contrived and subjective look at the life of a 25-year-old Thai prostitute in Bangkok's red-light district. It is bleak, shocking and, at times, tragic; most of all, it is a fascinating exercise in storytelling.

Although it is never actually stated or shown, it becomes clear that Aoi/ Chonchanakun is the centre-piece of O'Rourke's camera, as well as being his sexual compulsion. In making a 'factional' film about the woman he has paid for sex, the director has redefined the boundaries of the interviewer–interviewee relationship.

As he works his way through the emotional entanglement of his own relationship, O'Rourke takes more than just an arbitrary look at prostitution. Beneath his carefully measured narrative, the viewer can sense the intensity of a director beset by his own sexual illusions and guilt. It is this conflict—and O'Rourke's ability to harness it—that gives The Good Woman of Bangkok an energy found in few documentaries.

Some may find the premise of the film offensive, morally and ethically. O'Rourke is, after all, one of many seeking pleasure in a city where girls and young women are enslaved to prostitution by force, if not necessity. What's more, at the end he offers to buy Aoi a rice farm on the condition that she no longer sells her body. Is a film for a rice farm a fair deal?

To his credit, O'Rourke never tries to disguise his *modus operandi*. He sought a prostitute and found one; he watches tourists seek their prey at street-side bars; he films bizarre sex shows; and he lets the Video 8 camera roll on relentlessly in the hotel room as his subject bares her tattered soul in front of a mirror. He is both witness and accessory to the fact.

In title and accent, the film draws a parallel with Brecht's *The Good Person of Szechwan*, a play O'Rourke describes as 'an ironic parable about the impossibility of being good in an evil world'. Aoi, O'Rourke's good woman, is exposed for all her pathos, lost hope, wisdom and self-loathing. 'I have to close my eyes to force myself to do it for money', she says in one scene.

For a good part of the film, Aoi—who talks mostly in Thai, sometimes in broken English—is obviously spaced out from drugs or sheer exhaustion or both. There is nothing discreet about O'Rourke's style of interviewing her, nor his method of filming. At one point his camera pans over Aoi—her behind scantily clad by a towel—as she tries to sleep; she is also shown readjusting her glass eye.

The Good Woman of Bangkok was filmed over nine months, using the Rose Hotel as a base. Just how O'Rourke managed to put together the picture is a credit to his street nous and his ability to win the co-operation of his subjects. It seems odd, though, that for all of the project's candid honesty, it does not actually show Aoi, its centre-piece, working.

GREG KERR[2]

_____

[1] This character name is not given in the end credits but is given many times during the film in sub- and inter-titles.
[2] Extracted from Kerr's review in *Cinema Papers* (see References).

_____

References

'Dennis O'Rourke and The Good Woman of Bangkok', an interview with the film-maker by Andrew L. Urban, *Cinema Papers*, no. 84, August 1991, pp. 4–13.
'The Good Woman of Bangkok', a review by Greg Kerr, *Cinema Papers*, no. 86, January 1992, pp. 52–3.

Aoi (Yagwalak Chonchanakun).

ISABELLE EBERHARDT

Les Films Aramis[,] Seon Films [and] Flach Films present ISABELLE EBERHARDT. © 1991. A France–Australia Co-production. *Locations:* Algiers; Paris; Geneva. *Australian distributor:* Palace. *Video:* not released as yet. *Rating:* M. 35mm. 113 mins.

Producers: Jean Petit, Daniel Scharf. *Executive producer:* Jacques LeClere[1]. *Co-producers:* Jean-François LePetit, Isabelle Fauvel. *Scriptwriter:* Stephen Sewell. *Director of photography:* Manuel Teran. *Production designers:* Bryce Perrin, Geoffroy Larcher. *Costume designer:* Mic Cheminal. *Editor:* Ken Sallows. *Composer:* Paul Schutze. *Sound design:* Dean Gawen. *Sound recordist:* Bernard Aubouy. [*Sound editor:* not known. *Mixer:* not known.]

Cast

Mathilda May (Isabelle Eberhardt), Tcheky Karyo (Slimen), Peter O'Toole (Major Lyautey), Richard Moir (Conte), Arthur Dignam (Cauvet), Ben Smail (Hussein); Fouid Massah; Nabil Massad (Brahim), Wolfgang Harnisch (Trophimowsky); Rene Schoenend, David Pledger; Clement Mar [?]; Françoise [?]; Olivier Plindt; Claude Villers (Barracund).[2]

Isabelle Eberhardt (Mathilda May).

Major Lyautey (Peter O'Toole).

There have been many films about adventurers who journeyed to strange lands in search of diversion or forgetfulness, panacea or that peace which is oblivion. Isabelle Eberhardt was such a seeker, travelling to Algeria in search of one or two things which have become no less elusive over the past 92 or so years.

The film is set at the turn of the century when France was in the process of extending its dominion in North Africa. Isabelle (Mathilda May) leaves Paris and Geneva in search of a mysterious marquis, though she soon convinces herself that he has perished in the desert. She finds herself involved in the turmoil of Algiers, supporting—alternately, at times; simultaneously, at others—the Arabs and the French in their internecine conflict. She also writes short fiction, falls in love and finds time to search for the 'peace' of her 'soul', though what that might mean while she is alive is not at all clear.

Unfortunately, the search for the marquis is forgotten—not surprising, given the number of distractions here—and we do not learn whether that peace which she had valued so highly was ever attained or even attainable.

Ian Pringle, it would seem, planned to make a film about everything, or just about

everything, under the sun of Algiers (not to mention the shadows of Geneva and Paris). The thematic concerns encompass the search for identity and the creative constitution of the self; the nature and the rôle of the writer in a tumultuous world where values are compromised or surrendered; the issue of complicity in dishonourable political and military processes and in the brutality of colonisation; the paradox of tribal conflict among the indigenous people; the need for love and companionship; and the desire for oblivion under a sky which seems to be indifferent to the fate of such restless and tormented wanderers.

In this hodgepodge of a film, many strands are either abandoned, obscured or forgotten. The film lurches from one city to another, one sub-plot to another, while the really interesting material is submerged for significant periods.

Not all fails, though. The cinematography and art direction are often striking. The transitions from the darkness and shadows of Geneva (and rain), where Isabelle's father dies, and Paris to the brilliant, piercing light of Algiers, though familiar, do provide a dramatic analogy in relation to Isabelle's own journey through this world. The desert, and the structures that men erect against its

harshness, its alien aspects and inexorable winds, are highlighted in a number of memorable scenes. And a rather tired-looking Peter O'Toole, professional that he is, does what he can with dialogue that is too often stilted and banal.

It seems ironic, however, that the film should so undercut the figure who most represents the creative individual. Somewhere in this meandering film there is a fascinating story about a fascinating person that deserves to be told in more coherent and cogent terms.

RAYMOND YOUNIS[3]

---

1 As some credits are in capitals with no guide as how to reproduce then in upper-and-lower case, the spellings here of LeClere and LePetit are but guesses.
2 The credits were almost unreadable on the copy viewed, and the press material has many gaps.
3 Extracted from Younis' review in *Cinema Papers* (see References).

References

'Ian Pringle: In for the Long Haul', an interview with the director by Scott Murray, *Cinema Papers*, no. 81, December 1990, pp. 6–13.
'Isabelle Eberhardt', a review by Raymond Younis, *Cinema Papers*, no. 91, January 1993, pp. 50–1.

THE LAST DAYS OF CHEZ NOUS

Jan Chapman Productions presents the last days of chez nous. © 1991 Jan Chapman Productions Pty Limited and Australian Film Finance Corporation Pty Limited. *Location:* Sydney. Developed with the assistance of the Australian Film Commission and the Australian Broadcasting Corporation. Made with the participation of Australian Film Finance Corporation Pty Limited as part of the 1990 FFC Film Fund. *Australian distributor:* Hoyts. *Video:* not released as of July 1993. *Rating:* PG. 35mm. 93 mins.

Producer: Jan Chapman. *Associate producer:* Mark Turnbull. *Scriptwriter:* Helen Garner. *Director of photography:* Geoffrey Simpson. *Production designer:* Janet Patterson. *Costume designer:* Janet Patterson. *Editor:* Nicholas Beauman. *Composer:* Paul Grabowsky. *Sound recordist:* Ben Osmo. *Supervising sound editor:* Karin Whittington. *Sound editors:* Tim Jordan (dia.); Rick Lisle, John Penders, David Grusovin (asst). *Mixer:* Gethin Creagh.

Cast

Lisa Harrow (Beth), Bruno Ganz (JP), Kerry Fox (Vicki), Miranda Otto (Annie), Kiri Paramore (Tim), Bill Hunter (Beth's Father), Lex Marinos (Angelo), Mickey Camilleri (Sally), Lynne Murphy (Beth's Mother), Claire Haywood (Janet), Leanne Bundy (Susie), Wilson Alcorn (Cafe Dero), Tom Weaver (Thief), Bill Brady (Mayor), Eva di Cesare (Waitress), Danny Caretti (Waiter), Olga Sanderson (Singing Woman), Joyce Hopwood (Clinic Nurse), Steve Cox (Stranger), Harry Griffiths (Old Man Desert Tourist), Amanda Martin (Desert Waitress).

The Last Days of Chez Nous has a nuggety quality: a small, compact film which uncovers a motherload of sweet-and-sour nerve endings involving a rather quirky group of characters. Like most of Gillian Armstrong's films, narrative coherence tends to play second fiddle to the emotional incongruities of the central character. But with The Last Days of Chez Nous, although there is a strong sense that the film is driven along by the reminiscences of one character in particular, the dramatic and emotional patterns are dispersed and shaped by an ensemble of characters. If nothing else, the central focus of the film resides with how interpersonal relationships develop and change, and get chiselled out of a peculiar environment or setting.

In this case, the setting is an inner-city, part-family, part-share dwelling in which

Vicki (Kerry Fox), JP (Bruno Ganz) and Beth (Lisa Harrow).

Beth (Lisa Harrow), a writer of good repute, lives with her daughter, Annie (Miranda Otto), and her French lover, JP (Bruno Ganz). The household crew also includes a young lodger by the name of Tim (Kiri Paramore), and is only complete when Beth's younger sister, Vicki (Kerry Fox), returns home from a prolonged overseas trip.

There are a number of interesting things to be said about the spatial aspects of the house, and how characters are seen within the space(s). For one thing, characters are rarely seen on their own in any one part of the house; they are always with someone else. One major exception is in the film's opening when Vicki arrives to an empty house with the heart-shaped cake as her only welcome. After she takes a slice of the cake, she eventually makes her way to her bedroom, where she then pulls a photograph of a young man off the wall and rips it to pieces. It is only at this point that others burst onto the scene in a flurry of greetings. The quiet emptiness of the house is suddenly filled with gaiety, and so too is the emptiness of Vicki's heart.

There is a series of interchangeable associations which tend to slowly make their way to the surface of the film. For example, Vicki's return home is a result of a failed relationship while travelling overseas; Beth travels to the outback with her father (Bill Hunter) to resolve a long-existing emotional feud between them. But then, while Beth's relationship with her father improves, that

with JP is breaking down; and as Beth is travelling with her father, Vicki and JP become intensely involved with one another. In this respect, the characters can hardly ever be clear or sure of the paths they take or rôles they play.

Armstrong has succeeded in shaping for The Last Days of Chez Nous an odd, complicated balance of symmetrical and asymmetrical actions and events in order to juice the emotional grey areas without cheapening the dramatic situations.

RAFFAELE CAPUTO[1]

---

[1] Based on Caputo's review in *Cinema Papers* (see References).

References

'The Last Days of Chez Nous', a production report by Andrew L. Urban, *Cinema Papers*, no. 83, May 1991, pp. 18–22.

'Australian Films at Cannes', an overview by Jan Epstein with discussion on **The Last Days of Chez Nous**, *Cinema Papers*, no. 89, August 1992, pp. 22–5.

'The Last Days of Chez Nous: Gillian Armstrong', an interview with the director by Raffaele Caputo, *Cinema Papers*, no. 90. October 1992, pp. 4–8.

'The Last Days of Chez Nous', a review by Raffaele Caputo, ibid., pp. 52–3.

' "I like bold contemporary films…with an edge" ', an interview with director Gillian Armstrong by Mary Colbert, *Filmnews*, October 1992, pp. 11–12.

'The Last Days of Chez Nous', a review by Marg O'Shea, *Filmnews*, ibid., p. 16.

OVER THE HILL

Village Roadshow Pictures Limited in association with Rank Film Distributors Limited presents a Glasshouse Pictures Production. Over The Hill. © 1991 Australian Film Finance Corporation Pty Limited[,] Village Roadshow Pictures (Australia) Pty Limited [and] Over The Hill Pty Limited. Developed with the financial assistance of the Australian Film Commission. Made with the assistance of the Queensland Film Development Office. Made with the participation of Australian Film Finance Corporation Pty Limited. *Locations:* Glasshouse Mountains, Rainbow Beach; Gold Coast (Queensland); Alice Springs; Sydney; Bar Harbour, Maine (US). *Australian distributor:* Village Roadshow. Opened: 30 June 1992. *Video:* Applause (Roadshow Home Video). *Rating:* PG. 35mm. Panavision. 99 mins.

Producers: Robert Caswell, Bernard Terry. *Executive producers:* Greg Coote, Graham Burke. *Associate producer:* Liz Stroud. *Line producer:* Ross Matthews. *Scriptwriter:* Robert Caswell. Based on the book *Alone in the Australian Outback* by Gladys Taylor. *Director of photography:* David Connell. *Camera operator:* David Williamson. *Production designer:* Graham "Grace" Walker. *Costume designer:* Terry Ryan. *Editor:* Henry Dangar. *Composer:* David McHugh. *Sound recordist:* Gary Wilkins. *Sound editors:* Jeanine Chialvo (dia.); Penn Robinson (fx). *Mixers:* Phil Heywood, Martin Oswin.

Cast

Olympia Dukakis (Alma), Sigrid Thornton (Elizabeth), Derek Fowlds (Dutch), Bill Kerr (Maurie), Steve Bisley (Benedict), Martin Jacobs (Forbes), Gerry Connolly (Hank), Andrea Moor (Jan), Pippa Grandison (Margaret), Aden Young (Nick), Justine Anderson (Cashier), Gabriella Candida (First Receptionist), Rebecca Caswell (Waitress), Krystyna Dzierzanowski (Second Receptionist), Craig Elliott (First Hoon), Joy Irvine (Country Woman), Scott Johnson (Service Station Attendant), Anne Looby (Reporter), Tony Lynch (Third Hoon), Michael Ostapovitch (Second Hoon), Doug Scroope (Garageman).

'Over the hill': literally too old, seen better days, on the decline or downward bound (with not much hope of ascending again), nearer that threshold where the mind's vitality, the body's conflagrations, weaken and ebb; also, that time when, according to Gabriel Garcia Marquez, a person wanders or is supposed to wander around the dusty rooms with heavy, slippered feet, murmuring something about the way things were and having to put up with relatives who don't seem to listen or care, until the moment of death when everyone becomes attentive.

Over the Hill is an affirmation which is intended to refute the notion that ageing necessarily presupposes the decline of one's passions, desire for adventure and need for genuine companionship.

The plot is fairly simple: Alma (Olympia Dukakis) is encouraged to move, by her son, into a place with 'everything she needs'. Apparently, this is also what 'father' wanted. Alma will not have 'taxes' to pay. She moves.

Upon opening a window for the first time, all she can see is a brick wall in front of her. She is given a surprise birthday cake (she is sixty), but she goes to the front door and tosses it out into the snow. We cut to a plane which takes Alma to Australia. She is met there by her daughter, Elizabeth (Sigrid Thornton), who lives with a rather calculating, heartless man, who happens to be a politician. Alma hopes that the reunion will be successful.

Unfortunately, the film suggests Elizabeth is more concerned with her media image. She, it is clear, is preoccupied with appearances, with kowtowing to the cameras that seem to be perpetually at the entrance of her house. Alma is a burden and an unnecessary one at that. So Elizabeth and her husband decide to 'get rid' of her. Alma overhears (a significant point given that this is a political family), buys a supercharged Chevy and roars off into the bush.

The film does not only reveal the rather shallow and hypocritical life of the daughter and her enslavement. Alma, too, it is suggested, was once a pawn, but of another kind. Her struggle for independence complements the daughter's gradual process of enlightenment. Each will be the catalyst for the other.

Indeed, there is much to admire in the film, despite obvious flaws. One of the central characters, Dutch (Derek Fowlds), is another on an odyssey, and the two leading parts are played sympathetically and convincingly. Catalysts abound and processes of individuation reign (in mostly harsh and unforgiving conditions). The calm of the Pitjantjatjara people provides a still point of this turning world—they become monumental presences, figures of endurance and sincerity in a world of compromises and treachery.

Other elements are clearly derivative, some of the secondary characters are too shadowy and the resolution is somewhat predictable, but the central argument is put with some subtlety, and with a quiet insistence and sophistication.

RAYMOND YOUNIS[1]

---

[1] Extracted from Younis' review in *Cinema Papers* (see Reference).

Reference
'Over the Hill', a review by Raymond Younis, *Cinema Papers*, no. 89, August 1992, pp. 54–5.

Alma (Olympia Dukakis), Dutch (Derek Fowlds) and Maurie (Bill Kerr).

ROMPER STOMPER

Seon Films in association with the Australian Film Commission and Film Victoria. ROMPER STOMPER. © 1992 Romper Stomper Pty Ltd. Produced in association with the Australian Film Commission and Film Victoria. *Location:* Melbourne. *Australian distributor:* Roadshow. *Rating:* R. *Video:* Premiere. 35mm. 94 mins.

Producers: Daniel Scharf, Ian Pringle. *Associate producer:* Phil Jones. *Scriptwriter:* Geoffrey Wright. *Director of photography:* Ron Hagen. *Production designer:* Steven Jones-Evans. *Costume designer:* Anna Borghesi. *Editor:* Bill Murphy. *Composer:* John Clifford White. *Sound recordist:* David Lee. *Sound design:* Frank Lipson. *Sound editors:* Peter Burgess (ADR). *Mixers:* Steve Burgess, Roger Savage; Peter Palankay (music).

Cast

Russell Crowe (Hando), Daniel Pollock (Davey), Jacqueline McKenzie (Gabe), Alex Scott (Martin), Leigh Russell (Sonny Jim), Daniel Wylie (Cockles), James McKenna (Bubs), Samantha Bladon (Tracy), Josephine Keen (Megan), John Brumpton (Magoo), Eric Mueck (Champ), Frank Magree (Brett), Christopher McLean (Luke), Don Bridges (Harold), Jane Anderson (Jacqui), Stephen Hall (Fleo), Tony Lee (Tiger), Tri Phan (Nguyen), Thuan Le (Nguyen's Eldest Son), Minh Lu (Middle Son), Thach Le (Youngest Son), Yvonne Lawrence (Davey's Grandmother), Edwina Exton (Skinhead Girl), Angus Cummings (Roo), Craig Mercer (Chris).

Geoffrey Wright's **Romper Stomper** features a gang of neo-nazi hoodlums who, reviled by police, become social outcasts, spending most of their time vandalising, drinking, rooting and 'hanging out'. Wright likens the skinhead gang to a surrogate family with Hando (Russell Crowe) as its leader and 'father' figure; Davey (Daniel Pollock), his closest mate, alternating as 'brother' and 'son'; and a collection of motley blow-ins who hero worship Hando, like Peter Pan's boys.

Hando commands respect and instils a sense of purpose into the group. The skinheads' bonding ritual involves boozing, banging their women and affectionately brawling among themselves. Their comfort zone is fractured with the arrival of Gabe (Jacqueline McKenzie), who becomes Hando's lover. Unlike other skinhead molls, who are portrayed in the film as dumb and submissive, Gabe bunks the order by undermining Hando's power base.

At first she adopts a childlike demeanour, wooing him with her girlishness. But as their relationship develops, she takes on a motherly rôle, exampled in the scene where, after breaking into a warehouse, Gabe cooks for the gang, much to the disgust of Hando, who rejects her attempts at establishing a 'homely' environment by trashing her cooking. Unlike the other molls who simply flee when things start to turn nasty, Gabe enacts revenge when Hando finally dumps her by attacking him on peer and personal levels: snitching on the gang's whereabouts to the police and by seducing Davey, his ally.

In the dénouement of the film, Hando confronts Davey with a dilemma: loyalty to his male buddy, whom he has known through thick and thin, or loyalty to Gabe, whom he loves dearly. Hando cajoles; it is a case of better the devil you know than the devil you don't, entreating Davey, 'We're all we've got left, Davey.'

Like the skinheads, Gabe is also a social outcast, caught between fobbing off and being attracted to her father's incestuous advances, desiring love and acceptance, and yet overcome by suspicion and hatred.

Through anecdote, Wright evokes sympathy for the skinheads' plight: in most scenes, they appear like a bunch of aimless larrikins clinging to a cause. This neo-nazi thread, mostly visual, is never deeply explored. Wright uses it as a symbol of loyalty, supremacy and collectivism.

Rock-video-style editing, featuring 'wobblecam' and jump cuts, tends to distract the viewer from some of the film's more intense scenes, particularly during the film's set piece which involves a fight between the skinheads and the Vietnamese. Interestingly, the film's ugliest moments do not revolve around the skinheads but are set in Gabe's father's swanky house, a tribute to the excesses of success.

Romper Stomper is like peering through an eyeglass at some of the dross in society, ironically summed up by one skinhead comment: 'We came to wreck everything and ruin your life. God sent us.'

PAT GILLESPIE[1]

---

[1] Extracted from Gillespie's review in *Cinema Papers* (see References).

References

'Geoffrey Wright's **Romper Stomper**', a production report by Eva Friedman, *Cinema Papers*, no. 86, January 1992, pp. 6–11.

'Australian Films at Cannes', an overview by Jan Epstein with discussion on **Romper Stomper**, *Cinema Papers*, no. 89, August 1992, pp. 22–5.

'**Romper Stomper**', a review by Pat Gillespie, *Cinema Papers*, no. 91, January 1993, pp. 51–2.

'Stomping: Peter Galvin talks to Geoffrey Wright', an interview with the writer-director, *Filmnews*, November 1992, pp. 15–6.

'**Romper Stomper**', a review by Peter Galvin, *Filmnews*, ibid, p. 16.

'Violence and Redemption in **Romper Stomper**, **Autobus** and **Light Sleeper**', Bill Mousoulis, *Filmnews*, December 1992–January 1993, pp.2, 18.

Hando (Russell Crowe) and Gabe (Jacqueline McKenzie).

SECRETS

[Credits not checked[1].] A Beyond Films presentation of a Victorian International Pictures [Australia] and Avalon-NFU Studios [New Zealand] Co-production, with the participation of the Australian Film Finance Corporation and Film Victoria. SECRETS. © 1992. *Australian distributor:* Roadshow. *Video:* not released as of July 1993. *Rating:* M. 35mm. 91 mins.

Producer: Michael Pattinson. *Line producer:* Lynda House. *Executive producers:* David Arnell, Michael Caulfield, William T. Marshall. *Scriptwriter:* Jan Sardi. *Director of photography:* David Connell. *Production designer:* Kevin Leonard-Jones. *Costume designer:* Paul Sayers. *Editor:* Peter Carrodus. *Music:* Dave Dobbyn. *Sound recordist:* Ken Saville.

Cast

Beth Champion (Emily), Malcolm Kennard (Danny), Dannii Minogue (Didi), Willa O'Neill (Vicki), Noah Taylor (Randolf), Eddie Campbell (Emily's Father), Joan Watson (Randolf's Mother), Joan Reid (Sister Annuzia), Peter Vere-Jones (Jock).

Vicki (Willa O'Neill) and Randolf (Noah Taylor).

Secrets is set on the day The Beatles arrived in Melbourne in 1964. Five young characters are introduced through brief snatches of their respective lives as they individually react in different ways to the impending arrival of the Fab Four. One character, Danny (Malcolm Kennard), a die-hard Elvis fan, is seen hurling an egg at a billboard advertising the band's Australian tour. Another, Vicki (Willa O'Neill), a hairdresser's assistant, screams into a telephone at having won a ticket to the concert. The film intercuts these brief snatches with original archival footage and restaged scenes which place the characters strategically within the crowd gathered outside the Southern Cross Hotel.

After a confusing, riotous scuffle between police and the swelling crowd of fans, the five youths find themselves locked in the hotel's claustrophobic basement. The kids are all strangers to each other, and the basement—dark, sparse and closed-off—figures as a metaphor of discovery and interiority.

For **Secrets**, scriptwriter Jan Sardi and director Michael Pattinson, who together are old hands at the teen movie (**Moving Out**, 1983, and **Street Hero**, 1984), unashamedly borrow and attempt to cross-fertilise from two very specific American teen movies: the fast-paced, late-night favourite **I Wanna Hold Your Hand** (Robert Zemeckis, 1978) and John Hughes' peer-group soul-searcher, **The Breakfast Club** (1985). The former is an obsessional, hit-and-run farce about six New

Jersey teenagers attempting to crash the Ed Sullivan Show on the evening The Beatles are scheduled to appear. The latter, which concerns a group of teenagers detained at school for one whole day of the weekend, is a fine-line portrait of slightly varying social strata and nuances of personality that at a sensitive age are experienced as irreconcilable differences. Yet, through their experience on this day, they form a common bond.

But **Secrets** is neither. It is stuck in between, immobile. After the initial, expert economy in editing which links the characters to each other and to the frenetic excitement of a teen phenomenon, the film settles into a hardened, step-by-step, stripping away of an outward image. What The Beatles represents for each character is a catalyst for looking inward, particularly when and where it concerns sexual mores.

Danny, the anti-Beatles, is clearly set up as the symbolic 'other', who is both the one to challenge the others, and the one to be challenged. Yet, by evoking such an easy scapegoat, so to speak, the process of revealing oneself is a rudimentary switch of face values. Emily (Beth Champion), the innocent country girl, is rather more brazen than

the audience is first led to believe; Didi (Dannii Minogue), who looks the part of a spiderwoman, is actually a fourteen-year-old Catholic schoolgirl; Randolf (Noah Taylor), a wordly sophisticate who sports a Liverpool accent, is an inexperienced local boy; Vicki, who feigns virginity, is pregnant without knowing the father; and the older and confident Danny reveals an insecurity about himself which his staunch Elvis-against-Beatles stand covers over.

Secrets would have been a dramatically stronger and more sensitive film if the interplay between characters was less two-dimensional, and rather fixed its energy on the obsessional urges and drives of teenagers, the shades of sexual tensions and cultural prejudices which go to make up the nuances of personality.

RAFFAELE CAPUTO

---

[1] No video copy of the film was available for viewing.

Reference

'Secrets', a review by Mary O'Shea, *Filmnews*, December 1992–January 1993, p. 16.

MARK JOFFE

SPOTSWOOD

Meridian Films in association with Smiley Films present[s] Spotswood. *Alternative title:* The Efficiency Expert (US). © 1991 Australian Film Finance Corporation Pty Ltd and Meridian Films Pty Ltd. Developed with the assistance of the Australian Film Commission and Film Victoria. Made with the participation of Australian Film Finance Corporation Pty Limited as part of the 1990 FFC Film Fund. *Location:* Melbourne. *Australian distributor:* Hoyts. Opened: 22 January 1992. *Video:* Columbia-TriStar. *Rating:* PG. 35mm. 90 mins.

Producers: Richard Brennan, Timothy White. *Scriptwriters:* Max Dann, Andrew Knight. *Director of photography:* Ellery Ryan. *Camera operator:* Clive Duncan. *Production designer:* Chris Kennedy. *Costume designer:* Tess Schofield. *Editor:* Nicholas Beauman. *Composer:* Ricky Fataar. *Sound recordists:* Lloyd Carrick (location); Angus Robertson (post-sync dia.). *Supervising sound editor:* Karin Whittington. *Sound editors:* Gary O'Grady; Nick Breslin (post-sync dia.) *Mixer:* Gethin Creagh.

Cast

Anthony Hopkins (Wallace), Ben Mendelsohn (Carey), Alwyn Kurts (Mr Ball), Bruno Lawrence (Robert), John Walton (Finn), Rebecca Rigg (Cheryl), Toni Collette (Wendy), Russell Crowe (Kim), Angela Punch McGregor (Caroline), Daniel Wylie (Fletcher), John Flaus (Gordon), Gary Adams (Kevin), Jeff Truman (Ron), Toni Lamond (Mrs Ball), Jillian Murray (Ophelia), Jacob Kind (Marvin), Rosie Sturgess (Edna), Nathan Croft (Win), Leslie Baker (Gwen), Mickey Camilleri (Elsie), Amy Roberts (Ivy), Esme Melville (Rose).

Spotswood is set in the late 1960s, in the Melbourne industrial suburb of the same name, and centres on the life of a small moccasin factory, Ball's. The patriarch, Mr Ball (Alwyn Kurts), decides to call in Wallace (Anthony Hopkins), a 'time and motion' man, in a bid to modernise the factory. Wallace soon discovers that the business is running at a massive loss; the only possibility of turning the company around rests in reducing the workforce and increasing the productivity of the remaining staff.

Wallace—who prefers to be known as a productivity enhancement consultant—wishes to remain anonymous, but is soon introduced to all the staff. He enlists a young employee of the factory, Carey (Ben Mendelsohn), as an assistant, believing the young man will be eager to take the leap into management. But Carey is reluctant, and is only won over to the proposition when he realises he will be sharing a desk with the boss' youngest daughter, Cheryl (Rebecca Rigg), who is temporarily working at the factory as a secretary 'before she leaves to take up a career as a full-time model'.

Intercut with Wallace's trips to Ball's are scenes of his less-than-harmonious home life with wife Caroline (Angela Punch McGregor), and visits to Durmack's, a company where his consultation has resulted in the recommended shedding of 480 positions. The contrasts between the old management style of Ball's and the new management approach advocated by Wallace and his partner are what structure the film.

The film very nearly eschews the values of capitalism entirely, replacing them with a traditional working-class sense of community. The Social Club, with its climactic (and hilarious) slot-car race, provides an external focal point for this sentiment. The factory itself, and the staff canteen in particular, are equally important as sites of community.

It is significant that Wallace's conversion to a more ethical, compassionate view of management practices follows from his inability to maintain anonymity. He is drawn into the social as well as the economic life of Ball's, and the clear-cut distinction between the two which has been crucial to his handling of the dispute at Durmack's breaks down.

What the film finally offers is a catharsis, in which all the worst nightmares of the workers of Australia are exorcised. Unemployment is beaten by a more sympathetic approach by management, which finally recommends the formation of a co-operative venture, with workers as owners. The despised yuppie is cast out of the workers' paradise and into the hell of industrial confrontation. And the illusory lustre of the outside world is replaced by an even stronger sense of camaraderie and belonging. The possibility that this somewhat utopian vision is intended as a picture of innocence and opportunity lost, and not as a vision of how we might still be, is cast into doubt by the fact that, in that final shot, there is a third (and, according to Joffe, quite deliberate) figure—the West Gate Bridge, which was not opened until 1978.

KARL QUINN[1]

---

[1] Based on Quinn's review in *Cinema Papers* (see References).

References
'The Making of **Spotswood**', a production report by Andrew L. Urban, *Cinema Papers*, no. 83, May 1991, pp. 4–7.
'Anthony Hopkins', an interview with the actor by Andrew L. Urban, ibid., pp. 8–10.
'**Spotswood**', a review by Karl Quinn, *Cinema Papers*, no. 87, March–April 1992, pp. 65–6.
'The Making of **Spotswood**', an interview with joint producer Richard Brennan by Tina Kaufman, *Filmnews*, December 1991, pp. 11–12.
'**Spotswood**', a review by Peter Galvin, *Filmnews*, ibid., p. 16.

Carey (Ben Mendelsohn).

STAN AND GEORGE'S NEW LIFE

Margot McDonald and Brian McKenzie present in association with the Australian Film Commission STAN and GEORGE'S NEW LIFE. © 1990 Lea Films Pty Ltd. *Budget:* $1.2 million. *Locations:* Melbourne, Manangatang (Victoria); Ceduna (South Australia). *Australian distributor:* AFI/Fineline. *Video:* not released as of July 1993. *Rating:* PG. 35mm. 104 mins.

Producer: Margot McDonald. *Scriptwriters:* Brian McKenzie, Deborah Fox. *Director of photography:* Ray Argall. *Production designer:* Daryl Mills. *Costume designer:* Rose Chong. *Editor:* Edward McQueen-Mason. *Composer:* Michael Atkinson. *Sound recordist:* Lloyd Carrick. *Sound editors:* Livia Ruzic (dia.); Edward McQueen-Mason (fx). *Mixers:* Roger Savage, Steve Burgess.

Cast

Paul Chubb (Stanley Harris), John Bluthal (Stan Senior), Julie Forsyth (George), Margaret Ford (Sheila Harris), Roy Baldwin (Thomas Stearns), Bruce Alexander (Geoffrey), Beverly Gardiner (Receptionist), Shapoor Batliwalla (Grey Unit #1), Burt Cooper (Grey Unit #2), Kenneth MacLeod (Grey Unit #3), Dalibor Satalic (Horrie), Tibor Gyapjas (Wayne), Janne Coughlin (Tea Lady), John Murphy (Maintenance Man), Iris Shand (Roma), Jack Perry (Gordon), Robert Menzies (Gerald), Denzil Howson (Ces), George Zogopoupos (Drifter), Walter McKenzie (Stan & George's Son), Brian McLean (Young Boy), John Forsythe (Father).

B rian McKenzie is uncompromisingly on the side of underdogs and battlers. His **Stan and George's New Life** is a warm and joyful comedy which succeeds because the characters, without contrivance or sentimentality, and against all the odds, win a place for themselves in a world which scarcely acknowledges their existence.

Stanley Harris (Paul Chubb), a 40-year-old man living with his parents and working in his father's barber shop, desperately wishes to lead a life of his own. The opportunity comes when his eccentric father, Stan Senior (John Bluthal), an amateur meteorologist who makes his prognostications each day from his bed, shows his son an advertisement for a job as a clerk at the Weather Bureau.

At the Bureau, Stan is befriended by George (Julie Forsyth), a kind country girl who is intent on making a new life for herself in the city. At first, Stan is all at sea in his new job, but with George's help he soon adjusts, and even achieves modest success reading the weather reports for a radio station.

At the same time as their relationship develops, and they marry, the atmosphere in the office deteriorates. Bureaucrats in dark suits make mysterious visits to the office for unclear reasons, and discrepancies begin to appear in the reports received by George from weather stations which were previously reliable. Stan only has to look out of the window to know that the forecasts are wrong.

When George is fired one day for bringing these discrepancies to the attention of their increasingly harassed and distracted boss, Thomas Stearns (Roy Baldwin), the climate at home plummets. More people lose their jobs, and, as Stan begins to fear the loss of his too, he becomes more and more resentful of George's suspicions of a conspiracy.

McKenzie dwells lovingly and at length on his characters, delineating their peculiarities and their ordinariness with great attention to detail. He is helped by striking performances from his actors, particularly Chubb as the socially gauche Stan, and Forsyth (in her first film rôle) as the intelligent, more self-assured George. Their acting is subtle and touching.

McKenzie reserves his broadest strokes for Stan's bizarre parents: his ill-natured, pyjama-clad father locked into his obsession, the weather, and his batty, hymn-singing mother, Sheila Harris (Margaret Ford). Both Bluthal and Ford reinforce the film's off-beat appeal with fine support performances.

Nonetheless, McKenzie is careful not to let the film slip into farce. What he presents to his audience is sympathetic dark comedy which is rooted in reality, and quite distinct from the cruel irony and satire of the Barry Humphries' kind.

When McKenzie drifts from a study of character to a drama about ideas he half-switches genre and his touch is less sure. The narrative becomes episodic, the plot confused and a contrived coincidence serves little purpose other than to highlight its own artificiality. Fortunately, this lapse remains overshadowed by the success of the human drama.

JAN EPSTEIN[1]

---

[1] Extracted from Epstein's review in *Cinema Papers* (see References).

References

'Stan and George's New Life', a review by Jan Epstein, *Cinema Papers*, no. 90. October 1992, p. 55.

'Stan and George's New Life', a review by Barrett Hodsdon, *Filmnews*, August 1992, p. 13.

George (Julie Forsyth) and Stanley Harris (Paul Chubb).

STRICTLY BALLROOM

An M&A production. Strictly Ballroom. © 1992 M&A Film Corporation and Australian Film Finance Corporation. Developed with the assistance of New South Wales Film & Television Office. Made with the participation of Australian Film Finance Corporation. *Location:* Sydney. *Australian distributor:* Ronin. *Video:* Columbia Tristar. *Rating:* PG. 35mm. 94 mins.

   Producer: Tristram Miall. *Executive producer:* Antoinette Albert. *Line producer:* Jane Scott. *Scriptwriters:* Baz Luhrmann, Craig Pearce. Based on the N.I.D.A. stage production devised and developed by the original cast. *Director of photography:* Steve Mason. *Production designer:* Catherine A. Martin. *Costume designer:* Angus Strathie. *Choreographer:* John "Cha Cha" O'Connell. *Editor:* Jill Bilcock. *Composer:* David Hirshfelder. *Sound recordist:* Ben Osmo. *Sound editors:* Wayne Pashley, Julius Chan (fx); Antony Gray (dia). *Mixers:* Roger Savage, Ian McLoughlin, Phil Judd.

Cast

Paul Mercurio (Scott Hastings), Tara Morice (Fran), Bill Hunter (Barry Fife), Pat Thomson (Shirley Hastings), Gia Carides (Liz Holt), Peter Whitford (Les Kendall), Barry Otto (Doug Hastings), John Hannan (Ken Railings), Sonia Kruger (Tina Sparkle), Chris McQuade (Charm Leachman), Pip Mushin (Wayne Burns), Leonie Page (Vanessa Cronin), Antonio Vargas (Rico), Armonia Benedito (Ya Ya), Jack Webster (Terry), Lauren Hewett (Kylie), Steve Grace (Luke), Paul Bertram (J. J. Silvers), Di Emery (Waitress), Lara Mulcahy (Natalie), Brian M. Logan (Clarry), Michael Burgess (Merv), Todd McKenney (Nathan Starkey), Kerry Shrimpton (Pam Short).

While **Strictly Ballroom** loosely pays homage to 1940s dance musicals, the similarity stops with the ballgowns. Its call to fame is hype—a candid glimpse into the tacky, unnatural world of ballroom, but without insight.

   Director Baz Luhrmann islands a wan 'lurve' story, and spends a good part of the film toying superficially with people's bitchiness, obsessions with image, winning and peer groups. Comic relief is found in the film's caricatures, and lavish attention is paid to costuming and art direction.

   In the early scenes, the film uses pseudo-documentary face-to-camera interviews to introduce various characters including Doug (Barry Otto) and Shirley Hastings (Pat Thomson), parents of the promising Pan Pacific Grand Prix hopeful, Scott Hastings

Rico (Antonio Vargas) and Scott Hastings (Paul Mercurio).

(Paul Mercurio), and Australian Dance Federation President, Barry Fife (Bill Hunter).

   The plot crams in a plethora of clichés, ranging from unattractive dance novice who falls for heart-throb dancer, ambitious mother who will go to extreme lengths to make sure her baby wins, crushed father who realises his lost ambitions through his son, promising male dancer who bucks the system by dancing his own steps—the same male dancer who reaches maturity when he learns from a mentor, in this case flamenco teacher and dancer, Rico (Antonio Vargas)—to unattractive girl who blossoms into a beautiful woman under the gaze of 'lurve'. None of the dancers appear to have any substance, with the exception of Scott, who is singled out as a bit of a freak for wanting to explore new dance steps.

   The love story is a limp bridging device to hold together a number of vignettes. In one scene, Scott is taught the macho Spanish dance, the *paso doble*, by Fran's father. In one sense, the scene symbolises the imparting of strength and wisdom from the older bull to the younger, yet the scene disintegrates into cliché: ethnic family life and its down-to-earth values versus the tacky technicolour of the Australian ballroom life. Drama is an integral part of Spanish life, whereas the Australians introduce drama into their otherwise bland lives. It is the classic us-and-them scenario.

   Scott crosses the boundaries and effectively is shunned by his colleagues. After Scott and Fran's father 'bond' on the dance floor, the scene cuts to a long-shot showing the group partying and a train leaving frame, suggesting one journey ending and

another beginning. However, the rest of the film fails to explore the changes within Scott, preferring to wallow in the cosmetic build-up to the championships.

   Choreography throughout the film is chopped into fragments and edited to fit the film score instead of being allowed to explore its own visual rhythm. The dénouement of the film, the Pan Pacific Grand Prix dance championships, is where Scott and his new partner, Fran (Tara Morice), showcase their talents and get a second crack at winning. Ironically, the final dance sequence is so over-edited that one is left feeling frustrated, not elated. The flurry of quick cuts creates ambience, not resolution. One gets the impression that Scott hasn't challenged the system sufficiently to make change.

PAT GILLESPIE[1]

---

[1] No copy was available for viewing.
[2] Extracted from Gillespie's review in *Cinema Papers* (see References).

References

'Baz Luhrmann's **Strictly Ballroom**', a production report by Ronnie Taylor, including interviews with director Baz Luhrmann and actor Paul Mercurio, *Cinema Papers*, no. 88, May–June 1992, pp. 6–10.

'Australian Films at Cannes', an overview by Jan Epstein with considerable discussion on **Strictly Ballroom**, *Cinema Papers*, no. 89, August 1992, pp. 22–5.

'Strictly Ballroom', a review by Pat Gillespie, *Cinema Papers*, no. 91, January 1993, p. 52.

'**Strictly Ballroom**: Strictly a Success', Pauline Adamek, *Filmnews*, August 1992, pp. 5–6.

'**Strictly Ballroom**: Strictly Marketing', an interview with distributor Richard Payten by Tina Kaufman, *Filmnews*, *ibid.*, p. 6.

TURTLE BEACH

Village Roadshow Pictures [and] Regency International Pictures present a Roadshow, Coote and Carroll Production. Turtle Beach. © [no date given; atb 1991] Australian Film Finance Corporation Pty Ltd and Village Roadshow Pictures (Australia) Pty Ltd. *Locations:* Phuket (Thailand); Sydney. *Australian distributor:* Roadshow. *Video:* Roadshow. *Rating:* M. 35mm. 90 mins.

Producer: Matt Carroll. *Executive producers:* Graham Burke, Greg Coote. *Line producer:* Irene Dobson. *Scriptwriter:* Ann Turner. Based on the novel by Blanche d'Alpuget. *Director of photography:* Russell Boyd. *Camera operator:* David Williamson. *Production designer:* Brian Thomson. *Costume designer:* Roger Kirk. *Supervising film editor;* William Anderson. *Editors:* Lee Smith, Louise Innes. *Composer:* Chris Neal. *Sound recordist:* Ben Osmo. *Sound editors:* Tim Jordan (dia.); Wayne Pashley (fx). *Mixers:* Phil Judd; Steve Burgess.

Cast

Greta Scacchi (Judith), Joan Chen (Minou), Jack Thompson (Ralph), Art Malik (Kanan), Norman Kaye (Hobday), Victoria Longley (Sancha), Martin Jacobs (Richard), William McInnes (Minder), George Whaley (Bill), Andrew Ferguson (David), Daniel de Leur (Peter), Celia Wong (Amah), Monroe Reimers (Mohammed), Stuart Campbell (Nigel), Kee Chan (Behzed), Patrick Dickson (Julian), Francois Bocquet (French Reporter #1), Veronique Bernard (French Reporter #2), Sean Scully (Businessman #1), John Howitt (Businessman #2).

Turtle Beach is a momentous film, we are led to believe, given the political controversies that have erupted about its subject matter in the Department of Foreign Affairs. The film explores aspects of the refugee crisis in Malaysia in the 1970s. Some see the arrival of the refugees as a chance to vent their aggression and anger or to shed blood; some see business opportunities on the black market; some show concern, compassion and actually try to intervene; some claim that they feel compassion but are powerless to alter the circumstances; and, most chilling, some (quite a few) remain largely indifferent, distant and silent.

The film is set in Kuala Lumpur. Racial tension is ubiquitous and acts of brutality are common (between different races). One of the earliest and most resonant images, in fact, is that of a Chinese cook pummelling the carcass of a pig. Kuala Lumpur is clearly a maelstrom of tensions, enmities and strife.

Judith (Greta Scacchi) protects some Vietnamese boat people.

Into this environment, Judith (Greta Scacchi), reporter, is thrust (and almost trampled!). Ten years pass (she is separated and has custody of the children). She is told that the Vietnamese are treated like 'dogs' and the authorities would prefer to keep foreign reporters out. Her friend, Minou (Joan Chen), the president of a committee which is devoted to helping refugees, disappears. Judith leaves the children and returns to Malaysia.

The images of the authorities are not very encouraging. They seem to be corrupt, fond of money and quite brutal. Even worse, the villagers emerge as bloodthirsty killers who seem to have no qualms about dismembering refugees in the surf, nor are they averse to celebrating the discovery of a refugee's corpse rolling in the foam.

The lack of reasons given for such actions makes the killings more horrific (though the one reason that is suggested is not examined critically by the film-makers). There are potent, strident, harrowing images—the massacre itself at Turtle Beach (a resonant title), the state of the refugee camp with its enclosure for 'unaccompanied minors', a horrific bureaucratic name for children, we are reminded, whose parents perished in the waves.

But much detracts from the cogency of the whole: the screenplay (by Ann Turner) includes too much unnecessary dialogue, and characters too often state the obvious (e.g., Judith awakens from what was clearly a nightmare and her lover says, 'You had a

nightmare'); too often the dialogue consists of platitudes and unexamined clichés ('corruption at all levels'). The consequence is unfortunate: it seems that there is no real effort to penetrate the surfaces. (Indeed, the most forceful scenes, significantly, are those where image and music convey the meaning.) The editing is untidy to say the least and many transitions are handled awkwardly (signs of a very troubled post-production[1]).

Turtle Beach is most effective when it concentrates on the refugees and on the sacrifices that are demanded of the two women. Something positive does emerge, however, at the end, though the plight of the refugees remains uncertain, precarious and disquieting.

RAYMOND YOUNIS[2]

---

[1] The director, Stephen Wallace, was allegedly replaced during post-production and several new scenes were shot. Bruce Beresford directed some of these. As well, an additional writer was brought in to write linking material; in some cases this meant dubbing new lines over old lip movements. The first music score was also canned and a new one written.

[2] Based on Younis' review in *Cinema Papers* (see References).

References

'Turtle Beach', a review by Raymond Younis, *Cinema Papers*, no. 88, May–June 1992, pp. 53–4.

'Turtle Beach: Filmmaker's Licence?', Deborah Abraham and Peter Cronau, *Filmnews*, March 1992, p. 5.

UNTIL THE END OF THE WORLD

A Village Roadshow Pictures release. Jonathan Taplin and Anatole Dauman present Until the End of the World. © 1991 Australian Film Finance Corporation Pty Limited, Road Movies Filmproduction GmbH and Argos Films SA. Produced in association with Phanos Development. An Australian–German–French Co-production of Village Roadshow Pictures Pty Ltd, Road Movies Filmproduction GmbH and Argos Films SA. Made with the participation of Australian Film Finance Corporation Pty Limited. *Australian distributor:* Roadshow. *Video:* not released as of 1 July 1993. *Rating:* M. 35mm. 151 mins.

Producer: Jonathan Taplin. *Executive producer:* Anatole Dauman. *Producer:* Kim Vercera (Australia). *Executive producers:* Greg Coote (Australia), Jean-Pierre Spiri-Mercanton (France), Ulrich Felsberg (Germany). *Associate producers:* Julia Overton (Australia), Masa Mirage (Japan), Walter Donohue. *Scriptwriters:* Peter Carey, Wim Wenders. Based on an original idea by Wim Wenders and Solveig Dommartin. *Director of photography:* Robby Müller. *Production designer:* Thierry Flamand. *Costume designer:* Montserrat Casanova. *Editor:* Peter Przygodda. *Composer:* Graeme Revell. *Sound recordist:* Jean-Paul Mugel. *Sound Editor:* Barbara von Weitershausen. *Mixer:* Milan Bar.

Cast

Solveig Dommartin (Claire Tourneur), Pietro Falcone (Mario), Chick Ortega (Chico Rémy), Eddy Mitchell (Raymond Morret), William Hurt (Sam Farber, alias Trevor McPhee), Adelle Lutz (Makiko), Ernie Dingo (Burt), Sam Neill (Eugene Fitzpatrick), Ernest Berk (Anton Farber), Christine Osterlein (Irina Farber), Rüdiger Vogler (Phillip Winter), Elena Smirnova (Krasikova), David Gulpilil (David), Jeanne Moreau (Edith Farber), Lois Chiles (Elsa Farber), Lauren Graham (Heidi), Max Von Sydow (Henry Farber), Jimmy Little (Peter), Bart Willoughby (Ned), Justine Saunders (Maisie), Kylie Belling (Lydia), Rhoda Roberts (Ronda), Paul Livingston (Karl).

Until the End of the World is set in the near-future of 1999 with a wayward nuclear satellite hovering dangerously close to the Earth. Sam Farber (William Hurt), alias Trevor McPhee, an American with French–German parents, is a techno-industrial thief who has stolen a special camera his father had invented for the US government. The camera records pictures that can be eventually transmitted to blind people along with the bio-chemical experience of seeing. Farber's mother has been blind since she was eight years old, and he travels the world recording images of family members. In the meantime, he also tries to keep ahead of authorities and an Australian bounty hunter named Burt (Ernie Dingo).

While in France, Farber (as McPhee) encounters Claire Tourneur (Solveig Dommartin), who is married to a writer, Eugene (Sam Neill), but is a woman seemingly rootless and disillusioned with her life. Claire's brief encounter with the mysterious McPhee tends to give her an uncertain purpose, but he absconds believing her to be an agent in league with Burt. She becomes intrigued with Farber–intrigue bordering on obsession. With the help of her husband and a German detective, Phillip Winter (Rüdiger Vogler), Claire traces Farber's movements across the globe, culminating with the journey in the central Australian desert.

But when the rest of the world may have been destroyed by the malfunctioning satellite, the characters reach the home of Sam's parents, where Henry (Max von Sydow) and Edith Farber (Jeanne Moreau) have become family to the Aboriginal people in a remote area of the Australian outback. Henry Farber, the fugitive scientist who invented the camera, has built a high-tech, underground laboratory, and, with the images recorded by Sam, he fulfils the life-long ambition to give his wife the gift of sight.

After a few trials, the experiment is a success: Edith sees. But the physical and

Claire Tourneur (Solveig Dommartin) and Eugene Fitzpatrick (Sam Neill).

psychological effect takes its toll and Edith dies soon after. But Henry wants to further pursue his research, and with obsessive determination wishes to record dreams and childhood memories locked away in the unconscious. His Aboriginal family, however, already understand the danger and desert him. Undaunted, Henry continues to experiment, recording images from the minds of Claire and Sam as they sleep. As the couple view and review their dreams, their love for each other turns into a destructive narcissism. The film ends when Claire is saved from her morbid self-absorption by Eugene's story, given to her not through images, but in the traditional method of typewritten paper.

Wim Wenders has described **Until the End of the World** as 'the ultimate road movie', which is a statement not too extreme for the film is, after all, partly based on Homer's *Odyssey*, perhaps one of the earliest stories with something of a road theme.

The central characters of Sam Farber and Claire Tourneur are variations on the likes of the wayfaring Ulysses and the faithful Penelope. But, in this case, Claire is a restless, modern-day Penelope not content to wait it out on Ithaca. And Claire's husband, Eugene, is the film's voice-over narrator; in other words, an author–god who shapes the events of their journey (into a story).

Wenders' statement is all-embracing, yet it does the film little justice: **Until the End of the World** is also a detective film, a science-fiction adventure and a family melodrama. The film is characteristic of Wenders' exploration of dialectical polarities that so structures his *œuvre*–the desire for sight turning into blindness, selfless love turning into narcissism, aimless wandering as opposed to a homeland, and so on. The film churns out a myriad of thematic twists and ideas, but they are always at loose ends. Ironically, **Until the End of the World** is the ultimate Wenders film, but it is also his most æsthetically unsuccessful being too ambitious and too uncertain of its journey.

RAFFAELE CAPUTO

References

'Until the End of the World', director Wim Wenders interviewed by Ana Maria Bahiana, *Cinema Papers*, no. 88, May–June 1992, pp. 38–42.

'Reality's Crossroads', Robin Weston, *Filmnews*, October 1992, pp. 11, 12.

'Until the End of the World', a review by Jane Freebury, *Filmnews*, op. cit., pp. 16–17.

1993

*Nick (Alex Dimitriades) and Christina
(Claudia Karvan). Michael Jenkin's*
The Heartbreak Kid.

TRACEY MOFFATT

BeDevil

Southern Star Entertainment presents beDevil. © 1993 Australian Film Finance Corporation Pty Limited and Anthony Buckley Productions Pty Ltd. Script developed with the assistance of the Australian Film Commission. Made with the participation of Australian Film Finance Corporation Pty Limited as part of the 1992 FFC Film Fund. *Location:* Sydney (studio). *Filmed:* late 1992. *Australian distributor:* Ronin. *Video:* 21st Century–Ronin. *Rating:* PG. 35mm. 90 mins.

Producers: Anthony Buckley, Carol Hughes. *Scriptwriter:* Tracey Moffatt. *Director of photography:* Geoff Burton. *Production designer:* Stephen Curtis. *Costume designer:* Rosalea Hood. *Choreographer:* Juanita Parker. *Editor:* Wayne Le Clos. *Composer:* Carl Vine. *Sound recordist:* David Lee. *Sound editors:* Frank Lipson, Peter Burgess. *Mixers:* Peter Fenton, Ron Purvis.

Cast

'Mr Chuck': Diana Davidson (Shelley)[1], Jack Charles (Rick), Ben[2] Kennedy (Rick at 11 Years), Kenneth Avery (Rick at 7 Years); Daphne Byers, Lavina Phillips, Desarae Morgan (Rick's Sisters); Benjamin Collard (Swamp Ghost)

'Choo Choo Choo Choo': Pauline McLeod (Jack), Tracey Moffatt (Ruby), Banula Marika (Stompie), Auriel Andrews (Older Ruby), Mawuyul Yanthalawuy (Maudie), Cecil Parkee (Bob Malley), Lex Foxcroft (Old Mickey), Shaun Saunders (Ronnie), Christine Byers (Darlo), Colin Saunders (Podge)

'Lovin' the Spin I'm In': Lex Marinos (Dimitri), Dina Panozzo (Voula), Riccardo Natoli (Spiro), Debai Baira (Emelda), Pinau Ghee (Beba), Patricia Handy (Minnie), Luke Roberts (The Artist), John Conomos (Conos), Kee Chan (Fong).

BeDevil is an important though flawed addition to the non-naturalistic Australian cinema. It is a collection of three ghost stories which are drawn from indigenous (that is, Aboriginal) and settler cultures in Australia. The stories are quite separate entities and Moffatt has made no attempt to impose an overarching structure or a unifying logic.

The first story ('Mr Chuck') is set on an island with a swamp where an American soldier drowned. The island and a group of people seem to be bedevilled by the traces of his life, by the legacies of the past and by his unquiet ghost. The story suggests that the most stable structures may be constructed on troubled and troubling foundations.

The second story ('Choo Choo Choo Choo') concerns a group of workers on a railroad where an unseen train is heard every night passing through the territory. These people, who include the film-maker's mother, are bedevilled by the ghost train, which seems to suggest other places and other possibilities of existence beyond the desert.

The third story ('Lovin' the Spin I'm In') depicts the dislocation of urban existence through the bedevilment of a Greek merchant's son at a dockland where two ghostly lovers bring the promise of joy and liberty.

In each, plot is fractured, discontinuous, undermined. Colour, sound, gesture, motion and ambience bear the burden of signifying. Linear structures of narrative are dismantled by the proliferation of formalised signs, pregnant ellipses, multiplying tropes and resonances. Numerous discourses and images are deployed as if to suggest spaces in which multiple cultures co-exist and thrive as forms of potentiality or actuality. In this sense, the film is a homage to a burgeoning multi-culturalism that sustains and legitimises plurality (hence the connection between indigenous and non-indigenous sources of narrative).

Memory and the imagination suggest the importance of artifice and the rhetorical nature of the image. These stories are drawn from the childhood of the film-maker and, as such, are fantastically-stylised remnants of a reconstructed past in which the supernatural and the natural formed a seemingly-seamless whole. The process of reconstruction is thus implicitly celebrated in the film, but as something which transposes, fragments or erases parts of the remembered events, symbols, metaphors, myths. Though the stylisation often distances the viewer and consistently undermines the human dimensions of the drama, the film scintillates with cool, brilliant, æsthetically-heightened simulacra.

RAYMOND YOUNIS

---

1 The order follows that of the opening credits, with additions.
2 The opening credits have 'Benjamin'.

References
'BeDevil', writer–director Tracey Moffatt interviewed by John Conomos and Raffaele Caputo, *Cinema Papers*, no. 93, May 1993, pp. 26–32.
'46e International du Film de Cannes', an article by Jan Epstein, *Cinema Papers*, no. 94, August 1993, pp. 22–7.
'BeDevil', a review by John Wojdylo, *Cinema Papers*, no. 96, December 1993, pp. 46–7.
'BeDevil', a review by Deb Verhoeven, *Filmnews*, October 1993, p. 9.

Stompie (Banula Marika) in 'Choo Choo Choo Choo'.

BLACKFELLAS

Barron Films presents in association with Australian Film Commission[,] Australian Broadcasting Corporation [and] Australian Film Finance Corporation Pty Limited BLACKFELLAS. © 1992 Australian Film Finance Corporation Pty Limited, Australian Film Commission, Australian Broadcasting Corporation and Barron Films. *Alternative title:* 'Day of the Dog' (working). Script developed with the assistance of the Australian Film Commission. Made with the assistance of the Western Australian Film Council. Made with the participation of Australian Film Finance Corporation Pty Limited and Australian Film Commission. *Location:* Perth. *Filmed:* October–November 1991. *Australian distributor:* Ronin. *Video:* Ronin–21st Century. *Rating:* M. 35mm. 98 mins.

Producer: David Rapsey. *Executive producers:* Paul D. Barron, Penny Chapman. *Scriptwriter:* James Ricketson, in consultation with Archie Weller. Based on the book, *The Day of the Dog*, by Archie Weller. *Director of photography:* Jeff Malouf. *Camera operators:* Jeff Malouf, Brad Pearce. *Production designer:* Rob Ricketson. *Costume designer:* Ron Gidgup. *Editor:* Christopher Cordeaux. *Composer:* David Milroy. *Sound recordist:* Kim Lord. *Sound editors:* Lawrie Silvestrin (sup.); Peter Pritchard. *Mixer:* Kim Lord.

Cast

John Moore (Doug Dooligan), David Ngoombujarra (Floyd Davey), Jaylene Riley (Polly), Lisa Kinchela (Valerie), Julie Hudspeth (Mrs. Dooligan), John Hargreaves (Detective Maxwell), Ernie Dingo (Percy)[1]; Jack Charles (Carey), Michael Watson (Hughie), Judith Margaret Wilkes (Nanna), David Moran (Conway), Trevor Parfitt (Tiny), Attila Ozsdolay (Silver), Kelton Pell (Wilice), Latishia Kickett (Rebecca), Bruce Paterson (Tony Foley), Kevin Lewis (Young Floyd), Faatiga Iosia (Young Doug), Glenda Einder (Maureen Greyboy), Franklyn Nannup (Ray), John Pantelis (Mr. Bogdanovitch), Leslie Wright (Magistrate), Louie Mulladan (Old Aboriginal Man).

With good timing, James Ricketson's **Blackfellas** was released in the wake of Paul Keating's Mabo legislation, and during the Year of Indigenous Peoples. However, this story about black life on the margins is more than an issues film. It has much of the sweep and power of Greek tragedy, with a catharsis that avoids despair in a way that Bruce Beresford's **The Fringe Dwellers** (1986), for example, does not.

Doug Dooligan (John Moore) and Polly (Jaylene Riley).

The film relates how Doug Dooligan (John Moore), a young Aborigine just released from prison, is determined to go straight despite attempts by his best mate, Floyd Davey (David Ngoombujarra), to involve him in criminal activities. Based on Archie Weller's *The Day of the Dog*, **Blackfellas** is an insight into the pressures on urban Aborigines, and the difficulty of maintaining the Dreaming when they become locked into the vicious cycle of gaol and crime.

Ricketson and Weller developed the screenplay over a five-year period with the help of Perth's Nyoongah people. Many of them worked on the film, both behind and in front of the camera, and, although the film is marred by choppy editing at times, it is distinguished by its genuine black consciousness.

Blackfellas exorcises many of the demons that haunt films about Australian blacks, not the least being the perception that, except for a few (Ernie Dingo, David Gulpilil), Aborigines can't act. What is so startling about **Blackfellas** is the realisation that when blacks (many of whom have never acted before) have the opportunity to express their own culture, using their own vernacular, the awkwardness that comes from using white language disappears completely.

Both Moore and Ngoombujarra were nominated for awards at the 1993 AFI Awards, and Ngoombujarra won Best Supporting Actor. (Ricketson won Best Adapted Screenplay.) But other members of the black cast are also impressive, in particular Jaylene Riley, who makes her debut playing Doug's girlfriend, Polly; Lisa Kinchela as her sister, Valerie; and Trevor Parfitt as Tiny.

This time it is the white performers (Julie Hudspeth as Doug's mother and John Hargreaves as a belligerent detective) who appear stiff and unnatural. It may well be that, because black and white cultures are so far apart in Australia, it is not possible to make a film where black and white characters can comfortably inhabit the same cultural universe.

JAN EPSTEIN

---

[1] The first seven credits follow the order of opening credits; the rest are per the end credits.

References

'Films in Colour: or, Black and White Perspectives of Screenplay', an article by novelist Archie Weller, *Cinema Papers*, no. 87, March–April 1992, pp. 44–5.

'James Ricketson's **Day of the Dog** [Blackfellas]', picture preview, ibid., pp. 46–7.

'**Blackfellas**', a review by Karl Quinn, *Cinema Papers*, no. 96, December 1993, pp. 48–9.

'**Blackfellas**: a film that tackles the truth', a review by Martha Ansara, *Filmnews*, August 1993, p. 12.

EXCHANGE LIFEGUARDS

Beyond Films Limited presents Avalon Films presents EXCHANGE LIFEGUARDS. © 1992 Avalon Films. Made with the participation of Australian Film Finance Corporation Pty Limited. *Location:* Sydney. *Filmed:* 10 February–13 March 1992. *Australian distributor:* Beyond. *Video:* First Release. *Rating:* M. 35mm. 92 mins.

Producer: Phil Avalon. *Executive producers:* Hugh Begg, Ron Rheuben, Mikael Borglund, Ian Ingram, Gary Hamilton[1]; MPM and Beyond[2]. *Associate producer:* Dennis Kiely. *Scriptwriter:* Phil Avalon. *Additional dialogue:* Richard Carter. *Director of photography:* Martin McGrath. *Production designer:* Richard Hobbs. *Costume designer:* Jenny Campbell. *Editor:* Allan Trott. *Composer:* John Capek. *Sound recordist:* Bob Clayton. *Sound editors:* Ashley Grenville; Helen Brown (foley). *Mixers:* Phil Heywood, Martin Oswin.

Cast

Christopher Atkins (Bobby McCain), Julian McMahon (Mick Dooley), Rebecca Cross (Julie), Vanessa Steele (Charlene), Elliott Gould (Mike McCain), Richard Carter (Al Eastman), Amanda Newman-Phillips (Kylie), Christopher Pate (Richard Gray), Lois Larimore (Donna McCain), Brian M. Logan (Terry), Mark Hembrow (Max), Peter Gow (Tishi), Anthony Lawrence (Clint Eastman), Ann Brisk (Annie McCain), Elizabeth McIvor (Helen), Alan Glover (Rusty), Suzanne Butt (Karen West), The Fargone Beautie (Band), Craig Thomson (Tim), Lance Loughlin (Ginnie), Lyn Lovett (Mrs Bonnick), Chris Hession (Spy-Rollerblader), Graham Pugh (Taxi Driver), Fingers Demain (Press Man).

One of the truly iconic moments of 1970s American cinema is when, in Richard Rush's **Getting Straight** (1970), Harry Bailey (Elliott Gould) lectures a dazed and angry panel of academics about how Jordan Baker is a man and that Nick Carraway[3] is, therefore, gay. It is disappointing, then, to see Gould in a film as inconsequential as **Exchange Lifeguards**. Foreign actors at less than the pinnacles of their careers have often ventured to the antipodes at the offer of work, but there is something particularly sad in the way Gould walks through a part he knows is of no value whatsoever.

Gould plays Mike McCain, an American property developer who appears to be losing his marbles and becoming a late-age hippy. Far more into the spirit of slash-and-burn capitalism is his half-Aussie son, Bobby (Christopher Atkins). Conniving with the

Beach boy Mick Dooley (Julian McMahon) and resort developer Bobby McCain (Christopher Atkins).

dastardly Richard Gray (Christopher Pate), Bobby flies to Australia's Mullet Beach under the pretence of being an exchange lifeguard. There, he seeks to infiltrate and betray the resistance to his and Gray's plans for a hideous modern development.

True to genre, Bobby is seduced by the anti-development stance of his new-found mates ('Australia changes people …'), and finds true sex and surf. Mike is left with no option but to fly out to discover what has happened to his absent son. Not unexpectedly, Mike recovers his marbles (they were only taken away by bad drugs) and wins the day with an environment-friendly community development.

Producer Phil Avalon, the founder of the pioneering *Tracks* surfing magazine years ago, has preferenced the beach culture in other films, such as **Breaking Loose** (Rod Hay, 1988). But in this the characters are even less appealing than usual. The question one can't help asking is why any Australian film would wish to represent its citizens in so moronic a light.

Things aren't helped, either, by the resolutely-low aims of director Maurice Murphy, whose model is clearly the American teen sex comedy (minus the sex). Breasts are 'white pointers', dogs (when not farting) piss on bad guys and a good surfie is measured by the number of bikini bottoms accumulated in his sin-shack. Even when Bobby is handed some condoms by his mother-in-law, she surprisingly tells him: 'If you're going to lay anything, lay rubber first.'

The 'anything' is alarming, especially in a film which has a close-up of a dog licking a man's crotch.

It is hard to know where the film-makers felt the humour would come from. Everything is based on the most obvious caricature and there is not a single line of wit. Instead, one is accorded such lines as—

BOY: 'Think I'm okay?'

GIRL: 'Yes, but don't wet yourself.'

— all uttered by a cast which would be seriously challenged by a *Neighbours* audition.

Director Maurice Murphy has a reputation as one of Australia's best producer–directors of comedy on television. Film, so far, has not been a happy hunting-ground for him, **Exchange Lifeguards** having been preceded by **Fatty Finn** (1980) and **Doctors & Nurses: A Story of Hopes** (1981).

Despite extensive attempts to whip up enthusiasm at the thought of Christopher Atkins (star of **The Blue Lagoon**[4]) returning to this region, **Exchange Lifeguards** failed to get a national release, seemingly only exhibited in Avalon's turf of Sydney's northern beaches. The true fate for this tasteless tits, arse and double dog-fart flic was the video shelves.

SCOTT MURRAY

---

1 These are the executive producers as per the opening credits.
2 These are given as executive producers at the end of the film.
3 Characters in F. Scott Fitzgerald's *The Great Gatsby*.
4 **The Blue Lagoon** (Randall Kleiser, 1980).

FORTRESS

Davis Entertainment Company and Village Roadshow Pictures present a John Flock Production. FORTRESS[1]. ©1992 Fortress Films Limited. *Budget:* $15 million. *Location:* Movieworld Studios (Queensland). *Filmed:* November 1991–January 1992. *Australian distributor:* Roadshow. *Video:* Roadshow. *Rating:* M. 35mm. 91 mins.

Producers: John Davis, John Flock. *Executive producers:* Graham Burke, Greg Coote. *Co-producers:* Neal Nordlinger, Michael Lake. *Line producer:* Irene Dobson. *Associate producers:* Troy Neighbors, Steve Feinberg. *Scriptwriters:* Troy Neighbors, Steve Feinberg, David Venable, Terry Curtis Fox. Based on a story by Troy Neighbors, Steve Feinberg. *Director of photography:* David Eggby. *Production designer:* David Copping. *Costume designer:* Terry Ryan. *Visual effects supervisor:* Paul Gentry. *Special visual effects:* Praxis Film Works. *Editor:* Timothy Wellburn. *Composer:* Frederic Talgorn. *Sound recordist:* Paul Clark. *Sound editors:* Robert Mackston (sup.); Lewis Goldstein, Jon Johnston, James Matheny (dia.); Alan Howarth, Jason King, Lance Brown, Paul Menichini, George Nemzer, Tim Gedemer, John Chalfont, Anne Laing, Burke Greer, Randy Honaker; Virginia Ellsworth (sup. music); Bill Block (music). *Mixers:* Matthew Iadarola, Gary Gegan.

Cast

Christopher Lambert (John Brennick), Kurtwood Smith (Prison Officer Poe), Loryn Locklin (Karen Brennick), Clifton Gonzalez Gonzalez (Nino), Lincoln Kilpatrick (Abraham), Jeffrey Combs (D-Day), Tom Towles (Stiggs), Vernon Wells (Maddox), Carolyn Purdy-Gordon (Zed-10), Alan Zitner (Claustrophobic Prisoner), Denni Gordon (Karen's Cellmate), Eric Briant Wells (Border Guard), Dragicia Debert (Bio Scanner Guard), Heidi Stein (Pregnant Woman), Harry Nurmi (Guard #1), Peter Lamb (Guard #2), Troy Hunter (Guard #3), Peter Marshall (Travel Authorization Guard), Michael Simpson (Medical Trainee), Tracy Martin (Woman Prisoner), Annika Thomas (Brennick Baby), Sam Copping (Brennick–Age 3), Kiralee (Dream Girl).

What is the point of spending the first ten minutes of a futuristic action film showing off all the impressive, expensive sets of a privately-run, high-tech, underground prison if you're not going to have the common decency to blow them up in the last ten minutes? It's a tradition of action films bravely flouted by Stuart Gordon's **Fortress**.

There are a number of other traditions which fail to intimidate **Fortress** into submission: traditions such as taut action, believable sets, likeable characters, good effects and a decent level of firepower.

So what is the point of **Fortress**? A good laugh, apparently. **Fortress** is one of those glorious films that, in spite of its attempt at high-tech production values, sounds as if it was written during a pretty decent pot party.

John Brennick (Christopher Lambert) and his wife Karen (Loryn Locklin) get caught at a security checkpoint while trying to get to Canada. She is pregnant with their second child, a felony in the future as far as the population-control-crazy fascist government is concerned, even if the first child didn't live long.

Brennick ends up in a prison run by the Men-Tel Corporation and is thrown into a tiny cell. He is warned not to dream because Prison Officer Poe (Kurtwood Smith, so memorable as the draconian father in **Dead Poets Society**) has the ability to see into people's dreams and terminate them if they are about anything subversive, such as great sex.

Now, if you're going to have a high-tech film it has to be convincing, and **Fortress** isn't. It's a visual technological white elephant. The spherical surveillance cameras on the ceilings often move as though they are being pulled by an overworked strand of cotton wool thread, the video images thrown up in the central control room are of home movie standard, we get endless panning shots looking up and down a boring central shaft, the guns look plastic and, as if that wasn't bad enough, the prisoners even eat out of styrofoam containers.

Fortress would have been a total waste of time if it weren't for Poe, the whacky prison director. He has to be one of the biggest fruit-cakes ever to grace the cast of a prison movie. The guy is impotent, a by-product of being 'enhanced' by the Men-Tel Corporation, something which he apparently had no thundering objections to when he signed up for the programme. He also has major Oedipal problems with the matriarchal computer, which keeps telling him what to do. He can't hold his drink. He also has a liking for the foetal position. Fruitcake? About the only thing the guy doesn't do in the film is wear a dress.

The climax to **Fortress**, apart from being poorly shot and unexciting, is also just plain dumb. The place is not full of political prisoners or innocent citizens guilty of thought crime, but chock-full of murderers, rapists, armed robbers and so forth. So when Brennick & Co finally escape, having disabled the prison's security system, the rest of the population is presumably free to leave the place and work their way back into society. It's a morally-dubious note to end what is supposed to be a pretty straight action film.

Still, the potential for out-and-out comedy in **Fortress** is left untapped, which is good. If the makers had realised how funny it was going to turn out, they may have tried to turn it into an intentional comedy, which would have spoiled the effect.

JIM SCHEMBRI

---

[1] Under the word 'FORTRESS' is a bar code: '0 82430 96018 4 26 0 6': which could be argued by pedants to be part of the title.

References
'Fortress', joint producer John Flock interviewed by Marcial Coppolino, *Cinema Papers*, no. 89, August 1992, pp. 36–42.
'Fortress', a review by Jonathan Roper, *Cinema Papers*, no. 92, April 1993, pp. 49–50.

John Brennick (Christopher Lambert), a right-to-lifer on the run.

GREENKEEPING

Central Park Films in association with the Australian Film Commission presents GREENKEEPING. © 1992 Central Park Films. *Budget:* $0.84 million. *Location:* Sydney. *Filmed:* 23 September–18 October 1991. *Australian distributor:* Ronin. *Video:* 21st Century. *Rating:* PG. 16mm. 90 mins.

Producer: Glenys Rowe. *Scriptwriter:* David Caesar. *Director of photography:* Simon Smith. *Production designer:* Kerith Holmes. *Costume designer:* Tess Schofield. *Editor:* Mark Perry. *Composers:* David Bridle, John Phillips. *Sound recordist:* Liam Egan. *Sound editors:* Jeanine Chialvo (dia.); Liam Egan, David White, Counterpoint Sound. *Mixer:* Robert Sullivan.

Cast

Mark Little (Lenny), Lisa Hensley (Sue), Max Cullen (Tom)[1]; Jan Adele (Doreen), Gia Carides (Gina), Sid Conabere (Milton), Willie Fennell (Old Player), Kristoffer Greaves (Robbie), Tony Helou (Car Salesman), Connie Hobbs (Ruby), Harold Kissin (Joe), Rossi Koisis (Gina's Brother), Kazuhiro Muroyama (Rikyu), Robyn Nevin (Mum), David Phu An Chiem (Poker Machine Player), Grieg Pickhaver (Raffle Man), Raymond Poon (Rikyu's Friend), Leigh Russell (Dave), Rob Steele (Manager), Aer Vongphrachanh (Poker Machine Friend), David Wenham (Trevor), Frank Whitten (Dad), Zhang Yong (Chinese Musician).

Australian cinema includes a strand of film-making, often low-key, which pays affectionate tribute to the working-class Anglo-Australia of the 1950s and '60s. Brian McKenzie's **Stan and George's New Life** (1992) and Ray Argall's **Return Home** (1990) fit this category. So does Mark Joffe's **Spotswood** (1992) and Nadia Tass' **The Big Steal** (1990). David Caesar's **Greenkeeping**, his first feature, shares this same nostalgia for a simpler time and place.

Life gets out of control for Lenny (Mark Little), the not-so-bright greenkeeper of a Sydney bowls club, when all his stars cross at once. As well as the lawn turning brown for reasons he can't fathom or fix, his wife, Sue (Lisa Hensley), smokes dope all day, and is being hounded by dealers about her debts. When life at home becomes unbearable, Lenny makes gentle overtures to the club's waitress, Gina (Gia Carides), but these are rejected. As Pennant Day approaches, and tensions are heightened because of the likelihood of this year's trophy going to a

Japanese, the green looks browner the more Lenny waters it. To cap it off, a beady-eyed magpie takes pleasure in dive-bombing Lenny's head.

Despite its wandering plot and poor production values (blown up from 16mm, the colours look leached and grainy), **Green-keeping** is saved by its sympathetic, off-beat humour and fine acting from Little and Hensley, whose portraits of two latter-day Aussie battlers have charm and conviction.

However, not all the characters are drawn equally well. In contrast to the naturalism of the two leads, the minor characters (Sid Conabere and Max Cullen as two club members, and Robyn Nevin as Lenny's mother) lapse too easily into caricature and whimsy. Although this allows Caesar the opportunity to both jibe at RSL-type racism and underline what he sees as its essential benignity, the contrast jars nonetheless.

Though slight, **Greenkeeping** is genuinely oddball and appealing, the product of a non-conformist view of the world which sees meaning and humour in the mundane and ordinary. While it will never have great exposure (even on video, the definition and colour is poor), it represents a sub-genre of film-making that mourns the passing of the laconic stoicism of old Australia.

JAN EPSTEIN

---

[1] The first three credits follow the order of opening credits; the rest are per the end credits.

References

'David Caesar's **Greenkeeping**', a production report by Peter Galvin, *Cinema Papers*, no. 86, January 1992, pp. 21–3.

'David Caesar', an interview with the writer–director by Peter Galvin, ibid., pp. 23–6.

'**Greenkeeping**', a review by Karl Quinn, *Cinema Papers*, no. 95, October 1993, pp. 44–5.

Tom (Max Cullen) in the RSL club.

GROSS MISCONDUCT

R. A. Becker presents [a] PRO A PRO Films Production in association with David Hannay Productions and Underworld Productions. GROSS MISCONDUCT. © 1993 PRO Films (no. 1) Pty Limited [and] Australian Film Finance Corporation Pty Limited. Developed with the assistance of the Australian Film Commission. Made with the participation of Australian Film Finance Corporation Pty Limited. *Location:* Melbourne. *Filmed:* July–August 1992. *Australian distributor:* REP. *Video:* Columbia–Tristar–Hoyts. *Rating:* M. 35mm. 96 mins.

   Producers: David Hannay, Richard Sheffield-MacClure. *Executive producer:* Richard Becker. *Co-producers:* Gerard Maguire, Lance Peters. *Associate producer:* Rocky Bester. *Scriptwriters:* Lance Peters, Gerard Maguire. Based on the play, *Assault with a Deadly Weapon,* by Lance Peters. *Director of photography:* David Connell. *Production designer:* Jon Dowding. *Costume designer:* Aphrodite Kondos. *Editor:* Henry Dangar. *Composer:* Bruce Rowland. *Sound recordist:* Andrew Ramage. *Sound editors:* Tim Jordan (dia.); Nicki Roller (fx). *Mixer:* Phil Judd.

Cast

Jimmy Smits (Justin Thorne), Naomi Watts (Jennifer Carter), Sarah Chadwick (Laura Thorne), Adrian Wright (Kenneth Carter), Ross Williams (Guiderman), Paul Sonkkila (Rowland Curtis), Alan Fletcher (Henry Landers), Leverne McDonnell (Miriam McMahon), Beverley[1] Dunn (Judge Barlow), Nicholas Bell (Detective Matthews), Fiona Corke (Detective Coote), Brendon Suhr (Terry MacKnight[2])[3]; Tara Judah (Nancy Thorne), Goran Stamenkovic (Oliver Thorne); Susan Ellis, Edwina Exton, Bernadette Walsh, Peter Webb (Students); Paul Murphy (Dream Lover), Linda Cable (Club Singer), Angus Burchall (Drummer), Don Stevenson (Guitarist), Jeremy Alsop (Bass Player); Dimity Barber, Christine Brown (Girls in Club).

With George Miller's **Gross Misconduct**, we are hurled into the realm of the chaotic, free-for-all 'erotic thriller', a truly-international genre, and one especially popular in the video market. It incorporates a murder mystery, a courtroom drama, and a psychological exploration of 'aberrant' behaviour. Inevitably, it owes something to the 'Hitchcockian' legacy—but not so much to Hitchcock's own works as the more contemporary, kinetic, 'post-modern' reworkings of such narrative models in the

Professor and student: Justin Thorne (Jimmy Smits) and Jennifer Carter (Naomi Watts).

films of Brian De Palma and Dario Argento.

   In particular, **Gross Misconduct** shares with these contemporary thrillers a wilful, even paranoiac, tendency to strike out in every direction, hinting that every character who walks through a door is the person most likely to have committed the foulest imaginable crime. All it takes is a single cutaway to a sinister look or a mysterious gesture to make even the most seemingly-innocent character seem suspicious.

   The plot hook here is the current debate over sexual harassment and intimate relations between teachers and students in the tertiary arena, about which such prominent Australian literary figures as Helen Garner and Cassandra Pybus have written in recent years. Justin Thorne (Jimmy Smits) lectures on the Greek philosophy of love and Jennifer Carter (Naomi Watts) goes out of her mind with desire. After their sexual liaison takes place, a murder occurs, Jennifer develops amnesia, and Justin is pegged as the prime suspect. Miller evoked the 'politically-incorrect' terrain of the modern thriller—its exploration of taboo topics and 'dangerous' desires—when he referred in an interview on *The Movie Show* (SBS) to the 'hot, sexy' nature of his subject matter.

   But as soon as Miller and his writers approach the white-hot centre of this situation, the film becomes a crazy mess of innuendo, murder and perversion. The hysteria of the film prompted a like emotion in at least one reviewer (Peter Castaldi on the ABC television programme *Review*), who wildly castigated the film for exploiting unseemly fantasies of 'incest and child abuse'. One should perhaps not be so quick, however, to dismiss the film's broaching of the teacher–student taboo, since it is a recurring and even obsessive theme in Australian film and television, from **Fast Talking** (Ken Cameron, 1984) to **The Heartbreak Kid** (Michael Jenkins, 1993) and *Heartbreak High*.

   Gross Misconduct is indeed a strange and trashy artefact, which makes for curious, and sometimes inadvertently hilarious, viewing. Part of the discomfort of the film arises from the way Miller attempts to integrate into the general atmosphere of perversity and degradation a decent, old-fashioned human story of a marriage tested and fortified: somewhat unbelievably, Justin's wife, Laura (Sarah Chadwick), accepts him back after earlier throwing him out upon hearing of his teacherly infidelity.

   The film is styled like a tele-feature, and decked out with many familiar television faces. Most notably, it is one of those queerly-located 'mid-Pacific' movies which so many local critics love to hate—a mélange of American accents, real and faked, vying for attention with a touristic parade of local Aussie sites. There are more movies like this being made in Australia with each passing year of the 1990s, such as the Cynthia Rothrock action film, *Irresistible Force* (Kevin Hooks, non-theatrical, 1993). Most are modest, generic efforts which disappear to video without comment. **Gross Misconduct** suffered the misfortune of being plucked out of the pack and berated as a 'vulgar mistake', an exemplar of the kind of the film we should not be making in Australia. But, as a typical erotic thriller, it is no better and certainly no worse than a hundred similar titles from anywhere around the world.

ADRIAN MARTIN

---

[1] The opening credits drop the third e from Beverley.
[2] The press kit drops the 'a'.
[3] The first twelve credits follow the order of opening credits; the rest are per the end credits.

References

'Gross Misconduct', a production report by Andrew L. Urban, *Cinema Papers*, no. 91, January 1993, pp. 4–9.

'Gross Misconduct', a review by Greg Kerr, *Cinema Papers*, no. 95, October 1993, pp. 45–6.

THE HEARTBREAK KID

Ben Gannon presents THE HEARTBREAK KID[1]. © Australian Film Finance Corporation Pty Limited, View Films Pty Limited and Film Victoria. Script developed with the assistance of the Australian Film Commission. Produced with the assistance of Film Victoria. Made with the participation of Australian Film Finance Corporation Pty Limited. *Location:* Melbourne. *Filmed:* 7 September–19 October 1992. *Australian distributor:* Roadshow. *Opened:* 17 June 1993. *Video:* Roadshow. *Rating:* M. 35mm. 97 mins.

Producer: Ben Gannon. *Executive producer:* Andrea Asimow. *Co-producer:* Barbara Gibbs. *Scriptwriters:* Richard Barrett, Michael Jenkins. Based on the play by Richard Barrett. *Director of photography:* Nino Martinetti. *Production designer:* Paddy Reardon. *Costume designer:* Lisa Meagher. *Editor:* Peter Carrodus. *Composer:* John Clifford White. *Sound recordist:* John Phillips. *Sound editors:* Livia Ruzic (dia.); Gareth Vanderhope (fx). *Mixers:* Roger Savage, Steve Burgess.

Cast

Claudia Karvan (Christina), Alex Dimitriades (Nick), Nico Lathouris (George), Steve Bastoni (Dimitri), Doris Younane (Evdokia), George Vidalis (Vasili), Louise Mandylor (Eleni), William McInnes (Southgate), Jasper Bagg (Graham), Fonda Goniadis (Con), Vikash Prasad (Vikash), Bao Quach (Tran), Kathy Halliday (Maria), Chaka Johnson (Soula), Keith Iosifidis (Manolis), Perry Stamatopoulos (Kosta), Scott Major (Rivers), Vince Filomeno (Giordano), Scott Manic (Fight Boy), Jenny Athanasopoulos (Effie), Harry Shiamaris (Father Yanni), Maria Symeou (Antigone), Robin Cuming (Principal).

Michael Jenkins' The Heartbreak Kid, an adaptation of Richard Barrett's stage play, encapsulates the complexities of pursuing an independent lifestyle away from the rigours of family and cultural/ethnic ties. It is, for this reviewer, quite familiar in so many different personal ways: how many heartbreak kids have we met in our bi-cultural lives?

The Heartbreak Kid is a rich, multi-layered rites-of-passage examination of a Greek–Australian student, Nick (Alex Dimitriades), who falls in love with his Greek–Australian school teacher, Christina (Claudia Karvan). Both actors excel in their respective rôles and together they give a finely-calibrated performance of the deep-seated

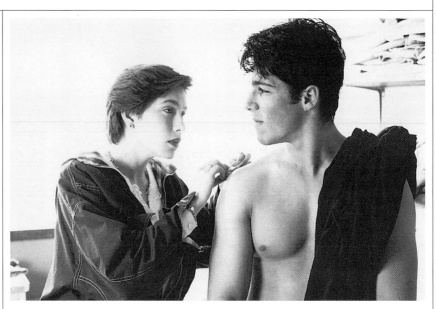

Teacher and student: Christina (Claudia Karvan) and Nick (Alex Dimitriades).

emotional undercurrents that are involved in such a dramatic situation.

The Heartbreak Kid succeeds partly because its two leading characters are in a fairly similar cauldron of emotional and ethnic turbulence. Christina is more orthodox (pardon the poor pun) in terms of cutting her middle-class ties with her overbearing parents (especially her dogmatic, sexist father) than is Nick, who is working class, a kid who lives for the pleasures of everyday life, music, soccer and sex. There is an admirable sexual honesty in the dawning relationship between Christina and Nick. But before they consummate their relationship in an apartment owned by one of Christina's girlfriends, Nick has to encourage Christina to make the leap into the thrilling realm of personal independence.

This part of the relationship is quite moving in contrast to so many 'multi-cultural' films that tend to elide the intricate tensions and ambiguities residing in such relationships. To see Christina in her car (after she has left her parents and her intended, conservative husband), carefree in the realisation that she is free from the stifling conflicting strictures of a traditional Greek–Australian home, is one of the film's finer moments.

I do not wish to make any ambitious claims for The Heartbreak Kid as some kind of benchmark production in the (in)visible history of Australian experimental and narrative mainstream films that represent the thematic, cultural and stylistic concerns of our 'multi-cultural' cinema. It is a fairly honest and modest work that knows its own conceptual and formal limits and strengths.

And the multiple-camera and vivid visual style of the film, with its apt hand-held camera scenes, gives The Heartbreak Kid the right kind of kinetic edge. It accentuates the dynamic character of Nick's world and personality and, at the same time, suggests the imminent consummation of the relationship between the teacher and her student.

The Heartbreak Kid is a film that does not seek solace in the convenient, but deadening, 'talking-head' formula that a large number of contemporary Australian films (that are adapted from another source) adopt. I can't say that I care for the television spin-off from The Heartbreak Kid, *Heartbreak High*, but I do think the film itself has something to offer anyone who cares for characters like Christina and Nick, and how they live their daily hybrid lives located between two different (but intricately-enmeshed) cultural worlds.

JOHN CONOMOS

---

[1] The title is a mix of upper and lower case.

References

'Coming of Age: Notes towards a Re-appraisal', an article by Raffaele Caputo, *Cinema Papers*, no. 94, August 1993, pp. 12–16.

'The Heartbreak Kid', co-writer–director Michael Jenkins interviewed by Pat Gillespie, ibid., pp. 18–21.

'The Heartbreak Kid', producer Ben Gannon interviewed by Pat Gillespie, ibid., p. 21.

'The Heartbreak Kid', a review by Pat Gillespie, ibid., pp. 43–4.

'The Heartbreak Kid', a review by Marg O'Shea, *Filmnews*, June 1993, p. 20.

D A V I D   P A R K E R

HERCULES RETURNS

Philm Productions presents HERCULES RETURNS. © 1992 Philm Productions Pty. Ltd. *Location:* Melbourne; 'Somewhere in Spain (in 1963)'. *Australian distributor:* Roadshow. *Video:* Roadshow. *Rating:* M. 35mm. 80 mins.

Producer: Philip Jaroslow. *Executive producer:* Peter Winter. *Scriptwriter:* Des Mangan. Developed from the live show, *Double Take Meet Hercules,* written and directed by Des Mangan. *Director of photography:* David Connell. *Production designer:* Jon Dowding. *Costume designer:* Aphrodite Kondos. *Editor:* Peter Carrodus. *Composer:* Philip Judd. *Sound recordist:* Lloyd Carrick. *Sound editors:* Bruce Emery (dia.); Gerry Long (foley); Gareth Vanderhope (fx). *Mixer:* Steve Burgess.

Cast

David Argue (McBain), Michael Carman (Kent), Mary Coustas (Lisa), Bruce Spence (Sprocket), Brendon Suhr (King), Nick Polites (Phone Executive), Lance Anderson (Wolf Whistler), Laurie Dobson (Barman), Richard Moss (Drunk), Burt Cooper (Frightened Man), Tom Coltraine (Kent Double).

Voices

Des Mangan (Hercules, Ted, Ursus, Machismo, Samson, Stretch, Dad, Testiculi), Sally Patience (Labia, Muriel, Fanny, Delilah), Matthew King (Charlie).

HERCULES RETURNS (Italian Film)[1] Senior Cinematographica (Rome)–Productares Exibidores Films S.S. (Madrid). An Italian–Spanish Co-production.

Director: Giorgio Capitani. *Producer:* Giorgio Cristallini. *Scriptwriters:* Sandro Continenza, Roberto Glanviti. Based on an original idea by Giorgio Cristallini. *Director of photography:* Carlo Bellero. *Camera operator:* Gaetano Valle. *Production designer:* G. F. Ramacci. *Costume designer:* Casa D'Arte, V. Ciarlo. *Editor:* Roberto Cinquini. *Composer:* Piero Unriliani. *Sound:* M. Del Pazzo, R. Cadner.

Cast

Alan Steel, Nadir Baltimor, Helene Chanel, Arnaldo Fabrizio, Valentine Macchi, Luciano Marin, Moira Orfei, Conrado San Martin, Attilio Tosato, Red Ross, Yan Lavor, Nino Del Fabro, Livio Lorenzon, Nino Marchetti, Elisa Montez, Maria Luisa Ponte, Carlo Tamberlani, Lia Zoppelli.

Double Take, the live comedy team which has had great success taking crappy old movies and redubbing them for laughs, has in Hercules Returns taken on one of John Steel's Hercules films of the early 1960s, Ercole, Sansone, Maciste, Ursus, Gli Invincibile (Hercules, Samson, Maciste and Ursus are Invincible, Giorgio Capitani, 1964). The fatal error with this transferring of a live theatrical idea to film is purely conceptual.

Double Take started out screening old movies and redoing the dialogue live from the back of the theatre. In one particularly-memorable season of *Double Take meets the Astro Zombies*, they not only wove a clever alternative plot to the original, but made great jokes about the bad film-making involved, about the ludicrousness of images (zombies with torches held to their foreheads) and bad continuity (a car jumps from one spot to another in one edit). Woody Allen did a similar thing with **What's up, Tiger Lily?** in 1966, so the prospect of lifting this idea to film had promise.

The all-encompassing problem with Hercules Returns, however, is that they try to explain why an old Italian Hercules film would be dubbed for laughs in the first place. This involves a modern-day intro with David Argue as McBain, a hapless film distribution executive with bad hair who works for the evil, cold Kent cinema chain.

McBain quits and hires an old movie theatre to show films in the old friendly way. He then recruits a projectionist friend called Sprocket (Bruce Spence) and a publicist, Lisa (Mary Coustas), and plans to screen Hercules on opening night.

On the night, however, they discover, like the dimwits they are, that the film is in Italian with no subtitles. So, they decide to improvise the voices and the sound effects from the projection booth. The premiere rolls ahead with the new voices, and intermittently we cut back to the projection booth to see shots of the trio mimicking the voices of Des Mangan, Sally Patience and Matthew King. We also get occasional shots of the first-night audience laughing their heads off.

Now, the important question arises: Why bother setting all this up? It is obvious that the dubbing of the old film has been painstakingly worked out, factoring in camera moves and acting gestures, so presenting it as if it is being improvised by way of explanation is simply dumb.

The idea would have been much better served by simply showing the film cold with its new voice track. As it is, there are only a few stretches that remain uninterrupted long enough for the crazy swing of the skills that have made Double Take famous to take effect.

There should have been some faith that the Double Take idea would hold on its own. For as that other comedy saying goes: 'If it ain't broke, don't fix it.' Well, it wasn't broke, and they tried to fix it, and they messed it up big.

JIM SCHEMBRI

---

[1] Even though the film does not credit it, the Italian film in question is **Ercole, Sansone, Maciste, Ursus, Gli Invincibile.**

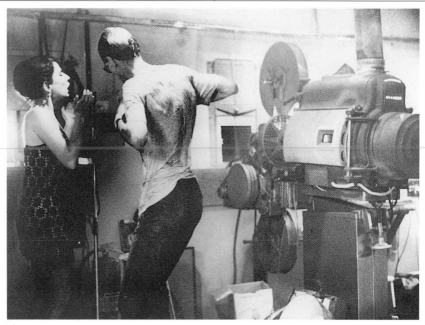

Lisa (Mary Coustas) and Sprocket (Bruce Spence) revoice a film.

LORENZO'S OIL

Universal Pictures presents a Kennedy Miller Film. © 1992 Universal City Studios, Inc. *Location:* Pittsburgh (US). *Filmed:* 9 September–12 December 1991. *Australian distributor:* UIP. *Opened:* March 1993.[1] *Video:* CIC. *Rating:* PG. 35mm. 135 mins.

Producers: Doug Mitchell, George Miller. *Executive producer:* Arnold Burk. *Associate producers:* Johnny Friedkin, Daphne Paris, Lynn O'Hare. *Scriptwriters:* George Miller, Nick Enright. *Director of photography:* John Seale. *Camera operator:* Brian W. Armstrong. *Production designer:* Kristi Zea. *Costume designer:* Colleen Atwood. *Editors:* Richard Francis-Bruce, Marcus D'Arcy, [Lee Smith[2]]. *Sound recordist:* Ben Osmo. *Sound design:* Lee Smith. *Sound editors:* Gareth Vanderhope; Livia Ruzic, Wayne Pashley (dia.); Steve Burgess, Jerry Long (foley); Annabelle Sheehan (ADR); Julius Chan (atmos.). *Mixers:* Roger Savage; Ian McLoughlin (addit.).

Cast

Nick Nolte (Augusto Odone), Susan Sarandon (Michaela Odone), Peter Ustinov (Professor Nikolais), Kathleen Wilhoite (Deirdre Murphy), Gerry Bamman (Doctor Judalon), Margo Martindale (Wendy Gimble), James Rebhorn (Ellard Muscatine), Ann Hearn (Loretta Muscatine), Maduka Steady (Omouri), Mary Wakio (Comorian Teacher), Don Suddaby (Don Suddaby), Colin Ward (Jack Gimble), La Tanya Richardson (Nurse Ruth), Jennifer Dundas (Nurse Nancy Jo), William Cameron (Pellerman), Becky Ann Baker (Pellerman's Secretary), Mary Pat Gleason (The Librarian), David Shiner (Clown), Ann Dowd (Pediatrician), Peter MacKenzie (Immunosuppression Doctor), Paul Lazar (Professor Duncan); Noah Banks, Billy Amman, Michael Haider, E. G. Daily, Christin Woodworth, Zack O'Malley Greenberg (Lorenzo).

Lorenzo Odone is a bright child who suddenly starts to show disturbing and violent behaviour. He is eventually diagnosed as suffering from ALD, an inborn error of metabolism which causes degeneration of the brain and inexorably progresses to death within two years.

Lorenzo's father, Augusto (Nick Nolte), is an official of the World Bank and his mother, Michaela (Susan Sarandon), is a determined and intelligent woman. Together they refuse to accept that there is nothing to be done for their child and they set out to discover all they can about the disease and Lorenzo's prognosis. They attend meetings of the families of other victims, but their activist work causes them to run foul of the ALD Foundation which urges caution. They embark on their own research and make certain discoveries about the power of oleic acid as a treatment, and then discover a further refinement which provides significant relief and appears to halt the progress of the disease. They do so despite the doubts of the medical fraternity but are unflagging in their devotion to Lorenzo's recovery. At the end of the film, after the medical breakthrough oil is tested and proved valuable, we are told that Lorenzo's Oil has produced great benefits for many similarly-afflicted children.

George Miller crossed over from medicine to the cinema via a short called *Violence in the Cinema ... Part 1* (1972) which revealed a somewhat pathological taste in its images. This pathology was continued in the first **Mad Max** movie (1979). **Lorenzo's Oil** would appear to mark one full circle in Miller's career. Only an MD could present this story with the lucid clarity that it contains. If that were all the film did, then it would have served a worthy if limited purpose. But this precision and attention to detail, a hallmark of Miller's work, is merely the start of a complex and profound film about human suffering and pain.

It is also determinedly not a film about grief and it has as little sentimentality as it is decently possible to present. The biggest moments which might have been milked for their emotion are avoided. The reunion with Omouri (Maduka Steady) takes place in long-shot. The breaking of the news about the diagnosis is followed by questions about the progress of the disease, a discreet moment as the couple walk back to reclaim their son and, in close-up, a mask of serenity, as the family reunite. What occurs though is even more unbearably emotional than all the cancer movies put together.

Finally, we are confronted with lives which must accept pain and loss, but also lives which must face the unbearable frustration of obsession. Slowly we discover a mother who can turn away from an almost lifeless child's body and intone, icy cold, 'Sometimes I wonder, my love, if people realise how incredible you truly are.' It is a stunning echo of her first words to Lorenzo as he emerges from school and she shouts for all to hear: 'Here he is ... the cleverest boy in the world!'

Miller and his co-scriptwiter Nick Enright have placed the weight of the film on Susan Sarandon's performance and she carries it with remarkable (though unrewarded) distinction. The director is less ably served by Nick Nolte's affecting Italian mannerisms and an Italian accent in a performance which is clearly beyond his range and technique. The inclusion of an actor of the calibre of Gian-Maria Volonte may have caused the film to be seen for the masterpiece it is, rather than as just a major work by our finest modern director, which, unfortunately, comes with one serious flaw.

GEOFF GARDNER

---

1 The film opened in the US in 1992.
2 The press kit, which in all other ways exactly matches the film's credits, also lists Lee Smith as an editor.

References
'Lorenzo's Oil', director–co-writer George Miller interviewed by Scott Murray, *Cinema Papers*, no. 92, April 1993, pp. 4–13, 60, 62.
'Lorenzo's Oil', a review by John Conomos, ibid., pp. 50–1.
'Miller's Way', an interview with George Miller by Mary Colbert, *Filmnews*, March 1993, pp. 5, 14.
'Lorenzo's Oil', a short review by Kathe Boehringer, ibid., p. 12.

Claiming for oneself: Augusto (Nick Nolte) and Michaela Odone (Susan Sarandon).

LOVE IN LIMBO

Beyond Films Limited presents Palm Beach Pictures presents Love in Limbo. © 1992 Palm Beach Pictures (WA) Pty Limited [and] Australian Film Finance Corporation Pty Limited. *Alternative title:* 'The Great Pretender' (working). Made with the assistance of the Western Australian Film Council. Made with the participation of Australian Film Finance Corporation Pty Limited as part of the 1991 FFC Film Fund. *Locations:* Perth, Kalgoorlie (WA). *Filmed:* June–July 1991. *Australian distributor:* Hoyts–Fox–Columbia–Tristar. *Opened:* 7 March 1993. *Video:* Triumph. *Rating:* M. 35mm. 102 mins.

Producer: David Elfick. *Co-producers:* Nina Stevenson, John Winter. *Scriptwriter:* John Cundill. *Director of photography:* Stephen F. Windon. *Camera operator:* Marc Spicer. *Production designer:* David McKay. *Costume designer:* Clarrissa Patterson. *Editor:* Stuart Armstrong. *Composer:* Peter Kaldor. *Sound recordist:* Guntis Sics. *Sound editors:* Karin Whittington (dia.); Julius Chan, Wayne Pashley (fx). *Mixer:* Phil Judd.

Cast

Craig Adams (Ken Riddle), Rhondda Findleton (Gwen Riddle), Martin Sacks (Max Wiseman), Aden Young (Barry McJannet), Maya Stange (Ivy Riddle), Samantha Murray (Maisie), Bill Young (Uncle Herbert), Russell Crowe (Arthur Baskin), Himself[1] (Little Willie Littlefield)[2]; Leith Taylor (Mrs Rutherford), Jill Perryman (Aunt Dorry), Paula Forrest (Miss Cornish), Robert Van Mackelenberg (Headmaster), Arianthe Galani (Mrs Costanides), Faye Metaxis (Mrs Laventis), Igor Sas (Maurice Hosking), Vincent Ball (Cyril Williams), Daina Reid (Brenda), Catherine Richardson (Irene), Pat Skevington (Head Manageress), Geoffrey Gibbs (Sir Harry Harvey-Watt), Margaret Ford (Dead Woman), Ramsay McLean (Dead Woman's Husband), George Shevtsov (Sid Leventine).

Celebrations are supposed to be loud and colourful, and David Elfick's **Love in Limbo** is. Celebrations are also supposed to be fun, and **Love in Limbo** is more fun than any local cinematic exercise in nostalgia since "Undercover", **Kitty and the Bagman** and **Eliza Fraser**[3]. It's like a fireworks display on film.

The decor is bright, the lighting high-key, the characters brash, the situations archetypal and the whole thing is assembled as an unashamed rhapsody celebrating a young man's first pubescent explorations of the glories of women.

Barry McJannet (Aden Young), Arthur Baskin (Russell Crowe) and Ken Riddle (Craig Adams).

Ken Riddle (Craig Adams), a student too preoccupied with puberty for his own good, is promptly dismissed from school for his erotic drawings and gets a position in his uncle's flourishing garment business. As luck would have it, one of the firm's senior employees is an attractive, ladykilling gad-about named Max Wiseman (Martin Sacks), eager to teach a lad like Ken about women.

Such contrivances are not liabilities in **Love in Limbo**; they are selling points. Also in the factory is a weedy, virginal Welsh git, Arthur Baskin (Russell Crowe), a well-built young stud, Barry McJannet (Aden Young), and a Greek woman with a daughter so beautiful Ken spends much of his time building fantasies around her.

If there is any real criticism of **Love in Limbo**—and that is pushing it for a film this full of charm—it is that it doesn't have much of a central plot. The film is basically a patchwork of vignettes nicely woven together by some neat narrative threads about Ken and his war widow mum, Ivy (Maya Stange), trying to move to the next stages of their lives.

The film's art direction (by David McKay) looks like a Norgen Vaas icecream counter. Exaggerated pastel colours reincarnate a glorious 1950s suburbia which has nothing to do with documentary recreation and everything to do with evoking a nostalgic memory that is universally pleasing.

The film uses humour to generate warmth, with practical jokes—such as the bogus STD test results scare—binding the small community of workers in the factory with laughter.

However, it does not shirk from the Freudian relationship between Ken and his attractive mother. He is protective of her, and becomes competitive with Max when he makes his play for her. Ken also finds her sexually alluring. While helping her out of her dress, he gets a psychologically-troubling but hormonally-pleasing glimpse of her bottom.

Of all the things celebrated in **Love in Limbo**, it is the romantic vision of a mythical Australia and the glory of its values that help give the film heart, however rose-coloured. There is male bonding through drinking, defiance of authority, larrikins, soft-hearted macho men and golden-hearted whores.

Surprisingly for a film this light, the film ends on an intelligently open-ended note by showing that, while her son still has a lot to learn, Ivy is not beyond maturing a little more herself. First she goes for security in a relationship, then for passion, and, finding satisfaction in neither, opts bravely to be on her own.

For a film which barely has a scene without a smile, to get away with such a turn is testament to Elfick's skill at blending comedy with drama without upsetting the film's upbeat cadence. It's a tough trick, beautifully pulled off.

JIM SCHEMBRI

1 Presumably the film-makers meant 'Little Willie Littlefield (Himself)'.
2 The first eight credits follow the order of the opening credits; the rest are in order of appearance.
3 "Undercover" (David Stevens, 1984), **Kitty and the Bagman** (Donald Crombie, 1983) and **A Faithful Narrative of the Capture, Sufferings and Miraculous Escape of Eliza Fraser** (Tim Burstall, 1976).

References
'David Elfick's **Love in Limbo**', a production report by Andrew L. Urban, *Cinema Papers*, no. 91, January 1993, pp. 24–8.
'Coming of Age: Notes towards a Re-appraisal', an article by Raffaele Caputo, *Cinema Papers*, no. 94, August 1993, pp. 12–16.
'**Love in Limbo**', a review by Karl Quinn, *Cinema Papers*, no. 94, August 1993, pp. 44–5.
'**Love in Limbo**', a review by Marg O'Shea, *Filmnews*, June 1993, p. 20.

MAP OF THE HUMAN HEART

Polygram presents a Working Title Films[,] Vincent Ward Films[,] Les Films Ariane[,] Sunrise Films [and] Map Films production of MAP OF THE HUMAN HEART. © 1992 Polygram Filmproduktion GmbH[–] Australian Film Finance Corporation Pty Limited. Script developed with the assistance of Australian Film Commission and New Zealand Film Commission. Made with the participation of Australian Film Finance Corporation Pty Limited. An Australia–Canada–France–UK co-production. *Locations:* Montréal, Canadian Arctic; the UK. *Filmed:* April–July 1991. *Australian distributor:* Hoyts. *Opened:* 22 April 1993. *Video:* First Release. *Rating:* M. 35mm. 109 mins.

Producers: Tim Bevan, Vincent Ward. *Co-producer:* Timothy White. *French co-producer:* Sylvanie Samderichin. *Canadian co-producers:* Linda Beath, Paul Saltzman. *Executive producers:* Graham Bradstreet, Harvey Weinstein, Bob Weinstein. *Associate producer:* Redmond Morris. *Scriptwriter:* Louis Nowra. Based on a story by Vincent Ward. *Director of photography:* Eduardo Serra. *Camera operators:* Pascal Ridao; David Worley (UK). *Production designer:* John Beard. *Costume designer:* Renee April. *Editors:* John Scott, George Akers. *Composer:* Gabriel Yared. *Sound recordist:* Pierre Camus. *Sound editors:* Andrew Plain (sup.); Anne Breslin, James Manche (fx); Livia Ruzic (dia.); Liz Goldfinch, Danielle Wiessner (ADR). *Mixers:* Gethin Creagh, Martin Oswin; Steve Burgess (foley).

Cast

Jason Scott Lee (Avik), Robert Joamie (Young Avik), Anne Parillaud (Albertine), Annie Galipeau (Young Albertine), Patrick Bergin (Walter Russell), Clotilde Coreau (Rainee), John Cusack (Mapmaker[1]), Jeanne Moreau (Sister Banville), Ben Mendelsohn (Farmboy), Jerry Snell (Boleslaw), Jayko Pitseolak (Avik's Grandmother), Matt Holland (Flight Navigator), Rebecca Vevee (Inuit Cook), Josape Kopalee (Inuit Elder), Reepah Arreak (Avik's Girlfriend), Monique Spaziani (Nurse Beatrice), Harry Hill (X-Ray Doctor), Anik Matern (Thelma), Marc Ruel (Photo Analyst), Tyley Ross (Photo Messenger), Charlotte Coleman (Julie).

Vincent Ward's Map of the Human Heart is a superbly-crafted narrative (told in flashback) about how an old Inuit Eskimo, Avik (Robert Joamie), was taken in 1931 to Montréal by a Canadian airman, Walter Russell (Patrick Bergin), for treatment for

Lovers across time: Albertine (Anne Parillaud) and Avik (Jason Scott Lee).

TB. At the hospital, Avik meets Albertine (Annie Galipeau), a half-breed Indian girl; ten years later, Avik (Jason Scott Lee) enrols in the Canadian Air Force in the hope of locating Albertine (Anne Parillaud) in Europe. The film finally culminates in Avik's encountering the daughter he never knew he had.

The title of Ward's intelligent and absorbing film resonates on several significant levels in terms of human character and conduct. Given the film's epic mode of storytelling—and Ward's directorial fluency as a storyteller is evident, time and again, throughout the film—the title itself speaks of the maps of love, human loss and the changing contours of cultural contact (that is, Avik's Eskimo identity and its implications of what it signifies in the encroaching wave of white colonisation).

Louis Nowra's intelligent and immensely-convincing script, with the playwright's familiar interest in marginalised characters trying to make sense of a world that has its own surreal logic, is manifested in the growing relationship between Avik and Albertine in hospital. She (like Avik) is displaced because of her fragmented individual iden-

tity—she wants to erase the stigma of being a half-breed—and both of them face the Christian missionary zeal that characterises the supervision of the hospital by nuns, and best expressed by Sister Banville (Jeanne Moreau).

To be a half-breed for Albertine is to die broke and bare-footed on the back of a horse (just as her father did). She dreams of owning a horse—a wish which finds its magical surreal moment later on where we encounter a black horse in Albertine and Walter's bedroom in England. This scene has a truly-surreal poetry, and it points to Ward's and Nowra's shared interest in creating a movie that attempts to go beneath the surface of everyday life to a deeper level of human reality.

The movie's intricate weaving of history, culture and human love (its uncharted intensities and mysteries) makes it an enthralling experience. Avik's love for Albertine takes him across several different countries, while his Eskimo world rapidly disintegrates. When Avik as an old man seeks a drink from an oil worker in a bar, the worker, while giving him a drink, tells Avik that all Eskimos are lazy, worthless alcoholics. Avik's wisdom in seeing beneath our maps of colonial expansion and superiority is predicated on a profound understanding that polycultural empathy and human love, and not indifference, deception and greed, should animate our world.

Map of the Human Heart is a finely-wrought film narrative that is supercharged with a poetic sensibility that captures the dramatic, thematic and stylistic nuances of its epic story material. Its charting of the overlapping connections between the map of one's ethnic and cultural landscape with that of the human heart (visibly rendered in several scenes where we see Avik and Albertine looking at a medical atlas of the human anatomy) is quite significant in this century of exiles and demographic turbulence.

JOHN CONOMOS

---

[1] The front credits opt for 'The Mapmaker'.

References
'Map of the Human Heart', a review by Anna Dzenis, *Cinema Papers*, no. 93, May 1993, pp. 48–9.
'Vincent Ward: Navigator of the Human Heart', an interview by Pauline Adamek, *Filmnews*, April–May 1993, pp. 9–10.
'Scriptwriters are Over-rated', an interview with scriptwriter Louis Nowra by Marg O'Shea, ibid., p. 11.

THE NOSTRADAMUS KID

Beyond Films presents a Roger Simpson and Roger Le Mesurier production. The Nostradamus Kid © 1992 Simpson Le Mesurier Films Pty Ltd [and] Australian Film Finance Corporation Pty Limited. Developed with the assistance of Film Victoria and the Australian Film Commission. Made with the participation of Australian Film Finance Corporation Pty Limited as part of the 1991 FFC Film Fund. *Location:* Sydney. *Filmed:* 14 October–6 December 1991. *Australian distributor:* Ronin. *Video:* 21st Century–Ronin. *Rating:* M. 35mm. 120 mins.

Producer: Terry Jennings. *Executive producers:* Roger Simpson, Roger Le Mesurier. *Scriptwriter:* Bob Ellis. *Director of photography:* Geoff Burton. *Production designer:* Roger Ford. *Assistant costume designer:* Louise Wakefield. *Editor:* Henry Dangar. *Composer:* Chris Neal. *Sound recordist:* David Lee. *Sound editors:* Jeanine Chialvo, Mark Perry (dia.); Penn Robinson (fx). *Mixers:* Peter Fenton, Ron Purvis, Martin Oswin.

Cast

Noah Taylor (Ken Elkin), Miranda Otto (Jennie O'Brien), Arthur Dignam (Pastor Anderson), Peter Gwynne (The Shepherd's Rod), Jack Campbell (McAlister), Erick Mitsak (Wayland), Loene Carmen (Meryl), Alice Garner (Esther Anderson), Lucy Bell (Sarai Anderson), Jeanette Cronin (Christy), Hec McMillan (Pastor Dibley), Colin Friels (American Preacher), Bob Maza (Black Man), Bartholomew Rose (Kavanagh), Robyn Gurney (Mrs. Elkin), Marie Lloyd (Mrs. Rod), Julie Godfrey (Meryl's Mum), Gregory Simpson (Mr. O'Brien), John Noble (General Booth), Jim McClelland (Magistrate), Bruno Baldoni (Italian Grocer), Alan Light (Brother Allison), Norm Galton (Bus Conductor), Carmel Mullin (Adventist Customer).

The Nostradamus Kid is one of those Australian movies which is more fun to argue about than to actually watch. Partly this is because of Ellis' stated indifference towards the craft of film directing—only the 10th most important ingredient in a successful movie, he reckons (below a solid script, canny casting, hiring a good director of photography and editor ...). This indifference shows: although it is his third film as a director, Ellis pays scant attention to visual style, story rhythm or proper guidance of the actors' performances.

The script is indeed the thing in The Nostradamus Kid. Ellis has often publicly placed himself in a tradition headed up by François Truffaut and Preston Sturges—neither of them, for most of their careers, 'showy' or flashily-visual directors. The references are astute: while Ellis emulates Truffaut's 'Antoine Doinel' cycle[1] by making a bittersweet, largely-autobiographical film (anyone even slightly familiar with the Ellis œuvre will recognise many of the individuals, incidents and attitudes portrayed), he also mimics Sturges' flair for brittly-humorous one-liners and socially-dynamic ensemble interaction.

Whatever its shortcomings, the film demands to be taken, warts and all, as Ellis's testament to himself and his distinctive sensibility. Ken Elkin (Noah Taylor) is a 'Nostradamus Kid' because, twice in his young life, he becomes obsessed with the notion that an apocalypse is imminent—firstly as a tormented soul at a Seventh Day Adventist camp in 1956, and secondly as a Sydney University student during the Cuban missile crisis of 1962. In both periods, Elkin fixates on dream-women: the shy Esther Anderson (Alice Garner) and the privileged Jennie O'Brien (Miranda Otto.)

It is easy to take The Nostradamus Kid as a fairly-straightforward exercise in misogyny. It tells a familiar story, a kind of Australian variation on a model Charles Bukowski fiction. Its key elements are a ragged, bohemian hero whose deepest personal relations are with other blokes; and the enigmatic women in his life who are rich, moralistic and treacherous, but endlessly desirable. Add to this brew a few stern, castrating father figures, loose jokes about rape, and the best friend, McAlister (Jack Campbell), who is also Ken's principal sexual rival, and you have one whopping great male fantasy of a movie.

Ultimately, however, the film's tone is more maudlin than aggro. Scenes in which Ellis allows Ken to castigate his enemies ('History will judge you harshly') or to receive fulsome praise from women ('You do it better than anyone') are welcome moments of ironic self-mockery. There is an uncharacteristically-defensive note, a nervous nod to feminist enlightenment in the (extremely clumsily-directed) scene in which Ken, absorbed as usual in himself and his own angst during the act of love, does not realise that Jennie has had her first orgasm.

Ellis mainly indulges a different sort of male fantasy: the sad song of the eternal 'little boy lost', forever mourning the passing of time and the waste of life's unfulfilled potentials. Such pathos can be found everywhere in those works of Australian culture created by men: we see variations of it in the writing of Barry Dickins, and the film and television work of Brian McKenzie. In Ellis' work across several media, this emotion has a boozy, bitter, wilfully 'politically-incorrect' edge to match the tear-soaked nostalgia and regret. Watching the increasingly-pained contortions of this uniquely-Aussie tradition in The Nostradamus Kid, one can only wonder whether it is fast approaching its historical and cultural use-by date.

ADRIAN MARTIN

---

[1] **Les Quatre Cents Coups** (1959), *Antoine et Colette* (short, 1962), **Baisers Volés** (1968), **Domicile Conjugal** (1970) and **L'Amour en Fuite** (1979), all starring Jean-Pierre Leaud. (Ellis has announced his intention to continue his screen autobiography with Noah Taylor as his *alter ego.*)

References

'Bob Ellis' The Nostradamus Kid', a production report by Andrew L. Urban, including interview with writer–director Bob Ellis, *Cinema Papers*, no. 86, January 1992, pp. 12–17.

'Coming of Age: Notes towards a Re-appraisal', article by Raffaele Caputo, *Cinema Papers*, no. 94, August 1993, pp. 12–16.

'The Nostradamus Kid', a review by Karl Quinn, *Cinema Papers*, no. 96, December 1993, pp. 50–1.

'The World According to Ellis', an article by Mary Colbert, *Filmnews*, November 1993, pp. 8–9.

Awaiting the end of time: Jennie O'Brien (Miranda Otto) and Ken Elkin (Noah Taylor).

DAVID ELFICK

NO WORRIES

Film Four International with the participation of British Screen presents [a] Palm Beach Pictures–Initial Films production in association with Southern Star Entertainment. No Worries. © 1992 Australian Film Finance Corporation Pty Limited, British Screen Finance Limited and Channel Four Television Company Limited. An Australia–United Kingdom co-production. Script developed with the assistance of the Australian Film Commission. Made with the participation of Australian Film Finance Corporation Pty Limited. *Locations:* Gilgandra shire, Sydney (New South Wales). *Filmed:* 17 February–16 April 1992. *Australian distributor:* Beyond. *Video:* Roadshow. *Rating:* G. 35mm. 92 mins.

Producers: David Elfick, Eric Fellner. *Executive producer:* Kim Williams. *Associate producers:* Nina Stevenson, John Winter. *Scriptwriter:* David Holman. Based on his play. *Director of photography:* Stephen F. Windon. *Camera operator:* Marc Spicer. *Production designer:* Michael Bridges. *Costume designer:* Clarrissa Patterson. *Editor:* Louise Innes. *Composers:* David A. Stewart, Patrick Seymour. *Sound recordist:* Guntis Sics. *Sound editor:* Karin Whittington (dia.). *Mixer:* Phil Judd.

Cast

The Bell Family: Amy Terelinck (Matilda), Geoff Morell (Ben), Susan Lyons (Ellen); Bundooma School: Geraldine James (Ann Marie O'Dwyer), David Kaff (Nathan Burke), Ashley Bindon (Raymond Drew), Anita Thompson (Laura Hay), Grant Noy ("Buddha" Ward), Joel Emerton (Kerry Hay), Amy Burnicle (Narelle), Brooke Lindsay (Tina), Nicole Johnson (Lisa); In the Country: John Hargreaves (Clive Ryan), Steven Vidler (Garry Hay), Gary Cooper (Tim Rush), Ray Barrett (Old Burkey), Harold Hopkins (John Burke), Annie Byron (Mrs Burke); City School: Bill Young (Mr Carmody), Ngoc Hanh Nguyen (Binh); In the City: Andrew Gilbert (Uncle Kev), Deborah Galands (Gina), Giau Van Tran (Hien), Jacqy Phillips (Maria), Jack Mayers (Mal).

The best thing about David Elfick's No Worries, which won first prize for Best Children's Film at the 1994 Berlin Festival, is that it isn't a 'children's' film at all. Children's film and television has come to a crossroads, because it is assumed that children don't need or desire to confront the major issues of our times. This has resulted in bland films which children themselves perceive as irrelevant to their lives.

No Worries is different. Through the eyes of Matilda Bell (Amy Terelinck), an 11-year-old girl living on a sheep farm in New South Wales, it takes an unsentimental look at the devastation caused by the latest drought to hit rural Australia, which was compounded by the recession and further aggravated by an uncompromising lack of sympathy from the banks.

Poverty on the land and banks go together, and No Worries makes it hard not to recall John Ford's classic The Grapes of Wrath (1940), particularly in the scenes which show the social upheaval affecting country people as families and rural communities collapse. Matilda and her family are, as No Worries shows when the film moves to Sydney, economic refugees, comparable not only to mid-west Americans going to California in the 1930s, but also to the economic refugees from Asia who escape to Australia, many by boat.

David Holman's script, loosely based on his 1986 play, translates these complex and adult issues effortlessly to the screen. The catastrophe wrought by drought is shown in many ways: mud dripping from a shower, sheep being shot, the awesome fury of a dust storm, tomatoes withering on the vine in Matilda's backyard. But the real power of the film comes from its focus on the resilience and courage of country Australia coping with disaster.

Elfick's direction is warm and assured, and the film is often humorous and always entertaining. The strong cast all give natural performances, particularly Susan Lyons as Matilda's mother, Geoff Morell as her father, and Geraldine James as the school teacher anxiously counting the dwindling number of children left to teach. But the most inspired acting comes from Amy Terelinck's central performance as Matilda, the tractor-driving, self-possessed country kid who's suddenly dispossessed and forced to make new alliances in the city.

No Worries tells its tale honestly and without histrionics. It has set a benchmark for children's films by realistically engaging with a major contemporary issue in Australia that has themes which are relevant for children everywhere.

JAN EPSTEIN

Reference
'No Worries Wins in Berlin; Now for Sydney ...', an interview with director David Elfick by Mary Colbert, *Filmnews*, March 1994, p. 16.

Ellen (Susan Lyons), Matilda (Amy Terelinck), Ben (Geoff Morell) and Binh (Ngoc Hanh Nguyen).

A N T O N I O   T I B A L D I

ON MY OWN

Ellepi Film s.r.l.[,] Alliance Communications [and] Rosa Colosimo Pty Ltd present a Leo Pescarolo production ON MY OWN. © 1991 Ellipi Film s.r.l.[,] Alliance Communications Corporation[,] Arto-pelli Motion Pictures Inc [and] Australian Film Finance Corporation Pty. Limited. Produced with the participation of RAI Radiotelevisione Italiana RAITRE, Australian Film Finance Corporation Pty. Limited, Arbo Film and Maran GmbH (Munich), Telefilm Canada and The Ontario Film Development Corporation. Made with the participation of Australian Film Finance Corporation Pty Limited, RAITRE, DGC/GCR and ACTRA. An Italy–Canada–Australia co-production. *Locations:* Toronto; London. *Filmed:* February–April 1991. *Australian distributor:* Ronin. *Opened:* 26 February 1993. *Video:* 21st Century. *Rating:* M. 35mm. 95 mins.

Producers: Leo Pescarolo, Elisa Resegotti. *Co-producers:* Stavros C. Stavrides, Will Spencer. *Executive producers:* Laël McCall, Rosa Colosimo. *Scriptwriters:* Gill Dennis, Antonio Tibaldi, John Frizzell. Based on a story by Antonio Tibaldi, Gill Dennis. *Directors of photography:* Vic Sarin; Ian Owles (London). *Production designer:* Bill Fleming. *Costume designer:* Kathy Vieira. *Editor:* Edward McQueen-Mason. *Composer:* Franco Piersanti. *Sound recordist:* Allan Scarth. *Sound editors:* Livia Ruzic (dia.); Craig Carter, Ross A. Porter (fx). *Mixers:* James Currie, John Simpson; Jason Russell (London).

Cast

Matthew Ferguson (Simon Henderson), Judy Davis (His Mother), David McIlwraith (His Father), Jan Rubes (The Colonel), Michele Melega (Shammas), Colin Fox (Palter), Nicholas Van Burek (Max Cobb), Rachel Blanchard (Tania), Lanna MacKay (Evi), Michael Polley (Soccer Coach), Colin Brezicki (Sawyers), James Mainprize (Computer Class Teacher), Norwich Duff (Classroom Teacher), Donald Ewer (Priest), Christopher Hicks (Henry Chase), Alberto Franceschetti (Alberto), Malcolm McClintock (Martin), Paul Brogren (Philibert), Terrence Bredin (Desk Clerk), Joanne Yeo (Psychiatric Nurse), Ranjeev Kimatrai (Shower Student).

Oᴺ **n My Own** tells the story of Simon Henderson (Matthew Ferguson), a boy being educated in a boarding school, who is first glimpsed waiting at a railway station for a train that will reunite him with his estranged parents for Christmas. His father,

Simon Henderson (Matthew Ferguson) and His Mother (Judy Davis).

however, welcomes him with the news that his mother has been hospitalised and will have to return to England. After a short and unhappy reunion, Simon returns early to school.

Simon makes the acquaintance of Max Cobb (Nicholas Van Burek), a boy whose brazen flouting of school rules is attractive. After a time, Simon's mother suddenly appears at the school and takes him away for an evening which ends in rancour between them, followed by a violent moment when his mother headbutts a hotel windowpane. Simon returns to school and sneaks out to participate in an evening of drinking and dancing with Max and Max's girlfriend. During a soccer match, he allows in his first goal for many matches and fails to break a record for keeping a clean sheet. Following the match, he loses his temper with teammates. This is quickly forgotten when he is summoned to talk to the headmaster, who tells him he must go to his mother in England and inadvertently lets Simon know that his mother is dead. After returning from the funeral, Simon declines to attend the school social. He dreams of his mother and at last becomes reconciled with her. He wakes up and heads for the social, his melancholy lifted.

It has to be said that this is an unassuming but not unpretentious film. It is determined to be low-key and wishes to present its characters and their emotions in a

subtle if not oblique manner, as well provide a degree of ambiguity about the relations between Simon, his parents and friends. It does make clear, even obvious, that Simon's hormones are coursing. But the determination to be low-key has the inevitable effect of producing a film lacking in emotional impact, thus failing to generate any sympathy for or complicity with the characters. There is no real drama occurring and there is an inevitability about the film's resolution. What interest there is tends to come from just a few moments of surprise. Things happen in the course of the narrative which are difficult to comprehend or assimilate in the circumstance. These moments are intriguing. Does a 17-year-old English–Canadian boy react with as much equanimity when his 35-year-old mother undresses in front of him and climbs naked into the double bed they will share? Surely a son sits next to his father in the church where they are attending the mother/wife's funeral. Such moments don't ring true, which is unfortunate in a film seeking to suggest some psychological insight and wishing to invoke some truthful elements of human experience.

GEOFF GARDNER

References
'On My Own', a review by Pat Gillespie, *Cinema Papers*, no. 95, October 1993, pp. 48–9.
'On My Own', a review by Jane Freeby, *Filmnews*, March 1993, p. 11.

JANE CAMPION

THE PIANO

CIBY 2000 presents a Jan Chapman Production. THE PIANO. © 1993 Jan Chapman Productions. Script developed with the assistance of the Australian Film Commission. Film developed with the assistance of New South Wales Film and Television Office. A French-financed Australia–New Zealand co-production. *Location:* New Zealand. *Australian distributor:* Miramax. *Video:* Touchstone. *Rating:* M. 35mm. 115 mins.

Producer: Jan Chapman. *Executive producer:* Alain Depardieu. *Associate producer:* Mark Turnbull. *Scriptwriter:* Jane Campion. *Director of photography:* Stuart Dryburgh. *Camera operator:* Alun Bollinger. *Production designer:* Andrew McAlpine. *Costume designer:* Janet Patterson. *Editor:* Veronika Jenet. *Composer:* Michael Nyman. *Sound designer:* Lee Smith. *Sound recordist:* Tony Johnson. *Sound editors:* Peter Townend (fx); Annabelle Sheehan (supervising ADR); Gary O'Grady, Jeanine Chialvo (dia.). *Mixers:* Gethin Creagh; Martin Oswin (fx).

Cast

Holly Hunter (Ada), Harvey Keitel (Baines), Sam Neill (Stewart), Anna Paquin (Flora), Kerry Walker (Aunt Morag), Genevieve[1] Lemon (Nessie), Tungia Baker (Hira), Ian Mune (Reverend), Peter Dennett (Head Seaman), Te Whatanui Skipwith (Chief Nihe), Peter Smith (Hone), Bruce Allpress (Blind Piano Tuner), Cliff Curtis (Mana), Carla Rupuha (Meni (Mission Girl)), Mahina Tunui (Mere[2] (Mission Girl))[2]), Hori Ahipene (Muturu), Gordon Hatfield (Te Kori), Mere Boynton (Chief Nihe's Daughter), Kirsten Batley (Marama), Tania Burney (Mahina), Annie Edwards (Te Tiwha), Harina Haare (Roimata), Christina Harimate (Parearau), Steve Kanuta (Amohia), P. J. Karauria (Taua), Sonny Kirikiri (Tame).

The critical backlash against Jane Campion's **The Piano** and its phenomenal international success has been ferocious. It is one of those movies that—in the time-honoured style of Australian film culture—no one can see very clearly, people reacting to it as either a blinding masterpiece or a hideous abomination. Indeed, one overseas visitor (Serge Grünberg from *Cahiers du Cinéma*) was moved to comment on the 'excess of dishonour' with which some Australians greeted the film, seeing in this a sign of our 'endemic cultural masochism' and our national 'contempt for everything indigenous'[3].

The Piano has suffered the severe misfortune of falling between two very different

Ada (Holly Hunter) and Flora (Anna Paquin).

kinds of cinema. For some, the tale of mute Ada (Holly Hunter) on a marshy New Zealand isle is clearly a 'period piece' in the manner of the Merchant–Ivory films, and thus needs to follow strict dramatic rules, in a relatively restrained and plausible manner. Perhaps because some of our own 'costume dramas' of the 1970s count among the dreariest made in the world, Australian film commentators tend to be extremely literal-minded in their prescriptions for this genre. Thus, angry reviewers (including Bob Ellis, Phillip Adams and John Slavin) have scoured **The Piano** for every last skerrick of narrative implausibility, obscure character motivation and historical anachronism.

One wonders, however, whether any of this fuss would have arisen if **The Piano** had come to us as a 'magic realist' art movie from overseas, signed by the likes of Emir Kusturica (**Arizona Dream**, 1993.) The majority of European critics have had no problem accepting Campion's film on this level, as obviously heightened, symbolic and 'irreal'. *Cahiers* even hailed it as a cross between Emily Brontë's *Wuthering Heights* and Kubrick's **2001: A Space Odyssey** (1968).

That the film has been so admired and appreciated by the French should not be surprising, since **The Piano**'s mix of high romanticism, melodrama, erotic perversity and stylistic modernism is closer to the work of André Téchiné (especially **Les Soeurs Brontës**, 1979) than anything in Australian cinema. The perversity—which is also a key feature of Campion's previous feature,

Sweetie (1989), and her short story, '*Big Shell*'[4]—has proved contentious. Some have protested that the relationship between Ada and Baines (Harvey Keitel) is a glorification of sexual harassment and rape. But, for Campion, sexual desire always detours through strange bargains, power games and unspoken understandings.

It is not a flawless movie. All the scenes involving Ada, her daughter Flora (Anna Paquin) and Baines are superb—stylistically bold, with always surprising rhythmic flows and performance gestures. But both the energy and the artistry dissipate whenever Ada's hapless, repressed husband Stewart (Sam Neill) appears, or when Campion cuts to a gaggle of Victorian nannies or a noble chorus of Maoris for dramatic counterpoint. The point of the latter element—the homology of collective, colonial tyranny with personal, patriarchal tyranny—is clear enough, but remains schematically sketched.

At its centre, however, **The Piano** is a commanding, passionate, poetic film. One would do an injustice to its artistic achievement and cultural significance if one did not consider it, at least in part, as a triumph of women's cinema—both in its intense intimacy with female psychology and sexuality, and its elaboration of what can be taken and celebrated as a 'female æsthetic'. Indeed, without wanting to be too dualistic and definitive about the masculine–feminine relation, it is hard not to read in the (mostly male) condemnation of **The Piano** a phobic fear of a new, powerfully-emerging cinema—a cinema in which the classical unities of plot, character and setting are shattered in a radical, expressionist rage.

ADRIAN MARTIN

1 Usually spelt 'Geneviève'.
2 The published script incorrectly gives the name as 'Mary (Mission Girl)'.
3 Serge Grünberg, 'Australia: From Desert to Hollywood', *Metro*, No. 100, December 1994.
4 Jane Campion, 'Big Shell', *Rolling Stone* (Australia), No. 426, Yearbook 1988, pp. 74–6.

References

'The Piano', writer–director Jane Campion interviewed by Miro Bilborough, *Cinema Papers*, no. 93, May 1993, pp. 4–8, 10–11.
'46e International du Film de Cannes', an article by Jan Epstein, with discussion of the film, *Cinema Papers*, no. 94, August 1993, pp. 22–7.
'The Piano', a review by Raymond Younis, *Cinema Papers*, no. 95, October 1993, pp. 50–1.
'Soundtracks', an article by Ivan Hutchinson, ibid., pp. 58–9.
'The Piano', a review by Mary Colbert, *Filmnews*, August 1993, p. 14.

RECKLESS KELLY

Warner Bros. presents a Serious Film.[1] RECKLESS KELLY. © 1993 Warner Bros., Serious Entertainment Pty Ltd, Roadshow Film Distributors Pty Ltd and Australian Film Finance Corporation Pty. Limited. Made with the participation of Australian Film Finance Corporation Pty Limited. *Locations:* Port Stephens, Broken Hill, Sydney (New South Wales); Gold Coast (Queensland); Los Angeles, Las Vegas, Hollywood. *Australian distributor:* Roadshow. *Opened:* 8 April 1993. *Video:* Roadshow. *Rating:* PG. 35mm. Panavision. 103 mins.

Producers: Yahoo Serious, Warwick Ross. *Executive producer:* Graham Burke. *Co-producer:* Lulu Serious. *Associate producer:* David Roach. *Line producer:* Tim Sanders. *Scriptwriter[s]:* Yahoo Serious [David Roach, Warwick Ross, Lulu Serious[2]]. *Director of photography:* Kevin Hayward. *Cameraman:* John Mahaffie.[3] *Camera operator:* John Mahaffie (Australia). [*Production designer:* not credited.] *Costume designer:* Sally Campbell. *Editors:* Yahoo Serious (supervising); David Roach (Australia); Larry Jordan (US digital). *Composers:* Anthony Marinelli, Tommy Tycho and Maurie Sheldon. *Sound recordists:* Tim Lloyd (Australia); Lee Orloff (US). *Sound editors:* Anthony Gray (dia.); Wayne Pashley (chief supervising fx); Julius Chan, John Penders (fx); Mike LeMaire (US sup.); Karola Stone, G. W. Davis, Edmund Chickelban (US).

Mixers: Phil Judd (Australia); Jeffrey J. Halboush, Greg P. Russell, Kevin E. Carpenter (US).

Cast

Yahoo Serious (Ned Kelly), Melora Hardin (Robin Banks), Alexei Sayle (Major Wib), Hugo Weaving (Sir John), Kathleen Freeman (Mrs Delance), John Panette (Sam Delance), Bob Maza (Dan Kelly), Martin Ferrero (Ernie the Fan), Anthony Ackroyd (Joe Kelly), Tracy Mann (Miss Twisty), Max Walker (Newsreader), Adam Bowen (Bank Teller Marcell); Warren Coleman, Tyler Coppin (Hollywood Bank Tellers); J. Andrew Prowse (Shorty), Don Stalings (Hank the Fan), Theresa Bell (Hollywood Outlaw), Paul Livingstone (Postman), Lulu Serious (Hollywood Supermarket Checkout), Russell Cheek (Bank Teller Gianni), Steven Cox (Bank Teller Wolfgang), Richard Carter (Police Sergeant (Australia), Clarence Felder (Hollywood Police Lieutenant), Gary Grossman (Las Vegas Sinner).

After his eccentric, yet attention-grabbing, debut feature, **Young Einstein** (1988), Yahoo Serious had substantial Hollywood backing to make this follow-up. Very loosely based on the story of the Ned Kelly myth about robbing from the rich to give to the poor, the film proceeds along fanciful lines, while pursuing strong contemporary themes.

As a comedy feature, **Reckless Kelly** takes early 1990s Australia, together with the issues of the day—the environment, corporate wealth and finance, nationalism, the Australian republican movement, Hollywood film-making and the star system—and holds them up to popular ridicule. In this objective, Yahoo Serious is at least true to the anti-authoritarian spirit of the Kelly Gang, to whom he dedicates the film.

The story revolves around a contemporary version of the Kelly gang and its ownership of the remote Reckless Island, which the one remaining member of the gang, Ned (Yahoo Serious), uses as a base for his bank robberies. Plugging into the Australian male ethos of beer and mates in the hotel environment, the island features the Glenrowan Hotel & Video Rental, which serves as the focus for a vaguely multi-cultural extended family, whose spokesperson is an Aborigine, Dan Kelly (Bob Maza).

Ned is very nearly caught and disposed of by a corporate-banking capitalist, Sir John (Hugo Weaving), and a buffoon-like British soldier, Major Wib (Alexi Sayle), who set out to dispose of Ned and his island by selling it to the Japanese. Ned moves to America to rob big banks, ends up in movies in Hollywood, meets the romantic interest, Robin Banks (Melora Hardin), and gets the money he needs to buy Reckless Island.

Loaded with sight gags, **Reckless Kelly** attracted little if any support from reviewers when it was released. Awkwardly constructed, its narrative sequences have the throwaway appeal of all good slapstick, with a strong Australian flavour. The acting and script editing do not, however, reflect such appealing attributes. This is unfortunate, because **Reckless Kelly** is one of those self-consciously rare films that positions an Australian experience at the forefront of the film. In an era of globalisation, this provides its own pleasures.

MARCUS BREEN

---

[1] An end credit reads: 'A Serious Entertainment Production'.
[2] The opening credits have Yahoo Serious as the sole scriptwriter. This is contradicted by the first of the roll credits at the end, which reads: 'Screenplay: Yahoo Serious, David Roach, Warwick Ross, Lulu Serious'.
[3] This is the only credit of its kind sighted in researching this book. It appears on the same opening credit as that of the DOP.

Reference
'Yahoo Serious: **Reckless Kelly**', an interview by Andrew L. Urban, *Cinema Papers*, no. 92, April 1993, pp. 30–5, 72.

Ned Kelly (Yahoo Serious) outside the Glenrowan Hotel & Video Rental.

THE REFRACTING GLASSES

Produced in association with the Australian Film Commission. THE REFRACTING GLASSES. © 1992 David Perry. *Locations:* Sydney; Moscow; Ukraine. *Australian distributor:* AFI. *Opened:* 30 July 1993. *Video:* AFI Distribution. *Rating:* M. 35mm. 104 mins.

Producer: David Perry. *Scriptwriter:* David Perry. *Directors of photography:* David Perry, Simon Smith; John Baird, Jim Powe (add.). *Computer animation:* Pavel Kyral. *Film animation:* David Perry. *Editor:* David Perry. *Sound recordist:* Liam Egan. *Sound editor:* David Perry (fx). *Mixer:* Phil Heywood.

Cast

David Perry (Constant Malernik), Tommy Thomas (Constant Malernik as a Child), Leon Teague (Constant in 1953), Taylor Owynns (VOG (the Voice Of God)), Lydia Fegan (Lydia), Alla Karihaloo (Alla), Iain Gardiner (Ern Malley), Skye Wansey (Ethel Malley); Celine Donegan, Richard Johnson, Riszard Ratajczak ("New Australians" in the Pub); Bobby Ferguson (Shostakovich in 1922), Phil Heywood (Vog's [sic] Producer), David Knight (Projectionist), John Baird (Constant's Camera Operator), Ross Carroll (Big Man in the Pub), Danny Gough (Barman), Ngaire Dignan (Timpanist/Artist); Paul Eichorn, Catherine Fairhall, Cameron Park, Paul Selwood (Workers in the Factory); Ludmilla Mishakova (Ludmilla), Ashley Bindon (Boy with the Cakes), Alex Marchevsky (Voice of V. E. Tatlin).

Davd Perry's **The Refracting Glasses** is a deftly-constructed, lyrical work that resonates across a number of important cultural, filmic and historical registers. It is a film that incorporates Perry's searching autobiographical quest to make sense of his life and times in the context of the major currents of European avant-garde art movements, the Russian Revolution and Australian socio-cultural history.

With characteristic fluency of audiovisual expression, Perry has shaped a moving and highly-informative work that deserves a wider audience, for in it the film-maker has given us a very rich and diverse film that draws upon Perry's life in Sydney since the 1950s as an independent film- and video-maker. Central to the thematic and formal concerns of **The Refracting Glasses** is Perry's non-didactic and courageous preoccupation in confronting his own æsthetic and political beliefs. To do this, Perry has constructed a playful, engaging narrative that features Constant Malernik, an artist and film-maker,

who is performed by Perry himself and represents a more exaggerated satirical version of the film-maker himself.

The Refracting Glasses is a highly-accessible and pleasurable film to watch—not least because Perry's bold mixed-media visual style successfully corresponds to the artistic and personal adventure of Perry's and partner Lydia Fegan's lives. (Fegan's journey to Russia signifies her own Russian ancestral history and her passion for Russian icon painting and culture.) The emphasis on displaying different styles of representation (computer and hand-drawn animation, documentary, mainstream feature performance and experimental 'hand-held' cinematography) attests to Perry's open-ended, risk-taking capacity to push the critical and formal limits of his art for the purpose of making significant, uncompromised personal cinema.

Here is a film that brims with so many ideas and engaging textual forms speaking of the intricate connections between art, revolution and politics. Importantly, **The Refracting Glasses**—an apt title that captures the prismatic complexities of 20th-century culture and life as refracted through the camera apparatus, art and political thought—represents an enthralling bricolage of computer and analogue images, sounds, painting, drawings and dramatised fiction (pivoting on the surreal implications of the celebrated literary hoax, the Ern Malley Affair). But central to this multifac-

eted poetic homage to the artists, film-makers and writers of 20th-century avant-garde art, experimental cinema and politics is the criss-crossing, discursive nature of Malernik's investigation into his own personal trajectory as an artist and film-maker—always questioning in a playful, instructive manner his own fascination for the materials, processes and forms of contemporary textual production.

While it eschews any kind of rigid adherence to fashionable theory templates of how such a film should be constructed, it is not afraid to explore the poetic potential of rubbing film against video, of painting against computers, of drawing against 'Voice-of-God' narrating (*viz* the Australian mainstream cinema). **The Refracting Glasses** lives up to its title: the incredible breadth of style, the lingering haunting computer-animated images of Tatlin's Monument to the Third International, the subtle stirring black-and-white and colour photography (the New York snow scenes are particularly vivid) and the apparition of Ern Malley (Iain Gardiner) hovering on the threshold of Malernik's studio all add up to a power of film-making seldom encountered these days.

JOHN CONOMOS

References
'The Refracting Glasses', a review by Anna Dzenis, *Cinema Papers*, no. 94, August 1993, pp. 44–5.
'Refracting Glasses [sic]', a review by Vikki Riley, *Filmnews*, July 1993, p. 12.

Constant in 1953 (Leon Teague).

THE SILVER BRUMBY

Media World Features presents the Silver Brumby. © 1992 Media World Features[–] Australian Film Finance Corporation Pty Limited. Made with the assistance of Film Victoria. Made with the participation of Australian Film Finance Corporation Pty Limited. *Locations:* Dinner Plain, Mt Hotham, Cobungra Station and Bindi, The High Country (Victoria). *Filmed:* 9 March–13 May 1992. *Australian distributor:* Roadshow. *Video:* Roadshow. *Rating:* G. 35mm. 104 mins.

Producers: Colin J. South, John Tatoulis. *Executive producer:* William T. Marshall. *Line producer:* Brian Burgess. *Associate producer:* Judy Malmgren. *Scriptwriters:* John Tatoulis, Jon Stephens. *Script consultant:* Elyne Mitchell. Based on the novel by Elyne Mitchell. *Director of photography:* Mark Gilfedder. *Camera operator:* Harry Panagiotidis. *Production designer:* Philip Chambers. *Costume designer:* Margot Lindsay. *Costume consultant:* Jane Hyland. *Horse master:* Evanne Chesson. *Editor:* Peter Burgess. *Composer:* Tassos Ioannides. *Sound recordist:* John Wilkinson. *Sound supervisor:* Peter Burgess. *Sound editors:* Glenn Newnham, Gavin Myers. *Mixers:* James Currie; Peter Best (asst).

Cast

Caroline Goodall (Elyne Mitchell), Russell Crowe (The Man), Ami Daemion (Indi Mitchell), Johnny Raaen (Jock), Buddy Tyson (Darcy), Graeme Fullgrabe (Auctioneer); Gary Amos, Murray Chesson, John Coles, Danny Cook, Peter Faithfull, Richard Faithfull, Charlie Harris, Cody Harris, Ken Mitchell, Kristen Olson, Helen Packer, Barry Stephan, David Storey, Harley Young (Riders).

The Man (Russell Crowe).

Just because a film is touted as being a 'children's film' doesn't mean it has to follow all the rules of a children's film. John Tatoulis' The Silver Brumby follows most of the rules dutifully and skilfully, and flouts one of them magnificently.

Most of the traditional elements and codes of your standard children's film are here: the mythical creatures; the classic conflict between man and nature; a sense of right and wrong; the inevitable, ever-useful theme of the child growing and learning about the realities of life, which are sometimes harsh.

Rules aside, The Silver Brumby looks exquisite. It's almost too good to be wasted on children. Writer Elyne Mitchell (Caroline Goodall)—on whose book the film is based—is trying to teach her daughter Indi

(Ami Daemion) to develop a relationship with her environment, which is more sensual than the merely functional one enjoyed by the stockmen who ride about in slow motion, their hats flapping, their stockwhips cracking, and their making repeated declarations of 'Yaaaaaaaaaah!'

Indi begins reading her mum's new manuscript about a marvellous silver brumby, a free and wild spirit roaming the high country, which captures the attentions of an intense young stockman (Russell Crowe).

The Man is not quite like other men of the high country. He is a harmonious portrait of the benign master, lying in its open spaces, like a large, free-range bed. Supine in a glistening stream, the camera glides over and past him, as if he is part of the stream. But the Silver Brumby defiantly presents itself to The Man as the one thing he can't have, so he promptly goes chasing it.

There are several ways this conflict can be interpreted: as man against beast, against nature, against woman, even against his own Id. But thematic and metaphysical analysis of the narrative isn't worth a boatload of gravy if the horses don't look good, and the horses in The Silver Brumby look absolutely grand. The animal photography is well above Disney standard, with some sweeping, single-take helicopter shots.

One of the distinct qualities of The Silver Brumby is its pronounced preference for the

visceral over the verbal. It is basically directed—reminiscent of some of the better scenes from the first Black Stallion[1] film—and much of Caroline Goodall's narration about what the horses are doing and feeling seems unnecessary; it was probably only included for the benefit of really young children.

The film's narrative alternates between Indi's reading about The Man's quest for the Silver Brumby and her life with Elyne in the high country. Just before The Man's climactic chase for the Brumby, however, the two parallel stories fuse so that Indi's fears for the Silver Brumby are brought into a reality over which she has no control.

A stunning helicopter shot shows the cliff over which the Silver Brumby commits a one-horse Thelma and Louise, but the ending is left deliciously ambivalent as Elyne fertilises the idea in Indi that the Silver Brumby may still somehow be alive. This way her daughter can retain at least one aspect of a childhood that is rapidly evaporating.

For those for whom it already has, the film is an opportunity to re-experience a magical innocence. To describe The Silver Brumby as a 'children's film' is an insult to its powerful evocation of the enchantment of myth.

JIM SCHEMBRI

---

[1] Black Stallion (Carroll Ballard, 1979).

CHRIS KENNEDY

THIS WON'T HURT A BIT!

Oilrag Productions presents This won't Hurt a Bit!. © Australian Film Finance Corporation Pty Limited and Oilrag Productions. Made with the participation of Australian Film Finance Corporation Pty Limited. *Alternative titles:* 'My Australian Dentist' and 'Le Dentiste' (working). *Locations:* Sydney; Portsmouth (UK); Paris. *Filmed:* June–August 1992. *Australian distributor:* Beyond Films. *Rating:* PG. *Video:* Triumph. 35mm. 82 mins.

Producers: Patrick Fitzgerald, Chris Kennedy. *Scriptwriter:* Chris Kennedy. *Director of photography:* Marc Spicer. *Production designer:* Ken Muggleston. *Costume designer:* Ruth Bracegirdle. *Editor:* Peter Butt. *Composer:* Mario Grigoriv. *Sound recordist:* David Glasser. *Sound editors:* Shawn Seet (foley); Jenny Ward (dia.). *Mixer:* Brett Robinson.

Cast

Greig Pickhaver (Gordon Fairweather), Jacqueline McKenzie (Vanessa Prescott), Maggie King (Mrs Prescott), Patrick Blackwell (Mr Prescott), Dennis Miller (Riley), Adam Stone (Farow), Gordon Chater (Dental Professor), Alwyn Kurts (Psychiatrist), Colleen Clifford (Lady Smith), Peter Browne (Railway Friend), Kate Smith (Dental Investigator), Lisa Peers (University Friend), Ralph Cotterill (Bank Manager), Ghandi McIntyre (Restaurateur), Brian Bird (Dental Prosthetist), Fiona Press (Wagga Girlfriend), Peter Borgonon (Solicitor), Peter Boswell (Interpol Officer), Marilyn Thomas (Matron), Brian McDermott (Policeman), Rowan Jackson (Dental Student).

Stereotypical, red-blooded Australians with Vegemite in their veins, zinc cream on their noses, Akubras on their heads and sucking on a tinnie of Fosters will find instant appeal in the notion behind Chris Kennedy's **This Won't Hurt a Bit!**.

Gordon Fairweather (Greig Pickhaver), a mentally-unstable runaway from an orphanage, bluffs his way into becoming a fully-unqualified dentist, complete with a bogusly-obtained degree. He promptly embarks on a trip to England where he sets up shop in Portsmouth, the place from where all the convicts were dispatched to Australia.

His plan is to wreak revenge on the English population for past injustices, both historical and personal. He wants to get them back for being responsible for his broken family. He also wants to get them back for Gallipoli. His plan is to do it in their mouths, with the aid of a dentist's drill, and move on before the authorities catch up with him.

Riley (Dennis Miller) and Gordon Fairweather (Greig Pickhaver).

It may only be a one-joke idea, but it's a great one. Pity, then, that the film sells itself so criminally short. The English make an irresistible first target, but why stop there? What about the French ... the Americans ... the Japanese?

The film does actually make it to France, but only in its closing minutes. Fairweather sets up shop, with a clear agenda to get them back for nuclear testing in the Pacific. It is a horrendously-unsatisfying way to end, unless there are sequels planned.

If the idea had been thought through a little more carefully and with a little more respect for where it could have led, it would not have wasted so much time with all the face-to-camera testimonials from psychiatrists talking about Fairweather's mental condition, teachers about his aptitude (or lack thereof), bank managers about his wealth, old mates from the orphanage about how he was the type of bloke who could 'fade into the background', and fraud investigators detailing their pursuit of him. This is all important information, to be sure, but it's background and delivered at too great a length at the expense of action.

And where is the action, the pay-off to the premise? In the surgery where Fairweather plies his craft, and in the homes of his patients. But we only get to know two: Lady Smith (Colleen Clifford), who displays stuffy Pommy dismay at the Aussie egalitarianism of Fairweather's surgery (a funny, neat archetypal clash of cultures); and Mr Prescott (Patrick Blackwell), who keeps coming back from Fairweather's surgery complaining of yet more work that needs to be done on his teeth while filling his family in on the latest news about Australia's droughts and flooding rain.

Gordon Fairweather could have been another Mick 'Crocodile' Dundee, or at least a worthy antithesis. Instead, the film's cursory and sometimes careless treatment of a brilliant comic idea leaves him merely a curious character who got away with a bit of mischief.

JIM SCHEMBRI

Reference
'This Won't Hurt a Bit!', a review by Raymond Younis, *Cinema Papers*, no. 96, December 1993, pp. 51–2.

WIND

Francis Ford Coppola presents a Mata Yamamoto production. WIND. ©1992 Filmlink International, Inc. Japan and The Wind Production Committee from American Zoetrope. A Co-production of Filmlink International, Inc. *Locations:* Perth; Newport, Utah, Hawaii (US). *Filmed:* February–May 1991. *Australian distributor:* Hoyts. *Opened:* 18 March 1993. *Video:* Columbia–Tristar–Hoyts. *Rating:* PG. 35mm. 125 mins.

Producers: Mata Yamamoto, Tom Luddy. *Executive producers:* Francis Ford Coppola, Fred Fuchs. *Associate producer:* Betsy Pollack. *Scriptwriters:* Rudy Wurlitzer, Mac Gudgeon. Story by Jeff Benjamin, Roger Vaughan, Kimball Livingston. *Director of photography:* John Toll. *Production designer:* Laurence Eastwood. *Costume designer:* Marit Allen. *Editor:* Michael Chandler; Mike Bradsell (addit.). *Composer:* Basil Poledouris. *Sound design:* Alan Spelt. *Sound recordist:* Drew Kunn. *Sound editors:* Frank Fulner, Patrick Dodd, Ewa Sztompke-Gatfield, Ann Kroeber, John Verbeck, Jeffrey Kroeber, Hugh Waddell. *Mixers:* Leslie Shatz, Alan Spelt, Marian Wallace; Jeffrey Stephens (music).

Cast

Matthew Modine (Will Parker), Jennifer Grey (Kate Bass), Cliff Robertson (Morgan Weld), Jack Thompson (Jack Neville), Stellan Skarsgård (Joe Heiser), Rebecca Miller (Abigail Weld), Ned Vaughn (Charley Moore), Peter Montgomery (T.V. Commentator), Elmer Ahlwardt (Sarge), Saylor Creswell (Butler), James Rebhorn (George), Michael Higgins (Artemus), Ron Colbin (Tad), Ken Kensei (Danny), Bill Buell (Swami), Tom Fervoy (Jeff), Ron Palillo (Tony), Matt Malloy (Lyle); Sailors: Mark Walsh (Spider), Kim Sheridan (Rubsey), Bruce Epke (Sheik), Sean Leonard (Mooney), Tom Darling (Otis), John Sangmeister (Skye), Stewart Silvestri (Tuck), Jay Brown (Hook), Mark McTeigue (Mac), Mark Richards (Bruno), Billy Bates (Cat).

Like most films about sport, **Wind** takes as its theme the triumph of one man over adversity, the main obstacle being not only the competition for the prize, but also the protagonist's struggle to overcome inner character flaws.

The protagonist in this case is Will Parker, played by the miscast but otherwise capable Matthew Modine. In the lead-up to the 30th America's Cup, Will is chosen as main tactician for the boat which will defend America's 130-year hold on the cup.

It is Will's lifelong dream come true, but to obtain it he must sacrifice the strong relationship he has with sailing partner and lover, Kate Bass (Jennifer Grey). Will's efforts to successfully defend America's hold on ocean sailing's greatest prize are doomed by his lack of inner strength and 'attitude'. He loses the Cup, and his woman, who goes to follow the career in aeronautical engineering she abandoned in order to bolster his dreams. The film suggests a link between Will's personal loss of integrity and inner weaknesses, and America's loss of the Cup, a thematic link which continues when Will finally 'finds' the ability to win again.

To win back the Cup, Will must discover the qualities within himself which will allow him to be a winner and a leader—he must take an inner journey. He partakes in the familiar American tradition and retreats to the wilderness. Will's 'version quest' takes place in Utah, where he finds Kate—living with another man, Joe Heiser (Stellan Skarsgård), and working in flat saltbed territory where distinct mountains create the wind that fuels his dreams and his ambition. Director Carroll Ballard introduces a mystical element in Will's growth from crew member to crew leader, as he communes with nature to find a rôle model on which to base his transformation. The native American mythic figure of Geronimo becomes Will's inspiration for the new boat—a tactic which, while interesting in its idea, doesn't quite pay off in the events of the film—lending perhaps a touch of insincerity and overloading the symbolism factor.

A noted cinematographer, Ballard displays an eye for landscape, picturesquely framing his characters amidst nature, visually highlighting the elements which make the sport of sailing unique—water and wind.

The film's most successful moments arise out his juxtaposition of human with nature. The scenes in Utah where Will and Joe contemplate building the perfect boat, framed in an above-ground pool with faux tropical palms tacked to the side, austere desert in the background, work with a wry humour and subtle visual flair to offset the personality struggles between the men and within themselves.

Joe is a passionate European aeronautical engineer, Kate is his assistant, and it is Joe, not Kate, who connects with Will in order to fulfil the dream of winning back the Cup. The relationship between the two men becomes a focal point for the film. In the friction between Joe's measured intellect and Will's burgeoning instinct, concerns such as individuality, self-respect, leadership and masculinity begin to take stronger symbolic form.

Mac Gudgeon was called in to rewrite the Australian sections, which are all too brief: Jack Thompson does an admirable job in a minor, but influential, rôle as the John Bertrand character, Jack Neville. An Australian audience would be hard pressed not to avoid a sense of irony, as the events of the 31st America's Cup Challenge are manipulated so that America's loss of the Cup to Australia is portrayed as the triumph of winning it back.

MONICA ZETLIN

References
'Wind', picture preview, *Cinema Papers*, no. 86, January 1992, p. 18.
'Wind', a review by Pat Gillespie, *Cinema Papers*, no. 94, August 1993, pp. 48–9.

Will Parker (Matthew Modine) and Kate Bass (Jennifer Grey).

*Bernadette (Terence Stamp). Stephan
Elliott's* **The Adventures of Priscilla,
Queen of the Desert.**

STEPHAN ELLIOTT

THE ADVENTURES OF PRISCILLA, QUEEN OF THE DESERT

Polygram Filmed Entertainment in association with the Australian Film Finance Corporation presents a Latent Image[−] Specific Films production. THE ADVENTURES OF [/] Priscilla [/] QUEEN OF THE DESERT. © 1994 Australian Film Finance Corporation Limited, Polygram Filmproduktion Gmbh, Latent Image Productions Pty Ltd and New South Wales Film and Television Office. Produced with the assistance and financial participation of New South Wales Film and Television Office. *Locations:* Sydney, Broken Hill (New South Wales); Kings Canyon, Alice Springs (Northern Territory). *Filmed:* 13 September–28 October 1993. *Australian distributor:* Roadshow. *Opened:* 15 September 1994. *Video:* Roadshow. *Rating:* M. 35mm. Dragarama. 99 mins.

Producers: Al Clark, Michael Hamlyn. *Executive producer:* Rebel Penfold-Russell. *Associate producer:* Sue Seeary. *Scriptwriter:* Stephan Elliott. *Director of photography:* Brian J Breheny. *Production designer:* Owen Paterson. *Costume designers:* Lizzy Gardiner, Tim Chappel. *Choreographer:* Mark White. *Editor:* Sue Blainey. *Composer:* Guy Gross. *Sound supervisor:* Phil Judd. *Additional sound design:* Guntis Sics. *Sound recordist:* Guntis Sics. *Sound editors:* Tim "Lobes" Colvin (fx); Angus "Goose" Robertson (dia.); Steve Burgess, Gerry Long (foley). *Mixer:* Phil Judd.

Cast

Terence Stamp (Bernadette), Hugo Weaving (Tick/Mitzi), Guy Pearce (Adam/Felicia), Bill Hunter (Bob)[1]; **Rebel Russell**[2] **(Logowoman), John Casey (Bartender), June Marie Bennett (Shirley), Murray Davies (Miner), Frank Cornelius (Piano Player), Bob Boyce (Petrol Station Attendant), Leighton Picken (Young Adam), Maria Kmet (Ma), Joseph Kmet (Pa), Alan Dargin (Aboriginal Man), Julia Cortez (Cynthia), Daniel Kellie (Young Ralph), Hannah Corbett (Ralph's Sister), Trevor Barrie (Ralph's Father), Ken Radley (Frank), Sarah Chadwick (Marion), Mark Holmes (Benjamin).**

Out of the closet and into the mainstream, this film raised gay culture to moderately-new heights of respectability in the suburbs of heterosexual Australia. It moved with great effect across the screens of North America and Europe, following on the heels of its glitzy precursor, **Strictly Ballroom** (Baz Luhrmann, 1992).

Playing along with antiseptic myths about the delights of the gay lifestyle, **The Adventures of Priscilla, Queen of the Desert** generously papers over the difficulties of homosexuality. It does this by literally dressing up the complexity of sexual politics in the 1990s, while boldly presenting the transvestite/trans-sexual life as normal. In this at least it succeeds and makes a consistently-assertive statement about life in the drag-lane.

Casting Terence Stamp as an ageing transvestite with an assiduous sense of purpose and deportment, the film found the mix of acting talent to satisfy its funders and the global audience. With Stamp's pre-history as an actor, his presence consolidated the film's ironic edge. Together with Hugo Weaving and Guy Pearce as the drag queens, the trio snapped, snarled and struggled their way from Sydney—Australia's gay heartland—through to the heterosexist wasteland of Alice Springs.

While it poses, in part at least, as a road movie, **Priscilla** flouts the bountiful optimism of a naïve Australia. Casting gay constraint (if ever such a thing existed) away, **Priscilla** reworks images of the Australian landscape in the frontier context of the Australian outback and desert. New heights of cinematic beauty are reclaimed, with the skill of an advertising executive looking for an award-winning image. The scenes of lengths of fabric trailing across and behind the bus, as it bounces over desert roads, give the red centre of Australia a feminine sense it has not previously experienced in Australian films.

The film takes its name from the bus on which the three leading characters travel from Sydney to Alice to perform a cabaret show. Overdressed in all the refinements of the æsthetic distortions of dress that make gay culture so alluring yet perverse, the bus is the perfect vehicle for the intensive dialogue that characterises marginalised, confident characters.

On concluding the trip and meeting the wife and young son of one of the trio—who, according to gay expectations, should have been childless and unmarried—the narrative tries to reconstitute itself as no longer a playful engagement with gay culture. Attempting to draw its audience into 'straight' dilemmas—am I gay or straight?—it fizzles rather than explodes in its celebration of difference.

MARCUS BREEN

---

[1] The order of first four credits follows that of the opening credits; the rest are as per order of appearance on end credits.

[2] As executive producer, Rebel Russell is called 'Rebel Penfold-Russell'.

References

'47e Festival international du Film, Cannes', an article by Jan Epstein, *Cinema Papers*, no. 100, August 1994, pp. 10–15.

'Stephan Elliott: **The Adventures of Priscilla, Queen of the Desert**', an interview with the writer–director by Jan Epstein, *Cinema Papers*, no. 101, October 1994, pp. 4–10, 86.

'Terence Stamp', an interview with the actor by Jan Epstein, ibid., p. 11.

'**The Adventures of Priscilla, Queen of the Desert**', a review by David Vallence and Monica Zetlin, ibid., pp. 62–3.

Bernadette (Terence Stamp), Felicia (Guy Pearce) and Mitzi (Hugo Weaving).

BAD BOY BUBBY

Bubby (Nicholas Hope) and cat.

A Fandango (Rome) [–] Bubby Pty Ltd (Adelaide) production of BAD BOY BUBBY. © 1993 Australian Film Finance Corporation Pty Limited[,] Fandago sri and Bubby Pty Ltd. *Alternative title:* 'Bubby' (working). Developed with financial assistance from the South Australian Government. Made in association with South Australian Film Corporation. Made with the participation of Australian Film Finance Corporation Pty Limited. *Location:* Adelaide. *Filmed:* 16 November 1992–30 January 1993. *Australian distributor:* Roadshow. *Video:* Roadshow. *Rating:* R. 35mm. Panavision. 113 mins.

Producers: Domenico Procacci, Giorgio Draskovic, Rolf de Heer. *Associate producer:* David Lightfoot. *Scriptwriter:* Rolf de Heer. *Director of photography:* Ian Jones. *Consulting directors of photography:* Ian Jones, Phil Dalwitz, Kim Vaniterous, Rick Martin, Clive Duncan, Ross Blake, Steve Arnold, David Burr, Gerard Thompson, Richard Michalak, John Chataway, Jeff Morrow, John Ogden, Barry Hellefen, Tibor Hegedes, John Armstrong, Ernie Clarke,

Brian Bossisto, Brigo Castello, Brendan Lavelle, Lisa Tomasetti, Harry Glynatsis, Walter Holt, Geoffrey Simpson, Steve McDonald, Roger Lanser, Simon Caromell, Richard Rees-Jones, David Foreman, Max Pepper. *Production designer:* Mark Abbott. *Costume designer:* Beverley Freeman. *Editor:* Suresh Ayyar. *Composer:* Graham Tardif. *Sound designer:* James Currie. *Sound recordist:* James Currie. *Sound editors:* James Currie (sup.); Suresh Ayyar, Jolie Chandler; John Simpson (foley). *Mixers:* James Currie; Tony Young (addit.).

Cast

Nicholas Hope (Bubby), Claire Benito (Mom), Ralph Cotterill (Pop), Carmel Johnson (Angel); Syd Brisbane (Yabba), Nikki Price (Screaming Woman), Ulli Brive (Robbed Woman), Audine Leith (Fondled Salvo), Natalie Carr (Cherie the Salvo), Lucia Mastrantone (Pizza Waitress), Jip de Heer (Treelopper), James Ammitzboll (Little), Grant Piro (Salesman), Dave Flannagan (Cops/Warder), Paul Philpot (Paul (Band) Singer), Todd Telford (Little Greg (Keyboards)), Paul Simpson (Big Greg (Drummer)), Stephen Smooker (Middle Greg (Bass)), Peter Monaghan (Steve (Guitarist)), Mark Brouggy (Mark (Roadie)), James Bonnifaco (Young Man), Emma West (Violinist), Bruce Gilbert (Dan), Michael Harber (Cop #2), Alan Holy (Cop #3).

Rolf de Heer's **Bad Boy Bubby** is a low-budget narrative film that displays a surreal-gothic understanding of the world and its underlying socio-cultural horrors.

The first part, which shows the deranged protagonist Bubby (Nicholas Hope) living in an incestuous relationship with his mother (Claire Benito), is a mini-film in itself: full of finely-observed and -performed pathological undercurrents, which constitute a daring black comedy of human depravity and psychosis (rarely seen in recent Australian film).

Bubby's psychosis mirrors the indifference, cruelty and absurdity of the world (something which is given its fuller narrative significance once Bubby leaves his stark domestic abode of residence). Bubby's phobic response to the world—he believes that if he ventures beyond his front door he will suffocate and die—is given a bizarre visual representation: every time his mother leaves their place she puts on a gasmask for his psychotic benefit. She also bathes, feeds and cleans him up after he shits himself: we have entered a transgressive world of mother–son

behaviour that would scare the life out of any recently-graduated social-worker student.

Though their place is orderly (up to a point), thanks to the mother's routine of trying to keep the place clean, it is nevertheless marked with the detritus of Bubby's pathology. He is transfixed by the notion that creatures, including human beings and cats, can actually breathe. He then clingwraps his cat to death—a fate that his parents later share. The scene depicting the clingwrapped corpses of Bubby's parents sitting on a divan is one that constitutes a post-Polanski rupture in Australian cinema—or, if you will, a scene that resembles a stark eerie performance by Joseph Beuys or Mike Kelly.

Bubby's capacity to repeat his parents' (and others') dialogue is indicative of his being located in a twilight zone of cybernetic and pathological dysfunction. He verbalises and acts out the social and psychological maladies that characterise our families and society. This has a particular dramaturgical and social resonance when we see Bubby leave his apartment to encounter a vast range of people on the outside: a carload of homophobic yahoos, a Salvation Army chorus singing in the street, a rock-and-roll band (of which he becomes their adopted 'Iggy Pop'-styled singer), the inmates of a dark, urine-infested police cell where he is raped by a naked prisoner, and so forth.

Bubby's adventures contain an epic sweep of an 18th-century picaresque novel. His various encounters cumulate into a flawed (but watchable) critique of one-dimensional society. Whether it is the familial, as represented by the repressive, cruel parents of Angel (Carmel Johnson) who mistreat her because of her obesity and independent frame of mind, or the police who do not comprehend Bubby's state of pathology, or the quadriplegic people who are hidden in institutions because we valorise the body as a perfect idealised thing in itself, this film offers numerous critical insights into our selves.

JOHN CONOMOS

References
'50a Mostra del Cinema del Venezia', an article by Peter Malone, *Cinema Papers*, no. 96, December 1993, pp. 42–4.
'Bad Boy Bubby', a review by Anna Dzenis, *Cinema Papers*, no. 101, October, 1994, pp. 63–4.
'Bad Boy Bubby', writer-director Rolf de Heer interviewed by Andrew L. Urban, *Cinema Papers*, no. 101, October, 1994, pp. 72–3.
'Bad Boy Bubby', actor Nicholas Hope interviewed by Andrew L. Urban, ibid., p. 73.

BODY MELT

Dumb Films presents in association with the Australian Film Commission and Film Victoria BODY melt. © 1993 Body Melt Pty Ltd. Produced in association with Australian Film Commission and Film Victoria. *Budget:* $1.6 million. *Locations:* Werribee, Melbourne. *Filmed:* October–November 1992. *Australian distributor:* Beyond. *Video:* not released as of 1 May 1995. *Rating:* R. 35mm. 80 mins.

Producers: Rod Bishop, Daniel Scharf. *Associate producer:* Lars Michalak. *Scriptwriters:* Philip Brophy, Rod Bishop. Based on four short stories by Philip Brophy. *Director of photography:* Ray Argall. *Camera operator:* Jennifer Meaney. *Production designer:* Maria Kozic. *Costume designer:* Anna Borghesi. *Editor:* Bill Murphy. *Composer:* Philip Brophy. *Sound designers:* Craig Carter, Philip Brophy. *Sound recordist:* Gary Wilkins. *Sound editors:* Craig Carter, James Harvey. *Mixer:* Steve Burgess.

Cast

The Police: Gerard Kennedy (Sam Phillips), Andrew Daddo (Johnno); Vimuville: Ian Smith (Dr. Carrera), Regina Gaigalas (Shann); Nowhere: Vince Gil (Pud), Neil Foley (Bob), Anthea Davis (Slab), Matt Newton (Bronto), Lesley Baker (Mack), Amy Grove-Rogers (Old Woman); 12 Pebbles Court: Adrian Wright (Thompson Noble), Jillian Murray (Angelica Noble), Ben Geurens (Brandon Noble), Amanda Douge (Elouise Noble); 11 Pebbles Court: Brett Climo (Brian Rand), Lisa McCune (Cheryl Rand); 10 Pebbles Court: Nick Polites (Sal Ciccone), Maurie Annese (Gino Argento); 9 Pebbles Court: William McInnes (Paul Matthews), Suzi Dougherty (Kate); More Police: Bill Young (Willie), Tommy Dysart (Sergeant), Stig Wemyss (Jordan), Matthew Green (Forensic Cop), Philip Green (Station Cop), Russell Allan (Patrol Cop 1), Lance Anderson (Patrol Cop 2).

'Now, I'm talking new drugs here. Not your '70s designer shit or your '80s ghetto powders. I'm talking fucking '90s cognition enhancers—designed to take your mind into new intra-phenomenological dimensions.' Willie (Bill Young) in **Body Melt**.

Like these new-age drugs, **Body Melt** is a film of the 1990s. It is pure cinema, visually and aurally exploding and imploding the limits of possibility. It is cerebral and visceral—fast, funny, clever and vile; an experience with a dialogue.

Writer, director, composer and co-sound designer Philip Brophy is a '90s multimedia

Pud (Vince Gil) and Bob (Neil Foley).

artist. His film credits include the shorts **No Dance** and **Salt, Saliva, Sperm and Sweat**, and he is a contributor of key theoretical writings in the areas of horrality and sonic cinema, all of which richly inform **Body Melt**.

Arriving in an Australian cinematic wasteland of coy, feel-good films, **Body Melt**'s critical reception was mixed. Screened at the 1994 Melbourne Film Festival and then for a season at the Valhalla, the film was marginalised as an alternative art-house work. Mainstream distributors wouldn't touch it and voices like those of former *The Age* critic Neil Jillett dismissed it as a lot of nonsense. In response to this, Adrian Martin, the new film critic of *The Age* and *The Week in Film* on Radio National, described **Body Melt** as 'undoubtedly the best Australian film of the year'. He argues that much of this neglect can be attributed to the film's 'accursed genre' and its evident adoration of trash culture.

Body Melt is indeed full of slime-soaked, oozing, bloodied corpses, runaway placentas, exploding penises, slashed wombs, mutating flesh, and other disturbed body parts which suffer a graphic and grisly demise. But it is also a film that very much understands its cultural place and moment, and drops many acerbic social observations in amongst the action, gore and splatter.

The ironic vision begins at Vimuville, a leisure resort/health farm, built on the site of an old chemical plant, and journeys across the recognisably-Australian landscape to a sterile, manicured housing estate, Homesville. Here in Pebbles Court four innocent families have been targeted for Vimuville drug testing. A complex narrative structure interweaves numerous stories across a panoramic sweep of extraordinary characters, action and culture. As Raffaele Caputo

described in *Cinema Papers*, this is 'the suburbia of television land'. Televisual icons and advertisements litter the screen. Gerard Kennedy (*Division 4*), Andrew Daddo (from the famous television family), Ian Smith (*Neighbours*), Lisa McCune and William McInnes (*Blue Heelers*) and Tiffany Lamb (*Paradise Beach*), amongst others, variously enact and bear witness to the dreams and fantasies of melodramas going horribly wrong.

This purvey of pop culture extends well beyond the creative casting. Nowhere, the outpost of Pud (Vince Gil) and his mixed-up mutant offspring is, thanks to Maria Kozic's inspired production design, like a contemporary pop museum with its Peters Ice Cream signs, purple arm chairs, Big M T-shirts, stuffed toys, Kiss masks, bubble lamps, resident kangaroo, and rambling mélange of related objects and artefacts—an ecstatic ode to a refined taste in 'tastelessness'.

In the end, this is a very funny film, and acknowledgments for this go all the way back to the witty Brophy–Rod Bishop script. In one of the final scenes, after a seriously-exploding Brian Rand (Brett Climo) has splattered the police station with green and yellow slime, in wanders Willie (Bill Young), the police forensic scientist, wearing his tie-dye T-shirt. He looks at Brian, then at his shirt, and exclaims, 'Got my fuckin' shirt on', before adding with glee, 'I can't help it. I love this fucking job.' **Body Melt**, like Willie, is a film that's seriously having fun.

ANNA DZENIS

References

'Melbourne Film Festival', a report by John Foam, *Cinema Papers*, no. 101, October, 1994, pp. 76–8.

'**Body Melt**', a review by Raffaele Caputo, *Cinema Papers*, no. 102, December, 1994, pp. 66–7.

BROKEN HIGHWAY

Black Ray Films presents in association with the Australian Film Commission and the Queensland Film Development Office BROKEN HigHWAY[1]. © 1993 Black Ray Films Pty. Ltd. Script developed with the assistance of New South Wales Film and Television Office. *Budget:* $1.35 million. *Location:* Port of Brisbane. *Filmed:* 25 May–10 July 1992. *Australian distributor:* Ronin. *Video:* 21st Century–Ronin. *Rating:* PG. 35mm. Black and white. Panavision. 98 mins.

Producer: Richard Mason. *Line producer:* Julie Forster. *Associate producers:* Gaby Mason, Meredith King. *Scriptwriter:* Laurie McInnes. *Director of photography:* Steve Mason. *Camera operators:* Steve Mason, Phil Cross. *Production designer:* Lesley Crawford. *Costume designer:* Lesley Crawford. *Editor:* Gary Hillberg. *Composer:* David Faulkner. *Audiographer:*[2] Penn Robinson. *Sound collaborator:* John Patterson. *Sound recordists:* Paul (Salty Dog) Brincat; John Dennison (foley); Tony Vaccher (ADR). *Sound editor:* Jeanine Chialvo (dia.). *Mixers:* Peter Fenton, Ron Purvis.

Cast

Aden Young (Angel), David Field (Tatts), William McInnes (Roger), Stephen Davies (Jack), Dennis Miller (Max), Kris McQuade (Woman), Peter Settle (Night Manager), Bill Hunter (Wilson), Claudia Karvan (Catherine), Norman Kaye (Kidd), Ashley Rycon (Girl at Caravan), Lachlan McInnes (Child in Car); Rola Thomas, Paula Zankay, Bob Mercer, Liam Mercer, Kim Sandeman, Chrissy Feld (Street Life).

Broken Highway arrived as one of a group of films touted as a particular kind of 'new wave' in Australian cinema. Peter Sainsbury, then principal adviser, Film Development, at the Australian Film Commission, spoke in the early 1990s of a slate of funded feature projects designed as 'marketable' films rather than commercial blockbusters, geared to new 'niche markets' within the burgeoning art-house exhibition sector. Moreover, the creativity and energy behind these films would be drawn from spaces in Australian cultural life hitherto neglected and made marginal—the enclaves of independent and experimental film-making, and intellectual cinema study. The relevant films include Ross Gibson's **Dead to the World** (1991, unreleased), Tracey Moffatt's **BeDevil** (1993), David Perry's **The Refracting Glasses** (1993), Solrun Hoaas' **Aya** (1991), John Hughes' *One Way Street: Fragments for Walter Benjamin* (documentary, 1992) and Susan Murphy Dermody's **Breathing Under Water** (1992).

Unlike these films, **Broken Highway** is neither highly intellectual nor intensely politically motivated. Writer–director Laurie McInnes has previously directed a highly-acclaimed, Cannes award-winning, quasi-experimental short, *Palisade* (1987). Her intricate, expressive concern with the possibilities of film language is, in **Broken Highway**, married to a particular form of drama, taking place entirely within the emotional registers of pain, loss, 'unfinished business', guilt and tormented memory. Yet it is not a melodrama: the proceedings have a hushed air and much of what interrelates and motivates the characters is left unspoken, as in the films of the Bresson-influenced Benoit Jacquot (such as **La Désenchantée**, 1990).

Angel (Aden Young) quits a life at sea and travels to Honeyfield in Queensland, carrying a bag of opium as a gift for the sinister landowner Kidd (Norman Kaye) from his recently-deceased acquaintance Max (Dennis Miller). Surrounded by a bunch of crazies who are morosely haunted by their dark past, Angel gravitates especially towards Catherine (Claudia Karvan.) In this psychodramatic tangle, each character seems to be the embodiment of someone else's lost mother, father or lover figure.

McInnes chooses to thin out this story material, expunging any violent or erotic content that might be deemed vulgar and sensationalist (a reticence shared by all the 'experimental features' cited above). It is a film of moody images and atmospheric

Angel (Aden Young) and Wilson (Bill Hunter).

soundscapes, at times strikingly realised, as in the remarkable scene of a night drive, where an object is glimpsed bursting into flames in the distance. But the dialogue is a problem for the actors, who struggle with such overstated and pseudo-poetic lines as 'You smell and your love smells' and 'You never seen glory. How can you hope to see a lost soul?'

The film has been greatly ridiculed for its qualities of obscurity (it is occasionally literally difficult to see or make out what is happening), emotional coldness and symbolic portentousness. Yet, given that McInnes clearly intended to make such a 'baroque' film on the levels both of style and dramatic content, it is possible to argue that **Broken Highway** is more 'of a piece', more coherent in its manner and sustained in its mood, than virtually all of the 'innovative' Australian films already mentioned.

Possibly the most interesting and successful aspect of the film is the unselfconscious way it filters the Australian landscape through an essentially-American sensibility. This tale of Gothic Queensland is basically an antipodean **Rumble Fish** (Francis Coppola, 1983) with a barrowfull of themes taken from the Sam Shepard school of modern melodrama (which has found its local variation in the plays of Daniel Keene, here a script consultant). With these influences come older references: Tennessee Williams, Orson Welles' **Touch of Evil** (1958), James Dean in **East of Eden** (Elia Kazan, 1955). The film doesn't know quite what to do with all this baggage, but it at least carries the load with ease and grace.

ADRIAN MARTIN

---

[1] The title is a mix of upper and lower case.
[2] The only known case of this form of credit.

References

'Broken Highway', picture preview, *Cinema Papers*, no. 92, April 1993, pp. 29–30.
'Broken Highway', writer-director Laurie McInnes interviewed by Lani Hannah, *Cinema Papers*, no. 93, May 1993, pp. 12–17, 58–9.
'46e International du Film de Cannes', an article by Jan Epstein, *Cinema Papers*, no. 94, August 1993, pp. 22–7.
'Broken Highway', a review by Dena Gleeson, *Cinema Papers*, no. 97–8, March 1994, pp. 48–9.
'The Craft of Cinematography', an article by Leilani Hannah and Raffaele Caputo, including an interview with director of photography Steve Mason, *Cinema Papers*, no. 99, June 1994, pp. 34–42, 84.
'Broken Highway', an interview with writer–director Laurie McInnes and some cast by Pauline Adamek, *Filmnews*, February 1994, p. 16.

COUNTRY LIFE

Australian Film Finance Corporation Limited presents a Dalton Films production. COUNTRY LIFE. © 1994 Australian Film Finance Corporation Limited [and] Dalton Films Pty Limited. Script developed with the assistance of Australian Film Commission. *Locations:* Maitland, Carcoar, Sydney (New South Wales). *Filmed:* 29 November 1993–24 January 1994. *Australian distributor:* UIP. *Video:* not released as of 1 May 1995. *Rating:* PG. 35mm. 95 mins.

Producer: Robin Dalton. *Line producer:* Adrienne Read. *Scriptwriter:* Michael Blakemore. Suggested by Anton Chekhov's *Uncle Vanya*. *Director of photography:* Stephen Windon. *Camera operator:* Marc Spicer. *Production designer:* Laurence Eastwood. *Costume designer:* Wendy Chuck. *Editor:* Nicholas Beauman. *Composer:* Peter Best. *Sound recordist:* Ben Osmo. *Sound editors:* Gary O'Grady (fx); Karin Whittington (dia.). *Mixer:* Phil Judd.

Cast

Sam Neill (Dr Max Askey), Greta Scacchi (Deborah Voysey), John Hargreaves (Jack Dickens), Kerry Fox (Sally Voysey), Michael Blakemore (Alexander Voysey), Googie Withers (Hannah), Patricia Kennedy (Maud Dickens), Ron Blanchard (Wally Wells), Robyn Cruze (Violet), Maurie Fields (Fred Livingstone), Bryan Marshall (Mr Pettinger); Tony Barry, Terry Brady (Loggers); Tom Long (Billy Livingstone), Rob Steele (James), Ian Bliss (David Archdale), Colin Taylor (Mr Wilson), Ian Cockburn (Mr Archdale), Reg Cribb (Vicar), Deran Scarr (Woman in Crowd), Owen Buik (Stationhand).

Michael Blakemore's Chekhov-inspired Country Life mirrors its precursor's fascination with a threatened bourgeoisie stifled by inactivity and ennui, but is unable to match the playwright's subtle and unique combination of comedy, pathos and tragedy. The characters and setting, 'suggested by' *Uncle Vanya*, provide the milieu for examining the effects of self-denial and lost or wasted opportunities.

At the end of World War I, an ageing Alexander Voysey (Blakemore), a retired drama critic based in London, returns to Australia and the family property of his deceased wife, with a second wife, Deborah (Greta Scacchi), who is strikingly beautiful and half his age. Alex had left his daughter, Sally (Kerry Fox), in Australia with his brother-in-law, Jack Dickens (John Hargreaves). Together they run the rural property of Canterbury, sending Alex 'his share' in the form of a monthly cheque. Completing this ensemble are Jack's mother, Maud (Patricia Kennedy), who reveres all things British; Wally Wells (Ron Blanchard), a lodger who pays his way in the form of odd jobs and haircuts rather than rent; and the local doctor, Max Askey (Sam Neill), a struggling alcoholic whose sympathetic attitude towards Aborigines and his conviction that Australian men should not have been sent to fight a European war rankle with the British colonialist and nationalist attitudes of the town.

Tensions rise from the moment the Voyseys arrive at Canterbury. Alex, convinced of his own self-importance, has meal times rearranged in line with his English lifestyle and midnight coffee brought to him by the pretty maid, Violet (Robyn Cruze), in an abortive attempt to satisfy his philanderous urges (he and Deborah sleep in separate rooms). Jack's envy of Alex and his work soon turns to hatred when he discovers Alex spends more time enjoying wine than theatre. Jack wants everything that Alex has but does not appreciate, including the bewitching Deborah, whose presence turns Jack into an embarrassing and awkward suitor.

However, Deborah hardly notices Jack's attentions as she has her own distraction: a growing attraction between herself and Dr Askey, who spends increasing amounts of time at Canterbury, letting his practice decline as he too becomes obsessed with what he cannot have. The tragic figure in this *ménage* is the plain-looking Sally, who confesses to Deborah she has secretly been in love with the doctor for six years. Sally is too naïve to realise that Deborah's offer to act as a go-between threatens to become, unintentionally, an act of betrayal.

Despite their solid performances, both Fox and Neill tend to elicit our pity rather than sympathy. The supporting cast, led by Googie Withers and Maurie Fields, is far more engaging and provides some of the film's delightfully-comic moments. Scacchi takes her time warming up to a rôle which is ultimately underwritten. It is Blakemore's Alex, with his pathetic machinations, who provides the greater insight into Deborah's emotional entrapment. Hargreaves' portrayal of Jack's breakdown in the final scenes is full of conviction but regrettably lacks any dramatic climax due to some unfortunate overplaying in the film's first half. In the attempt to transfer Chekhovian sensibility from the stage to screen, Blakemore's characters become one-dimensional.

FINCINA HOPGOOD

Reference
'Country Life', a review by Monica Zetlin, *Cinema Papers*, no. 101, October, 1994, p. 64.

Jack Dickens (John Hargreaves) and Deborah Voysey (Greta Scacchi).

THE CUSTODIAN

J. D. Productions presents THE CUSTO-DIAN. © 1993 Australian Film Finance Corporation Pty Limited[,] Australian Asset Management Limited [and] The Custodian Film Co Pty Ltd. Film developed with the assistance of The New South Wales Film & Television Office. Script developed with the assistance of the Australian Film Commission. Made with the participation of the Australian Film Finance Corporation Pty Limited. Financial assistance provided by Australian Asset Securities Ltd. *Location:* Sydney. *Australian distributor:* Beyond Films. *Video:* 21st Century–Ronin. *Rating:* M. 35mm. 109 mins.

Producer: Adrienne Read. *Executive producers:* Gary Hamilton, Mikael Borglund. *Co-producer:* Dimitra Meleti. *Scriptwriter:* John Dingwall. *Director of photography:* Steve Mason. *Production designer:* Philip Warner. *Costume designer:* Terry Ryan. *Editor:* Michael Honey. *Composer:* Phillip Houghton. *Sound designer:* Wayne Pashley. *Sound recordist:* Ben Osmo. *Sound editor:* Antony Gray (dia.). *Mixer:* Phil Judd.

Cast

Anthony LaPaglia (Quinlan), Hugo Weaving (Church), Barry Otto (Ferguson), Kelly Dingwall (Reynolds), Essie Davis (Jilly), Gosia Dobrowolska (Josie), Skye Wansey (Claire Ferguson), Christina Totos (Pixie Church), Naomi Watts (Louise), Joy Smithers (Helen Quinlan), Bill Hunter (Managing Director), Tim McKenzie (Beetson), Norman Kaye (Judge), Steven Grives (Brennan), Bogdan Koca (Psychologist), Russell Newman (Police Commissioner), Andrew Sharp (Ross Delhunty), Andrew S. Gilbert (Cameraman), Wayne Pygram (Detective Massey), Bob Baines (Detective Insp. Blewitt), Kee Chan (Chief Executive), Shane McNamara (Antonavitch), David Brown (Punk), Nan Vernon (Claire's Mother), Ken Snodgrass (Claire's Father).

Quinlan (Anthony LaPaglia) and Church (Hugo Weaving).

All the signs are there in the first 40 minutes of John Dingwall's **The Custodian** to point to a sweaty, top-notch cop thriller that Sidney Lumet (**Q & A**, **Serpico**, **Prince of the City**[1]) would have been proud of. It falls far short, however, of the heights it often looks like scaling. And it hurts.

Detective Quinlan (Anthony LaPaglia) is in an emotional crisis because of the breakup of his marriage, and in a moral crisis because all the cops around him are corrupt. His father was a straight beat cop, and Quinlan feels culpable if he doesn't do something. So he teams up with his partner in crime-fighting, Church (Hugo Weaving), and begins feeding information about the corruption to a tabloid television reporter, Reynolds (Kelly Dingwall), who in turn feeds it to Ferguson (Barry Otto), an internal affairs officer.

Things are shaping up nicely at this point, and this is when the film should hit third gear. But it keeps idling in second, occasionally slipping the clutch and grinding back into first.

A lot of the set-up in **The Custodian** makes for some spellbinding dramatic foreplay. There is an eerie intensity reminiscent of William Friedkin's underrated cop thriller **To Live and Die in LA** (1985) as Quinlan is assessed as psychologically unstable for promotion, discovers Church's scams, and descends into a corrupt mindset.

LaPaglia's performance as a cop whose life is one heart flutter away from shattering is powerful, alternating between understatement and emotional extreme. His low-key, monotonal declaration to Church that 'I want a piece of your pie, Frank' is typical of the weighty, hernia-inducing conviction he gives most of his dialogue.

But things start to spoil with the introduction of Reynolds, the current affairs reporter. Kelly Dingwall's performance is unforgivably wet, looking and sounding too much like an Internet nerd. He's meant to be tough but he couldn't scare a frog off a lily pad.

None of this is helped by the fact Reynolds is so stupid it makes one wonder how he managed to get a job, even in television. He is told emphatically by Quinlan not to contact Ferguson from his home number, else he'll reveal to the corrupt cops tapping his phone who Reynolds is feeding the information to.

But Reynolds promptly does. Realising his blunder, Reynolds is told by Quinlan to call Ferguson and warn him of the impending danger. Ferguson's not home, though, so his pregnant wife answers. Do you think he warns her? Once she is inevitably dispatched, Reynolds sobs to Quinlan: 'I killed her.'

In the climactic scene when Ferguson goes to shoot Church in the brain for the killing of his wife and unborn child, it is hard to shake the feeling that he is shooting the wrong person.

The ending of **The Custodian** is also troublesome. Quinlan, having cleaned out the trash in the force, is prepared to be thrown out with it, although he has enough evidence to clear himself. No understanding is given as to why he would commit such professional and personal self-immolation. The character arc doesn't make sense.

Besides, Quinlan has an attractive coffee-shop proprietor he could begin a new life with. But rather than serving as motivation for Quinlan's character, she is merely a convenient sex partner, and is treated as such. A tad more care should have given her, and the whole film a little more value.

JIM SCHEMBRI

---

[1] **Q & A** (1990), **Serpico** (1973) and **Prince of the City** (1981).

References

'The Custodian', writer–director John Dingwall interviewed by Andrew L. Urban, *Cinema Papers*, no. 95, October 1993, pp. 22–6.

'The Custodian', a review by Raymond Younis, *Cinema Papers*, no. 97–8, March 1994, pp. 50–1.

'The Custodian', a review by Annabelle Sheehan, *Filmnews*, April 1994, p. 12.

PAUL HARMON

DAVID O'BRIEN'S SHOTGUN WEDDING

Beyond Films presents a David Hannay–Charles Hannah Production. David O'Brien's [//] SHOTGUN WEDDING. © 1992 David Hannay Productions Pty. Limited [and] Australian Film Finance Corporation Pty. Limited. Produced by David Hannay Productions Pty. Limited. Developed with the assistance of Australian Film Commission. Made with the participation of Australian Film Finance Corporation Pty. Limited as part of the 1991 FFC Film Fund. *Budget:* $4.1 million. *Locations:* Warriewood Valley, Sydney (New South Wales). *Filmed:* 21 November 1991–6 December 1991. *Australian distributor:* REP. *Rating:* M. 35mm. 95 mins.

Producers: David Hannay, Charles Hannah. *Scriptwriter:* David O'Brien. *Director of photography:* Kim Batterham. *Camera operators:* Danny Batterham; Steve Arnold, Roger Lanser (add.). *Production designer:* Michael Philips. *Costume designer:* Clarrissa Patterson. *Editor:* Wayne Le Clos. *Composer:* Allan Zavod. *Sound recordist:* Ross Linton; Phil Keros (add.). *Sound designers:* John Dennison, Tony Vaccher, John Patterson. *Sound editors:* John Dennison, Tony Vaccher, John Patterson, Ross Chambers; Nicholas Holmes (dia.) [*Mixer:* not credited.]

Cast

Aden Young (Jimmy Becker), Zoë Carides (Helen Llewellyn), John Walton (Detective Frank Taylor), Marshall Napier (Detective Dave Green), John Clayton (Superintendent Church), Paul Chubb (Geoffrey Drinkwater), Yves Stening (Peter Bingham), Richard Healy (Brian Alcot), Andrew S. Gilbert (Bruce Llewellyn), Sean Scully (Detective Craig Haker), Vince Sorrenti (Detective Mario Bonelli), Jeff Truman (Detective Ted Jones), Mary Regan (Doctor Wainright), Bill Hunter (Police Commissioner Andrews[1]), Brian Adams (Doctor Craig Kelvin), Max Cullen (The Reverend Arthur Hickey)[2]; Garry Waddell (Nightclub Spruiker), Kathryn Chalker (Jody), Amanda McPaul (Trish), Frank Aldridge (Arnie), Leigh Martine (Ginfer), Paul Smith (Ralphie), Jandy Rainbow (Monique).

The challenge in making a geographically-inert film work is to keep the drama cooking and to expand the visual vocabulary of the setting so that people either don't notice or don't care that everything is basically happening in the one place.

Jocelyn Moorhouse did it superbly in **Proof** (1991), as did Phillip Noyce in **Dead Calm** (1989) and Peter Weir in **Green Card**

Police Commissioner Andrews (Bill Hunter), Superintendent Church (John Clayton) and The Reverend Arthur Hickey (Max Cullen).

(1991), which, by and large, took place in a cramped New York apartment which never seemed to run out of interesting nooks, crannies and corners for the actors to occupy.

The camera in **David O'Brien's Shotgun Wedding** is similarly restricted in where it can physically roam, but roam it does, capturing a rich and impressive variety of moods and atmospheres. The film's drama never quite keeps pace with the film's visual invention, but it does try.

As emphatically stated in its opening credits, **Shotgun Wedding** is not based on a true story, but is a fiction inspired by a real event in 1968. It basically takes place in a dilapidated farmhouse that is besieged by police and media when a desperate young ex-petty crook, Jimmy Becker (Aden Young), pretends to take his pregnant girlfriend, Helen Llewellyn (Zoë Carides), hostage to ward off the violent threats of a crooked cop, Frank Taylor (John Walton). To keep him at bay, Jimmy and Helen work out a nice little double act where she screams for her life as he threatens to shoot her.

Before Jimmy realises what he has started, he has been turned into a national hero, not so much for the nobility of his actions and on-air accusations of police corruption, but because he is great and easy copy. World-weary journalists exchange jokey, tabloid headline ideas and line up to file their copy from the local phone booth.

There is a subtle correlation between the framing of compositions and the progression of Jimmy's grasp of the situation he has created. Early on, when he is in control and has the media at his feet, the shots are expansive, emphasising the crowd that has gathered

for him, which is often shot with a long lens, adding an appropriate touch of documentary-like authenticity to the proceedings. The framing becomes much tighter as the cops get tough and Jimmy begins losing grip.

Performances are terrific throughout, especially from John Walton as Taylor who proves here, as he did in **"Undercover"** (David Stevens, 1984), that he is one of the most underrated and under-used of Australian actors.

Aden Young is convincingly twitchy and hyper as Jimmy, but the quality of his performance does not make up for the unfortunate shortcomings in Jimmy's characterisation. We simply get to know Jimmy too well, too soon. From the opening shots we see that he is sensitive, caring and deeply in love with the radiant Helen. So it's obvious from the word go that he is not capable of real violence. Some doubt about him could have made him a much more engaging figure to watch. When we are shown that he is holding a grenade during the wedding ceremony, we know too well that it's a dummy. It would have been nice to have worried about that.

JIM SCHEMBRI

---

1 Merely 'Commissioner Andrews' on head credits.
2 The first 15 credits follow the order of head credits; the rest as per order of appearance.

References
'Shotgun Wedding', a review by Raymond Younis, *Cinema Papers*, no. 100, August 1994, pp. 71–2.
'Shotgun Wedding', a review by Katie Hall, *Filmnews*, June 1994, p. 12.

FRAUDS

Live Entertainment and J & M Entertainment present a Latent Image production. FRAUDS. © 1992 Latent Image Productions Pty Limited [and] The Australian Film Finance Corporation. Developed with the assistance of New South Wales Film & Television Office. Made with the participation of Australian Film Finance Corporation Pty Limited. *Location:* Sydney. *Australian distributor:* Roadshow. *Video:* First release. *Rating:* M. 35mm. 90 mins.

Producers: Andrena Finlay, Stuart Quinn. *Executive producer:* Rebel Penfold-Russell. *Scriptwriter:* Stephan Elliott. *Director of photography:* Geoff Burton. *Camera operator:* David Williamson. *Production designer:* Brian Thomson. *Costume designer:* Fiona Spence. *Editor:* Frans Vandenburg. *Composer:* Guy Gross. *Sound recordist:* Ross Linton. *Sound editors:* Gary O'Grady (sup. fx); Gary Bell (fx); Tim Jordan (senior dia.); John Penders (dia.). *Mixers:* Jeffrey Perkins (sup.); Kurt Kassulke.

Cast

Phil Collins (Roland Copping), Hugo Weaving (Jonathan Wheats), Josephine Byrnes (Beth Wheats); Mitchell McMahon (Young Roland), Andrew McMahon (Young Matthew), Rebel Penfold[1] (Mother), Peter Mochrie (Michael), Helen O'Connor (Margaret), Colleen Clifford (Mrs. Waterson), Vincent Ball (Judge), Ghandi MacIntyre (Cartel Valuer), Christina Hammond (Detective Simms), Kee Chan (Detective Alan), Ian Cockburn (Matthew).

But for a poorly-judged opening sequence, the unnecessary appearance of a gun at the film's climax and a stupid schoolboy fight between Jonathan Wheats (Hugo Weaving) and Roland Copping (Phil Collins), Stephan Elliott's **Frauds** makes an admirable stab at oddball comedy, even though it suffers from too little comedy and too much Phil Collins.

It's usually a good thing when you're 20 minutes into a film and still not sure where it's heading. In the case of **Frauds**, this suspense is due not to any remarkably-eccentric narrative route or directorial style, but to a prologue that is too dramatic in tone for the well-decorated piece of fairyfloss that subsequently unspools.

During his disastrous birthday party to which nobody but his mum (Rebel Penfold) and brother Matthew (Andrew McMahon) come, a young Roland (Mitchell McMahon) dares Matthew to take a raft trip on a particularly-hazardous river, which inevitably ends in tragedy.

Years later, Roland is an enthusiastic insurance investigator, who likes catching people with fraudulent claims, and then blackmailing them. He uses the resulting avalanche of cash to finance a lifestyle that preserves the nursery-room mindset of his youth. He likes playing practical jokes on people and lives in a magnificently-decorated house that looks like a theme park.

Roland then happens upon the vulnerable suburban souls of Jonathan and Beth Wheats (Josephine Byrnes), whom he catches out in an insurance scam involving a silver service. He proceeds to bleed them of possessions, although his childlike mind is more interested in the game of blackmail than its spoils.

It is at this point you begin to twig that the wavelength the film is now transmitting on isn't the one it started out with. Wide-angle lenses, extreme close-ups, loud decor, occasional splotches of surrealism and the odd joke signal a high-concept, comic-book comedy which looks better than it feels, and a lot better than it sounds.

Roland's enigmatic presence and foggy intentions early on establish a lovely comic rhythm, producing some inventive comic moments. When two cops visit Beth to explain they probably won't find the cutlery set, she notices Roland has arranged a brightly-lit Christmas tree just behind them. She promptly throws up.

But as we see more and more of the Roland and the fantasy world he inhabits, he becomes less and less interesting, his enigma eroding through overexposure. The film also becomes less inventive. Thus it is during the climax in the funpark interior of Roland's house that a gun has to be produced, and a lame fistfight has to ensue between Roland and Jonathan in order to push the film to its figuratively and literally wet climax.

This is not helped by an off-key performance by Phil Collins. Collins does not have the screen presence or acting strength to give Roland the malicious streak that far too few of his delicious lines of dialogue suggest. Threatening to slice Beth vertically, he says how she'll never ride a bicycle again. A few dozen lines like that would have served the film much better.

Given all that, and forgiving a lot of it, **Frauds** does get away with more than it should, thanks to the intrigue of its premise, the splendour of its images and the fact that its scarce smattering of gags is enough, if only just.

JIM SCHEMBRI

---

[1] Rebel Penfold's credit as executive producer is given as 'Rebel Penfold-Russell'.

References
'Frauds', writer–director Stephan Elliott interviewed by Lani Hannah, *Cinema Papers*, no. 90, October 1992, pp. 44–9.
'46e International du Film de Cannes', an article by Jan Epstein, *Cinema Papers*, no. 94, August 1993, pp. 22–7.
'Frauds', a review by David Vallence, *Cinema Papers*, no. 101, October, 1994, p. 66.

Catching the crooked: Roland Copping (Phil Collins) and Beth Wheats (Josephine Byrnes).

HAMMERS OVER THE ANVIL

South Australian Film Corporation and Harvest Productions presents HAMMERS OVER THE ANVIL. © SAFC Productions Ltd, Harvey-Wright Enterprises Pty Ltd [and] Australian Film Finance Corporation Pty Limited. Script developed with the assistance of Australian Film Commission. Also developed with the assistance of Film Victoria. Made with the participation of Australian Film Finance Corporation Pty Limited as part of the 1991 FFC Film Fund. *Budget:* $4 million. *Filmed:* 11 October–29 November 1991. *Australian distributor:* Roadshow. *Video:* Roadshow. *Rating:* M. 35mm. 97 mins.

Producer: Ben Gannon. *Executive producers:* Gus Howard, Peter Gawler, Janet Worth. *Co-producer:* Peter Harvey-Wright. *Associate producer:* Barbara Gibbs. *Scriptwriters:* Peter Hepworth, Ann Turner. Based on the short stories by Alan Marshall. *Director of photography:* James Bartle. *Camera operator:* David Williamson. *Production designer:* Ross Major. *Costume designer:* Ross Major. *Editor:* Ken Sallows. *Composer:* Not Drowning, Waving. *Sound recordist:* Phil Tipene. *Sound editors:* Dean Gawen, Rex Watts, Paul Huntingford, Ashley Grenville. *Mixers:* James Currie, Peter D. Smith.

Cast

Charlotte Rampling (Grace McAlister), Russell Crowe (East Driscoll), Alexander Outhred (Alan Marshall), Frankie J. Holden (Dad), Jake D. Frost (Joe Carmichael), Alethea McGrath (Mrs Bilson), John Lee (McAlister), Frank Gallacher (Mr Thomas The Preacher), Amanda Douge (Nellie Bolster), Kirsty McGregor (Elsie Marshall), Daphne Grey (Mrs Herbert), Caroline Kemp (Lucy Taylor), Sam Nightingale (Freckles Jack), Syd Brisbane (Dave The Dance Caller), Peter Osborn (Father Finnegan), Wayne Pygram (Snarley Burns); Lachlan Fischer, John Francis, Hugh Gordon, Janet Gordon (Bungalow Bush+ Band); Brian Erskine, Matt Monroe (Pork Fair Bagpipers), Ian Welbourne (Cruel Boy).

Adapted from Alan Marshall's short-story collection of the same title, **Hammers Over the Anvil** interweaves an adulterous affaire with the trials of adolescence, and sets it against the social mores of the early 1900s.

Alexander Outhred plays 11-year-old Alan, who dreams of becoming a great horseman like his idol, East Driscoll (Russell Crowe), despite his crutches and leg brace, the legacy of infantile paralysis. With his best mate, Joe Carmichael (Jake D. Frost), Alan explores the adult world of sexual relations,

through innocent pecks exchanged with Joe's girlfriend to witnessing the seduction of teenager Nellie Bolster (Amanda Douge) by the sly local priest and blacksmith (Frank Gallacher). They also befriend the crazy old Mrs Bilson (Alethea McGrath), a hilarious and tragic character. Despite losing his mother as a young child, it is the inevitable death of Mrs Bilson which confronts Alan with his first experience of mortality and the loss of a friend.

These events frame the focus of the film's narrative: the immediate attraction between East and the newly-arrived wife of a wealthy landowner, Grace McAlister (Charlotte Rampling). Alan himself is strongly attracted to the elegant and yet strong-willed Grace. The trio become constant companions — the childless Grace drawn to the motherless Alan — and yet Alan remains the outsider on the fringes of an adult world, most clearly when he walks in on Grace and East in the stables and, concealed by the shadows, watches their lovemaking. The affaire ends tragically when a fall from a horse leaves East brain-damaged.

The film's strength lies in the rapport director Ann Turner encourages between the inexperienced Outhred and the expert ensemble cast, including some heated arguments with Alan's father (Frankie J. Holden). The photography is both expansive in its presentation of South Australia's Clare Valley and detailed in its inclusion of minutiæ which intensify the narration of significant events in Alan's life. As with her debut feature, **Celia** (1989), Turner presents us with a child's view of adult behaviour which is historically specific in its detail and yet timeless in its observations of human nature. The film's title, recalling the blacksmith's craft, represents the blows which mould a person as he or she passes through life, just as the hammer blows give shape to crude metal.

FINCINA HOPGOOD

References

'Ann Turner's **Hammers Over the Anvil**', a production report by Andrew L. Urban, *Cinema Papers*, no. 88, May–June 1992, pp. 12–14.

'Hammers Over the Anvil', a review by Fincina Hopgood, *Cinema Papers*, no. 101, October, 1994, pp. 66–8.

Grace McAlister (Charlotte Rampling) and Alan Marshall (Alexander Outhred).

D E A N   M U R P H Y

LEX AND RORY

The Globe Film Co. [and] Colorim International Releasing Corporation in association with Cinevision Australia. Lex and Rory[1]. © 1993 Lex and Rory Production Limited. Marketing assistance provided by Australian Film Commission and Film Victoria. *Location:* Albury (New South Wales). *Australian distributor:* Globe. *Video:* 21st Century. *Rating:* PG. 35mm. 95 mins.

[*Producer:* not credited.] *Executive producer:* Scott Andrews. *Associate producer:* Mal Bryning. *Associate director:*[2] Mal Bryning. *Scriptwriter:* Dean Murphy. *Director of photography:* Tim Smart. *Production designers:* Katie Wright, Dallas Olsen. [*Costume designers:* not credited; atb Katie Wright, Dallas Olsen.] *Editor:* John Leonard. *Composer:* Frank Strangio. *Sound supervisor:* Michael Slater. *Sound editors:* Scott Findlay (dia.); Antony Bohun (fx). *Mixer:* Michael Slater.

Cast

Angus Benfield (Lex), Paul Robertson (Rory), Fiona MacGregor (Dai), Wendy Holics (Nikki), Ashley Bindon (Jamie), Stewart Faichney (Gary Bryson), Carol Brand (Sue Bryson), Scott Goddard (Thomas), Scott Andrews (Jack #1), Dallas Olsen (Jack #2), Barbara Holics (College Principal), Dave Simpkins (Mr. Flavel), Katie Wright (Teacher); Rodney's Gang: Pat Giltrap (Rodney), Adam Carmody (Kenny), Anthony McKillop (Ocker); Judith Cary (Woman with Hose), Mick "Sammy" Kittelty (Cabbage Slapper), Karen Todd (Dai as a Child), Chris Brown (Student Dancer), Andrew Rhodes (Student Violator), Lucy Heal (T.V. Reporter), "Valley" (Mean Dog); Norman Yemm, Marcus Arnold (Derros on Steps); Wild Bill Murphy's Back Street Stumblers (Mouldey Fygge Jazz Band).

It is tempting, while watching this cliché-infested, wannabe teen romance fantasy, to judge not the film, but the heroic and genuinely-admirable production history behind it.

A couple of small-town dreamers from Albury–Wodonga fought hard to raise the artistic and financial support to turn their idea into a movie. Great. This is what true film-making is about and embodies the kind of spirit that any film industry needs and can always do with a lot more of.

That said, what of the film itself? Well: boy sees girl, boy wants girl, boy doesn't have balls to meet girl. So boy puts through a few phone calls to her under an alias and gets to know her telephonically. Boy ends up getting girl and credits roll before the film

Lex (Angus Benfield) and Rory (Paul Robertson).

actually gets a chance to do anything interesting.

For a film about teenagers, **Lex and Rory** is simply too slow. This is mainly due to the rather glaring fact that it has no third act. After his initial lustings, Lex (Angus Benfield) finally plucks up the courage to confront Dai (Fiona MacGregor) on the phone, and the rest of the film is basically a series of phone conversations. That's it.

The film is marred by some dreadful thematic exposition where characters, rather than speaking like characters, speak like scriptwriters discussing the subtext of what particular scenes are supposed to be about.

Hence, when Dai, in a half-hearted secondary story, confronts her stereotypically-demonic father (Stewart Faichney, who is sometimes shot like a demon) about not wanting to enter the car retail business because she wants to be a fashion designer, we get lines that sound like margin notes on a first draft:

'This is my life. It's my dream.'

'Maybe I have my own wishes and dreams. It is my life. Why can't you accept that? I don't want to do business, I want to do art.'

The private milieu Lex and Rory (Paul Robertson) inhabit is also off-key. The guys have a rumpus room which houses a computer, a pinball machine, a soft drink vending machine for Schweppes lemonade (thanks for the plug money), an immobile Porsche (thanks again) and a speaker phone courtesy of Telecom (and again). A few *Playboy*

magazines and girlie posters might have given the set some hormonal integrity.

Which leads to the important issue of boy talk. Even for two shy teenagers, Lex and Rory have the cleanest mouths since Disney put Kurt Russell on the payroll. There is one reference to wanting a 'furry collar for Freddie', and a few quips about 'getting a pro', but nothing more to indicate that these boys actually have genitalia that work.

Though much of the film's humour misfires—someone trying to eat off a turntable is about as inventive as the visual humour gets—some of it is memorable. Most of it is to do with Dai's younger brother Jamie (Ashley Bindon). His on-going battle with the school bullies forms a funny little subplot. The opening Nora Ephronesque exchange between the boys about looks and personality is promising, but these little nodes of humour never grow into anything strong enough to sustain a whole feature.

For most of the film the zappy red Porsche sits idly as the boys talk about life, desire and the future. Perhaps it is a symbol of the potential of youth yet to burgeon. It certainly serves as an apt symbol for the way the film just sits there, waiting for something better to happen.

JIM SCHEMBRI

---

[1] The 'and' is vertical, with the letters pointing left. Some press material incorrectly opted for an ampersand.

[2] Only known credit of its kind; immediately precedes director's credit.

LIGHTNING JACK

Village Roadshow Pictures presents a Lightning Ridge Village Roadshow Production. LIGHTNING JACK[1]. © 1992 Lightning Ridge Films Limited. Made with the support of the 5,860 unit holders of the Lightning Jack Film Trust. *Locations:* New Mexico, Arizona, Utah, Colorado (US); Queensland (Movieworld Studios). *Australian distributor:* Village Roadshow. *Video:* Roadshow. *Rating:* PG. 35mm. 98 mins.

Producers: Paul Hogan, Greg Coote, Simon Wincer. *Executive producers:* Graham Burke, Anthony Stewart. *Line producer:* Grant Hill. *Scriptwriter:* Paul Hogan. *Director of photography:* David Eggby. *Camera operators:* Buzz Feitshans, David Luckenbach. *Production designer:* Bernard Hides. *Costume designer:* Bruce Finlayson. *Editor:* O. Nicholas Brown. *Composer:* Bruce Rowland. *Sound recordists:* Bud Alper (US); Lloyd Carrick (Aust.). *Sound designer:* Tim Chau. *Sound editors:* Tim Chau (sup.); Peter Burgess, Livia Ruzic, Glenn Newnham, Glenn Martin, Gavin Myers, Frank Lipson; Roy Prendergast (music); Steve Burgess (foley). *Mixers:* Peter Fenton, Phil Heywood, Ron Purvis; Robin Gray (music).

Lightning Jack Kane (Paul Hogan) and Ben Doyle (Cuba Gooding Jr).

Cast

Paul Hogan (Lightning Jack Kane), Cuba Gooding Jr (Ben Doyle), Beverly D'Angelo (Lana), Kamala Dawson (Pilar), Pat Hingle (Marshall Kurtz), L. Q. Jones (Local Sheriff), Richard Riehle (Reporter), Frank McRae (Mr. Doyle), Max Cullen (Bart), Roy Brocksmith (Junction City Tailor), Douglas Stewart (Junction City Shopkeeper), Kevin O'Morrison (Old Guy in Alley), Mark Miles (Luke), Clif Stokes (Bully Cowboy), Bob Sorenson (Clem), Raymond O'Connor (Pat), Robert Guajardo (Bank Manager), Tom Noga (Bank Clerk), Ed Adams (Cole Younger), Bruce Miles (Third Man), Grace Keagy (Mrs. Franks), Jess Franks (Auctioneer), Kenny Jacobs (South Fork Bank Teller).

If **Lightning Jack** is remembered for anything, it will be for the floating for the first time of a film as a public company on the stock exchange, and for the money lost by thousands of small investors who punted on Paul Hogan piggybacking them to a fortune. Estimates at the time of writing have shares reduced to 7 per cent of their original value, a salutary reminder, if one is needed, that film-making is the biggest gamble of them all.

Hogan catapulted to superstardom after the international success of **Crocodile Dundee** (Peter Faiman, 1986), but it was

more than charisma that got him there. The script was good, too. And if the novelty of his rugged charm and laid-back humour was beginning to wear a tad thin in the more pedestrian "Crocodile" Dundee 2 (John Cornell, 1988), it was non-existent in **Almost an Angel** (John Cornell, US, 1990). In **Lightning Jack**, Hogan's particular brand of Australian affability is stretched to the point of no return. However, the film is saved from complete inconsequentiality by Hogan's co-star, Cuba Gooding Jr.

Gooding (**Boyz 'N' the Hood, A Few Good Men**[2]) plays Ben Doyle, the sidekick of Lightning Jack Kane (Hogan), and he proves himself a wonderful mime. Hogan's storyline has Doyle as a smart black man born dumb (i.e., mute), with the joke on Lightning Jack as a 'dumb' man who sees himself as smart. This involves Jack's adopting the rôle of mentor, and, in the course of inducting the young man into ways to woo women and rob banks, Doyle (amongst other generally-unfunny things) shoots himself in the foot, and gets frightened by a bear. American critics failed to see the joke and the film was panned for making Doyle into an 'Uncle Tom'.

However, Gooding's expressive face and talent for mime cannot make up for an aimless, meandering plot that lacks suspense or surprise, and has no resolution to speak of. It is also oddly bereft of any characters, apart

from Jack and Doyle, who are capable of engaging an audience. Jack himself is a tired variant of Mick Dundee, who is as misplaced in the west as Dundee seemed apposite in New York, where the notion of a simple Aussie bringing his bush survival skills to the most sophisticated city in the world was engaging and fresh.

Hogan's stated aim with **Lightning Jack** is to pay 'affectionate homage' to the Hollywood Western. The film adds little to the genre beyond the novelty of the idea that an Australian (Jack) wants desperately to become a legend of the American west. The fact that 'Jack' succeeds, where Hogan fails, only serves to illustrate the point that life rarely imitates art.

GEOFF GARDNER

---

1 There is a bolt of lightning between the two words.
2 **Boyz 'N' the Hood** (John Singleton, 1991) and **A Few Good Men** (Rob Reiner, 1992).

References

'Lightning Jack', director Simon Wincer interviewed by Scott Murray, *Cinema Papers*, no. 97–8, March 1994, pp. 4–10.
'Lightning Jack', a review by Emma Coller, *Cinema Papers*, no. 99, June 1994, pp. 69–70.
'Lightning Jack', a review by Raffaele Caputo, ibid., pp. 70–2.

BEN LEWIN

LUCKY BREAK

Australian Film Finance Corporation in association with Generation Films, Lewin Films and Pandora Cinema presents Lucky Break. © 1994 Australian Film Finance Corporation[,] Weis Films Pty Limited [and] Lewin Films Pty Limited. Marketing assistance provided by Film Victoria. This film was developed with the assistance of the NSW Film and TV Office[1]. Financed by Australian Film Finance Corporation. *Location:* Melbourne. *Australian distributor:* UIP. *Video:* Roadshow. *Rating:* M. 35mm. 90 mins.

Producer: Bob Weis. *Co-producer:* Judi Levine. *Line producer:* Lesley Parker. *Scriptwriter:* Ben Lewin. *Director of photography:* Vincent Monton. *Production designer:* Peta Lawson. *Costume designer:* Anna Borghesi. *Editor:* Peter Carrodus. *Composer:* Paul Grabowsky. *Sound rec-ordists:* John Phillips, Gary Wilkins. *Sound editors:* Livia Ruzic, Gavin Myers (dia.); Gareth Vanderhope (fx). *Mixer:* Roger Savage.

Cast

Gia Carides (Sophie), Anthony LaPaglia (Eddie), Rebecca Gibney (Gloria), Jacek Koman (Yuri), Sioban Turke (Kate), Lewis Fiander (Bruce Wrightman), Robyn Nevin (Anne-Marie LePine), Marshall Napier (George LePine), Mary-Anne Fahey (Myra), Michael Edward-Stevens (Benny), Steady Eddy (Nicholas), Michael Veitch (Dt Sgt Scott), Russell Fletcher (Det Tyrone), Nicholas Bell (Sophie's Doctor), Kurt Ludescher (Ernst), Max Bruch (Diamond Cutter), Lynda Gibson (Library Clerk), David Watson (Professor-type at Party), Kirk Alexander (Celebrant), Paul Karo (Defence Lawyer), Terry Norris (Judge), Alvin Chong (Chinese Doctor), Ernie Grey (Doctor at Wedding), Agnieszka Perepeczko (Woman at Wedding), Carolyn Bock (Hotel Hospitality Lady), Maggie Stevens (Mrs Wrightman), Cliff Ellen (Airline Porter), Alexandra Lewin (Music Student).

There are a lot of enticing 'what if's in Ben Lewin's muddled romantic comedy Lucky Break. What if a woman whose legs are debilitated by polio has an accident and breaks one? What if, with the plaster cast on her leg, people start treating her like a regular person who's merely had a skiing accident, and not like a full-time cripple? What if an attractive guy falls in love with her without knowing the truth? What if the theme got the respect it deserved?

Luscious though the premise is, the idea at the heart of Lucky Break only makes it half-way through before dying through lack of imagination.

Disabled since she was six, Sophie (Gia Carides) is a reluctant dreamer who spends a lot of her time in the library writing erotic prose for publication. Her inadvertent readings aloud attract Eddie (Anthony LaPaglia), a handsome jeweller. He is on the verge of marrying the strong-minded, beautiful Gloria (Rebecca Gibney), but finds Sophie's words a turn-on. After she has an accident which puts one of her legs in plaster, they steal away to an island where their romance progresses, although Gloria twigs that something is up.

All the elements are there to generate a lot more comedy and at least a little drama, but the film suffers from a lack of nerves and comic invention. The limited time Sophie has to engage Eddie in a relationship before her cast is removed is, surprisingly, not used to create any comic tension. She does not appear to have an agenda of things to achieve in this short time—such as sex—and the time passes far too uneventfully.

Tragically underdeveloped is Gloria, who for a few blissful moments shapes up as the chief drag engine for conflict and complication in Lucky Break. But though she finds out Sophie's secret, she does nothing with the information.

The film purports to deal with the issues of how we tend to judge and prejudge people by physical appearance, taking scant account of their inner qualities. Yet the physicality and sexuality of Gloria and Sophie (who, presumably, is a virgin) are not used to test Eddie's feelings. Things are kept light and easy and the dynamics between Sophie, Eddie and Gloria simply run out of puff.

So about half-way through the film, as Eddie and Sophie kiss in his jewellery store, it is almost out of necessity that a new plot twist literally comes walking through the door, in the form of the heavily-accented undercover police officer, Yuri (Jacek Koman), who suspects Eddie of dealing in stolen jewellery.

The film's crime-caper angle, to put it mildly, is terrible. A few tracking shots and the presence of a few cops, cars and guns fail to bring whatever intended action, humour and excitement they were supposed to.

For a comedy Lucky Break has a high rate of misfits, mainly due to misjudged pieces of slapstick. Only the comedy dealing with Sophie's situation work, such as her meeting with a handicapped friend, Nicholas (played by comedian Steady Eddy). He quickly susses out the lie she is spinning Eddie, but, rather than blow her cover, he begins to embarrass her by asking for details about her 'skiing accident'.

The simmering comic energy of this scene, however, is cut short in deference to a gag about men's toilet habits. It is typical of how the film continually points to its intrinsic merit before opting for something less.

JIM SCHEMBRI

---

[1] Usually 'New South Wales Film & Television Office'.

Reference
'Ben Lewin', writer–director Ben Lewin interviewed by Andrew L. Urban, *Cinema Papers*, no. 101, October 1994, pp. 38–42.

Sophie (Gia Carides), Eddie (Anthony LaPaglia) and Defence Lawyer (Paul Karo).

MARY

A Rosemary Blight production. MARY. © 1994 Australian Film Finance Corporation Limited, R. B. Films Pty Limited, Australian Film Commission, and New South Wales Film & Television Office. Produced and developed with the assistance and financial participation of the New South Wales Film and TV Office[1]. Developed with the assistance of the Australian Film Commission. Made with the assistance of the Sisters of Saint Joseph of the Sacred Heart. Financed by the Australian Film Finance Corporation Limited. *Locations:* Rome (Italy); New South Wales. *Australian distributor:* Ronin. *Video:* Ronin. *Rating:* PG. 35mm. 71 mins.

Producer: Rosemary Blight. *Consultant producer:* Bridget Ikin. *Scriptwriter:* Kay Pavlou. Based on an original concept by Julie Macken. *Director of photography:* Jan Kenny. *Production designer:* Angus Strathie. *Wardrobe supervisor:* Wendy Cork. *Editor:* Margaret Sixel. *Composer:* Douglas Stephen Rae. *Sound recordist:* Mark Blackwell. *Sound editors:* Mark Blackwell; Liam Egan (dia.). *Mixer:* Robert Sullivan.

Cast

Lucy Bell (Mary MacKillop[2]), Linden Wilkinson (Older Mary), Rebecca Scully-Webster (Young Mary), Brendan Higgins (Father Julian Woods), Brian Harrison (Bishop Shiel), Maureen Green (Sister Teresa), Brian McDermott (Bishop James Quinn), Stephen Leeder (Father Horan), Frank Garfield (Bishop Reynolds), Roslyn Oades (Sister Paula), Vanessa Downing (Mother (Flora MacKillop)), Dean Nottle (Governor's Gentleman), Lynne Porteous (Cook), Jan McDermott (Sister Clare), Nicholas Findlay (Thomas), Kye Clark (Donald MacKillop), Jaclyn Hewitt (Lexie MacKillop), Deborah Gallanos (Assistant Sister), Christen Cornell (Dying Miracle Woman), Ron Zines (Bishop Matthew Quinn).

Interviewees

Clare Dunn (Author, *No Plaster Saint*), Sister Marie Foale (Author, *The Josephite Story*), P. Peter Gumple S. J. (Saintmaker, Relator of Mary's Cause), Sister Margaret McKenna (Mary MacKillop Secretariat).

The beatification of Mary MacKillop[3] was completed by Pope John-Paul II in January 1995 in Sydney. Needless to say, the beatification generated a great deal of interest. This film seeks to retell the story of MacKillop's struggle to provide education for the poor, her struggles with the bishops and her (successful) appeals for help from Pope Pius IX, as well as the process by which her beatification was realised. The film is part documentary, part fiction. The combination may seem strange but it was necessitated by the low budget and the oversupply of information—after all, the story of MacKillop's life, death and beatification covers more than a century. The fictional sections dramatise scenes from her life; the documentary sections, with commentaries from Josephite sisters and representatives of the Vatican, provide bridging and informative guides to her character and achievement.

Writer–director Kay Pavlou has chosen wisely to adopt short, vivid tableaux. The approach generally eschews grand drama or epic sweep for a quiet, understated style which emphasises stillness, humility, reverence. The relative absence of irony at crucial stages will bother some viewers, and the simple and direct approach will not please others. But the simplicity of the film and the modesty of its approach—its refusal of the grand gesture or of the rhetorical flourish, with one or two exceptions—are in fact quite functional parts of the film's fabric, for they serve to heighten the sense of Mary's simple devotion to her calling, just as they serve to remind the hard-nosed modern sophisticate that her life was characterised by *sancta simplicitas*, a simplicity which might be considered holy.

There is no doubt that Pavlou can articulate sublime compositions and dramatic frames as two or three images in the film indicate (the 'crowning' of Mary and the shots of her body in the church). However, the tone which the director has chosen to adopt constantly emphasises some of the qualities and virtues for which the subject was beatified, and this is how it should be. In this sense, the film language reflects the ethos of the subject. The film also suggests, crucially, that the subject was not without faults, so it is quite untrue to claim that the film provides a hagiography. No doubt other more critical, deconstructive and expensive films will follow, but it is difficult to think of a more appropriate presentation of the subject in the year of her beatification. Certainly, Mary emerges as a determined, strong, devoted woman who was indefatigable in her work for the poor.

RAYMOND YOUNIS

---

1 Usually 'New South Wales Film & Television Office'.
2 McKillop's name on her birth certificate has no 'a'.
3 See footnote 2.
4 See footnote 2.

Reference

'Mary', a review by Peter Malone, *Cinema Papers*, no. 103, March, 1995, pp. 45–6, 48.

Mary MacKillop [4] (Lucy Bell) and Sister Paula (Roslyn Oades).

P . J . H O G A N

MURIEL'S WEDDING

A House & Moorhouse Films production. Muriel's Wedding. © 1994 Australian Film Finance Corporation Limited, House & Moorhouse Films Pty Ltd, Film Victoria and Peter Szabo & Associates, Pty. Ltd. Financed by the Australian Film Finance Corporation Limited in association with CiBy Sales. Developed and produced with the assistance of Film Victoria. Developed with the assistance of Film Queensland and the Pacific Film and Television Commission. Project developed with the assistance of Australian Film Commission. This film was produced with the assistance of New South Wales Film and Television Office. *Filmed:* 23 August–17 October 1993. *Australian distributor:* Roadshow. *Video:* Roadshow. *Rating:* M. 35mm. 101 mins.

Producers: Lynda House, Jocelyn Moorhouse. *Associate producers:* Michael D. Aglion, Tony Mahood. *Scriptwriter:* P. J. Hogan. *Director of photography:* Martin McGrath. *Camera operator:* David Williamson. *Production designer:* Patrick Reardon. *Costume designer:* Terry Ryan. *Editor:* Jill Bilcock. *Composer:* Peter Best. *Sound:* David Lee, Glenn Newnham, Livia Ruzic, Roger Savage. [*Sound recordist:* not credited; atb David Lee.] [*Sound editors:* not credited; atb Glenn Newnham, Livia Ruzic.] [*Mixer:* not credited; atb Roger Savage.]

Cast

Toni Collette (Muriel), Bill Hunter (Bill), Rachel Griffiths (Rhonda)[1]; Sophie Lee (Tania), Rosalind Hammond (Cheryl), Belinda Jarrett (Janine), Pippa Grandison (Nicole), Jeanie Drynan (Betty), Daniel Wyllie (Perry), Gabby Millgate (Joanie), Gennie Nevinson (Deidre), Matt Day (Brice), Chris Haywood (Ken Blundell), Daniel LaPaine (David Van Arkle)[2]; Susan Prior (Girl at Wedding), Nathan Kaye (Chook), Cecily Polson (Tania's Mother), Rob Steele (Higgins), Genevieve Picot (Store Detective), Richard Sutherland (Constable Saunders), Steve Smith (Constable Gillespie), Kate Saunders (Penelope), Dene Kermond (Malcolm), Jeamin Lee (Chinese Waitress), Jon-Claire Lee (Chinese Maitre D').

Muriel Heslop (Toni Collette) is an ugly duckling first glimpsed catching the bouquet at a friend's wedding. This event is quickly followed by Muriel being forced to give up the bouquet, the bridegroom having sex with a bridesmaid and Muriel being arrested for shoplifting.

In further quick succession, Muriel's father, Bill (Bill Hunter), bribes the police; the bride and her bridesmaids take off for a resort without the new husband; Bill stitch-

Cheryl (Rosalind Hammond), Bill (Bill Hunter), Muriel (Toni Collette), Janine (Belinda Jarrett) and Tania (Sophie Lee).

es up a land deal with Japanese businessmen; Muriel steals money from her mother and follows the other girls to a resort; there she runs into an old acquaintance, Rhonda (Rachel Griffiths), and together they win a talent contest doing a routine that mimics Muriel's beloved Abba; Muriel runs away to Sydney; Rhonda is diagnosed as having cancer; and Bill is arrested on corruption charges. Phew! … and there is a lot more to come.

The pace and the turn of events, many of them delightfully comic, are breathtaking, and the plot twists and turns relentlessly. It has to be said that there is a lot of script contrivance and coincidence, and not a few loose ends in the helter skelter of action. The film is not, of course, seeking to survive too much scrutiny as to how the characters and events race from A to Z. All of it is easily presented in a boisterous manner which wants to keep surprising the spectator with moments that mostly click but occasionally clink. It's a matter of judgement as to whether the best or the worst of these are the sudden sound of the strains of Abba's 'I Do, I Do, I Do, I Do' as Muriel starts her march down the aisle, or the sudden appearance of her husband as she rushes from her mother's funeral.

Elsewhere, there are similarly-mixed virtues in the presentation of the milieu of Muriel's family and their life in the resort of Porpoise Spit. This is the home territory of its writer–director, P. J. Hogan, and the background of petty corruption, familial betrayal and unthinking abuse is very clearly drawn. There is more than a hint of chilling accuracy in these scenes, though the portraits of Muriel's siblings are overdone to the point of rendering them half-witted. But there is also the portrait of Muriel's mother (Jeanie

Drynan), a bewildered and overweight matron turning a blind eye to her husband's corruption and infidelity, which is quite the most accomplished element of the film and is captured with unusual sympathy, especially given the larger-than-life representations of Muriel and Rhonda, to say nothing of the outright grotesqueries of the three bridesmaids.

It is worth pointing out that Jeanie Drynan has forsaken any effort at middle-aged glamour for a rôle that has more troubling truth to it than anything else in the film. This performance was overlooked in the AFI Awards, Drynan's peers preferring the rather more flamboyantly-raunchy, then cancer-stricken and wheelchair-bound rôle of Rhonda played by Rachel Griffiths.

At the end of the film Muriel and Rhonda shout goodbye to Porpoise Spit as they leave town in a taxi. The two cinderellas are leaving the ball and one gets the feeling that P. J. Hogan was invisibly driving the cab and urging them on to greater excess.

GEOFF GARDNER

---

1 First three actors in order of opening credits.
2 These eleven actors in order of appearance of 'main cast'; the rest in order of appearance from secondary cast.

References

'47e Festival international du Film, Cannes', an article by Jan Epstein, *Cinema Papers*, no. 100, August 1994, pp. 10–15.

'Muriel's Wedding', writer–director P. J. Hogan interviewed by Jan Epstein, *Cinema Papers*, no. 101, October 1994, pp. 28–32.

'Sydney Film Festival', a report by Raymond Younis, ibid., pp. 74–6.

'Muriel's Wedding', a review by David Vallence, *Cinema Papers*, no. 102, December, 1994, pp. 69–70.

NO ESCAPE

Columbia Tristar Film Distributors International presents in association with Allied Filmmakers a Pacific Western production.[1] © 1994 Allied Filmmakers N.V. *Alternative titles:* 'The Penal Colony' (working) and *Escape from Absalom* (video). *Budget:* $15 million. *Locations:* Queensland, New South Wales. *Filmed:* May 1993. *Australian distributor:* Hoyts. *Video:* Columbia–Tristar. *Rating:* M. 35mm. Panavision. 118 mins.

Producer: Gale Anne Hurd. *Executive producer:* Jake Eberts. *Co-producers:* Michael R. Joyce, James Eastep. *Scriptwriters:* Michael Gaylin, Joel Gross. Based on *The Penal Colony* by Richard Henley. *Director of photography:* Phil Meheux. *Production designer:* Allan Cameron. *Costume designer:* Norma Moriceau. *Editor:* Terry Rawlings. *Composer:* Graeme Revell. *Sound recordist:* Ben Osmo. *Sound editors:* Bob Risk (foley); Allan Killick (dia.). *Mixers:* Nicolas le-Messurier, Michael A. Carter; Peter Lacey (foley).

Cast

Ray Liotta (Robbins), Lance Henriksen (The Father), Stuart Wilson (Marek), Kevin Dillon (Casey); Kevin J. O'Connor[2], Don Henderson; Ian McNeice (King); Jack Shepherd; Michael Lerner (Warden), Ernie Hudson (Hawkins), Russell Kiefel (Iceman); Brian M. Loga, Cheuk-Fai Chan, Machs Colombani; Stephen Shanahan (Screaming Inmate), Dominic Bianco (Ralph), Justin Monjo (Technician #1), Brandon Burke (Technician #2), Stan Kouros (Nico); Ron Vreekin, Scott Lowe, Colin Moody, Richard Carter, Boris Brkic.

Set in a future where prisons are run by private corporations, No Escape takes as its premise a world where extreme circumstances create extreme communities. The film starts with a Blade Runner[3]-like opening sequence where the main character, Robbins (Ray Liotta), is introduced to a not-too-distant world of high-tech incarceration and advanced cruelty.

Robbins stands out from his fellow inmates with his daredevil defiance of authority and successful self-preservation techniques. He is a troubled soldier with a violent past, imprisoned because of his seemingly-unprompted murder of a commanding officer. It's not too long before Robbins quickly comes to the attention of the boss of the prison/corporation for his unsubservient attitude.

After a demonstration of his defiance, Robbins is released into a separate prison

Robbins (Ray Liotta) and The Father (Lance Henriksen).

world, Absolom—a tropical island where prisoners are abandoned and left to their own devices. The results are surveyed from afar by the nefarious corporation.

Taking more than just a similar name from another prison film set in the future, **Escape from New York** (John Carpenter, 1981), this film quickly sets up a society where investigating the primitive becomes an overriding theme.

The prisoners on the island are divided into two main tribes: the Outsiders, a cannibalistic collection of gangs led by wise-cracking, psychotic Marek; and the Insiders, a pastoralist commune of villagers led by the wise and noble man known as The Father (played with characteristic iciness by Lance Henriksen). First landing with the Outsiders, Robbins fights his way into the enclave of the Insiders, where he forms uneasy allegiances with the mysterious inhabitants of a community fortressed and organised around seemingly-democratic lines. There he meets the effete obese doctor, the upright lieutenant, the slightly-crazed inventor and the aforementioned mysterious The Father. Not one to join the herd, Robbins must negotiate lines of communication in order to live a common dream — escape.

In an increasingly-violent and ever-gory succession of fights, explosions, stabbings, guttings and decapitations, the inhabitants of this *Lord of the Flies* nightmare/paradise inch closer to the dream before mutual destruction.

Absolom is a world divided by dichotomies: primitive vs. civilised, innocent vs. guilty, freedom vs. incarceration. Like most dichotomies, what first appears as clearly opposing becomes muddied in its terms. As the main character, Robbins becomes a cipher for these often-frequented themes to be played out along the boundaries of the familiar. It is perhaps fitting then that, as an

actor, Ray Liotta lends a certain vacantness to his character. It starts with his see-through blue eyes and ends with his emotionless delivery. But it doesn't matter; the terrain is well-trodden enough to invest sufficient meaning.

Although the audience may know that the film was entirely shot in Queensland, the overriding Hollywoodness of the production means slight jarring occurs when the infrequent Australian accent is heard. Still, it is comforting to see the established faces of David Argue, Colin Moody and Chris Hargreaves amongst the imports.

No Escape is a B-grade movie with high production values. It's not only the setting which lends the more low-brow overtones, but also the cast. While they may have appeared in A-grade films, actors such as Lance Henriksen and Michael Lerner cannot help but make allusions to previous incarnations as character actors in less 'polished' movies. It is these aspects which probably 'save' **No Escape** from being another try-hard attempt by Hollywood to create a successful genre flick. It succeeds in its roughness and its outward simpleness in becoming an exciting and intriguing action parable about men placed in terrain which is both familiar and unknown.

MONICA ZETLIN

[1] A print of the film has not been sighted, so cannot say how the title is rendered. The title on the video version is 'ESCAPE FROM ABSOLOM'.
[2] Almost all the character names on the video copy are unreadable. No press book has been sighted.
[3] Blade Runner (Ridley Scott, 1982).

Reference
'The Penal Colony [No Escape]', a production report by Andrew L. Urban, *Cinema Papers*, no. 96, December 1993, pp. 28–30.

POLICE RESCUE

A Southern Star Xanadu Production and[1] the Australian Broadcasting Corporation and the Australian Film Finance Corporation. POLICE RESCUE[2]. © 1993 Australian Film Finance Corporation. Limited[,] Australian Broadcasting Corporation [and] Southern Star Entertainment Pty Limited. Made with the participation of Australian Film Finance Corporation Limited [and] Australian Broadcasting Corporation. *Location:* Sydney. *Filmed:* 30 August–1 October 1993. *Australian distributor:* UIP. *Video:* CIC. *Rating:* M. 35 mm. 93 mins.

Producers: John Edwards, Sandra Levy. *Executive producers:* Errol Sullivan, Penny Chapman. *Associate producer:* Wayne Barry. *Scriptwriter:* Debra Oswald. Based on a story by Debra Oswald, Sandra Levy, John Edwards. *Director of photography:* Russell Bacon. *Production designer:* Murray Picknett. *Costumes:* Wendy Falconer. *Editor:* Christopher Spurr. *Composer:* John Clifford White. *Sound recordist:* Peter Grace. *Sound editors:* Peter Hall (dia.); Fabian Sanjuro (fx). *Mixers:* Peter Purcell, Jonathan Hemming.

Cast

Gary Sweet ('Mickey' McClintock), Zoë Carides (Lorrie Gordon), Steve Bastoni ('Angel' Angelopoulos), John Clayton (Inspector Bill Adams), Tammy McIntosh (Kathy Orland), Jeremy Callaghan (Brian Morley), Belinda Cotterill (Sharyn Elliot), Sonia Todd (Georgia Rattray), Jeremy Sims (Terry), Cate Blanchett (Vivian), Paul Williams (Paul Skelton), Rel Hunt (Hugo), Damien Foley (Alex), Nash Edgerton (Alex's Mate), Steve Cox (Injured Fisherman), Tony Lynch (Body), Alan David Lee (Simmo); Richard Boue, Gillian Statham (Trainees); Keith Webster (Street Kid), Janet Foye (Val), Blazey Best (Kelly), Matt Reeder (Young Guy), Deanne Hardwick (Nerida).

Writing in *Sight and Sound*, on the occasion of the British release of **The Beverly Hillbillies, Maverick** and **The Flintstones**[3], David Marc argued that in each case the television series was superior to the film. What he valued about the films were the places they created: the 'cosmological space' where one could enter another universe or nostalgically revisit somewhere once familiar. What he found them unable to do—something television is so good at—was the plotting of multiple episodes, the long-term character development and the underestimated ability to tell a good story.

The same could be said about **Police Rescue**. The familiar characters—'Mickey' McClintock (Gary Sweet), Georgia Rattray (Sonia Todd) and 'Angel' Angelopoulos (Steve Bastoni)—are still with us. All the things that are normally wrong with the world of disasters and tragedies are still in need of their attention. The film has the usual excellent visual drama of space and distance as the camera spirals up endless stairwells and flies down impossibly-precipitous cliffs. The very impressive stunt work of the rescue team as they scale these impossible surfaces remains as exhilarating as ever. But something's also not quite right.

The narrative follows the popular convention where two stories intersect, collide and resolve each other. There is the adventure, the danger and excitement of the professional's story—the work of the group in public spaces—and there's the romance—the couple in the domain of private space.

In **Police Rescue**, the romantic interest is Lorrie Gordon (Zoë Carides), the newest member of the team. She is the classically-archetypal woman: all mystery and enigma. 'Mickey', of course, eventually falls in love with her, but not before Internal Affairs does some damage.

Lorrie is currently under investigation regarding her former partner (and lover) and his suspicious activities when they worked together in the Drug Squad. 'Mickey' knows this, but Lorrie doesn't, and she doesn't realise that he knows. We know, however, that the rescue team can only be as good as its weakest link. To get the job done, they're meant to trust each other, and their very lives depend on it. But the implications of a dirty cop, the eavesdropping and personal surveillance replace this trust with suspicion and deceit.

Circumstantial evidence eventually leads to Lorrie's suspension, and leaves the Rescue team momentarily pondering these moral dilemmas. All gets resolved, of course, in the final climactic scene where a suicidal father (Jeremy Sims) takes hostage an entire high-rise kindergarten, in a futile attempt to regain the custody of his daughter. In short, everyone has a chance to risk heroically his or her life, trust and mateship, but not really anything else before the conflict finally gets resolved.

The problem is that this is explicated in such a shorthand manner. There are just too many lengthy close-ups of 'Mickey' merely looking quizzical, contemplative or just plain wanton that stand in for what could be more poetically-persuasive cinematic moments. When you think of, for example, the Howard Hawks adventure/romance films like **Only Angels Have Wings** (1939) and **To Have and Have Not** (1944) and how richly and passionately Hawks crafted his *mise en scène* of group dynamics and camaraderie, you start to realise how empty many of these looks and exchanges in **Police Rescue** really are, how cinematically immature the film can appear.

Without the richness of a cumulative narrative that is the real privilege of serial television, without its dialectic of repetition and innovation, **Police Rescue** fails to transcend its origins and the greatness of serial television to become a film in its own right. It remains at best a slightly-longer television episode, lacking all the advantages of the shorter form.

ANNA DZENIS

1 In a brave attempt at grammar, the video slick changes 'and' for 'with'.
2 The video slick and many critics have incorrectly called the film, 'Police Rescue: The Movie'.
3 **The Beverly Hillbillies** (Penelope Sheeris, 1993), **Maverick** (Richard Donner, 1994) and **The Flintstones** (Brian Levant, 1994).

'Mickey' McClintock (Gary Sweet) and Lorrie Gordon (Zoë Carides).

THE ROLY POLY MAN

Rough Nut Productions in association with Kolapore Management. THE ROLY POLY MAN. © Australian Film Finance Corporation[,] New South Wales Film and Television Office [and] Rough Nut Productions Pty Limited. Produced with the assistance and financial participation of the New South Wales Film and Television Office. Made with the participation of Australian Film Finance Corporation. *Filmed:* 16 July–20 August 1993. *Australian distributor:* REP. *Video:* REP. *Rating:* M. Super 16. 91 mins.

Producer: Peter Green. *Line producer:* John Winter. *Executive producer:* Jonathan Shteinman. *Scriptwriter:* Kym Goldsworthy. *Director of photography:* Brian J Breheny. *Production designer:* Robert (Moxy) Moxham. *Costume designer:* Margot Wilson. *Editor:* Neil Thumpston. *Composer:* Dave Skinner. *Sound supervisors:* John Dennison, Tony Vaccher. *Sound recordists:* Guntis Sics; Paul (Salty Dog) Brincat (add.). *Sound editors:* John Patterson (fx); Tony Vaccher, Ross Brewer (dia.). *Mixers:* John Dennison, Tony Vaccher.

Cast

Paul Chubb (Dirk Trent), Les Foxcroft (Mickey), Susan Lyons (Sandra Burnett), Peter Braunstein (Detective McKenzie), Zoe Bertram (Laurel), Frank Whitten (Dr Henderson), Jane Harders (Jane Lewis), John Batchelor (Axel), Rowan Woods (Professor Wauchop), Valerie Bader (Hotel Manager), Sarah Lambert (Vicki Lane), Deborah Kennedy (Chantal), Jim Pike (Tony), Exploding White Mice (Thrash Rock Band), Barbara Stephens (Nun), Kylie Jane Green (School Girl), Bruce Venables (Security Guard), Laura Gabriel (Nurse), Marie Armstrong (Wife), Bill Vince (Husband), Robert Bruning (Garfield), Tony Poli (Gary), Daniel Wylie (Aggro Graffitist), Dorothy Blainey (Intact Graffitist), Jim Burnett (Tad Lewis).

Raymond Chandler must be spinning in his grave over Bill Young's low-budget private-detective comedy The Roly Poly Man, but whether his posthumous tumblings are due to his being upset or laughing too hard is tough to nail.

The Roly Poly Man is too clever not to be a homage to the screen adaptations of Chandler's classic, quick-witted private dick, Philip Marlowe. Yet its plot is far too outlandish and tangled for it not to be a satire of the film noir genre Chandler inspired. In particular, it seems to take great delight in extracting a sizeable consignment of mickey out of the unintelligible muddle that was

Howard Hawks' The Big Sleep (1946), which Chandler wrote but didn't understand.

The Roly Poly Man does have one major, and possibly inadvertent, advantage over that benchmark of film noir cinema—it actually makes sense. As wild as the plot gets, it all does tie together at the end, a result which may not only have been unintentional, but, given the energy of the narrative, irrelevant.

As Robert Altman illustrated with his shot at Chandler's Marlowe in The Long Goodbye (1973), the journey's the thing, not the arrival. Similarly, The Roly Poly Man takes its pleasures in testing out the stereotypical elements of the genre and playing with them while skating its way to a thunderously over-the-top ending.

The plot of The Roly Poly Man is so tangled people should get an award for understanding it on the first viewing. Indeed, to attempt to recite it here in any sort of detail would take until the next print run.

In a nutshell, it involves a slovenly private detective Dirk Trent (Paul Chubb) investigating a series of killings which involve people's heads exploding because leeches are feeding off tumours. He senses a conspiracy by Doctor Henderson (Frank Whitten) and with the help of his ageing, sprightly sidekick, Mickey (Les Foxcroft), and a morgue attendant, Sandra Burnett (Susan Lyons), goes 'a-sniffin' through seedy motels, various murders and the inevitable femme fatale.

As the lead, Chubb proves again what a neglected film comedy talent he is. He is fab-

ulous as the Philip Marlowe mutation, looking like 120 kilograms of sub-standard beef pressed into a 100 kilogram polyester bag, and sounding like a football fan on uppers, cracking wordplays, witticisms, similes and observations at every opportunity. His physical acting and pratfalls are straight out of the Jerry Lewis school.

The high levels of low-quality gore in the film, and its dabbling in science fiction (borrowing the look of the Mother Alien in Aliens (James Cameron, 1986) for its pig-blood-splattered finale) is a wonderfully-extreme and funny contrast to the dreary domestic pressures of Trent's private life, which are introduced through clever manipulation of the noir formula.

The Roly Poly Man comically reinterprets a classy genre with a resolute lack of class, both in its performances and its C-grade production values. It is so irresistible and entertaining that it is easy to forgive the film's budget-enforced grainy look and its total lack of visual flair. Still, when you are simultaneously tongue kissing a genre while kneeing it in the balls, such niceties take second place to getting good, cheap laughs en masse. It's not only a fair trade-off, but, given the bulk of golden, genre-busting gags on offer in The Roly Poly Man, quite a bargain.

JIM SCHEMBRI

Reference
'The Roly Poly Man', a review by Peter Malone, *Cinema Papers*, no. 101, October, 1994, p. 69.

Dirk Trent (Paul Chubb) and Sandra Burnett (Susan Lyons).

SIRENS

Giddy (Portia de Rossi), Sheela (Elle Macpherson), Pru (Kate Fischer) and Estella Campion (Tara Fitzgerald).

WMG with the participation of British Screen presents Sirens. © 1994 Australian Film Finance Corporation Pty. Limited, WMG Film GmbH, British Screen Finance Limited, Samson Productions Pty. Limited and Sarah Radclyffe Productions–Sirens Limited. Produced with the assistance of The New South Wales Film & Television Office. Made with the participation of Australian Film Finance Corporation Pty Limited. An Australia–United Kingdom co-production. *Locations:* Faulconbridge, Blue Mountains, Sofala (New South Wales). *Filmed:* April–May 1993. *Australian distributor:* Roadshow. *Video:* Touchstone. *Rating:* M. 35mm. 90 mins.

Producer: Sue Milliken. *Co-producer:* Sarah Radclyffe. *Executive producers:* Justin Ackerman, Hans Brockman, Robert Jones. *Scriptwriter:* John Duigan. *Director of photography:* Geoff Burton. *Camera operator:* Julian Penney. *Production designer:* Roger Ford. *Costume designer:* Terry Ryan. *Editor:* Humphrey Dixon. *Composer:* Rachel Portman. *Sound recordist:* David Lee. *Sound editors:* Alan Bell, Susan Midgley. *Mixers:* Dean Humphreys, Tim Cavagin.

Cast

Hugh Grant (Anthony Campion), Tara Fitzgerald (Estella Campion), Sam Neill (Norman Lindsay), Elle Macpherson (Sheela), Portia de Rossi (Giddy), Kate Fischer (Pru), Pamela Rabe (Rose Lindsay), Ben Mendelsohn (Lewis), John Polson (Tom), Mark Gerber (Devlin), Julia Stone (Jane), Ellis MacCarthy (Honey), Vincent Ball (Bishop of Sydney), John Duigan (Earnest Minister), Lexy Murphy (British Bulldog Girl), Scott Lowe (Station Master), Bryan Davis (Barman), Lynne Emanuel (Barmaid), Kitty Silver (Pub Woman 1), Carolyn Devlin (Pub Woman 2), Peter Campbell (Articulate Drunk).

It seems that when some film-makers reach a certain age they become very nostalgic for the great moments of 'sexual liberation' dotted throughout this century. Although this phenomenon is doubtless prompted by misty personal memories of the swinging 1960s. it is rarely this era which is directly represented. Rather, the '60s are displaced, projected backwards onto other mythical times and places. Thus, Philip Kaufman takes us back to the cavortings of Henry Miller and Anaïs Nin in **Henry & June** (1990), and Ken Russell takes it upon himself to film the collected works of D. H. Lawrence. John Duigan looks for a nationalist rôle model and finds it in the artist Norman Lindsay, whose 'radical' communal life in the country provides the inspiration for **Sirens**.

Duigan's previous project, an adaptation of Jean Rhys' *Wide Sargasso Sea*, relentlessly juxtaposed stiff, aristocratic, rationalist masculinity with magical, primitive, nature-loving femininity. Although **Sirens** is uncontestably a better-directed, more-coherent film than **Wide Sargasso Sea** (1993), it offers an almost identical, and equally static, bundle of themes and binary oppositions.

A repressed British couple, Anthony and Estella Campion (played with some charm by Hugh Grant and Tara Fitzgerald), become inexorably intoxicated by the sultry air surrounding Lindsay (Sam Neill) and his bevy of naked models (played by Elle Macpherson, Kate Fischer and Portia De Rossi.) Anthony is a priest—albeit a 'progressive' one, with a taste for modern art and contemporary philosophy—and so he engages Lindsay in debates that ponderously dramatise the concerns of the film. A token emblem of class conflict is added to the discussion via the proletarian interpolations of Pru (Fischer) .

Sirens is a film devoted to mellow, 'midway' compromises between all these extreme-positions, rather than melodramatic confrontation. It is, ultimately an extraordinarily-tame piece in which nothing much really happens. This is especially so on the sexual plane. Everything is fantasy, titillation, languorous craving—at least for the women characters, since (as Norman assures us) they are 'the embodiment of sexuality'. What makes the film such a 'retro' fantasy is that, even as it pretends to be a bold parable of female liberation, it tends to provide a very male-directed, blandly-voyeuristic view of women. And the liberation it offers is ambiguous, strictly conditioned: even Fitzgerald's single act of infidelity, it is suggested, may have been only a dream—a fantasy which serves merely to 'healthily' reintegrate her back into marriage with her still pretty stuffy husband at the end.

Duigan has defended the rather unsophisticated sexual politics of **Sirens** by claiming that he was trying to make a film true to Lindsay and the radical standards of the time, not those of our time. Hence the emphasis on female nudity, and the whole equation of women with landscape and nature, graphically illustrated by the final helicopter shot of all the story's female characters posing naked atop a rocky mountain.

Yet, on may levels, **Sirens** indeed betrays the workings of a 'sensitive new age guy's' unconscious imagination in the nervous 1990s. This is particularly evident in the film's representation of men and their sexuality. Mostly, the male characters (especially Lindsay) remain fully clothed and detached from the enactment of erotic scenarios. The one man who is elevated to the status of animalistic 'sex object' for the women, Devlin (Mark Gerber), is, very tellingly, blind—symbolically castrated, without true desire or a hungry 'male gaze'. It is as if Duigan wishes to ensure that there are no rapacious male lovers like Baines (Harvey Keitel) in **The Piano** (Jane Campion, 1993) around to mess up the film's schematic lesson of liberation.

ADRIAN MARTIN

Reference
'Sirens', a review by Lara Dunston, *Filmnews*, May 1994, p. 12.

SPIDER & ROSE

Australian Film Finance Corporation Limited presents a Dendy Films production. Spider & Rose[1]. © 1994 Australian Film Finance Corporation Limited and Dendy Films Pty Limited. Script developed with the assistance of the Australian Film Commission. [Made with the participation of Australian Film Finance Corporation Pty Limited as part of the 1993 FFC Film Fund.] *Location:* New South Wales. *Filmed:* 23 October–14 December 1993. *Australian distributor:* Dendy. *Video:* not released as of 1 May 1995. *Rating:* M. 35mm. 90 mins.

Producers: Lyn McCarthy, Graeme Tubbenhauer. *Line producer:* Julia Overton. *Scriptwriter:* Bill Bennett. *Director of photography:* Andrew Lesnie. *Production designer:* Ross Major. *Costume designer:* Ross Major. *Editor:* Henry Dangar. *Composer:* The Cruel Sea[2]. *Sound designers:* Syd Butterworth, Andrew Plain. *Sound recordist:* Syd Butterworth. *Sound editors:* Andrew Plain (sup.); Peter Townend (fx); Antony Gray (dia.). *Mixers:* Phil Heywood; Martin Oswin (asst.).

Cast

Ruth Cracknell (Rose), Simon Bossell (Spider), Max Cullen (Jack)[3]; Harry Tritton (Paddy), Heidi Lapaine (Nurse Maguire), Tina Bursill (Sister Abbott), Emily Dawe (Ambulance Officer), Marshall Napier (Henderson), Beth Champion (Nurse Price), Brian Vriends (Spider's Mate), Helen O'Connor (Distressed Mother), David Cockburn (Dying Boy), Bruce Venables (Semi-trailer Driver), Bruce Stratford (Hospital Sister), Lewis Fitz-Gerald (Robert), Jennifer Cluff (Helen), Nellie Bennett (Sarah), Henry Bennett (Miles); The Music Makers–Vivian Goulding, John Haberecht, William Kosseris, Barry Stutsel (Band); Bob Baines (Ambo Officer Muggle-ston).

In **Spider & Rose**, Bill Bennett seems to have hit upon the one important maxim he overlooked with **Backlash** (1986): just because roads are long, rambling and endless doesn't necessarily mean road movies have to be as well.

Indeed, while **Backlash** is a boring, incoherent, indulgent dirge about two cops and an Aboriginal murderer driving across the outback in search of a purpose, **Spider & Rose** is almost apologetically organised.

To accuse **Spider & Rose** of being predictable is like accusing a rocket launch of being loud. Character arcs are obvious from the word go, when the ageing Rose (Ruth Cracknell) is wheeled out of hospital and takes an instant dislike to Spider (Simon Bossell), the ambulance driver with whom

Spider (Simon Bossell) and Rose (Ruth Cracknell).

she is to spend the next six hours on her way home to her son's farm.

Of course, their initial friction will cause laughs before giving way to a close bonding. Of course, he will see in her values he doesn't have in his life, and vice versa. Of course, he'll help her out of her jam when son Robert (Lewis Fitz-Gerald) wants to slap her into a nursing home. And, of course, the road will be so busy serving as a symbolic and metaphoric organising principle for the drama of the journey that it will barely have time to fulfil its birthright as a surface for cars and trucks to drive on.

At first, Rose is a victim of the road, losing her husband in a horrific accident, the aftermath of which serves as a powerful opening to the film. She then becomes a prisoner of it, stuck in the ambulance with Spider. She subsequently asserts her independence by absconding with beekeeper Jack (Max Cullen), and later commandeering the driver's seat in the ambulance.

After an accident, Spider is injured and Rose becomes the full-time driver, now dominating the road, even stealing a tractor that all but prevents others from using the road. After being patronised by Robert, so accurately referred to by Jack as 'a shit', she takes to the open road on her own, with as much control over it as she now has over her life.

As cute and as neat as all this codification is, Bennett never allows any of it to appear contrived, or to be anything more than the type of subtext only overzealous film academics plump for in the small hours of the night.

The film is primarily about joy, and that is beautifully brought out through the chemistry between Bossell and Cracknell as they

play out the ironic central tension of a young man who has lived too much and of an old woman who has not lived enough.

At 22, Spider feels empty, having seen too much in his job, and suffering a trauma involving the death of a child, for which he blames himself. Rose, at 70, feels cheated by the death of her husband, and angrily protests any indignity that traditionally goes with old age, such as being made to ride in the back of an ambulance, or being moved into a nursing home by an ungrateful son.

Bossell makes a great foil, but **Spider & Rose** is Cracknell's film. Her feistiness and fondness for vibrators makes her the most attractive septuagenarian since Frances Sternhagen put her hand in Richard Farnsworth's lap in Rob Reiner's **Misery** (1990). In fact, when we see Rose finally using her vibrator, it gets a laugh because she is using it to massage her FEET.

When Spider quips to Rose, 'You're my kind of girl', he's not just speaking for himself.

JIM SCHEMBRI

---

[1] Some press and advertising materials mistakenly opt for 'and' instead of the correct ampersand.
[2] The end credits have 'original music composed by: James Cruickshank, Jim Elliott, Ken Carmody, Dan Rumour'.
[3] The first three credits follow the opening credits; the rest are per order of appearance.

References

'Bill Bennett's **Spider & Rose**', a report by John Conomos and Raffaele Caputo, *Cinema Papers*, no. 100, August 1994, pp. 40–4.
'**Spider & Rose**', a review by Lani Hannah, *Cinema Papers*, no. 102, December, 1994, pp. 71–2.

THE SUM OF US

Southern Star in association with the Australian Film Finance Corporation presents a Hal McElroy Southern Star production. THE SUM OF US. © 1994 The Australian Film Finance Corporation Limited [and] Southern Star Entertainment Pty Limited. Developed in association with The Great Sum Film Limited Partnership. *Budget:* $4 million. *Location:* Sydney. *Australian distributor:* UIP. *Video:* CIC. *Rating:* M. 35mm. 92 mins.

Producer: Hal McElroy. *Executive producers:* Errol Sullivan, Hal McElroy. *Co-executive producers:* Hal (Corky) Kessler, Donald Scatena, Kevin Dowling. *Line producer:* Rod Allan. *Scriptwriter:* David Stevens. Based on his play. *Director of photography:* Geoff Burton. *Camera operator:* Kathryn Milliss. *Production designer:* Graham (Grace) Walker. *Costume supervisor:* Louise Spargo. *Editor:* Frans Vandenburg. *Composer:* Dave Faulkner. *Sound recordist:* Leo Sullivan. *Sound editors:* John Patterson, Helen Brown (fx); John Dennison, Ross Brewer, Craig Butters (foley); Tony Vaccher, Ross Brewer (dia.). *Mixers:* John Dennison, Tony Vaccher.

Cast

Jack Thompson (Harry Mitchell), Russell Crowe (Jeff Mitchell), John Polson (Greg), Deborah Kennedy (Joyce Johnson), Joss Moroney (Young Jeff), Mitch Mathews (Gran), Julie Herbert (Mary), Des James (Football Coach), Mick Campbell (Footballer), Donny Muntz (Ferry Captain), Jan Adele (Barmaid), Rebekah Elmaloglou (Jenny), Lola Nixon (Desiree), Sally Cahill (Greg's Mother), Bob Raines (Greg's Father), Paul Feeman (George), Walter Kennard (Barman); Stuart Campbell, Graham Drake (Leather Men); Elaine Lee (Woman on Train), Ross Anderson (Gardener), Michael Burgess (Foreman), John Rhall (Dad's Brother), Helen Williams (Brother's Wife), Jan Merriman (Nurse).

The Sum of Us is a deeply-felt, daring and very funny film, which disarms homophobia by championing tolerance and humanistic values in the name of 'ocker' Australia. Adapted by David Stevens from his play of the same name, it focuses on the unconditional love of Harry Mitchell (Jack Thompson), a Sydney ferry captain, for his gay son, Jeff (Russell Crowe.)

From the outset, Stevens' sensitive, often bawdy screenplay turns stereotypes upside down. Harry is a lonely widower, an Australian ocker who just as readily dons an apron and housekeeps for his son as he downs a beer at the local pub. For his part, Jeff is a rugby-playing plumber whose bud-ding relationship with a spunky gardener, Greg (John Polson), is frustrated as much by Harry's well-meaning desire to play cupid as by Jeff's fear of rejection and need for old-fashioned intimacy and domesticity.

However, the lives of both father and son are changed permanently when Harry takes to computer dating, and romance in the form of Joyce Johnson (Deborah Kennedy) enters his life.

Intended as a tribute to the tolerance of ordinary Australia, **The Sum of Us** was originally set in Melbourne's western suburbs before Stevens took the play to the US, where it became a hit on Broadway. The film, however, relocates the play to Sydney, a move which further consolidates the Sydney-fication of Australia by merging the emblems of 'ockerdom'—beer drinking, football, weatherboard cottages, Hill's hoists, and shorts—with the iconography of the nation's 'capital'—the Harbour Bridge, Opera House, league clubs, gay mardi gras and ferries.

The blending works. Coupled with the Ken Done colours and saturated brightness of Geoff Burton's cinematography, it feels right to see these powerful Sydney icons as backdrops to Jack Thompson's flamboyant, outstanding performance as Harry, an ordinary bloke who happens to have a gay son.

The film's conceit is to pretend that Harry is an archetypal ocker, when quite clearly he is not. Harry is an exceptional man who not only tolerates his son's homosexuality, but cherishes him all the more because of it. By affirming the sustenance that can be derived from the familial and domestic—an affirmation which can transcend gender and sexual inclination—the film both cuts new ground and espouses traditional values.

Particularly moving are the grainy flashbacks to Harry's mother and her long-time companion, which remind audiences that everyone has the right to the comfort and solace that comes from loving another human being.

Incomprehensively, Thompson's luminous portrait of Harry failed to garner him a 1994 AFI Best Actor nomination. Instead, he was awarded the Raymond Longford Award for his contribution to Australian film-making over 25 years.

JAN EPSTEIN

References
'Geoff Burton: Cinematographer', an interview with the co-director by Leilani Hannah and Raffaele Caputo, *Cinema Papers*, no. 99, June 1994, pp. 43–6, 51.
'The Sum of Us', co-director Geoff Burton interviewed by Leilani Hannah and Raffaele Caputo, *Cinema Papers*, no. 100, August 1994, pp. 30–4, 82–3.
'The Sum of Us', a review by Alissa Tanskaya, ibid., pp. 72–3.
'Sydney Film Festival', a report by Raymond Younis, *Cinema Papers*, no. 101, October 1994, pp. 74–6.
'Melbourne Film Festival', a report by John Foam, ibid., pp. 76–8.

Family and mates: Harry (Jack Thompson) and Jeff Mitchell (Russell Crowe).

PAULINE CHAN

TRAPS

An Ayer Production. Traps. © 1993 Australian Film Finance Corporation Pty Limited and Ayer Productions Limited. Project developed with the assistance of Australian Film Commission. Produced with the assistance of Pacific Link Communication Japan. Produced with the financial assistance of the Queensland Government, PFTC and Film Queensland. Made with the participation of Australian Film Finance Corporation Limited. *Budget:* $3.5 million. *Locations:* Dau Tieng, Tay Ninh, Binh Ba, Vung Tau (Vietnam); Bingil Bay, Paronella Park, Innisfail (Queensland). *Australian distributor:* Ronin. *Video:* Ronin. *Rating:* M. 35mm. 100 mins.

Producer: Jim McElroy. *Line producer:* Tim Sanders. *Scriptwriters:* Robert Carter, Pauline Chan. Based on characters from the novel, *Dreamhouse,* by Kate Grenville. *Director of photography:* Kevin Hayward. *Production designer:* Michael Philips. *Costume designer:* David Rowe. *Editor:* Nicholas Beauman. *Composer:* Douglas Stephen Rae. *Sound recordist:* John Schiefelbein. *Sound editors:* Tim Jordan (dia.); Wayne Pashley, Peter Townend (fx). *Mixer:* Phil Judd.

Cast

Saskia Reeves (Louise Duffield), Robert Reynolds (Michael Duffield), Sami Frey (Daniel Renouard), Jacqueline McKenzie (Viola Renouard), Kiet Lam (Tuan), Hoa To (Tatie Chi); Nguyen Minh Tri (Thief), Thierry Marquet (Captain Brochard), Tran Duy An (Bao), Ho Thu Nga (Kim), Vu T. Le Thi (Bao's Mother), Nguyen Ngoc Dang (Bao's Grandfather), Jean Louis Beaulieu (French Officer), Claude Holweger (French Soldier), Tat Binh (Vietminh Captain), Trieu Xuan Sam (Vietminh in Hut), Ly Thai Dung (Vietminh Executioner).

Traps is the first English-speaking film to be shot in Vietnam since the opening of the country to contemporary western influence in the 1980s. Considering Australia's involvement in the Vietnam War, an Australian feature film about Vietnam is overdue. Yet Traps is disappointing, despite its handsome appearance, some fine performances and sympathetic direction by Pauline Chan, who was born and raised in Vietnam.

The film is set in Indochina in the 1950s, and, while it sheds interesting light on the struggle of the Vietminh (a coalition of nationalist and communist groups) to win the hearts of the Vietnamese people in the war against the French, it is primarily a vehicle to explore the struggle of a young English woman, Louise Duffield (Saskia Reeves), to liberate herself from the control of her husband, Michael (Robert Reynolds), an Australian journalist.

Traps is based on characters in Kate Grenville's *Dreamhouse*, a novel about a *ménage à quatre* set in Tuscany. The decision to transpose the setting is a congenial shift, and suits the film's theme of four people trapped by temperament and circumstance in Indochina before the fall of Dien Bien Phu.

Chan shows great flair for understanding women, and her female sensibility stands her in good stead for several powerful scenes between Louise and Viola Renouard (Jacqueline McKenzie), the daughter of a French plantation manager, when the pair are captured by communists. However, the film is let down in places by the script, in particular the characterisations of Michael and Daniel Renouard (Sami Frey) are two-dimensional.

Saskia Reeves delivers a finely-nuanced portrait of a woman forced in an extreme situation to fight for the right to see the world through her own eyes, both as a photographer and as the wife of a rigid 1950s man. Jacqueline McKenzie, as the difficult, resentful daughter chafing under her father's authority, is utterly convincing. Sami Frey, as the plantation manager and the villain of the piece, does a slick and professional job, but he is essentially a stereotype. The thoroughly unsympathetic portrait of Michael is diminished by lack of depth.

Although the last quarter of the film fails to maintain psychological tension and devolves into conventionality, the female line is consistently well-handled, and the lush photography and authentic settings make Traps worth seeing.

JAN EPSTEIN

References
'Traps', producer Jim McElroy and co-writer–director Pauline Chan interviewed by Sue Adler, *Cinema Papers*, no. 99, June 1994, pp. 4–8, 10.
'Traps', co-scriptwriter Robert Carter interviewed by Sue Adler, ibid., pp. 10–11.
'Traps', a review by Scott Murray, *Cinema Papers*, no. 101, October 1994, pp. 69–70.

Viola Renouard (Jacqueline McKenzie), Tuan (Kiet Lam) and Louise Duffield (Saskia Reeves).

Louise Duffield in a Vietnamese rubber plantation.

APPENDIX A
THE ANIMATED FEATURES OF YORAM GROSS

Dot and the Kangaroo (1977) was the first animated feature made by Yoram Gross since arriving in Australia in 1968. Like all his subsequent films (bar **The Magic Riddle** in 1991), **Dot and the Kangaroo** is a stylistic juxtaposition between live and animated action. For its time, this combination was essentially a process of experimentation in economic, technical and artistic fashions.

For example, the production of **Dot and the Kangaroo** did not enjoy the integrated services of a fully equipped studio in the manner which the Gross output has enjoyed since.[1] The execution of the cell drawings, as noted in *Australian Film 1900–1977: A Guide to Feature Film Production*, were 'sublet to various artists in Sydney, working separately in their own studios, rather than in a group "factory".[2] Given the already labour intensive aspect of animation, this required an unusual amount of production co-ordination. The use of live-action footage for a feature-length film certainly meant a reduction in time and labour expenses required for a fully animated film. But, unlike a fully animated film, this process also required a finely tuned consideration of photographing against a projected background (as opposed to one that is drawn), and of synchronising two distinct illusions of movement—one is recorded, the other is created.

If production logistics were not enough of a challenge, producers Yoram and Sandra Gross also sought to enter a somewhat closed market unaccustomed to the style of combining animated and live-action. By this time, the children's market for animated film was securely dominated by such well-established production houses as Disney and Hanna-Barbera. Disney, in particular, had long ago set the paradigm for children's entertainment with its fully animated, feature-length representations of classic fairytales or popular legends such as **Snow White and the Seven Dwarfs** (supervising director: David Hand, 1940), **Cinderella** (Wilfred Jackson, Hamilton Luske, Clyde Geronomi, 1950) and **Robin Hood** (Wolfgang Reitherman, 1973).[3] Disney's style of animation is determined by fantasy, and thus, in this sense, the 'reality' for and of children's entertainment is a world completely created, completely fantastical.

Animated works of the mixed media variety were certainly not the norm. Such films were and still are short-length, infrequent, specialist productions of political allegory and social satire.

Some of the animated works of Polish film-maker Walerian Borowczyk[4] are notable for this reason, and it is believed the early work of Dave and Max Fleischer also toyed with mixed media animation of a sort. Their work is frequently satirical and their development of the 'rotoscope' (an invention for tracing live-action into animation footage) is a variant on the actual combination of the two media. In a less-popular sense, the work could be seen as theoretical in approach, exploring abstract and conceptual ideas of colour, rhythm and figuration. New Zealand-born Len Lye, who pioneered the technique of painting images directly on to film in the 1930s, completed two works which combined live and animated action in this regard, **Rainbow Dance** (1936) and **Trade Tattoo** (1937). And generally the work is made by independent animators, student film-makers or artists dabbling with the craft, where they perform much of the work themselves, and the prospect of a commercial return is small if not altogether non-existent. The team of Jimmy Murakami and Fred Wolf from the mid-1960s, for instance, could only maintain a steady output of animated works by making commercials for television. The specialist attitude is further compounded by the occasional screenings of short animated films at film societies or festivals. (The latter is not an unfamiliar case for Yoram Gross prior to **Dot and the Kangaroo**, whose short films *The Politicians* and *To Nefertiti* were awarded prizes at the Sydney Film Festival in 1970 and 1971 respectively.)

Perhaps **Who Framed Roger Rabbit** (Robert Zemeckis, 1988) is the only film which catapulted the technique of combining live and animated action to landmark commercial proportions. But one could argue that Yoram Gross 'pioneered' the commercial viability of the technique despite the odds set against it. **Dot and the Kangaroo** went on to win a major prize at the Tehran Film Festival[5] and its successful release spawned a series of Dot films throughout the 1980s. By creating a niche in an exclusive market through the cost effectiveness of his technique, the operations of Yoram Gross have expanded in Australia as well as overseas, successfully marketing his product under the banner of 'family entertainment', enhanced by merchandising packages. Recently, **Blinky Bill** (1992) gained a considerable market boost with spin-off products like 'Blinky Bill' toys and souvenirs, and a promotional tie-in with the Australian branch of the family restaurant chain Pizza Hut.[6]

Ever since **Dot and the Kangaroo**, the name Yoram Gross has become synonymous with children's films. But what tends to be overlooked in this 'rags-to-riches' story is that much of the success is due to the specialist, experimental impulse of his films. For the film which followed **Dot and the Kangaroo**, **The Little Convict** (1979), a specially prepared kit to accompany the film is symptomatic of the educational value Gross places on his product. The printed kit details the basic principles of animation and was especially designed for easy comprehension by children. The kit includes a demonstration of a thaumatrope, a small disc with a drawing on either side and two pieces of string attached to the edges of the disc. When the disc is twirled by the strings, the eye perceives the two drawings as one. If nothing else, this simple explanation of the thaumatrope is indicative of the direct lineage the majority of Gross' work has to a history of scientific studies on early animation[7], extending further to experimental film practices of the 1920s.

This impulse has broadened the number of directions and concerns of films made for children. Offering product which is both entertaining and of educational value is one of the hallmarks of combining live and animated action. Gross' films therefore encapsulate the style of the documentary. In comparison, the Disney style is certainly naturalistic but can hardly lean toward the documentary. The live-action and animated combination of a Gross film has the desired purpose of weaving fictional-mythical elements with real elements in the subject of a lesson.

The Little Convict is essentially a history lesson on Australian settlement around which a story is built. The narrator, Rolf Harris in the guise of an itinerant artist, introduces the audience to real etchings and legends of early Australia. These real elements then magically dissolve into an animated equivalent which tells the story of Toby Nelson and his sister Polly, arriving in Australia as convicts who are put to work on a Government farm under the charge of sadistic troopers, Sergeant Bully Langden and Corporal Weazel Wesley. At intervals throughout the adventures of Toby and others, Rolf Harris suspends the story and offers a commentary on life in the penal colony as well as inviting the audience to sing along with a selection of Australian ballads.

In another example, **The Camel Boy** (1984), the story is based on the actual journeys into the

Australian desert by explorers at the beginning of the century. The film tells the story of a young Australian boy who, along with his father, captures camels for export to Arabia. The young boy befriends an old camel by the name of Binta, and circumstances take them on a journey to the exotic Arabian country of Bhustan. The fictional journey also involves a documentary journey which tells of how the camel came to feature in the Australian outback. Other films, the Dot series in particular, are similarly a mixture of fairytale fantasies and wondrous live-action footage into subjects about sea life (**Dot and the Whale**, 1986), the microscopic world of insects (**Dot and Keeto**, 1986) or a lesson on the conservation of the Australian bush or wildlife (**Dot and the Bunny**, 1984, and **Dot and the Koala**, 1986).

On a broadly thematic level, three elements tend to consistently emerge throughout the films of Yoram Gross. The first is the specifically Australian content of the stories, whether the subject is history, geography, legendary tales or the animal kingdom. The second is the consciously social and political overtones of the commentaries, which are often calls for respect and conservation of our eco-systems. And the third element is how each story revolves around displaced figures, i.e., characters that are forced from their homeland, or animals whose natural habitat is under threat. **Dot and the Smugglers** (1987) concerns shifty circus owners who use their travelling show as a front for a lucrative smuggling operation of rare wildlife species. In **Epic** (1985), the legend of Romulus and Remus is reinterpreted when a baby boy and his twin sister are orphaned through natural disaster, but are then rescued and reared by dingoes.

These thematic concerns are served well by the live and animated mix. More significantly, however, what intrigues by the combination of all these elements, especially in holding a little corner of the children's market, is the opportunity it offers in exploring and understanding cultural difference. The films are specifically Australian in content but also express a universal need in accommodating difference. The live Dot, for example, is a figure whose animated self is forever physically changing in order to understand the values and habits of the live environments in which her adventures are set. This is no better realised than in the sequel to **Dot and the Kangaroo, Around the World With Dot** (aka **Dot and Santa Claus**, 1982). This film features the mother kangaroo of the previous film and recaps the story of her lost joey. The film also introduces a Christmas theme in the form of a swagman who magically turns into Santa Claus. The pair embark on his sleigh to search the world for the lost joey. Their journey becomes a guided tour of people, places and customs, experiencing along the way the various Christmas traditions across the globe.

On a formal level, Gross' technique has a definite and complex affinity with film practices of the 1920s, when experimentation with the medium was rife among painters and musicians. A good deal of Gross' work tends to take up the practices of 'direct film' (not to be confused with the 'direct cinema' movement of the 1960s).

Sarah (1983), for instance, a story about the disruptive effects of war on family and environment, utilises World War II documentary footage and this seems etched with figures approximating soldiers going into battle. The example reminds one of the graphic cinema of Len Lye, who coined the term 'direct film', and was one of the first to experiment with the technique of directly applying paint, drawing or etching on the film stock. The significant aspect of this technique as practised by Lye is that it bypassed the photographic process. For Gross, however, the photographic process is certainly not one to reject.

In this respect, if one takes a film like **Epic**, Gross has closer affinities with the works of Fernand Léger and Hans Richter. The graphic figures and shapes or surroundings of **Epic** sometimes take on abstract dimensions of the calibre that take the film frame as a prime condition for creating effects—moving horizontally, vertically and in depth, while synchronising the movements to musical rhythms.

In **Dot and the Whale**, there are points in the film where the combination of live and animated material is composed within the frame as though it were a collage or Cubist painting. The contours and planes are so demarcated that the shapes cut away their representational anchor and tend to battle for the space of the frame. In debt to the film practices of the 1920s, experimental artist Stan VanDerBeek, in some of his films of the 1950s, incorporated collages with exposed film in similar vein and effect to that of **Dot and the Whale**. And like the earlier work of Lye, VanDerBeek also applied paint directly onto film. The technique is a form of animation directly applied to the celluloid strip. It is a technique VanDerBeek called 'time painting'.[8] But in a Gross film the frame as a whole has a sense of completeness in which the materials are in a dynamic, conflicting relationship with one another—a relationship that goes half-way into abstraction.

Most of all, however, from **Dot and the Kangaroo** right up to **Blinky Bill**, the live-action figure and/or background frequently and magically turns itself into its animated equivalent (and back again), which, as one of the major objectives of experimental cinema, signals the process itself, and confers the multitude of formal and plastic possibilities that are opened out. Only recently did Yoram Gross produce a fully animated film, **The Magic Riddle**. But the film still retains much of the earlier works' preoccupations. At the centre of the story, for example, is a young orphan girl, Cindy, who actually takes a self-reflexive journey into the world of the animated fairytale. The film is, after all, an amalgam of many favourite fairytale characters, from Cinderella to Pinocchio, Snow White to Little Red Riding Hood.

In an earlier version of this essay[9], it was suggested that a Gross feature may look quaint in comparison to the sophistication of something like **Who Framed Roger Rabbit**. But this is merely a preliminary knee-jerk reaction. The almost perfect, seamless integration of live and animated action in **Who Framed Roger Rabbit** could not allow for the worthwhile excursions into a number of artistic and cinematic forms of experimentation of a Gross feature. Gross compensates for the lack of sophistication by the distinctiveness with which each feature goes about combining the realities of live-action and animation. In this sense, Yoram Gross has blurred the conceptual distinctions between regular, mainstream animation and its experimental forms.

RAFFAELE CAPUTO

1 Today, the Yoram Gross Film Studios is a 1,400 square metre site located in the Sydney suburb of Camperdown. The studio employs more than 70 artists and technicians with full studio facilities, including three animation cameras, line-testing facilities, editing suites, a theatrette and recording studio.

2 Andrew Pike and Ross Cooper, *Australian Film: 1900–1977: A Guide to Feature Film Production*, Oxford University Press, in association with The Australian Film Institute, Melbourne, 1980. p. 404.

3 The only early challenge to Disney in feature animation came from Max and Dave Fleischer with **Gulliver's Travels** in 1939, which was a moderate success at the box office. But their follow-up film, **Mr Bug Goes to Town** (1941), died miserably and led to the take-over of their studio by Paramount. With the war in Europe, Disney had a near monopoly of the market and, although **Fantasia** (production supervisor: Ben Sharpstein, 1940) was a commercial flop, from the mid-1940s the Disney studio turned out animated features without interruption for well over a decade. United Pictures Association's **1001 Arabian Nights** (Jack Kinney, 1959) was the only challenge by an American studio since the Fleischers'. See Maurice Horn (ed.), *The World Encyclopedia of Cartoons*, Chelsea House, New York, 1980.

4 As is well known, Walerian Borowczyk was an animator from the late 1950s until the late 1960s when he finally turned to live-action feature films. **Goto, l'ile d'amour** (1968), **Blanche** (1970) and others are highly regarded films, but Borowczyk is also considered one of the most innovative animators of the post-war period. **Dom** (1958) and **Les Astronautes** (1959) are two of his works which combine animated and photographed images. The latter film was made in collaboration with Chris Marker. See Nicholas Thomas (ed.), *International Dictionary of Films and Filmmakers 2: Directors*, St James Press, London, 1991, pp. 84–86.

5 Pike and Cooper, p. 404.

6 *Variety*, February 25, 1991, pp. 53, 59.

7 The thaumatrope demonstration does honour to the heady days of 19th-century optical experiments to do with the illusion of continuous movement. Joseph Plateau and George Cruikshank are two (among many other) inventor-scientist-artist types who devised the 'phenakisti- scope' and 'zoetrope'. These devices employed the basic techniques of animation that have been practised ever since the first recorded public exhibition of animated drawings by Emile Reynaud's Théâtre Optique in 1892 (three years prior to Lumière's famous public exhibition of the cinématographe). The devices by Plateau and Cruikshank anticipate the Théâtre Optique by about seven decades. See Alexander Sesonske, 'The Origins of Animation', *Sight and Sound*, vol. 49, no.3, Summer 1980, and David Robinson, 'Animation: The First Chapter, 1833–1893', *Sight and Sound*, vol. 59, no.4, Autumn 1990.

8 See Parker Tyler, *Underground Film: A Critical History*, Penguin, London, 1974.

9 This is a revised and expanded version of an article which appeared in *Cinema Papers*, no. 86, January 1992, pp. 36–42.

RECENT SUPER 8 THEATRICAL FEATURES

LADYKILLER
BILL MOUSOULIS

[No opening production credit; atb Innersense Productions.] Ladykiller. © 1994 Innersense Productions. *Budget:* $2000. *Location:* Melbourne. *Filmed:* 7–25 March 1994. *Australian distributor:* Innersense Productions. *Video:* not released as of 1 May 1994. *Rating:* not rated. Super 8. 80 mins.

Producer: Bill Mousoulis. *Scriptwriter:* Bill Mousoulis. *Director of photography:* Laki Sideris. *Editor:* Bill Mousoulis. *Composer:* Mike Bellasmitchell. *Sound:* Tim Joy, John Humphries.

Cast

Rhys Muldoon (Chris), Catherine Hill (Susan), Angela Twigg (Helen), Mary Bellas (Mary), John Papanicolaou (John), Gerard Stainsby (Susan's Friend); Peter Roberts, Jennifer Doherty, Ben Rogan (Office Workers); Helena Pigrum (John's Girlfriend), Alex Newton (Boy), Perry Alexander (Boy's Father), Libby Stone (Susan's Neighbor), Steven Ram (Detective), Marc Laurence (Man on Street), George Manolis (John's Housemate), Eleni Lazaris (News Reader), Mike Bellasmitchell (Busker), Ian Poppins (Old Man), Michael Filippidis (Uni Tutor), Laki Sideris (Waiter); Nick Dimitriou, Gabriella Ilardi (Young Couple); Helen Hassoura (First Victim); Marcus Zerbini, Darron Davies, Bill Mousoulis, Maria Brkic, Sasha Brkic ([People] in Restaurant).

Chris (Rhys Muldoon) works in an office where his diligent skills are noticed, and he heads towards promotion. But behind his calm façade lies the fact he is a serial killer.

Also at work is Helen (Angela Twigg), a young woman whom Chris picks up after having murdered an unknown woman. His courtship is courteous and nonphysical. Helen is attracted to his quiet and seemingly sensitive nature, though she is also a little unnerved that he hasn't made a pass. That pass never comes, for Helen, too, is murdered.

Helen's friend, Susan (Catherine Hill), who is writing a book on serial killers, starts investigating Helen's death. Knowing he is being watched by Susan, Chris then commits a murder he knows will result in his arrest.

Intercut are other stories: of a child, with a penchant for cruelty to cats, who is physically and sexually abused by a father; of a young couple who break up in a park. Like Chris, who decided to take control of his own life 'as a project', after a hurtful relationship at age 20, so this young man vows to take control of his—another serial killer in the making?

OPEN CITY
BILL MOUSOULIS

Innersense Productions presents OPEN CITY. © 1993 Innersense Productions. *Budget:* $2000. *Location:* Melbourne. *Australian distributor:* Innersense Productions. *Opened:* 1 October 1993. *Video:* not released as of 1 May 1995. *Rating:* not rated. Super 8. 80 mins.

Producer: Bill Mousoulis. *Scriptwriter:* Bill Mousoulis. *Additional material:* John F. Howard. Based on an original idea by Andrew Preston. *Directors of photography:*[1] Con Filippidis, Clem Stamation. *Camera operators:*[2] Jenny Leach, Bill Mousoulis. *Editor:* Bill Mousoulis. *Sound:* Daniel Kotsonis, Rodney Bourke.

Cast

John F. Howard (James), Georgina Campbell (Christina), Claire Paradine (Julie), Peter Tsoukalas (George), Bruce Kane (Simon), John Penman (Jack), Anna Kotanidis (Anna), Harry Starverkos (Harry), Bill Jones (Bill); Peter Houghton, Mark Zenner, John Flaus, Meg Clancy, Daryl Pellizzer, George Glannopoulos, Nick Dimitriou, Pauline Webb, Mary Gotsis, Richard Hardman, Mira Rabadievska, Ian Poppins, Michael Kotanidis, Nick Kotanidis, Sarah Johnson, Jenny Leach, Leon Gotsis, Monica Mousoulis, Steven Ball, Con Filippidis, Michael Filippidis, Nicole Bensimon, Clem Stamation, Daniel Kotsanis.

James (John F. Howard), a foreign correspondent for *The Age* in Bosnia, becomes sick of the endless violence of the war, quits his job and returns home to Melbourne. He hooks back up with his ex-girlfriend, Christina (Georgina Campbell), a theatre set designer. But the initial peacefulness is replaced by an inner restlessness. So, when James meets Julie (Claire Paradine), a young writer, he engages in a sexual and intellectual relationship.

George (Peter Tsoukalas), an unemployed young Greek man, then enters the narrative. His and James' stories unfold together, firstly parallel, then perpendicular. Their paths ultimately cross in the final scene, on their way to different destinations: one open, the other closed.

Reference
'Open City = open cinema?', Michael Filippidis, *Filmnews*, September 1993, p. 18.

---

1 The film credit reads 'Lighting'.
2 The film credit reads 'Camera'.

Chris (Rhys Muldoon) and his final victim, Mary (Mary Bellas). Bill Mousoulis' Ladykiller.

James (John F. Howard) on his return to Melbourne from Bosnia. Bill Mousoulis' Open City.

A P P E N D I X   C
THEATRICAL VIDEO FEATURES

There are three known video features to have been theatrically released. There may be others, especially sex films such as **Arigato Baby**. Though **Arigato Baby** was legally shown in a Melbourne video sex cinema, other (X-rated) Australian sex films have also been shown, such as **Phone Sex Girls Australia** and **Bushwackers**. There is no known record of these films' release, as to screen them in original X-rated form is illegal (though tolerated). As well, most of the credits are pseudonymous.

ARIGATO BABY
GREG LYNCH

Juggernaught presents ARIGATO BABY. © 1990 Juggernaught Productions. *Location:* Melbourne. *Australian distributor:* Greg Lynch. *Rating:* R. *Video:* Greg Lynch. 80 mins.

Producer: Greg Lynch. *Executive producers:* Ken Hill, Eric Hill. *Scriptwriter:* A. J. Klitz. *Director of photography:* Jaque Rubin. *Editor:* Greg Lynch. *Composer:* Peter Doyle. *Sound:* Dreamtrak.

Cast: Yoko Atsumi (Yoko), Nicci Lane (Wendy), Adrian Wentworth (Adam); Mishi Marcos, Josephine Gomez (Parlor Girls); Jack F. Thornstein (Barman), Lupus Langrove (Barman).

Synopsis: Adam's sex adventures, which involve a contrast in values between Australian and Japanese culture.

BLOODLUST
RICHARD WOLSTENCROFT AND JON HEWITT

Windhover Productions present[s] BLOODLUST[1]. © 1991 Windhover Productions Pty Ltd. *Budget:* $75,000. *Locations:* Melbourne, Melton (Victoria). *Australian distributor:* Windhover Productions. *Video:* Damnation. *Rating:* R. 87 mins.

Producers: Richard Wolstencroft, Jon Hewitt. *Executive producers:* Robert Ruggi, Mark Spratt. *Scriptwriters:* Richard Wolstencroft, Jon Hewitt. *Director of photography:* Gary Ravenscroft. *Production designer:* Nicolas Barclay. *Costume designer:* Anne Liedel. *Editors:* Richard Wolstencroft, Jon Hewitt. *On-line editor:* Paul Jeffrey. *Music and fx:* Ross Hazeldine, Tom Fryer. *Sound recordist:* Angie Black. *Sound engineer:* David McCluney. [*Mixer:* not credited.]

Cast: Jane Stuart Wallace (Lear), Kelly Chapman (Frank), Robert James O'Neill (Tad), Phil Motherwell (Brother Bem), Paul Moder (Steig), James Young (Zeike), Max Crawdaddy (Deke), Ian Rilen (Dee; Happy), Colin Savage (Sonny), Big Bad Ralph (Butch; Bruno), Lex Middleton (Brother Bob), Michael Helms (Brother Thiatus), Esme Melville (Basket Lady), Michael Adams (Stoned Hippy), John Flaus (Mr Fetish), Troy Davies (Petrol Jack), Randall Berger (Car Salesman), Nick Ronan (Priest), Johnny L (Yamamoto Suit), Rick Masters (Cell Phone).

Synopsis: A schlock splatter movie about modern-day vampires.

MAD BOMBER IN LOVE
JAMES BOGLE

[Unchecked.] Pinchgut Productions. © 1991. *Location:* Sydney. Filmed: 5–20 August 1991. *Australian distributor:* Pinchgut Productions. *Video:* 21st Century. *Rating:* M. Betacam SP. 85 mins.

Producer: George Mannix. *Scriptwriters:* Peter Rasmussen, Leon Marvall, Martin Brown, George Mannix, James Bogle. *Director of photography:* John Brock. *Camera operators:* Toni Connolly, Martin Turner, Jon Cohen. *Production designer:* Martin Brown. *Wardrobe supervisor:* Terri Kibbler. *Editor:* Laura Zusters. *Composers:* Michael Roberts, Phil Rigger. *Sound recordist:* Nigel Brooks.

Cast: Rachel Szalay (Julia), Craig Pearce (Bernard), Alex Morgos (Gunther), Alan Lovell (Kevin), Zachery McKay (Bill), Laura Keneally (Mary Lou); Craig McLachlan, Anthony Ackroyd, Marcus Graham, Helen Jones, Paul Chubb, Max Cullen, Zoë Carides.

Synopsis: Bernard is a charming psychopath. When he moves into Julia's spare room, he falls in love. Everyone sharing your house can be difficult, but some men are murder to live with.

---

[1] The two Os overlap, like Olympic rings.

RECENTLY FILMED OR COMPLETED FEATURES AND TELE-FEATURES

The following list of films, with varyingly brief credits, covers (in the main) the period of 1992 to 1 May 1995. It is extracted from the research being done for the forthcoming companion volume to this book, which concentrates on tele-features and mini-series.

The list covers features destined for the cinema which have not as yet made it (or may never), plus features made specifically for video release or television. It is not intended to be complete, nor do the separate entries pretend to be comprehensive. This list is simply an interim aid while research continues.

The methodology of this appendix is different from that of the main portion of this book, mainly because few of the listed films have been yet sighted (many are still uncompleted) and, in most instances, the credits given come from secondary sources, not from the films themselves. (The printed titles, therefore, are no guarantee of what is or will be on the film or video.)

In the main, the credits and synopses have been taken from entries printed in the Production Survey published in each issue of *Cinema Papers*, the only regular listing of film and television production over the entire 1978–94 period, and by far the most comprehensive. Those brief entries, without cast details or synopses, generally come from the three editions of the invaluable *Get the Picture*, published by the Australian Film Commission. The fortnightly trade paper, *Encore*, has also been consulted.

Given the lesser emphasis accorded by film historians and critics to non-theatrical films, it is perhaps not surprising that the research so far published is sometimes contradictory or inaccurate. One sees the same film listed two or more times under different titles, understandable given the near frenzied way tele-features undergo title revisions.

Equally, films that start out as tele-features sometimes mutate into mini-series, just as a film intended for theatrical release may go first to video or television (or, in a couple of cases, nowhere known). Some films, in fact, may never have been completed, though each entry below taken from *Cinema Papers* is for a film the producer (or representative) has claimed to be already in production.

As well, some films that started out as more than 60 minutes may, in their final forms, have slipped under that feature-defining mark.

Unlike theatrical features, the date given here is the year of production (that is, principal photography).

All designations of film type ('tele-feature', 'feature-length pilot', etc.) come from the Production Survey entry in *Cinema Papers* supplied by the production company. While some films are perceived today as tele-features, some were once thought of by their producers and directors as potential theatrical features. Consequently, what some may consider a tele-feature has the notation 'Not theatrically released as of 1 May 1995' (i.e., in Australia). This is in no way an implied criticism, simply a statement of what the producer considered the project to be at the outset (each Production Survey form has a space where the type of project has to be clearly delineated by the production company). A theatrical release some time in the future may change how it is catalogued in future books.

Further research will inevitably correct some of what is given here, and it should be read accordingly.

ALEX
MEGAN SIMPSON

Isambard Productions and Total Film & Television in association with New Zealand Film Commission, New Zealand on Air and Australian Film Finance Corporation present Alex. © 1992 Australian Film Finance Corporation Pty Limited[,] New Zealand Film Commission [,] New Zealand On Air [and] Isambard Productions Limited. A New Zealand–Australia co-production. *Location:* Auckland (New Zealand). *Filmed:* September 1992. 105 mins. Feature released first to television in Australia, but with some overseas theatrical release.

Producers: Tom Parkinson, Phil Gerlach. *Line producer:* Tom Winley. *Associate producer:* Alan Withrington. *Scriptwriter:* Ken Catran. Based on the novel by Tessa Duder. *Director of photography:* Donald Duncan. *Production designer:* Kim Sinclair. *Costume designer:* Sara Beale. *Editor:* Tony Kavanagh. *Composer:* Todd Hunter. *Additional music:* Johanna Pigott. *Sound*

recordist: David Madigan. *Sound editors:* Ashley Grenville, Helen Brown. *Mixers:* Phil Heywood, Martin Oswin.

Cast: Lauren Jackson (Alex), Chris Haywood (Mr Jack), Josh Picker (Andy), Catherine Godbold (Maggie), Elizabeth Hawthorn (Mrs Benton), Bruce Phillips (Mr Archer), May Lloyd (Mrs Archer), Patrick Smith (Mr Benton), Rima Te Wiata (Female Commentator), Mark Wright (Male Commentator).

Synopsis: Winning has always been easy for Alex, a 15-year-old champion swimmer from the wrong side of the tracks. Then comes love and tragedy, and the loss of innocence.

ALL MEN ARE LIARS
GERARD LEE

Arenafilm. *Alternative title:* 'Goodnight Irene' (working). *Filmed:* 13 June–6 August 1994. Feature awaiting release as of 1 May 1995.

Producer: John Maynard. *Associate producer:* Robert Connolly. *Scriptwriter:* Gerard Lee. *Director of photography:* Steve Arnold. *Production designer:* Murray Pope. *Costume designer:* Wendy Chuck. *Editor:* Suresh Ayyar. *Sound recordist:* Greg Burgmann.

Cast: Toni Pearen, David Price, John Jarratt, Jamie Petersen, Carmen Tanti.

Synopsis: Mick, a 16-year-old country boy, cross dresses and joins an all-girl band in town for the local festival. He falls hopelessly in love with band member Angela, who is flirting with lesbianism. She's hot for Mick, not just because he's cute and talented but being a woman he's honest.

ANGEL BABY
MICHAEL RYMER

Astral Films. *Filmed:* March–April 1994. Feature awaiting release as of 1 May 1995.

Producers: Timothy White, Jonathan Shteinman. *Scriptwriter:* Michael Rymer. *Director of photography:* Ellery Ryan. *Production designer:* Chris Kennedy. *Costume designer:* Kerri Mazzocco. *Editor:* Dany Cooper. *Sound recordist:* John Phillips. *Sound editor:* Frank Lipsom.

Cast: John Lynch, Jacqueline McKenzie.

Synopsis: A roller-coaster journey to the fringes of the human psyche.

AUSTRALIAN NINJA
ADAM RAMOS, MICHELLE FIRMSTONE

Transworld International Pictures. 1992. 85 mins. Feature not theatrically released as of 1 May 1995.

Producers: Mario Difiori, Victor Sawicki. Scriptwriter: Adam Ramos.

Cast: Adam Ramos, Sandra Swan, Roy Fimmano.

Synopsis: The story of a private investigator, Cass Brown, who becomes romantically involved with Julia Swan, whom he has hired to work for him. The relationship is threatened by a villainous drug dealer and martial arts expert.

BABE: THE BRILLIANT SHEEP PIG
CHRIS NOONAN

Kennedy Miller. Feature in post-production as of 1 May 1995.

BACK OF BEYOND
MICHAEL ROBERTSON

Back of Beyond Films. Filmed: 12 September–15 October 1994. Budget: $3.8 million. Feature awaiting release as of 1 May 1995.

Producer: John Sexton. Executive producers: Doug Yellin, Gary Hamilton. Scriptwriters: Paul Leadon, Rick J. Sawyer, Anne Brooksbank. Director of photography: Stephen Dobson. Camera operator: Marc Spicer. Production designer: Ross Major. Editor: Tim Wellburn. Sound recordist: Guntis Sics. Sound editor: Gary O'Grady.

Cast: Paul Mercurio (Tom), Colin Friels (Connor), John Polson (Nick), Dee Smart (Charlie), Rebekah Elmaloglou (Susan), Bob Maza (Gilbert), Amy Miller-Porter (Rosie), Aaron Wilton (Ned), Terry Serio (Lucky), Glenda Linscott (Mary Margaret).

Synopsis: Outback Australia: an ancient land filled with infinite beauty and eternal mystery, the magical place where a young man's search for spiritual fulfilment becomes an emotional awakening of the heart and soul. It is a journey to back of beyond.

BEYOND THE RIM
CRAIG GODFREY

Pocketmoney Productions. Budget: $20,000. Filmed: April 1992. Feature not theatrically released as of 1 March 1995.

Producer: Craig Godfrey. Co-producer: Craig Godfrey. Line producer: Scott Goodman. Scriptwriter: Craig Godfrey. Director of photography: Craig Godfrey. Production designer: John Boling. Composer: Tony Francis. Sound recordist: Perry Dwyer.

Cast: Bill Conn (Jerome Ryan), Les Windspear (Jack), Kerry Laws (Lisa Ryan), Pamela John (Fenella Bailley), Ken Short (Henry Bourke).

Synopsis: A suicide turns out to be a murder uncovered by an unsuspecting hero who has visions through the dead man's glasses.

BIG IDEAS
MIKE SMITH

Robert Bruning Productions. Alternative title: 'High Hopes' (working). 1992. Tele-feature.

Producers: Robert Bruning, Adrienne Read. Scriptwriter: Peter Neale.

Cast: Justin Rosniak, Gosia Dobrowolska, Harold Hopkins.

Synopsis: An intrepid young entrepreneur takes on the bureaucracy in an ecological detective hunt.

BILLY'S HOLIDAY
RICHARD WHERRETT

Billy's Holiday. Feature awaiting release as of 1 May 1995.

Producer: Tristram Miall. Co-producer: Denis Whitburn. Scriptwriter: Denis Whitburn. Director of photography: Roger Lanser. Production designer: Michael Scott-Mitchell. Costume designer: Terry Ryan. Editor: Sue Blainey. Musical director: Peter Cobbin. Sound recordist: Guntis Sics.

Cast: Max Cullen, Kris McQuade, Tina Bursill, Drew Forsythe, Geneviève Lemon, Richard Roxburgh, Rachael Coopes.

Synopsis: In the eyes of his teenage daughter, Billy is a loser. And his girlfriend can't find the key to his heart. But when his pub jazz band takes off after Billy finds he has been magically blessed with the voice of his idol, the legendary Billie Holiday, life throws him some wild and wonderful curves. Fame, fortune—and Faust—turn Billy's world on its head.

BLACK NEON
JAMES RICHARDS, EDWARD JOHN STAZAK

Alternative title: 'Bouncers' (working). 1992. Feature not theatrically released as of 1 May 1995.

Producers: James Richards, Edward John Stazak. Scriptwriters: James Richards, Edward John Stazak.

Cast: James Richards, Edward John Stazak, Kristof Kacmarec.

Synopsis: The nightclub industry through the eyes of two tired nightclub bouncers.

BLACKWATER TRAIL
IAN BARRY

Rutherford Film Holdings. Feature in post-production as of 1 May 1995.

Producers: John Sexton, Julie Forster. Executive producers: Andrew Warren, Chris Brown. Scriptwriter: Andrew Russell. Director of photography: John Stokes. Production designer: Georgina Greenhill. Costume designer: Phillip Eagles. Editor: Tim Wellburn. Sound recordist: Paul 'Salty' Brincat.

Cast: Judd Nelson (Matt Curren), Dee Smart (Cathy), Mark Lee (Chris), Peter Phelps (Frank), Rowena Wallace (Beth), Gabrielle Fitzpatrick (Sandra), Daniel Roberts (Davies), Brett Climo (Father Michael).

Synopsis: Writer Matt Curren returns to the small town in Queensland, where he grew up, for the funeral of his old school friend, police detective Andy Green. At the funeral, Matt encounters his childhood sweetheart, Cathy, now married. Cathy insists that her brother, Andy, did not commit suicide, but was murdered. Matt is drawn into a dangerous web of cover-up and corruption that leads him closer and closer to the truth about his love for Cathy and the death of his best friend.

THE BOY WHO DARED TO DREAM
FRANK HOWSON

Boulevard Films. Feature not theatrically released as of 1 May 1995.

Producer: Frank Howson. Scriptwriter: Frank Howson. 1992/93.

CLOWNING AROUND
GEORGE WHALEY

Barron Films. Alternative title: 'Clowning Sim' (working). 1991. Shot as a feature but shown as a mini-series.

Co-producers: Paul Barron, Antonia Barnard. Scriptwriters: Tony Cavanaugh, Shane Brennan. Based on the novel Clowning Sim by David Martin. Director of photography: Laszlo Baranyai. Composer: Peter Best.

Cast: Clayton Williamson (Sim), Jean-Michel Dagory (Anatole), Ernie Dingo (Jack), Van Johnson (Neville Rathnow), Margaret Ford (Martha Rathnow).

Synopsis: Sim is a 13-year-old boy determined to become a famous clown. His dreams are treated by his foster parents, school acquaintances and welfare officers with amusement and indifference. He runs away and meets Anatole, an old clown.

CLOWNING AROUND ENCORE!
GEORGE WHALEY

Barron Films. Filmed: 21 September–15 November 1992. Sequel to above. Though first listed in reports as a feature, it is now considered a mini-series.

Producers: Julie Monton, Paul D. Barron. Executive producer: Paul D. Barron. Scriptwriters: John Coulter, Ranald Allan, Tony Cavanaugh. Based on the novel Clowning Sim by David Martin. Director of photography: Martin McGrath. Production designer: Herbert Pinter. Costume designer: Terri Lamera. Editor: Geoff Hall. Composer: Peter Best.

Cast: Clayton Williamson (Sim), Frederique Fouche (Eve), Ernie Dingo (Jack), Jean-Michel Dagory (Anatole), Heather Mitchell (Sarah).

Synopsis: Sim is now well established as a carpet clown with the Winter Circus in Paris. He still has ambitions. Being the world's greatest clown is not enough: he wants to own the world's greatest circus.

COME RAIN OR SHINE
FRANK HOWSON

Boulevard Films. 1991–92. Feature not theatrically released as of 1 May 1995.

Producer: Frank Howson. Scriptwriter: Frank Howson.

Cast: Joan Brockenshire, Tommy Dysart, Frank Howson, Adrian Wright, Kole Dysart.

COPS AND ROBBERS
MURRAY REECE

Isambard Productions–Total Film & Television. Alternative title: 'Kevin Rampenbacker and the Electric Kettle' (working). Filmed: October 1992. Feature not theatrically released as of 1 May 1995.

Producer: Tony Winley. *Executive producers:* Philip Gerlach, Tom Parkinson. *Scriptwriter:* Timothy Bean. *Director of photography:* Steve Arnold. *Production designer:* David McKay.

Cast: Grant Dodwell, Melissa Kounnas, Rima Te Wiata, Mark Wright, Gosia Dobrowolska.

Synopsis: A bankrupt man bungles his suicide attempt and embarks on a career of crime in this action-packed cops and robbers comedy involving murder, mayhem and marriage.

COSI
MARK JOFFE

Smiley Films. *Filmed:* 20 January–10 March 1995. Feature in post-production as of 1 May 1995.

Producer: Richard Brennan. *Executive producers:* Phaedon Vass, Harvey Weinstein, Bob Weinstein. *Associate producer:* Lyn Gailey. *Scriptwriter:* Louis Nowra. Based on his play. *Director of photography:* Ellery Ryan. *Production designer:* Chris Kennedy. *Costume designer:* Tess Schofield. *Editor:* Nicholas Beauman. *Sound recordist:* John Schiefelbein.

Cast: Ben Mendelsohn (Lewis), Barry Otto (Roy), Toni Collette (Julie), Jacki Weaver (Cherry), Pamela Rabe (Ruth), Paul Chubb (Henry), Colin Hay (Zac), David Wenham (Doug), Colin Friels (Errol), Aden Young (Nick), Rachel Grif-fiths (Lucy).

Synopsis: Lewis, a young university graduate, accepts a job directing psychiatric patients in a therapeutic drama course. His control is usurped by Roy, a manic depressive who demands that they stage an opera by Mozart, despite the fact that none of the patients can act, sing or speak Italian.

CRIME BROKER
IAN BARRY

John Sexton Productions–Channel Ten Network–Portman Entertainment (UK). *Filmed:* September 1992. Feature released first on television.

Producers: John Sexton, Andrew Warren, Kazuo Nakamura. *Executive producers:* Susumu Kondo, Hiroyuki Ikeda, Victor Glynn.

Cast: Jacqueline Bisset (Holly McPhee), Masaya Kato (Jin Okazki), John Bach (Frank McPhee), Sally Warwick (Belinda), Justin Lewis (Josh).

Synopsis: Holly McPhee sells crime. Hers is a double life. On the surface, she is the vision of respectability. The classic housewife, she keeps an immaculate Sydney home and is also a local magistrate. To ward off the tedium of her conventional lifestyle, Holly works as a 'crime broker' selling detailed criminal operations in the underworld marketplace. Things then get out of hand.

CRIME TIME
MARC GRACIE

Boulevard Films. 96 mins. Feature not theatrically released as of 1 May 1995.

Producer: Frank Howson. *Scriptwriter:* Bruce Venables.

Cast: Marcus Graham, Bruce Venables, Lucy Bell, David Argue, Steven Grives.

Synopsis: Policemen Robin Decker and John Little begin to realise that they are probably the only

two honest cops left in the force. The corruption goes all the way to the top. Decker comes up with a plan, while Little becomes increasingly concerned for their safety as they begin to turn up the heat and shake the tree.

THE CULT OF DEATH
GEOFFREY BROWN

1992. Feature not theatrically released as of 1 May 1995.

Producer: Geoffrey Brown. *Scriptwriter:* Derek Strahan.

Cast: Derek Strahan, Chris Lloyds.

Synopsis: When crusty Irish detective Tom Shanahan is assigned to investigate the bizarre murder of the lovely Luna, he has a hunch that he is dealing with more than the death of a high-class girl.

DAD AND DAVE ON OUR SELECTION
GEORGE WHALEY

Anthony Buckley Productions. *Filmed:* 31 October–18 December 1994. *Australian distributor:* Roadshow. Feature awaiting release as of 1 May 1995.

Producer: Anthony Buckley. *Co-producer:* Carol Hughes. *Executive producers:* Bruce Davey, Jonathan Shteinman. *Scriptwriter:* George Whaley. Based on the original novels by Steele Rudd. *Director of photography:* Martin McGrath. *Production designer:* Herbert Pinter. *Costume designer:* Roger Kirk. *Editor:* Wayne Le Clos. *Composer:* Peter Best. *Sound recordist:* Lloyd Carrick.

Cast: Leo McKern (Dad), Joan Sutherland (Mother); Geoffrey Rush, Cathy Campbell, John Gadden, Robert Menzies, Nicholas Eadie, Ray Barrett, Essie Davis, Barry Otto, David Field, Celie Ireland, Noah Taylor, Murray Bartlett.

Synopsis: A rural comedy based on the Steele Rudd novels, centred on the Rudd family as it battles to hang on to its 150-acre property in the face of drought, plagues of kangaroos and a takeover threat from a wealthy squatter.

DALLAS DOLL
ANN TURNER

Dallas Doll Productions. Feature not theatrically released as of 1 May 1995.

Producers: Ross Matthews, Ann Turner, Tatiana Kennedy. *Executive producer:* Penny Chapman. *Line producer:* Barbara Gibbs. *Associate producer:* Ray Brown. *Scriptwriter:* Ann Turner. *Director of photography:* Paul Murphy. *Production designer:* Marcus North. *Costume designer:* Rosalea Hood. *Editor:* Mike Honey. *Sound recordist:* Nick Wood.

Cast: Sandra Bernhard, Victoria Longley, Frank Gallacher, Jake Blundell, Ross Byrne, Douglas Hedge.

Synopsis: Nothing in the Sommers' family horoscope warned them to be wary of a stranger from a foreign land. Even teenage Rastus, obsessed by UFOs and with her telescope nightly trained to the stars, is unable to discover what fate has in store for the family. But on first sighting Dallas Adair, she and her faithful dog, Argus, know turbulent times are ahead.

DAWN OF THE DMFS
CHRIS SUMMERS

Black on Black. *Budget:* $50,000. Feature not theatrically released as of 1 May 1995.

Producers: Darrell Martin, Chris Summers. *Scriptwriter:* Chris Summers. *Director of photography:* Darrell Martin. *Production designer:* Stephen Radic. *Editor:* Chris Summers. *Composer:* Ian Kitney. *Sound recordist:* Rick Chandler.

Cast: Greg Christie (The Soldier), David Whiteley (The Businessman), Chris Summers (The Punk), Bernie Rhodes (Agent No. 1), Sharon Murakimi (Madam Doctor).

Synopsis: A 1950s-style, science-fiction, paranoia comedy about aliens who invade Earth with the plan of turning the entire population into incoherent, babbling Ediots.

DELIVER US FROM EVIL
RICHARD WOLSTENCROFT

Boulevard Films. 85 mins. 1991–92. Feature not theatrically released as of 1 May 1995.

Producer: Frank Howson. *Scriptwriter:* Michael Horowitz.

Cast: Totti Goldsmith, Lachy Hulme, Greg Parker, Dale Stevens, Paul Moder.

Synopsis: The story of a young couple who are terrorised by a stranger who has broken into their house. The intruder indulges in a series of mind games with the woman which leads to an explosive and surprising climax.

DE VIL'S TAS MANIA
DI NETTLEFOLD

Di Net Films. *Alternative title:* 'Three Cornered Island' (working). *Budget:* $250,000. *Filmed:* 10 February–20 March 1992. Feature not theatrically released as of 1 May 1995.

Producer: Di Nettlefold. *Scriptwriter:* Di Nettlefold. Based on the novel, *Three Cornered Island,* by Dorothy Halkerston. *Director of photography:* Peter Donnelly. *Production designer:* Di Nettlefold. *Editor:* Matthew Tucker. *Composer:* John Ertler. *Sound recordist:* Paul Clark.

Cast: David Burnett (Jack de Vils), Robyn Murray (Mary), Helen Mutkins (Julia), Sam Nettlefold (Dale), Charlotte Hurburgh (Eliza), Linzee Arnold (Burgess).

Synopsis: The fate and adventures of Jack de Vils and his mate, Dale, who have escaped from the local prison farm on the east coast of Tasmania.

THE DISTANT HOME
ROBERT MARCHAND

Robert Bruning Productions. 1991–92. Telefeature.

Producers: Robert Bruning, Adrienne Read. *Scriptwriter:* Tony Morphett.

DOT IN SPACE
YORAM GROSS

Yoram Gross Studios. 1994. 62 mins. Animated feature not theatrically released as of 1 May 1995.

Producer: Yoram Gross. *Executive producer:* Sandra Gross. *Scriptwriter:* John Palmer.

Voices: Robyn Moore, Keith Scott.

Synopsis: Dot resumes her adventures, this time in space, as she rescues a Russian dog from a malfunctioning satellite and has many adventures before returning safely to earth.

EBBTIDE
CRAIG LAHIFF

Genesis Films. *Budget:* $2.6 million. *Location:* Sydney. *Filmed:* late 1993. 35 mm. 94 mins. Feature not theatrically released as of 1 May 1995.

Producers: Craig Lahiff, Paul Davies, Helen Leake. *Scriptwriters:* Bob Ellis, Peter Goldsworthy, Warwick Hind.

Cast: John Waters, Harry Hamlin, Judy McIntosh, Susan Lyons, John Gregg, Frankie J. Holden.

Synopsis: Lawyer Jeff Warren takes over a compensation case after the sudden death of one of his legal partners. His subsequent investigations, and growing obsession with the enigmatic Ellen Fielding, compromise his values and his view of himself as a winner. His attempts to solve the complex intrigues lead him to be accused of murder.

ECONOMY CLASS
KEVIN CARLIN

Albert Street Productions–HSV Channel 7. Tele-feature.

Producer: Stephen Luby. *Scriptwriters:* Kevin Carlin, Stephen Luby.

EIGHT BALL
RAY ARGALL

Meridian Films. *Filmed:* 13 May–28 June 1991. 35mm. Feature that went straight to television.

Producer: Timothy White. *Executive producers:* Jill Robb, Bryce Menzies. *Scriptwriters:* Ray Argall, Harry Kirchner. *Director of photography:* Mandy Walker. *Production designer:* Kerith Holmes. *Costume designer:* Jane Hyland. *Editor:* Ken Sallows. *Composer:* Philip Judd. *Sound recordist:* Ian Cregan. *Sound supervisor:* Dean Gawen.

Cast: Matthew Fargher (Charlie), Angie Milliken (Julie), Paul Steven (Russell), Lucy Sheehan (Jacqui), Frankie J. Holden (Mal), Matthew Krok (Dougie), Ollie Hall (Biggs), Desmond Kelly (Bert).

Synopsis: Charlie is a young architect with seemingly everything going for him. Russell, the complete opposite, has just been released from prison. Their paths cross.

ENCOUNTERS
MURRAY FAHEY

Coventry Films. *Filmed:* 6 July–1 August 1993. Feature not theatrically released as of 1 May 1995.

Producer: Murray Fahey. *Scriptwriter:* Murray Fahey. *Director of photography:* Peter Borosh. *Production designer:* Robyn Monkhouse. *Editor:* Brian Kavanagh. *Composer:* Frank Strangio. *Sound recordist:* David Glasser. *Sound editors:* Dean Gawen, Rex Watts, Paul Huntingford. *Mixer:* Dean Gawen.

Cast: Kate Raison (Madaline Carr), Martin Sacks (Martin Carr), Martin Vaughan (Harris), Maggie Kirkpatrick (Aunt Helen), Vince Gil (Farmer Evans), John Krummel (Miles Franklin).

Synopsis: A suspense thriller in the Hitchcock tradition, about a woman haunted by her past and her search to discover the truth of what happened.

EPSILON
ROLF DE HEER

Epsilon. *Location:* Flinders Ranges (South Australia). Super 35. Feature awaiting release as of 1 May 1995.

Producers: Domenico Procacci, Rolf de Heer. *Co-producer:* Sean Cuddy, Digital Arts. *Associate producer:* Sharon Jackson. *Scriptwriter:* Rolf de Heer. *Director of photography:* Tony Clark. *Editor:* Tania Nehme. *Composer:* Graham Tardif. *Sound designer:* Peter D. Smith.

Cast: Ulli Birvé (She), Syd Brisbane (The Man).

Synopsis: An intergalactic love story about planet Earth.

EVERYNIGHT ... EVERYNIGHT
ALKINOS TSILIMIDOS

Rescued Films. 92 mins. Feature released in May 1995.

Producer: Alkinos Tsilimidos. *Scriptwriters:* Ray Mooney, Alkinos Tsilimidos.

Cast: David Field, Bill Hunter, Robert Morgan, Phil Motherwell, Jim Daley, Jim Shaw, Simon Woodward, Theodore Zakos.

Synopsis: Everynight ... Everynight is an indictment of systems—systems which are open to abuse and corruption; systems where police can behave like criminals and get away with it; systems which alienate and deprive people of their dignity to the extent that violence is a power-seeking device from men who have never known influence or affluence.

EXILE
PAUL COX

EXILE. © 1994 Illumination Films, Film Victoria [and] Australian Film Finance Corporation Pty Limited. Developed and produced with the assistance of Film Victoria. Made with the participation of Australian Film Finance Corporation Pty Limited. *Budget:* $2 million. *Location:* Freycinet National Park, Tasmania. *Filmed:* 15 March–17 April 1993. 35mm. 95 mins. Feature that went straight to video.

Producers: Santhana Naidu, Paul Ammitzboll, Paul Cox. *Executive producer:* William T. Marshall. *Scriptwriter:* Paul Cox. Based on the novel, *Priest Island,* by E. L. Grant Watson. *Director of photography:* Nino Martinetti. *Production designer:* Neil Angwin. *Costume designer:* Gosia Dobrowolska. *Editor:* Paul Cox. *Composer:* Paul Grabowsky. *Sound:* James Currie, Craig Carter. *Sound recordist:* James Currie. *Sound editors:* Craig Carter, James Currie. *Mixer:* James Currie.

Cast: Aden Young (Peter), Beth Champion (Mary), Claudia Karvan (Jean), Norman Kaye (Ghost), David Field (Timothy), Chris Haywood (Priest), Barry Otto (Sheriff), Hugo Weaving (Innes), Tony Llewellyn-Jones (Jean's Father), Nicholas Hope (MacKenzie).

Synopsis: In the 19th century, a young man is banished to an island after stealing a few sheep. There he lives, fighting the demons of his past and the ghosts of his present, until the arrival of a young woman.

FATAL PAST
CLIVE FLEURY

Phillip Emmanuel Productions. 1991–92. Feature not theatrically released as of 1 May 1995.

Producer: Phillip Emmanuel. *Scriptwriter:* Richard Ryan.

Cast: Kasia Figura, Costas Mandylor, Terence Cooper.

Synopsis: Costello is an underworld bodyguard. His employer, David Preston, is a shady entrepreneur. When Costello foils an attempt on Preston's life, he is rewarded with a job: 'babysitter' to Preston's mistress, Jennifer Lawrence.

THE FEDS
DAVID CAESAR

Crawfords Australia. *Filmed:* 1 March–2 April 1993. 16 mm. Tele-feature.

Producer: Jan Marnell. *Executive producer:* Bruce Gordon. *Associate producer:* Judith Bland. *Scriptwriters:* Vince Moran, John Reeves. *Director of photography:* Joseph Pickering. *Production designer:* Kerith Holmes. *Costume designer:* Sally Grigsby. *Editor:* Bill Murphy. *Composer:* Bruce Rowland. *Sound recordist:* John McKerron.

Cast: Sigrid Thornton (Christine McQuillan), Robert Taylor (Dave Griffin), Bruno Lawrence (Icehouse), Peter Hosking (Roland Cloke), Nicki Wendt (Melita Reale), Stephanie Chen (May Po), Rachel Griffiths (Angela Nraglia), Alex Menglet (Dr Steven Jellicoe), Lewis Fiander (Monk), Daniel Rigney ("Daisy").

Synopsis: The story involving Australia's premier law-enforcement body, the Federal Police. The action swings between Australia and Hong Kong in a world where the Triads and L'Honarata co-exist.

THE FEDS [VARIOUS]
DONALD CROMBIE, MICHAEL PATTINSON, AND OTHERS

Crawford Australia. *Filmed:* 30 May–11 November 1994. 16mm. Series of tele-features.

Producer: Jan Marnell. *Executive producers:* Bruce Gordon, John Kearney. *Scriptwriters:* Jan Sardi, Everett DeRoche, Vince Moran, Ian McFadyen, Patrick Edgeworth. *Directors of photography:* David Foreman, Roger Dowling. *Sound recordist:* John McKerrow. *Editors:* Bill Murphy, Denise Haratzis. *Production designer:* Paddy Reardon. *Costume designer:* Marion Boyce. *Composer:* Bruce Rowland. *Dialogue effects:* Bruce Climas. *Sound editors:* Stephen Vaughan, Michael Carden, Andrew Jobson.

Cast: Robert Taylor (Dave Griffin), Angie Milliken (Jo Moody), John Bach (Rainer Bass), Brian Vriends (Michael), Marcus Eyre (Blocker), Nell Feeney (Rose), Amanda Jane Bowden (Tina).

Synopsis: Experienced, likeable, all-too-human, a family man with a broken marriage, Superintendent Dave Griffin spearheads the Feds' battle against organised crime. Dave's regular partner is Detective Sergeant Jo Moody, a lawyer turned policewoman. Jo and Dave were lovers once. Now they are both striving to put the job first.

THE FLOOD
CHRIS THOMSON

Warner Bros. Television–The Wolper Organisation. 1992–93. Tele-feature.

Producer: Donna Kanter. *Scriptwriter:* David. J. Kinghorn.

GET AWAY GET AWAY
MURRAY FAHEY

Coventry Films. *Filmed:* January 1991–August 1992. Feature not theatrically released as of 1 May 1995.

Producer: Murray Fahey. *Scriptwriter:* Murray Fahey. *Director of photography:* Peter Borosh. *Editor:* Brian Kavanagh. *Composer:* Frank Strangio. *Sound recordist:* David Glasser.

Cast: Murray Fahey (Rick Carter), Annie Davies (Suzette), Ewan Campbell (Carltlemouth), Ned Manning (Bennytle), Rodd Hibbard (Darren the Cafe).

Synopsis: A paranoid bank teller meets a determined Frenchwoman, and on the way to Galarganbone they change each other's lives forever.

GINO
JACKIE MCKIMMIE

Filmside Productions. *Budget:* $2.8 million. *Filmed:* 5 April–16 May 1993. Feature not theatrically released as of 1 May 1995.

Producer: Ross Matthews. *Associate producer:* Sally Ayre-Smith. *Scriptwriters:* Vince Sorrenti, Larry Buttrose. *Director of photography:* Ellery Ryan. *Production designer:* Chris Kennedy. *Costume designer:* Anna Borghesi. *Editor:* Emma Hay. *Composer:* Roger Mason. *Sound recordist:* Ben Osmo.

Cast: Nick Bufalo (Gino Pallazetti), Zoë Carides (Lucia Petri), Bruno Lawrence (Joe Pallazetti), Rose Clemente (Rosa Pallazetti), Nico Lathouris (Rocco Petri).

Synopsis: Gino Pallazetti's life is simple: he's in love with Lucia, and his career as a stand-up comedian is about to take off.

GIRL
PETER THOMPSON

Phillip Emanuel Productions–Hips Film & Video Productions. *Budget:* $400,000. Feature in post-production as of 1 May 1995.

Producer: Phillip Emanuel. *Executive producer:* David Hannay. *Co-producer:* John Hipwell. *Scriptwriter:* Peter Thompson. *Director of photography:* Tim Smart. *Production designer:* Alex Zabotto-Bentley. *Editor:* Andrew Narozny. *Sound recordist:* Steven Best.

Cast: Karoline Hohlweg (Vali Martin), Kristy Pappas (Jeni Livieratos), Amelia Wong (Lin Hutchinson), Jamie Brindley (Susan Carmody), Jack Thompson (Victor Martin), Christine Kaman (Maria Martin), Mary Sitarenos (Despina Livieratos), Robert Forza (Jannis Livieratos), Maurie Annese (Georgio Livieratos), Justin D'Orazio (Michael Livieratos).

Synopsis: The story of four contemporary teenagers, three friends and one outsider, who enter a magazine photo competition. In consequence, one is propelled into an international modelling career.

GLAD RAGS
ROB STEWART

Nomad Films International. 16mm. Tele-feature.

Producer: Kate Faulkner. *Executive producer:* Doug Stanley. *Scriptwriter:* Trevor Todd. *Director of photography:* Alex McPhee. *Production designer:* Vicki Niehaus. *Composer:* Frank Strangio.

Synopsis: Glad Rags is a costume hire shop in a busy city. Lizzie Forbes lives above the shop which is run by her mother, Trish. Lizzie has a vivid imagination. She loves dressing up and fancies herself as an actress ... a spy ... or a detective, often with hilarious results.

GOD'S GIRLS
CHERIE NOWLAN

1992. Tele-feature.

Producer: Glenys Rowe. *Scriptwriter:* Cherie Nolan.

GOODFRUIT
STEPHEN PRODES, WILL USIC

Mezmo Pictures. 90 mins. In post-production as of 1 May 1995.

Producers: John Swaffield, Will Usic, Harriet Spalding. *Scriptwriter:* Will Usic.

Cast: Claudia Black, Chrissie Youhanna, Aaron Jeffrey, Vic Rooney, Calvin de Gray, Joshua Rosenthal, Peter Carmody.

Synopsis: A comedy–thriller centred on a young girl who holds the key to the whereabouts of a missing research project as she journeys through a hostile and confusing environment questioning her beliefs and learning to trust and believe in herself.

HALIFAX F.P. [VARIOUS]
PAUL MOLONEY, MIKE SMITH, STEVE JODRELL, SHIRLEY BARRETT, BRENDAN MAHER, MICHAEL CARSON

Simpson Le Mesurier Films. *Budget:* $7,800,000. 16mm. Series of tele-features.

Producers: Roger Le Mesurier, Roger Simpson. *Executive producer:* Ros Tatarka. *Scriptwriters:* Roger Simpson, Peter Kinloch, Mac Gudgeon, Keith Aberdein, Howard Griffiths. *Director of photography:* Craig Barden. *Production designer:* Tel Stolfo. *Costume designer:* Sandi Cichello. *Editor:* Anne Carter. *Sound recordist:* Andrew Ramage.

Cast: Rebecca Gibney (Jane Halifax).

Synopsis: Jane Halifax is a forensic psychiatrist whose specialty is the criminal mind.

HOTEL SORRENTO
RICHARD FRANKLIN

Bayside Pictures. *Locations:* Melbourne, Sorrento (Victoria). *Filmed:* 1993. 110 mins. Feature released in April 1995.

Producer: Richard Franklin. *Co-producer:* Helen Watts. *Scriptwriters:* Richard Franklin, Peter Fitzpatrick. Based on the play by Hannie Rayson. *Director of photography:* Geoff Burton. *Production designer:* Tracy Watt. *Costume designer:* Lisa Meagher. *Editor:* David Pulbrook. *Sound recordist:* Lloyd Carrick.

Cast: Caroline Gillmer (Hilary), Caroline Goodall (Meg), Joan Plowright (Marge), Ray Barrett (Wal), Nicholas Bell (Edwin), Ben Thomas (Troy), Tara Morice (Pippa), John Hargreaves (Dick).

Synopsis: Three sisters are reunited at their seaside family home by the disappearance of their father.

INHERIT THE STARS
ROBERT MARCHAND

1992. Tele-feature.

Producers: Robert Bruning, Tom Donald. *Scriptwriter:* Tony Morphett.

IRRESISTIBLE FORCE
KEVIN HOOKS

CBS Entertainment–Village Roadshow Pictures. 1993. Feature released straight to video.

Producer: Karlton Eastlake. *Scriptwriter:* Karlton Eastlake.

Cast: Cynthia Rothrock.

Synopsis: An action genre thriller.

JAILBIRDS RUN
KOJI WAKAMATSU

Right Vision Corporation–Village Roadshow Pictures. 1992–93. Feature not theatrically released as of 1 May 1995.

Producers: Kazunori Okada, Hisao Nabeshima. *Scriptwriters:* Toshiharu Maruuchi, Kazan Veno, Koji Wakamatsu.

JOH'S JURY
KEN CAMERON

ABC TV Drama–Southern Star Sullivan. 1992–93. Tele-feature.

Producer: Rod Allen. *Scriptwriter:* Ian David.

Cast: Simon Bossell, Penny Cook, Julie Hamilton, John Howard, Elaine Hudson, John Jarratt.

Synopsis: A dramatised documentary about the jury's deliberations in the trial of former Queensland premier, Sir Joh Bjelke-Petersen, who was charged with perjury.

JUSTIFIED ACTION
RENÉ NAGY JNR

Westworld Film Productions. *Budget:* $2.9 million. *Filmed:* 4 January–15 February 1993. Feature not theatrically released as of 1 May 1995.

Producer: René Nagy Jnr. *Executive producer:* Jack Samardzisa. *Associate producers:* Summer Nicks, Michael J. Knowles. *Scriptwriter:* Elliott A. McGarva. Based on a story by Elliott A. McGarva, Rene Nagy Jnr, Jack Samardzisa. *Director of photography:* Kevan "Loosey" Lind. *Production designer:* Wayne Deakin. *Costume designer:* Eva Maria Trust. *Editor:* Gary Woodyard.

Cast: Donald Swayze (Curtis Carter), Peter Phelps (Eddie Carter), Christina Ongley (Sarah Jordan), Mark Hembrow (Richard Carter), John Samaha (Vinny).

Synopsis: The head of international security for a multi-million dollar corporation and his estranged brother track down a Japanese businessman and avenge the murder of their older brother.

THE LAST MAN HANGED
LEWIS FITZ-GERALD

Bill Bennett Productions. 1992–93. Tele-feature.
Producer: Bill Bennett. *Scriptwriter:* Lewis Fitz-Gerald.

THE LIFE OF HARRY DARE
ALEKSI VELLIS

Infinity Pictures–South Australian Film Corp. *Budget:* $1.25 million. Feature awaiting release as of 1 May 1995.
Producer: Terry Charatsis. *Associate producer:* Barbara Gibbs. *Scriptwriter:* Gerald Thompson. *Director of photography:* Geoff Hall. *Camera operator:* Paul Meulenberg. *Production designer:* Ian Jobson. *Costume designer:* Beverley Freeman. *Editor:* Tony Paterson. *Sound recordist:* Bronwyn Murphy.
Cast: John Moore (Harry), Gordon Weetra (Harry, 8 years old), Aaron Wilton (Jim), Billy Trott (Jim in his twenties), Bobbi-Jean Henry (Jem), Francesca Cubillo-Alberts (Dulcie, 1965), Carole Frazer (Dulcie, 1978–80s), Bob Agius (Bert), Carrie Mellett (Anne), Ben Nelson (Johnny), Tony Briggs (Dan).
Synopsis: Harry Dare is the coolest Aboriginal detective there ever was. The man spent years restoring his VW Kombi only to have it stolen after its maiden voyage. Equipped with the detective kit bought by young son, Jim, father and son trek off to find the Kombi. Their search leads them to a relationship they never had, and to unravelling the mystery of Harry's father's disappearance many years ago. A comedy about discovery.

LILIAN'S STORY
JERZY DOMARADZKI

CML Films. *Filmed:* 20 March–14 May 1995. *Location:* Sydney. Feature in production as of 1 May 1995.
Producer: Marian Mcgowan. *Co-producer:* Mike Wilcox. *Executive producers:* David Court, Jeremy Bean. *Scriptwriter:* Steve Wright. Based on the novel by Kate Grenville. *Director of photography:* Slawomir Idziak. *Production designer:* Roger Ford. *Editor:* Lee Smith. *Sound recordist:* Ben Osmo.
Cast: Toni Collette (Lilian), Ruth Cracknell (Lilian), Barry Otto (Lilian's Father), Morgan Smallbone (F. J. Stroud); Susie Lindeman, John Flaus, Anne Louise Lambert.
The unconventional life of a legendary eccentric who recited Shakespeare for a dollar on the streets of Sydney and rode taxis for the price of a sonnet. Lilian's story is a celebration of being alive. Based on a novel by Kate Grenville.

LIVING COLOR
NEAL M. E. TAYLOR

Cinergy Motion Picture Entertainment. *Budget:* $2.5 million. *Filmed:* 5–21 January 1992. Feature not theatrically released as of 1 May 1995.
Producer: René Nagy Jnr. *Co-producer:* Summer Nicks. *Scriptwriter:* Neal M. E. Taylor. *Director of photography:* Nick Paton. *Production designer:* Kent Sherlock. *Editor:* Geoff Lamb. *Composer:* Shane Bryzak.

Cast: Derek Rucker (Dougle), Kim Denman (Molly), Michael Julian Knowles (Christian), Evelyn Taylor (Rachel), Scott Webb (Doctor).
Synopsis: Cat-and-mouse game between Molly, the young wife of Dougle, and Christian, a deranged killer out to be rid of all women because of his beliefs.

THE LONG LINE
AARON STEVENSON

Fatal Impact Productions. 1992. Feature not theatrically released as of 1 May 1995.
Producers: Aaron Stevenson, Gavin Pavey, Laurie Baston. *Scriptwriters:* Aaron Stevenson, Laurie Baston.
Cast: Rob Jealous, Lisa Heenan, Ross Simons.
Synopsis: Laurie Shields and his fiancée, Tracey, have their lives shattered when the psychotic Desmond declares war on the mental institution where Laurie works.

MERCY MISSION
ROGER YOUNG

Pahana Productions–Village Roadshow Pictures. 1992–93. Tele-feature.
Producer: Derek Kavanagh. *Scriptwriters:* Robert Benedetti, George Rubino.

METAL SKIN
GEOFFREY WRIGHT

Alternative title: 'Speed' (working). *Location:* Melbourne. *Filmed:* June–August 1993. Feature released in May 1995.
Producer: Daniel Scharf. *Line producer:* Elisa Argenzio. *Associate producer:* Jonathan Shteinman. *Scriptwriter:* Geoffrey Wright. *Director of photography:* Ron Hagen. *Production designer:* Steven Jones-Evans. *Editor:* Bill Murphy. *Composer:* John Clifford White.
Cast: Aden Young (Joe), Tara Morice (Savina), Nadine Garner (Roslyn), Ben Mendelsohn (Dazey), Chantal Contouri (Savina's Mother), Petru Gheor Hiu (Pop), Richard Sutherland (Rosco).
Synopsis: Tragedy comes inevitably in *Metal Skin*, a story about psycho Joe, an urban misfit who craves the respect of his peers on the streets and the love of a nice girl who secretly practises black magic.

MIGHTY MORPHIN POWER RANGERS
BRYAN SPICER

Tengu Productions. Feature in post-production as of 1 May 1995.
Producer: Suzanne Todd. *Co-producer:* David Coatsworth. *Executive producer:* Chris Meledandri. *Associate producers:* Jon Landau, Mike Levine. Based on the TV series. *Director of photography:* Paul Murphy. *Production designer:* Craig Stearns. *Costume designer:* Sanja Hays. *Editor:* Wayne Wahrman. *Sound recordist:* Bob Clayton.
Cast: Jason Frank (Tommy White Falcon), Steve Cardenas (Rocky Red Ape), Amy Jo Johnson (Kimberly Pink Crane), John Bosch (Adam Black Frog), Karan Ashley (Aisha Yellow Bear), David Yost (Billy Blue Wolf), Paul Freeman (Ivan Ooze), Juliette Cortez (Rita Repulsa), Gabrielle

Fitzpatrick (Dulcia), Paul Schrier (Bulk), Jason Narvey (Skull).
Synopsis: Zordon summons the Power Rangers to save the planet from the evil and destructive forces of Ivan and his army of monsters.

MUSHROOMS
ALAN MADDEN

Rosen Harper Entertainment. 92 mins. Feature awaiting release as of 1 March 1995.
Producer: Brian Rosen. *Executive producer:* Richard Harper. *Scriptwriter:* Alan Madden.
Cast: Julia Blake, Lynette Curran, Simon Chilvers.
Synopsis: A romantic black comedy about Minnie and Flo, widows in their mid-sixties, who become embroiled in a macabre plot when a corpse and a cop both decide to take refuge in the disused pawn shop that is their residence.

MY FORGOTTEN MAN
FRANK HOWSON

Boulevard Films. *Alternative titles:* 'Flynn' and 'Young Flynn' (working). 1993. Originally directed by Brian Kavanagh in 1989. Largely remade. Feature not theatrically released as of 1 May 1995.
Producer: Frank Howson. *Scriptwriters:* Frank Howson, Alister Webb. *Director of photography:* John Wheeler.
Cast: Guy Pearce (Errol Flynn), Claudia Karvan.
Synopsis: The story of Errol Flynn's early years, depicting his childhood in Tasmania and his wild teenage years in New Guinea. He was a thief, a liar, a gigolo, a gambler, a sailor, a street fighter and a soldier of fortune.

NAPOLEON
MARIO ANDREACCHIO

Film Australia–Furry Feature Films. 100 mins. Feature awaiting release as of 1 May 1995.
Producers: Mario Andreacchio, Michael Bourchier, Naonori Kawamura (Herald Ace). *Executive producers:* Ron Saunders, Masato Hara. *Line producer:* John Wild. *Scriptwriters:* Mario Andreacchio, Michael Bourchier, Steven J. Spears. *Director of photography:* Roger Dowling. *Production designer:* Vicki Niehus. *Editor:* Edward McQueen-Mason. *Sound designers:* James Currie, Craig Carter.
Synopsis: The story of a happy suburban puppy, Napoleon, unexpectedly transported into a natural bushland world.

THE NUN AND THE BANDIT
PAUL COX

Illumination Films. 1992. Feature that went straight to video.
Producers: Paul Ammitzboll, Paul Cox. *Scriptwriter:* Paul Cox. Based on the novel by E. L. Grant Watson. *Director of photography:* Nino Martinetti. *Composers:* Tom E. Lewis, Norman Kaye.
Cast: Gosia Dobrowolska (Sister Lucy), Chris Haywood (Michael Shanley), Victoria Eagger (Maureen), Charlotte Hughes Haywood (Julie Shanley), Tom E. Lewis (Bert Shanley), Norman Kaye (George Shanley).
Synopsis: Michael Shanley and his brothers are modern outlaws. But their plan to kidnap their

wealthy 14-year-old second cousin goes awry when her chaperoning nun refuses to abandon her charge.

OFFICIAL DENIAL
BRIAN TRENCHARD-SMITH

CNM Entertainment–Jeffrey Hayes Productions–Wilshire Court Productions. 1992–93. Tele-feature.

Producer: Darryl Sheen. *Scriptwriter:* Bryce Zabel.

OFFSPRING
RICHARD RYAN

Phillip Emmanuel Productions. *Budget:* $2.8 million. *Filmed:* April 1993. Feature not theatrically released as of 1 May 1995.

Producer: Phillip Emmanuel. *Co-producer:* David Hannay. *Line producer:* Stephen Jones. *Scriptwriter:* Richard Ryan. *Director of photography:* Julian Penney. *Production designer:* Laurence Eastwood. *Editor:* John Scott. *Sound recordist:* Syd Butterworth.

Cast: Chantal Contouri, Robert Mammone, Gabrielle Fitzpatrick.

Synopsis: Rosa is arrestingly beautiful, wealthy and sophisticated. She is consumed by a manic obsession to exact a calculated and brutal revenge upon her only daughter, Maria, a succesful international model who has recently made her debut as an actress.

POINT OF NO RETURN
VINCENT MONTON

Phillip Emanuel Productions–Hips Film & Video Productions. *Alternative title:* 'Countdown' (working). *Budget:* $500,000. Feature in post-production as of 1 May 1995.

Producer: Phillip Emanuel. *Executive producer:* David Hannay. *Co-producer:* John Hipwell. *Scriptwriter:* Vincent Monton. *Director of photography:* Louis Irving. *Production designer:* Neil Angwin. *Costume designer:* Aphrodite Kondos. *Editor:* Ted Ötton. *Composer:* Neil Sutherland. *Sound recordist:* Phil Sterling.

Cast: Marcus Graham (Grady/Christian), Nikki Coghill (Kate), Doug Bowles (O'Rourke), Stephen Whittaker (Kopinsky), John Arnold (Frank), Bruce Alexander (Detective Sergeant), George Vidalis (Keith), Andrew Curry (Jimmy), Jin Yi (Korean Diplomat), Roland Dantes (Large Asian Guy).

Synopsis: The story of Grady, an ex-soldier whose life has been disrupted and his emotions disturbed by his experiences both at war and most recently in prison. Grady escapes from police custody after attending the burial of his brother, Christian. His escape is successful and he returns to his home town to investigate Christian's murder. Grady turns to Kate, his ex-girlfriend, for help. They discover that Christian was betrayed by the people he trusted most.

THE PRESENCE
JOHN RHALL

All Action Films. 1992. Feature not theatrically released as of 1 May 1995.

Producer: John Rhall. *Scriptwriter:* John Rhall.

Cast: Louise McDonald, Nicola Ruscoe, Jason Crowe, John Rhall.

Synopsis: A modern-day ghost story set in a leafy suburb on Sydney's North Shore. A tale of a family who find that their newly-purchased home has a terrifying personality of its own.

RESISTANCE
PAUL ELLIOTT, HUGH KEAYS-BYRNE

Macau Light Film Corporation. 1991. Feature not theatrically released as of 1 May 1995.

Producers: Christina Ferguson, Pauline Rosenberg. *Scriptwriter:* Macau Collective.

Cast: Donal Gibson, Helen Jones, Lorna Lesley, Stephen Leeder, Kris McQuade.

Synopsis: A liberation epic dealing with military repression and resistance. Set in the near future in a country not unlike Australia.

ROUGH DIAMONDS
DONALD CROMBIE

Forest Home Films. *Filmed:* 1993. Feature awaiting release in Australia as of 1 May 1995.

Producer: Damien Parer. *Executive producers:* Damien Parer, Jonathan Shteinman. *Scriptwriters:* Donald Crombie, Christopher Lee. *Director of photography:* John Stokes. *Production designer:* Georgina Greenhill. *Costume designers:* Kim Sandeman, Chris Feld. *Editor:* Wayne Le Clos. *Composer:* Peter Martin. *Sound recordist:* John Schiefelbein.

Cast: Jason Donovan (Mike), Hayley Toomey (Sam), Jocelyn Rosen (Lisa), Angie Milliken (Chrissie), Kit Taylor (Les Finnigan), Lee James (Macka McKeegan), Jeffrey Hardy (Douglas McFarlane), Roger Ward (Merv Drysdale), Maurice Hughes (Jimmy Rawlins), Tim Gaffney (Doc).

Synopsis: Mike Tyrell's life changes when in a moment of inattention the cattle truck he is driving hits a car parked on the side of the road, belonging to Chrissie Bright, an ex-singer turned barrister's wife, on the run from suburban life.

SAY A LITTLE PRAYER
RICHARD LOWENSTEIN

Flying Films. *Alternative title:* 'Came Back to Show You I Could Fly' (working). 1992. Feature not theatrically released as of 1 May 1995.

Producer: Carol Hughes. *Scriptwriter:* Richard Lowenstein. Based on the novel *Came Back to Show You I Could Fly!*. *Director of photography:* Graeme Wood. *Production designer:* Chris Kennedy. *Costume designer:* Lynn-Maree Milburn. *Editor:* Lloyd Carrick. *Sound recordist:* Lloyd Carrick.

Cast: Fiona Rutelle (Angie), Sudi de Winter (Seymour), Lynne Murphy (Thelma), Mickey Camilleri (Seymour's Mum), Rebecca Smart (Lynne), Jill Forster (Mrs Easterbrook), Greg Carroll (Jake), Ben Mendelsohn (Nursery Boss), Phyll Bartlett (Op Shop Lady), Pepe Trevor (Shop Assistant), Roger Neave (Mr Easterbrook).

Synopsis: A skinny, introverted 11-year-old meets the young effervescent but drug-addicted Angie and enters her fantasy world. It is a relationship that offers strength to each, and through the highs and lows of a long hot summer they both gradually learn to face the truth about each other and themselves.

SEEING RED
VIRGINIA ROUSE

1993. Feature not theatrically released as of 1 May 1995.

Producers: Tony Llewellyn-Jones, Virginia Rouse. *Executive producer:* William T Marshall. *Associate producer:* Trish Carney. *Scriptwriter:* Roger Pulvers. Based on the story 'Red Herring' by Virginia Rouse. *Director of photography:* Ian Jones. *Production designer:* Virginia Rouse. *Costume designer:* Meg Gordon. *Editor:* Mark Atkin. *Composer:* Andrew Yencken. *Sound recordist:* Phillip Healy.

Cast: Zoë Carides (Red), Anne Louise Lambert (Amanda), Peta Toppano (Vivien), Tony Llewellyn-Jones (Duncan), George Spartels (Mark), Henri Szeps (Louie), John Mulock (Frank #1), David Wenham (Frank #2), David Field (William), Anthony Wong (Nguyen).

Synopsis: Writer Duncan and his son live alone. They are pursued from Sydney to Canberra and back by Red, Amanda, Vivien and the two Franks. The final coincidence foils the stockbroker, the thugs, the politicians and the editor–and hopefully ends the madness.

SEE JACK RUN
STEPHEN AMIS

A.F.M.S. Productions. *Budget:* $97,000. *Filmed:* August–September 1991. Tele-feature shot on video.

Producer: Roger Gough. *Line producer:* Christine Collins. *Associate producer:* Darrel Stokes, Martin Hunter, Christopher Hewitt. *Scriptwriters:* Stephen Amis, Robert Gough. Based on the play, *Who Cares*, by Gillian Wadds. *Director of photography:* Darrel Stokes. *Production designers:* Kim Bounds, Sally Shepherd. *Editor:* Robert Murphy. *Composer:* Barry Campbell.

Cast: Trent Mooney (Brian), Molly Brumm (Jan), Ellis Ebell (Colin), Elissa Holloway (Karen), Peter Docker (Steven), Kathy Thomaidis (Maria), John McCullough (Moss).

Synopsis: Urban teenage drama dealing with illiteracy, poverty and romance on both sides of the tracks.

THE SEVENTH FLOOR
IAN BARRY

Rutherford Films Holdings. *Location:* Sydney. *Filmed:* July 1993. 96 mins. Feature released first on television.

Producer: John Sexton. *Executive producers:* Victor Glynn, Chris Brown, Hiroyuki Ikeda, Susumu Kondo. *Scriptwriter:* Tony Morphett. *Director of photography:* Martin McGrath. *Production designer:* Roger Ford. *Costume designer:* Terry Ryan. *Editor:* Tim Wellburn. *Composer:* Roger Mason. *Sound recordist:* Guntis Sics.

Cast: Brooke Shields (Kate), Masaya Kato (Mitsura), Linda Cropper (Vivien), Craig Pearce (Ed).

Synopsis: When Kate's husband, Bill, dies, Kate takes his place as one of the three partners in a Sydney advertising agency. The two other partners, Ed and Vivien, introduce Kate to Mitsura, a design and computer whiz in the graphics department. With his help, Kate lands a major account. An envious Vivien blackmails Ed into forcing Kate out of the agency. Mitsura offers Kate his support. But his sweet demeanour cloaks a dark and dangerous personality.

SEX IS A FOUR LETTER WORD
MURRAY FAHEY

Winfalz Investments. *Alternative title:* 'Love Stories' (working). *Filmed:* 10 September–4 October 1994. *Budget:* less than $1 million. *Location:* Sydney. Feature awaiting release as of 1 May 1995.

Producer: Murray Fahey. *Scriptwriter:* Murray Fahey. D*irector of photography:* Peter Borosh. *Camera operator:* Peter Borosh. *Production designer:* Sean Callinan. *Costume designer:* Sean Callinan. *Editor:* Brian Kavanagh. *Composer:* Frank Strangio. *Sound recordist:* David Glasser.

Cast: Joy Smithers (Sylvia), Rhett Walton (Morris), Mark Lee (John), Tessa Humphries (Tracy), Timothy Jones (Tom), Miranda Otto (Viv), Jonathon Sammy-lee (Dan).

Synopsis: Sylvia is a love columnist. Tonight she has invited her friends over for drinks, dinner and conversation, the aim being to explore love experiences and sexuality for her new book, *Love Stories.* During the evening, relationships are formed, explored and destroyed.

SHINE
SCOTT HICKS

Momentum Films. Feature in production as of 1 May 1995.

Producer: Jane Scott. *Scriptwriter:* Jan Sardi. *Director of photography:* Geoffrey Simpson. *Musical director:* David Hirschfelder.

Cast: Geoffrey Rush, Lyn Redgrave, John Gielgud.

Synopsis: After succumbing to the pressure of his father's obsessive love and the fierce competition of the concert world as a child prodigy, David Helfgott makes a new beginning in London inspired by his passion for music and the woman he loves.

SIGNAL ONE
ROB STEWART

Canealian Productions. *Filmed:* April 1993. Feature not theatrically released as of 1 May 1995.

Producer: Phillip Avalon. *Executive producer:* Neal Gechtman. *Associate producer:* Dennis Kiely. *Scriptwriter:* Karl Shiffman. *Director of photography:* Martin McGrath. *Production designer:* Cathy Finlay. *Editor:* Tony Kavanagh. *Composer:* Art Phillips. *Sound recordist:* Art Phillips.

Cast: Christopher Atkins (Martin Bullet), Mark Jackson (Jack Moran), Virginia Hey (Toni), Richard Carter (O'Shaughnessy), Alfie Bell (Doug).

Synopsis: An Australian cop is teamed with an American law enforcer. The two detectives confront each other but prove their mettle against a dangerous crime syndicate.

SINGAPORE SLING (VARIOUS)
ROBERT MARCHAND AND OTHERS

Barron Films (Television). Series of tele-feature.

Producers: Julie Monton, Paul Barron. *Scriptwriter:* Robert Marchand.

SLOW NIGHT AT THE KUWAITI CAFE
MARC GRACIE

Boulevard Films. 1992. Feature not theatrically released as of 1 May 1995.

Producer: Frank Howson. *Scriptwriters:* Chris Thompson, Marc Gracie.

Cast: Michael Bishop, Tiriel Mora, Fiona Corke, Tanya Lacey.

Synopsis: A Vietnam veteran takes over the small Kuwaiti Cafe in downtown Melbourne and holds the manager hostage in the countdown to the Bush–Saddam confrontation. He attempts to divert the 'mother of all wars' in what proves to be a funny, sad and enlightening night at the Kuwaiti Cafe.

SNIPER
LUIS LLOSA

Baltimore Pictures. 1991–92. Feature not theatrically released as of 1 May 1995.

Producers: Bob Rosen, Jim Gorman. *Scriptwriters:* Michael Frost Beckner, Crash Leyland.

SPELLBINDER
NOEL PRICE

Film Australia. Tele-feature.

Producer: Noel Price. *Co-producer:* Polish Television. *Executive producer:* Ron Saunders. *Associate producer:* Dennis Kiely. *Scriptwriters:* Mark Shirrefs, John Thomson. *Director of photography:* Martin McGrath. *Production designer:* Nick McCallum. *Costume designer:* Julie Middleton. *Editor:* Pippa Anderson. *Sound recordist:* Paul Wyhowski.

Cast: Heather Mitchell (Ashka), Zbych Trofimiuk (Paul), Gosia Malgorzata (Riana), Andrzej Grabarczyk (Bron), Slawa Michalewska (Maran), Erlan Buchan (Jal), Julia Biczysko (Arla), Stanislaw Brejdygant (Summoner Toren), Rafal Zwierz (Gryvon).

STRANGERS IN CLOSE PROXIMITY
DAVID KERSTEN

Blue Goose Films. *Filmed:* September 1992. Feature not theatrically released as of 1 May 1995.

Producer: David Kersten. *Line producer:* Julianne Lawson. *Executive producer:* Michael O'Neill. *Scriptwriter:* David Kersten. *Director of photography:* Alex Catchpole. *Production designer:* Julianne Lawson. *Editor:* Mark Swan. *Composer:* Trojan Theatre.

STROKER
JOHN LAURIE

97 mins. Feature not theatrically released as of 1 May 1995.

Producer: John Laurie.

Cast: John Flaus, Belmont Holden, Rada Grmusa, Suzi Alesandra, Michael Barker, Ross McLeod.

Synopsis: Deranged patriarchy and doomed love in a post-Caligari underworld.

TALK
SUSAN LAMBERT

A Suitcase Films production in association with the Australian Film Commission. TALK. © 1993 Suitcase Films Pty. Limited. Script developed with assistance from Australian Film Commission. *Budget:* $1.2 million. *Location:* Sydney. *Filmed:* 1 March–2 April 1993. Super 16. Feature not theatrically released as of 1 May 1995.

Producer: Megan McMurchy. *Scriptwriter:* Jan Cornall. From an idea by Susan Lambert and Jan Cornall. *Director of photography:* Ron Hagen. *Production designer:* Lissa Coote. *Costume designer:* Clarrisa Patterson. *Editor:* Henry Dangar. *Composer:* John Clifford White. *Sound designers:* John Dennison, Tony Vaccher. *Sound recordists:* Tim Lloyd, Don Connolly. *Sound editors:* Tony Vaccher (dia.); John Patterson, John Dennison, Tony Vaccher (sd fx); John Dennison (foley). *Mixers:* John Dennison, Tony Vaccher.

Cast: Victoria Longley (Julia; Detective Julia), Angie Milliken (Stephanie; Detective Stephanie), Richard Roxburgh (Jack; Detective Harry), John Jarratt (Mac), Jacqueline McKenzie (The Girl); Ella-Mei Wong, Tenzing Tsewang, Kee Chan (Witnesses); Kerry Walker (Voice of the Witnesses), Aaron James (Detective).

Synopsis: A political thriller set on the Gold Coast.

TEMPTING A MARRIED MAN
ADAM LYNTON

1993. 100 mins. Feature not theatrically released as of 1 May 1995.

Producer: Adam Lynton. *Scriptwriter:* Adam Lynton. *Director of photography:* Adam Lynton. *Composer:* Adam Lynton.

Cast: Lile Hammond (Karen Scott), Tim Baker (Stan Scott), Theresa Huska (Peggy Lumet), Jay Gargett (Barbara Parker), Matt Pritchard (Harry Parker).

Synopsis: Three suspicious wives hire a prostitute to test their husbands' sexual loyalties.

TERRAIN
TERRY KYLE

Archipelago Films. *Filmed:* January–February 1994. Feature not theatrically released as of 1 May 1995.

Producers: Terry Kyle, Peter Gregory. *Associate producer:* Belinda Glaistner. *Scriptwriter:* Terry Kyle. *Director of photography:* Peter Gregory. *Production designer:* Adam Head. *Composer:* Craig Hanacek. BVU-SP. *Sound recordist:* Jeff Licence.

Cast: Jonathon Hardy (Ballard), Amanda Mires (Aria), Gerowyn Lacaze (Lear), Daniel Kealy (Joyner), Sallyanne Ryan (Manderson), Marc James (Felle)

Synopsis: Isolated on a remote planet, the crew of research station Orpheus are forced to confront the unknowability of each other and the hostile world they reside on.

THAT EYE THE SKY
JOHN RUANE

Entertainment Media. *Filmed:* 25 October–19 December 1993. Feature not theatrically released as of 1 May 1995.

Producer: Peter Beilby. *Co-producer:* Grainne Marmion. *Executive producers:* Fred Schepisi, Robert Le Tet, Tim Bevan. *Scriptwriters:* John Ruane, Jim Barton. Based on the novel, *That Eye the Sky,* by Tim Winton. *Director of photography:* Ellery Ryan. *Camera operator:* Mandy Walker. *Production designer:* Chris Kennedy. *Costume designer:* Vicki Friedman. *Editor:* Ken Sallows. *Sound recordist:* Lloyd Carrick.

Cast: Peter Coyote (Henry Warburton), Lisa Harrow (Alice Flack), Jamie Croft (Ort), Mark Fairall (Sam Flack), Amanda Douge (Tegwyn Flack), Louise Siversen (Mrs Cherry), Paul Sonkkila (Mr Cherry), Jeremy Dridan (Fat Cherry), Alelthea McGrath (Grammar).

Synopsis: A young boy struggles to free his father from a coma following a car accident.

TO THE POINT OF DEATH
CRAIG GODFREY

Pocket Money Productions. *Budget:* $80,000. *Filmed:* 7–24 November 1993. Feature not theatrically released as of 1 May 1995.

Producer: Craig Godfrey. *Co-producer:* Mark Tomlinson. *Scriptwriter:* Craig Godfrey. *Director of photography:* Mark Tomlinson. *Camera operators:* Mark Tomlinson, Craig Godfrey. *Production designers:* Jo Howie, Craig Godfrey. *Editor:* Ron McCullouch. *Composer:* Tony Francis. *Sound recordist:* George Goers.

Cast: Lorraine Merritt, Jon Sidney, Bill Pearson, Ian Lang, Kerry Laws, Tim Aris, David Noonan, Vick Hawkins, Jacqueline Kelly, Pam John, Gareth John.

Synopsis: Upset by an unfaithful fiancé, Cassie Kinsella retreats to a deserted beach town. It is winter. Only an eccentric anthropologist and an incestuous couple share the seclusion. Many murders later, Cassie is the target of a madman. Only a mental asylum can save her, maybe.

TUNNEL VISION
CLIVE FLEURY

Avalon Films. *Filmed:* 14 February–20 March 1994. *Australian distributor:* Beyond Films–Pro Films. Feature not theatrically released as of 1 May 1995.

Producer: Phillip Avalon. *Associate producers:* Phillip Bowman, Brenda Pam. *Scriptwriter:* Clive Fleury. *Director of photography:* Paul Murphy. *Production designer:* Phil Warner. *Costume designer:* Rosalea Hood. *Editor:* John Scott. *Composer:* David Hirschfelder. *Sound recordist:* John Schiefelbein.

Cast: Patsy Kensit (Kelly Wheatstone), Robert Reynolds (Frank Yanovitch), Rebecca Rigg (Helen Martelli), Gary Day (Steve Dogherty), Shane Briant (Kevin Bosey), Craig Breslin (Justin Monjo), David Woodley (David De Salvo), Vanessa Steele (Rachel Kossinger), Craig Ashley (Knowles), Jonathon Hardy (Henry Adams).

Synopsis: At the height of a murder investigation, Detective Frank Yanovitch is drawn into a web of deceit, jealousy and self-pity. His partner, Kelly Wheatstone, has her own agenda. The killer holds the ace card and decides to play the game on his terms.

TURNING APRIL
GEOFF BENNETT

Turning April Productions. *Filmed:* 27 February 1994–7 April 1995. Feature in post-production as of 1 May 1995.

Producers: Heather Ogilvie, Lael McCall. *Co-producer:* John Winter. *Executive producers:* Phil Gerlach, Robert Lantos. *Scriptwriter:* James W. Nichol. *Director of photography:* Steve Arnold. *Production designer:* Michael Philips. *Costume designer:* Clarrissa Patterson. *Editor:* Susan Shipton. *Sound recordist:* Bronwyn Murphy.

Cast: Tushka Bergen (April), Aaron Blabey (Leif), Dee Smart (Kyra), Tayler Kane (Donny), Justine Clarke (Rose), Bradley Byquar (Charlie), Christopher Morsley (Chappie), Kenneth Welsh (Father), Judi Farr (Mother).

The young wife of an ambitious bureaucrat, April is accidentally kidnapped by an inept street gang during a bungled robbery. Confinement turns to liberation as she comes to realize her young captors offer her a first taste of personal freedom and sexual awakening.

UNDER THE GUN
MATTHEW GEORGE

International Studio Pictures. 100 mins. Feature awaiting release as of 1 May 1995.

Producers: Paul Elliott Currie, Richard Norton. *Executive producer:* Fred Weintraub, Tom Kuhn. *Scriptwriter:* Matthew George.

Cast: Richard Norton, Robert Bruce, Peter Lindsey, Nicky Buckley, Kathy Long, Peter Cunningham, Stan Longinidis, Jane Badler, Tino Cenerano.

Synopsis: Under the Gun revolves around a nightclub owner attempting to unload his debt-ridden club on a night where everything that can go wrong does.

VACANT POSSESSION
MARGOT NASH

Wintertime Films. *Budget:* $1.54 million. *Filmed:* 8 November–17 December 1993. Feature awaiting release as of 1 May 1995.

Producer: John Winter. *Scriptwriter:* Margot Nash. *Director of photography:* Dion Beebe.

Cast: Pamela Rabe, John Stanton, Toni Scanlon, Linden Wilkinson, Rita Bruce, Olivia Patten.

Synopsis: Tessa returns to her childhood home—a house haunted by emotional memories. But how to return home all those years away? What's home after all? A house? A place? A family? Set on the shores of Botany Bay close to where Captain Cook landed, *Vacant Possession* tells a story of two families—one black, one white—both living in the shadow of the past. Weaving dream, memory and fantasy, it is the story of conflict and the complexities of reconciliation.

WHAT I HAVE WRITTEN
JOHN HUGHES

Early Works. *Budget:* $1.5 million. Feature in post-production as of 1 May 1995.

Producers: Peter Sainsbury, John Hughes. *Scriptwriter:* John A. Scott. Based on the novel, *What I Have Written,* written by John A. Scott. *Director of photography:* Dion Beebe. *Production designer:* Sarah Stollman.

Cast: Angie Milliken (Sorel Atherton / Gillian), Martin Jacobs (Christopher Houghton / Avery), Jacek Koman (Jeremy Fliszar), Gillian Jones (Catherine / Frances Bourin).

Synopsis: Fiction and reality become indistinguishable as one person's search for truth encounters another's realisation of desire. Based on John A. Scott's Premier's Award-winning novel.

YOU AND ME AND UNCLE BOB
ALISTER SMART

Robert Bruning Productions. 1992. Tele-feature. Feature not theatrically released as of 1 May 1995.

Producers: Robert Bruning, Adrienne Read. *Scriptwriter:* Rob George.

Cast: Melissa Jaffer, Brooke Anderson, David Kaff.

Synopsis: Two kids contrive to bring love to an unlikely older couple.

YOU CAN'T PUSH THE RIVER
LESLIE OLIVER

Sculpting Pictures. 1992. Feature not theatrically released as of 1 May 1995.

Producer: Robert Alcock. *Scriptwriters:* John Reddin, Leslie Oliver.

Cast: Nollaig O'Flannabhra, Antonia Punturiero, Kathryn Chalker.

Synopsis: Tony is a new boy in the school, dealing with his dislocation. Joe Glass, his teacher, is an Irishman who has travelled extensively, struggling to dispel his feelings of not belonging and of accepting his need to be part of someone, somewhere.

APPENDIX E
THE TWO GEORGE MILLER FILMOGRAPHIES

GEORGE MILLER

Born 1945, Brisbane. Graduated in medicine from University of NSW in 1970. Formed Kennedy Miller Production company with producer Byron Kennedy in 1979.

As director (features):
1979 **Mad Max**—also co-writer
1981 **Mad Max 2** (aka: **The Road Warrior**)— also co-writer
1983 **Twilight Zone: The Movie** (US)— 'Nightmare at 20,000 Feet' episode
1985 **Mad Max Beyond Thunderdome**— co-director (with George Ogilvie), also co-writer, a producer
1987 **The Witches of Eastwick** (US)
1993[1] **Lorenzo's Oil** (US)—also co-writer
Prod. **Contact** (US)

As director (other):
1972 *Violence in the Cinema … Part 1* (short)—also writer, actor
1973 *Devil in Evening Dress* (documentary)— also writer
1983 *The Dismissal* (mini-series)—a director, also an executive producer
1995 *The Century of Cinema: 40,000 Years of Dreaming* (feature documentary)— also writer

Also,
1973 *Frieze—An Underground Film* (short)— editor

1980 **The Chain Reaction**—second unit director, an associate producer
1984 *Bodyline* (mini-series)—a producer
1985 *The Cowra Breakout* (mini-series)— a producer
1985 *The Making of Mad Max Beyond Thunderdome* (documentary)— an executive producer
1987 *Vietnam* (mini-series)—a producer
1987 **The Year My Voice Broke**—a producer
1988 *The Dirtwater Dynasty* (mini-series)— a producer
1988 *Sportz Crazy* (documentary series)— a producer
1988 *The Clean Machine* (tele-feature)— a producer
1988 *The Riddle of the Stinson* (tele-feature)—a producer
1988 *Fragments of War: The Story of Damien Parer* (tele-feature)—a producer
1989 **Dead Calm**—a producer
1989 *Bangkok Hilton* (mini-series)— a producer
1991 **Flirting**—a producer
1995 **Babe: The Brilliant Sheep Pig**— a producer

GEORGE MILLER

Born 1943, Scotland. Moved to Melbourne as a child. Commenced work as television director at Crawford Productions in 1972.

As director (features):
1982 **The Man from Snowy River**
1984 **The Aviator** (Yugoslavia)
1986 **Cool Change**
1987 **Les Patterson Saves the World**
1987 **Bushfire Moon**
1990 **The Neverending Story II: The Next Chapter** (Germany)
1992 **Frozen Assets** (US)
1992 **Over the Hill**
1993 **Gross Misconduct**
1995 **Andre**

As director (other):
1976 *Cash and Company* (tele-series)
1978 *Against the Wind* (tele-series)
1979 *High Country* (documentary)
1980 *The Last Outlaw* (tele-series)
1983 *All the Rivers Run* (mini-series)
1984 *Five Mile Creek* (mini-series)
1985 *The Anzacs* (mini-series)
1985 *The Far Country* (mini-series)
1988 *Goodbye, Miss 4th of July* (tele-feature, US)
1989 *Spooner* (tele-feature, US)
1990 *A Mom for Christmas* (tele-feature, US)
Also,
1978 *The Making of Anna* (documentary)— actor
1979 **In Search of Anna**—assistant director

---

1 Released in Australia in 1994.

Australian Copyright Office, *Film and Copyright*, Sydney, 1990

Australian Council of Government Film Libraries, in association with the National Film & Sound Archive, *Focus on Reel Australia*, Canberra, 1990

Australian Film Commission, *Australian Film Data: Selected Film, Video and Television Statistics from the Australian Film Database*, Sydney, 1988

Peter Beilby (ed.), *Australian Motion Picture Year Book 1980*, Cinema Papers in association with the New South Wales Film Corporation, Melbourne, 1980

Peter Beilby (ed.), *Australian Motion Picture Year Book 1981/82*, Cinema Papers in association with the New South Wales Film Corporation, Melbourne, 1981

Peter Beilby and Ross Lansell (eds), *Australian Motion Picture Year Book 1983*, Four Seasons in association with Cinema Papers, Melbourne, 1982

Ina Bertrand (ed.), *Cinema in Australia: A Documentary History*, New South Wales University Press, Sydney, 1989

Annette Blonski, Barbara Creed and Freda Freiberg (eds), *Don't Shoot Darling!: Women's Independent Filmmaking in Australia*, Greenhouse Publications, Melbourne, 1987

Simon Brand, *The Australian Film Book: 1930–Today*, Dreamweaver Books, Sydney, 1985

Simon Brand, *Picture Palaces and Flea-Pits: Eighty Years of Australians at the Pictures*, Dreamweaver Books, Sydney, 1983

Nigel Buesst, *Melbourne Film Makers Resource Book*, printed with the assistance of Film Victoria, Melbourne, 1991

Al Clark (ed.), *The Film Yearbook: Volume Two*, Australian section edited by Tom Ryan, Currey O'Neil Ross, Melbourne, 1984

Al Clark (ed.), *The Film Yearbook 1985*, Australian section edited by Tom Ryan, Currey O'Neil Ross, Melbourne, 1984

Al Clark, *Making Prsicilla*, Penguin, Melbourne, 1994

Peter Coleman, *Bruce Beresford: Instincts of the Heart*, Angus & Robertson, Sydney, 1992

Diane Collins, *Hollywood Down Under: Australians at the Movies: 1896 to the Present Day*, Angus & Robertson Publishers, Sydney, 1987

Stephen Crofts, *Identification, Gender and Genre in Film: The Case of 'Shame'*, Australian Film Institute, Melbourne, 1993

John Cruthers (ed.), *Taking Care of Business: A Practical Guide to Independent Film and Video Production*, Volume 1: 'Production Budgeting and Accounting', written by John Cruthers, Andrew Scollo and (Janice) Digby Duncan; Volume 2: 'Case Studies in Independent Production', edited by John Cruthers; Volume 3: 'Marketing and Distribution', written by Jennifer Stott, Australian Film Television & Radio School and the Australian Film Commission, Sydney, 1988–89

Stuart Cunningham and Graeme Turner (eds), *Media in Australia: Industries, Texts, Audiences*, Allen & Unwin, Sydney, 1993

Rosemary Curtis and Shelley Spriggs (eds), *Get the Picture: Essential Data on Australian Film, Television and Video*, Australian Film Commission, Sydney, third edition and second revision of Spear edition, 1994

Jonathan Dawson and Bruce Molloy (eds), *Queensland Images in Film and Television*, University of Queensland Press, 1990

Susan Dermody and Elizabeth Jacka, *The Imaginary Industry: Australian Film in the Late '80s*, Australian Film Television & Radio School, Sydney, 1988

Susan Dermody and Elizabeth Jacka, *The Screening of Australia Volume 1: Anatomy of a Film Industry*, Currency Press, Sydney, 1987

Susan Dermody and Elizabeth Jacka, *The Screening of Australia Volume 2: Anatomy of a National Cinema*, Currency Press, Sydney, 1988

Bob Ellis, *The Inessential Ellis*, Angus & Robertson, Sydney, 1992

Sarah Ferber, Chris Healy and Chris McAuliffe, *Beasts of Suburbia: Reinterpreting Cultures in Australian Suburbs*, Melbourne University Press, Melbourne, 1994

Bryce Fraser, *The Macquarie Book of Events*, film section written by Graham Shirley, The Macquarie Library, Sydney, 1983

John Frow and Meaghan Morris (eds), *Australian Cultural Studies: A Reader*, Allen & Unwin, St Leonards, 1993

Ken G. Hall, *Australian Film: The Inside Story*, Summit Books, Sydney, 1980

Sandra Hall (consulting ed.), *Australian Film Index: A Guide to Australian Feature Films Since 1990*, Thorpe, Melbourne, 1992

Sandra Hall, *Critical Business: The New Australian Cinema in Review*, Rigby Publishers, Adelaide, 1985

William K. Halliwell, *The Filmgoers' Guide to Australian Films*, Angus & Robertson, Sydney, 1985

Peter Hamilton and Sue Mathews, *American Dreams: Australian Movies*, Currency Press, Sydney, 1986

Nick Herd, *Independent Filmmaking in Australia 1960–1980*, Australian Film, Television & Radio School, Sydney, 1983

Ivan Hutchinson, *Ivan Hutchinson's Movies on TV & Video*, The Five Mile Press, Melbourne, 1992

Anne Hutton (ed.), *The First Australian History and Film Conference Papers*, The History and Film Conference and the Australian Film and Television School, Sydney, 1982

Elizabeth Jacka, *The ABC of Drama: 1975–1990*, Australian Film Television & Radio School, Sydney, 1992

Karen Jennings, *Sites of Difference: Cinematic Representations of Aboriginality and Gender*, Australian Film Institute, Melbourne, 1993

Ross Jones, *Cut! Protection of Australia's Film and Television Industries*, The Centre for Independent Studies, NSW, 1991

Marcia Langton, *"Well, I Heard It on the Radio and I Saw It on the* Television ... ", Australian Film Commission, North Sydney, 1993

Wayne Levy, Graeme Cutts and Sally Stockbridge, *The Second Australian History and Film Conference Papers*, The History and Film Conference and the Australian Film and Television School, Sydney, 1984

Marion Marsh and Chris Pip (eds), *Women in Australian Film, Video and Television Production*, Australian Film Commission and the Australian Film Television & Radio School, Sydney, 1987

Adrian Martin, *Film—Matters of Style,* issue of *Continuum: The Australian Journal of Media and Culture*, Vol. 5, No. 2, Murdoch University, Perth, 1992

Adrian Martin, *Phantasms: The Dreams and Desires at the Heart of Our Popular Cinema*, McPhee Gribble, Melbourne, 1994

Sue Mathews, *35mm Dreams: Conversations with Five Australian Directors*, Penguin Books Australia, Melbourne, 1984

Brian McFarlane, *Australian Cinema 1970–1985*, William Heinemann Australia, Melbourne, 1987

Brian McFarlane, *Words and Images: Australian Novels into Film*, Heinemann Publishers in association with Cinema Papers, Melbourne, 1980

Brian McFarlane (ed.), *Literature/Film Quarterly: The Australian Cinema*, Salisbury State University, Salisbury,1993

Brian McFarlane and Geoff Mayer, *New Australian Cinema: Sources and Parallels in American and British Film*, Cambridge University Press, Melbourne, 1992

Jacqueline McKimmie, *Waiting: A Comedy of Errors and Expectations ...*, University of Queensland Press, St Lucia, 1993

Megan McMurchy and Jennifer Stott (eds), *Signs of Independents: Ten Years of the Creative Development Fund*, Australian Film Commission, Sydney, 1988

Jenny Middlemiss, *Guide to Film and Television Research*, Australian Film Television & Radio School, North Ryde, 1992

Albert Moran and Tom O'Regan (eds), *An Australian Film Reader*, Currency Press, Sydney, 1985

Albert Moran and Tom O'Regan (eds), *The Australian Screen*, Penguin Books Australia, Melbourne, 1989

Scott Murray (ed.), *Australian Cinema*, Allen & Unwin, Sydney, 1993 (revised edition in English of *Le Cinéma Australien;* refer Thoridnet)

Scott Murray (ed.), *Back of Beyond: Discovering Australian Film and Television*, Australian Film Commission, Sydney, 1988

Scott Murray (ed.), *The New Australian Cinema*, Thomas Nelson Australia in association with Cinema Papers, Melbourne, 1980

Andrew Pike and Ross Cooper, *Australian Film 1900–1977: A Guide to Feature Film Production*, Oxford University Press in association with the Australian Film Institute, Melbourne, 1980

Neil Rattigan, *Images of Australia: 100 Films of the New Australian Cinema*, Southern Methodist University Press, Dallas, 1991

Eric Reade, *The Australian Screen: A Pictorial History of Australian Film Making*, Lansdowne Press, Melbourne, 1975

Eric Reade, *Australian Silent Films*, Lansdowne Press, Melbourne, 1970

Eric Reade, *History and Heartburn: The Saga of Australian Film, 1896–1978*, Harper & Row, Sydney, 1979

Eric Reade, *The Talkies Era*, Lansdowne Press, Melbourne, 1972

Mary Anne Reid, *Long Shots to Favourites: Australian Cinema Successes in the 90s*, Australian Film Commission, North Sydney, 1993

Penny Ryan, Margaret Eliot and Gil Appleton (eds), *Women in Australian Film Production*, Women's Film Fund (Australian Film Commission) and the Australian Film Television & Radio School, Sydney, 1983

James Sabine (ed.), *A Century of Australian Cinema*, William Heinemann Australia, Port Melbourne, 1995

Lyndon Sayer-Jones, *Law Brief: The Australian Film and Television Industry in the Nineties: A Film Lawyer's Guide for Non Lawyers*, Trade News Corporation, Sydney, 1992

Kirsten Schou, *Policies for the Australian Film Industry: Part A: Rationale for assistance and direct government subsidy*, Australian Film and Television School, Sydney, 1982

Kirsten Schou, *The Structure and Operation of the Film Industry in Australia*, Australian Film and Television School, Sydney, 1982

John Shand and Tony Wellington, *Don't Shoot the Best Boy!: The Film Crew at Work*, Currency Press, Sydney, 1988

Sylvie Shaw, *No Koalas Please: Issues for Film-makers in Asia and Australia*, Asialink, Melbourne, 1990

Graham Shirley and Brian Adams, *Australian Cinema: The First Eighty Years*, Angus & Robertson in association with Currency Press, Sydney, 1983

Peta Spear (ed.), *Get the Picture: Essential Data on Australian Film*, Television and Video, Australian Film Commission, Sydney, 1989

John Stewart, *An Encyclopaedia of Australian Film*, Reed Books, Sydney, 1984

David Stratton, *The Avocado Plantation: Boom and Bust in the Australian Film Industry*, Pan Macmillan, Sydney, 1990

David Stratton, *The Last New Wave: The Australian Film Revival*, Angus & Robertson, Sydney, 1980

Claudine Thoridnet [and Scott Murray] (eds), *Le Cinéma Australien*, Centre Georges Pompidou, Paris, 1991

Victoria Treole (ed.), *Australian Independent Film*, Australian Film Commission, Sydney, 1982

John Tulloch, *Australian Cinema: Industry, Narrative and Meaning*, George Allen & Unwin Australia, Sydney, 1982

John Tulloch (ed.), *Conflict and Control in the Cinema: A Reader in Film and Society*, Macmillan, Melbourne, 1977

Graeme Turner, *National Fictions: Literature, Film and the Construction of Australian Narrative* (Second Edition), Allen & Unwin, St Leonards, 1993

David White, *Australian Movies to the World: The International Success of Australian Films Since 1970*, Fontana Australia, Sydney, and Cinema Papers, Melbourne, 1984

Andrée Wright, *Brilliant Careers: Women in Australian Cinema*, Pan Books, Sydney, 1986

A P P E N D I X   G

AUTHORS' INDEX

ACKNOWLEDGMENTS

The two people who helped most with the second edition of this book were Editorial Assistant Alissa Tanskaya and Proof-reader Arthur Salton.

Alissa not only marshalled and cajoled the army of writers, but pursued many an unpursuable still. Without her enthusiastic contribution, this edition might still be a work-in-progress.

Arthur has been the proof-reader (and de facto sub-editor) at *Cinema Papers* for nearly two decades. *Cinema Papers*, like this book, owes him a considerable debt of gratitude. It is hard to express the reassurance one gains from knowing Arthur will read and comment on a text before it heads off to the designer.

Almost all the photographs are from *Cinema Papers'* still library, an invaluable resource that made illustrating this book possible. The only exceptions are two stills from the Australian Film Institute.

When the publication of the first edition was mooted, a team of writers gathered to discuss the book's methodology: they were Ken Berryman, Rolando Caputo, Paul Harris, Adrian Martin and Tom Ryan. Many thanks for their initiating guidance. Kathy Bail was involved in the early discussions, while the book's first Editorial Assistant, Raffaele Caputo, was a major contributor.

Naturally, great appreciation goes to all those writers who contributed. Unlike many books where writers only cover films they love or films which are relevant to specific issues they wish to discuss, here there was a need to write at equal length about many unloved and unlovable films—a difficult task.

Working with Oxford University Press has been a joy. Peter Rose was enthusiastic from the outset, and has expertly guided two editions through its various stages. Geraldine Corridon skilfully oversaw various aspects of the production, as did Steve Randles the book's design, and Ruth Siems ably subbed the book (and even graciously put up with my insistence of the circumflex in rôle).

Finally, I happily record the great support of my wife, not only in her comments and contributions, but for keeping spirits high.

INDEX

This index covers all names, titles and organisations in the critical texts, plus certain categories in the credit blocks: namely, director; production companies; all the producers (executive, associate, etc., under the generic title 'producer'); scriptwriter; source writer (playwright, novelist, etc.) on whose work a screenplay has been based; director of photography (shortened to 'dop'); production designer; editor; and composer. Where a person fulfils more than one function, the entries are sorted to individual categories. For example:

Beresford, Bruce (director) 15n, **42**, **53**, **55**, **81**, 156, 173, 181, 184, **197**, 233, 245, 281, **331**, 331;
(scriptwriter) 42c, 53c, 197c

When two identical names appear after each other in the index (e.g., Ned Lander), that is because they are two different people (or because a degree of uncertainty about their identity/ies exists). Variants in a person's name (Greg and Gregory Coote) have been standardised to the most common form.

To distinguish the principal entry on each theatrical feature, the page number is given in bold (after both the film title and the director's name). Italicised page numbers refer to a photograph.

Additionally, there are three codes after some page numbers: 'c' indicates the entry is from the credits block, 'r' is for References and 'n' is for notes.

All entries have been sorted in strict alphabetical order, ignoring word breaks. Thus,

Dentiste', 'Le (see **This Won't Hurt a Bit!**)
De Palma, Brian 359
Depardieu, Alain (executive producer) 368c

All theatrical features are listed in bold; tele-features, documentaries, novels and mini-series, etc., in italics; working titles in single quotes. Titles of films known to be released or made after 1994 are given in italics. The abbreviation c. 1992—as in *Australian Ninja* (Adam Ramos, non-theatrical feature, c. 1992)—indicates the film was shot or completed in 1992.

M

X

Y

Z